SUPERSEDED

CORPORATE FINANCE:

PRINCIPLES AND PRACTICE

SECOND EDITION

by

WILLIAM J. CARNEY
Charles Howard Candler Professor of Law
Emory University

FOUNDATION PRESS
2010

THOMSON REUTERS

© 2005 THOMSON REUTERS/FOUNDATION PRESS
© 2010 By THOMSON REUTERS/FOUNDATION PRESS
      195 Broadway, 9th Floor
      New York, NY 10007
      Phone Toll Free 1–877–888–1330
      Fax (212) 367–6799
      foundation–press.com
Printed in the United States of America

ISBN 978–1–59941–608–3

Mat #40781494

To Jane

PREFACE TO THE SECOND EDITION

Teaching corporate finance in a law school is one of the more challenging pedagogical tasks confronting law teachers. There are too many choices confronting the teacher in this area, and none seems obviously superior to the others. A course can be law-oriented or finance-oriented. Among the difficulties with the law-oriented course is that it, too faces choices—which body of law? The traditional approach has been case law—appellate decisions applying legal principles are a safe and conventional choice. One difficulty with the case-law approach is that so much of corporate finance is simply contractual—constructing agreements that resolve the tensions between parties, such as the stockholder-bondholder conflict. Leading cases in some areas are simply old—these areas became settled law with the first authoritative pronouncement, after which drafters conformed their behavior to the announced rules. The other difficulty is that this approach gives little attention to the law as it is practiced—in deals and in documents. This book leans toward the deal side, particularly in the area of corporate debt and convertible securities. Contractual language should be seen and experienced.

Some casebooks in this field spend a good deal of time on the problems facing common stockholders, including the fiduciary duties from which shareholders benefit. While these are important, they are not emphasized here, in the expectation that they are covered in basic corporation courses, or in other courses such as mergers & acquisitions. Accordingly, there are no chapters on mergers and acquisitions in this book. The focus here (aside from finance) is on the contracting issues facing investors, from dilution of existing shareholders to imposition of greater risk on creditors.

The other difficulty with concentrating on the law is that it provides students with little theory about or understanding of the problems they are addressing when they function as transactional lawyers. Students approaching this course with a search for an overarching body of legal principles may be disappointed. The principles were found largely in their contracts course and to some extent in their corporations course. Here finance must play an organizing role. That is the approach of this book. My goal is that students will understand their clients' problems and see how standard drafting is designed to solve them.

Some teachers have employed finance textbooks addressed to business students to achieve this goal. Readings from this text are supplemented with cases and other materials prepared by the teacher. While I am sympathetic to this approach, I have never employed it, for several reasons. First, the finance is sometimes more technical than many law students are prepared for, which may limit enrollments to those with a prior background in finance or a strong taste for mathematics. Second, these texts are generally aimed at students who will make investment decisions within firms, which is not the focus best suited to law students. Third, the links between the finance theory and the cases may be harder to see, because the text authors had another audience in mind. This book is at least in part addressed to those teachers—I offer an alternative of less extensive (and less mathematical) discussion of finance problems and a greater integration with legal materials. At the same time, I hope the book is not intimidating to law teachers with less interest in the application of finance principles. Rather than use excerpts from the finance literature, in many cases I have attempted to present finance principles in my own words, in the hope that this presentation, with the law student reader in mind, may be somewhat more accessible if somewhat less technical.

I have retained the basic organizational approach in this edition, and aside from clean-up of obvious errors in the first edition, simply updated the materials where appropriate.

The book begins with an accounting chapter that inquires how we measure the output of a business. The approach here is to help students without an accounting background understand how to read financial statements, and how ratios can be used to evaluate the health of a business. Obviously accurate statements of earnings and cash flows are essential for the valuation material in Chapter Three. This accounting material re-emerges in the debt chapter, where covenants are frequently based on these same ratios. The book then proceeds to questions of how we maximize that value. Here contracting, on both common and preferred stock, as well as on debt, plays a critical role. I hope this will give students an understanding of the role that lawyers play in helping our economy create value, and an appreciation of the importance of their own role in that process.

Consistent with that approach, each chapter and each section generally begins with the finance theory, and only then proceeds to the cases. There are problems and questions to test students' understanding of the finance theory, but probably not as many as teachers accustomed to using a finance text might wish. Finally, the book places relatively more emphasis on contracting than other books, with generous samples of indenture language coupled with the discussion of finance theory. Hence the relevance of the title, "Principles and Practice."

As is customary in casebooks, I have taken certain liberties with judicial opinions. Citations are omitted without indication. Editing has removed sections of opinions important to the individual case but not to the pedagogical mission of this book. Formatting of headings follows a consistent approach in the book, which often will not be identical to the formatting in the original opinion.

WILLIAM J. CARNEY

ACKNOWLEDGMENTS

I thank George Shepherd and Robert Rhee who made painstaking efforts to find the glitches and typos in the first edition, of which there were many. Several classes of Emory Law students deserve my thanks for helpfully pointing out errors as well. The errors that remain are mine alone. Most importantly, I thank my wife Jane for her patience in once again putting up with my preoccupation with another book project.

With appreciation, this acknowledgment is made for the publishers and authors who gave permission for the reproduction of excerpts from the following materials:

American Bar Association

> Committee on Corporate Laws, Section of Business Law, American Bar Association, Report of the Committee on Corporate Laws, Vol. 34. The Business Lawyer, pp. 1867–68 (1979). Copyright 1979 © by The American Bar Association. Reprinted with permission. This information or any portion thereof may not be copied or disseminated in any form or by any means or stored in an electronic database or retrieval system without the express written consent of the American Bar Association.

> Jerome S. Katzin, Financial and Legal Problems in the Use of Convertible Securities, Vol. 24, The Business Lawyer, pp. 360–66 (1969). Copyright 1969 © by The American Bar Association. Reprinted with permission. This information or any portion thereof may not be copied or disseminated in any form or by any means or stored in an electronic database or retrieval system without the express written consent of the American Bar Association.

> Model Simplified Indenture, sections 6.01, 6.02, 6.05, and 7.01, in Vol. 38, The Business Lawyer, pp. 756–759 (1983). Copyright 1983 © by The American Bar Association. Reprinted with permission. This information or any portion thereof may not be copied or disseminated in any form or by any means or stored in an electronic database or retrieval system without the express written consent of the American Bar Association.

American Bar Foundation

> COMMENTARIES ON MODEL DEBENTURE INDENTURE PROVISIONS, pp. 324–26, 426–27 (1971).

American Economic Association

> John Lintner, Distribution of Incomes of Corporations Among Dividends, Retained Earnings, and Taxes, Vol. 46, American Economic Review, pp. 99–100, 102–106 (1956).

> Frank H. Easterbrook, Two Agency–Cost Explanations of Dividends, Vol. 74, American Economic Review, pp. 650–58 (1984).

Catholic University of America

William J. Carney, Signalling and Causation in Insider Trading, Vol. 36, Catholic University Law Review, pp. 877–883 (1987).

Dow Jones & Company, Inc.

Stocks Fall: Don't Fret, Wall Street Journal Eastern Edition, October 13, 2000, p. A18.

Credit Reports: Suddenly, Banks Are Acting a Lot Like Bond Markets, Wall Street Journal Eastern Edition, September 17, 2001, p. A1.

Are Markets Efficient?—Yes, Even If They Make Errors, by Burton G. Malkiel, Wall Street Journal, December 28, 2000, p. A10.

Are Markets Efficient?—No, Arbitrage Is Inherently Risky, by Andrei Shleifer, Wall Street Journal, December 28, 2000, p. A10.

Who Says You Can't Make Money Off Stalled Stocks?, Wall Street Journal Eastern Edition, October 8, 2002, p. D1.

Why Capital Structure Matters, by Michael Miliken, Wall Street Journal, April 21, 2009, p. A21.

Duke Law Publications

Randall S. Thomas and James F. Cotter, Measuring Securities Market Efficiency in the Regulatory Setting, Vol. 63, Issue 3, Law and Contemporary Problems, pp. 111–112 (2000).

Edward Elgar Publishing Ltd.

William J. Carney, Limited Liability, Vol. III, ENCYCLOPEDIA OF LAW AND ECONOMICS, pp. 669–671, 675–678 (2000).

Elsevier Inc. B.V.

Michael Jensen and William Meckling, Theory of the Firm: Managerial Behavior, Agency Costs and Ownership Structure, Vol. 3, Journal of Financial Economics, pp. 333–34 (1976).

Clifford W. Smith, Jr. and Jerold B. Warner, On Financial Contracting: An Analysis of Bond Covenants, Vol. 7, Journal of Financial Economics, pp. 117–119, 125–132, 134–144, 146, 148–149, and 151–152 (1979).

Eugene Fama and Kenneth R. French, Disappearing Dividends: Changing Firm Characteristics or Lower Propensity to Pay?, Vol. 60, Journal of Financial Economics, pp. 4–6, 15–17–19, and 34–40 (2002).

Emory University School of Law

Dennis F. Dunne, Stock Repurchase Agreements in Bankruptcy: A Tale of State Law Rights Discarded, Vol. 12, Bankruptcy Developments Journal, pp. 355, 382–395 (1996).

Loyola University of Chicago

> Mark Borelli, Market Making in the Electronic Age, Vol. 32, Loyola University of Chicago Law Journal, pp. 815–816, 819–827 (2001).

McGraw–Hill Companies

> Richard A. Brealey and Stewart C. Myers, PRINCIPLES OF CORPORATE FINANCE, at p. 717 (6th ed., 2000).

> Peter Coy, Commentary: Son, Don't Count on Double–Digit Stock Returns, Business Week June 26, 2000, at Midyear Investment Guide.

> Five Ways of Valuing Options, Business Week Online, July 19, 2002, at Daily Briefing.

New York Stock Exchange

> Listed Company Manual, § 703.02.

Northwestern University

> Marcel Kahan and Edward Rock, Hedge Fund Activism in the Enforcement of Bondholder Rights, Vol. 103, Northwestern Law Review, pp. 283–288.

University of Notre Dame

> William J. Carney and Leonard A. Silverstein, The Illusory Protections of the Poison Pill, Vol. 79, Notre Dame L. Rev., pp. 183–191 (2003).

Oxford University Press

> Andrei Shleifer, INEFFICIENT MARKETS: AN INTRODUCTION TO BEHAVIORAL FINANCE, pp. 10–16 (2000).

University of Pennsylvania Law School

> Michael L. Wachter, Takeover Defense When Financial Markets Are (Only) Relatively Efficient, Vol. 151, University of Pennsylvania Law Review, pp. 812–817 (2003).

> William J. Carney and Mark Heimendinger, Appraising the Non–Existent: The Delaware Courts' Struggle with Control Premiums, Vol. 15, University of Pennsylvania Law Review, pp. 845–847, 859–863 (2003).

RMA—The Risk Management Association

> RMA 2001 ANNUAL STATEMENT STUDIES© 2001 by RMA—The Risk Management Association. All rights reserved. No part of this table may be reproduced or utilized in any form or by any means, electronic or mechanical, including photocopying, recording or by any information storage or retrieval system without permission in writing from RMA—The Risk Management Association. Please refer to www.rmahq.org for further warranty, copyright and use of data information.

Syracuse University College of Law

> Rutherford B. Campbell, The Impact of Modern Finance Theory in Acquisition Cases, Vol. 53, Syracuse Law Review, pp. 4, 22, 41–41 (2003).

SUMMARY OF CONTENTS

PREFACE --- v
ACKNOWLEDGMENTS --- vii
TABLE OF CASES --- xxi

CHAPTER ONE Introduction -- 1

CHAPTER TWO Measuring Firm Output ----------------------- 4

1. Introduction --- 4
2. Forms of Financial Reports -- 10
   A. The Balance Sheet -- 10
   B. The Income Statement -- 26
   C. The Statement of Cash Flows --------------------------------------- 36
   D. The Statement of Changes in Stockholders' Equity ------------ 42
3. Analysis of Financial Statements -------------------------------------- 43
   A. Accounting Options -- 44
   B. Ratios -- 50
   C. The Analysis of Ratios -- 58

CHAPTER THREE Valuing Firm Output --------------------- 88

1. Introduction --- 88
2. Discounting and Present Value --- 90
   A. Compounding -- 90
   B. The Frequency of Compounding ----------------------------------- 93
   C. Present Values -- 95
   D. Annuities --- 98
   E. Valuing a Perpetuity -- 101
   F. Valuing Common Stock -- 101
   G. Valuing Investments with Different Cash Flows at Different
      Times -- 103
   H. Net Present Value --- 104
3. The Cost of Capital -- 106
   A. The Price of Risk -- 106
   B. Measurement of Risk—Of Expected Values and Standard Devi-
      ations -- 111
   C. Risk and Diversification --- 116
   D. Pricing Risk in Markets—The Capital Assets Pricing Model ----- 118
   E. Levered Betas and the Cost of Capital for Leveraged Firms ------ 128
   F. Challenges to CAPM -- 129
4. Efficient Capital Markets --- 131
   A. The ECMH Model --- 131
   B. Challenges to ECMH --- 135
   C. ECMH in the Courts -- 152

5. Valuation in the Courts --- 172
   A. CAPM in the Courts -------------------------------------- 172
   B. Minority Discounts, Control Premia and Leverage ------------ 194

CHAPTER FOUR Capital Structure --------------------------- 211

1. Introduction --- 211
2. The Range of Financial Choices ------------------------------- 212
3. Modigliani & Miller's Irrelevance Hypothesis ----------------- 226
4. The Real World -- 236
   A. Debt and Taxes --- 237
   B. Weighted Average Cost of Capital ------------------------ 238
   C. Debt and Agency Costs ---------------------------------- 243
5. Capital Structure in the Courts ------------------------------ 248
6. The Wages of Excessive Debt --------------------------------- 262
   A. Subordination -- 262
   B. Fiduciary Duties to Creditors --------------------------- 270
   C. Creditor Liability -------------------------------------- 279
   D. The Close Corporation and Disallowance of Interest Deductions -- 290
   E. Liability of Affiliated Parties under the "Deepening Insolvency" Doctrine --- 296
   F. Structural Response to the Threat of Insolvency ---------- 307

CHAPTER FIVE Common Stock ------------------------------- 309

1. Limited Liability of Stockholders ---------------------------- 309
2. The Problem of Dilution ------------------------------------- 313
   A. Preemptive Rights to Purchase a Portion of Any New Issue ----- 316
   B. Equitable Doctrines Governing Dilutive Stock Issues ------ 323
   C. Dilution as a Takeover Defense—The Poison Pill ---------- 328
   D. Creditor Protection: Legal Capital ---------------------- 346
   E. Public Securities Markets and Regulation ---------------- 351

CHAPTER SIX Corporate Debt ------------------------------ 364

1. Introduction --- 364
2. Contract Interpretation -------------------------------------- 371
3. Contract Terms -- 382
   A. Capital Structure: Restricting New Debt ----------------- 384
   B. Alteration of Risks ------------------------------------- 409
   C. Distributions -- 415
   D. Underinvestment—Asset Maintenance ---------------------- 420
   E. Conversion Rights as Substitutes for Covenants --------- 423
   F. Sinking Funds -- 424
   G. Call Protection -- 426
   H. Monitoring Compliance ---------------------------------- 433
   I. Amendments -- 435
   J. Enforcement of Covenant Breaches ----------------------- 445

4. The Indenture Trustee and the Trust Indenture Act ----------------------- 448
    A. The Nature of the Trustee and its Duties ------------------------ 448
    B. The Trustee's Duties in Default ------------------------------ 458
5. Capital Leasing --- 465
6. Asset Backed Financing --- 467

CHAPTER   SEVEN   Preferred Stock ---------------------------------- 477

1. Introduction -- 477
    A. Defining Preferred Stock ----------------------------------- 477
    B. The Uses of Preferred Stock -------------------------------- 481
2. Dividends -- 482
    A. The Varieties of Dividends --------------------------------- 482
    B. Straight and Cumulative Dividends ------------------------- 489
    C. Property Rights in Dividends ------------------------------- 494
3. Altering the Preferred Contract ------------------------------------- 508
    A. Voting Rules and Voting Rights ----------------------------- 508
    B. Dealing with the Class Veto Power ------------------------- 521
4. Board Duties --- 538
    A. Board Duties to Preferred Shareholders -------------------- 538
    B. Duties of a Preferred–Controlled Board ------------------- 548
5. Share Redemptions and Repurchases ----------------------------------- 565

CHAPTER   EIGHT   Options and Convertible Securities --------- 583

1. Introduction -- 583
    A. The Uses of Options and Option Theory -------------------- 583
    B. Real Options -- 586
    C. Long and Short Positions and Position Diagrams ----------- 587
2. How Options Operate --- 589
    A. Call Options -- 589
    B. Put Options --- 593
    C. Combining Options, Stocks and Bonds; Put–Call Parity ---------- 595
    D. Uses of Options --- 599
3. Valuation of Options --- 604
4. Disclosure Issues With Options -------------------------------------- 612
5. Convertible Securities and Deal Protection -------------------------- 616
    A. Destruction of the Option -------------------------------- 616
    B. Dilution of Option Rights -------------------------------- 631
6. Last Period Financing: Death Spirals -------------------------------- 687

CHAPTER   NINE   Dividends and Distributions ------------------- 707

1. Distributions and Investor Wealth ----------------------------------- 707
    A. Dividend Practices -- 707
    B. How Do Dividends Relate to Firm Value? ------------------- 715
    C. Explaining Dividend Practices ---------------------------- 720
    D. Alternative Explanations of Dividends. ------------------- 726
2. Restrictions on Dividends and Other Distributions to Shareholders 733

3. Board Discretion and Duties in Declaring Dividends ------------------- 753
4. Stock Dividends and Stock Splits ------------------------------------- 768
   A. The Economics of Stock Dividends and Stock Splits -------------- 768
   B. Accounting for Dividends and Splits--------------------------- 769
   C. Reverse Stock Splits -- 776
5. Stock Repurchases --- 788
   A. The Economics of Share Repurchases------------------------- 788
   B. Legal Authority for Share Repurchases-------------------------- 790
   C. Regulation of Share Repurchases ----------------------------- 791
   D. Duties in Share Repurchases--------------------------------- 818
6. Leveraged Buyouts--- 825
7. Spin–Offs and Tracking Stock --- 841
   A. Spin–Offs --- 841
   B. Tracking Stock--- 843

INDEX --- 845

TABLE OF CONTENTS

PREFACE v
ACKNOWLEDGMENTS vii
TABLE OF CASES xxi

CHAPTER ONE Introduction 1

CHAPTER TWO Measuring Firm Output 4

1. Introduction 4
2. Forms of Financial Reports 10
   A. The Balance Sheet 10
      i. Assets 11
      ii. Liabilities 12
      iii. Stockholders' Equity 13
         Bolt v. Merrimack Pharmaceuticals, Inc. 17
   B. The Income Statement 26
      In re Software Toolworks, Inc. 30
   C. The Statement of Cash Flows 36
   D. The Statement of Changes in Stockholders' Equity 42
3. Analysis of Financial Statements 43
   A. Accounting Options 44
   B. Ratios 50
      i. Profitability Ratios 51
      ii. Financial Leverage Ratios 53
      iii. Liquidity Ratios 54
      iv. Activity Ratios 55
      v. Market Value Ratios 56
   C. The Analysis of Ratios 58
      Appendix 2–A   Examples of Contingent Liability Statements ... 62
      Appendix 2–B   2001 Annual Statement Studies 71

CHAPTER THREE Valuing Firm Output 88

1. Introduction 88
2. Discounting and Present Value 90
   A. Compounding 90
   B. The Frequency of Compounding 93
   C. Present Values 95
   D. Annuities 98
   E. Valuing a Perpetuity 101
   F. Valuing Common Stock 101
   G. Valuing Investments with Different Cash Flows at Different
      Times 103
   H. Net Present Value 104

3. The Cost of Capital --- 106
   A. The Price of Risk --- 106
   B. Measurement of Risk—Of Expected Values and Standard Deviations --- 111
   C. Risk and Diversification -- 116
   D. Pricing Risk in Markets—The Capital Assets Pricing Model ----- 118
   E. Levered Betas and the Cost of Capital for Leveraged Firms ------ 128
   F. Challenges to CAPM --- 129
4. Efficient Capital Markets --- 131
   A. The ECMH Model --- 131
     Signalling and Causation in Insider Trading ----------------------- 131
   B. Challenges to ECMH -- 135
     Inefficient Markets: An Introduction to Behavioral Finance (2000), 10–16 --- 135
     Are Markets Efficient?—No, Arbitrage Is Inherently Risky ------- 140
     Are Markets Efficient?—Yes, Even if They Make Errors ----------- 141
     Takeover Defense When Financial Markets Are (Only) Relatively Efficient --- 144
   C. ECMH in the Courts -- 152
     West v. Prudential Securities, Incorporated ----------------------- 152
     Measuring Securities Market Efficiency in the Regulatory Setting --- 156
     In re Time Warner Securities Litigation ------------------------- 159
5. Valuation in the Courts -- 172
   A. CAPM in the Courts --- 172
     Cede & Co. and Cinerama, Inc. v. Technicolor, Inc. ---------------- 172
     Piemonte v. New Boston Garden Corp. --------------------------- 184
   B. Minority Discounts, Control Premia and Leverage ---------------- 194
     Rapid–American Corporation v. Harris -------------------------- 198
     Appraising The Non–Existent: The Delaware Courts' Struggle With Control Premiums --- 204

CHAPTER FOUR Capital Structure ------------------------------------- 211

1. Introduction --- 211
2. The Range of Financial Choices -- 212
   Eliasen v. Itel Corporation --- 218
3. Modigliani & Miller's Irrelevance Hypothesis ------------------------- 226
4. The Real World --- 236
   A. Debt and Taxes --- 237
   B. Weighted Average Cost of Capital -------------------------------- 238
   C. Debt and Agency Costs --- 243
     "Theory of the Firm: Managerial Behavior, Agency Costs and Ownership Structure" --- 244
5. Capital Structure in the Courts -- 248
   New England Tel. and Tel. Co. v. Department of Public Utilities ----- 248
   Heckman v. Ahmanson --- 256
6. The Wages of Excessive Debt --- 262
   A. Subordination --- 262
     In re Fett Roofing and Sheet Metal Co., Inc., Bankrupt ---------- 263
   B. Fiduciary Duties to Creditors ------------------------------------- 270

Credit Lyonnais Bank Nederland, N.V. v. Pathe Communications Co. ---- 271
C. Creditor Liability ---- 279
Krivo Industrial Supply Company v. National Distillers and Chemical Corporation ---- 279
D. The Close Corporation and Disallowance of Interest Deductions ---- 290
Fin Hay Realty Co. v. United States ---- 290
E. Liability of Affiliated Parties under the "Deepening Insolvency" Doctrine ---- 296
Official Committee of Unsecured Creditors v. R. F. Lafferty & Co. ---- 297
Trenwick America Litigation Trust v. Ernst & Young, L.L.P. ---- 302
F. Structural Response to the Threat of Insolvency ---- 307

CHAPTER FIVE Common Stock ---- 309

1. Limited Liability of Stockholders ---- 309
Limited Liability ---- 309
2. The Problem of Dilution ---- 313
A. Preemptive Rights to Purchase a Portion of Any New Issue ---- 316
Stokes v. Continental Trust Company ---- 317
B. Equitable Doctrines Governing Dilutive Stock Issues ---- 323
Katzowitz v. Sidler et al. ---- 323
C. Dilution as a Takeover Defense—The Poison Pill ---- 328
The Illusory Protections of the Poison Pill ---- 328
Moran v. Household International, Inc. ---- 335
D. Creditor Protection: Legal Capital ---- 346
E. Public Securities Markets and Regulation ---- 351
   i. The Federal Securities Laws in a Nutshell ---- 351
   ii. The New Issues Market ---- 355
   iii. Trading Markets ---- 359
   Market Making in the Electronic Age ---- 359

CHAPTER SIX Corporate Debt ---- 364

1. Introduction ---- 364
Credit Report: Suddenly, Banks Are Acting a Lot Like Bond Markets ---- 365
2. Contract Interpretation ---- 371
Sharon Steel Corporation v. The Chase Manhattan Bank, N.A. ---- 372
3. Contract Terms ---- 382
On Financial Contracting: An Analysis of Bond Covenants ---- 382
A. Capital Structure: Restricting New Debt ---- 384
On Financial Contracting: An Analysis of Bond Covenants ---- 384
Metropolitan Life Insurance Company v. RJR Nabisco, Inc. ---- 389
B. Alteration of Risks ---- 409
On Financial Contracting: An Analysis of Bond Covenants ---- 409
C. Distributions ---- 415
On Financial Contracting: An Analysis of Bond Covenants ---- 415
D. Underinvestment—Asset Maintenance ---- 420

On Financial Contracting: An Analysis of Bond Covenants ------- 420

E.   Conversion Rights as Substitutes for Covenants ------------------ 423
      On Financial Contracting: An Analysis of Bond Covenants ------- 423

F.   Sinking Funds -- 424
      On Financial Contracting: An Analysis of Bond Covenants ------- 424
      Principles of Corporate Finance, 6th Ed. (2000) ------------------ 425

G.   Call Protection --- 426
      Morgan Stanley & Co., Incorporated v. Archer Daniels Midland
        Company -- 426

H.   Monitoring Compliance --- 433
      On Financial Contracting: An Analysis of Bond Covenants ------- 433

I.   Amendments --- 435
      On Financial Contracting: An Analysis of Bond Covenants ------- 435
      Katz v. Oak Industries, Inc. ----------------------------------- 437

J.   Enforcement of Covenant Breaches ------------------------------ 445
      Hedge Fund Activism in the Enforcement of Bondholder Rights 445

4.   The Indenture Trustee and the Trust Indenture Act ------------------ 448

A.   The Nature of the Trustee and its Duties ---------------------- 448
      On Financial Contracting: An Analysis of Bond Covenants ------- 448
      Elliott Associates v. J. Henry Schroder Bank & Trust Co. --------- 450

B.   The Trustee's Duties in Default -------------------------------- 458
      LNC Investments, Inc. v. First Fidelity Bank, National Associa-
        tion -- 461

5.   Capital Leasing -- 465

6.   Asset Backed Financing --- 467
      Appendix 6–A   Moody's Investor Services ------------------------ 472
      Standard & Poors: -- 473
      Appendix 6–B   Revised Model Simplified Indenture ------------- 474

CHAPTER   SEVEN   Preferred Stock ---------------------- 477

1.   Introduction --- 477
A.   Defining Preferred Stock ------------------------------------- 477
B.   The Uses of Preferred Stock ---------------------------------- 481

2.   Dividends --- 482
A.   The Varieties of Dividends ------------------------------------ 482
      Arizona Western Insurance Company v. L. L. Constantin & Co. 483
      L.L. Constantin & Co. v. R.P. Holding Corp. ------------------ 485
B.   Straight and Cumulative Dividends --------------------------- 489
      Guttmann v. Illinois Central R. Co. ---------------------------- 489
C.   Property Rights in Dividends ---------------------------------- 494
      Hay v. Hay -- 494
      Smith v. Nu–West Industries, Inc. ---------------------------- 503

3.   Altering the Preferred Contract ------------------------------------ 508
A.   Voting Rules and Voting Rights ------------------------------- 508
      Elliott Associates, L.P. v. Avatex Corporation ----------------- 510
B.   Dealing with the Class Veto Power ---------------------------- 521
      Schreiber v. Carney -- 522
      Orban v. Field --- 531

4.   Board Duties -- 538
A.   Board Duties to Preferred Shareholders ---------------------- 538

Mary G. Dalton v. American Investment Company 538
  B. Duties of a Preferred–Controlled Board 548
     Baron v. Allied Artists Pictures Corporation 548
     Burton v. Exxon Corporation 555
5. Share Redemptions and Repurchases 565
    Gradient OC Master, Ltd. v. NBC Universal, Inc. 566

CHAPTER EIGHT Options and Convertible Securities 583

1. Introduction 583
  A. The Uses of Options and Option Theory 583
  B. Real Options 586
  C. Long and Short Positions and Position Diagrams 587
2. How Options Operate 589
  A. Call Options 589
     i. Long Positions in Call Options 590
     ii. Short Positions in Call Options 592
  B. Put Options 593
  C. Combining Options, Stocks and Bonds; Put–Call Parity 595
  D. Uses of Options 599
     Brane v. Roth 599
     Who Says You Can't Make Money Off Stalled Stocks? More
       Investors Use Options, Trading Upside for Steady Gains 601
3. Valuation of Options 604
4. Disclosure Issues With Options 612
  Five Ways of Valuing Options Of these possible methods, only one
    results in reliable, tamperproof, financial results 613
5. Convertible Securities and Deal Protection 616
  A. Destruction of the Option 616
     John Parkinson v. West End Street Railway Company 616
     Simons v. Cogan 618
     Andaloro v. PFPC Worldwide, Inc. 627
  B. Dilution of Option Rights 631
     HB Korenvaes Investments, L.P. v. Marriott Corporation .. 633
     Stephenson v. Plastics Corporation of America, Inc. 653
     Wood v. Coastal States Gas Corporation 662
     Coffman v. Acton Corporation 671
     CL Investments, L.P. v. Advanced Radio Telecom Corp. 676
6. Last Period Financing: Death Spirals 687
  Internet Library, Inc. v. Southridge Capital Management LLC ... 689
  GFL Advantage Fund, Ltd. v. Colkitt 692

CHAPTER NINE Dividends and Distributions 707

1. Distributions and Investor Wealth 707
  A. Dividend Practices 707
     Distribution of Incomes of Corporations Among Dividends,
       Retained Earnings, and Taxes 707
     Disappearing Dividends: Changing Firm Characteristics or
       Lower Propensity to Pay? 711
  B. How Do Dividends Relate to Firm Value? 715

C. Explaining Dividend Practices ---------------------------------- 720
    i. Clientele Effects and Expectations -------------------------- 720
    ii. Transaction Costs of Selling Shares ------------------------- 721
    iii. Taxes -- 722
    iv. Imperfect Capital Markets and the Signaling Value of
        Dividends -- 725
D. Alternative Explanations of Dividends. --------------------------- 726
    Two Agency–Cost Explanations of Dividends --------------------- 726
2. Restrictions on Dividends and Other Distributions to Shareholders 733
   Klang v. Smith's Food & Drug Centers, Inc. --------------------- 739
   Hullender v. Acts II --- 747
   *Stock Repurchase Agreements in Bankruptcy: A Tale of State Law
   Rights Discarded* -- 748
3. Board Discretion and Duties in Declaring Dividends --------------- 753
   Caleb & Co. v. E. I. Dupont de Nemours & Company -------------- 753
   Berwald v. Mission Development Company ------------------------ 757
   Smith v. Atlantic Properties, Inc. ---------------------------- 764
4. Stock Dividends and Stock Splits -------------------------------- 768
   A. The Economics of Stock Dividends and Stock Splits ------------ 768
   B. Accounting for Dividends and Splits ------------------------- 769
   C. Reverse Stock Splits -- 776
      Applebaum v. Avaya -- 777
5. Stock Repurchases --- 788
   A. The Economics of Share Repurchases -------------------------- 788
   B. Legal Authority for Share Repurchases ----------------------- 790
   C. Regulation of Share Repurchases ----------------------------- 791
      i. Market Repurchases -- 791
         *Securities and Exchange Commission v. Georgia–Pacific
         Corporation* --- 792
      ii. Going Private Transactions ------------------------------- 795
          Howing Co. v. Nationwide Corporation ------------------- 796
      iii. Repurchases During Hostile Tender Offers ---------------- 803
          AC Acquisitions Corp. v. Anderson, Clayton & Co. ------- 804
      iv. Targeted Repurchases ------------------------------------- 811
          Grobow v. Perot -- 811
   D. Duties in Share Repurchases --------------------------------- 818
      Nixon v. Blackwell --- 818
6. Leveraged Buyouts --- 825
   United States of America v. Tabor Court Realty Corp. ---------- 826
   Matter of Munford, Inc., d.b.a. Majik Market, Debtor --------- 836
7. Spin–Offs and Tracking Stock ------------------------------------ 841
   A. Spin–Offs --- 841
   B. Tracking Stock -- 843

INDEX --- 845

TABLE OF CASES

Principal cases are in bold type. Non-principal cases are in roman type. References are to Pages.

AC Acquisitions Corp. v. Anderson, Clayton & Co., 519 A.2d 103 (Del.Ch. 1986), 582, **804**

Advanced Communication Design, Inc. v. Follett, 615 N.W.2d 285 (Minn.2000), 196

Agnew v. American Ice Co., 2 N.J. 291, 66 A.2d 330 (N.J.1949), 493

Amalgamated Sugar Co. v. NL Industries, Inc., 644 F.Supp. 1229 (S.D.N.Y.1986), 345

Andaloro v. PFPC Worldwide, Inc., 830 A.2d 1232 (Del.Ch.2003), **627**

APL Corp. v. Johnson Controls, Inc., 85 Civ. 990 (E.D.N.Y. 1985), 345

Applebaum v. Avaya, Inc., 812 A.2d 880 (Del.Supr.2002), **777**

Arizona Western Ins. Co. v. L. L. Constantin & Co., 247 F.2d 388 (3rd Cir. 1957), **483**

Asarco Inc. v. Court, 611 F.Supp. 468 (D.N.J. 1985), 346, 479

Atlantic States Const., Inc. v. Beavers, 169 Ga.App. 584, 314 S.E.2d 245 (Ga.App. 1984), 195

Balsamides v. Protameen Chemicals, Inc., 160 N.J. 352, 734 A.2d 721 (N.J.1999), 196

Bank Leumi–Le–Israel, B. M., Philadelphia Branch v. Sunbelt Industries, Inc., 485 F.Supp. 556 (S.D.Ga.1980), 271

Baron v. Allied Artists Pictures Corp., 395 A.2d 375 (Del.Ch.1978), 555

Baron v. Allied Artists Pictures Corp., 337 A.2d 653 (Del.Ch.1975), 545, **548**

Basic Inc. v. Levinson, 485 U.S. 224, 108 S.Ct. 978, 99 L.Ed.2d 194 (1988), 791

Bassett v. United States Cast Iron Pipe & Foundry Co., 70 A. 929 (N.J.Ch.1908), 493

Bell v. Kirby Lumber Corp., 413 A.2d 137 (Del.Supr.1980), 204

Berwald v. Mission Development Co., 40 Del.Ch. 509, 185 A.2d 480 (Del. Supr.1962), **757**

Blitch v. Peoples Bank, 246 Ga.App. 453, 540 S.E.2d 667 (Ga.App.2000), 196, 197

Bolt v. Merrimack Pharmaceuticals, Inc., 503 F.3d 913 (9th Cir.2007), **17**

Brane v. Roth, 590 N.E.2d 587 (Ind.App. 1 Dist.1992), **599**

Broad v. Rockwell Intern. Corp., 642 F.2d 929 (5th Cir.1981), 625

Burton v. Exxon Corp., 583 F.Supp. 405 (S.D.N.Y.1984), **555**

Caleb & Co. v. E.I. DuPont de Nemours & Co., 615 F.Supp. 96 (S.D.N.Y.1985), **753**

Cavalier Oil Corp. v. Harnett, 564 A.2d 1137 (Del.Supr.1989), 194

Cede & Co. v. Technicolor, Inc., 1990 WL 161084 (Del.Ch.1990), **172**

Chandler & Co., In re, 230 N.Y.S.2d 1012 (N.Y.Sup.1962), 501

Charland v. Country View Golf Club, Inc., 588 A.2d 609 (R.I.1991), 195

Chesapeake Corp. v. Shore, 771 A.2d 293 (Del.Ch.2000), 789

CitX Corp., Inc., In re, 448 F.3d 672 (3rd Cir.2006), 301

Clarkson Co. Ltd. v. Shaheen, 660 F.2d 506 (2nd Cir.1981), 271

CL Investments, L.P. v. Advanced Radio Telecom Corp., 2000 WL 1868096 (Del. Ch.2000), **676**

Cofman v. Acton Corp., 958 F.2d 494 (1st Cir.1992), **671**

Cole Real Estate Corp. v. Peoples Bank & Trust Co., 160 Ind.App. 88, 310 N.E.2d 275 (Ind.App. 3 Dist.1974), 763

Condec Corp. v. Lunkenheimer Co., 43 Del. Ch. 353, 230 A.2d 769 (Del.Ch.1967), 480

Consolidated Rock Products Co. v. Du Bois, 312 U.S. 510, 61 S.Ct. 675, 85 L.Ed. 982 (1941), 470

Cort v. Ash, 422 U.S. 66, 95 S.Ct. 2080, 45 L.Ed.2d 26 (1975), 456, 457, 464

Crane Co. v. Westinghouse Air Brake Co., 419 F.2d 787 (2nd Cir.1969), 705

Credit Lyonnais Bank Nederland, N.V. v. Pathe Communications Corp., 1991 WL 277613 (Del.Ch.1991), **271**

C–T of Virginia, Inc., In re, 958 F.2d 606 (4th Cir.1992), 840

Dabney v. Chase Nat. Bank of City of New York, 196 F.2d 668 (2nd Cir.1952), 456

Dalton v. American Inv. Co., 490 A.2d 574 (Del.Ch.1985), **538,** 546

Davis v. Woolf, 147 F.2d 629 (4th Cir.1945), 278

Dodge v. Ford Motor Co., 204 Mich. 459, 170 N.W. 668 (Mich.1919), 761, 763

Dynamics Corp. of America v. CTS Corp., 637 F.Supp. 406 (N.D.Ill.1986), 345

Eliasen v. Itel Corp., 82 F.3d 731 (7th Cir.1996), **218,** 477

Elliott Associates v. J. Henry Schroder Bank & Trust Co., 838 F.2d 66 (2nd Cir.1988), **450**

Elliott Associates, L.P. v. Avatex Corp., 715 A.2d 843 (Del.Supr.1998), **510**

English v. Artromick Intern., Inc., 2000 WL 1125637 (Ohio App. 10 Dist.2000), 195, 196

Evergreen Valley Resort, Inc., In re, 23 B.R. 659 (Bkrtcy.D.Me.1982), 471

Federal Power Commission v. Hope Natural Gas Co., 320 U.S. 591, 64 S.Ct. 281, 88 L.Ed. 333 (1944), 248

Federal United Corp. v. Havender, 24 Del.Ch. 318, 11 A.2d 331 (Del.Supr.1940), 510

Fett Roofing & Sheet Metal Co., Inc., In re, 438 F.Supp. 726 (E.D.Va.1977), **263**

Fin Hay Realty Co. v. United States, 398 F.2d 694 (3rd Cir.1968), **290**

FMC Corp. v. Boesky, 852 F.2d 981 (7th Cir.1988), 260

FMC Corp. v. Boesky, 673 F.Supp. 242 (N.D.Ill.1987), 261

Gabelli & Co., Inc. v. Liggett Group Inc., 479 A.2d 276 (Del.Supr.1984), 761

Gelco Corp. v. Coniston Partners, 652 F.Supp. 829 (D.Minn.1986), 345

General Securities Corp. v. Watson, 477 S.W.2d 461 (Ark. 1972), 195

GFL Advantage Fund, Ltd. v. Colkitt, 272 F.3d 189 (3rd Cir.2001), **692**

Glassman v. Unocal Exploration Corp., 777 A.2d 242 (Del.Supr.2001), 510, 795

Goldman v. Postal Telegraph, 52 F.Supp. 763 (D.Del.1943), 530

Gottfried v. Gottfried, 73 N.Y.S.2d 692 (N.Y.Sup.1947), 762

Grace Bros., Ltd. v. Farley Industries, Inc., 264 Ga. 817, 450 S.E.2d 814 (Ga.1994), 795

Gradient OC Master, Ltd. v. NBC Universal, Inc., 930 A.2d 104 (Del.Ch.2007), **566**

Graves' Estate, In re, 221 Ill.App. 279 (Ill. App. 1 Dist.1921), 530

Gray v. President, etc., of Portland Bank, 3 Mass. 364 (Mass.1807), 316

Grobow v. Perot, 539 A.2d 180 (Del. Supr.1988), **811**

Guttmann v. Illinois Cent. R. Co., 189 F.2d 927 (2nd Cir.1951), **489**

Hariton v. Arco Electronics, Inc., 41 Del.Ch. 74, 188 A.2d 123 (Del.Supr.1963), 840

Harvard Industries, Inc. v. Tyson, 1986 WL 36295 (E.D.Mich.1986), 345

Hay v. Hay, 38 Wash.2d 513, 230 P.2d 791 (Wash.1951), **494**

HB Korenvaes Investments, L.P. v. Marriott Corp., 1993 WL 257422 (Del.Ch. 1993), **633**

Heckmann v. Ahmanson, 168 Cal.App.3d 119, 214 Cal.Rptr. 177 (Cal.App. 2 Dist. 1985), **256**

Hogle v. Zinetics Med., Inc., 63 P.3d 80 (Ut. 2002), 195

Horwitz v. Southwest Forest Industries, Inc., 604 F.Supp. 1130 (D.Nev.1985), 345

Hospes v. Northwestern Mfg. & Car Co., 48 Minn. 174, 50 N.W. 1117 (Minn.1892), 347

Howing Co. v. Nationwide Corp., 826 F.2d 1470 (6th Cir.1987), **796**

Hullender v. Acts II, 153 Ga.App. 119, 264 S.E.2d 486 (Ga.App.1980), **747**

Hunter v. Mitek Industries, Inc., 721 F.Supp. 1102 (E.D.Mo.1989), 195

Hurricane Elkhorn Coal Corp. II, In re, 19 B.R. 609 (Bkrtcy.W.D.Ky.1982), 471

Independence Tube Corp. v. Levine, 179 Ill. App.3d 911, 129 Ill.Dec. 162, 535 N.E.2d 927 (Ill.App. 1 Dist.1988), 195

In re (see name of party)

Internet Law Library, Inc. v. Southridge Capital Management, LLC, 223 F.Supp.2d 474 (S.D.N.Y.2002), **689**

Jedwab v. MGM Grand Hotels, Inc., 509 A.2d 584 (Del.Ch.1986), 546

J. I. Case Co. v. Borak, 377 U.S. 426, 84 S.Ct. 1555, 12 L.Ed.2d 423 (1964), 456, 464

Kaplan v. First Hartford Corp., 603 F. Supp. 2d 195 (D. Me. 2009), 195

Katz v. Oak Industries Inc., 508 A.2d 873 (Del.Ch.1986), **437**

Katzowitz v. Sidler, 24 N.Y.2d 512, 301 N.Y.S.2d 470, 249 N.E.2d 359 (N.Y.1969), **323**

Keller v. Wilson & Co., 21 Del.Ch. 391, 190 A. 115 (Del.Supr.1936), 508

Klang v. Smith's Food & Drug Centers, Inc., 702 A.2d 150 (Del.Supr.1997), **739**

Krivo Indus. Supply Co. v. National Distillers & Chemical Corp., 483 F.2d 1098 (5th Cir.1973), **279**

Langfelder v. Universal Laboratories, 68 F.Supp. 209 (D.Del.1946), 510

LaSalle Talman Bank, F.S.B. v. United States, 1999 WL 791080 (Fed.Cl.1999), 232

Law Debenture Trust Co. of New York v. Petrohawk Energy Corp., 2007 WL 2248150 (Del.Ch.2007), 447

L. L. Constantin & Co. v. R. P. Holding Corp., 56 N.J.Super. 411, 153 A.2d 378 (N.J.Super.Ch.1959), **485**

L & M Realty Corp. v. Leo, 249 F.2d 668 (4th Cir.1957), 268

LNC Inv., Inc. v. First Fidelity Bank, Nat. Ass'n, 935 F.Supp. 1333 (S.D.N.Y. 1996), **461**

Lohnes v. Level 3 Communications, Inc., 272 F.3d 49 (1st Cir.2001), 671

MacFarlane v. North American Cement Corp., 16 Del.Ch. 172, 157 A. 396 (Del.Ch. 1928), 546

Major's Furniture Mart, Inc. v. Castle Credit Corp., Inc., 449 F.Supp. 538 (E.D.Pa. 1978), 471

Matter of (see name of party)

McCann Ranch, Inc. v. Quigley–McCann, 276 Mont. 205, 915 P.2d 239 (Mont.1996), 195

Merrill Lynch, Pierce, Fenner & Smith, Inc. v. Curran, 456 U.S. 353, 102 S.Ct. 1825, 72 L.Ed.2d 182 (1982), 458

Metropolitan Life Ins. Co. v. Aramark Corp., 1998 WL 34302067 (Del.Ch.1998), 788

Metropolitan Life Ins. Co. v. RJR Nabisco, Inc., 716 F.Supp. 1504 (S.D.N.Y. 1989), **389,** 493

Miller v. Magline, Inc., 76 Mich.App. 284, 256 N.W.2d 761 (Mich.App.1977), 762

Minstar Acquiring Corp. v. AMF Inc., 621 F.Supp. 1252 (S.D.N.Y.1985), 345

Mohawk Carpet Mills v. Delaware Rayon Co., 35 Del.Ch. 51, 110 A.2d 305 (Del.Ch. 1954), 502

Moore v. New Ammest, Inc., 6 Kan.App.2d 461, 630 P.2d 167 (Kan.App.1981), 195

Moran v. Household Intern., Inc., 500 A.2d 1346 (Del.Supr.1985), **335,** 479

Morgan Stanley & Co., Inc. v. Archer Daniels Midland Co., 570 F.Supp. 1529 (S.D.N.Y.1983), **426**

Morris v. Cantor, 390 F.Supp. 817 (S.D.N.Y. 1975), 457

MT Properties, Inc. v. CMC Real Estate Corp., 481 N.W.2d 383 (Minn.App.1992), 195

Munford, Inc., Matter of, 97 F.3d 456 (11th Cir.1996), **836**

New England Tel. & Tel. Co. v. Department of Public Utilities, 327 Mass. 81, 97 N.E.2d 509 (Mass.1951), **248**

New York Credit Men's Adjustment Bureau v. Weiss, 305 N.Y. 1, 110 N.E.2d 397 (N.Y.1953), 278

Nixon v. Blackwell, 626 A.2d 1366 (Del. Supr.1993), **818**

North American Catholic Educational Programming Foundation, Inc. v. Gheewalla, 930 A.2d 92 (Del.Supr.2007), 278

Oakwood Homes Corp., In re, 340 B.R. 510 (Bkrtcy.D.Del.2006), 302

Offenbecher v. Baron Servs., 874 So. 2d 532 (Ala. Civ. App. 2002), 195

Official Committee of Unsecured Creditors v. R.F. Lafferty & Co., Inc., 267 F.3d 340 (3rd Cir.2001), **297**

Orban v. Field, 1997 WL 153831 (Del.Ch. 1997), **531**

Parkinson v. West End St. Ry. Co., 173 Mass. 446, 53 N.E. 891 (Mass.1899), **616**

Perlman v. Permonite Mfg. Co., 568 F.Supp. 222 (N.D.Ind.1983), 195

Piemonte v. New Boston Garden Corp., 377 Mass. 719, 387 N.E.2d 1145 (Mass. 1979), **184**

Piper v. Chris–Craft Industries, Inc., 430 U.S. 1, 97 S.Ct. 926, 51 L.Ed.2d 124 (1977), 456

PPI Enterprises (United States), Inc. v. Del Monte Foods Co., 2000 WL 1425093 (S.D.N.Y.2000), 547

Pueblo Bancorporation v. Lindoe, Inc., 63 P.3d 353 (Colo. 2003), 195

Pure Resources, Inc., Shareholders Litigation, In re, 808 A.2d 421 (Del.Ch.2002), 510

Rapid–American Corp. v. Harris, 603 A.2d 796 (Del.Supr.1992), **198**

Rauch v. RCA Corp., 861 F.2d 29 (2nd Cir. 1988), 521

Raytech Corp. v. White, 54 F.3d 187 (3rd Cir.1995), 842

R.D. Smith & Co., Inc. v. Preway Inc., 644 F.Supp. 868 (W.D.Wis.1986), 345

Reiss v. Financial Performance Corp., 97 N.Y.2d 195, 738 N.Y.S.2d 658, 764 N.E.2d 958 (N.Y.2001), 675

Rothschild Intern. Corp. v. Liggett Group Inc., 474 A.2d 133 (Del.Supr.1984), 521

Sanders v. Cuba R. Co., 21 N.J. 78, 120 A.2d 849 (N.J.1956), 493

Sanders v. Wang, 1999 WL 1044880 (Del.Ch. 1999), 675

Santa Fe Industries, Inc. v. Green, 430 U.S. 462, 97 S.Ct. 1292, 51 L.Ed.2d 480 (1977), 355

Schreiber v. Carney, 447 A.2d 17 (Del.Ch. 1982), **522**

Sharon Steel Corp. v. Chase Manhattan Bank, N.A., 691 F.2d 1039 (2nd Cir. 1982), **372,** 675

Shear v. Gabovitch, 43 Mass.App.Ct. 650, 685 N.E.2d 1168 (Mass.App.Ct.1997), 195

Siliconix Inc. Shareholders Litigation, In re, 2001 WL 716787 (Del.Ch.2001), 795

Simons v. Cogan, 542 A.2d 785 (Del.Ch. 1987), **618**

Sinclair Oil Corp. v. Levien, 280 A.2d 717 (Del.Supr.1971), 762

Smith v. Atlantic Properties, Inc., 12 Mass.App.Ct. 201, 422 N.E.2d 798 (Mass. App.Ct.1981), **764**

Smith v. Nu–West Industries, Inc., 2000 WL 1641248 (Del.Ch.2000), **503**

Software Toolworks Inc., In re, 50 F.3d 615 (9th Cir.1994), **30**

Solomon v. Pathe Communications Corp., 672 A.2d 35 (Del.Supr.1996), 510

Squires v. Balbach Co., 177 Neb. 465, 129 N.W.2d 462 (Neb.1964), 502

Stahl v. Apple Bancorp, Inc., 1990 WL 114222 (Del.Ch.1990), 345

Stephenson v. Plastics Corp. of America, 276 Minn. 400, 150 N.W.2d 668 (Minn. 1967), **653**

Stokes v. Continental Trust Co. of City of New York, 186 N.Y. 285, 78 N.E. 1090 (N.Y.1906), **317**

Tabor Court Realty Corp., United States v., 803 F.2d 1288 (3rd Cir.1986), **826**

Taylor v. Standard Gas & Elec. Co., 306 U.S. 307, 306 U.S. 618, 59 S.Ct. 543, 83 L.Ed. 669 (1939), 269

Telvest, Inc. v. Olson, 1979 WL 1759 (Del.Ch. 1979), 226, 478

Time Warner Securities Litigation, In re 9 F.3d 259 (2d Cir.1993) 511 U.S. 1017 (1994), 159

Touche Ross & Co. v. Redington, 442 U.S. 560, 99 S.Ct. 2479, 61 L.Ed.2d 82 (1979), 457, 464

Transamerica Mortg. Advisors, Inc. (TAMA) v. Lewis, 444 U.S. 11, 100 S.Ct. 242, 62 L.Ed.2d 146 (1979), 458

Trenwick America Litigation Trust v. Ernst & Young, L.L.P., 906 A.2d 168 (Del.Ch.2006), **302**

Trevor v. Whitworth, 1887 WL 10910 (HL 1887), 790

Tri–Continental Corp. v. Battye, 31 Del.Ch. 523, 74 A.2d 71 (Del.Supr.1950), 197, 203

United States v. ____(see opposing party)

Unocal Corp. v. Mesa Petroleum Co., 493 A.2d 946 (Del.Supr.1985), 345

Valuation of Common Stock of McLoon Oil Co., In re, 565 A.2d 997 (Me.1989), 195

Weinberger v. UOP, Inc., 457 A.2d 701 (Del. Supr.1983), 184, 192, 795

West v. Prudential Securities, Inc., 282 F.3d 935 (7th Cir.2002), **152,** 791

West Point–Pepperell, Inc. v. Farley Inc., 711 F.Supp. 1088 (N.D.Ga.1988), 346

White v. Perkins, 213 Va. 129, 189 S.E.2d 315 (Va.1972), 762

Winston v. Mandor, 710 A.2d 835 (Del.Ch. 1997), 546

Wood v. Coastal States Gas Corp., 401 A.2d 932 (Del.Supr.1979), **662**

Woodward v. Quigley, 257 Iowa 1077, 133 N.W.2d 38 (Iowa 1965), 195

Wouk v. Merin, 283 A.D. 522, 128 N.Y.S.2d 727 (N.Y.A.D. 1 Dept.1954), 501

CORPORATE FINANCE:

PRINCIPLES AND PRACTICE

CHAPTER ONE

INTRODUCTION

Few law school casebooks must "defend" or "sell" their subject's importance and relevance. Corporate Finance may be different. After all, this subject is taught in business schools, isn't it? And most law students came to law school because of a facility with words and perhaps a distaste for numbers. So why not leave finance to the MBAs? One answer might be that the subject is too important to leave to the MBAs. They may not always be around when you need them. Another reason is that successful business lawyers have to be able to understand their clients' (and prospective clients') businesses, so they can discuss how legal services can help them structure transactions to add value. The "rainmaker" in a law firm is generally a lawyer with a broad understanding of business as well as legal problems, who can relate to the clients' full range of concerns, and integrate that knowledge into the provision of legal services.

Corporate finance is about measuring, creating and protecting value. Lawyers engaged in a variety of practices might find these subjects useful. For example, if you are a personal injury lawyer and an insurance company offers your client either a lump sum settlement or a structured settlement, payable over time, how can you compare them, to ascertain that you're getting the best deal for your client? And can you explain to your client why one is better than the other, or the way in which your client should compare them? If you represent a party to a divorce, and the other party has a pension that will start paying in five years, how can you measure its value for purposes of a lump sum settlement? Suppose the other side offers a lump sum payment to be made in five years? What is it worth today, for purposes of settlement calculations?

Now suppose you represent a small business that has sought financing from a venture capitalist. The venture capitalist is prepared to invest a large sum of money in your client's business at a stated dividend rate on preferred stock. So far you know and understand the cost of obtaining this capital, right? But now suppose the venture capitalist also wants the right to convert the preferred stock into shares of common stock in your client over the next five years at a stated conversion price. Does this add to the cost? How much? And how can you begin to think about this issue with your client? If you want to represent your client effectively, you should at least know what questions to raise, and how to think about these issues.

This is all aside from the more conventional ways of thinking about corporate finance—about advising clients in the context of raising capital in public stock markets or by issuing corporate bonds. While the lawyer's job is generally thought of as writing the documents to implement plans put together by the client and its financial advisers, the lawyer who understands the underlying financial issues will be far better equipped to participate in these activities. With the passage of the Sarbanes–Oxley Act in 2002, which requires companies to maintain and assess internal financial controls, many directors are now learning more about accounting and finance. Having lawyers who also understand these areas will become even more important than it was in the past. Having a firm grounding in understanding what people value in financial transactions, and how value can be created, is essential to a successful practice. When we speak of the "stockholder-bondholder conflict," for example, we are speaking to the heart of drafting both bank loan agreements and bonds and debentures. Disclosures of the cost of employee stock options require some understanding of how to value them. You may even be surprised to learn that in some cases your understanding of finance will exceed that of some corporate executives.

Chapter Two introduces financial statements, assuming that the student has not had a previous accounting course. It will necessarily be an abbreviated introduction, but the object is not to produce accountants, but rather lawyers whose eyes do not glaze over when presented with financial statements. Understanding financial statements is critical, because they inform us about a company in a most basic way—what it owns, what it owes and what it earns (or loses), and how the shareholders are doing. The output of accounting is information that we need in order to be able to say something about the value of a business, the next subject of the book. In short, you can't think about value without having the numbers needed to calculate value. The focus of this chapter is on understanding the basic financial statements. Chapter Three covers the basics of valuation. This is perhaps the most financially-oriented chapter in the book, because it lies at the heart of the subject. We use cases only to examine how these techniques operate in the courts, not for any financial wisdom they might impart. This book will employ a certain amount of algebra, which is essential in the expression of some finance concepts. Nothing more than high school algebra is required. Thus far the book concentrates on basic theories about financial information and financial valuation that could appear in any corporate finance book, whether used in a business school or a law school. This is the prologue to the material that integrates legal doctrine with finance, in Parts III and IV.

In Parts III and IV we move into the value maximization inquiry, and the role that lawyers play. Part III examines capital structure, which includes the different kinds of financings firms can employ. It examines debt instruments in light of the stockholder-bondholder conflict, and the peculiar nature of preferred stock, so widely employed in venture capital financings. Convertible debt and options are also examined, in the light of both valuation models and the contractual doctrines we have previously seen. Having raised capital, Part IV examines how firms can distribute earnings, and what impact this may have on value.

This book differs from other law school corporate finance casebooks by putting first things first—an understanding of financial principles before proceeding to the legal doctrines involved. Second, it differs from other corporate finance casebooks in its emphasis on drafting and documentation. Having an understanding of how widely used forms respond to particular finance problems, as well as to the framework of legal doctrine, is one of the primary goals of this book. Finally, much in the style of business school texts, many of the chapters will contain questions and problems to test your understanding of the material.

This book is written in the aftermath of one of the great financial crises of history—the collapse of the subprime mortgage market and the bonds built on those mortgages. This led in turn to the collapse of several major investment banks, and the near-collapse and bailout of major commercial banks. None of that appears in this book, other than a brief section at the end of Chapter Six on asset backed financing. While it is an intensely interesting period of our history, it has little effect on the principles presented in this book.

CHAPTER TWO

MEASURING FIRM OUTPUT

1. INTRODUCTION

"Accounting is ... concerned with determining the value of assets and measuring income, but not in an economic sense. Accounting's primary role is recording and accounting for the receipt and disbursement of a limited (though very important) set of money-denominated assets. Primarily, accounting is designed to establish responsibility for these assets to reduce their theft and misuse, to provide records that help management determine the extent to which operations are conducted as expected, and to provide the records required by tax bureaus, regulatory agencies and other legal and quasi-legal authorities."

George H. Benston, Accounting Numbers and Economic Values, 27 Antitrust Bulletin 161, 165 (1982).

Businesses, which are an assemblage of human, tangible and intangible assets, require a way of expressing how well they function. This is necessary for a variety of reasons. First, from an organizational theory perspective, the agents who run the business must account to the owners of the business. Beyond this, there are a variety of other reasons why reporting is important. Taxes must be paid on income, and on payrolls; in some cases, regulation, whether rate regulation for some utilities or for landlords subject to rent control, may require accurate reports of the costs of providing goods or services; trustees must allocate between income and principal in some cases; buyers of businesses will require accurate accounting records of how profitable a business has been and of what it owns. Lenders may require compliance with certain minimum financial standards to assure the safety of their loans (covered in Chapter Six). Internally, accounting records provide managers with information about costs, inventories and sales that allow them to make more informed decisions about operating the business. Where managers are compensated on the basis of the profits the business produces, these profits must be accurately measured. The internal use of accounting is often described as managerial accounting, a subject we will not examine here. We are concerned with financial accounting, which produces reports that inform outsiders, such as investors and (prospective) creditors, about the condition of a business. In that sense, it is the foundation for the valuation material which follows in Chapter Three.

Accounting is the language of business, and of much financial analysis. For non-accountants, financial documents can appear to be written in a code. Too often in the practice of business law lawyers are unwilling or unable to engage in a close reading of financial statements that will give them a deeper understanding of their clients' business. In some cases a lack of such understanding can lead a lawyer drafting documents into serious errors that may prove harmful to clients. One writer claims that "The lawyer with the best book of clients is often the one who not only has strong technical legal skills, but also knows enough about business and finance to give clients confidence that their lawyer understands their circumstances and interests."* In this chapter we hope to introduce the student to a basic familiarity with financial statements, and to provide a beginning for further learning as one's career in the practice of business law (or business litigation) progresses.

If financial statements are to communicate clearly to a wide variety of users, a certain amount of standardization is necessary. This is complicated by the fact that a single method of accounting for all businesses may not provide the most useful information for some types of businesses. As a result, the accounting profession has provided sets of general principles (standards, rather than rules) that in some cases allow several approaches to accounting for transactions. In Statement of Financial Accounting Standards No. 2, the *Financial Accounting Standards Board* ("FASB") stated that "the better choice is one that, subject to considerations of cost, produces from among the available alternatives information that is most useful for decision making." Where this kind of variance is allowed, it becomes critical for the financial reports to reveal the choices made.

The general principles that govern accounting have been generated by a series of organizations over time. While the Securities and Exchange Commission has authority to establish accounting standards for use in reports filed with the SEC (under § 13 (b)(1)), it has exercised its authority with relative restraint, leaving development of standards to the profession. Regulation SX states requirements about the form and content of filings, and the SEC periodically provides policy statements in its Accounting Series Releases ("ASRs"), but to a large extent these reflect standards developed by the profession. Collectively, these standards are referred to as *Generally Accepted Accounting Principles* ("GAAP").**

The principal professional organization for accountants is the *American Institute of Certified Public Accountants* ("AICPA"). From 1939 to 1959 its Committee on Accounting Procedure issued Accounting Research Bulletins addressing specific problems. It was replaced by the *Accounting Principles Board* ("APB"), whose members were elected by the AICPA, which issued 31 opinions that were considered official and became part of GAAP.

---

* Robert B. Dickie, FINANCIAL STATEMENT ANALYSIS AND BUSINESS VALUATION FOR THE PRACTICAL LAWYER, xi (Chicago: American Bar Association, Section of Business Law, 1998).

** There is an effort to adopt *International Accounting Standards* ("IAS" also known as *International Financial Reporting Standards* ("IFRS")) that will be universally accepted in all financial markets. IFRS is currently in use in Europe, but it has not yet been accepted by the SEC, although on November 14, 2008, the SEC announced a "road map" for adoption of IFRS for use by U.S. issuers under its jurisdiction. If accepted, it would permit an issuer whose industry uses IFRS as the basis of financial reporting more than any other set of standards would be eligible to elect to use IFRS, beginning with filings in 2010. If milestones in the road map are met, it would require all U.S. issuers filing with the SEC to use IFRS by 2014.

Because of criticism of its lack of independence from AICPA, it was replaced in 1973 by Financial Accounting Standards Board ("FASB"), with representatives of the accounting profession, business, education and government. The accountants on this full-time board were required to sever their relations with their firms, and FASB was supported by a full-time research staff. FASB issues *Statements of Financial Accounting Standards* ("SFAS"). In 2002, in reaction to disclosures of a series of financial and accounting frauds at major corporations and charges that accountants had failed to discover and reveal these frauds, Congress passed the Sarbanes–Oxley Act, 107 P.L. 204, 116 Stat. 745, which created a new Public Company Accounting Oversight Board ("PCAOB") to govern the profession. The primary effect on accounting will be regulation of audits and auditing firms, leaving the development of GAAP to FASB.

The SEC has adopted its own accounting rules in Regulation S–X, 17 C.F.R. § 210.1–01 et seq. These rules focus primarily on the format of accounting statements for reports filed with the SEC.

In all cases, accounting entries are made when there is an "event," which generally means a "transaction" with a third party.

> "In accounting ... assets and liabilities generally are recorded when there is an arm's length, market transaction that is denominated in money terms. Cash receipts and disbursements are the principal transactions that give rise to accounting entries, since control over cash is particularly important and the amounts to record can be readily and objectively established. Where there is a change in legal title to goods or the establishment of a legal obligation to pay in the future (such as the receipt of inventory and the creation of an account receivable or the signing of a note payable), accounting entries are made."

George H. Benston, Accounting Numbers and Economic Values, 27 Antitrust Bulletin 161, 166 (1982).

There are a few basic principles that underlie all accounting that should be mentioned, at least briefly. First, assets are reported on a company's books at their historical cost and, with only minor exceptions, not at higher market values. This is called the *cost principle.* From it you can see that accounting is historical in its approach, recording prices at which value is exchanged in transactions. Accounting reports should be *reliable.* This means that they should be reasonably free from error, complete and verifiable. For public companies, this principle was reinforced by provisions of § 302 of the Sarbanes–Oxley Act, which requires *Chief Executive Officers* ("CEOs") and *Chief Financial Officers* ("CFOs") to certify the accuracy of corporate financial statements, and that the corporation has sufficient internal controls to assure accuracy. This principle is modified by the principle that accounting reports should be *cost effective,* and need only report *material* information—that is, information of a magnitude that it might influence a decision. As the General Counsel of a large corporation once remarked to the author, "we don't count pencils." Hence, many large companies will round numbers in their reports. Perhaps more importantly, even the auditor's opinion letter is not an absolute assurance of accuracy. Auditing involves sampling techniques to test the accuracy of financial statements, designed to provide "reasonable assurance" that the statements fairly present the firm's financial condition and results of operations.

Reports must be made for an *economic entity,* which means the entire enterprise. Typically this means that reports for a corporation and its subsidiaries are *consolidated* into a single report. In recent financial scandals such as Enron, controversy surrounded the use of "special purpose entities," that were allegedly separate from the main business, and allowed concealment of losses.

Sidebar: Consolidated Returns

Where a corporation owns 50% or more of the voting power of another corporation, it is deemed to have the power to control its affairs. Because of this control, while each separate corporation will prepare its own financial statements, the parent will prepare consolidated financial statements combining both entities. Where there are transactions between parent and subsidiary, these transactions are eliminated for consolidated reporting purposes. Thus sales of goods by the parent to the subsidiary are no longer treated as sales, since they are within the combined entity. Similarly, the parent's stock ownership in the subsidiary isn't an asset in the combined entity. Where an outside owns a minority interest in the subsidiary, that will not be eliminated, but will appear in the owners' equity part of the balance sheet as a separate entry for the "minority interest."

Where a corporation (now called the *investor*) owns less than 50% but more than 20% of the voting stock of another corporation (now called the *investee*), the returns are not consolidated. Instead, the parent uses the *Equity Method* of accounting, and enters its original investment in the subsidiary as an investment. Thereafter, the original investment is adjusted annually to reflect changes in the shareholders' equity of the investee. When dividends are paid on the investee's shares, the investor treats this as converting a part of the investment into cash.

If a corporation owns less than 20% of another's voting stock, it is carried on the balance sheet either as *Trading Securities*, if held with an intent to sell in the near term, or *Available-for-Sale Securities*, if held for another reason. Available-for-sale securities are recorded on the balance sheet at their *fair value*, which is their present market value. The portion of present market value that represents unrealized gains or losses is recorded as a net amount in a separate entry on the equity portion of the balance sheet until realized, rather than being recognized as current income or loss.

Financial reports are for *accounting periods,* which are typically yearly, and frequently quarterly or even monthly. (The SEC requires annual reports on Form 10–K and quarterly income statements on Form 10–Q.) Many corporations report on a calendar year basis, but others select a fiscal year ending on some other date, typically one that ends immediately after a busy period. Within each accounting period, all expenses incurred to generate reported income for the period must be *matched.* Corporations are required to use the accrual method of accounting. (Some partnerships, such as law firms, will use the cash method of accounting, in which revenues are only recognized when received.) Under the accrual method, the accountant attempts to allocate income to the period when earned, regardless of the time of receipt, and expenses to the period when incurred, regardless of the time of payment. Revenue is recognized when all of the activities associated with earning the revenue have been performed, such as delivery of goods or services. As a business continues across accounting periods, this method becomes more important if the firm has long-term projects that spread over several periods. The accrual method of accounting requires judgments to be made about when income should be recognized as earned, and when to recognize expenses as incurred. These judgments normally should be transparent; that is, the methods used for recognition should be described in accounting statements.* The failure to make these judgments transparent can lead to confusion on the part of readers of financial statements, and, in some cases, to charges of fraud. In some recent cases involving telecommunication firms, charges have been made that these firms engaged in "swaps" of capacity, in which the firm would recognize revenue from the "sale" of capacity in the current period and defer recognition of the costs of buying capacity until later periods.

Firms should report results on a *consistent* basis from one period to the next, and should prefer methods that will be *comparable* to those of other firms in the industry, thus facilitating comparisons. This is critical to

---

* In the next section we will examine the financial statements of Scientific–Atlanta, Inc. Footnote 1 to its financial statements is titled "Summary of Significant Accounting Policies," and, in accordance with accounting conventions, explains such matters as the treatment of revenue and expense recognition. It states in part:

"Revenue Recognition

"Scientific–Atlanta's revenue recognition policies are in compliance with Staff Accounting Bulletin No. 101 'Revenue Recognition in Financial Statements' issued by the Securities and Exchange Commission. Revenue is recognized at the time product is shipped or title passes pursuant to the terms of the agreement with the customer which include a standard right of return, the amount due from the customer is fixed and collectibility of the related receivable is reasonably assured. Revenue is recognized only when we have no significant future performance obligation. Our right of return policy, which is standard for virtually all sales, allows a customer the right to return product for refund only if the product does not conform to product specifications; the non-conforming product is identified by the customer; and the customer rejects the non-conforming product and notifies us within ten days of receipt.

"Revenues from progress-billed contracts are primarily recorded using the percentage-of-completion method based on contract costs incurred to date. Losses, if any, are recorded when determinable. Costs incurred and accrued profits not billed on these contracts are included in receivables. * * *"

analysts and investors, in determining how a company performed relative to others in the same industry.

All reports are on a *monetary* basis, which, in the U.S., means in dollars. U.S. companies with world-wide operations must convert their foreign currency transactions into dollars for purposes of financial statements.* These financial reports assume the entity is a *going concern,* that will continue to operate for the indefinite future. Transactions must be reported on a *conservative* basis; that is, if two methods of reporting a transaction are reasonable, accountants should use the more conservative one, that may understate rather than overstate profits, because understatement is likely to do less harm. For example, items held for sale, whether inventory or securities, must be valued generally at the lower of cost or market value.

Quick Check Question 2.1

Your client informs you that he has just bought a $100,000 dog. You ask him how and what he paid for it. He responds that he exchanged his two $50,000 cats for it. How should he book the transaction, if it is part of a business (perhaps dog-breeding)? What accounting principles are applicable?

One text makes the point that accounting is an art, not a science. While lawyers may think of GAAP as a single set of rules that must be followed, it is perhaps better to think of it as a set of standards that leave considerable discretion for management and its accountants to choose the method of reporting some transactions. Don't be shy when you find an entry that doesn't make sense to you. There are two possible approaches: first, read management's discussion and analysis (and footnote 1 to the financial statements) for an explanation of the treatment chosen; second, ask the accountants for their authority to use the treatment chosen, and if they believe it fairly presents the financial picture of the firm. When drawing contracts that depend on accounting numbers, ask the accountants what elections might disappoint your client.

The fact that accounting leaves discretion about how to report transactions raises one important issue: agency costs (discussed in Chapter Four, *infra*). While shareholders might prefer accounting choices that minimize taxes, managers often prefer choices that maximize stated net income, even if that also maximizes income taxes. Too many managers believe that investors focus on stated earnings per share, to the exclusion of the cash generated by the enterprise for the ultimate benefit of shareholders.

---

* Converting foreign currency transactions to dollars can cause profits to vary widely based in shifting currency rates. Thus, foreign profits as reported in the foreign currencies could remain stable, but result in either gains or losses when converted to dollars.

2.   FORMS OF FINANCIAL REPORTS

The Revised Model Business Corporation Act § 16.20(a) provides a legal introduction to financial reports:

> (a) A corporation shall furnish its shareholders annual financial statements, which may be consolidated or combined statements of the corporation and one or more of its subsidiaries, as appropriate, that include a balance sheet as of the end of the fiscal year, an income statement for that year, and a statement of changes in shareholders' equity for the year unless that information appears elsewhere in the financial statements. If financial statements are prepared for the corporation on the basis of generally accepted accounting principles, the annual financial statements must also be prepared on that basis.

Publicly traded companies are governed by the periodic reporting requirements of § 13 of the Securities Exchange Act. The central reporting requirement under that Act is Form 10–K, the annual report that must be filed with the SEC, the essence of which must be delivered to shareholders. Item 8 of Form 10–K requires financial statements meeting the requirements of Regulation S–X, 17 C.F.R. § 210.1 et seq., the SEC's accounting regulation. Rules 3.01, 3.02, 3.04 of Regulation S–X require filings to include balance sheets for the two most recent fiscal years, audited statements of income and cash flows for the three most recent fiscal years, and a statement of changes in stockholders' equity in periods between income statements required to be presented. Public companies' web sites frequently contain their financial statements. Many also link to the SEC's site that contains the financial reports of all companies filing reports with the SEC. These documents are filed electronically, on the SEC's Electronic Data Gathering and Retrieval ("EDGAR") system. You can locate it at: http:// www.sec.gov/edgar/searchedgar/webusers.htm.

You can also locate these filings on most companies' web pages under "investor information" or "SEC reports."

These requirements cover the four basic financial accounting reports: (1) the balance sheet; (2) the income statement; (3) the cash flow statement and (4) the statement of changes in stockholders' equity. We discuss each of these statements below.

A.   THE BALANCE SHEET

The balance sheet is typically the first statement described in texts on accounting, probably because it sets out the fundamental accounting equation:

$$Assets = Liabilities + Equity$$

This is another way of saying that all of the assets of a business are claimed by someone; when a business is dissolved, either creditors or "owners," whether proprietors, partners, members of a limited liability company ("LLC"), or stockholders, will receive a distribution of the remaining assets. A balance sheet reflects the firm's ownership of assets, and the claims against them, on a stated date. Typically firms create balance sheets at least annually, at the close of a fiscal year. (In some cases firms will choose a fiscal year ending on a date other than Dec. 31, because closing the books and taking inventory in the middle of a busy season may not be practicable.) In many cases balance sheets are presented in a format resembling a "T," which is the shape given to accounts in bookkeeping practice, as we will see, although in other cases the presentation is sequential. In all cases, the fundamental equation will hold, so that total assets are equaled by total claims on assets, of creditors and owners. Thus:

Balance Sheet
John Lawyer
December 31, 2004

Assets		Liabilities	
Current Assets	xx	Current Liabilities	xx
Long–Term Assets	xx	Long–Term Liabilities	xx
		Owners' Equity	xx
Total Assets	xxx	Total Liabilities & Equity	xxx

i. ASSETS

Until recently the question of what constituted "assets" raised few questions for most lawyers. Assets are the things owned by a business. A more careful specification might say it only includes probable future economic benefits owned or controlled by the business, that are obtained in a "transaction" to which accountants can attach a price. The recent Enron debacle involved the use of "special purpose entities" ("SPEs") or "special purpose vehicles" with which Enron engaged in purported transactions. A company that does business with an SPE may treat the SPE as if it were an independent, outside entity for accounting purposes if (1) an owner independent of the company makes a substantive equity investment of at least 3% of the value of the SPE's assets, (2) keeps that 3% at risk throughout the transaction, and (3) the independent owner exercises control of the SPE. If these conditions were not met, then Enron "owned" the assets of the SPE, and, correspondingly, was responsible for the liabilities of the SPE for accounting purposes.

Once an asset is recorded on the books of the company, generally no adjustments are made for future changes in market value (except, as noted in the sidebar, for securities in some cases). Thus, if a business had purchased land on Michigan Avenue immediately after the Chicago fire, or on Peachtree Street immediately after Sherman burned Atlanta, and continued to hold it, the land would be shown on the books at its original cost. There are two important exceptions to this rule: inventory should be recorded at the lower of cost or market. Marketable securities held for sale are reported at fair market value. Another important exception involves goodwill, but we will reserve discussion of this issue.

Assets are generally classified as either current or non-current. Current assets are those assets that either are cash or its equivalent, or are expected to be converted into cash within a year (the next accounting cycle) as a result of operations. Assets generally are listed on the balance sheet in order of liquidity, which means cash and equivalents (marketable securities) come first, followed by accounts receivable, inventory, and those prepaid expenses that are expected to be used within the year. (Prepaid expenses are treated as assets because they are a claim on someone else's assets, such as coverage by an insurance company, pre-paid rent, etc.) Non-current assets are all those assets not expected to be converted into cash within a year. Notwithstanding their relative lack of liquidity, they, too, are listed in order of liquidity, with long-term investments followed by equipment, buildings, and land, as a general ordering.

On the balance sheet of Scientific–Atlanta that follows, you will see an entry for "receivables," also known as "accounts receivable." This represents obligations of buyers of goods and services from the company for the goods the company has sold. Normally these amounts are due on a short cycle, perhaps thirty days or less. You will also note a deduction (allowance) for doubtful accounts, representing the company's best estimate of the amount of its receivables it will be unable to collect, generally based on past experience. The default rate on accounts receivable can vary considerably with the economy, and in some businesses estimating it is critically important. For example, if a bank concentrates on credit cards, the default rate on credit card debt can vary considerably over an economic cycle, and have a major effect on profits. In some cases this requires adjustments from experienced-based default rates to estimate the current risk of defaults.

ii. LIABILITIES

Liabilities can be defined as obligations to provide economic benefits to a third party in the future. This includes the obvious debts, such as accounts payable, promissory notes and long-term bonds. Typically liabilities involve obligations to pay money, but they may include a variety of other obligations as well. For example, in order to finance production, a manufacturer may sell inventory to a third party for current cash payments, with an agreement to repurchase the inventory in the future (an unconditional purchase obligation). Accounting treats this as essentially creation of a debt (which, incidentally, is secured by the inventory). A lawyer may accept a retainer in exchange for an agreement to perform specific legal services in the future. This is a legal obligation, and creates a liability in the same way. This is sometimes called "deferred revenue" or "unearned revenue." Other liabilities might include product warranty claims, product liability claims, and environmental clean-up obligations. In all cases, these obligations must be the result of a transaction-such as a court judgment in some cases. If uncertainty surrounds a liability, it may in some cases be treated as a contingent liability, and disclosed in the notes to the financial statements rather than as a balance sheet liability. Some leases are really disguised credit purchases of assets; this occurs when the lease is for most of the useful life of the asset, the lessee can purchase the asset at a bargain or nominal price at the end of the lease, and the present value of the lease payments equals 90% or more of the leased property's fair value. These are called "capital leases." The leased property is treated as a business asset and the lease payment obligations are shown as liabilities on the balance sheet.

As on the asset side, liabilities are classified as current or non-current, divided by whether they are payable within the current 12–month accounting cycle. Corporate bonds may represent both kinds of liabilities—the portion due and payable within the current accounting cycle will be listed as current, with the remainder being classified as long-term. Once again, liabilities in each category are listed in terms of their currency—that is, accounts payable, usually payable within 10–30 days after being incurred, are listed first, while taxes that may be payable later in the current accounting cycle are listed near the end of the list of current liabilities, along with the current portion of long-term debt. Because all liabilities are prior claims to those of stockholders in insolvency or bankruptcy, they are listed before equity.

iii. STOCKHOLDERS' EQUITY

This is the ownership interest of the stockholders, the final element in the balance sheet equation. (If this were another form of business, we might call it owners' equity or partners' equity.) The assets minus the liabilities produce the stockholders' portion of the balance sheet. In a corporation with preferred stock, the preferred stock will be listed first. Typically preferred stock will be listed at its par or nominal value, which generally corresponds closely to the amount actually received by the corporation for it, and generally to its liquidation value.* (There may be some adjustments to this, but we will not go into them here.) The common stock will be listed next. Again, the basic listing for the common stock will be for that portion of the sale price of the common represented by its par or nominal value or, in the case of no-par stock, that portion of the purchase price assigned to "capital" or "stated capital" or "paid-in capital." If shares were sold for more than their par or nominal value, or, in the case of no-par shares, for more than the amount assigned to capital, the balance will be assigned to "additional paid-in capital."**

The capital accounts will not remain static through the years. Because the common stockholders are the residual claimants after all creditors and

---

* This may not be the case in venture capital-financed firms, where holders of preferred stock may have the right to require the issuer to redeem a class or series of preferred stock at some premium or multiple of the par value under certain circumstances. See, e.g., Bolt v. Merrimack Pharmaceuticals, Inc. *infra* following the Scientific–Atlanta balance sheet (a redemption requirement, without any indication in the opinion about the relationship between par value and the redemption price).

** Older versions of the Model Business Corporation Act would call this "capital surplus."

preferred stockholders are paid, the value of their claims will fluctuate. If the corporation earns a profit and no dividends are paid, the common stockholders' claims will increase by the amount of that profit. This amount will be assigned to "retained earnings" (or, in lawyer's language, "earned surplus" under older versions of the Model Business Corporation Act). Similarly, if the corporation only has losses, the capital accounts will be diminished by the amount of the losses, which will be shown as a negative entry in the surplus account (or simply called accumulated deficit). Parentheses are used to designate negative amounts. To the extent dividends are paid, they also reduce the retained earnings account, so it becomes a running tally of the undistributed earnings, net of losses, over the years.

Below you will find the 2001 balance sheet of Scientific–Atlanta, which was filed with the SEC as part of its Form 10–K in the Summer of 2001. As you will see in greater detail later in this chapter, Scientific–Atlanta makes a variety of products for the cable television industry, notably set-top boxes. It no longer exists as a publicly traded company, having been acquired by Cisco Systems in 2006.

Scientific–Atlanta, Inc.
Consolidated Statements of Financial Position
June 29, 2001

		In Thousands	
Assets		2001	2000
Current assets			
Cash and cash equivalents		$ 563,322	$ 462,496
Short-term investments		191,001	61,481
Receivables, less allowance for doubtful accounts of $5,982,000 in 2001 and $4,134,000 in 2000		502,289	333,242
Inventories		201,762	209,916
Deferred income taxes		57,195	49,681
Other current assets		33,165	33,818
Total current assets		1,548,734	1,150,634
Property, plant and equipment, at cost			
Land and improvements		22,218	20,248
Buildings and improvements		67,946	40,915
Machinery and equipment		246,385	214,295
		336,549	275,458
Less–accumulated depreciation and amortization		108,934	96,209
		227,615	179,249
Goodwill and other intangible assets, net		81,491	7,475
Non-current marketable securities		17,159	381,983
Deferred income taxes		26,732	--
Other assets		101,097	60,119
Total Assets		$2,002,828	$1,779,460

Liabilities and Stockholders' Equity
    Current liabilities

Current maturities of long-term debt	$ 91	$ 386
Accounts payable	223,990	212,111
Accrued liabilities	164,991	149,402
Income taxes currently payable	5,051	18,264
Total current liabilities	394,123	380,163
Long-term debt, less current maturities	--	102
Deferred income taxes	--	114,428
Other liabilities	99,766	69,807
[Total Liabilities	493,889	564,500]*

Stockholders' equity
  Preferred stock, authorized 50,000,000
    shares; no shares issued
  Common stock, $0.50 par value,
    authorized 350,000,000 shares,
    issued 164,899,158 shares in 2001

and 159,971,077 shares in 2000	82,450	79,986
Additional paid-in capital	545,602	339,649
Retained earnings	935,038	607,822

Accumulated other comprehensive
  income (loss), net of taxes of
  $3,723,000 in 2001 and

$135,538,000 in 2000	(6,075)	221,141
	1,557,015	1,248,598

Less–Treasury stock, at cost (859,339
  shares in 2001 and 651,805 shares in

2000)	48,076	33,638
[Stockholders' Equity]	1,508,939	1,214,960
Total Liabilities and Stockholders' Equity	$2,002,828	$1,779,460

One of the items listed as an asset on Scientific–Atlanta's balance sheet is goodwill. Goodwill arises only in the acquisition of another business. Where the total purchase price for a business exceeds the fair market value of the tangible assets, the tangible assets will be assigned their fair market value on the buyer's books, and the balance of the purchase price will be assigned to an intangible asset—goodwill. Current accounting rules provide that goodwill can remain on the acquiring corporation's books as long as it is not "impaired." Under current rules, goodwill and intangible assets such as trademarks (think of the Coca–Cola name and marks) that have indefinite useful lives must be tested at least annually for impairment. If it is determined that the acquired business is no longer worth what the buying corporation paid for it, goodwill must be reduced to that extent. The Scientific–Atlanta entry is for "goodwill and other intangible assets", which may include such things as patents, trademarks, brand names, copyrights, licenses, franchises and research and development costs associated with new products or methods of production. If these intangibles are purchased from a third party, they will definitely be treated as capital assets, while if they are internally developed, GAAP is silent on their treatment, thus permitting capitalizing the costs of development. APB Opinion No. 17 does not encourage capitalizing such development expenditures. Other intangible assets are inextricably associated with the business, and may not be so readily bought and sold. "Going concern value," which represents the cost of assembling the assets and people necessary to a viable business, is never

* This is a heading that typically appears in balance sheets that is omitted in this one.

shown as an asset. Similarly, Coca–Cola's brand name (and its secret formula) are not shown as assets on the balance sheet, because they were internally developed. Funds expended to create these assets are charged as expenses to the period in which they are incurred.

You may wonder why Scientific–Atlanta's balance sheet shows an asset of $26,732,000 for deferred income taxes. How can income taxes ever be an asset? This situation can only exist where tax accounting treatment differs from that of financial accounting. Scientific–Atlanta accrues warranty expense at the time of sale. But the Internal Revenue Service does not recognize warranty expenses until actually expended.* As a result, income for tax purposes may exceed income for financial reporting purposes. In effect, from a financial reporting viewpoint, the company has "overpaid" its taxes for 2001, and as it later incurs parts of that warranty expense, it will obtain a deduction that will allow it to utilize that overpayment in future years. Hence, from the financial accounting perspective, this "overpayment" of "deferred income taxes" represents an asset that can be used to pay taxes in the future. Similarly, in some cases the tax laws permit "underpayment" in a current year, which creates a liability for future years. (This occurs, for example, when a corporation takes a larger deduction for depreciation expense for tax purposes than allowed by GAAP. In these cases, depreciation deductions in some future year will be smaller than had financial accounting standards been followed.)

Balance sheets sometimes show an asset called "Capital Leases." This is because some equipment is financed through leasing. An ordinary short-term lease would not create an asset entry, but simply an annual expense entry for the lease payments. But some leases look remarkably like long-term secured borrowing by a business. SFAS 13 provides that the lessee must capitalize the lease if *any* of the following criteria are met:

1. the lease contains a bargain purchase option, defined as a price so low that exercise of the option is almost certain;

2. the lease automatically passes title at the end of the lease to the lessee, without further payment;

3. the lease term is equal to at least 75% of the estimated useful life of the asset; or

4. the net present value of the lessee's minimum payments under the lease equals 90% or more of the fair market value of the asset at the beginning of the lease.

If any of these criteria are met, the lessee must capitalize the lease, and record the net present value of the payments to the lessor as both an asset and an offsetting liability on the balance sheet. The capitalization rate to be employed is the rate implicit in the lease. This is the rate that, when applied to the minimum lease payments plus the estimated fair market value at the end of the lease, results in a present value equal to the fair

---

* See Internal Revenue Code of 1986, § 461(h).

value of the leased property at the start of the lease. These leases are discussed in Chapter Six, Part 5.

One set of potentially important liabilities will not be revealed on the balance sheet. A company may have "contingent liabilities" if certain events occur, most frequently, if it loses pending litigation. These contingent liabilities are disclosed in the footnotes to the financial statements. We should emphasize that footnotes to financial statements are an integral part of the financial statements, and their disclosures are generally required by GAAP, although no particular format may be required. Footnote 3 to Scientific–Atlanta's financial statements contains the following disclosure:

> From time to time, we are involved in litigation and legal proceedings incident to the ordinary course of our business, such as personal injury claims, employment matters, contractual disputes and intellectual property disputes. We do not have pending any litigation or proceedings that management believes will have a material adverse effect, either individually or in the aggregate, upon us.

Not all such footnotes are so reassuring. We have included two such footnotes in Appendix 2–A, following this chapter, which illustrate the potential magnitude of contingent liabilities, and how they may threaten the very life of the company.

If a contingency is *probable*, and if the amount of the charge can be reasonably estimated, the company must take a charge against earnings in the current period. "Reasonably estimated" does not mean that it is possible to determine the amount with precision, but only that the company can determine a range, and can then report the amount within the range that seems most likely, or if no amount seems most likely, the lowest amount within the range. In the case of pending litigation, auditors will request an opinion of counsel about these matters. For guidance on responding to auditors' inquiries, the definitive statement is found in American Bar Ass'n, Statement of Policy Regarding Lawyers' Responses to Auditors' Requests for Information, 31 Bus. Law. 1709 (1976).

Bolt v. Merrimack Pharmaceuticals, Inc.

503 F.3d 913 (9th Cir.2007).

■ O'SCANNLAIN, CIRCUIT JUDGE:

We are called upon to interpret a corporation's articles of organization to decide whether it has an obligation to redeem certain shares of its stock.

Albert D. Bolt owns 52,488 shares of Series A Redeemable Preferred Stock ("Series A Stock") issued by Merrimack Pharmaceuticals, Inc. ("Merrimack"), a biotechnology company organized under the laws of Massachusetts. Bolt now wants to redeem those shares.

The relevant redemption provision of Merrimack's Restated Articles of Organization provides:

At any time from and after December 31, 1997, if the net worth of the Corporation, determined in accordance with generally accepted accounting principles and as shown on the balance sheet of the Corporation as of the end of the fiscal quarter then most recently ended, equals or exceeds five million dollars ($5,000,000.00), then upon the request of the holder of [the Series A] Preferred Stock, the Corporation shall redeem at the Redemption Price any and all shares of [the Series A] Preferred Stock which such holder, by such request, offers to the Corporation for redemption.

The following statement provides a snapshot of Merrimack's balance sheet as of December 31, 2001:

Assets	
Total assets	$11,331,070
Liabilities, Redeemable	
Convertible Preferred Stock and	
Stockholders' Deficit	
Total liabilities	$ 1,270,230
Redeemable convertible	
preferred stock:	
Series A redeemable preferred stock	$ 548,380
Series B convertible preferred stock	11,915,267
Total redeemable convertible	
preferred stock	$12,463,647
Total stockholders' deficit	($ 2,402,807)
Total liabilities, redeemable	
convertible preferred stock,	
and stockholders' deficit	$11,331,070

PricewaterhouseCoopers LLP audited Merrimack's financial statements, and opined that Merrimack's balance sheet referred to above "presents fairly, in all material respects, the financial position of Merrimack Pharmaceuticals, Inc. at December 31, 2001 in conformity with accounting principles generally accepted in the United States of America."

During 2001, Merrimack had issued 3,315,201 shares of Series B Redeemable Convertible Preferred Stock ("Series B Stock") with a book value of $11,915,267. The Series B Stock is redeemable at the option of the holder upon a "deemed liquidation," defined as (1) a merger with another company, after which the Merrimack stockholders would no longer hold a majority of the voting power, or (2) the sale of Merrimack's business assets. The Series B Stock appears in the "mezzanine" of the balance sheet, between the liabilities section and the stockholders' deficit (equity) section. *See* David R. Herwitz & Matthew J. Barrett, *Accounting for Lawyers* 505 (4th ed. 2006) (explaining that the "section between liabilities and equity on the balance sheet" is commonly referred to as the "mezzanine").

On April 11, 2001, and again on March 28, 2002, Bolt sent written requests to Merrimack for the redemption of his shares of Series A Stock. In a letter dated June 13, 2002, Merrimack rejected Bolt's demands for redemption. Bolt filed suit in federal district court seeking a declaratory judgment that Merrimack's net worth exceeded $5 million as of December 31, 2001. On cross-motions for summary judgment, the district court granted summary judgment for Bolt, concluding that Merrimack's net worth exceeded $5 million as of that date.

Merrimack timely appealed.

II

We are faced with the task of interpreting Merrimack's Restated Articles of Organization to determine if it indeed has an obligation to redeem the Series A Stock held by Bolt. The dispositive issue, of course, is whether Merrimack's net worth, determined in accordance with generally accepted accounting principles ("GAAP") and as shown on the balance sheet, equaled or exceeded $5 million as of December 31, 2001. The district court held that it did. We agree.

A

We must first determine the meaning of the term "net worth," the threshold yardstick to determine whether Merrimack has an obligation to redeem the Series A Stock as Bolt requests. Merrimack's Restated Articles of Organization fail to define that term. Nor does GAAP define that term. And no item on Merrimack's balance sheet is specifically labeled "net worth."

* * *

The common and well-established meaning of the term "net worth" is the difference between a corporation's total assets and its total liabilities.[2] Merrimack's total assets and total liabilities, as shown on its December 31, 2001 balance sheet, equal $11,331,070 and $1,270,230, respectively. Accordingly, employing the well-established meaning, Merrimack's net worth equals $10,060,840, well in excess of the $5 million threshold set by the Restated Articles of Organization.

Merrimack suggests that net worth is sometimes referred to as stockholders' equity. This reference is often accurate because a balance sheet generally involves only three basic accounting elements—assets, liabilities, and equity—and equity by definition equals the residual interest in the assets after subtracting liabilities.[4] Yet, under this reasoning, Merrimack's net worth would still exceed $5 million.

---

2. *See, e.g.,* Herwitz & Barrett, *supra,* at 3 ("The difference between what a business owns—its *assets*—and what it owes—its *liabilities*—represents its *net worth,* which accountants sometimes refer to as *equity.*"); Black's Law Dictionary (4th ed. 2004) (defining net worth as "[a] measure of one's wealth, usu. calculated as the excess of total assets over total liabilities"); *see also Am. Pac. Concrete Pipe Co., Inc. v. N.L.R.B.,* 788 F.2d 586, 590–91 (9th Cir. 1986) (calculating net worth for purposes of the Equal Access to Justice Act by "subtracting total liabilities from total assets"); *Overnite Transp. Co. v. Comm'r of Revenue,* 54 Mass. App. Ct. 180, 764 N.E.2d 363, 365 n.1 (Mass. App. Ct. 2002) (defining net worth for purposes of Massachusetts's tax revenue laws as "the book value of [the company's] total assets less its liabilities").

4. Elements of Financial Statements, Statement of Fin. Accounting Concepts No. 6 § 49, at 21 (Fin. Accounting Standards Bd. 1985) ("Equity or net assets is the residual interest in

But Merrimack goes further, arguing that the definition of net worth for purposes of its Restated Articles of Organization equals *only* Merrimack's total stockholders' deficit of $2,402,807, excluding Merrimack's total redeemable convertible preferred stock of $12,463,647. Merrimack contends that limiting the meaning of net worth to this amount is appropriate here because the Restated Articles of Organization point to net worth "as shown on the balance sheet" and call for no further calculations. While this argument has surface appeal, we ultimately are unpersuaded. The Restated Articles of Organization indeed point us to "net worth ... *as shown* on the balance sheet." (emphasis added.) But there is no item so labeled on the balance sheet involved here. Thus, such an interpretation of net worth is "shown" on the balance sheet only to the extent that we accept an additional premise necessary to connect it to the net worth reference in the Restated Articles of Organization. Either we accept Merrimack's premise that net worth is limited to total stockholders' equity (deficit) on the balance sheet, or we accept Bolt's premise that net worth is commonly defined as the difference between total assets and liabilities. Regrettably, the Restated Articles of Organization provide no further guidance as to the proper definition of the term. Given the common and well-established meaning of the term "net worth" as the difference between total assets and total liabilities, we cannot accept that the document reflects an intentionally narrower, more nuanced definition of that term that would equal only total stockholders' equity (deficit) simply because it employed the phrase "as shown on the balance sheet." We therefore decline to adopt Merrimack's definition here.

B

Nevertheless, our analysis does not end with our construction of the term "net worth." The Restated Articles of Organization specify that the balance sheet relied upon must be determined in accordance with GAAP.[6]

---

the assets of an entity that remains after deducting its liabilities.") [hereinafter "Concept No. 6"]; *id.* § 50, at 21 ("The equity or net assets of both a business enterprise and a not-for-profit organization is the difference between the entity's assets and its liabilities.").

6. Unfortunately, GAAP is not found in a single source. *See* Herwitz & Barrett, *supra*, at 182. Instead, in the United States, GAAP consists of a hodgepodge of accounting sources, which find their respective places in the hierarchical structure established by the American Institute of Certified Public Accountants ("AICPA"). *See* The Meaning of "Present Fairly in Conformity with Generally Accepted Accounting Principles" in the Independent Auditor's Report, Statement on Auditing Standards No. 69 § 7 (Am. Inst. of Certified Pub. Accountants 1992). There are five categories in the GAAP hierarchy. Officially established accounting principles, referred to as Category (a) authority, are the highest level and include the Financial Accounting Standards Board ("FASB") Statements of Financial Accounting Standards and Interpretations, Accounting Principles Board ("APB") Opinions, and AICPA Accounting Research Bulletins. *Id.* § 10. Moreover, Securities Exchange Commission ("SEC") rules and interpretative releases take an authoritative weight similar to Category (a) authority for companies registered with the SEC. Category (b) authority, the next highest level, consists of FASB Technical Bulletins and, if cleared by FASB, AICPA Industry Audit and Accounting Guides and AICPA Statements of Position. *Id.* The third level of authority, Category (c), consists of AICPA Accounting Standards Executive Committee Practice Bulletins that have been cleared by FASB and consensus positions of the FASB Emerging Issue Task Force.

If the balance sheet incorrectly reports total assets or total liabilities under GAAP, our determination of net worth necessarily would be affected.

To determine whether the balance sheet is prepared in accordance with GAAP, we do not take off our judicial black robes and reach for the accountant's green eyeshade. Rather, because " 'generally accepted accounting principles' are far from being a canonical set of rules that will ensure identical accounting treatment of identical transactions[, and] tolerate a range of 'reasonable' treatments," we generally defer to the professional judgment of the accountant who audited or prepared the financial statements, unless a GAAP authority *demands* a contrary accounting treatment.

1

Merrimack argues on appeal that the Series B Stock, which is presented in the mezzanine section of the balance sheet, is akin to a liability under GAAP authorities. Of course, if the Series B Stock were considered a liability, Merrimack's net worth would not equal or exceed $5 million. But Merrimack's balance sheet does not show the Series B Stock to be part of total liabilities. Nor do we believe that GAAP requires such accounting classification.

a

First, Merrimack claims to find support in Regulation S–X of the SEC, which requires certain stock to be presented on the balance sheet under the caption "redeemable preferred stock" and expressly prohibits including such stock under a general caption "stockholders' equity" or combined in a total with non-redeemable preferred stocks, common stocks, or other stockholders' equity. Regulation S–X, 17 C.F.R. § 210.5–02. That regulation applies to any class of stock with the following characteristics:

> (1) it is redeemable at a fixed or determinable price on a fixed or determinable date or dates, whether by operation of a sinking fund or otherwise; (2) it is redeemable at the option of the holder; or (3) *it has conditions for redemption which are not solely within the control of the issuer*, such as stocks which must be redeemed out of future earnings. Amounts attributable to preferred stock which is not redeemable or is redeemable solely at the option of the issuer shall be included under § 210.5–02.29 unless it meets one or more of the above criteria.

Id. § 210.5–02.28(a) (emphasis added).

Category (d), the fourth level of authority, consists of AICPA accounting interpretations and implementation guides published by the FASB staff, and practices that are widely recognized and prevalent either generally or in the industry. *Id.* In the absence of established accounting principles, auditors may consider accounting literature in the fifth and final level of authority, which includes FASB Statements of Financial Accounting Concepts; APB Statements; AICPA Issues Papers; International Accounting Standards of the International Accounting Standards Committee ("IASC"); Governmental Accounting Standards Board ("GASB") Statements, Interpretations, and Technical Bulletins; pronouncements of other professional associations or regulatory agencies; AICPA Technical Practice Aids; and accounting textbooks, handbooks, and articles. *Id.* § 11.

The parties do not dispute on appeal that Merrimack's Series B Stock falls within the scope of Regulation S–X and therefore is presented properly in the mezzanine section of the balance sheet. Merrimack, however, places great weight on the fact that Regulation S–X requires such stock to be presented "outside" of stockholders' equity, implicitly suggesting, Merrimack urges, that it should be considered akin to a liability for purposes of determining net worth.

In our view, Merrimack reads too much into Regulation S–X, which only requires that the Series B stock be *presented* in a separate caption in the mezzanine section of the balance sheet, not that such stock be *classified* as part of total liabilities. Indeed, in Accounting Series Release No. 268, the SEC expressly emphasized that these "rules are intended to highlight the future cash obligations attached to redeemable preferred stock through appropriate balance sheet *presentation* and footnote disclosure. They do not attempt to *deal with the conceptual question of whether such security is a liability*." Presentation in Financial Statements of Redeemable Preferred Stock, Accounting Series Release No. 268, [1937–1982 Transfer Binder] Fed. Sec. L. Rep. (CCH) ¶ 72,290, at 62,751 (July 27, 1979) (emphasis added). Accordingly, we are not persuaded that Regulation S–X requires the Series B Stock to be classified as part of total liabilities on the balance sheet for purposes of calculating net worth. By reporting the Series B Stock in the mezzanine section, the balance sheet properly followed the presentation requirements set forth in Regulation S–X, which forms part of GAAP.

b

Second, both parties claim to draw support from Accounting Standards No. 150. *See* Accounting for Certain Financial Instruments with Characteristics of both Liabilities and Equity, Statement of Fin. Accounting Standards No. 150 (Fin. Accounting Standards Bd. 2003) [hereinafter "Statement No. 150"]. We recognize, as does Merrimack, that Statement No. 150 was not effective until after the balance sheet involved in this case was prepared. However, we believe that this statement offers helpful guidance that confirms our conclusion. Statement No. 150 requires that a mandatorily redeemable financial instrument, defined as a financial instrument that "embodies an *unconditional* obligation requiring the issuer to redeem the instrument by transferring its assets at a specified or determinable date (or dates) or upon an event certain to occur," be reclassified as a liability. *Id.* § 9, at 10 (emphasis added). Even if Statement No. 150 applied in this case, the parties agree that it would not require the Series B Stock to be classified as a liability because redemption of that stock is *conditional* and expressly beyond the statement's scope. *See id.* at 5. A redeemable preferred stock conditioned "upon an event not certain to occur becomes mandatorily redeemable—*and, therefore, becomes a liability*—if that event occurs, the condition is resolved, or the event becomes certain to occur." *Id.* § 10, at 10 (emphasis added). Thus, while not applicable to the balance sheet at issue in this case, Statement No. 150's requirement that conditionally redeemable stock be classified as a liability upon the resolution of the conditional event suggests that under GAAP such stock, like the Series B Stock here, should not be classified as a liability before that event.

c

Finally, we have two additional GAAP authorities to consider. Merrimack points us to International Accounting Standards No. 32. *See* Financial Instruments: Disclosure and Presentation, International Accounting Standards No. 32 (Int'l Accounting Standards Bd. amended 2004) [hereinafter "International Standard No. 32"]. That standard provides that *conditionally* redeemable preferred stock, like the Series B Stock in this case, should be classified as a liability. While International Standard No. 32 is on point, we do not believe that it compels Merrimack to restate the Series B Stock, which is presented in the mezzanine section of the balance sheet, as part of total liabilities. International Accounting Standards fall on the lowest rung of the GAAP hierarchy in the United States. *See supra* n.6. Moreover, FASB, the organization charged with establishing GAAP in the United States, has expressly declined to adopt International Standard No. 32's position with respect to classifying conditionally redeemable preferred stock as a liability.

The parties also direct us to FASB's Concept No. 6. But we do not believe the conceptual definitions found therein require a conclusion that the Series B Stock must be classified as part of total liabilities, contrary to the presentation on Merrimack's balance sheet. Concept No. 6 defines "liabilities" as "probable future sacrifices of economic benefits arising from present obligations of a particular entity to transfer assets or provide services to other entities in the future as a result of past transactions or events," *id.* § 35, at 18, and "equity" as "the residual interest in the assets of an entity that remains after deducting its liabilities," *id.* § 49, at 21. Moreover, and more importantly, Concept No. 6 recognizes the conceptual difficulties with classifying certain hybrid securities like the Series B Stock at the nub of this case,[9] and instructs in such cases that the conceptual definitions are the starting point and "provide a basis for assessing, for example, the extent to which a particular application meets the qualitative characteristic of *representational faithfulness, which includes the notion of reporting economic substance rather than legal* form." *Id.* § 59, at 24 (emphasis added).

Merrimack argues that the Series B Stock should not be considered equity pursuant to Concept No. 6 because that stock is not a "residual interest." We appreciate, as do the parties, that the Series B Stock has a number of hybrid characteristics: Series B stockholders have (1) a right to

---

9. *Id.* § 55, at 23–24 ("Although the line between equity and liabilities is clear in concept, it may be obscured in practice. Applying the definitions to particular situations may involve practical problems because several kinds of securities issued by business enterprises seem to have characteristics of both liabilities and equity in varying degrees or because the names given some securities may not accurately describe their essential characteristics.... Preferred stock [for example] often has both debt and equity characteristics, and some preferred stocks may effectively have maturity amounts and dates at which they must be redeemed for cash.").

vote, together with the common stock as a single class, on all actions to be taken by the stockholders; (2) a right to elect one board member; (3) a dividend of four percent per annum of purchase price; (4) a liquidation preference before common stock, but after debts and liabilities and the Series A Stock preference; (5) a cash redemption right upon a "deemed liquidation" and at the election of the holder; (6) a right to convert such stock into common stock at any time according to a specified formula; (7) covenants and restrictions on certain actions by Merrimack; and (8) a preemptive right. However, while recognizing that the Series B Stock does not fit neatly into either the definition of liabilities *or* equity under Concept No. 6, we are unpersuaded that Merrimack's balance sheet, by not classifying that stock as part of total liabilities, is contrary to GAAP.

2

In sum, finding no GAAP authority that requires classifying Merrimack's Series B Stock as part of total liabilities, we defer to Pricewaterhouse-Cooper's conclusion that Merrimack's balance sheet "presents fairly, in all material respects, the financial position of Merrimack Pharmaceuticals, Inc. at December 31, 2001 in conformity with accounting principles generally accepted in the United States of America." We therefore agree with the district court's conclusion that Merrimack's balance sheet as of December 31, 2001 was determined according to GAAP.[10]

---

10. Merrimack's argument that the district court's decision must be interpreted to have concluded otherwise is unpersuasive. Merrimack selectively alters a quotation from the decision to assert that the district court ruled expressly, in direct conflict with Regulation S–X, that Merrimack's "argument that the Series B shares should be classified outside [equity] is an argument against generally accepted accounting principles." (alteration in brief) But the district court actually stated that the "Series B shares *must be classified as either an asset, a liability, or equity*. Defendant's argument that the Series B shares should be classified outside *those categories* is an argument against generally accepted accounting principles." (emphasis added.) Because FASB has expressly declined to expand on those three accounting elements on the balance sheet, Merrimack missteps by latching onto this statement to allege that the district court concluded that the balance sheet was not prepared in accordance with GAAP. *See* Statement No. 150, *supra*, §§ B56 & B57, at 47 ("Certain financial instruments were presented between the liabilities section and the equity section of the statement of financial position before the issuance of this Statement. *Because Concepts Statement 6 does not accommodate classification of items outside the elements of assets, liabilities, and equity, developing a model that would permit that practice would require the Board to define a new element of financial statements. The Board elected not to pursue that course of action, in part because, among other concerns, adding another element would set an undesirable precedent of adding elements whenever new instruments are created that are difficult to classify.* The Board instead elected to develop an approach that would address the issues related to determining the appropriate classification of financial instruments with characteristics of liabilities, equity, or both. . . ." (emphasis added)).

Nor is Merrimack's argument that the district court afforded no deference to PricewaterhouseCoopers, its auditors, of any moment. PricewaterhouseCoopers simply certified that the balance sheet—which reflects total assets of $11,331,070, total liabilities of $1,270,230, total redeemable convertible preferred stock of $12,463,647, and total shareholders' deficit of ($2,402,807)—presents Merrimack's financial position as of December 31, 2001 fairly in all material respects in accordance with GAAP. Even in a subsequent declaration submitted for purposes of this lawsuit, PricewaterhouseCoopers never opined that net worth equaled stockholders' equity or that the Series B Stock should be classified as a liability, but simply

Merrimack has an obligation to redeem Bolt's Series A Stock if its net worth equals or exceeds $5 million. Because we conclude that the term "net worth" for purposes of the Restated Articles of Organization should be given its well-established meaning as the difference between total assets and total liabilities, and because Merrimack's total assets and total liabilities equaled $11,331,070 and $1,270,230, respectively, as shown on the December 31, 2001 balance sheet calculated in conformity with GAAP, Merrimack's net worth exceeded $5 million. Accordingly, the district court's grant of summary judgment in favor of Bolt is AFFIRMED.

QUESTIONS

1. What does "mezzanine" mean in terms of balance sheet position of preferred stock?

2. Is stock that (1) promises a certain annual dividend rate and (2) a right to force the company to redeem it upon the occurrence of certain events more like a demand note or stock? Why?

3. Is this a drafting error on the part of lawyers? When Merrimack and Bolt entered into their agreement, Merrimack had a simple capital structure, with no other classes of preferred. Thus, increases in "net worth," absent new financings, could only have come from earnings (retained earnings) that belonged to the common stockholders. Bolt's $548,380 investment would have represented little more than 10% of "net worth" (defined as common stockholders' equity, if the $5 million net worth had been reached.)

4. Why would Merrimack agree to allow a stockholder to withdraw its capital upon the occurrence of certain events? Consider that Bolt may well have been an "angel investor" (an individual willing to make early-stage investments in technology companies before venture capitalists are willing to invest). Why should Bolt demand a right to exit from his investment at an earlier stage than other preferred stock investors?

5. Note the hierarchy of governing authority in the structuring of financial statements. Does the SEC rank lower than FASB for privately held companies? Why do International Accounting Standards ("IAS") rank even lower?

6. Would you expect a lawyer to be able to make the arguments in this case without expert assistance from accountants?

---

reaffirmed that "the classification of the Series B convertible preferred stock outside of permanent equity, or stockholder's [sic] equity (deficit) was presented in conformance with GAAP." As such, contrary to Merrimack's argument, we have no opinion by Pricewaterhouse-Coopers that net worth equals stockholders' equity to which to defer. Accordingly, we defer only to PricewaterhouseCoopers's conclusions that the balance sheet presents fairly in all material respects Merrimack's financial position as of December 31, 2001, in conformity with GAAP, and that the Series B Stock was properly presented outside of stockholders' equity in compliance with GAAP.

B. THE INCOME STATEMENT

Where the balance sheet is a snap-shot of a business at a particular moment, detailing what it owns and who has claims on it, the income statement is more like an historical novel. It begins on the first day of a fiscal year, and tells the reader how the corporation's balance sheet came to look the way it does at the end of the year. It is the link between two balance sheets. Many businesses produce income statements more frequently—corporations subject to SEC regulation must file quarterly income statements on Form 10-Q, and business may produce more frequent income statements for internal use.

Scientific–Atlanta, Inc.
Consolidated Statements of Earnings

(In Thousands, Except Per Share Data)	2001	2000	1999
Sales:	$2,512,016	$1,715,410	$1,243,473
Costs and expenses			
Cost of sales	1,718,160	1,212,655	888,162
[Gross margin on sales	793,856	502,755	355,311]
Sales and Administrative	222,027	177,588	162,017
Research and development	154,346	122,403	117,261
Stock compensation	10,778	--	--
[Operating Profit	406,705	202,764	76,033]
Interest expense	411	564	635
Interest income	(36,879)	(19,636)	(8,526)
Other (income) expense, net	(67,229)	(747)	(62,281)
Total costs and expenses	2,001,614	1,492,827	1,097,268
Earnings before income taxes	510,402	222,583	146,205
Provision for income taxes	176,728	66,775	43,862
Net earnings	$ 333,674	$ 155,808	$ 102,343
Earnings per common share			
Basic	$ 2.06	$ 0.99	$ 0.67
Diluted	$ 1.99	$ 0.94	$ 0.65
Weighted average number of common shares outstanding			
Basic	161,601	157,807	153,630
Diluted	167,688	164,895	157,130

Translating Financial Statements. Regulation S–K, Item 303, 17 C.F.R. 229.303, requires a company to provide "Management's Discussion and Analysis" of the company's financial statements. While the requirements in Item 303(b) are entitled "material changes" in the balance sheet and income statement, they provide for a textual discussion of each line of these statements. The footnotes below contain at least part of Scientific–Atlanta's discussion of various lines in its income statement. You will see how important it is to read these items to enhance your understanding of financial statements.

Scientific–Atlanta's "sales" represent the total revenues for the period.* The process of arriving at this number involves the principle mentioned earlier—that a business should not recognize revenues until either cash has been received or the right to a cash payment has arisen (the "completed contract method"). Thus, if Scientific–Atlanta ships some merchandise to customers that have a right to return the merchandise for 60 days, it has not "earned" the revenue until expiration of the 60 days. The merchandise has been shipped on what is the equivalent of "on consignment." If experience shows that returns average only 5%, then the company could book 95% of the revenue when shipment occurs. Methods of income recognition are required to be discussed in the first footnote to the financial statements.

Some income statements will insert a line after "cost of sales" (which is the cost of merchandise shipped or services rendered) called "gross margin on sales" or "gross profit."** We have inserted this line in Scientific–Atlanta's income statement for illustration. This number, by itself, has little significance for legal purposes, although it may be important in analyzing the results of operations. If, for example, the cost of sales is increasing as a percentage of gross sales, the resulting "gross margin" will be declining. This might be explained by rising costs of raw materials, competitive pressures on selling prices, or some similar factor. One item not shown separately on Scientific–Atlanta's income statement is the amount of "depreciation expense," or the amount charged against current income to represent the consumption of the value of long-term capital goods. This item is lumped with "depreciation and amortization expense" on Scientific–Atlanta's statement of cash flows, to be discussed in subsection C, which follows.

---

* "Sales of $2.5 billion in fiscal year 2001 increased 46 percent over the prior year. Domestic sales grew $779.3 million, or 57 percent, year over year. International sales increased 5 percent led by growth in Canada and Latin America.

"Subscriber product sales of $1.7 billion in fiscal year 2001 increased 100 percent over the prior year. During fiscal year 2001, we continued the rollout of advanced two-way digital cable systems, which are real-time, interactive digital networks designed to enable advanced services such as video-on-demand, e-mail and Web browsing. More than 4.8 million Explorer digital set-tops were shipped in fiscal year 2001, up from 1.9 million in fiscal year 2000. During fiscal year 2001, we increased the production capacity of our Explorer digital interactive set-tops in our Juarez facility from 1 million units per quarter to 1.5 million units per quarter. As previously announced, we do not expect to utilize all of this capacity in the first quarter of fiscal year 2002."

** "Cost of sales as a percent of sales decreased 2.3 percentage points in fiscal year 2001 from fiscal year 2000. We continue aggressively to reduce our costs through product design, procurement and manufacturing. Each generation of our custom ASICs (Application Specific Integrated Circuits) incorporates more functionality and helps us reduce the number of components in our digital set-tops. Our material costs have benefitted from the recent downturn in the electronics industry, which has reduced component costs and improved component availability. In addition, we have taken advantage of newly available e-commerce technology to reduce the cost of many of the commodity parts used in our products.

"Cost of sales as a percent of sales decreased 0.7 percentage points in fiscal year 2000 from fiscal year 1999, reflecting the economies of scale associated with increased manufacturing volumes, the continuing benefit from manufacturing in Juarez, Mexico and negotiated procurement savings."

Depreciation expense is a charge taken against current year's revenues to reflect the diminution in value of long-term assets used to produce income—those with an expected life of more than one accounting cycle.* These assets may diminish in value because they wear out from use, as in the case of many pieces of machinery, or because they become obsolete, as in the case of computers. An annual charge is taken, representing some proportion of the value of these assets (minus expected salvage value), each year of the expected useful life of the asset. These charges may not correspond exactly to the loss of market value of these assets, as we will discuss later. The term depletion refers to a similar process for wasting assets, such as minerals or oil and gas reserves. Where intangible assets have a finite life, they are amortized over their useful lives, a process similar to depreciation. Thus the book value of a patent that is purchased should be amortized over its remaining legal life (recall that the expenses of development of an invention are usually treated as a current expense, and thus give no book value to patents developed within a firm). On the other hand, an intangible asset such as goodwill has no definable useful life. Until 2001 GAAP required goodwill to be amortized over no more than forty years, but currently no fixed annual amortization is required. But if the value of goodwill has been demonstrably impaired, a one-time reduction in its book value (and a charge against current earnings) is required.

We have inserted a line after "Stock compensation" (an expense item for stock or option grants to employees, officers and directors) called "Operating Profit," which is frequently included in income statements. This is an important number for comparative purposes with other companies in the same business, because it is independent of such financial factors as interest expense and taxes, which will vary from firm to firm, even among firms making virtually identical products. In most cases this is useful because it summarizes all of the income available to pay claimants, whether creditors or shareholders, of the business. Analysts often use the term "EBIT" to describe this number, which is an acronym for "Earnings Before Interest and Taxes." In Scientific–Atlanta's case, there is significant

---

* "Research and development expenses were $154.3 million in fiscal year 2001, excluding the $10.8 million stock compensation charge discussed in Management's Discussion and Analysis of Consolidated Statements of Financial Position, up $31.9 million over fiscal year 2000 driven primarily by the development of international products and advanced digital set-tops. Research and development efforts in fiscal year 2001 continued to focus on the development of applications and enhancements to our interactive broadband networks. Research and development expenses were approximately 6 percent of sales in fiscal year 2001 and 7 percent and 9 percent of sales in fiscal years 2000 and 1999, respectively. We continue to invest in research and development programs to support existing products as well as future potential products and services for our customer base.

"Certain software development costs are capitalized when incurred and are reported at the lower of unamortized cost or net realizable value. Capitalization of software development costs begins upon the establishment of technological feasibility. The establishment of technological feasibility and the ongoing assessment of recoverability of capitalized software development costs requires considerable judgment by management with respect to certain external factors, including, but not limited to, anticipated future revenues, estimated economic life and changes in software and hardware technologies."

other non-operating income, so Operating Profit and EBIT are not identical.

Scientific–Atlanta had more interest income (in parentheses) than interest expense during the years 1999–2001, and some other income, apparently non-operating income (also shown in parentheses). Management's Discussion and Analysis discloses that the 2001 "other income" included a gain from the sale of investments in another company, offset by losses from some fixed assets and declines in the value of some other assets. Because these items were not directly related to operations, and are unlikely to be repeated annually, they were stated separately. After deducting all these expenses and a provision for anticipated 2001 taxes (to be paid in 2002), Scientific–Atlanta had net earnings of $333 million.* As is common, this is then stated on a per share basis, so investors can readily translate results into calculations about the value of Scientific–Atlanta's common stock. This number is "earnings per share" or "EPS."

Earnings per share are stated in a "basic" and "diluted" fashion. "Basic," in this context, refers to the average number of shares issued and outstanding during the year. "Fully diluted" uses both the "basic" number of shares, and the number of shares that would have been outstanding if all stock options were exercised, and all convertible securities were converted into common stock. This is an important distinction, because many younger corporations, particularly development-stage companies in high-technology industries, have used large amounts of stock options to compensate employees in lieu of cash.

In December of 2004, in FASB Statement No. 123R, the Financial Accounting Standards Board stated that in the future stock options would be expensed at "fair value." More details on this change, and on valuation methods, are provided in Chapter Eight, Part 4.

Sidebar: Extraordinary Items

There are two types of income statement items that require special treatment. Where a business has sold some operations during the year, a comparison with the previous years' earnings isn't possible without some adjustments. In these cases it is helpful to the reader to add a line to the income statement for "Discontinued Operations," and to place it below the line entitled "Net Income from Continuing Operations."

The other type of item is a non-recurring item. A company may sell a division for a price well in excess of its book value. This creates a

---

* "Net earnings were $333.7 million, or $1.99 per share in fiscal year 2001 as compared to $155.8 million, or $0.94 per share in fiscal year 2000. Earnings in fiscal year 2001 include an after-tax gain of $49.5 million from the sale of a portion of our investments in Bookham and Wink and a one-time, after-tax charge of $7.1 million related to the tender of shares held by minority shareholders of PowerTV. Excluding these items, net earnings were $291.3 million or $1.74 per share in fiscal year 2001."

profit for the company, but when was it earned? It was recognized in the current year, but the appreciation in the value of the business may have occurred over a period of years. Or a company may have suffered a major uninsured loss, perhaps through a 100–year flood of a plant, where it did not carry flood insurance. While this is truly a current event, to show this as a charge against operating income would distort comparisons with previous years. Thus, where these events occur, it is appropriate to add a line to the income statement to show "Net Income from Current Operations," and then disclose these extraordinary items below that line.

Finally, a company may decide to close a plant down rather than sell it. "In this case there is no transaction with which to recognize a loss, but assets have been removed from production, and most likely have lost much if not all of their value. In such cases companies take a one-time restructuring charge as an extraordinary item against earnings. While this has the effect of reducing current income, management has the ability to characterize this as an extraordinary item, and to limit public discussions to 'Net Income from Current Operations,' sometimes called 'pro forma earnings.' One difficulty here is that management may decide to write off 'too much,' thus making it easier to achieve higher earnings in later periods."

Sidebar: Modern Day Definitions

EBITDA

2001: Earnings Before Interest, Taxes, Depreciation and Amortization

2002: Earnings Because I Totally Duped Authorities

2003: Every Blessed Inside Trader & Director Arrested

SEC

2001: Securities and Exchange Commission

2002: Should've Evaluated Chairman

2003: Shabby Economic Custodians

FASB

2001: Financial Accounting Standards Board

2002: Failed At Showing Boondoggle

2003: Forget Any Statement's Believability

In re Software Toolworks, Inc.

50 F.3d 615 (9th Cir.1994).

■ HALL, CIRCUIT JUDGE

[Software Toolworks ("Toolworks") conducted a secondary public offering on behalf of its stockholders in July of 1990, in which stock was sold at $18.50 per share. After the offering the price of the stock declined steadily, to $5.40 per share on October 11, 1990. On that date a press release was issued announcing substantial losses and the price dropped to $2.375 per share. Investors filed class actions against Toolworks. Toolworks settled the litigation, but the suit continued against the underwriters, who, in order to prevail, were required to prove either "reasonable investigation" under section 11 of the Securities Act of 1933,* or "reasonable care" under section 12 of that act. The District court granted summary judgment to all defendant underwriters, and the plaintiffs appealed. The following excerpt deals only with the income recognition issue.]

The plaintiffs next assert that a material issue of fact exists regarding whether the Underwriters diligently investigated, or needed to investigate, Toolworks' recognition of OEM revenue on its financial statements. The plaintiffs claim that the Underwriters "blindly relied" on Deloitte in spite of numerous "red flags" indicating that the OEM entries were incorrect and that, as a result, the district court erred in granting summary judgment.

An underwriter need not conduct due diligence into the "expertised" parts of a prospectus, such as certified financial statements. Rather, the underwriter need only show that it "had no reasonable ground to believe, and did not believe ... that the statements therein were untrue or that there was an omission to state a material fact required to be stated therein or necessary to make the statements therein not misleading." The issue on appeal, therefore, is whether the Underwriters' reliance on the expertised financial statements was reasonable as a matter of law.

---

* Section 11 of the Securities Act of 1933, 15 U.S.C. § 77k, reads in relevant part as follows:

(a) In case any part of the registration statement, when such part became effective, contained an untrue statement of a material fact ..., any person acquiring such security ... may, either at law or in equity, in any court of competent jurisdiction, sue

(1) every person who signed the registration statement; * * *

(5) every underwriter with respect to such security. * * *

(b) Notwithstanding the provisions of subsection (a) no person, other than the issuer, shall be liable as provided therein who shall sustain the burden of proof—* * *

(3) that (A) as regards any part of the registration statement not purporting to be made on the authority of an expert, ... he had, after reasonable investigation, reasonable ground to believe and did believe, at the time such part of the registration statement became effective, that the statements therein were true ... (C) as regards any part of the registration statement purporting to be made on the authority of an expert (other than himself) or purporting to be a copy of or extract from a report or valuation of an expert (other than himself), he had no reasonable ground to believe and did not believe, at the time such part of the registration statement became effective, that the statements therein were untrue or that there was an omission to state a material fact required to be stated therein or necessary to make the statements therein not misleading.

Ed.

As the first "red flag," the plaintiffs point to Toolworks' "backdated" contract with Hyosung, a Korean manufacturer. During the fourth quarter of fiscal 1990, Toolworks recognized $1.7 million in revenue from an OEM contract with Hyosung. In due diligence, the Underwriters discovered a memorandum from Hyosung to Toolworks stating that Hyosung had "backdated" the agreement to permit Toolworks to recognize revenue in fiscal 1990. The plaintiffs claim that, after discovering this memorandum, the Underwriters could no longer rely on Deloitte because the accountants had approved revenue recognition for the transaction.

If the Underwriters had done nothing more, the plaintiffs' contention might be correct. The plaintiffs, however, ignore the significant steps taken by the Underwriters after discovery of the Hyosung memorandum to ensure the accuracy of Deloitte's revenue recognition. The Underwriters first confronted Deloitte, which explained that it was proper for Toolworks to book revenue in fiscal 1990 because the company had contracted with Hyosung in March, even though the firms did not document the agreement until April. The Underwriters then insisted that Deloitte reconfirm, in writing, the Hyosung agreement and Toolworks' other OEM contracts. Finally, the Underwriters contacted other accounting firms to verify Deloitte's OEM revenue accounting methods.

Thus, with regard to the Hyosung agreement, the Underwriters did not "blindly rely" on Deloitte. The district court correctly held that, as a matter of law, the Underwriters' "investigation of the OEM business was reasonable."

The plaintiffs next assert that the Underwriters could not reasonably rely on Deloitte's financial statements because Toolworks' counsel, Riordan & McKinzie, refused to issue an opinion letter stating that the OEM agreements were binding contracts. This contention has no merit because, contrary to the plaintiffs' assertions, Toolworks had never requested the law firm to render such an opinion. The plaintiffs attempt to infer wrongdoing in such circumstances is patently unreasonable. The district court correctly granted summary judgment in favor of the Underwriters on this issue.

Finally, the plaintiffs assert that, by reading the agreements, the Underwriters should have realized that Toolworks had improperly recognized revenue. Specifically, the plaintiffs claim that several of the contracts were contingent and that it was facially apparent that Toolworks might not receive any revenue under them. As the Underwriters explain, this contention misconstrues the nature of a due diligence investigation:

> [The Underwriters] reviewed the contracts to verify that there was a written agreement for each OEM contract mentioned in the Prospectus—not to analyze the propriety of revenue recognition, which was the responsibility of [Deloitte]. Given the complexity surrounding software licensing revenue recognition, it is absurd to suggest that, in perusing Toolworks' contracts, [the Underwriters] should have concluded that [Deloitte] was wrong, particularly when the OEM's provided written confirmation.

We recently confirmed precisely this point in a case involving analogous facts: "The defendants relied on Deloitte's accounting decisions (to recognize revenue) about the sales. Those expert decisions, which underlie the plaintiffs' attack on the financial statements, represent precisely the type of 'certified' information on which section 11 permits non-experts to rely." In re Worlds of Wonder Sec. Litig., 814 F. Supp. 850, 864–65 (N.D. Cal. 1993) ("It is absurd in these circumstances for Plaintiffs to suggest that the other defendants, who are not accountants, possibly could have known of any mistakes by Deloitte. Therefore, even if there are errors in the financial statements, no defendant except Deloitte can be liable under Section 11 on that basis.")

Thus, because the Underwriters' reliance on Deloitte was reasonable under the circumstances, the district court correctly granted summary judgment on this issue. See Toolworks I, 789 F. Supp. at 1498 ("Given the complexity of the accounting issues, the Underwriters were entitled to rely on Deloitte's expertise.").

The plaintiffs next attack the Underwriters' due diligence efforts for the period after Toolworks filed a preliminary prospectus and before the effective date of the offering.[2] During this time, several significant events transpired. First, Barron's published a negative article about Toolworks that questioned the company's "aggressive accounting." Second, in response to the Barron's article, the SEC initiated a review of Toolworks' prospectus. Third, Toolworks sent two letters responding to the SEC. And, fourth, Toolworks booked several consignment sales that made the company appear to have a prosperous quarter, thereby ensuring success of the offering.

The district court held that the Underwriters satisfied their due diligence obligations during this period primarily by relying on Toolworks' representations to the SEC. For the following reasons, we conclude that disputed issues of material fact exist regarding the Underwriters' efforts and, accordingly, we reverse and remand for a trial on the merits.

The plaintiffs first contend that the Underwriters should have done more to investigate the Barron's allegations of slumping sales and improper accounting. The Underwriters established, however, that they contacted a representative of Nintendo and several large retailers to confirm the strength of the market in response to the Barron's article. Moreover, as explained above, the Underwriters' reliance on Deloitte's accounting decisions was reasonable as a matter of law. Summary judgment was appropriate on this issue.

Next, the plaintiffs raise the issue of Toolworks' July 4, 1990 letter to the SEC, which described the company's June quarter performance. In the

---

2. The Underwriters' contention that the events of this period are inapplicable to sections 11 and 12(2) liability is clearly incorrect. Both statutory provisions require disclosure of information needed in order to make a prospectus truthful and not misleading. As the Underwriters' own experts testified, poor first quarter earnings prior to the effective date of the offering would definitely constitute material information and would have to be disclosed.

letter, Toolworks represented that, although preliminary financial data was not available, Toolworks anticipated revenue for the quarter between $21 and $22 million. The plaintiffs claim that Toolworks deliberately falsified these estimates and that the Underwriters knew of this deceit.

The Underwriters claim that they were not involved in drafting the July 4 SEC letter and that, as a result, they have no responsibility for its contents. The plaintiffs presented evidence, however, that the letter was a joint effort of all professionals working on the offering, including the Underwriters. In fact, a Riordan & McKinzie partner specifically testified that, "when the letter finally went to the SEC, all parties had been involved in the process of creating it. There had been conference calls discussing it and comments and changes made by a lot of different members of the working group." Others similarly testified that the Underwriters were actively involved in discussions of how to respond to the SEC's inquiries regarding the June quarter.

The Underwriters argue that, even if they participated in initial discussions about the letter, they never knew that Toolworks' financial data actually was available and that, as a result, they could not have known that the letter (and the prospectus) were misleading. Given the Underwriters participation in drafting both documents, however, we think this is an unresolved issue of material fact. A reasonable factfinder could infer that, as members of the drafting group, the Underwriters had access to all information that was available and deliberately chose to conceal the truth. We therefore hold that summary judgment was inappropriate on this issue.

After suffering lagging sales in the first two months of the June quarter, Toolworks booked several large consignment sales in late June, the quarter's final month, thereby enabling the company to meet its earning projections. Toolworks later had to reverse more than $7 million of these sales in its final financial statements for the quarter. The plaintiffs presented evidence that the Underwriters knew that Toolworks had performed poorly in April, that Toolworks had no orders for the month as of June 8, that the June quarter is traditionally the slowest of the year for Nintendo sales, and that the late June sales accounted for more revenue than the cumulative total of Toolworks' Nintendo sales for the prior two and a half months. For its due diligence investigation of these sales, however, the Underwriters did little more than rely on Toolworks' assurances that the transactions were legitimate. A reasonable inference from this evidence is that Toolworks fabricated the June sales to ensure that the offering would proceed and that the Underwriters knew, or should have known, of this fraud. As a result, we conclude that summary judgment regarding the Underwriters' diligence on this issue was also inappropriate. See Feit v. Leasco Data Processing Equip. Corp., 332 F. Supp. 544, 582 (E.D.N.Y. 1971) ("Tacit reliance on management is unacceptable; the underwriters must play devil's advocate.").

Thus, we hold that the district court properly granted summary judgment in favor of the Underwriters on the section 11 and 12[(a)](2) issues regarding their due diligence investigation into Toolworks' Nintendo sales practices and description of OEM revenue. The district court erred, however, by granting summary judgment on the section 11 and 12(2) claims regarding the July 4 SEC letter and Toolworks' June quarter results. We remand for a trial on the merits of those claims.

QUESTIONS

1. What legal doctrine would prevent the Hyosung contract from being a binding agreement in March, 1990?

2. If underwriters' counsel rather than the underwriters had conducted the due diligence, would the court have attached more weight to the argument that they were charged with knowledge of the non-binding nature of the Hyosung contract?

3. Would the officers & directors of Toolworks (who are also liable under § 11(a) of the Securities Act) be able to rely on the same defense as the underwriters with respect to the Hyosung contract? Suppose that Toolworks' lawyer is also a director?

4. What's a consignment sale contract? Why might it be misleading to include it in the June quarter sales?

5. Why does the court require the underwriters to investigate whether the consignment sale contracts in the June quarter were legitimate obligations, when it didn't require this for the Hyosung contract?

6. What would your obligations be as a lawyer representing the company in this offering with respect to the Hyosung contract, the revenue from which was reported as part of the audited financial statements? Issuers have no "reasonable investigation" defense under section 11.

7. Set out below is part of footnote 1 to Scientific–Atlanta's financial statements for the year ended June 29, 2001. How would you treat the Hyosung situation if this were the stated policy of Software Toolworks?

    "Revenue Recognition

    "Scientific–Atlanta's revenue recognition policies are in compliance with Staff Accounting Bulletin No. 101 'Revenue Recognition in Financial Statements' issued by the Securities and Exchange Commission. Revenue is recognized at the time product is shipped or title passes pursuant to the terms of the agreement with the customer which include a standard right of return, the amount due from the customer is fixed and collectibility of the related receivable is reasonably assured. Revenue is recognized only when we have no significant future performance obligation.

    "Our right of return policy, which is standard for virtually all sales, allows a customer the right to return product for refund only if the product does not conform to product specifications; the non-conforming product is identified by the customer; and the customer rejects the non-conforming product and notifies us within ten days of receipt.

"Revenues from progress-billed contracts are primarily recorded using the percentage-of-completion method based on contract costs incurred to date. Losses, if any, are recorded when determinable. Costs incurred and accrued profits not billed on these contracts are included in receivables. Unbilled receivables, which consist of retainage, were $443 at June 29, 2001 and $1,269 at June 30, 2000. It is anticipated that substantially all such amounts will be collected within one year."

C.   THE STATEMENT OF CASH FLOWS

Accrual accounting recognizes income when earned, regardless of when it is received. It also recognizes expenses when incurred, regardless of when paid. As a result, the income statement cannot accurately reflect the cash available to a business to pay its bills and to declare dividends to shareholders. When interest rates rose in the early 1980s, the distinction between available cash and stated earnings became painfully apparent. If a business had substantial short-term debt, its interest expense rose dramatically, and some businesses with substantial (but illiquid) net worth had trouble meeting their obligations. This led to a strong movement to provide investors with better information about the cash positions of companies. In December of 1987, FASB published *Statement of Financial Accounting Standards No. 95, Statement of Cash Flows*. This requires companies to provide a statement of cash flows in published financial statements. This statement is designed to show how much more (or less) cash a business has at the end of the year than it had at the beginning. In that sense, it is the accountants' response to "show me the money."

The first section of a cash flow statement shows the cash provided by operating activities. It begins with the net income from the income statement, and adds back the non-cash expenses, such as depreciation and amortization, discussed in more detail below. Second, it adjusts for changes in current assets that either increase or decrease cash. For example, a decrease in accounts receivable from the beginning of the year means that more receivables have been converted into cash. The same holds true for inventories. On the liabilities side, an increase in accounts payable means the company is holding its cash rather than paying its bills, so this is added to cash flows.

The next section deals with cash provided by investing activities. In some cases the company may sell a subsidiary or a plant, thus raising cash. In many cases, a company will invest in long-term assets, which decreases cash. In both cases these are measured from beginning to end of the year.

Finally, financing activities may be a source of cash. If the company sells stock or bonds during the year, the net increase in these accounts for the year contributes cash. On the other hand, the repayment of bonds as they come due and the repurchase of stock are a drain on cash, and similar adjustments are made.

We turn now to an actual Statement of Cash Flows. In the case of Scientific–Atlanta, the balance sheet tells us that it ended 2000 with $462 million cash, while it ended 2001 with an additional $101 million cash. But net earnings during 2001 were $333 million. What happened? This gets answered by the Statement of Cash Flows.

Scientific–Atlanta, Inc.
Consolidated Statements of Cash Flows

(In Thousands)	2001	2000	1999
Operating Activities:			
Net earnings	$333,674	$155,808	$102,343
Adjustments to reconcile net earnings to net cash provided by operating activities:			
(Gains) on marketable securities, net	(77,953)	(5,780)	(59,465)
Depreciation and amortization	66,342	50,707	46,075
Compensation related to stock benefit plans	26,296	20,779	9,720
Provision for doubtful accounts	1,866	(3,165)	(1,615)
Losses on sale of property, plant and equipment	2,740	2,396	4,436
(Gain) on sale of businesses, net	--	(6,527)	--
(Earnings) losses of partnerships, net	(257)	754	(6,023)
Changes in operating assets and liabilities, net of effects of acquisitions			
Receivables	(170,503)	(55,409)	(34,209)
Inventories	8,303	(28,308)	(29,809)
Deferred income taxes	(27,530)	(22,570)	(15,593)
Accounts payable and accrued liabilities	17,009	74,435	25,185
Other assets	(23,868)	(29,204)	(7,867)
Other liabilities	104,941	71,571	12,658
Exchange rate fluctuations, net	(2,181)	(3,266)	316
Net cash provided by operating activities	258,879	222,221	46,152
Investing Activities:			
Purchases of property, plant and equipment	(104,810)	(82,772)	(51,352)
Purchases of short-term investments	(129,520)	(60,628)	--
Tender for shares of PowerTV	(64,607)	--	--
Proceeds from the sale of businesses	--	68,606	--
Proceeds from the sale of investments	84,158	8,719	152,974
Other investments	(24,179)	(37,713)	4,952
Other	207	106	469
Net cash provided (used) by investing activities	(238,751)	(103,682)	107,043

Financing Activities:

Principal payments on long-term debt	(397)	(298)	(923)
Dividends paid	(6,458)	(5,541)	(4,618)
Issuance of stock	87,553	53,087	42,636
Treasury shares acquired	--	(3,745)	(65,228)
Net cash provided (used) by financing activities	80,698	43,503	(28,133)
Increase in cash and cash equivalents	100,826	162,042	125,062
Cash and cash equivalents at beginning of year	462,496	300,454	175,392
Cash and cash equivalents at end of year	$563,322	$462,496	$300,454

A business generates cash from several sources. We start with the net earnings for 2001, in the case of Scientific–Atlanta. These were, as noted, $333 million. We start with this number, and then make a series of adjustments. We begin with operating activities, proceed to investing activities, and then turn to financing activities.

Operating Activities. The adjustments here involve adding back non-cash expenses and deducting non-cash expenditures. On the expense side, we add back depreciation and amortization (book entries to reflect assumed reductions in the value of certain assets). When these assets were purchased or paid for, the company reduced its cash account (or incurred a liability) to pay for them. Now, when depreciation is expensed for a tangible capital asset, no cash is paid out—that was done when the asset was acquired. The depreciation expense simply represents a spreading of the initial purchase price as an expense for each accounting period in which the asset remains in use. The same is generally true for amortization, although, as discussed above, when an asset (such as goodwill) is impaired, it is often a one-time entry.

In Scientific–Atlanta's case, its assumed reserves for doubtful accounts were apparently too large in 2001, and the company recovered more cash from its accounts receivable than anticipated. Scientific–Atlanta added back $26.3 million in stock-based compensation, which was treated as an expense for income statement purpose. But the issuance of shares of the company's stock has no effect on its cash position. Scientific–Atlanta holds relatively high cash positions, together with short-term investments, totaling $754 million at the end of 2001. Cash can include "cash equivalents," which includes investments that can readily be converted into cash, such as Treasury bills, certificates of deposit, commercial paper and money market funds. These items, along with short-term investments, would normally be held "for sale" rather than for long-term investment, and accordingly unrealized gains or losses on their market value would be recorded in the income statement. To the extent these unrealized or "paper" gains are included in income, net earnings on the income statement are overstated for purposes of cash flows, so these gains are deducted from net earnings here. Similar reasoning accounts for entries for gains or losses on sales of businesses, and earnings or losses of partnerships in which the company has invested. The losses on sale of property, plant and equipment ($2.74

million) must have been losses for accounting purposes only, which nevertheless produced some cash for the business.

Operating activities can also shift amounts between various asset accounts. For example, when merchandise is sold but not yet paid for, it is included in sales (and thus has a positive effect on net earnings for the year). In Scientific–Atlanta's case, increasing sales led to a $170 million increase in receivables, which becomes a deduction from net earnings. Similarly, "other assets" were increased, which presumably were paid for in cash. On the other hand, inventories declined (apparently with increasing sales the company did not replace its inventory as rapidly as it consumed it), thus increasing cash. These inventories were used to generate sales (and net income), and thus a decline meant that some inventory was converted into cash during the year.

Liability accounts can have an effect on net cash flow as well. Thus, deferring payment of debts until a later period increases cash available this year. Thus accounts payable and accrued liabilities increased by $17 million over the year, and "other liabilities" (retirement and compensation) increased by $30 million. "Deferred income taxes" represent past deferrals that were paid this year, presumably because accelerated depreciation had run out on some equipment.

"Exchange rate fluctuations" describes adjustments made as a result of foreign operations. The results of these operations are translated into dollars at current exchange rates, presumably at the time entries for income or expense are accrued. If the foreign currencies received in payment for sales are less than the amount previously accrued in income, this requires a downward adjustment to earnings (the opposite is true for expenses).

Investing Activities. All investing activities consume cash, and don't show up on the income statement. The purchase of capital equipment is normally necessary to replace obsolete or worn-out equipment, as well as to support growth in sales or production of new products to replace older ones. Scientific–Atlanta spent $104 million of its cash in this way. It also spent $64 million on a tender offer for minority shares in PowerTV, a majority-owned subsidiary, giving Scientific–Atlanta 98% ownership of the subsidiary. Because of its highly liquid position, Scientific–Atlanta purchased $129 million in short-term investments, while selling $84 million of its investments in Bookham Technology plc, a UK based developer of optical equipment, and Wink Communications, Inc. It acquired another $24 million of investments (the "other investments" category, described in Management's Discussion and Analysis ("MD & A") as technology investments). You will find Scientific–Atlanta's 2002 MD & A in Appendix A at the end of the book.

Financing Activities. Scientific–Atlanta issued $87 million of common stock under its stock option plans, its 401(k) plan and its employee stock purchase plan. At the same time it paid a small amount of principal ($.4 million) on long-term debt (apparently eliminating all long-term debt) and $6.5 million in dividends.

Thus the Cash Flow Statement explains the sources of the $101 million increase in cash during 2001 for the company. While net profits were up $178 million, the cash picture was less rosy. As we will see when we analyze certain financial ratios, Scientific–Atlanta appears to have been conservatively financed, with considerable liquidity and reserves for any downturn in its business.

Sidebar: What Does the Cash Flow Statement Say?

Scientific–Atlanta's operating activities provided $258 million cash in 2001, compared to $222 million in 2000 and only $46 million in 1999. These results are pretty volatile, suggesting a business with real ups and downs. In 1999 Scientific–Atlanta spent $51 million on the purchase of capital goods, suggesting operations weren't generating enough cash to pay for growth. Where did the rest of the cash come from? Note that in 1999 the company sold $152 million of its investments. This may explain why the company retains a large amount of liquid investments that can be sold when operations don't produce enough cash. Does the cash shortage in 1999 suggest a company that could easily get into trouble? Or does it suggest a company that is growing and needs more cash to expand? Management's discussion and analysis reports that the $51 million of investing activities in 1999 was primarily for equipment and expansion of manufacturing capacity, primarily in Mexico. Investing activities in 2000 and 2001 were reportedly for the same purpose. When you examine the increase in cash provided by operating activities over the three years, it appears the cash was spent on expansion to increase profits and cash flows.

Your understanding of cash flows at this point should make it clear that net earnings isn't the last word on how well a company is doing. Scientific–Atlanta's Statement of Cash Flows provides more enlightening information. We know from that statement that the company increased its cash and equivalents by $100 million during 2001. But this doesn't exactly tell us how the company performed, because cash didn't just come from operations; it came from the sale of investments and issuance of new stock, to name two major sources, which together produced $190 million. At the same time, investing activities, such as purchases of plant and equipment and purchase of shares in another corporation, consumed $238 million, up $135 million from the previous year. Net cash provided by operating activities, $258 million, is probably a better measure of how it performed in 2001.

Frequently analysis begins with the income statement and makes some quick adjustments. One of the most frequently used is Earnings Before Interest and Taxes ("EBIT"). This is useful for comparison because net earnings are influenced strongly by these items, and they vary from one company to another, depending to a large extent on the capital structure of a company. Interest expense has nothing to do with the results of operations, so analysts often like to exclude them for comparative purposes. Because interest expenses are deductible for federal income tax purposes, they serve to reduce taxes. Thus these two items are often excluded, and EBIT is used as a substitute for net income in analysis. There are differences, however; Operating Profit does not include gains or losses from litigation, earnings from non-consolidated subsidiaries in which the company has a significant investment, interest revenues, and some other items included in EBIT.

Now we proceed one step further, and that much closer to "Net Cash Provided by Operating Activities." This is called Earnings Before Interest, Taxes, Depreciation and Amortization ("EBITDA"). This is sometimes simply called "cash flow." Recall that Depreciation is a bookkeeping entry for an expense that doesn't involve an expenditure. The same is true for Amortization. They recognize the reality that some assets are diminished in value over time, and exhausted in the production of income for the firm. But they aren't drains on cash. Hence, many analysts focus on EBITDA when trying to assess the value of a firm. Is this more useful and informative than EBIT? Keep in mind that while depreciation isn't a cash expenditure, any business will need to replace some equipment and other capital assets, probably on a regular basis, to keep operating profitably. If depreciation is pretty close to the cost of equipment replacement in the average year, then EBIT may be a better measure of what's left for investors (either creditors or stockholders) before taxes.* In 2001 amortization became an obsolete concept, because FASB eliminated the requirement that intangible assets be amortized. Instead FASB now requires an annual determination of whether and to what extent any intangible asset's value is "impaired," and an extraordinary deduction for the amount of the impairment.

Quick Check Question 2.2

Calculate the EBIT and EBITDA for Scientific–Atlanta. Which provides a better representation of the cash left for investors?

---

* Warren Buffett, the CEO of Berkshire–Hathaway and the most respected investor in the world, put it this way in one of his letters to his shareholders:

> Investors are often led astray by CEOs and Wall Street analysts who equate depreciation charges with the amortization charges we have just discussed. In no way are the two the same: With rare exceptions, depreciation is an economic cost every bit as real as wages, materials, or taxes. Certainly that is true at Berkshire and at virtually all the other businesses we have studied. Furthermore, we do not think so-called EBITDA (earnings before interest, taxes, depreciation and amortization) is a meaningful measure of performance. Managements that dismiss the importance of depreciation—and emphasize "cash flow" or EBITDA—are apt to make faulty decisions, and you should keep that in mind as you make your own investment decisions.

The Essays of Warren Buffett: Lessons for Corporate America, Compiled and Introduced by Lawrence A. Cunningham, 19 Cardozo L. Rev. 1, 179–80 (1997).

Sidebar: Free Cash Flow

Analysts employ a term not used in accounting statements to get at an essential feature of a firm's success: "free cash flow." This is cash flow less the cash needed to replace plant and equipment necessary to sustain current sales levels (but not to increase them). In essence, this is the cash over which management has discretion—to invest in expansion, pay off debt, or declare dividends. Depreciation, an artificial determination, is generally not used as a proxy for the cost of replacing equipment. For most purposes analysts ignore the fine distinction between cash needed to sustain existing businesses and cash used to expand the business. When cash flows exceed net investment (and dividend payments exceed proceeds from new stock issues), free cash flow is said to be positive, while free cash flow is negative when earnings don't cover investments (and new share issues exceed any dividend payments.)

Sidebar: The Cash Flow Cycle

There are different cash flows for companies at different stages in their lives and during a fiscal year. For example, a company that has just gone public might have raised more cash than it intends to use immediately, and may thus invest its surplus cash in short term securities. Amazon.com was a prominent example, borrowing hundreds of millions of dollars while maintaining large investments, while spending cash to develop its markets to the point where it could become profitable.

A typical manufacturing company will spend its cash to buy equipment and raw materials, and hire employees to begin production. At this point it becomes far less liquid, and has much of its capital tied up in illiquid investments, the value of which depends upon the market's acceptance of its products. If the products sell well, the company may convert much of its inventory and payroll expense into accounts receivable. While the company will hope these more liquid assets are valuable, uncertainty may remain. In the year following its 2001 financial statements Scientific Atlanta found that one major customer (and debtor), Adelphia, filed for Chapter 11 protection from its creditors while other cable operators faced hard, if not disastrous times, and cut back future orders.

The cycle may repeat if business is good. Good sales may require expansion, and all available cash may be reinvested, along with newly borrowed cash or the proceeds from stock sales.

D.   THE STATEMENT OF CHANGES IN STOCKHOLDERS' EQUITY

We've now seen three financial statements for Scientific–Atlanta. But one question remains: how have the stockholders fared in 2001? At this stage we know what net profits were from the income statement, and we know what dividends were from the Statement of Cash Flows (much smaller than profits). We also know from the Balance Sheet that Stockholders' Equity has increased from $1,248 million to $1,557 million. Is this, coupled with dividends the measure of stockholders' gains? (Recall that Scientific–Atlanta sold additional shares during the year.) This question about how stockholders fared is best answered by reference to a document sometimes called "Statement of Changes in Stockholders' Equity."

If we imagine a business where all of the capital was invested at its incorporation, and remained invested for years, the Statement of Changes in Stockholders' Equity would be a relatively simple document that would simply record each year's profits, minus any losses that might occur, less dividends paid. It is a cumulative account, and at the end of any year it explains the changes in the Retained earnings entry on the balance sheet. Set out below is the section of Scientific–Atlanta's Statement of Stockholders' Equity that gives us this information:

Scientific–Atlanta, Inc.
Consolidated Statements of Stockholders' Equity
and Comprehensive Income

(Dollars In Thousands, Except Per Share Data)	2001	2000	1999
Retained Earnings			
Balance, beginning of year	$607,822	$497,403	$399,678
Net income(a)	333,674	155,808	102,343
Issuance of a 2–for–1 stock split effected in the form of a stock dividend	—	(39,848)	—
Cash dividends ($0.04, $0.035 and $0.03 per share in fiscal years 2001, 2000 and 1999, respectively)	(6,458)	(5,541)	(4,618)
Balance, end of year	$935,038	$607,822	$497,403

Other sections of this statement show the number of new shares issued during the year and any shares repurchased during the year ("Treasury Shares"), which explain adjustments in the sections of the balance sheet for the "stated" or nominal value of issued shares, and in the "additional paid-in capital," which represents the price paid for shares in excess of their par or nominal value.

3. ANALYSIS OF FINANCIAL STATEMENTS

At this point, having read portions of Scientific–Atlanta's financial statements, there are a few observations you should be able to make without more. First, 2001 was a pretty good year for the company, perhaps a very good one. One way you know this is by looking at profits for the

previous year on its income statement, so you have a basis for comparison.*
Second, you can see from the balance sheet that the company seems to have
a lot of resources with which to pay its bills, since its current assets vastly
exceed its current liabilities. Because it has no long-term debt, it should be
able to withstand some hard times, and be able to borrow funds if
necessary, probably at a favorable interest rate. But these financial statements can tell analysts a lot more, and the purpose of this section is to give
you an introduction to the tools that permit an insightful reading of these
numbers. First, we will address some of the major options in accounting
treatment of various items that make comparisons somewhat difficult.

A.   Accounting Options

Accounting is not a single set of rigid rules that apply to all businesses
and all financial statements. It is, rather, a set of principles with a single
goal: to fairly describe the assets and results of operations of all firms. One
size would not fit all firms, so in some areas there are options about how to
treat certain items. Perhaps more importantly, these variances are crucial
in comparing the financial statements of companies, even when they are in
the same business. We explore some of the major ones that can have an
effect on financial results here.

Inventory Accounting. Recall that on the income statement the first
item listed is "cost of sales," sometimes called "cost of goods sold." This
records the cost of the materials that went into producing the goods that
were sold. These costs come from the inventory entry on the balance sheet,
which records the cost of inventory items at the price paid for each item.
Scientific–Atlanta has an inventory that consists of standard electronic
components, such as integrated circuits, wire, circuit boards, transistors,
capacitors and resistors. The market price of these items may vary considerably over time, and as a result, the inventory may include identical items
for which the cost to the company was quite different. Which ones were
selected to be used in the products sold in 2001? No company puts price
tags on its inventory so it will know the exact cost of each item used in the
products sold this year. That takes us back to the *materiality* principle
described in the introductory section of this chapter.

There are three widely recognized methods of handling inventory
accounting and the cost of goods sold. Two widely-used methods illustrate
the difference that a choice of method can make. The author spent part of
his youth working in a chain retail store. He was taught when serving as a
stock clerk** that new merchandise was always placed behind or under the
older merchandise—the goal was to get the older merchandise sold before it
became stale or shop-worn. (Hint: if you want the freshest milk in the dairy

---

* It may help you realize exactly how good 2001 was to know that net earnings for the
fiscal year ending June 28, 2002, fell to $104 million. Sales declined to $1,671 million, a decline
of 33% from 2001. Part of the decline in earnings was caused by a $55 million bad debt
expense taken in the fourth quarter of 2002 for the bankruptcy of Adelphia Communications,
a major customer.

** This was a promotion, of sorts, from serving in a janitorial capacity.

cooler at the supermarket, reach back as far as you can to see if you can find a bottle with a later expiration date.) One inventory method reflects this: First-in, First out ("FIFO"). One effect of this method is to provide a more realistic reflection of the current value of the inventory, since the remaining units are those most recently purchased.

One alternative is a method that goes completely against the actual handling of inventory. It treats the most recently purchased inventory as that which is first used to manufacture or sell goods. This is called Last-in, First-out ("LIFO"). The virtue of LIFO is that it matches current costs with current sales prices. Thus, it tells us more about the cost of replacing inventory than does FIFO. If inventory is never depleted to zero, the stated value of inventory on the balance sheet will get more and more out of alignment with current costs under conditions of inflation.

If price levels remain stable, the differences between FIFO and LIFO may be trivial. In those cases, comparing the results for Scientific–Atlanta with those of its major competitors won't be much influenced by whether they use the same method of inventory accounting. But in inflationary times, with price levels rising, it can make a large difference. Assume a business purchases one unit of stock every 2 months all year, and sells 4 units at the end of the year. In our example, the price of units doubles half way through the year:

Period	Purchases	Price	Sales	Price		Income
1	1 unit	$1.00	0	—		0
2	1 unit	$1.00	0	—		0
3	1 unit	$1.00	0	—		0
4	1 unit	$2.00	0	—		0
5	1 unit	$2.00	0	—		0
6	1 unit	$2.00	3 units	$2.00	=	$6.00

First In, First Out (FIFO) accounting produces the following result:

Income:	$6.00
Cost:	3.00
Net profit	$3.00

Last In, First Out (LIFO) accounting produces a very different result:

Income:	$6.00
Cost:	6.00
Net profit	$0.00

Both methods are permitted under GAAP. So is a third method, called the weighted average method. Because the business cannot identify which units were actually sold, it could use an average cost, which in our example would be $1.50 per unit. (If different quantities were purchased at different prices, the average would be weighted to reflect this.) Using the average cost method, the cost of goods sold would be 3 × $1.50 = $4.50, and the net profit would be $1.50 Companies are required to disclose how they account for inventory in Management's discussion and analysis.*

You can now see that choice of accounting method can make a big difference in stated profits. In the past, companies that wanted to show high profits preferred FIFO in inflationary periods, because it minimized the cost of goods sold and maximized stated profits. Ironically, it had the secondary effect of increasing taxable income. One suspects that managers choosing this method believed that investors valued stated earnings before taxes more than they valued cash flows.

Depreciation Accounting. Another area involving judgment is accounting for depreciation on long-term capital assets with a remaining life that exceeds the current accounting cycle. The one asset we exclude from depreciation is land, on the theory that its value is never consumed.** Most businesses know approximately how long a new asset will remain in productive use in their business. Some assets will have a "salvage value" at the end of their useful lives, and predictions can be made about that value. The difference between original cost and salvage value is the amount that will be consumed in producing income over a number of years. The next task is determining how to allocate that amount over the useful life of the asset.

There are several things to be noted here. The useful life for a business may not be the entire physical life of the asset. Rental car companies, for example, dispose of their vehicles after a year or two. A business may adopt a replacement cycle for computers, even though they still function. In the case of auto makers, they know the dies for body parts will be obsolete when the model they make reaches the end of its popularity in the market. When assets are purchased, the business must make an estimate of how long the useful life will be. This is necessarily an educated guess. One example can illustrate how businesses may differ in their approaches. In

---

* Scientific-Atlanta's disclosure is as follows:

Inventories are stated at the lower of cost (first-in, first-out) or market. Cost includes materials, direct labor, and manufacturing overhead. Market is defined principally as net realizable value. Inventories include purchased and manufactured components in various stages of assembly as presented in the following table:

	2001	2000
Raw Materials and Work-In-Process	$144,270	$163,969
Finished Goods	57,492	45,947
Total Inventory	$201,762	$209,916

** The author has a family member whose business is a minor exception to this rule. She and her husband raise sod. Each time a crop of sod is harvested, some portion of the productive soil is shipped in the roots of the crop. Thus, under tax laws, the business is permitted to "deplete" its investment in the land, on the theory that at some point the useful productivity of the land will be consumed. This is depletion similar to that employed in mining and oil and gas operations, where assumptions are made about the amount of the asset consumed each year.

the 1960s most businesses did not own their own computers, but relied on service companies that owned huge main-frame computers (less powerful than today's notebooks) for their data processing. A few large businesses were able to lease these behemoths. IBM leased computers at a monthly rate that allowed it to recover the selling price of the computer, plus an interest rate, over four years, assuming that the useful life cycle of a computer was four years. A competitor, Leasco Data Processing, operated by a young entrepreneur, Saul Steinberg, purchased computers from IBM and leased them at lower monthly rates! How could it do this? By depreciating the computers over five years, rather than four. Leasco and Steinberg were simply betting that computers had a longer useful life than IBM thought they did.

Sidebar: Why Depreciation Accounting May Not Coincide With Replacement Costs

Our examples assume that the full purchase price of an asset less its salvage value must be depreciated over the useful life of an asset. Thus, at the end of the life cycle, the firm will "possess" a sum equal to the original purchase price, so its financial statements reflect the consumption of that asset and leave a "reserve" with which to replace it. The underlying and unspoken assumption is that the firm leaves the depreciation "allowance" in a sock under the mattress. But what happens if the firm invests the cash represented by the depreciation expense annually at its current rate of return on capital?

Let's assume instead that the firm depreciates our $100 asset with no salvage value over 10 years, and compounds interest on each sum at 10%:

Year	Investment	Compounds to	Total
1	$10	$23.58	$23.58
2	10	21.44	45.02
3	10	19.49	64.51
4	10	17.72	82.23
5	10	16.11	98.34
6	10	14.64	112.98
7	10	13.31	126.29
8	10	12.10	138.39
9	10	11.00	149.39
10	10	10.00	159.39

Will it cost the firm $159.39 to replace the asset? No one can predict. In inflationary times, the cost may be higher, but some assets may decline in cost over time (think of computers and other electronics). So what can we say about the usefulness of depreciation accounting? First, it's better than no recognition at all of the cost of capital goods consumed in producing revenue. But the actual amounts spent on replacing capital goods are much better indicators of such costs.

(Note that the depreciation charge is taken at the end of each accounting period, so the last charge has no opportunity to earn interest.)

Once we have determined the amount to be depreciated and the useful life of the asset, we have to determine the method to allocate the total depreciation over this period. Accounting principles permit a variety of methods.

Straight line depreciation is probably the most common method. Thus, if we assume an asset with a 10 year life, an original cost of $100, and no salvage value, straight line depreciation is $10 per year. In many cases straight line probably creates more realistic annual statements of income. If the asset remains equally productive over its useful life, then using straight line depreciation results in a relatively consistent charge against revenues.

Not all assets depreciate in a manner that corresponds with straight line depreciation, however. Perhaps the best example would be a car rental company that owns vehicles which depreciate much more rapidly in the early years of use than in the later ones. Thus, if the average automobile has a useful life of ten years, a rental car company might decide to use straight line depreciation. But at the end of one year the market value of the car would have declined by a far greater percentage, as the company would discover when it resold it. Under these circumstances, straight line depreciation would not have provided a realistic account of the costs of operations during the year. Because of this, businesses are permitted to use one of several "accelerated depreciation" methods. The two most common ones are Sum of the Digits and Double Declining Balance depreciation.

We can illustrate Sum of the Digits as follows. This method involves adding up the number of years of the asset's useful life, and then using a fraction, the numerator of which in the first year is the number of years, and the denominator is the sum of the years. For example, the sum of the digits 1 to 10 inclusive is 55. If an asset has a ten year life, the depreciation schedule would be as follows:

Year 1	10/55	= 18.1%	$18.10	depreciation expense
Year 2	9/55	= 16.3%	$16.30	depreciation expense
Year 3	8/55	= 14.5%	$14.50	depreciation expense
Year 4	7/55	= 12.7%	$12.70	depreciation expense
Year 5	6/55	= 10.9%	$10.90	depreciation expense
Year 6	5/55	= 9.1%	$ 9.10	depreciation expense
Year 7	4/55	= 7.2%	$ 7.20	depreciation expense
Year 8	3/55	= 5.5%	$ 5.50	depreciation expense
Year 9	2/55	= 3.6%	$ 3.60	depreciation expense
Year 10	1/55	= 1.8%	$ 1.80	depreciation expense

Total depreciation: $99.70*

Double Declining Balance depreciation uses double the straight-line rate (10% in our example), and applies it to the declining balance:

---

* A rounding error explains the $0.30 discrepancy.

Year	Calculation	Depreciation Expense	Remaining Balance
1	$100 (.10 × 2)	$20.00	$80.00
2	$ 80 (.10 × 2)	16.00	64.00
3	$ 64 (.10 × 2)	12.80	51.20
4	$ 51.20 (.10 × 2)	10.24	40.96
5	$ 40.96 (.10 × 2)	8.19	32.77
6	$ 32.77 (.10 × 2)	6.55	26.22
7	$ 26.22 (.10 × 2)	5.24	20.98
8	$ 20.98 (.10 × 2)	4.20	16.78
9	$ 16.78 (.10 × 2)	3.36	13.42
10	$ 13.42 (.10 × 2)	2.68	10.74

It takes forever to depreciate the last $10.74 under this method. This may be acceptable if there's a salvage value that approximates $10. Otherwise, must keep on depreciating until it reaches the end, which is somewhere out near infinity. Firms sometimes shift to sum of the digits in the last few years to get rid of this amount. We should point out that variations on Declining Balance Depreciation permit using a lesser rate, such as 150% per year.

You can now see that the choice of depreciation method can have a major impact on costs and earnings, if depreciable assets are large in relation to the sales of the business. As a result, for readers to be able to compare the earnings of two firms in the same industry, it is important to know the method employed by each firm. Consistent with accounting practice, footnote 1 to Scientific–Atlanta's financial statements tells readers that depreciation uses "principally" the straight-line method.

Expense vs. Capitalization. Generally the choice between treating an expenditure as a current expense or a capital investment is fairly straightforward. If the outlay creates no value for the company beyond the current accounting cycle, it should be treated as a current expense. Capital expenditures create an asset that has value in later years, and thus should be treated as investments in a capital asset. Perhaps the best example of the dividing line involves expenditures on existing capital assets, such as machinery. Repairs are defined as expenditures to maintain the current usefulness of the machinery. A capital expenditure, on the other hand, adds something to the existing capacity of the machinery, by making it work faster, more accurately, or less expensively, for a period of time beyond the current accounting period.

Principles of conservatism have led the accounting profession to treat virtually all expenditures on intangibles as current expense items, even if they attempt to create long-term value. Thus, research and development costs are expensed currently, even if they may lead to valuable assets, such as patents or trade secrets. On the other hand, if intangibles are purchased, they will show up on the balance sheet at their cost.

Sidebar: Contracting for a Net Profit Interest

Lawyers frequently draw contracts that depend on a determination of net profits. Formerly such contracts were used by actors and writers working on Hollywood films. Humourist Art Buchwald agreed to take a percentage of net profits for his idea for the film Coming to America, a blockbuster starring Eddie Murphy. Sadly for Mr. Buchwald, Paramount Pictures reported that there were no profits on the film, which led to litigation over whether Paramount had understated revenues associated with the film and overstated costs assigned to it. You can imagine a client going to work to turn around a troubled subsidiary corporation, and contracting for a percentage of the profits if successful. You now know that simply stipulating that books be kept in accordance with GAAP isn't enough protection. In addition to assuring no changes from existing depreciation and amortization practices, you would want to protect your client's expectations by assuring that the parent corporation didn't raise expenses by assigning additional overhead from the parent to the subsidiary, or by engaging in parent-subsidiary dealings at the expense of the subsidiary's profits. Would this be enough? When businesses are sold, disagreements about future earnings, and thus the value of the business, are sometimes resolved by "earn-out" clauses, which provide for additions to the purchase price if the seller's optimistic projections about future profits are met. If you represent the seller, you would want to assure that expenses charged to the business do not increase to wipe out all profits. What protections would you want to write into such a contract?

B. RATIOS

These numbers get used for a variety of purposes. Financial analysts use them to determine the expected earnings and/or cash flows of a business for purposes of determining its value, as you will see in Chapter Three. One use of ratios in valuation is to place a variety of companies on a common basis—that is, financial ratios, that eliminate differences in size and type of business. Ratios also allow a comparative analysis of the same business over a series of years.

We can classify ratios into several categories. First, there are *profitability ratios*. These allow the analyst to look at returns against various measures—sales, assets, or equity. Next, there are *financial leverage ratios*. These analyze the capital structure of a firm, and measure its ability to pay its debts in a timely and certain fashion. These ratios are employed by creditors in analyzing whether to extend credit to an enterprise, and by attorneys drafting bond indentures, to provide bondholders with reasonable safeguards. Similarly, *liquidity ratios* examine a debtor's short-term ability to pay its debts, and are used for the same purposes. *Activity ratios*, also turn as *asset turnover ratios*, are used by lenders, primarily in secured lending based on receivables or inventory, to measure how efficiently the firm converts its assets into cash. *Market value ratios* measure the relationship between accounting measures of earnings and value to market value of the firm's securities. Where acronyms are employed by accountants and financial experts, we provide those as well. It's really embarrassing to have to ask what "EPS" is in the middle of a meeting with clients. (You will find a more complete set of ratios in Appendix 2–B to this Chapter.)

i. PROFITABILITY RATIOS

Earnings Per Share ("EPS"). This represents the most common statement of how well shareholders are doing. It shows how much of a company's earnings are available to common stockholders, after paying interest on debt, taxes and dividends on preferred stock.

$$\frac{\text{Net income (after preferred dividends)}}{\text{Weighted average outstanding shares during the period}}$$

Recall that Scientific–Atlanta reports this figure on both a "basic" (currently issued and outstanding) and a "diluted" basis, which includes shares to be issued upon exercise of outstanding options and conversion rights. This is required by GAAP. "Weighted average" means using the average of the number of shares outstanding at the beginning and end of the accounting period. The calculations are as follows:

Earnings per common share:	Basic		$2.06
	Diluted		$1.99
Basic: Net Earnings:		$333,674	= $2.0648
Average outstanding shares:		161,601	

Gross Profit Percentage. This is a measure of the business's profitability from selling its products, separate from its operating expenses (general, selling and administrative). It is expressed as a percentage for comparative purposes, on the theory that a company with a high gross profit percentage may enjoy some competitive advantage over the competition:

$$\frac{\text{Gross Profit (Margin) on Sales}}{\text{Sales}}$$

For Scientific–Atlanta, this ratio would be calculated as follows:

Sales		$2,512,016
Cost of Sales		− 1,718,160
Gross Margin on Sales		$ 793,856
Gross profit %:	$ 793,856	= 0.316
	$2,512,016	

Profit Margin. This is sometimes called return on sales, and measures how much of each sales dollar winds up as net income. This is a primary measure of a company's operating performance. It is represented by:

$$\frac{\text{Net income}}{\text{Sales}}$$

For Scientific–Atlanta, this would be calculated as follows:

Net Income (per income statement) $\underline{\$\ 333,674}$ $= 0.13283$
Sales $\$2,512,016$

Return on Sales ("ROS"). This is a measure of how much of each sales dollar becomes cash available to shareholders, a variant on the preceding measure ("Profit Margin"). It can be an important measure of an enterprise's efficiency, especially when compared to its competitors because it eliminates the variable of capital structure, which influences both interest and taxes. Here we measure:

$$\frac{\text{Earnings Before Interest and Taxes ("EBIT")}}{\text{Sales}}$$

For Scientific–Atlanta, this is:

Net Earnings for 2001: $333,674
Add back interest expense: 411
Add back provision for income taxes: $\underline{176,728}$
EBIT: $510,813 /$2,512,016 = 0.2039

Return on Assets ("ROA"). This measures the profitability of the business on the basis of the book value of all the assets employed. The weakness of this calculation is that the book value of assets may not be equivalent to the fair market value of the assets (in the case of appreciated land, for example). One advantage of this method is that it removes capital structure from calculations of profitability, when comparing different businesses in the same industry.

$$\frac{\text{Earnings Before Interest and Taxes ("EBIT")}}{\text{Average Total Assets*}}$$

For Scientific–Atlanta, this would be calculated as follows:

Net Earnings for 2001: $333,674
Add back interest expense: 411
Add back provision for income taxes: 176,728
EBIT: $510,813 /$2,512,016 = 0.2039

Generally "average total assets" is simply the average of the beginning and ending asset accounts for the accounting period.

Return on Equity ("ROE"). Where return on assets measures the return on capital contributed by both creditors and stockholders, return on equity focuses the calculation of profits as a percentage of stockholders' equity, which factors in capital structure, so that interest payments on bonds and other debt are factored in.

---

* Some investors simply use net income/average total assets, while others add interest expense back into net income when performing this calculation because they prefer to use operating returns before the cost of borrowing. The important fact is that comparable measures must be employed for comparators.

$$\frac{\text{Net Income}}{\text{Average Shareholders' Equity}}$$

For Scientific–Atlanta, this ratio is:

Average shareholders' equity is the average of ending equity for this year and last year.

2000:	$1,214,690
2001:	$1,508,939
Total:	$2,723,629/2 = $1,361,814

Net Income: $\frac{\$\ 333,674}{\$1,361,814}$ = 0.245

*Economic Value Added ("EVA®").** This is a measure of how much value managers have added to the firm's value. "In its simplest form, EVA is net operating profit after taxes less a charge for the capital employed to produce those profits." The capital charge is the required, or minimum, rate of return necessary to compensate all the firm's investors, debtholders as well as shareholders, for the risk of the investment.** Thus:

$$\frac{\text{Net Operating Profit After Taxes}}{\text{Cost of Capital}}$$

Because this is a complex calculation, as Stern Stewart describes it, it is generally not a calculation that anyone can make. In Chapter Three we will examine cost of capital more closely.

ii. FINANCIAL LEVERAGE RATIOS

Financial leverage ratios measure the extent to which a firm operates with creditors' funds, and thus presents a fundamental measure of capital structure. As you will see in Chapter Six, creditors will use these ratios to impose limits on the amount of new debt that a borrower can assume.

Debt to Total Assets Ratio ("Debt Ratio"). This describes the percentage of total assets supplied by creditors. The higher this ratio, the greater

---

* This is a proprietary system owned by Stern Stewart Management Services, Inc.

** "EVA is charged for capital at a rate that compensates investors for bearing the firm's explicit business risk. The assessment of business risk is based upon the Capital Asset Pricing Model [described in Chapter Three], which allows for a specific, market-based evaluation of risk for a company and its individual business units using the concept of 'beta.' In addition, the tax benefit of debt financing is factored into the cost of capital, but in such a way as to avoid the distortions that arise from mixing operating and financing decisions. To compute EVA, the operating profit for the company and for each of the units is charged for capital at a rate that blends the after-tax cost of debt and equity in the *target* proportions each would plan to employ rather than the actual mix each actually uses year-by-year. Moreover, operating leases are capitalized and considered a form of debt capital for this purpose. As a result, new investment opportunities are neither penalized nor subsidized by the specific forms of financing employed."

Joel M. Stern et al., "The EVA Financial Management System," 8, No. 2 JOURNAL OF APPLIED CORPORATE FINANCE 32, 40 (1995).

the burden of interest and debt repayments. This leads to two difficulties for a firm: a higher variance in returns to shareholders, and a greater probability of bankruptcy. A caution: like most ratios, it uses book values of assets, rather than fair market value. While this means the ratio isn't a perfect measure, it may not be as bad as first appears, because it's difficult to realize full market value in a distress sale.

$$\frac{\text{Total Debt}}{\text{Total Assets}}$$

For Scientific–Atlanta, this is:

Total Liabilities: $\underline{\$\ \ 493,889}$ =   0.246
Total Assets: $\$2,002,828$

Debt to Equity Ratio. This describes the proportions of assets contributed by creditors and shareholders. While this is not a significantly different measure of leverage from the Debt to Total Assets ratio, it is used a great deal to describe the leverage of a firm.

$$\frac{\text{Total Liabilities}}{\text{Total Equity}}$$

For Scientific–Atlanta, this is:

Debt (total liabilities): $\$493,889/\$1,508,939$ =   0.327

iii. LIQUIDITY RATIOS

Current Ratio. Current assets are defined as those assets that can reasonably be expected to be converted into cash within the current accounting cycle: cash and equivalents (liquid short-term securities), accounts receivable, inventory, and those prepaid expenses that are expected to be used within the year. Correspondingly, current liabilities are defined as those liabilities due and payable within the same cycle. Thus this ratio defines the relationship between current obligations and the assets available to meet them.

$$\frac{\text{Current Assets}}{\text{Current Liabilities}}$$

For Scientific–Atlanta, this is:

Current Assets: $\$1,548,734/\$394,123$ =   3.93

The difference between current assets and current liabilities is called *Working Capital*. If a firm's working capital is negative, it generally seeks long-term financing to remedy this condition.

Quick ("Acid–Test") Ratio. If a firm gets into trouble, its inventory may not be worth book value (customer unwillingness to buy is often the problem). Thus, creditors and managers may focus more intensively on the cash, cash equivalents (short-term securities) and accounts receivable as a measure of cash available to pay creditors:

$$\frac{\text{Cash} + \text{Short–Term Securities} + \text{Receivables}}{\text{Current Liabilities}}$$

For Scientific–Atlanta, this is:

Cash:	$ 563,322
Short-term securities:	191,001
Receivables:	502,289
Total:	$1,256,612/$394,123 = 3.188

Cash Ratio. In the very short run, the most certain assets creditors can count on are the firm's holdings of cash and equivalents. (Recall that Scientific–Atlanta wrote off $55 million of receivables on the bankruptcy of Adelphia Communications in 2002.)

$$\frac{\text{Cash} + \text{Short–Term Securities}}{\text{Current Liabilities}}$$

For Scientific–Atlanta, this is:

Cash & equivalents:	$ 563,322
Short-term investments:	191,001
	$ 754,323/$394,123 = 1.914

Times–Interest Earned (Interest Cover) Ratio. This measures the extent to which interest obligations are covered by earnings before interest and taxes (EBIT). This is a ratio that is frequently employed to protect creditors in loan agreements and bond indentures; when a debtor falls below a required coverage ratio, a default may be triggered unless the debtor can cure it within a brief time. (In some cases, this ratio is calculated on the basis of EBIT plus depreciation.)

$$\frac{\text{EBIT}}{\text{Interest}}$$

For Scientific–Atlanta, this is:

Net Earnings for 2001:	$ 333,674
Add back interest expense:	411
Add back provision for income taxes:	176,728
EBIT:	$ 510,813/$411 = 1242

iv. ACTIVITY RATIOS

Activity ratios are used primarily by lenders in making credit decisions.

Asset Turnover Ratio. This is the ratio of sales to average assets for the period, using beginning and ending balance sheets. It indicates how many dollars of revenue the company generates from each dollar of assets owned by the business. While generally squeezing more dollars of sales from assets would be seen as a sign of efficiency, it could also show a neglect of new investment to maintain long-term strength.

$$\frac{\text{Net Sales}}{\text{Average Total Assets}}$$

For Scientific–Atlanta, this ratio is calculated as follows:

Sales: $\dfrac{\$2,512,016}{\$1,891,144} = 1.329$

Receivables Turnover Ratio. This is the ratio of sales to average accounts receivable. This provides some measure of the liquidity of the accounts receivable. In some cases creditors may want to measure the ratio of credit sales to accounts receivable, but this test generally cannot be accomplished with publicly available financial statements.

$$\frac{\text{Sales}}{\text{Average Receivables}}$$

For Scientific–Atlanta, this is:

2000 Ending Receivables:	$ 333,242
2001 Ending Receivables:	502,289
Average Receivables:	$ 835,531/ 2 = $417,765
Sales:	$2,512,016/ $417,765 = 6.01

Inventory Turnover Ratio. Analysts perform a similar calculation involving the cost of goods sold for the year and the average inventory during the year (using opening and closing inventories).

$$\frac{\text{Cost of Goods Sold}}{\text{Average Inventory}}$$

For Scientific–Atlanta, this is:

2000 Ending Inventory:	$ 209,916
2001 Ending Inventory:	201,762
	$ 411,678/2 = $205,839 = Average Inventory
Cost of Sales:	$\dfrac{\$1,718,160}{\$ 205,839} = 8.347$
Average Inventory:	

v.   MARKET VALUE RATIOS

Price-Earnings Ratios. When you read stock price quotations in the financial pages of a newspaper, they typically report, in addition to current prices, information about earnings per share. Here, for example, is the report on its stock from THE WALL STREET JOURNAL of Friday, Sept. 6, 2002:

YTD % CHG	52–WEEK HI	LO	STOCK (SYM)	DIV	YLD %	PE	VOL 100s	CLOSE	NET CHG
-42.7	31.19	11.09	SciAtlanta SFA	.04	.3	21	12247	13.71	-0.22

"PE" stands for price-earnings ratio, perhaps the most common ratio used in finance, although not necessarily the most useful one. You should now understand the difficulty in equating all "net profits" of companies for comparative purposes. The price-earnings ratio is expressed simply:

$$\frac{\text{Market Price Per Share}}{\text{Earnings Per Share}}$$

For Scientific–Atlanta, this is:

Basic: $\dfrac{\$40.60}{\$\ 2.06}$ =   19.7

Diluted: $\dfrac{\$40.60}{\$\ 1.99}$ =   20.4

Earnings per share, as used in THE WALL STREET JOURNAL, is described as "the company's diluted per-share earnings, as available, for the most recent four quarters." Recall that Scientific–Atlanta reports earnings per share on both a "basic" and "diluted" basis, using the weighted average number of shares outstanding during the period in each case. This is required by GAAP. The higher this ratio, the greater the value apparently attached by the market to the prospect of growth in future earnings. As you will see in Chapter Three, this is a crude measure of a more sophisticated valuation technique widely used in finance, called discounted present value.

Dividend Yield. Recall that the stock price quotation shown above has a column for "YLD," or dividend yield. This is a measure of how much of the firm's earnings are paid to shareholders in the form of dividends, measured against the stock's market price.

$$\frac{\text{Dividend Per Share}}{\text{Stock Price}}$$

For Scientific–Atlanta, this is:

Dividend per share: $\dfrac{\$\ 0.04}{\$13.71}$ =   .0029
Stock price as of 9/13/02

Dividend Payout Ratio. This is another measure of how much of the firm's earnings are paid out to shareholders in the form of dividends.

$$\frac{\text{Dividends}}{\text{Earnings}}$$

For Scientific–Atlanta, this is:

Dividends: $\dfrac{\$\ 6,458}{\$333,674}$ =   0.019
Earnings:

Market to Book Ratio. This is the ratio of the stock's market price to the book value per share, which is calculated by using stockholders' equity divided by the number of outstanding shares.

$$\frac{\text{Stock Price}}{\text{Book Value Per Share}}$$

For Scientific–Atlanta, this is:

Stock price: $13.71
Book value: $1,508,939,000/164,899,158 = $ 9.15   =   1.55

Tobin's Q. James Tobin, an economist, developed a widely-used ratio of the market value of the company's debt and equity to the current replacement cost of its assets.* This ratio was developed because ratios of book to market value did not account for the real economic value of the asset employed in the business, especially where inflation had driven up the market value of assets. Where the value of a firm exceeds the current value of its assets, this suggests that the market believes management is adding value, and that there may be growth opportunities, if the market value attributed to expansion projects will exceed their cost. Thus the formula is:

$$\frac{\text{Market value of assets}}{\text{Estimated replacement cost}}$$

C.   THE ANALYSIS OF RATIOS

We've now reviewed a large number of ratios, and you should be able to calculate most of them for any set of financial statements. When you can do this, you're equipped to talk intelligently with financial analysts and accountants about these subjects. If you're drafting loan agreements or bond indentures, keep in mind that borrowers will want some protection against risky behavior by debtors that might jeopardize repayment. Specifying compliance with certain minimum ratios is one way to do this. If you're representing a client making an initial public offering, keep in mind that the underwriter, the supposed expert in setting the offering price, has incentives to underprice the offering (both to assure its success and lower the risk for the underwriter, and perhaps to provide benefits to favored customers by allocating bargain-priced shares to them). So how can you and your client know if the underwriter is underpricing the offering? You probably can't. But you and your client can marshal arguments for a higher price, based on comparisons of your company with comparable companies with established market prices.

And where do you find comparable companies? Until a few years the U.S. Census Bureau produced the "Standard Industrial Classification" ("SIC") system, for categorizing all companies. In 1997 the Census Bureau replaced the SIC with the "North American Industry Classification Sys-

---

* James Tobin, "A General Equilibrium Approach to Monetary Theory," 1 JOURNAL OF MONEY, CREDIT, AND BANKING 15 (Feb., 1969).

tem" ("NAICS"). The US NAICS Manual is published annually, with definitions for each industry classification. The manual is on the Census Bureau's web site at http://www.census.gov/eos/www/naics/. Below we offer a sample of the classification system found in this document, at www.census.gov/epcd/naiccod.txt. This system begins with broad two-digit classifications, and then adds more digits to refine it. Classes 31–33 are for manufacturing, for example. Where a business has multiple product lines, analysts may be forced to use three-digit categories, although adding more digits is always preferable for comparison purposes.

- 334 Computer and Electronic Product Manufacturing
- 3341 Computer and Peripheral Equipment Manufacturing
- 33411 Computer and Peripheral Equipment Manufacturing
- 334111 Electronic Computer Manufacturing
- 334112 Computer Storage Device Manufacturing
- 334113 Computer Terminal Manufacturing
- 334119 Other Computer Peripheral Equipment Manufacturing
- 3342 Communications Equipment Manufacturing
- 33421 Telephone Apparatus Manufacturing
- 334210 Telephone Apparatus Manufacturing
- 33422 Radio and Television Broadcasting and Wireless Communications Equipment Manufacturing
- 334220 Radio and Television Broadcasting and Wireless Communications Equipment Manufacturing
- 33429 Other Communications Equipment Manufacturing
- 334290 Other Communications Equipment Manufacturing

The following is Item 1 of Scientific–Atlanta's Form 10–K annual report for fiscal year 2001, filed with the SEC in August of 2001:

"Item 1. Business

"General

"Scientific–Atlanta, Inc. provides its customers with broadband transmission networks, digital interactive subscriber systems, content distribution networks and worldwide customer service and support. Established as a Georgia corporation in 1951, we have evolved from a manufacturer of electronic test equipment for antennas and electronics to a producer of a wide variety of products for the cable television industry, including digital video, voice and data communications products. On April 25, 2000, ViaSat, Inc. acquired our satellite network business, which constituted a substantial part of our satellite business. We retained our satellite television network business, which provides the content distribution networks. We now operate only in the Broadband segment.

"We are one of the leading providers of end-to-end networks used by programmers and cable operators to provide video, data, and voice services to their customers. These networks are comprised of equipment and software that reside at the programmer's facility, at the cable operator's headend (or "central office"), in the outside transmission plant (whether underground or aerial), and in the consumer's home. Our products include satellite communications equipment that transports programming from its source to geographically distributed headends, optical communications products that transport information within metropolitan areas to individual neighborhoods, and radio frequency electronics products that provide connectivity within the neighborhoods to each consumer's home. Increasingly, as these networks have transitioned to digital technology, our products have included integrated computer systems and software at the cable operators' headends. These systems manage video and data services to large networks, often comprising hundreds of thousands of consumers. Our products that reside in the consumer's home include digital interactive set-tops and high-speed cable modems.

"Our Explorer® digital set-tops, digital headends and cable modems are designed to enable subscribers to access new interactive television services to be developed by us and third parties, such as e-mail through cable television service, video-on-demand (VOD), Web browsing, various types of electronic commerce and other Internet Protocol (IP) services. Several of these advanced services, including e-mail, VOD, electronic commerce and Web browsing, have already been deployed on our networks. Sales of our Explorer digital set-tops constituted approximately 57 percent, 34 percent and 15 percent of Scientific–Atlanta's total sales in fiscal years 2001, 2000 and 1999, respectively."

Can you tell from this description which industrial classification most closely fits Scientific–Atlanta? To how many digits can you refine your attempt without more information? Each classification is hyperlinked to its definition. Thus, clicking on 334220 will reveal that this is Scientific–Atlanta's category:

"334220 Radio and Television Broadcasting and Wireless Communications Equipment Manufacturing

"This industry comprises establishments primarily engaged in manufacturing radio and television broadcast and wireless communications equipment. Examples of products made by these establishments are: transmitting and receiving antennas, cable television equipment, GPS equipment, pagers, cellular phones, mobile communications equipment, and radio and television studio and broadcasting equipment."

The next step in analysis is to find similar ratios for comparable companies. Perhaps the most widely-used publication is from the Risk Management Association, which publishes annually the RMA ANNUAL STATEMENT STUDIES. As of 2001, the Annual Statement Studies was published with the industries sorted by Standard Industrial Classification (SIC) codes, with a reference to the North American Industrial Classification System (NAICS) codes. RMA has since adopted the NAICS codes. In many respects, there are no significant differences between the two systems. The relevant pages from the RMA ANNUAL STATEMENT STUDIES 2001–2002 are set out in Appendix 2–B at the end of this chapter.

QUESTIONS

1. How do Scientific–Atlanta's financial leverage and liquidity ratios compare with these ratios for the rest of the industry group?

2. How profitable was Scientific–Atlanta in 2001, compared to the rest of the industry?

3. Insolvency. You are informed by your senior partner that when a corporation is in the "vicinity of insolvency," that its board of directors' duties shift, so it owes duties to creditors. Your law firm represents Amazon.com. Your senior partner hands you the following summary of Amazon's balance sheet for the year ending December 31, 2001. Is Amazon in the "vicinity of insolvency?" Do you need to know more before you can answer this question?

Amazon.com, Inc.
Summary Balance Sheet
December 31, 2001
(in thousands)

Assets	
Total Current Assets	$ 540,282
Total Assets	1,637,547
Liabilities	
Total Current Liabilities	921,414
Long-Term Debt	2,156,133
Stockholders' Deficit	
Common stock, par value $0.01	3,732
Additional paid-in capital	1,462,769
Deferred stock-based compensation	(9,853)
Accumulated other comprehensive loss	(36,070)
Accumulated deficit	(2,860,578)
Total Liabilities and stockholders' deficit	$1,637,547

APPENDIX 2–A

EXAMPLES OF CONTINGENT LIABILITY STATEMENTS

Owens–Corning 1996 Form 10–K, Notes to Financial Statements

21. Contingent Liabilities

ASBESTOS LIABILITIES

The Company is a co-defendant with other former manufacturers, distributors and installers of products containing asbestos and with miners and suppliers of asbestos fibers (collectively, the "Producers") in personal injury and property damage litigation. The personal injury claimants generally allege injuries to their health caused by inhalation of asbestos fibers from the Company's products. Most of the claimants seek punitive damages as well as compensatory damages. The property damage claims generally allege property damage to school, public and commercial buildings resulting from the presence of products containing asbestos. Virtually all of the asbestos-related lawsuits against the Company arise out of its manufacture, distribution, sale or installation of an asbestos-containing calcium silicate, high temperature insulation product, the manufacture of which was discontinued in 1972.

Status

As of December 31, 1996, approximately 157,900 asbestos personal injury claims were pending against the Company, of which 36,400 were received in 1996. The Company received approximately 55,900 such claims in 1995, and 29,100 in 1994.

Many of the recent claims appear to be the product of mass screening programs and not to involve malignancies or other significant asbestos related impairment. The Company believes that at least 40,000 of the recent claims involve plaintiffs whose pulmonary function tests (PFTs) were improperly administered or manipulated by the testing laboratory or otherwise inconsistent with proper medical practice, and it is investigating a number of testing organizations and their methods. In 1996 the Company filed suit in federal court against the owners and operators of certain pulmonary function testing laboratories in the southeastern U.S. challenging such improper testing practices. This matter is now in active pre-trial discovery.

During 1996 the Company was engaged in discussions with a group of approximately 30 leading plaintiffs' law firms to explore approaches toward resolution of its asbestos liability. The discussions involved the possible resolution of both pending claims and claims that may be filed in the future. The law firms involved in the talks agreed to refrain from serving any further asbestos claims on the Company unless they involved malignancies. This agreement, which expired as to certain of the firms on November 1, 1996, was extended until January 1, 1997, by firms representing a substantial majority of the cases historically filed by the group. This agreement may have impacted the number of cases received by the Company during the second, third and fourth quarters of 1996.

Through December 31, 1996, the Company had resolved (by settlement or otherwise) approximately 183,300 asbestos personal injury claims, including the dismissal in May 1996, for lack of medical proof, of approximately 15,000 maritime cases which named Owens Corning as a defendant, resulting in an 11,700 case reduction in the backlog after reduction for duplicate cases and cases previously settled. During 1994, 1995, and 1996, the Company resolved approximately 60,600 asbestos personal injury claims, over 99% without trial, and incurred total indemnity payments of $626 million (an average of about $10,300 per case).

The Company's indemnity payments have varied considerably over time and from case to case, and are affected by a multitude of factors. These include the type and severity of the disease sustained by the claimant (i.e., mesothelioma, lung cancer, other types of cancer, asbestosis or pleural changes); the occupation of the claimant; the extent of the claimant's exposure to asbestos-containing products manufactured, sold or installed by the Company; the extent of the claimant's exposure to asbestos-containing products manufactured, sold or installed by other Producers; the number and financial resources of other Producer defendants; the jurisdiction of suit; the presence or absence of other possible causes of the claimant's illness; the availability or not of legal defenses such as the statute of limitations or state of the art; whether the claim was resolved on an individual basis or as part of a group settlement; and whether the claim proceeded to an adverse verdict or judgment.

Insurance

As of December 31, 1996, the Company had approximately $329 million in unexhausted insurance coverage (net of deductibles and self-insured retentions and excluding coverage issued by insolvent carriers) under its liability insurance policies applicable to asbestos personal injury claims. This insurance, which is substantially confirmed, includes both products hazard coverage and primary level non-products coverage. Portions of this coverage are not available until 1997 and beyond under agreements with the carriers confirming such coverage. All of the Company's liability insurance policies cover indemnity payments and defense fees and expenses subject to applicable policy limits.

In addition to its confirmed primary level non-products insurance, the Company has a significant amount of unconfirmed potential non-products coverage with excess level carriers. For purposes of calculating the amount of insurance applicable to asbestos liabilities, the Company has estimated its probable recoveries in respect of this additional non-products coverage at $225 million, which amount was recorded in the second quarter of 1996. This coverage is unconfirmed and the amount and timing of recoveries from these excess level policies will depend on subsequent negotiations or proceedings.

Reserve

Prior to the second quarter of 1996 the Company's financial statements included a reserve for the estimated cost associated with asbestos personal injury claims that may be received through the year 1999. Such financial statements did not include any provision for the cost of unasserted claims which might be received in years subsequent to 1999 because management was unable to predict the number of such claims and other factors which would affect the cost of such claims. Throughout 1996, the Company continued to review the feasibility of making provision for the cost of unasserted asbestos personal injury claims with respect to claims which may be received by the Company during and after the year 2000. In conducting such review the Company took into account, among other things, the effect of recent federal court decisions relating to punitive damages and the certification of class actions in asbestos cases, the pendency of the discussions with the group of plaintiffs' law firms referred to above, the results of its continuing investigations of medical screening practices of the kind at issue in the federal PFT lawsuit, recent developments as to the prospects for federal and state tort reform, the continued rate of case filings at historically high levels, additional information on filings received during the 1993–1995 period and other factors. As a result of the review, the Company took a non-recurring, noncash charge to earnings of $1.1 billion in the second quarter of 1996. This charge represented the Company's estimate of the indemnity and defense costs associated with unasserted asbestos personal injury claims that may be received by the Company in years subsequent to 1999.

The combined effect of the $1.1 billion charge and the $225 million probable additional non-products insurance recovery was an $875 million charge in the second quarter of 1996.

The Company's estimated total liabilities in respect of indemnity and defense costs associated with pending and unasserted asbestos personal injury claims that may be received in the future, and its estimated insurance recoveries in respect of such claims are reported separately as follows:

	December 31, 1996	December 31, 1995
	(In millions of dollars)	
Reserve for asbestos litigation claims		
Current	$ 300	$ 250
Other	1,670	887
Total Reserve	1,970	1,137
Insurance for asbestos litigation claims		
Current	100	100
Other	454	330
Total Insurance	554	430
Net Asbestos Liability	$ 1,416	$ 707

The Company cautions that such factors as the number of future asbestos personal injury claims received by it, the rate of receipt of such claims, and the indemnity and defense costs associated with asbestos personal injury claims, as well as the prospects for confirming additional insurance, including the additional $225 million in non-products coverage referenced above, are influenced by numerous variables that are difficult to predict, and that estimates, such as the Company's, which attempt to take account of such variables, are subject to considerable uncertainty. The Company believes that its estimate of liabilities and insurance will be sufficient to provide for the costs of all pending and future asbestos personal injury claims that involve malignancies or significant asbestos-related functional impairment. While such estimates cover unimpaired claims, the number and cost of unimpaired claims are much harder to predict and such estimates reflect the Company's belief that such claims have little or no value. The Company will continue to review the adequacy of its estimate of liabilities and insurance on a periodic basis and make such adjustments as may be appropriate.

Management Opinion

Although any opinion is necessarily judgmental and must be based on information now known to the Company, in the opinion of management, while any additional uninsured and unreserved costs which may arise out of pending personal injury and property damage asbestos claims and additional similar asbestos claims filed in the future may be substantial over time, management believes that any such additional costs will not impair the ability of the Company to meet its obligations, to reinvest in its businesses or to take advantage of attractive opportunities for growth.

On October 5, 2000 Owens–Corning filed a petition for reorganization under Chapter 11 of the Bankruptcy Code.

General Motors Corporation, 2002 Form 10–K, Notes to Financial Statements:

NOTE 14. Pensions and Other Postretirement Benefits

GM has a number of defined benefit pension plans covering substantially all employees. Plans covering U.S. and Canadian represented employees generally provide benefits of negotiated, stated amounts for each year of service as well as significant supplemental benefits for employees who retire with 30 years of service before normal retirement age. The benefits provided by the plans covering U.S. and Canadian salaried employees and employees in certain foreign locations are generally based on years of service and compensation history. GM also has certain nonqualified pension plans covering executives that are based on targeted wage replacement percentages and are unfunded. Pension plan assets are primarily invested in equity and fixed income securities, U.S. Government obligations, commingled pension trust funds, insurance contracts, GM $1–2/3 par value common stock (valued at December 31, 2002 at approximately $30 million), and GM Class H common stock (valued at December 31, 2002 at $1.6 billion).

GM's funding policy with respect to its qualified pension plans is to contribute annually not less than the minimum required by applicable law and regulations. GM made pension contributions to the U.S. hourly and salary plans of $4.8 billion in 2002, no pension contributions in 2001, and contributions of $5.0 billion in 2000 (consisting entirely of GM Class H common stock contributed during the second quarter of 2000). In addition, GM made pension contributions to all other U.S. plans of $106 million, $99 million, and $69 million in 2002, 2001, and 2000, respectively.

Additionally, GM maintains hourly and salary benefit plans that provide postretirement medical, dental, vision, and life insurance to most U.S. retirees and eligible dependents. The cost of such benefits is recognized in the consolidated financial statements during the period employees provide service to GM. Postretirement plan assets in GM's hourly VEBA trust are invested primarily in equity securities, fixed income securities, and GM Class H common stock (valued at December 31, 2002 at approximately $200 million).

Certain of the Corporation's non-U.S. subsidiaries have postretirement plans, although most participants are covered by government-sponsored or administered programs. The cost of such programs generally is not significant to GM.

	U.S. Plans Pension Benefits		Non–U.S. Plans Pension Benefits		Other Benefits	
	2002	2001	2002	2001	2002	2001
Change in benefit obligations			(dollars in millions)			
Benefit obligation at beginning of year	$ 76,383	$76,131	$ 9,950	$ 9,911	$ 52,489	$ 49,889
Service cost	885	901	194	176	506	480
Interest cost	5,307	5,294	700	638	3,689	3,733
Plan participants' contributions	25	25	25	24	55	50
Amendments	83	33	31	2	--	--
Actuarial losses	3,678	152	1,040	346	3,802	1,582
Benefits paid	(6,463)	(6,321)	(641)	(549)	(3,392)	(3,173)
Curtailments, settlements, and other	216	168	830	(598)	80	(72)
Benefit obligation at end of year	80,114	76,383	12,129	9,950	57,229	52,489
Change in plan assets						
Fair value of plan assets at beginning of year	67,322	77,866	6,340	7,397	4,944	6,724
Actual return on plan assets	(4,933)	(4,444)	(329)	(391)	(150)	(479)
Employer contributions	4,906	99	258	224	1,000	--
Plan participants' contributions	25	25	25	24	--	--

Benefits paid	(6,463)	(6,321)	(641)	(549)	--	(1,300)
Curtailments, settlements, and other	3	97	290	(365)	--	--
Fair value of plan assets at end	60,860	67,322	5,943	6,340	5,794	4,945
Funded status	(19,254)	(9,061)	(6,186)	(3,610)	(51,435)	(47,544)
Unrecognized actuarial loss	36,212	21,207	3,802	1,808	13,540	8,902
Unrecognized prior service cost	6,002	7,174	691	740	(292)	249
Unrecognized transition obligation	--	--	46	54	--	--
Net amount recognized	$ 22,960	$19,320	$ (1,647)	$(1,008)	$(38,187)	$(38,393)
Amounts recognized in the consolidated balance sheets consist of:						
Prepaid benefit cost	$ 1	$ 7,006	$ 218	$ 521	$ --	$ --
Accrued benefit liability	(17,237)	(7,617)	(5,525)	(3,222)	(38,187)	(38,393)
Intangible asset	6,002	5,625	690	606	--	--
Accumulated other comprehensive income	34,194	14,306	2,970	1,087	--	--
Net amount recognized	$ 22,960	$19,320	$ (1,647)	$(1,008)	$(38,187)	$(38,393)

The projected benefit obligation, accumulated benefit obligation, and fair value of plan assets for pension plans with accumulated benefit obligations in excess of plan assets were $92 billion, $89 billion, and $66 billion, respectively, as of December 31, 2002, and $59 billion, $59 billion, and $48 billion, respectively, as of December 31, 2001.

	U.S. Plans Pension Benefits			Non–U.S. Plans Pension Benefits			Other Benefits		
Components of expense	2002	2001	2000	2002	2001	2000	2002	2001	2000
				(dollars in millions)					
Service cost	$ 885	$ 901	$ 900	$194	$176	$177	$ 506	$ 480	$ 448
Interest cost	5,307	5,294	5,425	700	638	630	3,688	3,733	3,346
Expected return on plan assets	(7,133)	(7,521)	(7,666)	(580)	(605)	(578)	(390)	(542)	(650)
Amortization of prior service cost	1,255	1,325	1,416	93	93	97	(14)	(45)	(42)
Amortization of transition obligation/(asset)	—	—	(48)	25	3	(17)	—	—	—
Recognized net actuarial loss/(gain)	733	82	8	62	(1)	2	320	96	70
Curtailments, settlements, and other	213	65	235	51	100	24	—	—	—
Net expense	$1,260	$ 146	$ 270	$545	$404	$ 335	$4,110	$3,722	$3,172
Weighted-average assumptions									
Discount rate	6.75%	7.25%	7.25%	6.23%	6.81%	7.06%	6.76%	7.25%	7.74%
Expected return on plan assets	10.0%	10.0%	10.0%	8.8%	8.9%	9.0%	7.9%	7.9%	8.1%
Rate of compensation increase	5.0%	5.0%	5.0%	3.4%	3.8%	4.0%	4.3%	4.7%	4.3%

For measurement purposes, an approximate 7.2% annual rate of increase in the per capita cost of covered health-care benefits was assumed for 2003. The rate was assumed to decrease on a linear basis to 5.0% through 2009 and remain at that level thereafter.

A one percentage point increase in the assumed health-care trend rate would have increased the Accumulated Postretirement Benefit Obligation (APBO) by $6.3 billion at December 31, 2002 and increased the aggregate service and interest cost components of non-pension postretirement benefit expense for 2002 by $523 million. A one percentage point decrease would have decreased the APBO by $5.3 billion and decreased the aggregate service and interest cost components of non-pension postretirement benefit expense for 2002, by $416 million.

GM sets the discount rate assumption annually for each of its retirement-related benefit plans at their respective measurement dates to reflect the yield of high quality fixed-income debt instruments.

GM's expected return on assets assumption is derived from a detailed periodic study conducted by GM's actuaries and GM's asset management group. The study includes a review of anticipated future long-term performance of individual asset classes and consideration of the appropriate asset allocation strategy given the anticipated requirements of the respective plans to determine the average rate of earnings expected on the funds invested to provide for the pension plan benefits. While the study gives appropriate consideration to recent fund performance and historical returns, the assumption is primarily a long-term, prospective rate. Based on its recent study, GM is revising its expected long-term return assumption for its U.S. plans effective January 1, 2003 to 9%, a reduction from its previous level of 10%.

The following table illustrates the sensitivity to a change in certain assumptions for U.S. pension plans (as of December 31, 2002 the Projected Benefit Obligation (PBO) for U.S. pension plans was $80.1 billion and the minimum pension liability charged to equity with respect to U.S. pension plans was $21.2 billion net of tax):

Change in Assumption	Impact on 2003 Pre–Tax Pension Expense	Impact on December 31, 2002 PBO	Impact on December 31, 2002 Equity (Net of tax)
25 basis point decrease in discount rate	+ $120 million	+ $1.9 billion	− $1.1 billion
25 basis point increase in discount rate	− $120 million	− $1.8 billion	+ $1.1 billion
25 basis point decrease in expected return on assets	+ $170 million	—	—
25 basis point increase in expected return on assets	− $170 million	—	—

These changes in assumptions would have no impact on GM's funding requirements.

The following table illustrates the sensitivity to a change in the discount rate assumption related to GM's U.S. OPEB plans (the U.S. APBO was a significant portion of GM's worldwide APBO of $57.2 billion as of December 31, 2002):

Change in Assumption	Impact on 2003 Pre–Tax OPEB Expense	Impact on December 31, 2002 APBO
25 basis point decrease in discount rate	+ $150 million	+ $1.6 billion
25 basis point increase in discount rate	− $140 million	− $1.5 billion

QUESTIONS

1.   What is a "defined benefit" pension plan?

2.   How large is the deficit in GM's funding for its pension obligations at the close of 2002?

3.   How does this compare to its 2002 net income of $1.736 billion?

4.   GM's Balance Sheet reveals a deduction from shareholders' equity of $22.762 billion, leaving a net stockholders' equity of $6.814 billion. Note that in calculating this deficit, GM has shown $17.954 billion in intangible assets, including goodwill of $6.992 billion. Goodwill is the cost of acquired businesses in excess of the fair value of their identifiable net assets. What does this tell you about the tangible net worth of GM?

5.   What are Post-retirement benefits other than pensions? Note that GM's balance sheet shows a deduction from shareholders' equity of $38.197 billion. Note that footnote 14 states that the total benefit obligation is $57.2 billion.

6.   In calculating the funding of its pension plans, GM assumes a certain rate of return on a portfolio consisting of "U.S. Government obligations, equity and fixed income securities, commingled pension trust funds, insurance contracts, GM $1–2/3 common stock ..., and GM Class H common stock...." In its 2001 annual report GM stated that returns on this portfolio are "below GM's long-term asset return assumption, in any 10–year period over the last 15 years, GM has achieved pension asset returns of 10% per annum or greater." Keep in mind that some of the highest returns in history were earned in the period 1985–2000, when the Dow rose from less than 1,500 to over 11,000. Further, long-term returns to broad stock market averages have been between 10–11% over the previous seventy years or more. Returns on corporate bonds had averaged 5.7% and long-term Treasury Bonds had averaged 5.2%. Would it make sense to use an assumed return of 10% on a portfolio of government and corporate bonds, stocks and GM stock? If so, why did GM reduce its assumed rate of return to 9% in its 2002 report? In an announcement in December, 2003, GM

stated that it intended "to reduce the GM pension funds' exposure to stocks in both U.S. and international markets, and increase investments in global bonds and other alternatives to stocks." "GM Says It Closed Gap in Pension Fund; 9% Return is Needed," WALL STREET JOURNAL, Dec. 15, 2003, C1. What do you think the shift from stocks to bonds is likely to do to expected returns on the portfolio?

7. Much of GM's non-pension benefit obligations are for health care for retirees. GM makes certain assumptions about rates of increase in health-care benefit costs through 2009. If GM's estimates are on the low side by one percent, what would this do to GM's currently estimated $38.187 billion obligation?

8. From Dec. 31, 2002 until Dec. 15, 2003, the Dow Jones Industrial Average rose from 8,341 to approximately 10,040, or approximately 20%. The GM press release quoted above stated that "Thanks to a $13.5 billion debt offering, improving stock-market conditions, and an expected $4.1 billion the company plans to contribute to the fund after selling its Hughes Electronics Co. subsidiary within the next few weeks, GM expects its pension obligations to be nearly fully funded by the end of this year. The forecast is based on an expected 18% annual return on assets at the end of the calendar year, at a discount rate of 6.25%." What does this say about the dependence of GM's pension funds on equity investments? After reading the next chapter, consider whether a discount rate of 6.25% is appropriate given the apparent riskiness of GM's pension investments.

APPENDIX 2–B

2001 ANNUAL STATEMENT STUDIES

by Risk Management Associates

DEFINITION OF RATIOS

INTRODUCTION

Below the common size balance sheet and income statement presented on each data page are series of ratios which have been computed from the financial statement data. Each ratio has three values: the upper quartile, median, and lower quartile. For any given ratio, these figures are calculated by first computing the value of the ratio for *each* financial statement in the sample. These values are then arrayed—"listed"—in an order from the strongest to the weakest. (We acknowledge that, for certain ratios, there may be differences of opinion concerning what is a strong or a weak value. RMA has resolved this problem by following general banking guidelines consistent with sound credit practice in its presentation of data.)

The array of values are then divided into four groups of equal size. The three points that divide the array are called quartiles—upper quartile, second quartile or median, and lower quartile. The upper quartile is that point at which 1/4 of the array of ratios falls between the strongest ratio and the upper quartile point. The median is the middle value and the lower quartile is that point at which 3/4's of the array falls between the strongest ratio and the lower quartile point. In many cases we take the average of two values to arrive at the quartile value. The median and quartile values will be shown on all *Statement Studies* data pages in the order indicated below. A sample is shown on the following page for illustrative purposes.

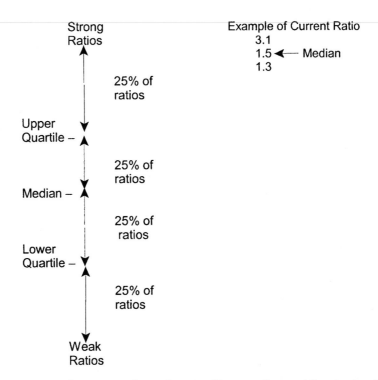

There are several reasons for using medians and quartiles instead of an average. One is to eliminate the influence which values in an "unusual" statement would have on an average. The method used more accurately reflects the ranges of ratio values than would a straight averaging method.

It is important to understand that the spread (range) between the upper and lower quartiles represents the middle 50% of all the companies in a sample. Ratio values greater than the upper or less than the lower quartiles, therefore, begin to approach "unusual" values.

For some ratio values, you will occasionally see an entry that is other than a conventional number. These unusual entries are defined as follows:

(1) *UND*—This stands for "undefined," the result of the denominator in a ratio calculation approaching zero.

(2) *NM*—This may occasionally appear as a quartile or median for the ratios sales/working capital, debt/worth, and fixed/worth. It stands for "no meaning" in cages where the dispersion is so small that any interpretation is meaningless.

(3) *999.8*—When a ratio value equals 1,000 or more, it also becomes an "unusual" value and is given the "999.8" designation. This is considered to be a close enough approximation to the actual unusually large value.

Important Notes:

- Throughout the *Statement Studies*, the ratio values have been omitted whenever there were less than ten statements in a sample. Occasionally, the number of statements used in a ratio array will differ from the number of statements in a sample because certain elements of data may not be present in all financial statements. **In these cases, the number of statements used is shown in parentheses to the left of the array.**

- For certain ratios **(Sales/Receivables, Cost of Sales/Inventory, Cost of Sales/Payables)** you will see two numbers, one in **BOLD** and one in regular type set. These ratios are generally called turnover ratios. The number in **BOLD** represents the **number of days** and the number in regular type set is the **number of times. Please see the definition of Sales/Receivables on the following pages for an excellent description of the two types of calculations and what each means.**

- In interpreting ratios, the "strongest" or "best" value is not always the largest numerical value, nor is the "weakest" always the lowest numerical value. The following description of each of the ratios appearing in the *Statement Studies* will provide details regarding the arraying of the values. The ratios in the *Statement Studies* are grouped into five principal categories: liquidity, coverage, leverage, operating, and specific expense items.

- **Inventory presentations** are based on fiscal year end point in time balances, not averages. In addition, our data capture does not permit us to know what method of inventory accounting (LIFO, FIFO for instance) was used.

The following ratios are contained in the *Statement Studies*:

LIQUIDITY RATIOS

Liquidity is a measure of the quality and adequacy of current assets to meet current obligations as they come due.

1. Current Ratio

Computation: Total current assets divided by total current liabilities.

$$\frac{\text{Total Current Assets}}{\text{Total Current Liabilities}}$$

Interpretation: This ratio is a rough indication of a firm's ability to service its current obligations. Generally, the higher the current ratio, the greater the "cushion" between current obligations and a firm's ability to pay them. The stronger ratio reflects a numerical superiority of current assets over current liabilities. However, the composition and quality of current assets is a critical factor in the analysis of an individual firm's liquidity.

The ratio values are arrayed from the highest positive to the lowest positive.

2. *Quick Ratio*

Computation: Cash and equivalents plus trade receivables divided by total current liabilities.

$$\frac{\text{Cash \& Equivalents} + \text{Trade Receivables} - \text{(net)}}{\text{Total Current Liabilities}}$$

Interpretation: Also known as the "ACID TEST" ratio, it is a refinement of the current ratio and is a more conservative measure of liquidity. The ratio expresses the degree to which a company's current liabilities are covered by the most liquid current assets. Generally, any value of less than 1 to 1 implies a reciprocal "dependency" on inventory or other current assets to liquidate short-term debt.

The ratio values are arrayed from the highest positive to the lowest positive.

3. *Sales/Receivables*

Computation: Net sales are divided by trade receivables.

$$\frac{\text{Net Sales}}{\text{Trade Receivables} - \text{(net)}}$$

In the contractor section both Accounts Receivable–Progress Billings and Accounts Receivable–Current Retention are included in the Receivables figure used in calculating the Revenues/Receivables and Receivables/Payables ratios.

Interpretation: This ratio measures the number of times trade receivables turn over during the year. The higher the turnover of receivables, the shorter the time between sale and cash collection. For example, a company with sales of $720,000 and receivables of $120,000 would have a sales/receivables ratio of 6.0, which means receivables turn over six times a year. If a company's receivables appear to be turning slower than the rest of the industry, further research is needed and the quality of the receivables should be examined closely.

A problem with this ratio is that it compares one day's receivables, shown at statement date, to total annual sales and does not take into consideration seasonal fluctuations. An additional problem in interpretation may arise when there is a large proportion of cash sales to total sales.

When the receivables figure is zero, the quotient will be undefined (UND) and represents the best possible ratio. The ratio values are therefore arrayed starting with undefined (UND) and then from the numerically highest to the numerically lowest value. The only time a zero will appear in the array is when the sales figure is low and the quotient rounds off to zero. By definition, this ratio cannot be negative.

Days' Receivables: The sales/receivables ratio will have a figure printed in bold type directly to the left of the array. This figure is the days' receivables.

Computation: The sales/receivables ratio divided into 365 (the number of days in one year).

$$\frac{365}{\text{Sales/Receivable ratio}}$$

Interpretation: This figure expresses the average time in days that receivables are outstanding. Generally, the greater number of days outstanding, the greater the probability of delinquencies in accounts receivable. A comparison of a company's daily receivables may indicate the extent of a company's control over credit and collections. The terms offered by a company to its customers, however, may differ from terms within the industry and should be taken into consideration.

In the example above, 365/6 = 61—i.e., the average receivable is collected in 61 days.

4. *Cost of Sales/Inventory*

Computation: Cost of sales divided by inventory.

$$\frac{\text{Cost of Sales}}{\text{Inventory}}$$

Interpretation: This ratio measures the number of times inventory is turned over during the year. High inventory turnover can indicate better liquidity or superior merchandising. Conversely it can indicate a shortage of needed inventory for sales. Low inventory turnover can indicate poor liquidity, possible overstocking, obsolescence, or in contrast to these negative interpretations a planned inventory buildup in the case of material shortages. A problem with this ratio is that it compares one day's inventory to cost of goods sold and does not take seasonal fluctuations into account. When the inventory figure is zero, the quotient will be undefined (UND) and represents the best possible ratio. The ratio values are arrayed starting with undefined (UND) and then from the numerically highest to the numerically lowest value. The only time a zero will appear in the array is when the cost of sales figure is very low and the quotient rounds off to zero.

Some service industries report data for cost of sales, while others do not. Note that in cases where the sample reporting it was insufficient, we have adjusted the data for cost of sales by putting it into operating expenses.

Please be aware, too, that our data collection process does not provide for differentiating the method of inventory valuation.

Days' Inventory

The post of sales/inventory ratio will have a figure printed in bold type directly to the left of the array. This figure is the days' inventory.

Computation: The cost of sales/inventory ratio divided into 365 (the number of days in one year).

$$\frac{365}{\text{Cost of Sales/Inventory ratio}}$$

Interpretation: Division of the inventory turnover ratio into 365 days yields the average length of time units are in inventory.

5. *Cost of Sales/Payables*

Computation: Cost of sales divided by trade payables.

$$\frac{\text{Cost of Sales}}{\text{Trade Payables}}$$

In the contractor section both Accounts Payable—Trade and Accounts Payable—Retention are included in the Payables figure used in calculating the Cost of Revenues/Payables and Receivables/Payables ratios.

Interpretation: This ratio measures the number of times trade payables turn over during the year. The higher the turnover of payables, the shorter the time between purchase and payment. If a company's payables appear to be turning more slowly than the industry, then the company may be experiencing cash shortages, disputing invoices with suppliers, enjoying extended terms, or deliberately expanding its trade credit. The ratio comparison of company to industry suggests the existence of these possible causes or others. If a firm buys on 30 day terms, it is reasonable to expect this ratio to turn over in approximately 30 days.

A problem with this ratio is that it compares one day's payables to cost of goods sold and does not take seasonal fluctuations into account. When the payables figure is zero, the quotient will be undefined (UND) and represents the best possible ratio. The ratio values are arrayed starting with undefined (UND) and then from the numerically highest to the numerically lowest value. The only time a zero will appear in the array is when the cost of sales figure is very low and the quotient rounds off to zero.

Days' Payables

The cost of sales/payables ratio will have a figure printed in bold type directly to the left of the array. This figure is the days' payables.

Computation: The cost of sales/payables ratio divided into 365 (the number of days in one year).

$$\frac{365}{\text{Cost of Sales/Payables ratio}}$$

Interpretation: Division of the payables turnover ratio into 365 days yields the average length of time trade debt is outstanding.

6. *Sales/Working Capital*

Computation: Net sales divided by net working capital (current assets less current liabilities equals net working capital).

$$\frac{\text{Net Sales}}{\text{Net Working Capital}}$$

Interpretation: Working capital is a measure of the margin of protection for current creditors. It reflects the ability to finance current operations. Relating the level of sales arising from operations to the underlying working capital measures how efficiently working capital is employed. A low ratio may indicate an inefficient use of working capital while a very high ratio often signifies overtrading-vulnerable position for creditors.

If working capital is zero, the quotient is undefined (UND). If working capital is negative, the quotient is negative. The ratio values are arrayed from the lowest positive to the highest positive, to undefined (UND), and then from the highest negative to the lowest negative.

COVERAGE RATIOS

Coverage ratios measure a firm's ability to service debt.

1. *Earnings Before Interest And Taxes (Ebit)/Interest*

Computation: Earnings (profit) before annual interest expense and taxes divided by annual interest expense.

$$\frac{\text{Earnings Before Interest \& Taxes}}{\text{Annual Interest Expense}}$$

Interpretation: This ratio is a measure of a firm's ability to meet interest payments. A high ratio may indicate that a borrower would have little difficulty in meeting the interest obligations of a loan. This ratio also serves as an indicator of a firm's capacity to take on additional debt.

Only those statements which reported annual interest expense were used in the calculation of this ratio. The ratio values are arrayed from the highest positive to the lowest positive and then from the lowest negative to the highest negative.

2. *Net Profit + Depreciation, Depletion, Amortization/Current Maturities Long–Term Debt*

Computation: Net profit plus depreciation, depletion, and amortization expenses, divided by the current portion of long-term debt.

$$\frac{\text{Net Profit + Depreciation, Depletion, Amortization Expenses}}{\text{Current Portion of Long–Term Debt}}$$

Interpretation: This ratio expresses the coverage of current maturities by cash flow from operations. Since cash flow is the primary source of debt retirement, this ratio measures the ability of a firm to service principal repayment and is an indicator of additional debt capacity. Although it is misleading to think that all cash flow is available for debt service, the ratio is a valid measure of the ability to service long-term debt.

Only data for *corporations* which have the following items were used;

(1) Profit or loss after taxes (positive, negative, or zero)

(2) A positive figure for Depreciation/Depletion/Amortization expenses

(3) A positive figure for current maturities of long-term debt

Ratio values are arrayed from the highest to the lowest positive and then from the lowest to the highest negative.

LEVERAGE RATIOS

Highly leveraged firms (those with heavy debt in relation to net worth) are more vulnerable to business downturns than those with lower debt to worth positions. While leverage ratios help to measure this vulnerability, it must be remembered that they vary greatly depending on the requirements of particular industry groups.

1. *Fixed/Worth*

Computation: Fixed assets (net of accumulated depreciation) divided by tangible net worth (net worth minus intangibles).

$$\frac{\text{Net Fixed Assets}}{\text{Tangible Net Worth}}$$

Interpretation: This ratio measures the extent to which owner's equity (capital) has been invested in plant and equipment (fixed assets). A lower ratio indicates a proportionately smaller investment in fixed assets in relation to net worth, and a better "cushion" for creditors in case of liquidation. Similarly, a higher ratio would indicate the opposite situation. The presence of substantial leased fixed assets (not shown on the balance sheet) may deceptively lower this ratio.

Fixed assets may be zero, in which case the quotient is zero. If tangible net worth is zero, the quotient is undefined (UND). If tangible net worth is negative, the quotient is negative. The ratio values are arrayed from the lowest positive to the highest positive, undefined, and then from the highest negative to the lowest negative.

2. *Debt/Worth*

Computation: Total liabilities divided by tangible net worth.

$$\frac{\text{Total Liabilities}}{\text{Tangible Net Worth}}$$

Interpretation: This ratio expresses the relationship between capital contributed by creditors and that contributed by owners. It expresses the degree of protection provided by the owners for the creditors. The higher the ratio, the greater the risk being assumed by creditors. A lower ratio generally indicates greater long-term financial safety. A firm with a low debt/worth ratio usually has greater flexibility to borrow in the future. A more highly leveraged company has a more limited debt capacity.

Tangible net worth may be zero, in which case the ratio is undefined (UND). Tangible net worth may also be negative which results in the quotient being negative. The ratio values are arrayed from the lowest to highest positive, undefined, and then from the highest to lowest negative.

OPERATING RATIOS

Operating ratios are designed to assist in the evaluation of management performance.

1. % *Profits Before Taxes/Tangible Net Worth*

Computation: Profit before taxes divided by tangible net worth and multiplied by 100.

$$\frac{\text{Profit Before Taxes}}{\text{Tangible Net Worth}} \times 100$$

Interpretation: This ratio expresses the rate of return on tangible capital employed. While it can serve as an indicator of management performance, the analyst is cautioned to use it in conjunction with other ratios. A high return, normally associated with effective management, could indicate an undercapitalized firm. Whereas, a low return, usually-an indicator of inefficient management performance, could reflect a highly capitalized, conservatively operated business.

This ratio has been multiplied by 100 since it is shown as a percentage.

Profit before taxes may be zero, in which case the ratio is zero. Profits before takes may be negative resulting in negative quotients. Firms with negative tangible net worth have been omitted from the ratio arrays. Negative ratios will therefore only result in the case of negative profit before taxes. If the tangible net worth is zero, the quotient is undefined (UND). If there are less than 10 ratios for a particular size class, the result is not shown. The ratio values are arrayed starting with undefined (UND), and then from the highest to the lowest positive values, and from the lowest to the highest negative values.

2. % *Profit Before Taxes/Total Assets*

Computation: Profit before taxes divided by total assets and multiplied by 100.

$$\frac{\text{Profit Before Taxes}}{\text{Total Assets}} \times 100$$

Interpretation: This ratio expresses the pre-tax return on total assets and measures the effectiveness of management in employing the resources available to it. If a specific ratio varies considerably from the ranges found in this book, the analyst will need to examine the makeup of assets and take a closer look at the earnings figure. A heavily depreciated plant and a large amount of intangible assets or unusual income or expense items will cause distortions of this ratio.

This ratio has been multiplied by 100 since it is shown as a percentage. If profit before taxes is zero, the quotient is zero. If profit before taxes is negative, the quotient is negative. These ratio values are arrayed from the highest to the lowest positive, and then from the lowest to the highest negative.

3.   *Sales/Net Fixed Assets*

Computation: Net sales divided by net fixed assets (net of accumulated depreciation).

$$\frac{\text{Net Sales}}{\text{Net Fixed Assets}}$$

Interpretation: This ratio is a measure of the productive use of a firm's fixed assets. Largely depreciated fixed assets or a labor intensive operation may cause a distortion of this ratio.

If the net fixed figure is zero, the quotient is undefined (UND). The only time a zero will appear in the array will be when the net sales figure is low and the quotient rounds off to zero. These ratio values cannot be negative.

They are arrayed from undefined (UND), and then from the highest to the lowest positive values.

4.   *Sales/Total Assets*

Computation: Net sales divided by total assets.

$$\frac{\text{Net Sales}}{\text{Total Assets}}$$

Interpretation: This ration is a general measure of a firm's ability to generate sales in relation to total assets. It should be used only to compare firms within specific industry groups and in conjunction with other operating ratios to determine the effective employment of assets.

The only time a zero will appear in the array will be when the net sales figure is low and the quotient rounds off to zero. The ratio values cannot be negative. They are arrayed from the highest to the lowest positive values.

EXPENSE TO SALES RATIOS

The following two ratios relate specific expense items to net sales and express this relationship as a percentage. Comparisons are convenient because the item, net sales, is used as a constant. Variations in these ratios are most pronounced between capital and labor intensive industries.

1.   *% Depreciation, Depletion, Amortization/Sales*

Computation: Annual depreciation, amortization, and depletion expenses divided by net sales and multiplied by 100.

$$\frac{\text{Depreciation, Amortization, Depletion Expenses}}{\text{Net Sales}} \times 100$$

2.   *% Officers', Directors', Owners' Compensation/Sales*

Computation: Annual Officers', Directors', Owners' Compensation divided by net I sales and multiplied by 100. Included here are total salaries, bonuses, commissions, and other monetary remuneration to all officers; directors; and/or owners of the firm during the year covered by the statement. This includes drawings of partners and proprietors.

$$\frac{\text{Officers', Directors', Owners' Compensation}}{\text{Net Sales}} \times 100$$

Only statements showing a positive figure for each of the expense categories shown above were used. The ratios are arrayed from the lowest to highest positive values.

Explanation of Noncontractor Balance Sheet and Income Data

Cash & Equivalents
All cash, marketplace, securities, near-cash items. Excludes sinking funds.

Trade Receivables-(net)
All accounts from trade, net of allow ance for doubtful accounts.

Inventory
Anything constituting inventory for the firm.

All Other Current
Any other current assets. Does not include prepaid items.

Total Current
Total of all current assets listed above.

Fixed Assets (net)
All property, plant, leasehold improvements and equipment, net of accumulated depreciation or depletion.

Intangibles (net)
Intangible assets, including goodwill, trademarks, patents, catalogs, brands, copyrights, formulas, franchises, and mailing lists, net of accumulated amortization.

All Other Non-Current
Prepaid items and any other non-current assets.

Total
Total of all items listed above.

ASSETS
Cash & Equivalents
Trade Receivables (net)
Inventory
All Other Current
Total Current
Fixed Assets (net)
Intangibles (net)
All Other Non-Current
Total

Notes Payable-Short Term
All short term note obligations, including bank and commercial paper. Does not include trade notes payable.

Current Maturities–L/T/D
That portion of long term obligations which is due within the next fiscal year.

Trade Payables
Open accounts due to the trade.

Income Taxes Payable
Income taxes including current portion of deferred taxes.

All Other Current
Any other current liabilities, including bank overdrafts and accrued expenses.

LIABILITIES
Notes Payable-Short Term
Cur. Mat.-L/T/D
Trade Payables
Income Taxes Payable
All Other Current
Total Current
Long Term Debt
Deferred Taxes
All Other Non-Current
Net Worth
Total Liabilities & Net Worth

Total Current
Total of all current liabilities listed above.

Long Term Debt
All senior debt, including bonds, debentures, bank debt, mortgages, deferred portions of long term debt, and capital lease obligations.

Deferred Taxes
All deferred taxes.

All Other Non-Current
Any other non-current liabilities including subordinated debt and liability reserves.

Net Worth
Difference between Total Liabilities and Total Assets. Minority interest is included here.

Total Liabilities & Net Worth
Total of all items listed above.

Net Sales
Gross sales, net of returns
and discounts allowed, if any.

Gross Profit
Net sales minus cost of sales.

Operating Expenses
All selling and general &
administrative expenses. Includes
depreciation, but not
interest expense.

INCOME DATA
Net Sales
Gross Profit
Operating Expenses
Operating Profit
All Other Expenses (net)
Profit Before Taxes

Operating Profit
Gross profit minus operating
expenses.

All Other Expenses (net)
Includes miscellaneous other income
and expenses (net), such as interest
expense, miscellaneous expenses
not included in general & administrative expenses, netted against recoveries, interest income, dividends
received and miscellaneous income.

Profit Before Taxes
Operating profit minus all other
expenses (net).

MANUFACTURING RADIO & TELEVISION BROADCASTING & COMMUNICATIONS EQUIPMENT SIC# 3663 (NAICS 33422)

Current Data Sorted By Assets							Comparative Historical Data	

						Type of Statement		
		8	14	4	1	Unqualified	32	36
	2	7				Reviewed	16	15
1	3	7	2			Compiled	11	10
1	1					Tax Returns	2	
1	4	6	2	3	5	Other	32	18
	15 (4/1-9/30/00)		57 (10/1/00-3/31/01)				4/1/96-3/31/97	4/1/97-3/31/98
0-500M	500M-2MM	2-10MM	10-50MM	50-100MM	100-250MM		ALL	ALL
3	10	28	18	7	6	NUMBER OF STATEMENTS	91	81
%	%	%	%	%	%	ASSETS	%	%
	6.5	6.9	16.9			Cash & Equivalents	11.6	10.3
	36.6	29.5	22.8			Trade Receivables - (net)	27.9	27.2
	22.0	32.8	23.0			Inventory	26.1	26.7
	1.0	2.0	6.0			All Other Current	3.5	3.4
	66.1	71.3	68.7			Total Current	69.1	67.6
	31.6	19.3	22.2			Fixed Assets (net)	22.4	22.2
	.3	3.5	4.6			Intangibles (net)	3.4	3.3
	2.0	5.9	4.5			All Other Non-Current	5.1	7.0
	100.0	100.0	100.0			Total	100.0	100.0
						LIABILITIES		
	8.9	11.0	5.2			Notes Payable-Short Term	6.7	6.2
	5.0	3.3	3.1			Cur. Mat.-L/T/D	3.0	2.5
	16.6	10.9	11.1			Trade Payables	12.6	10.7
	.0	.3	.1			Income Taxes Payable	.9	.6
	13.8	14.1	7.1			All Other Current	8.4	10.3
	44.4	39.6	26.6			Total Current	31.6	30.3
	12.3	12.3	10.0			Long Term Debt	11.3	10.5
	.1	2.6	1.2			Deferred Taxes	.7	1.8
	1.1	2.5	2.5			All Other Non-Current	3.7	3.3
	42.1	43.0	55.6			Net Worth	52.8	54.2
	100.0	100.0	100.0			Total Liabilities & Net Worth	100.0	100.0
						INCOME DATA		
	100.0	100.0	100.0			Net Sales	100.0	100.0
	49.5	35.4	39.0			Gross Profit	38.0	37.2
	42.0	28.5	36.9			Operating Expenses	30.6	30.8
	7.5	7.0	2.2			Operating Profit	7.4	6.4
	1.5	.7	-.9			All Other Expenses (net)	.9	1.0
	6.0	6.3	3.1			Profit Before Taxes	6.5	5.4
						RATIOS		
	2.8	2.9	4.5				3.6	4.0
	1.3	2.1	3.2			Current	2.3	2.6
	.8	1.4	1.6				1.5	1.7
	2.3	1.8	2.9				2.2	2.5
	.8	.9	1.8			Quick	1.1	1.3
	.4	.6	.9				.8	.8
28 12.9	40 9.1	51 7.2				Sales/Receivables	38 9.5	38 9.7
47 7.8	50 7.4	53 6.9					51 7.1	51 7.2
65 5.6	71 5.1	69 5.3					76 4.8	73 5.0
0 UND	45 8.2	61 6.0				Cost of Sales/Inventory	41 8.8	41 8.8
63 5.8	84 4.3	108 3.4					79 4.6	91 4.0
98 3.7	154 2.4	140 2.6					122 3.0	146 2.5
23 15.7	15 24.3	26 13.9				Cost of Sales/Payables	22 16.6	19 19.2
40 9.2	29 12.7	31 11.6					34 10.6	32 11.3
125 2.9	44 8.3	47 7.7					56 6.5	54 6.7
	5.0	3.9	2.3				3.1	3.1
	11.3	6.4	3.4			Sales/Working Capital	5.5	4.6
	-34.4	14.6	5.8				10.5	8.0
	12.9	33.5					15.8	19.8
	(25) 4.9	(14) 2.2				EBIT/Interest	(74) 4.5	(71) 5.6
	2	-4.3					1.9	1.6
	6.8					Net Profit + Depr., Dep.,	18.0	7.5
	(10) 2.9					Amort./Cur. Mat. L/T/D	(36) 5.1	(37) 4.0
	1.8						2.3	1.2
	.2	.2	.1				.2	.2
	.5	.3	.3			Fixed/Worth	.4	.3
	2.0	1.0	.5				.9	.7
	.5	.6	.4				.3	.3
	1.9	1.4	.6			Debt/Worth	.9	.7
	4.8	3.7	1.5				2.2	1.6
	38.1	67.0	43.3			% Profit Before Taxes/	45.5	37.0
	(26) 11.8	24.5	7.8			Tangible Net Worth	(85) 24.6	(75) 16.4
	8.4	4.5	-20.5				7.5	2.1
	16.3	26.9	28.8			% Profit Before Taxes/	24.4	18.5
	6.8	10.1	3.6			Total Assets	10.6	8.5
	2.7	1.3	-6.6				3.3	1.3
	UND	51.8	17.9				20.6	21.9
	13.1	18.7	9.3			Sales/Net Fixed Assets	10.1	9.8
	4.6	5.3	4.3				5.0	4.6
	2.8	2.5	1.9				2.7	2.4
	2.4	2.1	1.4			Sales/Total Assets	1.8	1.7
	1.5	1.4	1.0				1.2	1.2
	.6	.7				% Depr., Dep., Amort./	1.1	.9
	(27) 1.7	(14) 2.7				Sales	(77) 2.2	(72) 2.0
	2.6	3.9					3.7	4.2
						% Officers', Directors',	1.2	1.6
						Owners' Comp/Sales	(19) 5.4	(15) 4.3
							8.6	7.1
5082M	32269M	272905M	589962M	668461M	1315972M	Net Sales ($)	2852309M	2954165M
812M	13037M	137017M	432032M	442945M	1088764M	Total Assets ($)	2097630M	2317598M

© RMA 2001 M = $ thousand MM = $ million

See Pages 9 through 18 for Explanation of Ratios and Data

MANUFACTURING-RADIO & TELEVISION BROADCASTING COMMUNICATIONS EQUIPMENT SIC# 3663 (NAICS 33422)
Comparative Historical Data   Current Data Sorted By Sales

			Type of Statement						
33	29	27	Unqualified		1		4	8	14
19	11	9	Reviewed		1	1	4	3	
10	11	13	Compiled	2		3	4	3	1
1	2	2	Tax Returns		1		1		
27	21	21	Other	1	2	1	7	3	7
4/1/98-	4/1/99-	4/1/00-			15 (4/1-9/30/00)			57 (10/1/00-3/31/01)	
3/31/99	3/31/00	3/31/01							
ALL	ALL	ALL		0-1M	1-3MM	3-5M	5-10MM	10-25MM	25MM & OVER
90	74	72	NO. of STATEMENTS	3	5	5	20	17	22
%	%	%	ASSETS	%	%	%	%	%	%
12.0	11.3	10.7	Cash & Equivalents				4.5	10.0	15.2
26.2	25.3	26.8	Trade Receivables (net)				24.4	32.0	22.2
27.1	27.4	25.5	Inventory				32.2	29.4	20.7
2.7	4.5	3.7	All Other Current				2.1	3.6	6.2
68.0	68.6	66.7	Total Current				63.2	75.1	64.3
19.7	20.5	23.6	Fixed Assets (net)				26.7	16.9	21.1
4.8	3.9	5.2	Intangibles (net)				3.5	4.6	9.8
7.5	7.0	4.5	All Other Non-Current				6.7	3.5	4.8
100.0	100.0	100.0	Total				100.0	100.0	100.0
			LIABILITIES						
10.7	10.9	7.0	Notes Payable-Short Term				10.4	10.3	2.3
2.6	3.7	4.1	Cur. Mat.-L/T/D				5.1	2.0	3.7
13.3	15.1	11.5	Trade Payables				10.2	11.7	11.3
.6	.3	.2	Income Taxes Payable				.4	.0	.2
9.4	10.9	11.1	All Other Current				12.8	13.8	9.6
36.6	40.9	33.9	Total Current				38.9	37.8	26.1
12.5	13.7	12.1	Long Term Debt				18.2	8.5	9.5
.6	.7	1.5	Deferred Taxes				3.3	1.7	.5
4.8	3.0	2.4	All Other Non-Current				3.1	1.1	3.6
45.5	41.7	50.1	Net Worth				36.5	50.9	60.4
100.0	100.0	100.0	Total Liabilities & Net Worth				100.0	100.0	100.0
			INCOME DATA						
100.0	100.0	100.0	Net Sales				100.0	100.0	100.0
38.3	38.8	39.6	Gross Profit				41.1	36.2	33.0
32.1	34.1	33.0	Operating Expenses				32.3	35.0	25.5
6.2	4.7	5.6	Operating Profit				8.8	1.2	7.5
.6	2.2	1.4	All Other Expenses (Net)				4.4	-2.5	1.9
5.5	2.6	5.2	Profit Before Taxes				4.5	3.7	5.6
			RATIOS						
3.4	3.6	3.4					2.3	2.5	3.8
1.9	1.7	2.2	Current				1.6	2.4	2.9
1.3	1.2	1.3					.9	1.5	1.6
2.2	1.7	2.2					1.0	2.2	2.8
1.1	1.0	1.0	Quick				.7	1.3	1.2
.6	.5	.6					.5	.8	.8
38 9.5	37 10.0	44 8.3					40 9.1	48 7.6	49 7.5
46 7.9	49 7.4	51 7.1	Sales/Receivables				51 7.1	52 7.0	51 7.2
66 5.6	61 6.0	68 5.4					73 5.0	67 5.4	60 6.0
47 7.8	47 7.8	41 8.8					28 13.0	42 8.7	49 7.5
88 4.2	88 4.1	81 4.5	Cost of Sales/Inventory				84 4.8	91 4.0	64 4.4
150 2.4	135 2.7	138 2.6					166 2.2	143 2.5	111 3.3
18 20.5	21 17.6	20 17.9					16 23.0	22 16.7	22 16.8
35 10.4	39 9.4	31 11.8	Cost of Sales/Payables				35 10.5	29 12.7	33 11.1
66 5.5	61 5.5	45 8.0					51 7.1	37 9.7	55 6.6
3.6	3.5	3.0					4.0	3.6	2.8
6.0	6.4	5.6	Sales/Working Capital				9.0	6.0	4.2
11.6	23.2	11.4					-62.3	10.5	7.0
14.1	14.1	15.7					12.9	35.0	10.3
(72) 5.6	(61) 3.8	(59) 4.2	EBIT/Interest				(17) 4.9	(14) 4.6	(17) 2.9
1.6	.7	1.4					2.0	-1.6	1.1
5.3	6.8	8.2	Net Profit + Depr., Dep.,						20.0
(38) 3.0	(28) 2.3	(29) 2.8	Amort./Cur. Mat. L/T/D						(12) 2.9
1.3	1.2	.8							1.1
.2	.2	.2					.2	.2	.2
.4	.5	.4	Fixed/Worth				.7	.3	.3
.7	1.3	1.0					2.9	.7	.5
.5	.5	.4					1.0	.4	.3
1.3	1.5	1.0	Debt/Worth				2.1	1.0	.7
3.1	3.0	2.2					4.9	2.1	1.2
56.8	36.4	49.0					83.2	53.4	27.1
(79) 22.2	(65) 20.7	(69) 16.6	% Profit Before Taxes				(18) 22.1	16.1	(21) 15.9
10.0	1.5	2.8	Tangible Net Worth				3.9	-25.0	.2
21.9	17.3	23.1					29.4	19.4	17.8
10.2	9.2	.8	% Profit Before Taxes/Total				9.7	9.5	6.8
21.9	.6	1.0	Assets				.8	-6.0	1.9
27.9	26.0	26.6					35.4	28.2	12.2
10.4	12.1	9.6	Sales/Net Fixed Assets				10.9	18.2	9.2
6.0	5.4	5.1					4.2	5.3	5.2
2.5	2.5	2.6					2.7	3.0	1.9
2.0	1.9	.0	Sales/Total Assets				1.9	1.8	1.3
1.3	1.1	1.1					1.0	1.3	1.1
.9	.9	.7					.7	.6	2.1
(76) 2.4	(64) 2.2	(60) 2.1	% Depr., Dep., Amort./Sales				(19) 2.0	(15) 1.7	(17) 2.9
3.9	3.3	3.5					3.5		2.3	4.6
2.9	1.7	1.6							
(19) 4.7	(17) 4.1	(13) 4.1	% Officers', Directors',						
6.7	8.5	6.9	Owners' Comp/Sales						
3240742M	2135947M	2824651M	Net Sales ($)	1596M	9858M	20557M	148757M	265765M	2378118M
2540313M	1479632M	2114607M	Total Assets ($)	1376M	5183M	9904M	180203M	162640M	1755301M

© RMA 2001   M = $ thousand   MM = $ million
See Pages 9 through 18 for Explanation of Ratios and Data

MANUFACTURING-ELECTRONIC COMPONENTS, NEC SIC# 3679 (NAICS 33422, 33431, 334418)

Current Data Sorted By Assets							Comparative Historical Data	

							Type of Statement	
3	2	18	29	4	9	Unqualified		
2	9	29	5		1	Reviewed		
6	13	16	5	2	1	Compiled		
4	4					Tax Returns		
1	11	31	18	2	5	Other		
		57(4/1-9/30/00)		172 (10/1/00-3/31/01)				

							4/1/96-3/31/97	4/1/97-3/31/98
0-500M	500M-2MM	2-10MM	10-50MM	50-100MM	100-250MM		ALL	ALL
16	39	94	57	8	15	NO. OF STATEMENTS		
%	%	%	%	%	%	ASSETS	%	%
8.6	9.9	7.3	8.5		19.6	Cash & Equivalents	D	D
34.6	38.3	29.9	23.5		16.2	Trade Receivables - (net)	A	A
29.8	27.7	31.2	29.6		16.7	Inventory	T	T
1.7	1.8	1.2	4.6		3.9	All Other Current	A	A
74.7	77.7	69.6	66.4		56.5	Total Current		
17.1	15.0	21.8	22.6		23.3	Fixed Assets (net)	N	N
3.3	1.4	3.9	5.6		10.4	Intangibles (net)	O	O
4.8	5.8	4.7	5.4		9.8	All Other Non-current	T	T
100.0	100.0	100.0	100.0		100.0	Total		
						LIABILITIES	A	A
21.9	9.7	15.0	7.6		2.3	Notes Payable-Short Term	V	V
2.6	2.1	3.5	3.5		.9	Cur. Mat.-L/T/D	A	A
24.2	16.6	14.2	13.9		7.8	Trade Payables	I	I
.6		.4	.3	4	.2	Income Taxes		
						Payable	L	L
25.6	9.7	9.0	7.8		8.6	All Other Current	A	A
74.9	38.5	42.1	33.2		19.8	Total Current	B	B
12.1	7.5	11.3	16.2		16.9	Long Term Debt	I	I
0	.1	.3	.5		.8	Deferred Taxes	E	E
13.1	10.3	4.8	3.3		11.2	All Other Non-Current		
-.1	43.6	41.4	46.8		51.3	Net Worth		
100.0	100.0	100.0	100.0		100.0	Total Liabilities & Net Worth		
						INCOME DATA		
100.0	100.0	100.0	100.0		100.0	Net Sales		
43.2	35.5	30.0	29.6		37.2	Gross Profit		
39.9	30.7	26.3	25.0		34.5	Operating Expenses		
3.3	4.8	3.7	4.6		2.7	Operating Profit		
2.3	.6	.4	1.5		-2.0	All Other Expenses (net)		
1.0	4.1	3.3	3.1		4.6	Profit Before Taxes		
						RATIOS		
2.3	4.1	2.6	3.2		5.5			
1.2	2.2	1.6	2.2		3.7	Current		
1.1	1.3	1.2	1.5		2.2			
1.2	2.6	1.4	1.9		4.1			
.8	1.3	.8	1.1		1.6	Quick		
.3	.7	.6	.6		.8			
19 19.6	39 9.5	37 9.8	49 7.5		52 7.0			
34 10.9	56 6.5	48 7.6	57 6.4		63 5.8	Sales/Receivables		
45 8.0	72 5.1	57 6.4	73 5.0		65 5.6			
19 19.4	27 13.5	39 9.5	63 5.8		69 5.3			
47 1.8	51 7.1	70 5.2	94 3.6		110 3.3	Cost of Sales/Inventory		
74 4.9	86 4.2	104 3.5	128 2.9		125 2.9			
8 43.3	14 25.1	16 22.2	27 13.7		33 11.1			
33 11.0	33 11.0	29 12.5	42 8.6		42 8.7	Cost of Sales/Payables		
55 6.7	46 7.9	40 9.1	61 6.0		54 6.7			
7.8	4.1	4.7	3.0		7.1			
27.1	15.9	9.2	4.4		3.5	Sales/Working Capital		
116.7	13.0	17.4	7.6		5.6			
11.8	13.0	6.1	11.4		127.2			
(10) 2.6	(35) 3.7	(83) 2.8	(51) 3.2		(12) 4.3	EBIT/Interest		
.9	1.1	1.1	.6		-1.1			
		8.1	13.3			Net Profit + Depr., Dep.,		
		(39) 3.4	(19) 2.1			Amort./Cur. Mat. L/T/D		
		1.6	.3					
.2	.1	.3	.2		.3			
.3	.3	.6	.5		.3	Fixed/Worth		
NM	.8	1.2	1.2		1.1			
1.0	.5	.8	.4		.2			
2.0	1.3	1.7	1.2		.3	Debt/Worth		
NM	3.4	3.1	3.5		3.1			

0-500M	500M-2MM	2-10MM	10-50MM	50-100MM	100-250MM		ALL	ALL
			3/31/97	3/31/98			4/1/96-	4/1/97

16	39	94	57	8		15	NO. OF STATEMENTS		
%	%	%	%	%		%		%	%
99.5	52.5	36.1	32.2			35.8			
(12) 49.2	(37) 24.1	(87) 18.2	(51) 16.9			(13) 13.4	% Profit Before Taxes/Tangible		
3.7	5.1	4.4	2.6			-1.8	Net Worth		
29.1	21.9	14.0	14.0			18.1			
6.3	5.7	6.5	6.7			8.3	% Profit Before Taxes/Total		
-2.7	6	1.0	.2			-9.3	Assets		
63.1	62.7	28.5	18.0			6.6			
36.1	21.6	10.5	7.6			4.5	Sales/Net Fixed Assets		
17.2	10.5	5.6	4.0			3.6			
5.6	3.1	2.8	1.9			1.3			
3.9	2.5	2.1	1.5			.9	Sales/Total Assets		
3.1	2.0	1.7	1.1			.7			
	6	.7	1.4						
	(33) 1.5	(86) 1.9	(46) 2.6				% Depr., Dep., Amort./Sales		
	3.2	3.4	4.0						
	2.4	2.4							
	(18) 5.3	(30) 4.0					% Officers', Directors',		
	11.0	8.2					Owners' Comp/Sales		
17121M	119208M	1043752M	2100884M	927394M	2388250M		Net sales ($)		
4403M	47869M	461749M	1371782M	599612M	2609406M		Total Assets ($)		

    M = $ thousand   MM = $million

See Pages 9 through 18 for Explanation of Ratios and Data

MANUFACTURING-ELECTRONIC COMPONENTS, NEC SIC# 3679 (NAICS 33422, 33431, 334418)

Comparative Historical Data   Current Data Sorted By Sales

			Type of Statement						
76	60	65	Unqualified	2	3	2	6	19	33
43	36	45	Reviewed	1	6	4	12	20	2
23	18	43	Compiled	2	11	5	8	6	8
4	10	8	Tax Returns	2	4	1	1		
64	69	68	Other		6	11	16	13	21
4/1/98-	4/1/99-	4/11/00-			57(4/1-9/30/00)		172 (10/1/00-3/31/01)		
3/31/99	3/31/00	3/31/01		0-1 MM	1-3MM	3-5MM	5-10MM	10-25MM	25MM & OVER
ALL	ALL	ALL							
210	193	229	NO. OF STATEMENTS	8	30	26	43	58	64
%	%	%	ASSETS	%	%	%	%	%	%
7.8	8.1	9.0	Cash & Equivalents	9.8	9.2	6.8	8.2	10.6	
28.5	30.1	29.2	Trade Receivables-(net)	36.9	33.9	26.3	30.9	24.3	
29.3	28.7	29.0	Inventory	27.4	30.2	32.2	30.2	26.1	
1.7	2.2	2.6	All Other Current	1.0	2.2	1.5	1.4	5.4	
67.4	69.1	69.7	Total Current	75.0	75.5	66.9	70.7	56.5	
23.6	22.2	20.6	Fixed Assets (net)	15.3	20.3	23.3	19.5	22.0	
3.6	3.7	4.3	Intangibles (net)	1.9	1.4	3.1	5.8	5.9	
5.4	5.0	5.4	All Other Non-Current	7.8	2.9	6.7	4.0	5.7	
100.0	100.0	100.0	Total	100.0	100.0	100.0	100.0	100.0	
			LIABILITIES						
11.7	9.8	11.6	Notes Payable-Short Term	14.5	9.9	13.7	12.7	6.9	
3.5	3.7	3.2	Cur. Mat.-L/T/D	2.8	2.2	3.4	3.5	3.6	
13.5	15.8	15.0	Trade Payables	17.5	15.1	12.8	15.5	14.1	
.5	.3	.3	Income Taxes Payable	.4	2	.1	.4	.3	
11.3	8.9	10.0	All Other Current	11.3	8.9	10.0	8.6	8.7	
40.5	38.4	40.1	Total Current	46.4	36.3	40.0	40.8	33.5	
14.5	15.4	12.8	Long Term Debt	9.9	9.4	10.4	14.1	18.5	
.5	.6	.3	Deferred Taxes	.0	2	.2	.6	.4	
4.3	5.3	6.7	All Other Non-Current	15.8	11.5	3.5	2.5	5.8	
40.3	40.3	40.1	Net Worth	27.9	42.6	45.9	41.9	42.7	
100.0	100.0	100.0	Total Liabilities & Net Worth	100.0	100.0	100.0	100.0	100.0	
			INCOME DATA						
100.0	100.0	100.0	Net Sales	100.0	100.0	100.0	100.0	100.0	
32.6	32.2	32.0	Gross Profit	38.9	34.4	30.7	28.4	30.3	
30.3	27.8	28.0	Operating Expenses	38.2	28.8	28.1	23.7	24.7	
2.2	4.4	4.0	Operating Profit	.7	5.6	2.6	4.7	5.6	
4.4	1.4	.8	All Other Expenses (net)	.3	1.1	-.1	1.5	.8	
-2.1	3.0	3.1	Profit Before Taxes	.4	4.5	2.7	3.2	4.7	
			RATIOS						
2.8	2.8	3.1		3.7	4.0	2.9	2.8	4.1	
1.8	1.9	1.8	Current	1.9	2.2	1.7	1.8	2.2	
1.2	1.4	1.3		1.1	1.6	1.2	1.3	1.5	

4/1/98-	4/1/99-	4/11/00-			57(4/1-9/30/00)		172 (10/1/00-3/31/01)		
3/31/99	3/31/00	3/31/01		0-1 MM	1-3MM	3-5MM	5-10MM	10-25MM	25MM & OVER
ALL	ALL	ALL							
210	193	229	NO. OF STATEMENTS	8	30	26	43	58	64
%	%	%		%	%	%	%	%	%
1.5	1.7	1.7			2.3	2.2	1.2	1.6	1.8

			Ratio						
9	1.0	1.0	Quick	1.1	1.2	.8	1.0	1.1	
6	7	6		.6	.7	.6	.6	.6	
39 9.3	44 9.3	39 9.4	Sales/Receivables	36 10.1	35 10.3	39 9.3	37 9.7	47 7.8	
49 7.4	54 6.8	53 6.9		56 6.5	52 7.0	48 7.6	53 6.9	65 5.6	
62 5.9	65 5.6	65 5.6		83 4.4	16 5.5	57 16.4	64 5.7	69 5.3	
48 7.6	55 5.6	45 3.1	Cost of Sales/Inventory	19 19.2	37 9.9	40 9.1	45 8.0	62 5.9	
81 4.5	78 4.7	74 4.9		61 5.0	70 5.2	80 4.6	70 5.2	64 4.3	
116 3.1	110 3.3	112 3.3		114 3.2	98 3.7	114 3.2	112 3.3	120 3.0	
23 15.9	21 17.0	19 18.0	Cost of Sales/Payables	14 26.7	15 24.5	18 20.1	17 21.1	24 15.2	
31 11.7	37 10.0	33 10.8		38 9.5	32 11.4	30 12.4	32 11.4	40 9.2	
46 7.9	52 7.0	53 6.9		69 5.3	42 8.6	42 8.8	54 6.7	62 5.9	
4.2	4.0	3.7	Sales/Working Capital	3.8	3.9	4.2	4.6	3.3	
7.5	6.7	6.8		9.4	5.5	7.3	7.9	5.2	
20.9	12.4	15.1		41.9	11.3	25.8	15.3	9.9	
9.9	11.9	9.9	EBIT/Interest	9.1	13.5	12.0	6.3	17.1	
(193)3.7	(177)3.4	(199)3.0		(26) 2.6	(24) 2.8	(39) 2.8	(53) 3.0	(54) 3.9	
1.3	.8	1.0		.5	1.3	.1	1.5	.8	
9.4	10.2	9.8	Net Profit + Depr., Dep. Amort./Cur. Mat. L/T/D			9.0	8.9	20.2	
(85)2.8	(75)3.1	(73)3.0				(19) 2.3	(24) 4.3	(18) 2.0	
1.5	1.2	1.2				1.0	2.5	.9	
.3	.2	.2	Fixed/Worth	.1	.1	.2	.2	.3	
.6	.5	.5		.3	.4	.5	.5	.5	
1.4	1.5	1.2		1.0	1.0	1.0	1.4	1.3	
.8	.7	.5	Debt/Worth	.5	.3	.6	.7	.3	
1.6	1.4	1.6		2.3	1.4	1.4	1.8	1.4	
3.5	4.5	3.8		6.3	3.1	3.3	3.9	5.1	
39.7	41.3	43.4	% Profit Before Taxes/Tangible Net Worth	50.7	52.2	25.3	35.5	40.9	
(189)21.5	(178)20.4	(206)18.6		(27)15.4	(24)14.0	(41)10.3	(51)19.2	(57)25.9	
7.0	3.0	4.5		0	5.7	-2.1	4.8	10.0	
15.0	15.5	14.6	% Profit Before Taxes/Total Assets	17.2	18.3	15.3	12.2	15.9	
7.8	6.5	6.4		4.5	5.4	5.7	6.9	8.1	
1.7	-.2	0		-2.9	1.3	-1.5	1.5	-.9	
20.2	23.2	29.2	Sales/Net Fixed Assets	57.6	55.0	22.6	33.7	17.2	
9.9	11.5	11.3		21.1	18.5	10.0	9.8	6.7	
4.9	5.4	5.2		9.1	5.6	4.9	6.0	4.4	
2.6	2.6	2.6	Sales/Total Assets	2.9	3.2	2.4	2.9	1.9	
2.0	2.0	2.0		2.2	2.5	2.0	2.1	1.5	
1.4	1.4	1.4		1.5	1.7	1.5	1.5	1.1	
1.2	1.4	.7	% Depr., Dep. Amort./Sales	.7	.6	.9	.8	1	
(180)2.1	(167)2.3	(187)1.9		(25) 1.9	(23) 1.3	(41) 2.3	(51) 1.9	(45) 2.3	
3.5	3.7	3.5		3.7	2.0	3.8	2.9	4.4	
1.4	2.6	2.4	% Officers, Directors', Owners' Comp/Sales	4.7	2.2	3.4	1.2		
(62) 3.6	(57)4.9	(62)4.8		(12)9.3	(15) 5.0	(12) 7.2	(16) 3.7		
6.6	11.2	3.6		14.6	8.1	9.3	4.9		
6505761M	6108205M	6596599M	Net Sales ($)	5027M	55469M	102470M	298366M	927618M	5207649M
4235257M	4166684M	5094821M	Total Assets ($)	1673M	28892M	49204M	182963M	537099M	4294990M

© RMA 2001
M = $ thousand   MM = $ million
See Pages 9 through 18 for Explanation of Ratio and Data

CHAPTER THREE

VALUING FIRM OUTPUT

1. INTRODUCTION

A business is generally a combination of several assets. First, there are hard tangible assets that have been purchased in order to provide goods or services that the business can sell. What are they worth? In some cases the answer is easy: there may be a ready market for them. A car rental company, for example, owns a fleet of late model automobiles that can readily be sold in the used car market. There are publications that regularly survey the selling prices of used cars, both wholesale and retail, that can provide reasonably reliable information about the value of the fleet. In other cases assets are unique, as in the case of real estate and buildings. What is the value of an abandoned factory? It may depend on how readily adaptable it is to uses other than its former use, or whether there are other buyers who could operate it in its current use. How many such prospective buyers are there? Not as many as for used cars. And perhaps the prospective buyers have just completed construction or acquisition of their own new factories, and thus have no need for this one in the foreseeable future. Finally, the assets may be specific to the business or its location. A high speed newspaper press, weighing many tons, affixed to a concrete pad inside a building, may be useless unless there is another newspaper in the same area that requires increased press capacity. Refinery tanks may be useless to others if a refinery is to be closed. On the other hand, some real estate can be readily valued because its uses are varied and there are many prospective buyers for it. Thus, office buildings and warehouses are of general use to all types of businesses, and are sold with enough frequency that an informed appraiser can make an intelligent estimate of what such real property would bring in a sale. This value, significantly, depends to a large extent on what tenants would pay to rent the space, and the costs of maintaining and operating the building. The common link here is a reference to what an asset would bring if offered for sale in the relevant market. References are more or less easy depending upon the "thickness" of the market—the degree of frequency with which similar if not fungible assets are traded.

The courts frequently refer to "book value" as a measure of the value of a firm. Book value is an accounting artifact that frequently has no relationship to the economic value of a business. The book value of a company is a function of the value of its assets as recorded in its accounting records. Typically book value begins with the price paid for assets in arm's length transactions. In some cases, funds spent by the firm to create assets will be assigned as the book value of the asset thus created. At the moment of an arm's length purchase, there is generally good reason to believe that book value reflects fair market value for the acquired asset. But frequently book value begins to deviate from fair market value immediately after purchase. In some cases this is because the market value of such assets changes. The longer the asset has been held, the more likely such changes are to occur. Further, with inflation, all price levels rise, and the value of assets frequently rises above the original acquisition price. Depreciation offers another explanation for why asset values may diverge from market values. Many assets have a finite useful life, such as plant or equipment. They are either worn out or become economically obsolete over time. Depreciation is an annual charge designed to reflect that loss of value over the useful life of the asset. For a variety of reasons, this depreciation may not fairly reflect the actual loss of value.

Book value is a concept often extended from individual assets to the entire firm, and then to the shares of the firm. Thus, the book values of the individual assets may be summed up, and the firm's debts subtracted from them. The remaining value is described as the net book value of the firm, which reflects the book value of the shareholders' claims on these assets.* When the number of outstanding shares is divided into the net book value of the firm, the number is described as book value per share.** (This assumes that no shares of preferred stock are outstanding, with fixed claims, more or less like those of creditors.)

In addition to its hard assets, a business has a series of relationships that may generate value. It may be a computer software company with a large team of highly skilled and innovative software designers and programmers. What assurance do we have that these valuable assets, with their human capital, will not walk out the door?

All of this is just a way of saying that businesses are complex and varied. The first job of corporate finance, in determining values, is to find a common denominator that allows us to value all businesses. The common denominator, not surprisingly, is the amount of cash produced by the business. Investors who buy stocks in a corporation don't want to own their pro rata share of its tangible and intangible assets. What would you do with your 1/100,000,000th share of an aircraft hanger or a Boeing passenger jet, for example? Most of us don't know how to fly a jet, and it's much more convenient to book a seat with an established airline than jockey about flight times and destinations with all your co-owners of a jet. So we look for cash results from our investments, which we can convert into an array of goods and services when we want them. That cash, as you will see, may

---

* Book value is sometimes used as a proxy for replacement value of firm assets, particularly when analysts attempt to measure the ratio of the market value of a firm's stock to the replacement value of its assets. This concept was first developed by Nobel Laureate James Tobin, and is called "Tobin's Q." Because replacement value of assets is so difficult to measure, book value is often used as a substitute, acknowledging the infirmities of such a measure.

** If a firm has options to purchase additional shares outstanding, calculation of book value per share without taking into account the shares to be issued on exercise may be misleading. Sometimes book value is expressed on a "fully diluted" basis, as if the shares subject to issuance upon exercise of all options have been issued.

come in the form of dividend payments made by a corporation to its shareholders, by corporate offers to repurchase shares, or in the form of reinvestment in the corporation to cause the company to increase its earnings. In the latter case, you may not realize cash from your investment until you sell you shares.

2. DISCOUNTING AND PRESENT VALUE

A. COMPOUNDING

Businesses will produce different amounts of cash at different times. Making these amounts comparable is the task of anyone trying to value a business, or a particular security. We must begin our journey with the notion of the *opportunity cost of capital*. And this task begins with the concept of *compounding*.

If I have a dollar that I do not require for present consumption, I have a choice of investment opportunities. Most of these opportunities will produce regular payments, perhaps annually (although the payments may be semi-annually or quarterly). For convenience and simplicity we start with the assumption of annual payments. Here we should make the distinction between *simple interest* and *compound interest*. If a bank calculated interest only on one's original investment, you would be paid simple interest. Of course, the bank knows that if it calculated in this manner you would withdraw your money as soon as interest had been paid on your account, and redeposit the increased sum (perhaps with another bank). So the bank is forced by competition to calculate interest on the interest it has already paid into your account, thus paying interest on interest, or compound interest.

Assume that I have one dollar that I can invest at 10% interest for a five year period. If interest compounds annually at the end of each year, how much will I have at the end of five years? The solution is to multiply the year-end balance by the interest rate and add this to your principal amount, which in this case would result in 1.10. This is shown in the following table:

Table 3–1			
Compounding			
Year	**Balance at Start of Year**	**Interest Earned During Year**	**Balance at End of Year**
Year 1:	$1.00 ×	.10 = $.10	$1.10
Year 2:	$1.10 ×	.10 = $.11	$1.21
Year 3:	$1.21 ×	.10 = $.121	$1.33
Year 4:	$1.33 ×	.10 = $.133	$1.46
Year 5:	$1.46 ×	.10 = $.146	$1.61

This can be presented more formally. The nominal *future value* ("FV") of a sum(s) to be received with interest at the end of a year equals the sum multiplied by one plus the interest rate ®.

This is: FV = s (1 + r).

If interest will be compounded, that is, added to the sum, the value of s at the end of year 2 (V_2) is: $V_2 = (1 + r) (1 + r)$.

This in turn can be stated: $V_2 = (1 + r)^2$.

Similarly, the value of s at the end of year 5 = $V_5 = (1 + r)^5$.

Many books provide compound interest tables to show the amounts produced for various period at various interest rates, and financial calculators are programmed to provide these calculations. But even the simplest calculator can handle these calculations, by placing $1 + r$ in memory, and repeating the multiplication.* Multiply each year's starting balance by one plus the interest rate. Put this in memory and the process gets easier. Thus:

$1.00	×	1.10	=	$1.10
$1.10	×	1.10	=	$1.21
$1.21	×	1.10	=	$1.33
$1.33	×	1.10	=	$1.46
$1.46	×	1.10	=	$1.61

Table 3–2 shows the future value of $1.00 for different periods and different interest rates:

Table 3-2 Future Values of $1.00 Invested Today, Compounded Annually

Interest Rate, r

Year	3%	4%	5%	6%	7%	8%	9%	10%	12%	15%	20%	Year
1	1.030	1.040	1.050	1.060	1.070	1.080	1.090	1.100	1.120	1.150	1.200	1
2	1.061	1.082	1.102	1.124	1.145	1.166	1.188	1.210	1.254	1.323	1.440	2
3	1.093	1.125	1.158	1.191	1.225	1.260	1.295	1.331	1.405	1.521	1.728	3
4	1.126	1.170	1.216	1.262	1.311	1.360	1.412	1.464	1.574	1.749	2.074	4
5	1.159	1.217	1.276	1.338	1.403	1.469	1.539	1.611	1.762	2.011	2.488	5
6	1.194	1.265	1.340	1.419	1.501	1.587	1.677	1.772	1.974	2.313	2.986	6
7	1.230	1.316	1.407	1.504	1.606	1.714	1.828	1.949	2.211	2.660	3.583	7
8	1.267	1.369	1.477	1.594	1.718	1.851	1.993	2.144	2.476	3.059	4.300	8
9	1.305	1.423	1.551	1.689	1.838	1.999	2.172	2.358	2.773	3.518	5.160	9
10	1.344	1.480	1.629	1.791	1.967	2.159	2.367	2.594	3.106	4.046	6.192	10
11	1.384	1.539	1.710	1.898	2.105	2.332	2.580	2.853	3.479	4.652	7.430	11
12	1.426	1.601	1.796	2.012	2.252	2.518	2.813	3.138	3.896	5.350	8.916	12
13	1.469	1.665	1.886	2.133	2.410	2.720	3.066	3.452	4.363	6.153	10.700	13
14	1.513	1.732	1.980	2.261	2.579	2.937	3.342	3.797	4.887	7.076	12.840	14
15	1.558	1.801	2.079	2.397	2.759	3.172	3.642	4.177	5.474	8.137	15.410	15
16	1.605	1.873	2.183	2.540	2.952	3.426	3.970	4.595	6.130	9.358	18.490	16
17	1.653	1.948	2.292	2.693	3.159	3.700	4.328	5.054	6.866	10.760	22.190	17
18	1.702	2.026	2.407	2.854	3.380	3.996	4.717	5.560	7.690	12.380	26.620	18
19	1.754	2.107	2.527	3.026	3.617	4.316	5.142	6.116	8.613	14.230	31.950	19
20	1.806	2.191	2.653	3.207	3.870	4.661	5.604	6.727	9.646	16.370	38.340	20
25	2.094	2.666	3.386	4.292	5.427	6.858	8.623	10.830	17.000	32.920	95.400	25
30	2.427	3.243	4.322	5.743	7.612	10.060	13.370	17.450	29.960	66.210	237.40	30
40	3.261	4.780	7.040	10.286	14.972	22.885	31.647	45.265	93.056	267.88	1470.0	40
50	4.384	7.103	11.469	18.422	29.452	49.410	74.908	117.41	289.03	1083.9	9102.1	50

---

* Thus, enter 1.1; memory plus; multiply; memory recall; equal; multiply, etc., for the number of powers required for your calculation.

You can also use Microsoft Excel™ to perform these calculations. Here you enter the present value of the sum, the applicable interest rate, the recurring payment, and the number of periods. This is illustrated below:

The Rate at 10% would be entered as "0.1" for annual compounding. The number of periods would be annual or quarterly, as appropriate, and the payment would be the specified periodic amount. Present value would be the present value of the initial payment, while Type requires insertion of "1" if payments occur at the beginning of a period and "0" if they occur at the end of the period. When the entries are made the result is displayed after "Formula result =."

The future value concepts explained thus far involve an equation using future value, present value, the interest rate, and the number of periods. This can be expressed as:

$$FV = PV(1+r)^n$$

There is a handy rule of thumb you can use when you don't have a calculator or a compound interest table available. The *Rule of 72* tells you how long it will take to double your money at various interest rates. This requires you to divide the appropriate interest rate into 72 to learn the number of years required to double your money:

$$\text{Doubling Time} = \frac{72}{\text{Interest rate}}$$

This means that if your rate of return is 10%, your investment will double every 7.2 years.

Quick Check Question 3.1

You can test this formula by determining how long it will take your money to double at 8%, against the results in Table 3–2. How long will it take at 6%?

Quick Check Question 3.2

In 1737 Ben Franklin's Poor Richard's Almanac published the adage, "A penny saved is a penny earned."* What elements were missing from his statement? If Franklin had invested that penny at 6% interest compounded annually, what would the sum have been worth in 2000? (Hint: If you don't want to multiply 1+ interest rate 250 times or use Microsoft Excel™, you can use the compounding table and a pocket calculator to short-cut your calculations. Thus, if one cent compounds to 18.4 cents in 50 years, what will it do in 250?)

---

* This is a modern restatement. Franklin actually wrote "A penny saved is twopence clear" in 1737. Thanks to Muriee S. McClory.

B.   THE FREQUENCY OF COMPOUNDING

Interest rates on savings accounts are usually stated in the form of an *annual percentage rate*, with a certain frequency of compounding, such as monthly, quarterly, or semiannually. If you wanted to calculate compounded interest over shorter periods, such as a quarter or a month, you simply divide the stated (nominal) interest rate by the number of periods. Assume now that you can obtain a rate like the one employed in Table 3–1 from savings accounts. One bank offers you 10% interest, compounded quarterly, that is, 2.5% each quarter, while another offers 10.38%, compounded annually. Which account is best? Table 3–3 below shows the interest payments.

Table 3–3 Compounding Over Different Time Periods	Quarterly Compounding	Annual Compounding
Beginning Balance	$1,000.00	$1,000.00
Quarter 1:		
Interest: .025 × $1,000	25.00	0.00
Ending Balance	1,025.00	1,000.00
Quarter 2:		
Interest: .025 × $1,025.00	25.62	0.00
Ending Balance	1,050.62	1,000.00
Quarter 3:		

	Quarterly	Annual
Interest: .025 × $1,050.62	26.27	0.00
Ending Balance	1,076.89	1,000.00
Quarter 4:		
Interest: .025 × $1,076.89	26.91	
.1038 × $1,000.000		103.80
Ending Balance	$1,103.80	$1,103.80

Thus the interest payments at the end of the year are identical, even though the stated rates are not. The *effective annual rate* on both loans is 10.38%, if we define the effective annual rate as the rate of return received, calculated as if interest were only compounded annually.

Calculating the effective annual rate is surprisingly simple: you simply determine the *future value* (FV) you will have at the end of the year for each dollar invested, and subtract one from that amount. The general formula for the effective annual rate is:

$$\text{Effective annual rate} = \left(1 + \frac{\text{Annual Percentage Rate}}{N}\right)^m - 1$$

where M = number of periods in each year.

What this formula does is start with the familiar compounding formula of 1 + r (annual interest rate), divide the APR by the number of periods and compound 1 + the periodic APR (the smaller fractional interest rate for the period) by the number of periods. This is exactly the same as the calculations in Table 3–3. The result is then multiplied by a power of m to return us to a one-year period, and one is subtracted to return us from the multiplier formula to the effective annual rate obtained. Thus, in our example of quarterly compounding:

Effective annual rate = $(1 + 0.025)^4 - 1 = (1.025)^4 - 1 = 1.1038 - 1 = .1038$

The explanation for the identity of the effective annual rate in our two examples in Table 3–3, as you can see, is *timing*. Receiving interest payments earlier than year-end has the effect of increasing your return over the stated (nominal) interest rate, because the interest received now counts as part of the account for future interest payments. Put another way, "time is money," and sooner is always better than later, because it allows the investor to reinvest the payments that much sooner.

Quick Check Question 3.3

Assume your interest payments are compounded monthly in Table 3.3. What is your effective annual interest rate?

C.   Present Values

Our examination of compounding showed how much money you would have at some future date if you invested a certain sum today. We now turn to determining how much money you have to invest today in order to have a certain sum at some future date. In one sense, you already know the answer from our compounding. If we were to ask the present value of $1.61 to be received at the end of five years, discounted at 10%, Table 3–1 tells us that having $1.00 today is the equivalent of $1.61 in five years if the dollar is invested at 10%, compounded annually. Thus, we are just reversing the process used in section A to determine the compounded value of a sum in the future.

Recall in Table 3.1 that to determine the sum's value after one year we multiplied our dollar by 1.1. If we wanted to determine the present value of $1.10 to be received at the end of one year, we simply divide $1.10 by 1.1. Then the present value (PV) is given by:

$$PV = \frac{\$1.10}{1.1} = \$1.00$$

So the discount rate is simply one plus the interest rate, used as a divisor instead of as a multiplier. We can generalize this formula. Present value is the sum it would take now, invested at the interest rate r, to equal the sum to be received later. The formula becomes the reciprocal of the previous formula.

Thus, the present value (PV) of a sum(s) to be received at the end of year 1 is the sum divided by one plus the interest (discount) rate (r):

$$PV = \frac{s}{1 + r}$$

Now assume that you will receive one dollar at the end of one year. The formula, using 10% as the discount rate, is as follows:

$$PV = \frac{s}{1 + r} \quad = \quad \frac{\$1.00}{1 + .10} \quad = \quad \frac{\$1.00}{1.10} \quad = \quad \$0.909$$

And the present value of a sum to be received in year 2 is:

$$PV_2 = \frac{S}{(1+r)(1+r)} = \frac{S}{(1+r)^2} = \frac{\$1.00}{1.21} = \$0.826$$

While the present value of a sum to be received in year 5 is:

$$PV_5 = \frac{S}{(1+r)^5} = \frac{\$1.00}{1.61} = \$0.62$$

Stated another way, if you deposit $0.62, you can take home $1.00 at the end of five years. (To check this, compound $0.62 by the factor (1.611) shown in Table 3–2 for five years under the 10% column.) These are the kind of calculations that must be done with instruments such as $50.00 savings bonds, which pay $50 at maturity, to determine their present value. Similarly, U.S. Treasury Bonds are sometimes stripped of their interest coupons, and the resulting promise of a principal payment at some future date is sold separately, at its discounted present value. Implicit in this market price is a return of a percentage of the investment annually, compounded for the remaining life of the bond. Should it surprise you that the Internal Revenue Service regards this as equivalent to earned income on an annual basis?* Recall that the market value of your bond will increase by the amount of the effective discount rate annually.

Calculating present values is called discounting, and the interest rate used in this calculation is generally called the discount rate. The general formula for calculating the present value of a sum to be received one or more periods (n) in the future is as follows:

$$PV = \frac{S}{(1+r)^n}$$

where the interest rate r is expressed as a decimal.

Just as there are tables to show you the value of a sum to be received with compound interest in the future, there are tables to show you the discounted present value of these sums. If, for example, we were to discount all the future values shown in Table 3–2 to present value, using the interest (discount) rates shown on each column, each sum would discount to a present value of $1.00. Below we set out a comparable discounted present value table.**

---

* This is called "original issue discount" and is covered in 26 U.S.C. § 1272.

** Microsoft Excel™ will calculate present values, using the "NPV" function. For new users, hit the function key, "fx," in the toolbar, and search for "NPV." Having selected NPV, simply insert the discount rate in the first line and the expected payment in one of 29 periods.

Table 3-4 Discounted Present Values of $1.00 Received at End of Year

Discount Rate, r

Year	3%	4%	5%	6%	7%	8%	9%	10%	12%	15%	20%	Year
1	.971	.962	.952	.943	.935	.926	.917	.909	.893	.870	.833	1
2	.943	.925	.907	.890	.873	.857	.842	.826	.797	.756	.694	2
3	.915	.889	.864	.840	.816	.794	.772	.751	.712	.658	.579	3
4	.888	.855	.823	.792	.763	.735	.708	.683	.636	.572	.482	4
5	.863	.822	.784	.747	.713	.681	.650	.621	.567	.497	.402	5
6	.837	.790	.746	.705	.666	.630	.596	.564	.507	.432	.335	6
7	.813	.760	.711	.665	.623	.583	.547	.513	.452	.376	.279	7
8	.789	.731	.677	.627	.582	.540	.502	.467	.404	.327	.233	8
9	.766	.703	.645	.592	.544	.500	.460	.424	.361	.284	.194	9
10	.744	.676	.614	.558	.508	.463	.422	.386	.322	.247	.162	10
11	.722	.650	.585	.527	.475	.429	.388	.350	.287	.215	.135	11
12	.701	.625	.557	.497	.444	.397	.356	.319	.257	.187	.112	12
13	.681	.601	.530	.469	.415	.368	.326	.290	.259	.163	.093	13
14	.661	.577	.505	.442	.388	.340	.299	.263	.205	.141	.078	14
15	.642	.555	.481	.417	.362	.315	.275	.239	.183	.123	.065	15
16	.623	.534	.458	.394	.339	.292	.252	.218	.163	.107	.054	16
17	.605	.513	.436	.371	.317	.270	.231	.198	.146	.093	.045	17
18	.587	.494	.416	.350	.296	.250	.212	.180	.130	.081	.038	18
19	.570	.475	.396	.331	.277	.232	.194	.164	.116	.070	.031	19
20	.554	.456	.377	.312	.258	.215	.178	.149	.104	.061	.026	20
25	.478	.375	.295	.233	.184	.146	.116	.092	.059	.030	.010	25
30	.412	.308	.231	.174	.131	.099	.075	.057	.033	.015	.004	30
40	.307	.208	.142	.097	.067	.046	.031	.022	.011	.004	.0006	40
50	.228	.141	.087	.054	.034	.021	.013	.008	.003	.001	.0001	50

Quick Check Question 3.4

It is your brother's tenth birthday, and your grandparents give him a $10,000 savings bond that matures in eight years, when he is expected to begin college. Your brother writes down "$10,000" on his list of gifts received. How can you explain his error to him? Assuming the current interest rate paid on government bonds with an eight-year maturity is 7%, can you tell him what the present value of this gift is?

Note how little value is assigned to payments fifty years from now. If we use a 10% discount rate (pretty close to the long-run returns on stocks, as we will explore shortly), the value of $1.00 received in year 50 is less than one cent! If you received a series of $1.00 payments annually for fifty years, the discounted present value (the sum of the present values for years 1 through 50) is $9.914. (See the annuity table, Table 3–5, which follows.) If we promised a stream of $1.00 payments in perpetuity, the discounted present value increases, but only to $10.00! It seems human being don't attach much value to payments to be received a very long time in the future. While these are perfectly rational calculations for individuals and businesses making savings and borrowing decisions, do they leave something out if a government is trying to calculate long-term effects of actions? Note how little regard is shown in these calculations for those who follow us—our grandchildren, for example.

Quick Check Question 3.5

Your law school is engaged in a capital funds campaign. You read in the school paper that a prominent alumnus has pledged $1,000,000 in his will to support the law school. Assume the alum is now 65 years old, with a life expectancy of 85. If the appropriate discount rate is 7%, what is the present value of his pledge? How should the law school report it to other alumni?

D. Annuities

How would you value a corporate bond? A bond is a promise of a series of (annual)* interest payments, plus repayment of principal at the maturity of the bond, which can be anywhere from one year to 100 years (although 100–year bonds have been rarely seen). The easiest way to value a bond is to separate the payments. For example, if a $1,000 bond paid 10% interest annually at the close of each year (and 10% remained the appropriate discount rate), we could discount each interest payment to present value, using Table 3–4. We can also use Table 3–4 to value the repayment of principal (the "terminal payment"). Here are the results:

Year 1:	$100 ÷ 1.1000	= $90.91
Year 2:	$100 ÷ 1.2100	= $82.64
Year 3:	$100 ÷ 1.3310	= $75.13
Year 4:	$100 ÷ 1.4641	= $68.30
Year 5:	$100 ÷ 1.6105	= $62.09
Year 6:	$100 ÷ 1.7716	= $56.45
Year 7:	$100 ÷ 1.9487	= $51.32
Year 8:	$100 ÷ 2.1436	= $46.65
9 years	$100 ÷ 2.3579	= $42.41
10 years	$100 ÷ 2.5937	= $38.55
Total of interest payments:		614.45
Principal: $1,000 ÷ 2.5937		385.55
Discounted Present Value:		$1,000.00

Any stream of payments, such as that found in a bond, is called an *"annuity,"* although common usage frequently limits the term to annuity policies sold by insurance companies. As you can see, the present value of an annuity is simply the discounted present value of each payment, summed. The present value of an annuity of $1 per period for n years is expressed:

$$PV = \frac{1}{r} - \frac{1}{r(1 + r)^n}$$

Excel® can solve for this equation, using a 20 year annuity of a dollar discounted at 10% as follows:

---

* Bond interest may be paid semi-annually, but for our purposes we will assume annual payments in these examples.

```
Function Arguments

PV
        Rate  [        0.1        ]  = number
        Nper  [         20        ]  = number
        Pmt   [          1        ]  = number
        Fv    [          0        ]  = number
        Type  [          0        ]  = number
                                     = 8.51356372
Returns the future value of an investment based on periodic, constant payments and a constant
interest rate.

                  Rate is the interest rate per period.  For example, use 6%/4 for
                  quarterly payments at 6% APR.

Formula result = ($8.51)

                                              [ OK  ]  [ Cancel ]

Help on this function
```

One feature of present value calculations should be noted here. The higher the discount rate, the lower the present value of any obligation to make a fixed payment in the future, or a series of payments in an annuity. Thus, as interest rates rise in the economy, the market value of bonds declines. This risk of decline in value of an investment is called *interest rate risk*. It is a partial explanation of why investors insist on higher rates of return on long-term bonds than on short-term obligations. For example, over the period 1926–1997 the average yield on short-term Treasuries was 3.8%, while the average yield on long-term Treasuries was 5.2%. (You will find these returns in Table 3–6 in the next section.) You can view current interest rates, and a "yield curve" showing the relationship between bond duration and rates, on Bloomberg.com. As of this writing, the url is: http://www.bloomberg.com/markets/rates/index.html

Some issuers may wish to provide investors with lower inflation risk in order to get a lower interest rate on long-term debt, which they can do by using a variable interest rate. One form involves treasury Inflation–Indexed Securities, often called Treasury Inflation–Protected Securities or TIPS. Holders of TIPS receive interest payments every six months and a payment of principal when the security matures. The difference is this: Interest and redemption payments for TIPS are tied to inflation. As of 2004 the Treasury offered TIPS in five, ten and twenty-year maturities. The Treasury also offers I Bonds, with a 30–year maturity. I Bond interest rates have two parts: a fixed rate that lasts for 30 years, and an inflation rate that changes every six months.

We offer a brief annuity table to give you a look at these values.

Table 3-5 Present Value of an Annuity Payable at the end of Each Period for n Periods

Discount Rate, r

Year	3%	4%	5%	6%	7%	8%	9%	10%	12%	15%	20%	Year
1	0.971	0.961	0.952	0.943	0.934	0.925	0.917	0.909	0.892	0.869	0.833	1
2	1.913	1.886	1.859	1.833	1.808	1.783	1.759	1.735	1.690	1.625	1.527	2
3	2.829	2.775	2.723	2.673	2.624	2.577	2.531	2.486	2.401	2.283	2.106	3
4	3.717	3.629	3.546	3.465	3.387	3.312	3.239	3.169	3.037	2.855	2.588	4
5	4.580	4.451	4.329	4.212	4.100	3.992	3.889	3.790	3.604	3.352	2.990	5
6	5.417	5.242	5.075	4.917	4.766	4.622	4.485	4.355	4.114	3.784	3.325	6
7	6.230	6.002	5.786	5.582	5.389	5.206	5.033	4.868	4.563	4.160	3.604	7
8	7.020	6.732	6.463	6.209	5.971	5.746	5.534	5.334	4.967	4.487	3.837	8
9	7.786	7.435	7.107	6.801	6.515	6.246	5.995	5.759	5.328	4.771	4.031	9
10	8.530	8.111	7.721	7.360	7.023	6.710	6.417	6.144	5.650	5.018	4.192	10
11	9.253	8.761	8.306	7.886	7.498	7.139	6.805	6.495	5.937	5.233	4.327	11
12	9.954	9.385	8.863	8.383	7.942	7.536	7.160	6.813	6.194	5.420	4.439	12
13	10.635	9.985	9.393	8.852	8.357	7.903	7.486	7.103	6.423	5.583	4.532	13
14	11.296	10.563	9.898	9.295	8.745	8.244	7.786	7.366	6.628	5.724	4.610	14
15	11.937	11.118	10.379	9.712	9.107	8.559	8.060	7.606	6.810	5.847	4.675	15
16	12.561	11.652	10.837	10.105	9.446	8.851	8.312	7.823	6.974	5.954	4.729	16
17	13.166	12.165	11.274	10.477	9.763	9.121	8.543	8.021	7.119	6.047	4.774	17
18	13.753	12.659	11.689	10.827	10.059	9.371	8.755	8.201	7.249	6.128	4.812	18
19	14.323	13.133	12.085	11.158	10.335	9.603	8.950	8.364	7.365	6.198	4.843	19
20	14.877	13.590	12.462	11.469	10.594	9.818	9.128	8.513	7.469	6.259	4.869	20
25	17.413	15.622	14.093	12.783	11.653	10.674	9.822	9.077	7.843	6.464	4.947	25
30	19.600	17.292	15.372	13.764	12.409	11.257	10.273	9.426	8.055	6.566	4.978	30
40	23.114	19.792	17.159	15.046	13.331	11.924	10.757	9.779	8.243	6.641	4.996	40
50	25.729	21.482	18.255	15.761	13.800	12.233	10.961	9.914	8.304	6.660	4.999	50

Earlier we examined how a bond could be valued to maturity. Note that if our bond consists solely of ten interest payments of $100 each, our annuity table values this stream of payments at $614.40. If interest payments are traded separately from the principal obligation on the bond, this is the price at which they would trade. Thus, when U.S. Treasury obligations are "stripped" of the interest obligation, this is their value in the market. The "stripped" bond itself, now consisting only of the obligation to pay $1,000 at maturity, would trade for $386.00 (see the 10% column in Table 3–4). The implicit interest rate paid by the stripped Treasury would be 10%. Why would someone purchase such a stripped Treasury, especially when the IRS would impute interest income (original issue discount) at the 10% rate even though the holder was receiving no cash payments? Part of the answer has to be that some bond holders don't pay current taxes on their income. Tax-deferred retirement plans are probably the best example of this kind of investor.

Quick Check Question 3.6

Recall the calculation of the value of the 10-year bond in the example at the beginning of this section. If the market interest rate on such a bond drops to 8%, what is the Discounted Present Value of the bond?

E. Valuing a Perpetuity

So far we have dealt with finite payment streams, on the assumption that we know (presumably from their contract terms) that they will terminate on a date certain. A share of preferred stock may pay a regular dividend, for example. If the company is not in obvious trouble, and if the preferred shares are not redeemable at any particular time, how should we calculate the value of that stock? Similarly, the British government issued bonds in the 19th century that were not repayable at any particular time— they just paid a stated rate of interest. This is a special form of annuity, called a *"perpetuity."* We often calculate the value of shares of common stock on the same basis, with some modifications, because shares of common stock have no termination date on their rights, but continue as long as the business continues.

One could attempt to value a perpetuity by continuing to make annuity calculations for a very long period. But if you refer to Table 3–4, you will see that by the end of 50 years, using discount rates of 10% or higher, the incremental value of each new year's payment is only a fraction of one percent. In short, the discounted present value of later years becomes trivial. Examine the 10% column for 50 years, and compare the present value of this annuity with the results of the formula we are about to describe.

The simplest way to think about a perpetuity is to consider how much money you would have to invest at 10% to assure yourself an annual payment of $10.00. The answer is obvious: $100. (Note with a perpetuity you never get your principal back, so you don't have to worry about valuing a terminal payment, as you do with a bond.) (Now notice how close this answer is to the discounted present value of a 50–year annuity at 10%—the far distant future isn't worth much.) The general formula for valuing a perpetuity is simply to divide the annual payment by the discount rate. Thus:

$$\text{Present Value of a Perpetuity} = \frac{\text{Payment}}{\text{Discount Rate}} = PV = \frac{P}{r}$$

Quick Check Question 3.7

What is the value of a share of preferred stock carrying an $8.00 annual dividend, discounted at 7%, assuming it is neither redeemable by the company ("callable") nor subject to forced redemption by the holder? What if the discount rate is 10%?

F. Valuing Common Stock

Valuing common stock is a special case of valuing a perpetuity, for several reasons, some of which will be expanded upon later in this book.

The first difficulty, of course, is figuring out what to value. Do we value the firm's earnings, divided by the number of shares ("*earnings per share*" or "*EPS*")? Should we value dividends, on the assumption that the only earnings that matter to investors are the earnings they receive? Or is there some intermediate, more complex calculation? Unfortunately, it is the latter, which we've discussed in the preceding chapters' discussions of free cash flow.

The second difficulty is predicting the future earnings of the firm. For purposes of simplification these calculations begin with the assumption of level earnings. We will later introduce modifications of this assumption. Third, how long will the firm's earnings last? Again, for purposes of simplification, we assume these earnings will last forever. As we have seen, if they only last for 50 years, it won't make very much difference in our calculations. Again, there is no terminal payment for common stock, until the issuing corporation liquidates and distributes its remaining assets to its common stockholders, after it has satisfied all its other claimants or you sell your shares at some earlier date.

It is obvious to even the most casual observer that few firms actually expect to have level earnings forever. Assume, for example, that you buy a stock currently paying a cash dividend of $1.00 per year, that you expect to grow by 4% each year. If the market rate is 10% on this investment, you must discount a stream of future payments that grow at a 4% rate annually. This is sometimes called a "*growth annuity*." The formula for valuing such a growth annuity is set forth below:

$$\text{Present Value of a Growth Annuity} = \frac{\text{Initial Payment}}{\text{Discount Rate} - \text{Growth Rate}}$$

More formally: $PV = \dfrac{P}{r - g}$
where g = the growth rate.

Applied to our example: $PV = \dfrac{\$1.00}{.10 - .04} = \dfrac{\$1.00}{.06} = \$16.67$

Of course, not all stocks can be expected to have growing earnings indefinitely. Companies frequently experience a growth period early in their existence, or after introduction of a highly profitable new product. But over time competitors catch up with them, markets mature and become saturated with the products, and profits decline to more normal levels after a period of growth. In this event, we have two periods of calculations to consider. In the first period, we have earnings growing at 4% per year. You can find the nominal amounts of such earnings in the compound interest calculations in Table 3–2. Thus, if this year's earnings are expected to be $1.00, then next year's are expected to be $1.04, the third year's $1.0816, and so on. Each one of these nominal amounts would have to be discounted to present value, using our assumed 10% discount rate. Finally, after the growth period, we arrive at our assumed perpetuity for the rest of time. Just remember, this perpetuity doesn't kick in until we've finished the growth period, so if we use a present value for a perpetuity, we'll have to further discount it for its later starting date. (This is sometimes called the *"terminal value."*) The following example assumes a five-year growth period, followed by level earnings in perpetuity:

Year	Earnings ×	Discount Factor @ 10%	= Present Value
1	1.00	0.9091	$0.9091
2	1.04	0.8264	0.8595
3	1.0816	0.7513	0.8126
4	1.1249	0.6830	0.7683
5	1.17	0.6209	0.7264
	Subtotal:		4.0759
6	Perpetuity of $\dfrac{\$1.17}{.10} = \$11.70 \times 0.5645 =$		6.6046
	Total Present Value:		$10.6805

This is fairly standard methodology for experts in valuation proceedings. They routinely assume that growth will not go on indefinitely. Experts can (and will, depending on which side they represent) differ about the termination date for growing earnings, and about the rate of growth. You will observe this methodology in the Technicolor case in Part 5 of this Chapter.

G. VALUING INVESTMENTS WITH DIFFERENT CASH FLOWS AT DIFFERENT TIMES

Just like growing dividends, other investments may offer different cash flows at different periods. One of the nice things about present value calculations is that you can compare two investments with different cash flows in different periods and decide which one is better. Suppose, in the following example, that each investment will require $400,000 invested at the beginning of year one. Again, assume a discount rate of 10%. Here are the expected returns:

Project A: **Project B:**

End of Year	Return	End of Year	Return
1	$200,000	1	$100,000
2	150,000	2	100,000
3	150,000	3	325,000
Total:	$500,000	Total:	$525,000

Here are the discounted present values, using Table 3–4:

Project A:

End of Year	Return	×		NPV
1	$200,000	×	.9091	$181,920
2	150,000	×	.8264	123,960
3	150,000	×	.7513	112,695
Totals:				$418,575

Project B:

End of Year	Return	×		NPV
1	$100,000	×	.9091	$90,910
2	100,000	×	.8264	82,640
3	325,000	×	.7513	244,172
				$417,722

Thus Project A has the higher discounted present value, despite the higher nominal (undiscounted) value of Project B. These are the kinds of calculations that corporate executives must engage in when choosing between projects.

H.   NET PRESENT VALUE

Thus far we have not talked about why different discount rates might be used, but the answer is implicit in our previous discussions. Every time you are offered an investment opportunity, e.g., to receive a dollar (or any other sum) at some point in the future, you must forego some other investment that you could make. (We will return to the problem of the appropriate discount rate later on.) First, we examine the present value calculation for a single project with different cash flows in each period. Assume three investments in a project: Now, the end of year 1, and the end of year 2. Assume a cost of capital of 10%.

OUTLAYS:

Amount	End of Year	Present Value
$1,000,000	immediately	$1,000,000
200,000	1	181,820
300,000	2	247,920
		$1,429,740

Now assume net revenues after operating expenses of $200,000 at the end of the second year, and assume that for years 3–22 (20 years) net revenues are $300,000 annually. Finally, at the end of year 22, the salvage value of the assets brings in $100,000. The single payments are simply discounted to present value at 10% (See Table 3–4). The stream of payments is an 20–year annuity. Use the annuity table (Table 3–5), to calculate the present value of an annuity for 20 years discounted at 10%:

$$8.5136 \times \$300,000 = \$2,554,080$$

Because this payment won't start to be received until the end of year 3 it must also be discounted to present value at 10%. Using Table 3–4:

$$0.7513 \times \$2,554,080 = \$1,918,880.^*$$

RECEIPTS

Amount	End of Year	Discount Factor	Present Value
$200,000	2	0.8264	$165,280
2,554,080	3	0.7513	$1,918,880
100,000	22	0.1228	12,280
			$2,096,440

---

*   Microsoft Excel™ has a Net Present Value function. "NPV" asks the initial payments, the discount rate, and the expected payments over 29 periods (which can be any number of those periods). Payments are treated as negative amounts, e.g., (1000000).

Note that this is just a variation on the valuation of bonds, which also have different payments in different periods. But the important fact is that we have made the value of investments comparable to those for returns. And the present value of the returns exceeds the present value of the investments. That means we should invest in this project, assuming that we have used the correct discount rate. When the present value of returns exceeds that of investments, we say that the project has a positive *net present value*. Another way of stating this is that a manager should accept investment opportunities offering rates of return in excess of the opportunity cost of capital. If the present value of the returns were less than the present value of the funds to be invested, it would be described as having a negative net present value. The obvious conclusion is that a business should accept all projects with a positive net present value and reject all projects with a negative net present value.

Quick Check Question 3.8

A factory costs $400,000. You calculate that it will produce net cash after operating expenses of $100,000 in year 1, $200,000 in year 2, and $300,000 in year 3, after which it will shut down with zero salvage value. Calculate the net present value, using a 10% discount rate.

Sidebar: Alternative Valuation Methods: Payback Period

Companies sometimes use the *payback* period to calculate whether to accept or reject a project. This avoids the difficulties of NPV calculations. It simply calculates the number of years it takes for the initial investment to be repaid from project cash flows. Firms using this method pick an arbitrary period for the payback. This method gives equal weight to all cash flows received within the payback period, in contrast to NPV calculations. Because this method also cuts off later cash flows that occur after the payback period, it may undervalue a project that will have increasing cash flows in later years. If the payback period is too long, it will permit acceptance of projects that may have negative NPVs.

Sidebar: Alternative Valuation Methods: Internal Rate of Return

Different projects may all have positive net present values, and it is possible that some of them will have earlier payoffs than others. Thus, simply learning that two projects both have positive net present values may not be enough information, if the firm lacks sufficient capital to undertake both projects. (We ignore the possibility of raising additional capital in this example.) Under these circumstances, we might want to employ the *internal rate of return* ("IRR") approach. As one finance book puts it, "the IRR is about as close as you can get to the NPV without actually being the NPV." Simply put, the IRR is the discount rate at which net present value turns out to be zero. For our purposes, the best way to approximate the IRR is trial and error: simply employ a series of discount rates until you get close to a zero NPV. Financial calculators permit direct calculation of IRR, but we will not pursue that topic further here. There are two problems with IRR, however. First, if a project has initial positive cash flows, followed by periods of negative cash flows that require further investments, followed by more positive cash flows, the IRR can produce two different rates of return. In these cases IRR cannot be used. The next problem is that the IRR method assumes that disinvested funds are invested at the same rate of return as the rate on the project itself. The distortion is worse if the examined project has higher cash flows in its early years, since this assumes that more cash is reinvested at high rates of return that will probably not be available. Microsoft Excel™ can be used for these calculations. An example appears in Chapter Six, Part 1. Using Excel, compare the following projects:

Project:	A	B
Start (investment)	($400,000)	($400,000)
Year 1	$400,000	$50,000
Year 2	$100,000	$450,000
Year 3	0	$50,000
Net cash flows	$100,000	$150,000
Net Present Value @10%	$42,070	$49,930
IRR	21%	17%

Using net present value methodology, Project B produces a higher net present value, and should be selected. But IRR produces a dramatically different result. This is because the $400,000 cash flow in Year 1 for Project A is assumed to be reinvested at the same rate of return, while the first year for Project B is only $50,000.

Why is the IRR assumption unrealistic? If both A and B return more than the current 10% cost of capital for the company, it's unrealistic to assume that the cash flows can always be invested in new projects above the normal rate of return. The curious thing is how often finance professionals continue to use IRR, despite its widely publicized defects.

3. THE COST OF CAPITAL

A. THE PRICE OF RISK

The remaining question is how discount or interest rates are set. One can readily observe that interest rates have two components; one is compensation for the time value of money—for consumption deferred by the lender or investor. Generally we can isolate this by looking at the return on risk-free investments, such as short term Treasury bills. (This rate must also compensate for inflation.) One major study showed that the nominal average interest rate before inflation on Treasury Bills was 3.8% for the period 1926–1997. The real rate of return, after adjusting for inflation, was 0.7% on Treasury bills.*

The second part of the return demanded by investors is for the risk of non-payment (default). We'll turn in a moment to the economic principles underlying this, but it's also intuitive that people who lend (invest) money like to be repaid, and like it much more than non-payment! Thus, when we loan money to our bank in the form of a deposit in a savings account, we're so certain of repayment that we accept a low interest rate on savings accounts. But now think about lenders who have to worry more about repayment. Banks extend credit to a wide variety of customers through credit cards, often with very little investigation of the card holder's ability to repay, and little control over how wisely or foolishly the holder manages his or her finances, except to impose some credit limit on the cards. Banks can expect, on average, that a certain percentage of card holders will fail to repay their debts, and the bank will lose money on those accounts. It comes as no surprise to anyone that banks will set credit card interest rates to compensate themselves for this cost of doing business.

This basic principle applies to all those who invest, whether in loans, corporate bonds or stocks. Higher rates of return are demanded by investors for risky investments. A study by Ibbotson Associates showed the following rates of return through 1997:**

Table 3–6				
Returns to Asset Classes				
Asset Class	**Nominal Return**	**Real Return**	**Std. Deviation of Annual Returns**	**Risk Premium over Treasury Bills**
Short-term Treasury Bills	3.8%	0.7%	3.2%	0%
Intermediate–Term Treasury Bonds	5.3%	2.2%	5.7%	1.5%
Long–Term Treasury Bonds	5.2%***	2.1%	9.2%	1.4%
Corporate Bonds	5.7%	2.6%	8.7%	1.9%
Large–Company Stocks (S & P 500)	11%	7.9%	20.3%	7.2%
Small–Company Stocks	12.7%	9.6%	33.9%	8.9%

While the fact that investors demand higher returns to bear risk is intuitive, it can be explained in a more formal manner, as we do below. The

---

* Ibbotson Associates, STOCKS, BONDS, BILLS AND INFLATION: 1998 YEARBOOK.

** *Id.* All of the data except risk premia are taken from Table 2–1, p. 33.

*** A situation where the return on long-term bonds is lower than the rate on intermediate term bonds is surprising. This is called an inverted yield curve.

answer is found in the declining marginal utility of wealth. Assume a "fair" bet—the odds of winning are 50–50: a coin flip. The expected value of the bet is the weighted average of the expected returns. Assume you flip for a dollar. You can win $1.00 or lose $1.00. Thus, you wind up with either $2.00 or zero. The expected return is calculated as follows:

Outcome	Probability	Weighted Outcome
$0	0.5	$0
$2.00	0.5	$1.00
Expected outcome:		$1.00

If you play the game repeatedly, you come out where you started. Obviously this is not very interesting. But if you increase the stakes the game is more interesting, especially if you don't play an infinite number of games. Suppose, for example, you are offered a coin flip for next year's tuition—$25,000. The bet is still fair:

Outcome	Probability	Weighted Outcome
$0	0.5	$0
$50,000	0.5	$25,000
Expected outcome:		$25,000

While just as fair as the first bet, this one is more exciting because the consequences are more exciting. If you win, you have more money to live on next year. But if you lose, you defer graduation for a year while you earn the tuition. Underlying this observation is the notion of declining marginal utility of wealth, that first units of wealth have more value than later units. In this case, the first units enable you to attend law school next year, while the later units (if you win) enable you to buy a new car to drive to school. Most individuals would decline this bet, because they are risk averse. If you doubt this, observe the enormous size of the insurance industry, which is built on risk aversion.

Thus a fair bet for a large amount without compensation for risk isn't attractive to most people. This can be illustrated by the following figure. Assume that you have $10,000 more than tuition ($35,000). (Let's keep something to live on):

Figure 3-1

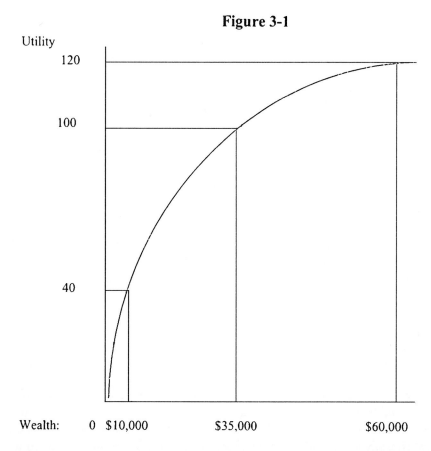

Utility

120

100

40

Wealth: 0 $10,000 $35,000 $60,000

Winning the bet increases your wealth from $35,000 to $60,000, which is a 71% gain. Losing decreases your wealth from $35,000 to $10,000, a 71% loss. In that sense the bet is "fair," and symmetrical. But notice the dramatically different impact on your personal utility. Winning increases your utility from 100 to 120. That's good, but it's only a 20% gain. On the other hand, losing decreases your utility from 100 to 40, which is a 60% loss. This illustrates the great truth of the declining marginal utility of wealth: first dollars are used to satisfy our most intense demands, normally for things like food, clothing and shelter, while later dollars are used to satisfy whatever demands we place less priority on. In order to induce most people to enter into a bet under these conditions, the payoffs from winning have to be increased—the expected returns—to the point where gains and losses in utility, not wealth, are at least equal. We illustrate that with Figure 3–2:

Figure 3-2

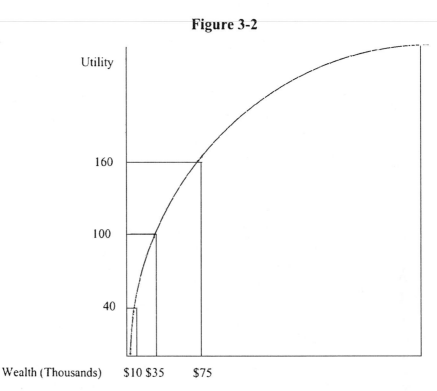

Wealth (Thousands) $10 $35 $75

Here the dollar returns are skewed. Winning increases your wealth from $35,000 to $75,000, which is a 115% gain. Losing remains the same as before, decreasing your wealth from $35,000 to $10,000, a 71% loss. But now the payoffs in utility are symmetrical—a gain or loss of 60 units of utility, so, given this utility function, you are able to accept this bet as a reasonably fair one.

Of course we can't graph the utility function of anyone. There is no theory to express the marginal utility of wealth for individuals, and thus their preference for (or aversion to) risk. We do know it exists, in part because we can observe it. Table 3–6 shows the rates of return that investors have demanded on risky investments over very long periods of time. As previously mentioned, the existence of large markets for insurance is compelling evidence of risk aversion.

Another measure of risk is shown by the Capital Market Line, used to demonstrate the returns investors expect on riskier stocks. Without going into the details of the theory behind this line (the "Capital Assets Pricing Model"), the line looks like this:

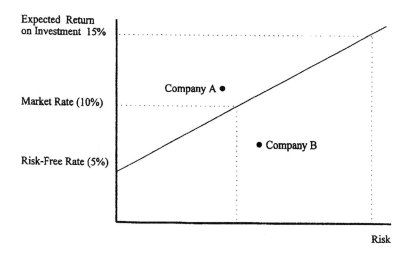

Expected Return
on Investment 15%

Company A •

Market Rate (10%)

• Company B

Risk-Free Rate (5%)

Risk

B. MEASUREMENT OF RISK—OF EXPECTED VALUES AND STANDARD DEVIATIONS

Thus far we have not discussed how risk is determined. We have proceeded as if the future payments to be received were certain. In fact, nothing is certain about future earnings except payments on government bonds, and that is because the government owns the presses that print money, and can always repay, in nominal currency, although it may be much depreciated through inflation of the currency. In discounting to present value, then, we are discounting "expected earnings" or "expected payments." The relative certainty (or uncertainty) of those expected payments determines the rate of return that investors will demand. There is no magic in this process. It normally represents the best estimates of informed individuals about the future success of a business. A large number of variables may influence actual future results, and any estimate about the future is necessarily just an educated guess, although our predictive ability is better in some cases than in others.

In the previous examples of coin flips, we examined possible outcomes in the simplest state of the world, with only two possible outcomes, heads or tails. In predicting the future performance of a company, far more outcomes are possible, and they are far more complex to determine. They depend on numerous variables, from those that affect the general economy to those outside forces that face the firm, such as competitors' success, costs of raw materials, and to forces within the firm, such as successful marketing, cost control, and management generally. For some firms in relatively stable businesses, this process is less difficult. Everyone will continue to consume groceries regardless of the state of the economy, for example, so grocery store chains can expect to be less impacted by general economic conditions than say, an automobile manufacturer. The range of possible outcomes for the grocery store chain is likely to be much smaller than for a car maker. Similarly, in such a business a dominant company in the industry may be subject to less pressure from competitors than smaller firms.* But in the end, the process of projecting the range and magnitude of possible outcomes is an educated (highly educated, one hopes) guess. These guesses are made internally by companies as they try to plan for future capital needs, manage their cash flows, and plan competitive strategies. They are also made by securities analysts. The analysts' projections generally result in estimates of a range of future profits, with the best estimate being the expected earnings.

In 1999 Amazon.com's stock traded as high as $110 per share. At the time Amazon.com was losing hundreds of millions of dollars per year. Part of the losses were the result of Amazon.com's spending huge amounts to develop the market for on-line books and other merchandise. How would one predict the value of a company that had never earned a profit, and didn't appear to be close to earning one? The answer, in truth, was anybody's guess. By early 2001 Amazon.com's stock was trading below $10 per share—a loss of over 90% of its earlier value. While it had earned a tiny profit for a little while, losses continued. Several consultants, writing for the large consulting firm McKinsey & Company, explored how investors might approach valuation of a company of such an uncertain future.** Part of the exercise was to determine if there was any possibility that the market values then being attributed to Amazon.com by the market might somehow be rational.

The authors began by imagining four possible scenarios for Amazon.com in the long-term future (2010), attributing a market value to each of them, and discounting those values to present value. Finally, they weighted the probabilities of each outcome to arrive at a possible expected value for the company. In the most optimistic scenario, they assume that Amazon.com is the next Wal–Mart, and that it dominates on-line sales of books and music, while producing higher margins, since it does not have to maintain the stores that conventional retailing requires. The second scenario assumes similar levels of sales, but lower margins, closer to those of traditional retailers. The third and fourth scenarios produced smaller sales and higher costs. The authors then assume that the middle two scenarios are the most likely ones. Ultimately, they attach only a 5% probability to the most optimistic scenario, a 35% probability to each of the middle two scenarios, and a 25% probability to the least optimistic scenario. This results in a market valuation not too far below the values at which Amazon.com traded in late 1999. The authors note the extreme range of possible outcomes, and the high degree of risk attached to such projections. Amazon seems to have justified the high stock prices observed in 1999,

---

* Unless, of course, the grocery chain faces competition from a new entrant, Wal–Mart, that appears able to obtain scale economies beyond those available to traditional grocery chains.

** Driek Desmet, Tracy Francis, Alice Hu, Timothy M. Koller and George A. Riedel, Valuing Dot–Coms, in VALUATION: MEASURING AND MANAGING THE VALUE OF COMPANIES 3d ed. 2000.

despite the drop in the overall market witnessed in 2008–2009. Here is a chart of the most recent ten years of stock prices for Amazon:*

Below, in Figure 3–3, we illustrate how probabilities might appear for a particular set of businesses. We might assume that Firm A is Wal–Mart, while Firm B is Amazon.com, and that we are trying to predict values in ten years.

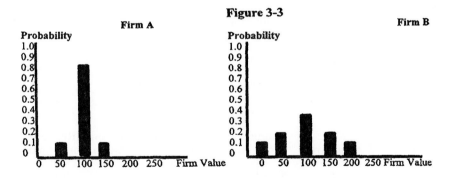

Figure 3-3

You can readily see that Firm B carries more risk, because the spread of possible outcomes is greater. These results can be converted into an "expected value" for each firm by weighting each outcome by its probability, and summing up the results, as illustrated on the following page:

* http://moneycentral.msn.com/investor/charts/chartdl.aspx?PeriodType=8&CP=0&PT= 8&CE=0&D3=0&D4=1&ViewType=0&D5=0&&ShowChtBt=Refresh+Chart&DateRange Form=1&ComparisonsForm=1&Symbol=AMZN&C9=2&DisplayForm=1 (last visited 6/29/09).

	Firm A				Firm B	
Outcome ×	**Probability**	**= Product**		**Outcome** ×	**Probability**	**= Product**
$0	0	$0		$0	.1	$0
50	.1	5		50	.2	10
100	.8	80		100	.4	40
150	.1	15		150	.2	30
200	0	0		200	.1	20
Expected Value:		$100		Expected Value:		$100

Thus both firms' earnings have an *expected value* of $100. This is another way of saying that the mean of the probable values for each firm is $100. In our example the median, or midpoint of the distributions, is also $100, but that is not a necessary relationship. This is just a first step in quantifying the relative riskiness of the two investments. The next step is to determine the *variance* of the expected earnings for each firm. We do this by measuring the deviations from the mean in each case, again using the weighting process. But in measuring deviations, we encounter a slight problem. Some deviations are less than $100 (and thus negative numbers), and other deviations exceed $100, and thus are positive numbers. If we sum up positive and negative numbers in this case, they will add up to zero. The obvious solution is to get rid of negative numbers, which we do by squaring all numbers to determine variance. Again, we weight results, as shown below in Table 3–7:

Table 3–7

Firm A

Outcome ×	Probability	Deviation from Mean	Deviation Squared	Probability times Deviation Squared
0	0	-100	0	0
50	.1	-50	2,500	250
100	.8	0	0	0
150	.1	+50	2,500	250
200	0	+100	0	0
Variance				500

Firm B

Outcome ×	Probability	Deviation from Mean	Deviation Squared	Probability times Deviation Squared
0	.1	-100	10,000	1,000
50	.2	-50	2,500	500
100	.4	0	0	0
150	.2	+50	2,500	500
200	.1	+100	10,000	1,000
Variance				3,000

We have now quantified the difference in *variance* of the expected earnings of the two firms. Variance is the expected squared deviation of the expected returns. But, because of the fact that we have squared our deviations in order to eliminate negative numbers, we have arrived at results that are out of scale with the original results. In order to eliminate this, we calculate the square root of each result:

Firm A: $\sqrt{500}$ = 22.36

Firm B: $\sqrt{3,000}$ = 54.77

The *standard deviation* of our results is simply defined as the square root of the variance. Statistics tells us that 68% of the results of any distribution of outcomes normally fall within one standard deviation of the mean, and 95% fall within two standard deviations. But, as Table 3–6 illustrated, we can carry our analysis a bit further, by converting each standard deviation into a percent of the mean (or expected value). In our example, Firm A's standard deviation is 22.36% of its expected value, while Firm B's standard deviation is 54.77% of its expected value.* This can now be related to the returns shown in Table 3–6, which show that investors demand progressively higher returns as they face higher standard deviations. In future examples, our equations will refer to standard deviation as "σ," or "sigma."

Sidebar: Is Standard Deviation An Accurate Measure of Risk Aversion?

Our model assumes that investors are just as averse to positive results that deviate from the mean as they are negative results. Obviously this is counterintuitive, and some studies by behavioral scientists suggest otherwise. These studies show that investors are irrationally attached to the status quo, and that they are more troubled by the possibility of a loss than they are elated by the prospect of a symmetrical gain. One form of this bias is called the "endowment effect." In experiments, people insist on a higher price to sell something they already own than they are willing to pay to buy the same item if they don't already own it. Because these experiments are always in artificial settings, there are skeptics about these results, but they are widely obtained.

Sidebar: Adjusting for Risk in Presentations to Venture Capitalists

Owners of development-stage companies (Amazon.com is an example) generally are faced with persuading venture capitalists of the expected value of their innovative business or invention. In biotechnology companies, the place to start at the end: what revenues are ultimately expected if the new drug is successful? Typically this process begins by looking at the total size of the market for drugs for the target ailment, and estimating the market share this drug is likely to obtain, given how it compares with existing drugs. From this one can estimate the typical royalty payments earned by drug development companies from the large pharmaceutical companies that typically take the drug through final human testing, Food & Drug Administration (FDA) approval, and marketing. One then calculates the lifetime of the expected income stream (the life of the patent less the years before the drug gets to market) to determine the total expected payoff. From this

---

* Add a footnote for STDEV in Excel—refer to current version.

we must subtract the expected costs of development to get the net payoff. (Recall Part 2.H above in this chapter, calculating net present value.)

But we've ignored risk entirely so far, and this is what will concern the venture capitalists, assuming the drug's laboratory and animal tests are satisfactory, the patent rights are secure, and management seems competent. There are three phases in human testing of drugs to satisfy the FDA, and something can go wrong—perhaps so wrong the drug won't ever succeed—at each stage. Thus, if there is an 80% chance of success at each stage, the prospects of success are $.8 \times .8 \times .8 = .51$. If the owners of the company think the ultimate net value of the drug is $500 million, they will argue that its worth is $255 million $((.51)(\$500 \text{ million}))$, discounted to present value. Venture capitalists asked to put up half of this amount may balk, since there is roughly a 50–50 chance they could lose it all. But the costs of each phase of testing are dependent on success in the preceding stage, so these costs should also be risk-adjusted. Thus, there is only a .8 probability that the second phase testing costs will be incurred, and a .64 probability that the third phase testing costs (the greatest expense) will be incurred. If these costs are thus risk-adjusted, and discounted to present value, along with the expected revenues, we have a presentation that venture capitalists will understand and appreciate.

C.   RISK AND DIVERSIFICATION

Our next task is to translate our measures of risk into the rates of return demanded by investors on increasingly risky stocks. Table 3–6 offered evidence that investors indeed demand higher returns, but offered no theory. We begin with the simple notion that diversification reduces risk: the axiom, known throughout history: "Don't put all your eggs in one basket." If one diversifies across different financial assets with different risk characteristics, one can reduce the total amount of risk faced. The first part of this strategy is easy: if you invest all your assets in a single firm, you run risks that you wouldn't run if you invested more widely. These include the risk that the top officer of the company may depart or die; that the company may engage in some illegal activity that damages its business; that a competitor may build a better mousetrap, and other events unique to that company. Thus, if a business is risky, such as biotechnology, where some companies may discover the "billion dollar molecule," and others go broke trying, the risks are quite high, as measured by standard deviations. Assume, for the moment, that you have $100,000 to invest, and that any given biotech company has a 50–50 chance of success on any given drug, and that these companies only make one drug each. If a drug succeeds, your investment is worth $400,000. Assuming that you believe a particular industry offers the opportunity for superior returns, you can avoid these risks by investing in several companies within the industry group.* If you invest in two companies in the same industry, splitting your investment equally between them, you reduce the variance of your expected returns substantially. This is illustrated by the following example:**

<table>
<tr><td colspan="4" align="center">**Table 3–8**</td></tr>
<tr><td colspan="4" align="center">**Single–Firm Probabilities**</td></tr>
<tr><td>**Outcome   x**</td><td>**Probability**</td><td>**Payoff**</td><td>**Rate of Return**</td></tr>
<tr><td>Drug fails</td><td>.5</td><td>0</td><td>-100%</td></tr>
<tr><td>Drug succeeds</td><td>.5</td><td>$400,000</td><td>+300%</td></tr>
<tr><td colspan="4" align="center">**Two–Firm Probabilities**</td></tr>
<tr><td>**Outcome   x**</td><td>**Probability**</td><td>**Payoff**</td><td>**Rate of Return**</td></tr>
<tr><td>All drugs fail</td><td>.25</td><td>0</td><td>-100%</td></tr>
<tr><td>One drug succeeds</td><td>.5</td><td>$200,000</td><td>+100%</td></tr>
<tr><td>Two drugs succeed</td><td>.25</td><td>400,000</td><td>+300%</td></tr>
</table>

The formula for the Expected Payoff is:

Expected Payoff = Sum of (Probability of Payoff) (Possible Payoff)

Applying this formula to a single drug, we find:

Expected Payoff = .5 × 0 + .5 × $400,000 = $200,000

Applying this formula to two drugs, we find:

Expected Payoff = .25 × 0 + .5 × $200,000 + .25 × $400,000 = $200,000

While both investment programs have the same expected value, the two-drug investment has a lower standard deviation—you can see this from the fact that a zero return's probability is reduced from .5 to .25.

The formula for the standard deviation is:

Standard deviation = Square Root of the sum of (Probability) (Possible Payoff—Expected Payoff)^2

Applying this formula to a single drug, we find:

$$\sigma = \sqrt{(.5)(0 - \$200,000)^2 + (.5)(\$400,000 - \$200,000)^2} = \$200,000$$

Applying this formula to two drugs, we find:

$$\sigma = \sqrt{(.25)(0-\$200,000)^2 + (.5)(\$200,000 - \$200,000)^2 + (.25)(\$400,000 - \$200,000)^2}$$
$$= \$141,421.$$

Thus diversification, simply across two stocks in the same industry, reduces the standard deviation of an investment from $200,000 to

* Companies are classified within Standard Industrial Classifications described in Chapter Two, Part 3.C.

** This is taken from Zvi Bodie & Robert C. Merton, FINANCE, 299–300 (2000).

118 CHAPTER THREE VALUING FIRM OUTPUT

$141,421. Why would any rational investor hold one of these stocks when she could hold two, and achieve the same expected return at lower risk? Once we realize this, it follows that markets will price stocks as if held by rational investors, who hold more than one stock, and demand a return based on the reduced risk that results from holding a diversified portfolio.

Of course, this is the weakest kind of diversification. One can invest in stocks that are uncorrelated with each other—that is—their outcomes are not influenced by the same factors, in much larger numbers. Like most activities, there are declining marginal returns from increasing diversification, but the following table, based on stocks traded on the New York Stock Exchange, illustrates the risk-reducing benefits of diversification. These results assume a randomly selected portfolio. "Volatility" is a synonym for standard deviation in this usage. Table 3–9 illustrates the reductions in volatility resulting from further diversification of a portfolio.

Table 3–9

Effects of Increasing Diversification on Return Volatility

Number of Stocks in Portfolio (1)	Average Volatility of Annual Portfolio Returns (2)	Ratio of Portfolio Volatility To Volatility of a Single Stock (3)
1	49.24%	1.00
2	37.36	0.76
4	29.69	0.60
6	26.64	0.54
8	24.98	0.51
10	23.93	0.49
20	21.68	0.44
30	20.87	0.42
40	20.46	0.42
50	20.20	0.41
100	19.69	0.40
200	19.42	0.39
300	19.34	0.39
400	19.29	0.39
500	19.27	0.39
1,000	19.21	0.39

Source: Meir Statman, "How Many Stocks Make a Diversified Portfolio?," 22 JOURNAL OF FINANCIAL AND QUANTITATIVE ANALYSIS 353–64 (1987), as reported in Zvi Bodie & Robert Merton, FINANCE, 301 (2000).

D. PRICING RISK IN MARKETS—THE CAPITAL ASSETS PRICING MODEL

We have shown in Part 3.A. of this chapter that the standard deviations of stocks are greater than those for government securities or corporate bonds. Indeed, the study by Ibbotson Associates summarized in Table 3–6 shows that small-company stocks are riskier than large-company stocks (as measured by the Standard & Poors 500 Stock Index). Table 3–9 shows how diversification can reduce the risk of holding single stocks.

Individual companies are subject to the particular risks that attend their particular circumstances: the quality of their management, the stability of their customers, the extent to which raw material prices may be more volatile than finished good prices, the exposure to new competition and new products, to name a few. But even with a group of high risk securities, risk can be reduced through diversification. Thus, if one holds a portfolio of ten securities, each with the same high degree of risk, it is likely that the portfolio will be less risky than the individual securities. This is because the performance of all stocks in the portfolio will not move exactly together. That is, their performance will not be perfectly (and positively) correlated.

If a sufficiently large number of stocks are held in the portfolio, the risk associated with individual firms can be nearly completely eliminated. Firm risk, or *unique risk*, also called *unsystematic risk* or *diversifiable risk*, stems from the fact that many of the perils that face an individual company are not faced by all other companies. Indeed, what is risk for one company may be an opportunity for another. Thus, in a properly diversified portfolio, individual firm risk, often called unsystematic risk, or the alpha factor in risk, is irrelevant. Hence this risk will have no impact on the market price of a security. Should it have an impact on the price one company is willing to pay for another? Can it? If you are a manager of a firm in a highly cyclical industry, and you know that managers tend to get fired when earnings are depressed, would you have incentives to have your firm diversify? Does this diversification benefit investors, or can they achieve the same results themselves?

There are also risks that are general to all securities, that are associated with the performance of the economy generally, and in the case of stocks, with the performance of the stock market. This risk, called *systematic risk* because it is associated with the economic system, cannot be eliminated through diversification, at least within that economic system. All stocks are subject to this risk. Thus market risk is important in valuing securities.

Not all stocks are similarly affected by market risk. Some stocks are relatively immune to the fluctuations of the business cycle, while others are severely impacted by it. Thus an investor must consider market risk when selecting the stocks that will comprise a portfolio. The sensitivity of an individual stock's return to market movements is called its beta. This is measured over time by measuring the returns to the particular stock against returns to a broad market portfolio, such as the Standard & Poor's 500 Stock Index, or the New York Stock Exchange Index.

Beta is measured by its relationship to market moves. Thus, if a stock's return is perfectly correlated with that of the market portfolio, it is said to have a beta of one. If the stock moves up (or down) in its return exactly one-half as much as the market portfolio moves, it has a beta of .5. Similarly, if its returns increase (or decrease) twice as much as those of the market, it has a beta of two. With this knowledge of the beta of particular securities, an investor can select exactly the degree of systematic risk he or she wishes. Beta is measured over time, by plotting the price movements of a broad market average, and then plotting the movements of individual stocks at each point. The beta is then estimated with a linear regression, by using a standard least-squares regression program to find the best fit between the points on a chart showing the price moves of the particular stock against the market. In many cases betas are measured by using monthly observations of the stock price and the market average for 60 months, although some calculations use 36 months.

There are several possible variables in this calculation. First, which maturity of U.S. Treasury security should one use to determine the risk-free rate? Typically the total returns on the Standard & Poor's 500 Index are used for the market rate of return. The index itself is often used for this purpose. You can locate the S & P 500 Index on any financial web page, such as Yahoo! Finance or CNN Finance. What is the return on this index? The simplest way to calculate it, although not the most accurate, is to use the price/earnings ratio and calculate the capitalization rate.

Sidebar: Calculating a Beta

The text above stressed the intuition behind beta. The actual definition of beta is

$$\beta_i = \frac{Cov(R_i, R_M)}{\sigma^2(R_M)} =$$

where $Cov(R_i, R_M)$ is the covariance between the return on asset i and the return on the market portfolio M and $\sigma^2(R_M)$ is the variance of the market.

Now we need only determine returns on a particular stock and on the market portfolio. Happily, most companies provide this information for us, at least on an annual basis, in their proxy statements or annual reports. See Schedule 14A, Item 8, and Regulation S–K, Item 402. (Some provide it only in graphs, and not tabular form.) Thus, for Tri–Valley Corporation, we find the following in the 2007 Annual Report on Form 10–K:

"Performance Graph The following table compares the performance of Tri–Valley Corporation's common stock with the performance of the Standard & Poors 500 Composite Stock Index and the Amex Oil Index from December 31, 2002 through December 31, 2007. The table shows the appreciation of our common stock relative to two broad-based stock performance indices. The information is included for historical comparative purposes only and should not be considered indicative of future stock performance. The table and graph compares the yearly percentage change in the cumulative total stockholder return on $100 invested in our common stock with the cumulative total return of the two stock indices. The stock performance graph assumes for comparison that the value of the Companys Common Stock and of each index was $100 on December 31, 2002 and that all dividends were reinvested. Past performance is not necessarily an indicator of future results.

	2002	2003	2004	2005	2006	2007
Tri–Valley Corporation	$100	$314	$874	$556	$678	$529
S & P 500 Index	$100	$128	$142	$149	$172	$182
AMEX Oil Index	$100	$129	$170	$236	$290	$387"

But to calculate covariance, we need more. Obviously Tri–Valley has outperformed the market and even the narrower AMEX Oil Index over this period. But is this because of higher volatility (greater risk) and the reward one would expect for risk? The easy way to determine the beta for a stock is to look it up on one of the web's financial pages. For example, you'll learn that Tri–Valley's stock symbol is "TIV." On the "Money" section on the lower right side of MSN's web page, insert "TIV" in the "Get Quote" box. When the Tri–Valley page pops up, you'll find its beta in the upper right hand corner, just below the blue line. As of February 17, 2009, MSN Money calculated its beta as 1.89. Just in case you think this is the last word, now go to Yahoo!'s Finance page. On the menu on the left side, under the "Comp heading, click on "Key Statistics." Here you will find "Trading Information" on the right side of the screen, and under it, "Stock Price History." The first item is "Beta," which, as of the same date, was calculated as 1.13. There are unrevealed premises in these calculations, so we cannot reconcile these two conflicting betas without more information about the periods used for each calculation.

The methodology involves calculating monthly returns on the stock and the index employed, and then calculating the covariance of the two. Typically the relationship between an individual stock and the market (covariance) is positive, so that when the index moves up, the stock generally also moves up. Recall our calculation of variance in Table 3–7. Variance is simply the sum of the squares of each deviation from an expected (mean) return. Standard deviations are the square roots of the variances. To calculate co-variance of Tri–Valley's stock and the market index, take each of the monthly returns and subtract each of them from the expected return on the stock. Then multiply these deviations together. When these deviations are multiplied for each period, calculate the sum of the multiplied deviations for all periods, and divide by the number of periods. This provides the average covariance for the entire period. To obtain the beta of Tri–Valley, one then divides Tri–Valley's covariance with the market return by the square of the variance of the market return. Symbolically this can be expressed as:

$$\beta_t = \frac{\sigma_{tm}}{\sigma^2 m}$$

Where t is Tri-Valley, σ_{tm} is the covariance between Tri-Valley's return and the market return, and $\sigma^2 m$ is the variance of the market return.

Betas are published by a number of brokerage and advisory services. Most of these require either that you have an account with the broker or subscribe to the advisory service. Some of these, such as Value Line Investment Survey, are available in most reference libraries. As described in the Sidebar, you can find betas at MSN Money. When you plug in the stock's symbol on the front page of MSN, it will take you to a summary page for the stock that will display the current stock price, a chart showing today's prices, and, in the upper right hand corner, the stock's beta.*

The final part of the story involves how returns to risk are set. We begin with the notion that two points on a graph are set—the return on a risk-free portfolio, consisting of government securities (Treasury Bills), and the return on a stock market portfolio, consisting of either the entire market or some portfolio large enough to represent the market. The previous table shows that the risk premium over Treasury Bills paid on common stocks is somewhere between 7.2% and 8.9% over the long term. This spread is not the result of a mathematical formula; it is simply a reflection of the prices investors demand for accepting risk.

This principle of substituting risk-free and risky investments can best be understood by examining the rates of return obtainable through substitution. The following example illustrates expected returns, assuming the risk-free Long–Term Treasury Bond rate is 5% and the return on large-company stocks is 10%:

Table 3–10

Returns on Portfolios Containing Risk–Free Treasuries and the Market Portfolio

% Treasury Bonds	Rate of Return	Weighted Return	% Common Stocks	Rate of Return	Weighted Return	Total Return
100	5%	5%	0	0%	0%	5%
75	5%	3.75%	25	10%	2.5%	6.25%
50	5%	2.5%	50	10%	5%	7.5%
25	5%	1.25%	75	10%	7.5%	8.75%
0	5%	0%	100	10%	10%	10%

* For example, for Pharmasset, Inc. (VRUS), this is displayed at http://moneycentral.msn.com/detail/stock_quote?Symbol=vrus (last visited 6/29/09).

Note that an investor can choose any set of expected returns between the risk-free rate (5%) and the market rate (10%) simply by mixing risky and risk-free investments in a portfolio. In doing so, the investor who moves from 100% Treasury Bills to a diversified common stock portfolio will move the expected return along a straight line between the two points we have defined. As risk moves up, expected returns also move up in a linear relationship. If an investor chooses a portfolio of common stocks that do not replicate the entire stock market, but are, for example, less risky, the investor's expected returns will decline in the same linear relationship. Thus, if the investor's stock portfolio has only 50% as much market risk as the entire market (a beta of 0.5), then the return the investor can expect is the same as that on a portfolio invested in 50% of a broad market portfolio and 50% in risk-free treasuries. Why is this so? Because financial markets are generally viewed as efficient, and if the stock portfolio with a beta of 0.5 returns more than the comparable mixed portfolio of 7.5%, investors will sell Treasuries and buy stocks with betas of 0.5, thus bidding up their prices until their expected returns decline to restore an equilibrium. Remember that as a stock price rises, its earnings, if stable, represent a smaller return on the investment. We earlier observed this relationship with bonds.

If investors can borrow at the risk-free rate, they can "leverage" their investments in risky stocks, and achieve returns higher than those offered by the market portfolio. This is easy to see: if an investor can borrow at 5% and invest at 10%, the 5% increment represents an increase in the total rate of return on the investors' own funds. If an investor can build a portfolio with funds borrowed at rates below the expected return on stocks, this provides an alternative to investing in stocks with greater market risk (beta). This substitute portfolio thus sets the ceiling and floor for expected returns on higher-beta stocks.

This can be illustrated by extending the previous table to show the results of investing borrowed money:

Table 3–11						
Returns on the Market Portfolio with Borrowing						
Stocks	% Return	Return on Equity	%Borrowed Funds*	Interest Rate	Interest Expense	Net Return
100	10%	10%	0%	5%	0	10%
125	10%	12.5%	25%	5%	1.25%	11.25%
150	10%	15%	50%	5%	2.5%	12.5%
175	10%	17.5%	75%	5%	3.75%	13.75%
200	10%	20%	100%	5%	5%	15%

Placed together and extended, these tables illustrate all of the possible combinations of risk and return. Overall, this line, called the "*Capital Market Line*" reflects a straight line from the risk-free rate of return to the

---

* In this context, "percent" denotes the percentage of equity borrowed.

return on the riskiest stocks available in the market. While the notion of borrowing at the risk-free rate is somewhat artificial, there appear to be enough borrowers who can obtain rates close to the risk-free rate, because stock prices do seem to be distributed along this security market line, which slopes upward and to the right. The Capital Asset Pricing Model ("CAPM") is illustrated in Figure 3–4, which follows, where the diagonal line represents the Capital Market Line. The logic of the model, combining risky and risk-free investments and borrowing as substitutes, suggests that all stocks must be priced along the capital market line.

Figure 3-4

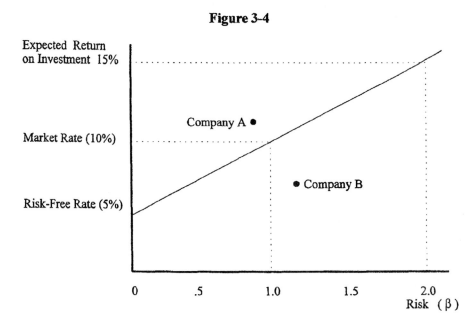

In the model shown above, the risk premium over the risk-free rate for holding the market portfolio is 5%. This is called the *"Equity Premium."*

We now come to a critical point in portfolio theory. An investor can earn any rate of return along the market line in one of two ways. First, an investor can hold a single risky stock with an expected return of 15%. In doing so, the investor would bear both the systematic risk of the market and the non-systematic risk of the individual stock. In short, in the example given in Table 3–9, the investor would be facing expected annual volatility of 49.21% rather than the 19.21% available from diversification. In that example the risk of holding a single stock is roughly 2½ times the risk of holding the market portfolio.

Unfortunately for our single-stock investor, there is no risk premium that compensates him or her for holding this risky investment. Rather, investors willing to bear the risk of such a portfolio will buy a market portfolio with leverage, as illustrated in Table 3–11, or they will buy a portfolio of stocks with a beta of 2.0, based on the relationships shown in Figure 3–4. You can see how this reduces the risk of holding a single stock portfolio.

The Capital Asset Pricing Model now enables us to predict the cost of equity capital for any company, if we know its beta. The formula is simply that the expected risk premium on a stock equals its beta times the expected market risk premium. Thus, for a company with a beta of 2.0, the risk premium is $2 \times 5\%$, or 10%. The company's cost of capital will thus be 15%, because it must also include the risk-free rate of return (5%).

We show two hypothetical stocks in Figure 3–4. Company A's stock is returning more than the market rate with a beta below 1.0. If investors observe this, they will sell other stocks (the market portfolio) and buy Company A's stock, thus driving its price up, and its expected return down. This continues until the expected returns from holding Company A stock reach the Capital Market Line. Conversely, Company B's stock is riskier, with a beta of approximately 1.5. Investors holding a stock with this beta will demand the risk-free rate (5%) plus 1.5 times the Equity premium (7.5%), for a total expected return of 12.5%. Investors owning Company B stock will sell this overpriced stock, thus driving its price down until the expected return on ownership reaches the Capital Market Line, or approximately 12.5%.

We can now state the equation that expresses the cost of capital for a firm:

Cost of Capital = Risk Free Return + (beta $\times$ equity premium)

In the case of Company B, this means C of C = $5\% + (1.5 \times 5\%) = 5\% + 7.5\% = 12.5\%$.

We can now make three statements:

1. Investors price stocks on the basis of their contribution to the risk of a diversified portfolio.

2. Investors are unwilling to pay for non-systematic risk, the unique risks associated with a single firm.

3. The Capital Market Line describes the expected returns investors will demand for all stocks in relation to their betas.

We must caution that this model, which is both simple and elegant, does not capture everything that goes on in stock markets. For a very long time returns of portfolios with different betas have fitted quite nicely with the Capital Market Line. But beginning in the 1960s the fit has been less perfect. Small stocks have outperformed large stocks, and so-called "value stocks," with a high ratio of book value to market value, have both outperformed the overall market. If beta was the only factor that explained differences in expected returns, this could not have happened. Does this mean that beta has no explanatory power any more? It seems unlikely. It may mean that other factors must be added to beta to make more accurate predictions of expected returns.

Experience with the bull market of the late 1990s and early 21st century reduced expected returns to stocks, as stock prices rose more rapidly than expected returns on stocks. While this turned out to be a speculative "bubble" that collapsed, returning stock prices to levels where expected risk premia are closer to historical averages, not everyone could predict this in 2000. Some observers believed there had been a permanent change in the market, and that the risk premium for stocks (the "equity premium") had been permanently reduced. Here is the view of a contemporary dissenter.

Peter Coy, Commentary: Son, Don't Count on Double–Digit Stock Returns, BUSINESSWEEK ONLINE: JUNE 26, 2000 ISSUE

For the past half-century, making money from stocks has been shockingly easy. From 1950 to 1999, real returns on the Standard & Poor's 500-stock index averaged 8.3% more than what you could have taken in on risk-free short-term debt.

However, if you're a 30–year–old who's not saving much because you're relying on making returns just as profitable as those of the past decades from now until you retire, think again—or you just might end up living on dog food and government cheese.

A new study called "The Equity Premium," available soon on the World Wide Web at www.ssrn.com, strengthens the case that the stock market gains of the past 50 years are unlikely to persist. It's by two leading finance scholars, Eugene F. Fama of the University of Chicago and Kenneth R. French of Massachusetts Institute of Technology.

RISKY BUSINESS. Fama and French argue that over the long run, stocks are likely to outperform risk-free debt by only 3% to 3.5% a year. (In the short run, the authors expect that number to be less than 1%, but Fama and French say that they're less confident about that statement, so let's leave it aside.)

Their approach differs from that of other bearish professors such as Yale University's Robert J. Shiller, author of Irrational Exuberance. Fama and French focus on trying to measure the true level of the equity risk premium, which is the extra return that investors demand to compensate them for the riskiness of holding stocks.

They note that from 1872 to 1949, stocks outperformed risk-free securities by only about 4% a year. From 1950 to 1999, the performance gap rose to 8.3%. Economists reason that the 8.3% must have been the premium that investors demanded in order to hold equities during that period. But Fama and French raise another possibility. Perhaps investors actually demanded a premium of only about 4%, as in the earlier period, and the rest was an unexpected bonus.

"GOOD SURPRISE." Their conclusion: Investors got lucky. The authors say that an unexpected flow of good news was largely responsible for the excellent performance of stocks over the past half-century. Says French: "In 1950, the Depression was not so far in the past. Over the next 50 years, the economy was far more productive than we had imagined. The info-tech revolution hit. We won the Cold War. You got good surprise after good surprise after good surprise." One indicator that stocks did better than expected is that average stock-market returns actually outpaced the average return on equity of companies over the 50–year period.

The bad thing about good surprises is that you can't count on them to keep happening. Fama and French estimate that in the future, stocks will return to more like their pre–1950 norm. Says French: "We're saying that if you're a pension fund, you ought to pencil in returns of 3% or 3.5% [above the risk-free rate] for the next 30 years."

French says the research results undermine the frequently stated prescription that long-term investors should hold only stocks. Are he and Fama too pessimistic? Maybe. However, even Jeremy J. Siegel, author of Stocks for the Long Run and a leading advocate of stocks in preference to bonds, says investors should prepare for much lower returns on stocks than the nominal 17% compound annual return they earned from 1982 to 1999. "Half of that would be on the aggressive side," he says.

Oh, well. It was a good half-century while it lasted.

––––––––––––

Mark Smith, **Stocks Fall: Don't Fret**, Wall Street Journal, Oct. 13, 2000, A18

The current sharp slide in the stock market has elicited a variety of explanations. We are told that investors fear a possible Gore presidency and a Democratic Congress. That Federal Reserve Monetary policy has been too tight, jeopardizing the prospects of a "soft landing." Or that a speculative bubble in technology stocks has finally burst. In each case it is assumed that something has changed drastically; somehow, for some very important reason, investors now look at the market very differently than they did a few months ago.

I believe this view reflects a fundamental misunderstanding of how stocks are valued. To get back to the basics, over the long run stocks are worth exactly (and only) an amount equal the discounted future value of the cash flows investors expect to receive from them. This is usually taken to mean both future dividends and share repurchases that put money back in the hands of stockholders.

What most analysts fail to understand when they breathlessly seek out dramatic reasons for major moves in the market is that in this model relatively minor changes in assumptions about interest rates, and the rate of future dividend increases, can create large shifts in theoretical stock valuations.

Take, for example, the 1987 crash. Immediately before the crash, dividends were roughly 3%, and interest rates 10%. (For purposes of simplicity, we shall ignore share repurchases.) This means that, given the assumptions of the model, investors before the crash were anticipating that future dividends would grow at a 7% annual rate.

What if investors became slightly more conservative? For example, as economist Merton Miller has pointed out, if investors in the fall of 1987 increased their forecast for interest rates by only 0.5%, and also reduced the rate at which they expected dividends to grow by a similar 0.5%, a whopping 25% drop in stock prices would have resulted. (In fact, the market fell by 22% on Oct. 19, 1987.)

At the time, all sorts of opinions were offered seeking to explain why the 1987 crash occurred. Many "experts" claimed that the collapse anticipated a serious recession, or some sort of financial crisis. When no such calamity developed, they were perplexed. They failed to grasp how small changes in projected interest rates and dividend increases can have a very large impact on stock prices. A seemingly catastrophic drop in the stock market need not predict a catastrophe for the economy as a whole.

Stocks are volatile today because much more emphasis than ever before is placed on predicting cash flows from businesses, particularly technology companies, that are growing very rapidly, and whose future cash flows are hard to accurately anticipate. Investor assumptions continuously change; each small change in assumptions is magnified into large swings in stock prices. There need be no overarching macroeconomic reason for this, such as unfavorable election results, Federal Reserve policy changes, etc. Instead, wide swings such as that which we are now experiencing are inevitable, and should not be seen as a source of great concern.

E.   LEVERED BETAS AND THE COST OF CAPITAL FOR LEVERAGED FIRMS

For an all-equity firm, determining the return demanded by investors is now relatively simple. Once we determine the risk-free rate, the market rate, and the beta of the particular firm, we can determine its cost of capital. All of this assumes agreement about the appropriate measure of returns, discussed in Chapter Two.

Betas for firms are quoted in various publications. So long as the firm's business mix remains stable, betas based on past relationships to the market are likely to be reliable. Betas are usually calculated on a monthly basis, comparing monthly rates of return with market returns over the period. Brokerage firms publish "beta books" using as many as 60 monthly observations to determine historical betas. The MSN Money page allows you to plug in a stock's symbol, and the next page, showing current prices, also displays the stock's beta. These published betas measure the stock's volatility in relation to the market, given whatever level of borrowing the company may have done. In short, beta measures the volatility of returns to stock regardless of firm leverage, rather than the volatility of returns on assets employed in the business.

Different companies have different amounts of leverage in their capital structures. When the equity premium is calculated based on rates of return to a broad market average such as the Standard & Poor's 500 Stock Index, the rate of return reflects the volatility (and risk) present in the average capital structure for these firms. When we calculate the cost of equity capital for an individual firm, is it necessary to adjust for the difference between its capital structure and the average capital structure of the market average? The answer has to be "no." If increased leverage increases the volatility (variance) of a particular firm's expected returns, that will be reflected in a higher beta for that firm.

If we are valuing an entire company, rather than simply the value of its equity, we may not want to value just its equity. Thus, if one company is considering buying another, valuing the entire target firm may make perfect sense. Capital structure is a separate choice that a buyer can make once it has determined to acquire another business. In this case, a prospective buyer wants to measure the risk of the target firm's business activities, not the risk introduced by its capital structure. Thus we are after the Beta of the firm's assets. Here is how you compute an unlevered beta for a company:

$$\text{Unlevered Beta} = \frac{\text{Leveraged Beta of the company}}{1 + (1 - \text{tax rate for company}) (\text{Percent debt/percent equity})}$$

Why do we introduce a tax rate into our calculation? Because interest payments on debt are a tax deduction, and thus reduce the cost of debt capital from the nominal cost of interest. Below we offer an example of this calculation:

Assumptions:

Levered beta:	1.2
Tax rate:	.40
Capital Structure:	30% debt, 70% equity

$$\text{Unlevered Beta} = \frac{1.2}{1 + (1-.40)(.30/.70)} = \frac{1.2}{1 + (.60)(.429)} = \frac{1.2}{1.257} = .95$$

This unlevered beta can now be applied, using CAPM, to determine the cost of capital for an entire company, based on its pre-debt payment cash flows. As a reality check, one can always determine the cost of equity capital in the normal manner, and add the cost of debt capital as observed in the market. Where debt is not trading at par, the market rate demanded by debt-holders should be used rather than the nominal rate of interest stated on bonds or debentures.

F. CHALLENGES TO CAPM

The Capital Asset Pricing Model thus predicts that all expected returns will lie along the diagonal line in the above figure. Early empirical studies confirmed that actual returns lie approximately along this line. See, e.g., E. F. Fama and J. D. MacBeth, Risk, Return, and Equilibrium: Empirical Tests, 81 J. Political Economy 607 (1973). There are two problems with the use of CAPM for valuations. The first one is relatively easy to explain and deal with. Actual performance of stocks does not perfectly match the performance predicted by CAPM. This is because the CAPM model predicts expected returns, assuming *all other things are equal*. But of course they are not equal. Different non-systematic factors influence the actual performance of individual companies. So we expect actual returns to cluster *around* but not on Capital Market Line. It is sufficient if the Capital Market Line is the best "fit" with this cluster. The fit has not been perfect, however. The slope of the risk-return relationship has never been as steep as predicted by the theory. That is, low-beta stocks have earned returns above the Capital Market Line while high-beta stocks have earned returns below it over very long periods. The actual line has flattened further in the past three decades, so that high-beta stocks underperform predicted returns by a significant amount.

Subsequent work has challenged this model more fundamentally, primarily by showing other relationships that influence stock valuations. More recently at least one study suggests these relationships have weakened or disappeared in the last thirty years, to be replaced by multiple variables. Fama and French, The Cross–Section of Expected Stock Returns, 47 Journal of Finance 427 (1992). Their study covered the period from 1963–1990 and included nearly all the stocks on the NYSE, AMEX and NASDAQ. The stocks were divided into ten groups by book/market ratios and were re-ranked annually. The lowest book/market stocks outperformed the highest book/market stocks 21.4% to 8% with each decile performing worse than the previous. Fama and French and others found that size, in the sense of market capitalization of a company, also matters. Fama and French, Size and Book-to-Market Factors in Earnings and Returns, 50 Journal of Finance 131 (1995). These studies have found that the smaller a firm's market capitalization, the greater the returns, compared to those predicted by beta alone. See also Josef Lakonishok and Alan C. Shapiro, Systematic Risk, Total Risk and Size as Determinants of Stock Market Returns, 10 Journal of Banking and Finance 115 (1986).

Stephen Ross and others have developed an alternative pricing model, called the Arbitrage Pricing Theory ("APT"). Stephen A. Ross, The Arbitrage Theory of Capital Asset Pricing, 13 Journal of Economic Theory 341 (1976); Richard W. Roll and Stephen A. Ross, The Arbitrage Pricing Theory Approach to Strategic Portfolio Planning, 51 Financial Analysts Journal 122 (1995). This theory argues that the risk and return of each stock depends partly on specific macroeconomic factors, such as the spread in yields between long-term government bonds and short-term Treasury bills, the interest rate, the change in the value of the dollar compared to a market basket of other currencies, changes in forecasts of Gross National Product, and changes in forecasts of inflation.* (The other part of the risk is non-diversifiable systematic risk.) APT also includes a joker—"noise," events that are unique to that company (which seems similar to nonsystematic risk). It is possible to estimate the effects of these factors on value, a task that we will not attempt here.

---

* These factors were not identified by Roll and Ross, but appear in E.J. Elton, M.J. Gruber and J. Mei, Cost of Capital Using Arbitrage Pricing Theory: A Case Study of Nine New York Utilities, 3 Financial Markets, Institutions, and Instruments 46 (1994).

4. Efficient Capital Markets

A. The ECMH Model

The model described above assumes that investors can select the stocks with the best risk-return relationships. It also assumes that these choices will drive the prices of other securities to offer comparable returns to comparable risks. We now explore why that phenomenon will generally occur.

Signalling and Causation in Insider Trading

by William J. Carney.
36 Cath. U.L. Rev. 863, 877–883 (1987).

A. Efficient Capital Market Theory

Theories and evidence about investor choices and behavior center on how participants in capital markets process new information. It would be redundant to repeat all of the evidence in support of what Michael Jensen has called one of the best established propositions in all of the social sciences: the Efficient Capital Markets Hypothesis. Beginning with research that established that stock price movements are unpredictable, researchers were able to infer that stock markets were efficient in a weak form—that nothing in the sequence of past stock prices enabled us to predict future price movements. From that, researchers proceeded to test stronger claims of market efficiency. The semi-strong form asserted that all publicly available information about issuers was reflected in stock prices, while the strong form asserted that all such information, public or not, was reflected.

Tests of the semi-strong form provide voluminous support for the hypothesis. There is, nevertheless, some contradictory evidence. Thus far, evidence does not support an alternative theory. Those who make general challenges to the semi-strong form may make anecdotal arguments, or argue that market participants sometimes play sub-games so that some stock prices inaccurately reflect "intrinsic values," or that bargains can be found in supposedly efficient markets. The most recent criticism, that of Gordon and Kornhauser,* appears merely to be that the tools used to test market efficiency are not necessarily accurate. But none of these studies challenge the general proposition that markets are effective, if not perfect, processors of information about the value of firms. Further, little evidence challenges the conclusion that markets are unbiased predictors of future values, and that is the most important feature of this literature for purposes of this Article.

---

* Jeffrey Gordon & Lewis Kornhauser, Efficient Markets, Costly Information and Securities Research, 60 N.Y.U.L. Rev. 761 (1985).

The strong form of the Efficient Capital Markets Hypothesis argues that stock prices reflect all available information about firms, so that gains are unavailable even to insiders. However, empirical tests have demonstrated that insiders do indeed earn above-normal returns on their trading. On the other hand, the semi-strong form now appears supported by this evidence, since the most recent study shows that it is unlikely that outsiders can gain from emulating insiders' trades.

The significance of these findings can be stated simply. Where stock markets are efficient, public announcements will immediately affect the price of a security, without the necessity of any trading, as traders rapidly adjust reservation prices to reflect the new information. Sophisticated traders will realize that there is little reason to trade on the basis of this announcement, to the extent the information contained in these filings is unambiguous in its significance to investors. Ambiguous information that is publicly available may have trading value, but it may require expenditures of considerable resources to enable traders to extract significance (and therefore value) from it.

Only unsophisticated traders might believe that they can win at this stage by "beating the market." They are naive to hold this belief, and can hardly be described as "prudent" in expending resources to trade on information that has no value. Sophisticated traders, on the other hand, can confidently alter their portfolios knowing that the market reflects all of this information. Indeed, that has been one of the goals of the securities laws—to build confidence in the securities markets.

B. The Mechanisms of Market Efficiency

The point here is not to test whether or not capital markets are efficient, but to examine the processes by which prices reflect information of various types. This Article will follow the model of Gilson and Kraakman,* which attempted to link the three forms of the Efficient Capital Markets Hypothesis with the mechanisms used to distribute information. As these authors pointed out, to say that sooner or later prices will reflect certain information is not by itself very interesting; the most critical question is "How long does it take?"

Weak form market efficiency presumes that information is readily available to all traders. This includes old information, such as price histories, as well as information about current events, such as important news items. Indeed, even news stories about particular firms affect prices too rapidly to support trading profits. In these instances, no particular trading seems required to move stock prices to adjust to new widely distributed information. Thus, public announcements of Federal Reserve Board policy changes can be met with instantaneous changes in the reservation prices of traders, just as major company announcements can. Gilson and Kraakman point out that where news is incomplete, uncertainty about future prospects will remain until events or announcements resolve

---

* Ronald Gilson & Reinier Kraakman, The Mechanisms of Market Efficiency, 70 Va. L. Rev. 549 (1984).

the uncertainty. During this period, a certain amount of trading activity will occur to fine-tune the price to reflect the consensus of traders' assessments.

Semi-strong form market efficiency shifts from "publicly distributed" information to "publicly available" information that is not known to all market participants. For example, experts pore over government filings by issuers, such as SEC reports, to analyze this information. The resulting market insights might be available only to such experts. Studies support the assertion that stock markets also reflect this information with such rapidity that no extraordinary trading profits are generally available. Since virtually all such disclosures are historical rather than forward-looking, they provide only weak insights about the future performance of a firm. Because this information is not readily available to all traders (at least in a useful form), price adjustments to such information rely on trading by a minority of market traders—informed professionals. Gilson and Kraakman explain this in terms of the trading volume controlled by market professionals, but volume arguments, standing alone, raise serious questions about market efficiency. The evidence to date suggests that all stocks with similar beta coefficients are treated as fungible by investors, so demand for any given security is perfectly elastic, absent special information about an issuer. In this context, volume is relevant to price only to the extent that it signals traders that someone is apparently acting on superior information.

Thus far, this Article has described the forms of market efficiency generally accepted by the SEC when designing an integrated disclosure system and rules governing shelf registrations. Here, there seems to be a consensus among lawyers and economists that markets are fully informed about the data disclosed. Investors can confidently rely on this information when trading in securities in efficient markets, without undertaking further analysis on their own. With respect to this data, at least, stocks are assumed to be fairly priced, in the sense that there is no systematic bias. Insiders who are aware of this information can trade freely on it, confident that the courts will not find any unlawful informational advantage over other market participants.

Moving from information that is publicly available to firm-specific information not formally announced or released, price adjustments become more complex, and less well documented. Market participants act as if markets are not efficient, and as if information can produce gains. This has been described as the paradox of efficient markets; in order for them to function, participants must disbelieve in the hypothesis. Expenditures on securities research may provide more or less perfect substitutes for much inside information. There are reports that traders and analysts spend as much as $600 million seeking information. Securities analysts attempt to duplicate inside information by researching sources identical or similar to those providing insiders with their insights. Suppliers, customers, and competitors are all potential sources.

ECMH depends critically on the correctness of certain assumptions, set out below. While this is a formal statement of the conditions, you can ask yourself how closely these conditions are likely to obtain in the real world.

Zero transaction costs in securities. Obviously transaction costs can never reach zero in markets; this is an idealization for modeling purposes. But they can be relatively low. When ECMH was first developed, trading costs were much higher than at present, in part because of fixed commissions mandated by the New York Stock Exchange. With the abolition of fixed commissions and the development of discount brokers, commissions at the retail level fell dramatically. For large institutional traders, block trades allow them to gain economies of scale, and in some cases they can trade directly with each other, thus bypassing brokerage costs altogether (and replacing them with their own search costs). More recently, the development of internet trading firms has dramatically lowered costs for retail investors. These costs have been reduced in part because of the development of automated systems to fill small orders on both exchanges and NASDAQ.

All available information is costlessly available to market participants. It is clear that inside information is not costlessly available to market participants, other than the insiders themselves (who are, in most instances, barred from trading on it). Empirical studies show that insiders continue to earn above-normal profits on their trades in their own companies' shares, demonstrating their informational advantage over other market participants. Information at the macro level—about the economy generally, for example, is generally universally and almost instantaneously known to all participants. Public news announcements generally provide costless and universal availability to all market participants. A widely cited description of how other information is made available to market participants is by Ronald J. Gilson and Reinier H. Kraakman, The Mechanisms of Market Efficiency, 70 Va. L. Rev. 549 (1984). These authors argue that the availability requirement is met when a significant subset of the market— informed traders—is aware of the information. Market professionals are the most active traders—a statement even more true today than in 1984— and presumably disseminate the essence of any news through their trading activities. Thus, it is marginal traders, who can invest large sums, who can move market prices, whose knowledge is probably sufficient to satisfy this condition.

Agreement on the implication of current information for stock prices. It is easy to see how traders will normally agree on the implications of business or financial news, such as reductions in unemployment, increased orders for capital goods by manufacturers, changes in interest rates, announcements of sales and earnings increases, and the like. Gilson and Kraakman point out that some information, such as an innovation, such as a new form of security, may create more difficulties in deciphering its meaning. In these cases markets may discount the value of the innovation until some traders can verify its value independently of the issuer's claims, which may be regarded as puffing.

Sufficient capital to engage in risky arbitrage. This was not a condition that was stated originally, but rather was posited by later critics of EMCH, such as Andre Shleifer, whose critique is set forth below.

B. CHALLENGES TO ECMH

Inefficient Markets: An Introduction to Behavioral Finance (2000), 10–16

By Andrei Shleifer.

Shortly after Jensen's announcement [that "there is no other proposition in economics which has more solid empirical evidence supporting it than the Efficient Markets Hypothesis"*], the EMH was challenged on both theoretical and empirical grounds. Although the initial challenges were primarily empirical, it is easier to begin by reviewing some potential difficulties with the theoretical case for the EMH and then turn to the evidence. * * *

To begin, it is difficult to sustain the case that people in general, and investors in particular, are fully rational. At the superficial level, many investors react to irrelevant information in forming their demand for securities; as Fischer Black put it, they trade on noise rather than information.** Investors follow the advice of financial gurus, fail to diversify, actively trade stocks and churn their portfolios, sell winning stocks and hold on to losing stocks thereby increasing their tax liabilities, buy and sell actively and expensively managed mutual funds, follow stock price patterns and other popular models. In short, investors hardly pursue the passive strategies expected of uninformed market participants by the efficient markets theory.

This evidence of what investors actually do is only the tip of the iceberg. Investors' deviations from the maxims of economic rationality turn out to be highly pervasive and systematic. As summarized by Kahneman and Riepe,*** people deviate from the standard decision making model in a number of fundamental areas. We can group these areas, somewhat simplistically, into three broad categories: attitudes toward risk, non-Bayseian expectation formation, and sensitivity of decision making to the framing of questions.

First, individuals do not assess risky gambles following precepts of von Neumann–Morgenstern rationality. Rather, in assessing such gambles, people look not at the levels of final wealth they can attain but at gains and losses relative to some reference point, which may vary from situation to situation, and display loss aversion—a loss function that is steeper than a

---

* Michael Jensen, Some Anomalous Evidence Regarding Market Efficiency, 6 J. Fin. Econ. 95 (1978).—Ed. Note: Not all references in this excerpt have been footnoted by the editor.

** Fischer Black, Noise, 41 J. Fin. 529 (1986).—Ed.

*** D. Kahneman & M. Riepe, Aspects of Investor Psychology, 24 J. Portfolio Mgt. 52 (1998).—Ed.

gain function. Such preferences—first described and modeled by Kahneman and Tversky in their "Prospect Theory"*—are helpful for thinking about a number of problems in finance. One of them is the notorious reluctance of investors to sell stocks that lose value, which comes out of loss aversion. Another is investors' aversion to holding stocks more generally, known as the equity premium puzzle.**

Second, individuals systematically violate Bayes rule and other maxims of probability theory in their predictions of uncertain outcomes. For example, people often predict future uncertain events by taking a short history of data and asking what broader picture this history is representative of. In focusing on such representativeness, they often do not pay enough attention to the possibility that the recent history is generated by chance rather than by the "model" they are constructing. Such heuristics are useful in many life situations—they help people to identify patterns in the data as well as to save on computation—but they may lead investors seriously astray. For example, investors may extrapolate short past histories of rapid earnings growth of some companies too far into the future and therefore overprice these glamorous companies without a recognition that, statistically speaking, trees do not grow to the sky. Such overreaction lowers future returns as past growth rates fail to repeat themselves and prices adjust to more plausible valuations.

Perhaps most radically, individuals make different choices depending on how a given problem is presented to them, so that framing influences decisions. In choosing investments, for example, investors allocate more of their wealth to stocks rather than bonds when they see a very impressive history of *long-term* stock returns relative to those on bonds, than if they only see the volatile *short-term* stock returns.

A number of terms have been used to describe investors whose preferences and beliefs conform to the psychological evidence rather than the normative economic model. * * * Less kindly, the investors whose conduct is not rational are described as "unsophisticated" or, following Kyle and Black, as "noise traders."

If the theory of efficient markets relied entirely on the rationality of individual investors, then the psychological evidence would by itself present an extremely serious, perhaps fatal, problem for the theory. But of course it does not. Recall that the second line of defense of the efficient markets theory is that the irrational investors, while they may exist, trade randomly, and hence their trades cancel each other out. It is this argument that the Kahneman and Tversky theories dispose of entirely. The psychological evidence shows precisely that people do not deviate from rationality randomly, but rather most deviate in the same way. * * * Investor sentiment

---

* Daniel Kahneman and Aaron Tversky, Prospect Theory: An Analysis of Decision under Risk, 47 Econometrica 263 (1979).—Ed.

** R. Mehra and E. Prescott, The Equity Premium: A Puzzle, 15 J. Monetary Econ. 145 (1985); S. Benartzi and R. Thaler, Myopic Loss Aversion and the Equity Premium Puzzle, 110 Q. J. Econ. 73 (1995).—Ed.

reflects the common judgment errors made by a substantial number of investors, rather than uncorrelated random mistakes.

Individuals are not the only investors whose trading strategies are difficult to reconcile with rationality. Much of the money in financial markets is allocated by professional managers of pension and mutual funds on behalf of individual investors and corporations. Professional money managers are of course themselves people, and as such are subject to the same biases as individual investors. But they are also agents who manage other people's money, and this delegation introduces further distortions into their decisions relative to what fully-informed sponsors might wish.* For example, professional managers may choose portfolios that are excessively close to the benchmark that they are evaluated against, such as the S & P 500 Index, so as to minimize the risk of underperforming this benchmark. They may also herd and select stocks that other managers select, again to avoid falling behind and looking bad. They may artificially add to their portfolios stocks that have recently done well, and sell stocks that have recently done poorly, to look good to investors who are getting end-of-year reports on portfolio holdings. There indeed appears to be some evidence of such window-dressing by pension fund managers. Consistent with the presence of costly investment distortions, pension and mutual fund managers on average underperform passive investment strategies. In some situations, they may be the relevant noise traders.

This brings us to the ultimate set of theoretical arguments for efficient markets, those based on arbitrage. Even if sentiment is correlated across unsophisticated investors, the arbitrageurs—who perhaps are not subject to psychological biases—should take the other side of unsophisticated demand and bring prices back to fundamental values. Ultimately, the theoretical case for efficient markets depends on the effectiveness of such arbitrage.

The central argument of behavioral finance states that, in contrast to the efficient markets theory, real-world arbitrage is risky and therefore limited. As we already noted, the effectiveness of arbitrage relies crucially on the availability of close substitutes for securities whose price is potentially affected by noise trading. To lay off their risks, arbitrageurs who sell or sell short over-priced securities must be able to buy "the same or essentially similar" securities that are not overpriced. For some so-called derivative securities, such as futures and options, close substitutes are usually available, although arbitrage may still require considerable trading. For example, the S & P 500 Index futures typically sell at a price close to the value of the underlying basket of stocks, since if the future sells at a price different from the basket, an arbitrageur can always buy whichever is cheaper and sell whichever is more expensive against it, locking in a safe profit. Yet in many instances, securities do not have obvious substitutes. Thus arbitrage does not help pin down price levels of, say, stocks and bonds as a whole. These broad classes of securities do not have substitute

---

* J. Lakonishok, Andre Shleifer and R. Vishny, The Structure and Performance of the Money Management Industry, BROOKINGS PAPERS ON ECONOMIC ACTIVITY MICROECONOMICS 339 (1992).—Ed.

portfolios, and therefore if for some reason they are mispriced, there is no riskless hedge for the arbitrageur. An arbitrageur who thinks that stocks as a whole are overpriced cannot sell short stocks and buy a substitute portfolio, since such a portfolio does not exist. The arbitrageur can instead simply sell or reduce exposure to stocks in the hope of an above-market return, but this arbitrage is no longer even approximately riskless, especially since the average return on stocks is high and positive. * * *

Even when individual securities have better substitutes than does the market as a whole, fundamental risk remains a significant deterrent to arbitrage. First, such substitutes may not be perfect, even for individual stocks. An arbitrageur taking bets on relative price movements then bears idiosyncratic risk that the news about the securities he is short will be surprisingly good, or the news about the securities that he is long will be surprisingly bad. Suppose, for example, that the arbitrageur is convinced that the shares of Ford are expensive relative to those of General Motors and Chrysler. If he sells short Ford and loads up on some combination of GM and Chrysler, he may be able to lay off the general risk of the automobile industry, but he remains exposed to the possibility that Ford does surprisingly well and GM or Chrysler do surprisingly poorly, leading to arbitrage losses. With imperfect substitutes, arbitrage becomes risky. Such trading is commonly referred to as "risk arbitrage," because it focuses on the statistical likelihood, as opposed to the certainty, of convergences of relative prices.

There is a further important source of risk for an arbitrageur, which he faces even when securities do have perfect substitutes. This risk comes from the unpredictability of the future resale price or, put differently, from the possibility that mispricing becomes worse before it disappears. * * *

An example may help illustrate the idea of risky and limited arbitrage. Consider the case of American stocks, particularly the large capitalization stocks, in the late 1990s. At the end of 1998, large American corporations were trading at some of their historically highest market values relative to most measures of the profitability. * * *

But what is an arbitrageur to do? If he sold short the S & P 500 Index at the beginning of 1998, when the price earnings multiple on the Index was at an already high level of 24, he would have suffered a loss of 28.6 percent by year end. In fact, if he sold short early on when the experts got worried, at the beginning of 1997, he would have lost 33.4 percent that year before losing another 28.6 percent the next. If he followed a more sophisticated strategy of selling short the S & P 500 at the beginning of 1998 and buying the Russell 200 Index of smaller companies as a hedge on the theory that their valuations by historical standards were not nearly as extreme, he would have lost 30.8 percent by the end of the year. Because the S & P 500 Index does not have good substitutes and relative prices of imperfect substitutes can move even further out of line, arbitrage of the Index is extremely risky. * * *

The bottom line of this work is that theory by itself does not inevitably lead a researcher to a presumption of market efficiency. At the very least, theory leaves a researcher with an open mind on the crucial issues.

QUESTIONS

1. Does it matter if many investors are irrational, if others are not? Economics teaches that there is a difference between average and marginal behavior. Does that apply here?

2. Does it matter if some professional traders engage in some of the same kinds of irrational behavior as individual investors, if others do not?

3. Does Shleifer offer an alternative theory to ECMH? Can one expect to explain the behavior of markets without a theory?

4. The primary test of a theory is its predictive power. Does Shleifer offer a theory that might predict outcomes?

5. Shleifer emphasizes the difficulties in arbitrage when the entire stock market is "mis-priced." What does he mean by mispricing? How can you tell when a market is overpriced?

6. Does Shleifer's critique hold as powerfully for individual stocks as it does for the stock market as a whole? What role does the availability of substitutes play in your answer? What is the role of derivatives such as SPDRs (warehouse receipts with a return that tracks the return of the S & P–500 index.)? (Similar SPDRs exist to track the S & P MidCap 400, nine different sectors of the S & P–500 (Select Sector SPDRs), and to track the Dow Jones Industrial Average (Diamonds).) Unlike index mutual funds, these securities can be sold short.

7. In Chapter Eight we will examine the claim that given the availability of any three of the four following financial instruments, the fourth instrument can be replicated: (1) a riskless zero-coupon bond; (2) a share of stock; (3) a call option on the stock and (4) a put option on the stock. What are the implications of this theorem for Shleifer's argument about the unavailability of substitutes?

8. Is Shleifer correct in arguing that close substitutes for individual stocks may be difficult to find? As you know, given the Capital Assets Pricing Model, an investor can assemble any desired portfolio from a combination of risky stocks and risk-free debt or risky borrowings. In the context of a portfolio, does choosing the particular stock to substitute for an overpriced one matter?

9. Shleifer argues that professional money managers are subject to the same biases as individual investors. What does this say about the effects of an education in economics and finance? Are professional money managers likely to have easy access (availability) to types of information that might influence their behavior in a different manner from that of the average investor?

Are Markets Efficient?—No, Arbitrage Is Inherently Risky

The Wall Street Journal, Thursday, December 28, 2000.*
By Andrei Shleifer.

* * *

To illustrate this point, consider how efficient markets theory goes wrong. One very clear example is the pricing of the shares of Royal Dutch and Shell. Royal Dutch and Shell are independently incorporated in the Netherlands and England, respectively. In 1907, they formed an alliance agreeing to merge their interests on a 60–40 basis while remaining separate and distinct entities. All their profits, adjusting for corporate taxes and control rights, are effectively split into these proportions.

Information clarifying the linkages between the two companies is widely available. This makes for an easy prediction for the efficient markets theory: If prices are right, the market value of Royal Dutch should always equal 1.5 times the market value of Shell. In this case, the efficient markets theory reflects the law of one price: Identical securities must sell at the same price in different markets. If not, there would be clear and easy arbitrage opportunities from dumping the relatively expensive stock and buying the cheaper one.

The nearby chart [not included—Ed.] shows the deviations of market values of Royal Dutch and Shell from the 60–40 parity from 1990 to 1999. In the early 1990s, Royal Dutch traded at a 5% to 7% discount from parity, while in the late 1990s it traded at up to a 20% premium. A closer look at the chart clarifies why the market doesn't bring the relative prices to efficiency.

A shrewd investor who noticed, for example, that in the summer of 1997, Royal Dutch traded at an 8% to 10% premium relative to Shell, would have sold short the expensive Royal Dutch shares and hedged his position with the cheaper Shell shares. Sadly for this investor, the deviation from the 60–40 parity only widened in 1998, reaching nearly 20% in the autumn crisis. This bet against market inefficiency lost money, and a lot of money if leveraged.

In this case, it is said that when Long Term Capital Management collapsed during the Russian crisis, it unwound a large position in the Royal Dutch and Shell trade. Smart investors can lose a lot of money at the times when an inefficient market becomes even less efficient. In fact, as the LTCM experience illustrates, their businesses might not survive long enough to see markets return to efficiency.

The inefficiency in the pricing of Royal Dutch and Shell is a fantastic embarrassment for the efficient markets hypothesis because the setting is the best case for that theory. The same cash flows should sell for the same price in different markets. It shows that deviations from efficiency can be

---

large and persistent, especially with no catalysts to bring markets back to efficiency. It also shows that market forces need not be strong enough to get prices in line even when many risks can be hedged, and that rational and sophisticated investors can lose money along the way, as mispricing deepens.

But if markets fail to achieve efficiency in this near-textbook case, what should we expect in more complicated situations, when the risks of arbitrage are greater? Who would dare to sell short Internet stocks to bring their prices down to earth when a company trading at five times its fundamental value can easily rise to 10 times its value? Or who would bet against the overpriced S & P 500 as a whole? What would have happened to the sellers of the market who heeded Alan Greenspan's concerns in 1996?

Are Markets Efficient?—Yes, Even if They Make Errors

By Burton G. Malkiel.
The Wall Street Journal, Thursday, December 28, 2000.*

There is an old story about a finance professor and a student who come upon a $100 bill lying on the ground. The student stoops to pick it up. "Don't bother," the professor admonishes. "If it were really a $100 bill, it wouldn't be there."

This story illustrates what financial economists mean by efficient markets. Markets can be efficient even if investors are subject to overconfidence and errors in judgement. Markets can be efficient even if they make errors in the valuation of individual stocks and exhibit greater volatility than can apparently be explained by fundamentals such as earnings and dividends.

Many of us economists who believe in this efficient market theory do so because we view markets as amazingly successful devices for reflecting new information rapidly and, for the most part, accurately. Above all, we believe that financial markets are efficient because they don't allow investors to earn above-average returns without taking above-average risks. In short, we believe that $100 bills are not lying around for the taking.

While the efficient market theory has been the mantra of my generation, it has come under increasing attack from a new breed of economists. Their work has emphasized psychological and behavioral elements of stock-price determination; they believe future stock prices are somewhat predictable on the basis of past stock-price patterns and certain "fundamental" valuation metrics.

In their view, value stocks—those with low ratios of stock prices to earnings and book values—are alleged to outperform growth stocks, while small-company stocks supposedly do better than large-capitalization stocks. They believe that stock prices sometimes underreact to news, creating some short-run momentum, as well as sometimes overreact to events, creating

---

price reversals that can be exploited by investors. Behavioralists also emphasize that the arbitrage activities of rational professional investors, who might be expected to bring stock prices back to fundamental values, are often impossible to execute and, in any event, risky and therefore limited.

These attacks on the efficient market theory are far from convincing. Some of the market patterns discovered may have rational causes; others may be spurious. But none of them are dependable in all time periods. And there is no evidence that rational investors can exploit any of the alleged mispricing in securities markets to earn above-average returns.

Many of the statistical patterns behaviorists emphasize could have rational as well as psychological explanations. Some long-run evidence suggests that growth stocks produce lower returns than value stocks. Behavioralists argue that this reflects investor overconfidence about optimistic growth forecasts and overpricing of growth stocks. But it is also possible that stocks selling at low valuations relative to their book values reflect some degree of financial distress and riskiness, so they should offer higher rates of return.

Behavioralists also believe stock prices exhibit reversals because individuals overreact to recent events. But reversals for the market as a whole could be caused by the tendency of interest rates and risk perceptions to fluctuate, meaning that stock prices are simply rationally adjusting to underlying economic conditions.

Many of the predictable patterns behaviorists claim to find in stock prices may be the result of endlessly mining the vast financial data banks now available until they cough up some seemingly significant, but wholly spurious, relationship. Moreover, findings of underreaction appear in the data about as frequently as overreaction and so could be random occurrences consistent with market efficiency. Many supposedly exploitable price patterns tend to become marginal or even disappear when alternative measurement approaches are used.

Even the strongest empirical regularities in the stock market aren't dependable. For example, small-cap stocks have historically outperformed large-cap stocks, while value stocks have outperformed growth stocks. But investors acting on that finding would have suffered very disappointing investment results indeed over this past decade of high-tech investment.

And what of the behavioral tenet that when psychological contagion pushes price-earnings ratios well above, and dividend yields well below, their historical averages, poor investment results must follow? An investor who followed that advice would have sold out in the mid–1990s when the stock market was less than half its present value. While the "Dogs of the Dow" strategy of buying the depressed highest dividend yields in the Dow worked brilliantly in back tests, when mutual funds were recently introduced based on that technique the dogs didn't hunt.

Finally, even if systematic pricing patterns persist over time, it may be impossible to exploit them. One pattern my colleagues at Princeton and I attempted to exploit was the overreaction phenomenon leading to return reversals. We simulated a strategy of buying those stocks with the poorest three-to five-year performance (the losers) and selling those stocks with the best three-to five-year performance (the winners). We found that statistical patterns of return reversals held up and were strongly significant: The losers later enjoyed better performance and the winners performed more poorly. What the losers did not produce, however, were excess returns: The returns for both groups were the same. There was statistical evidence of mean reversion but no inefficiency that could be exploited for gain.

As Richard Roll, a brilliant financial economist and active money manager, has said, "I have personally tried to invest money, my client's and my own, in every single anomaly and predictive result that academics have dreamed up. And I have yet to make a nickel on any of these supposed market inefficiencies. An inefficiency ought to be an exploitable opportunity. If there's nothing investors can exploit in a systematic way, time in and time out, then it's very hard to say that information is not being properly incorporated into stock prices. Real money investment strategies don't produce the results that academic papers say they should."

As further evidence of how difficult it is to outguess the collective wisdom of the market, consider the relative performance of index funds (that simply buy and hold the entire market portfolio) and active mutual-fund managers. While more than half the active managers are beating the indexes so far in 2000, the long-run results are devastating. Over the past three-year, five-year and 10–year periods, more than 75% of active managers underperformed index funds when both are measured after expenses. Those that do outperform in one period are not typically the ones who outperform in the next.

There are some exceptions like Peter Lynch and Warren Buffett, but you can count the truly outstanding long-term overachievers on the fingers of one hand. If markets were nearly as inefficient as some would believe, it would be easier for well paid professionals to profit at the expense of those who make systematic mistakes in processing information. As Rex Sinquefield, co-author of a thorough compendium of past stock returns, has said: "There are three classes of people who don't think markets work; the Cubans, the North Koreans and active money managers."

To be sure, we sometimes know in advance of isolated instances of mispricing. My favorite this year occurred when 5% of Palm Pilot shares were spun off by its parent 3Com, which retained the other 95%. The market immediately priced Palm Pilot shares at a valuation that made 3Com's ownership interest "worth" more than $50 billion, much more than the entire $28 billion market capitalization of the parent company. It was as if the operational component of 3Com had a negative value. The mispricing persisted for a while because not enough Palm Pilot shares were available for borrowing to effect a profitable arbitrage. But over time, and with more Palm shares available, the mispricing was corrected. The story illustrates that even occasional irrationality in market prices doesn't create a profitable trading opportunity.

In summary, I remain skeptical that markets are systematically irrational and that knowledge of such irrationalities can lead to profitable trading strategies. Indeed, the more potentially profitable a discoverable pattern is, the less likely it is to survive. This is the logical reason one should be cautious not to overemphasize apparent departures from efficiency.

It is always possible that new patterns will emerge and be discovered, but such patterns must be exploited immediately because they are unlikely to last. The advice I give my students is slightly different from that of the finance professor of the story: "If you see a $100 bill on the ground, pick it up right away because it surely won't be there for long."

QUESTION

1. Fred S. McChesney has written that "it takes a model to beat a model," citing George Stigler, The Theory of Price 7 (4th ed. 1987), who wrote: "Refutation requires a new theoretical model, testable implications that distinguish the newer from the older model, and statistical verification that the newer model out-performs the older one." McChesney, Contractarianism Without Contracts? Yet Another Critique of Eisenberg, 90 Colum. L. Rev. 1332, 1336, n. 20 (1990). Does Shleifer present a new model?

Takeover Defense When Financial Markets Are (Only) Relatively Efficient

By Michael L. Wachter.
151 U. Pa. L. Rev. 787, 812–817 (2003).

A.   Anomalies in the Fabric of Market Efficiency

The first of the three factors of importance determining whether market inefficiency is supportive of a management-discretion theory, and hence in the corporate law debate as a whole, is the role of anomalies or predictability in the fabric of market efficiency. There is growing consensus that there are anomalies represented by predictability in future returns that are not predicted by the theory. Perhaps the dominant position today, and the one taken in this Article, recognizes that anomalies or departures from efficiency exist, can persist for some time, and play a major role in the workings of financial markets and the overall economy. John Campbell, Andrew Lo, and A. Craig MacKinlay state that although predictability would have been seen as an outright rejection of market efficiency in the past, it may be a necessary component of market functioning since it rewards arbitrageurs for taking on dynamic risk.[72] Indeed, "predictability is the oil that lubricates the gears of capitalism," and departures from efficiency "play a major role in determining the nature of competition and

---

72.   See [John] Campbell et al., [The Econometrics of Financial Markets (1997)], at 80 ("A certain degree of predictability may be necessary to reward investors for bearing certain dynamic risks.").

the function of markets.''[73] If anomalies represent a regular feature of financial markets, it makes more sense to talk about relative efficiency where market efficiency serves the same function in financial markets that perfect competition serves in product markets: it is the ideal or benchmark against which departures are measured.[74]

The idea that financial markets are only relatively efficient is a middle-of-the-road position in the finance debate. On one side is the strict efficiency camp that argues that apparent departures from efficiency reflect nothing more than data limitations or problems in the precise specification of the theory. Markets get it right in pricing assets, only finance economists get it wrong when they use inadequate data or theories.[75] On the other side is the behaviorist camp that sees anomalies as representing true departures from efficiency and argues that the tests effectively refute ECMH/CAPM. It claims that once investor sentiment and behavior is incorporated into financial models, systematic, persistent, and significant deviations from efficiency become the norm.[76]

In the empirical finance literature, ECMH survives in much better form than does CAPM. As noted above,[77] the prevailing view is that the anomalies that exist in the data are consistent with the view that they represent a return to dynamic risk bearing. Consequently, the weak and semi-strong theories of market efficiency still hold in that informed traders cannot systematically outperform the market by making use of past price data or news announcements. In the strict efficiency camp, most examples of anomalies reflect bad econometrics rather than departures from ECMH. Even the behaviorists largely accept the conclusion that informed arbitrageurs cannot outperform the market once risk is taken into account. The reason is that absent a theory to predict investor sentiment, arbitrageurs not only take on considerable risk in attempting to profit from irrational investor behavior, but also often do not succeed.[78]

The CAPM component of market efficiency, however, does poorly in the account of any of the three camps. The central conclusion of CAPM involves the predictions of the slope of the security market line and the claim that the market capitalization rate of each company can be explained by its stock beta. The results show that the security market line has been

---

73. [Andrew W.] Lo & [A. Craig] MacKinlay, [A Non–Random Walk Down Wall Street (1999)] at 4.

74. See Campbell et al., supra note [72], at 24 (arguing that whereas perfect efficiency is an unrealistic benchmark, relative efficiency "may be a more useful concept than the all-or-nothing view taken by much of the traditional market-efficiency literature").

75. In a recent article, Eugene Fama claims that the long-term anomalies are a function of data sample and econometric technique and thus do not serve to reject the hypothesis of market efficiency. Eugene F. Fama, Market Efficiency, Long–Term Returns, and Behavioral Finance, 49 J. Fin. Econ. 283, 303–04 (1998).

76. For an example of such a theory, see Andrei Shleifer, Inefficient Markets: An Introduction to Behavioral Finance 112–53 (2000).

77. Supra text accompanying note 24.

78. Shleifer, supra note 76, at 13.

consistently too flat for several decades, indicating that certain classes of seemingly low-risk stocks have too high a return and that beta is a highly imprecise predictor of the future excess returns of individual stocks or portfolios of stocks.[79] Two major examples of these shortcomings are represented by the returns on small company stocks and on stocks with high book-to-market value.[80]

How does the strict efficiency camp deal with this apparent inconsistency? The major work on the topic is by Eugene Fama and Kenneth French.[81] They acknowledge the inconsistencies with the single risk factor (beta) specification of CAPM, but argue that the solution is to incorporate other risk factors into CAPM. In particular, they assert that stocks of smaller firms, or of firms with high book-to-market ratios, must earn higher returns because they are fundamentally riskier. The high stock returns of small companies and companies with high book-to-market ratios are actually capturing risk effects not otherwise captured by beta.[82] In the broader three-factor CAPM, they propose that the security market line is no longer too flat: the anomalies have been incorporated into the theory.[83]

But the fix has its costs. First, while it is possible to advance cogent explanations that the two factors serve as proxies for systematic risk, it cannot be proved. Yes, small size and high book-to-market ratios are correlated with distress risk, but there has been no direct evidence to support the assertion. This is measurement without a theoretical foundation. It leaves unanswered the question whether the two portfolios are measuring fundamental risk or something else. Second, even if one accepts the claim that the new factors capture risk, the alternative specifications of CAPM yield imprecise estimates of the cost of equity capital. Standard errors for the cost of equity capital of more than three percent are typical.[84] Fama and French note that these uncertainties result in estimates of the cost of equity that are "distressingly imprecise."[85]

The imprecision in estimates of the market capitalization rate are magnified in valuing the corporation. The higher the growth rate in the company's cash flow, the greater the sensitivity of the stock price to even small changes in the discount rate. Even a one standard deviation range in the cost of equity capital could generate a range for the correct stock price that could easily vary by 100% or more. In other words, with respect to

---

79. A textbook review of these points can be found in [Richard A.] Brealey & [Stewart C.] Myers, [Principles of Corporate Finance (6th ed. 2000)] at 199–205.

80. Id.

81. The Cross–Section of Expected Stock Returns, 47 J. Fin. 427 (1992).

82. Id. at 449–52.

83. The three-factor CAPM is still very much in the tradition of the original CAPM in that the single tradeoff is between risk and return. The other mean-variance theory is the Arbitrage Pricing Theory, first developed by Stephen A. Ross, and examined in his article, The Arbitrage Theory of Capital Asset Pricing, 13 J. Econ. Theory 341 (1976).

84. [Eugene F.] Fama & [Kenneth R.] French, [Industry Costs of Equity, 43 J. Fin. Econ. 153] at 178 [(1997)].

85. Id. The implication of the Fama and French article is that the mispricing can be quite large.

CAPM, reliable valuation estimates are simply not available given the current state of the theory. If corporate insiders believe that the market is incorrectly pricing their stock, they might actually be right.

While the testing of CAPM is primarily in a cross section, there are other anomalies that occur in the time-series context. Perhaps the most significant of these is the time-series change in either dividend/price ratios, or expected returns from holding stocks. In CAPM, the risk premium on stocks, and hence the market capitalization rate, should not vary over the business cycle. But, tests show that the underlying risk premium does appear to be time variant rather than stable as predicted by the theory.[86] If the risk premium on stocks varies cyclically, this will cause market capitalization rates for individual companies to increase during recessions and decrease during expansions.[87] An alternative explanation, also consistent with the data, and also unanticipated by the theory, is that the source of the anomaly is in changes in the expected growth rate of free cash flows rather than in the discount rate.[88] In other words, investors systematically overestimate future growth rates during expansionary periods and then underestimate future growth rates during contractionary periods. Here again, there is no consensus in the literature so that the results can be explained either as another anomaly, another source of imprecision in the original theory, or another variant of investor behavior theory.[89]

This time-series anomaly has importance for perhaps illuminating some of the historical dynamics in Delaware corporate law. The boom period of hostile tender offers which began in the late 1970s and continued at least until Paramount Communications, Inc. v. Time, Inc.,[90] provided management with more discretion to counter them.[91] Of course, hostile tender offers continue to this day, but their characteristics have changed considerably since that time. The 1970s and 1980s were years of abnormally low dividend/price or price/earnings multiples.[92] This is consistent with

---

86. This point is developed in John Y. Campbell & John H. Cochrane, By Force of Habit: A Consumption–Based Explanation of Aggregate Stock Market Behavior, 107 J. Pol. Econ. 205 (1999).

87. Id. at 235–37.

88. This can be seen from the constant

$$\underline{\text{grow}}\text{th formula} \qquad P_0 = \frac{DIV_1}{r\text{-}q}$$

where P_0 is the current stock price, $DIV<1>$ is the dividend expected at the end of the first year, r is the discount rate referred to above, and q is the constant growth rate in dividends. A percentage point increase in q thus has the same effect as a percentage point decrease in R. Brealey & Myers, supra note 36, at 67.

89. For a discussion of this literature, see Campbell et al., supra note [72], at 181–279.

90. 571 A.2d 1140 (Del. 1989).

91. Paramount provides a key example of this expansion in management discretion as it essentially refuted the Interco doctrine. The Interco doctrine is discussed supra text accompanying notes 20–22.

92. Hostile Takeovers and Junk Bond Financing: A Panel Discussion, in Knights, Raiders, and Targets: The Impact of the Hostile Takeover 13, 13 (John C. Coffee, Jr. et al. eds., 1988) (comments of Warren E. Buffett).

abnormally high-risk premiums and thus abnormally low stock prices, if abnormality is defined in terms of some average of historical dividend/price ratios. Hence, it is entirely consistent with Warren Buffett's comment at a 1985 symposium that, in his view, most public companies traded at a price below what the companies would be worth in a negotiated deal.[93]

It would be nice to be able to quantify the nature of the anomalies both as to the effect on stock prices and to the persistence of the mispricing. Unfortunately, this is not possible because of the large number of disparate anomalies and the range of possible outcomes. Even the two examples discussed above suggest that market anomalies might be quite large and persistent in their impact on the price of stocks, and thus on the market's valuation of the corporation. Of course, financial markets may in fact be more efficient than empirical tests validate. The tests may be flawed and the theory may be correct. At this point, however, such hope rests entirely on prior faith in market efficiency.

It is worth asking whether the evidence undercuts the existence of a correct fundamental value for the corporation. For example, do the behaviorists undercut CAPM/ECMH as a theory of valuation? Do they offer an alternative theory of valuation? The answer to both questions is "no." Even in the behaviorist literature, CAPM/ECMH is the theory against which anomalies are tested. The behaviorist claim is that markets are inefficient, but this means that stock prices are not those predicted by CAPM/ECMH.

At this point, the behaviorists do not offer an alternative theory. While behaviorists argue that investor sentiment and behavior drive stock prices,[94] they do not, and probably cannot, offer a systematic explanation for security prices based on investor sentiment and behavior. Many of the inefficiencies that arise eventually disappear, either because those who act inefficiently learn that their practices are costly, or arbitrageurs uncover the inefficiency and trade it away. In either case, valuation effects are transitory.

Consequently, when I speak of a "correct" capitalization rate or value of the corporation, the reference is to a value calculation consistent with CAPM/ECMH. I am assuming that markets, although not entirely efficient, are relatively efficient as defined by CAPM/ECMH. But I am also assuming that there can be differences in estimates of the future cash flows and appropriate market capitalization rate depending on the precise model of CAPM that is adopted and on knowledge of the appropriate risk factors. In this sense, there is no way of knowing with certainty the appropriate valuation at any point in time. In this setting, the next question is whether managers (or perhaps informed bidders) have better information than the market, where "better information" means a more reliable estimate of the

93. Id.

94. An excellent review on behavioral theories of finance is provided in Shleifer, supra note 76, at 112–74.

future returns on the company's stock (or, alternatively, a more precise estimate of the market capitalization rate).

NOTE

Henry Manne, one of the "fathers" of law and economics, commented on this debate in the June 13, 2006 issue of the Wall Street Journal (page A16). He noted that to a large extent both sides lacked a theory about how markets operated. He recounted F. A. Hayek's explanation in THE USE OF KNOWLEDGE IN SOCIETY (1945), where Hayek was arguing to counter socialist doctrine. Hayek argued that a centrally planned economy could never make economically efficient decisions because no central planner, or group of them could accumulate all the diffuse bits and pieces of information needed for a fully informed choice. Diffuses markets allow all participants to bring their particularized information to the price formation process. In 2004 financial journalist James Suroweicki wrote THE WISDOM OF CROWDS, that begins with a story of a contest at a county fair to guess the weight of an ox after slaughter and dressing. There were about 800 guesses by knowledge-able people as well as those with no experience. The average of all the guesses was 1,197 pounds, while the actual dressed weight was 1,198 pounds. Manne, following these writers, argues that stock market prices are weighted averages that reflect the same wisdom, made more accurate by the fact that only those with confidence in their information and judgments will make relatively large bets on a price. In this model, the "only requirements for these markets to work well are that the various traders be diverse and that their judgments be independent of each other."

NOTE

In Part 3 we examined the cost of equity capital by using a company's beta in CAPM. Now we have seen that not all experts place total confidence in market efficiency and CAPM. Given this debate among the experts, what is a manager (or a lawyer) to do? In many cases managers don't have to do these calculations when they are seeking new financing. They can simply refer to the market price of their stock, and conclude that new shares can be issued at that price (recall that the quantity of new shares to be issued shouldn't affect the price, because all shares are fungible in a diversified portfolio). They may have to price a new offering slightly below the market price, to account for the signal sent to the market, which is frequently that management has determined this is the best time to sell new shares, because the news about the company in the future may be less rosy than today's picture. The use of valuation models is more important in an initial public offering, where there is no market price for these shares to refer to. Even beta can't be determined directly, although the betas of similar firms in the same business can be observed.

In the late 1990s underwriters continued a long-standing tradition of underestimating the prices at which a initial public offering could be sold. This has several effects. First, the underwriter's risk of being unable to sell the entire offering is reduced, because all investors want a bargain. Second, because underwriters know the number of orders for the stock before committing to an offering price, they can price the offering so that not all demand for the stock at that price is satisfied, generally leading to a rise in the market price after completion of the offering. While this is frequently sold to issuers as a good thing, because it leads to happy investors, the other way of regarding it is that issuers were leaving money on the table, and unnecessarily diluting the investments of existing shareholders. Third, underpricing allowed underwriters to do favors for preferred customers by allocating part of a "hot issue" to these customers, who were generally individuals who could direct other business to the underwriter. This practice led to pressures on analysts employed by the underwriters to "hype" these securities, which in turn led to investment banking scandals at the end of the twentieth century. As the market for new issues began a tentative revival in 2001, some issuers began looking for ways to avoid these problems. Google was the most prominent, but not the only issuer, to attempt to use a Dutch Auction to obtain the best possible price for its shares under conditions of uncertainty.

In a Dutch auction, the offering price for shares is determined by the investors, who submit the highest price they're willing to pay and the number of shares they want at that price. The people who bid the highest (and, if they bid the same price, the earliest) get the first opportunity to buy the shares, which are then allocated in order from highest to lowest bid, until they're all gone. No matter what you bid, though, the price you pay is the lowest price that any investor who got shares bid. While this is the description of a dutch auction in the finance field, it is not an accurate description of the original dutch auction, which was used in some cases to market flowers and produce. The auctioneer would start the auction at a ridiculously high price, and gradually lower the price until bidders appeared. When enough bidders appeared to sell the entire lot of goods, all successful bidders would pay the same price. This type of auction is only practical when all bidders are in the same auction room (or perhaps electronically connected). When dispersed securities brokerage firms are soliciting individual customers by telephone, this type of Dutch Auction wouldn't work.

Google filed a registration statement for an initial public offering for its common stock in the Spring of 2004. In its first amendment to its registration statement, filed May 21, 2004, Google described the process by which interested investors would submit bids (which is a modified form of Dutch auction), and described the closing process as follows:

> "We expect that the bidding process will reveal a clearing price for the shares of Class A common stock offered in our auction. The clearing price is the highest price at which all of the shares offered (including shares subject to the underwriters' over-allotment option) may be sold to potential investors, based on bids in the master order book that have not been withdrawn or rejected at the time we and our underwriters close the bidding for our auction.

"The initial public offering price will be determined by the underwriters and us after the auction closes. We intend to use the auction clearing price as the principal factor to determine the initial public offering price and, therefore, to set an initial public offering price that is near or equal to the clearing price. However, we and our underwriters have the ability to set an initial public offering price that is below the clearing price. The other factors we may consider in determining our initial public offering price include:

"● Our goal of setting an initial public offering price that results in the trading price for our Class A common stock not moving significantly up or down relative to the market in the days following our offering.

"● The prices bid by professional investors.

"● Our assets, current or expected financial performance or book value.

"● Other established criteria of value."

Google's prospectus also warned investors about the risks of its form of offering:

"Risks Related to the Auction Process for Our Offering

"Our stock price could decline rapidly and significantly.

"Our initial public offering price will be determined primarily by an auction process conducted on our behalf by our underwriters. We believe this auction process will provide information with respect to the market demand for our Class A common stock at the time of our initial public offering. However, we understand that this information may have no relation to market demand for our Class A common stock once trading begins. We intend to use the auction clearing price as the principal factor to determine the initial public offering price and therefore to set an initial public offering price that is near or equal to the clearing price. If we satisfy the demand for our shares at or near the clearing price for the auction, market demand for our shares when trading begins in the public market may be significantly limited compared to demand experienced in an initial public offering priced in a more traditional manner. This or other factors could cause the price of our shares to decline following our initial public offering.

"The auction process for our public offering may result in a phenomenon known as the 'winner's curse,' and, as a result, investors may experience significant losses.

"The auction process for our initial public offering may result in a phenomenon known as the 'winner's curse.' At the conclusion of the auction, bidders that receive allocations of shares in this offering (successful bidders) may infer that there is little incremental demand for our shares above or equal to the initial public offering price. As a result, successful bidders may conclude that they paid too much for our shares and could seek to immediately sell their shares to limit their losses should our stock price decline. In this situation, other investors that did not submit successful bids may wait for this selling to be completed, resulting in reduced demand for our Class A common stock in the public market and a significant decline in our stock price. Therefore, we caution investors that submitting successful bids and receiving allocations may be followed by a significant decline in the value of their investment in our Class A common stock shortly after our offering.

"To the extent our auction process results in a lower level of participation by professional long-term investors and a higher level of participation by retail investors than is normal for initial public offerings, our stock price may decrease from the initial public offering price and be more volatile.

"Successful bidders hoping to capture profits shortly after our Class A common stock begins trading may be disappointed.

"As part of our auction process, we are attempting to assess the market demand for our Class A common stock and to set the size of the offering and the initial public offering price to meet that demand. During the bidding process, we and our managing underwriters will monitor the master order book to evaluate the demand that exists for our initial public offering. Based on this information, we and our managing underwriters may revise the price range for our initial public offering as described on the cover of this prospectus. In addition, we and the selling stockholders may decide to change the number of shares of Class A common stock offered through this prospectus. It is very likely that the number of shares offered by the selling stockholders will increase if the price range increases. In an auction process, this could result in a lower clearing price and increase the likelihood your bid may be successful if you do not reduce your bid price. This may also result in downward pressure on the offering price and the trading price of our stock in the public market once trading begins. Therefore, buyers hoping to capture profits shortly after our Class A common stock begins trading may be disappointed."

In the first days of 2010 Google's stock traded above $600, after the initial public offering at $100. Its price never fell below the public offering price.

C.   ECMH IN THE COURTS

West v. Prudential Securities, Incorporated

282 F.3d 935 (7th Cir.2002).

■ EASTERBROOK, CIRCUIT JUDGE.

According to the complaint in this securities-fraud action, James Hofman, a stockbroker working for Prudential Securities, told 11 of his customers that Jefferson Savings Bancorp was "certain" to be acquired, at a big premium, in the near future. Hofman continued making this statement for seven months (repeating it to some clients); it was a lie, for no acquisition was impending. And if the statement had been the truth, then Hofman was inviting unlawful trading on the basis of material non-public information. He is a securities offender coming or going, as are any customers who traded on what they thought to be confidential information—if Hofman said what the plaintiffs allege, a subject still to be determined. What we must decide is whether the action may proceed, not on behalf of those who received Hofman's "news" in person but on behalf of everyone who bought Jefferson stock during the months when Hofman was misbehaving. The district judge certified such a class, invoking the fraud-on-the-market doctrine of Basic, Inc. v. Levinson, 485 U.S. 224, 241–49, 99 L. Ed. 2d 194, 108 S. Ct. 978 (1988). Prudential asks us to entertain an interlocutory appeal under Fed. R. Civ. P. 23(f). For two reasons, this is an appropriate case for such an appeal, which we now accept.

* * *

Because the parties' papers have developed their positions fully, and the district court has set a trial date less than two months away, we think it best to resolve the appeal promptly, and thus we turn to the merits.

Causation is the shortcoming in this class certification. Basic describes a mechanism by which public information affects stock prices, and thus may affect traders who did not know about that information. Professional investors monitor news about many firms; good news implies higher dividends and other benefits, which induces these investors to value the stock more highly, and they continue buying until the gains are exhausted. With many professional investors alert to news, markets are efficient in the sense that they rapidly adjust to all public information; if some of this information is false, the price will reach an incorrect level, staying there until the truth emerges. This approach has the support of financial economics as well as the imprimatur of the Justices: few propositions in economics are better established than the quick adjustment of securities prices to public information. See Richard A. Brealey, Stewart C. Myers & Alan J. Marcus, Fundamentals of Corporate Finance 322–39 (2d ed. 1998).

No similar mechanism explains how prices would respond to non-public information, such as statements made by Hofman to a handful of his clients. These do not come to the attention of professional investors or money managers, so the price-adjustment mechanism just described does not operate. Sometimes full-time market watchers can infer important news from the identity of a trader (when the corporation's CEO goes on a buying spree, this implies good news) or from the sheer volume of trades (an unprecedented buying volume may suggest that a bidder is accumulating stock in anticipation of a tender offer), but neither the identity of Hofman's customers nor the volume of their trades would have conveyed information to the market in this fashion. No one these days accepts the strongest version of the efficient capital market hypothesis, under which non-public information automatically affects prices. That version is empirically false: the public announcement of news (good and bad) has big effects on stock prices, which could not happen if prices already incorporated the effect of non-public information. Thus it is hard to see how Hofman's non-public statements could have caused changes in the price of Jefferson Savings stock. Basic founded the fraud-on-the-market doctrine on a causal mechanism with both theoretical and empirical power; for non-public information there is nothing comparable.

The district court did not identify any causal link between non-public information and securities prices, let alone show that the link is as strong as the one deemed sufficient (by a bare majority) in Basic (only four of the six Justices who participated in that case endorsed the fraud-on-the-market doctrine). Instead the judge observed that each side has the support of a reputable financial economist (Michael J. Barclay for the plaintiffs, Charles C. Cox for the defendant) and thought the clash enough by itself to support class certification and a trial on the merits. That amounts to a delegation of judicial power to the plaintiffs, who can obtain class certification just by hiring a competent expert. A district judge may not duck hard questions by observing that each side has some support, or that considerations relevant to class certification also may affect the decision on the merits. Tough questions must be faced and squarely decided, if necessary by holding evidentiary hearings and choosing between competing perspectives.

Because the record here does not demonstrate that non-public information affected the price of Jefferson Savings' stock, a remand is unnecessary. What the plaintiffs have going for them is that Jefferson's stock did rise in price (by about $5, or 20% of its trading price) during the months when Hofman was touting an impending acquisition, plus a model of demand-pull price increases offered by their expert. Barclay started with a model devised by another economist, in which trades themselves convey information to the market and thus affect price. See Joel Hasbrouck, Measuring the Information Content of Stock Trades, 46 J. Fin. 179 (1991). Hasbrouck's model assumes that some trades are by informed traders and some by uninformed traders, and that the market may be able to draw inferences about which is which. The model has not been verified empirically. Barclay approached the issue differently, assuming that all trades affect prices by raising demand even if no trader is well informed—as if there were an economic market in "Jefferson Savings stock" as there is in dill pickles or fluffy towels. Hofman's tips raised the demand for Jefferson Savings stock and curtailed the supply (for the tippees were less likely to sell their own shares); that combination of effects raised the stock's price. Yet investors do not want Jefferson Savings stock (as if they sought to paper their walls with beautiful certificates); they want monetary returns (at given risk levels), returns that are available from many financial instruments. One fundamental attribute of efficient markets is that information, not demand in the abstract, determines stock prices. See Myron S. Scholes, The Market for Securities: Substitution Versus Price Pressure and the Effects of Information on Share Prices, 45 J. Bus. 179 (1972); Richard A. Brealey, An Introduction to Risk and Return from Common Stocks 15–18, 25–46 (2d ed. 1983). There are so many substitutes for any one firm's stock that the effective demand curve is horizontal. It may shift up or down with new information but is not sloped like the demand curve for physical products.

That is why institutional purchases (which can be large in relation to normal trading volume) do not elevate prices, while relatively small trades by insiders can have substantial effects; the latter trades convey information, and the former do not. Barclay, who took the view that the market for Jefferson Savings securities is efficient, did not explain why he departed from the normal understanding that information rather than raw demand determines securities prices.

Data may upset theory, and if Barclay had demonstrated that demand by itself elevates securities prices, then the courts would be required to attend closely. What Barclay did is inquire whether the price of Jefferson Savings stock rose during the period of additional demand by Hofman's customers. He gave an affirmative answer and stopped. Yet it is not possible to prove a relation between demand and price without considering other potential reasons. Was there perhaps some truthful Jefferson-specific information released to the market at the time? Did Jefferson perhaps move with the market? It rose relative to a basket of all financial institutions, but (according to Cox's report) not relative to a portfolio of Midwestern financial intermediaries. Several Missouri banks and thrifts similar to Jefferson Savings were acquired during the months in question, and these transactions conveyed some information about the probability of a deal involving Jefferson Savings. If the price of Jefferson Savings was doing just what one would have expected in the presence of this changing probability of acquisition, and the absence of any Hofman-induced trades, then the causal link between Hofman's statements and price has not been made out. By failing to test for and exclude other potential sources of price movement, Barclay undercut the power of the inference that he advanced.

Indeed, Barclay's report calls into question his belief that the market for Jefferson Savings stock is efficient, the foundation of the fraud-on-the-market doctrine. In an efficient market, how could one ignorant outsider's lie cause a long-term rise in price? Professional investors would notice the inexplicable rise and either investigate for themselves (discovering the truth) or sell short immediately, driving the price back down. In an efficient market, a lie told by someone with nothing to back up the statement (no professional would have thought Hofman a person "in the know") will self-destruct long before eight months have passed. Hofman asserted that an acquisition was imminent. That statement might gull people for a month, but after two or three months have passed the lack of a merger or tender offer puts the lie to the assertion; professional investors then draw more astute inferences and the price effect disappears. That this did not occur implies either that Jefferson Savings was not closely followed by professional investors (and that the market therefore does not satisfy Basic's efficiency requirement) or that something other than Hofman's statements explains these price changes.

The record thus does not support extension of the fraud-on-the-market doctrine to the non-public statements Hofman is alleged to have made about Jefferson Savings Bancorp. The order certifying a class is

reversed.

QUESTION

1. Judge Easterbrook seems to presume that the stock of Jefferson Savings Bancorp is efficiently priced, and suggests that the burden is on the plaintiff to show otherwise. Does behavioral economics suggest a different presumption?

How should one test whether the market for a particular stock is efficient? Consider the following:

Measuring Securities Market Efficiency in the Regulatory Setting

by Randall S. Thomas and James F. Cotter.
63, No. 3 L. & Contemp. Probl. 105 (2000).

C. Analyst Coverage as a Method of Measuring the Efficiency of Securities Markets

Analyst coverage is the most widely-accepted method of measuring when securities markets are efficient at processing information. Academic commentators have agreed that analyst coverage is an important mechanism for disseminating information to the market.[37] For example, Professor Coffee has claimed that analyst coverage is one of the key means for information to get out to the investing public.[38] Coffee states that "the analyst seems likely to become the critical mechanism of market efficiency because on-line computerization of the SEC-filed data makes access to such information both immediate and relatively costless to the analyst."[39]

---

37. See, e.g., Alan K. Austin & Clay B. Simpson, Interacting With Analysts, in The Art of Counseling Directors, Officers & Insiders 1998, at 91 (PLI Corp. Law & Practice Course Handbook Series No. 1083, 1998) (stating that "analyst coverage makes the market for the company's stock more efficient, by getting new information out to the public as it is released by the public"); Brad M. Barber et al., The Fraud-on-the-Market Theory and the Indicators of Common Stock Efficiency, 19 Iowa J. Corp. L. 285 (1994).

38. See John C. Coffee, Jr., Market Failure and the Economic Case for a Mandatory Disclosure System, 70 Va. L. Rev. 717, 723–24 (1984) (stating that "most accounts explaining the stock market's efficiency assign a substantial responsibility to the competition among analysts for securities information").

39. Id. at 723. According to Coffee, though, there are factors that constrain the analyst's ability to perform his function as effectively as possible. For example, because many people use securities research as the information gets passed along, it has a "public goods-like character." Id. at 726. This character, in turn, means that the analyst will not get the full economic benefit of his work and will, therefore, engage in less search and verification than the investing public desires. See id. Another problem that the analyst faces is the fact that he cannot contract on a bilateral basis and is, therefore, under-compensated, a fact that also operates as a disincentive. See id. at 727. Coffee argues that mandatory disclosure will alleviate these problems and allow analysts to perform their market function. See id. at 728. He states that mandated disclosure "reduces the market professional's marginal cost of acquiring and verifying information" and "increases the aggregate amount of securities research and verification provided." Id. at 729. As analysts begin to see more returns on their

Several empirical studies examine the equity analyst's role as an information producer and conduit for company information. For instance, Sok Te Kim, Je CAI Lin, and Myron Slovin examine the market response to analysts who initiate coverage on a company with a buy recommendation.[40] They find that despite slight differences between NYSE/AMEX and NAS-DAQ announcements, the private information disseminated by analysts who initiate coverage with a buy recommendation is reflected in stock prices in less than fifteen minutes.[41] Similarly, Carl Chen, James Wuh Lin, and David Sauer examine the "informational effect of earnings announcements on stock price changes," and how the number of analysts affect the extent of an earnings surprise and the lag for the information to be reflected in stock prices.[42] They show that the number of analysts significantly decreases the extent to which the market is "surprised" by the company's announced earnings (percent difference between the analysts' consensus estimate and the actual reported earnings).[43] Moreover, they show that the market adjusts more quickly to information releases as the number of analysts increases.[44] These studies do not, however, resolve the critical question of what level of analyst coverage is necessary to ensure that securities markets are efficient. As commentators on the earlier adoption of integrated disclosure noted, even if one accepts the claim that market efficiency justifies the use of simplified disclosure for the sale of securities of companies whose stock is traded in efficient markets, a question remains about where to draw the line for making this determination.[45]

Background of the Time Warner Case

In 1989 Time, Inc. and Warner Communications had negotiated a stock merger when Paramount made a $175 bid for Time, later raised to $200. Time's stock traded at $126 after the Warner merger was announced, but rose to $170 after Paramount announced its first bid, and ultimately reached $182.75. Time's board had previously considered Paramount as a merger partner and concluded that Warner was a better fit, and determined to complete the combination with Warner. Because a tender offer could be completed more rapidly (20 business days) than a merger, Time revised its deal with Warner into a cash tender offer for 51% of Warner's

work, there will be an influx of competitors into the field and the industry will therefore become more competitive. See id.

40. See Sok Te Kim et al., Market Structure, Informed Trading and Analysts' Recommendations, 32 J. Fin. & Quantitative Analysis 507, 513 (1997).

41. See id.

42. Carl R. Chen et al., Earnings Announcements, Quality and Quantity of Information, and Stock Price Changes, 20 J. Fin. Res. 483, 492 (1997).

43. See id.

44. See id.

45. See, e.g., Gordon & Kornhauser, supra note 18, at 813.

common, to be followed by a merger. Delaware courts sustained this as an informed good faith business judgment, and that Time's response was a measured one.

Time's financial advisers had indicated that Time–Warner stock might trade at $150–$175 post-merger, but that in the next several years might trade between $208–$402. Post-merger, the stock traded around $100–115, and Time–Warner carried $11 billion in debt, and was reporting losses after paying interest. At this time Time–Warner began to try to find "strategic partners" that would invest in some of its businesses, to raise funds to pay down the debt. This was not a great success, as you will see in the opinion.

In 1991 Time–Warner attempted to sell additional shares of stock to start to pay down the debt. Time believed that a large offering would drive down its stock price, and that its existing shareholders would thus suffer dilution of the value of their investments. You might ask why this should be. Does an additional "supply" of Time–Warner shares in the face of a downward sloping demand curve suggest this? Why would the demand curve for Time–Warner shares slope downward? Keep CAPM in mind when you think about this. Or was a large stock offering likely to send a signal to the market about Time–Warner's lack of success post-merger?

Time proposed a rights offering to its own shareholders—if there was going to be a bargain purchase, they would get the first opportunity to buy. It was intended to raise up to $3.5 billion, and to sell roughly 40% additional shares (34.5 million). The holder of each current share would get a right to buy 0.6 of a share. Each new whole share would be sold for as high as $105, if the offering were fully subscribed, and as low as $63 if it were not. This is a "Dutch Auction," in which the lowest price necessary to sell the entire offering becomes the price at which all securities offered are sold.* A shareholder wouldn't know in advance what the purchase price would be, or how many shares she would get. You would know that the purchase price would be lower than the previous market price.

Time–Warner shareholders reacted negatively to what they saw as a dilutive and therefore coercive offer. These rights weren't transferable, so if a shareholder didn't exercise, he or she suffered uncompensated dilution. The SEC even threatened to sue. Time–Warner withdrew this offer from registration with the SEC and proposed a new rights offering, at $80 per share. Obviously this was still dilutive, and still coercive, and created shareholder resentment. But shareholders could sell these rights, and if you

---

* In a Dutch auction, as pointed out in Part 4.B of Chapter Three, the offering price for shares is determined by the investors, who submit the highest price they're willing to pay and the number of shares they want at that price. The people who bid the highest (and, if they bid the same price, the earliest) get first dibs on the shares, which are then allocated in order from highest to lowest bid, until they're all gone. No matter what you bid, though, the price you pay is the lowest price that any investor who got shares bid. While this is the description of a dutch auction in the finance field, it is not an accurate description of the original dutch auction, which was used in some cases to market flowers and produce. The auctioneer would start the auction at a ridiculously high price, and gradually lower the price until bidders appeared. When enough bidders appeared to sell the entire lot of goods, all successful bidders would pay the same price.

chose not to exercise, you could get some compensation for the expected dilution by selling the rights. (In late July, 1991, the rights traded at $4.50 per Time–Warner share.)

In re Time Warner Securities Litigation

9 F.3d 259 (2d Cir.1993), certiorari denied, 511 U.S. 1017 (1994).

■ JON O. NEWMAN, CHIEF JUDGE:

* * *

Plaintiffs' complaint alleged that defendant Time Warner, Inc. and four of its officers had misled the investing public by statements and omissions made in the course of Time Warner's efforts to reduce its debt. The District Court dismissed the complaint with prejudice for failure to adequately plead material misrepresentations or omissions attributable to the defendants and for failure to adequately plead scienter. We hold that the complaint's allegations of scienter and certain of its allegations concerning omissions are adequate to survive a motion to dismiss, and we accordingly reverse the order of dismissal and remand.

Background

On June 7, 1989, Time, Inc. received a surprise tender offer for its stock from Paramount Communications. Paramount's initial offer was $175 per share, in cash, and was eventually increased to $200 per share. See Paramount Communications, Inc. v. Time Inc., 571 A.2d 1140, 1147–49 (Del. 1989). Time's directors declined to submit this offer to the shareholders and continued discussions that had begun somewhat earlier concerning a merger with Warner Communications, Inc. Eventually, Time and Warner agreed that Time would acquire all of Warner's outstanding stock for $70 per share, even though this acquisition would cause Time to incur debt of over $10 billion. Time shareholders and Paramount were unsuccessful in their effort to enjoin the Warner acquisition, which was completed in July 1989.

Thus, in 1989, Time Warner Inc., the entity resulting from the merger, found itself saddled with over $10 billion in debt, an outcome that drew criticism from many shareholders. The company embarked on a highly publicized campaign to find international "strategic partners" who would infuse billions of dollars of capital into the company and who would help the company realize its dream of becoming a dominant worldwide entertainment conglomerate. Ultimately, Time Warner formed only two strategic partnerships, each on a much smaller scale than had been hoped for. Faced with a multi-billion dollar balloon payment on the debt, the company was forced to seek an alternative method of raising capital—a new stock offering that substantially diluted the rights of the existing shareholders. The company first proposed a variable price offering on June 6, 1991. This proposal was rejected by the SEC, but the SEC approved a second proposal announced on July 12, 1991. Announcement of the two offering proposals caused a substantial decline in the price of Time Warner stock. From June 5 to June 12, the share price fell from $117 to $94. By July 12, the price had fallen to $89.75.

The plaintiff class, which has not yet been certified, consists of persons who bought Time Warner stock between December 12, 1990, and June 7, 1991. Their complaint, containing causes of action under sections 10(b) and 20(a) of the Securities Exchange Act, and state law, alleges that a series of statements from Time Warner officials during the class period were materially misleading in that they misrepresented the status of the ongoing strategic partnership discussions and failed to disclose consideration of the stock offering alternative. The parties have classified the challenged statements in two categories: (1) press releases and public statements from the individual defendants, (2) statements to reporters and security analysts emanating from sources within the company but not attributed to any identified individual. The statements, which we discuss in more detail below, consist of generally positive messages concerning the progress of the search for strategic partners, and imply to varying degrees that significant partnerships will be consummated and announced in the near future. None of the statements acknowledged that negotiations with prospective partners were going less well than expected or that an alternative method of raising capital was under consideration.

* * *

The District Court's opinion considered the two categories of misstatements in turn. As to the first category—attributed public statements by the individual defendants or the corporation—the Court agreed that defendants attempted to drum up enthusiasm for strategic partnerships and did not disclose either their difficulties in pursuing that course or the possibility of a stock offering. But the Court found that the statements were accurate when made, and that later events did not give rise to a duty to correct or update the statements. The Court also concluded that plaintiffs had not adequately pled scienter under any theory. As to the second category of statements, the Court ruled that Rule 9(b) required plaintiffs to allege the identity of the speakers. The Court further concluded that the defendants could not be held responsible for any of the unattributed statements and that in any event the statements were not actionable for the same reasons that the attributed statements were not actionable. * * *

Discussion

Cases of this sort present an inevitable tension between two powerful interests. On the one hand, there is the interest in deterring fraud in the securities markets and remedying it when it occurs. That interest is served by recognizing that the victims of fraud often are unable to detail their allegations until they have had some opportunity to conduct discovery of those reasonably suspected of having perpetrated a fraud. Consistent with that interest, modern pleading rules usually permit a complaint to survive dismissal unless, in the familiar phrase, "it appears beyond doubt that the plaintiff can prove no set of facts in support of his claim which would entitle him to relief."

On the other hand, there is the interest in deterring the use of the litigation process as a device for extracting undeserved settlements as the price of avoiding the extensive discovery costs that frequently ensue once a complaint survives dismissal, even though no recovery would occur if the suit were litigated to completion. It has never been clear how these competing interests are to be accommodated, and the adjudication process is not well suited to the formulation of a universal resolution of the tensions between them. In the absence of a more refined statutory standard than the vague contours of section 10(b) or a more detailed attempt at rule-making than the SEC has managed in Rule 10b–5, despite 50 years of unavailed opportunity, courts must adjudicate the precise cases before them, striking the balance as best they can.

* * *

To state a cause of action under Rule 10b–5, a plaintiff must plead that "in connection with the purchase or sale of securities, the defendant, acting with scienter, made a false material representation or omitted to disclose material information and that plaintiff's reliance on defendant's action caused [plaintiff] injury." The shortcomings of the complaint identified by the District Court were the failure to identify a false material representation or material undisclosed information, and the failure to adequately plead scienter. We find it convenient to consider first the so-called unattributed statements before turning to those for which Time Warner acknowledges responsibility.

I. Existence of an actionable misrepresentation or omission

* * *

B. Attributed statements and corporate press releases

We next focus on those statements as to which there is no issue of attribution. While plaintiffs claim that these statements were misleading, in that they exaggerated the likelihood that strategic alliances would be made, plaintiffs primarily fault these statements for what they did not disclose. The nondisclosure is of two types: failure to disclose problems in the strategic alliance negotiations, and failure to disclose the active consideration of an alternative method of raising capital. We have listed excerpts of the relevant statements in the margin.[3]

---

3. 1. "This company is worth a hell of a lot more than $200.00 a share. It was then. It is now." (Wall Street Journal, Feb. 7, 1990) (quoting defendant Levin).

2. "There may be four big industrial partners with one in Europe and two in Japan, or two in Europe and two in Japan and [an] American company." (Wall Street Journal, Nov. 1990) (exact date unspecified) (quoting defendant Ross).

3. The company would seek foreign investors to take a minority interest in subsidiaries as a means of alleviating debt without selling off assets. (Time Warner announcement, Nov. 19, 1990) (no direct quotation provided).

1. *Affirmative misrepresentations.* We agree with the District Court that none of the statements constitutes an affirmative misrepresentation. Most of the statements reflect merely that talks are ongoing, and that Time Warner hopes that the talks will be successful. There is no suggestion that the factual assertions contained in any of these statements were false when the statements were made. As to the expressions of opinion and the projections contained in the statements, while not beyond the reach of the securities laws, the complaint contains no allegations to support the inference that the defendants either did not have these favorable opinions on future prospects when they made the statements or that the favorable opinions were without a basis in fact.

2. *Nondisclosure of problems in the strategic alliance negotiations.* The allegations of nondisclosure are more serious. Plaintiffs' first theory of nondisclosure is that the defendants' statements hyping strategic alliances gave rise to a duty to disclose problems in the alliance negotiations as those problems developed. We agree that a duty to update opinions and projections may arise if the original opinions or projections have become misleading as the result of intervening events. But, in this case, the attributed public statements lack the sort of definite positive projections that might require later correction. The statements suggest only the hope of any company, embarking on talks with multiple partners, that the talks would go well. No identified defendant stated that he thought deals would be struck by a certain date, or even that it was likely that deals would be struck at all. These statements did not become materially misleading when the talks did not proceed well.[4]

---

4. The company "continues to have serious talks that could lead to the sale of five or six separate minority stakes in its entertainment subsidiaries next year." (Wall Street Journal, Nov. 30, 1990) (quoting defendant Ross).

5. The company "received and continues to receive many expressions of interest in forming joint ventures of all of its businesses from all over the world." (Time Warner press release, Dec. 3, 1990).

6. "Management of Time Warner also has had discussions with potential partners on the mutual advantages of strategic alliances formed at the subsidiary level." (1990 SEC 10–K Statement).

7. Ross and Nicholas "are excited by the possibilities for growth that will increase shareholder value, especially through strategic partnerships." (1990 Annual Report).

8. The company "was in talks with possible buyers of stakes in some of its entertainment businesses." (Ross, March 7, 1991).

9. Time Warner "was continuing talks with potential foreign partners.... We're not selling or buying.... We're partnering." (Nicholas, Mar. 15, 1991).

10. Time Warner is "currently engaged in nearly two dozen discussions in Europe and Asia that could link most of the world's entertainment and media companies in a complex web of relationships.... We are making alliances at the subsidiary level with the partners keeping their national identities and bringing their respective strengths to bear." (Business Week, May 13, 1991) (quoting defendant Ross).

11. "We are pursuing a number of innovative business ventures all over the world." (Time Warner public announcement, May 14, 1991).

4. Although the statements are generally open-ended, there is one sense in which they have a solid core. The statements represent as fact that serious talks with multiple parties

3. *Nondisclosure of alternative methods of raising capital.* Still more serious is the allegation of a failure to disclose the simultaneous consideration of the rights offering as an alternative method of raising capital. As an initial matter, of course, a reasonable investor would probably have wanted to know of consideration of the rights offering. Though both the rights offering and strategic alliances would have brought capital into the corporation, the two acts would have directly opposite effects on the price of Time Warner stock. A successful strategic alliance, simultaneously opening new markets and reducing debt, would have improved the corporation's expected profit stream, and should have served to drive up the share price. An offering of new shares, in contrast, would dilute the ownership rights of existing shareholders, likely decrease dividends, and drive down the price of the stock.

* * *

We have previously considered whether disclosure of one business plan required disclosure of considered alternatives in Kronfeld v. Trans World Airlines, Inc., 832 F.2d 726 (2d Cir. 1987), cert. denied, 485 U.S. 1007, 99 L. Ed. 2d 700, 108 S. Ct. 1470 (1988). In Kronfeld, the defendant, TWA's parent corporation, failed to disclose in the prospectus for a new issue of TWA stock that it was contemplating termination of its relationship with TWA. Because the prospectus discussed "in some detail the relationship between TWA" and the parent, we held that a fact question was presented as to whether it was materially misleading not to disclose the possibility of termination. In effect, the alternative, if disclosed, would have suggested to investors that the various guarantees extended from the parent to TWA might be meaningless. In the pending case, the District Court understood the obligation to disclose alternate business plans to be limited to the context of mutually exclusive alternatives. It is true that Kronfeld involved such alternatives—the TWA parent could not both maintain and terminate its relations with TWA—and that this case does not. Time Warner potentially could have raised all its needed capital from either strategic alliances or a rights offering, or it could have raised some part of the necessary capital using each approach.

We believe, however, that a disclosure duty limited to mutually exclusive alternatives is too narrow. A duty to disclose arises whenever secret information renders prior public statements materially misleading, not merely when that information completely negates the public statements. Time Warner's public statements could have been understood by reasonable investors to mean that the company hoped to solve the entire debt problem through strategic alliances. Having publicly hyped strategic alliances, Time Warner may have come under a duty to disclose facts that would place the statements concerning strategic alliances in a materially different light.

---

were ongoing. If this factual assertion ceased to be true, defendants would have had an obligation to update their earlier statements. But the complaint does not allege that the talks ever stopped or ceased to be "serious," just that they eventually went poorly.

It is important to appreciate the limits of our disagreement with the District Court. We do not hold that whenever a corporation speaks, it must disclose every piece of information in its possession that could affect the price of its stock. Rather, we hold that when a corporation is pursuing a specific business goal and announces that goal as well as an intended approach for reaching it, it may come under an obligation to disclose other approaches to reaching the goal when those approaches are under active and serious consideration. Whether consideration of the alternate approach constitutes material information, and whether nondisclosure of the alternate approach renders the original disclosure misleading, remain questions for the trier of fact, and may be resolved by summary judgment when there is no disputed issue of material fact. We conclude here only that the allegations in this complaint of nondisclosure of the rights offering are sufficient to survive a motion to dismiss.

II. Scienter

As an alternative basis for its dismissal order, the District Court found that plaintiffs had failed to adequately plead scienter. Scienter is a necessary element of every 10b–5 action, and though it need not be plead with "great specificity," the facts alleged in the complaint must "give[] rise to a 'strong inference' of fraudulent intent." We have recognized two distinct ways in which a plaintiff may plead scienter without direct knowledge of the defendant's state of mind. The first approach is to allege facts establishing a motive to commit fraud and an opportunity to do so. The second approach is to allege facts constituting circumstantial evidence of either reckless or conscious behavior. The District Court concluded that the complaint fell short under either approach.

A. Motive and opportunity

The difficulty with plaintiffs' motive and opportunity approach to scienter lies in the pleading of motive; no one doubts that the defendants had the opportunity, if they wished, to manipulate the price of Time Warner stock. Plaintiff's allegations concerning motive have shifted somewhat throughout the proceedings. Initially, plaintiffs emphasized that the defendants had embarked on a campaign to convince the public that Time Warner stock was worth in excess of $200 per share, so as to soften public criticism and avoid personal embarrassment stemming from their blocking of the Paramount tender offer. Plaintiffs now emphasize that defendants were motivated to misrepresent the status of the strategic alliance negotiations to avoid jeopardizing talks with prospective partners, and to withhold disclosure of consideration of the rights offering to maintain a high stock price prior to announcement of the new rights offering in order to lessen the dilutive effect. The complaint alleged the maintenance of an artificially high stock price, but relied on an inference for the motive of lessening the dilutive effect of the ultimately disclosed rights offering. The District Court found these proffered motives facially irrational, since Time Warner had no unilateral ability to cause prospective partners to invest and since, without strategic alliances, a rights offering, which would necessarily depress the stock price, was inevitable. Defendants make similar arguments on appeal; they also claim that these motive theories are too speculative.

Whether plaintiffs' motive allegations, with respect to nondisclosure of the rights offering, are adequate to survive a motion to dismiss is a close question. On the one hand, it is surely true, as the District Court noted, that strategic alliances could not be compelled and that, once the rights offering was announced, the price of Time Warner stock would inevitably drop. On the other hand, it is not clear, at least at this threshold stage of the lawsuit, that the defendants had nothing to gain by playing up strategic alliances while simultaneously keeping secret until the last moment the alleged active consideration of a rights offering. The unresolved issue is whether the effects of the alleged artificial raising of the stock price by the combination of the glowing reports of potential strategic alliances and the nondisclosure of the active consideration of a rights offering could reasonably have been expected by the company not to have been completely dissipated by the announcement of the rights offering, thereby enabling the company to set the rights offering price somewhat higher than would have been possible without the misleading statements and to lessen the dilutive effect of the offering.

Defendants ridicule plaintiffs' motive argument as "nonsensical," by arguing that the misleading statements about possible alliances all preceded the one-month period starting May 1, 1991, in which they are alleged to have been actively considering the rights offering. Thus, defendants contend, plaintiffs are alleging a conspiracy in which all of the overt acts occurred before the May 1 date that marks the start of the conspiracy. This argument is strong on rhetoric but insufficient to preclude all possibility of developing proof that a motive in fact existed. The pre-May 1 statements were not, as we have held, actionable when made. However, they arguably became misleading after May 1 when the rights offering was allegedly under active consideration and not disclosed. The failure to render the prior statements not misleading by disclosing consideration of the rights offering occurred after May 1. The close question is not whether any actionable nondisclosure occurred after May 1; the complaint adequately alleges that it did. The close question is whether the defendants are adequately alleged to have had a motive to benefit from the nondisclosure, thereby satisfying the scienter requirement.

The defendants are on somewhat sounder ground in faulting the plaintiffs for not articulating with either clarity or consistency their motive theory. Nevertheless, we think that a motive theory emerges with sufficient reasonable possibilities to withstand a motion to dismiss. With all inferences drawn in favor of the plaintiffs, it is arguable that the defendants acted in the belief that they could somewhat reduce the degree of dilution by artificially enhancing the price of the stock. This could have happened if (a) the statements about strategic alliances, which became misleading upon nondisclosure of consideration of the rights offering, artificially increased the stock price, and (b) the effect of that increase was not fully dissipated by the announcement of the rights offering.[5] If some artificial enhancement remained, the defendants would have been able to raise the needed capital at a higher rights offering price, thereby issuing fewer shares and lessening the dilutive effect (or raising more capital by issuing the same number of shares).

We recognize that the Supreme Court has proceeded on the assumption that "market professionals generally consider most publicly announced material statements about companies, thereby affecting stock market prices." See Basic, Inc., 485 U.S. at 247, n.24. Though confidence in the efficient markets hypothesis is not universally shared, see Donald C. Langevoort, Theories, Assumptions, and Securities Regulation: Market Efficiency Revisited, 140 U. Pa. L. Rev. 851 (1992),[6] we do not intend to permit a scienter allegation to survive dismissal on the vague possibility that some irrational share purchasers might not comprehend disclosures made in the normal course by a company that has fully and timely discharged all its disclosure obligations. But the allegations here are that a company has not discharged its disclosure obligations and has permitted prior statements (concerning strategic alliances) to become misleading by a material nondisclosure (of the active consideration of a dilutive rights offering). In such circumstances, we consider the pleading sufficient to survive dismissal because, however efficiently markets may be thought to work when disclosures are proper, it is not beyond doubt that they may not fully correct for prior misleading information once a necessary disclosure has been made. Though, in many circumstances, a truthful correction might be expected promptly to alert the market to errors in prior statements, whether those erroneous prior statements were made willfully or innocently, it is possible, in some circumstances, that the embellishments of a deliberately false statement and the manner of its dissemination might leave its effects lingering in the market for some time, despite a correcting statement. In a case like the pending one, however, the issue is not whether the misleading aspect of the prior statement in fact lingered; it is only

---

5. Presumably, announcement of a rights offering will tend to reduce a stock price by the extent to which the offering, if fully subscribed, dilutes the position of the original shareholders. For example, if a company with 1,000 outstanding shares selling at $100 a share raises $100,000 of new capital by a rights offering that issues 2,000 shares at a price of $50 a share, the original shareholders will own one-third (1,000 shares of 3,000 outstanding) of a company that should be worth $200,000, and the share price after the rights offering should be $66.67 ($200,000/3,000). The question is whether an artificial enhancement of the pre-rights offering price to, say, $150 per share, thereby creating a post-rights offering company "worth" $250,000 can result in a post-rights offering stock price of somewhere between $83.33 ($250,000/3,000) and $66.67. If so, the company might decide to set the rights offering price somewhat above $50 in the expectation that it could raise the needed $100,000 by issuing somewhat less than 2,000 shares, thereby somewhat reducing the dilutive effect of the offering.

6. Two critics have expressed their doubts in these colorful words: "If the efficient markets hypothesis was a publicly traded security, its price would be enormously volatile.... The stock in the [conventional] hypothesis ... crashed along with the rest of the market on October 19, 1987. Its recovery has been less dramatic than the rest of the market." Andrei Shleifer & Lawrence H. Summers, The Noise Trader Approach to Finance, J. Econ. Persp. 19 (Spring 1990).

whether the plaintiffs can show that the defendants had a motive not to promptly correct the misleading aspect of the prior statement. Whether such a motive existed depends not on what any member of this panel believes, but on what the plaintiffs can prove.

Since the laws of economics have not yet achieved the status of the law of gravity, we cannot say, on a motion to dismiss, that the plaintiffs cannot prove that a motive existed. What cannot be determined from the pleadings is whether, in this instance, the defendants acted to maintain the stock price at an artificially enhanced value in the hope that it would not descend all the way to its "true" value upon announcement of the fact—consideration of the rights offering—that rendered the prior statements misleading. Whether some focused preliminary discovery will permit the matter to be resolved adversely to the plaintiffs on a motion for summary judgment remains to be determined.

* * *

Conclusion

We reverse the order of the District Court dismissing counts one and two of the complaint, and affirm the order dismissing count three of the complaint. The case is remanded for further proceedings consistent with this opinion.

■ WINTER, CIRCUIT JUDGE, dissenting:

I respectfully dissent. In my view, Time Warner's purported scheme to float a variable-price rights offering at an artificially inflated price is at odds with many long-standing assumptions of the securities laws and thus does not suffice to establish scienter for purposes of a Rule 12(b)(6) motion. Moreover, it is expressly contradicted by the complaints.

I

First, the area of agreement. I agree that the allegation that Time Warner's failure to disclose active consideration of the variable-price rights offering was material in that it rendered prior statements arguably misleading. * * *

Because I view the complaints in a somewhat different light than my colleagues, I will set out in some detail what I regard to be the pertinent allegations. Time Warner had taken on considerable debt and had a balloon payment coming up. This was not news to the market for its shares. Over the course of time, various officers of Time Warner made statements regarding strategic alliance conversations and the benefits of such alliances. These benefits sometimes involved the penetration of new markets or the development of new products, frequently involved the infusion of cash that would be available to pay off the debt, and sometimes involved both. Analysts responded favorably, noting that they anticipated the consummation of strategic alliances, sales of Time Warner assets, or other "restructurings," any of which would enable the company to meet its debt payments.

Given the somewhat loose use of the term "dilution" in this litigation and my view of the scienter issue set forth infra, two matters must be emphasized. First, when a debt-ridden company raises cash by a strategic alliance, a sale of an asset, or a restructuring, the parties providing the cash will demand interests in the company that dilute the existing common shares in the sense that it will reduce their share of equity. Indeed, it is inconceivable that any strategic alliance could have been consummated by Time Warner without sharing, and diluting, equity interests. Second, investors who do not care about control also do not care about dilution. They care about share value, and that value may (in this case would) increase as a result of a diluting infusion of cash brought about by a strategic alliance or even by an issue of additional common stock.

* * *

However, the offering here was not your standard equity offering. The variable-price rights offering—although not consummated, it is the offering that allegedly rendered prior statements misleading—was restricted to existing shareholders. This was news in light of the prior statements because it indicated that outside capital was not available. It thus indicated that the only source of capital available for the debt payments were the locked-in shareholders of Time Warner who might lose all if the company defaulted on the debt. Moreover, the variable-price rights offering was dilutive but in a very different sense from that indicated by my colleagues. If all shareholders exercised their rights, each would purchase one new share for $105. If only 60% exercised the rights, those shareholders would purchase 1–2/3 shares for $63. As the complaints allege, therefore, the offering was coercive because shareholders hoping to minimize their losses would feel compelled to come up with fresh money. Unlike an infusion of capital from outside that would dilute but also benefit shareholders, this new issue of equity would necessarily lessen the value of the common shares because existing shareholders had either to put up more money or to incur a disproportionate loss in value. In light of the prior statements, therefore, active consideration of the variable-price option should have been disclosed under Kronfeld, 832 F.2d at 737.

My disagreement with my colleagues concerns the complaints' allegations with regard to scienter, or in this case the motive for the alleged failure to make timely disclosure. There is certainly no self-evident motive. The variable-price rights offering was a drastic step, to be sure, and very bad news, but the timing of the announcement seems rather irrelevant. The complaints allege that appellees failed to make early disclosure because of the fear that potential partners would be scared off by the bad news. That is implausible, however. News that Time Warner could raise fresh cash from its shareholders would be welcome news to potential partners concerned about the burden of debt. That news thus might cause negotiations close to agreement to succeed. It appears, however, that no alliance conversations were ever that close to an agreement.

The scenario relied upon by my colleagues to establish motive is that Time Warner management failed to disclose consideration of the variable-price rights offering to inflate the price at which that offering could be sold so that the dilutive effect would be minimized. The legal and logical flaws in this scenario seem rather plentiful. As a threshold matter, the complaints, as discussed infra, at times contradict it. * * *

Most important, the scenario is wholly implausible in light of the nature of the variable-price rights offering. Time Warner management was not seeking to minimize the dilutive effect on existing shareholders. To the contrary, as the complaints vigorously allege and as discussed supra, the variable-price rights offering created a disproportionate dilutive effect on non-exercising shareholders as a means of coercing shareholders to exercise the rights. The notion that the existing shareholders would continue to rely upon long-gone statements regarding fresh capital in the face of the coercive rights offering is entirely far-fetched. The complaints allege in great detail that the rights offering "shocked the investment community," was viewed by analysts as an admission that Time Warner was unable to find fresh money from outside, and had "angered" shareholders. How the management of Time Warner might have expected any other reaction, much less continued faith in weeks-old statements that outside capital was available, defies common sense. The very existence of the variable-price rights offering was a tangible, high-profile, and unmistakable negation of the earlier statements. That indeed is the reason that a failure to make timely disclosure is a material omission.

Moreover, the management of Time Warner knew at all pertinent times that such an offering had to be preceded by the filing of a registration statement with the SEC followed by a statutory waiting period. That registration statement would have to reveal the failure of the strategic alliance talks and the fact that holders of Time Warner's common shares who would not or could not come up with more money would find their interests diluted. That information would become public when filed, and investors would have several days to assimilate it before the rights offering could be sold. When it was filed on June 6, the registration statement, in the words of one complaint, "shocked the investment community," while by its own terms the registration statement could not be effective before June 17.

This scenario posits a management that expects that the disclosure of the failure of the strategic alliance conversations and resort to a coercive rights offering would not be fully assimilated by shareholders during the waiting period. It also posits that a substantial number of shareholders would continue to give credence to statements that were weeks old and flatly contradicted by the registration statement.

My colleagues express skepticism about the usefulness of the efficient market hypothesis (while quoting a rather uncritical acceptance of it by the Supreme Court) in Basic, Inc. v. Levinson, 485 U.S. 224, 246–27(1988). However, the notion that markets impound available information relatively promptly in share prices, at least in widely traded companies, pervades securities law. Most pertinent is the statutory provision for a waiting period after the filing of a registration statement. One purpose of the waiting period is to allow ample time for the information contained in the state-ment to be absorbed by investors. Indeed, that is why acceleration of the validity of a registration statement depends in part on whether the infor-mation contained in it has been widely disseminated.

In Texas Gulf Sulphur, we indicated that an insider might trade on previously confidential information within a reasonable period of time after information was disseminated on the Dow Jones tape. Although no doubt unintended, my colleagues' belief that the market cannot fully absorb what was headline information in the financial press over a period of many days would seem quite inconsistent with Texas Gulf Sulphur. Moreover, the SEC's adoption of Form S–3 was based on the view that filings with the SEC by widely traded companies are quickly absorbed in the price of shares.

Finally, although there are weak forms of the efficient market hypothe-sis, a fairly strong form has been adopted by the Supreme Court. See Basic, Inc., 485 U.S. at 246 ("Recent empirical studies have tended to confirm Congress' premise that the market price of shares traded on well-developed markets reflects all publicly available information. . . ."). Indeed, one of the striking ironies of my colleagues' ruling is that the complaints in the present matter stress the efficiency of the market for Time Warner shares and never allege even the possibility that the strategic alliance statements had, or could have had, a lingering effect after June 6. To the contrary, one complaint alleges that the market "reacted promptly to disclosure" that the quest for strategic partners had failed. While my colleagues suggest that the efficient market hypothesis is flawed, each of the complaints alleges it as an operative fact so far as Time Warner stock is concerned. Each complaint thus states that Time Warner stock "traded on an active and efficient market," or uses similar language. Of course, these allegations are intended to establish appellants' reliance upon the material omission. The result of the present ruling is that appellants are allowed to establish reliance in their pleadings by stressing the efficiency of the market in Time Warner's shares while establishing scienter by positing a market that cannot absorb a current registration statement's negation of weeks-old information. This inconsistency seems rather stark in light of the facts that the statements concerning strategic alliance conversations promised no success while the announcement of the variable-price rights offering unam-biguously disclosed the failure of those conversations. Nevertheless, plain-tiffs avoid dismissal on the claim that investors would continue to harbor unwarranted optimism as a result of the earlier statements notwithstand-ing the company's later straightforward admission of failure.

It is not my position that one must simply assume the efficiency of markets, although the strength of such an assumption is greatest in the case of widely traded companies, like Time Warner, whose affairs are closely followed in the financial press. However, allegations of delays in the absorption of information, the existence of "bubbles," or other inefficien-cies should be made with some precision. In the present matter critical ambiguities—as well as the internal contradiction concerning the issue of reliance noted above—shroud my colleagues' views of the operation of capital markets. For example, the present ruling suggests, as noted, that the legally designated waiting period is too short for the market to absorb information in a registration statement. If so, how can we be confident that disclosure on May 1 would have led to any greater absorption?

The only description given of the supposed imperfection is a suggestion that markets may work efficiently "when disclosures are proper [but] it is not beyond doubt that they may not fully correct for prior misleading information once a necessary disclosure has been made." (emphasis in original) I doubt the validity of this proposition. It appears to posit that if A, Inc. truthfully projects high earnings and later states, again truthfully, that it now expects only to break even, the market can absorb the downgrading. It also seems to posit that if A, Inc. falsely projects high earnings but later states truthfully that it now expects only to break even, the market cannot fully absorb the downgrading. This does not seem plausible to me.

Nor can I find an explanation of why the inefficiency of the market is only on the up rather than on the down side. Why doesn't the dashing of hopes as to strategic alliances and the adoption of a coercive, variable-price rights offering lead to overcorrection instead of undercorrection? More pertinently, why would Time Warner management expect—actually, count on—undercorrection?

Neither Time Warner nor its shareholders, who must pay the costs of defending and settling this action, profited from any delay in announcing the variable-price rights offering. The argument regarding a motive for such delay posits a scenario that is inconsistent with assumptions underlying securities law, statements in the complaint, and any plausible understanding of the operation of capital markets. I would affirm the dismissal of the complaint.

QUESTIONS

1. Does the majority suggest that all statements made must be updated when new information would make them no longer completely true?

2. Note that the Court concludes that consideration of a possible stock offering rather than strategic alliances would be material to investors. "An offering of new shares, in contrast [to a strategic alliance], would dilute the ownership rights of existing shareholders, likely decrease dividends, and drive down the price of the stock." If you represented Time–Warner, what arguments could you make that this wasn't so?

3. Note the dilution example in footnote 10 of the majority's opinion, quoted below. Do you see any logical flaws in employing this example in Time–Warner?

"Presumably, announcement of a rights offering will tend to reduce a stock price by the extent to which the offering, if fully subscribed, dilutes the position of the original shareholders. For example, if a company, with 1,000 outstanding shares selling at $100 a share raises $100,000 of new capital by a rights offering that issues 2,000 shares at a price of $50 a share, the original shareholders will own one-third (1,000 shares of 3,000 outstanding) of a company that should be worth $200,000, and the share price after the rights offering should be $66.67 ($200,000/3,000).''

4. How does Judge Winter distinguish types of dilution compared to the majority's approach?

5. Is there anything in particular about the Time–Warner Rights Offering that might make the above example realistic?

6. Plaintiff's scienter theory argued in part that management concealed plans for the rights offering because it didn't want to scare off potential strategic partners. How does the court react to this argument?

7. Plaintiff's scienter theory argues that management was motivated to maintain an artificially high market price so the asking price in the rights offering could be higher. What assumptions underlie this argument?

8. How does the court reconcile plaintiff's theory with ECMH?

9. Why does Judge Winter think the motive to artificially maintain the market price in advance of the rights offering is implausible?

NOTE

The Private Securities Litigation Reform Act of 1997 (PSLRA) (codified in part at 15 U.S.C. §§ 77z–1, 78u–4 and 78u–5), added sections 21D and 21E to the Securities Exchange Act. It applies to private class actions, and in fraud cases § 21D(b) requires the complaint to (1) "specify each statement alleged to have been misleading, the reason or reasons why the statement is misleading," and (2) "with respect to each act or omission alleged to violate this title, state with particularity facts giving rise to a strong inference that the defendant acted with the required state of mind." The Act also prohibits discovery until any motions on the pleadings have been disposed of.

5.   VALUATION IN THE COURTS

A.   CAPM IN THE COURTS

Cede & Co. and Cinerama, Inc. v. Technicolor, Inc.

Delaware Court of Chancery, 1990.
1990 WL 161084.

■ ALLEN, CHANCELLOR.

On January 24, 1983, MacAndrews and Forbes Group Incorporated ("MAF") (acting through a wholly owned subsidiary) completed the second step in its acquisition of Technicolor, Inc., a Delaware corporation. The transaction that occurred that day was a cash-out merger in which the 17.81% of the Technicolor common stock not owned by MAF was converted into a right to receive $23 in cash. The first step in this acquisition had been completed several weeks earlier by December 31, 1982, when MAF closed a public cash tender offer for up to all of the Technicolor common stock at $23.00. Both the merger and the predicate tender offer had been negotiated with and agreed to by the Technicolor board of directors, which was (with two arguable exceptions) free of any pre-existing entanglement or involvement with MAF or its principal stockholder, Ronald O. Perelman.

Pending in this court are two actions that arise out of that second-step merger. Plaintiff in each is Cinerama, Inc., the beneficial owner of some 201,200 shares of Technicolor common stock (4.4% of the outstanding stock). Cinerama elected to dissent from the merger and promptly filed the first of these actions which seeks a judicial appraisal of the fair value of its stock pursuant to Section 262 of the Delaware General Corporation Law.[1] The second action was filed on January 22, 1986. It is directed against individuals who comprised the Technicolor board of directors and against MAF and Mr. Perelman. * * *

* * * This opinion reflects the decision of the court on the issues raised in the first of these cases, which requires an appraisal of the "fair value" of petitioner's Technicolor stock "exclusive of any element of value arising from accomplishment or expectation of the merger." 8 Del. C. § 262(h).

The evidence in the appraisal case was structured around the elaborate testimony of dueling experts. Each expert employed a discounted cash flow analysis of Technicolor as of January 24, 1983, but significant methodological and input differences yielded radically different estimates of value. Petitioner's expert was Mr. John Torkelsen, a financial analyst in his own firm, Princeton Venture Research ("PVR"). He opined, for reasons in part described below, that his best estimation of the statutory fair value of Technicolor on a per share basis as of January 24, 1983 was $62.75. Respondent's principle expert was Professor Alfred Rappaport of Northwestern University Graduate Business School who also functions in a consulting firm, Alcar. Professor Rappaport stated his opinion that the statutory fair value of Technicolor on a per share basis as a going concern at the time of the merger was $13.14. The dynamics of litigation no doubt contribute to this distressingly wide difference.

For the reasons set forth below I conclude, attempting to consider all pertinent factors as of the date of the merger, exclusive of elements of value arising from the expectation or accomplishment of the merger, and acting within the confines of the record created by the parties at trial, that the fair value of a share of Technicolor stock for purposes of appraisal was $21.60. A fair rate of annual interest on this appraised value is fixed at 10.72%.

---

1. Cinerama's stock was held in street name through the nominee Cede & Co., which is therefore a nominal but necessary party to the appraisal action.

I.

Ronald Perelman's leveraged acquisition of Technicolor in the two-step transaction agreed upon on October 29, 1982, by the Technicolor board must rank as one of the most successful change of corporate control transactions in a decade that was to become first crowded and later littered with such transactions. MAF's $23 cash price represented a large (more than 100%) premium over the September 1982 market prices of Technicolor's stock. The $105 million stock acquisition cost was funded almost entirely with bank credit and other borrowings. Upon acquiring control of the company Mr. Perelman and his associates, Bruce Slovin and Robert Carlton began to dismember what they saw as a badly conceived melange of businesses. Within one year these entrepreneurs had sold several of those businesses for approximately $55.7 million in cash ($11 per share) and paid about half of the bank debt used to acquire the company. Remarkably, the sale of these businesses did not significantly alter Technicolor's positive cash flow. The remaining businesses (including importantly Technicolor's traditional business of theatrical film processing and a new business of producing videocassettes under contract with copyright owners) were apparently thereafter managed with skill and good luck. As modified during the course of MAF's ownership, Technicolor was later sold in an arm's length transaction to Carlton, PLC in 1988 for some $738 million in cash. In the annals of the effective uses of leverage, the account of MAF's original minimal cash contribution to the acquisition of Technicolor certainly deserves a place.

* * *

C. Technicolor's Stock Price

Technicolor's stock was traded on the New York Stock Exchange. It was widely held. There was no control block, or even any large stockholders....

On June 30, 1978, the end of its 1978 fiscal year, Technicolor's stock was trading on the New York Stock Exchange at $7.75. The following year, Technicolor's consolidated net income grew, climbing from $3.5 million in FY1978 to $7.9 million in FY1979. The company experienced a corresponding increase in its stock price to $10.333 on June 30, 1979. Consolidated net income more than doubled again in FY1980 to more than $17 million. Of that amount, however, about $9 million reflected the value of silver recovered from film processing. (Silver prices—and silver recovery profits— soared during the period because of an attempt by the Hunt Brothers to corner the silver market). Technicolor's stock price rose during that period, reaching $24.667 by June 30, 1980. The benefit from high silver reclamation profits was short-lived, however, as the silver market subsided in 1981.

Despite receiving abnormally high profits from the sale of silver in FY1981, Technicolor's consolidated net income stagnated during that period. As earnings stagnated and silver began to fall, Technicolor's stock, which reached a high of $28.50 on April 7, 1981, began to decline.

On June 4, 1981, Technicolor announced its decision to enter the One Hour Photo business. At the time of the announcement, Technicolor's stock was trading at $22.13. The stock market's reaction to the announcement was negative. By July 7, Technicolor's stock price had fallen to $18.63. The decline continued during the balance of 1981 and in 1982 as the company struggled and experienced a further drop in earnings. On June 30, 1982, the stock closed at $10.37. In September 1982, it reached $8.37 and at the end of that month stood at $11.25.

II.

A Preliminary: A Note on Judicial Method In this Appraisal Proceeding

In this case the expert opinions on value cover an astonishing range. Two experts looking at the same historic data and each employing a discounted cash flow valuation technique arrive at best estimates as different as $13.14 per share and $62.75 per share.[15]

In many situations, the discounted cash flow technique is in theory the single best technique to estimate the value of an economic asset. Prior to our Supreme Court's decision in Weinberger v. U.O.P., Del. Supr., 457 A.2d 701 (1983) however, that technique was not typically employed in appraisal cases in this jurisdiction. But with Weinberger's implicit encouragement this technique has become prominent. The DCF model entails three basic components: an estimation of net cash flows that the firm will generate and when, over some period; a terminal or residual value equal to the future value, as of the end of the projection period, of the firm's cash flows beyond the projection period; and finally a cost of capital with which to discount to a present value both the projected net cash flows and the estimated terminal or residual value.

* * *

While the basic three-part structure of any two DCF models of the same firm, as of the same date, will be the same, it is probably the case (and is certainly true here) that the details of the analysis may be quite different. That is, not only will assumptions about the future differ, but different methods may be used within the model to generate inputs. This fact has a significant consequence for the way in which this matter is adjudicated. Sub-parts of the DCF models used here are not interchangeable. With certain exceptions, each expert's model is a complex, interwoven whole, no part of which can be removed from that model and substituted into the alternative model.[16]

* * *

---

15. A significant part of this difference is accounted for by the differing discount rates used in the DCF models. If one substitutes the higher discount rate used by respondent's principal expert for the lower rate used by petitioner's expert and makes no other adjustment to either DCF model the difference reduces from $49.61 a share to $20.86.

16. The most notable exceptions are, the cost of capital component and, the long-term debt figure. They are free standing and may be adjusted without affecting other aspects of the model.

An appraisal action is a judicial, not an inquisitorial, proceeding. The parties, not the court, establish the record and the court is limited by the record created. The statutory command to determine fair value is a command to do so in a judicial proceeding, with the powers and constraints such a proceeding entails. Accepting that the expert testimony has been so structured as to largely foreclose the court from accepting parts of one DCF model and sections of the other, it follows that the court must decide which of the two principal experts has the greater claim overall to have correctly estimated the intrinsic value of Technicolor stock at the time of the merger. Having decided that question, it will be open to me to critically review the details of that expert's opinion in order to determine if the record will permit, and judicial judgment require, modification of any inputs in that model. What the record will not permit is either a completely independent judicially created DCF model[17] or a pastiche composed of bits of one model and pieces of the other.

III.

The estimation of the fair value as of January 24, 1983, of Technicolor of Professor Rappaport is, in my considered opinion, a more reasonable estimation of statutory fair value than is the alternative valuation of petitioner's expert. In reaching that judgment I have considered a large number of factors, none of which was itself decisive. Together these factors point overwhelmingly to this conclusion.

The following statement of the reasoning leading to this conclusion is in three principle parts reflecting the tripartite structure of the DCF model used by each witness. The first part treats the generation of net cash flows for the forecast period for the various Technicolor businesses and a particular legal question relating to cash flow projection upon which the parties divide. The second aspect of the DCF model—the terminal or residual value of the company at the conclusion of the forecast period—is treated. It is in connection with that aspect of the model that the methodological differences between the DCF methodology of Mr. Rappaport/Alcar and that of Mr. Torkelsen/PVR will be treated. Finally, the selection of an appropriate cost of capital/discount rate will be discussed.

----

17. For good reasons aside from technical competence, one might be disinclined to do so. Simply to accept one experts' view or the other would have a significant institutional or precedential advantage. The DCF model typically can generate a wide range of estimates. In the world of real transactions (capital budgeting decisions for example) the hypothetical, future-oriented, nature of the model is not thought fatal to the DCF technique because those employing it typically have an intense personal interest in having the best estimates and assumptions used as inputs. In the litigation context use of the model does not have that built-in protection. On the contrary, particularly if the court will ultimately reject both parties DCF analysis and do its own, the incentive of the contending parties is to arrive at estimates of value that are at the outer margins of plausibility—that essentially define a bargaining range. If it is understood that the court will or is likely to accept the whole of one witnesses testimony or the other, incentives will be modified. While the incentives of the real world applications of the DCF model will not be replicated, at least the parties will have incentives to make their estimate of value appear most reasonable. This would tend to narrow the range of estimates, which would unquestionably be a benefit to the process.

Differences in the witnesses treatment of each of these three principal components contributes to the vastly different estimations of value presented. As I have gone through the process of evaluation of the testimony, I have tried to roughly assess the extent to which particular differences in inputs contribute to the total difference. These assessments are not precise and in most instances (but not valuation of the videocassette business) play no real role in the evaluation of which experts' testimony presents the most reasonable estimation of statutory fair value. They do help to some extent to understand where in these competing models value is generated and to what extent. To that extent these calculations may highlight particularly important aspect of this dispute.

* * *

B.   Methodology and Residual Values

The most basic conceptual difference in the two DCF models used is this: Professor Rappaport assumes (and Mr. Torkelsen does not) that for every company its particular set of comparative advantages establish, as of any moment, a future period of some greater or lesser length during which it will be able to earn rates of return that exceed its cost of capital. Beyond that point, the company (as of the present moment of valuation) can expect to earn no returns in excess of its cost of capital and therefore, beyond that point, no additional shareholder value will be created. Professor Rappaport calls this period during which a company's net returns can be predicted to exceed its costs of capital, the company's "value growth duration," which is a coined term. While Professor Rappaport has copyrighted some software that employs this concept, the basic idea is not unique to him. It is an application of elementary notions of neo-classical economics: profits above the cost of capital in an industry will attract competitors, who will over some time period drive returns down to the point at which returns equal the cost of capital. At that equilibrium point no new competition will be attracted into the field. The leading finance text includes a reference to this concept of a future period beyond which there is no further value is created. See R. Brealey & S. Myers, Principles of Corporate Finance (3d ed. 1988) at 65–66. The existence of such a point in time does not mean that there is no value attributed to the period beyond that point, but rather that there is no further value growth.

I accept as sound (as a "technique . . . generally considered acceptable in the financial community" Weinberger at 713) the methodology of Professor Rappaport. Mr. Rappaport's method is in most respects conceptually similar to that employed by Mr. Torkelsen. Its distinctive feature—forecasting net cash flows for a "value growth duration" ("VGD") rather than a defined period (often 5 years)—is, however, difficult to apply here. There were no firms closely comparable to Technicolor in order to estimate VGD with confidence (in my opinion). The other principle movie labs were small departments of much larger motion picture studios. Nor when one looked for structurally similar firms from a financial point of view did a clear VGD pattern emerge. Ultimately, a 5 year VGD period was chosen for existing businesses and 7 years for videocassettes and OHP. It is unquestionably a weakness in the VGD aspect of Professor Rappaport's DCF analysis that no clear VGD could be generated for these businesses, but I am persuaded that Professor Rappaport is nevertheless in a position to make a responsible estimation.

In the final analysis, however, Professor Rappaport used a period to project Technicolor's most important net cash flows similar to that employed by Mr. Torkelsen (5 years). Therefore, the practical significance of this conceptual difference between the DCF model used by Rappaport and that used by Torkelsen is in connection with what each does with cash flows at the end of the projection period, that is how each creates the terminal or residual value component of his DCF analysis. To estimate residual value Rappaport capitalizes a constant (last forecasted year) cash flow; he assumes no new value creation beyond the forecast period (but nevertheless much of his total value is attributed to the residual value). In creating his estimation of residual value Torkelsen, on the other hand, increases the last forecasted year's net cash flows by 5% each year (for inflation) into infinity, before capitalizing those flows. The result—and this is the practical gist of this theoretical difference between the experts—is that Mr. Torkelsen assumes that Technicolor net profits (along with all other aspects of its cash flow) and its value will increase every year in perpetuity, while Professor Rappaport assumes there will come a time when, while it may make profits, Technicolor will not be increasing in value.

The absolute difference in the residual value of each model is large. That difference is attributable not simply to methodology but to three differences in the assumptions of the models: differing discount rates (see note 15 supra), the differing estimates of cash flows in the last year projected and the assumption by PVR of a net cash flow that is perpetually increasing at 5%, a stipulated rate of inflation. It is this last assumption that most pointedly relates to the differing DCF methodology of the witnesses. PVR's assumption of a 5% growth rate in cash flows after the projection period is striking when one recalls that PVR projects growth during the 5 year explicit forecast period in the critical film processing business at 2.3% (which I find to be less probable then Alcar's no growth assumption in that business). This 5% growth assumption adds very substantial additional value to the discounted present value of a share of Technicolor stock. That assumption alone contributes $16.56 in per share value (making all other assumptions PVR makes).

In estimating residual value, Professor Rappaport, capitalizes a constant (the last forecast year) cash flow, not a perpetually growing one. He asserts that this is consistent with an inflating (or deflating) future world because he posits that whatever the value of money and indeed whatever the size of the company's cash flows, the most reasonable assumption about the future is that there will be a future time at which the firm will not earn returns in excess of its cost of capital. That is if, after that point, one posits increased cash flows, due to inflation (or decreases due to deflation) his model stipulates off-setting increases (or decreases) in the firms overall cost of capital.

Neither approach can be said to be wrong as a matter of logic nor (aside from the "Perelman plan" assumption of PVR) is either methodology inconsistent with the record. Thus, methodology cannot be decisive on choice of the most dependable of the two opinions. The impacts of methodological differences are only expressed through specific application, which of course involves substantive assumptions about the business and its future. Thus, the financial impact of the most important methodological difference—the 5% growing cash flow—is itself derivative from the cash flows generated in the last year. That difference at $16.56 a share of present value is huge in this context, but it would be larger still, or smaller, if the net cash flows projected were different. That significant $16.56 per share difference is also affected by the discount rate.

Therefore, while I believe it is incumbent upon the court to examine the experts methods, where as here those methods each present a reasonable approach recognized in the world of financial analysis, other factors, such as the projection of future cash flows, the cost of capital and sources of corroboration are necessary in order to make the overall assessment concerning which opinion is more likely to estimate fair value as defined in Section 262.

C. Discounting With the Cost of Capital

The cost of capital supplies the discount rate to reduce projected future cash flows to present value. The cost of capital is a free-standing, interchangeable component of a DCF model. It also allows room for judicial judgment to a greater extent than the record in this case permits in other areas of the DCF models.

Professor Rappaport used two cost of capital rates. For most of the cash flows (notably film processing and videocassette) he used a weighted cost of capital of 20.4%; for One Hour Photo and two small related businesses he used 17.3%.

Professor Rappaport used the Capital Asset Pricing Model (CAPM) to estimate Technicolor's costs of capital as of January 24, 1983. That model estimates the cost of company debt (on an after tax basis for a company expected to be able to utilize the tax deductibility of interest payments) by estimating the expected future cost of borrowing; it estimates the future cost of equity through a multi-factor equation and then proportionately weighs and combines the cost of equity and the cost of debt to determine a cost of capital.

The CAPM is used widely (and by all experts in this case) to estimate a firm's cost of equity capital. It does this by attempting to identify a risk-free rate for money and to identify a risk premium that would be demanded for investment in the particular enterprise in issue. In the CAPM model the riskless rate is typically derived from government treasury obligations. For a traded security the market risk premium is derived in two steps. First a market risk premium is calculated. It is the excess of the expected rate of return for a representative stock index (such as the Standard & Poor 500 or all NYSE companies) over the riskless rate. Next the individual company's "systematic risk"—that is the nondiversified risk associated with the economy as a whole as it affects this firm—is estimated. This second element of the risk premium is, in the CAPM, represented by a coefficient (beta) that measures the relative volatility of the subject firm's stock price relative to the movement of the market generally. The higher that coefficient (i.e., the higher the beta) the more volatile or risky the stock of the subject company is said to be. Of course, the riskier the investment the higher its costs of capital will be.

The CAPM is widely used in the field of financial analysis as an acceptable technique for estimating the implicit cost of capital of a firm whose securities are regularly traded. It is used in portfolio theory and in capital asset budgeting decisions. See generally R. Brealey & S. Myers, Principles of Corporate Finance (3d ed. 1988) at pp. 47–66 and 173–196; V. Brudney & M. Chirelstein, Corporate Finance (3d ed. 1987) at pp. 75–113. It cannot, of course, determine a uniquely correct cost of equity. Many judgments go into it. The beta coefficient can be measured in a variety of ways; the index rate of return can be determined pursuant to differing definitions, and adjustments can be made, such as the small capitalization premium, discussed below. But the CAPM methodology is certainly one of the principle "techniques or methods ... generally considered acceptable [for estimating the cost of equity capital component of a discounted cash flow modeling] in the financial community ..." Weinberger v. UOP, Inc. at 713.

In accepting Professor Rappaport's method for estimating Technicolor's costs of capital, I do so mindful of the extent to which it reflects judgments. That the results of the CAPM are in all instances contestable does not mean that as a technique for estimation it is unreliable. It simply means that it may not fairly be regarded as having claims to validity independent of the judgments made in applying it.

With respect to the cost of capital aspect of the discounted cash flow methodology (in distinction to the projection of net cash flows and, in most respects, the terminal value) the record does permit the court to evaluate some of the variables, used in that model chosen as the most reasonable of the two (i.e., Professor Rappaport's) and to adjust the cost of capital accordingly. I do so with respect to two elements of Professor Rappaport's determination of costs of equity for the various Technicolor divisions. These businesses were all (excepting One Hour Photo, Consumer Photo Processing and Standard Manufacturing) assigned a cost of equity of 22.7% and a weighted average cost of capital of 20.4%. The remaining businesses were assigned a cost of equity of 20.4% and a weighted average cost of capital of 17.3%.

In fixing the 22.7% cost of equity for film processing and other businesses Professor Rappaport employed a 1.7 beta which was an estimate published by Merrill Lynch, a reputable source for December 1982. That figure seems intuitively high for a company with relatively stable cash flows. Intuition aside, however, it plainly was affected to some extent by the striking volatility in Technicolor's stock during the period surrounding the announcement of MAF's proposal to acquire Technicolor for $23 per share. Technicolor stock rapidly shot up to the $23 level from a range of $9 to $12 in which it traded for all of September and the first week of October. Technicolor stock was thus a great deal more volatile than the market during this period. Applying the same measure of risk—the Merrill Lynch published beta—for September yields a significantly different beta measurement: 1.27. Looking at other evidence with respect to Technicolor betas I conclude that 1.27 is a more reasonable estimate of Technicolor's stock beta for purposes of calculating its cost of capital on January 24, 1983, than 1.7, even though that latter figure represents a December 1982 estimation.

The second particular in which the record permits and my judgment with respect to weight of evidence requires a modification of Mr. Rappaport's cost of capital calculation relates to the so-called small capitalization effect or premium. This refers to an unexplained inability of the capital asset pricing model to replicate with complete accuracy the historic returns of stocks with the same historic betas. The empirical data show that there is a recurring premium paid by small capitalization companies. This phenomena was first noted in 1981 and has been confirmed. The greatest part of the additional return for small cap companies appears to occur in January stock prices. No theory satisfactorily explaining the phenomena has been generally accepted.

Professor Rappaport classifies Technicolor as a small capitalization company and expressed the view that its cost of equity would include a 4% premium over that generated by the CAPM.

The question whether the premium can be justified in this instance is difficult because of the inability of academic financial economists to generate an accepted theory of the phenomena. While Technicolor may qualify as a small cap company, the particulars of its situation are different from many small cap companies. It was an old, not a new company. It existed in a relatively stable industry—motion picture film processing. That industry was an oligopoly and Technicolor was a leader. It had "brand name" identification. Do these distinctive characteristics that Technicolor had in common with many giant capitalization companies, matter at all in terms of the "small cap" anomaly? One cannot say. Yet the impact of a 4% increase in the cost of equity (yielding a 3.44% increase in the cost of capital of the Film Processing & Videocassette divisions) would be material to the value of the company and the appraisal value of a share. In these circumstances, I cannot conclude that it has been persuasively shown that the statutory fair value of Technicolor stock would more likely result from the inclusion of a small capitalization premium than from its exclusion. In this circumstance, I conclude it should not be considered.

Thus, in summary, I find Professor Rappaport's calculation of a cost of capital follows an accepted technique for evaluating the cost of capital; it employs that technique in a reasonable way and, except for the two particulars noted above, in a way that is deserving of adoption by the court. Applying these adjustments they lead to a cost capital of 15.28% for the main part of Technicolor's cash flow and 14.13% for the One Hour Photo related cash flows.

Mr. Torkelsen suggests a range of discount rates from 9.96% (weighted average cost of capital of MAF) to 15% (the average cost of capital for all manufacturing companies). He uses a 12.50% rate (an average of these two) to generate the $62.75 figure which he presents as his best estimation of value. This technique of estimating a discount rate is decidedly less reliable than Professor Rappaport's technique. It is not an acceptable professional technique for estimating Technicolor's cost of capital to look to the cost of capital (CAPM derived) of the acquiring company. Mr. Torkelsen's alternative of the average of all industrial concerns is far too gross a number to use except where no finer determination is feasible, which is not the case here.

* * *

For the foregoing reasons, I conclude that Professor Rappaport's model presents a reasonable method to estimate the value of Technicolor on January 24 under either the assumption that the entity he valued is subject to the business plan of the Kamerman management, or that of the Perelman management; that the value of the Kamerman managed company as of January 24, 1983, is the relevant value here; that Professor Rappaport's opinion as to value is far more likely then that of Mr. Torkelsen to correctly estimate the fair value of Technicolor, excluding value arising only from the expectation or accomplishment of the merger, as of the date of the merger; and that that estimate of value as modified by adjustment to the discount rate as indicated above and to the long-term corporate debt figure, is reasonable and is determined as the fair value, as defined in our statute, of a share of Technicolor stock on that day. That value is $20.48 (see Stipulation of August 16, 1990) plus $1.12 adjustment for long-term debt or $21.60 per share.

* * *

A judgment order consistent with the foregoing may be submitted on notice.

QUESTIONS

1. What are the incentives of each expert in a case such as this? How would those incentives influence each expert's calculations of expected future cash flows and the cost of capital?

2. What are the three parts of discounted cash flow analysis described by the court?

3. Why do you suppose experts focus on the first 5–7 years before calculating a terminal value?

4. Why did the court prefer the September 1982 beta to the December 1982 beta?

5. What do Rappaport's calculations suggest about the cost of capital without a small cap premium?

6. What is the small cap premium? What does the court think of applying it to Technicolor?

7. Why does the court use a lower cost of capital for One Hour Photo (14.13%) than for the rest of Technicolor (15.28%)? What would cause it to make such a decision?

8. If experts determine the beta for Technicolor and then use CAPM to determine cost of capital, to what should they apply it?

NOTE

This opinion is just one of many in this case, which ultimately has become the Delaware version of Jarndyce v. Jarndyce in Dickens' Bleak House, which, coincidentally, involved a court of chancery, albeit in a different jurisdiction and with corruption never evident in the Delaware courts involved in corporate law. Chancellor Allen's decision, reported above, was reversed by the Delaware Supreme Court on the grounds that he had abdicated his judicial function when he decided to choose the best appraisal of the experts. Without detailing the entire procedural history of the case, it has been remanded to the Chancery Court by the Supreme Court on five occasions. The last (as of this writing) decision was reached by Chancellor Chandler (who replaced Chancellor Allen when he left the bench for a law teaching post) on December 31, 2003. 2003 Del. Ch. LEXIS 146. Recall that the merger called for cash payments of $23.00 per share. Chancellor Allen valued the shares at $21.60. After a nine day new trial Chancellor Chandler valued them at $23.22. Cinerama owned 201,200 shares. The net gain from the twenty year appraisal process over the merger consideration was thus $44,264. Chancellor Chandler summarized the problem as follows:

"Although 8 Del. C. § 262 requires this Court to determine 'the fair value' of a share of Technicolor on January 24, 1983, it is one of the conceits of our law that we purport to declare something as elusive as *the* fair value of an entity on a given date, especially a date more than two decades ago. Experience in the adversarial battle of the experts' appraisal process under Delaware law teaches one lesson very clearly: valuation decisions are impossible to make with anything approaching complete confidence. Valuing an entity is a difficult intellectual exercise, especially when business and financial experts are available to organize data in support of wildly divergent valuations for the same entity. For a judge who is not an expert in corporate finance, one can do little more than try to detect gross distortions in the experts' opinions. This effort should, therefore, not be understood, as a matter of intellectual honesty, as resulting in *the* fair value of a corporation on a given date. The value of a corporation is not a point on a line, but a range of reasonable values, and the judge's task is to assign one particular value within this range as the most reasonable value in light of all of the relevant evidence and based on considerations of fairness."

2003 WL 23700218, at *5– *6.

The players in the case are fascinating. The plaintiffs were represented by Milberg Weiss, the now-disgraced plaintiffs' law firm where several partners pleaded guilty to criminal charges for their conduct in cases, including misrepresenting facts about payments to lead plaintiffs to the courts. John Torkelson of Princeton Venture Research was described as the "house economist" for Milberg Weiss. Mr. Torkelson admitted that sometimes he was paid more than his hourly rate by Milberg Weiss in successful cases and received nothing in unsuccessful cases. Mr. Torkelson pleaded guilty to defrauding the Small Business Administration in an investment scheme in 2005 and was sentenced to five years imprisonment. "Federal Prosecutors Put Pressure on Milberg Weiss' Star Expert, Law.Com, June 9, 2006, at http://www.law.com/jsp/article.jsp?id=1149757526656 (last visited 6/30/2009).

———————

The following case describes the valuation methods used in Delaware before Weinberger v. UOP, Inc., 457 A.2d 701 (Del. 1983), and still in use in many courts.

Piemonte[18] v. New Boston Garden Corp.

377 Mass. 719, 387 N.E.2d 1145 (Mass. 1979).

■ WILKINS, JUSTICE:

The plaintiffs were stockholders in Boston Garden Arena Corporation (Garden Arena), a Massachusetts corporation whose stockholders voted on July 19, 1973, to merge with the defendant corporation in circumstances which entitled each plaintiff to "demand payment for his stock from the resulting or surviving corporation and an appraisal in accordance with the provisions of [G. L. c. 156B, §§ 86–98]." The plaintiffs commenced this action under G. L. c. 156B, § 90, seeking a judicial determination of the "fair value" of their shares "as of the day preceding the date of the vote approving the proposed corporate action." Each party has appealed from a judgment determining the fair value of the plaintiffs' stock. We granted the defendant's application for direct appellate review.

On July 18, 1973, Garden Arena owned all the stock in a subsidiary corporation that owned both a franchise in the National Hockey League (NHL), known as the Boston Bruins, and a corporation that held a

———

18. The fifteen plaintiffs collectively owned 6,289 shares in Garden Arena Corporation, representing approximately 2.8% of its 224,892 shares of outstanding stock.

franchise in the American Hockey League (AHL), known as the Boston Braves. Garden Arena also owned and operated Boston Garden Sports Arena (Boston Garden), an indoor auditorium with facilities for the exhibition of sporting and other entertainment events, and a corporation that operated the food and beverage concession at the Boston Garden. A considerable volume of documentary material was introduced in evidence concerning the value of the stock of Garden Arena on July 18, 1973, the day before Garden Arena's stockholders approved the merger. Each side presented expert testimony. The judge gave consideration to the market value of the Garden Arena stock, to the value of its stock based on its earnings, and to the net asset value of Garden Arena's assets. Weighting these factors, the judge arrived at a total, per share value of $75.27.[3]

In this appeal, the parties raise objections to certain of the judge's conclusions. We shall expand on the facts as necessary when we consider each issue. We conclude that the judge followed acceptable procedures in valuing the Garden Arena stock; that his determinations were generally within the range of discretion accorded a fact finder; but that, in three instances, the judge's treatment of the evidence was or may have been in error and, accordingly, the case should be remanded to him for further consideration of those three points.

General Principles of Law

The statutory provisions applicable to this case were enacted in 1964 as part of the Massachusetts Business Corporation Law. The appraisal provisions were based on a similar, but not identical, Delaware statute (Del. Code tit. 8, § 262). In these circumstances, consideration of the Delaware law, including judicial decisions, is appropriate, but in no sense should we feel compelled to adhere without question to that law, which has been in the process of development since our enactment of G. L. c. 156B in 1964. We do not perceive a legislative intent to adopt judicial determinations of Delaware law made prior to the enactment of G. L. c. 156B and certainly no such intent as to judicial interpretations made since that date.

The Delaware courts have adopted a general approach to the appraisal of stock which a Massachusetts judge might appropriately follow, as did the judge in this case. The Delaware procedure, known as the "Delaware block approach," calls for a determination of the market value, the earnings value, and the net asset value of the stock, followed by the assignment of a percentage weight to each of the elements of value. See generally, Note,

---

3. The judge determined the market value, earnings value, and net asset value of the stock and then weighted these values as follows:

	Value		Weight		Result
Market Value:	$ 26.50	×	10%	=	$ 2.65
Earnings Value:	$ 52.60	×	40%	=	$21.04
Net Asset Value:	$103.16	×	50%	=	$51.58
Total Value Per Share:					$75.27

Valuation of Dissenters' Stock under Appraisal Statutes, 79 Harv. L. Rev. 1453, 1456–1471 (1966).

* * *

Market Value

The judge was acting within reasonable limits when he determined that the market value of Garden Arena stock on July 18, 1973, was $26.50 a share. Each party challenges this determination. The plaintiffs' contention is that market value should be disregarded because it was not ascertainable due to the limited trading in Garden Arena stock. The defendant argues that the judge was obliged to reconstruct market value based on comparable companies, and, in doing so, should have arrived at a market value of $22 a share.

Market value may be a significant factor, even the dominant factor, in determining the "fair value" of shares of a particular corporation under G. L. c. 156B, § 92. Shares regularly traded on a recognized stock exchange are particularly susceptible to valuation on the basis of their market price, although even in such cases the market value may well not be conclusive. On the other hand, where there is no established market for a particular stock, actual market value cannot be used. In such cases, a judge might undertake to "reconstruct" market value, but he is not obliged to do so. Indeed, the process of the reconstruction of market value may actually be no more than a variation on the valuation of corporate assets and corporate earnings.

In this case, Garden Arena stock was traded on the Boston Stock Exchange, but rarely. Approximately ninety per cent of the company's stock was held by the controlling interests and not traded. Between January 1, 1968, and December 4, 1972, 16,741 shares were traded. During this period, an annual average of approximately 1.5% of the outstanding stock changed hands. In 1972, 4,372 shares were traded at prices ranging from $20.50 a share to $29 a share. The public announcement of the proposed merger was made on December 7, 1972. The last prior sale of 200 shares on December 4, 1972, was made at $26.50 a share. The judge accepted that sale price as the market price to be used in his determination of value.

The judge concluded that the volume of trading was sufficient to permit a determination of market value and expressed a preference for the actual sale price over any reconstruction of a market value, which he concluded would place "undue reliance on corporations, factors, and circumstances not applicable to Garden Arena stock." The decision to consider market value and the market value selected were within the judge's discretion.

Valuation Based on Earnings

The judge determined that the average per share earnings of Garden Arena for the five-fiscal-year period which ended June 30, 1973, was $5.26.

To this amount he applied a factor, or multiplier, of 10 to arrive at $52.60 as the per share value based on earnings.

Each party objects to certain aspects of this process. We reject the plaintiffs' argument that the judge could not properly use any value based on earnings and also reject the parties' various challenges to the judge's method of determining value based on earnings.

Delaware case law, which, as we have said, we regard as instructive but not binding, has established a method of computing value based on corporate earnings. The appraiser generally starts by computing the average earnings of the corporation for the past five years. Extraordinary gains and losses are excluded from the average earnings calculation. The appraiser then selects a multiplier (to be applied to the average earnings) which reflects the prospective financial condition of the corporation and the risk factor inherent in the corporation and the industry. In selecting a multiplier, the appraiser generally looks to other comparable corporations. Universal City Studios, Inc. v. Francis I. duPont & Co., [334 A.2d 216,] 219–221 (averaging price-earnings ratios of nine other motion picture companies as of date of merger); Gibbons v. Schenley Indus., Inc., [339 A.2d 460], 471 (using Standard & Poor's Distiller's Index as of date of merger); Felder v. Anderson, Clayton & Co., [39 Del. Ch. 76], 87 (averaging price-earnings ratios of representative stocks over previous five-year period because of recent boom in industry). The appraiser's choice of a multiplier is largely discretionary and will be upheld if it is "within the range of reason."

The judge chose not to place "singular reliance on comparative data preferring to choose a multiplier based on the specific situation and prospects of the Garden Arena." He weighed the favorable financial prospects of the Bruins: the popularity and success of the team, the relatively low average age of its players, the popularity of Bobby Orr and Phil Esposito, the high attendance record at home games (each home team retained all gate receipts), and the advantageous radio and television contracts. On the other hand, he recognized certain risks, the negative prospects: the existence of the World Hockey Association with its potential, favorable impact on players' bargaining positions, and legal threats to the players' reserve clause. He concluded that a multiplier of 10 was appropriate. There was ample evidentiary support for his conclusion. He might have looked to and relied on price-earnings ratios of other corporations, but he was not obliged to.

The judge did not have to consider the dividend record of Garden Arena, as the defendant urges. Dividends tend to reflect the same factors as earnings and, therefore, need not be valued separately. And since dividend policy is usually reflected in market value, the use of market value as a factor in the valuation process permitted the low and sporadic dividend rate to be given some weight in the process. Beyond that, the value of the plaintiffs' stock should not be depreciated because the controlling interests often chose to declare low dividends or none at all.

The judge did not abuse his discretion in including expansion income (payments from teams newly admitted to the NHL) received during two of the five recent fiscal years. His conclusion was well within the guidelines of decided cases. The Bruins first received expansion income ($2,000,000) during the fiscal year which ended on June 30, 1967, a year not included in the five-year average. The franchise received almost $1,000,000 more in 1970 and approximately $860,000 in 1972. This 1970 and 1972 income was reflected in the computation of earnings. Expansion income did not have to be treated as extraordinary income. The judge concluded that it did not distort "an accurate projection of the earnings value of Garden Arena" and noted, as of July 18, 1973, an NHL expansion plan for the admission of two more teams in 1974–1975 and for expansion thereafter.

Valuation Based on Net Asset Value

The judge determined total net asset value by first valuing the net assets of Garden Arena apart from the Bruins franchise and the concession operations at Boston Garden. He selected $9,400,000 (the June 30, 1973, book value of Garden Arena) as representing that net asset value. Then, he added his valuations of the Bruins franchise ($9,600,000) and the concession operation ($4,200,000) to arrive at a total asset value of $23,200,000, or $103.16 a share.[10]

The parties raise various objections to these determinations. The defendant argues that the judge included certain items twice in his valuation of the net assets of Garden Arena and that he should have given no separate value to the concession operation. The plaintiff argues that the judge undervalued both the Boston Garden and the value of the Bruins franchise.

The defendant objects to the judge's refusal to deduct $1,116,000 from the $9,400,000 that represented the net asset value of Garden Arena (exclusive of the net asset value of the Bruins franchise and the concession operation). The defendant's expert testified that the $9,400,000 figure included $1,116,000 attributable to the good will of the Bruins, net player investment, and the value of the AHL franchise. The judge recognized that the items included in the $1,116,000 should not be valued twice and seemingly agreed that they would be more appropriately included in the value of the Bruins franchise than in the $9,400,000. He was not plainly wrong, however, in declining to deduct them from the $9,400,000, because, as is fully warranted from the testimony of the defendant's expert, the judge concluded that the defendant's expert did not include these items in his determination of the value of the Bruins franchise. The defendant's expert, whose determination the judge accepted, arrived at his value of the Bruins franchise by adding certain items to the cost of a new NHL franchise, but none of those items included good will, net player investment, or the value of an AHL franchise. Acceptance of the defendant's argument would have resulted in these items being entirely omitted from the net asset valuation of Garden Arena.

---

10. $23,200,000/224,892 (the number of outstanding shares).

The plaintiffs object that the judge did not explicitly determine the value of the Boston Garden and implicitly undervalued it. Garden Arena had purchased the Boston Garden on May 25, 1973, for $4,000,000, and accounted for it on the June 30, 1973, balance sheet as a $4,000,000 asset with a corresponding mortgage liability of $3,437,065. Prior to the purchase, Garden Arena had held a long-term lease which was unfavorable to the owner of the Boston Garden.[13] The existence of the lease would tend to depress the purchase price.

The judge stated that the $9,400,000 book value "includes a reasonable value for Boston Garden" (emphasis supplied). He did not indicate whether, if he had meant to value the Boston Garden at its purchase price (with an adjustment for the mortgage liabilities), he had considered the effect the lease would have had on that price. While we recognize that the fact-finding role of the judge permits him to reject the opinions of the various experts,[14] we conclude, in the absence of an explanation of his reasons, that it is possible that the judge did not give adequate consideration to the value of the Garden property. The judge should consider this subject further on remand.

A major area of dispute was the value of the Bruins franchise. The judge rejected the value advanced by the plaintiffs' expert ($18,000,000), stating that "[a]lthough the defendant's figure of [$9,600,000] seems somewhat low in comparison with the cost of expansion team franchises, the Court is constrained to accept defendant's value as it is the more creditable and legally appropriate expert opinion in the record" (emphasis supplied). Although the choice of the word "constrained" may have been inadvertent, it connotes a sense of obligation. As the trier of fact, the judge was not bound to accept the valuation of either one expert or the other. He was entitled to reach his own conclusion as to value.

Because the judge may have felt bound to accept the value placed on the Bruins franchise by the defendant's expert, we shall remand this case for him to arrive at his own determination of the value of the Bruins franchise. He would be warranted in arriving at the same valuation as that advanced on behalf of the defendant, but he is not obliged to do so.

The defendant argues that, in arriving at the value of the assets of Garden Arena, the judge improperly placed a separate value on the right to operate concessions at the Boston Garden. We agree with the judge. The fact that earnings from concessions were included in the computation of earnings value, one component in the formula, does not mean that the value of the concessions should have been excluded from the computation of net asset value, another such component.

---

13. The lease, which ran until June 1, 1986, contained a fixed maximum rent and an obligation on the lessee to pay only two-thirds of any increase in local real estate taxes. In a period of inflation and rising local real estate taxes, the value of the lease to the lessor was decreasing annually.

14. The lowest value expressed by any expert for the plaintiffs was $8,250,000 (exclusive of mortgage liabilities), based on depreciated reproduction cost. The defendant offered no testimony concerning the value of the property on July 18, 1973.

The value of the concession operation was not reflected in the value of the real estate. Real estate may be valued on the basis of rental income, but it is not valued on the basis of the profitability of business operations within the premises. Moreover, it is manifest that the value of the concession operation was not included in the value placed on the Boston Garden. The record indicates that Garden Arena already owned the concession rights when it purchased the Boston Garden. The conclusion that the value of the concession operation was not reflected in the value of the Boston Garden is particularly warranted because the determined value of the right to operate the concessions ($4,200,000) was higher than the May 25, 1973, purchase price ($4,000,000) of the Boston Garden.

We do conclude, however, that the judge may have felt unnecessarily bound to accept the plaintiffs' evidence of the value of the concession operation. He stated that "since the defendant did not submit evidence on this issue, the Court will accept plaintiffs' expert appraisal of the value of the concession operation." Although the judge did not express the view that he was "constrained" to accept the plaintiffs' valuation, as he did concerning the defendant's valuation of the Bruins franchise, he may have misconstrued his authority on this issue. The judge was not obliged to accept the plaintiffs' evidence at face value merely because no other evidence was offered.

On remand, the judge should reconsider his determination of the value of the concession operation and exercise his own judgment concerning the bases for the conclusion arrived at by the plaintiffs' expert. However, the evidence did warrant the value selected by the judge, and no reduction in that value is required on this record.

Weighting of Valuations

The judge weighted the three valuations as follows:

Market Value	—	10%
Earnings Value	—	40%
Net Asset Value	—	50%

We accept these allocations as reasonable and within the range of the judge's discretion.

Any determination of the weight to be given the various elements involved in the valuation of a stock must be based on the circumstances. The decision to weight market value at only 10% was appropriate, considering the thin trading in the stock of Garden Arena. The decision to attribute 50% weight to net asset value was reasonably founded. The judge concluded that, because of tax reasons, the value of a sports franchise, unlike many corporate activities, depends more on its assets than on its earnings; that Garden Arena had been largely a family corporation in which earnings were of little significance; that Garden Arena had approximately $5,000,000 in excess liquid assets; and that the Garden property was a substantial real estate holding in an excellent location.

The judge might have reached different conclusions on this record. He was not obliged, however, to reconstruct market value and, as the defendant urges, attribute 50% weight to it. Nor was he obliged, as the plaintiffs argue, to consider only net asset value. Market value and earnings value properly could be considered in these circumstances.

Although we would have found no fault with a determination to give even greater weight to the price per share based on the net asset value of Garden Arena, the judge was acting within an acceptable range of discretion in selecting the weights he gave to the various factors.

* * *

Conclusion

We have concluded that the judge's method of valuing the Garden Arena stock was essentially correct. In this opinion, we have indicated, however, that the case should be remanded to him for clarification and further consideration on the record of three matters: his valuation of the Boston Garden, the Bruins franchise, and the concession operation.

So ordered.

QUESTIONS

1. What does the average earnings for the past five years tell us about expected future earnings? Would it make a difference if there was a trend, either up or down? Suppose, for example, that earnings had risen $1.00 per year for the past five years, from $3.26 to $7.26? Suppose an expert believed that earnings would continue to rise at this rate for the next five years, and then level off? If you used a capitalization rate of 10%, what earnings value would this produce for New Boston Garden Corp.?

2. When a court uses a multiple of earnings to determine earnings value, does this resemble any of the valuation techniques available in modern finance? If it differs, in what ways does it differ?

3. The trial court included income received from payments made by new teams admitted to the NHL in income. Why? Wasn't this extraordinary income that should be excluded, as the court's discussion of the Delaware approach suggests?

4. The trial court accepted the defendant's expert's valuation of $1,116,000 for the good will of the Boston Bruins, the "net player investment," and the value of the AHL franchise as part of the asset valuation. Are these tangible assets? How does good will add value to a business? If you represent the defendant, how would you argue this to the court?

5. The court held that it was not error to appraise the asset value of the concessions, while their earning power was already included in the calculation of earnings value. The concessions were valued at $4.2 million, roughly equal to the purchase price of the Boston Garden. Do

you suppose they represented comparable tangible assets? If not, are they likely to duplicate the earnings valuation of the business?

6. What is the court doing to determine the asset value of the Bruins' franchise? Does this duplicate either of the other approaches?

7. If the company was valued more for its assets than its earnings because of tax reasons, why didn't the market value it higher than the $26.50 price the court determined for market value?

8. The court uses the net book value of the Boston Garden Arena as its asset value. Is this a useful approach?

9. Why did the court say that in a family corporation earnings were of little significance?

10. What is the significance of the court's statement that Garden Arena had approximately $5 million in excess liquid assets?

11. Can you discern a principled way in which courts can decide how much weight to assign to each valuation method?

12. How can there be such large differences (from $26.50 to $103.16) in the valuation of the same company, depending on which valuation method is used?

13. Is the dissenting shareholder getting what his minority interest is worth, or a pro rata share of the value of the entire business?

14. If the company wasn't being managed to produce earnings, what was it producing for shareholders?

15. If the company wasn't being managed to produce earnings, and its asset value is twice its earnings value, why not rely exclusively on asset values?

16. If the company's favorable long-term lease on the Boston Garden depressed the sale price of the Boston Garden, did book value reflect the fair market value of the Arena?

NOTE

Professor Rutherford B. Campbell, Jr. has surveyed the valuation methods employed by the Delaware courts since the 1983 decision in Weinberger v. UOP, Inc., 457 A.2d 701 mandated the use of modern valuation methods, of the kind employed in the Technicolor decision. Having examined 76 post-Weinberger decisions, he concluded:

"The conclusions from the data are not very encouraging. In short, courts since *Weinberger* have, to a significant extent, failed to base their opinions on modern finance theory. For example, the data indicate that courts in only about one-third of their opinions relied on the discounted cash flow valuation methodology, the valuation method broadly approved in modern finance theory. The data show that other inappropriate and unsound methodologies, such as the weighted average method and asset valuations, continue to be used in a large percentage of all decisions."

Campbell, The Impact of Modern Finance Theory in Acquisition Cases, 53 Syracuse L. Rev. 1 (2003). Surprisingly, this remains true in Delaware as well as elsewhere, as Professor Campbell's research demonstrates:

TABLE 4: DELAWARE CASES: METHODOLOGIES ACCEPTED BY DELAWARE COURTS IN ALL CASES AFTER *WEINBERGER*

	Discounted Cash Flow	Asset Value*	Deal Value**	Comparative Ratio***	Weighted Average	Other
Percentage	49%	19%	5%	7%	14%	7%
Fraction	21/43	8/43	2/43	3/43	6/43	3/43

TABLE 5: NON–DELAWARE CASES: METHODOLOGIES ACCEPTED BY NON–DELAWARE COURTS IN ALL CASES AFTER *WEINBERGER*

	Discounted Cash Flow	Asset Value	Deal Value	Comparative Ratio	Weighted Average	Other
Percentage	9%	21%	0%	6%	50%	15%
Fraction	3/34	7/34	0/34	2/34	17/34	5/34

Professor Campbell offers the following explanations for this:

"The first factor involves the nature of the evidence that parties offer courts in valuation cases. Generally, when examining particular court opinions from the data, one finds too many courts overwhelmed by massive amounts of complex, tedious, technical valuation evidence offered by the parties, evidence that is often so dense that not even the best judges have any realistic chance of sorting through the testimony of the parties' experts and ultimately coming to a sensible conclusion.

"Part of the complexity that courts face in these decisions is due to the fact that courts usually are offered multiple valuation methodologies in each case. Thus, in [53] useable cases from the data, courts on average were presented a total of 2.4 evaluation methodologies per case. In 43% of the cases, courts were presented with a total of three or more valuation methodologies that they were required to sort through, and in only 23% of the cases were courts offered a single valuation methodology by the parties. Indeed, in 56% of the useable cases, at least one of the parties itself offered more than one valuation method to the court in support of its position on value.

---

* By this the author means liquidation value, which he criticizes as inappropriate for valuing a going concern.—Ed.

** By this the author means values of comparable companies based on acquisitions, which the author criticizes as including synergies from the combination.—Ed.

*** By this the author means a range of ratios used by the courts, such as price/earnings, EBIT/earnings or book/market values, each of which can produce a different value.—Ed.

"One should not be surprised to find that the parties as between themselves offer different methodologies to the court. Each party, operating under the flexibility of a *Weinberger* regime, will offer the court the valuation methodology that enhances its own chances of an outcome favorable to itself. One might expect that the methodology that supports the higher possible value (the plaintiff's position) and the lowest possible value (the defendant's position) are often different, and the data are consistent with that conclusion.

"For at least two reasons, a single party may feel it advantageous to offer the court more than one valuation methodology. First, a party may see its chances of a court's accepting its particular estimate of value enhanced if the party supports its valuation under multiple theories. So the party may say, essentially: 'I propose that the company is worth $100 per share, and here are three evaluation methodologies, each of which supports a valuation of at least $100 per share.' Alternatively, a party may have no good idea of which methodology is the court's favorite or may conclude from past decisions that the court uses different methodologies without any evidence of a discernable principle. Once again, therefore, a logical strategy in such a circumstance is for a party to present multiple methodologies in the hope that at least one of the methodologies will appeal to the court."

B.   MINORITY DISCOUNTS, CONTROL PREMIA AND LEVERAGE

In Cavalier Oil Corp. v. Hartnett, 564 A.2d 1137 (Del. 1989), the Delaware Supreme Court rejected the notion of a minority discount for shares owned by a person holding a small portion of the company's shares. It explained this in the following terms:

"Cavalier's final claim of error is directed to the Vice Chancellor's refusal to apply a minority discount in valuing Harnett's EMSI stock. Cavalier contends that Harnett's 'de minimus' (1.5%) interest in EMSI is one of the 'relevant factors' which must be considered under Weinberger's expanded valuation standard. In rejecting a minority or marketability discount, the Vice Chancellor concluded that the objective of a section 262 appraisal is 'to value the corporation itself, as distinguished from a specific fraction of its shares as they may exist in the hands of a particular shareholder' [emphasis in original]. We believe this to be a valid distinction.

"A proceeding under Delaware's appraisal statute, 8 Del. C. § 262, requires that the Court of Chancery determine the 'fair value' of the dissenting stockholders' shares. The fairness concept has been said to implicate two considerations: fair dealing and fair price. Weinberger v. UOP, Inc., 457 A.2d at 711. Since the fairness of the merger process is not in dispute, the Court of Chancery's task here was to value what has been taken from the shareholder: 'viz. his proportionate interest in a going concern.' Tri–Continental Corp. v. Battye, Del. Supr., 31 Del. Ch. 523, 74 A.2d 71, 72 (1950). To this end the company must be first valued as an operating entity by application of traditional value factors, weighted as required, but without regard to post-merger events or other possible business combinations. See Bell v. Kirby Lumber Corp., Del. Supr., 413 A.2d 137 (1980). The dissenting shareholder's proportionate interest is determined only after the company as an entity has been valued. In that determination the Court of Chancery is not required to apply further weighting factors at the shareholder level, such as discounts to minority shares for asserted lack of marketability.

* * *

"The application of a discount to a minority shareholder is contrary to the requirement that the company be viewed as a 'going concern.' Cavalier's argument, that the only way Harnett would have received value for his 1.5% stock interest was to sell his stock, subject to market treatment of its minority status, misperceives the nature of the appraisal remedy. Where there is no objective market data available, the appraisal process is not intended to reconstruct a pro forma sale but to assume that the shareholder was willing to maintain his investment position, however slight, had the merger not occurred. Discounting individual share holdings injects into the appraisal process speculation on the various factors which may dictate the marketability of minority shareholdings. More important, to fail to accord to a minority shareholder the full proportionate value of his shares imposes a penalty for lack of control, and unfairly enriches the majority shareholders who may reap a windfall from the appraisal process by cashing out a dissenting shareholder, a clearly undesirable result." 564 A.2d at 1144–45.

The cases in other jurisdictions are mixed on the application of a minority discount. For cases approving such a discount, see Moore v. New Ammest, Inc., 630 P.2d 167 (Kan. App. 1984); Perlman v. Permonite Mfg. Co. 568 F. Supp. 222 (N.D. Ind. 1983), aff'd, 734 F.2d 1283 (7th Cir. 1984) (applying Indiana law); Independence Tube Corp. v. Levine, 535 N.E.2d 927 (Ill. App. 1988); Atlantic States Construction, Inc. v. Beavers, 314 S.E.2d 245 (Ga. App. 1984); Shears v. Gabovitch, 685 N.E.2d 1168 (Mass. App. 1997); McCann Ranch, Inc. v. Quigley–McCann, 915 P.2d 239 (Mont. 1996). Contra: Woodward v. Quigley, 133 N.W.2d 38 (Ia. 1965); In re Valuation of Common Stock of McLoon Oil Co., 565 A.2d 997 (Me. 1989); MT Properties, Inc. v. CMC Real Estate Corp., 481 N.W.2d 383 (Minn. App. 1992); Charland v. Country View Golf Club, Inc., 588 A.2d 609 (R.I. 1991) and Hunter v. Mitek Industries, 721 F. Supp. 1102 (E.D. Mo. 1989) (applying Missouri law); Swope v. Siegel–Robert, Inc., 243 F.3d 486 (8th Cir.), cert. denied, 534 U.S. 887 (2001) (applying Missouri law); General Securities Corp. v. Watson, 477 S.W.2d 461 (Ark. 1972); Pueblo Bancorporation v. Lindoe, Inc., 63 P.3d 353 (Colo. 2003); Hogle v. Zinetics Med., Inc., 63 P.3d 80 (Ut. 2002); Kaplan v. First Hartford Corp., 603 F. Supp. 2d 195 (D. Me. 2009) (applying Maine law); Offenbecher v. Baron Servs., 874 So. 2d 532 (Ala. Civ. App. 2002). In many of these cases the decision seems to turn upon the statutory language: does the statute require compensation for a pro rata share of the entire corporation, or is the shareholder only entitled to be compensated for that which was taken from her? See, e.g., English v. Artromick International, Inc., 2000 WL 1125637 (2000) (applying a minority discount where statute required appraisal of "fair cash value" of shares, and distinguishing it from "fair value.")

Delaware's attempts to value the entire firm and to give a dissenting shareholder her pro rata share of the value of the entire firm are a clear rejection of the concept of a minority discount. The Revised Model Business Corporation presently takes a similar approach. Revisions to M.B.C.A. § 13.01(4) now define "fair value" for appraisal purposes as follows:

> "(4) 'Fair value' means the value of the corporation's shares determined:
> (i)   immediately before the effectuation of the corporate action to which the shareholder objects;
> (ii) using customary and current valuation concepts and techniques generally employed for similar businesses in the context of the transaction requiring appraisal; and
> (iii) without discounting for lack of marketability or minority status except, if appropriate, for amendments to the articles of incorporation pursuant to section 13.02(a)(5)."

This language has been adopted by eleven states that follow the Model Act approach. One court has used this approach, citing the Model Act, even where this language was not adopted by the state. Blitch v. Peoples Bank, 540 S.E.2d 667 (Ga. App. 2000). See, e.g., Advanced Communication Design, Inc. v. Follett, 615 N.W.2d 285 (2000). The decision seemed to confuse marketability discounts with minority discounts, holding that "a result that allows majority shareholders to reap a windfall by buying out dissenting or oppressed shareholders at a discount that encourages corporate squeeze-outs is contrary to the statutory purpose to provide a remedy to minority shareholders...."

Other courts have differed with both the Model Act drafters and Delaware on the question of a marketability (as opposed to a minority) discount in closely held corporations. In English v. Artromick International, Inc., 2000 WL 1125637, the court applied both minority and marketability discounts. The opinion noted that the valuation process permitted evidence of any factor that a reasonable person would take into consideration in determining value, and that a minority interest was such a factor. As for a marketability discount, the court distinguished the Ohio statute, which required payment of "fair cash value" from cases applying a "fair value" standard, and declined "to find that marketability discounts are either against public policy or are not relevant to valuing minority interest in freeze-out mergers." See also Balsamides v. Protameen Chemicals, Inc., 734 A.2d 721 (N.J. 1999), where the court ordered that the oppressed minority shareholder had the right to buy out the shares of the oppressing majority. Here the court applied a marketability discount, holding that because of the illiquid nature of the corporation's shares, their value was reduced, and a marketability discount should be applied to avoid unfairly burdening the oppressed shareholder making the purchase.

QUESTIONS

1. Note that until about 1999 the Revised Model Business Corporation Act, § 13.01(3), provided that " 'fair value' with respect to a dissenter's shares, means the value of the shares immediately before the effectuation of the corporate action...." Does this suggest a minority discount? But see current M.B.C.A. § 13.01(4)(iii). See also Blitch v. Peoples Bank, 540 S.E.2d 667 (Ga. App. 2000), cert. applied for (holding that minority discounts are not appropriate under the new Model Act language, and applying it to the former Model Act language).

2. Note also that Del. Gen. Corp. L. § 262(a) gives a dissenting shareholder the right "to an appraisal by the Court of Chancery of the fair value of his shares of stock...." Does this suggest a minority discount?

3. Does the type of transaction involved matter in determining value? For example, M.B.C.A. § 13.01(3) provides that value shall be determined as of a date immediately before the effectuation of the corporate action, "excluding any appreciation or depreciation in anticipation of the corporate action, unless exclusion would be inequitable." In adopting this language in 1977, the ABA Committee on Corporate Laws explained that this was intended to give courts the authority to award a higher value in freeze-out mergers. American Bar Association, Section of Corporation, Banking and Business Law, Committee on Corporate Laws, Changes in the Model Business Corporation Act Affecting Dissenters' Rights, 32 Bus. Lawyer 1855, 1864, 1874 (1977). What reasons might exist to justify a distinction between freeze-out mergers and other mergers?

4. In Tri–Continental Corp. v. Battye, 74 A.2d 71, 72 (Del.1950), the court read the similar language of the predecessor to Del. GCL § 262(a) to mean that "The basic concept of value under the appraisal statute is that the stockholder is entitled to be paid for that which has been taken from him, viz., his proportionate interest in a going concern." Is this consistent with the statutory language?

5. If all small lots of shares traded in market transactions carry a minority discount, did Hartnett pay a pro rata share of the value of the entire corporation when he purchased his EMSI stock?

6. If Hartnett purchased at a price reflecting a minority discount, what is the "fair value of his shares of stock"?

7. If an investor pays a control premium for shares, does payment of a proportionate share of firm value to minority shareholders deprive the minority shareholder of the benefit of its bargain? Does it make a difference whether the transaction is an arm's length merger with a third party or a take-out merger?

8. The Official Comment to the definition of fair value in M.B.C.A. § 13.01(3) states in part: "This definition thus leaves untouched the accumulated case law about market value, value based on prior sales,

capitalized earnings value, and asset value." Does this enshrine the Delaware Block approach?

9. Recall that Del. Gen. Corp. L. § 262(b) denies appraisal to shareholders of certain widely-traded companies if they receive shares of stock in either the surviving corporation (which would by definition be widely traded) or in another such company in a merger. This denial is justified in part on the basis that the unhappy shareholder can sell her shares into the market if displeased with the transaction. Manning, The Shareholder's Appraisal Remedy: An Essay for Frank Coker, 72 Yale L.J. 223 (1962). Is this treatment consistent with the approach in Cavalier Oil Corp. v. Hartnett?

Rapid–American Corporation v. Harris

603 A.2d 796 (Del.1992).

■ MOORE, JUSTICE.

This consolidated appeal challenges the results of a statutory appraisal of Rapid–American Corporation ("Rapid") which awarded certain dissenting shareholders $51.00 per share. * * *

Appellees and cross-appellants ("Harris"), owned 58,400 shares of Rapid before the merger. Harris brought a statutory appraisal action pursuant to 8 Del. C. § 262, contesting the merger consideration. The merger price included cash and securities worth approximately $28.00 per share. After a trial in the Court of Chancery, the court awarded Harris $51.00 per share plus simple interest.

Rapid now challenges the trial court's decision to award Harris $51.00 per share. It claims that the results of the appraisal are unrealistic because the $51.00 award represents a 200% premium over Rapid's unaffected market price at the time of the merger. Rapid maintains that the trial court's error was the result of its decision to adopt Harris' valuation technique. Rapid claims that Harris' appraisal methodology violated Delaware law.

Harris further claims that the trial court erred when it failed to include a "control premium" in its valuation of Rapid. Harris argues that the inclusion of a "control premium" was necessary to compensate Rapid's shareholders for their 100% ownership in three operating subsidiaries. * * *

After carefully examining the record, we affirm the trial court's decision to adopt Harris' valuation technique. Harris' methodology does not contravene Delaware law. * * *

Finally, we reverse the denial of a "control premium" to Harris. We find that the trial court had an affirmative duty to consider the nature of the enterprise as an element of its valuation. Rapid, as a parent company owning a 100% interest in three valuable subsidiaries, was entitled to an adjustment of its inherent value as a going concern to reflect the economic reality of its structure at the corporate level. The valuation technique the trial court applied artificially discounted Rapid's ownership interest in its subsidiaries and deprived all of Rapid's shareholders of fair value.

* * *

I.

The underlying facts of this case are not in serious dispute. Rapid was a publicly-held conglomerate receiving 99% of its net sales and most of its operating profits from three wholly-owned subsidiaries. These subsidiaries included the McCrory Corporation ("McCrory"), Schenley Industries, Inc. ("Schenley"), and McGregor–Duniger, Inc. ("McGregor"). Rapid and each subsidiary had a full and distinct set of executives and operating officers. All of the subsidiaries maintained independent financial reports and records.

* * *

A.

The merger transaction leading to the appraisal began in 1974. At that time, Riklis, Rapid's CEO and Chairman, began to purchase Rapid's shares in the open market through his interests in Kenton and AFC. Rapid also contemporaneously began to repurchase large blocks of its own shares. The repurchase program ultimately increased Riklis' control of Rapid's outstanding shares.

On April 11, 1980, Rapid announced that it had agreed to merge with Kenton into a newly reformed Rapid–American corporation. On the eve of the merger, Kenton and AFC controlled 46.5% of Rapid's outstanding stock. After the merger was effectuated on January 31, 1981, Rapid's shareholders received a compensation package worth approximately $28. The compensation included $45 principal in a newly-issued 10% sinking fund subordinated debenture, $3 in cash and an additional $.25. This nominal cash fee represented settlement consideration for certain pending derivative suits.

Rapid employed an independent Transaction Review Committee ("TRC") to evaluate the merger price. The TRC retained Bear Stearns & Co. to provide financial advice. The TRC also employed Standard Research Consultants ("SRC") to determine, among other things, the fairness of the proposed transaction to Rapid's shareholders. Arthur H. Rosenbloom, SRC's head consultant and expert witness at trial, led the investigation. The examination continued for approximately six months. SRC ultimately concluded that the $28.00 compensation package was fair to Rapid's shareholders.

SRC's valuation technique considered Rapid on a consolidated basis. It evaluated Rapid based on an analysis of earnings and dividends. SRC calculated price/earnings ratios for each subsidiary and adjusted its figures to include certain dividend ratios. It figured each subsidiaries' contribution to the parent's operating income for a set period of time to calculate

Rapid's ultimate value. SRC then tested its figures against various established financial ratios of similarly situated corporations.

Harris retained Willamette Management Associates, Inc. ("WMA") to evaluate the merger consideration. In contrast to SRC's technique, WMA separately evaluated each of Rapid's subsidiaries. * * *

* * * The court also faulted SRC for its decision not to treat Rapid on a debt-free basis. Finally, the court explicitly rejected SRC's valuation, and held that it violated Delaware law. The court found that SRC's valuation technique "determined the value of [Harris'] shares as freely trading minority shareholders instead of considering Harris' "proportionate (1.5%) [sic] interest in Rapid as a going concern. . . .

The court adopted a modified version of WMA's valuation technique in a highly detailed, forty-three page opinion. It then ruled that Rapid's fair value at the time of the merger was $51.00 per share. The trial court also awarded Harris 12.75% simple interest.

B.

The Court of Chancery adopted WMA's comparative analysis. It examined each of Rapid's subsidiaries as a separate entity. It then compared the subsidiaries to a group of comparable publicly-traded companies.

III.

We now consider the merits of Harris' cross-appeal. The trial court determined the publicly traded equity ("PTE") value of Rapid's shares after adopting WMA's "segmented" comparative valuation technique. The court, however, refused to add a "control premium" to the PTE for each of Rapid's operating subsidiaries. The court, citing Cavalier, reasoned that adding a "control premium" violated 8 Del.C. § 262 because it contravened the general proscription against weighing any additional factors affecting valuation "at the shareholder level."

Harris claims that the trial court's decision to exclude a "control premium" constituted legal error. He argues that the court should have considered and valued Rapid's 100% interest in its subsidiaries. Harris maintained that WMA's valuation technique only compared its subsidiaries' PTE's with the individual shares of similar corporations trading in the market. He notes that the market price of these comparable corporations are discounted and do not reflect a control premium. Harris concludes that the trial court effectively treated Rapid as a minority shareholder in its wholly-owned subsidiaries. Harris contends that the trial court gave the new, privately-held Rapid, a windfall at his expense.

Rapid claims that the trial court did not commit error. Rapid, citing to Cavalier and Bell, argues that the addition of a control premium violates Delaware law because it takes into account Rapid's liquidation value. In sum, Rapid assumes that it could not realize a "control premium" unless it was sold to a third party. Rapid also argues that Harris only owned 1.2% of its outstanding shares and factually was not entitled to realize a "control premium."

* * *

B.

This Court, in accordance with the statutory mandate, has consistently held that a dissenting stockholder in an appraisal action is only entitled to "that which has been taken from him [or, in other words] his proportionate interest in a going concern." Two distinct but related concepts emerge from the statutory scheme. First, a court cannot assign value to any "speculative" events arising out of the merger or consolidation. Second, the court must value the dissenter's proportionate interest in the corporation as a "going concern" taking into account all other "relevant factors" affecting value. In accordance with this principle, a court cannot adjust its valuation to reflect a shareholder's individual interest in the enterprise. As Cavalier succinctly states:

> The dissenting shareholder's proportionate interest is determined only after the company as an entity has been valued. In that determination the [trial court] is not required to apply further weighing factors at the shareholder level, such as discounts to minority shares or asserted lack of marketability.

Rapid, in apparent agreement with the trial court, seizes upon Cavalier, and argues that the phrase "such as" similarly prohibits a court from adding "a control premium" at the shareholder level. Rapid indicates that adding a control premium at the shareholder level violates this Court's decision in Bell. It reasons that a control premium typically only "arises out" of the merger and is not part of Rapid's going-concern value.

We disagree with the trial court's characterization of the "control premium" in this case as an impermissible shareholder level adjustment. Its reliance on Cavalier and Bell is misplaced. The "control premium" Harris urged the trial court to adopt represented a valid adjustment to its valuation model which "applied a [bonus] at the company level against all assets...."

C.

* * *

Tri–Continental recognized that a court had the authority to discount the value of the enterprise at the corporate level. The company appraised in Tri–Continental was a leveraged closed-end mutual fund. The court understood that the shares of a leveraged closed-end mutual fund ordinarily trade at a discount of its underlying assets. The court concluded:

> The full value of the corporate assets to the corporation is not the same as the value of those assets to the common stockholder because of the factor of discount. To fail to recognize this conclusion ... is to fail to face the economic facts and to commit error.

Cavalier also recognized the importance of assigning a realistic market value to the appraised corporation. Cavalier claimed that the Tri–Continental decision authorized shareholder level discounts to devalue the shares of the minority dissenters. The Court rejected that argument. It correctly interpreted Tri–Continental as standing for the proposition that an appraisal valuation must include consideration of the unique nature of the enterprise. It drew the important distinction between assigning value at the corporate level and the shareholder level. Id. Cavalier authorized corporate level discounting as a means of establishing the intrinsic value of the enterprise. The court, however, rejected shareholder level discounting. It found that an appraisal explicitly considering the minority discount at the shareholder level both injects speculative elements into the calculation, and more importantly:

> Fails to accord to a minority shareholder the full proportionate value of his shares [which] imposes a penalty for lack of control, and unfairly enriches the majority shareholders who may reap a windfall from the appraisal process by cashing out a dissenting shareholder, a clearly undesirable result.

Rapid misses the fundamental point that Harris was not claiming a "control premium" at the shareholder level. Harris urged the trial court to add a premium at the parent level to compensate all of Rapid's shareholders for its 100% ownership position in the three subsidiaries. WMA's valuation technique arrived at comparable values using the market price of similar shares. These shares presumptively traded at a price that discounted the "control premium."

The trial court's decision to reject the addition of a control premium within the WMA valuation model placed too much emphasis on market value. * * *

Rapid was a parent company with a 100% ownership interest in three valuable subsidiaries. The trial court's decision to exclude the control premium at the corporate level practically discounted Rapid's entire inherent value. The exclusion of a "control premium" artificially and unrealistically treated Rapid as a minority shareholder. Contrary to Rapid's arguments, Delaware law compels the inclusion of a control premium under the unique facts of this case.[17] Rapid's 100% ownership interest in its subsidiaries was clearly a "relevant" valuation factor and the trial court's rejection of the "control premium" implicitly placed a disproportionate emphasis on pure market value.

We also reject Rapid's implicit claim that the inclusion of a "control premium" violates our decision in Bell. Rapid seems to contend that a "control premium" is only payable when the corporation is liquidated. It

---

17. We are fully aware of the Court of Chancery's decision in Cede & Co. v. Technicolor, Inc., Del. Ch., Civ. A. No. 7129, Allen, C. (Oct. 19, 1990), which explicitly rejected the inclusion of a "control premium" in a calculation of the intrinsic value of dissenting shares. Id. at 50–52 & n.41. We note that Cede is factually distinguishable and did not consider a corporate level "control premium." We now express no view on the particular merits of the trial court's holding in Cede, a case in which an appeal is now pending before this Court.

concludes that the addition of a "control premium" incorrectly inflates Rapid's worth to an acquisition value instead of pricing its inherent value as a going concern.

We reject Rapid's arguments because Bell is easily distinguishable on its facts. Unlike Bell, the WMA valuation technique did not assume that an acquiror would liquidate Rapid. WMA's valuation technique added the "control premium" to reflect market realities. Rapid may have had a different value as a going concern if the court had considered that it enjoyed a 100% interest in its three major subsidiaries.

We recognize that the term "control premium" may be misleading here. The past decade has proven that an acquiror is often willing to pay a "control premium" in return for a majority interest in a corporation. Nonetheless, the WMA valuation technique utilized the control premium as a means of making its valuation more realistic. Under the circumstances presented here, the trial court was under a duty to assess the value of Rapid's full ownership in its subsidiaries.

Harris also argues that the control premium increases Rapid's fair value to $73.28 per diluted share, and urges us to adopt that sum on appeal. The trial court explicitly rejected the control premium without analysis. It now must reconsider that action. There is no basis for us to adopt Harris' claimed valuation.

Accordingly, we reverse the Court of Chancery and remand. The court must consider the "control premium," together with all other traditional valuation elements, and determine what, if any, additional value is to be ascribed to Harris' stock above the $51.00 per share initial finding.

NOTE

On remand, then Vice Chancellor Chandler added $22.29 as a control premium to the $51 valuation he had previously determined.

QUESTIONS

1. Why did both appraisers value the subsidiaries rather than Rapid as a whole?

2. What did the Chancery Court mean when it criticized the SRC report as valuing Harris' shares "as freely trading minority shareholders"?

3. What rationale supports WMA's addition of a control premium to the values it found for Rapid–American's subsidiaries? If Rapid had liquidated the subsidiaries and become the direct owner of their assets and businesses, does this mean the control premium would disappear?

4. If a control premium means that a controlling block of shares is worth more per share than a minority block, how can a 100% ownership carry a control premium?

5. Tri–Continental Corp. v. Battye, 74 A.2d 71 (Del. 1950), involved a discount of the asset value of a closed-end mutual fund. Closed-end mutual funds are organized like business corporations, in that they

issue shares that are subsequently traded in markets, in contrast to open-end funds, which continuously redeem and reissue shares. Closed-end funds' shares typically trade at prices that deviate from their "net asset value," which is their pro rata share of the investments owned by the funds. Where the investments are publicly traded securities, determining net asset value is a simple task; one performed daily by open-end funds. These deviations from net asset value for closed-end companies' shares generally are discounts from net asset value. Thus the value of a closed-end fund's assets in its hands is less than the value of the same assets in the market, and the Tri–Continental court recognized that this factor should be taken into account in an appraisal proceeding. How does this relate to a discussion of whether a shareholder in Rapid–American should be accorded a control premium?

6. What does the court mean when it says that Harris was not claiming a control premium at the shareholder level?

7. Bell v. Kirby Lumber Corp., 413 A.2d 137 (Del. 1980) involved a company where use of liquidation values was rejected by the Delaware Supreme Court, on the theory that the firm was to be valued as a going concern, with the expectation that it would continue, despite the fact that its liquidation value, according to asset appraisals, was over $600, while its value based on its income was approximately $150. Note that WMA's valuation added a control premium, but the court stated that this didn't involve a liquidation valuation, because WMA didn't assume that an acquiror was going to liquidate Rapid–American. From the perspective of the present shareholders of Rapid–American, isn't a sale of their entire interest to a new buyer equivalent to a liquidation?

Appraising The Non–Existent: The Delaware Courts' Struggle With Control Premiums

by William J. Carney and Mark Heimendinger.
152 U. Penn. L. Rev. 845 (2003).

Appraisal proceedings have hardly been the Delaware courts' finest moments. For decades these courts eschewed evidence based on widely accepted finance methodology, holding rather that determinations of value were questions of law and not fact.[1] It was not until 1983 that the Delaware Supreme Court permitted introduction of evidence obtained through modern valuation methods.[2] While the current methodology is generally market-based, the courts nevertheless continue to speak about value in ways that show a deep misunderstanding of valuation methodology, and distrust of market values.[3] Indeed, the Delaware Supreme Court has stated that

---

1. See, *e.g.* Francis I. duPont & Co. v. Universal City Studios, 312 A.2d 344, 348–49 (Del. Ch.1973), aff'd, 334 A.2d 216 (Del.1975). For a criticism of the former "Delaware Block" methodology, *see* David Cohen, Comment: Valuation in the Context of Share Appraisal, 34 Emory L.J. 117 (1985).

2. Weinberger v. UOP, Inc., Del. Supr., 457 A.2d 701 (1983).

3. While the market value of a company's stock does not necessarily accurately estimate such company's future cash flows, The Efficient Capital Markets Hypothesis ("ECMH")

"the 'market price of shares may not be representative of true value.' "[4] In Smith v. Van Gorkom, the Supreme Court criticized a board that relied on a 46% premium over the market because it was uninformed about "intrinsic value."[5] More recently the Supreme Court rejected an appraised valuation that was 200% above the pre-transaction market value, on the basis that the "trial court's decision to reject the addition of a control premium ... placed too much emphasis on market value."[6] The court criticized the Chancery Court's valuation as *too low*, because it failed to add a control premium to the market price of comparable companies to reach the asserted value of the whole firm, rather than the "discounted" market price of a small block of shares in the trading market. The pre-announcement market price was $17.25;[7] the consideration paid in the cash-out merger was worth approximately $28;[8] the appraised value initially determined by the Chancery Court was $51;[9] and the final value awarded after remand, including the control premium, was $73.29.[10] If a shareholder purchased shares immediately before the announcement, the gain was 325%. This bizarre result has received relatively little attention, except to the extent that it has become an accepted part of Delaware law.[11] While the Delaware courts appear to believe they are using the science of financial economics in their valuation efforts, their misunderstandings have led to windfalls for dissenting shareholders.

* * *

A. Common Sense About Control Premiums

We argue here that the received economic wisdom of courts may contain some fundamental misconceptions about value. The misunderstanding involved is an appealing one in part because control premiums are observed. It also has a certain intuitive quality that seems to confirm its

demonstrates that a certain deference needs to be given to market value. *See* Richard A. Brealey & Stewart C. Myers, Principles of Corporate Finance 368–374 (6th ed. 2000) (setting forth a caution to management to pay attention to market values in a chapter entitled "The Six Lessons of Market Efficiency"). We caution courts to head this advice.

4. Paramount Communications, Inc. v. Time Inc., Del. Supr., 571 A.2d 1140, 1150 n.12 (1989). While we do not argue that this statement is false, the statement fails to suggest any of the reasons for this shortcoming, such as the existence of material non-public information. *But see* Part IV(B); Daniel R. Fischel, Symposium: Management and Control of the Modern Business Corporation: Corporate Control Transactions: Market Evidence in Corporate Law, 69 U. Chi. L. Rev. 941 (2002) (arguing in favor of giving often conclusive weight on market evidence when valuing corporations).

5. 488 A.2d 858 (Del.1985). This misguided search for the Holy Grail of intrinsic value began with Tri–Continental Corp. v. Battye, 74 A.2d 71, 72 (Del. 1950).

6. Rapid-American Corp. v. Harris, 603 A.2d 796, 806 (Del. 1992).

7. Harris v. Rapid American Corp., 1992 Del. Ch. LEXIS 75, *7.

8. Harris v. Rapid American Corp., 1990 Del. Ch. LEXIS 166, *3.

9. *Id.* at *52.

10. 1992 WL 69614 at *13.

11. *But see* Richard A. Booth, Minority Discounts and Control Premiums in Appraisal Proceedings, 57 Bus. Law. 127 (2001).

truthfulness. Whenever control of a company is transferred, it is easy to observe that the transfer occurs at a price above the previous market value of the shares, assuming the market did not anticipate the transfer. A rich empirical literature demonstrates that these premiums exist, and they can be large. Michael Jensen estimated shareholder gains from mergers and acquisitions at $400 billion between 1977 and 1986, while Joseph Grundfest found total shareholder gains of $167 billion between 1981 and 1986, and a third study found premiums of $118.4 billion in the same period.[66] From this it is easy to see how one could conclude that such premiums inhere in all companies, and should be considered when valuing any particular company. The intuitive appeal stems from the desire to protect minorities from overreaching by majorities, and the apparent belief that whenever any shareholders receive something different in kind (shares rather than cash), there has been some element of overreaching or unfairness. We argue that absent an actual transfer of control, control premiums represent probabilities of a control transfer at a premium. Where the probability is close to zero, so is the premium.

Our reasons for suggesting this is a misunderstanding are relatively simple: control premiums only occur in transactions involving a transfer of control where there are thought to be gains from trade. These premiums are observed only because of a perception by the purchaser that the transaction offers some opportunity to create new value, not previously existing within the target firm.[67] Even if all values, both present and potential, are valued in the market price for the firm's shares, one would not expect to find a discernable control premium in a widely held firm that is well managed and appears to offer little probability of a transfer of control. Any small probability of a control transaction will already be reflected in the market price, because all shareholders expect to have an equal opportunity to share in such a premium, should it appear, absent a dominant shareholder.

66. Michael Jensen, The Takeover Controversy: Analysis and Guidance, 4 Midland Corp. Fin. J. 6 (1986); Joseph Grundfest & Bernard Black, Stock Market Profits from Takeover Activity Between 1981 and 1986: $167 Billion is a Lot of Money, Securities and Exchange Commission News Release, Sept. 28, 1987; Gregg A. Jarrell, James A. Brickely and Jeffry M. Netter, The Market for Corporate Control: The Empirical Evidence Since 1980, 2, No. 1 J. Econ. Persp. 49 (1988); further evidence of such premiums is offered in Lawrence A. Hamermesh, Premiums in stock for stock mergers and some consequences in the Law of Director Fiduciary Duties, in this symposium. 152 U. Pa. L. Rev. 881 (2003).

67. They are offered in public tender offers in order to overcome free rider problems. *See* Sanford J. Grossman & Oliver D. Hart, *Takeover Bids, the Free–Rider Problem, and the Theory of the Corporation*, 11 BELL J. ECON. 42, 42–43 (1980). In the case of a negotiated purchase of control from a single shareholder or a group, the premium is offered both to account for the private benefits control shareholders receive and to provide a price that at least meets their reservation price, but may well be higher because of the uncertainties of negotiating under conditions of bilateral monopoly. In Cooper v. Pabst Brewing Co., 1993 Del. Ch. LEXIS 91, *23, Vice Chancellor Hartnett rejected the blended value of a takeover bid as the measure of the target's value on the date of the merger, stating that it "is often an unreliable guide to the true market value because it may reflect a control premium and other factors connected with the acquiror's intentions but unrelated to the value of the firm as a going concern."

B. Stories of Separate Markets

We turn now to the academic discussion of the market for corporate control and the arguments that have flowed from it about control premiums. We argue that control premiums are reflected in all stock prices, as explained at the beginning of section A.

The phrase "market for corporate control" was introduced in 1965 by Manne's classic article.[68] Manne introduced the concept of a market for corporate control without claiming that it was somehow separate from the market for small lots of shares. He simply claimed that as management quality and effort declined, so did expected earnings, so that stock prices would decline relative to well-managed companies. This lower stock price would both facilitate and provide the impetus for takeovers, costly as they might be. As he pointed out "the potential return from the successful takeover and revitalization of a poorly run company can be enormous."[69] While other explanations of gains have since been offered, Manne's explanation remains a central one. It integrates control transactions with trading transactions in an important way. A takeover bid introduces important new information about the value of a firm—that someone, other than current management, believes it can produce greater cash flows for investors from the existing assets.[70] In the parlance of efficient market analysis, this is "news." The fact that a takeover bid is a low-probability event for many firms explains why even prices of badly managed firms do not rise to reflect the full value of a potential control premium; they reflect only its expected value under conditions of uncertainty.[71] Many firms are well-managed and consequently offer few potential gains in a takeover. In such a case both the probability of and expected gains from a takeover bid may be trivial. But in both cases, efficient markets should set prices to reflect the particular situation of each firm.

Not all scholars accept this view. One explanation of a lack of acceptance has been offered by Martin Shubik: "These assumptions [of efficient capital markets] are set up to rule out, by assumption, the possibility that the market for a few shares of the stock of a corporation and the market for control of a corporation may be fundamentally different markets."[72] Shubik elaborates his challenge to the law of one price:

68. Henry G. Manne, Mergers and the Market for Corporate Control, 73 J. Pol. Econ. 110 (1965). For a review of the impact of this and other articles of Manne's on thinking about takeover premiums, *see* William J. Carney, The Legacy of "The Market for Corporate Control" and the Origins of the Theory of the Firm, 50 Case Wes. Res. L. Rev. 215 (1999).

69. Manne, *supra* note 68, at 113.

70. The market price of the target's stock reflects the anticipated takeover bid in advance of its announcement. Michael Bradley, Interfirm Tender Offers and the Market for Corporate Control, 41 J. Bus. 345, 361–64 (1980).

71. *Id.*

72. Martin Shubik, Corporate Control, Efficient Markets, and the Public Good, in Knights, Raiders & Targets: The Impact of the Hostile Takeover 31, 32–33 (John C. Coffee, Jr., Louis Lowenstein and Susan Rose–Ackerman, eds. 1988).

"The lawyers may talk about a premium for control. But to a true believer of efficient markets, there cannot be a premium for control. If, in contradistinction to the adherents of the single, efficient market, we suggest that there are several more or less imperfect markets involving the market for a few shares, the market for control, the market for going-business assets, and the market for assets in liquidation, then we have a structure for interpreting what is going on in terms of arbitrage among these markets."[73]

Shubik's argument uses the term "market" loosely.[74] Stigler has described markets as a situation where prices of homogeneous goods are identical.[75] Discrete markets exist when different prices appear, which are generally not arbitraged away because of transaction costs, transportation costs, or cultural differences that inhibit complete arbitrage.[76] Significantly different prices are not observed for the same stock at the same time, except perhaps in the irrelevant sense of different reservation prices.[77] A takeover bid appears in the same market in which trading occurs, and the news of the bid instantaneously moves the market price to a new level, approximating traders' estimations of the bid's prospect for success, discounting for the time value of money and the probability of oversubscription and pro-rationing.[78] Thus there is no evidence of the simultaneous existence of market prices for control and for minority interests. This

---

73. Shubik, *supra* note 72, at 33. *See also* Lynn A. Stout, Are Takeover Premiums Really Premiums? Market Price, Fair Value, and Corporate Law, 99 Yale L.J. 1235 (1990). Shubik's language was quoted by Chancellor Allen in Paramount Communications, Inc. v. Time Incorporated, 571 A.2d 1140 (Del. Supr. 1989). n. 13; Fed. Sec. L. Rep. (CCH) ¶ 94,514. We believe Shubik is mistaken when he claims that true believers in efficient capital markets hold that there cannot be a control premium. *See* Manne, *supra* note 68. Shubik argues that when hostile takeovers occur, conditions approximating zero transaction costs in perfectly competitive markets no longer exist. Shubik, *supra* note 72, at 35–36. Of course he is right, but this only goes to the probability and size of a control premium. Because not all bad managers are removed by takeovers because of these costs does not necessarily mean there are separate markets.

74. One cannot be too critical of various uses of the term "market," however. Two distinguished economists have written: "The term ... market as commonly used is so turgid of meaning that we can not hope to explain every entity to which the name is attached in common or even technical literature." Armen Alchian and Harold Demsetz, Production, Information Costs, and Economic Organization, 62 Am. Econ. Rev. 777, 785 (1973).

75. George Stigler, THE THEORY OF PRICE 85 (3d ed. 1966).

76. Shubik correctly argues that the pool of purchasers of the assets of a firm may be different (thinner) than the pool of purchasers of its shares. In some cases, if there is only one prospective asset purchaser, conditions of bilateral monopoly exist, making prediction of control premiums impossible. But this does not address the probability of a transaction in control.

77. In that sense, investors are price-takers, not price searchers. Auctions exist to deal with the problem of heterogeneous goods, to allow efficient price-searching. The New York Stock Exchange is a "continuous auction market" to search for prices intertemporally, as "news" continuously alters reservation prices of both buyers and sellers.

78. This is not to say that markets operate with perfect efficiency in eliciting bids, anticipating the probability of bids, or the probable outcome of a bidder's interest. *See* Guhan Subramanian, The Drivers of Market Efficiency in *Revlon* Transactions, J. Corp. L. (forthcoming 2003).

demonstrates that the law of one price prevails at any one time, and that prices changes only when the probability of an event such as a change of control changes.[79]

Another version of the separate market story is offered without any attempt at a theory: it simply asserts that all publicly traded shares reflect an implicit minority discount.[80] Responding to an assertion without a theory is impossible, and probably not worthwhile. It is, unfortunately, the currently operative assumption of the Delaware courts.

While economists have developed sophisticated models demonstrating how arbitrage occurs between markets[81] none of that is necessary in this context, because only one market exists for the shares of each company.

NOTE

While this ends the more theoretical discussion of valuation, it does not end a discussion of alternative valuation methods lawyers may encounter. Let's start with two examples of the types of firms where standard DCF methodology may not inspire as much confidence. There are, of course, privately held firms where there is no established market price for shares. In many respects these shares could be described as unmarketable, because there can be no certainty of a willing buyer or seller being available at any given time. And even if there is a prospective counterparty for a transaction, whatever price is set for a one-time exchange can hardly be described as a market. The price will be the result of what economists describe as a bilateral monopoly situation, where the price that results from negotiations is indeterminate in advance. It depends on such things as the relative subjective valuations of the two parties; any pressures on one or the other to buy or to sell; the relative bargaining skills of each, and a variety of other circumstances.

The other example involves companies that are either seeking venture capital financing that expect to either sell shares to the public in the future or sell out to a larger company. And even for those that successfully offer shares to the public, that offering price may not inspire great confidence in the accuracy of the price. Consider that there are several hundred biotechnology companies traded in public markets that have no product to sell, and no certainty that they ever will! These companies generally are

---

79. Coates provides an expanded description of arbitrage under these conditions, pointing out that the presence of a controlling shareholder in the target means that market prices will also reflect the risk that a bidder will acquire control directly from the controlling shareholder and the probability that the new controlling shareholder will deal more or less fairly with the public minority shareholders. John C. Coates IV, "Fair Value" As An Avoidable Rule of Corporate Law: Minority Discounts in Conflict Transactions, 147 U. Pa. L. Rev. 1251, 1265, n. 46 (1999) (citing Lucian Ayre Bebchuk, Efficient and Inefficient Sales of Corporate Control, 109 Q. J. Econ. 957, 961–64 (1994)).

80. Shannon P. Pratt, et al., VALUING A BUSINESS 304–05 (3d ed. 1996). *See also* Coates, *supra* note 79, at 1265.

81. Shubik, *supra* note 72, at 36, citing Kenneth Arrow and G. Debreu, Existence of an Equilibrium for a Competitive Economy, 22 Econometrica 215 (1954).

somewhere in the process of clinically testing newly invented drugs in the hope that the drugs will be both effective and free of serious side effects. The odds against these companies are high. Potential sales are uncertain. The volume of such sales can only be an educated guess. The strength of competition that may develop before the drug is approved and for sale can't really be known. Recall the difficulties with projections for Amazon.com discussed in Section 3.B of this chapter.

What can analysts, venture capitalists and entrepreneurs do with these facts?

In the case of the closely held company, analysts may look at the value of the company's assets. Book values should be adjusted for the current market value of the assets. This is a floor on value, on the assumption that the assets are marketable. The author once was involved in the valuation of a furniture store, and learned that stores such as this were valued at the value of their inventory and furniture and fixtures. It was a commodity business, where customer relations did not offer much opportunity for exploitation.

A more common way is to use similar public companies as a reference point for valuation. Here the appraiser or analyst would look for smaller public companies in the same line of business. The appraiser would analyze how the market values these companies not only on a DCF basis, but also on other multiples, such as sales, cash flow and book value, as back-ups. All of these can be applied to the private company, but the appraiser must then discount the results to reflect the fact that public companies are traded in liquid markets.

Where a sale of the private company is involved, the appraiser may use a similar comparability method, looking at sale prices of public companies, and in some cases data bases may have information on sales of private companies.

Finally, appraisers may use a DCF methodology, but with a much higher capitalization rate than one would see for a public company

Venture capitalists looking at early stage biotech companies, as well as prospective underwriters and analysts looking at those companies that have gone public without sales or products must engage in a somewhat speculative enterprise. If a drug ultimately reaches the market after Food & Drug Administration (FDA) approval, how large will its sales be? This will depend on the disease or condition it addresses, how good the current and expected competitors are, the expected price of the drug, and when sales will start and peak. With all of this information in hand, the analyst can then project sales and profits for the drug, starting some year in the future. This expected profit stream must be discounted back to present value to reflect the delay in the start of revenues. At what discount rate? There are some rules of thumb used by analysts about discount rates for drugs at various points in clinical development that run as high as 35%. This discount rate reflects the relatively high degree of uncertainty that a drug will ever be successful.

CHAPTER FOUR

CAPITAL STRUCTURE

1. INTRODUCTION

We begin this chapter with some thoughts about methodology. One of the insights of economics has to do with the role of *substitutes*. Rival or competing products are described as substitutes. The *substitutability postulate* states that "for some more of any good, a person is willing to sacrifice some of any one, or group of goods."* Typically economists speak of rates of substitution—the number of units of another good one is willing to sacrifice in order to obtain one unit of the subject good. These rates are subjective to each individual, but are observable. In finance, virtually all financial instruments and arrangements are substitutes for each other— offering particular combinations of expected risks and returns.

This means that one way to examine what value certain securities or financial practices have is to look for substitutes. We did this, without explicit discussion, in Chapter Three in determining the cost of equity capital by examining at how you could construct a portfolio using risk-free government securities, risky common stock, and risky borrowings. Having determined the rates of return for various combinations, we could now determine the rates that investors would demand for stock portfolios with various levels of risk. This enabled us to derive the capital market line, along which all returns must lie. We also did this when we examined both the leveraged beta and the unlevered beta for a company's stock. We learned that adding debt to a firm's capital structure increases the variance of the value of its stock, and thus its beta.

So we begin by thinking of debt and equity as substitutes. Obviously common forms of debt, which are promises to pay a fixed sum on a specified date, together with period payments of interest, are quite distinct from common stock, a residual claim, entitled to all remaining assets on liquidation after all other claims are paid, and such dividends as the board may from time to time determine to declare. We can, as you will see, find an infinite variety of financial instruments in between these two extremes that blur the differences that initially seem so bright. The varieties are as numerous as different issuer circumstances, and as markets demand.

Why are there so many kinds of financial instruments that can be used to finance the same project? The short answer is that firms seeking to raise capital try to do so at the lowest possible cost, thus benefitting the residual claimants, the shareholders. This chapter explores both the variety of

---

* Armen A. Alchian & William R. Allen, UNIVERSITY ECONOMICS: ELEMENTS OF INQUIRY (3d ed.1972) 21.

instruments used to raise capital and the cost-saving reasons why firms choose one form of financing over others.

2.   The Range of Financial Choices

The range of instruments available to finance a business is as broad as the imaginations of investment bankers and attorneys. Often we think only of stock and bonds, which represents a useful division of categories between fixed and residual claims, but it includes enormous variety. We will explore some of the varieties in the chapters that follow, but here we will attempt only to list and describe some of the major subcategories. We hope at least to expand your vocabulary, but also to prepare you to think about the ways in which financial instruments can be tailored to deal with a variety of problems dealing with risk and return.

Warrants. If we were to start with the riskiest forms of investments in corporations, most would expect to start with common stock. Common stock, after all, represents the residual claim on the earnings and assets of the firm, after all other claimants have been paid off. But there are instruments that are even riskier than common stock, represented by options to purchase stock. Stock options are called ''warrants'' when they are issued by the company, and *''call options''* when written by others, as we will explore in Chapter Eight. An *American Option* is a right to purchase a share of common stock at a specified price over a specified period. Warrants typically are of this form. If the underlying stock price never exceeds the exercise price during the life of the warrant, the warrant expires and becomes worthless. Warrant holders have no rights to vote or receive earnings from the corporation—their rights are strictly contractual.

Common stock. While options and warrants may be the riskiest form of investment in a corporation, common stock is the starting point. Shareholders are generally regarded as the ''residual'' claimants on the firm, entitled to all income and assets after the rights of senior claimants (listed below) are satisfied. Because of their residual status, shareholders are also the ultimate repository of voting rights, with the right to vote for election (and removal) of directors and to vote upon fundamental changes in the corporate contract—charter amendments, mergers, sales of all assets, and liquidations and dissolution. Holders of common shares are the beneficiaries of fiduciary duties owed by directors, who generally must look out exclusively for the rights of the stockholders, as opposed to those of other claimants. Common shares may be issued in classes with different rights, such as non-voting common and voting common, or common with super-voting rights compared to other common shares.

Preferred stock. Start-up companies seeking outside equity financing (''angel capital'' at the earliest stage and ''venture capital'' later on) often issue preferred stock to the outside investors, while the founders retain the common stock. Start-ups ordinarily don't expect to have profits for a while, and don't expect to pay dividends for a while, so the type of preferred issued in these companies typically does not involve any fixed mandatory periodic dividend obligation, although it may be given the right to participate with the common should any dividends be declared. Preferred stock is also largely a creature of contract, with few if any rights created by law. In this case, the contract is the corporate charter. In most states corporate laws authorize the charter to create a class of "blank preferred" stock, which the board of directors can later subdivide into one or more series, and specify the rights and preferences as new series are authorized. See, e.g., Del. L. Ann. tit. 8, § 151(a); Rev. Model Bus. Corp. Act § 6.02. In these cases, when the board creates a new series of preferred and specifies its rights, it files a "certificate of designation" with the Secretary of State, which amends the charter to include its terms. Preferred used as start-up and venture capital financing may have voting rights identical to those of the common stock, and will generally be convertible into common stock if the company succeeds and makes a public offering of its common stock. Preferred stock used in so-called "poison pills," or shareholder rights plans, typically carries no fixed dividend right, other than the right to receive the same dividends as the common stock, and the same amounts on liquidation as the common stock.

Conventional forms of preferred stock carry a dividend right that represents a preference over the dividend rights of the common stock. Preferred stock dividends are in a specified amount, expressed either as a dollar amount or as a percentage of the original price (par value in most cases) of the preferred stock. As in the case of the common stock, receipt of dividends is not a property right of the preferred stock; it remains a decision of the board of directors whether to pay a dividend on the preferred. The only assurance that preferred shareholders have is that no dividends can be paid on the common unless and until a dividend is first paid on the preferred. "Straight" preferred stock, which is largely a financial instrument of the past, only prohibited paying a dividend on the common in any year that no dividend was paid on the preferred. Because this permits the board to pass on preferred stock dividends for a number of years, then pay a single dividend on the preferred and a large dividend of accumulated earnings to the common, wise investors avoid this form of preferred. Virtually all preferred is "cumulative," which means that when dividends are passed on the preferred, no dividend can be paid on the common until the accumulated "arrearages" are first paid on the preferred. Cumulative preferred stock typically has a liquidation preference in the amount of its par or nominal value, plus all arrearages in dividends. The voting rights of preferred stock are mostly a creature of contract. Publicly issued preferred stock frequently will have no voting rights in the ordinary course of business, but will obtain, by statute, at least, voting rights on any amendment of the terms of the preferred and, in some cases, on issuance of new classes or series of preferred having rights and preferences senior to those of the outstanding preferred. Publicly issued preferred stock frequently is granted the right, by contract, to elect some or all directors in the event that dividends are passed on the preferred for some specified number of periods. Preferred issued to venture capitalists will generally have full voting rights, equal to those of the common and will often have the right to elect a designated number of directors.

Participating preferred stock is a fairly rare type of preferred stock that gives holders the right to receive additional earnings payouts over and above the specified dividend rate under certain conditions. It is sometimes used in venture capital financing. It has the effect of allowing venture capitalists to participate in profits in excess of the specified dividends on the same basis as the common stockholders.

Convertible preferred is far less rare, and is commonly used in venture capital financing. A conversion feature allows the preferred stockholder to convert a share of preferred into a specified number of shares of common stock.

Floating rate preferred (sometimes called *"floaters"*) is a preferred stock with a dividend rate that varies with short-term interest rates. This paper is often issued by banks and sold to corporations with excess cash available for short-term investment, for which it makes an attractive alternative to short-term debt instruments, because of the dividends received deduction available to corporations. Where the rate was determined by weekly auctions, the market for this type of preferred collapsed in 2008.

Corporate Debt. While some small number of features of preferred stock are controlled by corporate law, corporate debt is truly a creature of contract. As a result, the number of permutations that debt can take is truly enormous, and we cannot discuss all of them here. We might note that in the case of many start-up corporations promoters borrow funds personally to invest in their business. While the promoters expect to repay these loans from the profits earned in the business, as far as contractual obligations are concerned, these remain the personal obligation of the promoter, and are not generally thought of as part of corporate finance. Promoters in start-up businesses that wish to borrow funds from banks are frequently required personally to guarantee the corporate obligation. While creditors are not thought of as "owners" of the business in the same way that shareholders are treated as owners, this distinction is more legal than economic.

Short-term debt is generally thought of as debt that comes due within one year from the time it is incurred. This kind of debt financing is typically used to finance current operations, often involving seasonal needs for cash, such as those of retail merchants that must build up inventory in advance of holiday sales. On the balance sheet this is classified as current debt (see Chapter Two), and long-term debt is often described as "funded debt."

Bank Loans. Bank lending plays a more important role in corporate finance in Europe than it does in the United States, but it nevertheless plays an important role here as well. But other institutions such as commercial finance companies and factors duplicate much of the financing available through banks. Bank loans may be term loans, repayable over a period generally less than ten years. Some of the forms of bank loans are described below. Interest rates may be fixed or may float with a reference rate, such as LIBOR (London Interbank Offered Rate), which is the interest rate at which major international banks lend dollars to each other. Yields on various U.S. Treasury securities are also used as reference points.

Accounts receivable financing is most often used by businesses facing short-term cash flow needs. Many lenders will lend as much as 75% of accounts receivable, but as accounts grow older, lenders will reduce the percentage of face value they will lend or, in some cases, will refuse to lend on them. This form of financing is a type of secured loan in which accounts receivable are pledged as collateral in exchange for cash. The loan is repaid within a specified short-term period as the receivables are collected. In other cases, finance companies may purchase the receivables, which does not create a liability on the debtor's books.

Inventory financing is similar to accounts receivable financing, except the business's current inventory is used as collateral for the secured loan. For retail inventory that retailers expect to sell quite currently, the borrower may be able to borrow 60–80% of a conservative valuation of the inventory. Manufacturers' inventories, consisting of component parts and unfinished materials, may fetch as little as 30%. The key factor is the merchantability of the inventory—how quickly and for how much money could the inventory be sold. Like receivable financing, this is current financing, and typically is used to purchase new inventory.

Businesses can also finance current transactions with a *line of credit* that sets a maximum amount of funds available from the bank, to be used when needed, for the ongoing working capital or other cash needs of a business. These credit lines are offered for renewable periods, which may range up to several years. Typically banks want the line to reach zero at some point during the year. Interest rates float at the current rate, and most lines of credit are secured by receivables or inventory. Established businesses with good cash flows and credit histories may be able to borrow on an unsecured basis. These commitments are sometimes called *"revolving credit facilities"* or *"revolvers."* A commitment fee may be assessed by the bank for making a line of credit available to the borrower, even if the full amount is never used. Interest accrues only on the amount actually borrowed.

Although *short-term commercial loans* are sometimes used to finance the same type of operating costs as a working capital line of credit, they differ from lines of credit in that a commercial loan is usually taken out for a specific expenditure (e.g., to purchase a specific piece of equipment or pay a particular debt), and a fixed amount of money is borrowed for a set time with interest paid on the lump sum. These loans are typically secured, and can be either short-term or for periods of three to five years.

Banks also make *longer-term loans*, often secured by more permanent capital goods of a business, such as plant and real estate. Interest rates typically float on these loans. Banks are limited by federal regulation to lend not more than 10% of their capital to any one borrower. Where a borrower's needs are larger than a bank's capacity, it frequently brings in additional banks to participate in the loan (a syndication). Similar loans are made by other financial institutions, such as pension funds and insurance companies.

A *letter of credit* guarantees payment upon proof that contract terms between a buyer and seller have been completed, often used to facilitate international credit purchases. A buyer of goods from a foreign seller purchases a letter of credit from its bank, in which the bank promises to pay to the seller a stipulated purchase price upon satisfactory delivery of the goods. The issuing bank typically delivers the purchase price to the seller's bank upon receipt of satisfactory documentation concerning the delivery of the goods.

Credit in Capital Markets. Over the past thirty years more corporate borrowers have been able to turn directly to capital markets for financing. U.S. markets are the most developed markets in the world for corporate debt.

Commercial paper involves short-term, unsecured promissory notes, typically with maturities of no more than nine months, to take advantage of securities law exemptions. Proceeds are typically used only for current transactions. More than 1,700 companies now issue commercial paper, with financial companies as the largest group of issuers. Issuers can market paper directly to buyers (other companies that invest short-term) or sell through a dealer, such as an investment bank or a subsidiary of a commercial bank, that resells in the commercial paper market. Paper is usually issued in denominations of $100,000 or more. The Federal Reserve Board publishes commercial paper rates for specific maturities. Commercial paper is rated by credit rating agencies, such as Moody's Investors Services and Standard and Poor's, Inc.

Structured Financing is frequently used by borrowers to obtain a lower interest rate than they could obtain on the basis of their overall credit ratings. The purpose is to use high-quality assets (such as accounts receivable) and to separate them from the risks of the borrower's overall business. This involves a sale of these assets to a *special-purpose vehicle* (*"SPV"*) (sometimes called a *"special purpose entity,"* or *"SPE"*), which in turn issues securities against the pool of assets. If the sale is a true sale for value and does not leave the borrower with unreasonably small capital, concerns about the potential bankruptcy of the operating business do not attach to the SPV, and the transaction is not a fraudulent conveyance or a voidable preference in bankruptcy.

Debentures. Unsecured corporate debt sold in public markets is generally called a debenture, although short-term debt may be called "notes." There is no legal or economic distinction between the two. In some cases debentures may be expressly subordinated to some other debt, such as debts owed general creditors. In such cases the risk attached to subordinated debt begins to approach the risks borne by stockholders, and higher interest rates will be required to attract investors. When the risk is sufficiently high the debt will not be rated as investment grade by the rating services, and will be called "high yield" debt or, in the vernacular, "junk bonds." Because of the requirements of the Trust Indenture Act of 1939, 15 U.S.C. § 15 USC § 77aaa et seq., all debentures sold in amounts in excess of $10 million must be issued pursuant to a trust indenture, which names a trustee to act as agent on behalf of the holders to enforce the terms of the contract. Indentures are written in standardized terms, as we shall see in Chapter Six. Some debentures are convertible into common stock, a subject examined in Chapter Eight. Like other loans, interest rates may be variable on debentures.

Bonds. Bonds are also promissory notes, with terms very much like those of debentures, except the term bond is typically used to describe obligations that are secured by collateral, which gives them a priority in bankruptcy, to the extent of the collateral, over unsecured claims. Like debentures, they are issued under a trust indenture. Sometimes the term "bond" is loosely used to describe unsecured debt, so the distinction becomes less important. In some cases a security interest in fixed assets that are specific to a business may be worth very little if the salvage value of the assets is low.

Capital Leases. Businesses frequently use long-term leases as an alternative to borrowing and purchasing assets. Typically these leases are for a significant portion of the expected economic life of the asset. Lease payments are calculated to return to the lender (either a commercial finance company or a subsidiary of a bank) the entire purchase price of the asset plus interest. At the termination of the lease, the lessee typically has the right to purchase the asset at a nominal price. Equipment leasing is an important form of corporate finance. Airlines frequently lease their aircraft, and shippers frequently lease rail cars. Other companies may lease vehicles. In some cases companies may sell assets and lease them back as a form of financing. Leasing fungible assets such as railroad cars or trucks eliminates much of the lessor's need to engage in a credit investigation of the lessee, because on default the lease terminates and the equipment can quickly be leased to others.

Leasing has some tax advantages over ownership. Normally the lessor obtains the depreciation deduction on the asset, and where the lessor's tax rate is higher than the lessee's, this has the net effect of reducing taxes. In some cases businesses may not be able to take full advantage of aggressive depreciation deductions available to others. Under the Internal Revenue Code it is possible to deduct more depreciation expense in the early years of the life of an asset than the company would like to report as an expense to investors. Thus, the company may choose to report financial results using "straight line" depreciation, in which it deducts an equal amount of depreciation expense in each year of the asset's useful life. At the same time, it may choose to use accelerated depreciation for tax purposes, which allows it to deduct more in the early years of the life of the asset. But if the company has "too many" such deductions, which are treated as "tax shelters," it may become subject to the alternative minimum tax, which is at a higher rate than taxes computed the regular way. But lease payments are not treated as a tax shelter, so the company can deduct the entire lease payment, and the lessor is not subject to the alternative minimum tax, thus reducing the total tax burden. You might wonder why lessees would care about the ability of lessors to take generous tax deductions, but there is an easy answer. In a world of competition lenders will be forced to give some of these tax breaks back to the lessees in the form of lower lease payments.

In some other nations leasing transactions have no effect on the balance sheet, but this is not the case in the United States. The Financial Accounting Standards Board (FASB) requires the present value of the lease payment obligations on "capital leases" be shown as a liability, and an equivalent amount be shown as an asset of the lessee. This applies only to "capital leases," which are those leases that meet any one of the four following requirements:

1. The lease transfers ownership to the lessee before the lease expires;

2. The lessee can purchase the asset for a bargain price when the lease expires;

3. The lease lasts for at least 75% of the asset's estimated useful economic life; or

4. The present value of the lease payments is at least 90% of the asset's value.

All other leases are operating leases, and do not require such balance sheet treatment.

The Internal Revenue Service is suspicious of capital leases, which allow the lessee to deduct the entire lease payment rather than just depreciation and interest on borrowed money. The IRS has standards to trying to distinguish a "real" lease from a disguised installment purchase or a secured loan arrangement. There are certain features of leasing arrangement that will cause the IRS to treat it as a loan rather than a lease:

1. Designating any part of the lease payment as "interest;"

2. Giving the lessee the option to acquire the asset for a nominal sum, such as $1, at the end of the lease term;

3. Front-end loading the lease payments, so the lessee has essentially "paid for" the equipment, and then continued to use it at a nominal cost;

4. Providing lease terms to assure the lessee remains solvent and credit-worthy, such as prohibitions on new borrowings;

5. Leasing highly specialized equipment of little value to other users.

Eliasen v. Itel Corporation

82 F.3d 731 (7th Cir.), cert. denied, 519 U.S. 965 (1996).

■ Posner, C.J.

Three years ago Itel Corporation, which owned all the common stock plus 78 percent of the Class B debentures of the Green Bay & Western

Railroad Company, sold the railroad. The owners of the remaining Class B debentures, who are the plaintiffs in this class action against Itel, claim to be entitled to share in the proceeds of the sale over and above the $1,000 face value of each debenture that they received when, in accordance with the terms of their debenture certificates, the debentures were repaid out of the proceeds of the sale. They argue that in refusing to honor their claim Itel has converted property that is rightfully theirs, in violation of both federal and state law under a variety of legal theories unnecessary to discuss. The district judge granted Itel's motion to dismiss, ruling that the debentures did not entitle the holders to more than $1,000 per debenture. If the ruling is correct, the suit has no merit and was properly dismissed without regard to the defendant's numerous other defenses. This is so even though the plaintiffs also complain about Itel's refusal, before it sold the railroad, to credit (more precisely, to cause the railroad, which it controlled, to credit) any of the railroad's income to the Class B debentures. But this complaint, at least as the plaintiffs formulated it in the district court—and it is too late for them to recast the theory of their case on appeal—hinges on their contention that they are the residual claimants to the proceeds of the sale. They say the residuum would have been greater had Itel properly applied the income to the improvement of the railroad rather than (as the plaintiffs allege it did) siphoning that income into the pockets of Itel's shareholders. If the debenture holders had no rights in the residuum, they were not harmed by the siphoning.

A debenture, as the word is normally used in the legal and financial communities of the United States, and as it was normally used a century ago as well, when the debentures involved in this suit were first issued, is a type of bond, specifically a bond unsecured by a lien. Richard A. Brealey & Stewart C. Myers, Principles of Corporate Finance 597 (4th ed. 1991); William Z. Ripley, Railroads: Finance & Organization 142 (1915). Ordinarily, when a corporation is sold, the proceeds above what is needed to pay off creditors, including bondholders—including therefore debenture holders—go to the shareholders, as the residual claimants to the corporation's assets. The plaintiffs argue that, contrary to the norm, the Class B debentures in the Green Bay & Western Railroad Company were intended to be the equivalent of shares of stock, while the shares of stock were intended to be the equivalent of debentures. They ask us to look behind the labels that these instruments bear to the economic reality.

Each debenture certificate is a contract between the railroad and the debenture holder, and parties to a contract can agree to use words in a nonstandard sense. But it does not help the plaintiffs' case that they are unable to direct us to any other instance in U.S. corporate history in which the word "debenture" has been used to denote an equity interest. Convertible debentures, that is, debentures convertible into stock upon the coming to pass of stated conditions, have by virtue of their conversion feature an equity hue; but the debentures issued by the Green Bay & Western Railroad are not convertible. A treatise gives an example of where the term "debenture" has been interpreted to mean preferred stock. 6 Fletcher Cyclopedia of the Law of Private Corporations § 2649.1, p. 27 (1989 rev. ed.). But there is much less space between a conventional debenture and preferred stock than between a conventional debenture and common stock, since preferred stock normally is "maxed out" at its stated par value, 11 id. at § 5303, p. 592, just like the Class B debentures if Itel's interpretation is accepted.

To determine whether the interpretation is correct requires an examination of the history and terms of the securities. The Green Bay & Western Railroad was created, under a different name, in 1866. It went broke ten years later and again in 1888, emerging from the second bankruptcy exactly one century ago, in 1896, with a radically new capital structure. The first mortgagees, who had foreclosed on the railroad's property, received all the capital stock of the new company—25,000 shares with a par value of $100 each. The second mortgagees and old shareholders received the Class B debentures—7,000 debentures each with a face value, as we have said, of $1,000—and also, in exchange for investing $600,000 of new money, 600 Class A debentures with a face value of $1,000 each. None of the three classes of securities specified either maturity dates or a fixed entitlement to income, and only the capital stock had voting rights.

Although the debentures do not create a fixed entitlement to interest or dividends, they do provide for the allocation of any annual dividends that the board of directors decides to declare. The dividends are to go to the holders of the Class A debentures until those investors have received 2.5 percent of the face value of the debenture, then to the shareholders until they have received 2.5 percent of the par value of their stock, and then to the holders of the Class A debentures and the shareholders, pro rata, until the two groups have received a total of 5 percent of the face value of the Class A debentures and of the par value of the stock. Any money left after these distributions is to go to the holders of the Class B debentures. In simplest terms, then, the Class B debenture holders are entitled to any dividends that exceed what is necessary to give the shareholders and the Class A debenture holders 5 percent of the face amount of their securities.

In the event of a sale or reorganization of the company, the Class B debenture certificate specifies the following distribution of the proceeds after payment of all liens and charges: the first $600,000 to the holders of the Class A debentures, the next $2.5 million to the shareholders, and either the rest—or the first $7 million of the rest—to the holders of the Class B debentures. Which it is the issue in this case.

Each Class B debenture certificate states that the Green Bay & Western Railroad Company

> certifies that this is one of a series of seven thousand of its Class B Debentures, in the sum of ONE THOUSAND DOLLARS each, aggregating in all the sum of Seven Million Dollars, *which sum of One Thousand Dollars will be payable to the bearer hereof* as follows: viz., only in the event of a sale or reorganization of the Railroad and property of said Company, and then only out of any net proceeds of

such sale or reorganization which may remain after payment of any liens and charges upon such railroad or property, and after payment of Six Hundred Thousand Dollars to the holders of a series of Debentures known as Class A, issued or to be issued, by said Company, and the sum of Two Million Five Hundred Thousand Dollars to and among the stockholders of said Company. *Any such net proceeds remaining after such payments shall be distributed pro rata to and among the holders of this series of Class B Debentures.* [Emphasis added].

Itel argues that the first clause that we have italicized makes clear that the only entitlement of the holders of Class B debentures is to $1,000 per debenture. The plaintiffs argue that the last sentence in the quoted passage, which we have also italicized, makes clear that any proceeds from a sale over and above all liens and charges, $600,000 to the holders of the Class A debentures, and $2.5 million to the shareholders, go to the holders of the Class B debentures, making them in effect the equity owners of the railroad. On Itel's reading the shareholders have a debt-like claim to the par value of their stock (the $2.5 million) that is subordinate only to the other creditor interests (including that of the Class A debentures) but they also have the normal equity interest, which comes into play after the Class B debenture holders are paid their $7 million.

The question of what happens after the Class B debenture holders receive the full face value of their debentures cannot arise unless at the time of sale or reorganization the net value of the company exceeds $10.1 million, the sum of the face or par values of the three classes of security. That happy eventuality must have seemed remote in 1896, for the debentures and other documents of the 1896 reorganization do not make clear provision for it. Nevertheless the presumption in 1896 as now was (is) that the residual, unprovided-for value of a corporation belongs to the shareholders rather than to the holders of debentures or other bonds. The first clause that we italicized in the Class B debenture reinforces the presumption, for it states flatly that the holder's right in the event of a sale or reorganization of the railroad is to receive the face amount of the debenture, $1,000. The sentence on which the plaintiffs rely can easily be read as merely specifying the mode of distribution among the Class B debenture holders in what must have seemed the likely event that the proceeds of the sale were insufficient to give them the full $7 million.

It is true that on Itel's interpretation the Class B debenture holders got very little in the reorganization. They got no right to any income unless the board of directors decided to declare a dividend larger than 5 percent of the combined face value of the Class A debentures and par value of the common stock, that is, more than 5 percent of $3.1 million ($155,000). And if the railroad was never sold or reorganized, the debenture holders would never get their principal back. But remember that the recipients of the Class B debentures were the junior mortgagees, and the shareholders, of a bankrupt railroad. They may have gotten little in exchange for the surrender of their interests in the railroad because those interests were worth little. The junior mortgagees had not been paid anything on their mortgages for the fourteen years preceding the reorganization. To the extent that these investors did not merely exchange their old interests for new ones but also contributed new value to the railroad, as they did, they were compensated by receiving Class A debentures. Those debentures were entitled to priority both in the distribution of the railroad's income and in the eventuality of a sale or reorganization. The new shareholders, having in their previous capacity as first mortgagees already foreclosed on the railroad, received both voting control and a bond-like entitlement to $2.5 million in the event that a sale or reorganization yielded net proceeds after all liens and charges of at least $3.1 million, plus (on Itel's interpretation) what must have seemed the remote possibility of an additional return should the railroad be sold and reorganized at a time when it had attained a net worth in excess of $10.1 million.

Itel's interpretation makes better economic sense than the plaintiffs' because it is more consistent with the creation and maintenance of proper incentives for operating the railroad in such a way as to maximize its value. (This is relevant because most commercial transactions are designed to be value-maximizing.) Only the shareholders had been given voting rights. Only the shareholders, therefore, could control the management of the corporation. If they had no right to any part of the gain from increasing the value of the corporation above $3.1 million, the level that would just cover their fixed entitlement to $2.5 million, they would have had little zeal for developing the railroad to the level it reached when it was sold in 1993. We do not know the sale price, because Itel sold the Green Bay & Western Railroad together with another railroad for a combined price of $64 million. The plaintiffs claim that $43 million is the minimum amount of the sale price fairly allocable to the Green Bay, which if so would entitle the Class B debenture holders, under the plaintiffs' theory of the case, to roughly $40 million. The plaintiffs, recall, own 22 percent of those debentures.

A corporate structure in which the bondholders, for that is what the plaintiffs think the shareholders are—holders of 25,000 bonds worth $100 apiece—have all the voting rights, and the shareholders, who are what the plaintiffs consider the Class B debenture holders to be, have no voting rights, is anomalous. See Frank H. Easterbrook and Daniel R. Fischel, "Voting in Corporate Law," 26 J. Law & Econ. 395, 403–05 (1983). And yet this inverted corporate structure would not be crazy if at the time it was created the possibility that the railroad would ever be worth at least $10.1 million was so remote that the shareholders, even if they were the residual claimants, would have no incentive to maximize the value of the railroad, beyond trying to create a cushion to protect their $2.5 million bond-like entitlement. As Easterbrook and Fischel point out, corporate indentures frequently shift voting rights to creditor groups when financial distress attenuates the shareholders' interests and makes the creditors the de facto residual claimants to the value of the corporation's assets. Throughout most of the history of the railroad it has been the Class B debenture holders who have been the real equity owners, because until the railroad attained a net value of $10.1 million (which for all we know has not yet occurred) any increase in value would enure to the benefit of those investors. But this is an argument for having given the Class B debenture holders the voting rights and hence control of the corporation, which the reorganization plan and the debenture certificates did not do. The only way to give the shareholders a robust incentive to maximize the railroad's value is to give them an equity kicker above the Class B debenture holders' entitlement, and so the debenture contract can be presumed to have done this.

[handwritten margin note: Then why not shareholders]

Another reason to doubt that the debenture holders received an equity interest is that the shareholders, being in control of the corporation as a consequence of their voting rights, could so easily circumvent that interest. Before a sale or reorganization of the railroad the value of the debentures would be depressed because the holders would have no right to force either a sale of the railroad or a declaration of dividends in an amount that would give any part of the railroad's income to the debenture holders. The owners of the stock could therefore buy up the debentures cheap, so that, when the railroad was sold, the stockholders (now also the debenture holders) would obtain the benefits of the equity interest nominally held, under the plaintiffs' interpretation, by the debenture holders. And indeed when Itel bought the railroad's common stock it also bought 78 percent of the Class B debentures.

So uncertain was the right of the debenture holders to income from the corporation that the Tax Court ruled, in a decision upheld by this court in Green Bay & W.R. Co. v. Commissioner, 147 F.2d 585 (7th Cir. 1945), that the railroad could not deduct payments to either class of debenture holders as interest. Instead it had to treat these payments for tax purposes as dividends (the term, as it happens, used in the debentures themselves). But this is just to say that the debenture holders have no interest entitlement. It does not address the question of their entitlement in the event of a sale. This is obvious from the fact that the court treated the Class A debenture holders the same as the Class B holders, even though it is indisputable that the former are entitled only to the face value of their debentures in the event of a sale.

* * *

Even if as we believe Itel has the better of the argument when consideration is limited to the text of the Class B debenture, should consideration be so limited? Since the debenture makes no explicit provision for the allocation of the net proceeds of sale above $10.1 million, and since the last sentence that we quoted from the debenture certificate, the sentence on which the plaintiffs pitch their case, provides at least some support for it, there is enough ambiguity to permit the consideration of extrinsic evidence, that is, evidence outside the text of the Class B debenture itself. Itel implicitly acknowledges this by pointing out that these debentures were issued in exchange for interests that probably had little value.

The first item of extrinsic evidence that the plaintiffs want us to consider is the text of the Class A debenture. It is almost identical to that of the Class B debenture, except that the first sentence of the Class A debenture, of course, states the entitlement of the holders of that debenture to their $1,000 rather than the entitlement of the Class B debenture holders to their $1,000. Like the Class B debenture, the Class A debenture goes on to specify the order of distribution, including the payment to the holders of the Class B debentures of the surplus over the Class A debenture holders' and the shareholders' entitlements. Since the first sentence of the Class A debenture does not mention the Class B debenture holders, there is nothing to qualify the last sentence—the sentence that taken by itself appears to give the entire surplus, with no $7 million cap, to those debenture holders. That sentence does not appear, however, in the description of the Class A debentures that appears in the articles of incorporation of the reorganized firm. And to the holder of a Class A debenture the only important thing is his entitlement, and not, after his entitlement has been satisfied, how any surplus above the amount necessary to satisfy it is to be divided between other classes of investor. It would be odd for the owner of a Class B debenture to look to the text of another debenture for the statement of his rights (though, granted, initially the holders of the two classes of debentures were the same people—the railroad's second mortgagees and former shareholders). No one reading the Class B debenture, with its flat statement that it entitles the holder to $1,000 if the railroad is ever sold or reorganized, would suppose that it entitled the holder to more—to almost six times as much, in fact, if the plaintiffs' estimate of the sale price of the railroad is correct.

The plaintiffs point to a series of statements that the railroad made, some in the two cases that we discussed, some in other cases, others in submissions to the SEC and the ICC, which the plaintiffs construe as admissions that the Class B debenture holders are the residual owners of the railroad. So far as appears, however, these statements (contradicted, incidentally, by others, which do refer to the $7 million cap) were made at a time when the railroad was worth less than $10.1 million, so that the question of the entitlement to any surplus value above that was academic. In the 1940s, when Biltchik and the tax case were decided, the market value of the Class B debentures was only $120, implying that the net worth of the railroad may have been as little as $3,940,000 ($.6 million plus $2.5 million plus 7,000 X $120). If so, the Class B debenture holders were the real equity owners, because, had the railroad been sold then at that price, they would have received the entire net proceeds minus the $3.1 million reserved for the Class A debenture holders and the shareholders.

Despite what we have just said, the value of the railroad cannot be inferred directly from the market value of the Class B debentures. That market value would have been depressed by the inability of the debenture holders to force a sale or a distribution of income to them. The court in Biltchik thought the railroad worth more, about $5 million—or so we infer from 26 N.W.2d at 635. This estimate may well have been more realistic. But it is still far below the point at which the Class B debenture holders would be paid in full in the event the railroad was sold.

The plaintiffs presented no evidence of the value of the railroad at any of the times when the statements on which they rely were made, although it appears that as late as 1986 the railroad was worth no more than $8.4 million. Itel had acquired its interest in the railroad—100 percent of the common stock and 78 percent of the Class B debentures—in 1978 for a total of $8 million. (Because it had bought securities of the railroad rather than the railroad itself, its purchase did not trigger the entitlement of the debenture holders to be paid out.) The plaintiffs' claim that the railroad was sold for at least $43 million in 1993 appears to be grossly exaggerated. Itel had paid $61 million for the Fox River Valley Railroad, the railroad it sold together with the Green Bay & Western Railroad for $64 million in 1993.

Remarks, even considered statements, that the Class B debenture holders were the real equity owners of the Green Bay, made at the time when they were the real though not formal equity owners, are not highly probative of what their status would be if the residual value of the railroad rose above the face amount of those debentures. The plaintiffs want a trial but have cited no evidence that would rebut the presumption from the text and history and economic logic of the Class B debenture that it caps the holders' entitlement at $7 million. No jury would be permitted to speculate that this debenture was really a share of stock.

Yet the thrust of our analysis has been that Itel was entitled to summary judgment, not that the complaint should have been dismissed for failure to state a claim. While a court, either the district court or the court of appeals, can grant summary judgment even though neither party has moved for it, it must not do so without giving the party against whom the court proposes to enter summary judgment notice of what is in store for that party. But this is not a problem here. The plaintiffs have laid out their extrinsic evidence—the evidence they think creates a triable issue—in full in their briefs in this court and Itel has explained why it thinks that the plaintiffs' evidence does not create a triable issue. This is equivalent to Itel's arguing that if it was not entitled to dismissal under Rule 12(b)(6) it was entitled to summary judgment. The plaintiffs had, and have availed themselves, of the opportunity to reply to the argument. In effect the parties have recast the issue on appeal as whether we should grant summary judgment for the defendant. We should and do. The judgment is therefore

Affirmed.

QUESTIONS

1. What priorities does Plaintiff argue for?
2. Does Plaintiff's argument give any meaning to the face value of the debentures?
3. What priorities does Itel argue for?
4. What does the plain language provide?

5. Does Itel's position give any meaning to the language that stockholders shall be paid $2.5 million?

6. Why does the court look at ancient history and describe the bankruptcy priorities in 1896?

7. Who stood last in line in the bankruptcy? Is this important to the court? Should it be?

8. Who had voting rights? Why is this relevant to determining priorities on payment?

9. If the B debentures only receive "dividends" after the A debentures and stock, what does this suggest?

NOTE

For a decision on whether preferred stock was really preferred stock or, as some commentators called it, "sham preferred," see Telvest v. Olson, 1979 WL 1759 (Del. Ch. 1979).

---

3.   MODIGLIANI & MILLER'S IRRELEVANCE HYPOTHESIS

As noted in the preceding section we observe a wide variety of financial instruments employed by corporations to raise capital, and a wide variety of capital structures, in terms of proportions of debt, preferred stock and common stock, in corporations. This phenomenon has persisted over long periods of time, with different market conditions and different tax structures. All of this suggests that capital structure must be useful in maximizing value for investors in firms. This intuition is sound: capital structure does matter. Nevertheless, we begin with the hypothesis that capital structure is irrelevant to firm value. This is widely known as Modigliani's and Miller's *Proposition I*.*

About $3 trillion in corporate debt was outstanding in 1996. That debt constituted 31% of the capital structure of U.S. companies.** The object of capital structure is to maximize the value of all securities representing ownership of the firm. To a large extent this process is expected to benefit stockholders. A standard example of how leverage is said to benefit stockholders is set out below:

THE NET INCOME PERSPECTIVE

The traditional method of analysis suggests that if the rate of interest on borrowings is lower than the rate of return demanded by investors in a

---

* Franco Modigliani and Merton Miller, The Cost of Capital, Corporation Finance and the Theory of Investment, 48 Am. Econ. Rev. 261 (1958).

** See Board of Governors of the Fed. Reserve Sys. of the United States, Flow of Funds Accounts: Flows and Outstandings of the Fourth Quarter 1996, at 63 tbl.L102 [hereinafter Fed. Reserve Funds Flows] (showing total debt of $2.966 trillion and total market value of equities of $6.713 trillion), as cited in Yakov Amihud, Kenneth Garbade, and Marcel Kahan, A New Governance Structure for Corporate Bonds, 51 Stan. L. Rev. 447 (1999).

firm's stock, the firm should borrow to finance new projects that are expected to return a rate equal to the discount rate applied by investors for stock. We illustrate this with the following example.

Firm One is an all equity firm with $100,000 invested, that has an expected return to shareholders of $12,000.

Firm Two has $50,000 equity and $50,000 borrowings, and would have an expected return to shareholders of $16,000:

Operating income	$12,000
less interest	− 4,000
Net Income	$8,000

The traditional approach looks only at net income, and valued earnings per share. Under this assumption, if Firm One and Firm Two are identical, the expected earnings of each should be capitalized at 12%.

Equity of Firm One: $\dfrac{\$12,000}{.12}$ = $100,000

Equity of Firm Two: $\dfrac{\$8,000}{.12}$ = $66,666

Thus, if Firm Two has $66,666 worth of common stock plus $50,000 in debt, it must be worth $116,666, or considerably more than Firm One. Notice that this approach focuses on the net income available for the shareholders, which intuitively seems like the appropriate way to value the firm's stock. But this misses the important point that the expected earnings associated with the shares of Firm Two are more volatile than those of Firm One, because of the fixed demands of creditors for their interest payments, regardless of whether the firm has a good year or not. We can illustrate this as follows. Assume the following situations for the leveraged and unleveraged firm:.

FIRM ONE

	Bad Year	Normal Year	Good Year
Assumed net earnings	$2,000	$12,000	$22,000
Earnings to shareholders	$2,000	$12,000	$22,000

FIRM TWO

	Bad Year	Normal Year	Good Year
Assumed gross earnings	$2,000	$12,000	$22,000
Interest	(4,000)	(4,000)	(4,000)
Earnings to shareholders	($2,000)	$8,000	$18,000

Note how leverage increases the variance of expected returns for stockholders in Firm Two. Thus leverage increases variance, and thus risk. Investors seek higher returns for higher risk. This can be illustrated by assuming each of the above returns occurs for investors in each firm:

		Net Profit	Rate of Return (on equity)
Firm One:			
	Bad	$2,000	2%
	Normal	$12,000	12%
	Good	$22,000	22%
Firm Two:			
	Bad	($2,000)	–4%
	Normal	$8,000	16%
	Good	$18,000	36%

A firm with half as much stock as before, and an equal amount of debt, faces a doubling of its variance. If the normal year is a 12% return on Firm One's equity and a 16% return on Firm Two's Equity, look at what happens in a bad year, when Firm One's earnings drop by 83%. Firm Two's earnings drop by 125%. And in a good year, Firm One's earnings increase from normal by 83%, where Firm Two's earnings increase by 125%.

But this misses the cost of default risk, the probability that it will be unable to repay its obligations on Firm Two's debt. If bankruptcy occurs, creditors seize Firm Two's assets to pay off the debt. Creditors rarely get full payment, and bankruptcy itself imposes transaction costs that creditors bear. Assume now that investors recognize that shares of Firm Two are riskier than shares of Firm One, and demand a 14% return on them:

Revised Equity of Firm Two: $\dfrac{\$8,000}{.14}$ = $57,143

So, when Firm Two's $50,000 debt is added, Firm Two is still worth $107,143, or more than Firm One. This suggests that there are still gains from leveraging, from a shareholder perspective. For a long time this represented the conventional wisdom in finance. But in 1958 an analytical revolution began as described below.

THE NET OPERATING INCOME APPROACH (Modigliani and Miller)

The Net Income Approach suggests that leverage increases the value of the firm's shares. It also suggests that investors don't recognize that they are bearing as much risk as they really are. Why should you pay more for a leveraged firm when you can do it yourself? This is the great insight of Modigliani and Miller's irrelevance hypothesis.* Its approach focuses not on

---

* Franco Modigliani and Merton H. Miller, The Cost of Capital, Corporation Finance and the Theory of Investment, 48 AMERICAN ECONOMIC REVIEW 261 (1958). This is also called M&M Proposition One.

net income available to shareholders, but rather on net operating income of the firm, before any payments of interest to creditors.

Assumptions: Because Modigliani and Miller's thesis is primarily a heuristic, designed to enable us to see certain essential features, it abstracts from real-world conditions.* For example, it assumes a world of:

1. no taxes

2. no difference in borrowing costs between corporations and shareholders,** and

3. low transaction costs, so investors can readily shift between investments.

Assume you have $100,000 cash to invest, and you can borrow another $100,000 at 8%. Now assume that there are two firms, each earning $12,000, with a current market value of $100,000 each. This means investors demand a 12% return on the cash flows and have capitalized earnings at 12%.

Choice One: An unleveraged investment. You get expected 12% rate of return ($12,000 on $100,000)

Choice Two: A leveraged investment. You invest $50,000 equity in each of two identical firms. You borrow $100,000 at 8% to buy the balance of the equity in both firms. Results:

$$\begin{array}{rl} \$24,000 & \text{total income} \\ -\ \underline{8,000} & \text{interest} \\ \$16,000 & \text{net income} \end{array}$$

In Choice Two, you get an expected 16% rate of return on your $100,000. This is called "home made leverage." Note that you have paid $100,000 for the equity under either Choice One or Choice Two. If you see a certain similarity to our example in the Net Income approach, it is not coincidental. Thus an investor can personally borrow money to buy a larger amount of equity, and get the expected 16% return by personally bearing the higher risk. So an investor wouldn't pay more than $100,000 for Firm Two's equity, because she can "home-make" the same set of results.

---

* It's not clear M&M intended it to be this way. Assuming away taxes may have been an error. The title of their subsequent article adjusting for taxes suggests this: Corporate Income Taxes and the Cost of Capital: A Correction, 53 AMERICAN ECONOMIC REVIEW 422 (1963).

** This may surprise many readers. On May 25, 2004 Yahoo! disclosed the following rates:

AAA corporate bonds:
10 years—5.21%;
20 years—6.17%

Home mortgages:
15 years—5.05% minimum, 5.57% average;
30 years—5.36% minimum, 6.13% average.

Unfortunately, bond and mortgage durations are not quoted on a comparable basis.

On this basis, this is the calculation:

Revised Valuation of Choice Two: $\dfrac{\$16{,}000}{.16}$ $=$ $\$100{,}000$

So we are back to having equity worth $100,000. Any rate below 16% doesn't fully compensate investors for the riskiness of shares in this firm. If, for example, in our Net Income Approach, investors had capitalized the net income of the leveraged Firms in Choice Two at 14%, leaving the stock in these two firms with a value of $114,285, while Firm One's equity was only valued at $100,000, this condition could not persist. Owners of equity in the Firms in Choice Two should sell their shares, borrow money, and buy shares in Firm One. In the process they bid down the price of the shares of the Firms in Choice Two. If they ultimately demand a 16% return on the equity of the Firms in Choice Two equity, which is the same return they can get by borrowing themselves:

Revised Equity of Choice Two: $\dfrac{\$16{,}000}{.16}$ $=$ $\$100{,}000$

This process is called arbitrage, and occurs when similar goods carry different prices in different markets. The other way to look at the problem is that you can spend your $100,000 in either firm, but in Firm Two you decide to invest $50,000 in stock and $50,000 in debt.

Choice Three Investment:

Return on Equity:	$50,000	@	16%	=	$8,000
Return on Debt:	$50,000	@	8%	=	$4,000
Total Return:					$12,000

Your exposure to risk in both firms is identical, so you would expect to get the same return, with one exception: Firm Two has expected bankruptcy costs (which you personally have in Firm One).

As the risk of default rises with increasing leverage, both bondholders and stockholders demand higher rates of return. Thus the same cash flows to stockholders are discounted at higher rates, to leave firm value stable. This can be graphed as follows:

Figure 4–1

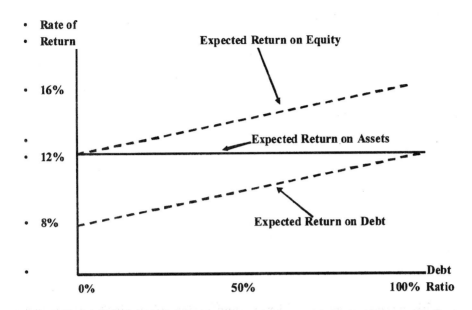

This leads us to *M&M's Proposition II,* which is that the expected rate of return on the common stock on the common stock of a levered firm increases in proportion to the debt-equity ratio of the firm. The expected return on equity required by investors will start to rise with any increase in leverage, because leverage increases the variance of expected returns. Figure 4–1 demonstrates that in efficient capital markets, where the return on firm assets is 12% under any capital structure, gains from increased leverage in the stated rate of return on equity are accompanied by gradually rising interest costs for the firm. As the percentage of debt in the capital structure increases, the rate of increase in interest rates accelerates, as creditors must now be compensated for default (bankruptcy) risk. At extreme levels of risk, the expected return on equity rises more slowly, because debt holders are taking on part of the risk. But in all cases, the expected returns to the firm remain constant.

The One–Owner Corporation Example

We will look at the problem another way. Assume that you have $50,000 to invest, and a corporation with a value of $100,000 (earning $12,000) is for sale. Assume that either you or the corporation can borrow $50,000 @ 8% interest. If the corporation borrows the money, it will buy back half of its stock, and you will buy the other shares for your $50,000. If you borrow the money, you'll buy all the stock for $50,000. As the following example shows, you should be indifferent as between these choices:

	Choice One	**Choice Two**
Gross income	$12,000	$12,000
Firm interest expense	0	-4,000
Net firm profits	$12,000	$8,000
Less interest paid by shareholder	-$4,000	0
Net available to shareholder	$8,000	$8,000

Thus the investor will be indifferent about who borrows the money. If there is risk of default, the investor might prefer having the firm borrow, because the stockholder has limited liability. But if the investor can get the bank to lend on the security of the stock, without recourse, there isn't any difference.

This is Modigliani and Miller's *"Proposition I,"* that a firm cannot change the total value of its securities just by splitting its cash flows into different streams through different securities. The consequence of this Proposition I is that the value of a firm's investments is independent of the type of financing used to engage in these projects.

How is this proposition greeted in the courts? One example is found in LaSalle Talman Bank, F.S.B. v. United States, 45 Fed. Cl. 64 (Ct. Claims, 1999). This case was brought against the government for a regulatory "taking," in that savings and loan associations, also known as "thrifts," were forced by a change in regulations either to seek new capital by selling more shares or by merging. This was caused when new laws reversed the previous practice of allowing treatment of goodwill (remember this intangible asset that represents the amount paid for a business in excess of the value of its tangible assets?) as an asset for purposes of calculating debt-equity ratios for thrifts, which were required to maintain a certain level. Prior to this time regulatory authorities had encouraged solvent thrifts to purchase insolvent ones, and to treat the price, to the extent it exceeded the net assets of the acquired thrift, as goodwill (called "regulatory goodwill"), and the equivalent of a tangible asset for regulatory purposes. Once this rule was reversed, many thrifts, including the plaintiff, found themselves in noncompliance with the new minimum capitalization rules, and were forced to seek either new financing or a merger partner. It's worth noting that banking regulation sets maximum levels of leverage for banks and thrifts, based on their capital. Regulated financial institutions are among the most highly leveraged of institutions, being able to borrow over ten times their capital. Hundreds of suits were brought in the Court of claims, and summary judgment was granted on the merits in the lead case. What follows is a discussion of the damage issue, and how a thrift might have been injured by a reduction in leverage:

"The Value of Leverage

"The assumption behind plaintiff's presentation is that one reason supervisory goodwill has value is that it permits leveraging, i.e., using this capital to attract disproportionately more in low-interest deposits, which in turn permit lending at higher yields. Defendant offered Professor Merton Miller, a Nobel Prize-winning economist, to rebut this assertion.

"Although Professor Miller may be a brilliant academic, his generalized theories bear little relation to the specific context of the savings and loan industry. For example, his assertion that leverage does not provide a thrift with any net benefit cannot be squared with the real world. Professor Miller testified that leverage exacerbates a company's potential losses as well as its profits. This is true. But his conclusion that leverage has no net value is based on the assumption that the probability of negative and positive interest rate spreads is equal, and hence that it is equally likely that a thrift will garner negative and positive net earnings. Although there have been periods when the interest rate spread has been negative—the early 1980s is an obvious example—these periods are exceptions to the normal, positive spread that forms the foundation for the entire savings and loan industry. As Professor James testified, if a positive interest rate spread was not the norm, the thrift industry would not exist. Indeed, the industry is viable because positive interest rate spreads are the norm.

"During trial, it became apparent that Professor Miller refuses to acknowledge this position because he cannot accept that supervisory goodwill had value. He testified: 'Phasing out supervisory goodwill is not the same as taking a chicken farm. A chicken farm is a valuable asset.' Of course, if supervisory goodwill was not a valuable asset, there would have been no need for Talman to replace it either by issuing preferred stock or agreeing to be acquired by ABN AMRO. But that was not the case. Professor Miller's testimony was skewed by his refusal to recognize that supervisory goodwill did have value. Moreover, Professor Miller's hypothesis that leverage has no value, which underlies the first of the Modigliani & Miller propositions,* is premised upon numerous assumptions which he did not establish, including that capital markets are perfectly efficient and individual investors can borrow at the same rate as financial institutions."

Id. at 79.

QUESTIONS

1. What is the court's essential challenge to Professor Miller's analysis?
2. If you were taking the position in court that leverage has no value, given this court's reaction to Professor Miller's testimony, how could you improve the odds of persuading a court of Professor Miller's position?

Why Capital Structure Matters

Companies that repurchased stock two years ago are in a world of hurt.

By MICHAEL MILKEN

---

* These propositions are widely known as the "M&M" propositions. Proposition II is that the expected rate of return on equity increases in proportion to the debt-equity ratio, which is discussed later in this Part.

The Wall Street Journal, April 21, 2009, page A21

Thirty-five years ago business publications were writing that major money-center banks would fail, and quoted investors who said, "I'll never own a stock again!" Meanwhile, some state and local governments as well as utilities seemed on the brink of collapse. Corporate debt often sold for pennies on the dollar while profitable, growing companies were starved for capital.

If that all sounds familiar today, it's worth remembering that 1974 was also a turning point. With financial institutions weakened by the recession, public and private markets began displacing banks as the source of most corporate financing. Bonds rallied strongly in 1975–76, providing underpinning for the stock market, which rose 75%. Some high-yield funds achieved unleveraged, two-year rates of return approaching 100%.

The accessibility of capital markets has grown continuously since 1974. Businesses are not as dependent on banks, which now own less than a third of the loans they originate. In the first quarter of 2009, many corporations took advantage of low absolute levels of interest rates to raise $840 billion in the global bond market. That's 100% more than in the first quarter of 2008, and is a typical increase at this stage of a market cycle. Just as in the 1974 recession, investment-grade companies have started to reliquify. Once that happens, the market begins to open for lower-rated bonds. Thus BB- and B-rated corporations are now raising capital through new issues of equity, debt and convertibles.

This cyclical process today appears to be where it was in early 1975, when balance sheets began to improve and corporations with strong capital structures started acquiring others. In a single recent week, Roche raised more than $40 billion in the public markets to help finance its merger with Genentech. Other companies such as Altria, HCA, Staples and Dole Foods, have used bond proceeds to pay off short-term bank debt, strengthening their balance sheets and helping restore bank liquidity. These new corporate bond issues have provided investors with positive returns this year even as other asset groups declined.

The late Nobel laureate Merton Miller and I, although good friends, long debated whether this kind of capital-structure management is an essential job of corporate leaders. Miller believed that capital structure was not important in valuing a company's securities or the risk of investing in them.

My belief—first stated 40 years ago in a graduate thesis and later confirmed by experience—is that capital structure significantly affects both value and risk. The optimal capital structure evolves constantly, and successful corporate leaders must constantly consider six factors—the company and its management, industry dynamics, the state of capital markets, the economy, government regulation and social trends. When these six factors indicate rising business risk, even a dollar of debt may be too much for some companies.

Over the past four decades, many companies have struggled with the wrong capital structures. During cycles of credit expansion, companies have often failed to build enough liquidity to survive the inevitable contractions. Especially vulnerable are enterprises with unpredictable revenue streams that end up with too much debt during business slowdowns. It happened 40 years ago, it happened 20 years ago, and it's happening again.

Overleveraging in many industries—especially airlines, aerospace and technology—started in the late 1960s. As the perceived risk of investing in such businesses grew in the 1970s, the price at which their debt securities traded fell sharply. But by using the capital markets to deleverage—by paying off these securities at lower, discounted prices through tax-free exchanges of equity for debt, debt for debt, assets for debt and cash for debt—most companies avoided default and saved jobs. (Congress later imposed a tax on the difference between the tax basis of the debt and the discounted price at which it was retired.)

Issuing new equity can of course depress a stock's value in two ways: It increases the supply, thus lowering the price; and it "signals" that management thinks the stock price is high relative to its true value. Conversely, a company that repurchases some of its own stock signals an undervalued stock. Buying stock back, the theory goes, will reduce the supply and increase the price. Dozens of finance students have earned Ph.D.s by describing such signaling dynamics. But history has shown that both theories about lowering and raising stock prices are wrong with regard to deleveraging by companies that are seen as credit risks.

Two recent examples are Alcoa and Johnson Controls each of which saw its stock price increase sharply after a new equity issue last month. This has happened repeatedly over the past 40 years. When a company uses the proceeds from issuance of stock or an equity-linked security to deleverage by paying off debt, the perception of credit risk declines, and the stock price generally rises.

The decision to increase or decrease leverage depends on market conditions and investors' receptivity to debt. The period from the late–1970s to the mid–1980s generally favored debt financing. Then, in the late '80s, equity market values rose above the replacement costs of such balance-sheet assets as plants and equipment for the first time in 15 years. It was a signal to deleverage.

In this decade, many companies, financial institutions and governments again started to overleverage, a concern we noted in several Milken Institute forums. Along with others, including the U.S. Chamber of Commerce, we also pointed out that when companies reduce fixed obligations through asset exchanges, any tax on the discount ultimately costs jobs. Congress responded in the recent stimulus bill by deferring the tax for five years and spreading the liability over an additional five years. As a result, companies have already moved to repurchase or exchange more than $100 billion in debt to strengthen their balance sheets. That has helped save jobs.

The new law is also helpful for companies that made the mistake of buying back their stock with new debt or cash in the years before the market's recent fall. These purchases peaked at more than $700 billion in 2007 near the market top—and in many cases, the value of the repurchased stock has dropped by more than half and has led to ratings downgrades. Particularly hard hit were some of the world's largest companies (i.e., General Electric, AIG, Merrill Lynch); financial institutions (Hartford Financial, Lincoln National, Washington Mutual); retailers (Macy's, Home Depot); media companies (CBS, Gannett); and industrial manufacturers (Eastman Kodak, Motorola, Xerox).

Without stock buybacks, many such companies would have little debt and would have greater flexibility during this period of increased credit constraints. In other words, their current financial problems are self-imposed. Instead of entering the recession with adequate liquidity and less debt with long maturities, they had the wrong capital structure for the time.

The current recession started in real estate, just as in 1974. Back then, many real-estate investment trusts lost as much as 90% of their value in less than a year because they were too highly leveraged and too dependent on commercial paper at a time when interest rates were doubling. This time around it was a combination of excessive leverage in real-estate-related financial instruments, a serious lowering of underwriting standards, and ratings that bore little relationship to reality. The experience of both periods highlights two fallacies that seem to recur in 20–year cycles: that any loan to real estate is a good loan, and that property values always rise. Fact: Over the past 120 years, home prices have declined about 40% of the time.

History isn't a sine wave of endlessly repeated patterns. It's more like a helix that brings similar events around in a different orbit. But what we see today does echo the 1970s, as companies use the capital markets to push out debt maturities and pay off loans. That gives them breathing room and provides hope that history will repeat itself in a strong economic recovery.

It doesn't matter whether a company is big or small. Capital structure matters. It always has and always will.

Mr. Milken is chairman of the Milken Institute.

4.   THE REAL WORLD

No one challenges the logic of the M&M thesis. But even M&M acknowledge that we observe the use of debt and preferred stock in capital structures, and that these capital structures vary across firms. Explaining why this happens involves relaxing the assumptions of the M&M thesis.

A.   DEBT AND TAXES

First let's relax the "no taxes" assumption and introduce taxes at current maximum rates. For individuals, assume that the marginal income tax rate is approximately 40% on income over $250,000. For corporations, assume that the top marginal rate is approximately 35%.* Using the same example as before, assume that each firm dividends all its income to shareholders, and that the shareholders also own the debt in Firm Two

Firm One is an all equity firm with $100,000 invested and expected return of $12,000.

	Corporate Level	Shareholder Level		
		Payments	Taxes @ 40%	Net
Net corporate income	$12,000			
Less corporate taxes @ 35%:	(4,200)			
Corporate income after taxes	$7,800			
Dividend to shareholders	($7,800)	$7,800	($3,120)	$4,680

Firm Two has $50,000 equity and $50,000 borrowings with an expected return to shareholders of $8,000.

	Corporate Level	Investor Level		
		Payments	Taxes @ 40%	Net to s/h
Operating income	$12,000			
less interest	(4,000)	$4,000	($1,600)	$2,400
Net Income	$8,000			
Less corporate taxes @ 35%	(2,800)			
Corporate income after taxes	$5,200			
Dividend to shareholders	($5,200)	$5,200	($2,080)	$3,120
Totals:		$9,200	($3,680)	$5,520

Thus owning all of the debt and equity in a leveraged firm increases total after tax wealth of shareholders from $4,680 to $5,520, an increase of approximately 18%. This is because every dollar paid as interest reduces corporate taxes by 35%. Thus, in Firm Two, the interest tax shield is .35 times the interest payments, or .35 x $4,000 = $1,400. These are funds that are available to shareholders (or to the firm for expansion) not

---

* We have ignored the choice between individual debt and corporate debt in these examples. If individual taxpayers can obtain more tax benefits from interest deductions than can corporations, then individual borrowing may be preferable. But if some shareholders pay no current taxes on corporate income (as in the case of non-profit organizations and pension plans where all taxes are paid by plan beneficiaries on a deferred basis), then corporate borrowing is clearly preferable. Thus, in our example, if an individual can borrow the same $50,000 at 8%, the individual interest expense deduction is $1,600 at 40%, or more than the corporate deduction of $1,400. For investors in lower brackets, corporate borrowing will be more attractive. For a considerable period the top marginal Federal Income Tax rate was 39.6% for individuals. Rates began a decline in the Bush administration, but when state income taxes are added, marginal rates for many individuals are at or above 40%. At present top Federal marginal rates for individuals are very close to those for corporations. Politics being what it is, there is no assurance that top marginal individual rates will not rise again.

available in an all-equity firm. Naturally, investors will capitalize this additional after-tax income. The "tax shield" for debt thus raises the value of the leveraged firm. At what rate would investors capitalize these savings? Investors generally use a firm's beta to determine the riskiness of its earnings in a diversified portfolio. But we all know that nothing is more certain than death and taxes. Tax rates may vary somewhat over time, but corporate tax rates have been quite stable over a long period. So as long as the firm expects to earn at least enough to cover its interest payments, the tax deduction becomes quite certain, and should thus be capitalized at a relatively low rate. The most common assumption used in capitalizing these deductions is that they are as certain as the interest payments on the debt, so that the interest rate creditors charge is the appropriate capitalization rate. Thus, in our previous example, if debt carries an 8% interest rate, we would capitalize it as follows:

$$\text{PV Tax Shield} \ = \ \frac{\$1,400}{.08} \ = \ \$17,500$$

Quick Check Question 4.1

In 2003 the Federal Income Tax rate on dividends received by individuals was reduced to 15%. What effect would this have on the incentives of corporations to pay interest rather than dividends? In the two firms shown above, what would the net payments to investors be under the new laws?

This tax shield explained part of the attraction of the leveraged buyouts ("*LBOs*") of the 1980s. Firms that carried too little debt lost the tax savings associated with debt. In some cases bidders were able to make an offer based on the capitalized value of the cash flows of a leveraged firm, including the discounted present value of the tax shield, which was greater than the current market value of the target firm.

The LBO phenomenon was not without some missteps, however. Some LBOs of the 1980s were too highly leveraged, and the debtors defaulted. This suggests that there is an optimal amount of debt—the most that can be borne with minimal bankruptcy costs. Even taking taxes into consideration, Modigliani and Miller recognized that the tax subsidy did not counsel an all-debt capital structure, because of the introduction of bankruptcy costs.*

B.   WEIGHTED AVERAGE COST OF CAPITAL

Corporate managers need to know the cost of capital so they can determine whether new projects are positive net present value projects—

---

* Franco Modigliani and Merton H. Miller, Corporate Income Taxes and the Cost of Capital: A Correction, 53 AMERICAN ECONOMIC REVIEW 422, 442 (1963).

whether they will return profits at least equal to the firm's cost of capital. Lawyers may need to know the cost of capital for other purposes. Public utilities, for example, are allowed to recover their cost of capital as part of the rates regulators permit them to charge. There may be instances in corporate disclosure documents describing new projects where the lawyers should ask corporate officials if they have undertaken these calculations, and how they have done so. As we pointed out in Chapter Three, in an all-equity firm with traded shares, it's pretty easy to calculate the firm's cost of capital. One simply needs to know the earnings per share and the market value of shares, and divide earnings by the market value of the shares. You get to the same place by dividing earnings per share by the stock price. (Here we ignore various measures of earnings such as EBITDA, and the effect of "fully diluting outstanding shares by the number of optioned shares not yet exercised.")

Very few firms are all equity. (The exceptions are high technology companies just developing products, but they often don't have earnings to use as a basis for these calculations.) M&M taught us that the value of a firm is the value of its business. One way to determine this is to sum up the market value of its debt and the market value of its equity. Now, if we know its earnings before interest, we know its earnings, right? All we need to do now is divide earnings before interest by the market value of debt and equity.

We can be a little more specific in calculating a cost of capital for a firm. We may know, for example, what the firm currently pays for its borrowings. So we now know the cost of debt. Any beta we calculate for the firm's stock will reflect the greater riskiness introduced by the presence of debt. Betas observed in the market thus reflect not only the volatility of the company's business, but also its capital structure. The latter factor is sometimes called "financial risk." Thus a glance at betas for firms with similar businesses may reveal widely different betas, depending upon their capital structure. If we know the risk-free rate, the equity premium and the firm's beta, we can calculate the cost of equity capital (which we can also do by taking EPS and the stock price). Assume now that the firm has an 8% cost of debt, which represents 50% of the market value of its securities, and a cost of equity of 15% for the other 50% of the market value of its securities.

Typically experts will compute the *Weighted Average Cost of Capital* ("*WACC*") by calculating separate costs of debt and equity, and weighting each in proportion to its role in the firm's capital structure. This can be expressed as follows:

$$\text{WACC} = \left(\frac{\text{Value of Debt}}{\text{Value of Firm}} \times \text{interest rate}\right) + \left(\frac{\text{Value of Equity}}{\text{Value of Firm}} \times \text{capitalization rate}\right)$$

In more traditional notation:

$$\text{WACC} = \left(\frac{D}{V} \times r_D\right) + \left(\frac{E}{V} \times r_E\right)$$

Where r = interest rate or rate of return. Thus, if a firm with a total market value of its debt and equity of $100 million is paying 8% for debt, which accounts for 50% of its capital structure and trades at face value, and if the cost of equity capital is 15%, the weighted average cost of capital can be calculated as follows:

$$\text{WACC} = \frac{(\$50{,}000{,}000 \times .08)}{\$100{,}000{,}000} + \frac{(\$50{,}000{,}000 \times .15)}{\$100{,}000{,}000} = (.5 \times .08) + (.5 \times .15) = .115$$

We have omitted one item from this calculation: as we have previously noted, interest costs are deductible for a firm, and thus increase the cash available to pay to equity investors. Thus the true WACC should be the weighted average cost of equity and the weighted average after-tax cost of debt. In the previous example, if the firm's tax rate is 35%, we calculate the after-tax cost of debt as follows:

After tax cost of debt = $(r_D)(1 - T_C)$

where T_C is the corporation's tax rate.

Thus, where the cost of debt is .08 and the tax rate is .35, the cost of debt is shown as follows:

$$r_D = (.08)(.65) = .052.$$

Our previous calculation for a firm with 50% debt in its capital structure would now be as follows:

$$\text{WACC} = \frac{(\$50{,}000{,}000 \times .052)}{\$100{,}000{,}000} + \frac{(\$50{,}000{,}000 \times .15)}{\$100{,}000{,}000} = (.5 \times .052) + (.5 \times .15) = .101$$

NOTE: CAPITAL STRUCTURE, RELEVERAGING AND FINANCING DECISIONS

Recapco has an all-equity capital structure, of 1,000,000 shares of common stock with net earnings of $10 million, a market value of $100 per share, and an aggregate market value of $100 million. Assume the market rate of return is 10%. Further assume that Recapco is a no-growth company. The interest rate on Treasury securities is 6%, and the market capitalization rate is 10%. Recapco's earnings after taxes are $10 million, or $10.00 per share. Assume there are no transaction costs in effecting the recapitalization. Assume a corporate tax rate of 35%.

Now assume that Recapco can borrow $100 million at 8% interest, and invest it in a project earning $8.5 million in perpetuity. Is this a good investment?

One's first reaction might be that any time you can invest someone else's money (the creditors) at a return greater than the cost of the funds, this is a no-brainer, and obviously a net present value project. But keep in mind that the relevant cost of capital is the weighted average cost of capital, which, with these numbers, is 10%. If the project only returns 8.5%, it's a negative net present value project for the firm. Why does the firm's cost of capital rather than the project's cost become the relevant number? Keep in mind that borrowing so much money increases the risk borne by the shareholders. In this case, risk is increased and the shareholders would demand a risk-adjusted return *above* the 10% they are currently earning. While the borrowings coupled with the returns on the new project, after interest expense, would contribute $500,000 to net earnings available to shareholders, that would not be sufficient to compensate them for the increased risk, as reflected in the higher beta, higher discount rate for share earnings, and thus the market price would decline.

We can demonstrate this as follows. If the T-bill rate is 6%, and the market return is 10%, the Equity Premium is 4%. Obviously an unlevered Recapco in this example has a beta of one. What happens if we introduce 50% leverage? Now we need to relever our beta calculations. Start with the notion that both stockholders and creditors receive a share of the firm's cash flow. Typically the debtholders' claims are much more secure, which is to say that they have a very low variance. Many analysts assume that corporate debt has a beta of zero, especially for large blue-chip companies. For our purposes, let's assume a beta of 0.2 for the debt.

If you owned a portfolio of all the firm's securities, its beta would be equivalent to the beta of its assets. Assuming our new project has the same beta as existing projects, in our example the beta of Recapco's assets remains one. And if investors required a 10% return on its assets before the borrowing, they will collectively require a 10% return after the borrowing. Necessarily, then, the beta of a portfolio of all the firm's securities has to have a beta of one. But if we assume that the debt has a beta of 0.2 (because it must be repaid with certainty, and isn't very risky), you can readily see what will happen to the beta of the stock—it must increase. The equation that expresses this relationship is

$$\beta equity = \beta asset + (\beta asset—\beta debt)debt/equity$$

Thus, if the original beta of the assets was 1.0, and remains that after the financing, we solve as follows:

$$\beta equity = 1.0 + (1.0 - 0.2)(50/50) = 1.0 + (0.8/1) = 1.0 + 0.8;$$

$$\beta equity = 1.8$$

And now we can calculate the return demanded on Recapco's stock as follows:

$$R = 6\% + 4\% (1.8) = 13.2\%.$$

Now we can see that our project provides an additional $500,000 for the common stockholders, after interest is paid. If we capitalize $10.5 million at 13.2%, we obtain:

$$\frac{\$10,500,000}{.132} = \$79,545,454$$

So our investment decision turned out to be a poor one, if we invested in a project returning only 8%. Note that we have omitted the tax benefits of leverage in these calculations. If Recapco now has an interest expense of

$8,000,000 on its borrowings, this is deductible. Assuming the corporate tax rate is 35%, this produces a tax saving for the company of $8,000,000 x 0.35 = $2,800,000. Adding this saving to net income produces the following calculation for the value of the firm's equity:

$$\frac{\$13,475,000}{.132} = \$102,083,333$$

This illustrates the power of the "tax subsidy" or "tax shield" for corporate debt. Absent taxes, this isn't a good deal for shareholders. With taxes, it's acceptable. But would the shareholders be even better off if the firm borrowed funds to create leverage and tax deductions and bought back half of its shares at the market price of $100?

Unleveraging

Recall in Chapter Three that Time–Warner decided to issue new shares in order to retire debt. Time was extremely heavily indebted, which meant that the interest rates on its debt were quite high in relation to the overall return on the company's assets. At a time when Time's stock was trading at $117, Time announced two proposed offerings to its shareholders, the first in the form of a Dutch auction and the second at $80 per share. With stock trading at $117, do you wonder why Time's board felt it necessary to offer new shares at such a low price? Note that with very high interest rate debt, the tax shield of debt is quite large. This example will explore that question. Assume that Recapco's capital structure includes 1,000,000 shares of common stock, with a total market value of $100,000,000 ($100 per share) and $100,000,000 of debt with an 8% interest rate (with face and market value identical). Recapco proposes a recapitalization in which it will sell new shares of stock to redeem all of its debt at its face value, with no premium. At this time, before the recapitalization, the interest rate on Treasury securities is 6%, and the market capitalization rate is 10%. Recapco's earnings after interest and taxes are $10 million, or $10.00 per share. We will assume there are no transaction costs in effecting the recapitalization. Assume a corporate tax rate of 35%.

1. *What is the beta of Recapco's shares before the repurchase? What will its beta be after the new offering?*

The first part is easy. The market capitalization rate is 10%, and Recapco stock currently returns 10%, so its beta must be one.

The second part applies our formula for an unleveraged beta from Part 3.E of Chapter Three:

Unlevered Beta $= \dfrac{\text{Leveraged Beta of the company}}{1 + (1\text{--tax rate for company}) (\text{Percent debt / percent equity})}$

In this case:

$$\text{Unlevered Beta} = \frac{1.0}{1 + (1-.35)(50/50)} = \frac{1.0}{1 + (.65)(1)} = \frac{1}{1.65} = .606$$

2. *What will net earnings after interest and taxes be after the redemption?*

Recapco had $18 million earnings before interest payments and federal income taxes before. Now it lacks the $8 million interest expense, but it also lacks the .35% interest deduction, which produced $2,800,000 in tax savings. So we must reduce the $18 million by $2.8 million, to $15.2 million.

3. *How many shares will Recapco have to issue to raise the $100 million needed to redeem the debt?*

Recall that Recapco's beta is now .606. Now we need to calculate what return investors will demand on a stock with this beta. Recall the cost of capital equation from Part 3.D of Chapter Three:

Cost of Capital = Risk Free Return + (beta × equity premium)

In Recapco's case, this means:

Cost of Capital = .06 + (.606 × .04) = .06 + (.024) = .084

This means it will take $100,000,000 × .084, or $8.4 million in earnings on common stock, to raise the $100 million to repurchase the debt. (Since Recapco is losing its debt shield, do you begin to see a problem?) Recall that Recapco now has only $15.2 million in after-tax earnings, so that the new investors will demand $8,400,000/$15,200,000 = 55.3% of all earnings available to the common stock. This means the ratio of new common to old common will be as follows:

$$\text{Ratio of } \frac{\text{new}}{\text{old}} \text{ commonstock} = \frac{.553}{.447} = 1.237$$

This means that 1,237,000 new common shares must be issued to raise $100 million.

4. *What do you expect the market price of Recapco's shares will be after the recapitalization?*

This is the easy part. Earnings of $15,200,000 are divided by 2,237,000 shares, to determine earnings per share of $6.80 per share. Divide this by Recapco's cost of capital: $6.80/.084 = $80.96. Multiplied by 2,235,000 shares, Recapco now has a total market value of $180,952,380. Recall that it was worth $200 million before we began.

What's happened here? The primary factor is that Recapco lost a tax shield worth $2,800,000. If we capitalize the tax shield at the unleveraged cost of capital, we get $2,800,000/.084 = $33,333,333. So what may be good for consumers, paying off debt, isn't always so great for corporations and their shareholders.

C. DEBT AND AGENCY COSTS

Differences in tax treatment of interest and dividends aren't the entire explanation for the use of debt. Debt existed in capital structures before income taxes were introduced in 1913. At least since Adam Smith, economists have observed that corporate managers don't always behave as shareholders would like.* Managers may not work as hard as shareholders would prefer. Funds may be spent wastefully on benefits for managers—high salaries, fancy offices, corporate jets, etc. And profits may be reinvested in negative net present value projects. Thus, if the firm's cost of capital is 10%, managers should never reinvest in projects with an expected return below 10%, because shareholders can invest for themselves at 10%.

Jensen & Meckling formally modeled the agency cost problem identified by Adam Smith. They argued that a manager's decisions diverged from those of an owner-manager, because the manager did not bear the full costs of his decisions, nor obtain the full benefit of them. They then described some of the devices designed to reduce these divergences, such as monitoring (by outside accountants and directors, for example) and bonding (often in the form of incentive compensation). Even where these devices are successful, they are also costly, leading the authors to the conclusion that there were irreducible costs associated with the agency relationship, and that they were the sum of the costs of divergence from the owners' goals plus the monitoring and bonding costs incurred.

"Theory of the Firm: Managerial Behavior, Agency Costs and Ownership Structure"

By Michael Jensen and William Meckling.
3 Journal of Financial Economics 305, 333–34 (1976).

"In general if the agency costs engendered by the existence of outside owners are positive it will pay the absentee owner (i.e., shareholders) to sell out to an owner-manager who can avoid these costs. This could be accomplished in principle by having the manager become the sole equity holder by repurchasing all of the outside equity claims with funds obtained through the issuance of limited liability debt claims and the use of his own personal wealth. This single-owner corporation would not suffer the agency costs associated with outside equity. Therefore there must be some compelling reasons why we find the diffuse-owner corporate firm financed by equity claims so prevalent as an organizational form.

"An ingenious entrepreneur eager to expand, has open to him the opportunity to design a whole hierarchy of fixed claims on assets and earnings, with premiums paid for different levels of risk. Why don't we observe large corporations individually owned with a tiny fraction of the

---

* "The directors of such companies, however, being the managers of other people's money than of their own, it cannot well be expected that they should watch over it with the same anxious vigilance with which the partners in a private copartnery frequently watch over their own. Like the stewards of a rich man, they are apt to consider attention to small matters as not for their master's honor, and very easily give themselves a dispensation from having it. Negligence and profusion, therefore, must always prevail, more or less, in the management of the affairs of such a company." Adam Smith, THE WEALTH OF NATIONS (1976, Cannan edition, 1937), p. 700.

capital supplied by the entrepreneur in return for 100 percent of the equity and the rest simply borrowed?* We believe there are a number of reasons: (1) the incentive effects associated with highly leveraged firms, (2) the monitoring costs these incentive effects engender, and (3) bankruptcy costs.

* * *

"We don't find many large firms financed almost entirely with debt type claims (i.e., non-residual claims) because of the effect such a financial structure would have on the owner-manager's behavior. Potential creditors will not loan $100,000,000 to a firm in which the entrepreneur has an investment of $10,000. With that financial structure the owner-manager will have a strong incentive to engage in activities (investments) which promise very high payoffs if successful even if they have a very low probability of success. If they turn out well, he captures most of the gains, if they turn out badly, the creditors bear most of the costs."

Jensen and Meckling illustrated their point with a figure that showed the situation facing a 100% owner-manager of a firm. Under these conditions the manager had to choose the level of effort he would expend, and efforts he would make to economize on non-essential fringe benefits, whether comfortable offices, excess staff to serve him, or company club memberships and cars (all lumped under the heading of non-pecuniary benefits, which we will call "shirking"). In the 100% ownership situation, the manager was forced to internalize all shirking costs, in the form of a direct loss of net income. (This is demonstrated by the budget line facing the owner-manager.) In their example, they then demonstrate the effects of a sale of part of the business to a passive outsider who takes no precautions to limit shirking expenses. Now the manager's situation changes: the budget line facing the manager shifts to a more horizontal slope, because the manager no longer pays for all costs of shirking, but only a fraction of them, while retaining 100% of the benefits of shirking. David Haddock calls this the "rube model" of investing. It is illustrated in Figure 4–3, below, drawn from Jensen & Meckling's article. The "indifference curves" show in this figure represent the theoretical trade-offs an individual would make between two goods (in this case, oversimplified, between wealth and leisure). The truth behind these curves is found in the declining marginal utility of any single good, when compared with others.

---

* This was written before the widespread appearance of Leveraged Buy–Outs in the 1980s, where capital structures approaching 100% were observed.—Ed.

Figure 4-3

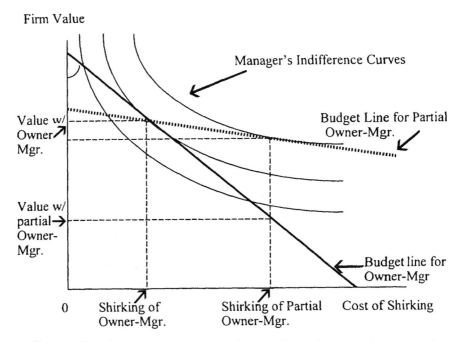

Once a firm has growth opportunities and needs more financing than the owner-manager can supply, the owner-manager faces a dilemma. If investors (and markets) are rational, they will anticipate the increased shirking of the owner-manager, and will value the company on the reduced basis shown above. For the owner-manager, selling off part ownership of the company under these conditions means that he will receive a disappointing amount for the sale of say, one-half of the shares in the business. One solution, of course, is for the manager to finance expansion with his own funds. This may be impractical for several reasons. The obvious one is that the manager may not have sufficient funds to finance a large (and potentially profitable) expansion. Although the manager could personally borrow additional funds, pledging his interest in the business as well as his personal assets, he may be reluctant to incur that much risk, by placing all his eggs in one basket.

One major solution to this valuation problem is to use outside debt financing by the corporation. Because of limited liability, the manager will not bear the increased risks of this financing. But debt, as we shall see, is a powerful disciplinary tool. Creditors, whether banks or public investors, are not naive. If the manager is left unconstrained, creditors will wish to compensate themselves ex ante for the high risk of default on firm loans with a high interest rate (which may itself increase the risk of default). In a default, the creditors will capture all firm assets, leaving the original owner-manager with worthless stock. The manager can undertake certain actions to assure outside investors that he will not increase agency costs as much as anticipated, and thus attempt to reduce interest costs. These include limits on salaries and dividends, covenants against increasing the riskiness of the firm's activities, and performance measures that must be met to avoid default. Performance measures, of course, require outside monitoring, usually in the form of audited financial statements (see Chapter Two). Some of these are costs that would also be incurred with the use of outside equity. In both cases, outside investors, whether stockholders or creditors, would probably prefer some outsiders on the board of directors to serve as monitors (and, in today's world, as an audit committee of the board).

All of this leads us to a few general observations:

1. Agency costs rise with the use of outside equity.

2. Outside debt financing reduces agency costs because of the discipline imposed, and because the owner/manager still bears the agency costs imposed on residual claimants.

3. Agency costs of debt rise with increasing use of debt (e.g., owner/managers are tempted to take higher risks because shareholders capture all the gains while bondholders suffer a large share of the losses).

Figure 4–4, also drawn from Jensen & Meckling's article, illustrates the relationships between agency costs, outside equity and outside debt:

Figure 4-4

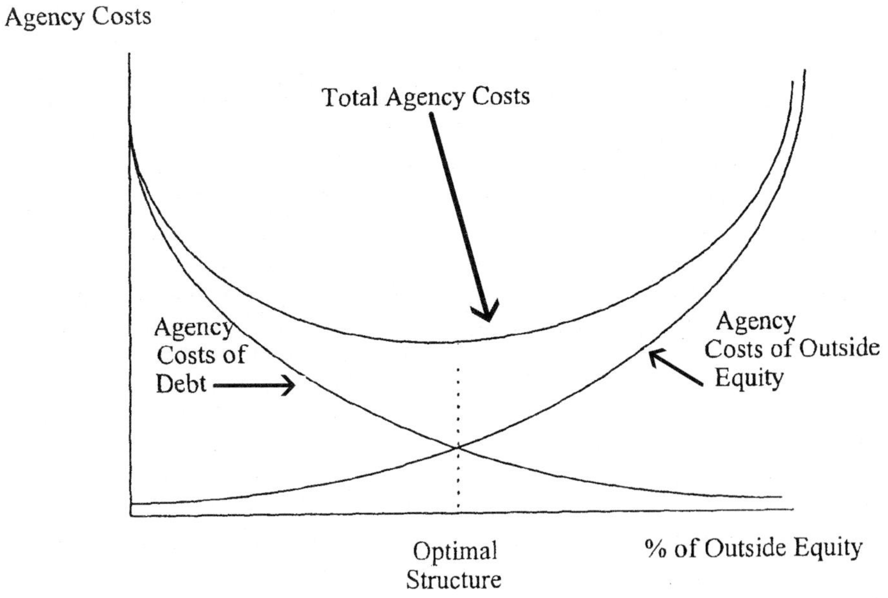

Agency Costs

Total Agency Costs

Agency Costs of Debt →

Agency Costs of Outside Equity

Optimal Structure

% of Outside Equity

Jensen and Meckling had thus laid the theoretical foundation that explained many of the LBOs of the 1980s. Agency costs of outside equity had apparently increased during 1960s and 1970s with creation of conglomerates. All too often, managers were reinvesting free cash flows in new projects that were negative net present value projects rather than paying funds to shareholders. Debt provided a discipline for managers—the obligation to pay interest and repay principal or default and lose control of the firm. A new set of entrepreneurs arose to provide 100% ownership of the equity of these firms. Generally, they formed relatively small investment partnerships to raise the capital for a leveraged buyout. Often, in order to reduce agency costs, they required managers of the acquired firm to invest heavily—all of their available wealth—in the equity of the acquired firm. Not all firms were appropriate subjects for this kind of financing. The best candidates possessed stable cash flows that reduced some of the risk of high leverage. Ideally, they also had fungible assets, that provided collateral that can be resold at a high percentage of value by creditors in the event of a default. Many were mature businesses, with few opportunities for reinvesting capital in positive net present value projects.

5.   CAPITAL STRUCTURE IN THE COURTS

As a preface to the following case, it should be noted that Federal Power Commission v. Hope Natural Gas Co., 320 U.S. 591 (1944), set the constitutional constraints on regulation of rates of public utilities. It held that in serving the public in a regulated industry, the company was entitled to recover its costs, which included the cost of capital. Regulatory bodies operating under this constraint have generally taken the position that the public is not obligated to pay for unnecessary costs incurred by utilities.

New England Tel. and Tel. Co. v. Department of Public Utilities

Supreme Judicial Court of Massachusetts, Suffolk.
327 Mass. 81, 97 N.E.2d 509 (1951).

■ QUA, C.J.

This is a suit in equity brought by the plaintiff, hereinafter called the company, under G.L. (Ter. Ed.) c. 25, § 5, n1 praying for the annulment of, or other relief from, an order of the department dated March 18, 1949, in a proceeding known as D.P.U. 8181, which disallowed a schedule of rates and charges filed by the company on April 21, 1948. . . .

* * *

When this present suit came on for hearing before the single justice of this court, the company and the department presented a stipulation wherein the company waived all issues except those relating to the adequacy of the return and the rate of return allowed by the department, including as still open the subsidiary issues (a) of adequate return upon stock capital, (b) of a safe ratio of debt capital to total capital, and (c) of the right of the company to earnings upon reinvested surplus. This stipulation included an agreement as to certain facts, among them being that the average 1949 Massachusetts intrastate rate base upon which the company was entitled to a fair return was $238,264,400, if the company was not entitled to earnings upon surplus reinvested in its plant, or $244,185,500, if the company was entitled to such earnings; that the company's total capitalization, not including surplus, was $410,570,100, consisting of long term debt of $135,000,000, advances from the American Telephone and Telegraph Company of $120,000,000, and common stock amounting to $155,570,100, making a ratio of debt capital to total capital of 62.1%; that the surplus was $9,585,000; that the composite cost of existing long term debt was 3.613% as found by the department, which (according to the stipulation and the findings) could be reduced to 3.45%[2] upon the acquisition of new debt capital at slightly lower cost; and that the composite return on the rate base resulting from the department's order would be 4.887% if the company was not entitled to earnings on reinvested surplus and 4.768% if the company was so entitled. Reference will be made to other facts agreed in so far as becomes necessary. It was further agreed that the case should be presented to the single justice upon the pleadings, the facts agreed, and the evidence presented to the department bearing upon rate of return for the determination of the issues "by the court upon its own independent judgment as to both law and fact."

* * *

It is elementary that the fixing of rates is not a proper judicial function. On the other hand, where a rate established by a public regulatory body is attacked as confiscatory the Constitution of this Commonwealth and seemingly still that of the United States require that there be a full opportunity for judicial review as to both fact and law. * * * It is the contention of the company here that the rates set up by the order of the department of March 18, 1949 (the 5% rates), do not permit a fair return upon the property of the company devoted to the public service and are confiscatory. That issue is before us in all its aspects. It was said, however, in St. Joseph Stock Yards Co. v. United States, 298 U.S. 38, 53, that "the court will not interfere with the exercise of the rate-making power unless confiscation is clearly established."

The Factual Background of the Case.

Certain undisputed facts form the background of the case and will in large measure determine the outcome. They are established by a plenitude of figures, charts, and testimony, but their substance may be stated in simple language. The company is one of the associated companies of the Bell system. Of its stock 68.9% is held by the American Telephone and Telegraph Company. During and since World War II there has been an immense increase in the demand for the company's telephone service. The company has greatly increased its facilities but nevertheless by the summer

---

2. This percentage assumes a debt ratio of approximately 45% which the department found to be safe, as hereinafter appears.

of 1948 shortly before the hearings began before the department it had not yet been able to catch up with the accumulated applications for service. To enable the company to expand its plant to meet the vast public demand, and in accordance with a custom in the Bell system, the American Telephone and Telegraph Company has advanced to the company on unsecured demand notes at 2.75% the sum of $120,000,000, which amounts to between a quarter and a third of the total capitalization of the company. This money was advanced in the expectation that it would be repaid in accordance with the custom in the system out of new issues of securities by the company. The company is under an absolute obligation to repay these advances but can do so only by means of acquiring new permanent capital either in the form of additional debt capital through bond issues or in the form of additional stock capital through stock issues. But the experts who testified were in agreement, and we suppose it is matter of common knowledge, that the proportion of debt capital cannot be extended indefinitely without adversely affecting the credit of the company, injuring the market for its stock, and to some degree that for its bonds also. It would seem that the company, with a ratio of 62.1% of debt capital to total capital, is already top heavy with debt, and that a substantial part of the new capital required must be raised by the sale of stock, how much will be a subject of discussion later in this opinion. And at this time, when it has become necessary to raise a substantial amount of new capital through an issue of stock, we are confronted with the further undoubted facts that high costs of operation since the war have greatly impaired the company's earning capacity relative to the capital invested, so that the dividends upon the stock have decreased from 6% to 4.25%, and as the hearing before the department approached its end the stock, of which the par value is $100, had fallen in the market so that it was hovering around $80 to $85. Moreover, the company is a New York corporation and under New York law cannot issue new stock at less than par. Such in rough outline was the situation with which the company and the department had to deal. The expert witness called by the Attorney General in behalf of the public conceded that the company was faced with a very serious financial problem to which he could see no answer except in some way to increase earnings.

Theories of Rate Making.

The department approached the problem by way of its so called theory of "prudent investment" upon which it and its predecessor commissions have for many years relied in ascertaining the property "actually used or useful for the convenience of the public." As applied to this case the department describes its method in these words, "our method is to ascertain, through appropriate steps, the value of the company's investment in gross intrastate plant in Massachusetts, to deduct therefrom the amount of the company's corresponding depreciation reserve, and to add thereto the amount of working capital, if any, required by the company in its intrastate operations." Application of this method led to the finding of the rate base of $238,264,400, and as hereinbefore stated the parties have now agreed upon this figure, subject to an increase to $244,185,500, if the company is entitled to earnings upon its reinvested surplus.

In determining the fair rate of return upon the rate base the department adopted the "cost of capital" method. As to debt capital this means that the company is entitled to earnings which will pay its actual interest obligations as they accrue on existing debt capital and upon new debt capital required in the immediate future, and as to stock capital, according to a statement of the department in the early part of its decision, it means "the amount which the company would have to pay in order to 'hire' its equity capital under current conditions," subject to the important consequence, which the department apparently recognizes, that commonly a company cannot issue new stock which will have a preferred position over stock already outstanding, and that the rate must therefore be sufficient to pay the same dividends upon all the stock that are required to enable the company to sell new stock.

* * *

Cost of Debt Capital.

In following the department's theories, no particular difficulty is encountered in ascertaining the probable total cost of debt capital after the acquisition of $120,000,000 of required new capital. We understand the stipulation of the parties and the pleadings to mean that the total cost of debt capital would then be 3.45%, if the debt ratio were reduced to 45%, and would be slightly higher if the debt ratio were reduced to 35%.

Cost of Stock Capital. Debt Ratio.

It is in determining the cost of stock capital that serious difficulty arises. In this connection debt ratio becomes a matter of more importance and has greater effect upon the cost of obtaining new capital. The company contended that in order to restore a sound capital structure it was necessary that enough of the required new capital should be in the form of stock capital to reduce the debt ratio to not more than 35%. The department, while recognizing the necessity of reducing the present debt ratio, was of opinion that a reduction to 45% would be safe. The company further contends that debt ratio is a matter for the exclusive determination of the management of the company. As to this last contention, we agree of course that a public regulatory board cannot assume the management of the company and cannot under the guise of rate making interfere in matters of business detail with the judgment of its officers reached in good faith and within the limits of a reasonable discretion. But we think that in this instance, in the circumstances now existing and especially in proceeding upon the "cost of capital" theory, the debt ratio is not a matter of that kind. This company is in effect seeking additional capital and higher rates in order to obtain and support such additional capital. Debt ratio substantially affects the manner and cost of obtaining new capital. It seems to us that to say the department could not even consider debt ratio would be to blind its eyes to one of the elements in the problem before it. From the standpoint of the company it might be better to have no debt capital at all. An honest board of directors might think so, and at least from the standpoint of loyalty to the company's interests it would be difficult to say that they had abused their discretion. Yet the evidence shows that such a decision under present conditions might well double or even triple the cost of new capital and increase correspondingly the burden laid upon the public for obtaining it. Surely the department could give consideration to this matter. There was a great deal of evidence on the point which we cannot undertake to summarize here. It included opinion evidence and comparisons with the debt ratios in other companies, not all of which, it is true, were wholly comparable. It appeared, however, beyond question that under conditions existing at the time of the hearing before the department, owing partly to the tax laws and to the increasing aggregations of capital in the hands of insurance companies and savings institutions, which are restricted in their stock investments, debt capital was very plentiful and cheap, while stock capital was difficult to obtain and comparatively expensive. The department also took into consideration the increased Federal income taxes and the State franchise tax incident to new stock capital. These might well amount to millions of dollars annually and might seriously increase the cost to the public of stock capital compared to that of debt capital. We think that the department could properly consider these additional taxes as elements in the problem before it. Upon all the evidence, and remembering that the burden of proof is upon the company, we are not prepared to say that the refusal of the department to adjust its rates to a reduction in the debt ratio all at once under particularly adverse conditions from the high point of 62.1% to an ideal ratio of 35% or lower and the department's adoption of the figure of 45% were in themselves unlawful or confiscatory.

* * *

We are unable, however, to follow the finding of the department that a 6% return on stock capital is adequate. We find no evidence to support the proposition that under the prevailing conditions new stock capital could be had at all unless the rate of return thereon was substantially increased above this figure. Several expert witnesses of undoubted competency testified upon the point most elaborately and after careful study and research. They differed somewhat as to the rate of return on stock capital necessary to sell new stock. The lowest estimate was that of the witness called by the Attorney General in the interest of the public, who testified that 8% would be required at a 45% debt ratio. Estimates of experienced witnesses called by the company, some of them, so far as appears, wholly disinterested, were somewhat higher and were based upon a debt ratio of only 35%. All witnesses agreed that the price of the stock must go substantially above par in the market before an issue of new stock could be sold. At the time this testimony was given the stock was selling substantially below par. Even the witness called in behalf of the public testified in substance that in order to float an issue of new stock the intrinsic worth of the stock ought to approach $120 a share, and that increased earnings were necessary. Indeed, the department itself did not attempt to find in the face of this evidence that new stock capital could be obtained at a 6% return. Its finding was that such return was "fair, reasonable, adequate for the company's needs, and likely under normal and representative conditions to maintain the price of the common stock at or above its par of 100." This may or may not be true, but it does not reach to the real point. The question was not what return might maintain the stock at par in some hoped for representative period. The question was a much more immediate and practical one. Here is one of our greatest and most necessary public utilities. It cannot be permitted to fail in its service to the public. It was legally and morally bound to increase its service to meet an insistent public demand. It did so by borrowing $120,000,000 on demand notes from a source which fortunately was available to it. It must repay this money in the near future. It cannot expect to retain this borrowed money indefinitely as part of its capital structure. Its only means of repayment is by obtaining new capital. Concededly it must not increase its debt ratio. It must therefore sell a substantial amount of stock. On the evidence it can do this only if it is allowed a return on stock capital substantially larger than the 6% allowed by the department. On this part of the case we agree with the following two paragraphs taken from the opinion of the dissenting member of the department.

"The fact is, that the investors of New England have apparently lost confidence in these securities. This is indeed unfortunate, but it is true. The stock, which is listed in Boston and New York, is currently selling at about 82, and has not been above 90 in a year or more. The majority has adopted a so-called 'historical basis' of arriving at the cost of equity capital, losing sight of the fact that this company is going to be compelled to float new issues, not in the period of from 1938 to 1946, and certainly not in 1925, but now and on the present market. No witness anywhere in the record, including the Commonwealth's own witness, Whiteside, testified that the company could acquire new equity capital at less than 8 per cent. . . .

"The company has been receiving revenues under an emergency rate increase since July, 1947, of about $5,000,000 in excess of its prior '1946' rates. We are now informed that this emergency increase is to be cancelled but that, on the other hand, an increase of almost exactly the same amount over the prior '1946' rates will restore the company's earnings to the point where its stock will go up some twenty points on the market. I feel this is a peculiar logic and one which is lacking in realism. Neither my own observations nor the testimony before us cause me to believe that any such result will follow."

It is repeatedly stated or implied in the decided cases, so far as we know without contradiction, that one of the constitutional rights of a regulated utility is the right to earn a sufficient return to maintain its credit and to obtain additional capital when needed to enable it to serve its public. It is sometimes added that earnings should be sufficient to enable something to be passed to surplus. . . . The department made no provision for surplus. If the "cost of capital" theory on which the department purported to proceed requires the cost of stock capital to be ascertained by reference to some supposedly normal period and in disregard of the stubborn facts existing in the period when the capital must be raised, instead of by reference to "the amount which the company would have to pay in order to 'hire' its equity capital under current conditions" as stated in the department's own definition of that theory, the theory must give way to the extent necessary to afford the utility its constitutional rights. Stated in a different way, if rates are to be fixed on a "cost of capital" theory so that a return of only 3.45% is allowed on debt capital, the theory must be consistently applied, and a sufficient return must be allowed on stock capital so that in fact necessary stock capital can be acquired. We do not see that the situation is materially altered by the hope or even expectation that the American company will take the full 68.9% to which it is entitled out of any new stock issue. It is not bound to take any and might not do so. Moreover, if it took its full share, the necessity for selling a large block to the general public would still exist. For the reasons above set forth, we are forced to conclude that the allowance of only a 6% return on stock capital, where less than 3 ½% has been allowed on debt capital, and the resulting overall return on both kinds of capital is only 4.887%, if surplus is not entitled to earnings, and 4.768% if surplus is entitled to earnings, was confiscatory and unlawful. It seems proper to add that if we turn away from the method and consider only the result reached, an examination of the decisions of regulatory boards and of courts convinces us that an overall return of approximately 4.8% on the rate base is considerably below that which is reasonably expected and is generally being allowed on the capital of public utilities used and useful in the public service.

Although it is beyond our power to fix rates and we certainly have no desire to attempt that task, yet it is our duty to draw to the best of our ability the line where confiscation begins, and in the circumstances of this case, in order to make our decision as useful as possible and not merely the starting point of a series of attempts to ascertain by the method of trial and error just what figure this court would allow to stand, it seems that we should state where in our judgment on the evidence before us that line must be drawn. As previously stated, there is no dispute as to the cost of debt capital. But on all the evidence, and we have nothing else to go by, it is our opinion that a return of nothing less than 8.5% will suffice to attract new stock capital at a debt ratio of 45% and to enable the company to restore its credit and properly to capitalize its new construction. This is somewhat less than the company asserted and introduced evidence to prove that it must have and is only one half of one per cent more than the expert witness called by the Attorney General testified to be necessary. It should produce an overall composite net return on all capital devoted to the public service (disregarding for the moment surplus reinvested in the business) of 6.23%, as appears below:

45% debt capital × 3.45% net return	=	1.55% net return on whole capital
55% stock capital × 8.5% net return	=	4.68% net return on whole capital
Composite net return on total of both kinds of capital		6.23%.

In our opinion therefore a net return of less than 8.5% on stock capital or less than 6.23% on the sum of both kinds of capital is below the level where confiscation begins. It does not follow that a considerably higher return might not fall within the range of reason and might not have been allowed by the department, but our duty is performed by marking the line of confiscation.

* * *

QUESTIONS

1. Why do you suppose the Department uses the cost of debt and equity separately to determine the cost of capital?

2. In determining the cost of debt, does the Department use the current yield demanded by investors on its debt or the face amount of the interest obligation? Why?

3. What rate of return is used to calculate a cost of equity capital, some historic figure or current costs of equity?

4. What method did the Department and the witnesses appear to use in determining the cost of equity capital?

5. The court said "the return to the equity owner should be commensurate with returns on investments in other enterprises having comparable risks." How would you suggest identifying stocks of such companies?

6. Why do you suppose the Department of Public Utilities Argued that the cost of capital should be determined on the basis of a hypothetical capital structure with 40% debt?

7. Has the Court ignored the effect of taxes on optimal capital structure? What treatment would you argue for if you represented the Department?

NOTE

Walt Disney Productions was not in favor on Wall Street in 1984. In January, the Wall Street Journal's "Heard on the Street" column reported that despite a lack of enthusiasm from analysts for the stock, considerable buyer interest indicated that the company might be a takeover target. The attraction, it speculated, was replacement of current management. At this time the President and Chief Executive Officer was Ronald Miller, a former college football star who married Walt Disney's daughter. By March, a Business Week article noted that Disney might be an attractive takeover target because of two underutilized assets: Disney's film library and its real estate holdings. Here we might include the Disney characters, which later became the subject of enormously successful marketing. As Fred McChesney has noted, these are unique assets, the value of which is extraordinarily difficult to determine without an auction. McChesney, Transaction Costs and Corporate Greenmail: Theory, Empirics and a Mickey Mouse Case

Study, 14 Managerial and Decision Economics 131 (1993). Perhaps indicative of Disney's problems was the fact that it had no takeover defenses in place that might delay or fend off a first bidder and allow the company to conduct an auction if necessary.

With Disney stock trading in the 50s in the early part of 1984, Saul Steinberg, through the Reliance Group, began acquiring the stock of Disney, as described in the decision reported below. One of the responses described below was Disney's agreement to purchase Arvida corporation, which was 70% owned by the Bass Brothers, who, as a result, owned 5.5% of Disney's stock. While one motivation for the acquisition may have been to interest the Bass Brothers in serving as a counter-weight to Steinberg, and perhaps to serve as a "white knight" to keep control in friendly hands, one analyst approved of the combination of land-rich Disney with an experienced Florida developer as "an eminently logical move for Disney."

Heckman v. Ahmanson

168 Cal. App.3d 119, 214 Cal. Rptr. 177 (Cal. App. 1985).

■ JOHNSON, ASSOCIATE JUSTICE.

Plaintiffs, stockholders in Walt Disney Productions, are suing to recover the payoff in the greenmailing[1] of Disney. Defendants are the Disney directors who paid the greenmail and the "Steinberg Group" to whom the money, approximately $325 million, was paid.

Plaintiffs obtained a preliminary injunction which, in effect, imposes a trust on the profit from the Disney–Steinberg transaction, approximately $60 million, and requires the Steinberg Group to render periodic accountings of the disposition of the entire proceeds. The Steinberg Group appeals from this preliminary injunction. We affirm.

As will be discussed more fully below, if plaintiffs prove the Steinberg Group breached a fiduciary duty to the corporation and its shareholders in the sale of stock to the corporation the plaintiffs would be entitled to a constructive trust upon the profits of that sale. Plaintiffs have established a reasonable probability of proving breach of fiduciary duties by the Steinberg Group. The trial court could reasonably conclude from the evidence a preliminary injunction was necessary to prevent the dissipation or disappearance of the profit during the pendency of the action and the balance of hardships involved in granting or denying the injunction incline in plaintiffs' favor.

---

1. A greenmailer creates the threat of a corporate takeover by purchasing a significant amount of the company's stock. He then sells the shares back to the company at a premium when its executives, in fear of their jobs, agree to buy him out. For further discussion of greenmail see, Lowenstein, Pruning Deadwood In Hostile Takeovers: A Proposal For Legislation (1983) 83 Colum. L. Rev. 249, 311 & fn. 249; Greene & Junewicz, A Reappraisal Of Current Regulation Of Mergers And Acquisitions (1984) 132 U. Pa. L. Rev. 647, 706–707.

Facts and Proceedings Below

In March 1984 the Steinberg Group purchased more than two million shares of Disney stock. Probably interpreting this as the opening shot in a takeover war, the Disney directors countered with an announcement Disney would acquire Arvida Corporation for $200 million in newly-issued Disney stock and assume Arvida's $190 million debt.[3] The Steinberg Group countered this move with a stockholders' derivative action in federal court to block the Arvida transaction. Nonetheless, on June 6, 1984, the Arvida transaction was consummated.

Undeterred by its failure to halt Disney's purchase of Arvida, the Steinberg Group proceeded to acquire some two million additional shares of Disney stock, increasing its ownership position to approximately 12 percent of the outstanding Disney shares. On June 8, 1984, the Steinberg Group advised Disney's directors of its intention to make a tender offer for 49 percent of the outstanding shares at $67.50 a share and its intention to later tender for the balance at $72.50 a share. The directors' response was swift. On the evening of the same day, the directors proposed Disney repurchase all the stock held by the Steinberg Group. Agreement was reached on June 11.

Under the agreement with the Steinberg Group, Disney purchased all the stock held by the group for $297.4 million and reimbursed the estimated costs incurred in preparing the tender offer, $28 million, for a total of $325.4 million, or about $77 per share. The Steinberg Group garnered a profit of about $60 million. In return, the Steinberg Group agreed not to purchase Disney stock and to dismiss its individual causes of action in the Arvida litigation. It did not dismiss the derivative claims.

Disney borrowed the entire sum necessary to repurchase its shares. This transaction, coupled with the debt assumed in the Arvida purchase, increased Disney's total indebtedness to $866 million, two-thirds of Disney's entire shareholder equity. Upon the announcement of its agreement with the Steinberg Group, the price of Disney stock dropped below $50 per share. Thus, the Steinberg Group received a price 50 percent above the market price following the transaction.

The gravamen of the action against the Steinberg Group is that it used its tender offer and the Arvida litigation to obtain a premium price for its shares in violation of its fiduciary duties to Disney and the other shareholders. The complaint seeks, among other things, rescission of Disney's repurchase agreement with the Steinberg Group, an accounting and a constructive trust upon all funds the Steinberg Group received from Disney.

---

3. Like the puff fish, a corporate delicacy will often attempt to avoid being swallowed up by making itself appear less attractive to a potential predator. See, Lowenstein, supra, at p. 313; Nathan & Sobel, Corporate Stock Repurchases in the Context of Unsolicited Takeover Bids (1980) 35 Bus. Law. 1545, 1547 & fn. 2; Rosenzweig, The Legality of "Lock–Ups" [etc.] (1983) 10 Sec. Reg. L. J., 291, 299; Prentice, Target Board Abuse of Defensive Tactics [etc.] (1983) J. Corp. L. 337, 341, 343; Greene & Junewicz, supra, 132 U. Pa. L. Rev. at p. 702.

After due notice and hearing, the trial court issued a preliminary injunction enjoining the Steinberg Group from transferring, investing or disposing of the profit[4] from its sale of Disney stock except in accordance with the standards applicable to a prudent trustee under Civil Code section 2261. The injunction also requires the Steinberg Group to notify plaintiffs and the court of every change in the form or vehicle of investment of the entire proceeds of the repurchase agreement. The injunction became effective upon plaintiffs' posting an undertaking in the sum of $1 million.

Discussion

* * *

II.   Plaintiffs Demonstrated a Reasonable Probability of Success on the Merits Entitling Them to a Constructive Trust Upon the Profits the Steinberg Group Received From Its Sale of Disney Stock.

A.   Liability of the Steinberg Group as an Aider and Abettor of the Disney Directors' Breach of Fiduciary Duty.

Although we have found no case in which a greenmailer was ordered to return his ill-gotten gains, precedent for such a judgment exists in California law.

In Jones v. H. F. Ahmanson & Co. (1969) 1 Cal.3d 93, 108–109 [81 Cal.Rptr. 592, 460 P.2d 464], our Supreme Court adopted the shareholders' Magna Carta set forth in Pepper v. Litton (1939) 308 U.S. 295 [84 L.Ed. 281, 60 S.Ct. 238]:

"A director is a fiduciary.... So is a dominant or controlling stockholder or group of stockholders.... Their powers are powers of trust...." "He who is in such a fiduciary position cannot serve himself first and his cestuis second. He cannot manipulate the affairs of his corporation to their detriment and in disregard of the standards of common decency and honesty.... He cannot use his power for his personal advantage and to the detriment of the stockholders.... For that power is at all times subject to the equitable limitation that it may not be exercised for the aggrandizement, preference, or advantage of the fiduciary to the exclusion or detriment of the cestuis. Where there is a violation of these principles, equity will undo the wrong or intervene to prevent its consummation." The ultimate question "is whether or not under all the circumstances the transaction carries the earmarks of an arm's length bargain."

Ahmanson involved a scheme in which the majority stockholders set up a holding company in a manner which made the minority shares unmarketable. The court held the facts alleged in the complaint stated a cause of action for breach of fiduciary duty. "[Defendants] chose a course of action

---

4. The profit, for purposes of the preliminary injunction, was defined as the difference paid by defendants for the stock, approximately $63.25 per share, and the total amount received under the repurchase agreement, approximately $77.50 per share, together with income earned on that amount from the date of receipt. This totals approximately $60 million.

in which they used their control of the Association to obtain an advantage not made available to all stockholders. They did so without regard to the resulting detriment to the minority stockholders and in the absence of any compelling business purpose.''

While there may be many valid reasons why corporate directors would purchase another company or repurchase the corporation's shares, the naked desire to retain their positions of power and control over the corporation is not one of them.[5]

If the Disney directors breached their fiduciary duty to the stockholders, the Steinberg Group could be held jointly liable as an aider and abettor. The Steinberg Group knew it was reselling its stock at a price considerably above market value to enable the Disney directors to retain control of the corporation. It knew or should have known Disney was borrowing the $325 million purchase price. From its previous dealings with Disney, including the Arvida transaction, it knew the increased debt load would adversely affect Disney's credit rating and the price of its stock. If it were an active participant in the breach of duty and reaped the benefit, it cannot disclaim the burden. "Where there is a common plan or design to commit a tort, all who participate are jointly liable whether or not they do the wrongful acts.''

The Steinberg Group contends there was no evidence presented to the trial court that the repurchase agreement was motivated by the Disney directors' desire to perpetuate their own control instead of a good faith belief the corporate interest would be served thereby.

At this point in the litigation, it is not necessary the court be presented with a "smoking gun.'' We believe the evidence presented to the court was sufficient to demonstrate a probability of success on the merits. The acts of the Disney directors—and particularly their timing—are difficult to understand except as defensive strategies against a hostile takeover. The Steinberg Group began acquiring Disney stock in March 1984. In May 1984 the Disney directors announced Disney would acquire Arvida and its $190 million debt. Trying to make the target company appear less attractive is a well-recognized defensive tactic by a board seeking to retain control. Furthermore, the Steinberg Group announced its tender offer for 49 percent of the outstanding Disney shares on June 8, 1984. Immediately following this announcement, the Disney directors began negotiations to repurchase the Steinberg Group's stock and reached an agreement on the repurchase two days later.

Once it is shown a director received a personal benefit from the transaction, which appears to be the case here, the burden shifts to the director to demonstrate not only the transaction was entered in good faith, but also to show its inherent fairness from the viewpoint of the corporation and those interested therein. The only evidence presented by the Disney

---

5. We recognize the Disney directors were not parties to the proceedings on the preliminary injunction nor this appeal and have not had the opportunity to tell their side of the story.

directors was the conclusory statement of one of its attorneys that "[the] Disney objective in purchasing [the] stock was to avoid the damage to Disney and its shareholders which would have been the result of [the] announced tender offer." This vague assertion falls short of evidence of good faith and inherent fairness.

* * *

The order granting a preliminary injunction is affirmed.

QUESTIONS

1. The court characterizes the repurchase price ($77.50 per share) as 50% above the market price following the transaction. Is this a fair characterization of the economics of the transaction? What kind of a profit did Steinberg earn over his costs?

2. What theories seem to be involved in the plaintiff's claim?

3. Why would additional borrowings to repurchase shares necessarily hurt stockholders and cause the stock price to fall?

4. This litigation was settled by Steinberg for $21.1 million. Do the theories expressed by the court suggest serious liability exposure?

5. In the settlement, Disney paid $24.2 million. Can you think of a reason why? Who would get this sum?

6. Subsequent to the greenmail transaction, the Bass Brothers (greenmailers themselves) acted as a "white knight" and acquired 24% of Disney. This was followed by new management (end of Walt Disney's son-in-law), led by Michael Eisner. Revenues tripled from 1984 to 1990, and Earnings went from $97.8 million in 1984 to $824 million in 1990. Eisner introduced the extension of the Disney characters as marketing tools, including all the Disney merchandise and stores, and acquired a movie studio that produced films for adults. The stock had more than doubled in value to over $135 by 1991, and return on equity rose from 8% in 1984 to 25% in 1990. The stock doubled again by 1996, and again by 2000. Does this provide a basis for concluding that paying greenmail to Steinberg was good for Disney shareholders? Thereafter, the stock price did not increase through early 2004. Michael Eisner's leadership was questioned by Roy Disney and another board member, and Comcast made an uninvited bid for Disney. Despite some opposition from institutional investors, Eisner was reelected to the Disney Board, although he was removed as Chairman.

NOTE

FMC Corporation v. Boesky, 852 F.2d 981 (7th Cir.1988), involved a suit brought by FMC against Ivan Boesky and his associates. Boesky was perhaps the most notorious insider trader of the 1980s, obtaining information about impending corporate takeovers and takeover defenses from investment bankers serving as advisers to these corporations.

FMC's management determined, with advice from its investment bankers, to engage in a recapitalization that would double the percentage of stock held by managers and FMC's Thrift Plan, which was presumably controlled by management, from roughly 20% to 40%. This would be coupled with changes in FMC's charter that would give management a veto power over future mergers. The plan called for an exchange of all existing FMC common stock for a combination of new shares and cash. Public shareholders would be offered $70 cash plus one new share for each existing share, while managers would receive 5.67 new shares and no cash. The fairness of these ratios depended on Goldman Sachs' calculation that each new share would trade for approximately $15, so that each group would receive a value of $85 per share. Boesky learned of this plan and begin buying FMC shares, which forced FMC to announce its plan earlier than it had intended. After the board approved the transaction, the market price of FMC stock rose above $85 for the proposed 5.67 shares, thus calling into question Goldman's $85 per share valuation. Goldman told the FMC board that it would have to increase the cash to be offered public shareholders, because Goldman now believed the new shares would trade for over $17. Boesky learned of this and bought nearly 10% of FMC's stock, which he sold at a profit of $20 million when FMC announced that the cash portion of the offer would be increased from $70 to $80.

In its complaint against Boesky, FMC alleged that it was injured because it was forced to pay an additional $220 million to its public shareholders to consummate the recapitalization, and that Boesky had engaged in illegal insider trading. The trial court dismissed the complaint, unable to find an injury to FMC from the insider trading (although there was little doubt that some shareholders might have a claim). The trial court held that the payment to its own shareholders did not injure FMC, because the recapitalization was essentially "a distribution of part of FMC's assets to the owners of those assets in exchange for their giving up a part of their equity interest to management," FMC Corp. v. Boesky, 673 F. Supp. 242, 250 (N.D. Ill. 1987). The court held that this was simply a redistribution of corporate assets among shareholders, and that "where the shareholders decide to distribute to themselves the assets of the corporation on a pro rata basis, absent an erosion of the asset base in such a manner as to impinge upon the rights of creditors, no one has been harmed, so the corporation has suffered no injury." The majority of the court of appeals disagreed, finding that the confidential plans about the recapitalization were corporate property that Boesky had misappropriated, and that the very act of misappropriation of its property rights was an injury to the corporation, and remanded. In this way the majority avoided the question of whether there were any monetary damages connected with the injury.

Judge Manion dissented, and took on the monetary injury question much more directly:

"FMC may be irritated, but it has not been injured. Individual shareholders who sold low may have been injured—and management shareholders who bought higher than they would have liked may think of themselves as injured—but they are not parties, and FMC has no standing to sue on their behalf.

"FMC claims that Boesky's misdeeds caused it to pay an additional $235 million to recapitalize. But that additional payment was to its shareholders. As with any corporation, FMC's assets belong to its shareholders, and a transfer from the corporation's treasury to the shareholders damages no one. As Judge Williams stated in her opinion, 'the economic effect of the transaction can therefore properly be viewed as a distribution of part of FMC's assets to the owners of those assets in exchange for their giving up a part of their equity interest to management.' 673 F. Supp. at 250.

"FMC's management obviously preferred the original plan proposed before Boesky's interference, but ... FMC could have but chose not to abandon the recapitalization. Instead, as the majority acknowledges in footnote 11, FMC's board (and management) maintained that the recapitalization was good for the company and its shareholders because it would lead to a higher return on equity. The recapitalization was approved by both the board and the shareholders after Boesky 'manipulated' the price. Thus, according to the face of the complaint, the entire injury FMC claims to have suffered, including the additional expenses incurred after Boesky's involvement, was merely the cost of FMC's choice to finance future opportunities other than through retained earnings. See D. Fischel, The Law and Economics of Dividend Policy, 67 Va. L. Rev. 699, 701–02 (1981). In his concurrence, Judge Ripple well captures the essence of FMC's position when he writes that 'the alleged ... injury to FMC for purposes of Article III standing, however, is that the structure of the corporation was changed.... It is the corporation itself that is vitally affected by the change in its structure.' In my view, varying the proportion of debt to equity or otherwise changing a company's capital structure does not affect its value. See F. Modigliani and M. Miller, The Cost of Capital, Corporation Finance and the Theory of Investment, 48 Am. Econ. Rev. 261, 268–71 (1958). As Judge Williams stated, 'it is difficult to articulate FMC's injury when all of the shareholders benefitted from the transaction, and there are no allegations of harm to creditors of FMC.' 673 F. Supp. at 251. With no injury to be found anywhere, the district judge properly found no constitutional standing and thus properly declined to call upon pendent jurisdiction to consider whether there were well-pleaded state law claims."

---

6. THE WAGES OF EXCESSIVE DEBT

The most obvious cost of excessive debt is bankruptcy, as we have noted above. But excessive debt, or at least an unusually large proportion of debt in a capital structure, also leads to certain legal consequences.

A. SUBORDINATION

Bankruptcy Code, 11 U.S.C. § 510.   Subordination

(a) A subordination agreement is enforceable in a case under this title to the same extent that such agreement is enforceable under applicable nonbankruptcy law.

(b) For the purpose of distribution under this title, a claim arising from rescission of a purchase or sale of a security of the debtor or of an affiliate of the debtor, for damages arising from the purchase or sale of such a security, or for reimbursement or contribution allowed under section 502 on account of such a claim, shall be subordinated to all claims or interests that are senior to or equal the claim or interest represented by such security, except that if such security is common stock, such claim has the same priority as common stock.

(c) Notwithstanding subsections (a) and (b) of this section, after notice and a hearing, the court may—

(1) under principles of equitable subordination, subordinate for purposes of distribution all or part of an allowed claim to all or part of another allowed claim or all or part of an allowed interest to all or part of another allowed interest; or

(2) order that any lien securing such a subordinated claim be transferred to the estate.

In re Fett Roofing and Sheet Metal Co., Inc., Bankrupt

438 F. Supp. 726 (E.D. Va. 1977), affirmed 605 F.2d 1201 (4th Cir. 1979).

■ CLARKE, J.

This matter comes before the Court on the appeal by plaintiff from an order of United States Bankruptcy Judge Hal J. Bonney, Jr., which dismissed plaintiffs' complaint, subordinated the note claims of the plaintiff to the claims of all other creditors and set aside deeds of trust which purported to secure the note claims. Appellant contends that the Bankruptcy Judge's findings of fact and conclusions of law were completely erroneous and that appellant's claims against the bankrupt should be reinstated.

The Facts

The record below discloses that the bankrupt, Fett Roofing and Sheet Metal Co., Inc., was owned and run prior to 1965 by plaintiff herein, Donald M. Fett, Sr., as a sole proprietorship. During 1965, Mr. Fett incorporated his business, transferring to the new corporation assets worth $4,914.85 for which he received 25 shares of stock. The stated capital of the corporation was never increased during the course of the corporation's existence. Mr. Fett was the sole stockholder and also the president of the corporation. The roofing business continued to be run completely by Mr. Fett much as it had been prior to its incorporation. In short, Fett Roofing was a classic "one-man" corporation. Over the years, plaintiff advanced money to his business as the need arose. Three of these transactions made in 1974, 1975 and 1976 involved the transfer to the corporation of $7,500, $40,000 and $30,000, respectively. In each instance plaintiff borrowed from the American National Bank, made the funds available to his business and took back demand promissory notes. On April 6, 1976, at a time his business had become insolvent, plaintiff recorded three deeds of trust intended to secure these notes with the realty, inventory, equipment and receivables of Fett Roofing and Sheet Metal Co., Inc. The deeds were backdated to indicate the dates on which the money had actually been borrowed. On November 8, 1976, an involuntary petition in bankruptcy was filed.

After a trial in which both sides presented considerable evidence and the plaintiff personally testified regarding his claim, Judge Bonney made the following findings of fact.

1.   The bankrupt was undercapitalized at its inception in 1965, and remained undercapitalized throughout its existence. The capital necessary for the operation and continuation of its business was provided by the complainant in the form of so-called loans on an "as-needed" basis. Promissory notes, including the three involved herein, were given to the complainant in the course of such transactions.

2.   The three deeds of trust which purport to secure the said notes were all back-dated to create the impression that they were executed contemporaneously with the advance of funds and the giving of the notes; all three were in fact executed and recorded during the first week of April 1976, when the notes were, by their terms, past due.

3.   The purpose of the deeds of trust was to delay, hinder, and defraud the creditors of the bankrupt, and to give the complainant a preference over them, in the event a liquidation of assets became necessary.

4.   Complainant was in sole control of the affairs of the bankrupt, and was its sole stockholder. His interests were at all times identical to and indistinguishable from that of the bankrupt; he was the alter ego of the bankrupt.

5.   At the time these three deeds of trust were executed and recorded, the bankrupt was, and for several months had been, unable to meet its obligations as they came due in the ordinary course of business. Many of the debts listed in the schedules filed by the bankrupt were incurred and delinquent prior to April 1976.

6.   Complainant knew that his corporation was insolvent no later than February 1976.

Based on these findings, Judge Bonney concluded that the advances made by plaintiff to his corporation were actually contributions to capital, not loans, and that claims based on them therefore should be subordinated to those of all the other creditors of the bankrupt. The Judge further found that even if the transfers had been bona fide loans, the deeds of trust intended to secure them would have been null and void as having been given with actual intent to delay, hinder and defraud creditors in violation of § 67d(2)(d) of the Bankruptcy Act, 11 U.S.C. § 107(d)(2)(d). In addition, Judge Bonney determined that such loans were given in fraud of creditors under state law and therefore were voidable under § 70(e) of the Bankruptcy Act, 11 U.S.C. § 110(e).

Because we have concluded that the Bankruptcy Judge was correct in his determination that the plaintiff's transfers of money to his corporation were capital contributions and not loans we do not consider the soundness of the last two legal findings.

The Law

* * *

Although the Court is not bound by the Bankruptcy Judge's conclusions of law and is free to make its own legal deductions, an analysis of the particular facts of this case and the relevant authorities clearly shows that the determination that plaintiff made capital contributions to the bankrupt rather than loans is legally sound.

A director, officer, majority shareholder, relatives thereof or any other person in a fiduciary relation with a corporation can lawfully make a secured loan to the corporate beneficiary. However, when challenged in court a fiduciary's transaction with the corporation will be subjected to "rigorous scrutiny" and the burden will be on him "... not only to prove the good faith of the transaction but also to show its inherent fairness from the viewpoint of the corporation and those interested therein." Pepper v. Litton, 308 U.S. 295, 84 L. Ed. 281, 60 S.Ct. 238 (1939).

Where a director or majority shareholder asserts a claim against his own corporation, a bankruptcy court, sitting as a court of equity, will disregard the outward appearances of the transaction and determine its actual character and effect.

> Similar results have properly been reached in ordinary bankruptcy proceedings. Thus, salary claims of officers, directors and stockholders in the bankruptcy of "one-man" or family corporations have been disallowed or subordinated where the courts have been satisfied that allowance of the claims would not be fair or equitable to other creditors. And that result may be reached ... where on the facts the bankrupt has been used merely as a corporate pocket of the dominant stockholder, who, with disregard of the substance or form of corporate management, has treated its affairs as his own. And so-called loans or advances by the dominant or controlling stockholder will be subordinated to claims of other creditors and thus treated in effect as capital contributions by the stockholder not only in the foregoing types of situations but also where the paid-in capital is purely nominal, the capital necessary for the scope and magnitude of the operation of the company being furnished by the stockholder as a loan.

Pepper v. Litton, supra 308 U.S. at 308–310.

The record on this appeal reveals the bankrupt to have been a large construction contractor requiring ample amounts of capital. As indicated above, the corporation was capitalized at slightly under $5,000 when it was created in 1965. No increment to this initial amount was ever formally made. According to the schedule filed with the Bankruptcy Judge, the bankrupt's debt to secured creditors alone stood at $413,000. This is a debt-to-equity ratio of over 80 to 1. While this fact by itself will not serve to convert what is otherwise a bona fide loan into a contribution to capital, it does cast serious doubt on the advances by a person in plaintiff's special situation being considered debt rather than equity. The fact that no evidence was adduced by plaintiff to show that the "borrowings" in question were formally authorized by the corporation or that interest was ever paid on them, coupled with the undisputed day-in-and-day-out control over corporate affairs wielded by plaintiff, as president and sole stockholder leave little doubt that plaintiff, ignoring corporate formalities, was infusing new capital into his business and avoiding such necessities as charter amendment or the issuance of new stock. The record discloses that the funds transferred to the corporations were used to finance the acquisition of equipment and material necessary to the functioning of the business. Although one of the advances was used to pay a bona fide tax liability, this does not affect its character as a capital contribution under the particular circumstances of this case. The fact that plaintiff at various times characterized these advances as "re-capitalization" can only reinforce a conclusion which consideration of the entire record makes inevitable.

The Courts of this circuit have had no reluctance to pierce through surface appearances in these matters and distinguish contributions to capital from genuine loans.

* * *

Similarly in L & M Realty Corp. v. Leo, 249 F.2d 668 (4th Cir. 1957), the Court of Appeals subordinated the claim of a principal shareholder, noting:

> While the amounts thus advanced were treated by the stockholders as loans to the corporation and it was not contemplated that stock was to be issued in payment of them, it is clear that they were not loans in the ordinary sense and were not intended to be paid in ordinary course, as were the claims of other creditors. The corporation was not adequately capitalized, the advancements were made shortly after it was organized and no steps were ever taken looking to their repayment. They were made in approximately equal amounts by the two stockholders owning the corporation, who actually paid other creditors in priority to themselves year after year, no interest was ever paid on them and the evidence is that the money was advanced as loans rather than as subscription to stock in the thought that this would be helpful for income tax purposes. In such situation, while the loans are not to be treated as investments in stock, it is clear that they were capital contributions to a corporation inadequately capitalized and that, having been made by the two stockholders, who completely owned and controlled the corporation, they should be subordinated to the claims of other creditors.

Although the advances contested here were made well after the corporation was created, there is evidence in the record that plaintiff had "loaned" the bankrupt money over the years and that the transfers here in issue were only the latest in a series of contributions made necessary by the corporation's grossly inadequate capitalization. Since these three transactions were "part of a plan of permanent personal financing," the fact that they did not occur at the outset of corporate existence is not crucial and the claims based on them are properly subordinated to those of other creditors.

Since the transfers made by plaintiff to the bankrupt were, in contemplation of law, capital contributions the deeds of trust purporting to secure these advances were properly set aside since there was in fact "no debt to be secured."

As the cases make clear, no one fact will result in the determination that putative loans are actually contributions to capital. The Court is guided by equitable principles that look to the result of the transaction as well as to the formal indicia of its character. A person in the special position of the plaintiff "... cannot by the use of the corporate device avail himself of the privileges normally permitted outsiders in a race of creditors." It is not necessary that fraud, deceit or calculated breach of trust be shown. Where, as here, a corporate insider, indeed the corporate alter ego, has so arranged his dealings with his corporate principal that he achieves an unfair advantage over outside creditors dealing at arms length, the Court will subordinate his claim to theirs.

In summary, the Court has accepted the Bankruptcy Judge's findings of fact pertaining to the nature of the advances made by plaintiff and the nature of the corporation as plaintiff's alter ego, as supported by substantial evidence and not clearly erroneous. Further, it finds ample support in the facts and in the relevant authorities for treating plaintiff's advances to the bankrupt as contributions to capital and not as loans.

For the foregoing reasons, the Order appealed from is AFFIRMED.

QUESTIONS

1. When the court says an insider such as a director, officer or majority shareholder owes a duty of fairness when lending on a secured basis to the corporation "and those interested therein," who else is interested?

2. If the sole shareholder makes an initial secured loan to the corporation at the time of incorporation, and if the loan is disclosed to subsequent creditors doing business with the corporation, what complaint of unfairness might they have?

3. The court states that shareholder loans to a company will be subordinated when paid-in capital is "purely nominal, the capital necessary for the scope and magnitude of the operation of the company being furnished by the stockholder as a loan." Does this formula provide any guidance for clients? Isn't all capital, both equity and debt, "necessary" for the scope and magnitude of the operation?

4. The court notes that the secured debt: equity ratio at the time of bankruptcy was 80:1. Is this the right time to test the ratio to determine whether the shareholder's loans were in fact a capital contribution rather than *bona fide* loans?

5. The court notes that the proceeds of the loans were used to finance the acquisition of equipment and material necessary to the functioning of the business. Why should the use of proceeds be relevant to the characterization of the loans?

6. Many parent-subsidiary corporations have centralized cash management programs, designed to make efficient use of the cash of the several corporations owned by a parent. In these cases, when one corporation has cash and another needs cash, a transfer is made by the parent from the cash-rich subsidiary to the cash-poor subsidiary. Book entries are made for both subsidiaries, and typically interest is charged to the receiving corporation at rate the parent has obtained on any bank loans it may have. What precautions would you advise the parent to observe in order to avoid subordination of loans should one subsidiary sink into bankruptcy? How much should other corporations be allowed to advance to a cash-needy member of the corporate group?

7. In L & M Realty Corp. v. Leo, 249 F.2d 668 (4th Cir.1957), the Court of Appeals called attention to the fact that the stockholders thought loans would be helpful for tax purposes. Is this a sign of an intention to contribute to capital? If so, why?

8. Recall the capital structure of New England Telephone & Telegraph Co. v. Department of Public Utilities, *supra,* where the capital structure was: long-term debt, $135 million, AT & T advances $120 million on demand notes at low interest rates, and common stock $155 million. If New England Telephone's rates remained too low and AT & T declined to purchase new securities to refinance the demand notes, would this be grounds for subordination of AT & T's advances to the claims of general creditors?

9. Assume your client and two friends wish to incorporate a new business and minimize federal income taxes by financing with as much debt as possible. How would you advise them to structure the capital in order to avoid both subordination to other creditors and disallowance of the interest paid deduction by the Internal Revenue Service, which you can assume is a decision that will parallel that of subordination? Consider the following issues:

    a. If total capital required for all eventualities currently foreseeable is $300,000, but it is expected that $150,000 of that amount is required for only part of the year, when inventories must be built up for seasonal sales, how much could they safely put up as loans?

    b. Should each shareholder make the loans at the time of incorporation, or only as needed?

    c. Can you advise the shareholders how the loans should be structured, e.g., maturities, interest rates, pledges to secure them?

    d. Should each shareholder make a loan in proportion to his or her stock ownership? If not, why not? If not, how do you address their desire to be equal investors in the enterprise?

10. If all claims sold to investors other than management in an LBO are contractually attached to each other ("stapled") so that each investor owns a pro rata share of each class of claim, from senior debt to common stock, what effect would this have on the risk of subordination? Should it?

11. If all claimants hold identical stapled packages of securities, and if the LBO is highly leveraged, what will this do to the likelihood that the Internal Revenue Service will disallow some of the interest deductions and treat interest payments as dividends to stockholders?

NOTE

Subordination often occurs in cases where a parent has claims against a subsidiary corporation in bankruptcy or reorganization. The most famous of these is Taylor v. Standard Gas & Electric Co., 306 U.S. 307 (1939). Standard, the parent of Deep Rock Oil Corporation, had thinly capitalized its subsidiary when it purchased the assets of an existing business. Standard had "dominated" Deep Rock in the way most parent corporations do, by seeing that officers of the subsidiary reported to officers of the parent. Undercapitalization meant that Deep Rock required a continuing series of advances from the parent, which kept a running account of the balance, and charged Deep Rock interest on the balance. (Note that such cash management programs are common in parent-subsidiary relationships.) As Deep Rock's debts increased, Standard caused it to seek new financing, which ultimately turned out to be available only if Standard forgave some of its debts, which it did in exchange for preferred stock, and if Standard furnished additional funds to pay off a mortgage on the property. When Deep Rock entered bankruptcy reorganization, Standard filed a claim for the $9 million balance in the open account, which was compromised at $5 million. The District Court and Court of Appeals approved a plan of reorganization recognized Standard's claim, only to be reversed by the Supreme Court, on the grounds of equitable subordination. The court's justification was stated as follows:

> Petitioners invoke the so-called instrumentality rule—under which, they say, Deep Rock is to be regarded as a department or agent of Standard,—to preclude the allowance of Standard's claim in any amount. The rule was much discussed in the opinion below. It is not, properly speaking, a rule, but a convenient way of designating the application in particular circumstances of the broader equitable principle that the doctrine of corporate entity, recognized generally and for most purposes, will not be regarded when to do so would work fraud or injustice.

An interesting discussion of these issues can be found in Robert Clark, The Duties of the Corporate Debtor to Its Creditors, 90 Harv. L. Rev. 505 (1977).

Quick Check Question 4.2

It is almost always the case that a parent can borrow more cheaply than its subsidiaries, if for no other reason than it generally holds a more diversified portfolio of income-producing activities and assets. It is also true that a parent can minimize aggregate borrowing costs for all subsidiaries by serving as an internal banker, taking surplus funds from some subsidiaries and advancing them to others. Under these circumstances, assuming (1) undercapitalization will always be determined in hindsight and (2) a result-oriented court can nearly always justify concluding that the parent "dominated" the subsidiary, if a parent corporation wishes to operate a centralized cash management program with its subsidiaries, where the parent furnishes advances obtained either from its own or borrowed cash, what would you advise the parent to do to protect against equitable subordination?

Subordination of shareholders' claims as creditors is not the only bankruptcy risk that confronts lending shareholders. Consider section 548(a) of the Bankruptcy Code:

§ 548.   Fraudulent transfers and obligations

(a)(1) The trustee may avoid any transfer of an interest of the debtor in property, or any obligation incurred by the debtor, that was made or incurred on or within one year before the date of the filing of the petition, if the debtor voluntarily or involuntarily—

(A) made such transfer or incurred such obligation with actual intent to hinder, delay, or defraud any entity to which the debtor was or became, on or after the date that such transfer was made or such obligation was incurred, indebted; or

(B)(i) received less than a reasonably equivalent value in exchange for such transfer or obligation; and

(ii)(I) was insolvent on the date that such transfer was made or such obligation was incurred, or became insolvent as a result of such transfer or obligation;

(II) was engaged in business or a transaction, or was about to engage in business or a transaction, for which any property remaining with the debtor was an unreasonably small capital; or

(III) intended to incur, or believed that the debtor would incur, debts that would be beyond the debtor's ability to pay as such debts matured.

B.   FIDUCIARY DUTIES TO CREDITORS

While it is clear that directors owe duties to creditors when the corporation is in bankruptcy, they may also owe duties at some time before bankruptcy. Several courts have held that once a corporation becomes insolvent, directors owe fiduciary duties to creditors.*

Credit Lyonnais Bank Nederland, N.V. v. Pathe Communications Co.

1991 WL 277613 (Del.Ch.1991).

■ ALLEN, CHANCELLOR:

This is an action under Section 225 of the Delaware General Corporation Law seeking a judicial determination of the persons who constitute the lawfully elected board of directors of MGM–Pathe Communications Co. ("MGM") a Delaware corporation. The principal plaintiff is Credit Lyonnais Bank Nederland ("CLBN" or "the Bank"), a major lender both to MGM and to MGM's parent Pathe Communications Corp. ("PCC"). By reason of claimed defaults by PCC on loans from CLBN that were secured by PCC's controlling block of MGM stock, CLBN now claims to be the legal (registered) owner of that controlling stock interest, at least for purposes of voting it.

Defendants are PCC and three individuals, Giancarlo Parretti, Maria Cecconi and Yoram Globus, each of whom CLBN purported to remove from the MGM board on June 16, 1991. Giancarlo Parretti had for several years been the dominant factor in the ownership and management of PCC. In November 1990, he caused PCC to acquire MGM. Maria Cecconi is Mr. Parretti's partner and wife. Yoram Globus, formerly controlled PCC (then called Cannon Films, Inc.) and continued to work for the firm after Parretti acquired control of it by 1989. Parretti and Globus appear to have had a productive working relationship.

[Giancarlo Parretti became the manager and major shareholder of Cannon Group, Inc., which ultimately became PCC. The Bank became PCC's principal lender. Parretti wanted to see PCC make bigger budget motion pictures, and ultimately engaged in a leveraged buyout of MGM, financed by the Bank to a large extent. This transaction closed on Nov. 1, 1990. Parretti's efforts to sell MGM assets were insufficient to pay down the amount of debt anticipated by the LBO financing, and the Bank ultimately promised to lend $125 million for working capital, on the understanding that an existing $186 million working capital liability would be paid off. Parretti and MGM failed to pay off the prior obligation, and the Bank thus was not obligated to fund the working capital loan. But MGM's working capital situation was desperate, and only five months after the acquisition, its trade creditors forced it into a chapter 7 proceeding in bankruptcy court. The bank officers who supervised the Bank's loans to Parretti and MGM were Francois Gille and Alexis Wolkenstein, who met with Parretti after the bankruptcy filing. Parretti agreed to step down from

---

* Clarkson Co. Ltd. v. Shaheen, 660 F.2d 506 (2d Cir.1981), cert. denied 455 U.S. 990 (1982); Bank Leumi-Le-Israel, B.M. v. Sunbelt Industries, Inc., 485 F.Supp. 556 (S.D.Ga.1980).

his position as chairman and chief executive officer in order to solve the current problems.

To replace Parretti with competent management, Gille and Wolkenstein identified Alan Ladd, a well-known film executive who had previously served as chairman and chief executive officer of MGM–United Artists, as the candidate to serve in the same role at MGM. A new chief operating officer would also be appointed by the bank. Ladd and Jay Kanter would make up an executive committee of the board of directors of MGM, and the executive committee would be given full operating authority, with the board (consisting of three other directors in addition to the bank's two nominees) having limited authority to approve extraordinary transactions. Parretti ultimately agreed to the proposed arrangement, which was formalized in a "Corporate Governance Agreement" ("CGA") and a "Voting Trust Agreement," by which CLBN would be given the right to vote the controlling shares of PCC and MGM.

From the beginning, Parretti sought to subvert the Corporate Governance Agreement, insisting that MGM officials who were to report to Ladd and Charles Meeker, who was named as chief operating officer, report also to Parretti and his executives. Gille agreed to the appointment of Parretti's associate Liliana Avincola to the position of secretary of MGM for the purpose of apprising PCC officers of the executive committee's activities. In the course of taking control, Ladd and Meeker learned that things were worse at MGM than the Bank had realized. An agreement by which MGM had licensed its film library to Reteitalia to raise cash had a "put" arrangement, by which the licensee could, after evaluating the films it received, require MGM to unwind the agreement within twelve months and return $100 million. Gille and Wolkenstein warned Parretti that he must fully cooperate in carrying out the Corporate Governance Agreement, but at the same time Parretti and his lieutenants, PCC's chief financial officer, Aurelio Germes, Mr. Hamburger, PCC's and MGM's general counsel, were meeting with Theodore Cohen, PCC's corporate counsel, to seek ways to challenge the validity of the agreement. Hamburger advised Parretti that the Corporate Governance Agreement might conflict with the provisions of a consent decree with the SEC settling previous fraud charges, and with the provisions of the Foreign & Corrupt Practices Act, section 13(b)(2) of the Securities Exchange Act, that requires the board to maintain a system of internal accounting controls.

On June 14 the Parretti members of the board met, which the CLBN directors, Ladd and Kanter pointedly did not attend, since there was no agenda for the meeting. Without them the board lacked a quorum, but that did not prevent them from attempting to act. It adopted purported resolutions stating the priority of the earlier consent decree and the Foreign & Corrupt Practices Act over any governance arrangement, disapproved contracts for Ladd's nominees for various positions, and authorized Parretti to take all actions with respect to a certain PCC property that Parretti wanted to sell to MGM, over Ladd's objections. Finally, the three directors purported to divest MGM's investment in UIP, a foreign movie consortium, when

Ladd and the executive committee had declined to take such action at that time. The court concluded that the participants knew it was not a valid board meeting, but wanted to give the impression that it was in order to allow Parretti to gain more power than allowed in the Corporate Governance Agreement.

Immediately thereafter Parretti left for Paris, where he informed Gille of the board's actions, and the opinion of his counsel that the Corporate Governance Agreement was invalid. Further, he stated that PCC had governance rights in MGM, and that if Ladd and Kanter missed another board meeting, he would have them removed from the board.

In response, CLBN took actions according to the arrangements supporting the Corporate Governance Agreement. CLBN broke the escrow that held the Voting Trust Agreement, and proceeded to register the Voting Trust Agreement with MGM, caused the PCC shares in MGM to be transferred into its name as voting trustee, and executed a shareholders' consent purporting to remove Parretti, Globus and Cecconi from the MGM board and replacing them with Meeker, Meyer and Jones.]

II.

* * *

For the reasons set forth below I conclude that Giancarlo Parretti was guilty of material breaches of the Corporate Governance Agreement. I conclude as a consequence that the action of CLBN in purporting to exercise its rights under the Voting Rights Agreement and the Voting Trust Agreement was valid and effective corporate action. Moreover, I conclude that CLBN did not itself breach its agreements with Mr. Parretti or his affiliates or behave towards him in an inequitable or unfair way. Thus I will dismiss the defendants' counterclaims with prejudice.

* * *

I believe that, in the circumstances, the bank's election to remove the defendants from office was a reasonable one, even if one assumes that Mr. Parretti was at all times operating with subjective good faith under the Corporate Governance Agreement. However, upon consideration of the evidence, I am required to conclude that Giancarlo Parretti did not act with that degree of good faith that contracting parties are entitled to expect and demand.

More specifically, I conclude that he breached the foundational obligation implicit in every contract, to refrain from acting with respect to the subject matter of his contract so as to deny or materially impair the value bargained for by his promisee. * * *

A. Giancarlo Parretti Failed to Comply "In Form and Substance" with the Corporate Governance Agreement.

1. Mr. Parretti's rights and obligations under the CGA.

In a simple single transaction contract the obligations of the parties are usually discreet and easily identified: to render a single performance or to pay a stated price, for example. When a contract contemplates not a single performance or set an identified performance but contemplates an on-going relationship of some sort, difficulties in defining contractual obligations at the outset will increase. As the scope or time-frame of the contractual relation is extended, the express allocation of risks of future contingencies becomes more difficult. In only a moderately complex or extend [sic—extended?] contractual relationship, the cost of attempting to catalog and negotiate with respect to all possible future states of the world would be prohibitive, if it were cognitively possible.[44] In such contracts some things must be left to the good faith of the parties.

* * *

Generally speaking, contracting parties are, to a large extent, entitled to act selfishly to promote their own interests under the contract. While in a relational contract it may be short-sighted and bad business to do so, they generally are entitled to push their claims of entitlement under a contract in an attempt to maximize their self-interest. But while contracting parties are not fiduciaries for each other, there are outer limits to the self-seeking actions they may take under a contract. Where one party's actions are such as to deprive the other of a material aspect of the bargain for which he contracted, the first party will be found to have violated that elemental obligation of all contracting parties to deal with each other in good faith and to deal fairly with each other with respect to the subject matter of the contract. That is the case here.

2. Mr. Parretti Breached An Obligation to Act in Good Faith and Deal Fairly with MGM and CLBN.

* * *

I do not conclude lightly or easily that the covenant of good faith and fair dealing was violated here. The entire course of conduct of defendant up to and including the June 15 Paris meeting does, however, force me to that conclusion. That is, I conclude that no reasonable negotiator who consented to the mid-April agreements (including the CGA) could have concluded, if all of the actions of Mr. Parretti and his agents up to June 15 were considered, that such action would constitute compliance "in form and substance" with the CGA.

* * *

The Cohen legal memos and the assertion by Parretti that the CGA was invalid most pointedly demonstrate the final bankruptcy of the governance structure that the CGA had contemplated. With these charges and with the assertion of the right to throw Ladd off the board, Mr. Parretti deliberately pushed matters to a crisis. The Bank might have responded by a partial or total capitulation (i.e., consent to Ladd's removal) or by removing Mr. Parretti. Mr. Parretti no doubt fostered the hope of the

---

44. See Goetz and Scott, Principles of Relational Contracts, 67 Va. L. Rev. 1089, text at n. 4 (1981).

former outcome. He had some ground for that hope. The Bank's relationship with Ladd was not of long standing and was not financially involved as was its relationship with Mr. Parretti. One imagines that Mr. Parretti understood that he was pushing the CGA to a crisis but that he misunderstood in what direction CLBN would jump, if it were pushed to do so.

One need not psychoanalyze Mr. Parretti, however, to conclude that his actions sought to deprive Mr. Ladd of the power for which he and CLBN had contracted and did so to a material extent. To conclude that the covenant of good faith and fair dealing has been breached, we need not conclude that the breaching party actually intended to violate a contract right. "Subterfuges and evasions violate the obligation of good faith in performance even though the actor believes his conduct to be justified." Restatement (Second) of Contracts § 205 (Comment d) (1981). The question is not whether Mr. Parretti believed that his pushing, his threats and his lack of candor constituted evasions of his contractual obligations under the CGA, the question is whether they objectively were. For the reason set forth above, I conclude that they were.

* * *

III. The Claim that CLBN and Ladd Violated Mr. Parretti's Rights and the Issue of Credibility.

* * *

C. The weight of the credible evidence establishes that neither the Ladd management team nor CLBN breached a fiduciary duty or a duty of good faith and fair dealing owed to Mr. Parretti and PCC.

Defendants complain that the members of the Ladd management group were committed to preventing Parretti from regaining control of MGM because they realized that Mr. Parretti would promptly remove them from office. Parretti says they did two things that breached their fiduciary duty to PCC as the 98.5% shareholder of MGM. First they entered into certain severance agreements with certain members of the Ladd team, which were triggered by Parretti's regaining control. Defendants assert that these payments represented a tax upon the shareholders' exercise of their right to elect the board and thus constituted a breach of duty. Second, Parretti claims that the executive committee—with whom the Bank chose to share its contractual power to veto asset sales—delayed and impeded the sale of MGM's interest in UIP, a foreign movie distribution consortium, as well as other transactions.

The first point need not delay one for long. I find no evidence of bad faith in Mr. Ladd's decision to cause MGM to enter these employment contracts. * * *

I turn then to the second aspect of the argument that Mr. Ladd was disloyal to PCC in its capacity as MGM's stockholder by failing to facilitate sale transactions that Parretti sought in order to help him regain control. (In fact those proposed transactions were too little, too late in any event).

It is true that a conflict emerged between Mr. Parretti and Mr. Ladd. If this conflict was not inevitable under the CGA, it was at all events quite likely. I pass over the question whether the existence of this conflict affects the availability of the business judgment form of judicial review of controversial executive committee decisions. Under any approach, I find that the executive committee decisions were valid and did not represent a breach of duty. Mr. Meekers' testimony presents persuasive evidence that the Ladd management group acted prudently with respect to these transactions from the point of view of MGM.

In these circumstances where the company was in bankruptcy until May 28 and even thereafter the directors labored in the shadow of that prospect, Mr. Ladd and his associates were appropriately mindful of the potential differing interests between the corporation and its 98% shareholder. At least where a corporation is operating in the vicinity of insolvency, a board of directors is not merely the agent of the residue risk bearers, but owes its duty to the corporate enterprise.[55]

---

55.   The possibility of insolvency can do curious things to incentives, exposing creditors to risks of opportunistic behavior and creating complexities for directors. Consider, for example, a solvent corporation having a single asset, a judgment for $51 million against a solvent debtor. The judgment is on appeal and thus subject to modification or reversal. Assume that the only liabilities of the company are to bondholders in the amount of $12 million. Assume that the array of probable outcomes of the appeal is as follows:

	Expected Value
25% chance of affirmance ($51mm)	$12.75
70% chance of modification ($4mm)	2.8
5% chance of reversal ($0)	0
Expected Value of Judgment on Appeal	$15.55

Thus, the best evaluation is that the current value of the equity is $3.55 million. ($15.55 million expected value of judgment on appeal, $12 million liability to bondholders). Now assume an offer to settle at $12.5 million (also consider one at $17.5 million). By what standard do the directors of the company evaluate the fairness of these offers? The creditors of this solvent company would be in favor of accepting either a $12.5 million offer or a $17.5 million offer. In either event they will avoid the 75% risk of insolvency and default. The stockholders, however, will plainly be opposed to acceptance of a $12.5 million settlement (under which they get practically nothing). More importantly, they very well may be opposed to acceptance of the $17.5 million offer under which the residual value of the corporation would increase from $3.5 to $5.5 million. This is so because the litigation alternative, with its 25% probability of a $39 million outcome to them ($51 million—$12 million $39 million) has an expected value to the residual risk bearer of $9.75 million ($39 million × 25% chance of affirmance), substantially greater than the $5.5 million available to them in the settlement. While in fact the stockholders' preference would reflect their appetite for risk, it is possible (and with diversified shareholders likely) that shareholders would prefer rejection of both settlement offers.

But if we consider the community of interests that the corporation represents it seems apparent that one should in this hypothetical accept the best settlement offer available providing it is greater than $15.55 million, and one below that amount should be rejected. But that result will not be reached by a director who thinks he owes duties directly to shareholders only. It will be reached by directors who are capable of conceiving of the corporation as a legal and economic entity. Such directors will recognize that in managing the business affairs of a solvent corporation in the vicinity of insolvency, circumstances may arise when the right (both

The Ladd management was not disloyal in not immediately facilitating whatever asset sales were in the financial best interest of the controlling stockholder. In managing the business affairs of MGM, Mr. Ladd, and those he appointed owed their supervening loyalty to MGM, the corporate entity.[56] It was not disloyal for them to consider carefully the corporation's interest in the UIP transaction, in the UK cinemas sale and in other proposed transactions. This I conclude they did. Mr. Parretti had gotten himself into a corner. He needed to liquidate assets to raise capital. Ladd and his team could reasonably suspect that he might be inclined to accept fire-sale prices. But the MGM board or its executive committee had an obligation to the community of interest that sustained the corporation, to exercise judgment in an informed, good faith effort to maximize the corporation's long-term wealth creating capacity.

* * *

Therefore, having heard the lengthy testimony in this case, I conclude that Giancarlo Parretti and PCC had by June 16, 1991 failed to comply with the CGA "in form and substance," as the Summary Agreement required and that, as a result, the bank was legally entitled at that time to exercise its rights under the Voting Trust Agreement. The action it purported to take in removing Messrs. Parretti and Globus and Ms. Cecconi was valid and effective action. Moreover, I conclude that the allegations of the defendants' counterclaim have not been proven and that pleading will be dismissed with prejudice.

Plaintiffs may submit a form of implementing order on notice.

QUESTIONS

1. An electric utility that generates power at wholesale and sells it under long-term supply contracts to consumer utilities at a price related to market prices for wholesale electricity had entered into a long-term requirements contract for coal to fuel its generators. The price is fixed, at a price that seemed favorable when the utility signed it. Since that time, however, the price of natural gas, a substitute fuel for electric generation, has fallen, forcing the market price of coal down. With that downward shift, the measuring wholesale price for electricity that the company receives has declined. The company now loses money on all its power sales, and if the wholesale price remains low, the company will lose money for the balance of the term of its requirements contracts—the next 15 years. While its assets are currently in excess of its liabilities, and its current net worth is substantial, it seems probable that within the next ten years it will exhaust its net worth with

---

the efficient and the fair) course to follow for the corporation may diverge from the choice that the stockholders (or the creditors, or the employees, or any single group interested in the corporation) would make if given the opportunity to act.

56. But cf. Blasius Industries Inc. v. Atlas Corp., Del. Ch., 564 A.2d 651 (1988) (board action intended to impede stockholder exercise of statutory franchise right is suspect even if taken in good faith effort to promote corporate welfare).

operating losses. Is the company currently in the vicinity of insolvency? What advice would you give to the board if it is considering payment of a dividend? See Del. G.C.L. §§ 170, 173–174 and Rev. Model Bus. Corp. Act §§ 6.40 & 8.33. How would you determine bankruptcy insolvency? What would you capitalize?

2. Your client is a company that once produced products that contained asbestos. While it stopped using asbestos as an ingredient many years ago, in recent years a number of plaintiffs have brought suit alleging that the company's products caused them injury. The incubation period on asbestos-related injury, particularly mesothelioma and lung cancer, is often 25 to 40 years. At the moment there are only a few hundred suits, but the numbers are growing rapidly. Nationally there are over 600,000 suits pending against other companies. A substantial number of defendant companies have already been forced into bankruptcy. Is the company currently in the vicinity of bankruptcy? The board of directors would like to engage in a spin-off, in which it would place an important segment of its business in a separate subsidiary, and then declare a dividend of the subsidiary's stock to the company's shareholders. What advice would you give the board? Would you like an expert opinion about the expected costs of all asbestos claims? How much confidence would you have in such an opinion? Would the lawyer who responds to the auditors' request for an opinion about the likelihood of contingent liabilities from litigation and pending claims be a person qualified to give such an opinion and provide protection for the directors?

NOTE

The difficulty with this line of cases is that the courts have been unclear about when duties shift to creditors. In one case, the court held that even if the "corporation was technically solvent but insolvency was approaching and was then only a few days away, defendants, as officers and directors, were, in effect, trustees by statute for the creditors."[*] Another court referred to the triggering event as "when a corporation becomes insolvent, *or in a failing condition* ..."[**] Finally, in Credit Lyonnaise, Chancellor Allen stated that "where a corporation is operating *in the vicinity of insolvency*, a board of directors is not merely the agent of the residue risk bearers...." The difficulty with these tests is that they require the board to predict insolvency, and to determine that uncertain period when the corporation is in its "vicinity."

The Delaware Supreme Court acknowledged this indeterminacy in North American Catholic Educational Programming Foundation, Inc. v. Gheewalla, 930 A.2d 92, 99 (2007). That case held that creditors have no

---

[*] New York Credit Men's Adjustment Bureau v. Weiss, 305 N.Y. 1, 110 N.E.2d 397, 398 (1953).

[**] Davis v. Woolf, 147 F.2d 629, 633 (4th Cir.1945).

ability to bring a direct action for any breach of duty by the directors, even during insolvency.

Second, the courts have not defined "insolvency" with precision. There are two forms of insolvency: (1) when a corporation is unable to pay its bills as they come due ("equity insolvency") and (2) when a corporation's liabilities exceed its assets ("bankruptcy insolvency"). These two distinct forms of insolvency are not always recognized as distinct by the courts.

In view of the uncertainty in the definition of insolvency, cautious directors might wish to regard themselves as owing fiduciary duties to both creditors and shareholders upon the occurrence of or even the imminence of, either form of insolvency. Chancellor Allen suggests the difficulties facing directors in resolving the conflicts that might arise between them. There are no legal guidelines about how directors might resolve these conflicts.

There is a well-known conflict between stockholders and creditors that we will examine in more detail in Chapter Six, explained in footnote 55 of the Credit Lyonnaise opinion. Once creditors have entered into a contract that specifies an interest rate, they have contracted to receive a limited amount of compensation for the risk of non-payment they currently expect to face. If the corporation thereafter increases the riskiness of its business or financial structure, that will harm the creditors by imposing uncompensated risk on them. On the other hand, where an enterprise is thinly capitalized, this may benefit the shareholders. This is because the shareholders are in essence risking creditors' money on ventures from which shareholders, not creditors, will be the primary beneficiaries if the gamble is successful. Shareholders may increase the risk of the business by reducing the shareholders' equity investment in the company, by increasing its indebtedness, or by engaging in riskier projects than before. These are the events that are frequently protected against in bond indentures.

C. Creditor Liability

Krivo Industrial Supply Company v. National Distillers and Chemical Corporation

483 F.2d 1098 (5th Cir.1973).

■ Roney, Circuit Judge:

Plaintiffs, ten creditors of a now reorganized corporation, individually sued National Distillers and Chemical Corp., the major creditor of that corporation, on their debts. Finding that the cases all involved common questions of law and fact, the District Court consolidated them for trial on the single issue of liability. The issue of damages was severed and was reserved for subsequent proceedings. The alleged liability of National Distillers was predicated upon the rule that, when one corporation controls and dominates another corporation to the extent that the second corporation becomes the "mere instrumentality" of the first, the dominant corporation becomes liable for those debts of the subservient corporation attributable to an abuse of that control. After hearing plaintiffs' evidence, the District Court granted a directed verdict in favor of National Distillers. We affirm, finding that the evidence was insufficient to establish a jury question as to the presence of the requisite degree of control.

I.   The Law

* * *

The "Instrumentality" Doctrine

We note at the outset that the case before us involves only the question of National Distillers' liability under the "instrumentality" theory. It involves no question of fraud, deceit, or misrepresentation. Nor does it involve charges that National Distillers received large amounts of security for small debt and made excessive, overreaching profits through foreclosure. Hence, we must examine the evidence exclusively within the framework of the narrow rule of corporation law known as the "instrumentality" doctrine.

Basic to the theory of corporation law is the concept that a corporation is a separate entity, a legal being having an existence separate and distinct from that of its owners. This attribute of the separate corporate personality enables the corporation's stockholders to limit their personal liability to the extent of their investment. But the corporate device cannot in all cases insulate the owners from personal liability. Hence, courts do not hesitate to ignore the corporate form in those cases where the corporate device has been misused by its owners. The corporate form, however, is not lightly disregarded, since limited liability is one of the principal purposes for which the law has created the corporation.

One of the most difficult applications of the rule permitting the corporate form to be disregarded arises when one corporation is sought to be held liable for the debts of another corporation. * * * The rationale for holding the dominant corporation liable for the subservient corporation's debts is that, since the dominant corporation has misused the subservient corporation's corporate form by using it for the dominant corporation's own purposes, the debts of the subservient corporation are in reality the obligations of the dominant corporation. In these cases, "the courts will look through the forms to the realities of the relation between the companies as if the corporate agency did not exist and will deal with them as the justice of the case may require." Here, then, the corporate form of the subservient corporation is disregarded so as to affix liability where it justly belongs. Plaintiffs' claim in this case is based on this second theory of liability.

* * *

... [T]wo elements are essential for liability under the "instrumentality" doctrine. First, the dominant corporation must have controlled the subservient corporation, and second, the dominant corporation must have proximately caused plaintiff harm through misuse of this control.

In considering the first element, that of control, the courts have struggled to delineate the kind of control necessary to establish liability under the "instrumentality" rule. Two problem areas have persistently troubled the process of ascertaining the extent of control. First, to what extent is stock ownership critical, and second, how much weight should be given to the existence of a creditor-debtor relationship in those cases where the debtor corporation is alleged to be the "instrumentality" of its creditor?

* * *

As with stock ownership, a creditor-debtor relationship also does not per se constitute control under the "instrumentality" theory. The general rule is that the mere loan of money by one corporation to another does not automatically make the lender liable for the acts and omissions of the borrower. The logic of this rule is apparent, for otherwise no lender would be willing to extend credit. The risks and liabilities would simply be too great. Nevertheless, lenders are not automatically exempt from liability under the "instrumentality" rule. If a lender becomes so involved with its debtor that it is in fact actively managing the debtor's affairs, then the quantum of control necessary to support liability under the "Instrumentality" theory may be achieved.

An examination of "instrumentality" cases involving creditor-debtor relationships demonstrates that courts require a strong showing that the creditor assumed actual, participatory, total control of the debtor. Merely taking an active part in the management of the debtor corporation does not automatically constitute control, as used in the "instrumentality" doctrine, by the creditor corporation.

The broad scope permitted creditors to institute various restrictions on the activities of their debtors is exemplified by Chicago Mill & Lumber Co. v. Boatmen's Bank, 234 F. 41 (8th Cir. 1916). In Chicago Mill & Lumber Co., a bank lent large sums of money to a mill and land company. To protect its investment, the bank had its assistant cashier elected president of the debtor company. The manager of the company testified that he took his directions from either the president of the bank or the assistant cashier who headed the company. After the company went into bankruptcy, a creditor sued the bank on the theory that the bankrupt company had been merely a department of the bank and that the bank's arrangements for monitoring the activities of its debtor entitled the plaintiff to a jury determination of whether or not the company was in fact controlled by the bank.

Affirming the District Court's directed verdict in favor of the bank on the issue, the Eighth Circuit accorded great importance to the fact that "the bank was a large creditor, and as such largely interested in the prosperity of the company, and most naturally should desire to keep an oversight over its doings." 234 F. at 46. Referring to various statements attributed to bank personnel indicating that the bank owned the company or was conducting the company's business in the bank's behalf, the Court stated:

> Comprehensively speaking, they are all easily and naturally refera-ble to a legitimate and customary practice of keeping an oversight by a creditor over the business, management, and operations of a debtor of doubtful solvency. All the facts of this case and all the reasonable inferences deducible from them would not, in our opinion, have war-ranted a jury in finding ... that the [bank] was carrying on the business of the [company] as a part of its own....

* * *

In summary, then the control required for liability under the "instru-mentality" rule amounts to total domination of the subservient corpora-tion, to the extent that the subservient corporation manifests no separate corporate interests of its own and functions solely to achieve the purposes of the dominant corporation. As Professor Fletcher states:

> The control necessary to invoke what is sometimes called the "instrumentality rule" is not mere majority or complete stock control but such domination of finances, policies and practices that the con-trolled corporation has, so to speak, no separate mind, will or existence of its own and is but a business conduit for its principal.

1 W. Fletcher, supra, § 43 at 204–205. No lesser standard is applied in "instrumentality" cases involving a creditor-debtor relationship. As the Court said in In re Kentucky Wagon Mfg. Co., 3 F. Supp. 958, 963 (W.D. Ky. 1932), aff'd, 71 F.2d 802 (6th Cir.), cert. denied, Laurent v. Stites, 293 U.S. 612, 55 S. Ct. 142, 79 L. Ed. 701 (1934), "it is to be noted that it is not 'controlling influence' that is essential. It is actual control of the action of the subordinate corporation."

In addition to actual and total control of the subservient corporation, the "instrumentality" rule also requires that fraud or injustice proximately result from a misuse of this control by the dominant corporation. Berger v. Columbia Broadcasting System, Inc., supra; see National Bond Finance Co. v. General Motors Corp., supra. Alabama emphatically rejects actual fraud as a necessary predicate for disregarding the corporate form, holding instead that courts may decline to recognize corporate existence whenever recognition of the corporate form would extend the principle of incorpo-ration "beyond its legitimate purposes and [would] produce injustices or inequitable consequences."

This is the better rule, for the theory of liability under the "instrumen-tality" doctrine does not rest upon intent to defraud. It is an equitable doctrine that places the burden of the loss upon the party who should be responsible. The basic theory of the "instrumentality" doctrine is that the debts of the subservient corporation are in reality the obligations of the dominant corporation.

II. The Factual Background

* * *

Brad's Machine Products, Inc., was a California corporation that began its existence as a machine shop in Stanton, California. Employing approximately 25 persons, Brad's was owned by John C. Bradford and his wife Nola. In addition to the machine business, Bradford's investments included a championship quarter horse, racing boats, airplanes, an Arizona bar, an Alabama motel, Florida orange groves, and oil wells. In addition, Bradford, a country and western singer, formed a motion picture company, Brad's Productions, Inc., through which he produced a film that featured him as a singer. All of these investment activities were funded by his income from the machine shop.

The record shows that Bradford was an able and inventive machinist and that the California operation had been profitable. In 1966, Bradford saw potential profit in the munitions industry, so he employed Arnold Seitman to guide his entry into the Government contracting system. Seitman had previously supervised government contracting for a company in Gadsden, Alabama, and he soon obtained for Brad's a 2.7 million dollar contract for the production of M–125 fuses, the principal component of which was brass.

* * *

For a brief time, Brad's appeared to prosper. Bradford's wide-ranging investments, however, soon became a severe financial drain on the Brad's operation. One subsidiary, a Gadsden box plant that made wooden boxes for shells, alone lost over one million dollars. By the end of 1968, Brad's was headed for financial distress.

The M–125 booster fuse assembly was the major product manufactured by Brad's, accounted for ninety percent of its gross sales, and required substantial quantities of brass rods. In the beginning Brad's had purchased its brass requirements from three sources: Revere Brass Company, Mueller Brass Company, and Bridgeport Brass Company. Brad's principal source of supply was Bridgeport, and Brad's was one of Bridgeport's larger customers. Bridgeport is a division of the defendant, National Distillers and Chemical Corporation.

In early 1969, Bridgeport was shipping approximately $400,000–$500,000 worth of brass rod to Brad's every month. In March, 1969, Brad's owed Bridgeport approximately $1,000,000 and Bridgeport, at the request of Brad's, agreed to convert this arrearage to a promissory note. On March 28, 1969, Bridgeport accepted Brad's note, secured by (1) the personal guaranties of John C. Bradford, Chairman of the Board and sole stockholder of Brad's, and his wife and (2) a mortgage on real property owned by J–N Industries, Inc., a subsidiary of Brad's located in Tucson, Arizona. The note was payable at the rate of $40,000 per month, plus interest on the unpaid balance, and it contained a "balloon agreement" under which the final payment in March of 1970 would equal the unpaid balance. * * *

In connection with the agreement for deferred payment, Brad's and Bridgeport entered into a "financing and loan agreement." Under this agreement, Bridgeport agreed to continue to supply Brad's with brass rod, so long as Brad's paid for current brass shipments within fifteen or sixteen days (with a ten day grace period). Despite this condition, by the end of July, 1969, Bridgeport permitted Brad's to build up an additional $630,000 in brass rod accounts payable.

On August 1, 1969, Bradford, Brad's President E. J. Huntsman, and Brad's Comptroller Roy Compton, went to New York to confer with representatives of National Distillers, including Assistant General Counsel and Secretary John F. Salisbury. The representatives of Brad's stated that its current financial situation precluded continued operation unless it received additional assistance, including working capital. They blamed the unsuccessful attempts to diversify Brad's as the reason for the company's financial straits. Moreover, they needed immediate assistance because the Government had threatened to cancel the current fuse contract if the financial condition of Brad's continued to worsen. Bradford offered to put up all the assets he and the company had in exchange for the additional funds and for National Distillers' intervention with the Government on behalf of Brad's.

At the close of the August 1, 1969, meeting, National Distillers and Brad's reached an oral agreement in line with Bradford's requests. National Distillers was to (1) provide internal financial management assistance to help Brad's eliminate costly waste, (2) lend Brad's another $600,000 in cash, (3) defer payment on the $630,000 accounts receivable, (4) help Brad's and Bradford liquidate unprofitable holdings to provide more capital for Brad's, and (5) intervene with the Government to prevent cancellation of the current fuse body contract. Brad's and Bradford personally were to assign to National Distillers as collateral the various interests accumulated during the attempted diversification.

Salisbury immediately telephoned a Government official in Birmingham, Alabama, whose job included monitoring for the Defense Contract Administration Service the financial ability of Brad's to perform its Government contracts, and assured him of National Distillers' intent to aid Brad's. * * * To help the financial management at Brad's, Leon Rudd, one of National Distillers' "Internal Auditors" was sent to Gadsden to oversee its finances and to establish control procedures for managing cash and investments. Finally, Salisbury assigned one of his assistants to help him and Brad's dispose of the assets assigned to National Distillers and other assets not so assigned. Under the terms of several agreements, both formal and informal, National Distillers agreed that any income or proceeds from these unassigned assets would be used for certain designated purposes in aid of Brad's other creditors and then either would revert to Brad's or to Bradford or would belong to National Distillers outright.

Rudd remained with Brad's for fifteen months, during which National Distillers loaned Brad's an additional $169,000 in cash and deferred another $667,131.28 in accounts payable by Brad's to Bridgeport. Despite these transfusions, Brad's ceased its operations in December, 1970. These suits resulted from debts left unpaid by Brad's.

III.   The Decision

After a comprehensive review of the testimony and exhibits presented by the plaintiffs in the District Court, and viewing the evidence in the light most favorable to the plaintiffs, we conclude that the evidence was not "of such quality and weight that reasonable and fair-minded men in the exercise of impartial judgment might reach different conclusions," on the issue of control. Keeping in mind that the kind of control prerequisite to liability under the "instrumentality" rule is actual, operative, total control of the subservient corporation, the evidence here was wholly insufficient to support a jury decision that Brad's had "no separate mind, will or existence of its own and [was] but a business conduit" for National Distillers. The evidence is overwhelming that Brad's maintained a separate, independent corporate existence at all times. Hence, the motion for a directed verdict in favor of defendants was properly granted.

In cases involving the "instrumentality" rule, we must take a broad approach to the question of control, examining all of the plaintiffs' evidence to ascertain if the allegedly subservient corporation in fact had no separate corporate purposes or existence. In the case before us, plaintiffs presented evidence of (1) National Distillers' ownership of majority control of Brad's, (2) National Distillers' view of its relationship to Brad's, (3) the scope of National Distillers' control over Brad's, and (4) the alleged exploitation of Brad's supposedly wrought through abuses of that control.

* * *

2.   According to plaintiffs, the evidence shows that National Distillers believed that it had the power to control Bradford and his corporation and acted accordingly. A careful examination of this evidence, however, makes clear that National Distillers considered control of Brad's to be, at most, only partly shared between National Distillers and Brad's.

First, a letter from National Distillers' Salisbury to the general manager of the movie company, Brad's Productions, Inc., stated: "As I am sure you are aware, National Distillers and Chemical Corporation has taken an active role in the management and control of Brad's Machine Products, Inc., and various other undertakings of John C. Bradford." This letter, however, is not inconsistent with National Distillers' argument, which we conclude is correct, that the evidence shows that Brad's voluntarily shared control with National Distillers. The letter does not say that National Distillers had taken control of Brad's; rather, it states only that National Distillers had "taken an active role in the management and control of Brad's."

* * *

Third, plaintiffs quote Seitman's testimony that states that Salisbury at one time threatened to "fire" both Seitman and Bradford and run the

Brad's operation itself. A complete reading of Seitman's testimony indicates that he believed that National Distillers' so-called power or authority to "fire" lay in its "control of the purse strings." Seitman testified that National Distillers could not "have told Brad's who its officers were to be," and he then stated that he understood Salisbury to mean that National Distillers would cease extending credit to Brad's if certain contracts were not fulfilled. Thus, it is plain that National Distillers could have "fired" Brad's personnel only by cutting off credit or loans, thereby putting Brad's out of business. The record contains no evidence showing that National Distillers conceived that it could have directed or implemented the replacement and selection of management personnel, absent credit control.

3. As to the scope of National Distillers' alleged control, the evidence shows only that National Distillers' activities were narrowly restricted to safeguarding its interests as a major creditor of Brad's, that National Distillers participated in the corporate decision-making at Brad's only to a limited degree, and that at no time did National Distillers assume actual, participatory, total control of Brad's.

The thrust of plaintiffs' contention here is that Leon Rudd, who was sent to the Gadsden plant by National Distillers in August, 1969, and who remained until late November, 1970, actively dominated the Brad's decision-making apparatus during his stay.

A reading of the testimony, especially that of the Brad's comptroller Compton, compels a conclusion that Rudd's activities were much more circumscribed than appellants argue. Rudd, an internal auditor employed by National Distillers, was transferred to Brad's in response to John Bradford's request for assistance in establishing a system of internal controls. Rudd was not thrust upon Brad's unwanted or unneeded.

Because many of the financial problems at Brad's had been precipitated by improvident investments and uncontrolled spending, Rudd immediately moved to put himself in the position of monitoring Brad's cash outlays. According to Compton's testimony, Rudd suggested, and they all "readily agreed," that no purchase orders be sent out without his prior approval. Also, Rudd's signature was made mandatory on all checks from the Brad's accounts. From these "controls," plaintiffs would extrapolate the theory that National Distillers, through Rudd, was in charge of Brad's. Such a conclusion is untenable.

First, the evidence showed that, in fact, Rudd's prior approval of purchase requisitions was not always necessary for purchases. At the trial, several of plaintiffs' purchase orders, put in evidence for other purposes, were shown to have been made up and sent out without Rudd's approval.

Second, assuming that Rudd in fact enjoyed such an all-powerful veto over purchases, this power was never exercised where Brad's proper business purposes were involved. Rather, Rudd voiced his displeasure only when expenditures were contemplated that were unrelated to the Brad's machine shop operation.

Third, Rudd's powers were essentially negative in character. The testimony showed that his function was to monitor the finances and to help Compton fend off aggressive, unhappy creditors. Although plaintiffs contend that Rudd "participated in the management" of Brad's, the evidence shows that he did so only in a limited sense. Only those decisions having an immediate effect on Brad's financial position were subject to Rudd's primary attention. He attended management meetings solely in that capacity. The record contains no evidence that he was ever substantially involved in personnel or production decisions. Rudd left the delicate task of renegotiating Government contracts to Compton. (After a Government contract had been completed, Government officials often reviewed the profits of the contracting firm, seeking the return of "excess profits").

Fourth, Rudd's position as a required signatory on all checks drawn against the Brad's general account provides little support for plaintiffs' theory. Besides Rudd's signature, the checks also required one other signer from Brad's. Hence, Rudd again had but a veto power.

Plaintiffs argue that Rudd, using his power as a required signatory, expanded his powers into management (1) by negotiating and consummating settlements of disputed claims and (2) by designating the order in which creditors were to be paid. Once again, Compton's uncontradicted testimony illuminates the extent of Rudd's "control." Because Brad's had always been short of working capital, the practice had developed of writing checks to creditors as soon as a particular bill came due and then retaining the checks until there was money in the Brad's account to pay the checks. As could be expected, irate creditors often called upon Compton to pay up. When Rudd arrived, he and Compton worked together handling creditors. Compton testified that theirs was a cooperative effort but that, since Rudd was more skilled in dealing with creditors, he had the final decision as to which creditors were paid. The factors they considered included (1) the amount of money in the account, (2) the importance of the creditor to the continued operation of the plant, (3) the age of the bill, and (4) the urgency or fervor of a particular creditor's demand. In addition, Rudd often spoke with these creditors, attempting to forestall or to settle their demands.

Rudd's activities while at Brad's simply do not amount to active domination of the corporation. His job was to provide internal financial management assistance and all that he did was in keeping with this mission. Although he kept a fairly tight rein on disbursements, the evidence shows that his role was that of providing a centralized control over purchases and disbursements. His job was two-fold: (1) to eliminate costly duplication, e.g., multiple orders of the same supply, and (2) to eliminate all disbursements not directly and immediately related to the machine shop business. These controls were strong, and Rudd was not afraid to exercise his power, but we cannot conclude from the evidence before us that his activities could justify a jury verdict that found control. Rudd limited the scope of his position to overseeing the finances of Brad's. Neither he nor anyone else from National Distillers or from Bridgeport Brass had much, if any, influence, let alone control, over other key areas of managerial decision-making at Brad's.

In addition to Rudd's activities, plaintiffs argue that other National Distillers personnel exercised control over Brad's outside investments and production.

First, they contend that Salisbury and an assistant made the final decisions as to which assets of the "mini-conglomerate" to retain and which to liquidate. Compton testified that these efforts stemmed from Bradford's earlier request for management assistance from National Distillers and that all the proceeds were returned to Brad's to provide working capital. Although National Distillers' personnel apparently did make the final decision on the disposition of these assets, in many cases this power may be traced to the transaction in which they were assigned to National Distillers for precisely such a disposition.

Second, Compton also testified that a vice president of Bridgeport, Al Jones, visited Brad's on a weekly basis for five or six months, offering his advice and assistance wherever the production personnel at Brad's might need it. Nowhere in the record is it indicated that Jones ever exercised any control over the production process. To the contrary, his function was that of a consultant, checking data and offering his analysis. Compton specifically testified that neither Rudd nor Jones was concerned with production quantity.

These activities of both Rudd and the other are not sufficient to establish the degree of control requisite to "instrumentality" rule liability. The evidence shows that, at most, National Distillers shared managerial responsibility for some but not all aspects of the Brad's operation. That is not enough.

4. Finally, plaintiffs contend that control was shown indirectly by proving abuses of the Brad's corporation by National Distillers that could have been accomplished only with the requisite control.

First, plaintiffs complain that Rudd did not exercise his supposed veto enough. They point to Rudd-approved disbursements for a new house for Bradford, for a Mercedes automobile for the Bradford family, and for racing boats. Plaintiffs argue that these examples represent the abuse of power and control by National Distillers. In view of Rudd's limited functions at Brad's, the only fair inference that can be drawn from this configuration of "abuses of control" is that, in fact, Rudd had very little control over John Bradford.

* * *

After considering the plaintiffs' evidence in the most favorable light, it is plain that Brad's never became an "instrumentality" of National Distillers. Although National Distillers' position as a major creditor undoubtedly vested it with the capacity to exert great pressure and influence, we agree with the District Court that such a power is inherent in any creditor-debtor relationship and that the existence and exercise of such a power, alone, does not constitute control for the purposes of the "instrumentality" rule. Plaintiffs had to show the exercise of that control in the actual operation of the debtor corporation. Accordingly, because plaintiffs failed to produce substantial evidence of such actual operative total control, we affirm the directed verdict granted by the District Court.

Because we hold that plaintiffs failed to establish the requisite degree of control, we do not reach the question of whether the case should have been tried before a judge or before a jury.

Costs will be taxed to appellants.

AFFIRMED.

QUESTIONS

1. Why does Bridgeport Brass keep shipping brass to Brad's on open account?

2. While the court does not reach the question of whether dominating a corporation so it becomes a mere "instrumentality" proximately caused injury to plaintiffs, what kinds of injury can you imagine would persuade a court that dominance caused injury?

3. As part of the August 1, 1969 deal, Brad's pledged its plant and equipment to National Distillers, thus giving National a priority over general creditors. Why wouldn't a court focus on this as inequitable conduct that constituted an abuse of National's dominance of Brad's?

4. Note that part of the August 1, 1969 agreement provided that "National Distillers agreed that any income or proceeds from these unassigned assets would be used for certain designated purposes in aid of Brad's other creditors and then either would revert to Brad's *or would belong to National Distillers outright*." (emphasis supplied) If National sells assets of Brad's that aren't pledged to it, and retains the proceeds, what kind of claim might other creditors of Brad's make?

5. If you represented National Distillers in the August 1, 1969 negotiations, exactly what would your goals be in committing to "provide internal financial management assistance to help Brad's eliminate costly waste"? In order to avoid potential charges of domination of the debtor sufficient to make it a mere instrumentality, what would you like the agreement to provide in this area?

6. What does the court think that National's credit manager, Zimmerman, meant when he said that National "had the power, authority to fire Bradford and run him off"?

7. Would it have mattered if the August 1, 1969 agreement had given National Distillers the power "to fire Bradford and run him off"?

8. The court notes that Rudd's powers "were essentially negative in character." Why would this matter if he had a veto power over all purchase orders and all checks? Isn't this veto power the substantial equivalent of the power to make affirmative decisions?

9. Suppose you represent a bank that proposes to lend to a corporation already in some financial difficulty. The bank proposes to lend by obtaining a security interest in the debtor's accounts receivable. Each day the debtor will report its sales and deliver a form of assignment of the account to the bank, giving the bank the right to collect the account. As customers pay their bills, the borrower deposits the funds into a specialized "lock-box" account under the bank's control, which the bank can use to reduce the size of the loan. New sales by the debtor increase the amount the debtor can borrow, by as much as 80% of the face amount of the account. Does this arrangement give the bank life and death control over the debtor? Should you worry that this is a form of dominance?

10. Rudd, who had to approve all purchase orders and had the power to veto checks by refusing to co-sign, apparently allowed Brad's to purchase a home, a Mercedes and racing boats for Bradford. Why does the court reject the argument that this is an abuse of Brad's corporation in which National Distillers was complicit?

D. THE CLOSE CORPORATION AND DISALLOWANCE OF INTEREST DEDUCTIONS

Fin Hay Realty Co. v. United States

398 F.2d 694 (3d Cir.1968).

■ FREEDMAN, CIRCUIT JUDGE.

We are presented in this case with the recurrent problem whether funds paid to a close corporation by its shareholders were additional contributions to capital or loans on which the corporation's payment of interest was deductible under § 163 of the Internal Revenue Code of 1954.[1]

The problem necessarily calls for an evaluation of the facts, which we therefore detail.

Fin Hay Realty Co., the taxpayer, was organized on February 14, 1934, by Frank L. Finlaw and J. Louis Hay. Each of them contributed $10,000 for which he received one-half of the corporation's stock and at the same time each advanced an additional $15,000 for which the corporation issued to him its unsecured promissory note payable on demand and bearing interest at the rate of six per cent per annum. The corporation immediately purchased an apartment house in Newark, New Jersey, for $39,000 in cash. About a month later the two shareholders each advanced an additional $35,000 to the corporation in return for six per cent demand promissory notes and next day the corporation purchased two apartment buildings in East Orange, New Jersey, for which it paid $75,000 in cash and gave the

---

1. Section 163(a) provides: "There shall be allowed as a deduction all interest paid or accrued within the taxable year on indebtedness."

seller a six per cent, five year purchase money mortgage for the balance of $100,000.

Three years later, in October, 1937, the corporation created a new mortgage on all three properties and from the proceeds paid off the old mortgage on the East Orange property, which had been partially amortized. The new mortgage was for a five year term in the amount of $82,000 with interest at four and one-half per cent. In the following three years each of the shareholders advanced an additional $3,000 to the corporation, bringing the total advanced by each shareholder to $53,000, in addition to their acknowledged stock subscriptions of $10,000 each.

Finlaw died in 1941 and his stock and notes passed to his two daughters in equal shares. A year later the mortgage, which was about to fall due, was extended for a further period of five years with interest at four per cent. From the record it appears that it was subsequently extended until 1951. In 1949 Hay died and in 1951 his executor requested the retirement of his stock and the payment of his notes. The corporation thereupon refinanced its real estate for $125,000 and sold one of the buildings. With the net proceeds it paid Hay's estate $24,000 in redemption of his stock and $53,000 in retirement of his notes. Finlaw's daughters then became and still remain the sole shareholders of the corporation.

Thereafter the corporation continued to pay and deduct interest on Finlaw's notes, now held by his two daughters. In 1962 the Internal Revenue Service for the first time declared the payments on the notes not allowable as interest deductions and disallowed them for the tax years 1959 and 1960. The corporation thereupon repaid a total of $6,000 on account of the outstanding notes and in the following year after refinancing the mortgage on its real estate repaid the balance of $47,000. A short time later the Internal Revenue Service disallowed the interest deductions for the years 1961 and 1962. When the corporation failed to obtain refunds it brought this refund action in the district court. After a nonjury trial the court denied the claims and entered judgment for the United States. From this judgment the corporation appeals.

This case arose in a factual setting where it is the corporation which is the party concerned that its obligations be deemed to represent a debt and not a stock interest. In the long run in cases of this kind it is also important to the shareholder that his advance be deemed a loan rather than a capital contribution, for in such a case his receipt of repayment may be treated as the retirement of a loan rather than a taxable dividend.[6] There are other instances in which it is in the shareholder's interest that his advance to the corporation be considered a debt rather than an increase in his equity. A loss resulting from the worthlessness of stock is a capital loss under § 165(g), whereas a bad debt may be treated as an ordinary loss if it qualifies as a business bad debt under § 166. Similarly, it is only if a

---

6. The partial retirement of an equity interest may be considered as essentially equivalent to a dividend under § 302, while the repayment of even a debt whose principal has appreciated is taxed only as a capital gain under § 1232.

taxpayer receives debt obligations of a controlled corporation[7] that he can avoid the provision for nonrecognition of gains or losses on transfers of property to such a corporation under § 351.[8] These advantages in having the funds entrusted to a corporation treated as corporate obligations instead of contributions to capital have required the courts to look beyond the literal terms in which the parties have cast the transaction in order to determine its substantive nature.

In attempting to deal with this problem courts and commentators have isolated a number of criteria by which to judge the true nature of an investment which is in form a debt: (1) the intent of the parties; (2) the identity between creditors and shareholders; (3) the extent of participation in management by the holder of the instrument; (4) the ability of the corporation to obtain funds from outside sources; (5) the "thinness" of the capital structure in relation to debt; (6) the risk involved; (7) the formal indicia of the arrangement; (8) the relative position of the obligees as to other creditors regarding the payment of interest and principal; (9) the voting power of the holder of the instrument; (10) the provision of a fixed rate of interest; (11) a contingency on the obligation to repay; (12) the source of the interest payments; (13) the presence or absence of a fixed maturity date; (14) a provision for redemption by the corporation; (15) a provision for redemption at the option of the holder; and (16) the timing of the advance with reference to the organization of the corporation.

While the Internal Revenue Code of 1954 was under consideration, and after its adoption, Congress sought to identify the criteria which would determine whether an investment represents a debt or equity, but these and similar efforts have not found acceptance. It still remains true that neither any single criterion nor any series of criteria can provide a conclusive answer in the kaleidoscopic circumstances which individual cases present.

The various factors which have been identified in the cases are only aids in answering the ultimate question whether the investment, analyzed in terms of its economic reality, constitutes risk capital entirely subject to the fortunes of the corporate venture or represents a strict debtor-creditor relationship. Since there is often an element of risk in a loan, just as there is an element of risk in an equity interest, the conflicting elements do not end at a clear line in all cases.

In a corporation which has numerous shareholders with varying interests, the arm's-length relationship between the corporation and a shareholder who supplies funds to it inevitably results in a transaction whose form mirrors its substance. Where the corporation is closely held, however, and the same persons occupy both sides of the bargaining table, form does

---

7. While not all debt obligations qualify for the desired tax treatment, equity interests can never qualify.

8. A taxpayer might wish to avoid § 351 when he transfers depreciated property to the corporation and seeks to recognize the loss immediately and also when the transferred property is to be resold by the corporation but will not qualify for capital gains treatment in the hands of the corporation.

not necessarily correspond to the intrinsic economic nature of the transaction, for the parties may mold it at their will with no countervailing pull. This is particularly so where a shareholder can have the funds he advances to a corporation treated as corporate obligations instead of contributions to capital without affecting his proportionate equity interest. Labels, which are perhaps the best expression of the subjective intention of parties to a transaction, thus lose their meaningfulness.

To seek economic reality in objective terms of course disregards the personal interest which a shareholder may have in the welfare of the corporation in which he is a dominant force. But an objective standard is one imposed by the very fact of his dominant position and is much fairer than one which would presumptively construe all such transactions against the shareholder's interest. Under an objective test of economic reality it is useful to compare the form which a similar transaction would have taken had it been between the corporation and an outside lender, and if the shareholder's advance is far more speculative than what an outsider would make, it is obviously a loan in name only.

In the present case all the formal indicia of an obligation were meticulously made to appear. The corporation, however, was the complete creature of the two shareholders who had the power to create whatever appearance would be of tax benefit to them despite the economic reality of the transaction. Each shareholder owned an equal proportion of stock and was making an equal additional contribution, so that whether Finlaw and Hay designated any part of their additional contributions as debt or as stock would not dilute their proportionate equity interests. There was no restriction because of the possible excessive debt structure, for the corporation had been created to acquire real estate and had no outside creditors except mortgagees who, of course, would have no concern for general creditors because they had priority in the security of the real estate. The position of the mortgagees also rendered of no significance the possible subordination of the notes to other debts of the corporation, a matter which in some cases this Court has deemed significant.

The shareholders here, moreover, lacked one of the principal advantages of creditors. Although the corporation issued demand notes for the advances, nevertheless, as the court below found, it could not have repaid them for a number of years. The economic reality was that the corporation used the proceeds of the notes to purchase its original assets, and the advances represented a long term commitment dependent on the future value of the real estate and the ability of the corporation to sell or refinance it. Only because such an entwining of interest existed between the two shareholders and the corporation, so different from the arm's-length relationship between a corporation and an outside creditor, were they willing to invest in the notes and allow them to go unpaid for so many years while the corporation continued to enjoy the advantages of uninterrupted ownership of its real estate.

It is true that real estate values rose steadily with a consequent improvement in the mortgage market, so that looking back the investment now appears to have been a good one. As events unfolded, the corporation reached a point at which it could have repaid the notes through refinancing, but this does not obliterate the uncontradicted testimony that in 1934 it was impossible to obtain any outside mortgage financing for real estate of this kind except through the device of a purchase money mortgage taken back by the seller.

It is argued that the rate of interest at six per cent per annum was far more than the shareholders could have obtained from other investments. This argument, however, is self-defeating, for it implies that the shareholders would damage their own corporation by an overcharge for interest. There was, moreover, enough objective evidence to neutralize this contention. The outside mortgage obtained at the time the corporation purchased the East Orange property bore interest at the rate of six per cent even though the mortgagee was protected by an equity in excess of forty per cent of the value of the property.[14] In any event, to compare the six per cent interest rate of the notes with other 1934 rates ignores the most salient feature of the notes—their risk. It is difficult to escape the inference that a prudent outside businessman would not have risked his capital in six per cent unsecured demand notes in Fin Hay Realty Co. in 1934. The evidence therefore amply justifies the conclusion of the district court that the form which the parties gave to their transaction did not match its economic reality.

It is argued that even if the advances may be deemed to have been contributions to capital when they were originally made in 1934, a decisive change occurred when the original shareholder, Finlaw, died and his heirs continued to hold the notes without demanding payment. This, it is said could be construed as a decision to reinvest, and if by 1941 the notes were sufficiently secure to be considered bona fide debt, they should now be so treated for tax purposes. Such a conclusion, however, does not inevitably follow. Indeed, the weight of the circumstances leads to the opposite conclusion.

First, there is nothing in the record to indicate that the corporation could have readily raised the cash with which to pay off Finlaw's notes on his death in 1941. When Hay, the other shareholder, died in 1949 and his executor two years later requested the retirement of his interest, the corporation in order to carry this out sold one of its properties and refinanced the others. Again, when in 1963 the corporation paid off the notes held by Finlaw's daughters after the Internal Revenue Service had disallowed the interest deductions for 1961 and 1962 it again refinanced its real estate. There is nothing in the record which would sustain a finding that the corporation could have readily undertaken a similar financing in 1941, when Finlaw died even if we assume that the corporation was able to undertake the appropriate refinancing ten years later to liquidate Hay's interest. Moreover, there was no objective evidence to indicate that in 1941 Finlaw's daughters viewed the notes as changed in character or in security,

---

14. The corporation purchased the property for $175,000 and the sellers took back a purchase money mortgage of $100,000.

or indeed that they viewed the stock and notes as separate and distinct investments. To indulge in a theoretical conversion of equity contributions into a debt obligation in 1941 when Finlaw died would be to ignore what such a conversion might have entailed. For Finlaw's estate might then have been chargeable with the receipt of dividends at the time the equity was redeemed and converted into a debt. To recognize retrospectively such a change in the character of the obligation would be to assume a conclusion with consequences unfavorable to the parties, which they themselves never acknowledged.

The burden was on the taxpayer to prove that the determination by the Internal Revenue Service that advances represented capital contributions was incorrect. The district court was justified in holding that the taxpayer had not met this burden.

The judgment of the district court will be affirmed.

NOTE

In an apparent attempt to bring more clarity to this area, in 1969 Congress enacted 26 U.S.C. § 385:

§ 385. Treatment of certain interests in corporations as stock or indebtedness.

(a) Authority to prescribe regulations. The Secretary is authorized to prescribe such regulations as may be necessary or appropriate to determine whether an interest in a corporation is to be treated for purposes of this title as stock or indebtedness (or as in part stock and in part indebtedness).

(b) Factors. The regulations prescribed under this section shall set forth factors which are to be taken into account in determining with respect to a particular factual situation whether a debtor-creditor relationship exists or a corporation-shareholder relationship exists. The factors so set forth in the regulations may include among other factors:

(1) whether there is a written unconditional promise to pay on demand or on a specified date a sum certain in money in return for an adequate consideration in money or money's worth, and to pay a fixed rate of interest,

(2) whether there is subordination to or preference over any indebtedness of the corporation,

(3) the ratio of debt to equity of the corporation,

(4) whether there is convertibility into the stock of the corporation, and

(5) the relationship between holdings of stock in the corporation and holdings of the interest in question.

(c) Effect of classification by issuer.

(1) In general. The characterization (as of the time of issuance) by the issuer as to whether an interest in a corporation is stock or

indebtedness shall be binding on such issuer and on all holders of such interest (but shall not be binding on the Secretary).

(2) Notification of inconsistent treatment. Except as provided in regulations, paragraph (1) shall not apply to any holder of an interest if such holder on his return discloses that he is treating such interest in a manner inconsistent with the characterization referred to in paragraph (1).

(3) Regulations. The Secretary is authorized to require such information as the Secretary determines to be necessary to carry out the provisions of this subsection.

In the years since 1969 the Treasury tried to adopt regulations and gave up the effort. Readers cannot rely on the list of factors in section 385 as the exclusive factors to be considered. The Senate Committee Report on the Tax Reform Act of 1969 stated: "It is not intended that only these factors be included in the guidelines [to be adopted by the Treasury] or that, with respect to a particular situation, any of these factors must be included in the guidelines, or that any of the factors which are included by statute must necessarily be given any more weight than other factors added by the regulations."

QUESTIONS

1. The court held that arms' length lenders would not have loaned money to a business with the risks it faced for 6% interest. Is there any evidence to support this conclusion?

2. Was it realistic to make these demand notes under the circumstances existing in 1934?

3. Real estate investors typically borrow as much of the purchase price of property as they can manage. Is this evidence that the loans that enable the corporation to purchase its properties were really equity?

4. Suppose three entrepreneurs approach you about starting a corporate business. They each propose to put in $50,000 for stock. They discuss each lending the corporation another $100,000, but instead decide that each will personally guarantee a $100,000 part of a bank loan to be obtained by the corporation. Assuming that the corporation requires the entire $450,000 to begin business, and that the corporation could obtain no credit without the shareholders' guarantees, is it likely that the interest paid by the corporation to the bank will be deductible?

E. Liability of Affiliated Parties under the "Deepening Insolvency" Doctrine

Those who assist a debtor in obtaining borrowings beyond its ability to repay may at first think of themselves as simply prolonging the life of the debtor, and thus giving it a chance to recover from any disasters that have placed it in a precarious financial position. Recently a number of courts have recognized the tort of "deepening insolvency" to hold participants liable to a bankrupt debtor's estate for the damages thus caused by increased indebtedness. The following discussion involves claims brought against attorneys and investment bankers who arranged the public marketing of additional debt by an insolvent debtor. Other cases have involved accounting firms, and in some cases commercial banks that served as depositories for funds.

Official Committee of Unsecured Creditors v. R. F. Lafferty & Co.

267 F.3d 340 (3d Cir.2001).

■ FUENTES, CIRCUIT JUDGE:

[This case involved charges of a Ponzi scheme,* in which the family controlling the debtor corporations caused them to issue huge amounts of debt securities, which were then taken at least in part as salaries and other compensation by some of the defendants. Walnut Equipment Leasing Company experienced financial difficulties, and created a Special Purpose Entity, Equipment Leasing Corporation of America ("ELCOA") to raise capital through debt sales to acquire equipment leases from Walnut. Fraud in the offer and sale of these securities was alleged, in the form of fraudulent financial statements by both companies. Among the alleged participants in the fraud were a law firm controlled by the majority shareholder of Walnut, William Shapiro, their accountant, Cogen Sklar,

---

* Carlo "Charles" Ponzi was an Italian immigrant who lived in Boston, and was considering publishing a magazine. He had written about the publication to a person in Spain, who replied and included an international postal reply coupon, which Ponzi could take to his local post office to exchange for stamps to be used to mail the magazine to Spain. Ponzi discovered that the coupon had cost the equivalent of one cent, but was exchangeable in the U.S. for six one-cent stamps. Eureka! Ponzi thought he had found the ultimate arbitrage opportunity. In order to finance this activity, he sought funds from local investors, promising a 50% return on borrowed funds within 90 days. Not unreasonable, since he could earn a 600% return with every dollar invested in postal reply coupons overseas. But the transaction costs of arbitrage were higher than he anticipated—there were long delays in transferring currency abroad, and unexpected red tape in dealing with various postal organizations. But Ponzi bragged about his scheme, and investors lined up at the door to invest with him. While he promised to repay funds with 50% interest in 90 days, in fact he repaid it in 45 days. Unfortunately, he did this with funds received from later investors. Word of these returns spread, and he was soon taking in a million dollars a week. His newly hired staff was kept so busy they were storing investors' cash in closets, desk drawers and wastebaskets. Within six months, Ponzi was living the life of a millionaire. While authorities were suspicious, no investor filed a complaint, because all had been repaid. A newspaper story questioning the legitimacy of his business led Ponzi to offer to have his books audited. Within hours of the story a run on his business occurred, but he was able to repay all of the investors who appeared, which restored confidence in the business. This continued until the auditors declared that his business was bankrupt, and it collapsed. Over 40,000 people had invested with him. He was prosecuted for fraud and sentenced to five years in federal prison, of which he served three and one-half, and was then sentenced to an additional seven to nine years in Massachusetts. While out on bond pending an appeal, Ponzi finally did what most good swindlers do much earlier—he ran and disappeared, turning up under another name in Florida to conduct a land swindle After another conviction, he was transferred to Massachusetts to serve his sentence. Upon deportation to Italy in 1934, he still had many fans who gave him an enthusiastic send-off.—Ed.

LLP, and their underwriters, R. F. Lafferty & Co. and Liss Financial Services, Inc. The Court of Appeals held that Pennsylvania courts would recognize a claim for "deepening insolvency." Part of the discussion involved whether this was a claim to be brought by the bankrupt estate or by the creditors.]

We agree with the District Court's evaluation. With the exception of a single federal securities law claim, the Committee brought only state common law claims on behalf of the Debtors. According to the Amended Complaint, the defendants (including Lafferty), through their alleged fraud and participation in the scheme, injured the Debtors by "wrongfully expand[ing] the [D]ebtors' debt out of all proportion of their ability to repay and ultimately forc[ing] the [D]ebtors to seek bankruptcy protection." In other words, the Committee alleges an injury to the Debtors' corporate property from the fraudulent expansion of corporate debt and prolongation of corporate life. This type of injury has been referred to as "deepening insolvency." As far as the state law claims are concerned, it is clear that, to the extent Pennsylvania law recognizes a cause of action for the Debtors against Lafferty, the Committee can demonstrate the injury required for standing to sue in federal court. Given Lafferty's arguments, the standing analysis then consists of three inquiries: (1) whether the Committee is merely asserting claims belonging to the creditors, (2) whether "deepening insolvency" is a valid theory giving rise to a cognizable injury under Pennsylvania state law, and (3) whether, as Lafferty contends, the injury is merely illusory.

* * *

B. Whether "deepening insolvency" is a valid theory that gives rise to a cognizable injury under state law

Having established that the Committee brought claims on behalf of the Debtors, rather than the creditors, we must now determine whether the alleged theory of injury—"deepening insolvency"—is cognizable under Pennsylvania law. Neither the Pennsylvania Supreme Court nor any intermediate Pennsylvania court has directly addressed this issue. In the absence of an opinion from the state's highest tribunal, we must don the soothsayer's garb and predict how that court would rule if it were presented with the question. Indeed, because no state or federal courts have interpreted Pennsylvania law on this subject, we will rely predominantly on decisions interpreting the law of other jurisdictions and on the policy underlying Pennsylvania tort law to make this prediction.

Drawing guidance from these authorities, we conclude that, if faced with the issue, the Pennsylvania Supreme Court would determine that "deepening insolvency" may give rise to a cognizable injury. First and foremost, the theory is essentially sound. Under federal bankruptcy law, insolvency is a financial condition in which a corporation's debts exceed the fair market value of its assets. Even when a corporation is insolvent, its corporate property may have value. The fraudulent and concealed incurrence of debt can damage that value in several ways. For example, to the extent that bankruptcy is not already a certainty, the incurrence of debt can force an insolvent corporation into bankruptcy, thus inflicting legal and administrative costs on the corporation. See Richard A. Brealey & Stewart C. Myers, Principles of Corporate Finance 487 (5th ed. 1996) ("[B]y issuing risky debt,[a corporation] give[s] lawyers and the court system a claim on the firm if it defaults."). When brought on by unwieldy debt, bankruptcy also creates operational limitations which hurt a corporation's ability to run its business in a profitable manner. Aside from causing actual bankruptcy, deepening insolvency can undermine a corporation's relationships with its customers, suppliers, and employees. The very threat of bankruptcy, brought about through fraudulent debt, can shake the confidence of parties dealing with the corporation, calling into question its ability to perform, thereby damaging the corporation's assets, the value of which often depends on the performance of other parties. In addition, prolonging an insolvent corporation's life through bad debt may simply cause the dissipation of corporate assets.

These harms can be averted, and the value within an insolvent corporation salvaged, if the corporation is dissolved in a timely manner, rather than kept afloat with spurious debt. As the Seventh Circuit explained in Schacht v. Brown:

> [C]ases [that oppose "deepening insolvency"] rest[ ] upon a seriously flawed assumption, i.e., that the fraudulent prolongation of a corporation's life beyond insolvency is automatically to be considered a benefit to the corporation's interests. This premise collides with common sense, for the corporate body is ineluctably damaged by the deepening of its insolvency, through increased exposure to creditor liability. Indeed, in most cases, it would be crucial that the insolvency of the corporation be disclosed, so that shareholders may exercise their right to dissolve the corporation in order to cut their losses. Thus, acceptance of a rule which would bar a corporation from recovering damages due to the hiding of information concerning its insolvency would create perverse incentives for wrong-doing officers and directors to conceal the true financial condition of the corporation from the corporate body as long as possible.

711 F.2d 1343, 1350 (7th Cir.1983) (citations omitted) (emphasis added).

Growing acceptance of the deepening insolvency theory confirms its soundness. In recent years, a number of federal courts have held that "deepening insolvency" may give rise to a cognizable injury to corporate debtors. See, e.g., id. (applying Illinois law and holding that, where a debtor corporation was fraudulently continued in business past the point of insolvency, the liquidator had standing to maintain a civil action under racketeering law); Hannover Corp. of America v. Beckner, 211 B.R. 849, 854–55 (M.D.La.1997) (applying Louisiana law and stating that "a corporation can suffer injury from fraudulently extended life, dissipation of assets, or increased insolvency"); Allard v. Arthur Andersen & Co., 924 F.Supp. 488, 494 (S.D.N.Y.1996) (applying New York law and stating that, as to suit brought by bankruptcy trustee, "[b]ecause courts have permitted recovery under the 'deepening insolvency' theory, [defendant] is not entitled to summary judgment as to whatever portion of the claim for relief represents damages flowing from indebtedness to trade creditors"); In re Gouiran Holdings, Inc., 165 B.R. 104, 107 (E.D.N.Y.1994) (applying New York law, and refusing to dismiss claims brought by a creditors' committee because it was possible that, "under some set of facts two years of negligently prepared financial statements could have been a substantial cause of [the debtor] incurring unmanageable debt and filing for bankruptcy protection"); Feltman v. Prudential Bache Securities, 122 B.R. 466, 473 (S.D.Fla. 1990) (stating that an " 'artificial and fraudulently prolonged life . . . and . . . consequent dissipation of assets' constitutes a recognized injury for which a corporation can sue under certain conditions", but concluding that there was no injury on the facts). Some state courts have also recognized the deepening insolvency theory. See, e.g., Herbert H. Post & Co. v. Sidney Bitterman, Inc., 219 A.D.2d 214, 639 N.Y.S.2d 329 (N.Y.App.Div. 1st Dep't 1996) (applying New York law and allowing a malpractice claim for failing to detect embezzlement that weakened a company, which already was operating at a loss, thereby causing default on loans and forcing liquidation); Corcoran v. Frank B. Hall & Co., 149 A.D.2d 165, 175, 545 N.Y.S.2d 278 (N.Y.App.Div. 1st Dep't 1989) (applying New York law and allowing claims for causing a company to "assume additional risks and thereby increase the extent of its exposure to creditors").

Significantly, one of the most venerable principles in Pennsylvania jurisprudence, and in most common law jurisdictions for that matter, is that, where there is an injury, the law provides a remedy. * * * Thus, where "deepening insolvency" causes damage to corporate property, we believe that the Pennsylvania Supreme Court would provide a remedy by recognizing a cause of action for that injury.

* * *

We pause here to consider the 19th century case of Patterson v. Franklin, 176 Pa. 612, 35 A. 205 (1896), an arguably applicable decision of the Pennsylvania Supreme Court. In Patterson, an assignee standing in the shoes of an insolvent corporation brought suit against the incorporators, claiming that they had allegedly made false representations in the statement of incorporation. Id. at 206. Apparently, the false representations had allowed the corporation to contract more debts. Id. On these allegations, the Pennsylvania Supreme Court affirmed the dismissal of the assignee's claims, reasoning that, because the assignee had alleged that the corporation had benefitted from the representations, there was no viable cause of action. Id. In our view, Patterson is not controlling here. The Patterson court never expressly considered the "deepening insolvency" theory, as the opinion does not indicate that the assignee presented any version of that argument to the court. In fact, it seems that the assignee in Patterson had not even alleged an injury to the corporation at all:

> The fraud was perpetrated for its benefit. It was a gainer, not a loser because of it. It was given a considerable credit by the statement to which, as it is alleged, it had no claim whatever.

Id. (emphasis added). Thus, given the allegations in the case, it was perfectly reasonable for the court in Patterson to affirm the dismissal. See also Kinter v. Connolly, 233 Pa. 5, 81 A. 905, 905 (1911) (rejecting receiver's claim on behalf of the corporation against the directors for fraudulent statements that induced parties to do business with the corporation because "there [was] no averment that any act or omission of those of the defendants who demur caused loss or injury to the [corporation].").

Our reading of Patterson is informed in part by its age. In the hundred-plus years between that decision and the present, the business practices of corporations in the United States have changed quite dramatically. Likewise, society's understanding of corporate theory has grown. Therefore, we decline to draw any broad principle from Patterson, a decision which did not directly address "deepening insolvency."

In sum, we believe that the soundness of the theory, its growing acceptance among courts, and the remedial theme in Pennsylvania law would persuade the Pennsylvania Supreme Court to recognize "deepening insolvency" as giving rise to a cognizable injury in the proper circumstances.

* * *

QUESTIONS

1. What does the court mean by "fraudulent debt"?

2. What is wrong with prolonging a corporation's life?

3. How could issuing more debt, which may "deepen" insolvency, prolong a corporation's life?

4. If you are a shareholder in a potentially or actually insolvent corporation that lacks funds to pay employee salaries, would you want to persuade them to take notes in lieu of salary? If so, why?

5. Is postponing a bankruptcy filing in the interests of the corporation? Do you have to decide who is the "corporation" before you can answer this question?

NOTE

The Third Circuit declined to expand its Lafferty holding in In re: CitX Corporation, Inc. v. Detweiler, 448 F.3d 672 (3d Cir.2006). In CitX the debtor was alleged to have falsified its financial statements to deceive its accounting firm and obtain "clean" financial statements that allowed it to raise new capital through fraudulent stock sales. The court affirmed the district court's dismissal of a negligent misrepresentation claim against the accounting firm on the basis that the claim of fraudulent stock sales did not allege harm to the creditors or CitX. stating that "[a]ssuming for the sake of argument that Detweiler's financial statements allowed CitX to raise over one million dollars, that did nothing to 'deepen' CitX's insolvency. Rather, it lessened CitX's insolvency. Before the equity infusion, CitX was

$2,000,000 in the red (using round numbers for ease of discussion). With the added $1,000,000 investment, it was thereby insolvent only $1,000,000. This hardly deepened insolvency." 448 F.3d at 677. Note that the fraudulent stock offering increased CitX's contingent liabilities by $1,000,000, although this would not have been recorded on the books (and even then only in a footnote) until a claim was brought on behalf of the defrauded stockholders. Once this happened, CitX would have remained $2,000,000 in the red. How does this differ from Lafferty?

Other federal courts have extended Lafferty's reasoning to other states. OHC Liquidation Trust v. Credit Suisse First Boston, 340 B.R. 510 (Bankr. D. Del. 2006) held, on a motion to dismiss, that the Supreme Courts of Delaware, New York and North Carolina would recognize a claim of deepening insolvency. The opinion contains an extensive discussion of the origins and dubious development of the doctrine. Vice Chancellor Strine rejected this suggestion for Delaware later that year, as you will read below.

Trenwick America Litigation Trust v. Ernst & Young, L.L.P.

906 A.2d 168 (Del. Ch. 2006).

■ STRINE, VICE CHANCELLOR.

[On motion to dismiss the complaint.]

This case is unusual. The primary defendants in this case were directors of a publicly listed insurance holding company. All but one of the eleven directors was an independent director. The other director was the chief executive officer of the holding company.

In 1998, the holding company embarked on a strategy of growth by acquisition. Within a span of two years, the holding company acquired three other unaffiliated insurance companies in arms-length transactions. The two transactions at issue in this case involved the acquisition of publicly-traded entities and were approved by a vote of the holding company's stockholders. The holding company's stockholder base was diverse and the company had nothing close to a controlling stockholder.

In connection with the last acquisition, the holding company redomiciled to Bermuda, for the disclosed reason that tax advantages would flow from that move. Consistent with the objective of reducing its tax burden, the holding company reorganized its subsidiaries by national line, creating lines of United States, United Kingdom, and Bermudan subsidiaries. As a result of that reorganization, the holding company's top U.S. subsidiary came to be the intermediate parent of all of the holding company's U.S. operations. The top U.S. subsidiary also continued and deepened its role as a guarantor of the holding company's overall debt, including becoming a primary guarantor of $260 million of a $490 million line of credit, a secondary guarantor of the remainder of that debt, and assuming the holding company's responsibility for approximately $190 million worth of various debt securities. Nonetheless, after that reorganization, the financial statements of just the top U.S. subsidiary indicated that it had a positive asset value of over $200 million.

In 2003, the holding company had to place its insurance operations in run-off globally. The holding company and its top U.S. subsidiary filed for bankruptcy. The cause of the failure was that the claims made by the insureds against the holding company's operating subsidiaries (including the insureds of the companies it had acquired) exceeded estimates and outstripped the holding company's capacity to service the claims and its debt.

The reorganization plan for the top U.S. subsidiary resulted in the creation of a Litigation Trust. That Trust was assigned all the causes of action that the U.S. subsidiary owned.

The Litigation Trust then brought this case. The essential premise of its claims is that the majority independent board of the holding company engaged in an imprudent business strategy by acquiring other insurers who had underestimated their potential claims exposure. As a result of that imprudent strategy, the holding company and its top U.S. subsidiary were eventually rendered insolvent, to the detriment of their creditors. Not only that, because the top U.S. subsidiary took on obligations to support its parent's debt and actually assumed some of that debt, the top U.S. subsidiary and its creditors suffered even greater injury than the holding company and its creditors.

* * *

[The court examined and rejected claims that the board had breached duties to creditors because Trenwick America was insolvent at the time of the reorganization, and that the Trenwick directors enriched themselves through the reorganization.]

D. Delaware Law Does Not Recognize A Cause Of Action For So–Called "Deepening Insolvency"

In Count II of the complaint, the Litigation Trust seeks to state a claim against the former Trenwick America directors for "deepening insolvency." The Count consists of the following cursory allegations:

From 2000 until 2003, these [Trenwick America] Defendants fraudulently concealed the true nature and extent of [Trenwick America's] financial problems by expanding the amount of debt undertaken by [Trenwick America].

The [Trenwick America] Defendants knew that [Trenwick America] would not be able to repay this increased debt, but fraudulently represented to creditors and other outsiders that the debt would be repaid.

By these actions, [Trenwick America's] officers and directors prolonged the corporate life of [Trenwick America] and increased its insolvency, until [Trenwick America] was forced to file for bankruptcy on August 20, 2003.

As a result of [those] actions, [Trenwick America] suffered damages to be proven at trial, which [the Litigation Trust] is entitled to recover.

The concept of deepening insolvency has been discussed at length in federal jurisprudence, perhaps because the term has the kind of stentorious academic ring that tends to dull the mind to the concept's ultimate emptiness.

Delaware law imposes no absolute obligation on the board of a company that is unable to pay its bills to cease operations and to liquidate. Even when the company is insolvent, the board may pursue, in good faith, strategies to maximize the value of the firm. As a thoughtful federal decision recognizes, Chapter 11 of the Bankruptcy Code expresses a societal recognition that an insolvent corporation's creditors (and society as a whole) may benefit if the corporation continues to conduct operations in the hope of turning things around.[103]

If the board of an insolvent corporation, acting with due diligence and good faith, pursues a business strategy that it believes will increase the corporation's value, but that also involves the incurrence of additional debt, it does not become a guarantor of that strategy's success. That the strategy results in continued insolvency and an even more insolvent entity does not in itself give rise to a cause of action. Rather, in such a scenario the directors are protected by the business judgment rule. To conclude otherwise would fundamentally transform Delaware law.

The rejection of an independent cause of action for deepening insolvency does not absolve directors of insolvent corporations of responsibility. Rather, it remits plaintiffs to the contents of their traditional toolkit, which contains, among other things, causes of action for breach of fiduciary duty and for fraud. The contours of these causes of action have been carefully

---

103. *See, e.g., Kittay v. Atlantic Bank of N.Y. (In re Global Servs.)*, 316 B.R. 451, 460 (Bankr. S.D.N.Y. 2004) ("The fiduciaries of an insolvent business might well conclude that the company should continue to operate in order to maximize its 'long-term wealth creating capacity,' or more generally, its enterprise value. In fact, chapter 11 is based on the accepted notion that a business is worth more to everyone alive than dead."). *See also NLRB v. Bildisco & Bildisco*, 465 U.S. 513, 528, 104 S.Ct. 1188, 79 L. Ed. 2d 482 (1984) ("The fundamental purpose of reorganization is to prevent a debtor from going into liquidation, with an attendant loss of jobs and possible misuse of economic resources."); *In re RSL Com Primecall, Inc.*, 2003 WL 22989669, at * 8 (Bankr. S.D.N.Y. Dec. 11, 2003) ("It has never been the law in the United States that directors are not afforded significant discretion as to whether an insolvent company can 'work out' its problems or should file a bankruptcy petition."); *Steinberg v. Kendig (In re Ben Franklin Retail Stores, Inc.)*, 225 B.R. 646, 655 (Bankr. N.D. Ill. 1998) (noting there is no duty "to liquidate and pay creditors when the corporation is near insolvency, provided that in the directors' informed, good faith judgment there is an alternative"), *aff'd in part & rev'd in other part*, 2000 WL 28266 (N.D. Ill. 2000); H.R. REP. No. 95–595, at 220 (1977), *as reprinted in* 1978 U.S.C.C.A.N. 1978, 5963, 6179 ("The premise of a business reorganization is that assets that are used for production in the industry for which they are designed are more valuable than those same assets sold for scrap ... It is more economically efficient to reorganize than to liquidate, because it preserves jobs and assets.").

shaped by generations of experience, in order to balance the societal interests in protecting investors and creditors against exploitation by directors and in providing directors with sufficient insulation so that they can seek to create wealth through the good faith pursuit of business strategies that involve a risk of failure. If a plaintiff cannot state a claim that the directors of an insolvent corporation acted disloyally or without due care in implementing a business strategy, it may not cure that deficiency simply by alleging that the corporation became more insolvent as a result of the failed strategy.

Moreover, the fact of insolvency does not render the concept of "deepening insolvency" a more logical one than the concept of "shallowing profitability." That is, the mere fact that a business in the red gets redder when a business decision goes wrong and a business in the black gets paler does not explain why the law should recognize an independent cause of action based on the decline in enterprise value in the crimson setting and not in the darker one. If in either setting the directors remain responsible to exercise their business judgment considering the company's business context, then the appropriate tool to examine the conduct of the directors is the traditional fiduciary duty ruler. No doubt the fact of insolvency might weigh heavily in a court's analysis of, for example, whether the board acted with fidelity and care in deciding to undertake more debt to continue the company's operations, but that is the proper role of insolvency, to act as an important contextual fact in the fiduciary duty metric. In that context, our law already requires the directors of an insolvent corporation to consider, as fiduciaries, the interests of the corporation's creditors who, by definition, are owed more than the corporation has the wallet to repay.[104]

In this case, the Litigation Trust has not stated a viable claim for breach of fiduciary duty. It may not escape that failure by seeking to have this court recognize a loose phrase as a cause of action under our law, when that recognition would be inconsistent with the principles shaping our state's corporate law. In so ruling, I reach a result consistent with a growing body of federal jurisprudence, which has recognized that those

---

104. *See, e.g., Prod. Res. Group*, 863 A.2d at 791 (Del. Ch. 2004) ("When a firm has reached the point of insolvency, it is settled that under Delaware law, the firm's directors are said to owe fiduciary duties to the company's creditors. This is an uncontroversial proposition and does not completely turn on its head the equitable obligations of the directors to the firm itself. The directors continue to have the task of attempting to maximize the economic value of the firm. That much of their job does not change. But the fact of insolvency does necessarily affect the constituency on whose behalf the directors are pursuing that end. By definition, the fact of insolvency places the creditors in the shoes normally occupied by the shareholders—that of residual risk-bearers. Where the assets of the company are insufficient to pay its debts, and the remaining equity is underwater, whatever remains of the company's assets will be used to pay creditors, usually either by seniority of debt or on a pro rata basis among debtors of equal priority.") (internal citations omitted); *Angelo, Gordon & Co. v. Allied Riser Comm. Corp.*, 805 A.2d 221, 229 (Del. Ch. 2002) ("Even where the law recognizes that the duties of directors encompass the interests of creditors, there is room for application of the business judgment rule."); *Geyer v. Ingersoll Publ'ns Co.*, 621 A.2d 784, 787 (Del. Ch. 1992) ("[W]hen the insolvency exception [arises], it creates fiduciary duties for directors for the benefit of creditors."); *see generally* Laura Lin, *Shift of Fiduciary Duty Upon Corporate Insolvency: Proper Scope of Directors' Duty to Creditors*, 46 VAND. L. REV. 1485 (1993).

federal courts that became infatuated with the concept, did not look closely enough at the object of their ardor.[105] Among the earlier federal decisions embracing the notion—by way of a hopeful prediction of state law—that deepening insolvency should be recognized as a cause of action admittedly were three decisions from within the federal Circuit of which Delaware is a part.[106] None of those decisions explains the rationale for concluding that deepening insolvency should be recognized as a cause of action or how such recognition would be consistent with traditional concepts of fiduciary responsibility. In a more recent decision, the Third Circuit has taken a more skeptical view of the deepening insolvency concept,[107] a view consistent with the outcome reached in this decision. In fact, many of the decisions that seem to embrace the concept of deepening insolvency do not clarify whether the concept is a stand-alone cause of action or a measurement of damages (the extent of deepening) for other causes of action.[108]

---

105. Good examples of this jurisprudence include: *Bondi v. Bank of America Corp. (In re Parmalat)*, 383 F. Supp.2d 587 (S. D. N. Y. 2005) (explaining that "[i]f officers and directors can be shown to have breached their fiduciary duties by deepening a corporation's insolvency, and the resulting injury to the corporation is cognizable . . . that injury is compensable on a claim for breach of fiduciary duty" and declining to recognize a separate tort for deepening insolvency under North Carolina law); *Alberts v. Tuft (In re Greater Southeast Community Hosp. Corp.)*, 333 B. R. 506, 517 (Bankr. D.C. 2005) ("Recognizing that a condition is harmful and calling it a tort are two different things. The District of Columbia courts have not yet recognized a cause of action for deepening insolvency, and this court sees no reason why they should. . . . There is no point in recognizing and adjudicating 'new' causes of action when established ones cover the same ground. The Trust's duplicative claims will be dismissed."); *In re Vartec Telecom, Inc.*, 335 B. R. 631, 641, 644 (Bankr. N. D. Tex. 2005) (describing recent cases and the trend to decline recognizing deepening insolvency as a separate tort because the injury caused is substantially duplicated by torts already in existence); *In re Global Servs.*, 316 B. R. at 459 ("The distinction between 'deepening insolvency' as a tort or damage theory may be one unnecessary to make. Prolonging an insolvent corporation's life, without more, will not result in liability under either approach. Instead, one seeking to recover for 'deepening insolvency' must show that the defendant prolonged the company's life in breach of a separate duty, or committed an actionable tort that contributed to the continued operation of a corporation and its increased debt.") (citations omitted); Sabin Willet, *The Shallows of Deepening Insolvency*, 60 Bus. LAW. 549 (2005) (providing detailed reasons not to recognize deepening insolvency as a cause of action). *See also In re CitX Corp., Inc.*, 448 F.3d 672, 679 n.11 (3d Cir. 2006) (rejecting, as without basis in reason, a request to hold that a claim of negligence will sustain a cause of action for deepening insolvency under Pennsylvania law).

106. *See Official Comm. of Unsec. Creditors v. R.F. Lafferty*, 267 F.3d 340 (3d Cir. 2001) (recognizing deepening insolvency as a valid cause of action under Pennsylvania law where defendants used fraudulent financial statements to raise capital in the debtor's name, thereby deepening debtor's insolvency and causing bankruptcy); *OHC Liquidation Trust v. Credit Suisse First Boston (In re Oakwood Homes Corp.)*, 340 B.R. 510, 2006 WL 864843, at * 16–17 (Bankr. D. Del. 2006) (holding that Delaware, New York, and North Carolina would recognize the cause of action); *In re Exide Technologies, Inc.*, 299 B.R. 732 (Bankr. D. Del. 2003) ("based on the Third Circuit's decision in *Lafferty* and the Delaware courts' policy of providing a remedy for an injury, I conclude that Delaware Supreme Court would recognize a claim for deepening insolvency when there has been damage to corporate property").

107. *See In re CitX Corp.*, 448 F.3d at 680 n.11.

108. *E.g., Lafferty*, 267 F.3d at 351, *clarified by, CitX*, 448 F.3d 672 at 677 (explaining that in *Lafferty* "we did describe deepening insolvency as a 'type of injury,' and a 'theory of injury' but that "we never held it was a valid theory of damages for an independent cause of action.") (citations omitted).

F. STRUCTURAL RESPONSE TO THE THREAT OF INSOLVENCY

When companies are highly leveraged, the risk of bankruptcy obviously rises, and the expected costs of bankruptcy increase. Bankruptcy is not a zero-sum game, in which wealth is shifted from shareholders to creditors. The litigation and transaction costs of bankruptcy can be substantial, so that whatever creditors receive is worth less than the value of the company pre-bankruptcy. One study found that bankruptcy costs consumed about three percent of the debtor's estate. Stephen J. Carroll et al., RAND Inst. for Civil Justice, Asbestos Litigation Costs and Compensation 72 (2002). In the face of this fact, it should hardly be surprising that under some circumstances both issuers and lenders would seek ways to diminish bankruptcy costs.

The leveraged buyout movements of the 1980s and the early years of the 21st century represented the most extreme examples of the widespread use of leverage in capital structures. Both LBO buyers of firms and their lenders recognized the bankruptcy risks, and often attempted to provide incentives for these lenders to abstain from putting troubled debtors into Chapter 11 reorganization. One way to do this was to provide the LBO lenders with a large portion of the equity in the acquired or refinanced firm. Under ordinary circumstances this would not prevent bankruptcy initiatives from creditors, because the LBO lenders could sell either the stock they received or the debt instruments they had acquired. The solution in some cases was to "staple" the debt and equity together (called "strip financing"),* so there would be few possible gains for a creditor to push a debtor into bankruptcy. On the other hand, making creditors into shareholders would reduce shareholder incentives to undertake risky projects at the expense of creditors.

In 2003–04 this concept was transferred to public issues of securities. First developed in Canada, the securities are known there as "Income Trusts," while in the United States they are known as "Income Deposit Securities" ("IDS") or Enhanced Income Securities ("EIS"). Like the earlier LBO packages, they combine a company's common stock with units of high-yield debt (low grade bonds). The attraction is the offer of relatively high yields, required for junk bonds, plus, in some cases, the issuers' commitment to pay out a certain percentage of free cash flow as a dividend. Issuers are characterized by high cash flows and little need for new capital investments, so that much of the issuer's free cash flow can be paid out. Many of these are companies in stable businesses with few growth prospects. At a time when long-term U.S. Treasuries were yielding slightly

---

* Michael C. Jensen, Agency Costs of Free Cash Flow, Corporate Finance, and Takeovers, 76, No. 2 Am. Econ. Rev. (Papers and Proceedings) 323, 325–26 (1986). Strip financing was involved in most of the LBOs of the early 1980s, but declined thereafter, replaced by public debt. The loss of the monitoring of financial institutions caused by this shift is one of the explanations for the higher default rate on these later deals. Steven N. Kaplan & Jeremy C. Stein, The Evolution of Buyout Pricing and Financial Structure (Or, What Went Wrong) in the 1980s, in Donald C. Chew, Ed., THE NEW CORPORATE FINANCE: WHERE THEORY MEETS PRACTICE, 600, 609 (2000).

more than 4%, these securities were offering 8% to 11%. The value of these securities, like any debt securities, is vulnerable to interest rate changes. Nevertheless, they have attracted many individual investors seeking higher yields in a low-interest rate environment, especially those approaching retirement.

As of this writing, the tax treatment of these instruments is not resolved. As we observed in Part 6.D, the Internal Revenue Service could deny interest deductions for the payments on the bond part of these instruments, if it concludes that they are truly equity securities. That would increase the tax liabilities of the issuers, and reduce their ability to pay the promised high rates of "interest." Typically this has not been a concern for public corporations.

CHAPTER FIVE

COMMON STOCK

1. LIMITED LIABILITY OF STOCKHOLDERS

This section does not review the exceptions to shareholder limited liability, which have been covered briefly in Chapter Four, and in all basic corporations casebooks under the "veil piercing" heading. Rather it examines the rationales for limited liability.

Limited Liability

By William J. Carney.
III Encyclopedia of Law and Economics (2000) 659.

8. LIMITED LIABILITY AND THE SUPPLY OF CAPITAL

The principal argument in favor of limited liability stems from the common law rule of liability for partners—joint and several liability—in which any one partner may be held liable for the entire amount of the firm's debt. This appears to be the general European rule as well. Under these conditions there are three economic arguments in favor of limited liability: (1) it fosters economic growth by encouraging investors to take risks; (2) it facilitates the efficient spreading of risks among corporations and their voluntary creditors; and (3) it avoids the enormous litigation costs that would be required for creditors to seek recovery from shareholders.

* * *

9. ENCOURAGING RISKY INVESTMENTS

It has long been argued that joint and several unlimited liability would discourage wealthy investors from investing in risky enterprises, particularly when they intended to play a passive role where they could not monitor and supervise the firm's risky activities. This is supported by one study that suggests that the choice of limited liability is positively correlated with the wealth of owners.

9.1 Encouraging Diversification by Wealthy Investors

Limited liability permits the diversification which is necessary to risk minimization in a specialized firm, where passive investors specialize in risk-bearing, and not monitoring of management. Under joint and several liability, wealthy investors would be the first targets of firm creditors upon failure, and thus would be forced to forego the benefits of diversification in order to concentrate their investments to allow them to monitor effectively. Indeed, diversification would increase the expected risk of wealthy share-

holders; the maximum possible loss is invariant with diversification, but its probability increases with diversification.

One result of unlimited liability might be larger firms engaged in more diversified activities, to protect shareholders from personal losses. This diversification would, of course, be limited by the increasing agency costs associated with management of conglomerates, and the costs of using internal capital markets, with their limited monitoring ability, rather than external markets. Because such diversification and increase in size would convey more benefits on wealthy investors under a joint and several liability regime, the benefits of this strategy would not be symmetrically distributed across investors, which could lead to constituency effects, in which wealthy investors would specialize in owning large diversified firms. Such diversification at the firm level is generally inefficient because investors can home-make their own diversification, absent unlimited liability rules.

9.2 Reducing Shareholder Monitoring of Co–Owners

A joint and several liability rule would force shareholders to monitor not only firm activities, but also the wealth of their fellow shareholders, which leads to excessive monitoring costs. The result would be higher costs and lower returns to equity, which would limit the supply of equity for industry. One article rejects this, arguing that shareholders would not need to increase monitoring of either firms or fellow shareholders, since share prices in efficient markets provide them with all required information. But other authors respond that joint and several liability of shareholders would destroy efficient capital markets, because the value of shares would be a function of the expected cash flows of the business and the wealth of each individual buyer, and of expected fellow shareholders.

* * *

14. LIMITED LIABILITY IN CONTRACT

Early literature concentrated on limited liability for contract obligations. It may be that these writers thought tort liability was trivial. It was only later that writers, recognizing that liabilities for mass torts that could bankrupt even large firms, turned to analysis of the impact of limited liability on tort risks.

14.1 The Theory of Limited Liability in Contract

In a perfect capital market with zero transaction costs the value of the firm and its optimal investment policy would not be affected by the liability rule chosen. Unlimited liability would reduce creditors' risks and the interest rates and other contractual protections demanded, and increase returns to shareholders to compensate for this risk. Firms that choose a limited liability regime will face higher borrowing costs, although it is argued that trade creditors typically fail to incur the transaction costs to investigate credit risk. In the case of one-shareholder corporations with little capital, creditors will either charge higher interest rates for risky loans or insist on personal guarantees, so that credit terms are invariant to the liability rule. If we introduce transaction costs, where lenders are uncertain about the extent of shirking and risky behavior by owners with limited liability they may increase interest costs to the point where owners prefer to finance without borrowings at the firm level. This analysis has been extended to stock insurance companies: if shareholder liability is limited, policyholders will presumably recognize the risk they bear and pay less for policies. Insurers can bond against risky investments by writing participation rights into insurance policies. They can also submit to regulation that assures minimum capital and constrains risky investments.

Under an unlimited liability regime, Leebron argues that shareholders would probably prefer to borrow using their interest in the firm as collateral, because they would each only be liable for their own borrowing (pro rata), while if the firm borrows, each would be liable for everyone's borrowings (joint & several). Corporate borrowing with limited liability is equivalent to nonrecourse borrowing by shareholders who pledge their shares as collateral, but the transaction costs of such borrowing would be higher, because so many lenders would have to investigate the firm in markets with large numbers of potential lenders. Limited liability creates a state of the world where the worst possible state of the world is known to all investors, both creditors and shareholders, while unlimited liability does not allow shareholders the same certainty.

The evidence from 18th and 19th century Scottish banking is consistent with this model. Shareholders in unlimited liability banks earned higher returns than shareholders in limited liability banks. Despite such differences in returns, in small firms risk aversion leads to a preference for limited liability, especially as firm projects grow riskier, according to a study of German firms.

14.2   The Cost of Limited Liability in Contract

There are at least three costs borne by firm owners for achieving limited liability, at least two of which apply to both contract and tort liability. First, under limited liability, voluntary creditors will impose higher costs on firms (see above). Second, in many legal regimes, tax costs will be higher for limited liability, because the entity may be treated as separate, although this is not a necessary condition for limited liability. In the United States the development of the Limited Liability Company and Limited Liability Partnership have eliminated the tax cost for closely held enterprises in recent years. Third, in most legal systems except the United States, forming a limited liability entity will subject the firm to extensive public disclosures. This apparently is designed to provide potential creditors with information about the firm's capital where unlimited liability is not available. While Posner argues that creditors are the most efficient risk-bearers Easterbrook & Fischel reject this, arguing that the evidence is otherwise: creditors accept lower returns because they prefer less risk, presumably because they are not the least cost monitors of firms. Johnsen argues that creditors accept lower returns because they monitor only the value of debtors' assets in alternative and less specialized uses, rather than in the present use, which is left to shareholders. Recent literature on domination of large corporations by big banks in Germany and Japan has raised the question of whether at least some creditors are superior monitors of firms, but fails to bring any evidence to bear on the subject.

Some authors treat small trade creditors as if they were involuntary creditors, because they face high transaction costs in assessing the riskiness of their credit extensions. These arguments ignore both the ability of trade creditors to monitor current payments on a monthly or more frequent basis and their ability to free ride on the negative covenants imposed by larger creditors with scale economies in negotiating credit contracts. Further, they ignore the ability of many trade creditors to bear risk by diversifying their customer base.

The costs of limited liability imposed on creditors depend on capital structure; thus, secured creditors monitor assets, not firms, so their monitoring costs are not increased by limited liability. To the extent that limited liability imposes unmonitored risk on creditors, it has been suggested that increasing the tax on firm profits and paying subsidies to creditors can solve the risky behavior problem. The creditor subsidy will reduce interest costs to the firm, while raising managerial efforts, thus leaving managers better off, because managers exert less effort when liability is limited. A similar suggestion has been made with respect to the level of taxation of profits on U.S. financial institutions, to reduce incentives to take risks. The difficulty with these proposals is that profits taxes do not distinguish returns to risk from returns to superior management.

14.3   The Benefits of Limited Liability in Contract

Many of the benefits of limited liability in contract are related to capital markets. With limited liability, investors have the ability to diversify their investments in shares of corporations. This is true in part because without limited liability, for a wealthy investor, each investment would increase the risk of being held personally liable for the debts of a failed firm. It is also true because it reduces the need for any shareholder to monitor management for risky choices. It also seems likely that given modern techniques for reporting financial results of firms, that monitoring shareholder wealth is more costly than monitoring firm wealth. Evans and Quigley argued that unlimited liability was observed in Scottish banking at a time when it was cheaper to monitor shareholder wealth than bank solvency. Finally, limited liability reduces the transaction costs of collection.

15.   LIMITED LIABILITY IN TORT

Limited liability's externalization creates three problems: (1) firms make excessively risky decisions because they do not consider externalized costs; (2) corporations fail to insure fully; and (3) product costs do not reflect full social costs. Many early authors apparently believed that the problem of tort liability under a limited liability system was not a serious one, either because they felt that other parts of the legal system had dealt with the principal forms of business accidents, through workers' compensation, unemployment insurance, and mandatory automobile insurance, or because they focused on the large publicly held corporation, where the risk that individual tort liability would bankrupt a firm seemed trivial. For this reason, much of the early literature focused on contract liability. The development of the mass tort, stemming either from industrial accidents or strict products liability, has changed the analysis.

2.   THE PROBLEM OF DILUTION

Dilution means having claims that are relatively smaller because some class of security is issued to another. Generally we think of dilution when more shares of the same class are issued to others. Simple dilution is involved where a person owns 10 out of 100 outstanding shares, and the company issues another 100 shares to third parties. Your claim has been diluted from 10% to 5% of the shares. Your voting power is less, and your share of profits and assets is less. Are you worse off? If any consideration was received for the shares, you own a smaller *percentage* of a bigger pie.

The examples below assume that investors require a 10% return on an investment in common stock. This means you can calculate the value of a share of common stock by taking the earnings per share and multiplying them by 10.

> Example (1): Corporation A earns profits of $100 per year. Corporation A has 100 shares of common stock outstanding, with a market value of $10 per share (total $1,000). Corporation A sells 100 new shares of common stock for $10 per share. The expected return on the new capital is the same as on the existing capital. Thus 200 shares will earn $200. Each common share will earn $1.00, and the value of the shares will be $10 each, and the value of the firm will be $2,000.

Value of A's outstanding common stock:	100 shares	@ $10 =	$1,000
New issue of common stock:	100 shares	@ $10 =	1,000
New value of A's stock:	200 shares	@ $10 =	$2,000

This means the value of each share has been maintained, and earnings per share are the same. So while your voting interest has been diluted, and your ownership *percentage* has been diluted, your investment's *value* hasn't been diluted.

> Example (2): Corporation A has outstanding 100 shares of common stock selling for $10 per share. A's expected return in a year is $100, or 10%. A gives away 100 shares of new common stock [to others]. Assuming there is no change in A's profitability, the expected per-share return on existing common will be diluted by 50% (200 shares will earn the same total amount as 100 shares did before the share issuance).

Investors still demand a 10% return on their stock, so that a company that earns $100 will be valued at $1,000, regardless of the number of shares outstanding. Issuing 100 new shares for no consideration cuts earnings per share in half, from $1.00 per share to $.50.

Value of A's common stock:	100 shares	@ $10 =	$1,000
New issue of common stock:	100 shares	@ $ 0 =	0
New value of A's stock:	200 shares	@ $ 5 =	$1,000

This means the value of each outstanding share has been cut in half. Both your voting and economic percentage, as well as your value, have been diluted. Intermediate cases, where new shares are issued for less than $10 and more than zero, are perhaps the most common cause of dilution of a shareholder's investment. The cost to an existing investor of the issuance of cheap stock to third parties can be expressed as follows:

$$L = ma - \frac{(mx + p)}{x + d} \quad (a)$$

where L = existing shareholders' loss through dilution;

m = market price of a share before issuance;

a = a shareholder's share ownership at the time new shares are issued;

x = shares outstanding before dilutive issuance;

d = number of shares issued in dilutive distribution; and

p = proceeds from sale of new shares.

Generally, we would predict that no shareholder would consent ex ante to a system that allows dilutive issuance of new shares to others. Provisions requiring that par value be paid for shares represented one form of protection of shareholders against such dilution, but these provisions have become much weaker over time. Modern statutes generally permit the authorization of shares with no par value, and all permit the use of very low par values (e.g., one cent, or even a fraction of a cent), thus rendering the constraints of par value meaningless. This relaxation of formal requirements has been replaced with a more general statutory duty. M.B.C.A. § 6.21(b) delegates the power to issue new shares to the board of directors, and § 6.21(c) requires the board to determine that the consideration to be received is adequate. Delaware G.C.L. § 152 is essentially the same. M.B.C.A. § 6.21(a) allows articles of incorporation to reserve this power to the shareholders. This would still allow a majority of shareholders to authorize issuance of shares for less than fair market value, because the Model Act provides that shareholder action is by plurality of a quorum, see, e.g., M.B.C.A. § 7.25(a), while Delaware G.C.L. § 216 provides for a majority of a quorum. Shareholder control of new issues can also be achieved in either Delaware or a Model Act state by not authorizing more shares than are originally intended to be issued in the articles of incorporation, so that amendment of the articles of incorporation is required each time. Here voting standards are stricter, requiring a majority of the shares entitled to vote. M.B.C.A. § 10.03(e) and Del. G.C.L. § 242(b)(2). In all cases, charters can provide for supermajority voting on authorizing new shares, providing even stricter minority protection. Unless self-dealing by the majority is involved (for which special legal standards apply), minority shareholders can generally rely on the self-interest of the majority to avoid dilution of the value of their shares.*

NOTE: DILUTION BY DESIGN

It is not uncommon to set up rules for "penalty dilution" in some enterprises. This often occurs where anticipated investment is sequential or uncertain in amount. Here the initial group of investors may each agree to invest a certain sum in an enterprise. But because not all of the funds are needed immediately to fund the project—which might be built, developed or acquired in stages—they agree to contribute some initial sum, and agree either to make specified payments over time, perhaps on a schedule, or perhaps agree that the firm may simply issue a call on them from time to time. What happens if an investor fails to pay his or her agreed share at some later date? This may occur because the investment no longer looks so rosy, or because the investor now has found a higher-yielding project for the remaining funds. In some cases it may be that if the investor fails to contribute, the remaining investors will feel compelled to do so. If things have gone badly, and more money is needed to salvage some part of the investment, the non-contributing investor may benefit from the investments of the others, at no cost to him.

Assume, for example, a $1,000,000 investment that has gone bad, so that creditors will claim one-half of the firm's assets, leaving only $500,000 for the original investors if no new funds are put in. But if an additional $1,000,000 is invested, the investment will be worth $1,750,000, thus salvaging $250,000. If 100 original units were sold at $10,000 each, consider the options:

(i) Another 100 units are sold at $10,000 each. At the end, 200 units will share a net worth of $1,750,000, or $8,750 per unit. An investor would thus have a loss of $2,500 ($1,250 on both his original and his new unit). A rational investor who owns one unit, looking out exclusively for his own interest, will decline to invest a fresh $10,000 to buy another unit worth $8,750, hoping that others will do so. In this case the "free rider" only loses $1,250 of his original investment.

(ii) 133.33 new units are offered at $7,500 each. At the end of the day, 233.33 units will share a value of $1,750,000, or $7,500 per unit.

---

* In the early 21st century the stock market for newly public high-tech companies experienced a serious decline, with the NASDAQ composite index falling from over 5,000 to below 1,500. With it, the hopes of many small development stage companies also dropped, because their values were based on anticipation of an initial public offering at a high price. These development stage companies typically seek new financing from venture capitalists in several rounds before making an initial public offering. With the drop in public market stock prices, venture capitalists revised downward their estimates of the value of these development stage companies as well. The result of this was that later rounds of financing could only be completed at prices lower than those of previous rounds, when investors were more sanguine. These "down rounds" resulted in dilution of the book value of the earlier investors.

The investor is now indifferent: he can invest another $10,000, and own 2.333 units worth a total of $17,500. He has lost $2,500. If he fails to invest, his original unit is worth $7,500, and his loss is $2,500.

(iii) 200 new units are offered at $5,000 each. At the end of the day, 300 units will share a value of $1,750,000, or $5,833 per unit. The investor who buys two new units has invested $20,000 for a total of three units worth $17,500. He has lost $2,500. If he fails to invest, his original unit is worth $5,833, and his loss is $4,167. The free rider is still better off than his original situation, which was a $5,000 loss.

(iv) Now let's make it really tough and offer 400 new units at $2,500 each. We now have the same value of $1,750,000, shared by 500 units, each worth $3,500. The investor who buys four new units has now invested $20,000, and has five units worth $17,500. He, too, has lost $2,500. But our free rider's unit is now worth $3,500, so he has lost $6,500.

The moral of the story is that penalty dilution doesn't work until the offering price of new units is less than the fair market value of the current units.

Under what circumstances could investors use penalty dilution? If they had not agreed in advance to its use, could a corporation or a limited partner just decide to use it? What justifications could you give? Recall the Time–Warner case in Part 4.C of Chapter Three? In order to assure the sale of large amounts of new shares to pay down its huge debt, Time–Warner was required to use a Dutch auction to make an offer that present shareholders could not refuse.

The other prominent use of dilution is as a takeover defense. The standard poison pill (or shareholder rights plan) defense involves a promise to issue new shares of common stock at a price well below market value, to all shareholders except an uninvited bidder for control that acquires a specified percentage of the company's shares. The typical poison pill makes numerous new shares available to the other shareholders at a price that is typically 50% of fair market value. Such rights are addressed in Chapter Five, Part 2.C.

A.   PREEMPTIVE RIGHTS TO PURCHASE A PORTION OF ANY NEW ISSUE

The doctrine of preemptive rights is a creation of common law courts in the United States. *Gray v. Portland Bank*, 3 Mass. 364 (1807), created the doctrine. *Gray* held that since the power to authorize new shares resided in the shareholders, they had an equitable interest in new shares when created. (This was back in the days of special charters, when all authorized shares had to be subscribed for before beginning business, and the charter, as a contract between shareholders and the state, could only be amended by (i) unanimous consent of shareholders and (ii) consent of the legislature.) The *Gray* majority reasoned that, like partners, only the shareholders had the right to admit new owners, and that the value of shares in the hands of later shareholders benefitted from the investments of the earlier stockholders. The court held that corporation "held" its authorized but unissued shares in trust for its shareholders, subject to their paying for them. (This is really saying that the new investment is really a business opportunity that belongs to the original stockholders.) A concurring judge used the partnership and business opportunity analogy, and also natural law:

> "Whenever a partnership adopts a project ... it must be for the benefit of all the partners, in proportion to their respective interests. Natural justice requires that the majority should not have authority to exclude the minority." 3 Mass. at 383.

Stokes v. Continental Trust Company

Court of Appeals of New York.
78 N.E. 1090 (N.Y. 1906).

■ JUDGES: VANN, J. HAIGHT, J. (dissenting). CULLEN, CH. J., WERNER and HISCOCK, JJ., concur with VANN, J.; WILLARD BARTLETT, J., concurs with HAIGHT, J.; O'BRIEN, J., absent.

■ VANN, J.

[Plaintiff sued to compel a corporation to issue at par the number of shares to which he allegedly was entitled by virtue of his preemptive rights to a new stock issue, and in case such shares could not be delivered, for damages. The trial court found in favor of the plaintiff, but the Appellate Division reversed.]

* * * [T]he question presented for decision is whether according to the facts found the plaintiff had the legal right to subscribe for and take the same number of shares of the new stock that he held of the old?

The subject is not regulated by statute and the question presented has never been directly passed upon by this court, and only to a limited extent has it been considered by courts in this state.

* * *

The leading authority is Gray v. Portland Bank, decided in 1807 and reported in 3 Mass. 364. * * * The court held that stockholders who held old stock had a right to subscribe for and take new stock in proportion to their respective shares. As the corporation refused this right to the plaintiff he was permitted to recover the excess of the market value above the par value, with interest. In the course of its argument the court said: "A share in the stock or trust when only the least sum has been paid in is a share in the power of increasing it when the trustee determines or rather when the cestuis que trustent agree upon employing a greater sum. * * * A vote to increase the capital stock, if it was not the creation of a new and disjointed capital, was in its nature an agreement among the stockholders to enlarge their shares in the amount or in the number to the extent required to effect that increase. * * * If from the progress of the institution and the expense incurred in it any advance upon the additional shares might be obtained in the market, this advance upon the shares relinquished belonged to the whole, and was not to be disposed of at the will of a majority of the stockholders to the partial benefit of some and exclusion of others."

This decision has stood unquestioned for nearly a hundred years and has been followed generally by courts of the highest standing. It is the foundation of the rule upon the subject that prevails, almost without exception, throughout the entire country.

* * *

In the case before us the new stock came into existence through the exercise of a right belonging wholly to the stockholders. As the right to increase the stock belonged to them, the stock when increased belonged to them also, as it was issued for money and not for property or for some purpose other than the sale thereof for money. By the increase of stock the voting power of the plaintiff was reduced one-half, and while he consented to the increase he did not consent to the disposition of the new stock by a sale thereof to Blair & Company at less than its market value, nor by sale to any person in any way except by an allotment to the stockholders. The increase and sale involved the transfer of rights belonging to the stockholders as part of their investment. The issue of new stock and the sale thereof to Blair & Company was not only a transfer to them of one-half the voting power of the old stockholders, but also of an equitable right to one-half the surplus which belonged to them. In other words, it was a partial division of the property of the old stockholders. The right to increase stock is not an asset of the corporation any more than the original stock when it was issued pursuant to subscription. The ownership of stock is in the nature of an inherent but indirect power to control the corporation. The stock when issued ready for delivery does not belong to the corporation in the way that it holds its real and personal property, with power to sell the same, but is held by it with no power of alienation in trust for the stockholders, who are the beneficial owners and become the legal owners upon paying therefor. The corporation has no rights hostile to those of the stockholders, but is the trustee for all including the minority. The new stock issued by the defendant under the permission of the statute did not belong to it, but was held by it the same as the original stock when first issued was held in trust for the stockholders. It has the same voting power as the old, share for share. The stockholders decided to enlarge their holdings, not by increasing the amount of each share, but by increasing the number of shares. The new stock belonged to the stockholders as an inherent right by virtue of their being stockholders, to be shared in proportion upon paying its par value or the value per share fixed by vote of a majority of the stockholders, or ascertained by a sale at public auction. While the corporation could not compel the plaintiff to take new shares at any price, since they were issued for money and not for property, it could not lawfully dispose of those shares without giving him a chance to get his proportion at the same price that outsiders got theirs. He had an inchoate right to one share of the new stock for each share owned by him of the old stock, provided he was ready to pay the price fixed by the stockholders. If so situated that he could not take it himself, he was entitled to sell the right to one who could, as is frequently done. Even this gives an advantage to capital, but capital necessarily has some advantage. Of course, there is a distinction when the new stock is issued in payment for property, but that is not this case. The stock in question was issued to be sold for money and was sold for money only. A majority of the stockholders, as part of their power to increase the stock, may attach reasonable conditions to the disposition thereof, such as the requirement that every old stockholder electing to take new stock shall pay a fixed price therefor, not less than par, however, owing to the limitation of the statute. They may also provide for a sale in parcels or bulk at public auction, when every stockholder can bid the same as strangers. They cannot, however, dispose of it to strangers against the protest of any stockholder who insists that he has a right to his proportion. Otherwise the majority could deprive the minority of their proportionate power in the election of directors and of their proportionate right to share in the surplus, each of which is an inherent, preemptive and vested right of property. It is inviolable and can neither be taken away nor lessened without consent, or a waiver implying consent. The plaintiff had power, before the increase of stock, to vote on 221 shares of stock, out of a total of 5,000, at any meeting held by the stockholders for any purpose. By the action of the majority, taken against his will and protest, he now has only one-half the voting power that he had before, because the number of shares has been doubled while he still owns but 221. This touches him as a stockholder in such a way as to deprive him of a right of property. Blair & Company acquired virtual control, while he and the other stockholders lost it. We are not discussing equities, but legal rights, for this is an action at law, and the plaintiff was deprived of a strictly legal right. If the result gives him an advantage over other stockholders, it is because he stood upon his legal rights, while they did not. The question is what were his legal rights, not what his profit may be under the sale to Blair & Company, but what it might have been if the new stock had been issued to him in proportion to his holding of the old. The other stockholders could give their property to Blair & Company, but they could not give his.

A share of stock is a share in the power to increase the stock, and belongs to the stockholders the same as the stock itself. When that power is exercised, the new stock belongs to the old stockholders in proportion to their holding of old stock, subject to compliance with the lawful terms upon which it is issued. When the new stock is issued in payment for property purchased by the corporation, the stockholders' right is merged in the purchase, and they have an advantage in the increase of the property of the corporation in proportion to the increase of stock. When the new stock is issued for money, while the stockholders may provide that it be sold at auction or fix the price at which it is to be sold, each stockholder is entitled to his proportion of the proceeds of the sale at auction, after he has had a right to bid at the sale, or to his proportion of the new stock at the price fixed by the stockholders.

We are thus led to lay down the rule that a stockholder has an inherent right to a proportionate share of new stock issued for money only and not to purchase property for the purposes of the corporation or to effect a consolidation, and while he can waive that right, he cannot be deprived of it without his consent except when the stock is issued at a fixed price not less than par and he is given the right to take at that price in proportion to his holding, or in some other equitable way that will enable him to protect his interest by acting on his own judgment and using his own resources. This rule is just to all and tends to prevent the tyranny of majorities which needs restraint, as well as virtual attempts to blackmail by small minorities which should be prevented.

* * *

Haight, J. (dissenting). I agree that the rule that we should adopt is that a stockholder in a corporation has an inherent right to purchase a proportionate share of new stock issued for money only, and not to purchase property necessary for the purposes of the corporation or to effect a consolidation. While he can waive that right he cannot be deprived of it without his consent, except by sale at a fixed price at or above par, in which he may buy at that price in proportion to his holding or in some other equitable way that will enable him to protect his interest by acting on his own judgment and using his own resources. I, however, differ with Judge Vann as to his conclusions as to the rights of the plaintiff herein. Under the findings of the trial court the plaintiff demanded that his share of the new stock should be issued to him at par, or $100 per share, instead of $450 per share, the price offered by Blair & Company and the price fixed at the stockholders' meeting at which the new stock was authorized to be sold. This demand was made after the passage of the resolution authorizing the increase of the capital stock of the defendant company and before the passage of the resolution authorizing a sale of the new stock to Blair & Company at the price specified. After the passage of the second resolution he objected to the sale of his proportionate share of the new stock to Blair & Company and again demanded that it be issued to him, and the following day he made a legal tender for the amount of his portion of the new stock at $100 per share. There is no finding of fact or evidence in the record showing that he was ever ready or willing to pay $450 per share for the stock. He knew that Blair & Company represented Marshall Field and others at Chicago, great dry goods merchants, and that they had made a written offer to purchase the new stock of the company provided the stockholders would authorize an increase of its capital stock from five hundred thousand to a million dollars. He knew that the trustees of the company had called a special meeting of the stockholders for the purpose of considering the offer so made by Blair & Company. He knew that the increased capitalization proposed was for the purpose of enlarging the business of the company and bringing into its management the gentlemen referred to. There is no pretense that any of the stockholders would have voted for an increase of the capital stock otherwise than for the purpose of accepting the offer of Blair & Company. All were evidently desirous of interesting the gentlemen referred to in the company, and by securing their business and deposits increase the earnings of the company. This the trustees carefully considered, and in their notice calling the special meeting of the stockholders distinctly recommended the acceptance of the offer. What, then, was the legal effect of the plaintiff's demand and tender? To my mind it was simply an attempt to make something out of his associates, to get for $100 per share the stock which Blair & Company had offered to purchase for $450 per share; and that it was the equivalent of a refusal to pay $450 per share, and its effect is to waive his right to procure the stock by paying that amount. An acceptance of his offer would have been most unjust to the remaining stockholders. It would not only have deprived them of the additional sum of $350 per share, which had been offered for the stock, but it would have defeated the object and purpose for which the meeting was called, for it was well understood that Blair & Company would not accept less than the whole issue of the new stock. But this is not all. It appears that prior to the offer of Blair & Company the stock of the company had never been sold above $450 per share; that thereafter the stock rapidly advanced until the day of the completion of the sale on the 30th of January, when its market value was $550 per share; but this, under the stipulation of facts, was caused by the rumor and subsequent announcement and consummation of the proposition for the increase of the stock and the sale of such increase to Blair & Company and their associates. It is now proposed to give the plaintiff as damages such increase in the market value of the stock, even though such value was based upon the understanding that Blair & Company were to become stockholders in the corporation, which the acceptance of plaintiff's offer would have prevented. This, to my mind, should not be done. I, therefore, favor an affirmance.

QUESTIONS

1. What business reasons motivated the increase in authorized stock and the sale to Blair & Co.?

2. Do you have any reason to believe that $450 per share was an unfairly low price for the sale of new shares in Continental Trust Company?

3. Would it have been fair to other shareholders to allow Stokes to purchase newly issued shares at their par value of $100?

4. Assuming the shares of Continental had a fair market value of $450, and could have been sold for that price to Blair, how much of a loss would the other Continental shareholders have suffered if Stokes were allowed to purchase 221 new shares at their par value of $100? (See the dilution formula that precedes this opinion. Note that you can't simply use Stokes' bargain purchase ($450–$100) for his 221 shares, because the dilution reduces the value of all shares below $450.)

5. Why would the other shareholders vote to dilute their own share of ownership by selling new shares to Blair at $450?

6. What effect would honoring Stokes' preemptive rights be likely to have on Blair's interest in acquiring one-half of the total shares of Continental?

7. Does the majority opinion suggest any limits on the preemptive rights doctrine that might provide a way for Blair and the other shareholders to avoid Stokes' claims? If so, how would you suggest restructuring the transaction if you represented Blair or the majority of the shareholders?

NOTES

In the early 20th century some statutes required preemptive rights unless the corporation opted out of them in its articles of incorporation. Normally preemptive rights are interpreted as granting to shareholders the right to buy at the same price that is offered to others. The difficulties with preemptive rights are at least two-fold. First, they make no sense in publicly held corporations, where shareholders generally regard themselves as holding a claim of a certain value, not of a certain proportion of the total claims against the corporation. Second, where preemptive rights exist, they are often ignored for innocent reasons of ignorance. The modern approach is exemplified by M.B.C.A. § 6.30(a) which provides no preemptive rights unless provided in the articles of incorporation. But a simple statement in the articles that "the corporation elects to have preemptive rights" gets shareholders a standard form set of preemptive rights, unless the articles of incorporation vary them. M.B.C.A. § 6.30(b).

The Stokes case stated that the preemptive right exists to purchase shares "for money only and not to purchase property...." This doctrine is embodied in a standard exception to preemptive rights for "shares sold otherwise than for money" in M.B.C.A. § 6.30(b)(3)(iv).

The most difficult question is what is the law trying to protect with preemptive rights? At the beginning of the doctrine, capital structures were likely to be relatively simple, so preemptive rights protected shareholders from dilution both of their investment and their voting power. But as companies began to issue several classes of stock, it became more difficult to apply the doctrine. Thus, shares might have a preference on income with no voting rights. Or they might be secondary on income (e.g., more common, when preferred is outstanding) but have voting rights. One early author noted the difficulties. Alexander Hamilton Frey, Shareholders' Preemptive Rights, 38 Yale L. J. 563, 566–68 (1929):

> Thus, as to dividend payments alone, there are today four groups of shares: (1) common, *i.e.,* unpreferred and unlimited, (2) participating preferred, *i.e.,* preferred and unlimited, (3) non-participating preferred, *i.e.,* unpreferred and limited, and (4) deferred, *i.e.,* unpreferred and limited. Obviously, shares may be created having with respect to capital distributions any one of these four combinations of incidents, depending upon whether the share is preferred or unpreferred, limited or unlimited, as to capital distributions. And as each one of these four types as to dividend payments may be combined with any one of the four as to capital distributions, sixteen different groups of shares are possible, taking into consideration only the presence or absence of a preference or limitation, both as to dividend payments and capital distributions.

When only those other share incidents thus far invented are applied to each of these groups, the number of possible classes of shares becomes staggering. For example, each group may be voting or non-voting, and even voting rights may be of a number of different classes; voting may be cumulative or non-cumulative.... * * * When confronted with such a maze of possible classes of shares, how is the proportionate claim of any given shareholder to shares of a particular class to be determined in relation to shareholders of other classes. When shares have certain incidents in common but are not identical, how is the relative importance of specific incidents to be evaluated in determining the proportionate distribution of new shares to the respective existing shareholders?

Quick Check Question 5.1

How does the Model Business Corporation Act deal with these issues? See M.B.C.A. § 6.30. How does Delaware deal with these issues? See Del. GCL § 102(b)(3).

Another difficult question involves curing violations of preemptive rights. A violation represents a chose in action, which is not automatically assigned when a shareholder with a claim sells her shares. Thus, claims of violations of preemptive rights represent contingent claims against the corporation. Once discovered, if these violations are material, they must be disclosed in the company's financial statements, where they represent a cloud on the value of the title of existing shareholders, and a barrier to new financings at attractive prices for existing shareholders. Existing shareholders cannot necessarily waive past violations of preemptive rights, unless they were the shareholders whose rights were violated at the time. Where shareholders are numerous or much time has passed since the violation, absent a short statute of limitations on such claims, they can be difficult to cure or resolve.

Similar problems face holders of securities convertible into common stock. If debt securities or preferred stock are convertible into a specified number of common shares, an implicit price is set by the conversion ratio. Whenever companies issue new shares, these conversion rights become diluted in much the same way as existing stock. We will examine the contractual solutions to this problem in Chapter Eight, Part 5.

B. EQUITABLE DOCTRINES GOVERNING DILUTIVE STOCK ISSUES

Katzowitz v. Sidler et al.

Court of Appeals of New York.
249 N.E.2d 359 (1969).

■ JUDGES BURKE, SCILEPPI, BERGAN, BREITEL and JASEN concur with JUDGE KEATING; CHIEF JUDGE FULD dissents and votes to affirm on the opinion at the Appellate Division.

■ KEATING, J.

Isador Katzowitz is a director and stockholder of a close corporation. Two other persons, Jacob Sidler and Max Lasker, own the remaining securities and, with Katzowitz, comprise Sulburn Holding Corp.'s board of directors. Sulburn was organized in 1955 to supply propane gas to three other corporations controlled by these men. Sulburn's certificate of incorporation authorized it to issue 1,000 shares of no par value stock for which the incorporators established a $100 selling price. Katzowitz, Sidler and Lasker each invested $500 and received five shares of the corporation's stock.

The three men had been jointly engaged in several corporate ventures for more than 25 years. In this period they had always been equal partners and received identical compensation from the corporations they controlled. Though all the corporations controlled by these three men prospered, disenchantment with their inter-personal relationship flared into the open in 1956. * * *

In December of 1961 Sulburn was indebted to each stockholder to the extent of $2,500 for fees and commissions earned up until September, 1961. Instead of paying this debt, Sidler and Lasker wanted Sulburn to loan the money to another corporation which all three men controlled. Sidler and Lasker called a meeting of the board of directors to propose that additional securities be offered at $100 per share to substitute for the money owed to the directors. The notice of meeting for October 30, 1961 had on its agenda "a proposition that the corporation issue common stock of its unissued common capital stock, the total par value which shall equal the total sum of the fees and commissions now owing by the corporation to its * * * directors". (Emphasis added.) Katzowitz made it quite clear at the meeting that he would not invest any additional funds in Sulburn in order for it to make a loan to this other corporation. The only resolution passed at the meeting was that the corporation would pay the sum of $2,500 to each director.

With full knowledge that Katzowitz expected to be paid his fees and commissions and that he did not want to participate in any new stock issuance, the other two directors called a special meeting of the board on December 1, 1961. The only item on the agenda for this special meeting was the issuance of 75 shares of the corporation's common stock at $100 per share. The offer was to be made to stockholders in "accordance with their respective preemptive rights for the purpose of acquiring additional working capital". The amount to be raised was the exact amount owed by the corporation to its shareholders. The offering price for the securities was 1/18 the book value of the stock. Only Sidler and Lasker attended the special board meeting. They approved the issuance of the 75 shares.

Notice was mailed to each stockholder that they had the right to purchase 25 shares of the corporation's stock at $100 a share. The offer was to expire on December 27, 1961. Failure to act by that date was stated to constitute a waiver. At about the same time Katzowitz received the notice, he received a check for $2,500 from the corporation for his fees and commissions. Katzowitz did not exercise his option to buy the additional shares. Sidler and Lasker purchased their full complement, 25 shares each. This purchase by Sidler and Lasker caused an immediate dilution of the book value of the outstanding securities.

On August 25, 1962 the principal asset of Sulburn, a tractor trailer truck, was destroyed. On August 31, 1962 the directors unanimously voted to dissolve the corporation. Upon dissolution, Sidler and Lasker each received $18,885.52 but Katzowitz only received $3,147.59

The plaintiff instituted a declaratory judgment action to establish his right to the proportional interest in the assets of Sulburn in liquidation less the $5,000 which Sidler and Lasker used to purchase their shares in December, 1961.

Special Term (Westchester County) found the book value of the corporation's securities on the day the stock was offered at $100 to be worth $1,800. The court also found that "the individual defendants * * * decided that in lieu of taking that sum in cash [the commissions and fees due the stockholders], they preferred to add to their investment by having the corporate defendant make available and offer each stockholder an additional twenty-five shares of unissued stock." The court reasoned that Katzowitz waived his right to purchase the stock or object to its sale to Lasker and Sidler by failing to exercise his pre-emptive right and found his protest at the time of dissolution untimely.

The Appellate Division (Second Department), two Justices dissenting, modified the order of Special Term. The modification was procedural. The decretal paragraph in Special Term's order was corrected by reinstating the complaint and substituting a statement of the parties' rights. On the substantive legal issues and findings of fact, the Appellate Division was in agreement with Special Term. The majority agreed that the book value of the corporation's stock at the time of the stock offering was $1,800. The Appellate Division reasoned, however, that showing a disparity between book value and offering price was insufficient without also showing fraud or overreaching. Disparity in price by itself was not enough to prove fraud. The Appellate Division also found that the plaintiff had waived his right to object to his recovery in dissolution by failing to either exercise his pre-emptive rights or take steps to prevent the sale of the stock.

The concept of pre-emptive rights was fashioned by the judiciary to safeguard two distinct interests of stockholders—the right to protection against dilution of their equity in the corporation and protection against dilution of their proportionate voting control. After early decisions, legislation fixed the right enunciated with respect to proportionate voting but left to the judiciary the role of protecting existing shareholders from the dilution of their equity.

It is clear that directors of a corporation have no discretion in the choice of those to whom the earnings and assets of the corporation should be distributed. Directors, being fiduciaries of the corporation, must, in issuing new stock, treat existing shareholders fairly. Though there is very little statutory control over the price which a corporation must receive for new shares the power to determine price must be exercised for the benefit of the corporation and in the interest of all the stockholders.

Issuing stock for less than fair value can injure existing shareholders by diluting their interest in the corporation's surplus, in current and future earnings and in the assets upon liquidation. Normally, a stockholder is protected from the loss of his equity from dilution, even though the stock is being offered at less than fair value, because the shareholder receives rights which he may either exercise or sell. If he exercises, he has protected his interest and, if not, he can sell the rights, thereby compensating himself for the dilution of his remaining shares in the equity of the corporation.

When new shares are issued, however, at prices far below fair value in a close corporation or a corporation with only a limited market for its shares, existing stockholders, who do not want to invest or do not have the capacity to invest additional funds, can have their equity interest in the corporation diluted to the vanishing point.

The protection afforded by stock rights is illusory in close corporations. Even if a buyer could be found for the rights, they would have to be sold at an inadequate price because of the nature of a close corporation. Outsiders are normally discouraged from acquiring minority interests after a close corporation has been organized. Certainly a stockholder in a close corporation is at a total loss to safeguard his equity from dilution if no rights are offered and he does not want to invest additional funds.

Though it is difficult to determine fair value for a corporation's securities and courts are therefore reluctant to get into the thicket, when the issuing price is shown to be markedly below book value in a close corporation and when the remaining share-holder-directors benefit from the issuance, a case for judicial relief has been established. In that instance, the corporation's directors must show that the issuing price falls within some range which can be justified on the basis of valid business reasons. If no such showing is made by the directors, there is no reason for the judiciary to abdicate its function to a majority of the board of stockholders who have not seen fit to come forward and justify the propriety of diverting property from the corporation and allow the issuance of securities to become an oppressive device, permitting the dilution of the equity of dissident stockholders.

The defendant directors here make no claim that the price set was a fair one. No business justification is offered to sustain it. Admittedly, the stock was sold at less than book value. The defendants simply contend that, as long as all stockholders were given an equal opportunity to purchase additional shares, no stockholder can complain simply because the offering dilutes his interest in the corporation.

The defendants' argument is fallacious.

The corollary of a stockholder's right to maintain his proportionate equity in a corporation by purchasing additional shares is the right not to purchase additional shares without being confronted with dilution of his existing equity if no valid business justification exists for the dilution.

A stockholder's right not to purchase is seriously undermined if the stock offered is worth substantially more than the offering price. Any purchase at this price dilutes his interest and impairs the value of his original holding. "A corporation is not permitted to sell its stock for a legally inadequate price at least where there is objection. Plaintiff has a right to insist upon compliance with the law whether or not he cares to exercise his option. He cannot block a sale for a fair price merely because he disagrees with the wisdom of the plan but he can insist that the sale price be fixed in accordance with legal requirements." Judicial review in this area is limited to whether under all the circumstances, including the disparity between issuing price of the stock and its true value, the nature of the corporation, the business necessity for establishing an offering price at a certain amount to facilitate raising new capital, and the ability of stockholders to sell rights, the additional offering of securities should be condemned because the directors in establishing the sale price did not fix it with reference to financial considerations with respect to the ready disposition of securities.

Here the obvious disparity in selling price and book value was calculated to force the dissident stockholder into investing additional sums. No valid business justification was advanced for the disparity in price, and the only beneficiaries of the disparity were the two director-stockholders who were eager to have additional capital in the business.

It is no answer to Katzowitz' action that he was also given a chance to purchase additional shares at this bargain rate. The price was not so much a bargain as it was a tactic, conscious or unconscious on the part of the directors, to place Katzowitz in a compromising situation. The price was so fixed to make the failure to invest costly. However, Katzowitz at the time might not have been aware of the dilution because no notice of the effect of the issuance of the new shares on the already outstanding shares was disclosed. In addition, since the stipulation entitled Katzowitz to the same compensation as Sidler and Lasker, the disparity in equity interest caused by their purchase of additional securities in 1961 did not affect stockholder income from Sulburn and, therefore, Katzowitz possibly was not aware of the effect of the stock issuance on his interest in the corporation until dissolution.

No reason exists at this time to permit Sidler and Lasker to benefit from their course of conduct. Katzowitz' delay in commencing the action did not prejudice the defendants. By permitting the defendants to recover their additional investment in Sulburn before the remaining assets of Sulburn are distributed to the stockholders upon dissolution, all the stockholders will be treated equitably. Katzowitz, therefore, should receive his aliquot share of the assets of Sulburn less the amount invested by Sidler and Lasker for their purchase of stock on December 27, 1961.

Accordingly, the order of the Appellate Division should be reversed, with costs, and judgment granted in favor of the plaintiff against the individual defendants.

QUESTIONS

1. If you think of this as penalty dilution, could the defendants argue that the offer wasn't unfair to Katzowitz?

2. What does it mean that the book value of Sulburn's shares was $1,800 at the time the stock was offered to the three shareholders?

3. Is book value the ultimate test of the price at which shares should be offered in a corporation? Why or why not?

4. If you represented Katzowitz at the time new shares were offered at $100 each, how would you advise him assuming he did not have a pressing need for the $2,500 he had just received from Sulburn? Why?

5. The court states that preemptive rights were created by the courts to protect two distinct rights of shareholders—their equity in the corporation and their proportionate voting control. Which is more important here?

6. If shares had been offered to each shareholder at $1,800 per share, would Katzowitz have any complaint?

7. If the existing shares of Sulburn were worth $1,800, what is the amount of damages Katzowitz has suffered because of his failure to purchase? (Hint: see the formula preceding the *Stokes* case.)

8. Is this an offer that normally a shareholder like Katzowitz can't refuse? If so, can you think of any justification for allowing directors to make such an offer?

9. If the right to purchase shares for $100 that are worth $1,800 is offered, and Katzowitz chooses not to exercise these rights, is there any other way he can obtain value from the right? If so, why didn't he do so?

10. If you represent a minority investor about to buy shares in a newly organized company, can you think of ways to give someone in Katzowitz's position a veto power of the price of new issues?

C.   DILUTION AS A TAKEOVER DEFENSE—THE POISON PILL

The Illusory Protections of the Poison Pill

by William J. Carney and Leonard A. Silverstein.
79 Notre Dame Law Review 101 (2003).

I. THE OPERATION OF A RIGHTS PLAN

Rights are issued as pro rata distributions to all common stockholders.[11] The right is typically the right to purchase one unit of a new series of

---

11. The date of the declaration of the dividend of rights is generally called the "Record Date" or the "Rights Dividend Declaration Date."

preferred stock.[12] The preferred stock unit has rights that are essentially equivalent to those of the common, with minor distinctions.[13] These rights are exercisable at the projected "long term value" of the common stock—the price the stock is predicted to reach at the end of the ten year life of the rights—a price typically three to five times higher than the current market price of the common stock.[14] To reach these valuations, financial advisers to the adopting company's board are required to make heroic assumptions about growth rates for company profits—typically in excess of 17% per year compounded for the ten year life of the rights plan.[15]

These rights are initially "stapled" to the common stock, in the sense that they can only be transferred with the common stock, and are not immediately exercisable on issue.[16] The rights separate from the common stock certificates and rights certificates are issued and become transferable apart from the common stock on a "Distribution Date." This occurs when a bidder appears, either by making a tender offer for a significant block of target shares, typically 30%,[17] or by becoming an "Acquiring Person" by acquiring a somewhat smaller block, typically 15% on the "Acquisition Date."[18] This makes it more difficult for a bidder to make a tender offer for

---

12. While there are no legal barriers to using whole shares of preferred, many companies lack sufficient authorized but unissued shares to accomplish this, and thus use fractions of a share.

13. Each unit has the same dividend and liquidation rights as the common, with the theoretical difference that the preferred's rights to payment are "prior" to those of the common, to satisfy what are thought to be legal requirements of a priority of some kind.

14. See, e.g., Wachtell, Lipton, Rosen & Katz, *The Share Purchase Rights Plan* (1996), *reprinted in* Ronald J. Gilson & Bernard S. Black, THE LAW AND FINANCE OF CORPORATE ACQUISITIONS: 1999 SUPPLEMENT 10, 15 and Martin Lipton & Erica H. Steinberger, 1 TAKEOVERS & FREEZEOUTS § 6.03[4][b][i], at 6–61 (Release 27, 1999). A recent study of 341 rights plans adopted in 1998 showed median exercise prices were 5.1 times the price of the common stock at the time of the announcement, but only 3.5 times the high stock price for the 12 months preceding adoption of the rights plan, suggesting that declining stock prices may be a primary motivating factor in the adoption of rights plans. Houlihan Lokey Howard & Zukin, *Stockholder Rights Plan Study* 4 (1999).

15. The implied annual growth rate for earnings required to achieve these valuations was 17.7%. *Id.*

16. By the terms of the rights agreement, the rights are initially represented by the common stock certificates, which will contain a notation to this effect.

17. In some plans the rights separate ten days after the date of first announcement that the bidder either acquires the triggering amount of shares or announces a tender offer that would result in such ownership. Wachtell, Lipton, Rosen & Katz, *supra* note 14 at 15.

18. A survey of rights plans adopted in 1998 found thresholds ranging from 10% to 35%, with a median of 15% and a mean of 16%. Houlihan Lokey Howard & Zukin, *supra* note 14 at 2. In 1999 the triggers may have been somewhat lower. More than 75% of the firms adopting or amending rights plans in 1999 set the trigger at or below 15%, with two-thirds of all adopting firms selecting the 15% level. Pat McGurn, *Guest Features–Poison Pills: The Storm of 1999 Trickles into 2000*, INVESTOR RELATIONS BUSINESS, Mar. 20, 2000, in LEXa package that includes both the common stock and the rights because those who hold rights certificates are no longer necessarily identical with the shareholders. Prior to the Acquisition Date, the rights are redeemable for a nominal amount.[19]

The board's power to redeem the rights for a nominal amount generally terminates on the Acquisition Date.[20] This prevents a bidder that has taken a substantial position from waging a proxy fight to replace the board with new members, who will redeem the rights using its newly acquired shares to win the contest.[21]

More importantly, at the Acquisition Date, the rights are no longer exercisable to acquire a preferred stock unit at an unrealistic price—it was never contemplated that the preferred stock rights would be exercised on their original terms.[22] In the event the bidder acquires a specified substantial block and becomes an "Acquiring Person," the rights "flip in" and become exercisable for the target's common stock (the "flip-in") at a discount, typically 50% of current market value.[23] The exercise price for the preferred becomes the exercise price for multiple shares of common stock. Thus, if the exercise price was $100 per unit of preferred, the holder of a right now has the right to purchase common stock with a market value (pre-Acquisition Date) of $200 for $100.[24] The key to the operation of this

IS/NEWS/ALLNWS. The ISS Study shows that approximately 95 out of 115 plans used a 15% threshold, while approximately ten set the threshold at 10%. ISS Study, *supra* note 1.

19. *Id.* at 16.

20. *Id.*

21. It does not prevent a bidder who has not yet reached the triggering amount from waging such a proxy fight, however, as AT & T did in its fight for control of NCR, and as Farley Industries did in its successful attempt to take over West Point–Pepperell, a fabric manufacturer. This threat was the inspiration for the "dead hand" pill, that attempted to protect the tenure of incumbent directors who were not otherwise protected by provisions for a staggered board, removal only for cause, and prohibitions against board-packing.

22. The Internal Revenue Service has concluded that the probability of exercise of these rights is so remote that the distribution of the rights as a dividend does not constitute the distribution of stock or property to shareholders, and thus has no tax consequences— shareholders do not realize any taxable income on the receipt of rights. Rev. Rul. 90–11, 1990– 1 C.B. 10.

23. Thus the holder of a right would obtain the right to purchase $200 worth of target common stock at an exercise of price of $100. See Wachtell, Lipton, Rosen & Katz, *supra* note 14 at 15 and 1 Lipton & Steinberger, *supra* note 14 at § 6.03[4][b][i], at 6–62.

24. Because companies may lack sufficient authorized but unissued shares of common stock to honor the rights, some plans now provide for a flip-in to be exercisable in "common stock equivalents," which are generally preferred share units with terms comparable to common stock. The number of preferred units is increased, so the exercise obtains for the rights holder a number of units equal to the number of shares of common stock that two times the exercise price could acquire. Because "blank check" preferred shares can be divided by the board into as many units as the board determines, and because these preferred units are the economic equivalent of the common stock, there is no limit to the number of shares that can be issued on exercise of the rights. See Wachtell, Lipton, Rosen & Katz, *supra* note 14 at 37 (Section 11(a) of the Rights Plan). Another solution provided by many rights plans is to allow the board to exchange the rights for one share of common stock. This avoids forcing shareholders to pay cash to exercise the rights. The difficulty, as we will show, is that the plan is discrimination against the bidder—rights are void in the bidder's hands.

These rights have an important anti-destruction provision—a merger of the target into the bidder does not destroy the rights—they "flip over" to become exercisable in the bidder's common stock, on the same bargain basis as the flip-in rights—a 50% discount, using the same exercise price. Thus the dilution of the bidder's shareholders is identical, whether the flip-in or flip-over rights are triggered.[25]

II.   THE IMPACT OF A RIGHTS PLAN

A.   *Introductory Problems*

We now examine how a rights plan would operate if triggered. We begin with a simple observation: a rights plan can only dilute the investment that a bidder has already made when it crosses the threshold that triggers the rights. If the threshold is 15%, that is the most that can be taken from a bidder through dilution, hardly enough, by itself, to deter a determined bidder prepared to pay a premium for a target it perceives to be undervalued. Because most rights plans only provide a 50% discount from market price, they will not appropriate all of the bidder's initial investment.

One of the difficulties in examining the operation of rights plans is that none have operated. In the 1980s Sir James Goldsmith acquired a sufficient amount of the stock of Crown Zellerbach Corporation to make its flip-over rights non-redeemable, but did not engage in a self-dealing event, such as a takeout merger, that allowed exercise of the flip-over rights.[26] No flip-in plan has ever been deliberately triggered,[27] although the authors experienced a close call in one case, and there have been a few other apparently inadvertent triggering events.[28] Several uncertainties present themselves in

---

smaller number of dilutive shares issued reduces the dilution of the bidder's investment. See Table 5, *infra.* Finally, many rights plans provide that in the event the issuer lacks sufficient shares to honor all the rights, it will be obligated to pay rights holders "damages"—the difference between the value of what they receive on exercise and the value of what they were entitled to. To avoid insolvency issues, these obligations are generally conditioned on availability of sufficient cash, and create a continuing obligation to pay cash as it becomes legally available for payment.

25. See text *infra* at Part II.B.7. Both the flip-in and flip-over rights have antidilution protection for rights holders of the type commonly found in convertible securities and options.

26. See Carney *supra* note 4 at 264. The earliest rights plans lacked a flip-in feature; they only operated if the bidder engaged in a merger or other business combination with the target.

27. 1 Arthur Fleischer, Jr. and Alexander R. Sussman, TAKEOVER DEFENSE, § 5.02[A], 5–18 to –19 (6th ed. 2002).

28. In our case, the investor that crossed the triggering threshold also failed to file a timely Schedule 13D, so there was no public announcement of the acquisition of the amount that would have constituted it an "Acquiring Person," which allowed a settlement. Among the issuers that experienced inadvertent triggering events are Pediatrix Medical Group, Michel Chandler, *Shareholder Nearly Triggers a Poison Pill at Ailing Pediatrix*, MIAMI HERALD, Sept. 21, 1999, C3; Newcor, Inc., News Digest, RUBBER & PLASTICS NEWS, July 24, 2000, p. 4; *Worldtex,*

assessing the impact of a rights plan. If the rights plan flips in, will rights holders exercise immediately or will they wait until immediately before expiration, as rational holders of conventional options will do? While shares should be valued on a fully diluted basis in efficient markets, uncertainty about the target's receipt of cash and its investment or disposition by the target could influence the market value of its stock after the flip-in, and thus the cost of acquisition. We discuss this issue in sections II.B.2 and II.B.6, *infra*.

Because of the lack of operational experience, several other questions cannot be answered definitively. What will a target do with proceeds received from the exercise of the rights? If rights are exercised, the target would receive cash representing a multiple of the aggregate market value of its current equity, and would be unlikely to have any massive positive net present value projects in which to invest. In essence, it will probably hold cash or equivalents. If the proceeds are simply held by the target, the bidder can recapture them upon obtaining 100% control. If they are distributed to other shareholders in a discriminatory manner, the bidder's dilution losses are increased. We explore this in Part II.B.6, *infra*. Similarly, what if rights are not exercised immediately, but are only exercised after the bidder has increased its ownership beyond the minimum amount required to trigger the rights? The obvious answer is that this means the bidder has a larger investment subject to dilution, and thus larger losses. This is also explored in Part II.B.6.

B.   Calculating Bidder Dilution

We begin our discussion of bidder dilution with a caution: it is only half the picture. Too often analysis stops with an observation that a hostile bidder's initial investment will be massively diluted by crossing the threshold that permits exercise of the flip-in rights. While this is true, it gives an incomplete picture of the costs imposed by a rights plan on a determined bidder; it is a static rather than a dynamic analysis. As we noted earlier, the typical rights plan's flip-in rights are triggered by a 15% acquisition. If a bidder's initial investment is totally destroyed by the exercise of the rights, the rights plan has added only 15% to the bidder's costs of a total acquisition. Dilution is never 100% because the bidder remains the owner

Inc., Business Briefs, THE CHARLOTTE OBSERVER, Mar. 29, 2000, LEXIS: News: Allnews; Illini Bank, Craig Woker, *Illinois Bank Sweeps Legal Doubleheader*, THE AMERICAN BANKER, Mar. 3, 2000, 5; Rawlings Sporting Goods Co. Inc., Al Stamborski, *Rawlings and 2 Investors Avoid Triggering Poison Pill*, ST. LOUIS POST DISPATCH, May 7, 1999, C11; BJ Services, David Ivanovich, *BJ Services Swallows Poison Pill; Takeover Defense Set Off by Mistake*, THE HOUSTON CHRONICLE, Jan. 7, 1994, Business Section, 1. Harold Simmons did trigger separation of a flip-in, flip-over plan of NL Industries in the 1980s, by acquiring 20% of its shares, but the flip-in rights did not become exercisable until occurrence of a business combination or the bidder's increase in its holdings by more than 1%. Amalgamated Sugar Co. v. NL Industries, 644 F. Supp. 1229 (S.D.N.Y. 1986). Newell Cos. announced that it would swallow a poison pill of Wm. E. Wright Co., but there is no indication whether it was a flip-in pill. *Newell to Swallow "Poison Pill,"* CHICAGO TRIBUNE, Oct. 21, 1985, Business Section, 3.

of some diminished percentage of the outstanding shares, so the bidder's actual losses (added costs) will be somewhat less.[29]

We begin our analysis by examining the operation of a typical preferred stock rights plan, with flip-in rights triggered at the 15% level, with the rights exercisable at a 50% discount from market price. We assume that rights have been issued at an exercise price four times the current (pre-bid) market price of the common stock. We further assume immediate exercise of the rights, and receipt of the proceeds by the target. We will then show that triggering flip-in rights at the minimum ownership level is a dominant strategy, because triggering with the bidder owning larger amounts always puts more of the bidder's investment at risk—at least until unrealistically high levels of ownership are attained. Table 1 below sets out the assumptions in our examples:

Table 1. Assumptions for a Typical Preferred Stock Rights Plan	
1. Target shares outstanding:	1,000,000
2. Pre-bid market price per share:	$ 10.00
3. Bidder's per share cost for the first 15%:	$ 15.00[30]
4. Expected takeover bid price per share:	$ 15.00
5. Exercise price for preferred stock rights:	$ 40.00
6. Assumed market value per share of target shares for calculating common stock acquisition price:	$ 15.00
7. Flip-in trigger:	15%
8. Flip-in discount:	50%
9. Shares issuable per right if the market price is $15 (*$80/15*):	5.3333333

1. The Operation of a Flip–In Rights Plan

We now assume that a bidder acquires the minimum amount of shares necessary to trigger the rights, so that shares now trade on a fully diluted basis. Because the bidder receives no rights and suffers dilution, its percentage ownership is severely diluted, from 15% to 2.7%. But, unlike prior examples, we assume that the bidder is determined, and then proceeds to acquire the remaining public shares at the takeover premium of 50% over the pre-bid value of the target.

Table 2 shows the bidder's costs of a complete acquisition using these assumptions:

Table 2. Bidder's Cost of Acquisition Using a Minimum Purchase With a Preferred Stock Rights Plan	
Bidder's initial acquisition of 150,000 shares @ $15.00	$ 2,250,000

---

29. It is impossible for a rights plan to destroy the bidder's entire investment, because whatever the percentage, the bidder retains some shares in the target.

30. This is a simplifying assumption; it is likely that the bidder's average cost per share for the first 15% will be less than $15 per share. The differences in results are modest, however. *See infra*, Part II.B.4.

Rights flip in for 5.3333333333 shares for 850,000 rights—
Shares Outstanding:

New shares	4,533,333.333	
Original shares	1,000,000	
Total shares	5,533,333.333	
Proceeds of exercise: *(850,000 × $40)*:	$34,000,000	
Market's estimate of value of target:	$49,000,000	
Value per fully diluted share *($49,000,000/5,533,333)*:	$ 8.855421	
Value of bidder's 150,000 shares:	$ 1,328,313	
Bidder's dilution losses:	$ 921,688	
Bidder's cost for remaining shares *(5,383,333 × $8.855422)* =		47,671,688
Total Cost to Bidder:		$49.921,688
Less: Dividend of cash proceeds of rights exercise		34,000,000
Net Cost to Bidder:		$15,921,688

If we assume that the proceeds of exercise of the rights have been retained intact by the target, once the bidder has gained control it can capture the $34,000,000 proceeds, leaving a net cost of $15,921,688. The dilution loss, $921,688, represents 41% of the bidder's initial investment.[31] Put another and more dynamic way, it represents 9.2% of the target's pre-bid value, or 6.1% of the bidder's original estimate of the cost of an acquisition, absent the rights plan. Premiums of this general magnitude are supported by studies of the premiums added to the cost of acquisitions by the presence of rights plans.[32]

31. If the proceeds were immediately dividended by the target before the bidder completed the acquisition, the bidder would receive a small portion (2.71%) of the $34,000,000 dividend. This would amount to $921,400, virtually eliminating the dilution of its investment (but not its ownership percentage) previously suffered. This is explored *infra* in Part II.B.6.

32. The presence of a rights plan increased premiums by almost 8% of firm value, as reported in Georgeson & Company Inc.'s study of premiums obtained by companies with and without pills for the period 1992–1996. Georgeson & Co., *Mergers & Acquisitions: Poison Pills and Shareholder Value, 1992–1996,* http://www.georgeson.com/pdf/M&Apoisonpill.pdf. (visited 6/11/03). An earlier study found bid improvements of 14% for targets with pills that were subsequently taken over. Office of the Chief Economist, Securities and Exchange Commission, *The Effects of Poison Pills on the Wealth of Target Shareholders,* 41 (1986). This study examines early versions of rights plans in a small sample, given the date of the study. A Morgan Stanley study of deals between 1988 and 1995 reports gains to firms with pills of approximately 16%. Mark S. Porter, *Poison Pills Add Premium to Deal Pricing,* 10 No. 31 INVESTMENT DEALERS' DIGEST 2 (Aug. 4, 1997); John C. Coates IV, *Empirical Evidence on Structural Takeover Defenses: Where Do We Stand?,* 54 U. MIAMI L. REV. 783, 794, text at n. 44 (2000). Coates notes an update that produced similar results. *Id.* At n. 45, citing Kenneth A. Bertsch, *Poison Pills,* Investor Responsibility Research Center, Corporate Governance Series 1998 Background Report E at 21 (Jun. 25, 1998). Comment & Schwert, *supra* note 1, at 30–31, also find premium increases in this range. These percentage gains are higher than the dilution inflicted by our model. This may be a result of the issuance of more shares than our model suggests. A magazine reported a Morgan Stanley study of acquisitions since 1997 showed a median premium for firms with pills of 35.9% vs. 31.9% for firms without pills. *Daily Briefing: The Bids Sure Are Getting Hostile,* BUSINESS WEEK ONLINE, Jan. 4, 2002, LEXIS. Table 3 demonstrates how increasing the number of shares issued can increase bidder dilution.

The expected cost of a rights plan to a bidder is the bidder's cost per share times the number of shares held by the bidder, minus the post-issue (fully diluted) market value of the target's shares held by the bidder, which is a function of the market value of the entire company divided by the post-issue number of target shares. This can be expressed as equation (1):

$$L = ca - \frac{(mx + p)}{x + d} \quad (a)$$

where L = bidder's loss through dilution; c = bidder's average pre-trigger cost per share; m = pre-trigger market price; a = bidder's share ownership at the time flip-in rights are triggered; x = shares outstanding before dilutive issuance; d = number of shares issued in dilutive distribution; p = proceeds from exercise of rights $(x-a)e$; and e = exercise price of rights.

Equation (1) expresses the obvious truth that the bidder's loss can be no more than the bidder's investment in the target (ma) at the time the rights become exercisable, ameliorated by the new value received upon exercise of the rights (p), and limited by the fact that the bidder will retain some percentage ownership in the firm absent issuance of an infinite number of new shares at a zero exercise price.

Moran v. Household International, Inc.

500 A.2d 1346 (Del.1985).

■ McNEILLY, JUSTICE:

This case presents to the Court for review the most recent defensive mechanism in the arsenal of corporate takeover weaponry—the Preferred Share Purchase Rights Plan ("Rights Plan" or "Plan"). The validity of this mechanism has attracted national attention. Amici curiae briefs have been filed in support of appellants by the Security and Exchange Commission ("SEC")[1] and the Investment Company Institute. An amicus curiae brief has been filed in support of appellees ("Household") by the United Food and Commercial Workers International Union.

In a detailed opinion, the Court of Chancery upheld the Rights Plan as a legitimate exercise of business judgment by Household. Moran v. Household International, Inc., Del. Ch., 490 A.2d 1059 (1985). We agree, and therefore, affirm the judgment below.

I

The facts giving rise to this case have been carefully delineated in the Court of Chancery's opinion. A review of the basic facts is necessary for a complete understanding of the issues.

---

1. The SEC split 3–2 on whether to intervene in this case. The two dissenting Commissioners have publicly disagreed with the other three as to the merits of the Rights Plan. 17 Securities Regulation & Law Report 400; The Wall Street Journal, March 20, 1985, at 6.

On August 14, 1984, the Board of Directors of Household International, Inc. adopted the Rights Plan by a fourteen to two vote.[2] The intricacies of the Rights Plan are contained in a 48–page document entitled "Rights Agreement." Basically, the Plan provides that Household common stockholders are entitled to the issuance of one Right per common share under certain triggering conditions. There are two triggering events that can activate the Rights. The first is the announcement of a tender offer for 30 percent of Household's shares ("30% trigger") and the second is the acquisition of 20 percent of the Household's shares by any single entity or group ("20% trigger").

If an announcement of a tender offer for 30 percent of Household's shares is made, the Rights are issued and are immediately exercisable to purchase 1/100 share of new preferred stock for $100 and are redeemable by the Board for $.50 per Right. If 20 percent of Household's shares are acquired by anyone, the Rights are issued and become non-redeemable and are exercisable to purchase 1/100 of a share of preferred. If a Right is not exercised for preferred, and thereafter, a merger or consolidation occurs, the Rights holder can exercise each Right to purchase $200 of the common stock of the tender offeror for $100. This "flip-over" provision of the Rights Plan is at the heart of this controversy.

Household is a diversified holding company with its principal subsidiaries engaged in financial services, transportation and merchandising. HFC, National Car Rental and Vons Grocery are three of its wholly-owned entities.

Household did not adopt its Rights Plan during a battle with a corporate raider, but as a preventive mechanism to ward off future advances. The Vice–Chancellor found that as early as February 1984, Household's management became concerned about the company's vulnerability as a takeover target and began considering amending its charter to render a takeover more difficult. After considering the matter, Household decided not to pursue a fair price amendment.[3]

In the meantime, appellant Moran, one of Household's own Directors and also Chairman of the Dyson–Kissner–Moran Corporation, ("D–K–M"), which is the largest single stockholder of Household, began discussions concerning a possible leveraged buy-out of Household by D–K–M. D–K–M's financial studies showed that Household's stock was significantly undervalued in relation to the company's break-up value. It is uncontradicted that Moran's suggestion of a leveraged buy-out never progressed beyond the discussion stage.

---

2. Household's Board has ten outside directors and six who are members of management. Messrs. Moran (appellant) and Whitehead voted against the Plan. The record reflects that Whitehead voted against the Plan not on its substance but because he thought it was novel and would bring unwanted publicity to Household.

3. A fair price amendment to a corporate charter generally requires supermajority approval for certain business combinations and sets minimum price criteria for mergers.

Concerned about Household's vulnerability to a raider in light of the current takeover climate, Household secured the services of Wachtell, Lipton, Rosen and Katz ("Wachtell, Lipton") and Goldman, Sachs & Co. ("Goldman, Sachs") to formulate a takeover policy for recommendation to the Household Board at its August 14 meeting. After a July 31 meeting with a Household Board member and a pre-meeting distribution of material on the potential takeover problem and the proposed Rights Plan, the Board met on August 14, 1984.

Representatives of Wachtell, Lipton and Goldman, Sachs attended the August 14 meeting. The minutes reflect that Mr. Lipton explained to the Board that his recommendation of the Plan was based on his understanding that the Board was concerned about the increasing frequency of "bust-up"[4] takeovers, the increasing takeover activity in the financial service industry, such as Leucadia's attempt to take over Arco, and the possible adverse effect this type of activity could have on employees and others concerned with and vital to the continuing successful operation of Household even in the absence of any actual bust-up takeover attempt. Against this factual background, the Plan was approved.

Thereafter, Moran and the company of which he is Chairman, D–K–M, filed this suit. On the eve of trial, Gretl Golter, the holder of 500 shares of Household, was permitted to intervene as an additional plaintiff. The trial was held, and the Court of Chancery ruled in favor of Household. Appellants now appeal from that ruling to this Court.

II

The primary issue here is the applicability of the business judgment rule as the standard by which the adoption of the Rights Plan should be reviewed. Much of this issue has been decided by our recent decision in Unocal Corp. v. Mesa Petroleum Co., Del. Supr., 493 A.2d 946 (1985). In Unocal, we applied the business judgment rule to analyze Unocal's discriminatory self-tender. We explained:

> When a board addresses a pending takeover bid it has an obligation to determine whether the offer is in the best interests of the corporation and its shareholders. In that respect a board's duty is no different from any other responsibility it shoulders, and its decisions should be no less entitled to the respect they otherwise would be accorded in the realm of business judgment.

Other jurisdictions have also applied the business judgment rule to actions by which target companies have sought to forestall takeover activity they considered undesirable. * * *

This case is distinguishable from the ones cited, since here we have a defensive mechanism adopted to ward off possible future advances and not a mechanism adopted in reaction to a specific threat. This distinguishing factor does not result in the Directors losing the protection of the business

---

4. "Bust-up" takeover generally refers to a situation in which one seeks to finance an acquisition by selling off pieces of the acquired company.

judgment rule. To the contrary, pre-planning for the contingency of a hostile takeover might reduce the risk that, under the pressure of a takeover bid, management will fail to exercise reasonable judgment. Therefore, in reviewing a pre-planned defensive mechanism it seems even more appropriate to apply the business judgment rule. See Warner Communications v. Murdoch, D. Del., 581 F. Supp. 1482, 1491 (1984).

Of course, the business judgment rule can only sustain corporate decision making or transactions that are within the power or authority of the Board. Therefore, before the business judgment rule can be applied it must be determined whether the Directors were authorized to adopt the Rights Plan.

III

Appellants vehemently contend that the Board of Directors was unauthorized to adopt the Rights Plan. First, appellants contend that no provision of the Delaware General Corporation Law authorizes the issuance of such Rights. Secondly, appellant, along with the SEC, contend that the Board is unauthorized to usurp stockholders' rights to receive hostile tender offers. Third, appellants and the SEC also contend that the Board is unauthorized to fundamentally restrict stockholders' rights to conduct a proxy contest. We address each of these contentions in turn.

A.

While appellants contend that no provision of the Delaware General Corporation Law authorizes the Rights Plan, Household contends that the Rights Plan was issued pursuant to 8 Del. C. §§ 151(g) and 157. It explains that the Rights are authorized by § 157[7] and the issue of preferred stock underlying the Rights is authorized by § 151.[8] Appellants respond by making several attacks upon the authority to issue the Rights pursuant to § 157.

---

7. The power to issue rights to purchase shares is conferred by 8 Del. C. § 157 which provides in relevant part:

> Subject to any provisions in the certificate of incorporation, every corporation may create and issue, whether or not in connection with the issue and sale of any shares of stock or other securities of the corporation, rights or options entitling the holders thereof to purchase from the corporation any shares of its capital stock of any class or classes, such rights or options to be evidenced by or in such instrument or instruments as shall be approved by the board of directors.

8.   8 Del. C. § 151(g) provides in relevant part:

> When any corporation desires to issue any shares of stock of any class or of any series of any class of which the voting powers, designations, preferences and relative, participating, optional or other rights, if any, or the qualifications, limitations or restrictions thereof, if any, shall not have been set forth in the certificate of incorporation or in any amendment thereto but shall be provided for in a resolution or resolutions adopted by the board of directors pursuant to authority expressly vested in it by the provisions of the certificate of incorporation or any amendment thereto, a certificate setting forth a copy of such resolution or resolutions and the number of shares of stock of such class or series shall be executed, acknowledged, filed, recorded, and shall become effective, in accordance with § 103 of this title.

Appellants begin by contending that § 157 cannot authorize the Rights Plan since § 157 has never served the purpose of authorizing a takeover defense. Appellants contend that § 157 is a corporate financing statute, and that nothing in its legislative history suggests a purpose that has anything to do with corporate control or a takeover defense. Appellants are unable to demonstrate that the legislature, in its adoption of § 157, meant to limit the applicability of § 157 to only the issuance of Rights for the purposes of corporate financing. Without such affirmative evidence, we decline to impose such a limitation upon the section that the legislature has not. Compare Providence & Worcester Co. v. Baker, Del. Supr., 378 A.2d 121, 124 (1977) (refusal to read a bar to protective voting provisions into 8 Del. C. § 212(a)).

As we noted in Unocal:

> [O]ur corporate law is not static. It must grow and develop in response to, indeed in anticipation of, evolving concepts and needs. Merely because the General Corporation Law is silent as to a specific matter does not mean that it is prohibited.

Secondly, appellants contend that § 157 does not authorize the issuance of sham rights such as the Rights Plan. They contend that the Rights were designed never to be exercised, and that the Plan has no economic value. In addition, they contend the preferred stock made subject to the Rights is also illusory, citing Telvest, Inc. v. Olson, Del. Ch., C.A. No. 5798, Brown, V.C. (March 8, 1979).

Appellants' sham contention fails in both regards. As to the Rights, they can and will be exercised upon the happening of a triggering mechanism, as we have observed during the current struggle of Sir James Goldsmith to take control of Crown Zellerbach. See Wall Street Journal, July 26, 1985, at 3, 12.* As to the preferred shares, we agree with the Court of Chancery that they are distinguishable from sham securities invalidated in Telvest, *supra*. The Household preferred, issuable upon the happening of a triggering event, have superior dividend and liquidation rights.**

Third, appellants contend that § 157 authorizes the issuance of Rights "entitling holders thereof to purchase from the corporation any shares of its capital stock of any class ..." (emphasis added). Therefore, their contention continues, the plain language of the statute does not authorize Household to issue rights to purchase another's capital stock upon a merger or consolidation.

---

* At the time of adoption of the rights plan, the Household common stock was trading in the range of $30–33. Because each 1/100 had the same dividend and liquidation rights as the common, it was highly unlikely that any shareholder would ever exercise rights to purchase the preferred stock. Rights in Crown Zellerbach preferred were not exercised after Sir James Goldsmith's acquisition of its common stock.—Ed.

** Each 1/100 of a share of preferred stock had the same dividend and liquidation rights as the common stock, except (to the extent this is possible), they were prior and superior to the rights of the common stock.—Ed.

Household contends, inter alia, that the Rights Plan is analogous to "anti-dilution" provisions which are customary features of a wide variety of corporate securities. While appellants seem to concede that "anti-destruction" provisions are valid under Delaware corporate law, they seek to distinguish the Rights Plan as not being incidental, as are most "anti-destruction" provisions, to a corporation's statutory power to finance itself. We find no merit to such a distinction. We have already rejected appellants' similar contention that § 157 could only be used for financing purposes. We also reject that distinction here.

"Anti-destruction" clauses generally ensure holders of certain securities of the protection of their right of conversion in the event of a merger by giving them the right to convert their securities into whatever securities are to replace the stock of their company. See Broad v. Rockwell International Corp., 5th Cir., 642 F.2d 929, 946, cert. denied, 454 U.S. 965 (1981); Wood v. Coastal States Gas Corp., Del. Supr., 401 A.2d 932, 937–39 (1979); B.S.F. Co. v. Philadelphia National Bank, Del. Supr., 204 A.2d 746, 750–51 (1964). The fact that the rights here have as their purpose the prevention of coercive two-tier tender offers* does not invalidate them.

* * *

Having concluded that sufficient authority for the Rights Plan exists in 8 Del. C. § 157, we note the inherent powers of the Board conferred by 8 Del. C. § 141(a), concerning the management of the corporation's "business and affairs" (emphasis added), also provides the Board additional authority upon which to enact the Rights Plan. Unocal, 493 A.2d at 953.[11]

B.

Appellants contend that the Board is unauthorized to usurp stockholders' rights to receive tender offers by changing Household's fundamental structure. We conclude that the Rights Plan does not prevent stockholders from receiving tender offers, and that the change of Household's structure was less than that which results from the implementation of other defensive mechanisms upheld by various courts.

Appellants' contention that stockholders will lose their right to receive and accept tender offers seems to be premised upon an understanding of the Rights Plan which is illustrated by the SEC amicus brief which states:

---

*When a bidder makes a tender offer (an invitation to shareholders to tender their shares) at an attractive price above the current market price, and assures those who do not tender that the bidder will engage in a "freeze-out" merger at a lower price, public shareholders may well feel that they are coerced into accepting the offer.—Ed.

11.   8 Del. C. § 141(a) provides:

(a) The business and affairs of every corporation organized under this chapter shall be managed by or under the direction of a board of directors, except as may be otherwise provided in this chapter or in its certificate of incorporation. If any such provision is made in the certificate of incorporation, the powers and duties conferred or imposed upon the board of directors by this chapter shall be exercised or performed to such extent and by such person or persons as shall be provided in the certificate of incorporation.

"The Chancery Court's decision seriously understates the impact of this plan. In fact, as we discuss below, the Rights Plan will deter not only two-tier offers, but virtually all hostile tender offers."

The fallacy of that contention is apparent when we look at the recent takeover of Crown Zellerbach, which has a similar Rights Plan, by Sir James Goldsmith. Wall Street Journal, July 26, 1985, at 3, 12. The evidence at trial also evidenced many methods around the Plan ranging from tendering with a condition that the Board redeem the Rights, tendering with a high minimum condition of shares and Rights, tendering and soliciting consents to remove the Board and redeem the Rights, to acquiring 50% of the shares and causing Household to self-tender for the Rights. One could also form a group of up to 19.9% and solicit proxies for consents to remove the Board and redeem the Rights. These are but a few of the methods by which Household can still be acquired by a hostile tender offer.

In addition, the Rights Plan is not absolute. When the Household Board of Directors is faced with a tender offer and a request to redeem the Rights, they will not be able to arbitrarily reject the offer. They will be held to the same fiduciary standards any other board of directors would be held to in originally approving the Rights Plan.

In addition, appellants contend that the deterrence of tender offers will be accomplished by what they label "a fundamental transfer of power from the stockholders to the directors." They contend that this transfer of power, in itself, is unauthorized.

The Rights Plan will result in no more of a structural change than any other defensive mechanism adopted by a board of directors. The Rights Plan does not destroy the assets of the corporation. The implementation of the Plan neither results in any outflow of money from the corporation nor impairs its financial flexibility. It does not dilute earnings per share and does not have any adverse tax consequences for the corporation or its stockholders. The Plan has not adversely affected the market price of Household's stock.

Comparing the Rights Plan with other defensive mechanisms, it does less harm to the value structure of the corporation than do the other mechanisms. Other mechanisms result in increased debt of the corporation. See Whittaker Corp. v. Edgar, *supra*, (sale of "price asset"), Cheff v. Mathes, *supra*, (paying greenmail to eliminate a threat), Unocal Corp. v. Mesa Petroleum Co., *supra*, (discriminatory self-tender).

There is little change in the governance structure as a result of the adoption of the Rights Plan. The Board does not now have unfettered discretion in refusing to redeem the Rights. The Board has no more discretion in refusing to redeem the Rights than it does in enacting any defensive mechanism.

The contention that the Rights Plan alters the structure more than do other defensive mechanisms because it is so effective as to make the corporation completely safe from hostile tender offers is likewise without merit. As explained above, there are numerous methods to successfully launch a hostile tender offer.

C.

Appellants' third contention is that the Board was unauthorized to fundamentally restrict stockholders' rights to conduct a proxy contest. Appellants contend that the "20% trigger" effectively prevents any stockholder from first acquiring 20% or more shares before conducting a proxy contest and further, it prevents stockholders from banding together into a group to solicit proxies if, collectively, they own 20% or more of the stock.[12] In addition, at trial, appellants contended that read literally, the Rights Agreement triggers the Rights upon the mere acquisition of the right to vote 20% or more of the shares through a proxy solicitation, and thereby precludes any proxy contest from being waged.[13]

Appellants seem to have conceded this last contention in light of Household's response that the receipt of a proxy does not make the recipient the "beneficial owner" of the shares involved which would trigger the Rights. In essence, the Rights Agreement provides that the Rights are triggered when someone becomes the "beneficial owner" of 20% or more of Household stock. Although a literal reading of the Rights Agreement definition of "beneficial owner" would seem to include those shares which one has the right to vote, it has long been recognized that the relationship between grantor and recipient of a proxy is one of agency, and the agency is revocable by the grantor at any time. Henn, Corporations § 196, at 518. Therefore, the holder of a proxy is not the "beneficial owner" of the stock. As a result, the mere acquisition of the right to vote 20% of the shares does not trigger the Rights.

The issue, then, is whether the restriction upon individuals or groups from first acquiring 20% of shares before waging a proxy contest fundamentally restricts stockholders' right to conduct a proxy contest. Regarding this issue the Court of Chancery found:

> Thus, while the Rights Plan does deter the formation of proxy efforts of a certain magnitude, it does not limit the voting power of individual shares. On the evidence presented it is highly conjectural to assume that a particular effort to assert shareholder views in the election of directors or revisions of corporate policy will be frustrated by the proxy feature of the Plan. Household's witnesses, Troubh and Higgins described recent corporate takeover battles in which insurgents holding less than 10% stock ownership were able to secure corporate control through a proxy contest or the threat of one.

---

12. Appellants explain that the acquisition of 20% of the shares trigger the Rights, making them non-redeemable, and thereby would prevent even a future friendly offer for the ten-year life of the Rights.

13. The SEC still contends that the mere acquisition of the right to vote 20% of the shares through a proxy solicitation triggers the rights. We do not interpret the Rights Agreement in that manner.

We conclude that there was sufficient evidence at trial to support the Vice–Chancellor's finding that the effect upon proxy contests will be minimal. Evidence at trial established that many proxy contests are won with an insurgent ownership of less than 20%, and that very large holdings are no guarantee of success. There was also testimony that the key variable in proxy contest success is the merit of an insurgent's issues, not the size of his holdings.

IV

Having concluded that the adoption of the Rights Plan was within the authority of the Directors, we now look to whether the Directors have met their burden under the business judgment rule.

The business judgment rule is a "presumption that in making a business decision the directors of a corporation acted on an informed basis, in good faith and in the honest belief that the action taken was in the best interests of the company." Aronson v. Lewis, Del. Supr., 473 A.2d 805, 812 (1984) (citations omitted). Notwithstanding, in Unocal we held that when the business judgment rule applies to adoption of a defensive mechanism, the initial burden will lie with the directors. The "directors must show that they had reasonable grounds for believing that a danger to corporate policy and effectiveness existed.... [T]hey satisfy that burden 'by showing good faith and reasonable investigation....'" In addition, the directors must show that the defensive mechanism was "reasonable in relation to the threat posed." Unocal, 493 A.2d at 955. Moreover, that proof is materially enhanced, as we noted in Unocal, where, as here, a majority of the board favoring the proposal consisted of outside independent directors who have acted in accordance with the foregoing standards. Then, the burden shifts back to the plaintiffs who have the ultimate burden of persuasion to show a breach of the directors' fiduciary duties.

There are no allegations here of any bad faith on the part of the Directors' action in the adoption of the Rights Plan. There is no allegation that the Directors' action was taken for entrenchment purposes. Household has adequately demonstrated, as explained above, that the adoption of the Rights Plan was in reaction to what it perceived to be the threat in the market place of coercive two-tier tender offers. Appellants do contend, however, that the Board did not exercise informed business judgment in its adoption of the Plan.

Appellants contend that the Household Board was uninformed since they were inter alia, told the Plan would not inhibit a proxy contest, were not told the plan would preclude all hostile acquisitions of Household, and were told that Delaware counsel opined that the plan was within the business judgment of the Board.

As to the first two contentions, as we explained above, the Rights Plan will not have a severe impact upon proxy contests and it will not preclude all hostile acquisitions of Household. Therefore, the Directors were not misinformed or uninformed on these facts.

Appellants contend that Delaware counsel did not express an opinion on the flip-over provision of the Rights, rather only that the Rights would constitute validly issued and outstanding rights to subscribe to the preferred stock of the company.

To determine whether a business judgment reached by a board of directors was an informed one, we determine whether the directors were grossly negligent. Smith v. Van Gorkom, Del. Supr., 488 A.2d 858, 873 (1985). Upon a review of this record, we conclude the Directors were not grossly negligent. The information supplied to the Board on August 14 provided the essentials of the Plan. The Directors were given beforehand a notebook which included a three-page summary of the Plan along with the articles on the current takeover environment. The extended discussion between the Board and representatives of Wachtell, Lipton and Goldman, Sachs before approval of the Plan reflected a full and candid evaluation of the Plan. Moran's expression of his views at the meeting served to place before the Board a knowledgeable critique of the Plan. The factual happenings here are clearly distinguishable from the actions of the directors of Trans Union Corporation who displayed gross negligence in approving a cash-out merger.

In addition, to meet their burden, the Directors must show that the defensive mechanism was "reasonable in relation to the threat posed". The record reflects a concern on the part of the Directors over the increasing frequency in the financial services industry of "boot-strap" and "bust-up" takeovers. The Directors were also concerned that such takeovers may take the form of two-tier offers.[14] In addition, on August 14, the Household Board was aware of Moran's overture on behalf of D–K–M. In sum, the Directors reasonably believed Household was vulnerable to coercive acquisition techniques and adopted a reasonable defensive mechanism to protect itself.

V

In conclusion, the Household Directors receive the benefit of the business judgment rule in their adoption of the Rights Plan.

The Directors adopted the Plan pursuant to statutory authority in 8 Del. C. §§ 141, 151, 157. We reject appellants' contentions that the Rights Plan strips stockholders of their rights to receive tender offers and that the Rights Plan fundamentally restricts proxy contests.

The Directors adopted the Plan in the good faith belief that it was necessary to protect Household from coercive acquisition techniques. The Board was informed as to the details of the Plan. In addition, Household has demonstrated that the Plan is reasonable in relation to the threat posed. Appellants, on the other hand, have failed to convince us that the Directors breached any fiduciary duty in their adoption of the Rights Plan.

---

14. We have discussed the coercive nature of two-tier tender offers in Unocal, 493 A.2d at 956, n.12. We explained in Unocal that a discriminatory self-tender was reasonably related to the threat of two-tier tender offers and possible greenmail.

While we conclude for present purposes that the Household Directors are protected by the business judgment rule, that does not end the matter. The ultimate response to an actual takeover bid must be judged by the Directors' actions at that time, and nothing we say here relieves them of their basic fundamental duties to the corporation and its stockholders. Their use of the Plan will be evaluated when and if the issue arises.

Affirmed.

NOTE ON RIGHTS PLANS

Flip-over rights, of the kind employed by Household, were approved in Horwitz v. Southwest Forest Industries, Inc., 604 F.Supp. 1130 (D. Nev. 1985). Flip-in plans were approved in APL Corp. v. Johnson Controls, Inc., 85 Civ. 990 (E.D.N.Y. 1985) (applying Wisconsin law); Gelco Corp. v. Coniston Partners, 652 F.Supp. 829 (D. Minn.1986); affirmed in part and vacated in part, 811 F.2d 414 (8th Cir.1987) and Harvard Industries, Inc. v. Tyson, [1986–87 Decisions] Fed. Sec. L. Rep. (CCH) ¶ 93,064 (E.D. Mich. 1986).

A flip-in plan, of the kind described in Carney & Silverstein, *supra*, was first approved in Delaware in Stahl v. Apple Bancorp, Inc., [1990 Decisions] Fed. Sec. L. Rep. (CCH) ¶ 95,412 (1990). Unlike the plan in *Moran*, this plan expressly excluded from the definition of beneficial ownership possession of revocable proxies obtained through a public proxy solicitation. The Chancery Court concluded that the poison pill was not an invalid infringement on shareholders' voting rights, because it left the holder of a number of shares less than the triggering percentage free to solicit proxies to remove the board and replace them with directors with the power to redeem the rights. It held that the minor restrictions imposed on a bidder, such as entering into agreements with other shareholders to serve on the board or to share expenses were immaterial. Still, the court cautioned that "It is troubling in either context if the side in control of the levers of power employs them with respect to an election to coerce its opposition to restrict its legitimate electioneering activities." 1990 WL 114222 at *5.

On the other hand, flip-in rights plans have been questioned more closely by the courts, since they can dilute the investment of the bidder in the target, and thus deter takeover bids altogether. Several courts have applied the "heightened scrutiny" of Unocal Corp. v. Mesa Petroleum Co., 493 A.2d 946 (Del. 1985), to closely examine whether the terms of the flip-in represented an overreaction to possible threats. Dynamics Corp. of America v. CTS Corp., 637 F.Supp. 406 (N.D. Ill.), aff'd, 794 F.2d 250 (7th Cir.1986), reversed on other grounds, 481 U.S. 69, 107 S. Ct. 1637 (1987); and R. D. Smith & Co., Inc. v. Preway, Inc., 644 F.Supp. 868 (W.D.Wis. 1986).

Other courts have examined whether rights plans that exclude bidders represent an unlawful discrimination. See The Amalgamated Sugar Company v. NL Industries, 644 F.Supp. 1229 (S.D.N.Y. 1986) (applying New Jersey law), which followed Minstar Acquiring Corp. v. AMF Inc., 621

F.Supp. 1252 (S.D.N.Y.1985) and Asarco Inc. v. Court, 611 F.Supp. 468 (D.N.J.1985). It was followed in West Point–Pepperell, Inc. v. Farley, Inc., 711 F.Supp. 1088 (N.D.Ga.1988).

Legislatures have responded to the questions raised by rights plans in a variety of ways. In every case where a rights plan was invalidated by a court as in excess of statutory authority, the statute was later amended to authorize such discriminatory features. Even states that did not experience such rulings took steps to amend their statutes.

D.   CREDITOR PROTECTION: LEGAL CAPITAL

Legal capital, the assignment of a nominal ("par") value to shares, had its origins in the era of special chartering, when a charter was a contract between the sovereign and promoters. In exchange for a monopoly franchise, the sovereign extracted a commitment for enough capital to accomplish the enterprise. The charters provided that shares must have a nominal value, and that the nominal value of all authorized shares was equal to the amount of capital stock authorized by the sovereign. This nominal value was called "par value." Before the franchise was valid, all shares had to be subscribed for, and a minimum amount paid in for these shares. Shareholders were liable for the balance of the subscription. Hence the state assured that in exchange for a monopoly franchise, the promoters would actually raise the capital to conduct the business, which was, in the eighteenth and early nineteenth century, a quasi-public enterprise with natural monopoly characteristics, such as bridges, toll roads, canals, mills, and finally railroads.

Americans grew accustomed to obtaining charters from the state for incorporation, which carried privileges of monopoly and limited liability. More conventional business corporations, such as the New England woolen and cotton mills, lacked the natural monopoly elements, and thus were not given exclusive franchises. But the use of requirements of minimum subscribed capital continued. Whether this was simply legislative inertia or a more conscious use of legal capital requirements for creditor protection is less obvious.

In the nineteenth century states began to pass General Corporation Laws, by which anyone could obtain the privilege of limited liability. Competition from low-cost states drove special chartering out of business. In the process, this eliminated the notion of a bargain with the state over the amount of capital committed to a business, and the original purpose of minimum capital commitments disappeared. The notions of minimum capital committed to a business, as a way of protecting those dealing with the corporation, developed during the nineteenth century. But some states continued to regulate the conditions on which limited liability could be obtained. Early restrictions included minimum capital, and limits on the capitalization of firms in some states (a populist reaction to fear of large accumulations of capital). This continued until the middle of the twentieth century and later. For example, Sec. 51 of M.B.C.A. (1950) required payment of $1,000 before business could begin, and did not disappear until the 1968 revision of the M.B.C.A.

The European approach has been to require minimum capital to begin a corporation, and to adopt rules designed to preserve it. The European Community's Second Directive, Art. 6, § 1 requires minimum capitalization of €25,000. Some member states have more stringent requirements. At least 25% of the subscription price for shares must be paid at the time of incorporation. EC Second Directive, Art. 9, § 1. Where shares were issued for non-cash asset contributions, independently appointed experts were required to appraise the value of assets under Art. 3 of the EC First Directive.

The practical need for these kinds of rules disappeared in the U.S. with the advent of general corporation laws in the middle of the 19th century. But rules about par value being the minimum amount that could be paid for a share persisted, a form of "path dependence," or inertia of legal doctrine. These same rules about par value and a requirement that payment of the full par value of shares was an obligation of a shareholder became a creditor protection device that was thought to disclose to creditors how much shareholders had invested in the business.

Note the limits on the value of this information: First, it only tells creditors how much shareholders originally invested (or committed to invest), not what their investment is currently worth. Second, the usefulness of par value depends on what shareholders gave up in exchange for shares. If they gave cash in the amount of par value, it is at least an accurate history of the value contributed, which is all accounting purports to accomplish. If they gave assets valued at inflated prices, it is not necessarily even accurate history.

Judicial doctrines developed to deal with the second problem. Where investors contributed over-valued assets, the shares were considered "watered" to the extent of the overstatement of the value of the assets. Where investors received shares for no consideration, these were called "bonus" shares. In each case, shareholders were liable, either to the company or to creditors, for the difference. Various theories were used to rationalize holding shareholders liable.

The "Trust Fund" Theory. This theory held that the corporation held its capital in trust for the benefit of creditors of the corporation. Shareholders who failed to pay in the full value of shares were also trustees to the extent of their underpayments. This doctrine was properly rejected as pure fiction in *Hospes v. Northwestern Mfg. & Car Co.*, 48 Minn. 174, 50 N.W. 1117 (1892). The court recognized that corporations hold their capital for the benefit of shareholders, not for the benefit of creditors.

The "Misrepresentation" Theory. This theory held that only those creditors who were deceived by the overstatement of capital and who relied on it in extending credit were entitled to make a claim. The difficulty with this theory is that after a few years of operations, which could involve profits, losses, or changes in asset values not reflected in accounting statements, no one should be deceived or rely on original contributions, and few creditors really look to this as any indication of a company's well-being. Issues of deceit are now more commonly and easily dealt with under securities laws.

The "Statutory Obligation" Theory. This holds that purchasing shares for less than par value creates a statutory obligation to pay the difference to creditors when the firm is insolvent. Some states still attempt to deal with the watered stock problem with statutory prohibitions of use of some suspect forms of consideration for shares. These states prohibit corporations from accepting either promissory notes or promises of future services for shares. Prior to 1980, M.B.C.A. § 19 followed this approach. It is still employed in Delaware, in Del. G.C.L. § 152 (shares shall be deemed fully paid and nonassessable if "(1) the entire amount of such consideration has been received by the corporation in the form of cash, *services rendered*, personal property....") (emphasis added). Other statutes made it clear that failure to pay full value didn't make shareholders liable as partners, but only liable for the balance of their subscription. See M.B.C.A. § 23, 1st ¶ (1950). This is reflected today in M.B.C.A. § 6.22(a):

> "A purchaser from a corporation of its own shares is not liable to the corporation or its creditors with respect to the shares except to pay the consideration for which the shares were authorized to be issued (section 6.21) or specified in the subscription agreement (section 6.20)."

The "Watered Stock" Theory. When shares were issued for assets the real value of which was less than the par value of the shares, the shares were said to be "watered." The origins of the phrase lie in cattle markets, where sharp sellers would cause their cattle to drink heavily before weighing. These shares could be treated as being sold for less than fair value. Most modern statutes require boards of directors to determine the value of consideration received for shares, and provide that in the absence of actual fraud, the board's determination shall be conclusive. See Del. G. C. L. § 152 and M.B.C.A. § 6.21(c).

The "Sweat Equity" Problem.

In many start-ups one person, A, will furnish the capital while the other, B, furnishes the efforts. In a partnership, if they want a 50–50 arrangement for splitting profits and losses, that's what they get by default, regardless of disparity in capital contributions. Uniform Partnership Act ("UPA"), § 18(a). Partners also get equal voting rights regardless of capital, unless they agree otherwise. UPA § 18(e). In contrast, in a corporation, both dividends and votes are proportional to capital invested.

How can A and B agree to take equal shares for their contributions to a corporation? Formerly, as a relic of the use of par value for protecting against watered stock, M.B.C.A. § 18 (1950) prohibited issuance of shares for either promissory notes or promises of future services. Thus shares to the laboring partner, B, would be invalidly issued, and if the shares have par value, the laboring partner, B, would have to pay at least par for them. But the contractual solution has always been easy: par value can be set at a low number, perhaps one cent per share or less. Under these circumstances, B could pay the nominal par value for his shares and A could pay a higher price. The excess of A's contribution would be capital surplus under M.B.C.A. § 2(m) (1950). The down side of this occurs if there is a sudden change of circumstances. For example, if the corporation were to be quickly dissolved (perhaps because of deadlock), B would get one-half of the remaining capital—a windfall.

There are solutions:

1. Have A & B each buy voting common shares for a low par value, and have A lend the balance of the capital to the firm. This protects him in dissolution. But it gives A more of the profits and assets on dissolution than B would get. To the extent that the vast majority of A's and B's total contributions are represented by A's claim as a creditor, this may create the danger of piercing the corporate veil under some circumstances, or at least subordination of A's claim to those of other creditors. (See Chapter Four, Part 6.)

2. Have A & B each buy voting common shares for a low par value, and have A buy nonvoting shares, either preferred or common, with the balance of his capital. The preferred has a dividend and liquidation preference that gives A more than B, just as in a loan. But the dividend rate can be made quite small. The liquidation preference has to be at least the amount invested to protect A's investment in dissolution.

3. Have A and B buy separate classes of common, each for the same price per share. Thus B would have fewer shares than A. But B's shares can be given more votes per share, so their voting power is equal. This protects A in dissolution, but A gets a higher dividend payment (more shares) than B. This can be equalized with a higher dividend rate on the B shares. A may want protection against early dissolution, if A & B hold equal amounts of stock. A may lend part of the capital to the business. A may take back preferred stock for part of his investment— perhaps non-voting, so their votes are equal. Or B's shares may be placed in escrow until B has worked for the firm for a specified time. Or A's debt or preferred may be convertible into common stock.

From 1950 on, the Model Act contemplated that the price paid for shares, at least up to their par value, should be preserved as a permanent fund, which could not be invaded for the benefit of shareholders. It became, in effect, a "cushion" for creditors—an assurance that shareholders would leave in place their original capital contributions. M.B.C.A. § 17 (1950) provided that "shares having a par value may be issued for such consideration expressed in dollars, *not less than the par value thereof*, as shall be fixed from time to time by the board of directors." Further, it provided that the amount paid for shares represented by their par value became the "stated capital" of the corporation, which could not be invaded by shareholders. Additional sums paid for shares were designated as "capital surplus," M.B.C.A. § 18 (1950). This was identical to Del. G.C.L. § 153. Dividends could only be paid out of "earned surplus," the accumulated earnings of the company, minus accumulated losses and accumulated dividends paid. Similarly, Delaware G.C.L. § 153 provides that shares with par value cannot be issued for less than par and § 154 provides that with respect to par value shares, the board can determine that only the part of the purchase price up to par value shall be allocated to stated capital.

But all these solutions involve transaction costs to contract around the statutory rule. Since 1978, the Model Business Corporation Act (currently M.B.C.A. § 6.21(b)) has rejected this older approach:

> "(b) The Board of directors may authorize shares to be issued for consideration consisting of any tangible or intangible property or benefit to the corporation, including cash, *promissory notes*, services performed, *contracts for services to be performed*, or other securities of the corporation." (Emphasis added)

These forms of "sweat equity" may have value to the corporation, and permit people to earn their way into ownership. At the same time, the Model Act eliminated all vestiges of par value and legal capital. The Official Comments to § 6.21 give the reason for this change:

> "Practitioners and legal scholars have long recognized that the statutory structure embodying 'par value' and 'legal capital' concepts is not only complex and confusing but also fails to serve the original purpose of protecting creditors and senior security holders from payments to junior security holders. Indeed, to the extent security holders are led to believe that it provides this protection, these provisions may be affirmatively misleading."

The 1978 amendments to the Model Act admitted that par value had not provided any real creditor protection, and abandoned this as a means of providing disclosure of a fund. M.B.C.A. § 6.01 is silent on par value. M.B.C.A. § 6.01(b) has the only requirements:

> "The articles of incorporation must authorize (1) one or more classes of shares that together have unlimited voting rights, and (2) one or more classes of shares (which may be the same class or classes as those with voting rights) that together are entitled to receive the net assets of the corporation upon dissolution."

Thus, under the Model Act, par value has been abolished, and the obligation to pay for shares is generally purely contractual, and not statutory. See M.B.C.A. § 6.22:

§ 6.22.   Liability of Shareholders

(a) A purchaser from a corporation of its own shares is not liable to the corporation or its creditors with respect to the shares except to pay the consideration for which the shares were authorized to be issued (Section 6.21) or specified in the subscription agreement (Section 6.20).

(b) Unless otherwise provided in the articles of incorporation, a shareholder of a corporation is not personally liable for the acts or debt of the corporation except that he may become personally liable by reason of his own acts or conduct.

Thus the Model Act leaves creditors to protect themselves in dealing with corporations in the same way they protect themselves when dealing with partnerships or individuals—determine what the real assets of the borrower are before lending.

In Chapter Nine, Part 2 we will examine how legal capital rules have required shareholders to leave capital in the firm on a continuing basis, by restricting distributions to shareholders, whether in the form of dividends, distributions in partial liquidation (return of capital) or share repurchases. It is worth noting that the European Union imposes legal capital restrictions similar to those of the 1950 M.B.C.A. and the Delaware act. For a criticism of these rules see Luca Enriques and Jonathan R. Macey, Creditors Versus Capital Formation: The Case Against the European Legal Capital Rules, 86 Cornell Law Review 1165 (2001). As of this writing, the author is informed that the European rules are being reconsidered.

E.   Public Securities Markets and Regulation

i.   THE FEDERAL SECURITIES LAWS IN A NUTSHELL

After the great stock market crash of 1929, Congress began to hold hearings about the causes of the crash. While many economists today believe that the crash was caused to a large extent by the monetary policies of the Federal Reserve Bank, which shrank the money supply by one-third, that was not the common view in 1929 and thereafter. The view was that Wall Street was the source of the crash, and that practices on Wall Street needed to be changed. These hearings focused on several so-called problems: (1) excessive speculation by ignorant investors; (2) manipulation of prices on established markets by market insiders; and (3) excessive use of credit in buying stocks.

Congress responded with a series of laws during the 1930s. We will address only the first two of these laws—the Securities Act of 1933, 15 U.S.C. § 77a et seq. (the "Securities Act") and the Securities Exchange Act of 1934, 15 U.S.C. § 78a et seq. (the "Exchange Act"). These two laws were important parts of Franklin D. Roosevelt's "New Deal" legislation of the 1930s.

The Securities Act was adopted within the first 100 days of the New Deal, and thus illustrates the importance that Congress and the President attached to reforming the securities markets. A principal justification for the Securities Act was to fill in the gap left by state regulation that could not reach transactions that occurred across state lines very effectively. Congress used the state laws (as well as certain provisions of the English Companies Act) as a model for the Securities Act. But Congress had to decide which model of state regulation to use: (1) merely prohibiting fraud in offering and selling securities; (2) requiring a registration and full disclosure to investors, or (3) providing that the government would judge the merits of offerings, and determine which could be sold to the public. Congress chose a combination of (1) and (2). The philosophy was one of full disclosure. The Securities Act contains an Appendix that states what a registration statement must contain, and it is a long and detailed list of disclosures about a business. These requirements were drawn from the "best practices" of reputable Wall Street underwriting firms of the time. Today's descendant of that appendix is Form S–1, adopted under the Securities Act for offerings of securities to the public. Its content basically traces that of Appendix A, and has been elaborated over the years to accommodate new disclosure requirements as new frauds have occurred, or as activists have sometimes demanded more disclosures. Its outline later became the genesis of the idea that all of this information (except that unique to the offering) should be regularly updated by issuers.

The coverage of the Securities Act (and of the Securities Exchange Act) is a combination of specified financial instruments that are easily recognized, and of more "open-ended" terms designed to cover evasions and innovations that might later develop.

The heart of the Securities Act is section 5, 15 U.S.C. § 77e, which requires that securities be registered before they may be offered or sold. The prospectus that is part of the registration statement must be delivered to all prospective buyers. The Act also applies to all those who assist an issuer in distributing its securities to the public, defined as "underwriters." Section 5 is enforced by provisions in section 12, 15 U.S.C. § 77*l*, that make those who offer and sell without registration liable to buyers, for the full amount of the sale price. It is also enforced by provisions in section 11, 15 U.S.C. § 77k, that make both the offering company, its directors, significant officers, as well as underwriters, liable for any false or misleading statements in the registration statement. The Securities Act is *not* a "merit" statute—it permits anyone to offer any kind of security to the public, so long as they make full disclosure about its merits and risks.

Congress recognized that the registration process would be time-consuming and expensive, and so it provided a series of exemptions from the registration requirements. These took two forms—exemptions for classes of securities, largely in section 3, 15 U.S.C. § 77c, and exemptions for particular transactions in securities, also found in section 3, but most importantly in section 4, 15 U.S.C. § 77d. The class exemptions were generally available where some other set of laws was likely to provide investors with equivalent protection—such as bank deposits, insurance policies, securities issued with the approval of regulatory agencies or the courts. The transaction exemptions contained some recognition that other laws might provide protections—as in the case of an offering made entirely within a single state, where state securities laws would apply and could be enforced effectively. In addition, these exemptions recognized that in some cases investors either did not need the protection of the securities laws, because they were capable of protecting themselves, or in some cases, the cost of protection was just too high, given the amounts being offered. Finally, the SEC has formalized exemptions for offerings to non-U.S. persons that take place entirely outside the United States, provided precautions are taken to assure that these securities do not flow back into the

United States immediately, and the non-U.S. investors bear the risks of investment before resales can occur in the U.S.

In some cases, U.S. exemptions have been vague and confusing. Section 4(2) of the Securities Act provides an exemption from registration for "transactions by an issuer not involving any public offering." In its first decision interpreting this language, the U.S. Supreme Court held that the exemption only applied where the offerees were able to "fend for themselves," in terms of being able to obtain the same information that registration would have provided, and being able to evaluate the merits and risks of the investment. This vague standard created conflicting interpretations in the lower courts, and, with the SEC staff taking a most aggressive approach to the gradual narrowing of this exemption. Beginning in the 1970s the SEC recognized that it had closed off access to capital for some smaller offerings, and began a program of introducing "safe harbors" by rule-making. The most notable attempt to do so is Regulation D, 17 C.F.R. 230.501 et seq., which has three exemptive rules. First, for offerings under $1 million, a flat exemption is provided, if the issuer complies with applicable state law requirements. For offerings up to $5 million, an exemption is available for up to 35 persons, provided that they receive the same sort of information that would have been provided by a registration statement. In addition, the offering may include any number of "accredited investors," a group which includes certain financial institutions and wealthy individuals. Finally, for offerings in excess of $5 million, the conditions are the same as for smaller offerings, but the issuer must also be satisfied that the buyers are sufficiently experienced in business and financial matters that they can judge the merits and risks of the investment. Because this requirement introduces the same subjective judgments that previously plagued this area, most issuers attempting such an exempt offering will limit their sales to "accredited investors" that can be identified with bright line tests.

The Continuous Reporting System in the U.S.

While the Securities Act of 1933 focused on the initial issue and distribution of securities, the Securities Exchange Act of 1934 focused on the provision of information about companies whose shares are traded. The Act requires companies whose shares are traded on a national exchange or are widely held (by 500 or more shareholders) to register with the SEC by providing comprehensive information about the company and its securities under section 12, 15 U.S.C. § 78l. (This information is comparable to that required in a Securities Act registration statement, except, of course, there is no description of an offering.) The SEC is empowered by section 13, 15 U.S.C. § 78m, to adopt regulations concerning periodic reports, and requires the filing of an annual report on Form 10–K that updates the original registration. The company-oriented information is an update of that information provided in a prospectus on Form S–1, previously described. In addition, registered companies are required to file quarterly financial reports on Form 10–Q, containing income statements for the quarter and "Management's Discussion and Analysis" in the same form described in the prospectus requirements on Form S–1. Finally, SEC Form 8–K requires filings within four days after a list of events, whenever they occur:

Item 1.01	Entry into a Material Definitive Agreement.
Item 1.02	Termination of a Material Definitive Agreement.
Item 1.03	Bankruptcy or Receivership.
Item 2.01	Completion of Acquisition or Disposition of Assets.
Item 2.02	Results of Operations and Financial Condition.
Item 2.03	Creation of a Direct Financial Obligation or an Obligation under an Off–Balance Sheet Arrangement of a Registrant.
Item 2.04	Triggering Events That Accelerate or Increase a Direct Financial Obligation or an Obligation under an Off–Balance Sheet Arrangement.
Item 2.05	Costs Associated with Exit or Disposal Activities.
Item 2.06	Material Impairments [of the value of assets].
Item 3.01	Notice of Delisting or Failure to Satisfy a Continued Listing Rule or Standard; Transfer of Listing.
Item 3.02	Unregistered Sales of Equity Securities.
Item 3.03	Material Modification to Rights of Security Holders.
Item 4.01	Changes in Registrant's Certifying Accountant.
Item 4.02	Non-Reliance on Previously Issued Financial Statements or a Related Audit Report or Completed Interim Review.
Item 5.01	Changes in Control of Registrant.
Item 5.02	Departure of Directors or Principal Officers; Election of Directors; Appointment of Principal Officers.
Item 5.03	Amendments to Articles of Incorporation or Bylaws; Change in Fiscal Year.
Item 5.04	Temporary Suspension of Trading Under Registrant's Employee Benefit Plans.
Item 5.05	Amendments to the Registrant's Code of Ethics, or Waiver of a Provision of the Code of Ethics.
Item 7.01	Regulation FD Disclosure.
Item 8.01	Other Events.

The SEC was given authority, for any corporation seeking proxies from its shareholders to be voted at a shareholders' meeting, to set the terms of those disclosures, by section 14 of the Exchange Act, 15 U.S.C. § 78n. These regulations specify the information required to be distributed to shareholders, including an annual report that includes most of the information in the annual report filed with the SEC on Form 10–k, and require companies to include certain shareholder proposals in the company's proxy materials.

The antifraud provisions of the Exchange Act cover a wide range of actions. Section 9, 15 U.S.C. § 78i, covers some of the manipulations that had been observed in the 1920s, and prohibits them. Section 10(b), 15 U.S.C. § 78j(b), the general antifraud provision, was originally part of section 9 of the bill, and was described as a catch-all, to cover manipulations and frauds not expressly prohibited. It gave the SEC authority to adopt rules to prevent fraud and manipulation, and the SEC adopted Rule

10b–5, 17 C.F.R. 240.10b–5, in 1942. From those beginnings has grown an enormous body of law. In Santa Fe Industries v. Green, 430 U.S. 462, 97 S.Ct. 1292, 51 L.Ed.2d 480 (1977), the Supreme Court outlined the limits of Rule 10b–5. The case involved a cash-out merger that was allegedly unfair and a breach of fiduciary duty, which the plaintiffs claimed constituted "fraud" under Rule 10b–5. In rejecting plaintiffs' claim, the Court stated:

> "The language of § 10(b) gives no indication that Congress meant to prohibit any conduct not involving manipulation or deception. Nor have we been cited to any evidence in the legislative history that would support a departure from the language of the statute. 'When a statute speaks so specifically in terms of manipulation and deception, * * * and when its history reflects no more expansive intent, we are quite unwilling to extend the scope of the statute * * *.' Thus the claim of fraud and fiduciary breach in this complaint states a cause of action under any part of Rule 10b–5 only if the conduct can be fairly viewed as 'manipulative or deceptive' within the meaning of the statute. * * *

> "It is also readily apparent that the conduct alleged in the complaint was not 'manipulative' within the meaning of the statute. Manipulation is 'virtually a term of art when used in connection with securities markets.' The term refers generally to practices, such as wash sales, matched orders, or rigged prices, that are intended to mislead investors by artificially affecting market activity. * * * Indeed, nondisclosure is usually essential to the success of a manipulative scheme."

ii. THE NEW ISSUES MARKET

Corporations can issue stock or debt in a variety of transactions. Small businesses typically issue securities in negotiated transactions, to persons known to the promoters of the business. In many cases these investors expect to participate actively in the operation of the business. Their negotiations are face to face, and may include, in addition to the price and terms of the securities, agreements over the role these investors will play in the management of the business. This may involve a position on the board of directors of the corporation, or full-time employment with the corporation.

As corporations grow larger and need capital beyond the means of those actively involved in the business, it may seek what is called a "private placement" of additional securities. In some cases the corporation may deal with a "venture capital" firm, which seeks investments in promising young businesses likely to offer securities to the public at a later date. Venture capital firms often raise their capital from financial institutions, pension plans, university endowments, as well as from wealthy investors willing to take the high risks associated with new ventures. Venture capitalists negotiate directly with start-up firms, and typically put start-ups under pressure to succeed within a few years, by taking preferred stock. If the business does not succeed, preferred stock gives the venture capitalist a priority over the original investors, who hold stock, in the liquidation of the firm. If the business succeeds, these securities typically have conversion rights—to convert the preferred stock into common stock of the corporation, to allow the venture capitalist to share in the growth in value of the firm. Typically the issuing corporation hopes to offer its securities to the public within a few years, and to register the venture capitalist's securities for sale to the public. If it fails to do so, the venture capitalist typically obtains a "put" right—to resell the securities to the issuing corporation. In some instances, that would be likely to require dissolution of the firm.

Other corporations will seek a private placement with a group of wealthy investors, often individuals who are able to bear the risks of the enterprise. They are sometimes described as "angel" investors, and invest at an early stage, before venture capital financing. In many cases these investors will be located by investment bankers, who know investors likely to be interested in such investments. The investment bankers will insist on the production of a "private placement memorandum" that describes the business fully, including its past history, its present situation, and its potential for the future. This private placement memorandum will contain the financial statements of the business for the past several years, as well as details about the business experience and background of those involved in the business. These investors will often buy common stock in the corporation, but they will frequently insist on rights that will enable them to liquidate their investment in a few years. These rights often include the right to insist that the corporation register their shares for public offering at some time in the future (see the description of public offerings below).

Larger corporations may undertake a private placement of debt securities with large financial institutions. These may involve offerings of $100 million or more. The financial institutions generally include insurance companies, pension funds, mutual funds, and the like. Typically these investors will designate one of their group to serve as the lead investor, to secure the information required to evaluate the investment, and to negotiate the terms of the investment.

Investment bankers play a role in these offerings. For a fee, they will provide advice about methods of financing, or act as middleman in private placements. But the most visible role of investment bankers occurs in the public offering process. In the typical corporate public offering, officials of a corporation approach an investment banker and explain their business and its need for funds. In an initial public offering (or "IPO") the terms of the offering are typically negotiated with the investment banker. After an initial evaluation of the corporation and its prospects, if the investment banker determines that the corporation represents a promising investment opportunity, it will enter into a tentative agreement to underwrite the corporation's securities. This tentative agreement is called a "letter of intent." It is an agreement that is binding only in limited respects. The investment banker does not make a binding commitment to underwrite the securities, but only to use its best efforts to secure financing. The only binding part of the letter of intent is the allocation of expenses of the offering, whether or not it proceeds.

The underwriter can agree to underwrite the offering in two ways. The first is called a "firm underwriting," and involves a commitment to take the securities and pay for them, regardless of the underwriter's ability to resell them at the public offering price. Underwriters will only commit to this form of offering where they feel confident that the offering will be well received by investors. The underwriters do not commit in advance to pay a specific price for the shares. Instead, they and the issuer's representatives conduct "road shows" before interested institutional investors, seeking to determine investor interest and at what price the shares can be marketed. Only then is a "price amendment" to the registration filed with the SEC, finalizing the price. In other cases, where they are less confident, underwriters will only commit to a "best efforts" (now euphemistically called a "registered direct") offering, in which they only commit to use their best efforts to sell the securities as agents on behalf of the issuer. In these cases investment bankers function in an agency capacity, and do not commit their own capital to the offering.

Once the letter of intent is signed, the issuer and the underwriter begin the preparation of a "registration statement," which includes a disclosure document called a "prospectus." This registration statement will be filed with the Securities Exchange Commission (SEC) in Washington, where it will be reviewed by the SEC staff for completeness and fairness of presentation. The period during which the SEC staff reviews the registration statement is one in which the issuer and underwriter are legally prohibited from selling the securities, but are permitted to offer them. It is called the "waiting period."

The issuer may shop for a variety of investment banks to participate in the underwriting, with a bank with the most financial heft serving as the "lead underwriter," which does most of the preparatory work, while the other investment bankers in the syndicate bear part of the risk of the offering, in return for part of the underwriting commissions. These additional underwriters will sign an "agreement among the underwriters," in which they agree to underwrite specific portions of the offering, thus limiting their liability to fixed amounts. The second level of marketing involves getting the prospectus portion of the filed registration statement into the hands of prospective investors. Investment bankers use this "preliminary prospectus," for use in soliciting their own customers to buy part of the offering. During the waiting period the syndicate members solicit indications from their customers of their interest in buying these securities, and communicate this interest to the managing underwriter.

The SEC staff reviews the registration statement for completeness and fairness of presentation. It does not verify the facts stated in the registration statement; that is the responsibility of the issuer and underwriter, and is enforced by civil liability provisions in the Securities Act. Typically the staff is not fully satisfied with the manner of disclosure, and writes the issuer a "letter of comments" detailing its concerns. The issuer is expected to make appropriate revisions in the registration statement to satisfy the

SEC staff's concerns. When an amendment is filed with the SEC staff, it is typically reviewed quickly, and if the staff is satisfied, the issuer is notified.

At this time the managing underwriter is in possession of information about the probable success of the offering, from the indications of investor interest obtained from the selling dealers. Only now does the underwriter make a commitment to a firm underwriting by signing a binding underwriting agreement. At this point the underwriter not only knows the extent of investor interest, but knows how the securities market has performed since it made its initial commitment in a letter of intent. It can now set the price on common stock to reflect the prices of comparable stocks available in the market. Indeed, the underwriter has an incentive to set the offering price on the low side, to make it easier to sell the offering, and to reduce the underwriter's risk of failure. If the public offering price is perceived by investors to represent a bargain, the offering will be oversubscribed, and will become a "hot issue." This means the issuer has not obtained the highest price it might have obtained, and has "left money on the table."* Once it has set the price, the registration statement is amended to reflect this price, and the SEC staff permits the registration statement to become "effective." Effectiveness means that the securities can be sold, and typically the selling dealers send their customers memoranda confirming the sale of the securities to them at the final price. Customers are expected to pay for the securities within three business days, and the underwriter typically commits to pay the issuer the proceeds of the offering immediately thereafter.**

An alternative system of underwriting has developed in the past twenty-five years in the U.S. in response to competitive pressures from European capital markets. The registration process for new offerings in the U.S. is both time-consuming and costly. It is not unusual for the SEC staff to take 30 days to review and comment upon a registration statement. In the meantime the issuer and underwriter may offer, but they cannot sell, the securities. In times of volatile interest rates this can mean that issuers attempting to raise capital through debt offerings will find that interest rates have risen before they can complete their sales. In response to this many larger American companies whose names were recognized in Europe sought to raise capital in European capital markets, where less regulation meant quicker access to funds when interest rates were favorable.

In response, the SEC developed an alternative method of registration for larger companies with access to foreign capital markets. Under this technique, the U.S. company may file a registration statement for a large

---

* In 2004 Google announced its intention to engage in an IPO in a radically altered form, using a "Dutch Auction" in which it would ask interested investors to offer the highest price they were willing to pay for its stock. Once enough investors had made bids to buy all of the offered shares, all successful (high) bidders would be sold shares at the lowest price of any successful bid. The Dutch Auction proposed by Google is discussed more fully in Chapter Three, Part 4.B.

** Securities Exchange Act Rule 15c6–1, 17 C.F.R. 240.15c6–1, requires brokers and dealers to pay funds and deliver securities no later than the third business day after the date of the contract.

amount of securities which it does not commit to offer currently. The registration statement is approved by the SEC staff of an offering "for the shelf," which means for future use. Then, when market conditions appear favorable, the issuer need only amend the registration statement to name the underwriter for an offering, to specify the price and amount of the registered securities to be sold. This amendment process can take place in a few days rather than in weeks or months, and the issuer can take advantage of the current interest rates or stock prices, as the case may be.

In these "shelf" offerings underwriters function differently than in the traditional "syndicated" offering described earlier. Because of the speed demanded by the issuer, the underwriter will commit to buy the entire offering without first soliciting enough buyers to be certain the entire offering can be resold. Thus the underwriter bears true underwriting risk, and may be unable to resell the entire offering at a profit. But U.S. capital markets are sufficiently well developed that this is a very small risk in most cases, since hundreds of millions of dollars of high quality bonds can generally be resold to financial institutions in a few hours.

iii. TRADING MARKETS

Market Making in the Electronic Age

by Mark Borrelli.
32 Loyola University of Chicago Law Journal 815 (2001).

I. Introduction

In 1974, an investor making his first purchase of stock might look in the newspaper and see that IBM, one of the hottest technology stocks of the day, is trading at $230. The investor might then call a stockbroker to place an order to purchase 500 shares. The investor's broker would call a representative of the firm on the floor of the New York Stock Exchange, who would find someone else on the floor of the exchange willing to execute, or "fill," the order. The transaction might cost the investor $200, and be filled at a price of $230¼. Although the novice investor may not think about the manner in which his broker fills the order, the investor's brokerage firm has a duty of "best execution," i.e., an obligation to fill the investor's order in a manner most favorable to the investor, including obtaining the best price.

In 2000, the same investor, now much more seasoned, pulls up a real-time quote for Cisco Systems, one of the day's hottest technology stocks, through an online brokerage account. He sees that the stock is trading at 30 "bid," 30¼ "offer," and places a buy order for 500 shares through his online account, which is executed almost immediately at the offer price of 30¼. As the stock is a Nasdaq stock, the order will not be routed to the floor of an exchange. It may not even make it to one of the dealers who collectively "make" the Nasdaq market. The broker-dealer with whom the customer places the order may itself sell the customer the stock, at 30¼, which is the best offer price currently shown on the Nasdaq market. The customer pays a commission of only \$9.99 for the trade. Two seconds after his order is executed, however, an order to sell 500 shares at 30⅛ goes unfilled. The investor, now much more familiar with best execution, questions whether he should have been able to buy these 500 shares at 30⅛.

* * *

B.   History of United States Securities Markets

The NYSE traces its history to the "Buttonwood Agreement" of 1792, where twenty-four brokers agreed to trade securities under a buttonwood tree on Wall Street. A formal organization, the New York Stock & Exchange Board, was formed in 1817. At this time, stocks were traded one at a time as the president of the Board called their names. In 1863, the market changed its name to the NYSE. In 1871, the system of trading changed, so that all stocks were traded simultaneously and the brokers for a particular stock stood in one location. Companies must meet certain financial criteria and satisfy other requirements to list their shares on the NYSE.

Historically, the NYSE was considered the most prestigious and liquid market in existence, although Nasdaq would clearly dispute that claim today. Nasdaq had humble beginnings, having arisen out of a study conducted by the SEC in the early 1960s. The study, which was released in 1963, recommended the development of an automated system to address "fragmentation" in the over-the-counter ("OTC") market. The OTC market is used to describe any off-exchange trading. Trading began on the Nasdaq on February 8, 1971, when the system displayed quotes for 2,500 securities.

At its inception, Nasdaq was nothing more than a system within the OTC market, created and operated by the NASD, through which quotes could be displayed. Trades were made exclusively through phone calls between broker-dealers. In 1975, Nasdaq established listing standards which began to distinguish it from the rest of the OTC market. Although many investors view Nasdaq as a stock exchange, it [remained] part of the OTC market until 2006. * * * There are two tiers within Nasdaq: the Global Market and the SmallCap Market. The Nasdaq Global Market has more stringent listing standards and is a more liquid market than the SmallCap market.

The American Stock Exchange ("Amex") was once the world's second largest floor-based exchange, after the NYSE. Amex uses a specialist system like that of the NYSE, but has much more lenient listing requirements. There are also several regional exchanges in the United States. Stocks that cannot satisfy the listing requirements of the exchanges or Nasdaq can be traded through the NASD's OTC bulletin board, which provides real-time quotations but has no listing standards. In January 1999, the Commission approved rule changes by the NASD that limited bulletin board stocks to those of issuers that were current in their periodic filings under the Exchange Act. The lowest tier in the United States securities markets is the "pink sheets," which were formerly a list of quotations printed on pink paper and disseminated daily by the National Quotation Bureau, Inc.*

C. Agency and Dealer Markets

While there are numerous exchanges and systems that can now be classified as "securities markets," the mechanics of trade execution is best understood by comparing the differences between the two dominant markets: the NYSE and Nasdaq. The NYSE is the most prominent example of an agency market, i.e., a market that charges a fee for bringing buyers and sellers together and matching their orders. Nasdaq is a dealer market, in which broker-dealers execute trades as principals and are compensated by profits on the trades. However, the NYSE, while it is classified as an agency market, has characteristics of a dealer market, and Nasdaq functions at times as an agency market.

1. New York Stock Exchange

Trading on the floor of the NYSE is essentially an auction in which agents of buyers and sellers gather at a "trading post" and a "specialist" facilitates the auction. The NYSE is a continuous auction market in which orders can be executed any time the exchange is open. The continuous market auction can be distinguished from a call auction market, where, at certain points in the trading day, all open orders are executed when the auction is "called." However, the NYSE uses the call auction feature at the beginning of trading on the exchange and in limited circumstances, such as when large order imbalances arise or trading in a stock is temporarily halted.

Brokerage firms route NYSE orders either to the specialist's post, through an automated order delivery system known as SuperDot, or to a "floor broker" on the floor of the exchange. There are two primary types of floor brokers: "commission brokers," who work for a broker-dealer and execute orders for its customers, and "independent floor brokers," who work for themselves. Independent floor brokers execute orders for firms that do not have commission brokers or orders which a broker-dealer's commission brokers are too busy to handle. Brokers who gather at a trading post are known as the "crowd." The specialist posts the bid and offer prices of the trading crowd at the specialist's post.

If an order is routed directly to the specialist through the SuperDot system, the specialist, acting as an agent for the party placing the order, finds a broker in the crowd willing to buy or sell the stock while seeking to obtain "price improvement," i.e., a better price for the customer than the current bid, in the case of a sale, or offer, in the case of a buy. The specialist also acts as an agent when a floor broker has a customer limit order that cannot be executed at the current market level and leaves the

---

* Brokers can trade securities of companies not registered under Section 12 of the Securities Exchange Act, but only if equivalent information is available to the public. Securities Exchange Act Rule 15c2–11, 17 C.F.R. 240.15c2–11.—Ed.

order with the specialist for later execution.* The specialist has no direct involvement in approximately seventy-five percent of orders, for which prices are established by brokers in the trading crowd shouting out bids and offers for the stock, a process known as "open outcry."

A key function of a specialist is to fulfill his or her obligation to maintain "fair and orderly" markets. As part of this obligation, specialists try to ensure that changes in stock prices are small from one trade to the next, even if the price is moving dramatically overall. Temporary imbalances between buy and sell orders have the potential to cause large price variations between consecutive transactions. Accordingly, when such an imbalance occurs, specialists buy or sell for their own account to maintain order in the market. Specialists profit both from their receipt of commissions on orders for which they act as agent, and from trading for their own account.

2. Nasdaq

The theory behind the Nasdaq market is that several broker-dealers will act as market makers by providing quotes under which they will buy or sell a particular stock. The competition among the market makers is designed to produce the market price for the security. Broker-dealers can participate in Nasdaq as either an order entry firm or a market maker. Order entry firms can access quotes of market makers and participate in Nasdaq's automated services, but they do not enter quotes for securities. On the other hand, market makers place bids and offer quotes for the securities in which they make markets.

Market participants in Nasdaq enter or access quotes through a workstation, the latest version of which is known as "Nasdaq Workstation II." Participants can view quotes for any Nasdaq stocks and enter quotes and orders through the Nasdaq workstation. The Workstation II display has two parts. The top portion is used to monitor market information for selected stocks. It has a "Market Minder" window, through which broker-dealers can monitor the inside quotes and last sale information for selected stocks, and a "Dynamic Quote Window," which shows the inside bid and offer, last sale, the day's price change, the day's high and low, and a short sale indicator for selected stocks. The bottom portion of the Workstation display contains the Nasdaq Quotation Montage, which shows market maker identification symbols ("MMIDs") for market makers and other participants quoting prices, and the market participants' quote, including the number of shares, next to the MMID. Market participants' bids and offers are ranked first by price and then by time.

Nasdaq has numerous rules governing the conduct of market makers. For example, Nasdaq market makers must observe Nasdaq's normal trading hours, must maintain "two-sided," i.e., bid and offer, quotations on the securities in which they make markets, and must maintain quotations

---

* A limit order is a customer order at a specified price, rather than at the best price the broker can currently obtain in the market.—Ed.

which are "reasonably related to the prevailing market." Nasdaq also seeks to maintain orderly markets by prohibiting market makers from "locking" or "crossing" the market. A market maker "locks" the market when it enters a bid quotation which is equal to the ask quotation of another market maker, or an offer quotation which is equal to the bid quotation of another market maker. A market maker "crosses" the market when it enters a bid quotation which is higher than the offer quotation of another market maker, or an ask quotation which is lower than the bid quotation of another market maker.

D. Electronic Communication Networks

An electronic communications network ("ECN") is an electronic system that collects buy and sell orders for securities and allows the orders to be executed against each other. ECNs do not generally "make markets" in the sense of acting as a principal on trades; instead, they act purely as agents by bringing buyers and sellers together. ECNs place limitations on the parties who may subscribe to their system, and typically charge an access fee. ECNs display subscriber orders, much like Nasdaq displays market maker quotes.

Instinet, the first ECN, actually predates Nasdaq. Instinet was founded in 1969 as a means of allowing institutional money managers to trade directly with each other. In addition to the development of the Internet and communications technology, the development of ECNs was spurred by the SEC's adoption of its Order Handling Rules in September 1996. While the Order Handling Rules were adopted partially to address perceived problems created by the rise of ECNs, they actually created an explosion in ECN activity by sanctioning the role of ECNs in order executions, subject only to the condition that they open their book of orders to the larger market beyond their subscribers.

CHAPTER SIX

CORPORATE DEBT

1. INTRODUCTION

Much of what we will discuss in this chapter involves publicly-issued debt, in the form of bonds and debentures. (See the discussion in Chapter Four, Part 2 of the types of corporate debt.) But it is important to note that most of the problems we deal with here, and the contractual approaches we will observe, also are employed in privately negotiated loan agreements. Indeed, in some cases the restraints on debtors may be tighter in loan agreements, because both parties recognize the opportunity for renegotiation should it seem appropriate under changed circumstances. Creditors that are repeat players in loan markets have incentives to maintain a reputation for commercial reasonableness, and a willingness to accommodate debtors when their circumstances change. Renegotiation is far more difficult in public debt markets, as we shall observe.

Why do corporations borrow both from banks and other financial institutions as well as borrow through public markets? Banks and financial institutions, after all, are intermediaries—they pay interest on the money they possess, and then re-lend to corporate borrowers. Larger corporations use banks mostly for short-term financing, for seasonal working capital, or for bridge loans before more permanent financing is obtained. Frequently corporations that expect to have frequent short-term needs will obtain a line of credit on which they can draw as needed. To assure the bank that this is not really long-term financing, banks frequently require that this line be paid down to zero at least once a year. In some cases these loans will be secured by accounts receivable, and the banks will frequently lend up to 80% of the receivables, assuming they are of good quality. Interest rates on receivables financing are relatively high because of the expenses involved in monitoring the receivables. An alternative is to sell the receivables to a factor, a commercial lender specializing in such transactions. Some banks and finance companies will lend on inventory, but this presents a problem of valuation. Suppose, for example that Scientific Atlanta had a large inventory of set-top boxes and several major customers failed? Or suppose the set-top boxes were not able to handle high definition signals, and the government mandated a switch to high definition? Or worse, suppose television manufacturers decided to integrate high definition cable access equipment into television sets? These things have actually happened to Scientific Atlanta in the past decade.

In many countries, notably Germany and Japan, most corporate borrowing is through large banks, and public debt markets play a relatively small role in debt financing. The United States is different, and many corporations offer debt in public securities markets by registering the offering with the SEC. Until the 1980s smaller American corporations were largely excluded from the public debt market and relied more on bank financing, which made growth more difficult. The advent of junk bonds in the early 1980s improved the access of smaller companies to public debt markets, and decreased their reliance on banks. Many American corporations offer debt to institutions in what the securities laws often characterize as a private offering, but it can be semi-public, in the sense that debt may be offered to large numbers of institutional investors. If this debt is not registered under the securities laws, it may trade in a separate market maintained for institutional buyers under Securities Act Rule 144A, called "PORTAL."

[handwritten margin notes: - bonds make growth easier - probably lower interest rates - more $ @ one time - pay off over long periods of time]

For most public companies the cost of issuing underwritten public debt has dropped dramatically over the past 25 years. Underwriting commissions have fallen precipitously, as competition among underwriters has increased. In late 2003 Altria Group (formerly Phillip Morris) borrowed $500 million on five-year notes at an underwriting cost of 0.6%, while it paid 0.65% to borrow $1 billion on ten-year notes. At the same time Zions Bancorporation was borrowing $150 million on three-year notes at an underwriting cost of 0.15%, and Citigroup was paying 0.35% to borrow one billion Euros on ten-year notes. Stated interest rates ran from 2.7% on the Zions Bancorporation three-year notes to 7% on Altria's ten-year notes. This was a time of historically low interest rates.

Credit Report: Suddenly, Banks Are Acting a Lot Like Bond Markets

By Greg Ip, Wall Street Journal, Sept. 17, 2002, A1.

* * *

Banks traditionally have been the institutions that take a long-term view of a company's prospects, management and ability to repay a debt. By contrast, the fast-paced, fickle bond market can change its mind in an instant about a company's creditworthiness and how much to charge. But many borrowers are finding that banks' loan business has come to look a lot like the markets.

Burned by costly lending decisions a decade ago, banks increasingly look to the impatient and unforgiving public markets to guide how much to lend and under what terms. The good news is, credit is available. The bad news is, it's often at a high price.

* * *

... At the beginning of the 1990s, many banks were unable or unwilling to lend. They were burdened with bad loans to commercial real estate, leveraged buyouts or developing nations, and also were under pressure from regulators to boost their capital. Their reluctance hastened the growth of bond and commercial-paper markets as a source of credit for corporations.

Now many companies' credit ratings have slipped so much that borrowing that way is impractical—while banks are healthier and able to lend.

Scarred by Early '90s

But when banks lend now, they don't behave the same way. Scarred by their early–1990s experience, they often don't hold onto loans, especially those to lower-quality companies. Increasingly, banks sell pieces of their loans to other banks, to specialized investment funds, insurance companies or to other institutional investors. As a result, the loans are subject to all the pricing and other tactics of the markets. And the banks are acting less like lenders and more like middlemen between borrowers and investors.

* * *

There are two markets for big corporate loans. One is for high-quality companies. Here, relationships still matter, and banks may lend at lower rates than capital markets would dictate because they hope to get fees from the borrowers for other services.

The other tier—called "leveraged loans"—involves companies rated below investment grade or nearly so. "That part of the market behaves very much like any other capital market," says Tom Okel, global head of loan syndications at Bank of America.

The terms of leveraged loans are strongly linked to where the companies' securities trade. Borrowers' fortunes are continuously re-evaluated by the markets for bonds, stocks, and "credit derivatives"—essentially insurance that banks take out to protect against a default. When a bank is about to make a loan, it can get snapshot of how these markets are judging the company's creditworthiness, and use this snapshot to guide its own decision.

* * *

Traditionally, bank loans and lines of credit have differed from bonds in a number of ways, such as by carrying a floating interest rate, not a fixed one. Another difference is that a typical bank line of credit lets the client borrow as much or as little as it wants up to a ceiling, and to repay early with little or no penalty. But beyond those basic differences, banks' increasing syndication of their loans is blurring some of the distinctions between loans and bonds. The banks now often split loans into pieces and sell chunks off, to such a degree that a bank may have only a small part, if any, left on its books.

* * *

Bank loans and pieces of them now change hands in an increasingly active secondary market. Its daily turnover of about $500 million is puny next to the stock and bond markets, but up 15–fold from a decade earlier, according to Credit Suisse First Boston. When a company sets out to borrow now, its lenders can see how this secondary market is valuing its old loans, and adjust terms of this new borrowing accordingly.

———

Since the collapse of the credit markets in late 2008 bank lending to business has been reported to be greatly curtailed. Certainly several major banks collapsed and were rescued with federal funds. But a study in October of 2008 for the Federal Reserve Bank of Minneapolis found no significant decline in lending to corporations.*

———

We now provide a brief description of some of the conventions of public debt. Corporate Debt is issued in denominations of $1,000, but quoted as $100 (to save column space in newspapers). Where debt offerings exceed $10 million and are offered to the public, the offered bonds or debentures must be issued subject to an indenture of trust, to solve collective action problems (and to comply with the Trust Indenture Act of 1939). If a debtor defaults, having thousands of bondholders race to the courthouse to get paid first doesn't make any more sense here than in bankruptcy. The indenture contains the terms of the obligations. A bank trust department is typically named as trustee for the bondholders to enforce the terms of the indenture, and to monitor the debtor's compliance with its covenants.

Most corporate debt that is publicly held is rated for safety by a bond rating agency. Moody's Investors' Services, Standard & Poors, and Fitch's, are among the major rating services. Appendix 6–A contains the rating categories employed by Moody's and Standard and Poors.

Recall that in Chapter Three, Part 2.D we discussed how to value bonds. Under the heading of "annuities" we noted that a bond is a fixed annuity for a stated number of years, plus a repayment of principal ("terminal payment") at maturity, and that we can simply sum the present value of these payments to obtain the value of a bond. Of course, to do this we have to know the discount rate. Unfortunately, you can't get this from the quotes on bonds in the newspaper. Here is what you could get from the Wall Street Journal on Dec. 6, 2002:

U.S. Exchange Bonds

---

4 p.m. ET Thursday, December 5, 2002

Explanatory Notes

———

* V.V. Chari et al., Facts and Myths about the Financial Crisis of 2008, Federal Reserve Bank of Minneapolis, Working Paper 666 (October, 2008) at http://www.minneapolisfed.org/research/WP/WP666.pdf (last visited 2/19/09).

For New York and American Bonds

Yield is Current Yield

cv—Convertible bond. **cf**—Certificates. **cld**—Called. **dc**—Deep discount. **f**—Dealt in flat. **Il**—Italian lire. **kd**—Danish kroner. **m**—Matured bonds, negotiability impaired by maturity. **na**—No accrual. **r**—Registered. **rp**—Reduced principal. **st**—Stamped. **t**—floating rate. **wd**—When distributed. **ww**—With warrants. **x**—Ex interest. **xw**—Without warrants. **zr**—Zero coupon. **vj**—In bankruptcy or receivership or being reorganized under the Bankruptcy Act, or securities assumed by such companies.

NEW YORK BONDS

Corporation Bonds

BONDS	CUR YLD	VOL	CLOSE	NET CHG
AES Cp 4½ 05 cv	22		33.63	−0.38
AES Cp 8s 8	17.2	43	46.50	−0.50
AMR 9s 16	18.0	350	50	−0.63
ANR 7s 25	8.0	4	88	4.00

The first observation is that the interest rate and year of maturity follow the codes. Thus the first AES bond listed carries a 4½% coupon rate, and matures in 2005. While bonds are sold in denominations of $1,000, they are quoted in units of $100, perhaps because of the constraints of newspaper columns. Thus the AES 8% bond quoted above traded at $465.00, not $46.50. The current yield displayed above is simply the interest payment/bond price. Thus, for the AES 8% bond, a payment of $80 per year, divided by $465, produces a current yield of 17.2043%. One element is missing here: the "yield to maturity." That takes into account the all-important final payment of principal, when the bond matures. This is also the "internal rate of return" previously discussed briefly in Chapter Three, Part 2.H. Typically this calculation is performed on a financial calculator or spreadsheet program. The basic approach requires finding the discount rate (yield) for the payment stream (including principal) that produces the current market price for the bond. Microsoft Excel™ has such a function. In the case of the AES 8% bonds due in 2008, the calculation is shown below:

	A	B	C	D
1	Initial payment (at end of 2003)	−46.50		
2	end of 2004 payment	8.00		
3	end of 2005 payment	8.00		
4	end of 2006 payment	8.00		
5	end of 2007 payment	8.00		
6	end of 2008 payment	108.00		
7	IRR	26.94%		

The formula entered in cell B7 is =IRR((B1:B6)). Note that the entry in cell B1 is the initial investment, and we assume interest payments at the end of the following year. Without a financial calculator or spread-sheet program, this is a trial and error process. Let's assume the year is 2005, and the ANR 7s due in 2025 are quoted at 88 ($880). What yield to maturity does this price produce?

We can start by using an 8% discount rate, and calculating a 20–year annuity of the interest payments of $70. (Table 3–5 in Chapter Three, Part 2.D contains the annuity table.) At 8%, we multiply the payment by 9.8181. Then we discount the final principal payment by 8% for 20 years (using a factor of 0.2145), as shown in Table 3–4, in Chapter Three, Part 2.C:

$$\begin{array}{rcll} \$70 & \times\ 9.8181 & = & \$687.27 \\ \$1000 & \times\ 0.2145 & = & \underline{\$214.50} \\ & & & \$901.77 \end{array}$$

Because this amount exceeds the market price by $21.77, we know the actual yield to maturity is higher than 8%. If we use a discount rate of 8.1%, we obtain an annuity multiplier of 9.7527, resulting in the following calculations:

$$\begin{array}{rcll} \$70 & \times\ 9.7527 & = & \$682.69 \\ \$1000 & \times\ 0.2108 & = & \underline{\$210.80} \\ & & & \$893.49 \end{array}$$

If we had calculated the yield to maturity using a discount rate of 8.25%, we would have reached $879.23.* This suggests the yield to maturity is slightly less, perhaps 8.24% or 8.23%.

Using a single discount rate is sometimes criticized as unrealistic, because investors demand higher interest rates for longer-term investments, to compensate for inflation risk. One could attempt to discount each bond payment at the rate appropriate for that maturity, but this would unduly complicate the calculations. Instead, we offer only an example of what is generally called the "yield curve" for different maturities of U.S. treasury bonds, taken from the Wall Street Journal of June 8, 1999, p. C23. Keep in mind that this is a drawing derived from the chart shown there, not an actual reproduction. You can find a current yield curve at http://www.bloomberg.com/markets/rates/index.html.

There is one problem with relying on bond prices and yields quoted in the newspapers. These prices only reflect bonds traded on exchanges, and most bonds are not traded in this manner. Because the vast majority of bonds are bought by financial institutions, there is very little trading. What little trading that occurs often takes place away from the exchanges,

---

* Annuity tables for a wide variety of discount rates can be found in THORNDIKE ENCYCLOPEDIA OF BANKING AND FINANCIAL TABLES, available in most libraries.

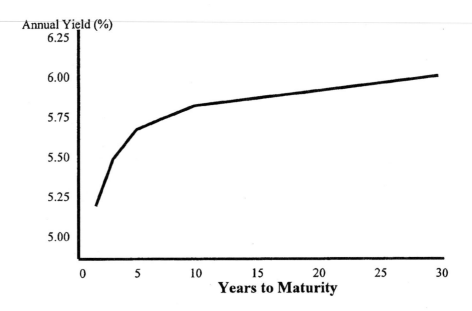

sometimes through securities dealers, but also on PORTAL, which is reserved for Qualified Institutional Buyers.

We have introduced the range of debt instruments available for financing in Chapter Four. We turn now to the fundamental problem in corporate borrowing: the stockholder-bondholder conflict. Creditors make decisions about whether to lend, how much to lend, and what interest rate to demand for a loan based on the debtor's prospects of repayment. These decisions are made at the time that credit is extended. The problem is that loans are not a one-day occurrence, but may remain outstanding for years. And things may change. Fundamentally, debtors will want to increase the riskiness of a business after they've borrowed at a fixed rate. Why? Because this becomes a "heads I win, tails you lose" type of game once the borrowing has occurred, and the creditor is locked in to a fixed interest rate for a fixed term.

Let's begin with a simple example. Assume $10,000 raised through sale of common stock, and $100,000 raised through sale of bonds @ 8%. Thus interest expense is $8,000 per year.

					Weighted			Weighted
Firm		Weighted	To		Value To	To		Value To
Earnings	Prob.	Value	Bondholders	Prob.	Bondholders	Stockholders	Prob.	Stockholders
$6,000	0.1	$600	$6000	0.1	$600	0	0.1	0
$10,000	0.8	$8,000	$8000	0.8	$6,400	$2,000	0.8	$1,600
$14,000	0.1	$1,400	$8000	0.1	$800	$6,000	0.1	$600
Expected Value	1.0	$10,000		1.0	$7,800		1.0	$2,200

Strategy I—Low Risk:

Firm Earnings	Prob.	Weighted Value	To Bondholders	Prob.	Weighted Value To Bondholders	To Stockholders	Prob.	Weighted Value To Stockholders
Strategy II—High Risk:								
$2,000	0.4	$800	$2,000	0.4	$800	0	0.4	0
$10,000	0.2	$2,000	$8,000	0.2	$1,600	$2,000	0.2	$400
$18,000	0.4	$7,200	$8,000	0.4	$3,200	$10,000	0.4	$4,000
Expected Value	1.0	$10,000		1.0	$5,600		1.0	$4,400

This allows us to see how choosing the risky project doubles the expected value of returns for shareholders, while reducing the expected value of returns for bondholders by $2,200. In both cases, however, the expected value of the total results for the firm remains the same, at $10,000. Note that the high risk strategy drops expected returns to bondholders from 7.8% to 5.6%, notwithstanding the 8% coupon rate. (For this example we assume that any default on the bonds isn't recoverable in bankruptcy.) But the high risk strategy raises stockholders' expected returns from 22% to 44%. Obviously, once the interest rate and the amount of the creditor's fixed claims are fixed, shareholders can gamble at least in part with creditors' money, because creditors will suffer losses in the worst case scenario. As we know from M&M, if bondholders recognize these risks in advance they will demand a higher interest rate to compensate for this risk.

How does this gambling occur? Obviously firms can choose risky projects, such as taking all of the firm's wealth and placing it all on one bet at a casino—a not entirely irrational choice if leverage is sufficiently high. (That explains the shift of duties from shareholders to creditors in firms teetering "in the vicinity of insolvency," as pointed out in Chapter Four.) But it doesn't exhaust the ways this can occur. Adding additional debt to the firm's capital structure has the same effect, since it reduces the probability of full repayment to the first creditor. Worse, the second creditor might obtain a security interest in firm assets, and thus gain a priority in bankruptcy over the first creditor. Shareholders can achieve the same effect by withdrawing their own capital, which will also make the firm more highly leveraged, and allow the shareholders to gamble with creditors' money. Related to this is the problem of "underinvestment"—in order to fund distributions to shareholders, the firm may neglect maintenance on its plant and equipment, or new investments needed to maintain the current business.

2. Contract Interpretation

When corporations turn to public markets they sell either bonds or debentures (see Chapter Four). As described more fully in Part 4, the terms of the bonds (used generically here to describe both bonds and debentures) are set in an indenture of trust. The indenture names a trustee to monitor compliance with the terms of the indenture and to take enforcement actions on behalf of the bondholders. When corporations borrow directly from banks and other financial institutions they enter into loan agreements that contain many of the same terms as indentures. In this chapter we will concentrate on publicly issued debt and the indentures that control their terms.

Because the stockholder-bondholder conflict is well known, the terms of bond indentures have been the subject of elaborate drafting to control the problem. The "bible" in this area was created in 1965, by a committee of bond lawyers representing issuing corporations and purchasing financial institutions. American Bar Foundation, COMMENTARIES ON THE MODEL DEBENTURE INDENTURE PROVISIONS 1965, MODEL DEBENTURE INDENTURE PROVISIONS—ALL REGISTERED ISSUES AND CERTAIN NEGOTIABLE PROVISIONS WHICH MAY BE INCLUDED IN A PARTICULAR INCORPORATING INDENTURE (1971) (hereinafter "Commentaries"). A later edition was published in 1977. In 1983 the ABA published the Model Simplified Indenture, 38 Bus. Law. 741 (1983), and in 2000 published the Revised Model Simplified Indenture, 55 Bus. Law. 1115 (2000). The simplified indentures lack the elaborate covenants found in the original document. To illustrate the general contents of an indenture, the Table of Contents from the Revised Model Simplified Indenture is set out in Appendix 6–B. Part 3 contains sample covenants, drawn largely from the Commentaries, to illustrate contractual resolutions of various parts of the stockholder-bondholder conflict.

NOTE

The following case arises largely because of the volatility of interest rates in the late 1970s and early 1980s. Inflation had raged in the late 1970s, reaching historic highs by early 1981. The Federal Reserve Bank responded with an increase in interest rates to dampen demand, and it caused the prime rate (banks' rates to their best customers) to rise to 18% for a brief period. The timing of this series of transactions was undoubtedly influenced by former section 337 of the Internal Revenue Code of 1954(eliminated in 1986), which allowed for a tax-free sale of assets if a corporation adopted a plan of liquidation and proceeded to liquidate pursuant to the plan within a twelve-month period.

Sharon Steel Corporation v. The Chase Manhattan Bank, N.A.

691 F.2d 1039 (2d Cir. 1982), cert. denied, 460 U.S. 1012 (1983).

■ WINTER, J.

This is an appeal by Sharon Steel Corp. ("Sharon") and UV Industries, Inc. ("UV"), trustees of the UV Liquidating Trust (collectively the "UV Defendants") from grants of a directed verdict and summary judgment by the United States District Court for the Southern District of New York ... in favor of the Trustees of certain UV indentures ("Indenture Trustees") and intervening holders of debentures issued pursuant to certain of those indentures ("Debentureholders").... Judge Werker held that UV's liquidation and unsuccessful attempt to assign its public debt to Sharon rendered UV liable for the principal and accrued interest on the debentures. The Indenture Trustees and Debentureholders cross-appeal from other parts of the judgment.

We affirm in part and reverse in part.

BACKGROUND

1. The Indentures

Between 1965 and 1977, UV issued debt instruments pursuant to five separate indentures, the salient terms of which we briefly summarize. In 1965, UV issued approximately $23 million of 5⅜% subordinated debentures due in 1995, under an indenture naming The Chase Manhattan Bank, N.A. ("Chase") as the trustee ("First Chase Indenture"). The current principal amount of the debentures outstanding under that indenture is approximately $14 million.

* * *

[Other bond issues were also described.]

The debentures, notes and guaranties are general obligations of UV. Each instrument contains clauses permitting redemption by UV prior to the maturity date, in exchange for payment of a fixed redemption price (which includes principal, accrued interest and a redemption premium) and clauses allowing acceleration as a non-exclusive remedy in case of a default. The First Chase Indenture,[4] The Port Huron Lease Guaranty, the Union

---

4. Section 13.01 of the First Chase Indenture reads as follows:

Nothing in this Indenture or any of the Debentures contained shall prevent any merger or consolidation of any other corporation or corporations into or with the Company, or any merger or consolidation of the Company (either singly or with one or more corporations), into or with any other corporation, or any sale, lease, transfer or other disposition of all or substantially all of its property to any corporation lawfully entitled to acquire the same or prevent successive similar consolidations, mergers, sales, leases, transfers or other dispositions to which the Company or its successors or assigns or any subsequent successors or assigns shall be a party; provided, however, and the Company covenants and agrees, that any such consolidation or merger of the Company or any such sale, lease, transfer or other disposition of all or substantially all of its property, shall be upon the condition that the due and punctual payment of the principal of, interest and premium, if any, on, all of the Debentures, according to their tenor, and the due and punctual performance and observance of all the terms, covenants and conditions of this Indenture to be kept or performed by the Company shall, by an indenture supplemental hereto, executed and delivered to the Trustee, be assumed by any corporation formed by or resulting from any such consolidation or merger, or to which all or substantially all of the property of the Company shall have been sold, leased, transferred or otherwise disposed of (such corporation being herein called the "successor corporation"), just as fully and effectively as if the successor corporation had been the original party of the first part hereto, and such supplemental indenture shall be construed as and shall constitute a novation thereby releasing the Company (unless its identity be merged into or consolidated with that of the successor corporation) from all liability upon, under or with respect to any of the covenants or agreements of this Indenture but not, however, from its liability upon the Debentures. After the execution and delivery of the supplemental indenture referred to in the preceding paragraph, any order, certificate, resolution or other instrument of the Board of Directors or officers of the Company may be made by the like board or officers of the successor corporation. The Trustee shall receive an Officers' Certificate that the foregoing

Planters Lease Guaranty, the Manufacturers Indenture and the U.S. Trust Indenture each contains a "successor obligor" provision allowing UV to assign its debt to a corporate successor which purchases "all or substantially all" of UV's assets. If the debt is not assigned to such a purchaser, UV must pay off the debt. While the successor obligor clauses vary in language, the parties agree that the differences are not relevant to the outcome of this case.

2. The Liquidation of UV

During 1977 and 1978, UV operated three separate lines of business. One line, electrical equipment and components, was carried on by Federal Pacific Electric Company ("Federal"). In 1978, Federal generated 60% of UV's operating revenue and 81% of its operating profits. It constituted 44% of the book value of UV's assets and 53% of operating assets. UV also owned and operated oil and gas properties, producing 2% of its operating revenue and 6% of operating profits. These were 5% of book value assets and 6% of operating assets. UV also was involved in copper and brass fabrication, through Mueller Brass, and metals mining, which together produced 13% of profits, 38% of revenue and constituted 34% of book value assets and 41% of operating assets. In addition to these operating assets, UV had cash or other liquid assets amounting to 17% of book value assets.

On December 19, 1978, UV's Board of Directors announced a plan to sell Federal. On January 19, 1979, the UV Board announced its intention to liquidate UV, subject to shareholder approval. On February 20, 1979, UV distributed proxy materials, recommending approval of (i) the sale of Federal for $345,000,000 to a subsidiary of Reliance Electric Company and (ii) a Plan of Liquidation and Dissolution to sell the remaining assets of UV over a 12–month period.[9] The proceeds of these sales and the liquid assets were to be distributed to shareholders. The liquidation plan required "that at all times there be retained an amount of cash and other assets which the [UV Board of Directors] deems necessary to pay, or provide for the payment of, all of the liabilities, claims and other obligations ..." of UV. The proxy statement also provided that, if the sale of Federal and the liquidation plan were approved, UV would effect an initial liquidating distribution of $18 per share to its common stockholders.

On March 26, 1979, UV's shareholders approved the sale of Federal and the liquidation plan. The following day, UV filed its Statement of Intent to Dissolve with the Secretary of State of Maine, its state of incorporation. On March 29, the sale of Federal to the Reliance Electric subsidiary for $345 million in cash was consummated. On April 9, UV

conditions are complied with, and an Opinion of Counsel that any such indenture supplemental hereto complies with the foregoing conditions and provisions of this Section 13.01. Subject to the provisions of Section 10.01, such Officers' Certificate and Opinion shall be full warrant to the Trustee for any action taken in reliance thereon.

9. Completion of the Liquidation Plan within 12 months was necessary for tax reasons. If so completed, UV would avoid recognition of any taxable gain on the sale of Federal and its other assets and UV shareholders could treat liquidation distributions as capital gains rather than ordinary income. [These tax rules were repealed in 1986.—Ed.]

announced an $18 per share initial liquidating distribution to take place on Monday, April 30.

The Indenture Trustees were aware that UV contemplated making an $18 per share liquidating distribution since at least February 20, 1979 (the date the proxy materials were distributed). On April 26, representatives of Chase, Manufacturers and U.S. Trust met with UV officers and directors and collectively demanded that UV pay off all the debentures within 30 days or, alternatively, that UV establish a trust fund of $180 million to secure the debt. There was testimony that at least one of the Indenture Trustees threatened to sue to enjoin UV from paying the $18 liquidating distribution on the grounds that a liquidating distribution prior to payment of US's debts would violate Maine law, which provides, as to a liquidating corporation, that:

> *After* paying or adequately providing for the payment of all its obligations, the corporation shall distribute the remainder of its assets . . . among its shareholders . . .

Me. Rev. Stat. Ann. Tit. 13–A, § 1106(4) (1971) (emphasis added).

The outcome of this meeting was an "Agreement for Treatment of Certain Obligations of UV Industries, Inc.," dated April 27, 1979, between UV and the Indenture Trustees ("April Document"). Under the April Document, UV agreed, *inter alia*, to set aside a cash fund of $155 million to secure its public debt and to present a proposal for the satisfaction and discharge of that debt to the Indenture Trustees within 90 days. The Indenture Trustees agreed not to seek an injunction against the payment of the $18 per share liquidating distribution. The April Document provided that all obligations thereunder would terminate upon the payment of UV's public debt or upon UV's abandonment of the plan of liquidation.

On July 23, 1979, UV announced that it had entered into an agreement for the sale of most of its oil and gas properties to Tenneco Oil Company for $135 million cash. The deal was consummated as of October 2, 1979 and resulted in a net gain of $105 million to UV.

sold oil properties

3.   The Sale to Sharon Steel

In November, 1979, Sharon proposed to buy UV's remaining assets. Another company, Reliance Group (unrelated to Reliance Electric), had made a similar offer. After a brief bidding contest, UV and Sharon entered into an "Agreement for Purchase of Assets" and an "Instrument of Assumption of Liabilities" on November 26, 1979. Under the purchase agreement, Sharon purchased all of the assets owned by UV on November 26 (*i.e.*, Mueller Brass, UV's mining properties and $322 million in cash or the equivalent) for $518 million ($411 million of Sharon subordinated debentures due in 2000—then valued at 86% or $353,460,000—plus $107 million in cash). Under the assumption agreement, Sharon assumed all of UV's liabilities, including the public debt issued under the indentures. UV thereupon announced that it had no further obligations under the indentures or lease guaranties, based upon the successor obligor clauses.

Sharon bought remaining assets and assumed the obligation of debt

[handwritten margin note: Trustees refused to sign obligation + fees]

On December 6, 1979, in an attempt to formalize its position as successor obligor, Sharon delivered to the Indenture Trustees supplemental indentures executed by UV and Sharon. The Indenture Trustees refused to sign. Similarly, Sharon delivered an assumption of the lease guaranties to both Chase and Union Planters but those Indenture Trustees also refused to sign.

4.   The Proceedings in the District Court

By letters dated December 24, 1979, Chase, U.S. Trust and Manufacturers issued virtually identical notices of default as a result of UV's purported assignment of its obligations to Sharon. Each demanded that the default be cured within 90 days or that the debentures be redeemed. Chase and U.S. Trust brought separate actions in New York County Supreme Court against UV and Sharon for redemption of the debentures; Manufacturers subsequently initiated a similar lawsuit. On December 26, 1979, Sharon initiated this action against Chase, U.S. Trust and Manufacturers.

* * *

A jury trial was held during April and early May, 1981, at which Sharon submitted voluminous testimony and other evidence. The Indenture Trustees and Debentureholders moved for a directed verdict, and on May 11, 1981, the District Court granted the motion and dismissed Sharon's claims. The Indenture Trustees and Debentureholders subsequently moved for summary judgment on their claims and counterclaims, which was granted on June 2, 1981. A judgment encapsulating these determinations was filed on August 18, 1981.

* * *

Sharon and the UV Defendants appeal various portions of [the] judgment. The Indenture Trustees and Debentureholders cross-appeal from the denial of the redemption premium. The Debentureholders cross-appeal from the denial of legal fees and expenses to be paid by UV and Sharon, rather than from the class recovery.

DISCUSSION

1.   The Successor Obligor Clauses

[handwritten margin note: successor obligor clauses not taken to jury = q of law not fact]

Sharon Steel argues that Judge Werker erred in not submitting to the jury issues going to the meaning of the successor obligor clauses. We disagree.

[handwritten margin note: boiler plate language]

Successor obligor clauses are "boiler plate" or contractual provisions which are standard in a certain genre of contracts. Successor obligor clauses are thus found in virtually all indentures. Such boiler plate must be distinguished from contractual provisions which are peculiar to a particular indenture and must be given a consistent, uniform interpretation. As the American Bar Foundation *Commentaries on Indentures* (1971) ("*Commentaries*") state:

Since there is seldom any difference in the intended meaning [boiler plate] provisions are susceptible of standardized expression. The use of standardized language can result in a better and quicker understanding of those provisions and a substantial saving of time not only for the draftsman but also for the parties and all others who must comply with or refer to the indenture, including governmental bodies whose approval or authorization of the issuance of the securities is required by law. *Id.*

Boiler plate provisions are thus not the consequence of the relationship of particular borrowers and lenders and do not depend upon particularized intentions of the parties to an indenture. There are no adjudicative facts relating to the parties to the litigation for a jury to find and the meaning of boiler plate provision is, therefore, a matter of law rather than fact.

Moreover, uniformity in interpretation is important to the efficiency of capital markets. As the Fifth Circuit has stated:

Uniformity needed in capital markets

A large degree of uniformity in the language of debenture indentures is essential to the effective functioning of the financial markets: uniformity of the indentures that govern competing debenture issues is what makes it possible meaningfully to compare one debenture issue with another, focusing only on the business provisions of the issue (such as the interest rate, the maturity date, the redemption and sinking fund provisions in the conversion rate) and the economic conditions of the issuer, without being misled by peculiarities in the underlying instruments.

Broad v. Rockwell International Corp., 642 F.2d 929, 943 (5th Cir.), *cert. denied*, 454 U.S. 965, 102 S. Ct. 506, 70 L. Ed. 2d 380 (1981).

Whereas participants in the capital market can adjust their affairs according to a uniform interpretation, whether it be correct or not as an initial proposition, the creation of enduring uncertainties as to the meaning of boiler plate provisions would decrease the value of all debenture issues and greatly impair the efficient working of capital markets. Such uncertainties would vastly increase the risks and, therefore, the costs of borrowing with no offsetting benefits either in the capital market or in the administration of justice. Just such uncertainties would be created if interpretation of boiler plate provisions were submitted to juries sitting in every judicial district in the nation.

Sharon also argues that Judge Werker erred in rejecting evidence of custom and usage and practical construction as to the meaning of the successor obligor clauses. While custom or usage might in some circumstances create a fact question as to the interpretation of boiler plate provisions, the evidence actually offered by Sharon simply did not tend to prove a relevant custom or usage. Sharon's experts both conceded that so far as the meaning of successor obligor clauses and the language "all or substantially all" are concerned, the UV/Sharon transaction was unique. Their testimony was thus limited to use of such clauses and such language in very different contexts. Because context is of obvious and critical importance to the use of particular language, the testimony offered did not tend to prove or disprove a material fact.

* * *

We turn now to the meaning of the successor obligor clauses. Interpretation of indenture provisions is a matter of basic contract law. As the *Commentaries* at 2 state:

> The second fundamental characteristic of long term debt financing is that the rights of holders of the debt securities are largely a matter of contract. There is no governing body of statutory or common law that protects the holder of unsecured debt securities against harmful acts by the debtor except in the most extreme situations ... The debt securityholder can do nothing to protect himself against actions of the borrower which jeopardize its ability to pay the debt unless he ... establishes his rights through contractual provisions set forth in the ... indenture.

Contract language is thus the starting point in the search for meaning and Sharon argues strenuously that the language of the successor obligor clauses clearly permits its assumption of UV's public debt. Sharon's argument is a masterpiece of simplicity: on November 26, 1979, it bought everything UV owned; therefore, the transaction was a "sale" of "all" UV's "assets." In Sharon's view, the contention of the Indenture Trustees and Debentureholders that proceeds from earlier sales in a predetermined plan of piecemeal liquidation may not be counted in determining whether a later sale involves "all assets" must be rejected because it imports a meaning not evident in the language.

Sharon's literalist approach simply proves too much. If proceeds from earlier piecemeal sales are "assets," then UV continued to own "all" its "assets" even after the Sharon transaction since the proceeds of that transaction, including the $107 million cash for cash "sale," went into the UV treasury. If the language is to be given the "literal" meaning attributed to it by Sharon, therefore, UV's "assets" were not "sold" on November 26 and the ensuing liquidation requires the redemption of the debentures by UV. Sharon's literal approach is thus self-defeating.

The words "all or substantially all" are used in a variety of statutory and contractual provisions relating to transfers of assets and have been given meaning in light of the particular context and evident purpose. *See Campbell v. Vose*, 515 F.2d 256 (10th Cir. 1975) (transfer of sole operating asset held to be a sale of all or substantially all of the corporation's assets even though two-thirds of asset book value in the form of bank balances, promissory notes and an investment portfolio was retained); *Atlas Tool Company v. Commissioner*, 614 F.2d 860 (3d Cir. 1980). ("Substantially all" requirement is chiefly determined by the transfer of operating assets). Sharon argues that such decisions are distinguishable because they serve the purpose of either shareholder protection or enforcement of the substance of the Internal Revenue Code. Even if such distinctions are valid, these cases nevertheless demonstrate that a literal reading of the words "all or substantially all" is not helpful apart from reference to the underlying purpose to be served. We turn, therefore, to that purpose.

Sharon argues that the sole purpose of successor obligor clauses is to leave the borrower free to merge, liquidate or to sell its assets in order to enter a wholly new business free of public debt and that they are not intended to offer any protection to lenders. On their face, however, they seem designed to protect lenders as well by assuring a degree of continuity of assets. Thus, a borrower which sells all its assets does not have an option to continue holding the debt. It must either assign the debt or pay it off. As the *Commentaries* state at 290:

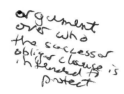
argument over who the successor obligor clause is intended to protect

> The decision to invest in the debt obligations of a corporation is based on the repayment potential of a business enterprise possessing specific financial characteristics. The ability of the enterprise to produce earnings often depends on particular assets which it owns. Obviously, if the enterprise is changed through consolidation with or merged into another corporation or through disposition of assets, the financial characteristics and repayment potential on which the lender relied may be altered adversely.

The single reported decision construing a successor obligor clause, *B.S.F. Company v. Philadelphia National Bank*, 42 Del. Ch. 106, 204 A.2d 746 (1964), clearly held that one purpose of the clause was to insure that the principal operating assets of a borrower are available for satisfaction of the debt.

Sharon seeks to rebut such inferences by arguing that a number of transactions which seriously dilute the assets of a company are perfectly permissible under such clauses. For example, UV might merge with, or sell its assets to, a company which has a minuscule equity base and is debt heavy. They argue from these examples that the successor obligor clause was not intended to protect borrowers from the kind of transaction in which UV and Sharon engaged.

We disagree. In fact, a substantial degree of protection against diluting transactions exists for the lender. Lenders can rely, for example, on the self-interest of equityholders for protection against mergers which result in a firm with a substantially greater danger of insolvency. So far as the sale of assets to such a firm is concerned, that can occur but substantial protection exists even there since the more debt heavy the purchaser, the less likely it is that the seller's equityholders would accept anything but cash for the assets. A sale to a truly crippled firm is thus unlikely given the self-interest of the equityholders. After a sale, moreover, the lenders would continue to have the protection of the original assets. In both mergers and sales, complete protection against an increase in the borrower's risk is not available in the absence of more specific restrictions, but the self-interest of equityholders imposes a real and substantial limit to that increase in risk. The failure of successor obligor clauses to provide even more protection hardly permits an inference that they are designed solely for the benefit of borrowers.

[handwritten margin note: difference between selling off in ordinary course of business v. intentional piece-meal liquidation]

Sharon poses hypotheticals closer to home in the hope of demonstrating that successor obligor clauses protect only borrowers: *e.g.*, a transaction involving a sale of Federal and the oil and gas properties in the regular course of UV's business followed by an $18 per share distribution to shareholders after which the assets are sold to Sharon and Sharon assumes the indenture obligations. To the extent that a decision to sell off some properties is not part of an overall scheme to liquidate and is made in the regular course of business it is considerably different from a plan of piecemeal liquidation, whether or not followed by independent and subsequent decisions to sell off the rest. A sale in the absence of a plan to liquidate is undertaken because the directors expect the sale to strengthen the corporation as a going concern. A plan of liquidation, however, may be undertaken solely because of the financial needs and opportunities or the tax status of the major shareholders. In the latter case, relatively quick sales may be at low prices or may break up profitable asset combinations, thus drastically increasing the lender's risks if the last sale assigns the public debt. In this case, for example, tax considerations compelled completion of the liquidation within 12 months. The fact that piecemeal sales in the regular course of business are permitted thus does not demonstrate that successor obligor clauses apply to piecemeal liquidations, allowing the buyer last in time to assume the entire public debt.

[handwritten margin note: successor liability does not apply in intentional piece-meal liquidation]

We hold, therefore, that protection for borrowers as well as for lenders may be fairly inferred from the nature of successor obligor clauses. The former are enabled to sell entire businesses and liquidate, to consolidate or merge with another corporation, or to liquidate their operating assets and enter a new field free of the public debt. Lenders, on the other hand, are assured a degree of continuity of assets.

* * *

Of the contending positions, we believe that of the Indenture Trustees and Debentureholders best accommodates the principal interests of corporate borrowers and their lenders. Even if the UV/Sharon transaction is held not to be covered by the successor obligor clauses, borrowers are free to merge, consolidate or dispose of the operating assets of the business. Accepting Sharon's position, however, would severely impair the interests of lenders. Sharon's view would allow a borrowing corporation to engage in a piecemeal sale of assets, with concurrent liquidating dividends to that point at which the asset restrictions of an indenture prohibited further distribution. A sale of "all or substantially all" of the remaining assets could then be consummated, a new debtor substituted, and the liquidation of the borrower completed. The assignment of the public debt might thus be accomplished, even though the last sale might be nothing more than a cash for cash transaction in which the buyer purchases the public indebtedness. The UV/Sharon transaction is not so extreme, but the sale price paid by Sharon did include a cash for cash exchange of $107 million. Twenty-three percent of the sale price was, in fact, an exchange of dollars for dollars. Such a transaction diminishes the protection for lenders in order to facilitate deals with little functional significance other than substituting a new debtor in order to profit on a debenture's low interest rate. ~~We hold,~~ ~~therefore, that boiler plate successor obligor clauses do not permit assign-~~ ~~ment of the public debt to another party in the course of a liquidation~~ ~~unless "all or substantially all" of the assets of the company at the time the~~ plan of liquidation is determined upon are transferred to a <u>single purchas-</u> er.

at the time of liquidation is determined is key

The application of this rule to the present case is not difficult. The plan of liquidation was approved by UV's shareholders on March 26, 1978. Since the Indenture Trustees make no claim as to an earlier time, *e.g.*, the date of the Board recommendation, we accept March 26 as the appropriate reference date. The question then is whether "all or substantially all" of the assets held by UV on that date were transferred to Sharon. That is easily answered. The assets owned by UV on March 26 and later transferred to Sharon were Mueller Brass, certain metals mining property, and substantial amounts of cash and other liquid assets. UV's Form 10–K and Sharon's Form S–7 state that Mueller Brass and the metals mining properties were responsible for only 38% of UV's 1978 operating revenues and 13% of its operating profits. They constitute 41% of the book value of UV's operating properties. When the cash and other liquid assets are added, the transaction still involved only 51% of the book value of UV's total assets.

Since we do not regard the question in this case as even close, we need not determine how the substantiality of corporate assets is to be measured, what percentage meets the "all or substantially all" test or what role a jury might play in determining those issues. Even when the liquid assets (other than proceeds from the sale of Federal and the on and gas properties) are aggregated with the operating properties, the transfer to Sharon accounted for only 51% of the total book value of UV's assets. In no sense, therefore, are they "all or substantially all" of those assets. The successor obligor clauses are, therefore, not applicable. UV is thus in default on the indentures and the debentures are due and payable. For that reason, we need not reach the question whether the April Document was breached by UV.

does not answer q of how much is "all or substantially all"?

* * *

CONCLUSION

We affirm Judge Werker's dismissal of Sharon's amended complaint and award of judgment to the Indenture Trustees and Debentureholders on their claim that the debentures are due and payable. We reverse his dismissal of the claim for payment of the redemption premium and his award of the interest earned on the $155 million fund. We affirm his granting of attorney's fees and expenses to the Debentureholders out of the judgment recovered. The Indenture Trustees shall be awarded their full costs. The Debentureholders shall be awarded one-half their costs.

QUESTIONS

1. Why did UV insist on assigning the obligations of the debentures, rather than paying them off?

2. Is interpretation of a successor obligor clause a question of fact or law?

3. What relevance does evidence of custom and usage have to interpretation of contracts?

4. Why wasn't evidence of custom and usage about interpretation of successor obligor clauses admissible?

5. Sharon argues that the assumption clause is for the exclusive benefit of the debtor, because it would allow sales to less solvent buyers that would assume the obligations of the indenture. What is Judge Winter's response to that argument?

6. Suppose the shareholders get cash plus assumption of the indebtedness represented by the indentures. What protects the debenture holders?

7. What is evidence of practical construction of a contract?

8. Was evidence of practical construction of the successor obligor clause properly admissible?

9. Note that Sharon bought everything UV had left, including its cash. Why does the court reject Sharon's literal interpretation of "all or substantially all" assets?

10. Why does the court restrict its analysis only to operating assets?

11. Why does the court relate the measuring date for "all" assets to March 26, 1978?

3. CONTRACT TERMS

Here we begin the integration of the theory and practice of contracting about corporate debt. We have briefly described the stockholder-bondholder conflict in Part 2 of this chapter, and now we expand on the nature of the conflict and explore the types of contract terms used to protect bondholders. As you review these materials, keep in mind the types of financial ratios described in Chapter Two, Part 3.C and Appendix 2–B.

On Financial Contracting: An Analysis of Bond Covenants

Clifford W. Smith. Jr. and Jerold B. Warner.
7 Journal of Financial Economics 117 (1979).

* * *

1. Introduction and summary

* * *

In this paper, we examine how debt contracts are written to control the bondholder-stockholder conflict. We investigate the various kinds of bond covenants which are included in actual debt contracts. A bond covenant is a provision, such as a limitation on the payment of dividends, which restricts the firm from engaging in specified actions after the bonds are sold.

Our description of the specific provisions in debt contracts is based primarily on an American Bar Foundation compendium entitled *Commentaries on Indentures*. This volume contains both the standardized provisions which arc included in the debt contract (the "boilerplates") and a practitioner-oriented discussion of their use.

one concern might be the amount of dividend paid to stockholders

1.1. Sources of the bondholder-stockholder conflict

Corporations are "legal fictions which serve as a nexus for a set of contracting relationships among individuals". To focus on the contract between the bondholders and the corporation, we assume that costs of enforcing other contracts are zero. For example, we assume that contracts between stockholders and, managers costlessly induce managers to act as if they own all the firm's equity.

The corporation has an indefinite life and the set of contracts which comprise the corporation evolves over time: as the firm's investment opportunity set changes decisions are made about the real activities in which the firm engages and the financial contracts the firm sells. With risky bonds outstanding, management, acting in the stockholders' interest, has incentives to design the firm's operating characteristics and financial structure in ways which benefit stockholders to the detriment of bondholders. Because investment, financing, and dividend policies are endogenous, there are four major sources of conflict which arise between bondholders and stockholders:

Dividend payment. If a firm issues bonds and the bonds are priced assuming the firm will maintain its dividend policy, the value of the bonds is reduced by raising the dividend rate and financing the increase by reducing investment. At the limit, if the firm sells all its assets and pays a liquidating dividend to the stockholders. the bondholders are left with worthless claims.

dividends

Claim dilution. If the firm sells bonds, and the bonds are priced assuming that no additional debt will be issued, the value of the bondholders' claims is reduced by issuing additional debt of the same or higher priority.

more debt

Asset substitution. If a firm sells bonds for the stated purpose of engaging in low variance projects and the bonds are valued at prices commensurate with that low risk. the value of' the stockholders' equity rises and the value of the bondholders' claim is reduced by substituting projects which increase the variance rate.[4]

riskier investments/ projects

Underinvestment. Myers (1977) suggests that a substantial portion of the value of the firm is composed of intangible assets in the form of future

---

4. The mere exchange of low-risk assets for high-risk assets does not alter the value of the firm if both assets have the same net present values. However, stockholders will have incentives to purchase projects with negative net present values if the increase in the firm's variance rate from accepting those projects is sufficiently large. Even though such projects reduce the total value of the firm, the value of the equity rises.

investment opportunities. A firm with outstanding bonds can have incentives to reject projects which have a positive net present value if the benefit from accepting the project accrues to the bondholders.

The bondholder-stockholder conflict is of course recognized by capital market participants. Rational bondholders recognize the incentives faced by the stockholders. They understand that after the bonds are issued, any action which increases the wealth of the stockholders will be taken. In pricing the bond issue, bondholders make estimates of the behavior of the stockholders, given the investment, financing, and dividend policies available to the stockholders. The price which bondholders pay for the issue will be lower to reflect the possibility of subsequent wealth transfers to stockholders.[5]

indentures factor these risks into the price of the bond

* * *

2. A description and analysis of bond covenants

We group observed covenants into four categories: production investment covenants, dividend covenants, financing covenants, and bonding covenants. Our discussion of the covenants covers all the restrictions reported in *Commentaries;* we have not singled out only particular types of covenants for discussion.

A.   CAPITAL STRUCTURE: RESTRICTING NEW DEBT

On Financial Contracting: An Analysis of Bond Covenants

Clifford W. Smith. Jr. and Jerold B. Warner.
7 Journal of Financial Economics 117 (1979).

* * *

2.3.   Bond covenants restricting subsequent financing policy

2.3.1.   Limitations on debt and priority

Description. In section I we discussed the stockholders' incentives to reduce the value of the outstanding bonds by subsequently issuing additional debt of higher priority, thereby diluting the bondholders' claim on the assets of the Firm. Covenants suggested in *Commentaries* limit stockholders actions in this area in one of two ways: either through a simple prohibition against issuing claims with a higher priority or through a restriction on the creation of a claim with higher priority unless the existing bonds are upgraded to have equal priority. The latter restriction requires, for example, that if secured debt is sold after the issuance of the bonds, the existing

---

5. Similarly, the value of the common stock at the time the bonds are issued will be higher to reflect possible transfers which shareholders will be able to effect. However, this is not to suggest that there is always a positive price at which the bonds can be sold. If the probability of a complete wealth transfer to stockholders prior to required payments to bondholders is 1, then the bonds will sell for a zero price.

bondholders must have their priority upgraded and be given an equal claim on the collateral with the secured debtholders.

In addition to restricting the issuance of debt of higher priority, there are sample covenants in *Commentaries* restricting the stockholders' right to issue any additional debt. Issuance of new debt can be subject to aggregate dollar limitations. Alternatively, issuing debt can be prohibited unless the firm maintains minimum prescribed ratios between (1) net tangible assets and funded (i.e., long-term) debt, (2) capitalization and funded debt, (3) tangible net worth and funded debt, (4) income and interest charges (referred to as earnings tests), or (5) current assets and current debt (referred to as working capital tests). There are also provisions requiring the company to be free from debt for limited periods (referred to as "clean-up" provisions). Combinations of two or more of these limitations are sometimes included in the indenture agreement.

It is important to note the scope of the restrictions imposed through the covenants limiting the issuance of additional debt. In addition to money borrowed, the covenants also apply to other liabilities incurred by the firm. Other debt-like obligations which can be limited by the covenants are: (1) assumptions or guarantees of indebtedness of other parties, (2) other contingent obligations which are analogous to, but may not technically constitute, guarantees; (3) amounts payable in installments on account of the purchase of property under purchase money mortgages, conditional sales agreements or other long-term contracts; (4) obligations secured by mortgage on property acquired by the company subject to the mortgage but without assumption of the obligations.

Since the claims of the firm in subsidiary corporations are like that of a stockholder, if a subsidiary issues debt or preferred stock the coverage afforded the bondholders of the parent firm is reduced. Thus the limitations on debt usually apply to the debt of the consolidated firm.

Analysis. Our analysis suggests that it is generally not optimal to prevent all future debt issues. If, as the firm's opportunity set evolves over time, new investments must be financed by new equity issues or by reduced dividends, then with risky debt outstanding part of the gains from the investment goes to bondholders, rather than stockholders. Those investments increase the coverage on the debt, and reduce the default risk borne by the bondholders. To the extent such reductions are unanticipated, they result in an increase in the value of outstanding bonds at the expense of the stockholders. So a prohibition of all debt issues would reduce the value of the firm because wealth maximizing stockholders would not take all positive net present value projects. The possibility of asset substitution increases the costs of outright prohibition on debt issues and makes variance-reducing positive net present value projects less attractive. However, our analysis suggests that contractually agreeing to have *some* degree of restriction on future debt issues is in the interests of the firm's owners. By merely restricting the total amount of all debt which can be issued, the perverse investment incentives associated with debt . . . are limited.

Financing-policy covenants also impact on investment incentives in other ways. In section 2.1. we discussed the direct limitations on financial investments included in bond covenants. Financial investments can also be restricted through the debt covenant. For example, when debt is limited to a specific percentage of net tangible assets, financial investments are sometimes excluded from the definition of net tangible assets for purposes of the covenant. This definition allows the firm to hold a portion of its assets as financial investments, but requires the firm to reduce the debt and its capital structure to do so, thus controlling the asset substitution problem associated with financial investments.

* * *

2.3.2. *Limitations on rentals, lease, and sale-leasebacks*

Description. *Commentaries* offers alternative restrictions on the stockholders' use of lease or rental contracts. The covenant typically restricts the firm from the sale-leaseback of property owned prior to the date of the indenture. Some covenants also exclude individual leases or sale-leasebacks below a specified dollar total. Lease payments can also be limited to a fraction of net income. Finally, leasing and renting can be controlled through the debt covenant by capitalizing the lease liability and including it in both the long-term debt definition and asset definitions. In this case the covenant specifies the procedure for computing the capitalized value of the asset and liability.

Analysis. Continued use of leased or rented assets by the firm is contingent on making the lease or rental payments. These payments represent liabilities to the firm, and are a claim senior to that of the debtholders: such obligations reduce the value of the outstanding bondholders' claim. For this reason, the Costly Contracting Hypothesis predicts restrictions on the stockholders' subsequent use of leases in the indenture agreement. However, we are unable to explain the specific form which the restriction will take for a particular set of firm characteristics.

NOTE: SAMPLE COVENANTS

The covenants we now treat are generally described as "negative covenants," because of the limitations they impose on debtors. Set out below are several versions of covenants based on *Commentaries*, Section 10–11, which restricts "funded debt." "Funded Debt" is defined as follows:

" 'Funded Debt' means any obligation payable more than one year from the date of determination thereof, which under GAAP is shown on the balance sheet as a liability, including obligations under capital leases, but excluding items customarily reflected below current liabilities, such as deferred federal taxes on income and other reserves."

§ 10–11 Limitations on Additional Funded Debt.

The Company shall not, and shall not permit any Subsidiary to, create, incur, assume or issue, directly or indirectly, or guarantee or in any manner become, directly or indirectly, liable for or with respect to the payment of any Indebtedness, except for:

(1) Indebtedness under the Debentures and this Indenture;

(2) Indebtedness of the Company and any Subsidiary not otherwise referred to in this Section ____ outstanding on the Date of Issue (specifically including the full amount available to the Company or its Subsidiary pursuant to the loan agreements referred to in clauses (i) and (ii) of the definition of "Senior Indebtedness" contained in Section ____ hereof);

(3) Indebtedness (plus interest, premium, fees and other obligations associated therewith), that, immediately after giving effect to the incurrence thereof, does not cause the ratio of Funded Debt to Consolidated Tangible Net Worth plus Shareholder Subordinated Debt to exceed 7:1; or

(4) any deferrals, renewals, extensions, replacements, refinancings or refundings of, or amendments, modifications or supplements to, Indebtedness incurred under clauses (2) or (3) above, whether involving the same or any other lender or creditor or group of lenders or creditors, provided that any such deferrals, renewals, extensions, replacements, refinancings, refundings, amendments, modifications or supplements (i) shall not provide for any mandatory redemption, amortization or sinking fund requirement in an amount greater than or at a time prior to the amounts and times specified in the Indebtedness being deferred, renewed, extended, replaced, refinanced, refunded, amended, modified or supplemented, (ii) shall not exceed the principal amount (plus accrued interest and prepayment premium, if any) of the Indebtedness being renewed, extended, replaced, refinanced or refunded and (iii) shall be subordinated to the Debentures at least to the extent and in the manner, if at all, that the Indebtedness being renewed, extended, replaced, refinanced or refunded is subordinated to the Debentures.

A Variation on ABF Model Covenants, § 10–11, Sample Covenant 1: Limitations on Incurrence of Debt.

(a) The Company will not, and will not permit any Subsidiary to, incur any Debt, other than Intercompany Debt, that is subordinate in right of payment to the Notes, if, immediately after giving effect to the incurrence of such Debt and the application of the proceeds thereof, the aggregate principal amount of all outstanding Debt of the Company and its Subsidiaries on a consolidated basis determined in accordance with GAAP is greater than 60% of the sum of (i) the Company's Adjusted Total Assets as of the end of the most recent fiscal quarter prior to the incurrence of such additional Debt and (ii) the increase in Adjusted Total Assets since the end of such quarter (including any increase resulting from the incurrence of additional Debt).

(b) The Company will not, and will not permit any Subsidiary to, incur any Debt if the ratio of Consolidated Income Available for Debt

Service to the Annual Service Charge on the date on which such additional Debt is to be incurred, on a pro forma basis, after giving effect to the incurrence of such Debt and to the application of the proceeds thereof would have been less than 1.5 to 1.

(c) The Company will not, and will not permit any Subsidiary to, incur any Debt secured by any mortgage, lien, charge, pledge, encumbrance or security interest of any kind upon any of the properties of the Company or any Subsidiary ("Secured Debt"), whether owned at the date hereof or hereafter acquired, if, immediately after giving effect to the incurrence of such Secured Debt and the application of the proceeds thereof, the aggregate principal amount of all outstanding Secured Debt of the Company and its Subsidiaries on a consolidated basis is greater than 40% of the sum of (i) the Company's Adjusted Total Assets as of the end of the most recent fiscal quarter prior to the incurrence of such additional Debt and (ii) the increase in Adjusted Total Assets since the end of such quarter (including any increase resulting from the incurrence of additional Debt).

(d) The Company will at all times maintain an Unencumbered Total Asset Value in an amount not less than 150% of the aggregate principal amount of all outstanding unsecured Debt of the Company and its Subsidiaries on a consolidated basis.

For purposes of the foregoing provisions regarding the limitation on the incurrence of Debt, Debt shall be deemed to be "incurred" by the Company or a Subsidiary whenever the Company or such Subsidiary shall create, assume, guarantee or otherwise become liable in respect thereof.

There are other negative covenants designed to protect against senior debt, that is, debt that is secured by the assets of the firm.

Variation on Model Covenants, § 10–10: Negative Pledge.

Neither the Company nor any Subsidiary will create, assume or suffer to exist any Lien on any asset now owned or hereafter acquired by it, except:

(a) Liens in favor of the Banks securing the Loans hereunder;

(b) Liens for taxes or assessments or other government charges or levies if not yet due and payable or if due and payable if they are being contested in good faith by appropriate proceedings and for which appropriate reserves are maintained;

(c) Liens imposed by law, such as mechanic's, materialmen's, landlord's, warehousemen's and carrier's Liens, and other similar Liens, securing obligations incurred in the ordinary course of business which are not past due for more than 30 days, or which are being contested in good faith by appropriate proceedings and for which appropriate reserves have been established;

(d) Liens under workmen's compensation, unemployment insurance, social security or similar legislation;

(e) Liens, deposits or pledges to secure the performance of bids, tenders, contracts (other than contracts for the payment of money), leases (permitted under the terms of this Agreement), public or statutory obligations, surety, stay, appeal, indemnity, performance or other similar bonds, or other similar obligations arising in the ordinary course of business;

(f) judgment and other similar Liens arising in connection with court proceedings; provided that the execution or other enforcement of such Liens is effectively stayed and the claims secured thereby are being actively contested in good faith and by appropriate proceedings;

(g) easements, rights-of-way, restrictions and other similar encumbrances which, in the aggregate, do not materially interfere with the occupation, use and enjoyment by the Company or any such Subsidiary of the property assets encumbered thereby in the normal course of its business or materially impair the value of the property subject thereto;

(h) Liens securing obligations of such a Subsidiary to the Company or another such Subsidiary;

(i) Liens set forth in Schedule III; and

(j) Liens not otherwise permitted by the foregoing clauses of this Section securing indebtedness in an aggregate principal amount at any one time outstanding not to exceed 30% of Consolidated Tangible Net Worth.

Tangible Net Worth is a defined term. Here is a sample:

" 'TANGIBLE NET WORTH' means, as of any date, the difference of (i) Net Worth, minus (ii) to the extent included in determining the amount under the foregoing clause (i), the net book value of goodwill, cost in excess of fair value of net assets acquired, patents, trademarks, tradenames and copyrights, treasury stock and all other assets which are deemed intangible assets under Generally Accepted Accounting Principles."

Metropolitan Life Insurance Company v. RJR Nabisco, Inc.

716 F. Supp. 1504 (S.D.N.Y. 1989).

■ WALKER, J.

I. INTRODUCTION

The corporate parties to this action are among the country's most sophisticated financial institutions, as familiar with the Wall Street investment community and the securities market as American consumers are with the Oreo cookies and Winston cigarettes made by defendant RJR Nabisco, Inc. (sometimes "the company" or "RJR Nabisco"). The present action traces its origins to October 20, 1988, when F. Ross Johnson, then the Chief Executive Officer of RJR Nabisco, proposed a $17 billion leveraged buy-out ("LBO") of the company's shareholders, at $75 per share.[1] Within a few days, a bidding war developed among the investment group led by Johnson and the investment firm of Kohlberg Kravis Roberts & Co. ("KKR"), and others. On December 1, 1988, a special committee of RJR Nabisco directors, established by the company specifically to consider the competing proposals, recommended that the company accept the KKR proposal, a $24 billion LBO that called for the purchase of the company's outstanding stock at roughly $109 per share.

The flurry of activity late last year that accompanied the bidding war for RJR Nabisco spawned at least eight lawsuits, filed before this Court, charging the company and its former CEO with a variety of securities and common law violations. The Court agreed to hear the present action—filed even before the company accepted the KKR proposal—on an expedited basis, with an eye toward March 1, 1989, when RJR Nabisco was expected to merge with the KKR holding entities created to facilitate the LBO. On that date, RJR Nabisco was also scheduled to assume roughly $19 billion of new debt. After a delay unrelated to the present action, the merger was ultimately completed during the week of April 24, 1989.

Plaintiffs now allege, in short, that RJR Nabisco's actions have drastically impaired the value of bonds previously issued to plaintiffs by, in effect, misappropriating the value of those bonds to help finance the LBO and to distribute an enormous windfall to the company's shareholders. As a result, plaintiffs argue, they have unfairly suffered a multimillion dollar loss in the value of their bonds.[4]

* * *

Although the numbers involved in this case are large, and the financing necessary to complete the LBO unprecedented, the legal principles nonetheless remain discrete and familiar. Yet while the instant motions thus primarily require the Court to evaluate and apply traditional rules of equity and contract interpretation, plaintiffs do raise issues of first impression in the context of an LBO. At the heart of the present motions lies plaintiffs' claim that RJR Nabisco violated a restrictive covenant—not an explicit covenant found within the four corners of the relevant bond indentures, but rather an *implied* covenant of good faith and fair dealing—

---

1. A leveraged buy-out occurs when a group of investors, usually including members of a company's management team, buy the company under financial arrangements that include little equity and significant new debt. The necessary debt financing typically includes mortgages or high risk/high yield bonds, popularly known as "junk bonds." Additionally, a portion of this debt is generally secured by the company's assets. Some of the acquired company's assets are usually sold after the transaction is completed in order to reduce the debt incurred in the acquisition.

4. Agencies like Standard & Poor's and Moody's generally rate bonds in two broad categories: investment grade and speculative grade. Standard & Poor's rates investment grade bonds from "AAA" to "BBB." Moody's rates those bonds from "AAA" to "Baa3." Speculative grade bonds are rated either "BB" and lower, or "Ba1" and lower, by Standard & Poor's and Moody's, respectively. *See, e.g., Standard and Poor's Debt Rating Criteria* at 10–11. No one disputes that, subsequent to the announcement of the LBO, the RJR Nabisco bonds lost their "A" ratings. [See Appendix 6–A at the end of this chapter.—Ed.]

not to incur the debt necessary to facilitate the LBO and thereby betray what plaintiffs claim was the fundamental basis of their bargain with the company. The company, plaintiffs assert, consistently reassured its bondholders that it had a "mandate" from its Board of Directors to maintain RJR Nabisco's preferred credit rating. Plaintiffs ask this Court first to imply a covenant of good faith and fair dealing that would prevent the recent transaction, then to hold that this covenant has been breached, and finally to require RJR Nabisco to redeem their bonds.

RJR Nabisco defends the LBO by pointing to express provisions in the bond indentures that, *inter alia*, permit mergers and the assumption of additional debt. These provisions, as well as others that could have been included but were not, were known to the market and to plaintiffs, sophisticated investors who freely bought the bonds and were equally free to sell them at any time. Any attempt by this Court to create contractual terms *post hoc*, defendants contend, not only finds no basis in the controlling law and undisputed facts of this case, but also would constitute an impermissible invasion into the free and open operation of the marketplace.

For the reasons set forth below, this Court agrees with defendants. There being no express covenant between the parties that would restrict the incurrence of new debt, and no perceived direction to that end from covenants that are express, this Court will not imply a covenant to prevent the recent LBO and thereby create an indenture term that, while bargained for in other contexts, was not bargained for here and was not even within the mutual contemplation of the parties.

II. BACKGROUND

* * *

A. The Parties:

Metropolitan Life Insurance Co. ("MetLife"), incorporated in New York, is a life insurance company that provides pension benefits for 42 million individuals. According to its most recent annual report, MetLife's assets exceed $88 billion and its debt securities holdings exceed $49 billion. MetLife is a mutual company and therefore has no stockholders and is instead operated for the benefit of its policyholders. MetLife alleges that it owns $340,542,000 in principal amount of six separate RJR Nabisco debt issues, bonds allegedly purchased between July 1975 and July 1988. Some bonds become due as early as this year; others will not become due until 2017. The bonds bear interest rates of anywhere from 8 to 10.25 percent. MetLife also owned 186,000 shares of RJR Nabisco common stock at the time this suit was filed.

RJR Nabisco, a Delaware corporation, is a consumer products holding company that owns some of the country's best known product lines, including LifeSavers candy, Oreo cookies, and Winston cigarettes. The company was formed in 1985, when R. J. Reynolds Industries, Inc. ("R. J. Reynolds") merged with Nabisco Brands, Inc. ("Nabisco Brands"). In 1979, and thus before the R. J. Reynolds–Nabisco Brands merger, R. J. Reynolds acquired the Del Monte Corporation ("Del Monte"), which distributes canned fruits and vegetables. From January 1987 until February 1989, co-defendant Johnson served as the company's CEO. KKR, a private investment firm, organizes funds through which investors provide pools of equity to finance LBOs.

B.   The Indentures:

The bonds implicated by this suit are governed by long, detailed indentures, which in turn are governed by New York contract law. No one disputes that the holders of public bond issues, like plaintiffs here, often enter the market after the indentures have been negotiated and memorialized. Thus, those indentures are often not the product of face-to-face negotiations between the ultimate holders and the issuing company. What remains equally true, however, is that underwriters ordinarily negotiate the terms of the indentures with the issuers. Since the underwriters must then sell or place the bonds, they necessarily negotiate in part with the interests of the buyers in mind. Moreover, these indentures were not secret agreements foisted upon unwitting participants in the bond market. No successive holder is required to accept or to continue to hold the bonds, governed by their accompanying indentures; indeed, plaintiffs readily admit that they could have sold their bonds right up until the announcement of the LBO. Instead, sophisticated investors like plaintiffs are well aware of the indenture terms and, presumably, review them carefully before lending hundreds of millions of dollars to any company.

Indeed, the prospectuses for the indentures contain a statement relevant to this action:

> The Indenture contains no restrictions on the creation of unsecured short-term debt by [RJR Nabisco] or its subsidiaries, no restriction on the creation of unsecured Funded Debt by [RJR Nabisco] or its subsidiaries which are not Restricted Subsidiaries, and no restriction on the payment of dividends by [RJR Nabisco].

Further, as plaintiffs themselves note, the contracts at issue "[do] not impose debt limits, since debt is assumed to be used for productive purposes."

1.   The relevant Articles:

A typical RJR Nabisco indenture contains thirteen Articles. At least four of them are relevant to the present motions and thus merit a brief review.

* * *

Article Ten addresses a potential "Consolidation, Merger, Sale or Conveyance," and explicitly sets forth the conditions under which the company can consolidate or merge into or with any other corporation. It provides explicitly that RJR Nabisco "may consolidate with, or sell or convey, all or substantially all of its assets to, or merge into or with any other corporation," so long as the new entity is a United States corporation, and so long as it assumes RJR Nabisco's debt. The Article also requires that any such transaction not result in the company's default under any indenture provision.

2. The elimination of restrictive covenants:

In its Amended Complaint, MetLife lists the six debt issues on which it bases its claims. Indentures for two of those issues—the 10.25 percent Notes due in 1990, of which MetLife continues to hold $10 million, and the 8.9 percent Debentures due in 1996, of which MetLife continues to hold $50 million—once contained express covenants that, among other things, restricted the company's ability to incur precisely the sort of debt involved in the recent LBO. In order to eliminate those restrictions, the parties to this action renegotiated the terms of those indentures, first in 1983 and then again in 1985.

MetLife acquired $50 million principal amount of 10.25 percent Notes from Del Monte in July of 1975. To cover the $50 million, MetLife and Del Monte entered into a loan agreement. That agreement restricted Del Monte's ability, among other things, to incur the sort of indebtedness involved in the RJR Nabisco LBO. In 1979, R. J. Reynolds—the corporate predecessor to RJR Nabisco—purchased Del Monte and assumed its indebtedness. Then, in December of 1983, R. J. Reynolds requested MetLife to agree to deletions of those restrictive covenants in exchange for various guarantees from R. J. Reynolds. A few months later, MetLife and R. J. Reynolds entered into a guarantee and amendment agreement reflecting those terms. Pursuant to that agreement, and in the words of Robert E. Chappell, Jr., MetLife's Executive Vice President, MetLife thus "gave up the restrictive covenants applicable to the Del Monte debt ... in return for [the parent company's] guarantee and public covenants."

MetLife acquired the 8.9 percent Debentures from R. J. Reynolds in October of 1976 in a private placement. A promissory note evidenced MetLife's $100 million loan. That note, like the Del Monte agreement, contained covenants that restricted R. J. Reynolds' ability to incur new debt. In June of 1985, R. J. Reynolds announced its plans to acquire Nabisco Brands in a $3.6 billion transaction that involved the incurrence of a significant amount of new debt. R. J. Reynolds requested MetLife to waive compliance with these restrictive covenants in light of the Nabisco acquisition.

In exchange for certain benefits, MetLife agreed to exchange its 8.9 percent debentures—which *did* contain explicit debt limitations—for debentures issued under a public indenture—which contain no explicit limits on new debt. An internal MetLife memorandum explained the parties' understanding:

> [MetLife's $100 million financing of the Nabisco Brands purchase] had its origins in discussions with RJR regarding potential covenant violations in the 8.90% Notes. More specifically, *in its acquisition of Nabisco Brands, RJR was slated to incur significant new long-term debt, which would have caused a violation in the funded indebtedness incurrence*

tests in the 8.90% Notes. In the discussions regarding [MetLife's] willingness to consent to the additional indebtedness, *it was determined that a mutually beneficial approach to the problem* was to 1) agree on a new financing having a rate and a maturity desirable for [MetLife] and 2) modify the 8.90% Notes. The former was accomplished with agreement on the proposed financing, while the latter was accomplished by [MetLife] agreeing to substitute RJR's public indenture covenants for the covenants in the 8.90% Notes. In addition to the covenant substitution, RJR has agreed to "debenturize" the 8.90% Notes upon [MetLife's] request. This will permit [MetLife] to sell the 8.90% Notes to the public.

3.   The recognition and effect of the LBO trend:

Other internal MetLife documents help frame the background to this action, for they accurately describe the changing securities markets and the responses those changes engendered from sophisticated market participants, such as MetLife and Jefferson–Pilot. At least as early as 1982, MetLife recognized an LBO's effect on bond values.[14] In the spring of that year, MetLife participated in the financing of an LBO of a company called Reeves Brothers ("Reeves"). At the time of that LBO, MetLife also held bonds in that company. Subsequent to the LBO, as a MetLife memorandum explained, the "Debentures of Reeves were downgraded by Standard & Poor's from BBB to B and by Moody's from Baal to Ba3, thereby lowering the value of the Notes and Debentures held by [MetLife]."

MetLife further recognized its "inability to force any type of payout of the [Reeves'] Notes or the Debentures as a result of the buy-out [which] was somewhat disturbing at the time we considered a participation in the new financing. However," the memorandum continued,

> our concern was tempered since, as a stockholder in [the holding company used to facilitate the transaction], we would benefit from the increased net income attributable to the continued presence of the low coupon indebtedness. The recent downgrading of the Reeves Debentures and the consequent "loss" in value has again raised questions regarding our ability to have forced a payout. *Questions have also been raised about our ability to force payouts in similar future situations, particularly when we would not be participating in the buy-out financing.*

Id. (emphasis added). In the memorandum, MetLife sought to answer those very "questions" about how it might force payouts in "similar future situations."

---

14. MetLife itself began investing in LBOs as early as 1980. *See* MetLife Special Projects Memorandum, dated June 17, 1989, attached as Bradley Aff. Exh. V, at 1 ("[MetLife's] history of investing in leveraged buyout transactions dates back to 1980; and through 1984, [MetLife] reviewed a large number of LBO investment opportunities presented to us by various investment banking firms and LBO specialists. Over this five-year period, [MetLife] invested, on a direct basis, approximately $430 million to purchase debt and equity securities in 10 such transactions . . .").

A method of closing this apparent "loophole," thereby forcing a payout of [MetLife's] holdings, would be through a covenant dealing with a change in ownership. Such a covenant is fairly standard in financings with privately-held companies ... It provides the lender with an option to end a particular borrowing relationship via some type of special redemption ... *Id.*, at 2 (emphasis added).

A more comprehensive memorandum, prepared in late 1985, evaluated and explained several aspects of the corporate world's increasing use of mergers, takeovers and other debt-financed transactions. That memorandum first reviewed the available protection for lenders such as MetLife:

Covenants are incorporated into loan documents to ensure that after a lender makes a loan, the creditworthiness of the borrower and the lender's ability to reach the borrower's assets do not deteriorate substantially. *Restrictions on the incurrence of debt*, sale of assets, mergers, dividends, restricted payments and loans and advances to affiliates *are some of the traditional negative covenants that can help protect lenders in the event their obligors become involved in undesirable merger/takeover situations.*

The memorandum then surveyed market realities:

Because almost any industrial company is apt to engineer a takeover or be taken over itself, *Business Week* says that investors are beginning to view debt securities of high grade industrial corporations as Wall Street's riskiest investments. In addition, *because public bondholders do not enjoy the protection of any restrictive covenants*, owners of high grade corporates face substantial losses from takeover situations, if not immediately, then when the bond market finally adjusts.... There have been 10–15 merger/takeover/LBO situations where, *due to the lack of covenant protection, [MetLife] has had no choice but to remain a lender to a less creditworthy obligor....* The fact that the quality of our investment portfolio is greater than the other large insurance companies ... may indicate that we have negotiated better covenant protection than other institutions, thus generally being able to require prepayment when situations become too risky ... [However,] a problem exists. And *because the current merger craze is not likely to decelerate* and because there exist vehicles to circumvent traditional covenants, the problem will probably continue. Therefore, *perhaps it is time to institute appropriate language designed to protect Metropolitan from the negative implications of mergers and takeovers.* (emphasis added).[15]

---

15. During discovery, MetLife produced from its files an article that appeared in *The New York Times* on January 7, 1986. The article, like the memoranda discussed above, reviewed the position of bondholders like MetLife and Jefferson–Pilot:

"Debt-financed acquisitions, as well as those defensive actions to thwart takeovers, have generally resulted in lower bond ratings ... Of course, a major problem for debtholders is that, compared with shareholders, they have relatively little power over management decisions. *Their rights are essentially confined to the covenants restricting, say, the level of debt a company can accrue.*"

Indeed, MetLife does not dispute that, as a member of a bondholders' association, it received and discussed a proposed model indenture, which included a "comprehensive covenant" entitled "Limitations on Shareholders' Payments." As becomes clear from reading the proposed—but never adopted—provision, it was "intend[ed] to provide protection against all of the types of situations in which shareholders profit at the expense of bondholders." *Id.* The provision dictated that the "corporation will not, and will not permit any subsidiary to, directly or indirectly, make any shareholder payment unless ... (1) the aggregate amount of all shareholder payment during the period [at issue] ... shall not exceed [figure left blank]." The term "shareholder payments" is defined to include "restructuring distributions, stock repurchases, debt incurred or guaranteed to finance merger payments to shareholders, etc."

Apparently, that provision—or provisions with similar intentions— never went beyond the discussion stage at MetLife. That fact is easily understood; indeed, MetLife's own documents articulate several reasonable, undisputed explanations:

> While it would be possible to broaden the change in ownership covenant to cover any acquisition-oriented transaction, *we might well encounter significant resistance in implementation with larger public companies* ... With respect to implementation, we would be faced with the task of imposing a non-standard limitation on potential borrowers, *which could be a difficult task in today's highly competitive marketplace. Competitive pressures notwithstanding, it would seem that management of larger public companies would be particularly opposed to such a covenant since its effect would be to increase the cost of an acquisition* (due to an assumed debt repayment), a factor that could well lower the price of any tender offer (thereby impacting shareholders).

The November 1985 memorandum explained that

> obviously, our ability to implement methods of takeover protection will vary between the public and private market. In that public securities do not contain any meaningful covenants, it would be very difficult for [MetLife] to demand takeover protection in public bonds. Such a requirement would effectively take us out of the public industrial market. A recent *Business Week* article does suggest, however, that there is increasing talk among lending institutions about requiring blue chip companies to compensate them for the growing risk of downgradings. *This talk, regarding such protection as restrictions on future debt financings, is met with skepticism by the investment banking community which feels that CFO's are not about to give up the option of adding debt and do not really care if their companies' credit ratings drop a notch or two.*

The Court quotes these documents at such length not because they represent an "admission" or "waiver" from MetLife, or an "assumption of risk" in any tort sense, or its "consent" to any particular course of conduct—all terms discussed at even greater length in the parties' submissions. Rather, the documents set forth the background to the present action, and highlight the risks inherent in the market itself, for any investor. Investors as sophisticated as MetLife and Jefferson–Pilot would be hard-pressed to plead ignorance of these market risks. Indeed, MetLife has not disputed the facts asserted in its own internal documents. Nor has Jefferson–Pilot—presumably an institution no less sophisticated than Met-Life—offered any reason to believe that its understanding of the securities market differed in any material respect from the description and analysis set forth in the MetLife documents. Those documents, after all, were not born in a vacuum. They are descriptions of, and responses to, the market in which investors like MetLife and Jefferson–Pilot knowingly participated.

These documents must be read in conjunction with plaintiffs' Amended Complaint. That document asserts that the LBO "undermines the foundation of the investment grade debt market ...," that, although "the indentures do not purport to limit dividends or debt ... such covenants were believed unnecessary with blue chip companies ...", that "the transaction contradicts the premise of the investment grade market ..."; and, finally, that "this buy-out was not contemplated at the time the debt was issued, contradicts the premise of the investment grade ratings that RJR Nabisco actively solicited and received, and is inconsistent with the understandings of the market ... which plaintiffs relied upon."

Solely for the purposes of these motions, the Court accepts various factual assertions advanced by plaintiffs: first, that RJR Nabisco actively solicited "investment grade" ratings for its debt; second, that it relied on descriptions of its strong capital structure and earnings record which included prominent display of its ability to pay the interest obligations on its long-term debt several times over; and third, that the company made express or implied representations not contained in the relevant indentures concerning its future creditworthiness. In support of those allegations, plaintiffs have marshaled a number of speeches made by co-defendant Johnson and other executives of RJR Nabisco.[18] In addition, plaintiffs rely on an affidavit sworn to by John Dowdle, the former Treasurer and then Senior Vice President of RJR Nabisco from 1970 until 1987. In his opinion, the LBO "clearly undermines the fundamental premise of the company's bargain with the bondholders, and the commitment that I believe the company made to the bondholders ... I firmly believe that the company made commitments ... that require it to redeem [these bonds and notes] before paying out the value to the shareholders."

---

18. *See, e.g.*, Address by F. Ross Johnson, November 12, 1987, P. Exh. 8, at 5 ("Our strong balance sheet is a cornerstone of our strategies. It gives us the resources to modernize facilities, develop new technologies, bring on new products, and support our leading brands around the world."); Remarks of Edward J. Robinson, Executive Vice President and Chief Financial Officer, February 15, 1988, P. Exh. 6, at 1 ("RJR Nabisco's financial strategy is ... to enhance the strength of the balance sheet by reducing the level of debt as well as lowering the cost of existing debt."); Remarks by Dr. Robert J. Carbonell, Vice Chairman of RJR Nabisco, June 3, 1987, P. Exh. 10, at 5 ("We will not sacrifice our longer-term health for the sake of short term heroics.").

III.   DISCUSSION

At the outset, the Court notes that nothing in its evaluation is substantively altered by the speeches given or remarks made by RJR Nabisco executives, or the opinions of various individuals—what, for instance, former RJR Nabisco Treasurer Dowdle personally did or did not "firmly believe" the indentures meant. The parol evidence rule bars plaintiffs from arguing that the speeches made by company executives prove defendants agreed or acquiesced to a term that does not appear in the indentures. In interpreting these contracts, this Court must be concerned with what the parties intended, but only to the extent that what they intended is evidenced by what is written in the indentures.

[handwritten margin note: parol evidence limited to 4 corners of document — no ambiguity]

The indentures at issue clearly address the eventuality of a merger. They impose certain related restrictions not at issue in this suit, but no restriction that would prevent the recent RJR Nabisco merger transaction. The indentures also explicitly set forth provisions for the adoption of new covenants, if such a course is deemed appropriate. While it may be true that no explicit provision either permits or prohibits an LBO, such contractual silence itself cannot create ambiguity to avoid the dictates of the parole evidence rule, particularly where the indentures impose no debt limitations.

Under certain circumstances, however, courts will, as plaintiffs note, consider extrinsic evidence to evaluate the scope of an implied covenant of good faith. However, the Second Circuit has established a different rule for customary, or boiler plate, provisions of detailed indentures used and relied upon throughout the securities market, such as those at issue. Thus, in *Sharon Steel Corporation v. Chase Manhattan Bank, N.A.*, 691 F.2d 1039 (2d Cir. 1982), Judge Winter concluded that

> boiler plate provisions are ... not the consequences of the relationship of particular borrowers and lenders and do not depend upon particularized intentions of the parties to an indenture. There are no adjudicative facts relating to the parties to the litigation for a jury to find and the meaning of boiler plate provisions is, therefore, a matter of law rather than fact. Moreover, uniformity in interpretation is important to the efficiency of capital markets ... Whereas participants in the capital market can adjust their affairs according to a uniform interpretation, whether it be correct or not as an initial proposition, the creation of enduring uncertainties as to the meaning of boiler plate provisions would decrease the value of all debenture issues and greatly impair the efficient working of capital markets ... Just such uncertainties would be created if interpretation of boiler plate provisions were submitted to juries sitting in every judicial district in the nation.

Id. at 1048. *See also Morgan Stanley & Co. v. Archer Daniels Midland Co.*, 570 F. Supp. 1529, 1535–36 (S.D.N.Y. 1983) (Sand, J.) ("[Plaintiff concedes that the legality of [the transaction at issue] would depend on a factual inquiry ... This case-by-case approach is problematic ... [Plaintiff's theory] appears keyed to the subjective expectations of the bondholders ... and reads a subjective element into what presumably should be an objective determination based on the language appearing in the bond agreement.''); *Purcell v. Flying Tiger Line, Inc.*, No. 84–7102, at 5, 8 (S.D.N.Y. Jan. 12, 1984) (CES) (''The Indenture does not contain any such limitation [as the one proposed by plaintiff].... In light of our holding that the Indenture unambiguously permits the transaction at issue in this case, we are precluded from considering any of the extrinsic evidence that plaintiff offers on this motion ... It would be improper to consider evidence as to the subjective intent, collateral representations, and either the statements or the conduct of the parties in performing the contract.'') (citations omitted). Ignoring these principles, plaintiffs would have this Court vary what they themselves have admitted is ''indenture boiler plate,'' to comport with collateral representations and their subjective understandings.

A. *Plaintiffs' Case Against the RJR Nabisco LBO:*

1. Count One: The implied covenant:

In their first count, plaintiffs assert that defendant RJR Nabisco owes a continuing duty of good faith and fair dealing in connection with the contract [i.e., the indentures] through which it borrowed money from MetLife, Jefferson–Pilot and other holders of its debt, including a duty not to frustrate the purpose of the contracts to the debtholders or to deprive the debtholders of the intended object of the contracts—purchase of investment-grade securities.

> In the ''buy-out,'' the company breaches the duty [or implied covenant] of good faith and fair dealing by, *inter alia*, destroying the investment grade quality of the debt and transferring that value to the ''buy-out'' proponents and to the shareholders.

In effect, plaintiffs contend that express covenants were not necessary because an *implied* covenant would prevent what defendants have now done.

A plaintiff always can allege a violation of an express covenant. If there has been such a violation, of course, the court need not reach the question of whether or not an *implied* covenant has been violated. That inquiry surfaces where, while the express terms may not have been technically breached, one party has nonetheless effectively deprived the other of those express, explicitly bargained-for benefits. In such a case, a court will read an implied covenant of good faith and fair dealing into a contract to ensure that neither party deprives the other of ''the fruits of the agreement.'' Such a covenant is implied only where the implied term ''is consistent with other mutually agreed upon terms in the contract.'' In other words, the implied covenant will only aid and further the explicit terms of the agreement and will never impose an obligation '' 'which would be inconsistent with other terms of the contractual relationship.' '' *Id.* (citation omitted). Viewed another way, the implied covenant of good faith is breached only when one party seeks to prevent the contract's performance or to withhold its benefits. As a result, it thus ensures that parties to a contract perform the substantive, bargained-for terms of their agreement.

In contracts like bond indentures, "an implied covenant ... derives its substance directly from the language of the Indenture, and 'cannot give the holders of Debentures any rights inconsistent with those set out in the Indenture.' *[Where] plaintiffs' contractual rights [have not been] violated, there can have been no breach of an implied covenant.*"

* * *

The appropriate analysis, then, is first to examine the indentures to determine "the fruits of the agreement" between the parties, and then to decide whether those "fruits" have been spoiled—which is to say, whether plaintiffs' contractual rights have been violated by defendants.

The American Bar Foundation's *Commentaries on Indentures* ("the *Commentaries*"), relied upon and respected by both plaintiffs and defendants, describes the rights and risks generally found in bond indentures like those at issue:

> The most obvious and important characteristic of long-term debt financing is that the holder ordinarily has not bargained for and does not expect any substantial gain in the value of the security to compensate for the risk of loss ... The significant fact, *which accounts in part for the detailed protective provisions of the typical long-term debt financing instrument*, is that *the lender (the purchaser of the debt security) can expect only interest at the prescribed rate plus the eventual return of the principal.* Except for possible increases in the market value of the debt security because of changes in interest rates, the debt security will seldom be worth more than the lender paid for it ... It may, of course, become worth much less. Accordingly, the typical investor in a long-term debt security is primarily interested in every reasonable assurance that the principal and interest will be paid when due.... Short of bankruptcy, the debt security holder can do nothing to protect himself against actions of the borrower which jeopardize its ability to pay the debt unless he ... establishes his rights through contractual provisions set forth in the debt agreement or indenture.

Id. at 1–2 (1971) (emphasis added).

A review of the parties' submissions and the indentures themselves satisfies the Court that the substantive "fruits" guaranteed by those contracts and relevant to the present motions include the periodic and regular payment of interest and the eventual repayment of principal. ("The Issuer covenants ... that it will duly and punctually pay ... the principal of, and interest on, each of the Securities ... at the respective times and in the manner provided in such Securities ..."). According to a typical indenture, a default shall occur if the company either (1) fails to pay principal when due; (2) fails to make a timely sinking fund payment; (3) fails to pay within 30 days of the due date thereof any interest on the date; or (4) fails duly to observe or perform any of the express covenants or agreements set forth in the agreement. Plaintiffs' Amended Complaint nowhere alleges that RJR Nabisco has breached these contractual obligations; interest payments continue and there is no reason to believe that the principal will not be paid when due.

It is not necessary to decide that indentures like those at issue could never support a finding of additional benefits, under different circumstances with different parties. Rather, for present purposes, it is sufficient to conclude what obligation is *not* covered, either explicitly or implicitly, by these contracts held by these plaintiffs. Accordingly, this Court holds that the "fruits" of these indentures do not include an implied restrictive covenant that would prevent the incurrence of new debt to facilitate the recent LBO. To hold otherwise would permit these plaintiffs to straightjacket the company in order to guarantee their investment. These plaintiffs do not invoke an implied covenant of good faith to protect a legitimate, mutually contemplated benefit of the indentures; rather, they seek to have this Court create an additional benefit for which they did not bargain.

Although the indentures generally permit mergers and the incurrence of new debt, there admittedly is not an explicit indenture provision to the contrary of what plaintiffs now claim the implied covenant requires. That absence, however, does *not* mean that the Court should imply into those very same indentures a covenant of good faith so broad that it imposes a new, substantive term of enormous scope. This is so particularly where, as here, that very term—a limitation on the incurrence of additional debt—has in other past contexts been expressly bargained for; particularly where the indentures grant the company broad discretion in the management of its affairs, as plaintiffs admit; particularly where the indentures explicitly set forth specific provisions for the adoption of new covenants and restrictions; and *especially* where there has been no breach of the parties' bargained-for contractual rights on which the implied covenant necessarily is based. While the Court stands ready to employ an implied covenant of good faith to ensure that such bargained-for rights are performed and upheld, it will not, however, permit an implied covenant to shoehorn into an indenture additional terms plaintiffs now wish had been included.

Plaintiffs argue in the most general terms that the fundamental basis of all these indentures was that an LBO along the lines of the recent RJR Nabisco transaction would never be undertaken, that indeed *no* action would be taken, intentionally or not, that would significantly deplete the company's assets. Accepting plaintiffs' theory, their fundamental bargain with defendants dictated that nothing would be done to jeopardize the extremely high probability that the company would remain able to make interest payments and repay principal over the 20 to 30 year indenture term—and perhaps by logical extension even included the right to ask a court "to make sure that plaintiffs had made a good investment." *Gardner*, 589 F. Supp. at 674. But as Judge Knapp aptly concluded in *Gardner*, "Defendants ... were under a duty to carry out the terms of the contract, but not to make sure that plaintiffs had made a good investment. The former they have done; the latter we have no jurisdiction over." *Id*. Plaintiffs' submissions and MetLife's previous undisputed internal memoranda remind the Court that a "fundamental basis" or a "fruit of an agreement'' is often in the eye of the beholder, whose vision may well change along with the market, and who may, with hindsight, imagine a different bargain than the one he actually and initially accepted with open eyes.

The sort of unbounded and one-sided elasticity urged by plaintiffs would interfere with and destabilize the market. And this Court, like the parties to these contracts, cannot ignore or disavow the marketplace in which the contract is performed. Nor can it ignore the expectations of that market—expectations, for instance, that the terms of an indenture will be upheld, and that a court will not, *sua sponte*, add new substantive terms to that indenture as it sees fit. The Court has no reason to believe that the market, in evaluating bonds such as those at issue here, did not discount for the possibility that any company, even one the size of RJR Nabisco, might engage in an LBO heavily financed by debt. That the bonds did not lose any of their value until the October 20, 1988 announcement of a possible RJR Nabisco LBO only suggests that the market had theretofore evaluated the risks of such a transaction as slight.

The Court recognizes that the market is not a static entity, but instead involves what plaintiffs call "evolving understanding[s]." Just as the growing prevalence of LBO's has helped change certain ground rules and expectations in the field of mergers and acquisitions, so too it has obviously affected the bond market, a fact no one disputes. To support their argument that defendants have violated an implied covenant, plaintiffs contend that, since the October 20, 1988 announcement, the bond market has "stopped functioning." They argue that if they had "sold and abandoned the market [before October 20, 1988], the market, if everyone had the same attitude, would have disappeared." What plaintiffs term "stopped functioning" or "disappeared," however, are properly seen as natural responses and adjustments to market realities. Plaintiffs of course do not contend that no new issues are being sold, or that existing issues are no longer being traded or have become worthless.

To respond to changed market forces, new indenture provisions can be negotiated, such as provisions that were in fact once included in the 8.9 percent and 10.25 percent debentures implicated by this action. New provisions could include special debt restrictions or change-of-control covenants. There is no guarantee, of course, that companies like RJR Nabisco would accept such new covenants; parties retain the freedom to enter into contracts as they choose. But presumably, multi-billion dollar investors like plaintiffs have some say in the terms of the investments they make and continue to hold. And, presumably, companies like RJR Nabisco need the infusions of capital such investors are capable of providing.

Whatever else may be true about this case, it certainly does not present an example of the classic sort of form contract or contract of adhesion often frowned upon by courts. In those cases, what motivates a court is the strikingly inequitable nature of the parties' respective bargaining positions. Plaintiffs here entered this "liquid trading market," with their eyes open and were free to leave at any time. Instead they remained there notwithstanding its well understood risks.

Ultimately, plaintiffs cannot escape the inherent illogic of their argument. On the one hand, it is undisputed that investors like plaintiffs recognized that companies like RJR Nabisco strenuously opposed additional restrictive covenants that might limit the incurrence of new debt or the company's ability to engage in a merger. Furthermore, plaintiffs argue that they had no choice other than to accept the indentures as written, without additional restrictive covenants, or to "abandon" the market.

Yet on the other hand, plaintiffs ask this Court to imply a covenant that would have just that restrictive effect because, they contend, it reflects precisely the fundamental assumption of the market and the fundamental basis of their bargain with defendants. If that truly were the case here, it is difficult to imagine why an insistence on that term would have forced the plaintiffs to abandon the market. The Second Circuit has offered a better explanation: "[a] promise by the defendant should be implied only if the court may rightfully assume that the parties would have included it in their written agreement had their attention been called to it ... *Any such assumption in this case would be completely unwarranted.*" *Neuman v. Pike*, 591 F.2d 191, 195 (2d Cir. 1979) (emphasis added, citations omitted).

In the final analysis, plaintiffs offer no objective or reasonable standard for a court to use in its effort to define the sort of actions their "implied covenant" would permit a corporation to take, and those it would not.[28] Plaintiffs say only that investors like themselves rely upon the "skill" and "good faith" of a company's board and management, and that their covenant would prevent the company from "destroy[ing] ... the legitimate expectations of its long-term bondholders."As is clear from the preceding discussion, however, plaintiffs have failed to convince the Court that by upholding the explicit, bargained-for terms of the indenture, RJR Nabisco has either exhibited bad faith or destroyed plaintiffs' *legitimate*, protected expectations.

* * *

2. Count Five: In Equity:

Count Five substantially restates and realleges the contract claims advanced in Count I. Along with these repetitions, plaintiffs blend in allegations that the transaction "frustrates the commercial purpose" of the parties, under "circumstances [that] are outrageous, and ... it would [therefore] be unconscionable to allow the 'buy-out' to proceed ..." Those very issues—frustration of purpose and unconscionability—are equally matters of contract law, of course, and plaintiffs could just as easily have advanced them in Count I. Indeed, to some extent plaintiffs did advance

---

28. Under plaintiffs' theory, bondholders might ask a court to prohibit a company like RJR Nabisco not only from engaging in an LBO, but also from entering a new line of business-with the attendant costs of building new physical plants and hiring new workers—or from acquiring new businesses such as RJR Nabisco did when it acquired Del Monte.

these claims in that Count. ("RJR Nabisco owes a continuing duty . . . not to frustrate the purpose of the contracts . . ."). For present purposes, it makes no difference how plaintiffs characterize their arguments. Their equity claims cannot survive defendants' motion for summary judgment.

In their papers, plaintiffs variously attempt to justify Count V as being based on unjust enrichment, frustration of purpose, an alleged breach of something approaching a fiduciary duty, or a general claim of unconscionability. Each claim fails. First, as even plaintiffs recognize, an unjust enrichment claim requires a court first to find that "the circumstances [are] such that in equity and good conscience the defendant should make restitution." Plaintiffs have not alleged a violation of a single explicit term of the indentures at issue, and on the facts alleged this Court has determined that an implicit covenant of good faith and fair dealing has not been violated. Under these circumstances, this Court concludes that defendants need not, "in equity and good conscience," make restitution.

Second, in support of their motions plaintiffs claim frustration of purpose. Yet even resolving all ambiguities and drawing all reasonable inferences in plaintiffs' favor, their claim cannot stand. A claim of frustration of purpose has three elements:

> First, the purpose that is frustrated must have been a principal purpose of that party in making the contract. . . . The object must be so completely the basis of the contract that, as both parties understand, without it the transaction would make little sense. Second, the frustration must be substantial. It is not enough that the transaction has become less profitable for the affected party or even that he will sustain a loss. The frustration must be so severe that it is not fairly to be regarded as within the risks that he assumed under the contract. Third, the non-occurrence of the frustrating event must have been a basic assumption on which the contract was made.

Restatement (Second) of Contracts, 265 comment a (1981). * * * Similarly, there is no indication here that an alleged refusal to incur debt to facilitate an LBO was the "essence" or "principal purpose" of the indentures, and no mention of such an alleged restriction is made in the agreements. Further, while plaintiffs' bonds may have lost some of their value, "discharge under this doctrine has been limited to instances where a virtually cataclysmic, wholly unforeseeable event *renders the contract value- less to one party.*" That is not the case here. Moreover, "the frustration of purpose defense is not available where, as here, the event which allegedly frustrated the purpose of the contract . . . was clearly foreseeable." Faced with MetLife's internal memoranda, plaintiffs cannot but admit that "Met-Life has been concerned about 'buy-outs' for several years." Nor do plaintiffs provide any reasonable basis for believing that a party as sophisticated as Jefferson–Pilot was any less cognizant of the market around it.

Third, plaintiffs advance a claim that remains based, their assertions to the contrary notwithstanding, on an alleged breach of a fiduciary duty. Defendants go to great lengths to prove that the law of Delaware, and not New York, governs this question. Defendants' attempt to rely on Delaware law is readily explained by even a cursory reading of *Simons v. Cogan*, 549 A.2d 300, 303 (Del. 1988), the recent Delaware Supreme Court ruling which held, *inter alia*, that a corporate bond "represents a contractual entitlement to the repayment of a debt and does not represent an equitable interest in the issuing corporation necessary for the imposition of a trust relationship with concomitant fiduciary duties." Before such a fiduciary duty arises, "an existing property right or equitable interest supporting such a duty must exist." *Id.* at 304. A bondholder, that court concluded, "acquires no equitable interest, and remains a creditor of the corporation whose interests are protected by the contractual terms of the indenture." *Id.* Defendants argue that New York law is not to the contrary, but the single Supreme Court case they cite—a case decided over fifty years ago that was not squarely presented with the issue addressed by the *Simons* court-provides something less than dispositive support. *See Marx v. Merchants' National Properties, Inc.*, 148 Misc. 6, 7, 265 N. Y. S. 163, 165 (1933). For their part, plaintiffs more convincingly demonstrate that New York law applies than that New York law recognizes their claim.[33]

Regardless, this Court finds *Simons* persuasive, and believes that a New York court would agree with that conclusion. In the venerable case of *Meinhard v. Salmon*, 249 N.Y. 458, 164 N.E. 545 (1928), then Chief Judge Cardozo explained the obligations imposed on a fiduciary, and why those obligations are so special and rare:

> Many forms of conduct permissible in a workaday world for those acting at arm's length, are forbidden to those bound by fiduciary ties. A trustee is held to something stricter than the morals of the market place. Not honesty alone, but the punctilio of an honor the most sensitive, is then the standard of behavior. As to this there has developed a tradition that is unbending and inveterate. Uncompromising rigidity has been the attitude of courts of equity when petitioned to undermine the rule of undivided loyalty ... Only thus has the level of conduct for fiduciaries been kept at a level higher than that trodden by the crowd.

Id. at 464 (citation omitted). Before a court recognizes the duty of a "punctilio of an honor the most sensitive," it must be certain that the complainant is entitled to more than the "morals of the market place," and the protections offered by actions based on fraud, state statutes or the panoply of available federal securities laws. This Court has concluded that

---

33. The indenture provision designating New York law as controlling, *see supra* n.10, would, one might assume, resolve at least the issue of the applicable law. In quoting the relevant indenture provision, however, plaintiffs omit the proviso "except as may otherwise be required by mandatory provisions of law." Defendants, however, fail to argue that the internal affairs doctrine, which they assert dictates that Delaware law controls this question, is such a "mandatory provision of law." Nor do defendants respond to plaintiffs' reliance on *First National City Bank v. Banco Para El Comercio*, 462 U.S. 611, 621, 77 L. Ed. 2d 46, 103 S. Ct. 2591 (1983) ("Different conflicts principles apply, however, where the rights of third parties *external* to the corporation are at issue.") (emphasis in original, citation omitted). Ultimately, the point is academic; as explained below, the Court would grant defendants summary judgment on this Count under either New York or Delaware law.

the plaintiffs presently before it—sophisticated investors who are unsecured creditors—are not entitled to such additional protections.

Equally important, plaintiffs' position on this issue—that "A Company May Not Deliberately Deplete its Assets to the Injury of its Debtholders,"—provides no reasonable or workable limits, and is thus reminiscent of their implied covenant of good faith. Indeed, many indisputably legitimate corporate transactions would not survive plaintiffs' theory. With no workable limits, plaintiffs' envisioned duty would extend equally to trade creditors, employees, and every other person to whom the defendants are liable in any way. Of all such parties, these informed plaintiffs least require a Court's equitable protection; not only are they willing participants in a largely impersonal market, but they also possess the financial sophistication and size to secure their own protection.

Finally, plaintiffs cannot seriously allege unconscionability, given their sophistication and, at least judging from this action, the sophistication of their legal counsel as well. Under the undisputed facts of this case, this Court finds no actionable unconscionability.

* * *

QUESTIONS

1. Are indenture terms negotiated by issuers with anyone, or are they simply contracts of adhesion?

2. Is interpretation of debenture indenture terms a question of fact or law?

3. Why does the court suggest that uniform interpretation of boiler plate language in indentures is important?

4. Is parole evidence admissible on the intent of the parties to a debenture indenture? Should it matter whether the covenants are in publicly issued debt or in a negotiated bank loan agreement? Is it likely that interpretation of the intent of the parties in loan agreements would provide precedent for interpretation of public debt?

5. Does silence in the contract about LBOs create an ambiguity in the contract calling for parole evidence about the intent of the parties?

6. Is there an implied covenant of good faith that issuing corporations won't harm the value of the bonds?

7. Where an indenture is silent on whether the issuing corporation can take a certain action, what is the legal rule?

8. What is an implied covenant of good faith?

9. How does an implied covenant of good faith differ from a fiduciary duty?

10. What elements are required for a claim of frustration of purpose? Why aren't they present here?

NOTE

RJR Nabisco bonds dropped about 20% in value on the announcement by RJR Nabisco officials that they were considering a leveraged buyout, amounting to a $1 billion loss. Kenneth Lehn & Annette Poulsen, Contractual Resolution of Bondholder–Stockholder Conflicts in Leveraged Buyouts, 34 J. L. & Econ. 645, 646 (1991) One study found that restructurings such as LBOs resulted in average bondholder losses of 2.5%. Paul Asquith & Thierry A. Wizman, Event Risk, Wealth Redistribution and the Return to Existing Bondholders in Corporate Buyouts, 27 J. Fin. Econ. 195 (1991)

After the buyout RJR had outstanding indebtedness of $29 billion, and a debt-equity ratio of 23:1. In January of 1991 RJR settled its litigation with MetLife and Jefferson Pilot by exchanging their debt for new equity and some new debt. In March and April of 1991, KKR's principals realized that RJR would default on its debt unless restructuring were undertaken. In March RJR made offerings of common stock and new debt, raising $1.5 billion. Several high-interest junk bond issues were repurchased in the market, reducing outstanding junk bonds from $4.8 billion to $1.7 billion over the next eight months. Another debt issue was repurchased through an exchange offer for a combination of new preferred stock and cash. The cash for these transactions was raised from the sale of Del Monte for $5.7 billion. A new loan allowed RJR to redeem an issue of increasing rate notes held by institutions. In October, 1991 RJR made an exchange offer of its common stock for the preferred that it had issued a few months earlier in its debt retirement program. By December 1991 RJR's debt was reduced below $15 billion, and it lost its junk bond rating, which further reduced its interest costs.

The aftermath of LBOs was a series of changes in indenture provisions. Here is a sample indenture provision from APOGENT Technologies, Inc. dated Oct. 10, 2001 (note: "CODES" is an acronym for Senior Convertible Contingent Debt Securities):

SECTION 11.1. REPURCHASE RIGHTS.

* * *

(b) Change of Control Put.

In the event that a Change in Control shall occur, each Holder shall have the right (each, a "CHANGE OF CONTROL REPURCHASE RIGHT" and, together with the Optional Repurchase Right, each a "REPURCHASE RIGHT"), at the Holder's option, but subject to the provisions of Section 11.2 hereof, to require the Company to repurchase, and upon the exercise of such right the Company shall repurchase, all of such Holder's CODES not theretofore called for redemption, or any portion of the principal amount thereof that is equal to $1,000 or an integral multiple thereof as directed by such Holder pursuant to Section 11.3 (provided that no single CODES may be repurchased in part unless the portion of the principal amount of such CODES to be Outstanding after such repurchase is equal to $1,000 or an integral multiple thereof), on the date (the "CHANGE OF

CONTROL REPURCHASE DATE'' and, together with the Optional Repurchase Date, each a ''REPURCHASE DATE'') that is a Business Day no earlier than 30 days nor later than 60 days after the date of the Company Notice at a purchase price in cash equal to 100% of the principal amount of the CODES to be repurchased (the ''CHANGE OF CONTROL REPURCHASE PRICE'' and, together with the Optional Repurchase Price, each a ''REPURCHASE PRICE''), plus accrued and unpaid Interest (including Contingent Interest) to, but excluding, the Change of Control Repurchase Date; provided, however, that installments of Interest (including Contingent Interest) on CODES whose Stated Maturity is prior to or on the Change of Control Repurchase Date shall be payable to the Holders of such CODES, or one or more Predecessor Securities, registered as such on the relevant Regular Record Date according to terms and the provisions of Section 2.1 hereof.

Another approach appears in the indenture of L 3 Communications Holdings, Inc., dated Dec. 20, 2001:

SECTION 1.1 DEFINITIONS.

''Adjusted Interest Rate'' means, with respect to any Reset Transaction, the rate per annum that is the arithmetic average of the rates quoted by two Reference Dealers selected by the Company or its successor as the rate at which interest on the Securities should accrue so that the Fair Market Value, expressed in Dollars, of a Security immediately after the later of:

(1) the public announcement of such Reset Transaction; or

(2) the public announcement of a change in dividend policy in connection with such Reset Transaction;

will most closely equal the average Trading Price of a Security for the 20 Trading Days preceding the date of public announcement of such Reset Transaction; provided that the Adjusted Interest Rate shall not be less than 4.00% per annum.

* * *

''Interest Rate'' means, (a) if a Reset Transaction has not occurred, 4.00% per annum, or (b) following the occurrence of a Reset Transaction, the Adjusted Interest Rate related to such Reset Transaction to, but not including the effective date of any succeeding Reset Transaction.

* * *

''Reset Transaction'' means: (i) a merger, consolidation or statutory share exchange to which the entity that is the issuer of the Common Stock into which the Securities are then convertible is a party, (ii) a sale of all or substantially all the assets of that entity, (iii) a recapitalization of that Common Stock or (iv) a distribution described in Section 12.4(d), in each case if after the effective date of the transaction or distribution the Securities would be convertible into:

(1) shares of an entity the common stock of which had a Dividend Yield for the four fiscal quarters of such entity immediately preceding the public announcement of such transaction or distribution that was more than 2.5% higher then the Dividend Yield on the Common Stock (or other common stock then issuable upon conversion of the Securities) for the four fiscal quarters preceding the public announcement of such transaction or distribution; or

(2) shares of an entity that announces a dividend policy prior to the effective date of such transaction or distribution which policy, if implemented, would result in a Dividend Yield on such entity's common stock for the next four fiscal quarters that would result in such a 2.5% increase.

Quick Check Question 6.1

If you represented a lender considering a large loan to Scientific Atlanta (see the financial statements in Chapter Two), what types of restrictions on new debt would you want to see? Do any of the financial ratios in Appendix 2-B seem promising measures of the limits you might want to impose?

B.   ALTERATION OF RISKS

On Financial Contracting: An Analysis of Bond Covenants

Clifford W. Smith. Jr. and Jerold B. Warner.
7 Journal of Financial Economics 117 (1979).

* * *

2.1.1.   *Restrictions on investments*

Description. Bond covenants frequently restrict the extent to which the firm can become a claimholder in another business enterprise. That restriction, known as the "investment" restriction, applies to common stock investments, loans, extensions of credit, and advances. Alternative forms of this covenant suggested in *Commentaries* either (1) flatly prohibit financial investments of this kind, (2) permit these financial investments only if net tangible assets meet a certain minimum. or (3) permit such investments subject to either an aggregate dollar limitation or a limitation representing a prespecified percentage of the firm's capitalization (owners' equity plus long-term debt).

Analysis. We suggest that stockholders contractually restrict their ability to acquire financial assets in order to limit their ability to engage in asset substitution after the bonds are issued. However, the inclusion of the investment covenant imposes opportunity costs. First, if there are economies of scale in raising additional capital, or costs associated with changing dividends, then allowing the purchase of financial assets can reduce these costs. Second, if a firm is involved in merger activities, the purchase of equity claims of the target firm prior to the merger can also provide benefits. Thus, the Costly Contracting Hypothesis* predicts that bond contracts of firms involved in merger activities, for which the opportunity cost of restricting 'investments' is therefore high, will contain less restrictive investment covenants. However, our analysis does not predict which of the above forms the investment restriction will take.

2.1.2.   Restrictions on the disposition of assets

Description. "The transfer of the assets of the obligor substantially as an entirety can be restricted by a standard boilerplate. The contract can also require that the firm not 'otherwise than in the ordinary course of business, sell, lease, transfer, or otherwise dispose of any substantial part of its properties and assets, including ... any manufacturing plant or substantially all properties and assets constituting the business of a division, branch, or other unit operation'. Another restriction is to permit asset disposition only up to a fixed dollar amount, or only so long as (1) the proceeds from the sale are applied to the purchase of new fixed assets, or (2) some fraction of the proceeds is used to retire the firm's debt."

Analysis. The Costly Contracting Hypothesis suggests that restrictions on the sale of substantial units of the firm's assets are observed because, in general, the proceeds if assets are sold piecemeal will be less than if sold as a going concern. By imposing the higher cost of piecemeal sale, this covenant also raises the cost to stockholders of substituting variance increasing assets for those currently owned by the firm.

One cost associated with flat prohibitions on the sale of particular assets rises from the fact that the firm is not permitted to divest itself of those assets whose value to others is greater than the value to itself. Thus the restriction which permits asset sale if the proceeds are applied to the purchase of new fixed assets lowers this opportunity cost. However, a provision which permits such asset exchange is costly because it allows for the possibility of obtaining variance increasing negative net present value assets in the exchange. The stipulation that a fraction of the proceeds from the sale of assets be used for the retirement of the firm's debt makes asset substitution more expensive for stockholders by requiring a concurrent increase in the coverage on, and thus the value of, the outstanding debt.

2.1.3.   Secured debt

Description. Securing debt gives the bondholders title to pledged assets until the bonds are paid in full. Thus, when secured debt is issued the firm cannot dispose of the pledged assets without first obtaining permission of the bondholders.

---

* The authors pose two competing hypotheses: (1) Modigliani & Miller's "Irrelevance Hypothesis," described in Chapter Four, that capital structure doesn't matter, and (2) the "Costly Contracting Hypothesis," "that control of the bondholder-stockholder conflict through financial contracts can increase the value of the firm."—Ed.

Analysis. We suggest that the issuance of secured debt lowers the total costs of borrowing by controlling the incentives for stockholders to take projects which reduce the value of the firm; since bondholders hold title to the assets, secured debt limits asset substitution. Secured debt also lowers administrative costs and enforcement costs by ensuring that the lender has clear title to the assets and by preventing the lender's claim from being jeopardized if the borrower subsequently issues additional debt. In addition, collateralization reduces expected foreclosure expenses because it is less expensive to take possession of property to which the lender already has established title.

However, secured debt involves out of pocket costs (e.g. required reports to the debt-holders, filing fees. and other administrative expenses). Securing debt also involves opportunity costs by restricting the firm from potentially profitable dispositions of collateral.

The Costly Contracting Hypothesis leads to two predictions about the use of secured debt. First, if the firm goes into bankruptcy proceedings and the collateral is judged necessary for the continued operation of the firm, the bankruptcy judge can prohibit the bondholders from taking possession of the property. Thus for firms where liquidation is more likely than reorganization (e.g., for smaller firms), the issuance of secured debt will be greater. Second. we would expect more frequent use of secured debt the less specialized the firm's resources. To the extent that assets (such as a patent right) are highly specialized and firm-specific, their value is greater to the firm than in the market place. Consequently, it will be costly to the stockholders if they dispose of such assets in order to engage in asset substitution. The more specialized the assets, the more costly is asset substitution to stockholders, the tighter the implicit constraint on asset sale, and thus the less likely is the use of secured debt.

2.1.4. *Restrictions on mergers*

Description. Some indenture agreements contain a flat prohibition on mergers. Others permit the acquisition of other firms provided that certain conditions are met. For example, *Commentaries* suggests restrictions in which the merger is permitted only if the net tangible assets of the firm, calculated on a post-merger basis, meet a certain dollar minimum, or are at least a certain fraction of long-term debt. The merger can also be made contingent on there being no default on any indenture provision after the transaction is completed.

The acquisition and consolidation of the firm into another can be permitted subject to certain requirements. For example, the corporation into which the company is merged must assume all of the obligations in the initial indenture. Article 800 of the American Bar Foundation *Model Debenture Indenture Provisions* also requires that there be no act of default after completion of the consolidation, and that the company certify that fact through the delivery to the trustee of an officer's certificate and an opinion of counsel.

Analysis. Since the stockholders of the two firms must approve a merger, the market value of the equity claims of both the acquired and acquiring firm must be expected to rise or the merger will not be approved by stockholders of the respective firms. A merger between two firms usually results in changes in the value of particular classes of outstanding claims because both the asset and liability structure of the resulting firm differ from that of the predecessor firms. The effects of a merger on the value of particular claims depend upon: (1) the degree of synergy brought about by the merger, (2) the resources consumed in accomplishing the merger, (3) the variance rates of the pre-merger firms' cash flows, (4) the correlation coefficient between the merged firms' cash flows, and (5) the capital structure (i.e., ratio of face value of debt to market value of all claims) of the respective firms. A merger Leaves the value of outstanding, debt claims unaffected if (1) the merger involves no synergy, (2) there are no transactions costs, (3) the pre-merger firm's cash flows have equal variance rates, (4) the correlation coefficient between the merged firms' cash flows is + 1, and (5) the pre-merger firms have the same capital structure.

With no contractual constraints against mergers, the value of the bondholders' claims can be reduced due to the effect of a difference in variance rates or a difference in capital structures. Our analysis implies, then, that merger restrictions limit the stockholders' ability to use mergers to increase either the firm's variance rate or the debt to asset ratio to the detriment of the bondholders. Note that to the extent that synergistic mergers are prevented by this covenant, the firm suffers an opportunity loss.

* * *

2.4.3.   Callability provisions

Description. The firm's right to redeem the debentures before maturity at a stated price is typically included in the Indenture agreement. Without the inclusion of the callability provision in the indenture agreement, a debenture holder cannot be compelled to accept payment of his debenture prior to its stated maturity date. In the usual case, the call price is not constant over the life of the bonds. The redemption price in a callable bond normally is initially set equal to the public offering price plus one year's interest on the bond. The schedule of call prices then typically scales the call premium to zero by a date of one year prior to the maturity of the bonds, although it is sometimes as early, as two to five years prior to maturity.

Analysis. We have suggested that if agency costs of equity are zero and recapitalization of the firm is costless, the firm will accept all projects with positive net present values and thus the stockholder-bondholder conflict of interest will be solved. One cost of buying out bondholders in a recapitalization results from the additional premium the bondholders demand for the firm to repurchase the bonds. **Since** the firm cannot vote bonds which it repurchases, a bilateral monopoly results from the attempt to repurchase the outstanding bonds. With a bilateral monopoly it is indeterminate how the gains will be divided between stockholders and bondholders. As Bodie/Taggart (1978) and Wier (1978) argue, a call provision places an upper limit on the gains which the bondholders can obtain. Wier notes further that if side payments can be negotiated costlessly, then the bondholder monopoly is unimportant from the standpoint of the value of the firm; the callability provision merely redistributes the property rights to the monopoly from bondholders to stockholders. Implicit in the argument that the call provision affects the total value of the firm is the notion that the bilateral monopoly implies real resource expenditures on negotiation.

It should also be noted that our argument cannot represent the only reason for callable bonds: after all, government bonds are often callable but there is no obvious investment incentive problem which such a provision addresses.

Variation on Model Covenants, § 8–1: Company May Consolidate or Merge Only on Certain Terms.

The Company shall not consolidate with or merge into any other corporation or convey, transfer or lease its properties and assets substantially as an entirety to any Person, and the Company shall not permit any Person to consolidate with or merge into the Company, unless:

(a) in case the Company shall consolidate with or merge into another corporation or convey, transfer or lease its properties and assets substantially as an entirety to any Person, the corporation formed by such consolidation or into which the Company is merged or the Person which acquires by conveyance or transfer, or which leases, the properties and assets of the Company substantially as an entirety shall be a corporation organized and existing under the laws of the United States of America, any State thereof or the District of Columbia and shall expressly assume, by an indenture supplemental hereto, executed and delivered to the Trustee, in form reasonably satisfactory to the Trustee, the due and punctual payment of the principal of (and premium, if any) and interest, if any, on all the Outstanding Securities of all series and the performance of every covenant of this Indenture on the part of the Company to be performed or observed;

(b) immediately after giving effect to such transaction, no Event of Default, and no event which, after notice or lapse of time or both, would become an Event of Default, shall have happened and be continuing; and

(c) if a supplemental indenture is required in connection with such transaction, the Company shall have delivered to the Trustee an Officers' Certificate and an Opinion of Counsel, each stating that such consolidation, merger, conveyance, transfer or lease and such supplemental indenture comply with this Article and that all conditions precedent herein provided or relating to such transaction have been complied with.

Variation on Model Covenants, § 8–2: Successor Corporation Substituted.

Upon any consolidation by the Company with or merger by the Company into any other corporation or any conveyance, transfer or lease of the properties and assets of the Company substantially as an entirety in accordance with Section ___ the successor corporation formed by such consolidation or into which the Company is merged or to which such conveyance, transfer or lease is made shall succeed to, and be substituted for, and may exercise every right and power of, the Company under this Indenture with the same effect as if such successor corporation had been named as the Company herein, and thereafter, the predecessor corporation shall be relieved of the performance and observance of all obligations and covenants under this Indenture and the Securities (and any Coupons appertaining thereto), including but not limited to the obligation to make payment of the principal of (and premium, if any) and interest, if any, on all the Outstanding Securities of all series (and any Coupons appertaining thereto), and, in the event of such conveyance, transfer or lease, may be liquidated and dissolved.

Model Covenants, § 10–13: Restrictions on Dispositions of Assets.

Subject to the provisions of Section ___, the Company will not convey, transfer or lease, any substantial part of its assets unless, in the opinion of the Board of Directors of the Company, such conveyance, transfer or lease, considered together with all prior conveyances, transfers and leases of assets of the Company, would not materially and adversely affect the interest of the Holders of the Notes or the ability of the Company to meet its obligations as they become due.

Variation on Model Covenants, § 10–16: Investments.

The Company will not make, or permit any of its Subsidiaries to make, any loan or advance to any Person or purchase or otherwise acquire, or permit any such Subsidiary to purchase or otherwise acquire, any capital stock, assets, obligations or other securities of, make any capital contribution to, or otherwise invest in, or acquire any interest in, any Person (all such transactions being herein called "Investments"), except:

(a) Investments in Liquid Assets;

(b) Investments in the Company or any or its Consolidated Subsidiaries;

(c) Investments in accounts, contract rights and general intangibles (as defined in the Uniform Commercial Code) or notes or other instruments receivable, arising from the sale, lease or other furnishings of goods or services by the Company or any Subsidiary in the ordinary course of its business;

(d) Investments in equity interests (including stocks and convertible debt securities) of corporations which do not become Consolidated Subsidiaries made with the proceeds of the issuance of stock by the Company;

(e) Acquisitions permitted by Section ___;

(f) Investments (including stocks, equity interests and convertible debt securities) of corporations that do not become Consolidated Subsidiaries made with the proceeds of the sale or other disposition of any capitalized

Investment permitted by clause (d), providing the Company gives the Banks notice of such Investment under this clause; and

(g) additional Investments not exceeding in the aggregate at any one time outstanding $20,000,000.

C.   DISTRIBUTIONS

On Financial Contracting: An Analysis of Bond Covenants

Clifford W. Smith. Jr. and Jerold B. Warner.
7 Journal of Financial Economics 117 (1979).

* * *

2.1.6.   *Covenants which indirectly restrict production/investment policy*

Stockholder use (or misuse) of production/investment policy frequently involves not some action, but the failure to take a certain action (e.g., failure to accept a positive net present value project). Because of this, investment policy can be very expensive to monitor, since ascertaining that the firm's production/investment policy does not maximize the firm's market value depends on magnitudes which are costly to observe. Solutions to this problem are not obvious. For example, if the indenture were to require the bondholders (rather than the stockholders) to establish the firm's investment policy, the problem would not be solved; the bondholders, acting in their self interest, would choose an investment policy which maximized the value of the bonds, not the value of the firm. In addition, there are other costs associated with giving bondholders a role in establishing the firm's investment policy. For instance, as we discuss in section 3, legal costs can be imposed on bondholders if they are deemed to have assumed control of the corporation.*

However, direct restrictions on the stockholder's choice of production/investment policy are only one way to limit the projects in which the firm can engage. Covenants constraining the firm's dividend and financing policies can also be written in a way which serves a similar function, since the firm's production/investment, dividend, and financing policies are linked through the cash flow identity. If direct restrictions on production/investment policy were sufficiently expensive to enforce, dividend and financing policy covenants would be the only efficient way of constraining the firm's actions.

2.2.   *Bond covenants restricting the payment of dividends*

Description. Cash dividend payments to stockholders, if financed by a reduction in investment, reduce the value of the firm's bonds by decreasing the expected value of the firm's assets at the maturity date of the bonds, making default more likely. Thus, it is not surprising that bond covenants

---

* See Chapter Four, Part 6.C, for treatment of lender liability.—Ed.

frequently restrict the payment of cash dividends to shareholders. Since the payment of dividends in cash is just one form which distributions to stockholders can take, actual dividend covenants reflect alternative possibilities. For example, if the firm enters the market and repurchases its own stock the coverage on the debt decreases in exactly the same way as it would if a cash dividend were paid, The constraints discussed in *Commentaries* relate not only to cash dividends, but to "all distributions on account of or in respect of capital stock . . . whether they be dividends. redemptions. purchases, retirements, partial liquidations or capital reductions and whether in cash, in kind, or in the form of debt obligations of the company".

The dividend covenant usually establishes a limit on distributions to stockholders by defining an inventory of funds available for dividend payments over the life of the bonds. The inventory is not constant: rather, it is allowed to change as a function of certain variables whose values can be influenced by the stockholders. * * * Hence the inventory of funds is a positive function of the earnings which the firm has accumulated, a positive function of the extent to which the firm has sold new equity claims. and a negative function of the dividends paid since the bonds were issued. . . .

The payment of a dividend is not permitted if its payment would cause the inventory to be drawn below zero. The inventory can become negative if the firm's earnings are negative. In that case. no dividend is permitted. However, stockholders are not required to make up the deficiency. * * *

Analysis. This form of dividend covenant has several interesting features. The dividend restriction is not an outright prohibition on the payment of dividends. In fact, the stockholders are permitted to have any level of dividends they choose, so long as the payment of those dividends is financed out of new earnings or through the sale of new equity claims. The dividend covenant acts a restriction not on dividends *per se*, but on the payment of dividends financed by issuing debt or by the sale of the firm's existing assets, either of which would reduce the coverage on, and thus the value of, the debt.

* * *

By placing a maximum on distributions, the dividend covenant effectively places a minimum on investment expenditures by the owners of the firm, as Myers and Kalay (1979) argue. This reduces the underinvestment problem discussed by Myers, since so long as the firm has to invest, profitable projects are less likely to be turned down.

While having a tight dividend constraint controls the stockholders incentives associated with the dividend payout problem, there are several associated costs. An outright prohibition on dividends or allowing dividends but setting k^* less than one increases the probability that the firm will be forced to invest when it has no available profitable projects. Investment in

---

* The symbol k in this article represents a fraction between zero and one multiplied by the sum of earnings, proceeds from the sale of stock, plus a cushion known as the "dip."—Ed.

securities of other firms is not always possible, since purchases of capital market instruments (which in the absence of corporate taxes have zero net present value) are frequently prohibited by the investments covenant we discussed in section 2.1. Even if financial investments are not restricted, Kalay argues that if the firm pays income taxes on its earnings, the taxation of the returns from the financial assets makes them negative net present value projects.

The tighter restriction on dividends implied by a lower k also increases the stockholders' incentives to engage in asset substitution, and increases the gain to the firm's shareholders from choosing high variance, negative net present value projects. Assume that negative net present value projects generate negative accounting earnings. Then ... the inventory available for dividends will be reduced by taking such a project. The lower the value of k, the smaller the reduction in the inventory. To the extent that dividends transfer wealth to stockholders, the marginal impact of lowering k is thus to increase the gain (or decrease the loss) to shareholders from accepting such projects. However. as we discuss below, a lower k also confers benefits, since it reduces the stockholders' incentive to engage in "creative accounting" to increase reported earnings.

If it is costly to restrict dividends, not all debt instruments will include a dividend restriction. Dividend covenants would be expected only if there are offsetting benefits. One prediction of our analysis is that the presence of a dividend covenant should be related to the maturity of the debt. Thus, short-term debt instruments (such as commercial paper) are less likely to contain dividend restrictions than long-term debt; if liquidation of the firm's assets within a short period of time is sufficiently costly to the shareholders, they are better off not selling the firm's assets for cash in order to pay themselves a dividend. This implicit constraint on dividend payout becomes less restrictive the longer the time to maturity of the debt, and the cost-offsetting benefits of an explicit dividend constraint thus become greater as a function of maturity.

Evidence. Kalay develops and tests a number of propositions about how the dividend constraint will be set. He argues that the shareholders' incentive to sell assets for cash is greater the higher the fraction of the firm consisting of debt: the higher that fraction, the greater the potential wealth transfer to stockholders. Consistent with the argument that the dividend constraint involves costs, he finds a significant negative cross-sectional relationship between the dividends which can be paid out under the constraint and the firm's debt/equity ratio.

Kalay also reports that firms do not always pay out all of the dividends to which they are entitled under the indenture agreement. He argues that firms maintain such an "inventory of payable funds" because having an inventory reduces the probability that the firm will be unable to pay dividends and thus be forced to invest when there are temporarily no profitable investment projects. However, if stockholders maintain an inventory and fail to pay out all funds available for dividends, wealth transfers from bondholders are foregone. On this basis, Kalay posits that the shareholders' incentive to maintain an inventory is lower the higher the firm's leverage. That proposition is consistent with his finding that there is a significant negative relationship between the firm's debt/equity ratio and the (size adjusted) "inventory of payable funds".

2.2.1. Control of investment incentives when the inventory is negative

Throughout the above analysis we have assumed that the inventory of funds available for the payment of dividends . . . is positive. If the firm has been experiencing negative earnings, the inventory can become negative; with a negative inventory, no dividends can be paid. The negative earnings which lead to a dividend prohibition are likely to be associated with a fall in the value of the firm, and an increase in both its debt/equity ratio and the probability of default on its debt. Hence at the times when a dividend prohibition comes into play, the firm is also likely to be faced with greater incentives to engage in asset substitution and claim dilution.

When the firm is doing poorly, the dividend constraint is not capable of controlling the investment and financing policy problem induced by the presence of risky debt. But the direct limitations on production/investment policy we discussed in section 2.1 can limit the stockholders' actions when the inventory for payment of dividends is negative. In addition, financing policy covenants not only address the claim dilution problem, but independently reinforce the effect of the dividend covenant in restricting production/investment policy.

As you review these covenants, recall our review of financial ratios in Chapter Two, and the availability of Risk Management Associates' Annual Statement Studies for most of the North American Industry Classification System. An astute representative of an issuer should be aware of what ratios are reasonable for a lender or an underwriter to demand for firms in that industry.

Sample Covenant: Current Ratio.

The Company shall maintain at all times a ratio of Consolidated Current Assets to Consolidated Current Liabilities of not less than 1.75 to 1.

Sample Covenant: Leverage Ratio.

The Company shall maintain at all times a ratio of Total Liabilities to Consolidated Tangible Net Worth of not greater than 1 to 1.

Sample Covenant: Minimum Consolidated Tangible Net Worth.

The Company will at no time permit Consolidated Tangible Net Worth to be less than the sum of (i) $288,981,000 plus (ii) 50% of consolidated net income of the Company and its Consolidated Subsidiaries for the period from January 31, 1993 through the end of the Company's then most recent fiscal quarter (treated for this purpose as a single accounting period) plus (iii) 50% of the net proceeds received by the Company from the issuance and sale subsequent to January 30, 1993 of shares of any class of the capital stock of the Company; provided, however, that in the event the Company incurs a net loss in one or more of its fiscal quarters ending after January 30, 1993, the results of such quarter or quarters shall be excluded in calculating consolidated net income of the Company and its Consolidated Subsidiaries pursuant to clause (ii) above.

Variation on ABF Model Covenants, § 10–12: Restrictions on Dividends, Redemptions, etc.

(a) The Company will not:

(1) declare or pay any dividend or make any other distribution on any Equity Securities of the Company, except dividends or distributions payable in Equity Securities of the Company, or

(2) purchase, redeem or otherwise acquire or retire for value any Equity Securities of the Company, except (and provided all other covenants of this Indenture are complied with) Equity Securities acquired upon conversion thereof into other Equity Securities of the Company or pursuant to an insurance funded buy-sell agreement covering the death or disability of a shareholder of the Company, or pursuant to a buy-sell agreement during the life time of a shareholder of the Company if purchased under a debt obligation which is Subordinated Indebtedness of the Company with a minimum term of five years with equal annual payments (a "Buy–Sell Debt Obligation"), or

(3) permit a Subsidiary to purchase, redeem or otherwise acquire or retire for value any Equity Securities of the Company,

if, upon giving effect to such dividend, purchase, redemption or the acquisition, the aggregate amount expended for all such purposes subsequent to December 31, 1995 would exceed the sum of

(1) 50% of the Consolidated Net Income accumulated subsequent to December 31, 1995;

(2) the aggregate of the net proceeds received by the Company or a Wholly–Owned Subsidiary from the sale or issuance after December 31, 1995 (other than to a Subsidiary or upon the Conversion of Equity Securities or Indebtedness or the Company or a Wholly–Owned Subsidiary) of Equity Securities of the Company, said net proceeds being deemed for the purposes of this Section to equal the aggregate of (a) the cash, if any, received by the Company or a Wholly–Owned Subsidiary from such sale or issue, plus (b) the value of any consideration, other than cash, received by the Company or a Wholly–Owned Subsidiary from such sale or issue, as determined by resolution of the Board of Directors; and

(3) the net proceeds (as above defined) received by the Company or a Wholly–Owned Subsidiary from the issuance or sale (other than to the Company or a Subsidiary) of any convertible Indebtedness of the Company which Indebtedness has been converted into Equity Securities of the Company after December 31, 1995.

(b) The Company will not (1) declare or pay any dividend or make any other distribution, other than a Regular Dividend, on any Equity Securities of the Company, except dividends or distributions payable in Equity Securities of the Company, or (2) purchase, redeem or otherwise acquire or retire for value any Equity Securities of the Company, except Equity Securities acquired upon conversion thereof into other Equity Securities of the Company or pursuant to an insurance funded buy-sell agreement covering the death or disability of a shareholder of the Company, or pursuant to a Buy–Sell Debt Obligation, (3) or, except as permitted by Section ___ herein, permit a Subsidiary to purchase, redeem or otherwise acquire or retire for value any Equity Securities of the Company, if, upon giving effect to such dividend, distribution, purchase, redemption or other acquisition, the Consolidated Tangible Net Worth of the Company would be reduced to less than an amount equal to 150% of the aggregate principal amount of Debentures and all Parity Indebtedness then outstanding.

(c) The provisions of this Section ___ shall not prevent (1) the payment of annual year-end bonuses to key employees, executive officers and shareholder employees of the Company pursuant to the bonus plan described in and consistent with the restrictions in Section ___ hereof, (2) the payment of any dividend within 60 days after the date of declaration thereof, if at such date such declaration complied with the foregoing provisions, although the dividends so paid shall be considered in determining subsequent restrictions under this Section or (3) the acquisition or retirement of any Equity Securities of the Company by exchange for, or upon conversion of, or out of the proceeds of the substantially concurrent sale (other than to a Subsidiary) of, other Equity Securities of the Company, and no effect shall be given to any such acquisition or retirement or the proceeds of any sale, conversion or exchange in any computation made under this Section. A certificate of a firm of independent certified public accountants shall be conclusive evidence of the amount of accumulated Consolidated Net Income and the amount of Consolidated Tangible Net Worth.

D. UNDERINVESTMENT—ASSET MAINTENANCE

On Financial Contracting: An Analysis of Bond Covenants

Clifford W. Smith. Jr. and Jerold B. Warner.
7 Journal of Financial Economics 117 (1979).

* * *

2.1. *Restrictions on the production/investment policy*

The stockholders' production/investment decisions could be directly constrained by explicitly specifying the projects which the firm is allowed to undertake. Alternatively, if it were costless to enforce, the debt contract could simply require the shareholders to accept all projects (and engage in only those actions) with positive net present values. Although certain covenants directly restrict the firm's investment policy, debt contracts discussed in *Commentaries* do not generally contain extensive restrictions of either form.

* * *

2.1.5. Covenants requiring the maintenance of assets

Description. The covenants we have discussed constrain production/investment policy by prohibiting certain actions. However, the firm's operating decisions can also be limited by *requiring* that it take certain actions, that it invest in certain projects, or hold particular assets. Examples of such covenants are those requiring the maintenance of the firm's properties and maintenance of the firm's working capital (i.e., current assets less current liabilities). *Commentaries* offers covenants which require the firm to maintain working capital above a certain minimum level. Frequently, activities such as mergers are made contingent upon the maintenance of working capital

Analysis. While a covenant can require that the firm maintain its properties, such a covenant will not have much impact if it is expensive to enforce. However, if the maintenance is performed by an independent agent, enforcement costs are expected to be lower and such a restriction will be effective. For example, in the shipping industry. where maintenance services are typically provided through third parties, bond covenants frequently explicitly include service and dry-docking schedules in the indenture.

We suggest that the working capital requirement is included because any violation of the covenant provides a signal to the lender. This signal can result in renegotiation of the debt contract, an alternative preferable to default when bankruptcy is more costly than renegotiation. This hypothesis is consistent with the interpretation of the working capital covenant in *Commentaries* (p. 453): "If a breach of the covenant occurs, the lender is in a position to use this early warning to take whatever remedial action is necessary."

ABF Model Covenants, § 10–5: Maintenance of Properties.

The Company will cause all its properties used or useful in the conduct of its business to be maintained and kept in good condition, repair and working order and supplied with all necessary equipment and will cause to be made all necessary repairs, renewals, replacements, betterments and improvements thereof, all as in the judgment of the Company may be necessary so that the business carried on in connection therewith may be properly and advantageously conducted at all times; provided, however, that nothing in this Section shall prevent the Company from discontinuing the operation and maintenance of any of its properties if such discontinuance is, in the judgment of the Company, desirable in the conduct of its business and not disadvantageous in any material respect to the Debentureholders.

ABF Model Covenants, § 10–6: Statement as to Compliance.

The Company will deliver to the Trustee, within 90 days after the end of each fiscal year, a written statement signed by the President or a Vice President of the Company, stating, as to each signer thereof, that:

(1) a review of the activities of the Company during such year and of performance under this Indenture has been made under his supervision; and

(2) to the best of his knowledge, based on such review, the Company has fulfilled all its obligations under this Indenture throughout such year, or, if there has been a default in the fulfillment of any such obligation, specifying each such default known to him and the nature and status thereof.*

ABF Model Covenants, § 10–7: Corporate Existence.

Subject to Article 8, the Company will do or cause to be done all things necessary to preserve and keep in full force and effect its corporate existence, rights (charter and statutory) and franchises; provided, however, that the Company shall not be required to preserve any right or franchise or any minor business activity if the Board of Directors shall determine that the preservation thereof is no longer desirable in the conduct of the business of the Company and that the loss thereof is not disadvantageous in any material respect to the Debentureholders.

Variation on ABF Model Covenants, § 10–9: Insurance.

The Company will at all times cause all buildings, plants, equipment and other insurable properties owned or operated by it or any Subsidiary to be properly insured and kept insured with responsible insurance carriers, against loss or damage by fire and other hazards, to the extent that such properties are usually insured by corporations owning or operation plants and properties or a similar character in the same localities; provided, however, that nothing in this Section shall prevent the Company or any Subsidiary from maintaining any self-insurance program covering minor risks if adequate reserves are maintained in connection with such program.

A variation on ABF Model Covenants, § 10–9: Sample Covenant 6.

The Company shall obtain and deliver to the Trustee, for the benefit of the Debentureholders during the term of the Debentures, a life insurance

---

* This is contemplated by § 314(a)(2) of the Trust Indenture Act, but no rules adopted by the SEC implement it.

"Sec. 314(a) Each person who, as set forth in the registration statement or application, is or is to be an obligor upon the indenture securities covered thereby shall—

* * *

"(2) to file [sic] with the indenture trustee and the Commission, in accordance with rules and regulations prescribed by the Commission, such additional information, documents, and reports with respect to compliance by such obligor with the conditions and covenants provided for in the indenture, as may be required by such rules and regulations, ..."

—Ed.

policy from an insurer acceptable to the Trustee insuring in the amount of the lesser of (i) $1,000,000 or (ii) the maximum amount of insurance that can be maintained with an annual premium of Seven Thousand Five Hundred Dollars ($7,500) on the life of Peter Pflaum, on which the Debentureholders are the primary beneficiaries and payees (the "Key-man Insurance"). The Company shall be named as a secondary beneficiary in accordance with the distribution provisions set forth below. The Company shall maintain such Key-man Insurance in full force and effect throughout the term of the Debentures and this Indenture.

E. CONVERSION RIGHTS AS SUBSTITUTES FOR COVENANTS

Chapter Eight will treat options and convertible securities more thoroughly, but it is important to note the role conversion features play in providing some form of protection for bondholders. Typically where convertible features are included, there are relatively few negative covenants. Often the convertible feature signals relatively risky debt, for which the issuer will pay a relatively low current interest rate, in exchange for the conversion feature. Conversion features are an important part of a related type of security—preferred stock, as well. Particularly when venture capitalists receive preferred stock, they expect no current dividends, because the company has no current earnings, and is "burning cash" in an effort to develop a viable business. Accordingly, the principal protection for venture capitalists (aside from seats on the board of directors and voting rights) is the conversion feature.

On Financial Contracting: An Analysis of Bond Covenants

Clifford W. Smith. Jr. and Jerold B. Warner.
7 Journal of Financial Economics 117 (1979).

* * *

2.4.2. *Convertibility provisions*

Description. A convertible debenture is one which gives the holder the right to exchange the debentures for other securities of the company, usually shares of common stock and usually without payment of further compensation. * * *

Analysis. Jensen/Meckling (1976) and Mikkelson (1978) discuss the use of convertible debt as a way to control aspects of the bondholder-stockholder conflict of interest. With non-convertible debt outstanding the stockholders have the incentive to take projects which raise the variability of the firm's cash flows. The stockholders can increase the value of the equity by adding a new project with a negative net present value if the firm's cash flow variability rises sufficiently. The inclusion of a convertibility provision in the debt reduces this incentive. The conversion privilege is like a call option written by the stockholders and attached to the debt contract. It reduces the stockholders' incentive to increase the variability of the firm's cash flows, because with a higher variance rate, the attached call option becomes more valuable. Therefore the stockholders' gain from increasing the variance is smaller with the convertible debt outstanding than with nonconvertible debt.

However, not all debt contracts include a convertibility provision since it is costly to do so. For example, the underinvestment problem is exacerbated with convertible debt outstanding.

F. SINKING FUNDS

On Financial Contracting: An Analysis of Bond Covenants

Clifford W. Smith. Jr. and Jerold B. Warner.
7 Journal of Financial Economics 117 (1979).

* * *

2.4. *Bond covenants modifying the pattern of payoffs to bondholders*

There are several provisions which specify a particular pattern of payoffs to bondholders in a way which controls various sources of stockholder-bondholder conflict of interest.

2.4.1. *Sinking funds*

Description. A sinking fund is simply a means of amortizing part or all of an indebtedness prior to its maturity. A sinking fund bond is like an installment loan.[44] In the case of a public bond issue, the periodic payments can be invested either in the bonds which are to be retired by the fund or in some other securities. The sinking fund payments can be fixed, variable or contingent. For the years 1963–1965, 82 percent of all publicly-offered issues included sinking fund provisions.

Analysis. A sinking fund affects the firm's production/investment policy through the dividend constraint.... [I]f a sinking fund is included in the indenture, principal repayment, P, will be positive prior to the maturity date of the bond; the book value of the assets of the firm can decline over the life of the bond issue without violating the dividend constraint. A sinking fund reduces the possibility that the dividend constraint will require investment when no profitable projects are available. One potential cost associated with the dividend constraint is thus reduced.

Myers (1977) has suggested that sinking funds are a device to reduce creditors' exposure in parallel with the expected decline in the value of the assets supporting the debt. Myers' analysis implies that sinking funds would be more likely to be included in debt issues (1) the higher the

---

44. In a private placement, the amortization may simply require periodic partial payments to the holder. An alternative to a sinking fund is to provide for serial maturities with part of the issue maturing at fixed dates. This practice is rarely used in the corporate bond market presumably because with fewer identical contracts, maintenance of a secondary market in the bond contracts is more expensive.

fraction of debt in the capital structure, (2) the greater the anticipated future discretionary investment by the firm and (3) the higher the probability that the project will have a limited lifetime. One industry which illustrates an extreme of the last of these characteristics is the gas pipeline industry. The sinking fund payments required in some gas pipeline debentures are related to the remaining available gas in the field.

Not all debt issues have sinking funds; their exclusion from some contracts can be explained by anticipated costs which sinking funds can impose on the trustee if there is a default. Although the application of sinking fund monies is set forth in the covenant, should default occur the applicable law is not clear. Even where only one series of bonds is involved, application of funds to the retirement of specific bonds with knowledge of a default might involve participation by the trustee in an unlawful preference for which the trustee might be held liable.

Principles of Corporate Finance, 6th Ed. (2000)

By Richard A. Brealey and Stewart C. Myers.
§ 24.5   Repayment Provisions.

Sinking Funds

The maturity date of the Ralston Purina bond is June 1, 2016, but part of the issue is repaid on a regular basis before maturity. To do this, the company makes a regular repayment into a *sinking fund*. If the payment is in the form of cash, the trustee selects bonds by lottery and uses the cash to redeem them at their face value. Instead of paying cash, the company can buy bonds in the marketplace and pay these into the fund. This is a valuable option for the company. If the price of the bond is low, the firm will buy bonds in the market and hand them to the sinking fund; if the price is high, it will call the bonds by lottery.

Generally, there is a mandatory fund which *must* be satisfied and an optional fund which can be satisfied if the borrower chooses. For example, Ralston Purina *must* contribute at least $13.5 million each year to the sinking fund but has the option to contribute a further $13.5 million.

As in the case of Ralston Purina, most "sinkers" begin to operate after about 10 years. For lower-quality issues the payments are usually sufficient to redeem the entire issue in equal installments over the life of the bond. In contrast, high-quality bonds often have slight sinking fund requirements with large balloon payments at maturity.

We saw earlier that interest payments provide a regular test of the company's solvency. Sinking funds provide an additional hurdle that the firm must keep jumping. If it cannot pay the cash into the sinking fund, the lenders can demand their money back. That is why long-dated, low-quality issues usually involve larger sinking funds.

Unfortunately, a sinking fund is a weak test of solvency if the firm is allowed to repurchase bonds in the market. Since the *market* value of the debt must always be less than the value of the firm, financial distress reduces the cost of repurchasing debt in the market. The sinking fund, then, is a hurdle that gets progressively lower as the hurdler gets weaker.

G. CALL PROTECTION

Corporate bonds, like home mortgages, may be written for relatively long periods, generally as much as 25–30 years, although a few have been even longer. If bonds carry a fixed rate, the bond becomes a bet on interest rates between borrower and lender. If interest rates rise, the borrower wins the bet, because it remains able to employ the borrowed funds at the lower interest rate originally negotiated. On the other hand, if interest rates fall, the lender wins, since it obtains a rate higher than current market rates. All of this goes into the process of setting the yield curve, which generally requires a higher interest rate for long-term debt. If the borrower has the ability to prepay the debt when interest rates fall, the bet becomes more one-sided, and presumably would have called for a higher initial interest rate to compensate for the lost opportunity for the lender. Similarly, as we shall see, corporate bonds contemplate this same problem. Where the bonds can be prepaid (called) by the issuer, limits are usually placed on the ability to call the bonds. In some instances the bonds may not be called for the first few years; in others, a "call premium" (a prepayment penalty) may be imposed; often this declines over time. In the case that follows, Archer Daniels Midland Co. borrowed by selling debentures in 1981, at the time of the worst inflation in our nation's recent history. Because most participants in credit markets probably believed that interest rates were bound to come down from the 16% ADM was forced to pay, ADM was forced to offer a substantial prepayment penalty. Set out below is the call premium schedule (based on the par value of the bonds):

Year	Percentage	Year	Percentage
1981	115.500%	1991	107.750%
1982	114.725	1992	106.975
1983	113.950	1993	106.200
1984	113.175	1994	105.425
1985	112.400	1995	104.650
1986	111.625	1996	103.875
1987	110.850	1997	103.100
1988	110.075	1998	102.325
1989	109.300	1999	101.550
1990	108.525	2000	100.775
		and thereafter at 100%	

Morgan Stanley & Co., Incorporated v. Archer Daniels Midland Company

570 F. Supp. 1529 (S.D.N.Y. 1983).

■ SAND, D.J.

This action ... arises out of the planned redemption of $125 million in 16% Sinking Fund Debentures ("the Debentures") by the defendant ADM

Midland Company ("ADM") scheduled to take place on Monday, August 1st, 1983. Morgan Stanley & Company, Inc. ("Morgan Stanley") brings this suit under § 10(b) of the Securities Exchange Act of 1934 and 316(b) of the Trust Indenture Act of 1939, and other state and federal laws, alleging that the proposed redemption plan is barred by the terms of the Indenture, the language of the Debentures, and the Debenture Prospectus. Plaintiff contends, in addition, that the failure on the part of ADM to reveal its intention to redeem the Debentures, as well as its belief that such redemption would be lawful under the terms of the Indenture Agreement, amounts to an intentional, manipulative scheme to defraud in violation of federal and state securities and business laws. Morgan Stanley seeks a preliminary injunction enjoining ADM from consummating the redemption as planned, and, after full consideration on the merits, permanent injunctive relief barring the proposed transaction and damages. Both parties have pursued an expedited discovery schedule and now cross-move for summary judgment.

FACTS

In May, 1981, Archer Daniels issued $125,000,000 of 16% Sinking Fund Debentures due May 15, 2011. The managing underwriters of the Debenture offering were Goldman Sachs & Co., Kidder Peabody & Co. and Merrill Lynch, Pierce, Fenner & Smith, Inc.

* * *

The Indenture provides, in relevant part:

"The Debentures may be redeemed . . . at the election of the Company as a whole or from time to time in part, at any time, . . . provided, however, that prior to May 15, 1991, the Company may not redeem any of the Debentures pursuant to such [prepayment] option from the proceeds, or in anticipation, of the issuance of any indebtedness for money borrowed by or for the account of the Company or any Subsidiary (as defined in the Indenture) or from the proceeds, or in anticipation of a sale and leaseback transaction (as defined in Section 1008 of the Indenture), if, in either case, the interest cost or interest factor applicable thereto (calculated in accordance with generally accepted financial practice) shall be less than 16.08% per annum."

* * *

The proceeds of the Debenture offering were applied to the purchase of long-term government securities bearing rates of interest below 16.089%.

ADM raised money through public borrowing at interest rates less than 16.08% on at least two occasions subsequent to the issuance of the Debentures. On May 7, 1982, over a year before the announcement of the planned redemption, ADM borrowed $50,555,500 by the issuance of $400,000,000 face amount zero coupon debentures due 2002 and $100,000,000 face amount zero coupon notes due 1992 (the "Zeroes"). The Zeroes bore an effective interest rate of less than 16.08%. On March 10,

1983, ADM raised an additional $86,400,000 by the issuance of $263,232,500 face amount Secured Trust Accrual Receipts, known as "Stars," through a wholly-owned subsidiary, Midland Stars Inc. The Stars carry an effective interest rate of less than 16.08%. The Stars were in the form of notes with varying maturities secured by government securities deposited by ADM with a trustee established for that purpose. There is significant dispute between the parties as to whether the Stars transaction should be treated as an issuance of debt or as a sale of government securities. We assume, for purposes of this motion, that the transaction resulted in the incurring of debt.

In the period since the issuance of the Debentures, ADM also raised money through two common stock offerings. Six million shares of common stock were issued by prospectus dated January 28, 1983, resulting in proceeds of $131,370,000. And by a prospectus supplement dated June 1, 1983, ADM raised an additional $15,450,000 by issuing 600,000 shares of common stock.

Morgan Stanley, the plaintiff in this action, bought $15,518,000 principal amount of the Debentures at $1,252.50 per $1,000 face amount on May 5, 1983, and $500,000 principal amount at $1,200 per $1,000 face amount on May 31, 1983. The next day, June 1, ADM announced that it was calling for the redemption of the 16% Sinking Fund Debentures, effective August 1, 1983. The direct source of funds was to be the two ADM common stock offerings of January and June, 1983. The proceeds of these offerings were delivered to the Indenture Trustee, Morgan Guaranty Trust Company, and deposited in a special account to be applied to the redemption. The amount deposited with the Indenture Trustee is sufficient to fully redeem the Debentures.

* * *

Plaintiff's allegations can be reduced to two general claims: First, plaintiff contends that the proposed redemption is barred by the express terms of the call provisions of the Debenture and the Indenture Agreement, and that consummation of the plan would violate the Trust Indenture Act of 1939, and common law principles of contract law. The plaintiff's claim is founded on the language contained in the Debenture and Trust Indenture that states that the company may not redeem the Debentures "from the proceeds, or in anticipation, of the issuance of any indebtedness ... if ... the interest cost or interest factor ... [is] less than 16.08% per annum." Plaintiff points to the $86,400,000 raised by the Stars transaction within 90 days of the June 1 redemption announcement, and the $50,555,500 raised by the Zeroes transaction in May, 1982—both at interest rates below 16.08%—as proof that the redemption is being funded, at least indirectly, from the proceeds of borrowing in violation of the Debentures and Indenture agreement. The fact that ADM raised sufficient funds to redeem the Debentures entirely through the issuance of common stock is, according to the plaintiffs, an irrelevant "juggling of funds" used to circumvent the protections afforded investors by the redemption provisions of the Debenture. Plaintiff would have the Court interpret the provision as barring redemption during any period when the issuer has borrowing at a rate lower than that prescribed by the Debentures, regardless of whether the direct source of the funds is the issuance of equity, the sale of assets, or merely cash on hand.

The defendant would have the Court construe the language more narrowly as barring redemption only where the direct or indirect source of the funds is a debt instrument issued at a rate lower than that it is paying on the outstanding Debentures. Where, as here, the defendant can point directly to a non-debt source of funds (the issuance of common stock), the defendant is of the view that the general redemption schedule applies.

direct v. indirect source of $ argument

* * *

According to Morgan Stanley, the fact that the Debentures were trading at levels above the call price prior to the redemption announcement bolsters the argument that the investing public thought it was protected against early redemption. The plaintiff asserts that it would not have bought the Debentures without what it perceived to be protection against premature redemption.

ADM contends that plaintiff's allegations of securities fraud stem in the first instance from its strained and erroneous interpretation of the redemption language. Defendant argues that the redemption language itself—a boilerplate provision found in numerous Indenture Agreements—was sufficient disclosure. Moreover, defendant asserts that it had no plan or scheme at the time the Debentures were issued to exercise its call rights in conjunction with speculation in government securities or otherwise and that the provision existed solely to offer the issuer "financial flexibility." More important, defendant contends that its view of the Debenture language was the one commonly accepted by both bondholders and the investing public. In support of this contention, defendant points to the only case directly to address the issue, Franklin Life Insurance Co. v. Commonwealth Edison Co., 451 F. Supp. 602 (S.D. Ill. 1978). Franklin held, with respect to language almost identical to that contained in the ADM Debentures, that a redemption directly funded through equity financing was not prohibited despite contemporaneous borrowing by the issuer.

Defendant contends that it first seriously contemplated redemption in the Spring of 1983 upon the suggestion of Merrill Lynch, one of its investment bankers. Merrill Lynch had received legal advice that a redemption transaction of the sort contemplated was proper under the language of the Debenture and the analysis of the Court in Franklin. Moreover, the defendant asserts that Morgan Stanley itself was fully aware of this interpretation of the redemption language, although it may have disagreed with it. ADM explains the high price at which the Debentures were trading prior to the redemption announcement not as a reflection of investors' belief that the Debentures were not currently redeemable, but rather as a reflection of the belief that ADM itself, or some other interested buyer, might seek to purchase the Debentures through a tender offer or other financial transaction.

DISCUSSION

* * *

With respect to the likelihood of success on the merits, defendant's interpretation of the redemption provision seems at least as likely to be in accord with the language of the Debentures, the Indenture, and the available authorities than is the view proffered by the plaintiff. We first note that the one court to directly address this issue chose to construe the language in the manner set forth in this action by the defendant. *Franklin Life Insurance Co. v. Commonwealth Edison Co.*, 451 F. Supp. 602 (S.D. Ill. 1978). While plaintiff is correct in noting that this Circuit is not bound by this decision, and while this case can no doubt be distinguished factually on a number of grounds, none of which we deem to be of major significance, *Franklin* is nevertheless persuasive authority in support of defendant's position.

Defendant's view of the redemption language is also arguably supported by *The American Bar Foundation's Commentaries on Model Debenture Indenture Provisions* (1977), from which the boilerplate language in question was apparently taken verbatim. In discussing the various types of available redemption provisions, the Commentaries state:

> Instead of an absolute restriction [on redemption], the parties may agree that the borrower may not redeem with funds borrowed at an interest rate lower than the interest rate in the debentures. Such an arrangement recognizes that funds for redemption may become available *from other than borrowing*, but correspondingly recognizes that the debenture holder is entitled to be protected for a while against redemption if interest rates fall and the borrower can borrow funds at a lower rate to pay off the debentures.

Id. at 477 (emphasis added). We read this comment as pointing to the source of funds as the dispositive factor in determining the availability of redemption to the issuer—the position advanced by defendant ADM.

Finally, we view the redemption language itself as supporting defendant's position. The redemption provision in the Indenture and the Debentures begins with the broad statement that the Debentures are "subject to redemption ... at any time, in whole or in part, at the election of the company, at the following optional Redemption Price...." Following this language is a table of decreasing redemption percentages keyed to the year in which the redemption occurs. This broad language is then followed by the narrowing provision "provided, however ... the Company may not redeem any of the Debentures pursuant to such option from the proceeds, or in anticipation, of the issuance of any indebtedness" borrowed at rates less than that paid on the Debentures.

While the "plain meaning" of this language is not entirely clear with respect to the question presented in this case, we think the restrictive phrasing of the redemption provision, together with its placement after broad language allowing redemption in all other cases at the election of the company, supports defendant's more restrictive reading.

Morgan Stanley asserts that defendant's view would afford bondholders no protection against redemption through lower-cost borrowing and would result in great uncertainty among holders of bonds containing similar provisions. In its view, the "plain meaning" of the redemption bondholders of these bonds and the investment community generally, is that the issuer may not redeem when it is contemporaneously engaging in lower-cost borrowing, regardless of the source of the funds for redemption. At the same time, however, the plaintiff does not contend that redemption through equity funding is prohibited for the life of the redemption restriction once the issuer borrows funds at a lower interest rate subsequent to the Debenture's issuance. On the contrary, plaintiff concedes that the legality of the redemption transaction would depend on a factual inquiry into the magnitude of the borrowing relative to the size of the contemplated equity-funded redemption and its proximity in time relative to the date the redemption was to take place. Thus, a $100 million redemption two years after a $1 million short-term debt issue might be allowable, while the same redemption six months after a $20 million long-term debt issue might not be allowable.

This case-by-case approach is problematic in a number of respects. First, it appears keyed to the subjective expectations of the bondholders; if it appears that the redemption is funded through lower-cost borrowing, based on the Company's recent or prospective borrowing history, the redemption is deemed unlawful. The approach thus reads a subjective element into what presumably should be an objective determination based on the language appearing in the bond agreement. Second, and most important, this approach would likely cause greater uncertainty among bondholders than a strict "source" rule such as that adopted in Franklin, *supra*.

Plaintiff's fear that bondholders would be left "unprotected" by adoption of the "source" rule also appears rather overstated. The rule proposed by defendant does not, as plaintiff suggests, entail a virtual emasculation of the refunding restrictions. An issuer contemplating redemption would still be required to fund such redemption from a source other than lower-cost borrowing, such as reserves, the sale of assets, or the proceeds of a common stock issue. Bondholders would thus be protected against the type of continuous short-term refunding of debt in times of plummeting interest rates that the language was apparently intended to prohibit. Moreover, this is not an instance where protections against premature redemption are wholly absent from the Debenture. On the contrary, the Debentures and the Indenture explicitly provide for early redemption expressed in declining percentages of the principal amount, depending on the year the redemption is effected.

At this early stage of the proceedings, on the record before us, and for all the reasons outlined above, we find that plaintiff has failed to show a sufficient likelihood of its success on the merits of its contract claims as to entitle it to preliminary injunctive relief.

QUESTIONS

1. Why were the ADM debentures trading at $1,252.50 when Morgan Stanley bought them on May 5, 1983?

2. Can you calculate the current yield on the bonds at this price?

3. What is the call price on these bonds?

4. Why do you suppose Morgan Stanley bought these bonds at such a premium?

5. What's the purpose of prohibiting redemption from the proceeds of a lower-interest bond issue?

6. This debenture indenture allowed redemption on 60 days' notice beginning in 1981, with call premiums starting at 115% of par, and declining to nearly par in 2000. How can this be consistent with the prohibition at issue in this case?

7. Does the market price for the debentures support Morgan's argument that there was a common understanding that this language didn't allow redemption where a debtor had sold large amounts of new debt at lower interest rates?

8. How can you tell if the debentures were being redeemed "from the proceeds" of any lower cost debt? ADM had raised $86 million from the Stars just 90 days before, and $50 million from the zeroes in May 1982?

9. What's unclear about the redemption language?

10. How can you tell if a redemption is from the proceeds of a particular financing? All money is fungible.

11. The court points to *Commentaries* for support for this position. Do they really support it?

12. How does the court find help in the structure of the redemption provision?

13. Morgan claims it's not arguing that a debtor can never redeem when its new borrowings are at lower rates. What, exactly, is its argument?

14. Why does the court reject Morgan's suggested reading of this clause?

15. ADM was borrowing at 16% and investing in risk-free government securities at lower rates. How could such a strategy make sense?

16. How badly did Morgan Stanley do with its investment?

NOTE

In theory, a firm attempting to maximize shareholder value should call bonds as soon as the market price of the bonds exceeds the call price, because this signals that the company could refinance its debt at lower current interest rates. But even in the absence of call protection in indenture covenants, companies do not always do this immediately. Two explanations have been offered. First, the company incurs new transactions costs when issuing new debt to replace older debt, so that it makes sense to wait until the market price of outstanding bonds is at least equal to the sum of these transactions costs and the redemption price. There is a second explanation: When interest rates and bond prices are volatile, an issuer has no assurance that bond prices will remain above this sum during the time necessary to complete the redemption process. Typical bond issues give bondholders about thirty days to surrender the bond and receive the call price in cash. During this period bond prices may decline below the call price, in which case the firm has paid too much to redeem bonds that it could have repurchased more cheaply in the market. Because of these two problems, issuers typically do not call bonds until the market price exceeds the call price by some amount sufficient not only to cover the transaction costs of the call but also sufficient to reduce the probability of a price drop below the market price.

① transaction cost
② volatility
don't redeem right away

H.   MONITORING COMPLIANCE

On Financial Contracting: An Analysis of Bond Covenants

Clifford W. Smith. Jr. and Jerold B. Warner.
7 Journal of Financial Economics 117 (1979).

* * *

25.   Covenants specifying bonding activities by the firm

Potential bondholders estimate the costs associated with monitoring the firm to assure that the bond covenants have not been violated, and the estimate is reflected in the price when the bonds are sold. Since the value of the firm at the time the bonds are issued is influenced by anticipated monitoring costs. it is in the interests of the firm's underwriters to include contractual provisions which lower the costs of monitoring. For example, observed provisions often include the requirement that the firm supply audited annual financial statements to the bondholders. Jensen/Meckling call these expenditures by the firm bonding costs.

2.5.1.   Required reports

Description. Indenture agreements discussed in *Commentaries* normally commit the company to supply financial and other information for as long as the debt is outstanding. Typically, the firm agrees to supply the following types of information: (1) all financial statements, reports. and proxy statements which the firm already sends to its shareholders: (2) reports and statements filed with government agencies such as the SEC or Public Utility Commissions; (3) quarterly financial statements certified by a financial officer of the firm and (4) financial statements for the fiscal year audited by an independent public accountant.

Analysis. Our analysis suggests that bondholders find financial statements to be useful in ascertaining whether the provisions of the contract have been (or are about to be) violated. If the firm can produce this information at a lower cost than the bondholders (perhaps because much of the information is already being collected for internal decision making), it pays the firm's stockholders to contract to provide this information to the bondholders. The market value of the firm increases by the reduction in agency costs.

Jensen/Meckling (1976) and Watts (1977) point out that firms have the incentive to provide financial statements which have been audited by an external accounting firm if the increase in the market value of the bonds is greater than the present value of the auditing fees, net of any nominal benefits which accrue in internal monitoring. If bonding activities which are related to the bondholder-stockholder conflict involve incremental costs, then since the conflict increases with the debt in the firm's capital structure, the use of externally audited financial statements should be positively related to the firm's debt/equity ratio. Auditing expenditures should be associated with the extent to which covenants are specified in terms of accounting numbers from financial statements.

* * *

2.5.4. *The required purchase of insurance*

Description. Indenture agreements frequently include provisions requiring the firm to purchase insurance. The sample covenants in *Commentaries* specify that the firm will purchase insurance to substantially the same extent as its competitors. The stockholders sometimes retain the right to self-insure if the plan is certified by an actuary. Typically, the indenture requires the firm to maintain liability insurance.

Analysis. In a world with perfect markets, there is no corporate demand for insurance; the corporate form effectively hedges insurable risk. Our analysis suggests that the corporate purchase of insurance is a bonding activity engaged in by firms to reduce agency costs between bondholders and stockholders (as well as between the managers and the owners of a corporation). If insurance firms have a comparative advantage in monitoring aspects of the firm's activities, then a firm which purchases insurance will engage in a different set of activities from a firm which does not.

For example, a frequently purchased line of corporate insurance is boiler insurance. Insurance companies hire and train specialized Inspectors to monitor the operation and maintenance of boilers, and the loss control program which is provided by the insurance company constrains the actions of the stockholders and managers of the firm. A covenant requiring the purchase of insurance gives stockholders the incentive to engage in the optimal amount of loss control projects. If the purchase of a sprinkler system were a positive net present value project it could still be rejected by stockholders of a levered firm because it reduces the variance rate of the firm's cash flows and thereby increases the value of the debt. But if the firm is contractually required to purchase insurance and if the insurance industry is competitive, the firm has the incentive to take any loss control project where the present value of the premium reductions is greater than the cost of the project. With the purchase of insurance the corporation's cash flow variability is unaffected by the purchase of loss control projects.

I. AMENDMENTS

On Financial Contracting: An Analysis of Bond Covenants

Clifford W. Smith. Jr. and Jerold B. Warner.
7 Journal of Financial Economics 117 (1979).

* * *

3.3. *Default remedies*

The debt contract typically gives the firm a strong incentive to live up to the restrictive covenants: any breach of the covenants is considered an act of default. Not only is the firm normally required to report any such breach, but the lender is given the right to engage in certain actions (e.g., seizure of collateral, acceleration of the maturity of the debt) to protect his interest.

3.3.1. *Renegotiation*

Description. Since actions such as the seizure of collateral consume real resources, the debt contract is often renegotiated in order to eliminate the default. In public debt issues the contract can be changed by the use of a supplemental indenture. The supplement must be approved by the bond-holders, and must meet the requirements of the [Trust Indenture Act].

Changes in the specific covenants cannot usually be made without the consent of the holders of two-thirds in principal amount of the outstanding debt (the firm itself is not allowed to vote any debt it holds). Moreover, the consent of 100 percent of the debtholders is required in order to change the maturity date or principal amount of the bonds. In private placements involving few lenders, renegotiation is typically easier.

Analysis. The seemingly lower renegotiating costs of privately placed debt issues further reinforce our earlier predictions that such private placements will contain tighter restrictions on the firm's behavior than will public issues.

3.3.2. *Bankruptcy*

Description. Should renegotiation fail, a default also gives the lender the right to put the firm into legal bankruptcy proceedings. Several features of the bankruptcy process bear on the enforcement of debt contracts. For example, since the bankruptcy process gives the firm temporary protection from acts of foreclosure and lien enforcement, some enforcement mechanisms are no longer available to the lender.

Analysis. Our theory suggests that it is more efficient to have some ambiguities in the initial debt contract, and to let them be resolved in bankruptcy should default ever occur. Since it is the firm's owners who bear the total costs associated with enforcing the debt contract, it is in their interests to find the most efficient balance between expenditures on drafting the debt contract and expected legal expenditures in bankruptcy. In a world where contracting is costly, that balance will imply less than complete specification of the payoff to be received by claimholders in every possible future state of the world.

As Warner (1977) discusses, bankruptcy courts recognize the priorities specified in the firm's debt agreements in only a limited sense. There are many cases where "junior" claimants are compensated before claimants "senior" to them are paid in full. Since "priorities" are not always enforced, it will not always pay the firm to indicate the priority of a given debt issue with much specificity (e.g., creditor A is forty-seventh in line)....

The power to amend the indenture is constrained by Section 316 of the Trust Indenture Act, 15 U.S.C. § 77ppp:

§ 316.   Directions and waivers by bondholders; prohibition of impairment of holder's right to payment; record date

(a) *Directions and waivers by bondholders.* The indenture to be qualified—

(1) shall automatically be deemed (unless it is expressly provided therein that any such provision is excluded) to contain provisions authorizing the holders of not less than a majority in principal amount of the indenture securities or if expressly specified in such indenture, of any series of securities at the time outstanding (A) to direct the time, method, and place of conducting any proceeding for any remedy available to such trustee, or exercising any trust or power conferred upon such trustee, under such indenture, or (B) on behalf of the holders of all such indenture securities, to consent to the waiver of any past default and its consequences; or

(2) may contain provisions authorizing the holders of not less than 75 per centum in principal amount of the indenture securities or if expressly specified in such indenture, of any series of securities at the time outstanding to consent on behalf of the holders of all such indenture securities to the postponement of any interest payment for a period not exceeding three years from its due date.

For the purposes of this subsection and paragraph (3) of subsection (d) of section 315, in determining whether the holders of the required principal amount of indenture securities have concurred in any such direction or consent, indenture securities owned by any obligor upon the indenture securities, or by any person directly or indirectly controlling or controlled by or under direct or indirect common control with any such obligor, shall be disregarded, except that for the purposes of determining whether the indenture trustee shall be protected in relying on any such direction or consent, only indenture securities which such trustee knows are so owned shall be so disregarded.

(b) *Prohibition of impairment of holder's right to payment.* Notwithstanding any other provision of the indenture to be qualified, the right of any holder of any indenture security to receive payment of the principal of and interest on such indenture security, on or after the respective due dates expressed in such indenture security, or to institute suit for the enforcement of any such payment on or after such respective dates, shall not be impaired or affected without the consent of such holder, except as to a postponement of an interest payment consented to as provided in paragraph (2) of subsection (a), and except that such indenture may contain provisions limiting or denying the right of any such holder to institute any such suit, if and to the extent that the institution or prosecution thereof or the entry of judgment therein would, under applicable law, result in the surrender, impairment, waiver, or loss of the lien of such indenture upon any property subject to such lien.

Katz v. Oak Industries, Inc.

508 A.2d 873 (Del. Ch. 1986).

■ ALLEN, CHANCELLOR.

A commonly used word—seemingly specific and concrete when used in everyday speech—may mask troubling ambiguities that upon close examination are seen to derive not simply from casual use but from more fundamental epistemological problems. Few words more perfectly illustrate the deceptive dependability of language than the term "coercion" which is at the heart of the theory advanced by plaintiff as entitling him to a preliminary injunction in this case.

Plaintiff is the owner of long-term debt securities issued by Oak Industries, Inc. ("Oak"), a Delaware corporation; in this class action he seeks to enjoin the consummation of an exchange offer and consent solicitation made by Oak to holders of various classes of its long-term debt. As detailed below that offer is an integral part of a series of transactions that together would effect a major reorganization and recapitalization of Oak. The claim asserted is in essence, that the exchange offer is a coercive device and, in the circumstances, constitutes a breach of contract. This is the Court's opinion on plaintiff's pending application for a preliminary injunction.

I.

The background facts are involved even when set forth in the abbreviated form the decision within the time period currently available requires.

Through its domestic and foreign subsidiaries and affiliated entities, Oak manufactures and markets component equipments used in consumer, industrial and military products (the "Components Segment"); produces communications equipment for use in cable television systems and satellite television systems (the "Communications Segment") and manufactures and markets laminates and other materials used in printed circuit board applications (the "Materials Segment"). During 1985, the Company has terminated certain other unrelated businesses. As detailed below, it has now entered into an agreement with Allied–Signal, Inc. for the sale of the Materials Segment of its business and is currently seeking a buyer for its Communications Segment.

Even a casual review of Oak's financial results over the last several years shows it unmistakably to be a company in deep trouble. During the period from January 1, 1982 through September 30, 1985, the Company has experienced unremitting losses from operations; on net sales of approximately $1.26 billion during that period it has lost over $335 million. As a result its total stockholders' equity has first shriveled (from $260 million on 12/31/81 to $85 million on 12/31/83) and then disappeared completely (as of 9/30/85 there was a $62 million deficit in its stockholders' equity accounts). Financial markets, of course, reflected this gloomy history.[2]

Unless Oak can be made profitable within some reasonably short time it will not continue as an operating company. Oak's board of directors, comprised almost entirely of outside directors, has authorized steps to buy the company time. In February, 1985, in order to reduce a burdensome annual cash interest obligation on its $230 million of then outstanding debentures, the Company offered to exchange such debentures for a combination of notes, common stock and warrants. As a result, approximately $180 million principal amount of the then outstanding debentures were exchanged. Since interest on certain of the notes issued in that exchange offer is payable in common stock, the effect of the 1985 exchange offer was to reduce to some extent the cash drain on the Company caused by its significant debt.

About the same time that the 1985 exchange offer was made, the Company announced its intention to discontinue certain of its operations and sell certain of its properties. Taking these steps, while effective to stave off a default and to reduce to some extent the immediate cash drain, did not address Oak's longer-range problems. Therefore, also during 1985 representatives of the Company held informal discussions with several interested parties exploring the possibility of an investment from, combination with or acquisition by another company. As a result of these discussions, the Company and Allied–Signal, Inc. entered into two agreements. The first, the Acquisition Agreement, contemplates the sale to Allied–Signal of the Materials Segment for $160 million in cash. The second agreement, the Stock Purchase Agreement, provides for the purchase by Allied–Signal for $15 million cash of 10 million shares of the Company's common stock together with warrants to purchase additional common stock.

The Stock Purchase Agreement provides as a condition to Allied–Signal's obligation that [holders of] at least 85% of the aggregate principal

---

2. The price of the company's common stock has fallen from over $30 per share on December 31, 1981 to approximately $2 per share recently. The debt securities that are the subject of the exchange offer here involved (see note 3 for identification) have traded at substantial discounts.

amount of all of the Company's debt securities shall have tendered and accepted the exchange offers that are the subject of this lawsuit. Oak has six classes of such long term debt.[3] If less than 85% of the aggregate principal amount of such debt accepts the offer, Allied–Signal has an option, but no obligation, to purchase the common stock and warrants contemplated by the Stock Purchase Agreement. An additional condition for the closing of the Stock Purchase Agreement is that the sale of the Company's Materials Segment contemplated by the Acquisition Agreement shall have been concluded.

Thus, as part of the restructuring and recapitalization contemplated by the Acquisition Agreement and the Stock Purchase Agreement, the Company has extended an exchange offer to each of the holders of the six classes of its long-term debt securities. These pending exchange offers include a Common Stock Exchange Offer (available only to holders of the 9–5/8% convertible notes) and the Payment Certificate Exchange Offers (available to holders of all six classes of Oak's long-term debt securities). The Common Stock Exchange Offer currently provides for the payment to each tendering noteholder of 407 shares of the Company's common stock in exchange for each $1,000 9–5/8% note accepted. The offer is limited to $38.6 million principal amount of notes (out of approximately $83.9 million outstanding).

The Payment Certificate Exchange Offer is an any and all offer. Under its terms, a payment certificate, payable in cash five days after the closing of the sale of the Materials Segment to Allied–Signal, is offered in exchange for debt securities. The cash value of the Payment Certificate will vary depending upon the particular security tendered. In each instance, however, that payment will be less than the face amount of the obligation. The cash payments range in amount, per $1,000 of principal, from $918 to $655. These cash values however appear to represent a premium over the market prices for the Company's debentures as of the time the terms of the transaction were set.

The Payment Certificate Exchange Offer is subject to certain important conditions before Oak has an obligation to accept tenders under it. First, it is necessary that a minimum amount ($38.6 million principal amount out of $83.9 total outstanding principal amount) of the 9–5/8% notes be tendered pursuant to the Common Stock Exchange Offer. Secondly, it is necessary that certain minimum amounts of each class of debt securities be tendered, together with consents to amendments to the underlying indentures.[4] Indeed, under the offer one may not tender securi-

---

3. The three classes of debentures are: 13.65% debentures due April 1, 2001, 10–1/2% convertible subordinated debentures due February 1, 2002, and 11–7/8% subordinated debentures due May 15, 1998. In addition, as a result of the 1985 exchange offer the company has three classes of notes which were issued in exchange for debentures that were tendered in that offer. Those are: 13.5% senior notes due May 15, 1990, 9–5/8% convertible notes due September 15, 1991 and 11–5/8% notes due September 15, 1990.

4. The holders of more than 50% of the principal amount of each of the 13.5% notes, the 9–5/8% notes and the 11–5/8% notes and at least 66–2/3% of the principal amount of the

ties unless at the same time one consents to the proposed amendments to the relevant indentures.

The condition of the offer that tendering security holders must consent to amendments in the indentures governing the securities gives rise to plaintiff's claim of breach of contract in this case. Those amendments would, if implemented, have the effect of removing significant negotiated protections to holders of the Company's long-term debt including the deletion of all financial covenants. Such modification may have adverse consequences to debt holders who elect not to tender pursuant to either exchange offer.

Allied–Signal apparently was unwilling to commit to the $15 million cash infusion contemplated by the Stock Purchase Agreement, unless Oak's long-term debt is reduced by 85% (at least that is a condition of their obligation to close on that contract). Mathematically, such a reduction may not occur without the Company reducing the principal amount of outstanding debentures (that is the three classes of outstanding notes constitute less than 85% of all long-term debt). But existing indenture covenants (See Offering Circular, pp. 38–39) prohibit the Company, so long as any of its long-term notes are outstanding, from issuing any obligation (including the Payment Certificates) in exchange for any of the debentures. Thus, in this respect, amendment to the indentures is required in order to close the Stock Purchase Agreement as presently structured.

Restrictive covenants in the indentures would appear to interfere with effectuation of the recapitalization in another way. Section 4.07 of the 13.50% Indenture provides that the Company may not "acquire" for value any of the 9–5/8% Notes or 11–5/8% Notes unless it concurrently "redeems" a proportionate amount of the 13.50% Notes. This covenant, if unamended, would prohibit the disproportionate acquisition of the 9–5/8% Notes that may well occur as a result of the Exchange Offers; in addition, it would appear to require the payment of the "redemption" price for the 13.50% Notes rather than the lower, market price offered in the exchange offer.

In sum, the failure to obtain the requisite consents to the proposed amendments would permit Allied–Signal to decline to consummate both the Acquisition Agreement and the Stock Purchase Agreement.

* * *

II.

* * *

As amplified in briefing on the pending motion, plaintiff's claim is that no free choice is provided to bondholders by the exchange offer and consent solicitation. Under its terms, a rational bondholder is "forced" to tender

---

13.65% debentures, 10–1/2% debentures, and 11–7/8% debentures, must validly tender such securities and consent to certain proposed amendments to the indentures governing those securities.

and consent. Failure to do so would face a bondholder with the risk of owning a security stripped of all financial covenant protections and for which it is likely that there would be no ready market. A reasonable bondholder, it is suggested, cannot possibly accept those risks and thus such a bondholder is coerced to tender and thus to consent to the proposed indenture amendments.

It is urged this linking of the offer and the consent solicitation constitutes a breach of a contractual obligation that Oak owes to its bondholders to act in good faith. Specifically, plaintiff points to three contractual provisions from which it can be seen that the structuring of the current offer constitutes a breach of good faith. Those provisions (1) establish a requirement that no modification in the term of the various indentures may be effectuated without the consent of a stated percentage of bondholders; (2) restrict Oak from exercising the power to grant such consent with respect to any securities it may hold in its treasury; and (3) establish the price at which and manner in which Oak may force bondholders to submit their securities for redemption.

III.

* * *

I turn first to an evaluation of the probability of plaintiff's ultimate success on the merits of his claim. I begin that analysis with two preliminary points. The first concerns what is not involved in this case. To focus briefly on this clears away much of the corporation law case law of this jurisdiction upon which plaintiff in part relies. This case does not involve the measurement of corporate or directorial conduct against that high standard of fidelity required of fiduciaries when they act with respect to the interests of the beneficiaries of their trust. Under our law—and the law generally—the relationship between a corporation and the holders of its debt securities, even convertible debt securities, is contractual in nature. Arrangements among a corporation, the underwriters of its debt, trustees under its indentures and sometimes ultimate investors are typically thoroughly negotiated and massively documented. The rights and obligations of the various parties are or should be spelled out in that documentation. The terms of the contractual relationship agreed to and not broad concepts such as fairness define the corporation's obligation to its bondholders.[7]

Thus, the first aspect of the pending Exchange Offers about which plaintiff complains—that "the purpose and effect of the Exchange Offers is to benefit Oak's common stockholders at the expense of the Holders of its debt"—does not itself appear to allege a cognizable legal wrong. It is the obligation of directors to attempt, within the law, to maximize the long-run interests of the corporation's stockholders; that they may sometimes do so

---

7. To say that the broad duty of loyalty that a director owes to his corporation and ultimately its shareholders is not implicated in this case is not to say, as the discussion below reflects, that as a matter of contract law a corporation owes no duty to bondholders of good faith and fair dealing. Such a duty, however, is quite different from the congeries of duties that are assumed by a fiduciary.

"at the expense" of others (even assuming that a transaction which one may refuse to enter into can meaningfully be said to be at his expense) does not for that reason constitute a breach of duty. It seems likely that corporate restructurings designed to maximize shareholder values may in some instances have the effect of requiring bondholders to bear greater risk of loss and thus in effect transfer economic value from bondholders to stockholders. But if courts are to provide protection against such enhanced risk, they will require either legislative direction to do so or the negotiation of indenture provisions designed to afford such protection.

The second preliminary point concerns the limited analytical utility, at least in this context, of the word "coercive" which is central to plaintiff's own articulation of his theory of recovery. If, pro arguendo, we are to extend the meaning of the word coercion beyond its core meaning—dealing with the utilization of physical force to overcome the will of another—to reach instances in which the claimed coercion arises from an act designed to affect the will of another party by offering inducements to the act sought to be encouraged or by arranging unpleasant consequences for an alternative sought to be discouraged, then—in order to make the term legally meaningful at all—we must acknowledge that some further refinement is essential. Clearly some "coercion" of this kind is legally unproblematic. Parents may "coerce" a child to study with the threat of withholding an allowance; employers may "coerce" regular attendance at work by either docking wages for time absent or by rewarding with a bonus such regular attendance. Other "coercion" so defined clearly would be legally relevant (to encourage regular attendance by corporal punishment, for example). Thus, for purposes of legal analysis, the term "coercion" itself—covering a multitude of situations—is not very meaningful. For the word to have much meaning for purposes of legal analysis, it is necessary in each case that a normative judgment be attached to the concept ("inappropriately coercive" or "wrongfully coercive", etc.). But, it is then readily seen that what is legally relevant is not the conclusory term "coercion" itself but rather the norm that leads to the adjectives modifying it.

In this instance, assuming that the Exchange Offers and Consent Solicitation can meaningfully be regarded as "coercive" (in the sense that Oak has structured it in a way designed—and I assume effectively so—to "force" rational bondholders to tender), the relevant legal norm that will support the judgment whether such "coercion" is wrongful or not will, for the reasons mentioned above, be derived from the law of contracts. I turn then to that subject to determine the appropriate legal test or rule.

Modern contract law has generally recognized an implied covenant to the effect that each party to a contract will act with good faith towards the other with respect to the subject matter of the contract. The contractual theory for this implied obligation is well stated in a leading treatise:

> If the purpose of contract law is to enforce the reasonable expectations of parties induced by promises, then at some point it becomes necessary for courts to look to the substance rather than to the form of the agreement, and to hold that substance controls over form. What courts

are doing here, whether calling the process "implication" of promises, or interpreting the requirements of "good faith", as the current fashion may be, is but a recognition that the parties occasionally have understandings or expectations that were so fundamental that they did not need to negotiate about those expectations. When the court "implies a promise" or holds that "good faith" requires a party not to violate those expectations, it is recognizing that sometimes silence says more than words, and it is understanding its duty to the spirit of the bargain is higher than its duty to the technicalities of the language. Corbin on Contracts (Kaufman Supp. 1984), § 570.

It is this obligation to act in good faith and to deal fairly that plaintiff claims is breached by the structure of Oak's coercive exchange offer. Because it is an implied contractual obligation that is asserted as the basis for the relief sought, the appropriate legal test is not difficult to deduce. It is this: is it clear from what was expressly agreed upon that the parties who negotiated the express terms of the contract would have agreed to proscribe the act later complained of as a breach of the implied covenant of good faith—had they thought to negotiate with respect to that matter. If the answer to this question is yes, then, in my opinion, a court is justified in concluding that such act constitutes a breach of the implied covenant of good faith.

With this test in mind, I turn now to a review of the specific provisions of the various indentures from which one may be best able to infer whether it is apparent that the contracting parties—had they negotiated with the exchange offer and consent solicitation in mind—would have expressly agreed to prohibit contractually the linking of the giving of consent with the purchase and sale of the security.

IV.

Applying the foregoing standard to the exchange offer and consent solicitation, I find first that there is nothing in the indenture provisions granting bondholders power to veto proposed modifications in the relevant indenture that implies that Oak may not offer an inducement to bondholders to consent to such amendments. Such an implication, at least where, as here, the inducement is offered on the same terms to each holder of an affected security, would be wholly inconsistent with the strictly commercial nature of the relationship.

Nor does the second pertinent contractual provision supply a ground to conclude that defendant's conduct violates the reasonable expectations of those who negotiated the indentures on behalf of the bondholders. Under that provision Oak may not vote debt securities held in its treasury. Plaintiff urges that Oak's conditioning of its offer to purchase debt on the giving of consents has the effect of subverting the purpose of that provision; it permits Oak to "dictate" the vote on securities which it could not itself vote.

The evident purpose of the restriction on the voting of treasury securities is to afford protection against the issuer voting as a bondholder in favor of modifications that would benefit it as issuer, even though such changes would be detrimental to bondholders. But the linking of the exchange offer and the consent solicitation does not involve the risk that bondholder interests will be affected by a vote involving anyone with a financial interest in the subject of the vote other than a bondholder's interest. That the consent is to be given concurrently with the transfer of the bond to the issuer does not in any sense create the kind of conflict of interest that the indenture's prohibition on voting treasury securities contemplates. Not only will the proposed consents be granted or withheld only by those with a financial interest to maximize the return on their investment in Oak's bonds, but the incentive to consent is equally available to all members of each class of bondholders. Thus the "vote" implied by the consent solicitation is not affected in any sense by those with a financial conflict of interest.

In these circumstances, while it is clear that Oak has fashioned the exchange offer and consent solicitation in a way designed to encourage consents, I cannot conclude that the offer violates the intendment of any of the express contractual provisions considered or, applying the test set out above, that its structure and timing breaches an implied obligation of good faith and fair dealing.

One further set of contractual provisions should be touched upon: Those granting to Oak a power to redeem the securities here treated at a price set by the relevant indentures. Plaintiff asserts that the attempt to force all bondholders to tender their securities at less than the redemption price constitutes, if not a breach of the redemption provision itself, at least a breach of an implied covenant of good faith and fair dealing associated with it. The flaw, or at least one fatal flaw, in this argument is that the present offer is not the functional equivalent of a redemption which is, of course, an act that the issuer may take unilaterally. In this instance it may happen that Oak will get tenders of a large percentage of its outstanding long-term debt securities. If it does, that fact will, in my judgment, be in major part a function of the merits of the offer (i.e., the price offered in light of the Company's financial position and the market value of its debt). To answer plaintiff's contention that the structure of the offer "forces" debt holders to tender, one only has to imagine what response this offer would receive if the price offered did not reflect a premium over market but rather was, for example, ten percent of market value. The exchange offer's success ultimately depends upon the ability and willingness of the issuer to extend an offer that will be a financially attractive alternative to holders. This process is hardly the functional equivalent of the unilateral election of redemption and thus cannot be said in any sense to constitute a subversion by Oak of the negotiated provisions dealing with redemption of its debt.

Accordingly, I conclude that plaintiff has failed to demonstrate a probability of ultimate success on the theory of liability asserted.

QUESTIONS

1. In analyzing whether Oak's tender offer violates the covenant that Oak may not vote its own debentures, the court concludes that the votes

will only be by "those with a financial interest to maximize return on their investment...." Is that the same as saying that Oak isn't effectively voting the bonds?

2. Why, in the context of rejecting the argument that Oak is not voting Notes that it holds (when they are tendered), does the court emphasize that the "incentive to consent is equally available to all members of each class of bondholders?"

3. Why does the court hold that the tender offers don't violate the implied covenant of good faith and fair dealing with respect to provisions requiring redemption at stated prices? Are the noteholders coerced into consenting and tendering by the threat of losing all the covenants?

4. The court concludes that the exchange offer leaves the Noteholders free to reject the offer, and that it would fail if it didn't reflect a premium over the market. Do you agree?

5. If Noteholders are told the company will fail if it doesn't get the $15 million from the stock sale, what would they do? Does the amendment request then become coercive because it eliminates financial covenants? Or does it just eliminate hold-outs who want to free ride and let other Noteholders solve Oak's solvency problem?

6. If the Trust Indenture Act (and the Oak indentures) permitted indenture amendments to relieve Oak of part of its payment obligations on the Notes on some supermajority vote (perhaps 75%), would this restructuring have been conducted differently?

7. If Oak had simply offered payments to the bondholders to consent to amendments to the indentures to eliminate the financial covenants and the requirements of pro rata repurchase, would the result have been the same?

J. Enforcement of Covenant Breaches

Hedge Fund Activism in the Enforcement of Bondholder Rights

Marcel Kahan and Edward Rock.
103 Northwestern Law Review 281 (2009).

In the past, many violations of bondholder rights have remained undetected and unsanctioned. This historic underenforcement problem was rooted in the collective action problems facing bondholders, in the lack of substantial incentives for the indenture trustee—the supposed bondholder representative—to represent bondholder interests vigorously, in contractual provisions in the bond indenture—the document that governs most bondholder rights—that provide little help in detecting violations and impose barriers on the ability of bondholders to enforce their rights, and in the relatively accommodating attitude of insurance companies and mutual funds—the traditional holders of corporate bonds.

With the rise of hedge funds, however, this historic underenforcement problem has given way to a new enforcement paradigm. Unlike traditional investors, activist hedge funds look for bonds where companies have violated, have arguably violated, or are about to violate some contractual provisions; buy up a large quantity of the issue; and then aggressively enforce their rights. Hedge funds have been able to greatly ameliorate the historic underenforcement problem because they have the sophistication to detect potential violations, the financial resources to acquire substantial amounts of a single bond issue, and the willingness to take on issuers; perhaps most importantly, they have decided to pursue, and become experienced in pursuing, this strategy.

Yet not all is peachy-keen, and not just for the companies that find themselves the unexpected targets of activism. Hedge funds are obviously motivated by the desire to make money, and how much money they make from this strategy depends on the remedy afforded to bondholders for violations of their rights. But as we show, this remedy scheme entails its own imperfections. In particular, the standard remedy for covenant violations—acceleration—can, depending on extraneous circumstances, result in payoffs that are significantly larger or significantly smaller than the harm related to the violations.

In those circumstances where the payoff exceeds the harm, and thus produces a windfall, activist bondholders have incentives to enforce their rights aggressively, leading to overenforcement. * * *

In the short run, it is likely that selective enforcement has resulted in a disequilibrium between indenture covenants—which were drafted with the expectation that they would be underenforced—and the actual, much higher level of selective enforcement. In the long run, we would expect the market to adjust to reach a new equilibrium that is likely to be more efficient than the old underenforcement equilibrium. This new equilibrium may entail less stringent and more carefully drafted covenants.

* * *

In this Part, we provide some examples to illustrate the nature and scope of recent bondholder activism. * * *

2. Spectrum Brands.—In January 2007, Sandell, Sandelman, and Xerion—three hedge funds—sent a notice of default to Spectrum Brands alleging that the company's borrowing under its Revolving Credit Facility violated the indenture for Spectrum's 8-1/2% Senior Subordinated Notes. Spectrum took the unusual step of filing with the SEC its own lengthy analysis of the indenture provision, explaining why no such violation had occurred. Apparently, however, Spectrum was not sure it would prevail. Two months later, on March 12, it announced that it had entered into an Exchange and Forbearance Agreement with Sandell and Sandelman. According to that agreement, the company agreed to offer to exchange the 8-1/2% Senior Subordinated Notes for new Toggle PIK Exchange Notes due

2013,[17] with an initial interest rate of 11%—which was to increase semi-annually to 15.25% unless redeemed—in exchange for a waiver of any defaults under the 8–1/2% notes.

* * *

2. KCS Energy.—7–1/8% Senior Notes by KCS Energy, Inc. contained a change of control repurchase right that was triggered when a majority of the directors of the "Company" were neither "nominated for election or elected" with the "approval" of a majority of KCS's premerger directors. On July 12, 2006, KCS merged into Petrohawk Energy Corp., with Petro-hawk surviving the merger. Prior to the merger, the board of KCS adopted a resolution "confirming and approving" the nomination and election of all the postmerger directors.[23] But only four of nine members of the postmerger board of Petrohawk (the "Company" for purposes of the indenture) were actual premerger directors of KCS. A group of note holders, reportedly organized by W.R. Huff Asset Management (a firm specializing in high yield bonds), replaced the indenture trustee and instructed the new trustee to file a suit arguing that the merger constituted a change of control. The court ruled in favor of Petrohawk, reasoning that the note holders were "attempting to exploit imprecise contract drafting" and to "use a technicality" to obtain a benefit. [Law Debenture Trust Company of New York v. Petrohawk Energy Corp., 2007 WL 2248150 (Del.Ch. 2007).]

The authors also describe numerous cases where issuers violated indenture terms through delinquent SEC filings. In UnitedHealth Group Inc. v. Wilmington Trust Co., 548 3d Cir. 1124 (8th Cir. 2008), United failed to file timely quarterly financial reports with the SEC on Form 10–Q, because it was conducting an investigation of allegedly backdated stock options, which could cause it to restate its financial statements. United did communicate with investors about the reasons for its delay, and provided its best estimate of what its earnings were, without any adjustment that might result from any required restatement. (It turned out that there was only a 1% difference.) Hedge funds that held the bonds filed a notice of default with United, alleging a violation of an indenture covenant. United subsequently filed suit against the indenture trustee seeking a declaratory judgment that it was not in violation of the covenant, which read as follows:

> So long as any of the Securities remain Outstanding, *the Company shall cause copies of all current, quarterly and annual financial reports on Forms 8–K, 10–Q and 10–K, respectively, and all proxy statements, which the Company is then required to file with the [Securities and*

---

17. For $1,000 in old notes, holders were to receive $950 in new notes and a $50 cash consent payment.

23. Law Debenture Trust Co. of N.Y. v. PetroHawk Energy Corp., No. Civ. A. 2422–VCS, 2007 WL 2248150, at 10 (Del. Ch. Aug. 1, 2007).

Exchange] Commission pursuant to Section 13 or 15(d) of the Exchange Act to be filed with the Trustee and mailed to the Holders of such series of Securities at their addresses appearing in the Security Register maintained by the Security Registrar, in each case, within 15 days of filing with the Commission. The Company shall also comply with the provisions of TIA [Trust Indenture Act] ss. 314(a).

The hedge funds urged that this meant that United was required to make timely filings, in accordance with the SEC regulations, and to mail copies of these filings within fifteen days of the scheduled date of the filings. The court rejected this argument, concluding that the indenture did not require SEC filings at any particular time, but only required mailing to the noteholders within fifteen days of the actual date of filing.

---

4.   The Indenture Trustee and the Trust Indenture Act

A.   The Nature of the Trustee and its Duties

On Financial Contracting: An Analysis of Bond Covenants

Clifford W. Smith, Jr. and Jerold B. Warner.
7 Journal of Financial Economics 117 (1979).

* * *

3.2.   The role of the trust indenture and the trustee

Description. Debt contracts discussed in *Commentaries* typically appoint an independent trustee to represent the bondholders and act as their agent in covenant enforcement. This is done under a device known as a corporate trust indenture, which specifies the respective rights and obligations of the firm, the individual bondholders, and the trustee. Although the trustee is an agent of the bondholders, in practice he is actually compensated by the firm.

Analysis. If the firm's debt is not held by a single borrower, then a number of problems related to enforcement of the debt contract arise. For example, any individual's holdings of the firm's debt may be so small that no single bondholder has much incentive to expend resources in covenant enforcement. But it is not the case that individual bondholders necessarily expend "too few" resources in covenant enforcement. If the number of bondholders is small, then there can actually be overinvestment in enforcement in the sense that there is either a duplication of effort, or that creditors expend resources which simply result in change in the distribution of the proceeds. Our analysis implies that the firm's owners offer a contract which appoints a trustee to help assure that the optimal amount of covenant enforcement will take place.

Having the firm pay the trustees directly solves the "free-rider" problem which would be inherent in making individual bondholders pay the trustee for enforcing the covenants. However, after the bonds have been sold the stockholders have an incentive to bribe the trustee so that they can violate the debt covenants. There are several factors which prevent such bribery from taking place.

Bribing the trustee is expensive if the trustee's reputation has significant value in the marketplace. *Ex ante*, it is in the interests of the firm's owners to choose an "honest" trustee—that is, one who is expensive to bribe. This is because the value of the firm at the time it issues the debt contract reflects the probability of covenant enforcement. To the extent that enforcement by an "honest" trustee reduces the problems of adverse borrower behavior induced by risky debt, the value of the firm is higher. Our analysis therefore implies that those chosen as trustees stand to lose much if they are caught accepting bribes. In fact, the indenture trustee is "generally a large banking institution", which has significant revenues from activities unrelated to being a trustee and which also depends on the market's perception of its trustworthiness. Furthermore, the behavior of the trustee is restricted by both trust and contract law.

The Trust Indenture Act of 1939

This statute was designed to address conflicts of interest between the indenture trustee and the debtor corporation that Congress believed were likely to cause indenture trustees to act in a manner disloyal to bondholders in matters of enforcement. In one sense this is not a surprising problem: it is the debtor that selects the trustee to represent the bondholders before the bonds are offered to the public. The trustee is likely to be a bank with which the issuing corporation already has banking relationships, and might be a creditor of the debtor, and thus have a conflict of interest about whom to prefer if the debtor gets in trouble.

The Trust Indenture Act applies to all debt issues in excess of $10 million (by exempting those issued pursuant to an indenture for $10 million or less). Trust Indenture Act, § 304(a)(9), 15 USC § 77ddd(a)(9). It mandates the use of an indenture for the issuance of debt. Trust Indenture Act, § 305(b)(1)(A), 15 USC § 77eee(b)(1)(A) (registered securities); § 306(c), 15 USC § 77fff(c) (unregistered). The contents of the proposed indenture must be approved by the SEC to ensure that they meet requirements of the Act. Trust Indenture Act, § 305(a), 15 USC § 77eee(a) (registered); § 307(a), 15 USC § 77ggg(a) (unregistered).

Trustees must meet certain minimum qualification standards. Trustees must have capital & surplus of at least $150,000 (a number that has not changed since 1939). Section 310(a)(2), 15 USC § 77jjj(a). Further, trustees may not have specified conflicting interests once the debtor is in default,*

---

* Until 1990 the Act prohibited such conflicts of interest at any time. One assumes Congress concluded that potential conflicts of interest were of little concern before default, when the Trustee's duties were routine and ministerial.

such as being a trustee under another indenture for the same debtor (Section 310(b)(1), 15 USC § 77jjj(b)(1)); being an underwriter for a debt issue of the same issuer (Section 310(b)(2), 15 USC § 77jjj(b)(2)); or controlling the debtor, by owning 10% or more of the debtor's voting securities, (Section 310(b)(4), 15 USC § 77jjj(b)(4)); or holding other debt of the debtor that is in default (10% of such issue) (Section 310(b)(8), 15 USC § 77jjj(b)(8)).

There are mandatory terms and duties that must be contained in the indenture. The trustee must report to the bondholders annually concerning any change in its eligibility to serve as trustee, the amount owed it by the debtor. Section 313(a), 15 USC § 77mmm(a). There are limits on the exculpation that may be given the trustee. Section 315(d), 15 USC § 77oooo(d). In the event of default, the trustee must notify the bondholders, Section 315(b), 15 USC § 77oooo(b), and take such actions as a prudent person would take in the conduct of his own affairs. Section 315(c), 15 USC § 77oooo(c).

The Act also Regulates the terms of the indenture concerning amendment: the indenture can't be amended to change rights to payment of interest, unless holders of 75% of debt consent, and interest can't be delayed for more than 3 years. Section 316(a)(2), 15 USC § 77ppp(a)(2). Any other limits on payment obligations require the consent of the holder (unanimous consent). Section 316(b), 15 USC § 77ppp(b).

Elliott Associates v. J. Henry Schroder Bank & Trust Co.

838 F.2d 66 (2d Cir. 1988).

■ ALTIMARI, CIRCUIT JUDGE:

This appeal involves an examination of the obligations and duties of a trustee during the performance of its pre-default duties under a trust indenture, qualified under the Trust Indenture Act of 1939 (the "Act"). The instant action was brought by a debenture holder who sought to represent a class of all debenture holders under the trust indenture. The debenture holder alleged in its complaint that the trustee waived a 50–day notice period prior to the redemption of the debentures and did not consider the impact of the waiver on the financial interests of the debenture holders. The debenture holder alleged further that, had the trustee not waived the full 50–day notice period, the debenture holders would have been entitled to receive an additional $1.2 million in interest from the issuer of the debentures. The debenture holder therefore concludes that the trustee's waiver was improper and constituted a breach of the trustee's duties owed to the debenture holders under the indenture, the Act and state law.

The district court dismissed the debenture holder's action after conducting a bench trial and entered judgment in favor of the defendants. The district court held that the trustee's waiver did not constitute a breach of any duty owed to the debenture holders—under the indenture or otherwise—because, as the court found, a trustee's pre-default duties are limited to those duties expressly provided in the indenture. We agree with the district court that no breach of duty was stated here. Accordingly, we affirm the district court's decision dismissing the action.

FACTS and BACKGROUND

Appellant Elliott Associates ("Elliott") was the holder of $525,000 principal amount of 10% Convertible Subordinated Debentures due June 1, 1990 (the "debentures") which were issued by Centronics Data Computer Corporation ("Centronics") pursuant to an indenture between Centronics and J. Henry Schroder Bank and Trust Company ("Schroder"), as trustee. Elliott's debentures were part of an aggregate debenture offering by Centronics of $40,000,000 under the indenture which was qualified by the Securities Exchange Commission ("SEC") pursuant to the Act.

The indenture and debentures provided, inter alia, that Centronics had the right to redeem the debentures "at any time" at a specified price, plus accrued interest, but the indenture also provided that, during the first two years following the issuance of the debentures, Centronics' right to redeem was subject to certain conditions involving the market price of Centronics' common stock. To facilitate its right to redeem the debentures, Centronics was required to provide written notice of a proposed redemption to the trustee and to the debenture holders. Section 3.01 of the indenture required that Centronics give the trustee 50–day notice of its intention to call its debentures for redemption, "unless a shorter notice shall be satisfactory to the trustee." Section 3.03 of the indenture required Centronics to provide the debenture holders with "at least 15 days but not more than 60 days" notice of a proposed redemption.

At the option of the debenture holders, the debentures were convertible into shares of Centronics' common stock. In the event Centronics called the debentures for redemption, debenture holders could convert their debentures "at any time before the close of business on the last Business Day prior to the redemption date." Subject to certain adjustments, the conversion price was $3.25 per share. The number of shares issuable upon conversion could be determined by dividing the principal amount converted by the conversion price. Upon conversion, however, the debentures provided that "no adjustment for interest or dividends [would] be made."

Debenture holders were to receive interest payments from Centronics semi-annually on June 1 and December 1 of each year. Describing the method of interest payment, each debenture provided that the Company will pay interest on the Debentures (except defaulted interest) to the persons who are registered Holders of Debentures at the close of business on the November 15 or May 15 next preceding the interest payment date. Holders must surrender Debentures to a Paying Agent to collect principal payments. To insure the primacy of the debenture holders' right to receive interest, the indenture provided that "notwithstanding any other provision of this Indenture, the right of the Holder of a Security to receive payment of . . . interest on the Security . . . shall not be impaired.''

In early 1986, Centronics was considering whether to call its outstanding debentures for redemption. On March 12, 1986, Centronics' Treasury Services Manager, Neil R. Gordon, telephoned Schroder's Senior Vice President in charge of the Corporate Trust Department, George R. Sievers, and informed him of Centronics' interest in redeeming the debentures. Gordon told Sievers that Centronics "was contemplating redemption" of all of its outstanding debentures, subject to SEC approval and fluctuations in the market for Centronics' common stock. Specifically addressing the 50–day notice to the trustee requirement in section 3.01 of the indenture, Gordon asked Sievers how much time "Schroder would need once the SEC had Centronics' registration materials and an actual redemption date could therefore be set.'' Sievers responded that "Schroder would only need [one] week'' notice of the redemption. Sievers explained that this shorter notice would satisfy section 3.01 because Centronics was proposing a complete rather than a partial redemption, and because there were relatively few debenture holders. Sievers explained that the shorter notice therefore would provide it with sufficient time to perform its various administrative tasks in connection with the proposed redemption.

Shortly thereafter, on March 20, 1986, Centronics' Board of Directors met and approved a complete redemption of all of its outstanding debentures and designated May 16, 1986 as the redemption date. On April 4, 1986—42 days prior to the redemption—Centronics' President, Robert Stein, wrote Schroder and informed the trustee that "pursuant to the terms of the Indenture, notice is hereby given that the Company will redeem all of its outstanding 10% Convertible Subordinated Debentures due June 1, 1990, on May 16, 1986.'' Centronics then proceeded to file registration materials with the SEC in order to receive clearance for the redemption. Schroder was furnished with copies of all the materials Centronics had filed with the SEC.

On May 1, 1986, the SEC cleared the proposed redemption. On that same day, pursuant to section 3.03 of the indenture, Centronics gave formal notice of the May 16, 1986 redemption to the debenture holders. In a letter accompanying the Notice of Redemption, Centronics' President explained that, as long as the price of Centronics' common stock exceeded $3.75 per share, debenture holders would receive more value in conversion than in redemption. In the Notice of Redemption, debenture holders were advised, inter alia, that the conversion price of $3.25 per share, when divided into each $1,000 principal amount being converted, would yield 307.69 shares of Centronics common stock. Based upon the April 30, 1986 New York Stock Exchange closing price of $5 3/8 per share of Centronics' common stock, each $1,000 principal amount of debenture was convertible into Centronics common stock having an approximate value of $1,653.83. Debenture holders were advised further that failure to elect conversion by May 15, 1986 would result in each $1,000 principal amount debenture being redeemed on May 16 for $1,146.11, which consisted of $1,000 in principal, $100 for the

10% redemption premium, and $46.11 in interest accrued from December 1, 1985 (the last interest payment date) to May 16, 1986 (the redemption date). Finally, the notice of redemption explained that accrued interest was not payable upon conversion:

> *No adjustments for Interest or Dividends upon Conversion.* No payment or adjustment will be made by or on behalf of the Company (i) on account of any interest accrued on any Debentures surrendered for conversion or (ii) on account of dividends, if any, on shares of Common Stock issued upon such conversion. Holders converting Debentures will not be entitled to receive the interest thereon from December 1, 1985 to May 16, 1986, the date of redemption. (emphasis in original).

On May 15, 1986, the last day available for conversion prior to the May 16, 1986 redemption, Centronics' common stock traded at $6 5/8 per share. At that price, each $1,000 principal amount of debentures was convertible into Centronics' common stock worth approximately $2,038. Thus, it was clear that conversion at $2,038 was economically more profitable than redemption at $1,146.11. Debenture holders apparently recognized this fact because all the debenture holders converted their debentures into Centronics' common stock prior to the May 16, 1986 redemption.

Elliott filed the instant action on May 12, 1986 and sought an order from the district court enjoining the May 16, 1986 redemption. Elliott alleged in its complaint that Schroder and Centronics conspired to time the redemption in such a manner so as to avoid Centronics' obligation to pay interest on the next interest payment date, i.e., June 1, 1986. This conspiracy allegedly was accomplished by forcing debenture holders to convert prior to the close of business on May 15, 1986. Elliott contended that, as part of this conspiracy, Schroder improperly waived the 50–day notice in section 3.01 of the indenture and thus allowed Centronics to proceed with the redemption as planned. Elliott claimed that Schroder waived the 50–day notice without considering the impact of that waiver on the financial interests of the debenture holders and that the trustee's action in this regard constituted, inter alia, a breach of the trustee's fiduciary duties. Finally, Elliott alleged that, had it not been for the trustee's improper waiver, debenture holders would have been entitled to an additional payment of $1.2 million in interest from Centronics.

* * *

The district court decided this matter on the basis of the papers filed. The parties stipulated to the facts, as summarized above, and submitted affidavits of experts in the field who provided opinions on the custom and practice in the financial community relevant to the issues in the case. The district court filed its decision on March 17, 1987 in which it denied Elliott's motion for class certification and granted Schroder and Centronics' motions to dismiss. The district court also denied Schroder's and Centronics' motions for costs and attorneys' fees.

DISCUSSION

The central issue on this appeal is whether the district court properly held that the trustee was not obligated to weigh the financial interests of the debenture holders when it decided on March 12, 1986 to waive Centronics' compliance with section 3.01's 50-day notice requirement. We agree with the district court's conclusion that the trustee was under no such duty.

At the outset, it is important to sort out those matters not at issue here. First, Elliott does not dispute that Centronics complied in all respects with the indenture's requirement to provide notice of redemption to the debenture holders. Elliott's claim only challenges the sufficiency of the notice to the trustee and the manner in which the trustee decided to waive that notice. Moreover, Elliott does not dispute that Schroder's actions were expressly authorized by section 3.01, which specifically allows the trustee discretion to accept shorter notice of redemption from Centronics if that notice was deemed satisfactory. * * * Rather, Elliott's claim essentially is that the trustee was under a duty—implied from the indenture, the Act or state law—to secure greater benefits for debenture holders over and above the duties and obligations it undertook in the indenture.

No such implied duty can be found from the provisions of the Act or from its legislative history. Indeed, section 315(a)(1) of the Act allows a provision to be included in indentures (which was incorporated into the indenture at issue here) providing that

> the indenture trustee shall not be liable except for the performance of such duties [prior to an event of default] as are specifically set out in [the] indenture.

Moreover, when the Act was originally introduced in the Senate by Senator Barkley, it provided for the mandatory inclusion of a provision requiring the trustee to perform its pre-default duties and obligations in a manner consistent with that which a "prudent man would assume and perform." However, the version of the Act introduced in the House of Representatives by Representative Cole excluded the imposition of a pre-default "prudent man" duty on the trustee. After extensive hearings on the House and Senate versions of the Act, during which representatives of several financial institutions expressed concern over the imposition of pre-default duties in excess of those duties set forth expressly in the indenture, Congress enacted the present version of section 315 of the Act. Thus, it is clear from the express terms of the Act and its legislative history that no implicit duties, such as those suggested by Elliott, are imposed on the trustee to limit its pre-default conduct.

It is equally well-established under state common law that the duties of an indenture trustee are strictly defined and limited to the terms of the indenture, although the trustee must nevertheless refrain from engaging in conflicts of interest.

In view of the foregoing, it is no surprise that we have consistently rejected the imposition of additional duties on the trustee in light of the special relationship that the trustee already has with both the issuer and the debenture holders under the indenture. As we recognized in Meckel [v. Continental Resources Co., 758 F.2d 811 (2d Cir. 1985)],

> an indenture trustee is not subject to the ordinary trustee's duty of undivided loyalty. Unlike the ordinary trustee, who has historic common-law duties imposed beyond those in the trust agreement, an indenture trustee is more like a stakeholder whose duties and obligations are exclusively defined by the terms of the indenture agreement.

758 F.2d at 816. We therefore conclude that, so long as the trustee fulfills its obligations under the express terms of the indenture, it owes the debenture holders no additional, implicit pre-default duties or obligations except to avoid conflicts of interest.

holding

Our analysis here is therefore limited to determining whether the trustee fulfilled its duties under the indenture. As set forth above, section 3.01 requires that, when the company intends to call its debentures for redemption, it must provide the trustee with 50–day notice of the redemption, "unless a shorter notice shall be satisfactory to the trustee." Section 3.02 of the indenture sets forth the manner in which the trustee selects which debentures are to be redeemed when the company calls for a partial redemption. The American Bar Foundation's Commentaries on Model Debenture Indenture Provisions (1971) (the "Commentaries") explains that "notice of the Company's election to redeem all the debentures need not be given to the Trustee since such a redemption may be effected by the Company without any action on the part of the Trustee...." Id. at § 11–3, p. 493. Thus, it appears that section 3.01's notice requirement is intended for the trustee's benefit to allow it sufficient time to perform the various administrative tasks in preparation for redemption. While compliance with a full notice period may be necessary in the event of partial redemption, the full notice may not be required in the event of a complete redemption. We find that, although the trustee may reasonably insist on the full 50–day notice in the event of a complete redemption, it nevertheless has the discretion to accept shorter notice when it deems such shorter notice satisfactory.

administrative tasks

* * *

CONCLUSION

In view of the foregoing, we affirm the judgment of the district court which dismissed Elliott's action. * * *

QUESTIONS

1. What was the debenture holder's complaint?
2. What was the redemption price for a $1,000 debenture?
3. Why does the court note the redemption value on the last day, May 15?
4. What was the conversion value on May 15?

5. Have debenture holders received adequate protection against premature redemption?

6. The court quotes the *Commentaries* to the effect that when all debentures are called, notice need not be given to the Trustee. How does this relate to the Company's obligation to give advance notice? Don't debenture holders have independent rights to advance notice?

7. How much notice to debenture holders was required before redemption?

NOTE

The *Elliott Associates* opinion contains at least two characterizations of the Trustee's position: (1) a mere stakeholder, with duties limited to those specified in the indenture, and (2) a trustee, with duties of loyalty to the bondholders, citing Dabney v. Chase National Bank, 196 F.2d 668 (2d Cir. 1952). But other courts have used at least two other characterizations: (3) a full trustee, with full duties to act as a "prudent man" and (4) an agent for the bondholders, with some fiduciary duties. See Smith, Case & Morrison, The Trust Indenture Act of 1939 Needs No Conflict of Interest Resolution, 35 Bus. Law. 161, n. 30 (1979). The authors observe that originally the trustee was employed simply to serve as mortgagee for secured debt, and that the role has grown from that simple beginning. The trust was an obvious device to borrow to describe the trustee's role, since it held liens on (or title to) property for the benefit of bondholders. But from the beginning the indenture severely limited the duties and liabilities of the indenture trustee. One might ask whether bailee would be a more accurate description of the trustee's role, but for the troublesome problem that in a bailment legal title to property does not pass, as it does in a mortgage (except in lien theory states).

The availability of private rights of action under the securities laws has varied considerably over the years, with changes in the approach of the Supreme Court. In J. I. Case Co. v. Borak, 377 U.S. 426, 84 S. Ct. 1555 (1964), the Court held that "It appears clear that private parties have a right under Section 27 [of the Securities Exchange Act] to bring suit for violation of Section 14(a) of the Act." Section 27 merely provides that "the district courts ... shall have exclusive jurisdiction of violations of this title ... and of all suits in equity and actions at law brought to enforce any liability or duty created by this title...." Under that reasoning, private rights of action would exist for violations of all sections of the '34 Act. The court reasoned that private litigants would serve as "private attorneys general" to supplement the enforcement activities of the SEC, which lacked to resources to detect all violations.

The broad rationale of Case v. Borak was rejected in Piper v. Chris–Craft Industries, Inc., 430 U.S. 1, *supra*. Rather than follow the reasoning of Case v. Borak, that Section 27 of the Exchange Act created actions for all violations of the securities laws, the Court held that the doctrines of Cort v. Ash, 422 U.S. 66, 78 (1975) would govern. In this instance, it held that the

Williams Act was adopted to protect investors, not defeated tender offerors, and that such bidders did not have a private right of action. The opinion limited its impact in a footnote that stated "[n]or is the target corporation's standing to sue in issue in this case." 430 U.S. at 42, n. 29.

In 1975, the date of Morris v. Cantor, 390 F. Supp. 817 (S.D.N.Y. 1975), the first case implying a private right of action under the Trust Indenture Act, the Supreme Court decided Cort v. Ash, 422 U.S. 66 (1975), which provided a four-factor test:

A. Whether the plaintiff was one of the class for whose special benefit the statute was enacted;

B. Whether there was any indication of legislative intent, either explicit or implicit, to create a remedy or to deny one;

C. Whether it is consistent with the underlying purpose of the legislative scheme to imply such a remedy for the plaintiff; and

D. Whether the cause of action is one traditionally relegated to state law.

One could conclude, without reading Judge Mukasey's opinion in the following case, that this would probably be fatal to an analysis of suits against an indenture trustee.

The approach of Case v. Borak was also expressly rejected in Touche Ross & Co. v. Redington, 442 U.S. 560 (1979), which involved an unsuccessful attempt to imply a private right of action under section 17(a) of the Exchange Act, which requires registered securities brokers and dealers to file reports with the SEC. The court held that the implied cause of action in Case v. Borak was derived from section 14, not section 27. The court stated "We do not now question the actual holding of that case, but we decline to read the opinion so broadly that virtually every provision of the securities acts gives rise to an implied private cause of action. * * * To the extent our analysis in today's decision differs from that of the Court in Borak, it suffices to say that in a series of cases since Borak we have adhered to a stricter standard for the implications of private causes of action, and we follow that stricter standard today."

The Touche Ross opinion even cast doubt on the vitality of the Cort v. Ash test, since the court said the four factors mentioned there were merely ways to determine Congressional intent. 99 S.Ct. at 2489. The court said: "Indeed, the first three factors discussed in Cort—the language and focus of the statute, its legislative history, and its purpose, see 422 U.S. at 78— are ones traditionally relied upon in determining legislative intent. Here, the statute by its terms grants no private rights to any identifiable class and proscribes no conduct as unlawful. And the parties as well as the Court of Appeals agree that the legislative history of the 1934 Act simply does not speak to the issue of private remedies under Section 17(a). At least in such a case as this, the inquiry ends there: the question whether Congress either expressly or by implication intended to create a private right of action, has been definitively answered in the negative." 99 S.Ct. at 2489.

Shortly thereafter the Court refused to create a private right of action for damages under the antifraud provisions of the Investment Advisers Act of 1940, in Transamerica Mortgage Advisors, Inc. v. Lewis, 444 U.S. 11, 100 S.Ct. 242, 62 L.Ed.2d 146 (1979), although it did allow equitable relief for rescission. The majority opinion focused on the legislative history and the language of the act exclusively, and rejected the suggestion in Cort v. Ash that it was relevant to examine the utility of a private remedy to the enforcement scheme as evidence of legislative intent. 100 S.Ct. at 249. In dissent, Justice White argued that the decision could not be reconciled with earlier decisions.

In a case arising under the Commodity Exchange Act, the Court has taken a more generous approach toward implied causes of action, simply holding that where lower courts have implied private rights of action under general antifraud language in the statute prior to Congressional amendment of the statute, Congress has indicated its approval of an implied right of action. Merrill Lynch, Pierce, Fenner & Smith v. Curran, 456 U.S. 353, 102 S.Ct. 1825, 72 L.Ed.2d 182 (1982). Four justices—Powell, Rehnquist, Burger & O'Connor, dissented from the holding, indicating the uncertainty surrounding rules in this area.

B. The Trustee's Duties in Default

Until a default, the indenture trustee's duties are minimal in most indentures. Set out below is the definition of default from the American Bar Association's Model Simplified Indenture:

Section 6.01. Events of Default.

An "Event of Default" occurs if:

(1) the Company fails to pay interest on any Security when the same becomes due and payable and such failure continues for a period of [30] days;

(2) the Company fails to pay the Principal of any Security when the same becomes due and payable at maturity, upon redemption or otherwise;

(3) the Company fails to comply with any of its other agreements in the Securities or this Indenture and such failure continues for the period and after the notice specified below;

(4) the Company pursuant to or within the meaning of any Bankruptcy Law:

(A) commences a voluntary case,

(B) consents to the entry of an order for relief against it in an involuntary case,

(C) consents to the appointment of a Custodian of it or for all or substantially all of its property, or

(D) makes a general assignment for the benefit of its creditors; or

(5) a court of competent jurisdiction enters an order or decree under any Bankruptcy Law that:

(A) is for relief against the Company in an involuntary case,

(B) appoints a Custodian of the Company or for all or substantially all of its property, or

(C) orders the liquidation of the Company, and the order or decree remains unstayed and in effect for 60 days.

* * *

A Default under clause (3) is not an Event of Default until the Trustee or the Holders of at least [25]% in Principal amount of the Securities notify the Company and the Trustee of the Default and the Company does not cure the Default, or it is not waived, within [60] days after receipt of the notice. The notice must specify the Default, demand that it be remedied to the extent consistent with law, and state that the notice is a "Notice of Default."

As in most installment payment agreements, the indenture gives the Trustee the power to accelerate upon default:

Section 6.02.   Acceleration.

If an Event of Default occurs and is continuing, the Trustee by notice to the Company, or the Holders of at least 25% in Principal amount of the Securities by notice to the Company and the Trustee, may declare the Principal of and accrued and unpaid interest on all the Securities to be due and payable. Upon such declaration the Principal and interest shall be due and payable immediately.

These provisions are required by section 317(a) of the Trust Indenture Act.*

Recognizing that trustees may have weak incentives to enforce the indenture in the event of default, the Trust Indenture Act, section 316(a), provides that an indenture shall be deemed to provide a right for bondholders to enforce.** The Model Indenture contains complying provisions:

---

* (a) The indenture trustee shall be authorized—

(1) in the case of a default in payment of the principal of any indenture security, when and as the same shall become due and payable, or in the case of a default in payment of the interest on any such security, when and as the same shall become due and payable and the continuance of such default for such period as may be prescribed in such indenture, to recover judgment, in its own name and as trustee of an express trust, against the obligor upon the indenture securities for the whole amount of such principal and interest remaining unpaid; . . . .

** § 316(a)(1) contains the following:

"The indenture to be qualified—

(1) shall automatically be deemed (unless it is expressly provided therein that any such provision is excluded) to contain provisions *authorizing the holders of not less than a majority in principal amount* of the indenture securities or if expressly specified in such indenture, of any series of securities at the time outstanding (A) *to direct the time, method and place of conducting any proceeding for any remedy*

Section 6.05. Control by Majority.

The Holders of a majority in Principal amount of the Securities may direct the time, method and place of conducting any proceeding for any remedy available to the Trustee or exercising any trust or power conferred on the Trustee. However, the Trustee may refuse to follow any direction that conflicts with law or this Indenture, is unduly prejudicial to the rights of other Securityholders, or would involve the Trustee in personal liability or expense for which the Trustee has not received a satisfactory indemnity.

Section 6.06. Limitation on Suits.

A Securityholder may pursue a remedy with respect to this Indenture or the Securities only if:

(1) the Holder gives to the Trustee notice of a continuing Event of Default;

(2) the Holders of at least 25% in Principal amount of the Securities make a request to the Trustee to pursue the remedy;

(3) the Trustee either (i) gives to such Holders notice it will not comply with the request, or (ii) does not comply with the request within [15 or 30] days after receipt of the request; and

(4) the Holders of a majority in Principal amount of the Securities do not give the Trustee a direction inconsistent with the request prior to the earlier of the date, if ever, on which the Trustee delivers a notice under Section 6.06(3)(i) or the expiration of the period described in Section 6.06(3)(ii).

A Securityholder may not use this Indenture to prejudice the rights of another Securityholder or to obtain a preference or priority over another Securityholder.

Section 315(a)(1) of the Act allows a provision in the indenture that the trustee shall not be liable except for breach of duties specifically set out in the indenture. In the event of default, the trustee must notify the bondholders, and take such actions as a prudent person would take in the conduct of his own affairs. Section 315(b) and (c) 15 USC § 77oooo(b) & (c). The Model Simplified Indenture provides the following language:

Section 7.01. Duties of Trustee.

(a) If an Event of Default has occurred and is continuing, the Trustee shall exercise such of the rights and powers vested in it by this Indenture, and use the same degree of care and skill in their exercise, as a prudent person would exercise or use under the circumstances in the conduct of its own affairs.

(b) Except during the continuance of an Event of Default:

---

available to such trustee, under such indenture, or (B) on behalf of the holders of all such indenture securities, to consent to the waiver of any past default and its consequences;. . . ." [Emphasis supplied.]

(1) The Trustee need perform only those duties that are specifically set forth in this Indenture and no others. * * *

LNC Investments, Inc. v. First Fidelity Bank, National Association

935 F. Supp. 1333 (S.D.N.Y. 1996).

■ MUKASEY, U.S. DISTRICT JUDGE:

Plaintiffs LNC Investments, Inc. and Charter National Life Insurance Company invested in an equipment trust (the "Trust") established by defendant First Fidelity with Eastern Airlines in 1986. Plaintiffs have sued several trustees for violation of the Trust Indenture Act's ("TIA") prudent person requirement, breach of the Indenture's prudent person requirement, and breach of fiduciary duties under the Indenture and New York common law. * * *

First Fidelity and Eastern established the Trust in 1986 pursuant to a Secured Equipment Indenture and Lease Agreement. The Trust sold certificates to investors, used the proceeds to buy airplanes from Eastern, and then leased those planes back to the airline. Eastern's lease payments enabled the trust to repay principal and interest to certificate holders. The terms of the Trust, and the responsibilities of the various parties, were defined by the "Secured Equipment Indenture and Lease Agreement," dated November 15, 1986, and a "Second Supplemental Indenture," dated February 18, 1987 (together, the "Indenture").

The Trust issued three series of trust certificates, with declining rights of priority to payment, graduated interest rates and increasingly distant maturity dates. A different trustee was appointed to protect the rights of the investors in each series. Midlantic Bank served as First Series Trustee, United Jersey Bank ("UJB") as Second Series Trustee, and National Westminster Bank, N.J. ("NatWest"), as Third Series Trustee from the date of the Second Supplemental Indenture until August 31, 1990, when it resigned and was succeeded by Shawmut. Shawmut served as Third Series Trustee for the remainder of the life of the trust. The Indenture appointed First Fidelity as the "Collateral Trustee," and First Fidelity so served for the duration of the trust. * * *

On March 9, 1989, Eastern filed for bankruptcy protection under Chapter 11 of the Bankruptcy Code. The filing resulted in an automatic stay of all actions or claims against Eastern, and prevented the Trust from recovering the airplanes—the trust collateral. Just before Eastern filed for bankruptcy, an independent appraiser valued the airplanes at approximately $682 million and cautioned that their value would decline rapidly in the near future. A year-and-a-half later, on November 14, 1990, the trustees moved to lift the stay. By the time the stay was lifted on January 18, 1991, the value of the collateral aircraft had plummeted, leaving the certificate holders undersecured. Second series certificate holders will receive only part of their principal and no interest, and third series certificate holders will receive neither principal nor interest.

[Plaintiffs contend that these losses could have been prevented if the trustees had requested a lifting of the stay when bankruptcy first was declared.] The trustees' failure to do so, plaintiffs maintain, breached: (1) the prudent man requirement of the TIA, (2) the prudent man requirement of the agreement, §§ 9.02 and 9A.01 of the Indenture, and (3) fiduciary duties under the Indenture and New York common law.

* * *

III.

* * *

The threshold issue is whether the TIA creates a private right of action. Although the parties have not disputed this issue, the answer cannot be taken for granted, and an affirmative answer is necessary to support jurisdiction. Because the "prudent man" section of the TIA does not include language to the effect that aggrieved persons may sue, the statute does not create an express right of action. The court may infer, however, that the right exists. Zeffiro v. First Pennsylvania Banking, 623 F.2d 290, 295–99 (3d Cir. 1980) (applying the test of Cort v. Ash, 422 U.S. 66, 45 L. Ed. 2d 26, 95 S. Ct. 2080 (1975), and concluding that a right of action may be inferred under § 315(c) of the TIA), cert. denied, 456 U.S. 1005 (1982). . . . In Zeffiro, the Third Circuit set forth a full and persuasive analysis of why the right to sue should be inferred. Zeffiro, 623 F.2d at 295–99. The Second Circuit recently has cited Zeffiro with approval, and acknowledged that it "established a private cause of action under the [TIA]." Bluebird Partners, L.P. v. First Fidelity Bank, N.A., 85 F.3d 970, 974 (2d Cir. 1996).

Both text and legislative history support the inference that Congress intended to permit debenture holders to sue in federal court. Section 302(a) of the TIA declares that the purpose of the Act is to serve the "national public interest and the interest of investors in notes, bonds, debentures, evidences of indebtedness, and certificates of interest or participation therein." A private right of action for investors helps to achieve that purpose.

Moreover, § 315(d) of the TIA, part of the same section as the prudent man requirement, states that "the indenture to be qualified shall not contain any provisions relieving the indenture trustee from liability for its own negligent action, its own negligent failure to act, or its own willful misconduct," except under specified circumstances. That section reflects Congress' awareness that the trustee may be sued for negligence or willful misconduct by those injured by that conduct. See Morris N. Simkin, The Central Bank Case: A Warning Light for Indenture Trustees, N.Y. L.J., Oct. 21, 1993, at 1 (citing § 315(d) to support the proposition that "the TIA was amended in the Trust Indenture Reform Act of 1990 to clarify that there is a private cause of action for its violation."). Section 315(d), however, does not change the source of the § 315(c) right of action; it is implied, not express.

Section 315(e) of the TIA, also part of the same section as the prudent man requirement, explains the circumstances under which a court may require one of the parties to "any suit against the trustee for any action taken or omitted by it as trustee," to post an undertaking and explicitly refers to suits instituted by "any indenture security holder, or group of indenture security holders." The quoted language does not appear to refer to the sole express private cause of action under the TIA, § 323, because that section imposes liability only for material misstatements or omissions in a report filed with the SEC. A reference to § 323 more likely and more precisely would refer to material misstatements or omissions, rather than to actions taken or omitted. If the quoted language does not refer to § 323, that language is over-broad unless indenture security holders—that is, private parties—may sue the trustee for actions taken or omitted.

It is significant also that once an indenture has been registered with the SEC, that agency is unable to enforce the TIA. Section 309 of the Act states that SEC is not empowered "to conduct an investigation or other proceeding for the purpose of determining whether the provisions of an indenture which has been qualified under this subchapter are being complied with, or to enforce such provisions." The SEC's only affirmative powers lie in qualifying indentures and receiving the required reports. That Congress intended the SEC to have only a minimal enforcement role is confirmed by the legislative history, which recites that

> the Commission will have no powers with respect to enforcement of the provisions of the indenture. After the indenture has been executed it will be enforceable only by the parties like any other contract.

S. Rep. No. 248, 76th Cong., 1st Sess. 2 (1939). If private parties may not sue to enforce the statute, and the SEC is explicitly barred from doing so, the command in § 315(c) of the TIA that the trustee shall exercise the care of a "prudent man" is simply an exhortation that no one can enforce. I refuse to read what Congress passes and the President signs as a sermon or a cheer, rather than a law.

Finally, it is important to note that the jurisdictional section of the Act, § 322(b), authorizes federal jurisdiction for "actions brought to enforce any liability or duty created by" the Act. The generality of that section suggests that its application is not limited to the single section of the Act, § 323(a), that expressly grants a private right of action. 15 U.S.C. § 77www(a) (1994) (imposing civil liability for material misstatements and omissions in a report filed with the SEC); see 9 Louis Loss & Joel Seligman, Securities Regulation 4455 (3d ed. 1990) (stating that a private right of action under the TIA was created first by implication, "then in 1990 by amendment of § 322(b) to create a private cause of action for enforcement of mandatory indenture terms."). If Congress created jurisdiction to enforce that duty only, the words "any liability or duty" in § 322 would be misleading. Again, I refuse to interpret the words of Congress in a way that does not cohere with the rest of the statute, or with common sense. By phrasing the jurisdictional grant so generally, and by isolating that grant in its own section rather than including it in § 323, Congress indicated that other duties imposed by the statute also may be enforced by private parties.

QUESTIONS

1. Why would plaintiffs wish to sue under the Trust Indenture Act, rather than for breach of the terms of the Indenture under state law?

2. The court cites § 302 of the Trust Indenture Act, the purpose recital, that the purpose is to "serve the national public interest and the interest of investors in notes, bonds, debentures...." In the context of a statute that sets requirements for trustees and mandates contents for trust indentures, how persuasive is this general statement as to Congress' intent to grant a private right of action?

3. Why do investors need a private right of action under the Trust Indenture Act? Wouldn't they already have a negligence action under common law rules when a trustee violates its duty of care?

4. Judge Mukasey relies on an amendment to section 322 of the Trust Indenture Act to demonstrate Congressional intent to create a private right of action. In J. I. Case Co. v. Borak, 377 U.S. 426 (1964), the Court relied on similar language in section 27 of the Securities Exchange Act of 1934 to imply a cause of action to enforce the antifraud provisions with respect to proxy solicitations. Section 27 provides that "the district courts ... shall have exclusive jurisdiction of violations of this title ... and of all suits in equity and actions at law brought to enforce any liability or duty created by this title...." The approach of Case v. Borak was rejected in Touche Ross & Co. v. Redington, 442 U.S. 560 (1979). The court stated "We do not now question the actual holding of that case, but we decline to read the opinion so broadly that virtually every provision of the securities acts gives rise to an implied private cause of action. * * * To the extent our analysis in today's decision differs from that of the Court in Borak, it suffices to say that in a series of cases since Borak we have adhered to a stricter standard for the implications of private causes of action, and we follow that stricter standard today." Can you distinguish the language in section 322 of TIA from that of section 27 of the Exchange Act? Does Judge Mukasey attempt to do so?

5. If Congress intended to create private rights of action under TIA for violation of its mandatory provisions, why didn't it say so?

6. Is Judge Mukasey correct when he argues that the TIA's mandatory indenture language requirement would be toothless if investors can't sue under the Act, because the SEC is barred from enforcing indenture terms?

7. In Cort v. Ash, 422 U.S. 66 (1975) the court imposed a four-factor test for determining Congressional intent to provide a private action. Has Judge Mukasey examined the various parts of that test?

5.   Capital Leasing

Leasing transactions are alternatives to buying assets. In the short-term setting, the reasons for leasing are obvious—the transaction costs of a short-term rental will be lower than the cost of buying the asset and reselling it. These leases are called "operating" leases or "true" leases, as opposed to the "capital" leases discussed below. The lessor is better able to locate others interested in such assets than a buyer attempting to resell the asset would be in most cases. Further, if the lessor specializes in a certain type of equipment, its volume purchases will give it more bargaining power than individual buyers would have. In these cases the lessor typically is responsible for maintenance of the equipment, so the short-term lessee does not have to acquire the skills to maintain it. The short-term lessee does not have to tie up a large amount of capital, but simply to make the rental payments for the rental period. Many trucks are rented short-term by users that may have seasonal needs during busy periods. Heavy construction equipment can be rented for the duration of a project. In these "operating leases" the lessor typically keeps an inventory of the equipment available. In some leases the term may be extended, but the lessee will have a cancellation option. In effect this type of lease gives the lessee some protection against rental increases during the lease term. In effect this becomes an option to lease over the full term (more of options in Chapter 8). Short-term rentals will be at higher rates per period than long-term leases, in part because the lessor has to take into account expected periods when the equipment may not be leased. You see examples of this kind of equipment leasing on a daily basis—U–Haul and Ryder trucks, as well as auto rental and leasing companies are prime examples.

The analysis of long-term leases is quite different. Here buying rather than leasing is a real option. In this case the most direct comparison is between a lease and borrowing the money to buy the asset. These leases are called "capital" or "financial" leases. Typically these leases extend over much of the economic life of the asset. These leases generally are on a "net" basis, which means that the lessee bears all the costs of maintaining the asset. Not surprisingly, this turns the lease into a purely financial transaction from the lessor's perspective, and introduces finance companies such as GE Capital into the leasing business. Typically the lessee selects the desired equipment from the dealer or manufacturer, and then negotiates lease terms with the leasing company, which enters into the purchase contract for the equipment. Major airlines obtain most of their planes through this type of lease.

The Modigliani–Miller hypothesis tells us that the value of an asset does not change depending on the means used to finance it. Why, then, would leasing rather than borrowing on a secured basis make sense? In some cases taxes provide an explanation, where the lessor can make better use of a tax deduction than the lessee. For example, if a lessee has large amounts of tax-favored income, such as income from tax-free municipal bonds, or the benefits of accelerated depreciation, it may encounter the Alternative Minimum Tax. If so, it must add back its tax-favored items to its otherwise taxable income, and pay a tax based on the higher of taxes calculated in the regular way or 20% of the amount of income with the add-backs. In the latter case, accelerated depreciation deductions may be of less value to a lessee than to a lessor. With a purchase, the buyer can only deduct the allowed depreciation each year plus interest on any borrowings to finance the purchase; with a lease, it can deduct the entire amount of the lease payment. In effect this turns principal amortization into a current expense item. Second, the lease allows the lessee to finance the entire amount of the purchase rather than the smaller fraction it might be able to finance through secured lending.

A second reason why a company might decide to lease rather than borrow and purchase has to do with the treatment of leases on the lessee's balance sheet. In an operating lease the lessee is not thought of as the "owner" of the equipment, and is not thought of as having incurred a "debt" for the lease payments. As a result, the lease payments show up in income statements, but lease obligations don't show up as liabilities of the company. Similarly, the leased equipment doesn't show up as an asset of the business. To the extent that a company uses a large amount of operating leases, it is committing a substantial amount of its future cash flows to lease payments, which is no different from borrowing. Many loan agreements and indentures will treat many such leases in the same manner as additional borrowings, in terms of negative covenants against excessive new debt.

A sophisticated reader should react that this justification for leasing makes no sense. Won't efficient capital markets recognize what's going on, and treat the lease obligations just like debt? Obviously creditors negotiating new loans should recognize these leases as equivalent to debt, if they engage in any due diligence. But what about the effect of these leases on stock valuations? Excluding them from the balance sheet improves debt-equity ratios, and understates the riskiness of the company's stock. Are analysts likely to overlook these obligations when calculating financial ratios for a company? If this were a widespread and systematic error, that would be surprising, and would provide an arbitrage opportunity. Can some companies slip under the radar for a while? Very possibly.

There are limits to this explanation, because GAAP requires enterprises to classify some leases as "capital leases," in which case the transaction is treated as a purchase of the asset and incurrence of indebtedness. The asset is carried on the lessee's balance sheet at its cost (and is thereafter depreciated by the lessee), and the present value of the lease payments (which includes the imputed interest expense) is carried as a liability. Statement of Financial Accounting Standards No. 13 requires treatment of a lease as a capital lease when *any one* of the following tests is met:

(1) The lease transfers ownership of the property to the lessee before the lease expires;

(2) The lessee can purchase the leased asset at a bargain price at the expiration of the lease;

(3) The lease term last for at least 75% of the asset's estimated economic life; or

(4) The present value of the minimum lease payments is at least 90% of the asset's fair value.

6. ASSET BACKED FINANCING

Corporations can, of course, borrow funds on a secured basis—that is, by pledging assets to secure the promised payments. While secured loans have priority over unsecured debt in bankruptcy, to the extent of the collateral, this distinction is sometimes more formal than real. Strategic behavior by junior creditors in bankruptcy reorganization under Chapter 11 of the Bankruptcy Code can cost secured creditors a significant amount during the course of administration. To this extent, the value of a security interest is reduced, and secured lenders will compensate in advance by demanding higher interest rates, approaching those on unsecured debt.

Even corporations with weak credit ratings may have some assets that produce reliable cash flows. Financial institutions flirting with insolvency may hold residential or commercial real estate mortgages, or equipment leases. Manufacturing or retailing corporations may hold trade receivables, credit card receivables or automobile loans, to name a few forms of liquid assets. It is important that there be sufficient separate financial obligations to provide diversification, so the default of a single debtor won't have a material adverse effect on the expected payments. Thus a single equipment lease wouldn't be a good candidate for securitization. Further, it's possible that even a pool of some kinds of such leases might not work, simply because in hard economic conditions multiple lessees might default. Consider airplane leases as an example. If an airline defaults, what happens to its planes? Frequently other airlines are also facing difficulties, so leasing them to another airline may not be possible. Despite these difficulties, airplane leases have been securitized. Often the types of assets used in this type of financing have well-established records for reliability of payments. If they were used for secured financing by a weak borrower, interest rates would be much higher than if they were used by a strong borrower.

The object of the exercise, then, is to cause the weak borrower to transfer these assets to a stronger borrower that can minimize the cost of borrowing. This requires a sale by the weak borrower (called the "Originator") to a separate legal entity (the "Special Purpose Entity" or "SPE").* The SPE is typically organized solely for the purpose of this transaction, and buys the financial assets from the Originator.

The SPE pays for the financial assets by issuing its own securities, either into public markets or in private placements to institutional buyers.

---

* These entities are also called "Special Purpose Vehicles" or "SPVs."

Whatever they are called, these securities are debt-like. And because the SPE has no other obligations, they are free of the risks faced by the Originator, and thus allow the SPE to sell its own debt securities at lower interest rates than the Originator could achieve. This allows the SPE to pass this benefit on to the Originator in the purchase price for the financial assets, because the SPE's cash flows allow it to service more debt than the Originator could have.

Use of an SPE has other benefits for the Originator. It converts one liquid asset (receivables, etc.) into a slightly more liquid asset (cash). Since both are current assets, this is by itself not a major benefit for the Originator's balance sheet or its credit-worthiness. But if the Originator had borrowed on a secured basis against these financial assets, it would have incurred debt, which would appear on the balance sheet, worsening its debt-equity ratio and raising its fixed charges. A sale to the SPE, however, keeps this debt off the Originator's balance sheet, which is a clear benefit. (All of this analysis changes, of course, if the sale is not a "true" sale, as discussed below.) Consider the following example, of a company that either borrows against or sells $100 million in accounts receivable:

Original Balance Sheet

Balance Sheet
LeverCo.
($millions)

Assets		Liabilities	
Cash	$100	Current liabilities	$100
Receivables	$100	Long-term liabilities	$100
Plant & Equipment	$200	Total liabilities	$200
		Shareholders' Equity	$200
Total Assets	$400	Total Liabilities + Equity	$400
Current ratio:	2:1		
Debt-equity ratio:	1:1		

Now assume that Leverco borrows against its receivables on a secured basis, and is able to borrow 100% of their value:

Balance Sheet with Borrowing
LeverCo.
($millions)

Assets		Liabilities	
Cash	$200	Current liabilities	$200
Receivables	$100	Long-term liabilities	$100
Plant & Equipment	$200	Total liabilities	$300
		Shareholders' Equity	$200
Total Assets	$500	Total Liabilities + Equity	$500
Current ratio:	3:2		
Debt-equity ratio:	3:2		

Now assume that Leverco sells its receivables to an SPE:

Balance Sheet with Sale
LeverCo.
($millions)

Assets		Liabilities	
Cash	$200	Current liabilities	$100
Receivables	0	Long-term liabilities	$100
Plant & Equipment	$200	Total liabilities	$200
		Shareholders' Equity	$200
Total Assets	$400	Total Liabilities + Equity	$400
Current ratio:	2:1		
Debt-equity ratio:	1:1		

There are several benefits from this difference between borrowing and selling. First, for companies with existing debt, borrowing may cause them to be in violation of covenants (note that borrowing increases LeverCo's debt-equity ratio, while selling receivables leaves ratios as they were before), while selling debt for cash should not cause any difficulties. (Covenants may prohibit asset sales, of course.) Second, in terms of ratio analysis, prospective creditors will be more willing to extend new credit to Leverco if it sells receivables rather than borrows against them on a secured basis. Third, where lenders to the Originator must worry about the Originator's credit risk and engage in a thorough credit investigation, that task falls away when the financial assets are separated from the Originator. As firms become more highly leveraged and edge closer to a real risk of insolvency, there is reason to believe that the risk that the Originator may not be completely candid about its problems increases.* Now, when the receivables are sold to an SPE with no other assets or liabilities, investors only need to know the quality of the receivables. In some cases, especially where there are doubts, Originators may seek credit enhancement in the form of overcollateralization or a letter of credit from a bank.

The SPE's debt can be structured into a series of classes with different rights and priorities. When its debt is structured in this way, the classes are called "tranches." One way is according to maturity: Class A receives all principal payments until it is fully paid; Class B then receives all principal payments in the same manner, and so on. Class A thus becomes relatively short-term debt with the greatest assurance of repayment, and will carry the lowest interest rate, while rates demanded by investors for successive tranches will rise. The other way to structure these tranches is by providing specific payment obligations on each class, with Class A being paid the amounts due it on each payment date, and then Class B being paid to the extent funds are available, and so on. Again, Class A will be the most secure and carry the lowest interest rate. When the securities are sold in public markets, they are generally rated by one of the bond rating agencies,

---

* This is a "last period" problem for desperate managers. For a discussion of this problem in the context of securities fraud, see Jennifer Arlen and William J. Carney, Vicarious Liability for Fraud on Securities Markets: Theory and Evidence, 1992 U. Ill. L. Rev. 691.

and the top tranche will receive a very high investment grade rating. This rating means that regulated buyers such as insurance companies can purchase the securities. Commercial banks got more favorable treatment for holding AAA-rated bonds of this type than for holding home mortgages, which encouraged the growth of this business.

The key to the success of structured financing is the ability to separate the SPE and its assets from the Originator and its creditors. Should the Originator find itself in bankruptcy reorganization, its creditors may make two types of arguments to reach the assets of the SPE. First, they may argue that the Originator's transfer of the financial assets was a fraudulent conveyance. In most cases this is a relatively easy argument to defeat, because the SPE will have paid the issuer all the proceeds from its own issue of securities, which is powerful evidence of the fair market value of the financial assets.

The second challenge to the transaction may come under the doctrine of substantive consolidation. Where there is unified operation of a parent and subsidiary corporations, courts may ignore the separate legal entities and treat all related corporations as part of a single debtor. Consolidated Rock Products Co. v. Du Bois, 312 U.S. 510 (1941). One key to avoiding this problem is to make certain that the SPE is "bankruptcy remote" from the Originator. If the SPE is controlled by the Originator, it may be tempted to cause the SPE to enter Chapter 11 at the same time as the Originator, in order to bring more assets into the debtor's estate through consolidation. One solution is that the charter or other organizing document of the SPE provide against voluntary filings, by requiring approval of independent directors of the SPE. Recall from Credit Lyonnais Bank Nederland, N.V. v. Pathe Communications, *supra* Chapter Four, Part 6.B, that directors of an insolvent parent will owe fiduciary duties to the parent's creditors as well as its shareholders. For an example of a director's causing an SPE to enter Chapter 11 along with the Originator, see the description of the Days Inn of America case in Steven L. Schwarcz, Structured Finance § 2:2.1 (3d ed. 2002, 2003).

The other key to avoiding consolidation is to assure that the financial assets are truly separated from the Originator, by a "true sale."* Part of the difficulty arises here because the Originator may "over-collateralize" the SPE, by giving it more financial assets than may be needed to pay off the SPE's obligations, in order to enhance the SPE's creditworthiness and reduce the interest rate to be paid by the SPE. Of course, if there are assets remaining after the SPE has repaid all its obligations, the Originator will want them returned. But this creates difficult questions of whether the transaction was a "true sale" or merely a secured loan by the Originator, so the assets remain part of the Originator's bankrupt estate. In this case the SPE simply becomes a creditor of the bankrupt estate, to share in the assets as a secured creditor. Because of the automatic stay of all collection proceedings, at the very least this imposes a delay on collection of the

---

* The Originator also wants this transaction treated as a sale rather than a secured loan to improve its own balance sheet, as shown in the examples given above.

financial assets. For example, it would not be surprising for the Originator to warrant to the SPE the quality of the financial assets, but if the Originator goes the next step to guarantee payment of the receivables, the Originator has retained the risks of an owner, and the transaction may be treated as a secured loan. Major's Furniture Mart, Inc. v. Castle Credit Corp., 449 F.Supp. 538 (E.D. Pa. 1978), *affirmed* 602 F.2d 538 (3d Cir. 1979). And if the Originator retains the right to surplus collections from the financial assets, after the SPE has paid off its debts and earned some agreed-upon return, the transaction may be treated as a secured loan. In re Evergreen Valley Resort, Inc., 23 B.R. 659, 661–62 (Bankr. D. Me. 1982); In re Hurricane Elkhorn Coal Corp. 19 B.R. 609, 617 (Bank. W.D. Ky. 1982), rev'd on other grounds, 763 F.2d 188 (6th Cir. 1985).

A full treatment of this subject can be found in Steven L. Schwarcz, *supra*, from which much of this discussion is drawn. Having listed other factors that influence whether a true sale has occurred, Schwarcz writes: "It is rare in modern commercial transactions for all the factors favoring a true bankruptcy sale to be met. There is inevitably a question of balance." *Id.* at 4:6.

We should note that mortgage pools were securitized in similar offerings that failed in 2008. These mortgage-backed securities suffered major defaults of mortgagors, particularly where mortgages were secured by subprime loans. These securities were originated in many cases by federally sponsored agencies such as the Federal National Mortgage Association ("Fannie Mae"), founded in the 1930s to buy mortgages from lenders, and Federal Home Loan Mortgage Corporation ("Freddie Mac"), founded in 1968 for the same purpose. In both cases these entities were sponsored by the U.S. government, but later sold their shares to investors, with the Government retaining control of appointment of the board of directors. They both sold mortgage-backed securities to investors in public markets. By the 1970s other private entities began entering the field, so that few lenders continued to hold the loans they originated, but rather sold them to agencies, banks, investment banks and others, such as Countrywide Finance, that packaged them and sold mortgage-backed securities. As in the case of SPEs, these securities were sold in tranches, with the first tranche structured so that these investments were paid first, were the most secure, and achieved the highest ratings from the ratings services (see Appendix 6–A, following this section). The rating agencies turned out to be terribly mistaken on the quality of many of these securities, and their value collapsed when willing buyers suddenly disappeared. The rating services based their ratings of these bonds on their past experience with other asset categories, apparently not recognizing that the subprime mortgages placed in these pools were generally of much lower quality than the other asset categories with which they were familiar. It was this crisis that was one of the major causes of the financial crisis of 2008, which required major government intervention in capital markets to prevent a collapse of the banking system.

APPENDIX 6-A

MOODY'S INVESTOR SERVICES

Aaa—Bonds which are rated Aaa are judged to be of the best quality. They carry the smallest degree of investment risk and are generally referred to as "gilt edge." Interest payments are protected by a large or by an exceptionally stable margin and principal is secure. While the various protective elements are likely to change, such changes as can be visualized are most unlikely to impair the fundamentally strong position of such issues.

Aa—Bonds which are rated Aa are judged to be of high quality by all standards. Together with the Aaa group they comprise what are generally known as high grade bonds. They are rated lower than the best bonds because margins of protection may not be as large as in Aaa securities or fluctuation of protective elements may be of grater amplitude or there may be other elements present which make the long term risks appear some-what greater than in Aaa securities.

A—Bonds which are rated A possess many favorable investment attributes and are to be considered as upper medium grade obligations. Factors giving security to principal and interest are considered adequate but elements may be present which suggest a susceptibility to impairment sometime in the future.

Baa—Bonds which are rated Baa are considered medium grade obligations, i.e., they are neither highly protected nor poorly secured. Interest payment and principal security appear adequate for the present but certain protective elements may be lacking or may be characteristically unreliable over any great length of time. Such bonds lack outstanding investment characteristics and in fact have speculative characteristics as well.

Ba—Bonds which are rated Ba are judged to have speculative elements; their future cannot be considered as well-assured. Often the protection of interest and principal payments may be very moderate, and thereby not well safeguarded during both good and bad times over the future. Uncertainty of position characterizes bonds in this class.

B—Bonds which are rated B generally lack characteristics of the desirable investment. Assurance of interest and principal payments or of maintenance of other terms of the contract over any long period of time may be small.

Caa—Bonds which are rated Caa are of poor standing. Such issues may be in default or there may be present elements of danger with respect to principal or interest.

Ca—Bonds which are rated Ca represent obligations which are speculative in a high degree. Such issues are often in default or have other marked shortcomings.

C—Bonds which are rated C are the lowest rated class of bonds, and issues so rated can be regarded as having extremely poor prospects of ever attaining any real investment standing.

STANDARD & POORS:

AAA—Debt rated "AAA" has the highest rating assigned by Standard & Poor's. Capacity to pay interest and repay principal is extremely strong.

AA—Debt rated "AA" has a very strong capacity to pay interest and repay principal and differs from the higher rated issues only in small degree.

A—Debt rated "A" has a strong capacity to pay interest and repay principal although it is somewhat more susceptible to the adverse affects of changes in circumstances and economic conditions than debt in higher rated categories.

BBB—Debt rated "BBB" is regarded as having an adequate capacity to pay interest and repay principal. Whereas it normally exhibits adequate protection parameters, adverse economic conditions or changing circumstances are more likely to lead to a weakened capacity to pay interest and repay principal for debt in this category than in higher rated categories.

BB, B, CCC, CC, C—Debt rated "BB", "B", "CCC", "CC" and "C" is regarded, on balance, as predominantly speculative with respect to capacity to pay interest and repay principal in accordance with the terms of the obligation. "BB" indicates the lowest degree of speculation and "C" the highest degree of speculation. While such debt will likely have some quality and protective characteristics, these are outweighed by large uncertainties or major risk exposures to adverse conditions.

APPENDIX 6–B

REVISED MODEL SIMPLIFIED INDENTURE

Table of Contents

ARTICLE 1   **Definitions and Rules of Construction; Applicability of the Trust Indenture Act**

Section 1.01	Definitions
Section 1.02	Other Definitions
Section 1.03	Rules of Construction
Section 1.04	Trust Indenture Act

ARTICLE 2   **The Securities**

Section 2.01	Form and Dating
Section 2.02	Execution and Authentication
Section 2.03	Agents
Section 2.04	Paying Agent to Hold Money in Trust
Section 2.05	Securityholder Lists
Section 2.06	Transfer and Exchange
Section 2.07	Replacement Securities
Section 2.08	Outstanding Securities
Section 2.09	Treasury Securities Disregarded for Certain Purposes
Section 2.10	Temporary Securities
Section 2.11	Global Securities
Section 2.12	Cancellation
Section 2.13	Defaulted Interest

ARTICLE 3   **Redemptions**

Section 3.01	Notice to Trustee
Section 3.02	Selection of Securities to be Redeemed
Section 3.03	Notice of Redemption
Section 3.04	Effect of Notice of Redemption
Section 3.05	Deposit of Redemption Price
Section 3.06	Securities Redeemed in Part

ARTICLE 4   **Covenants**

Section 4.01	Payment of Securities
Section 4.02	SEC Reports
Section 4.03	Compliance Certificate
Section 4.04	Notice of Certain Events

ARTICLE 5   **Successors**

Section 5.01	When Company May Merge, etc.
Section 5.02	Successor Corporation Substituted

ARTICLE 6   **Defaults and Remedies**

Section 6.01	Events of Default
Section 6.02	Acceleration
Section 6.03	Other Remedies
Section 6.04	Waiver of Past Defaults
Section 6.05	Control by Majority

Section 6.06   Limitation on Suits
Section 6.07   Rights of Holders to Receive Payment
Section 6.08   Priorities
Section 6.09   Undertaking for Costs
Section 6.10   Proof of Claim
Section 6.11   Actions of a Holder

ARTICLE 7   **Trustee**
Section 7.01   Duties of Trustee
Section 7.02   Rights of Trustee
Section 7.03   Individual Rights of Trustee; Disqualification
Section 7.04   Trustee's Disclaimer
Section 7.05   Notice of Defaults
Section 7.06   Reports by Trustee to Holders
Section 7.07   Compensation and Indemnity
Section 7.08   Replacement of Trustee
Section 7.09   Successor Trustee by Merger, etc.
Section 7.10   Eligibility
Section 7.11   Preferential Collection of Claims Against Company

ARTICLE 8   **Satisfaction and Discharge**
Section 8.01   Satisfaction and Discharge of Indenture
Section 8.02   Application of Trust Funds
Section 8.03   Reinstatement
Section 8.04   Repayment to Company

ARTICLE 9   **Amendments**
Section 9.01   Without Consent of Holders
Section 9.02   With Consent of Holders
Section 9.03   Compliance with Trust Indenture Act and Section 12.03
Section 9.04   Revocation and Effect of Consents and Waivers
Section 9.05   Notice of Amendment; Notation on or Exchange of Securities
Section 9.06   Trustee Protected

ARTICLE 10   **Conversion**
Section 10.01   Conversion Right and Conversion Price
Section 10.02   Conversion Procedure
Section 10.03   Fractional Shares
Section 10.04   Taxes on Conversion
Section 10.05   Company to Reserve Common Stock
Section 10.06   Adjustment for Change in Capital Stock
Section 10.07   Adjustment for Rights Issue
Section 10.08   Adjustment for Other Distributions
Section 10.09   Adjustment for Common Stock Issue
Section 10.10   Adjustment for Convertible Securities Issue
Section 10.11   Current Market Price
Section 10.12   When De Minimis Adjustment May Be Deferred
Section 10.13   When No Adjustment Required
Section 10.14   Notice of Adjustment
Section 10.15   Voluntary Reduction

Section 10.16   Notice of Certain Transactions
Section 10.17   Reorganization of the Company
Section 10.18   Company Determination Final
Section 10.19   Trustee's Disclaimer

ARTICLE 11   **Subordination**
Section 11.01   Securities Subordinated to Senior Debt
Section 11.02   Securities Subordinated in Any Proceeding
Section 11.03   No Payment on Securities in Certain Circumstances
Section 11.04   Subrogation
Section 11.05   Obligations of the Company Unconditional
Section 11.06   Trustee and Paying Agents Entitled to Assume Payments Not Prohibited in Absence of Notice
Section 11.07   Satisfaction and Discharge
Section 11.08   Subordination Rights Not Impaired by Acts or Omissions of the Company or Holders of Senior Debt
Section 11.09   Right to Hold Senior Debt
Section 11.10   No Fiduciary Duty of Trustee or Securityholders to Holders of Senior Debt
Section 11.11   Distribution to Holders of Senior Debt
Section 11.12   Trustee's Rights to Compensation, Reimbursement of Expenses and Indemnification
Section 11.13   Exception for Certain Distributions
Section 11.14   Certain Definitions

ARTICLE 12   **Miscellaneous**
Section 12.01   Notices
Section 12.02   Communication by Holders with Other Holders
Section 12.03   Certificate and Opinion as to Conditions Precedent
Section 12.04   Statements Required in Certificate or Opinion
Section 12.05   Rules by Trustee and Agents
Section 12.06   Legal Holidays
Section 12.07   No Recourse Against Others
Section 12.08   Duplicate Originals
Section 12.09   Variable Provisions
Section 12.10   Governing Law

CHAPTER SEVEN

PREFERRED STOCK

1. INTRODUCTION

A. DEFINING PREFERRED STOCK

Preferred stock is generally thought of as a class of stock having some preference over common stock—typically preferences as to dividends and payments on liquidation. The important observation is that preferred stock's terms are generally not set by law, but by contract, which is ultimately found in a company's charter. Delaware's statute, quoted below in part, is typical of statutes authorizing preferred stock.

§ 151. Classes and series of stock; redemption; rights, etc.

(a) Every corporation may issue 1 or more classes of stock or 1 or more series of stock within any class thereof, any or all of which classes may be of stock with par value or stock without par value and which classes or series may have such voting powers, full or limited, or no voting powers, and such designations, preferences and relative, participating, optional or other special rights, and qualifications, limitations or restrictions thereof, as shall be stated and expressed in the certificate of incorporation or of any amendment thereto, or in the resolution or resolutions providing for the issue of such stock adopted by the board of directors pursuant to authority expressly vested in it by the provisions of its certificate of incorporation.

See also Revised Model Bus. Corp. Act § 6.01(a).

The statute says nothing about "preferred" shares–only that a corporation may issue one or more classes of stock, leaving the determination of all rights and preferences to the corporate drafters. See also M.B.C.A. § 6.01(a). The default rule in both Delaware and Model Act jurisdictions is that each share has one vote, unless otherwise provided in the certificate or articles of incorporation. Del. G.C.L. § 212(a); M.B.C.A. § 7.21(a). Traditionally preferred stock has possessed a preference as to dividends over the common—recognizing, of course, that the declaration and payment of dividends is within the business judgment of the board of directors. See, e.g. Delaware G.C.L. § 170 and M.B.C.A. § 6.40(a) and Chapter Nine, *infra*. Typically the only real commitment of the corporation is that it will not pay any dividends on junior securities, such as common stock, unless and until it has paid the stated dividend on the preferred stock. Thus the dividend obligation is a conditional one—much like the "dividend" obligation on the Class A and Class B debentures in Eliasen v. ITEL Corporation, 82 F.3d 731 (7th Cir. 1996), in Chapter Four, Part 2. For a public company, the pressure to declare preferred dividends on a regular basis is considerable, because of the loss of reputation for reliability among investors in preferred stock that would result from passing a dividend. Thus preferred dividends are not a binding legal obligation: like dividends on common, they only become a corporate obligation when they are declared by the board of directors.

Preferred stock must be part of the authorized shares of a corporation, expressed in its articles (or certificate) of incorporation. It may be authorized at any time—upon creation of the corporation, or at some later date. Because the dividend rate required on the preferred is influenced somewhat by prevailing interest rates, it is often necessary to defer specifying the dividend rate until such time as the corporation contemplates preferred stock financing. Accordingly, the charter must be amended at that time to tailor the terms of the preferred to the current demands of the market. One of the great innovations of corporate law in the late 1960s was the development of so-called "blank check preferred," sometimes called simply "blank preferred." Both the Delaware statute and the Revised Model Business Corporation Act were amended to permit companies to authorize preferred stock "in blank," leaving it to the board of directors to fill in the terms at some later date by a board resolution and the filing of a "certificate of designation" or "articles of amendment" to the articles of incorporation. See Del. G.C.L. § 151 and Rev. Model Bus. Corp. Act § 6.02.

The amorphous nature of preferred stock is exemplified by the differences between the Delaware Chancery Court and the Delaware Supreme Court on this matter. In Telvest, Inc. v. Olson, 1979 WL 1759 (Del. Ch. 1979), the board of Outdoor Sports Industries, Inc. ("OSI") used a previously authorized class of blank check preferred stock to create a new series of preferred stock that was issued as a stock dividend to the common stockholders. The reason for the issuance was to create a new takeover defense against a threatening potential bidder for control. The principal feature of the preferred was that it required an 80% vote of the class, voting separately, to approve any merger or other major transaction with anyone owning 20% or more of its stock—a so-called "shark repellent" amendment. The preferred's economic rights were merely nominal–it had no specified dividend right, except the right to receive a dividend equal to those paid on the common stock, and to receive an amount in liquidation equal to that paid on a share of common stock. In both cases, the preferred was to receive that payment "before" the common stock. In rejecting the board's authority to use the blank check preferred stock in this way, Vice Chancellor Brown wrote:

> I am not persuaded by this reasoning at this point. In the first place, OSI's certificate of incorporation allows its directors, by resolution, to fix voting rights and preferences as to preferred stock only. There is some question as to whether the First Series Preferred is really preferred stock. It is entitled to a dividend only when the common stock is entitled to a dividend. The amount of its dividend must be the same as the common stock dividend. On dissolution, it receives only that amount received by the common stock. The only

difference is that in either event the First Series Preferred is entitled to be paid this identical sum first. As to the dividend aspect, a corporation cannot validly declare a dividend without setting aside sufficient funds to pay all dividends so declared. Wilmington Trust Co. v. Wilmington Trust Co., Del. Ch., 15 A.2d 665 (1940). As to dissolution rights, the funds to pay the First Series Preferred will have to be available by virtue of the fact that the amount per share is determined by dividing remaining net assets by the total number of First Series Preferred plus common shares. Thus any supposed preference as to dividends or liquidation rights seems illusory at best. If any preference is created, it would seem to lie almost entirely in the voting rights. In this regard, Starring v. American Hair & Felt Co., Del. Ch., 191 A.887 (1937) casts some doubt on the proposition that a stock can be classified as "special" or "preferred" under § 151 solely because it is given a favored voting position.

The opinion also expressed doubt that the voting rights of the common stockholders could be limited (by in effect giving a veto power to holders of 20% of the preferred) without a vote of the common stockholders, and expressed doubt about whether the filing of a certificate of designation of the rights and preferences of the preferred constituted a valid amendment of the certificate of incorporation. The second leg of the Vice Chancellor's opinion cast doubt that the board could in effect amend the certificate of incorporation by filing a certificate of designation on the rights of the preferred. The Delaware General Assembly quickly eliminated those doubts by adding a new sentence at the end of § 151(g): "When any certificate filed under this subsection becomes effective, it shall have the effect of amending the certificate of incorporation...."

The Telvest reasoning was applied under New Jersey law in Asarco Inc. V. Court, 611 F. Supp. 468, 479 (D.N.J. 1985), where Judge Debevoise wrote:

> The [Telvest] Court dismissed OSI's argument that the stock issuance was authorized by Section 151 of the Delaware General Corporation Law, which, like Section 14A:7–2 of the New Jersey Business Corporation Act, permits a board of directors, by resolution, to issue preferred stock and to set voting rights and preferences thereon by resolution if authorized to do so by the company's certificate of incorporation.
>
> The reasoning in Telvest is sound and is persuasive in this case. It leads to the conclusion that in adopting the voting provisions of Asarco Series C Preferred Stock, Asarco's Board of Directors exceeded the authority which the New Jersey Business Corporation Act conferred upon them. Thus issuance of the stock would be unlawful.

But the Delaware Supreme Court was not persuaded by Telvest. In Moran v. Household International, Inc., 500 A.2d 1346 (Del. 1985), the court rejected the plaintiff's so-called "sham preferred" argument based on the Telvest decision in the following terms:

Secondly, appellants contend that § 157 does not authorize the issuance of sham rights such as the Rights Plan. They contend that the Rights were designed never to be exercised, and that the Plan has no economic value. In addition, they contend the preferred stock made subject to the Rights is also illusory, citing Telvest, Inc. v. Olson, Del. Ch., C.A. No. 5798, Brown, V.C. (March 8, 1979).

Appellants' sham contention fails in both regards. As to the Rights, they can and will be exercised upon the happening of a triggering mechanism, as we have observed during the current struggle of Sir James Goldsmith to take control of Crown Zellerbach. See Wall Street Journal, July 26, 1985, at 3, 12. As to the preferred shares, we agree with the Court of Chancery that they are distinguishable from sham securities invalidated in Telvest, *supra*. The Household preferred, issuable upon the happening of a triggering event, have superior dividend and liquidation rights.

500 A.2d at 1351. The court's distinction is elusive, to say the least. The Household preferred (or 1/100 of a share) had a dividend identical to that of the common stock in amount, and the amount to be paid as a preference on liquidation was identical to that to be paid to the common. The only distinction is that the preferred is to be paid "first."

While approximately 85% of all poison pill plans employ preferred stock of this variety, there appear to have been remarkably few challenges based on whether the stock is truly "preferred." Other challenges to rights plans, where successful on other grounds, such as discrimination among common stockholders, have generally been legislatively reversed.

In some situations corporations that have become takeover targets have issued a new series of preferred stock, with a class veto power over mergers with a major shareholder, to a friendly corporation. Would this violate any duties owed by management to the common stockholders? See Condec Corp. v. Lunkenheimer Co., 230 A.2d 769 (Del. Ch. 1967), holding that issuing shares solely to dilute the control of a hostile bidder was a violation of management's duties, absent a threat to the company from the presence of a new shareholder.

PROBLEM

When El Paso Company found itself faced with a hostile bid from Burlington Industries, the board used authorized but unissued blank check preferred stock to issue a dividend of one new preferred share for every twenty shares of common stock. The new preferred carried an 8% cumulative dividend, and a stated liquidation preference of $25 per share over the common. Like the OSI stock, it had supermajority voting rights, requiring a 90% vote to approve a merger with an interested stockholder if the holder failed to assure that the merger would be on terms at least as favorable as the tender offer. Preferred shareholders also were granted the right to vote for one-third of the board of directors, although interested stockholders were denied the vote. Would this provision pass muster under the Telvest standard?

B. THE USES OF PREFERRED STOCK

Preferred stock serves a wide variety of purposes in corporate finance. As you will see, law plays a minor role in the structure of preferred stock; contractual arrangements play the major role, and the task of the courts is most often interpretation of the contract.

For development stage companies seeking venture capital financing, preferred is almost always the form in which venture capital is invested. Development stage companies are busy consuming capital, not earning profits, and thus do not anticipate being able to pay dividends until after the business becomes profitable. While the preferred stock typically carries a stated dividend rate, there is no expectation that the issuer will declare any dividends (and probably could not legally do so in states with legal capital rules discussed in Chapter Nine). As a result the dividends will accrue and accumulate ("cumulative dividends") as an obligation to be paid before any payments can be made to the common. On sale of the company, the dividend arrearages will also be paid first. On conversion of the preferred stock into common, a typical feature, the arrearages entitle the preferred holders to additional shares of common. Typically this kind of preferred stock will have voting rights, giving the venture capitalists a significant voice in the corporation, and will be convertible into common stock, which will occur automatically when the company has a public offering of its common stock. The preferred is typically issued at the valuation agreed upon for the common, and is convertible at that price, no matter how high the valuation of the common rises.

For companies that are already public, preferred stock is a tax favored form of investment. Under Internal Revenue Code of 1986 § 243, if stock is owned by another corporation, 70% of dividends received are deductible by the recipient in all cases; if the recipient owns 20% or more of the stock, 80% of the dividends are deductible, while they are 100% deductible if the recipient corporation owns 80% or more of the stock. Accordingly, for financial institutions that invest in income-producing securities, preferred stock has a tax advantage over corporate bonds, the interest on which is taxable as income to the recipient. Insurance companies are major investors in preferred securities.

From the issuer's standpoint, preferred stock is attractive because it can represent "permanent" capital that need never be redeemed, in contrast to debt which must be paid off or refinanced at current interest rates. (Some preferred will be redeemable, however.) In the 1980s, when some companies were acquired on a highly leveraged basis, buyers sometimes used preferred stock of the acquired company as part of the purchase price, because it did not create the same risk of default that bonds might create.*

---

* Another way in which LBO buyers avoided default risk was to issue debt that paid no current interest, but simply paid a face amount at maturity, so that the market value of the bond was discounted well below its face value ("deep discount debt" or "zero coupon debt.") In the alternative, LBO buyers sometimes employed debt where interest could be paid with

In other cases regulated companies use preferred stock as part of their capital structure because additional equity capital is required, but the holders of common stock may not wish to relinquish voting control. In these cases preferred stock may not have voting rights, unless dividends are missed.

In the venture capital setting, the venture capitalists that purchase preferred stock are typically given a right to insist on redemption after the passage of some period of time, during which it is expected that the company will either be successful and offer its common stock to the public (in which case the preferred automatically converts to common stock) or will recognize its failure. This "put" right will probably bankrupt the company, and is designed to give the venture capitalists a priority over the common stockholders in liquidation.

2. DIVIDENDS

A. THE VARIETIES OF DIVIDENDS

The so-called "straight" preferred stock (non-cumulative) dividend is almost never observed in practice. A dividend provision of this kind would simply state the annual (or semi-annual or quarterly) dividend rate, and provide that no dividends could be paid on the common until the annual, etc. dividend was paid. But what of next year? This year's missed dividend obligation would be gone, and in order to pay a dividend on the common stock next year, the corporation would only have to pay next year's preferred dividend. Indeed, one can imagine the directors (elected by common stockholders) passing on preferred dividends for as long as ten years, then declaring a single year's dividend on the preferred, and distributing the accumulated earnings from the past ten years to the common stockholders. For this reason virtually all preferred stock dividend rights in public corporations are cumulative, in the sense that no dividend can be paid on the common until arrearages on preferred stock dividends have first been paid.

Over history most preferred stock dividends have been set as either a stated dollar amount or a stated percentage of the par or nominal value of the shares. More recently preferred stock dividends, like interest rates on corporate loans, have been set at variable rates. Beginning in the early 1980s a number of major issuers sold adjustable rate preferred stock, with the dividend rate set to an objective measure of interest rates, frequently the highest of the Treasury bill rate, the ten-year constant maturity rate for Treasury bonds and the twenty-year constant maturity rate for Treasury bonds, plus or minus a specified number of basis points. (A basis point is 1/100th of one percent.)

---

additional bonds, rather than cash ("Payment in Kind" or "PIK" debt). Some LBO buyers also employed PIK preferred. These patterns were repeated in the first years of this century.

If quarterly adjustments were desired in the market, shorter adjustments might also be desirable. Issuers began to issue preferred with rates reset every 49 days, or at other periods. In some cases the process of setting rates varied, and these shares became known as "Auction Rate" preferred stock. In this case when a new dividend period started, each holder of preferred (which is sold in large units) indicated to the transfer agent whether it wished to continue to hold the preferred at whatever rate was set, or wished to set a minimum rate that it would accept, so that if the reset rate was below the minimum, it would sell its shares. The transfer agent (usually a bank) accepted bids for rates not only from existing holders of preferred, but also from potential buyers. Those holders who bid the lowest rates necessary to sell all of the preferred became the new preferred stockholders. All holders earned the highest rate necessary to sell the issue. This market collapsed in February 2008 when no one would buy these securities, and at this writing the auction market remains frozen.

Just as with common stock, directors are vested with broad discretion about whether to declare dividends on the preferred stock. As with common stock dividends, judicial review of the exercise of this discretion is generally governed by the business judgment rule, absent some conflict of interest.

Arizona Western Insurance Company v. L. L. Constantin & Co.

247 F.2d 388 (3d Cir. 1957).

■ BIGGS, C.J.

Arizona Western Insurance Company (Arizona) instituted this suit against L. L. Constantin & Co. (Constantin) to recover dividends on 10,000 shares of preferred stock in Constantin held by Arizona and authorized by the December 2, 1952 amendment to Constantin's certificate of incorporation. This provided in pertinent part that "The holders of the preferred stock shall be entitled to receive, and the Company shall be bound to pay thereon, but only out of the net profits of the Company, a fixed yearly dividend of Fifty Cents (50 cents) per share, payable semi-annually." An identical provision appeared in the preferred stock certificate. Arizona was the record holder of the stock from on or about October 1, 1954 to on or about February 1, 1956.

Constantin's Board of Directors on December 28, 1954 adopted a resolution which read: "Resolved, that a dividend be declared on preferred stock at the interest rate of 5% to all * * * stockholders of record on December 30, 1954, payable January 15, 1955." At the declared rate Arizona as the holder of 10,000 shares of preferred stock was entitled to dividends of $5,000. Constantin paid dividends on certain shares of its preferred stock but nothing was paid on the shares held by Arizona.

In 1955 no dividend was paid to any holder of preferred stock. After a demand for dividends Arizona instituted suit on the basis of diversity. * * * The third count alleged that under the terms of Constantin's amended certificate of incorporation and the preferred stock certificate, Constantin was bound to pay to Arizona out of net profits a fixed yearly dividend of 50 cents per share, payable semi-annually, and that net profits were available for the payment of such a dividend. Arizona alleged that it demanded payments of the dividends, that payment was refused and that it is entitled to a judgment in the amount of $5,000 plus interest for the dividend declared in 1954 and not paid to Arizona and to a judgment in the amount of $5,000 plus interest for the unpaid dividend which, it is alleged, Constantin was bound to pay in 1955, there being net profits available.

Constantin answered in substance that ... while admitting the declaration of a dividend on December 28, 1954, Constantin denied that any dividend had been declared in 1955, and denied also that any dividends were due in 1955 as a matter of right.

* * *

Constantin's motion for summary judgment, or judgment on the pleadings in the alternative, with respect to the third count of the amended complaint, was granted, and Arizona's cross-motion for summary judgment addressed to the third count was denied. The court below handed down no opinion explaining the reasons which caused it to take the action it did on the motions directed to the third count but on the occasion of oral argument on the motions the court expressed the view that "notwithstanding the provision in the certificate of incorporation, a dividend should be payable only when declared in the discretion and judgment of the Board of Directors."

* * *

Constantin contends that if this court compels the payment of a dividend, absent fraud or bad faith on the part of the Board of Directors, it will be interfering in the management and internal affairs of the corporation; that the compelling of a payment of a dividend would change the status of Arizona from a shareholder to a creditor; and that a suit to compel a declaration of a dividend is a class action and Arizona does not allege that it sues on behalf of other stockholders similarly situated.

* * *

The language employed by the Court of Chancery in Stevens v. United States Steel Corp., 68 N.J.Eq. 373, 377–378, 59 A. 905, 907 is pertinent. The Vice–Chancellor said: "Subject, of course, to provisions in the charter, and also to the by-laws of the Company, it is for the directors to say whether profits shall be distributed to the stockholders, or retained for the purpose of the corporate business." In Wilson v. American Ice Co., D.C. 1913, 206 F. 736, 738, the United States District Court for the District of New Jersey stated, "It is well settled, that in the absence of statutory provisions, the granting of dividends from the profits of a trading corporation is in the discretion of the directors, subject to the intervention of a court of equity for improper refusal."

* * *

We appreciate the reluctance of courts to construe provisions relative to the declaration of dividends in such a way as to hold that the directors are bound in certain circumstances to declare dividends. But the shareholder has the right to have his contract enforced, and, if the contract as expressed in the certificate of incorporation and the stock certificate, require the construction that dividends are mandatory under specified circumstances the courts can adopt no other construction of the contract between the corporation and the stockholder.

The amended certificate of incorporation in the case at bar provides in pertinent part that, "The holders of the preferred stock shall be entitled to receive, and the Company shall be bound to pay thereon, but only out of the net profits of the Company, a fixed yearly dividend of fifty cents (50 cents) per share, payable semi-annually." Identical language is found in the preferred stock certificate. Words could not more clearly or plainly manifest that Constantin agreed to be bound to pay dividends where net profits were available for the purpose. We will not hold that the words were employed as a bait to prospective purchasers of preferred stock.

L.L. Constantin & Co. v. R.P. Holding Corp.

56 N.J. Super. 411; 153 A.2d 378 (1959).

■ COLIE, J.S.C.

L.L. Constantin & Co., a New Jersey corporation, filed a complaint against R.P. Holding Corp., Charles Denby, Continental Bank & Trust Co. as receiver of Inland Empire Insurance Co., and Royal American Insurance Co., seeking a declaratory judgment stating the rights and obligations of the parties hereto in connection with preferred stock issued by the plaintiff corporation. Royal American Insurance Co. has not answered and a default has been taken against it.

The controversy between the plaintiff and defendants arises from the legal effect of an amendment on December 23, 1952 of the certificate of incorporation which read, so far as pertinent:

> "By authorizing the issuance of fifty thousand (50,000) shares of preferred stock having a par value of Ten dollars ($10.00) each. The holders of the preferred stock shall be entitled to receive, and the Company shall be bound to pay thereon, but only out of the net profits of the Company, a fixed yearly dividend of fifty cents (50 cents) per share, payable semi-annually. The said dividend shall be cumulative. Preferred stockholders shall have no voting rights. The stock shall be redeemable on and after January 2nd, 1955, at Ten dollars and fifty cents ($10.50) per share."

An identical legend appears upon the face of each preferred stock certificate.

[The court recited the holding in the previous litigation, and determined that there was no collateral estoppel in this action, because R. P.

Holding Corp. and its co-defendants were not parties to the previous litigation. Further, *res judicata* was not applicable here.]

* * *

[In 1956 Constantin's board passed the following resolution:]

"The holders of the preferred stock shall be entitled to receive (cumulative) dividends, as and when declared by the Board of Directors, out of its surplus or net profits, as determined pursuant and subject to the provisions of the General Corporation Law of the State of New Jersey, at the rate of 50 cents per annum * * *."

New preferred stock certificates were printed bearing, *inter alia*, the above language.

At the pretrial conference, the complaint was amended to allege that

"the corporate by-laws in article 7, provide that dividends are to be declared by the Board of Directors when expedient, and that unless the directors declare a dividend, the same does not become due and payable."

[The defendants all purchased their stock after these actions were taken.]

* * *

Standing alone, the 1952 amendment providing that "the holders of the preferred stock shall be entitled to receive, and the company shall be bound to pay * * *" presents no problem for construction. There is no ambiguity which would entitle this court to construe the above quoted direction. As the Court of Appeals said: "Words could not more clearly or plainly manifest that Constantin agreed to be bound to pay dividends where net profits were available for the purpose." However, the contract between Constantin and its preferred shareholders is to be found not alone in the language of the 1952 amendment but in the entire certificate of incorporation, as amended, and the applicable provisions of the statute in force at the time of incorporation, *i.e.*, 1947. The General Corporation Act provides that "the business of every corporation shall be managed by its board of directors * * *," and "unless otherwise provided in the certificate of incorporation, or in a by-law adopted by a vote of at least a majority of the stockholders." *R.S.* 14:8–20, from which the last quote is borrowed, reads:

"14:8–20. Working capital; directors may vary; dividends

Unless otherwise provided in the certificate of incorporation, or in a by-law adopted by a vote of at least a majority of the stockholders, the directors of every corporation organized under this title may, in their discretion, from time to time, fix and vary the amount of the working capital of the corporation and determine what, if any, dividends shall be declared and paid to stockholders out of its surplus or net profits. Dividends may be declared and paid in capital stock with or without par value."

The legislative history behind the enactment of *R.S.* 14:8–20 demonstrates that the declaration of dividends has had the attention of the Legislature, and its attempts to limit control over dividends were deemed unsatisfactory and ended, for the time being, in the enactment last quoted. The prior legislative attempts have been commented upon by our courts in no flattering terms. " * * * [T]he legislative experiment, in controlling the discretion of the managers of corporations in respect of the distribution of profits was somewhat dangerous, and brought about a situation which was liable to be productive of mischief, and exposed corporations to malicious and injurious attacks." *Stevens v. United States Steel*, 68 *N.J. Eq.* 373 (*Ch.* 1905). "Naturally, the amount needed for the legitimate purposes of the company's business must be determined by the directors, who are intrusted with the management of the company." *Murray v. Beattie Mfg. Co.*, 79 *N.J. Eq.* 604 (*E. & A.* 1911).

Public policy with respect to corporate management has been established by the mandate of the Legislature to be that "the business of every corporation shall be managed by its board of directors" and that "the directors of every corporation * * * may * * * determine what, if any, dividends shall be declared and paid to stockholders out of its surplus or net profits." Recognizing that the situation might arise in which this public policy might not be in the best interests of the corporation and its shareholders, the Legislature provided a means to permit the corporation to act contrary to such public policy. The device employed was to qualify the imposed discretion in the directors by providing that it could be avoided, but only where "otherwise provided in the certificate of incorporation, or in a by-law adopted by a vote of at least a majority of the stockholders * * *."

Article 7 of Constantin's by-laws reads:

"The Board of Directors shall by vote declare dividends from the surplus profits of the Corporation whenever, in their opinion, the condition of the Corporation's affairs will render it expedient for such dividend to be declared."

It is, in part, the inconsistency between the discretion imposed on the directors as to dividends and the mandatory declaration allegedly provided for in the 1952 amendment that requires judicial construction as between the charter, the by-laws and the statute. It may be conceded at the outset that where inconsistency exists between by-laws and certificate of incorporation, the latter ordinarily governs and it would seem more so where, as here, the conflict arose some years after the enactment of the by-law. However, the provision in the quoted by-law is consistent with *R.S.* 14:8–20 which vested discretion in the directors as to dividend declarations, and the fact that Article 7 of the by-laws was not amended when the 1952 amendment was adopted is some evidence that the 1952 amendment was not intended to divest the directors of discretion.

Can it be said that the statement that "the holders of the preferred stock shall be entitled to receive, and the Company shall be bound to pay * * *" meets the requirements of "unless otherwise provided in the certificate of incorporation, or in a by-law * * *" of Constantin? This court must answer that question in the negative. The statute is clear that the corporate business is to be managed by its directors and that, unless otherwise provided in the charter or by-law the directors may, in their discretion determine what if any dividends shall be declared and paid. In such an important area of corporate policy as is the discretion of the board of directors as to declaration of dividends little should be left to implication. It is only by implication that the language "entitled to receive * * * and bound to pay" can be said to override the statutory discretion embodied in *R.S.* 14:8–20.

* * *

In light of the statutory provisions, the language of Article 7 of the by-laws and the well-settled attitude of the courts against implied repealers and the absence of a "clear and peremptory" denial of the directors' statutory right to discretionary control of dividends, the court holds that the amendment of 1952 does not make the payment of a dividend mandatory, if net profits are available therefor.

QUESTIONS

1. How would a court be likely to decide the dispute over Constantin's dividend obligations under RMBCA §§ 6.40 and 8.01(b)?

2. How would the Delaware courts be likely to decide this question under Del. Gen. Corp. L. §§ 141 and 170?

3. Why would a company commit to a preferred stock with a dividend that was mandatory if earned? Why not issue corporate bonds instead?

4. Assuming that there is an ambiguity in the Constantin language governing dividends on the preferred stock, would the following provisions resolve that ambiguity?

> "The holders of first preferred shares will be entitled to receive semiannually or quarterly all net earnings of the corporation determined and declared as dividends in each fiscal year up to but not exceeding ___ percent per annum on all outstanding first preferred shares before any dividend will be set apart or paid upon any other shares of the company."

1A FLETCHER CORPORATION FORMS ANNOTATED § 905 (1999 Rev. Vol.)

> "Dividends upon the Series B Preferred Stock shall be paid out of funds legally available therefore, annually beginning on August 1, 2001, at the rate per annum of $.27 per share (annually the 'Mandatory Dividend' and collectively the 'Mandatory Dividends'). In addition, commencing on August 1, 2001, the holders of Series B Preferred Stock shall be entitled to receive, out of funds legally available therefore, additional annual dividends at the rate per annum of $.27 per share (the 'Elective Dividend' and collectively the 'Elective Dividends'), when, as and if declared by the Board of Directors. Elective and Mandatory Dividends (the 'Series B Accru-

ing Dividends') shall accrue from day to day, whether or not earned or declared, and shall be cumulative, from August 1, 2001.''

Articles of Incorporation of The Catalog.Com Inc.

B. STRAIGHT AND CUMULATIVE DIVIDENDS

Guttmann v. Illinois Central R. Co.

189 F.2d 927 (2d Cir.), certiorari denied, 342 U.S. 867 (1951).

■ FRANK, CIRCUIT JUDGE.

The trial court's findings of facts—which are amply supported by the evidence and unquestionably are not "clearly erroneous"—establish that the directors acted well within their discretion in withholding declarations of dividends on the non-cumulative preferred stock up to the year 1948. In so holding, we assume, *arguendo*, that, as plaintiff insists, the standard of discretion in weighing the propriety of the non-declaration of dividends on such preferred stock is far stricter than in the case of non-declaration of dividends on common stock. For, on the facts as found and on the evidence, we think the directors, in not declaring dividends on the preferred in the years 1937–1947, adopted a reasonable attitude of reluctant but contingent pessimism about the future, an attitude proper, in the circumstances, for persons charged, on behalf of all interests, with the management of this enterprise.[2]

The issue, then, is whether the directors could validly declare a dividend on the common stock in 1950 without directing that there should be paid (in addition to preferred dividends on the preferred for that year) alleged arrears of preferred dividends, the amount of which had been earned in 1942–1947 but remained undeclared and unpaid. To put it differently, we must decide whether (a) the directors had the power to declare such alleged arrears of dividends on the preferred and (b) whether they 'abused' their discretion in declaring any dividend on the common without ordering the payment of those alleged arrears.[*]

---

2. That the directors were not acting in the interest of the common stockholders in disregard of the interest of the preferred appears from the following: The Union Pacific Railroad holds about 25% of the outstanding common stock (i.e., 348,700 shares out of a total of 1,357,994) and was therefore pretty obviously in control of the Board of Directors. Yet, that same Railroad holds about 52% of the outstanding preferred shares (i.e., 98,270 out of a total of 186,457). Union Pacific would plainly be better off if the plaintiff were successful in this suit.

The interest of the public was involved in the reduction of funded debt. For railroads with excessive fixed charges, in periods of stress tend to skimp maintenance and not to improve service.

[*] The Certificate of Incorporation provided: "The preferred stock shall be preferred both as to dividends and assets and shall be entitled to receive out of the surplus or net profits of the Company, in each fiscal year, dividends at such rate or rates, not exceeding seven per cent, per annum, as shall be determined by the Board of Directors in connection with the issue of the respective series of said stock and expressed in the stock certificates therefor, before any

Our lode-star is Wabash Railway Co. v. Barclay, 280 U.S. 197, which dealt with the non-cumulative preferred stock of an Indiana railroad corporation. There were no controlling Indiana decisions or statutes on that subject. The United States Supreme Court was therefore obliged to interpret the contract according to its own notions of what the contract meant. We have a similar problem here, since there are no Illinois decisions or statutory provisions which control or guide us. Absent such decisions and statutes, we must take the Wabash opinion as expressing the correct interpretation of the rights of non-cumulative preferred stockholders of this Illinois company. For the difference between the language of the preferred stock here and that in Wabash seems to us to be of no moment.

In the Wabash case, plaintiffs, holders of non-cumulative preferred stock, sought an injunction preventing the defendant railroad company from paying dividends on the common stock unless it first paid dividends on the non-cumulative preferred to the extent that the company, in previous years, had had net earnings available for that payment and that such dividends remained unpaid. The Court decided against the plaintiffs. It spoke of the fact that, in earlier years, "net earnings that could have been used for the payment were expended upon improvements and additions to the property and equipment of the road"; it held that the contract with the preferred meant that "if those profits are justifiably applied by the directors to capital improvements and no dividend is declared within the year, the claim for that year is gone and cannot be asserted at a later date." We take that as a ruling that the directors were left with no discretion ever to pay any such dividend. For if they had had that discretion, it would surely have been an "abuse" to pay dividends on the common while disregarding the asserted claim of the non-cumulative preferred to back dividends. Indeed, the plaintiff in the instant case contends that a payment of common dividends, whenever there is such a discretion, constitutes an unlawful "diversion"; and such a "diversion" would be an "abuse" of discretion.[6]

Plaintiff, however, seeks to limit the effect of the Wabash ruling to instances where the net earnings, for a given year, which could have been paid to the non-cumulative preferred, have once been expended justifiably for "capital improvements" or "additions to the property or equipment." He would have us treat the words "non-cumulative" as if they read "cumulative if earned except only when the earnings are paid out for

dividends shall be paid upon the common stock, but such dividends shall be non-cumulative. No dividends shall be paid, declared, or set apart for payment on the common stock of the Company, in any fiscal year, unless the full dividend on the preferred stock for such year shall have been paid or provided for. Whenever in any year the dividend paid on such preferred stock is less in amount that the full dividend payable on all such stock outstanding, the dividends paid shall be divided between the series of such stock outstanding in the same proportion to the aggregate sums which would be distributable to the preferred stock of each of such series if full dividends were paid thereon."—Ed.

6. This becomes the more evident when it is noted that the plaintiff asserts that "non-cumulative" means in effect, "cumulative if earned." For directors have no discretion to pay common dividends without paying arrears of cumulative preferred dividends.

capital additions." He argues that the Wabash ruling has no application when net earnings for a given year are legitimately retained for any one of a variety of other corporate purposes, and when in a subsequent year it develops that such retention was not necessary. We think the attempted distinction untenable. It ascribes to the Supreme Court a naive over-estimation of the importance of tangibles (because they can be touched and seen) as contrasted with intangibles. Suppose the directors of a corporation justifiably invested the retained earnings for the year 1945 in land which, at the time, seemed essential or highly desirable for the company's future welfare. Suppose that, in 1948, it turned out that the land so purchased was not necessary or useful, and that the directors thereupon caused it to be sold. Plaintiff's position compels the implied concession that the proceeds of such a sale would never be available for payment of so-called arrears of unpaid non-cumulative preferred dividends, and that the directors would forever lack all discretion to pay them.[7] We fail to see any intelligible difference between (1) such a situation[8] and (2) one where annual earnings are properly retained for any appropriate corporate purpose, and where in a later year the retention proves wholly unnecessary.[9] There is no sensible ground for singling out legitimate capital outlays, once made, as the sole cause of the irrevocable destruction of the claims of the preferred. We do not believe that the Supreme Court gave the contract with the preferred such an irrational interpretation. It simply happened that in the Wabash case the earnings had been used for capital additions, and that, accordingly, the court happened to mention that particular purpose. Consequently, we think that the Court, in referring to that fact, did not intend it to have any significance. We disregard the decisions of the New Jersey courts, and the decision of the Ninth Circuit, since we think they are at odds with the rationale of the Wabash decision.

Here we are interpreting a contract into which uncoerced men entered. Nothing in the wording of that contract would suggest to an ordinary wayfaring person the existence of a contingent or inchoate right to arrears of dividends.[13] The notion that such a right was promised is, rather, the

---

7. Were plaintiff to contend that the proceeds of such a sale are available for preferred dividends he would logically be required to contend that reserves for depreciation of capital assets are similarly available. For such reserves constitute, in effect, a repayment of investment in capital.

8. Or one where, in our supposititious case, the corporation, no longer needing the land, could easily sell it at a handsome figure.

9. The attempted distinction would also come to this: (a) The noncumulative preferred irrevocably loses all rights to a dividend as of a given year, if the earnings for that year are invested in fixed capital, but (b) has an inchoate right in the form of a sort of contingent credit if those earnings are reasonably retained for future investments which are never made and which thereafter show up as wholly unnecessary. This is to say that the preferred take the risk of loss of a dividend as of a year in which it is earned when there is a reasonable need for a present capital investment, but no such risk if there is a present reasonable likelihood of a need for such an investment in the future, which later appears undesirable. We see no rational basis for such a distinction.

13. Berle, a most brilliant legal commentator on corporate finance, who may be credited with the authorship of plaintiff's basic contention, admitted that "popular interpretation,"

invention of lawyers or other experts, a notion stemming from considerations of fairness, from a policy of protecting investors in those securities.
But the preferred stockholders are not—like sailors or idiots or infants—
wards of the judiciary. As courts on occasions have quoted or paraphrased
ancient poets, it may not be inappropriate to paraphrase a modern poet,
and to say that "a contract is a contract is a contract." To be sure, it is an
overstatement that the courts never do more than carry out the intentions
of the parties: In the interest of fairness and justice, many a judge-made
legal rule does impose, on one of the parties to a contract, obligations which
neither party actually contemplated and as to which the language of the
contract is silent. But there are limits to the extent to which a court may go
in so interpolating rights and obligations which were never in the parties'
contemplation. In this case we consider those limits clear.

In sum, we hold that, since the directors did not "abuse" their
discretion in withholding dividends on the non-cumulative preferred for
any past years, (a) no right survived to have those dividends declared, and
(b) the directors had no discretion whatever to declare those dividends
subsequently.

From the point of view of the preferred stockholders, the bargain they
made may well be of a most undesirable kind. Perhaps the making of such
bargains should be prevented. But, if so, the way to prevent them is by
legislation, or by prophylactic administrative action authorized by legislation, as in the case of the S. E. C. in respect of securities, including
preferred stocks, whether cumulative or non-cumulative, issued by public
utility holding companies or their subsidiaries. The courts are not empowered to practice such preventive legal medicine, and must not try to revise,
extensively, contracts already outstanding and freely made by adults who
are not incompetents.

Affirmed.

QUESTIONS

1. What justifies passing preferred non-cumulative dividends when the
   company has sufficient profits to declare and pay them?

2. Is there any limit on the kinds of investments of profits a company can
   make when it passes on preferred dividends?

3. Does this mean the board has complete discretion about paying preferred non-cumulative dividends, as long as it acts in good faith?

4. Why doesn't the court exercise its equitable powers to provide some
   rights to passed dividends, when past profits are available?

---

including that of "investors and businessmen," holds "non-cumulative" to mean "that
dividends on non-cumulative preferred stock, once passed or omitted, are 'dead': can never be
made up." See Berle, Non-Cumulative Preferred Stock, 23 Columbia Law Review (1923) 358,
364–365.

5. Does the statement of the board's discretion to omit dividends on preferred stock differ in any significant way from the rule for common stock, that you can discern?

6. Recall the rules of interpretation for corporate bonds set forth in Metropolitan Life Insurance Company v. RJR Nabisco, Inc., 716 F.Supp. 1504 (S.D.N.Y. 1989) in Chapter Five, Part 3.A. Does this opinion suggest rules governing interpretation of preferred stock contracts are closer to those of corporate debt or common stock? Does any rationale suggest itself for such an approach?

NOTE ON SANDERS v. CUBA RAILROAD CO.

Judge Frank's opinion in the *Guttmann* case refers to some New Jersey decisions disregarded by the court. In 1956, the New Jersey Supreme Court rejected an opportunity to conform its rule to that of the *Guttmann* and *Wabash Railway* decisions. In Sanders v. Cuba Railroad Co., 120 A.2d 849 (N.J. 1956), the corporation had paid no preferred stock dividends from 1933 through 1955, although it had been profitable for the years 1941–48 and 1951–52, and had substantial accumulated earned surplus (retained earnings). After expressing some confusion over the plaintiffs' claim for relief, the court stated:

"The rights of the holders of the non-cumulative preferred stock rest generally (apart from statutory restrictions) upon the terms of the defendant's certificate of incorporation. See *Ballantine, Corporations*, 516, 517 (1946). Those terms conferred priority rights over common stockholders when there were annual net profits from which dividends could properly be declared. *Agnew v. American Ice Co.*, 2 *N.J.* 291, 298 (1949). If there were no such profits in a given year, then no dividends could be paid to the preferred stockholders with respect to that year, then or thereafter. If, however, there were such profits the board of directors still had broad discretionary power to withhold any declaration of dividends and retain the profits as part of the corporation's working capital. If during a later year the corporation earned net profits and its board of directors wished to declare dividends to both the non-cumulative preferred stockholders and the common stockholders, the question would then be presented as to whether the preferred stockholders were entitled to receive the earlier dividends (which were passed though they could have been paid from the annual net profits) before the common stockholders received any dividends. This question finds neither a clear nor a specific answer in the defendant's certificate of incorporation, and its determination, in an appropriate case, will involve full consideration of the precise language of the certificate and the present scope and effect of New Jersey's so-called 'Cast Iron Pipe Doctrine' or dividend credit rule. See *Bassett v. United States Cast Iron Pipe & Foundry Co.*, 74 *N.J. Eq.* 668 (*Ch.* 1908), affirmed 75 *N.J. Eq.* 539 (*E. & A.* 1909); *Agnew v. American Ice Co., supra.*

"It may be acknowledged that New Jersey's dividend credit rule has not generally been accepted by the other states or in the federal courts. In the recent case of *Guttmann v. Illinois Central R. Co.*, Judge Frank expressed the view that nothing in the terms of the ordinary non-cumulative preferred stock contract points to 'a contingent or inchoate right to arrears of dividends' and that the contrary notion is an invention 'stemming from considerations of fairness, from a policy of protecting investors in these securities.' There seems to be little doubt that equitable factors did play a significant part in the development of New Jersey's doctrine. In the *Wabash Railway* case, *supra*, Justice Holmes stated that there was a common understanding that dividends which were passed (though there were profits from which they could have been declared) were forever gone insofar as non-cumulative preferred stock was concerned; but he referred to no supporting materials and there are those who have suggested a diametrically opposite understanding. See *Lattin, Non–Cumulative Preferred Stock*, 25 *Ill. L. Rev.* 148, 157 (1930). This much is quite apparent—if the common stockholders, who generally control the corporation and will benefit most by the passing of the dividends on the preferred stock, may freely achieve that result without any dividend credit consequences, then the preferred stockholders will be substantially at the mercy of others who will be under temptation to act in their own self-interest. While such conclusion may sometimes be compelled by the clear contractual arrangements between the parties there is no just reason why our courts should not avoid it whenever the contract is silent or is so general as to leave adequate room for its construction. In any event, New Jersey's doctrine has received wide approval in legal writings and there does not seem to be any present disposition in this court to reject it or limit its sweep in favor of the Supreme Court's approach in the *Wabash Railway* case. See *Frey, The Distribution of Corporate Dividends*, 89 *U. Pa. L. Rev.* 735, 750 (1941); *Berle, Non–Cumulative Preferred Stock*, 23 *Col. L. Rev.* 358 (1923); *Lattin, supra*."

QUESTIONS

1. The New Jersey Supreme Court justifies the dividend credit rule because any other rule leaves preferred shareholders at the mercy of the directors elected by the common. What situation concerns the court?

2. How can prospective investors in preferred shares protect themselves from adverse actions by directors who are aggressively representing the common shareholders?

3. Is there reason to fear that companies will overreach preferred shareholders? Who are the typical buyers of preferred stock?

C. PROPERTY RIGHTS IN DIVIDENDS

Hay v. Hay

38 Wash.2d 513; 230 P.2d 791 (1951).

■ DONWORTH, J.:

The liquidating trustees of The Big Bend Land Company, a Washington corporation, instituted this action to secure a declaratory judgment construing Article VI of its amended articles of incorporation. The question presented is whether the holders of cumulative preferred stock upon liquidation of the corporation are entitled to be paid accrued dividends from the corporate assets before the common stockholders become entitled to participate in the distribution thereof, the corporation having no earned surplus or net profits.

The trial court entered a judgment declaring that the amended articles of incorporation required that the holders of the cumulative preferred stock receive from the assets of the corporation, so far as they might reach, an amount equal to six per cent per annum computed on the par value of each share from the date of issuance thereof to date of liquidation (January 18, 1947), and that the holders of the common stock were not entitled to receive any distribution of assets until payment of the six per cent per annum accrued dividend to the preferred stockholders had been fully made. The defendant Edward T. Hay, individually and as administrator of the estate of Fayette H. Imhoff, deceased, has appealed.

* * *

Prior to December 27, 1921, the capital stock of The Big Bend Land Company consisted entirely of common stock. On that date Article VI of the articles of incorporation was amended to read as follows:

"Amended Article VI

"The amount of the capital stock of this Corporation is One Million Five Hundred Thousand ($1,500,000) Dollars, divided into fifteen thousand (15,000) shares of the par value of One Hundred ($100) Dollars each.

"The stock of this Corporation is divided into two classes, namely: common stock in the amount of eighty-five hundred (8500) shares of the par value of One Hundred ($100) Dollars each, and preferred stock in the amount of sixty-five hundred (6500) shares of the par value of One Hundred ($100) Dollars each.

"The terms on which these two classes of stock are created and the particular character of the preference of the preferred stock and the conditions and limitations applying thereto and to the common stock are as follows:

"(a) The holders of the preferred stock shall be entitled to receive, when and as declared by the Board of Trustees of this Corporation, cumulative dividends thereon from the date of issuance of said preferred stock at the rate of six (6%) per cent per annum and no more, payable out of the surplus profits of this Corporation annually on the 31st day of December of each year before any dividend shall be paid or set apart for the common stock. Dividends on the preferred stock shall be cumulative, so that if in any year dividends amounting to six (6%) per cent shall not have been paid on such stock the deficiency shall be paid before any dividend shall be declared or paid upon or set apart for the common stock. . . .

"(b) This Corporation may at any time, or from time to time as shall be permitted under the laws of the State of Washington, redeem the whole or any part of its preferred stock on any annual dividend date by paying therefor in cash One Hundred and one and 50/100 ($101.50) Dollars per share, and all accrued unpaid dividends thereon at the date fixed for such redemption. . . .

"(c) Out of any surplus profits of the Corporation remaining after the payment of full dividends on the preferred stock for all previous dividend periods and after full dividends thereon for the then current annual dividend period shall have been declared and paid in full or provided for, then, and not otherwise, dividends may be declared upon the common stock.

"(d) In the event of any liquidation, dissolution or winding up of the Corporation the holders of the preferred stock shall be entitled to be paid in full the par value thereof, *and all accrued unpaid dividends thereon* before any sum shall be paid to or any assets distributed among the holders of the common stock, but after payment to the holders of the preferred stock of the amounts payable to them as hereinbefore provided, the remaining assets and funds of the Corporation shall be paid to and distributed among the holders of the common stock."

* * *

We have italicized the words which constitute the crux of this controversy.

There are no corporate creditors involved. The holders of the preferred stock have received from the liquidating trustees the par value thereof. No dividends on the cumulative preferred stock have ever been declared or paid. No surplus profits are available with which to pay the accumulated dividends. There is a substantial amount of assets on hand, but they would all be absorbed if they should be applied in payment of accrued dividends on the preferred stock.

Appellant takes the position that the phrase "all accrued unpaid dividends" means that before there can be a dividend there must be surplus profits, and that, since none ever existed, the right to such dividends never accrued and therefore none are payable. * * *

On the other hand, it is the contention of respondents that subdivisions (a), (b), and (c) of Amended Article VI of the articles of incorporation relate to the payment of dividends to preferred stockholders out of surplus profits *while the corporation is a going concern*, but that subdivision (d) authorizes the payment of accumulated and unpaid dividends out of assets *upon liquidation of the corporation*, even though there be no surplus profits available. They argue that, the corporation being in the process of liquidation, there can be no impairment of its capital and, therefore, there is no longer any purpose in restricting the payment of dividends to surplus profits.

It seems clear, even without reference to the decisions of other courts of last resort hereinafter cited, that the two classes of stockholders contracted between themselves with respect to the division of the assets in case of liquidation. Their agreement was that the preferred stockholders should receive the par value of their stock plus an amount equal to "all accrued unpaid dividends thereon" before any assets should be distributed to the common stockholders.

It should be noted that the articles contain no condition to the effect that the surplus profits must be equal to, or greater than, the total of all accrued unpaid dividends before such distribution could be made. The parties were contracting with reference to a possible future liquidation, a situation where the statutory prohibition (Rem. Rev. Stat., § 3823) against declaration of dividends out of capital had no application.

Appellant's construction of the subparagraph (d) of Amended Article VI as being subject to an implied condition (applicable only to a going concern) that such cumulative dividends are payable only out of surplus profits, is contrary to the fundamental concept of the law of corporations. Appellant's construction of subparagraph (d) is based upon a failure to recognize the vital distinction between a corporation which is a going concern and one which is in liquidation. The reference to "all accrued and unpaid dividends" in subparagraph (d) is the only practical yardstick by which the total share of the assets (which the preferred stockholders were to receive upon liquidation) could be measured. At the time the amended article was drafted and adopted, the quoted phrase was the most definite way that the preferential rights of the preferred stockholders could have been described. It stated the method by which the amount distributable to the preferred stockholders could be computed in the event of a liquidation in the future.

The decisions bearing on this subject were formerly in direct conflict, but the great weight of authority presently supports the interpretation of subparagraph (d) adopted by the trial court in this case. 12 Fletcher, Cyclopedia, Corporations (Rev. & Perm. ed.) 198, § 5449.

* * *

Reference has previously been made to Rem. Rev. Stat., § 3823, which was in effect when the articles of incorporation here involved were amended. This statute provides:

> "It shall not be lawful for the trustees to make any dividend except from the net profits arising from the business of the corporation, nor divide, withdraw, or in any way pay to the stockholders, or any of them, any part of the capital stock of the company, nor to reduce the capital stock of the company unless in the manner prescribed in this chapter, or the articles of incorporation or by-laws; and in case of any violation of the provisions of this section, the trustees, under whose administration the same may have happened, except those who may

have caused their dissent therefrom to be entered at large on the minutes of the board of trustees at the time, or were not present when the same did happen, shall, in their individual or private capacities, be jointly or severally liable to the corporation and the creditors thereof in the event of its dissolution, to the full amount so divided, or reduced, or paid out: *Provided, that this section shall not be construed to prevent a division and distribution of the capital stock of the company which shall remain after the payment of all its debts upon the dissolution of the corporation* or the expiration of its charter. . . ." (Italics ours.)

This statutory enactment forbidding the declaration of dividends except from net profits specifically provides that it shall not be construed to prevent a distribution of assets upon a dissolution after the payment of corporate debts. Appellant construes this statute as applying to the very situation to which the statute says it shall have no application. This is directly contrary to its express provision. There is nothing unusual in § 3823—practically all states have statutes forbidding the declaration of dividends out of capital assets while the corporation is a going concern. Section 3823 has no bearing upon the problem involved here.

Being of the opinion that Rem. Rev. Stat., § 3823, expressly provides that it has no application to this case and also that, according to the great weight of authority, respondents are entitled under the provisions of subparagraph (d) to receive a sum equal to all accrued unpaid dividends as well as the par value of their cumulative preferred stock in the liquidation of this corporation before appellants shall be entitled to participate therein, we affirm the judgment of the trial court.

■ GRADY, J. (dissenting)

* * *

The problem presented has caused the courts much difficulty, arising out of determining what are "accrued dividends," "cumulative dividends," "accumulated dividends," or "unpaid dividends," as those words are used in articles of incorporation. The courts do not seem to have had much trouble when questions arose in the ordinary course of business of a corporation, but differences of opinion arose when on liquidation preferred stockholders sought to have a preference in the distribution of assets to reimburse them, because in certain years the corporation had earned no net profits out of which dividends could be declared or paid.

One school of thought is of the view that a dividend can come into being and exist only by affirmative declaration of the trustees of a corporation, and then only if the corporation has on hand surplus net profits earned in the transaction of its business. If net profits, or a surplus, never existed, the right to a dividend never accrued, and that which never accrued cannot be demanded out of the capital account on liquidation. This was the view of the chancellor of Delaware in *Penington v. Commonwealth Hotel Const. Corp.*, 17 Del. Ch. 188, 151 Atl. 228.

Another school of thought is that dividends, if not regularly paid out of available earnings, may be amassed or stored up, whether earned or not earned, at regular dividend dates, and, in the absence of a controlling statute, may be paid out of assets when the corporation is liquidated if the articles of incorporation so provide. This idea found expression in *Penington v. Commonwealth Hotel Const. Corp.*, 17 Del. Ch. 394, 155 Atl. 514, 75 A. L. R. 1136. Three judges of the court disagreed with the chancellor. Two believed his views were correct and consistent with the better and more logical reasoning. The cases cited in the majority opinion follow the reasoning of the three judges.

* * *

It seems to me apparent that whoever prepared subdivisions (a), (b), (c), and (d) of the amended articles of incorporation was familiar with the rules of law relating to the rights of holders of common and preferred stock and desired to follow Rem. Rev. Stat., § 3823. . . .

The statute contains two inhibitions: (1) against making any dividend, except from net profits arising from the business; (2) against any division, withdrawal, or payment to the stockholders of any part of the capital stock of the corporation. By the proviso, the capital stock remaining after debts are paid may be divided among the stockholders when the corporation is dissolved or its charter expires. The subjects of the two inhibitions are wholly unrelated. The first relates to dividends and forbids the making of any, except from net profits. No dividend can be made out of assets, and any article of incorporation construed as so providing would be contrary to the statute and void. The second relates to the assets of the corporation and forbids any division thereof, except on dissolution or expiration of the charter.

Making dividends and dividing assets are two different things. A dividend can never be made unless there are in existence net or surplus profits derived out of the current business done by the corporation. The capital stock or assets of The Big Bend Land Company belong to the common stockholders. The preferred stockholders had either loaned money to the corporation and received in payment shares of preferred stock or had become purchasers of such stock. The common stockholders could have received dividends as and when they were made by the trustees out of net profits and secondary to preferred stockholders. The latter could have received dividends from the same source, but on an annual percentage basis.

If at the end of any year net profits had not been earned out of which the dividends could have been made in whole or in part, then the preferred stockholder had a preference whereby he would be entitled to such dividends as soon as there were net profits available. In the case of the common stockholder, he would not necessarily be paid a dividend, even though there might be available net profits therefor, but the preferred stockholder became entitled to dividends annually *if* there were net profits out of which they could be made. If such dividends were made, but were not paid to the stockholder, or if he chose to leave them with the corporation, he would have a preference right over common stockholders later to have them paid to him. Such dividends would be property of the corporation, and when ultimately paid would not be as dividends, but as corporate funds. Such payment would not be a violation of Rem. Rev. Stat., § 3823. Dividends as such are not made when a corporation is liquidated and dissolved. They are only made while it is doing business.

It seems to me that the purpose of subdivision (d), when considered along with all of the other subdivisions of Amended Article VI and Rem. Rev. Stat., § 3823, was to provide that, when the corporation was liquidated and dissolved, the preferred stockholders were entitled to have a redemption made of their stock and to receive any dividends which had at any time been made by the trustees out of net profits but had not been paid to them, before any should be paid to or any assets distributed among the holders of the common stock. I can find nothing in subdivision (d) that authorizes the making of dividends out of assets upon liquidation and dissolution.

* * *

I think a reading of the whole of Amended Article VI in connection with Rem. Rev. Stat., § 3823, must convince one that the dividends referred to in subdivision (d) can mean only those that may have been once lawfully made by the board of trustees out of surplus profits, but which had not been paid to the preferred stockholders. If we do otherwise, we must accuse the corporation of adopting a tricky device to favor preferred stockholders and deprive the common stockholders of their property. Granting that if in any year or years no net profits are earned, dividends have nevertheless "accrued" and during successive years have "accumulated" and may be paid at some future time, they can only be paid out of surplus profits and not out of capital. If the corporation is liquidated and does not have on hand any net or surplus profits, then there is nothing out of which the "dividends" can be paid. This was the view of the court in *Michael v. Cayey–Caguas Tobacco Co.*, 190 App. Div. 618, 180 N. Y. Supp. 532, especially when fortified by a statute the same as Rem. Rev. Stat., § 3823. The court said:

> "Since no profits have been made, and so no dividends were or could have been declared, it is difficult to understand how eight per centum annual dividends could have accumulated during these intervening years to be now paid out of 'surplus assets and funds' or 'surplus profits,' to wit, the amount remaining after payment of debts and repayment of capital. No such sum exists. The amount now on hand is not profits, but is capital.... There being no accumulated profits, when the preferred stockholders received the full par value of their stock they had received all that they were entitled to, in view of the fact that the amount remaining in the hands of the company was not sufficient to pay the par value of the common stock."

QUESTIONS

1. The dissenting judge stated that "the capital stock or assets of The Big Bend Land Company belong to the common stockholders." What does he mean by this?

2. The dissenting judge also stated that if there were profits and "dividends were made, but were not paid to the stockholder ... he would have a preference right over common stockholders later to have them paid to him. Such dividends would be the property of the corporation, and when ultimately paid would not be as dividends, but as corporate funds." What does he mean by this?

3. The dissenting judge interpreted the language of the relevant charters as requiring payment on dissolution of only declared but unpaid dividends. If declared dividends are a liability of the company, how meaningful is such a provision?

4. Modern statutes, such as the RMBCA, contain no legal capital requirements: shares need not have par value, no part of the price paid for shares must be segregated as "capital," and prohibitions on dividends under § 6.40(c) are couched solely in terms of insolvency, rather than impairment of "capital." What effect would incorporation under such a statute have on the reasoning of the two sides in this case?

5. If you wished to draft language for a corporate charter that would convince a court that undeclared past dividends were intended to be paid on liquidation, how would you write it?

NOTE

The debate about undeclared dividend arrearages on liquidation continued in Wouk v. Merin, 283 App. Div. 522, 128 N.Y.S.2d 727 (1954), where the majority held that where the governing language provided that the preferred shareholders were to receive the par value of their shares, together with "any arrearage of dividends to which the holders of such preferred stock may be entitled," they were not entitled to arrearages where the board had not declared dividends. This interpretation missed a critical legal point—had the dividends been declared, they would have become debts of the corporation, and the preferred shareholders would have claimed as creditors, not as shareholders. See William Meade Fletcher, 12 Fletcher Cyclopedia on the law of Private Corporations § 5322 (1995 Rev.). Thus the court's interpretation leaves the language devoid of meaning. In Matter of Dissolution of Chandler & Co., 230 N.Y.S.2d 1012 (N.Y.Sup. 1962), the charter provided that preferred shareholders were entitled to "One Hundred Dollars ($100), and also accrued dividends, before any amount shall be paid on account of the Second Preferred Stock and Common Stock." The court held that cumulative dividends "accrued" regardless of declaration. In distinguishing Wouk v. Merin, the court noted that the dissolution language there provided for payment of "any arrearage of dividends to which the holders of such preferred may be entitled."

> "Apparently, as the dissenting opinion notes ... had the dissolution clause contained the phrase 'together with any accumulated dividends due thereon' in lieu of the language actually employed as above quoted, it was conceded that the preferred stockholders would have been

entitled to accumulated dividends which accrued, by mere lapse of time."

230 N.Y.S.2d at 1017.

Mohawk Carpet Mills v. Delaware Rayon Co., 110 A.2d 305 (Del. Ch. 1954) held that where the charter provided for payment of par value to the preferred shareholders, such a provision was "clearly exhaustive." To the same effect is Squires v. The Balbach Company, 129 N.W.2d 462 (Neb. 1964), which reviews a large body of precedent.

The conflicting judicial decisions in this area demonstrate the need for clear drafting. Some examples of preferred stock liquidation provisions are set out below. Do they clearly resolve any potential ambiguity about the right of preferred shareholders to receive undeclared dividends, whether from profits or not, on liquidation?

Here is the approach of Deere & Co.:

"2.2   DEFINITIONS

"2.21 The term 'arrearages,' whenever used in connection with dividends on any share of preferred stock, shall refer to the condition that exists as to dividends, to the extent that they are cumulative (either unconditionally, or conditionally to the extent that the conditions have been fulfilled), on such share which shall not have been paid or declared and set apart for payment to the date or for the period indicated; but the term shall not refer to the condition that exists as to dividends, to the extent that they are non-cumulative, on such share which shall not have been paid or declared and set apart for payment.

2.4   LIQUIDATION RIGHTS

"2.41 In the event of any liquidation, dissolution or winding up of the corporation, whether voluntary or involuntary, the holders of preferred stock of each series shall be entitled to receive the full preferential amount fixed by the certificate of incorporation or any amendment thereto, or by the resolutions of the board of directors providing for the issue of such series, including any arrearages in dividends thereon to the date fixed for the payment in liquidation, before any distribution shall be made to the holders of any stock junior to the preferred stock. After such payment in full to the holders of the preferred stock, the remaining assets of the corporation shall then be distributable exclusively among the holders of any stock junior to the preferred stock outstanding, according to their respective interests."

Here is the provision of ADOLOR CORPORATION:

"4. Preference on Liquidation. In the event of the voluntary or involuntary liquidation, dissolution or winding up of the Corporation, holders of each series of Preferred Stock will be entitled to receive the amount fixed for such series plus, in the case of any series on which dividends will have been determined by the board of directors to be cumulative, an amount equal to all dividends accumulated and unpaid thereon to the date of final distribution whether or not earned or declared before any distribution shall be paid, or set aside for payment, to holders of Common Stock.''

Here is the provision for Krispy Kreme:

''SECTION 6. LIQUIDATION, DISSOLUTION OR WINDING UP. Upon any liquidation, dissolution or winding up of the Corporation, no distribution shall be made (1) to the holders of shares of stock ranking junior (either as to dividends or upon liquidation, dissolution or winding up) to the Series A Preferred Stock unless, prior thereto, the holders of shares of Series A Preferred Stock shall have received $1.00 per share, plus an amount equal to accrued and unpaid dividends and distributions thereon, whether or not declared, to the date of such payment; . . .''

And here is the provision for EOG RESOURCES, INC.:

''6. Liquidation Preference.

''(a) Upon the dissolution, liquidation or winding up of the Corporation, voluntary or involuntary, the holders of the then outstanding shares of Series B Senior Preferred Stock shall be entitled to receive and be paid out of the assets of the Corporation available for distribution to its stockholders, before any payment or distribution of assets shall be made on the Common Stock, the Junior Preferred Stock or any other class of stock of the Corporation ranking junior to the Series B Senior Preferred Stock upon liquidation, the amount of $1,000.00 per share, plus an amount equal to the sum of all accrued and unpaid dividends (whether or not earned or declared) on such shares to the date of final distribution.''

Smith v. Nu–West Industries, Inc.

2000 WL 1641248, affirmed, 781 A.2d 695 (Del. Supr. 2001).

■ CHANDLER, CHANCELLOR.

Plaintiff Roger B. Smith, and the class of Nu–West Class A preferred shareholders he represents, seeks a summary judgment determination on Count I of the complaint, alleging that Nu–West Industries (''defendant'' or ''Nu–West'') failed to pay the proper redemption price for all outstanding shares of Nu–West's Class A preferred shares. Nu–West and the other named defendants also moved for summary judgment on Count I. Plaintiff alleges that defendants miscalculated the amount of allegedly accrued but unpaid dividends owed on the Class A preferred stock. Defendants claim that Nu–West's certificate of incorporation plainly states that dividends were not payable for the period in question and, hence, were also not accruing during this period and should be excluded from the redemption price. For the reasons I set forth below, I grant plaintiff's motion for summary judgment.

I.

* * *

On December 13, 1996, Nu–West redeemed its Class A preferred stock at a price of $100 per share plus accrued and unpaid dividends of $71.50 per share, for a total of $171.50 per share. It is undisputed that dividends on Nu–West Class A preferred accumulated at the annual rate of $11 per share. To calculate the redemption price, Nu–West included $66 per share for dividends accrued during each of the six fiscal years ending June 30, 1990, through June 30, 1995, together with $5.50 per share for dividends accrued during the last six months of calendar year 1995. The redemption price did not include any payment for the dividend allegedly accruing during the period from January 1, 1996, through December 13, 1996.

On the redemption date, former plaintiff Shapiro was the record and beneficial owner of 1,126 shares of Class A preferred stock. When he received notice of Nu–West's intent to redeem the Class A preferred shares at $171.50, Shapiro questioned Nu–West's failure to include in the redemption price dividends accrued from January 1, 1996, through December 13, 1996. Nu–West responded that dividends do not accrue daily, but rather, accrue in full only at the end of each full fiscal year according to its interpretation of its certificate of incorporation. Shapiro believed that the redemption price should have included an additional $10.43 per share to account for the dividends accruing from January 1, 1996, through the date of redemption, December 13, 1996. * * * Ultimately, as noted above, Smith, the beneficial owner of 18,500 Class A preferred shares as of the redemption date, was substituted for Shapiro as the named plaintiff and the class of Class A preferred shareholders was certified.

II.

* * *

The issue the parties present for decision is the question of whether the provisions of Nu–West's certificate of incorporation provide for daily accrual of preferred dividends or annual accrual of preferred dividends. I find that there are no disputes of material fact and that the class of plaintiffs are, as a matter of law, entitled to an additional $10.43 per share. Thus, plaintiffs motion for summary judgment on the Count I of the complaint is granted. As discussed more fully below, Nu–West's certificate of incorporation clearly, and unambiguously, mandates a finding that dividends accrue daily and are payable at the time of redemption.

A.   The Certificate of Incorporation

As to the dividends associated with the Class A preferred shares, the relevant certificate sections provide:

(B)   Dividends and Distributions

(a) From the issuance date of the Class A Preferred Stock(the "Class A Preferred Issuance Date") until the end of the first full fiscal year of the Corporation, dividends shall begin to accrue and shall be payable only to the extent of Excess Cash Flow (as hereinafter defined) for such period, and unpaid dividends for such period shall not be cumulative.

(b) For the second full fiscal year of the Corporation after the Class A Preferred Issuance Date, cash dividends shall be payable only to the extent of Excess Cash Flow for such period and shall be cumulative only to the extent of the Adjusted Net Income (as hereinafter defined) for such period.

(c) For the third and each subsequent full fiscal year of the Corporation after the Class A Preferred Issuance Date, cash dividends shall be payable only to the extent of Excess Cash Flow for each such period and unpaid dividends for each such period shall be cumulative.

In the event of redemption, the certificate expressly provides that "dividends shall cease to accrue from and after the Class A Redemption Date designated in the notice of redemption."

Several other certificate provisions also address the treatment of Class A preferred shares. Article IV, § 2(1)(E)(1) notes that the Class A preferred is subject to being exchanged, at the option of Nu–West, for Nu–West's 11% Subordinated Debentures due June 1, 2002. In that event, the notice of exchange was required to state, among other things, "that dividends on the shares of Class A preferred Stock to be exchanged *will cease* to accrue *on such Exchange date.*" Moreover, the certificate provides that from, and after, the Exchange Date *"the right to receive dividends* [on Class A preferred] *shall cease to accrue."* Similarly, on the dissolution, liquidation, and winding up of Nu–West, holders of Class A preferred are entitled to receive $100 per share "plus a sum equal to all cumulative dividends on such shares accrued and unpaid thereon to the date of final distribution."

B. Summary of the Arguments

Plaintiff, in supporting his motion, argues that the certificate of incorporation, when read as a whole, clearly indicates that dividends for the preferred stock accrue on a daily basis. Moreover, in advancing this argument in both his brief and at the presentation of his motion, the plaintiff emphasized the distinction between the concepts of when dividends "accrue" and when they are "payable."

Defendants oppose plaintiff's motion and seek summary judgment in their favor. The gist of their argument is that the certificate of incorporation provides that dividends for preferred shares accrue to, and are payable to, shareholders at the end of the fiscal year only. In other words, defendants argue that when the certificate says "payable" it means both payable and accrued.

C. Application of the Law to the Undisputed Facts

The parties' motions ask the Court to interpret the provisions of Nu–West's Certificate of Incorporation related to preferred stock dividends.

The Certificate is interpreted using standard rules of contract interpretation which require a court to determine from the language of the contract the intent of the parties. In discerning the intent of the parties, the Certificate should be read as a whole and, if possible, interpreted to reconcile all of the provisions of the document.

If no ambiguity is present, the court must give effect to the clear language of the Certificate. A contract is not rendered ambiguous simply because the parties do not agree upon its proper construction. Rather, a contract is ambiguous only when the provisions in controversy are reasonably or fairly susceptible of different interpretations or may have two or more different meanings. . . . The true test is not what the parties to the contract intended it to mean, but what a reasonable person in the position of the parties would have thought it meant.[11]

At the very root of this controversy is the distinction between when, and how, dividends accrue and when they are *payable*. The defendants argue that the concepts are one and the same. I do not agree. Three concepts are important when discussing dividends for preferred stock.[12] First, there is the concept of when these dividends are *payable*. Generally, preferred shareholders benefit from a stated and fixed dividend rate, annual or otherwise, which is payable (i.e., the shareholder actually receives the dividend) only when the corporation has a stated level of earnings to pay the dividend. Often, a corporation's articles of incorporation will provide that where there are insufficient earnings or other funds to actually pay a preferred dividend, that dividend will *cumulate*. In the simplest of terms, this means the fixed dividend from the prior period is added to that of the current period. This cumulating will continue until there are funds to pay the dividends. Finally, there is the separate question of when does the shareholder's rights to a dividend accrue? A shareholder's rights to receive a dividend will vest at a particular time. At the time the rights vest, the corporation may, or may not, have the funds to pay the dividend. These are distinct concepts in the area of preferred stock dividends and care should be taken not to confuse them. This case thus reduces to a single question: When did Nu–West's shareholders' rights to a preferred dividend vest or accrue?

To answer this question, I must look to the terms of the certificate. First, I know when the preferred dividends are *payable*. Article IV, § 2(1)(B)(1)(a–c) provides that dividends are only payable to the extent of excess cash flow during the fiscal year. To the extent the excess cash flow at the end of the fiscal year is insufficient, the $11.00 dividend is not paid in that period and cumulates, or rolls forward, into the next year. This section establishes an annual system where at the end of each fiscal year either the dividend is paid or it cumulates.

---

11.   Kaiser Aluminum Corp. v. Matheson, Del. Supr., 681 A.2d 392, 395 (1996) (internal citations and quotations omitted).

12.   See Penington v. Commonwealth Hotel Const. Corp., Del. Supr., 17 Del. Ch. 394, 155 A. 514 (1931) and Garrett v. Edge Moor Iron Co., Del. Ch., 22 Del. Ch. 142, 194 A. 15 (1937).

The difficulty arises where there is an extraordinary event that disrupts the annual cycle. Here we are faced with the redemption of an entire class of preferred stock before the completion of a full annual cycle. The question now becomes whether, and to what extent, the shareholders' rights to that fixed $11.00 dividend have vested or accrued. If the rights do not accrue until the end of the fiscal year, as urged by the defendants, then the shareholders are not entitled to any part of the dividend. If the rights accrue daily from the first day of the fiscal year, as argued by the plaintiffs, then the shareholder will be entitled to a portion of the dividend.

While Nu–West's certificate is clear on when these preferred dividends are payable and that they cumulate if unpaid, the certificate is silent on whether the shareholders' rights to the dividends accrue daily up to the date of redemption. Mindful of this Court's duty to seek the intent of the parties from reading the contract as a whole, I find that other provisions of the certificate would lead a "reasonable person in the position of the parties" to conclude that the parties' intended the preferred dividends to accrue daily.

First, Article IV, § 2(1)(D)(5) clearly states that "dividends shall cease to accrue from and after the Class A Redemption Date designated in the notice of redemption." Logically, dividends can only cease to accrue "from and after the Class A Redemption Date" if they have been accruing continuously up to that date.

Second, Article IV, § 2(1)(E)(2)(iii) states that dividends will "cease to accrue" on the Exchange Date when preferred shares are exchanged for debt. This Exchange Date is an "extraordinary" event and not altogether different conceptually from a redemption. Likewise, Article IV, § 2(1)(G)(1) provides that upon dissolution, liquidation, and winding up, Class A preferred shareholders are entitled to receive "all cumulative dividends ... accrued and unpaid thereon to the date of final distribution." The date of final distribution may or may not occur at the end of a fiscal year.

III.

Reading the certificate of incorporation as a whole, I conclude that a reasonable person in the position of the parties would conclude that the preferred dividend accrues daily until the occurrence of an extraordinary event stops the accrual—here the redemption of the shares. I do not find that the certificate is ambiguous, nor do I find the terms in conflict. Rather, the provisions are quite clear on their face and act in concert to compel this result. It is only in applying those provisions to this specific fact situation—redemption—that a problem in interpretation arises. While the drafters were, quite simply, less clear than they could have been, the certificate as a whole fills in any minor gaps.

The facts in this case are undisputed and clear. The parties do not contest any fact, so they are entitled to a ruling, as a matter of law, as to whether dividends accrue daily or annually. Nu–West's certificate of incorporation clearly, and unambiguously, mandates a finding that dividends accrue daily and are payable at the time of redemption.

I grant plaintiff's motion for summary judgment and deny defendants' motion for summary judgment. The defendants are directed to pay an additional $10.43 per share for each Class A preferred share redeemed.

QUESTIONS

1. When do preferred shareholders have a legal right to cumulative preferred dividends absent a redemption or liquidation?

2. Assuming cumulative preferred dividends are earned but not declared, what rights do preferred shareholders have to dividends absent a redemption or liquidation?

3. Absent a declaration of cumulative preferred dividends, what does it mean to say these dividends accrue?

4. On similar facts, what would the results be under the language governing preferred stock of Deere & Co., Adolor Corporation, Krispy Kreme and EOG Resources, Inc.?

3. ALTERING THE PREFERRED CONTRACT

A. VOTING RULES AND VOTING RIGHTS

NOTE ON STATUTORY INTERPRETATION IN DELAWARE

The doctrine of independent legal significance in Delaware is the ultimate expression of the enabling act approach to corporation statutes. It began to develop as a result of the great depression of the 1930's, when a great many companies had passed on cumulative preferred dividends. The result was that enormous arrearages had built up that must be paid in full before any dividends could be paid on the common stock. As a result, common stock offerings were extremely difficult, since these companies could offer no promise of dividends for a very long period. In Keller v. Wilson, 21 Del. Ch. 391, 190 A. 115 (1936), the court considered a plan of recapitalization that would exchange old preferred shares and their arrearages for a new class of preferred. A similar arrangement was made for a second class of preferred, called class A. The vote in favor of the recapitalization was approved by the overwhelming vote of each class. The Delaware statute in effect at the time permitted amendments that affected the rights of classes if approved by the holders of a majority of the shares of each affected class. Yet One holder of Class A stock brought suit to enjoin the recapitalization. The court noted the conventional rule that dividends do not become a liability of the corporation until declared (and none of these dividends were declared), and noted the need for corporate flexibility. While conceding that these dividends were not vested property rights because they had not been declared, there were elements of an estoppel theory in the court's opinion—that the cumulative feature of the dividends was an inducement that caused investors to purchase the class. While they could not legally become vested property rights until a fund of retained profits existed from which they could be paid, "... it is difficult to perceive the justice of permitting the corporation to destroy the opportunity to create the fund by action under a subsequent amendment to the law which, when the corporation was formed and the stock issued, did not permit of such destruction." 190 A. at 124.

The final passages of the opinion were a ringing defense of property rights:

> "It may be conceded, as a general proposition, that the State, as a matter of public policy, is concerned in the welfare of its corporate creatures to the end that they may have reasonable powers wherewith to advance their interests by permitting adequate financing. It may also be conceded that there has been an increasing departure from the conception which formerly prevailed when the right of individual veto in matters of corporate government operated as a dangerous obstruction to proper functioning. But in determining whether the rights of the complainants herein are such as ought to be regarded a property rights, all aspects of the question must be considered to ascertain what is conducive to the best interests of society. The State is concerned also with the welfare of those who invest their money, the very essence of generation, in corporate enterprises. Some measure of protection should be accorded them. While many interrelations of the State, the corporation, and the shareholders may be changed, there is a limit beyond which the State may not go. Property rights may not be destroyed; and when the nature and character of the right of a holder of cumulative preferred stock to unpaid dividends, which have accrued thereon through passage of time, is examined in a case where that right was accorded protection when the corporation was formed and the stock was issued, a just public policy, which seeks the equal and impartial protection of the interests of all, demands that the right be regarded as a vested right of property secured against the destruction by the Federal and State Constitutions."

190 A. at 124–25. The court enjoined the recapitalization.

This ringing defense of cumulative dividend arrearages as vested property rights lasted four years. Federal United Corporation faced a similar problem, but rather than use a recapitalization, engaged in a merger with a wholly owned subsidiary, as a result of which the old preferred and its arrearages were canceled and replaced by new preferred in the merged entity, together with some common stock. The preferred shareholders were induced to vote for the merger in part by the corporation's promise that dividend payments on the new preferred would begin immediately. The court noted that the preferred shareholders were protected by their appraisal rights, and that the preferred shareholders bought their shares subject to the provisions of Delaware law permitting mergers upon satisfaction of certain conditions. Because of this, there was no vested property right that could permit preferred shareholders to object to a merger, when their financial interests were protected by appraisal. "There is a clear distinction between the situations recognized by the General law and the modes of procedure applicable to each of them; and we think that the strictness of the view of the merger provisions of the law entertained by the Chancellors below was, perhaps, induced by overlooking the distinction, so that it was assumed that to attempt to accomplish by merger that which could not be done by mere charter amendment, was a perversion of the statute in an effort to escape the reach of the decision in the Keller case." Federal United Corporation v. Havender, 24 Del. Ch. 318, 11 A.2d 331, 342–43 (Del. 1940).

The doctrine underlying this decision was articulated more clearly by Judge Leahy in Langfelder v. Universal Laboratories, Inc., 68 F.Supp. 209 (D. Del.1946) (applying Delaware law), involving another merger that eliminated arrearages on cumulative dividends. The opinion stated in part, reconciling the opinions in Keller v. Wilson and Federal United Corporation v. Havender:

> "Under Delaware law, accrued dividends after the passage of time mature into a debt and cannot be eliminated by an amendment to the corporate charter under Sec. 26 of the Delaware Corporation Law. But the right to be paid in full for such dividends, notwithstanding provisions in the charter contract, may be eliminated by means of a merger which meets the standard of fairness. The rationale is that a merger is an act of independent legal significance, and when it meets the requirements of fairness and all other statutory requirements, the merger is valid and not subordinate or dependent upon any other section of the Delaware Corporation Law."

The doctrine of independent legal significance may be under attack in Delaware. In the takeover area, the Delaware Supreme Court has held that a bidder owes no fiduciary duties of fairness to public shareholders of a target company in a tender offer, *Solomon v. Pathe Communications Corp.*, 672 A.2d 35 (Del. 1996), and as a follow-up, during a cash-out merger of the minority, owes no such duties in a short form merger where the majority shareholder owns 90% of the stock of the subsidiary, so that no vote of either the board or the minority stockholders of the subsidiary is required. *Glassman v. Unocal Exploration Corporation*, 777 A.2d 242 (Del. 2001). Some Delaware judges have expressed concern that this elevates form over substance, and at least one judge has attempted to impose fiduciary-like duties on a dominant shareholder when it makes a tender offer for the remaining shares. *In re Pure Resources, Inc. Shareholders Litigation*, 808 A.2d 421, 442–47 (Del. Ch. 2002).

While the following case involves interpretation of preferred stock provisions, it raises the interesting question of the interrelationship between statutes and contracts.

Elliott Associates, L.P. v. Avatex Corporation

715 A.2d 843 (Del. 1998.)

■ VEASEY, CHIEF JUSTICE:

In this case of first impression, we hold that certain preferred stockholders have the right to a class vote in a merger where: (1) the certificate

[handwritten margin notes: Class vote / 1. expressly stated ~ A of I / 2. merger nullifies protections / 3. material + adv impact]

of incorporation expressly provides such a right in the event of any "amendment, alteration or repeal, whether by merger, consolidation or otherwise" of any of the provisions of the certificate of incorporation; (2) the certificate of incorporation that provides protections for the preferred stock is nullified and thereby repealed by the merger; and (3) the result of the transaction would <u>materially and adversely affect the rights</u>, preferences, privileges or voting power of those preferred stockholders. In so holding, we distinguish prior Delaware precedent narrowly because of the inclusion by the drafters of the phrase, "whether by merger, consolidation or otherwise."

Facts

Defendant Avatex Corporation ("Avatex") is a Delaware corporation that has outstanding both common and preferred stock. The latter includes two distinct series of outstanding preferred stock: "First Series Preferred" and "Series A Preferred." Plaintiffs in these consolidated cases are all preferred stockholders of defendant Avatex. The individual defendants are all members of the Avatex board of directors.

Avatex created and incorporated Xetava Corporation ("Xetava") as its wholly-owned subsidiary on April 13, 1998, and the following day announced its intention to merge with and into Xetava. Under the terms of the proposed merger, Xetava is to be the surviving corporation. Once the transaction is consummated, Xetava will immediately change its name to Avatex Corporation. The proposed merger would cause a conversion of the preferred stock of Avatex into common stock of Xetava. The merger will effectively eliminate Avatex' certificate of incorporation, which includes the certificate of designations creating the Avatex preferred stock and setting forth its rights and preferences. The terms of the merger do not call for a class vote of these preferred stockholders. Herein lies the heart of the legal issue presented in this case.

Plaintiffs filed suit in the Court of Chancery to enjoin the proposed merger, arguing, among other things, that the transaction required the consent of two-thirds of the holders of the First Series Preferred stock. Defendants responded with a motion for judgment on the pleadings, which the Court of Chancery granted, finding that the provisions governing the rights of the First Series Preferred stockholders do not require such consent.

The plaintiffs allege that, because of Avatex' anemic financial state, "all the value of Avatex is [currently] in the preferred stock." By forcing the conversion of the preferred shares into common stock of the surviving corporation, however, the merger would place current preferred stockholders of Avatex on an even footing with its common stockholders. In fact, the Avatex preferred stockholders will receive in exchange for their preferred stock approximately 73% of Xetava common stock, and the common stockholders of Avatex will receive approximately 27% of the common stock of Xetava.

Under the terms of the Avatex certificate of incorporation, First Series stockholders have no right to vote except on:

> (a) any "amendment, alteration or repeal" of the certificate of incorporation "whether by merger, consolidation or otherwise," that
>
> (b) "materially and adversely" affects the rights of the First Series stockholders.

The text of the terms governing the voting rights of the First Series Preferred Stock is set forth in the certificate of designations as follows:

> Except as expressly provided hereinafter in this Section (6) or as otherwise ... required by law, the First Series Preferred Stock shall have no voting rights....
>
> So long as any shares of First Series Preferred Stock remain outstanding, the consent of the holders of at least two-thirds of the shares of the First Series Preferred Stock outstanding at the time (voting separately as a class ...) ... shall be necessary to permit, effect or validate any one or more of the following: ...
>
> (b) The amendment, alteration or repeal, whether by merger, consolidation or otherwise, of any of the provisions of the Restated Certificate of Incorporation or of [the certificate of designations] which would materially and adversely affect any right, preference, privilege or voting power of the First Series Preferred Stock or of the holders thereof....[6]

* * *

---

6. In addition, Section 4 of the Avatex certificate of incorporation provides, in relevant part:

> So long as any of the preferred stock remains outstanding, the consent of the holders of at least a majority of all outstanding shares of preferred stock ... shall be necessary for effecting or validating any amendment, alteration or repeal of any of the provisions of this Article [including certain board resolutions] which increase or decrease the par value of the preferred stock or would adversely affect the rights or preferences of the preferred stock, or of the holders thereof....

See also 8 Del. C. § 242(b)(2) (providing by statute a class vote in certain circumstances). When an amendment to a certificate of incorporation is sought to be effected under that section:

> The holders of the outstanding shares of a class shall be entitled to vote as a class upon a proposed amendment, whether or not entitled to vote thereon by the certificate of incorporation, if the amendment would increase or decrease the aggregate number of authorized shares of such class, increase or decrease the par value of the shares of such class, or alter or change the powers, preferences, or special rights of the shares of such class so as to affect them adversely.

Id. Because the merger here implicates a different statute (8 Del. C. § 251, which does not itself require a class vote), the provisions of Section 242 are not implicated, the two statutes being of independent legal significance. See Warner Communications Inc. v. Chris–Craft Indus., Inc., Del. Ch., 583 A.2d 962, 970, aff'd, Del. Supr., 567 A.2d 419 (1989). Likewise, Section 4 of the Avatex certificate is not applicable. Similarly, the Avatex Series A Preferred

This appeal, then, reduces to a narrow legal question: whether the "amendment, alteration or repeal" of the certificate of incorporation is caused "by merger, consolidation or otherwise" thereby requiring a two-thirds class vote of the First Series Preferred stockholders, it being assumed for purposes of this appeal that their rights would be "materially and adversely" affected. The Court of Chancery answered this question in the negative. Although we respect that Court's craftsmanlike analysis, we are constrained to disagree with its conclusion.

Relying primarily on *Warner Communications Inc. v. Chris–Craft Industries Inc.*,[16] the Court of Chancery held that it was only the *conversion* of the stock as a result of the merger, and not the *amendment, alteration or repeal* of the certificate, that would adversely affect the preferred stockholders. It is important to keep in mind, however, that the terms of the preferred stock in *Warner* were significantly different from those present here, because in *Warner* the phrase "whether by merger, consolidation or otherwise" was not included. The issue here, therefore, is whether the presence of this additional phrase in the Avatex certificate is an outcome-determinative distinction from *Warner*.

In *Warner,* the question was whether the Series B preferred stock of Warner Communications, Inc. had the right to a class vote on a proposed merger of Warner with Time, Inc. (renamed Time Warner Inc.) and TW Sub, its wholly-owned subsidiary. As the first step in a two-step transaction, Time had acquired approximately 50% of Warner's common stock in a tender offer. The second step was the "back-end" merger in which TW Sub was merged into Warner, which survived as a wholly-owned subsidiary of Time. The Warner common stock not held by Time was converted into cash, securities and other property. In the merger, the Warner Series B preferred would be converted into Time Series BB preferred stock. The parties stipulated that the Warner Series B stockholders would thereby be adversely affected.

The Chancellor held that the drafters of the Warner Series B certificate of designations did not intend for two-thirds of the Series B stockholders to have a veto over every merger in which their interest would be adversely affected because the right to vote was conferred expressly (as it must under Delaware law), and "only in narrowly defined circumstances ... not present here." The two provisions in the certificate of designations involved in *Warner* were as follows. Section 3.3 provided:

> So long as any shares of Series B Stock shall be outstanding and unless the consent or approval of a greater number of shares shall then be required by law, ... the affirmative vote or written consent of the holders of at least two-thirds of the total number of the then outstand-

---

stock, which is not implicated in this appeal, has the right to a two-thirds class vote if the corporation seeks to "amend, alter, repeal or waive" any provision of the certificate of incorporation. But the additional language of the First Series Preferred, "whether by merger, consolidation or otherwise," significantly is missing from the rights granted to the Series A Preferred.

16. 583 A.2d 962.

ing shares of Series B Stock ... voting as a class, shall be necessary to alter or change any rights, preferences or limitations of the Preferred Stock so as to affect the holders of all such shares adversely....

Section 3.4 provided:

So long as any shares of Series B Stock shall be outstanding and unless the consent or approval of a greater number of shares shall then be required by law, without first obtaining the consent or approval of the holders of at least two-thirds of the number of shares of the Series B Stock ... the Corporation shall not (i) *amend, alter or repeal any of the provisions of the Certificate of Incorporation or By-laws of the Corporation so as to affect adversely* any of the preferences, rights, powers or privileges of the Series B Stock or the holders thereof....

We note again that nowhere in the Series B certificate of designations was found the phrase "by merger, consolidation or otherwise," which is the key phrase in the present case. Nevertheless, the heart of the Warner rationale, which we must address here, is that it was not the amendment, alteration or repeal of the Warner certificate that adversely affected the Warner Series B stock. The Chancellor held that it was only the conversion of the Warner Series B Preferred to Time Series BB Preferred that caused the adverse effect, and, moreover, that the conversion was permissible under 8 Del. C. § 251, which (unlike 8 Del. C. § 242) does not require a class vote on a merger. Further, the Chancellor held that no contractual protection of the Warner Series B stock provided for a class vote on a merger. The Chancellor summarized his rationale in Warner as follows:

1. Section 3.4(i) does not create a right to a class vote on the proposed merger despite the fact that Warner's certificate of incorporation is being amended in the merger because, in the circumstances, the amendment itself will not "adversely affect" the Series B Preferred.

2. The same reasoning that supports the conclusion that the proposed merger does not trigger a class vote under Section 3.4(i) requires an identical conclusion with respect to 3.3(i).

3. If the amendment of Warner's certificate does not trigger the class vote provisions of either 3.4(i) or 3.3(i), the dispositive question becomes whether the merger itself may trigger that result under the language of Section 3.3(i). Stated differently, the core issue here may be said to be whether the predicate words of Section 3.3(i), "alter or change," are to be read to include "convert pursuant to a merger." I conclude that Section 3.3(i) does not create a right to a class vote on a merger that will convert the Series B Preferred stock into other securities, other property or cash.

In more detail, he continued:

Section 3.4(i) provides a right to a series vote ... in the event of a charter amendment that amends, alters or repeals any provision of the certificate of incorporation so as to adversely affect the Series B Preferred or its holders.

Warner will be the surviving corporation in the proposed merger. Its charter will be amended in the merger.... Nevertheless, Section 3.4(i) does not, in my opinion, grant a right to a series vote in these circumstances because the adverse effect upon defendants is not caused by an amendment, alteration or repeal of any provision of Warner's certificate of incorporation. Rather it is the conversion of the Warner Series B Preferred into Time Series BB Preferred that creates the adverse effect. * * *

This conclusion is further supported by a review of other provisions of the certificate of designation.... The drafters did expressly address the possibility of a merger in connection with the very question of a class vote by the preferred and adopted the limited protection afforded by Section 3.4(iii):

> Without ... consent ... of the Series B Stock ... the Corporation shall not ... (iii) be a party to any transaction involving a merger, consolidation or sale ... in which the shares of Series B Stock ... are converted into the right to receive equity securities of the surviving, resulting or acquiring corporation ... unless such corporation shall have, after such merger, consolidation or sale, no equity securities either authorized or outstanding ... ranking prior, as to dividends or in liquidation, to the Series B Stock or to the stock of the surviving, resulting or acquiring corporation issued in exchange therefor.

Plaintiffs here argue that *Warner* is distinguishable for three reasons: (1) the fact that the words "whether by merger, consolidation or otherwise" were not present in the Warner Series B certificate; (2) in *Warner,* unlike here, the preferred stockholders did not remain as stockholders of the surviving corporation, whose certificate arguably was amended and on which the preferred stockholders in *Warner* were relying for a right to a class vote; and (3) in *Warner,* unlike here, the merger was not an attempt simply to change the rights of the preferred stock, but rather there was economic and business substance to that transaction beyond an effort to do indirectly what could not be done directly.

In our view, only the first reason is valid in this appeal. * * *

The relevant statutory provisions are found in Sections 251(b) and 251(e) of the Delaware General Corporation Law ("DGCL"), which provide, in pertinent part:

§ 251. Merger or consolidation of domestic corporations.

* * *

(b) The board of directors of each corporation which desires to merge or consolidate shall adopt a resolution approving an agreement of merger or consolidation. The agreement shall state: (1) The terms and conditions of the merger or consolidation; (2) the mode of carrying the same into effect; (3) in the case of a merger, such amendments or changes in the certificate of incorporation of the surviving corporation as are desired to be effected by the merger, or, if no such amendments or changes are desired, a statement that the certificate of incorporation of the surviving corporation shall be its certificate of incorporation; (4) in the case of a consolidation, that the certificate of incorporation of the resulting corporation shall be as is set forth in an attachment to the agreement; (5) the manner of converting the shares of each of the constituent corporations into shares or other securities of the corporation surviving or resulting from the merger or consolidation and, if any shares of any of the constituent corporations are not to be converted solely into shares or other securities of the surviving or resulting corporation, the cash, property, rights or securities of any other corporation or entity which the holders of such shares are to receive in exchange ...; and (6) such other details or provisions as are deemed desirable....

* * *

(e) In the case of a merger, the certificate of incorporation of the surviving corporation shall automatically be amended to the extent, if any, that changes in the certificate of incorporation are set forth in the agreement of merger.

In short, Section 251 of the DGCL describes three ways that a merger or consolidation can affect the certificate of a constituent corporation:

(1) Section 251(b)(3) Amendments. First, the merger agreement may call for amendments to the pre-existing certificate of the surviving corporation.

(2) Displacement and Substitution by Merger. Second, the merger can designate the certificate of one of the constituent corporations as the certificate of the surviving entity, and thereby render the certificate of every other constituent corporation a legal nullity.

(3) Displacement and Substitution via Consolidation. Finally, in the case of a consolidation, the certificate of the resulting corporation displaces and renders a legal nullity the certificate of every disappearing constituent corporation.

In speaking of the "amendment, alteration or repeal" of the Avatex certificate by "merger, consolidation or otherwise," the drafters must have been referring to some or all of the events permitted by Section 251. Therefore, Section 251 provides the relevant backdrop for the interpretation of the First Series Preferred voting rights.

Avatex argued below, and the Court of Chancery appears to have agreed, that *only* a Section 251(b)(3) Amendment to the surviving corporation's charter amounts to an "amendment, alteration or repeal" within the meaning of the provisions defining the voting rights of the preferred stockholders. Accordingly, the argument runs, these provisions would apply *only* in the circumstance (not present here) where Avatex survives the merger and its certificate is amended thereby. Since the proposed merger with Xetava does not contemplate any such amendments to the disappearing Avatex certificate, the argument goes, the transaction can go forward without a First Series class vote.

The difficulty with this reading is that it fails to account for the word *consolidation,* which appears in the phrase "by merger, consolidation or otherwise." A consolidation cannot entail a Section 251(b)(3) Amendment because in a consolidation there is no "surviving corporation" whose pre-existing certificate is subject to amendment. The resulting corporation in a consolidation is a completely new entity with a new certificate of incorporation. All the certificates of the constituent corporations simply become legal nullities in a consolidation. In short, Avatex' proposed reading of the relevant provisions would render the word *consolidation* mere surplusage, and is problematic for that reason.[37]

Although the transaction before us is not a consolidation, the drafters' use of the word *consolidation* is significant. They must have intended the First Series Preferred stockholders to have the right to vote on at least some mergers or other transactions whereby the Avatex certificate—and indeed, Avatex itself—would simply disappear. Consolidation, by definition, implicates the disappearance of all constituent corporations. Here, Avatex disappears, just as it would in a consolidation. Under the terms of the proposed merger, Xetava will be the surviving entity and, since Avatex will cease its independent existence, its certificate becomes a legal nullity, as defendants concede. In our view, this constitutes a repeal, if not an amendment or alteration. Thus, the proposed merger is potentially within the class of events that trigger First Series Preferred voting rights.

The first question is: What will happen as a result of the merger to the "rights, preferences, privileges or voting power" of the Avatex First Series Preferred stock as set forth in the existing Avatex certificate? They disappear when the preferred stockholders of Avatex become common stockholders of Xetava under its certificate that does not contain those protections. We assume, as did the trial court, that their elimination would affect the First Series Preferred stockholders adversely.

The second question is: What act or event will cause this adverse effect if the merger is consummated? The trial court held that, "as in Warner," the adverse effect on the plaintiffs "will not flow from any 'amendment, alteration or repeal' of the First Series Certificate (however accomplished) but from the conversion into common stock of the First Series Preferred in the Proposed Merger." The Court so held notwithstanding that it had noted the distinguishing language of the certificate here—not present in *Warner*—"whether by merger, consolidation or otherwise." But the Court dismissed this distinction by concluding that this "language only modifies the phrase 'amendment, alteration and repeal' and does not independently create a right to a class vote in the case of *every merger*." But that is not

---

37. *See Sonitrol Holding Co. v. Marceau Investissements,* Del. Supr., 607 A.2d 1177, 1184 (1992) (under "cardinal rule of contract construction," court should give effect to all contract provisions).

the issue here where there is no contention that the First Series Preferred have a right to a class vote on *every merger.*

* * *

In our view, the Court of Chancery misapplied *Warner's* holding that "the amendment contemplated [as a 'housekeeping' measure post-merger] is necessitated by the merger [and the] amendment, like the conversion, flows from the merger and is not a necessary condition of it." This was the case in *Warner,* but is not here. The error of the trial court here was in its conclusion that the observation in *Warner* quoted above "is at least equally apposite here, where *Avatex* is to be merged with and into Xetava and will simply cease to maintain a separate corporate existence as a matter of law, without the necessity of any amendment, alteration or repeal" of the certificate.

In our view, the merger does cause the adverse effect because the merger is the corporate act that renders the Avatex certificate that protects the preferred stockholders a "legal nullity," in defendants' words. That elimination certainly fits within the ambit of one or more of the three terms in the certificate: *amendment* or *alteration* or *repeal*. The word *repeal* is especially fitting in this context because it contemplates a nullification, which is what defendants concede happens to the Avatex certificate.

* * *

In our view, the rights of the First Series Preferred are expressly and clearly stated in the Avatex certificate. The drafters of this instrument could not reasonably have intended any consequence other than granting to the First Series Preferred stock the right to consent by a two-thirds class vote to any merger that would result in the elimination of the protections in the Avatex certificate if the rights of the holders of that stock would thereby be adversely affected. The First Series Preferred stock rights granted by the corporate drafters here are the functional equivalent of a provision that would expressly require such consent if a merger were to eliminate any provision of the Avatex certificate resulting in materially adverse consequences to the holders of that security.

The drafters were navigating around several alternatives. First, all parties agree that pure amendment protection available to the First Series Preferred stockholders as granted by Section 242(b)(2) of the DGCL and Section 4 of the certificate does not—absent the very phrase at issue here— apply to this merger. Although *Warner* was decided after the Avatex certificate of designations became effective, *Warner* clearly supports this view and it continues to be valid precedent for that proposition. Second, all parties agree that if Avatex would have been the survivor, and its certificate were amended in the merger as contemplated by 8 *Del. C.* § 251(c)(3), the First Series Preferred would have the right to consent by two-thirds class vote. * * *

If Section 6 of the certificate does not guarantee a class vote to the First Series Preferred in this merger, what could it conceivably be interpreted to mean? Defendants argue that the certificate can be construed to apply *only* in the second instance noted above—namely, in the case where Avatex is the survivor and *its* certificate is amended, altered or repealed, as contemplated by Section 251(b)(3). But, as plaintiffs point out, this cannot be the *only* outcome the drafters intended because the certificate grants the First Series Preferred this protection in a consolidation where Section 251(b)(3) does not apply. Because the word *consolidation* is included, it cannot reasonably be argued that the protections of Section 6 of the certificate applicable to the First Series Preferred are confined to a Section 251(b)(3) amendment. Therefore, the term *consolidation* cannot be ignored or wished away as surplusage, as defendants argue. It is well established that a court interpreting any contractual provision, including preferred stock provisions, must give effect to all terms of the instrument, must read the instrument as a whole, and, if possible, reconcile all the provisions of the instrument.

Conclusion

The Court of Chancery held, and defendants contend on appeal that *Warner* compels a different result from that which we reach because *Warner* held that there it was only the stock conversion, not the amendment that adversely affected the preferred. But the short answer here is that the language of the First Series Preferred stock is materially different from the language in *Warner* because here we have the phrase, "whether by merger, consolidation or otherwise." This provision entirely changes the analysis and compels the result we hold today. Here, the repeal of the certificate and the stock conversion cause the adverse effect.

It is important to place what we decide today in proper perspective. The outcome here continues a coherent and rational approach to corporate finance.[51] The contrary result, in our view, would create an anomaly and could risk the erosion of uniformity in the corporation law. The Court of Chancery was mindful of this concern in referring to our general observations in *Kaiser* that the courts should avoid creating enduring uncertainties as to the meaning of boilerplate provisions in financial instruments. To be sure, there are some boilerplate aspects to the preferred stock provisions in the Avatex certificate and those found in other cases. But one is struck by the disuniformity of some crucial provisions, such as the differences that

---

51. *See* [Richard M.] Buxbaum, [*Preferred Stock–Law and Draftsmanship*, 42 Cal. L. Rev.], at 243 [(1954)]:

> PREFERRED STOCK is an anomalous security. It is a debt security when it claims certain absolute rights.... It is an equity security when it tries to control the enterprise through a practical voting procedure or to share in excess distributions of corporation profits. Of course, a share of preferred stock is actually a composite of many rights.

> * * *

> The primary source of a share's legal rights is the share contract. There is no ideal preferred stock but only a collection of attributes which the share contract says makes up a share of preferred stock. The share contract, in turn, is found in the articles of incorporation and the applicable state statutes.

(footnotes omitted).

exist when one compares the provisions in *Warner* and *Sullivan* with those presented here. That lack of uniformity is no doubt a function of (a) the adaptations by different drafters of some standard provisions; (b) negotiations by preferred stock investors seeking certain protections; (c) poor drafting; or (d) some combination of the above. The difference between the provisions in the Warner certificate and the Avatex provisions are outcome-determinative because we find there is no reasonable interpretation of the Avatex certificate that would deny the First Series Preferred a class vote on an "amendment, alteration or repeal ... by merger, consolidation or otherwise" of the protective provisions of the Avatex certificate.

The path for future drafters to follow in articulating class vote provisions is clear. When a certificate (like the Warner certificate or the Series A provisions here) grants only the right to vote on an amendment, alteration or repeal, the preferred have no class vote in a merger. When a certificate (like the First Series Preferred certificate here) adds the terms "whether by merger, consolidation or otherwise" and a merger results in an amendment, alteration or repeal that causes an adverse effect on the preferred, there would be a class vote. When a certificate grants the preferred a class vote in any merger or in any merger where the preferred stockholders receive a junior security, such provisions are broader than those involved in the First Series Preferred certificate. We agree with plaintiffs' argument that these results are uniform, predictable and consistent with existing law relating to the unique attributes of preferred stock.

The judgment of the Court of Chancery is reversed and the matter is remanded for further proceedings consistent with this Opinion.

QUESTIONS

1. Does the court's interpretation give meaning to the words "amendment, alteration or repeal" as the exception to the denial of voting rights for the First Series Preferred?

2. Is there an alternative reading of section 6(b) of the certificate of designation that gives meaning to this language *and* to the phrase, "whether by merger, consolidation, or otherwise ...."?

3. What is a "consolidation"? It is not a defined term in the Delaware General Corporation Law. It nearly always appears as part of the phrase "merger or consolidation." The only statutory hint appears in § 252(c)(5). How does the court describe a consolidation?

4. The court rejected Avatex's argument that § 251(b)(3) provides that only a merger in which Avatex is the surviving corporation would amend or alter the certificate of incorporation and require a preferred shareholder vote. The court rejects this argument because it ignores the language in the charter that states "by merger, *consolidation* or otherwise." (Emphasis added) How does this effect the case?

5. Should it matter that, to the author's knowledge, no corporation has engaged in a "consolidation" in over thirty years, because this method

has been replaced by the triangular merger, in which a new subsidiary is created?

6. Would the result have been different under the Revised Model Business Corporation Act, which has no provisions for consolidation? See RMBCA §§ 10.04 and 11.04. See also Cal. Corp. Code § 1202(b).

NOTE

A different result was reached in Rothschild International Corp. v. Liggett Group, Inc., 474 A.2d 133 (Del. 1984), where preferred shares were eliminated in a merger for $70 each, which was $30 below their liquidation preference. The court held that a merger that converted their shares into cash was not a liquidation, and that the investors took their preferred shares with notice that a merger could alter their rights without their consent, if they had no voting rights in the transaction. To the same effect is Rauch v. RCA Corp., 861 F.2d 29 (2d Cir. 1986 (applying Delaware law).

B. Dealing with the Class Veto Power

While Section 251 of Del. G.C.L. creates no preferred class voting rights in mergers, in contrast to charter amendments, The Model Act provides an integrated approach to charter amendments and mergers. See M.BC.A. §§ 10.04 & 11.04(f). These voting rules are mandatory, unlike many other provisions of the Model Act. Model Act § 10.04(a)(5) only requires a class vote when another class of preferred is created if the rights or preferences of the new class are "prior or superior" to the shares of the existing class. For many drafters, however, compliance with the New York Stock Exchange's requirements will require additional protection, as set out below.

New York Stock Exchange, Listed Company manual, ¶ 313.00(C):

Increase in Authorized Amount or Creation of a Pari Passu Issue—

An increase in the authorized amount of a class of preferred stock or the creation of a pari passu issue should be approved by a majority of the holders of the outstanding shares of the class or classes to be affected. The Board of Directors may increase the authorized amount of a series or create an additional series ranking pari passu without a vote by the existing series if shareholders authorized such action by the Board of Directors at the time the class of preferred stock was created. *50%*

Creation of a Senior Issue—

Creation of a senior equity security should require approval of at least two-thirds of the outstanding preferred shares. The Board of Directors may create a senior series without a vote by the existing series if shareholders authorized such action by the Board of Directors at the time of the existing series of preferred stock was created. A vote by an existing class of preferred stock is not required for the creation of a senior issue if the existing class has previously received adequate *67%*

notice of redemption to occur within 90 days. However, the vote of the existing class should not be denied if all or part of the existing issue is being retired with proceeds from the sale of the new stock.

Alteration of Existing Provisions—

Approval by the holders of at least two-thirds of the outstanding shares of a preferred stock should be required for adoption of any charter or by-law amendment that would materially affect existing terms of the preferred stock. If all series of a class of preferred stock are not equally affected by the proposed changes, there should be a two-thirds approval of the class and a two-thirds approval of the series that will have a diminished status. The charter should not hinder the shareholders' right to alter the terms of a preferred stock by limiting modification to specific items, e.g., interest rate, redemption price.

These provisions make it clear that preferred stock can play an important role in corporate transactions. Where classes of preferred stock are relatively small, this may mean that investors with a minor stake in the company can exercise a veto power over major transactions. One solution to this is to create a holding company with a simple one-stock structure, that can engage in future financing and merger transactions without seeking approval of preferred stockholders of the subsidiary. The following case illustrates the difficulties that can arise in the initial step of creating the holding company structure.

As a mechanical matter, creating a holding company structure typically involves having the current (operating) company create a wholly-owned subsidiary (ultimately the holding company), which in turns creates its own wholly-owned subsidiary. Both subsidiaries are capitalized with nominal amounts. At this point shareholders in the operating company are asked to approve a merger with the second-level subsidiary, in which the common stockholders will exchange their shares for stock in the holding company. At the end of the transaction the operating company will be the surviving corporation in the merger with the second-level subsidiary, which will retain the original charter, preferred shares and debts of the operating company. New financings and transactions can occur at the holding company level without any vote of the holders of the preferred shares.

Schreiber v. Carney

447 A.2d 17 (Del. Ch.1982).

■ HARTNETT, VICE CHANCELLOR.

In this stockholder's derivative action, Leonard I. Schreiber, the plaintiff, brought suit on behalf of defendant—Texas International Airlines, Inc. ("Texas International"), a Delaware corporation, challenging the propriety of a loan from Texas International to defendant Jet Capital Corporation ("Jet Capital"), the holder of 35% of the shares of stock of Texas International. Also joined as individual defendants were Texas International's board of directors—several of whom also served on Jet Capital's board of directors. The matter is presently before the Court on cross-motions for summary judgment. Defendants' motion is based on their contention that there has been no showing of waste and that plaintiff lacks standing to bring this suit. Plaintiff's motion is based on his contention that the transaction was tainted by vote-buying and is therefore void. For the reasons set forth below, both motions must be denied.

I

The essential facts are undisputed. The lawsuit arises out of the corporate restructuring of Texas International which occurred on June 11, 1980. The restructuring was accomplished by way of a share for share merger between Texas International and Texas Air Corporation ("Texas Air"), a holding company formed for the purpose of effectuating the proposed reorganization. Texas Air is also a Delaware corporation. At the annual meeting held on June 11, 1980 the shareholders voted overwhelmingly in favor of the proposal. As a result the shareholders of Texas International were eliminated as such and received in trade for their stock an equal number of shares in Texas Air. Texas International in turn became a wholly-owned subsidiary of Texas Air.

Prior to the merger Texas International was engaged in the airline business servicing the cities of Houston and Dallas, Texas. All concede that the purpose of the merger was to enable Texas International—under a new corporate structure—to diversify, to strengthen itself financially and in general to be transformed into a more viable and aggressive enterprise. According to the proxy statement issued in connection with the merger, management indicated that although there were no commitments at that time, it was actively considering the possibility of acquiring other companies engaged in both related as well as unrelated fields.

During the formulation of the reorganization plan, management was confronted with an obstacle, the resolution of which forms the basis for this lawsuit, because Jet Capital, the owner of the largest block of Texas International's stock, threatened to block the merger. Jet Capital's veto power resulted from a provision in Texas International's Certificate of Incorporation which required that each of its four classes of stock participate in the approval of a merger. At that time, Texas International's four classes of outstanding stock consisted of 4,669,182 shares of common stock and three series of convertible preferred stock; 32,318 shares of Series A stock, 66,075 shares of Series B stock and 2,040,000 shares of Series C stock. According to the Certificate of Incorporation a majority vote was required of both the common stockholders and the Series A preferred stockholders voting as separate classes. Similarly, a majority vote was required of the Series B and Series C preferred stockholders, but voting together as a single class. Because Jet Capital owned all of the Series C preferred stock—the larger class—it was in a position to block the merger proposal. Jet Capital indicated that although the proposal was indeed beneficial to Texas International and the other shareholders, it was nevertheless compelled to vote against it because the merger, if approved, would impose an intolerable income tax burden on it. This was so because the merger had an adverse impact on Jet Capital's position as the holder of certain warrants to purchase Texas International's common stock which would expire in 1982. There were warrants outstanding for the purchase of 1,029,531 shares of Texas International common stock at $4.18 per share and, of these, Jet Capital owned sufficient warrants to acquire 799,880 shares of Texas International's common shares. As the holder of these warrants, Jet Capital was faced with three alternatives.

The first alternative for Jet Capital was for it to participate in the merger and exchange its Texas International warrants for Texas Air warrants. However, according to an Internal Revenue Service ruling obtained by management, each holder of an unexercised Texas International warrant would be deemed to have realized taxable income from the merger as if the warrant had been exercised. Thus, it was estimated that Jet Capital would incur an $800,000 federal income tax liability. Because Jet Capital was a publicly held company, its management could not justify the assumption of such a tax liability and, therefore, did not consider this a viable alternative.

The second alternative was for Jet Capital to exercise the warrants prematurely. The merger would then be tax free to it as it would be to the other shareholders. This, however, was also not deemed to be feasible because Jet Capital lacked the approximately three million dollars necessary to exercise the warrants. Jet Capital's assets—other than its Texas International stock—were worth only $200,000. In addition, borrowing money at the prevailing interest rates in order to finance an early exercise of the warrants was deemed prohibitively expensive by the management of Jet Capital. In any event, this alternative was considered to be imprudent because the early exercise of the warrants posed an unnecessary market risk because the market value of Texas International's stock on the date of the early exercise might prove to be higher than that on the expiration date. As a result, this alternative was also not considered viable.

The third and final alternative was for Jet Capital to vote against the merger and thus preclude it. Given these alternatives, Jet Capital obviously chose to oppose the restructuring.

In order to overcome this impasse, it was proposed that Texas International and Jet Capital explore the possibility of a loan by Texas International to Jet Capital in order to fund an early exercise of the warrants. Because Texas International and Jet Capital had several common directors, the defendants recognized the conflict of interest and endeavored to find a way to remove any taint or appearance of impropriety. It was, therefore, decided that a special independent committee would be formed to consider and resolve the matter. The three Texas International directors who had no interest in or connection with Jet Capital were chosen to head up the committee. After its formation, the committee's first act was to hire independent counsel. Next, the committee examined the proposed merger and, based upon advice rendered by an independent investment banker, the merger was again found to be both a prudent and feasible business decision. The committee then confronted the "Jet Capital obstacle" by considering viable options for both Texas International and Jet Capital and, as a result, the committee determined that a loan was the best solution.

After negotiating at arm's length, both Texas International and Jet Capital agreed that Texas International would loan to Jet Capital $3,335,000 at 5% interest per annum for the period up to the scheduled 1982 expiration date for the warrants. After this period, the interest rate would equal the then prevailing prime interest rate. The 5% interest rate was recommended by an independent investment banker as the rate necessary to reimburse Texas International for any dividends paid out during this period. Given this provision for anticipated dividends and the fact that the advanced money would be immediately paid back to Texas International upon the exercise of the warrants, the loan transaction had virtually no impact on Texas International's cash position.

As security Jet Capital was required to pledge all of its Series C preferred stock having a market value of approximately 150% of the amount of the loan. In addition, Jet Capital was expected to apply to the prepayment of the loan any after tax proceeds received from the sale of any stock acquired by Jet Capital as a result of the exercise of the 1982 warrants.

The directors of Texas International unanimously approved the proposal as recommended by the committee and submitted it to the stockholders for approval—requiring as a condition of approval that a majority of all outstanding shares and a majority of the shares voted by the stockholders other than Jet Capital or its officers or directors be voted in favor of the proposal. After receiving a detailed proxy statement, the shareholders voted overwhelmingly in favor of the proposal. There is no allegation that the proxy statement did not fully disclose all the germane facts with complete candor.

The complaint attacks the loan transaction on two theories. First, it is alleged that the loan transaction constituted vote-buying and was therefore void. Secondly, the complaint asserts that the loan was corporate waste. In essence, plaintiff argues that even if the loan was permissible and even if it was the best available option, it would have been wiser for Texas International to have loaned Jet Capital only $800,000—the amount of the increased tax liability—because this would have minimized Texas International's capital commitment and also would have prevented Jet Capital from increasing its control in Texas International on allegedly discriminatory and wasteful terms. Plaintiff also points out that the 5% interest rate on the loan was only equal to the amount of dividends Texas International would have been expected to pay during the period between the time of the early exercise and the date the warrants expired. Jet Capital, therefore in effect it is urged, received an interest free loan for the nearly two-year period preceding the 1982 warrant expiration date.

* * *

IV

* * *

It is clear that the loan constituted vote-buying as that term has been defined by the courts. Vote-buying, despite its negative connotation, is simply a voting agreement supported by consideration personal to the stockholder, whereby the stockholder divorces his discretionary voting power and votes as directed by the offeror. The record clearly indicates that Texas International purchased or "removed" the obstacle of Jet Capital's opposition. Indeed, this is tacitly conceded by the defendants. However, defendants contend that the analysis of the transaction should not end here because the legality of vote-buying depends on whether its object or purpose is to defraud or in some manner disenfranchise the other stockholders. Defendants contend that because the loan did not defraud or disenfranchise any group of shareholders, but rather enfranchised the other shareholders by giving them a determinative vote in the proposed merger, it is not illegal per se. Defendants, in effect, contend that vote-buying is not void per se because the end justified the means. Whether this is valid depends upon the status of the law.

The Delaware decisions dealing with vote-buying leave the question unanswered. In each of these decisions, the Court summarily voided the challenged votes as being purchased and thus contrary to public policy and in fraud of the other stockholders. However, the facts in each case indicated that fraud or disenfranchisement was the obvious purpose of the vote-buying.

* * *

The present case presents a peculiar factual setting in that the proposed vote-buying consideration was conditional upon the approval of a majority of the disinterested stockholders after a full disclosure to them of all pertinent facts and was purportedly for the best interests of all Texas International stockholders. It is therefore necessary to do more than merely consider the fact that Jet Capital saw fit to vote for the transaction after a loan was made to it by Texas International. As stated in Oceanic Exploration Co. v. Grynberg, Del. Supr., 428 A.2d 1 (1981), a case involving an analogous situation, to do otherwise would be tantamount to "[d]eciding the case on . . . an abstraction divorced from the facts of the case and the intent of the law."

A review of the present controversy, therefore, must go beyond a reading of Macht v. Merchants Mortgage & Credit Co., [Del. Ch. 194 A. 19 (1937)] *supra*, and consider the cases cited therein. There are essentially two principles which appear in these cases. The first is that vote-buying is illegal per se if its object or purpose is to defraud or disenfranchise the other stockholders. A fraudulent purpose is as defined at common law, as a deceit which operates prejudicially upon the property rights of another.

The second principle which appears in these old cases is that vote-buying is illegal per se as a matter of public policy, the reason being that each stockholder should be entitled to rely upon the independent judgment of his fellow stockholders. Thus, the underlying basis for this latter principle is again fraud but as viewed from a sense of duty owed by all stockholders to one another. The apparent rationale is that by requiring each stockholder to exercise his individual judgment as to all matters presented, "[t]he security of the small stockholders is found in the natural disposition of each stockholder to promote the best interests of all, in order to promote his individual interests." In essence, while self interest motivates a stockholder's vote, theoretically, it is also advancing the interests of the other stockholders. Thus, any agreement entered into for personal gain, whereby a stockholder separates his voting right from his property right was considered a fraud upon this community of interests.

The often cited case of Brady v. Bean, 221 Ill. App. 279 (1921), is particularly enlightening. In that case, the plaintiff—an apparently influential stockholder—voiced his opposition to the corporation's proposed sale of assets. The plaintiff feared that his investment would be wiped out because the consideration for the sale appeared only sufficient enough to satisfy the corporation's creditors. As a result and without the knowledge of the other stockholders, the defendant, also a stockholder as well as a director and substantial creditor of the company, offered to the plaintiff in exchange for the withdrawal of his opposition, a sharing in defendant's claims against the corporation. In an action to enforce this contract against the defendant's estate, the Court refused relief stating:

> "Appellant being a stockholder in the company, any contract entered into by him whereby he was to receive a personal consideration in return for either his action or his inaction in a matter such as a sale of all the company's assets, involving, as it did, the interests of all the stockholders, was contrary to public policy and void, it being admitted that such contract was not known by or assented to by the other stockholders. The purpose and effect of the contract was apparently to influence appellant, in his decision of a question affecting the rights and interests of his associate stockholders, by a consideration which was foreign to those rights and interests and would likely to induce him to disregard the consideration he owed them and the contract must, therefore, be regarded as a fraud upon them. Such an agreement will not be enforced, as being against public policy." (emphasis added) 221 Ill. App. at 283.

In addition to the deceit obviously practiced upon the other stockholders, the Court was clearly concerned with the rights and interests of the other stockholders. Thus, the potential injury or prejudicial impact which might flow to other stockholders as a result of such an agreement forms the heart of the rationale underlying the breach of public policy doctrine.

An automatic application of this rationale to the facts in the present case, however, would be to ignore an essential element of the transaction. The agreement in question was entered into primarily to further the interests of Texas International's other shareholders. Indeed, the shareholders, after reviewing a detailed proxy statement, voted overwhelmingly in favor of the loan agreement. Thus, the underlying rationale for the argument that vote-buying is illegal per se, as a matter of public policy, ceases to exist when measured against the undisputed reason for the transaction.

Moreover, the rationale that vote-buying is, as a matter of public policy, illegal per se is founded upon considerations of policy which are now outmoded as a necessary result of an evolving corporate environment. According to 5 Fletcher Cyclopedia Corporation (Perm. Ed.) § 2066:

> "The theory that each stockholder is entitled to the personal judgment of each other stockholder expressed in his vote, and that any agreement among stockholders frustrating it was invalid, is obsolete because it is both impracticable and impossible of application to modern corporations with many widely scattered stockholders, and the courts have gradually abandoned it."

In addition, Delaware law has for quite some time permitted stockholders wide latitude in decisions affecting the restriction or transfer of voting rights. In Ringling Bros., Etc., Shows, Inc. v. Ringling, Del. Supr., 53 A.2d 441 (1947), the Delaware Supreme Court adopted a liberal approach to voting agreements which, prior to that time, were viewed with disfavor and were often considered void as a matter of public policy. In upholding a voting agreement the Court stated:

> "Generally speaking, a shareholder may exercise wide liberality of judgment in the matter of voting, and it is not objectionable that his motives may be for personal profit, or determined by whims or caprice, so long as he violates no duty owed his fellow stockholders." (citation omitted)

The Court's rationale was later codified in 8 Del. C. § 218(c), which permits voting agreements.

Recently, in Oceanic Exploration Co. v. Grynberg, Del. Supr., 428 A.2d 1 (1981), the Delaware Supreme Court applied this approach to voting trusts. The Court also indicated, with approval, the liberal approach to all contractual arrangements limiting the incidents of stock ownership. Significantly, Oceanic involved the giving up of voting rights in exchange for personal gain. There, the stockholder, by way of a voting trust, gave up his right to vote on all corporate matters over a period of years in return for "valuable benefits including indemnity for large liabilities." 428 A.2d at 5.

Given the holdings in Ringling and Oceanic it is clear that Delaware has discarded the presumptions against voting agreements. Thus, under our present law, an agreement involving the transfer of stock voting rights without the transfer of ownership is not necessarily illegal and each arrangement must be examined in light of its object or purpose. To hold otherwise would be to exalt form over substance. As indicated in Oceanic more than the mere form of an agreement relating to voting must be considered and voting agreements in whatever form, therefore, should not be considered to be illegal per se unless the object or purpose is to defraud or in some way disenfranchise the other stockholders. This is not to say, however, that vote-buying accomplished for some laudable purpose is automatically free from challenge. Because vote-buying is so easily susceptible of abuse it must be viewed as a voidable transaction subject to a test for intrinsic fairness.

V

Apparently anticipating this finding, plaintiff also attempts to cast the loan agreement as one seeking to accomplish a fraudulent purpose. As indicative of fraud, plaintiff points to the fact that no other warrant holder was given a similar loan to enable an early exercise of the warrants. However, despite this contention, I am satisfied that, based on the record, there is no evidence from which an inference of a fraudulent object or purpose can be drawn.

As to the other warrant holders who did not get a loan, they were merely the holders of an expectant and contingent interest and, as such, were owed no duty by Texas International except as set forth in the warrant certificates. FOLK, The Delaware General Corporation Law, Little, Brown (1972) § 155, p. 126. In any event, the record fails to show any evidence that Texas International's ultimate decision to fund Jet Capital's early exercise of the warrants was motivated and accomplished except with the best interests of all Texas International stockholders in mind.

VI

I therefore hold that the agreement, whereby Jet Capital withdrew its opposition to the proposed merger in exchange for a loan to fund the early exercise of its warrants was not void per se because the object and purpose of the agreement was not to defraud or disenfranchise the other stockholders but rather was for the purpose of furthering the interest of all Texas International stockholders. The agreement, however, was a voidable act. Because the loan agreement was voidable it was susceptible to cure by shareholder approval. Michelson v. Duncan, Del. Supr., 407 A.2d 211 (1979). Consequently, the subsequent ratification of the transaction by a majority of the independent stockholders, after a full disclosure of all germane facts with complete candor precludes any further judicial inquiry of it.

* * *

VIII

In summary plaintiff's motion for summary judgment on the grounds that the transaction before the Court was permeated by vote-buying and was therefore void or voidable is denied. Defendants' motion for summary judgment on the grounds that plaintiff lacks standing to bring this suit or on the grounds that there is no factual basis for a claim of waste is denied.

It is so ordered.

NOTE

In Goldman v. Postal Telegraph, Inc., 52 F.Supp. 763 (D. Del.1943), the court sustained what was in effect a payment to holders of common stock to secure their consent to a liquidating asset sale. The suit was brought by a holder of preferred stock, who complained that the proceeds of the sale were less than the liquidation claims of the preferred, but that, in the vote submitted to the shareholders to approve the sale, it was proposed to amend the company's charter to provide that the preferred stockholders would receive stock of the buyer at a formula that left approximately 16% of the sale proceeds for the common stockholders. If the company had been liquidated, the plaintiff complained, the common stockholders would have received nothing. Accordingly, he argued that this amendment was simply a payment to the common stockholders to secure their votes, which were necessary to approve the sale. The court dismissed the complaint, stating:

> "The reality of the situation confronting Postal's management called for some inducement to be offered the common stockholders to secure their favorable vote for the plan. * * * The fact is something had to induce the common stockholders to come along. This court and the Delaware courts have recognized the strategic position of common stock to hamper the desires of the real owners of the equity of a corporation, and the tribute which common stock exacts for its vote under reclassification and reorganization."

If a class of preferred is held by widely dispersed investors, determining the outcome of a probable vote will create much greater uncertainty. Fortunately, many classes of preferred are not so widely held, but are generally held by corporate institutional investors, so that such bargaining may be feasible in a surprisingly large number of cases. For the use of special classes or series of preferred to create voting road blocks to acquisitions, see Telvest v. Olson, *supra*, Part 1.A of this chapter. For academic discussion of this question, see, e.g., Robert Clark, Vote Buying and Corporate Law, 29 Case W. Res. L. Rev. 776 (1979) and Henry G. Manne, Some Theoretical Aspects of Share Voting: An Essay in Honor of Adolf A. Berle, 64 Colum. L. Rev. 1427 (1964).

QUESTIONS

1. What is the effect of this merger on the veto power of Jet Capital in the future?

2. Would this approach work under the Model Act and the Delaware Act?

3. In Section IV of its opinion, the Schreiber court discussed the holding in Brady v. Bean, 221 Ill. App. 279 (1921), where a shareholder who was also a creditor of the corporation, seeking to cause the corporation to sell its assets, offered to share his gains as a creditor with another shareholder if he would drop his opposition and vote in favor of the dissolution. The court characterizes this as causing a potential injury to other shareholders, because the motivating force was a creditor's claim, "a consideration which was foreign to those rights and interests [of the

other stockholders]." How does this differ from the interests of Jet Capital? Are warrants to purchase stock claims that are foreign to the rights of the shareholders? Are they foreign if the warrant-holder can purchase shares at a price below the current market price, and thus would dilute the investment of the existing shareholders?

4. How would the Schreiber court have decided Brady v. Bean? Why?

5. Recall that the Revised Model Business Corporation Act gives separate voting rights as a voting group to classes or series of stock in certain mergers. Could you restructure the transaction that Texas International wishes to engage in under the Model Act, using a share exchange, to avoid Jet Capital's veto power?

Orban v. Field

1997 WL 153831 (Del.Ch. 1997).

■ ALLEN, CHANCELLOR.

This is a stockholders' suit brought by certain holders of common stock of Office Mart Holdings Corp. ("Office Mart"). The suit arises out of a series of transactions culminating in a June 23, 1992 stock-for-stock merger between Office Mart and a subsidiary of Staples, Inc. The first of the transactions was a November 15, 1991 recapitalization in which, in exchange for forgiveness of principal and interest of outstanding notes, Office Mart creditors accepted a package of securities including common stock warrants and a new Series C Preferred stock. The second step was board action of May 1992 facilitating the exercise of certain warrants held by the holders of preferred stock. The concluding transaction was the merger with Staples. In that merger, various classes of Office Mart preferred stock were entitled to liquidation preferences that together exceed the value of the consideration paid. Thus, the Office Mart common stock received no consideration in the merger. The merger was an arm's-length transaction and it is not contended in this suit that the price paid by Staples was not a fair price or the best price reasonably available.

In summary, the claims made are now two. First, it is asserted that the Office Mart board breached its duty to the common stock by facilitating steps that enabled the holders of preferred stock to exercise warrants that enabled the preferred to overcome a practical power that the common held to impede the closing of the merger. This claim in essence asserts that the board, which was controlled by holders of preferred stock, exercised corporate power against the common and in favor of the preferred and, thus, breached a duty of loyalty to the common. * * *

* * *

Extensive discovery has now occurred and an amended complaint, which no longer contains claims concerning undisclosed negotiations, has been filed. Defendants have moved for summary judgment.

For the reasons that follow, I conclude that no fact material to the appropriate legal analysis is in dispute and that defendants are entitled to judgment as a matter of law. With respect to the first claim, I conclude that there is no evidence upon which a fact finder could conclude that the board's actions (as explained below) in facilitating the exercise by holders of preferred stock of their legal rights to exercise warrants represented a disloyal act towards the common stock. Even assuming, as I do, that in facilitating the exercise of the warrants in these circumstances (where the warrants were used to overcome Mr. Orban's resistance to the merger) the board has a burden to establish either the reasonableness of its actions or its fairness, the record is in my judgment, entirely consistent with that conclusion and wholly inconsistent with the opposite conclusion.

* * *

I. Relevant Facts

George Orban, the principal plaintiff in this action, founded Office Mart in 1987; served as its CEO until 1989; and as a director until March 1992. From 1987 to 1992, Office Mart developed and operated a chain of ten "WORKplace" office supply superstores in and around Tampa, Florida. The company was, however, never well capitalized. That fact became rather quickly apparent when the company sought to expand into the California market in 1988, from which it was forced to retreat.

Capital structure: Initially, the company was capitalized largely with equity in the form of voting preferred stock from institutional investors. Mr. Orban, who in this litigation, characterizes himself as a "venture capitalist," invested only approximately $15,000 in exchange for which he received all of the common stock. (Later other employees of the firm came to hold modest amounts of the common as well). The substantial capital; came in several tranches from financial institutions. 2,422,750 shares of Series A preferred stock were issued in 1987 to raise $2,950,000 in initial capital. In May 1988, an additional $17,084,080 was raised by the private placement of 6,833,632 shares of Series B preferred stock.

All classes of equity voted together. Mr. Orban was the largest holder of common stock, however, he held only 14.32% of the total voting power. Series A and Series B preferred stockholders held 22.59% and 63.18%, respectively, of the company's total voting rights. Both classes of preferred stock were convertible into common stock and entitled to vote on an as-converted basis, both had anti-dilution rights and possessed liquidation preferences payable in the event of a merger. The common stock, of course, had no such rights.

Continuing need for long term capital: Relatively early on, by June 1989, Office Mart's board was forced to conclude that it either had to find additional capital to pursue an aggressive growth strategy, or had to sell the company. At that point, Mr. Orban resigned as CEO and Stephen Westerfield agreed to assume the duties of CEO. He had had no prior involvement with Office Mart [although he was an experienced former president of another company]. Mr. Westerfield began taking steps to address these issues. The investment banking firm of Donaldson Lufkin & Jenrette was hired to assist in these efforts, but no potential investors or acquirors were identified and the financial position of the company continued to worsen.

Recognizing that it would be difficult for Office Mart to borrow necessary capital from commercial lenders, the company began to consider means to attract additional capital from the company's current investors. In April 1990, a group of Series B stockholders (including affiliates of Prudential Insurance, and Manufacturers Hanover Bank) provided the company with a $5.2 million line of credit in consideration of the issuance by the company of its 13% secured notes and warrants to acquire 40% of the company's fully diluted equity shares, exercisable at a price of $1.39 per share. The notes matured in three years (due on March 31, 1993) but could be prepaid at par plus accrued interest.

Office Mart began to draw down its credit facility shortly after its establishment. The company had difficulty from the beginning in meeting the interest payments on the debt. In order to ameliorate this situation in January 1991, an agreement was reached with creditors pursuant to which the company's interest obligations were deferred, in consideration of the grant of additional common stock warrants. The warrants covered common stock equal to 1.75% of total equity for each quarter of interest deferred, for a maximum of up to 10.575% of total equity. Despite the credit facility and deferred interest agreement, Office Mart continued to have financial difficulties throughout 1991.

The recapitalization: On September 5, 1991, Mr. Westerfield recommended that a recapitalization plan be adopted in order to eliminate the debt burden on the company's balance sheet. During a telephone meeting on September 27, 1991, Mr. Westerfield expressed his opinion that the recapitalization was necessary for the company to continue as a going concern; the board approved a proposed recapitalization plan at that time. On November 14, 1991, the Board again unanimously voted on the terms of the recapitalization, authorizing the company's officers to effectuate the transaction on the following day. At that meeting, Mr. Westerfield informed the Board that "there was no significant activity" with respect to efforts that had been made to locate potential investors or buyers of the company.

The material elements of the recapitalization plan: First, a new senior, nonconvertible Series C Senior Cumulative Redeemable Preferred Stock was created.[5] In exchange for 5.2 million shares of the Series C preferred stock and 2,136,976 new shares of common stock (equal to more than half

---

5. In the event of a liquidation or merger of the company, the new Series C preferred stock would entitle its owners to receive an initial preference of $7.5 million and a secondary preference of $1.5 million to be paid only after $12 million had been distributed to the A and B preferred stockholders. After the satisfaction of the secondary preference, the remaining proceeds would first go to the A and B preferred stockholders in order to meet their still unpaid liquidation preferences. The common stockholders would not receive any distributions until all of these preferences had been satisfied in full.

of all then outstanding common stock and equal to 10% of the fully diluted equity of the company), the holders of the debt agreed to its cancellation and released the company from the repayment of the $5.2 million principal amount and $607,800 in accrued interest. Finally, the company reduced the exercise price on the warrants issued to the creditors in connection with the original extension of the $5.2 million credit, from $1.39 to $0.75 per share.

Mr. Orban voted in favor of the recapitalization as a member of the Board and, subsequently, in his capacity as a Series A preferred stockholder. Although the common stockholders never were asked to approve the recapitalization plan in a shareholders' vote, it went into effect on November 15, 1991.[6]

As a result of the recapitalization plan, the following changes in the company's capital structure were to be made. As to Mr. Orban, his combined ownership of common and preferred stock was diluted from 13.27% to 2.54%. As to the common stockholders as a group, since the total number of shares of common stock outstanding had been increased from 1,548,411 to 3,683,387 shares, the percentage of voting power held by the holders of the pre-recap common was reduced from 14% to less than 3%. As to the former creditors, the recapitalization was structured to provide them with a potential for 50% voting interest in the company, with the Series A and B preferred stockholders now capable of voting 10.54% and 36.92% of the equity respectively, and with the remainder 3% voted by the common stockholders.

[Shortly after the recapitalization Westerfield began his search for an investor. His efforts resulted in an offer from Office Depot valuing the company at approximately $30 million. The board rejected the offer and instructed management to keep negotiating and to solicit offers from others. No other offers had been received within two months, and the board instructed Westerfield to renew negotiations for an improved offer with Office Depot. Shortly after the board meeting, Staples, concerned that Office Depot might acquire the company, expressed interest in acquiring Office Mart. By February 22, Staples had agreed to acquire Office Mart for Staples Stock valued at $35 million, based on the current price of Staples' stock.]

The Staples proposal was for a merger qualifying as a tax free merger and for "pooling of interests" accounting treatment. In order to assure that the transaction qualified for pooling of interest treatment, Staples demanded a contract clause requiring that holders of each class of Office Mart stock approve the transaction with a 90% vote.

* * *

---

6. This Court has determined that the common stockholders were not legally entitled to vote as a class on the recapitalization plan. *See Orban,* Mem. Op. at 19. The plan was approved by the Board and holders of Class A and B preferred stock which together constituted a majority of the total voting power of the company.

Third, the parties had to agree upon a stock allocation date upon which to determine the proportionate distribution of the Staples shares to Office Mart stockholders. Due to the fact that the total consideration was of less value than the total preferred stock preferences, as of the date of the letter agreement, this issue was particularly important to the common stockholders. The common stockholders could only receive merger consideration if the value of the Staples shares exceeded $35,062,470—the total amount of preferences to which the preferred were entitled—on the stock allocation date. The Board elected the date of May 29, the date of the signing of the definitive merger agreement. In hindsight, we know that the stock allocation date was inconsequential for the common stockholders because they would not have received merger proceeds on any of the possible stock allocation dates.

[The Staples agreement was conditioned not only on a 90% vote of all shares eligible to vote, but also on the approval of 90% of the shares of each class. Because Mr. Orban held more than 10% of the common stock, and expressed opposition to a merger in which the common would receive nothing, the board met with him in a series of unsuccessful negotiations to resolve the dispute.]

Dilution of Mr. Orban's common stock interest: Instead of continuing negotiations with Mr. Orban, the Board removed the impediment to the closure of the transaction by facilitating the exercise of warrants to acquire common stock by the Series A and B stockholders.

Several steps were required to effectuate this readjustment of proportionate ownership. First, the company's certificate of incorporation had to be amended to increase the authorized common stock from 25 to 56 million and preferred stock shares from 15 to 16.175 million. Second, to compensate for the issuance of additional shares, the Board adjusted the conversion ratio of the Series A and B and proportionately increase the number of warrants held by the holders of Series C preferred. Third, the Board proportionately reduced the exercise price of the warrants from $.75 to $.28726 in order to maintain the total exercise price of $6.4 million. Finally, the Board authorized the redemption of 2,089,714 shares held by Series C preferred stockholders, on a non-pro rata basis. In doing so, the company extended sufficient consideration to the Series C holders ($3,013,995) to enable them to exercise warrants to permit them, as a group, to hold more than 90% of Office Mart's outstanding common stock. The aggregate effect of these steps was to assure that Mr. Orban was entitled to vote less than 10% of the company's common stock.

The merger: When Office Mart and Staples entered into the definitive merger agreement on May 29, 1992, the agreement received the approval of 90% of each class of outstanding stock. As of May 29, the stock valuation date, the 1,093,750 shares of Staples common stock were worth a total of $31,992,188. When the transaction closed on June 23, that amount was used to allocate the merger proceeds to be distributed to each class of Office Mart stock in accord with the preferences of the preferred stockholders.

Since the merger consideration was insufficient to satisfy all of the contractual preferences of Office Mart's preferred stockholders, Mr. Orban and the other common stockholders received no proceeds. It might be noted, however, that Mr. Orban would have received no proceeds from the merger even if the recapitalization and related transactions had never occurred.

* * *

II. Analysis

Plaintiffs contend that the Board breached its fiduciary duty of loyalty to the common stockholders by facilitating the exercise of legal rights of preferred stockholders in transactions aimed at eliminating the leverage of the common stockholders by diluting their ownership interest below 10%.[23] The basic theory of Mr. Orban's case is that although the common stock was practically under water (i.e., valueless in a liquidation context) as of the spring of 1992, when evaluating the merger consideration in relation to the preferred stock preferences, *the pooling provision requiring a 90% approval vote of each class of stock gave Mr. Orban stock a certain value.* That value was destroyed when the Board took actions to assist the preferred stockholders to exercise their warrants, diluting the plaintiffs' common stock interest below 10%.

In response, defendants contend that the contested actions taken by the Board did not constitute any breach of fiduciary duty because they were legal and necessary to effectuate a merger in the best interest of the company. Further, defendants argue that the business judgment rule should apply to all of the challenged acts of the Board because the directors neither stood on both sides of the transactions nor received distinct personal benefits from such transactions.[24] According to defendants, all of the challenged acts of the Board were approved by a fully informed majority of disinterested directors and then ratified by an informed majority of the stockholders. *Williams v. Geier,* Del. Supr., 671 A.2d 1368 (1996).*

For purposes of this motion for summary judgment, I will assume that the business judgment rule is not applicable to the actions challenged by Mr. Orban's breach of fiduciary duty claim. Unquestionably in this instance the board of directors exercised corporate power—most pointedly in authorizing a non-pro-rata redemption of preferred shares for the purpose of funding the exercise by holders of preferred stock of warrants to buy

---

23. There is no claim that the Board engaged in fraud or that the merger itself was not in the best interests of the corporation.

24. Defendants stress that the fact that a director represents a large shareholder of the company is insufficient alone to find that a director was interested in the transaction. *See Citron v. Fairchild Camera and Instrument Corp.,* Del. Supr., 569 A.2d 53, 65 (1989). Although this is true even where other shareholders are in potential conflict with the affiliated shareholder, it is inapplicable if there had been special treatment of the affiliated shareholders, as is alleged in this case. *Id.*

* In addition to Orban, the other three directors were Westerfield, alleged by Orban to have a conflict because of his right to severance payments on a sale or merger, and two officers of corporate owners of Series B preferred stock.—Ed.

common stock. That act was directed against the common stock who found themselves with a certain leverage because of the requirements for pooling treatment. A board may certainly deploy corporate power against its own shareholders in some circumstances—the greater good justifying the action—but when it does, it should be required to demonstrate that it acted both in good faith and reasonably. See Phillips v. Insituform, Inc., Del. Ch., C.A. No. 9173, Allen, C. (Aug. 27, 1987); *Unocal Corp. v. Mesa Petroleum Co.,* Del. Supr., 493 A.2d 946 (1985); *see also Unitrin, Inc. v. American General Corp.,* Del. Supr., 651 A.2d 1361 (1995). The burden is upon defendants, the party moving for summary judgment, to show that their conduct was taken in good faith pursuit of valid ends and was reasonable in the circumstances.

While such a test is inevitably one that must be applied in the rich particularity of context, it is not inconsistent with summary adjudication where no material facts are in dispute or disputed facts may be assumed in favor of non-movant. In my opinion, the record established, satisfies the defendants' burden.

As a preliminary matter, it is important to note that there is no evidence, or even remaining allegation, that the November recapitalization was part of a scheme to deprive the common stockholders of consideration in the subsequent merger. The recapitalization was legally effectuated by the Board, validly altering the existing ownership structure of the company. Certainly, when viewed as an isolated event, the recapitalization was fair, authorized appropriately, and if it were to be tested under a fairness test, it would satisfy that standard.

The subsequent conduct of the Board, while requiring a more involved analysis, was, in my opinion, fair as a matter of law as well.

Duty of loyalty: Dilution of Mr. Orban's common stock interest: Once Orban attempted to use a potential power to deprive the transaction of pooling treatment, the Board was inevitably forced to decide whether it would support the common stock's (Mr. Orban's) effort to extract value from the preferred position or whether it would seek to accomplish the negotiated transaction, which it believed to be the transaction at the highest available price.

Certainly in some circumstances a board may elect (subject to the corporation's answering in contract damages) to repudiate a contractual obligation where to do so provides a net benefit to the corporation. To do so may in some situations be socially efficient. *See, e.g.,* Richard Craswell, *Contract Remedies, Renegotiation, and the Theory of Efficient Breach,* 61 S. CAL. L. REV. 629 (1988). But it would be bizarre to take this fact of legal life so far as to assert, as Mr. Orban must, that the Board had a duty to common stock to refrain from recognizing the corporation's legal obligations to its other classes of voting securities.[26]

To resolve this situation, the Board decided not to negotiate with Mr. Orban, but rather to effectuate the transaction as intended, respecting the

---

26. In economic terms, Mr. Orban's position does not represent an allocatively efficient transaction, the presence of which may make efficient breach socially desirable. Rather, it

preferential rights of the preferred stockholders. In my opinion, it cannot be said that the Board breached a duty of loyalty in making this decision. Whereas the preferred stockholders had existing legal preferences, the common stockholders had no legal right to a portion of the merger consideration under Delaware law or the corporate charter. The Staples' transaction appeared reasonably to be the best available transaction. Mr. Orban's threat to impede the realization of that transaction by the corporation was thwarted by legally permissible action that was measured and appropriate in the circumstances.

* * *

Based on the foregoing, defendants' motion for summary judgment is granted.

QUESTIONS

1. What was the nature of Orban's complaint that the board acted in a self-interested way to favor the preferred shareholders? Was it the recapitalization? Was it the repurchase of preferred shares?

2. Westerfield, as holder of a severance agreement, was to receive a cash payment from Office Mart under his agreement at the merger closing. Orban objected to the payment as "waste" in a part of the opinion omitted here. Is Westerfield's situation any different from that of the creditors and preferred stockholders?

3. If the board owes fiduciary duties to all shareholders, did it owe any duty to allocate some part of the merger consideration to the common stockholders, in exchange for their (diluted) veto power, as "tribute," in the words of the district judge in Goldman v. Postal Telegraph, Inc.?

4. Does this decision give a preferred-controlled board the power to ignore the welfare of the common in a merger?

5. If Orban had dissented from the merger and demanded the appraised fair value of his shares, would he have a better case than this complaint about fiduciary duties?

4. BOARD DUTIES

A. BOARD DUTIES TO PREFERRED SHAREHOLDERS

Mary G. Dalton v. American Investment Company

490 A.2d 574 (Del. Ch. 1985).

■ BROWN, CHANCELLOR.

This action is brought by certain preferred shareholders of American Investment Company, a Delaware corporation. The suit charges that the

---

could be preferable to deny the preferred their full liquidation preference (or the fullest amount of it available) only on the assumption that, as a practical matter, Office Mart would not be required to repair the loss with damages.

individual defendants, in their capacity as the board of directors of American Investment Company (hereafter "AIC"), breached the fiduciary duty owed by them to the plaintiffs during the course of a merger whereby AIC was merged into Leucadia American Corp., a wholly-owned subsidiary of Leucadia, Inc. ("Leucadia"). In that merger, the common shareholders of AIC were eliminated from their equity position in the corporation at a price of $13 per share. However, the preferred shareholders of AIC were not cashed out, but were left as preferred shareholders of the corporation surviving the merger. Plaintiffs contend that AIC's board looked only to the interests of the common shareholders in seeking a merger partner for AIC and, by so doing, unfairly froze the preferred shareholders into the post merger AIC as completely controlled by Leucadia. Thus, the suit is unusual in that the plaintiff shareholders are complaining about being unfairly frozen in as shareholders as opposed to the more normal shareholder lament that they were unfairly cashed out.

The plaintiffs also contend that the benefit allegedly given to them in the merger—an increase in their preferred dividend percentage plus the creation of a sinking fund and a plan for the mandatory redemption of the preferred shares—was wrongfully accomplished since it was done without their approval. They say that this constituted a change which adversely affected their existing preference rights and that as a consequence they were entitled to vote as a class on the merger proposal. They say that the failure of the defendants to permit them to vote as a class rendered shareholder approval of the merger illegal and wrongfully forced them into their present predicament. Under either theory plaintiffs seek a recovery of money damages against the individual defendants as well as against Leucadia indirectly through its subsidiary, AIC.

* * *

I.

* * *

Aside from operating the insurance companies, AIC was in the business of consumer finance. In essence, it borrowed money wholesale in order to lend it at retail rates through a chain of offices scattered throughout the country. It is my impression that consumer finance was the primary business of AIC during the 1970's.

[During the late 1970s AIC found that rising interest rates were squeezing its profits. As a consumer finance company, it borrowed money at wholesale (at presumably low rates) and lent at retail (presumably at significantly higher rates). By late 1980 the prime rate (at which banks lend to their best customers) reached 18%, and other interest rates, as well as dividend rates on newly issued preferred stock, were correspondingly high. In 1977 the AIC board retained Kidder, Peabody & Co., Inc. ("Kidder Peabody") to seek a prospective purchaser or merger partner.]

* * *

Kidder, Peabody sent out many letters and pursued numerous merger candidates. Eventually, in 1978, Household Finance Corporation ("HFC") came forth with an offer to acquire all outstanding shares of AIC. The offer of HFC was $12 per share for the common stock and $25 per share for the two series of preferred stock. At the time Kidder, Peabody had valued AIC's common stock within a range of $9 to $11, and the $12 figure offered by HFC approximated the then book value of the common shares. At the $25 redemption and liquidation value, the price offered for the preferred shares represented their book value also. The preferred shares were trading for about $9 per share at the time.

This offer by HFC was approved as fair by Kidder, Peabody and was accepted by AIC's board. It was also approved overwhelmingly by AIC's shareholders, both common and preferred. However, the United States Department of Justice entered the picture and sought to prohibit the acquisition by HFC on antitrust grounds. Ultimately, the acquisition of AIC by HFC was enjoined by the federal courts and HFC's merger proposal was terminated.

[Thereafter AIC's President, Brockmann, took an active role in seeking a new buyer. Because HFC's $12 price was approximately the book value of AIC's stock at the time of its offer, Brockman used book value to suggest a floor for any new offers, in part because AIC's book value per share was rising to $13.50 even as its business deteriorated. HFC's offer of $25 for preferred stock trading at $9 was regarded as a "Christmas present" for the preferred shareholders. Brockman never suggested a $13.50 price for the stock, but the HFC total bid was approximately $75 million, which was well known by market participants.]

* * *

In February, 1980, Leucadia, a company also in the consumer finance business, submitted a written offer to AIC whereby it proposed to acquire all common shares of AIC for $13 per share. The proposal contained no offer for the preferred shares but rather it proposed to leave them in place. Later, presumably as a result of Brockmann's suggestion that something should be done for the holders of the preferred, Leucadia revised its proposal by offering to make available to AIC's preferred shareholders immediately following the merger a Leucadia debenture worth 40% of the face value of the preferred shares, with interest at 13%, which could be exchanged for the preferred shares. Still later, however, because of declining economic conditions, Leucadia withdrew its offer altogether.

In August, 1980, Leucadia reappeared. This time it offered $13 per share for all outstanding shares of AIC's common stock and offered further to increase the dividend rate on the preferred shares from 5 1/2% to 7%. In addition, and again because of Brockmann's expression of concern for the preferred shareholders, Leucadia added a "sweetener" in the form of a sinking fund to redeem the preferred shares over a period of 20 years at the rate of 5% each year. Any such redemptions were to continue to be made by lot as provided by AIC's original preference designations, but subject, however, to the added proviso that any market purchases or other acquisitions of preferred shares made during a given year could be credited against the annual 5% redemption requirement.

Kidder, Peabody opined that this offer was fair to AIC and its shareholders, stressing the fairness of the price to the common (AIC was trading for $11 per share on the day prior to the announcement of the approval of the merger in principle) and the safety that the proposal would provide to the rights of the preferred. The board of AIC accepted the offer and, when put to the vote of the shareholders, it was overwhelmingly approved by AIC's common shareholders and was approved unanimously by the holders of the other series of preferred stock. However, the holders of the Series B preferred, including the plaintiffs, voted some 170,000 of the 280,000 Series B shares against the proposal. Nonetheless, with all shares being accorded an equal vote, the plan of merger was adopted and AIC was merged into Leucadia American Corp., the wholly-owned subsidiary of Leucadia, with the name of the surviving corporation being changed to AIC. The former common shareholders of AIC were cashed out at $13 per share. Leucadia became the owner of all of AIC's common stock while the preferred shareholders were continued on as shareholders of AIC, albeit at the increased dividend rate and with the added redemption and sinking fund provisions.

Other relevant factors may be summarized as follows. On the same day that Leucadia submitted the offer that was ultimately accepted by AIC, another company, Dial Financial Corporation, still another company engaged in the consumer finance business, also submitted a merger proposal to AIC. The offer of Dial Financial Corporation (hereafter "Dial") was $13.50 per share for the common stock and nothing for the preferred other than the creation of a sinking fund for redemption purposes. The AIC board considered both offers but opted to take the Leucadia offer even though it was 50 cents per share lower for the common stock because the board viewed Leucadia's offer to be better from the standpoint of the preferred shareholders and because it avoided potential antitrust problems since Dial was a direct competitor of AIC in certain market areas.

* * *

II.

Addressing first the plaintiffs breach of fiduciary duty claims, it is their contention that the individual defendants, in their capacity as directors, owed a duty of fair dealing to all shareholders of AIC, both the common and the preferred, in negotiating and agreeing to any plan of merger. They say, however, that the defendant directors violated this duty to the extent that it was owed to the preferred shareholders once the HFC proposal had aborted. They charge that the defendants did so following the cancellation of the HFC offer by discreetly seeking to channel the whole of any prospective purchase price toward the payment for the common shares of AIC alone, and to the deliberate exclusion of the preferred shares.

[Plaintiffs argued that Brockmann sought to capture the whole of any $75 million offer for the common stockholders but suggesting book value as a floor on any bid, which would result in common shareholders receiving the entire purchase price to the exclusion of any benefit for the preferred.]

* * *

Plaintiffs say that this was wrong. They argue that even though they were minority preferred shareholders of AIC, they were nonetheless entitled to the protections of the fiduciary duty of fairness imposed upon those who were in a position to guide the fortunes of the corporation. They contend that the recent decision in *Weinberger v. UOP, Inc.*, Del. Supr., 457 A.2d 701 (1984) makes it clear that they were owed a duty of fair dealing by AIC's board in its search for financial assistance for the company through the merger route. They say that our law is well established that where the real and only purpose of a merger is to promote the interests of one class of shareholders to the detriment, or at the expense, of another class of minority shareholders, the duty to deal fairly with all shareholders is violated and the merger transaction itself is rendered improper.

* * *

In response, the defendants take the position that the arguments of the plaintiffs ignore the economic and legal realities of the situation. They point out first that the preference rights applicable to the Series B preferred were negotiated in 1961 as a result of arms-length bargaining surrounding the purchase of the two insurance companies by AIC. They suggest that if the original preferred shareholders failed to negotiate for redemption or other rights in the event of a merger or sale of substantial assets, they had nobody to blame but themselves. Defendants suggest that the Series B shareholders were probably unable to get such rights because they traded them off in order to get what was then a highly favorable 5 1/2% dividend rate, guaranteed indefinitely. But, say the defendants, the fact that what had been a good deal in 1961 had turned sour by 1980— when interest rates were hovering near 20%—did not impose a fiduciary duty on AIC's board to get the Series B preferred shareholders out of that deal, or to negotiate a new deal for them.

In short, defendants argue that the rights of preferred shareholders are contract rights and that as against the rights of the common shareholders they are fixed by the contractual terms agreed upon when the class of preferred stock is created. Since the preferred shareholders had no contractual right to be bought out as part of the acquisition of AIC by Leucadia— either at par value or at any other price—defendants argue that the board of AIC had no fiduciary duty to bargain on their behalf in an effort to obtain a cash-out deal for them also.

* * *

III.

Having considered the foregoing arguments in light of the evidence, I am satisfied that the answer to the plaintiffs' charges of breach of fiduciary duty lies somewhere between the legal positions advocated by the parties, and that it turns on the factual determination of whether or not Leucadia's offer was made in response to a solicitation by Brockmann and the other directors defendants. I find on the evidence that it was not, and accordingly I rule in favor of the defendants on this point.

As framed, the issue appears to be a troublesome one on the surface. However, it can be placed in perspective if certain factors are first weeded out. To begin with, I have no doubt that Brockmann and the AIC board were attempting to invite an offer of $13.50 for the common stock while at the same time they were seeking nothing specific for the preferred shares. One could scarcely reach any other conclusion. I am convinced also that they well suspicioned that if a third party offered anything near that amount for the common stock there would be little, if anything, offered for the preferred. I think that the inference to be drawn from the evidence on this point clearly preponderates in favor of the plaintiffs.

* * *

Given that Brockmann's approach of alluding to the book value of the common shares can, in the context of matters, be reasonably interpreted as a solicitation for an offer for the common shares only without a corresponding offer for the preferred, what the plaintiffs proceed to do in their argument is to then assume that the Leucadia offer was made in response to that solicitation and as a direct result of it. Because only if that were so can the plaintiffs establish that the predicament in which they now find themselves was caused by the conduct of the AIC directors, and only then would we reach the legal question of whether or not it was a breach of the fiduciary duty owed by the directors to the preferred shareholders for them to have engaged in such conduct.

I find that we do not have to reach this legal question because the inference of causal connection which the plaintiffs attempt to draw from the sequence of events as they happened is adequately rebutted by the direct evidence offered by Leucadia. When the trimmings of precedent and fiduciary duty are brushed aside, plaintiffs' argument, reduced to its simplest terms, is (1) that between the HFC proposal in 1978 and the Leucadia merger in 1980 the price per share for the common stock was increased from $12 to $13 per share while the preferred shareholders went from $25 per share to no cash consideration whatever, and (2) that during the interval between the two events Brockmann and the AIC board were soliciting offers at book value, or $13.50, for the common shares while seeking nothing for the preferred. From these two premises plaintiffs proceed to the conclusion that the difference between the HFC and Leucadia proposals was necessarily a direct result of the efforts by the AIC board to increase the cash consideration from the common stock with knowledge that such an increase would be at the expense of the preferred shares.

Having thus bridged the gap to arrive at this factual conclusion, plaintiffs then plug it into the legal principle which holds that it is improper for those in a fiduciary position to utilize the merger process solely to promote the interests of one class of shareholders to the detriment, and at the expense, of the members of a minority class of shareholders. Thus plaintiffs reach their final position that they have been injured momentarily by the failure of the defendant directors to adhere to their fiduciary duty to deal fairly with all shareholders in a merger context.

The weakness in the plaintiffs' argument, as I see it, is making the factual assumption that because Brockmann's solicitation of an offer from Leucadia and the subsequent Leucadia offer crossed each other, the latter must have been a direct result of the former. It is the "but for" assumption. It is an argument that "but for" Brockmann's solicitation of an offer for the common stock alone with nothing sought for the preferred, Leucadia would likely have followed HFC's lead and proposed a buy-out of both classes of stock at a price of something less than $13 per share for the common and at a price either equating or approaching the liquidation value of the preferred. In addition to being speculative, such a proposition does not comport with the evidence.

The evidence indicates that the Leucadia offer was formulated and put forth by two of Leucadia's principle officers and shareholders, Ian M. Chumming and Joseph S. Steinberg. * * *

Overall, Steinberg's testimony indicates that Leucadia had its own economic justification for not cashing out the preferred shareholders, that Leucadia was advised by its attorneys that it was not legally necessary that the preferred shares be bought out, and that Leucadia reached its decision to offer to purchase the common shares only for its own reasons and not because of anything said by Brockmann or anyone else on behalf of AIC.

Accordingly, I find on the evidence that Leucadia's offer in the form in which it was put forth was not made in direct response to a veiled solicitation by Brockmann. Rather, I find that the Leucadia offer was made by knowledgeable and experienced businessmen who chose to take advantage of an existing situation of which they were well aware for business reasons peculiar to the interests of their company. Thus, I cannot find that the terms of the merger which left the plaintiffs as continuing preferred shareholders of AIC were brought about as a result of any breach of fiduciary duty on the part of the defendant directors of AIC, even assuming without deciding that the conduct of Brockmann and the AIC board in seeking a merger partner in the manner they did would have constituted a breach of fiduciary duty owed to AIC's preferred shareholders.

* * *

For the reasons given, judgment will be entered in favor of the defendants.

QUESTIONS

1. Why would Leucadia not be interested in purchasing the preferred stock at this time?

2. Does the court intimate that the directors owed duties to the preferred to see that it was sold along with the common?

3. If the preferred has no right to be redeemed, should it have a right to be purchased along with the common? Is this a form of interference with prospective advantage?

4. If you represent the AIC board when it is considering a sale of the company, and you have advised it that the holders of the Series B Preferred have no right to redemption, what would you advise the board about its duties to the Series B Preferred?

5. If no bid has yet been received, could the board seek a buyer solely for the common?

6. If the board has already received a bid for both preferred and common, does that place a limit on what it can ask for with respect to the common thereafter?

7. If the board has not received any offers but judges that the entire company is worth $75 million, must it seek to include the preferred in any sale? Must it seek $25 for a stock trading at $9? If it obtains such an offer, would the common stockholders have a claim against the board for not seeking more for the common?

NOTE

Preferred stock is everywhere seen as the oddest of hybrids, between debt and common stock. Despite that, the rights of preferred shareholders are generally seen as contractual, rather than deriving from fiduciary duties.* The standard recital of the courts is that "it is well established that the rights of preferred stockholders are contract rights."** Noting that preferred contract rights are protected in a limited way by the implied covenant of good faith and fair dealing, Vice Chancellor Jacobs stated that "[t]o allow a fiduciary claim to coexist in parallel with an implied contractual claim, would undermine the primacy of contract law over fiduciary law in matters involving the essentially contractual rights and obligations of preferred shareholders."*** The flintiness of the law in this area was famously demonstrated in *Havender v. Federal United Corp.*, where the Delaware Supreme Court permitted the destruction of accrued arrearages on preferred stock, because the statute permitting exchanges of securities in mergers antedated the issuance of the preferred and was thus part of the shareholders' contract.**** Notwithstanding these rules, exceptions have been carved that cast doubt on the basic nature of the relationship of preferred stock to the corporation, its managers, and common shareholders. In *Baron v. Allied Artists Pictures Corp.* the court held that the board had

---

* Victor Brudney, Contract and Fiduciary Duty in Corporate Law, 38 B. C. L. Rev. 595, 649–51 (1997) (noting the exceptions to the doctrine).

** Baron v. Allied Artists Pictures Corporation, 337 A.2d 653, 657 (Del. Ch. 1975).

*** Gale v. Bershad, 23 Del. J. Corp. L. 1294, 1306 (Del. Ch. 1998).

**** 11 A.2d 331, 342–43 (Del. 1940).

"a fiduciary duty to see that the preferred dividends [which were in arrears] are brought up to date as soon as possible in keeping with prudent business management."* The greatest confusion arises, predictably, in connection with acquisition and sale transactions. The blurring of the lines between contract and fiduciary duties is quite ancient here. In 1928 preferred shareholders complained that a merger agreement did not provide them with a fair amount of the purchase price, pleading that it was "grossly unfair and fraudulent with respect to the preferred stockholders...."** The court saw its duty to determine whether the terms of the merger were "so grossly unfair and inequitable to the preferred stockholders ... as to be a fraud upon them and entitle them to equitable relief."*** While the opinion did not invoke fiduciary duties, they were invoked by Chancellor Allen in 1986, when he explained that while stated preferences were strictly governed by contract, but "where however the right asserted is not to a preference as against the common stock but rather a right shared equally with the common, the existence of such right and the scope of the correlative duty may be measured by equitable as well as legal standards," and that a claim to a fair allocation of merger proceeds "fairly implicate fiduciary duties and ought not be evaluated wholly from the point of view of the contractual terms of the preferred stock designations."**** Imposing a duty of "fair sharing" on directors is such an open standard that room for litigation should always exist. At about the same time, the court addressed the complaint of preferred shareholders left behind in their corporation when the common stock was acquired. In the face of defendants' claim that preferred stockholders were limited to their contract rights and preferred stockholders' claims of a breach of fiduciary duties owed them, Chancellor Brown, in Solomonic fashion, ruled that "the answer ... lies somewhere between the positions advocated by the parties...."***** The court then engaged in a fact-intensive analysis of whether the terms of the acquisition were initiated by the buyer or the seller. The resulting body of law is something less than clear, and invited further litigation.

Winston v. Mandor, 710 A.2d 835 (Del. Ch. 1997), involved a series of transactions in which a controlling common shareholder caused the corporation to purchase troubled real estate investments owned by the shareholder at an allegedly sweetheart price. This was followed by a transfer of the corporation's original properties to a newly created subsidiary and a spin-off of the shares of the subsidiary as a dividend to the common stockholders, leaving the convertible preferred stockholders with claims against a very different and allegedly inferior pool of assets. The preferred

---

* 337 A.2d 653, 660 (Del. Ch. 1975). One can question whether this duty runs to the preferred shareholders, or to the common, who had lost board control when dividends fell in default.

** MacFarlane v. North American Cement Corp., 157 A. 396, 397 (Del. Ch. 1928).

*** Id. at 399.

**** Jedwab v. MGM Grand Hotels, Inc., 509 A.2d 584, 594 (Del. Ch. 1986).

***** Mary G. Dalton v. American Investment Co., 490 A.2d 574, 582 (Del. Ch. 1985).

shareholders had no voting rights on the transactions, and thus the court held they had no claim that a shareholder vote was required for the spin-off, as a sale of substantially all assets under Del. GCL § 271. As for claims of breach of the board's fiduciary duty to the preferred stockholders, the court stated "... the corporation's duties and obligations to preferred stockholders include fiduciary responsibilities where their acts extend beyond the bounds of the contractual relationship contemplated by the certificate [of incorporation]. When, however, the corporate actions complained of are expressly contemplated by a certificate, the duties and obligations of the corporation and its preferred stockholders are governed exclusively by their contract. And so it is here." The court noted that the sale of substantially all assets and a dividend to common shareholders were covered by conversion and price adjustment provisions of the certificate of incorporation.

PPI Enterprises (U.S.) Inc. v. Del Monte Foods Company, 2000 WL 1425093 (S.D.N.Y. 2000) involved a financially troubled preferred shareholder, PPI, which was attempting to sell its preferred stock to satisfy its liability under a lease that it had broken. It was a party to a shareholders' agreement with Del Monte that required Del Monte's consent to a transfer, which was not forthcoming. Del Monte did agree, however, to provide financial information to PPI and its creditor. PPI then filed for protection under Chapter 11 of the bankruptcy laws, and Del Monte offered PPI $1 million for its shares. The complaint alleged that in response to questions Del Monte replied that it was not contemplating any sale of the company, and that Del Monte asserted the stock was worthless. At a later stage, PPI's creditor entered the bidding for the Del Monte preferred, and before the auction was over, Del Monte had bid $10.15 million, although it was ultimately outbid by the creditor. Within three months Del Monte was sold for a price well above the values it had provided PPI, and PPI's buyer sold the stock for $33 million. PPI's complaint alleged breach of the shareholders' agreement, negligent misrepresentation, fraud, and breach of a fiduciary duty owed by Del Monte to its preferred shareholder. In dismissing the fiduciary duty claim, the court stated:

> PPIE claims that Del Monte owed it the "highest obligations and fiduciary duties" because PPIE was a shareholder in Del Monte. Despite the diligent efforts of counsel, the parties have not uncovered a single Maryland case which has held that a corporation owes a fiduciary duty to its shareholders. Courts in other jurisdictions that have considered the proposition have concluded that no such fiduciary duty exists. See, e.g., State Teachers Retirement Bd. v. Fluor Corp., 566 F.Supp. 939, 944 (S.D.N.Y. 1982). The task of creating a new cause of action under the corporation law of Maryland is something for the Maryland courts or legislature to do rather than a federal court sitting in New York in diversity jurisdiction. See id. Absent a showing by PPIE that an action exists in Maryland against the corporation for the misconduct alleged in the second claim of this complaint, this court will not imply such a cause of action.

Id. at *29–*30.

B.   DUTIES OF A PREFERRED-CONTROLLED BOARD

It has long been the convention, although not required by corporation laws, for preferred stockholders, who normally have no rights to elect directors, to gain such rights when dividends are passed. This rule finds a modern expression in rules of the New York Stock Exchange.

New York Stock Exchange Listed Company Manual, § 313.00(C)

(C) Preferred Stock, Minimum Voting Rights Required

Preferred stock, voting as a class, should have the right to elect a minimum of two directors upon default of the equivalent of six quarterly dividends. The right to elect directors should accrue regardless of whether defaulted dividends occurred in consecutive periods.

The right to elect directors should remain in effect until cumulative dividends have been paid in full or until non-cumulative dividends have been paid regularly for at least a year. The preferred stock quorum should be low enough to ensure that the right to elect directors can be exercised as soon as it accrues. In no event should the quorum exceed the percentage required for a quorum of the common stock required for the election of directors. The Exchange prefers that no quorum requirement be fixed in respect to the right of a preferred stock, voting as a class, to elect directors when dividends are in default.

One might ask what purpose is served by requiring that preferred shareholders be allowed to elect a minority of the board of a financially troubled corporation. Obviously these directors cannot control corporate action, even by veto, unless supermajority voting requirements are in effect for the board, which would be a rarity in a public corporation. But they can serve as gadflies, raising questions about corporate policies and the use of free cash flow. It may even be possible for them to search independently for prospective buyers for the corporation, which would be likely to put pressure on management to restore dividend payments and clear up arrearages as quickly as possible. In some cases where troubled corporations seek new financing through a preferred stock investment, it may be the case that investors will insist on board control in the event that preferred stock dividends are passed.

Read Del. G.C.L. § 170.

Baron v. Allied Artists Pictures Corporation

337 A.2d 653 (Del. Ch. 1975).

■ BROWN, VICE CHANCELLOR.

Plaintiff originally brought suit as a stockholder of the defendant Allied Artists Pictures Corporation, a Delaware corporation, (hereafter "Allied") to have the 1973 election of directors declared illegal and invalid and to have a master appointed to conduct a new election pursuant to 8

Del.C. §§ 225 and 227. He has since filed a second action seeking the same relief as to the 1974 election of directors, and the two causes have been consolidated for decision based upon the cross-motions of the parties for summary judgment. Both sides to the controversy agree that there is no material dispute of fact and that the matter is a proper one for determination by summary judgment.

Plaintiff charges that the present board of directors of Allied has fraudulently perpetuated itself in office by refusing to pay the accumulated dividend arrearages on preferred stock issued by the corporation which, in turn, permits the preferred stockholders to elect a majority of the board of directors at each annual election so long as the dividend arrearage specified by Allied's certificate of incorporation exists. Defendants contend that the recent financial history and condition of the corporation has justified the nonpayment of the preferred dividend arrearages, at least to the present, and they further ask that the plaintiff's claims be dismissed because they constitute a purchased grievance.

By way of background, Allied was originally started in the mid–1930's as Sterling Pictures Corporation and later changed its name to Monogram Films under which it gained recognition for many B-pictures and western films. In the early 1950's it changed its name to the present one. Around 1953, with the advent of television, it fell upon hard times. Being in need of capital, Allied's certificate of incorporation was amended in 1954 to permit the issuance of 150,000 shares of preferred stock at a par value of $10.00, with the dividends payable quarterly on a cumulative basis. The amended language of the certificate provides that the preferred shareholders are entitled to receive cash dividends "as and when declared by the Board of Directors, out of funds legally available for the purpose. . . ." The amended certificate further provides that

> ". . . in case at any time six or more quarterly dividends (whether or not consecutive) on the Preferred Stock shall be in default, in whole or in part, then until all dividends in default on the Preferred Stock shall have been paid or deposited in trust, and the dividend thereon for the current quarterly period shall have been declared and funds for the payment thereof set aside, the holders of the Preferred Stock, voting as a class, shall have the right, at any annual or other meeting for the election of directors, by plurality vote to elect a majority of the Directors of the Corporation."

In addition, the amended certificate requires that a sinking fund be created as to the preferred stock into which an amount equal to ten per cent of the excess of consolidated net earnings over the preferred stock dividend requirements for each fiscal year shall be set aside. From this sinking fund the preferred stock is to be redeemed, by lot, at the rate of $10.50 per share.

Thereafter, as to the preferred stock issued under the 1954 offering, regular quarterly dividends were paid through March 30, 1963. Subsequently, Allied suffered losses which ultimately impaired the capital represented by the preferred stock as a consequence of which the payment of dividends became prohibited by 8 Del.C. § 170. Allied has paid no dividends as to the preferred shares since 1963. By September 1964 the corporation was in default on six quarterly dividends and thus the holders of the preferred stock became entitled to elect a majority of the board of directors. They have done so ever since.

As of December 11, 1973 election of directors, Kalvex, Inc. owned 52 per cent of the outstanding preferred stock while owning only 625 shares of Allied's 1,500,000 shares of common stock. Since the filing of the first action herein Kalvex has taken steps to acquire a substantial number of common shares or securities convertible into the same. Thus unquestionably Kalvex, through its control of the preferred shares, is in control of Allied, although its holdings are said to represent only 7 ½ per cent of the corporation's equity.

Plaintiff points out that the defendant Emanual Wolf, as director, president and chief executive officer of Allied at an annual salary of $100,000, is also president and chief executive officer of Kalvex. Defendant Robert L. Ingis, a director, vice-president and chief financial officer of Allied, is the executive vice-president of Kalvex. Defendants Strauss and Prager, elected as directors by the preferred shareholders, are also vice-presidents of Allied. Of the four directors nominated by management to represent the common stockholders, and duly elected, two serve Allied at salaried positions and two serve as counsel for Allied receiving either directly or through their firms substantial remuneration for their efforts. Plaintiff asserts that for fiscal 1973, the officers and directors of Allied, as a group, received $402,088 in compensation.

Returning briefly to the fortunes of the corporation, in 1964 Allied was assessed a tax deficiency of some $1,400,000 by the Internal Revenue Service. At the end of fiscal 1963, it had a cumulative deficit of over $5,000,000, a negative net worth of over $1,800,000 and in that year had lost more than $2,700,000. As a consequence Allied entered into an agreement with the Internal Revenue Service to pay off the tax deficiency over a period of years subject to the condition that until the deficiency was satisfied Allied would pay no dividends without the consent of Internal Revenue.

Thereafter Allied's fortunes vacillated with varying degrees of success and failure which, defendants say, is both a hazard and a way of life in the motion picture and theatrical industry. Prior to fiscal 1973 there were only two years, 1969 and 1970, when its preferred capital was not impaired. But plaintiff points out that in 1970 the preferred capital surplus was $1,300,000 at a time when the preferred dividend arrearages were only $146,500. And, while recognizing that Allied suffered net income loss of over $3,000,000 in the following year, 1971, plaintiff further points out that during several years between 1964 and 1973 the corporation had, on occasion, sufficient net income to contribute to the sinking fund or to pay the dividend arrearages. Defendants argue that when viewed overall it was not until the end of the fiscal year terminating June 30, 1973 that Allied had, for the first time, a capital surplus available for preferred dividends, and that this surplus was only $118,000, or less than half of the amount necessary to liquidate the preferred dividend arrearage. (If this constitutes a dispute of fact, I do not consider it to be material for the purpose of this decision.)

Starting with 1972, Allied's financial condition began to improve substantially. It acquired the rights to, produced and distributed the film "Cabaret," which won eight Academy Awards and became the largest grossing film in Allied's history up to that time. It thereafter took a large gamble and committed itself for $7,000,000 for the production and distribution of the film "Papillon." In his initial litigation plaintiff complained vigorously of this, but he has since abandoned his objection since "Papillon" proved to be even a greater financial success than "Cabaret." For fiscal 1973 Allied had net income in excess of $1,400,000 plus a $2,000,000 tax carry-over remaining from its 1971 losses. Presumably its financial situation did not worsen prior to the December 11, 1974 election of directors although unquestionably it has gone forward with financial commitments as to forthcoming film releases.

Throughout all of the foregoing, however, the Internal Revenue agreement, with its dividend restriction, persisted. Prior to the 1973 election the balance owed was some $249,000 and as of the 1974 election, one final payment was due, which presumably has now been made. Prior to the 1973 election, Allied was in default on forty-three quarterly preferred dividends totaling more than $270,000. By the time of the 1974 election, the arrearages exceeded $280,000.

Without attempting to set forth all of the yearly financial data relied upon by the plaintiff, his position is, quite simply, that for one or more years since the preferred shareholders have been in control of Allied the corporate financial statements show that there was either a net income for the preceding fiscal year or a capital surplus at the end of the preceding fiscal year in an amount larger than the accumulated preferred dividend arrearages, and that consequently the board of directors elected by the preferred shareholders, being only a caretaker board, had a duty to use such funds to pay the dividend arrearage, and also the balance due on the Internal Revenue agreement, if necessary, and to thereupon return control of the corporation to the common stockholders at the next annual election. Specifically, plaintiff charges that the corporation had both the legal and financial capability to pay off the Internal Revenue obligation and the dividend arrearage prior to both the 1973 and 1974 annual election of directors which, had it been done, would have prevented the preferred shareholders, as controlled by Kalvex, from reelecting a majority of the board. Thus, plaintiff seeks the Court to order a new election at which Allied's board of directors will be elected by the common stockholders.

Plaintiff stresses that he is not asking the Court to compel the payment of the dividend arrearages, but only that a new election be held because of the preferred board's allegedly wrongful refusal to do so. Since the certificate of incorporation gives preferred shareholders the contractual right to elect a majority of the directors as long as dividends are six quarters in arrears, plaintiff, in effect, is asking that this contractual right be voided because of the deliberate refusal of the preferred shareholders to see themselves paid as soon as funds became legally available for that purpose.

Plaintiff has cited a wealth of authorities standing for various accepted propositions of corporate law, the most prominent of which hold that incumbent directors cannot issue stock without consideration or otherwise manipulate corporate machinery so as to maintain or perpetuate control in a particular group of stockholders. Although plaintiff contends that in principle this is what the defendants are doing here, he offers no authorities which apply this prohibition to a factual situation such as the present one.

Despite the approach that plaintiff attempts to take, I fail to see how his relief can be granted without reaching the question of whether the dividend arrearages should have been paid. While preferences attaching to stock are the exception and are to be strictly construed, it is well established that the rights of preferred stockholders are contract rights. In Petroleum Rights Corporation v. Midland Royalty Corp., 19 Del. Ch. 334, 167 A. 835 (1933) a somewhat similar provision of the corporate charter extended to preferred shareholders the right to elect a majority of the board when six quarterly dividends became in arrears, which right continued *"so long as the surplus ... applicable to the payment of dividends shall be insufficient to pay all accrued dividends."* The Chancellor there held that as long as there was the prescribed default in dividends and the surplus remained insufficient, the preferred stockholders were entitled to elect a majority of the board. It was argued to him that this right of election and control was limited by the language "so long as the surplus ... shall be insufficient" and that the accumulation of a surplus sufficient to pay all accrued dividends constituted a condition subsequent, the existence of which would forthwith defeat the right to elect control. This view was rejected, on the theory that if accepted it would mean that the sole purpose of such a scheme would be to put the preferred in control to force a payment of passed dividends once a dividend fund became available. The Chancellor concluded that a shift of control should not be made to turn on the personal interests of the preferred shareholders in dividends alone but, in addition, on the consideration that if surplus fell below unpaid dividends the time had arrived to try a new management. 167 A. 837. He also stated as follows at 167 A. 836:

> "... if the surplus does in fact exceed the six quarterly dividends in arrear and the preference stock should elect a majority of the board and the board should resolve not to pay the dividends, the right of the preference stock to continue to elect a majority of the board would undoubtedly terminate."

I interpret this to mean that the contractual right to elect a majority of the board continues until the dividends can be made current in keeping with proper corporate management, but that it must terminate once a fund becomes clearly available to satisfy the arrearages and the preference board refuses to do so. Plaintiff seeks to limit this requirement to a mere mathematical availability of funds, and indeed the charter language in *Petroleum Rights* may have intended such a result. Here, however, Allied's charter, and thus its contract with its preferred shareholders, does not limit the right merely until such time as a sufficient surplus exists, as it did in *Petroleum Rights*, but rather it entitles the preferred shareholders to their dividends only "as and when declared by the Board of Directors, out of funds legally available for the purpose." This obviously reposes a discretion in Allied's board to declare preferred dividends, whether it be a board elected by the common or by the preferred shareholders.

The general rule applicable to the right to receive corporate dividends was succinctly stated by Justice Holmes in Wabash Ry. Co. v. Barclay, 280 U.S. 197, 203, 50 S. Ct. 106, 107, 74 L. Ed. 368 (1930):

> "When a man buys stock instead of bonds he takes a greater risk in the business. No one suggests that he has a right to dividends if there are no net earnings. But the investment presupposes that the business is to go on, and therefore even if there are net earnings, the holder of stock, preferred as well as common, is entitled to have a dividend declared only out of such part of them as can be applied to dividends *consistently with a wise administration of a going concern*."

Although one purpose of allowing the preferred to elect a majority of the board may be to bring about a payment of the dividend delinquencies as soon as possible, that should not be the sole justification for the existence of a board of directors so elected. During the time that such a preference board is in control of the policies and business decisions of the corporation, it serves the corporation itself and the common shareholders as well as those by whom it was put in office. Corporate directors stand in a fiduciary relationship to their corporation and its shareholders and their primary duty is to deal fairly and justly with both.

The determination as to when and in what amounts a corporation may prudently distribute its assets by way of dividends rests in the honest discretion of the directors in the performance of this fiduciary duty. Before a court will interfere with the judgment of a board of directors in refusing to declare dividends, fraud or gross abuse of discretion must be shown. And this is true even if a fund does exist from which dividends could legally be paid. As stated by the Chancellor in Eshleman v. Keenan, *supra*, at 194 A. 43:

> "That courts have the power in proper cases to compel the directors to declare a dividend, is sustained by respectable authorities. But that they should do so on a mere showing that an asset exists from which a dividend may be declared, has never, I dare say, been asserted anywhere. In such a case a court acts only after a demonstration that the corporation's affairs are in a condition justifying the declaration of the dividend as a matter of prudent business management and that the withholding of it is explicable only on the theory of an oppressive or fraudulent abuse of discretion."

Plaintiff here appears to be asking that an exception be carved from these well established principles where the nonpayment of dividends and arrearages results in continued control by the very board which determines not to pay them. As I understand his argument, he asks for a ruling that a board of directors elected by preferred shareholders whose dividends are in arrears has an absolute duty to pay off all preferred dividends due and to return control to the common shareholders as soon as funds become legally available for that purpose, regardless of anything else. Thus, in effect, he would have the court limit the discretion given the board by the certificate of incorporation, and make the decision to pay arrearages mandatory upon the emergence of a lawful financial source even though the corporate charter does not require it (as perhaps it did in *Petroleum Rights*). He has offered no precedent for such a proposition, and I decline to create one.

Plaintiff's attempt to distinguish his action by asserting that he does not seek to compel the payment of the dividend arrearages, but only to return control to the common stockholders, has a hollow ring. In either case the basic question is whether or not the board has wrongfully refused to pay dividends even if funds did exist which could have been used for such purpose. The established test for this is whether the board engaged in fraud or grossly abused its discretion. The mere existence of a legal source from which payment could be made, standing alone, does not prove either.

When the yearly hit-and-miss financial history of Allied from 1964 through 1974 is considered along with the Internal Revenue obligation during the same time span, I cannot conclude, as a matter of law, that Allied's board has been guilty of perpetuating itself in office by wrongfully refusing to apply corporate funds to the liquidation of the preferred dividend arrearages and the accelerated payment of the Internal Revenue debt. Thus I find no basis on the record before me to set aside the 1974 annual election and to order a new one through a master appointed by the court.

* * *

It is clear, however, that Allied's present board does have a fiduciary duty to see that the preferred dividends are brought up to date as soon as possible in keeping with prudent business management. This is particularly true now that the Internal Revenue debt has been satisfied in full and business is prospering. It cannot be permitted indefinitely to plough back all profits in future commitments so as to avoid full satisfaction of the rights of the preferred to their dividends and the otherwise normal right of the common stockholders to elect corporate management. While previous limitations on net income and capital surplus may offer a justification for the past, continued limitations in a time of greatly increased cash flow could well create new issues in the area of business discretion for the future.

* * *

Plaintiff's motion for summary judgment is denied. Defendants' motion for summary judgment is granted. Order on notice.

QUESTIONS

1. Why does the plaintiff point to the salaries the Kalvex personnel receive from Allied as part of his case? Is it plausible that Kalvex is passing on dividends just so its own officers can enjoy salaries from Allied?

2. Baron argues that during several years Allied had net income from which it could have paid dividends. Ignoring limits imposed by the agreement with the Internal Revenue Service, how could it have lawfully paid dividends under Del. G.C.L. § 170?

3. If the Board owed duties to the Common as well as the preferred, how does it satisfy those duties when considering preferred dividends? Suppose the board approves a risky project with huge potential payoffs for the common stockholders, but with a limited (or no) upside for the preferred?

4. What must a plaintiff show in order to challenge a board's failure to pay preferred dividends?

5. How does this standard compare with the business judgment rule standard for ordinary dividends on the common?

6. If the preferred directors were doing so well, why would Baron, a common stockholder, want to remove them? Remember, Allied has just had two big hit movies? Would it matter that Baron has only recently purchased his common stock? See *Baron v. Allied Artists Pictures Corp.*, 395 A.2d 375, 378 (Del. Ch. 1978):

> "Allied also points to the fact that Baron did not purchase his 10 shares of stock until the fall of 1973, and thus after he was aware of the pertinent matters relating to the preferred shareholders' control of Allied. This was also after two similar actions had been brought by one Bruce D. Stuart one of Baron's lawyers who Baron later admitted was acting on his behalf in so doing. Stuart purchased his shares the day before he verified his complaint in the first action brought by him. At the time Baron was employed as the manager of a Los Angeles movie theatre at a salary of $180 per week. His other means were not substantial. Thus, in addition to contending that Baron's claims fall into the category of a purchased grievance (an argument made by Allied but not decided in these actions in view of the decision made on the merits), Allied doubts that it could have been Baron himself who was financing the 'cross-country multicourt litigation' against it."

Burton v. Exxon Corporation

583 F. Supp. 405 (S.D.N.Y. 1984).

■ GOETTEL, D.J.:

This is a class action brought by plaintiff John R. Burton on behalf of himself and all other similarly situated holders of $7 Cumulative Second

Preferred Stock of the European Gas & Electric Company ("Eurogasco") against Eurogasco, the Exxon Corporation ("Exxon"), R. F. Dilworth, D. G. Gill, and W. W. Stewart. The plaintiff alleges that the defendants breached their fiduciary duties to the Second Preferred stockholders, and seeks various forms of equitable relief. Briefly stated, the plaintiff argues that the defendants engaged in a course of conduct which depleted the assets of Eurogasco to the detriment of the plaintiff class. From 1977 through 1980, Eurogasco received over $9 million in compensation for the nationalization of its properties in Hungary. Eurogasco's Board of Directors used this money to pay dividend arrearages on the First Preferred Stock owned by Exxon and the excess money was deposited with Exxon. The plaintiff argues that instead of engaging in self-dealing the defendants could have invested the entire fund so as to enable Eurogasco to make payments to the plaintiff class. The plaintiff seeks an order requiring Exxon to return to Eurogasco the sum of $8,641,147, which represents the dividends paid to Exxon plus the profit Exxon has made on the dividends. In addition, the plaintiff seeks an order enjoining the defendants from dissolving Eurogasco without complying with Eurogasco's Certificate of Incorporation and Delaware law. This matter having come on for trial, this opinion will constitute the Court's findings of facts and conclusions of law under Fed. R. Civ. P. 52(a).

FACTS

I. The Parties

Eurogasco is a corporation duly organized and existing under the laws of the State of Delaware, with its principal place of business at 1251 Avenue of the Americas, New York, New York. Eurogasco has issued an outstanding 22,100 shares of $7 Cumulative First Preferred Stock, Series A (the "First Preferred"), 7,336 shares of $7 Cumulative Second Preferred Stock, Series A (the "Second Preferred") and 2,098,600 shares of common stock (the "Common Stock"). The founders of Eurogasco took Second Preferred stock, and sought a larger investor, ultimately Exxon, to fund operations by purchasing the First Preferred.

The majority stockholder in Eurogasco is Exxon. * * * It owns 22,100 shares (100%) of the First Preferred, 1,945 shares (26.5%) of the Second Preferred, and 1,908,190 shares (90.9%) of the Common Stock of Eurogasco.

In addition to Exxon, Eurogasco has approximately 150 public stockholders. Of those public stockholders, approximately 120 are holders of the Second Preferred. John R. Burton ("Burton") owns and, at all times pertinent to this action, has owned 10 shares of the Second Preferred. Burton is a citizen of the State of Ohio.

At all times pertinent to this action, R. F. Dilworth ("Dilworth"), D. G. Gill ("Gill"), and W. W. Stewart ("Stewart") constituted the entire Board of Directors of Eurogasco. Dilworth and Gill were directors of Eurogasco during the period 1977–1981. Stewart served as a director from December 29, 1977, when he replaced P. W. Moyer as director, through 1981.

II. Background of Eurogasco

[Eurogasco was organized under Delaware law in 1931 for the production and sale of oil and natural gas in Hungary, Austria and Czechoslovakia. The timing was not propitious: its business activities were interrupted in the late 1930s by Nazi occupation and World War II. During the war Eurogasco lost all of its Austrian properties. The end of the war was followed by the partitioning of Europe, that resulted in the nationalization of Eurogasco's Hungarian and Czech properties. This was the end of Eurogasco's active conduct of its business, and the start of its efforts to be compensated for its taken properties. In the 1950s it negotiated a recovery from the Austrian government for its seized properties, and realized $979,702 from the Austrian government in 1961–64.

Recovery with respect to nationalized properties in Hungary and Czechoslovakia was more difficult. In the period 1959–67 it received $987,201 from Hungarian assets in the United States. In 1973, after an agreement between Hungary and the United States, Hungary made a series of payments to the U.S. Treasury. From these sums Eurogasco was paid $9,060,128 during 1977–1980. This was the end of the payments.]

* * *

Eurogasco used the payments referred to above to repay its indebtedness to Exxon, and to pay dividends.

III. Exxon's Interest in Eurogasco

Exxon had no role in Eurogasco's formation. When Eurogasco was formed, its promoters took Second Preferred stock. The First Preferred stock was reserved for later issuance and was designed to serve as an inducement to an outside investor who could supply the capital needed to fund Eurogasco's operations. Exxon was approached to fulfill this role. Commencing in 1933, Exxon made a series of loans and capital contributions to Eurogasco.

* * *

The Fourth Article of Eurogasco's Certificate of Incorporation provides that when accrued dividend arrearages on the First Preferred and the Second Preferred remain unpaid, the exclusive right to vote for Eurogasco's directors (and, except as otherwise provided in the Certificate of Incorporation or applicable statute, on all other corporate questions) is vested in the holders of the First Preferred and the Second Preferred, voting as one class. Thus, for more than forty years, because Eurogasco has consistently failed to pay dividends on its preferred shares and Exxon has owned more than 80% of those shares, Exxon has controlled Eurogasco.

* * * Since 1977, all Eurogasco directors have been employees of Exxon or its affiliates. All of Eurogasco's current officers and directors are employees of Exxon.

* * *

IV.   Actions by the Board of Directors

During the period 1977–1980, the Board of Directors took several actions that, the plaintiff claims, constituted a breach of the defendants' fiduciary duties.

A.   The Dividend Payments

Eurogasco's stockholders have the following rights to dividend payments pursuant to the Certificate of Incorporation and the Certificate of Designation.

[The First Preferred had a preference for its cumulative dividends over all other classes of stock, while the Second Preferred was entitled to cumulative dividends of $7 per share, subordinated to the rights of the First Preferred. No dividends could be paid on the common stock until all preferred dividends, including those for the current period, were paid to the First and Second Preferred holders.

Eurogasco paid no dividends from its creation in 1931 through 1976, leaving it with arrearages of $6,498,975 on the First Preferred and $2,332,771 on the Second Preferred. Eurogasco received $9,060,128 under the Claims Agreement from 1997–1980, and had interest income of $823,297, for a total income of $9,883,425. During this period Eurogasco paid dividends of $4,139,800 on the First Preferred to Exxon. In each case this reduced Eurogasco's stockholders' equity to an amount no greater than $85,000 above the minimum required by its charter.]

Eurogasco's payments of accrued dividends to Exxon were in full compliance with the preference provisions set forth in Eurogasco's Certificate of Incorporation and Certificate of Designation.

As of December 31, 1980, the accrued dividend arrearages on the First Preferred amounted to $2,861,950, and the accrued dividend arrearages on the Second Preferred amounted to $2,499,665. As of December 31, 1981, the accrued dividend arrearages on the First Preferred amounted to $3,171,305, and the accrued dividend arrearages on the Second Preferred amounted to $2,602,369.

The plaintiff claims that the payments of dividends to Exxon, the First Preferred stockholder, were self-dealing and constituted a breach of the defendants' fiduciary duty. As discussed below, the Court concludes that the payments were not in violation of the defendants' fiduciary duty.

* * *

C.   Decision to Seek Dissolution

In or around March 1981, Eurogasco's Board of Directors determined that Eurogasco's continuation served no useful purpose, and therefore deemed it advisable that Eurogasco should be dissolved. Pursuant to Article Fourth of the Certificate of Incorporation, however, Eurogasco cannot voluntarily dissolve, liquidate or wind up its affairs without the consent of at least two-thirds of both the First Preferred and Second Preferred, each voting as a separate class, either in writing or at a special meeting called for that purpose. The directors decided, therefore, to obtain a stockholder vote on whether Eurogasco should be dissolved. [The proxy statement disclosed that available funds were insufficient to satisfy the claims of the First Preferred, which meant nothing would be left for the Second Preferred. While all of the First Preferred, voted in favor of dissolution, few shares of the Second Preferred voted for it, with most shareholders abstaining, which counted as "no" votes. Of the 7,336 shares of Second Preferred, only 2,808 voted in favor, and 244 shares voted "no," while approval of the holders of two-thirds of the class was needed. Burton then filed suit to enjoin dissolution, while Exxon filed a petition to dissolve in the Delaware Chancery Court.]

* * *

As discussed below, the Court concludes that it will not grant an injunction.

EVALUATION OF THE BOARD OF DIRECTORS' ACTIONS

* * *

II. The Legal Standard By Which to Test the Transactions

Exxon is the majority stockholder of Eurogasco. It nominates all the members of Eurogasco's Board of Directors whose membership during the period of the challenged transactions consisted entirely of officers, directors, or employees of Exxon or affiliates of Exxon. The status of a majority stockholder or parent corporation carries with it a fiduciary duty with respect to the minority stockholders of the subsidiary. Thus, by reason of Exxon's status and domination, it is clear that Exxon owed Eurogasco a fiduciary duty. As part of this fiduciary duty, Exxon and Eurogasco's Board of Directors were required to be fair in their dealings insofar as those dealings affected the interests of the minority stockholders.

In the absence of divided interests, the judgment of the majority stockholders and/or the board of directors "is presumed made in good faith and inspired by a bona fides of purpose". But when the stockholders or directors, who control the making of a transaction and its terms, are on both sides, then the presumption and deference to sound business judgment are no longer present. Intrinsic fairness is then the criterion. Thus, there are two tests which have been applied by the Delaware courts to determine the limits of fairness in parent-subsidiary's or majority stockholder-subsidiary's business dealings.

* * *

If there is no proof of self-dealing, the business judgment standard is the proper standard by which to evaluate the transactions. Under the business judgment rule a court will not interfere with the judgment of a board of directors unless there is a showing of fraud or gross abuse of discretion.

III. Application of the Appropriate Legal Standard to the Contested Transactions

A.   The Dividend Payments

During the period of 1977–1980, Eurogasco's Board of Directors declared and paid dividends totaling $4,139,800 to Exxon, the First Preferred stockholder. The plaintiff argues that this decision must be evaluated by the intrinsic fairness test. The defendants argue that the business judgment rule should be applied, but as a back-up argument urge that the decision passes muster under either test.

A decision to declare a dividend is a matter ordinarily addressed to the discretion of the board of directors. The Delaware courts have permitted directors wide latitude in making this decision, which is considered a routine matter. The decision, thus, enjoys a presumption of sound business judgment which will not be disturbed by a court in the absence of a disabling factor, *i.e.*, fraud or gross abuse of discretion.

The intrinsic fairness test, however, can be applied to a dividend declaration made by a dominated board. If the dividend is in essence self-dealing, then the intrinsic fairness test is the proper standard by which to evaluate the dividend payments.

It must be determined whether the dividend payments by Eurogasco were, in essence, self-dealing by Exxon. There appears to be no Delaware case directly on point. However, the court in *Sinclair Oil, supra,* 280 A.2d [717] at 721, put forth a hypothetical case dealing with a dividend declaration by a dominated board:

> Suppose a parent dominates a subsidiary and its board of directors. The subsidiary has outstanding two classes of stock, X and Y. Class X is owned by the parent and Class Y is owned by minority stockholders of the subsidiary. If the subsidiary, at the direction of the parent, declares a dividend on its Class X stock only, this might well be self-dealing by the parent. It would be receiving something from the subsidiary to the exclusion of and detrimental to its minority stockholders. This self-dealing, coupled with the parent's fiduciary duty, would make intrinsic fairness the proper standard by which to evaluate the dividend payments.

Id. at 721. Comparing this hypothetical with the case at bar, it would seem that the Delaware courts would apply the intrinsic fairness test to evaluate the dividend payments by Eurogasco to Exxon.

At the direction of Exxon, Eurogasco declared a dividend on its First Preferred stock only. The dividends resulted in great sums of money being transferred from Eurogasco to Exxon. Not a penny of this sum was received by the Second Preferred stockholders of Eurogasco. Exxon received $4,139,800 in dividend payments from Eurogasco to the exclusion of, and detriment to, the minority stockholders. Thus, the intrinsic fairness test should be applied.

The defendants argue, however, that the facts in this case require a different result. They argue that before a plaintiff can invoke the intrinsic fairness test, the parent must usurp for itself a benefit to which the minority stockholders might otherwise have had a right. In the instant case, the defendants point out that the holders of the Second Preferred had no right to recover any dividends between 1977 and 1980 because the dividends on the First Preferred were in arrears. Thus, argue the defendants, the directors did not opt to pay dividends to the exclusion of, or detriment to, the minority stockholders, since one cannot be harmed by the nonreceipt of something to which one is not entitled. The Court disagrees.

In determining whether self-dealing has occurred the test is not whether the minority stockholders were entitled to the item transferred but whether the minority stockholders were excluded from, or damaged by, the transfer from the subsidiary to the parent or majority stockholder. Here, the minority stockholders were excluded from the money consequences of the dividend declaration and this was to their detriment because the declaration depleted much of Eurogasco's cash flow. The fact that the plaintiff class was not entitled to a dividend declaration due to the small amount of available cash in comparison to the huge arrearages on the First Preferred is important only in so far as deciding whether the dividend decision was intrinsically fair. In conclusion, the decision to pay dividends to the First Preferred stockholder, Exxon, must be tested under the intrinsic fairness standard.

The intrinsic fairness test shifts the burden of proof to the defendants to demonstrate the intrinsic fairness of the dividend declaration. The Court concludes that the defendants have met this burden as demonstrated by the following facts.

Eurogasco received its first payment under the Claims Agreement, in the amount of $4,768,901, in September 1978. After receipt of this payment, the directors recognized the need to satisfy the company's income tax liability and to discharge its remaining indebtedness to Exxon. When evaluating the alternative uses for the remaining money, Gill understood and counseled his fellow directors, that they had to "lean over backwards to be fair" to all stockholders in light of the fact that the directors were employees of the First Preferred stockholder.

Gill testified that when the directors voted in December 1977 on how to apply the remainder of the funds available, the following factors were considered:

(1) In Gill's judgment as a specialist in international claims, the amount and timing of additional payments to Eurogasco on its Hungarian claims, beyond those received in August 1977, were subject to substantial uncertainty. * * * By December 1977, Gill and Eurogasco's other directors estimated—fairly accurately as it turned out—that, in addition to the $4.7 million that Eurogasco had then received, Eurogasco would probably receive an additional $3.5 to $4 million from the United States Treasury and that such amount would be paid within the next three years. However, there was no certainty that their funds would be paid so rapidly.

(2) Eurogasco owed its First Preferred stockholder $6.5 million in accrued unpaid dividends. Under Article Fourth of Eurogasco's Certificate of Incorporation, the satisfaction of these dividend arrearages had absolute priority over any payments toward arrearages of the Second Preferred stock or any other payments on the Common Stock.

* * *

(4) Based on the limited funds Eurogasco had received and the then-prevailing interest rate, a decision not pay to dividends until sufficient amounts had accumulated to cover the arrearages on the First Preferred and Second Preferred would have meant that the First Preferred would have been required to wait until the next century to receive any payments on its arrearages.

(5) Unlike the situation with large companies which could spread the risk over a large number of oil and gas ventures, the limited funds in Eurogasco's treasury made it in Gill's view extremely imprudent for Eurogasco to gamble by investing those funds in any such ventures.

Eurogasco's circumstances led to the conclusion that retention of Eurogasco's funds was not a reasonable course to adopt, and that the company should instead begin to pay off the arrearages on the First Preferred in accordance with the provisions of the Certificate of Incorporation. As of December 29, 1977, Eurogasco's sole assets were the funds that it had on deposit with Exxon as a consequence of the September payment from the United States Treasury, and Eurogasco's claim and expectation that it would receive additional payments pursuant to the Hungarian Claims Agreement. On December 29, 1977, Eurogasco's Board declared a dividend in the amount of $3,134,250, all of which was paid to the First Preferred stockholder. This was disclosed to the plaintiff and all other stockholders no later than April 21, 1978, the date of Eurogasco's 1977 Annual Report.

* * *

The plaintiff contends that instead of paying dividends on the First Preferred in 1977–1980, Eurogasco should have retained and invested that money until such time as the amount in the treasury was sufficient to pay the dividend arrearages attributable to both the First Preferred and Second Preferred. It is true that Eurogasco's Certificate of Incorporation does not require the payment of dividends on preferred shares even when arrearages exist and thus the decision to declare dividends is discretionary. However, for two reasons it would have been unwise and unfair of Eurogasco to refuse to pay Exxon, the First Preferred stockholder, its long overdue dividends, in order to create a fund for the eventual compensation of stockholders with inferior rights.[6]

---

6. The Court also notes a third reason why the plaintiff's suggestion is not a viable one. This reason has to do with the other group of excluded stockholders—the holders of the Common Stock. If Eurogasco was required to retain the funds until it could pay money to the

First, there was substantial uncertainty with regards to future payments under the Claims Agreement and to future interest rates. The plaintiff argues that if the Board had invested the money received under the Claims Agreement or placed the money on deposit with Exxon at the interest rates that Eurogasco was then earning on its Exxon account, such funds would have grown to an amount such that Eurogasco's assets at year-end 1984 would have exceeded the total amount of First Preferred dividend arrearages and liquidation preferences.

However, as the defendants point out, using the interest rate prevailing in 1977, it would have taken until the year 2024 for Eurogasco's funds to accumulate to the point where all arrearages of the First and Second Preferred could be paid. Even had Eurogasco's directors in 1977 been able to peer through the uncertainties of the amount and timing of any future claims payments and predict the future precisely, under the then-prevailing interest rate, Eurogasco would not have had enough money to pay off the arrearages on the Second Preferred until the year 2000. Beyond that, if the directors had also been able to foresee that interest rates in 1978–1983 would reach levels double or triple their level in 1977, they would still have found that the payoff date for the Second Preferred arrearages remained 14 years away, in 1991.

Considering the uncertainties in this situation, it would have been unwise to hold the funds with the expectation of paying off the arrearages on the preferred shares. Although the future proved that such a course might have been profitable, hindsight should not be used now to find that the actions taken were unfair.

The second reason for not following the plaintiff's suggestion is that, if Eurogasco's Board of Directors had adopted this course, Exxon would have had strong grounds for challenging the decision.

> Courts have the power in proper cases to compel the directors to declare a dividend.... In such a case a court acts only after a demonstration that the corporation's affairs are in a condition justifying the declaration of the dividend as a matter of prudent business management and that the withholding of it is explicable only on the theory of an oppressive or fraudulent abuse of discretion.

Eshleman v. Keenan, 22 Del. Ch. 82, 194 A. 40, 43 (Del. Ch. 1937), *aff'd,* 23 Del. Ch. 234, 2 A.2d 904 (Del. 1938). Here, Eurogasco has been defunct for thirty years, with no operations or business other than to collect on its claim. It had never paid any dividends and had by 1977 accumulated nearly $6.5 million in dividend arrearages on the First Preferred. In keeping with prudent business management, the board of directors does have a fiduciary duty to see that preferred dividend arrearages

---

holders of the Second Preferred, why should it not also be required to retain the funds until it could pay dividends to the holders of the Common Stock.

The Second Preferred may have preferences over the Common Stock. These preferences, however, do not guarantee the payment of dividends. In this regard, the Second Preferred stockholders are on the same footing with the Common Stock stockholders.

are brought up to date as soon as possible. *Baron, supra,* 337 A.2d at 660. A long drawn out and unjustified freezing of liquid assets by the board of directors would have justified intervention by the court in order to protect the preferred stockholder's equity.

If the positions were reversed, *i.e.,* Exxon owned all the Second Preferred shares and the plaintiff class owned the First Preferred shares, and if Eurogasco followed the suggestion of the plaintiff, the plaintiff would probably be in court today arguing that the defendants breached their fiduciary duty by not declaring a dividend. The declaration of dividends on the First Preferred is not unfair just because the First Preferred stock was owned by Exxon. "Granted, the fact that the parent owes a fiduciary duty to its subsidiary, the duty does not require self-sacrifice from the parent." *Getty Oil, supra,* 267 A.2d at 888.

In conclusion, we are satisfied that, in the present circumstances, Exxon has carried its burden to show the intrinsic fairness of the dividend declarations.

* * *

In conclusion, the defendants did not breach their fiduciary duties and thus, the plaintiff class is not entitled to any recovery.

QUESTIONS

1. Note that of the 7,336 shares of Second Preferred, only 2,808 voted, while two-thirds approval was needed. In seeking shareholder approval of dissolution, why didn't Eurogasco's board make any special effort to persuade the holders of the Second, when it knew it needed a 2/3 vote to approve dissolution?

2. The court stated that where a parent owns all of one class and the minority owns another class, a dividend on the parent's class is self-dealing. Suppose the parent owns all of the common and a class of preferred is publicly held. Does this mean each dividend on the common is self-dealing, subject to challenge by the preferred?

3. Suppose the parent owns all of a class of voting preferred and the public holds common, is every dividend on the preferred subject to challenge as self-dealing?

4. Exxon argued that self-dealing only exists when the parent receives something to which the minority shareholders had a right. Here, Exxon argued that the 1st Preferred had an absolute priority on dividends, to which the 2d Preferred had no right. How did the court respond to this argument?

5. If, in December 1977 the Eurogasco Board believed that it had between $8.2 and $8.7 million available for shareholders, and the arrearages on the 1st Preferred were $6.5 million, why wasn't approximately $2 million left for the arrearages on the 2d Preferred?

6. The plaintiff argued that the board should reinvest the funds received until they were sufficient to pay off the 2d Preferred as well as the 1st Preferred. Why does the court reject this argument?

7. What does the court mean when it says that the test of fairness is not denial of a minority's right, but damages to the minority from an exclusion?

8. Is it fair to characterize a contractually subordinate class of security holders as a minority? Did holders of the Second Preferred voluntarily assume the risk that they might not receive anything on liquidation? Who were these holders?

9. If Eurogasco had delayed paying off the First Preferred dividends until 2024 in order to pay the Second Preferred, what compound rate is the court assuming for interest on its invested funds. At that rate, what is the discounted present value of the arrearages?

---

5. SHARE REDEMPTIONS AND REPURCHASES

The use of any long-term agreement, whether for debt or preferred stock, assigns interest rate risks. If a preferred stock is issued during a period of low interest rates and rates subsequently rise, the corporation has won the bet, and the preferred stock will trade below its original issue price. On the other hand, if preferred stock is issued during a period of high interest rates and correspondingly high dividend rates, the investors have won the bet as dividend rates decline. The preferred stock, just like a bond, will trade above its original issue price. As in the case of corporate debt, issuing corporations may find that a fixed dividend rate set years before has become quite costly as interest and dividend rates decline in the market. Just as in the case of corporate debt, issuing corporations frequently address this issue by providing that the preferred is redeemable by the corporation, or "callable." Typically, as in the case of corporate debt, the redemption price will be set at a price above the liquidation value of the preferred, thus providing a "call premium."

The flip side of the coin is sometimes found in venture capital financing, where the holders of convertible preferred stock are given the right to "put" the stock to the issuing corporation, at a price that is designed to provide the shareholders with a substantial return on their capital. Typically these put rights are triggered by a failure of the corporation to meet certain milestones, primarily engaging in an initial public offering of the common at a minimum valuation that also assures the preferred stockholders of a profit on conversion of their preferred into common stock. While these put rights exist in a number of preferred stock issues, they are rarely exercised, because the issuing corporation will, in all likelihood, lack the funds to repurchase the preferred, especially if it has been unable to engage in an initial public offering.

Gradient OC Master, Ltd. v. NBC Universal, Inc.

930 A.2d 104 (Del. Ch. 2007).

■ PARSONS, VICE CHANCELLOR.

This dispute involves challenges by holders of two classes of senior preferred stock of ION Media Networks, Inc. ("ION" or the "Company") to an exchange offer being made to those stockholders as one of several transactions provided for under a Master Transaction Agreement ("MTA") to restructure the Company's ownership and capital structure. Defendants are ION, its directors, NBC Universal, Inc. ("NBCU") and Citadel Investment Group LLC and an affiliate, CIG Media, LLC, (collectively, "CIG"). ION, NBCU and CIG are parties to the MTA. Plaintiffs assert that the exchange offer violates Delaware's prohibition against coercive or misleading offers to stockholders and also improperly extracts value from minority shareholders for the benefit of a majority or controlling shareholder, namely, NBCU, CIG or both of them. * * *

* * * For the reasons stated below, I conclude that plaintiffs have not shown a reasonable likelihood of success on the merits as to their claims for wrongful coercion based on, among other things, the elevation feature of the exchange offer, under which if less than 90% of the senior preferred shares participate in the exchange, preferred stock of NBCU and CIG junior to plaintiffs' stock will be elevated to subordinated debt with priority over plaintiffs' preferred shares. * * *

I. FACTS AND PROCEDURAL HISTORY

A. Background

* * *

Plaintiffs in C.A. No. 3021 are a group of investors holding $13\frac{1}{8}\%$ Cumulative Junior Exchangeable Preferred Stock, currently accruing dividends at $14\frac{1}{4}\%$ ("$14\frac{1}{4}\%$ Preferred Stock" or "Preferred Stock") of ION. Plaintiffs appear to be six different hedge funds. * * *

ION, a Delaware corporation, is a network television broadcasting company that owns the largest television station group in the United States, operating approximately 60 television stations. The company, renamed in February, 2006 from Paxson Communications, Inc., reaches around 90 million households through reruns of shows such as "Mama's Family" and "The Wonder Years." In 1999, ION and NBCU's predecessor entered into an agreement whereby NBCU invested approximately $415 million in ION in exchange for 41,500 shares of 8% Series B convertible exchangeable preferred stock, warrants to purchase up to a total of over 32 million shares of Class A common stock, and registration rights under the Securities Act.

On or around November 7, 2005, ION and NBCU entered into additional agreements to restructure NBCU's investment in the Company and to settle certain litigation that had arisen between them relating to the NBCU preferred shares. As part of the settlement, NBCU acquired contractual provisions related to its preferred shares that required ION to obtain NBCU's consent before engaging in, among other things, certain financial transactions. NBCU also received an 18–month transferable call option from Lowell Paxson and certain affiliates controlled by him that, if exercised, would trigger a sale of the rest of the Company and give NBCU a controlling block of Class A and B common stock and the right to designate a nominee to purchase those shares. The call option was set to expire on May 6, 2007.

At some point, ION and NBCU determined that certain rules promulgated by the Federal Communications Commission ("FCC") would prohibit NBCU from exercising the call right, leading NBCU to seek a third party to which it could transfer the call right before it expired. In the latter part of 2006, NBCU and Citadel engaged in discussions and negotiations with each other with a view toward proposing a comprehensive recapitalization transaction to ION, including a transfer of NBCU's call option to CIG. From NBCU's perspective, in addition to facilitating a transfer of the option, "a fundamental component of the transaction that ultimately was proposed with Citadel was to reduce the fixed claims or functional leverage on [ION's] balance sheet."

B. ION's Board of Directors Explores Restructuring

ION had a complex capital structure and was considered overly leveraged. As of March 31, 2007, the Company had $1.1 billion in senior secured debt; the 14¼% Preferred Stock, with an aggregate liquidation preference and accumulated dividends of $640 million; a series of 9¾% Series A Convertible Preferred Stock (the "9¾% Preferred Stock") with an aggregate liquidation preference and accumulated dividends of $175 million; and a series of 11% Series B Convertible Exchangeable Preferred Stock (the "Series B Preferred Stock") with an aggregate liquidation preference and accumulated dividends of $706 million.

Under a previous refinancing of senior debt obligations in December, 2005, the Company was permitted to incur up to approximately $650 million of subordinated debt that could be available for use in a future recapitalization. In April, 2006, the Company retained UBS Securities LLC ("UBS") to advise it on financial strategies. In June, 2006, ION's Board created a special committee of independent directors to explore the Company's strategic options (the "Special Committee"). The following month, the Special Committee retained Lazard Freres & Co. LLC ("Lazard") as its financial advisor and Pillsbury Winthrop as its legal advisor. In the fall of 2006, ION's management publicly announced that the Company's highly leveraged position was hampering their ability to progress and the Board needed to modify its capital structure to improve liquidity and reduce obligations.

The Senior Preferred Stock had mandatory redemption dates in November and December 2006. ION did not redeem the shares. As a result, the two classes of Senior Preferred Stock, including the 14¼% Preferred Stock, each elected two directors to the Board. They took office in April 2006.

C.   ION's Negotiations with NBCU and Citadel

On January 17, 2007, Citadel and NBCU, substantial holders of ION preferred stock, jointly proposed an equity restructuring transaction to ION (the "CIG/NBCU Proposal"). The proposal contemplated a tender offer by the Company for the Class A common stock at a price in the range of $1.41 per share in cash. The proposal also called for an exchange offer, which provided holders of the 14¼% Preferred Stock the opportunity to exchange their securities for subordinated debt at a ratio of 70% of the face amount. If more than 90% of Senior Preferred Stock participated in the exchange offer, CIG and NBCU would remain at the bottom of the capital structure and receive preferred stock that was mandatorily convertible into common stock. The proposal also included a so-called Contingent Exchange ("Contingent Exchange" or "Elevation") that would permit CIG and NBCU to exchange up to $470 million of their preferred stock for subordinated debt if less than 90% of Senior Preferred Stock participated in the exchange offer. As participation in the exchange offer increased, CIG and NBCU would exchange a proportionally decreasing amount of preferred stock. According to Citadel and NBCU, their proposal would reduce fixed claims in the capital structure by approximately $300 million and recurring fixed charges by approximately $50 million.

After evaluating Citadel's and NBCU's proposal, ION's Special Committee and Board concluded that the proposal was unacceptable without significant improvements. Between January and the end of April, 2007, the Special Committee and its advisors had numerous discussions with representatives of NBCU and Citadel about their proposal. After extensive negotiations, and a couple of revised proposals, Citadel and NBCU had made the following concessions, many of which benefited Senior Preferred Stockholders:

- CIG, rather than ION, would make the tender offer for non-Paxson common stock.

- CIG, which held significant amounts of 14¼% and 9¾% Preferred Stock, agreed to participate fully in the Exchange Offer on the same terms offered to the other Preferred Stockholders, for an aggregate principal amount of $66.8 million of subordinated debt.

- CIG agreed to invest $100 million in ION.

- The initial recovery for the holders of 14¼% Preferred Stock was raised from 70% to 80% of the face amount.

- To ensure that the securities offered in the exchange would trade at par, the coupon on the notes being offered was increased from 7% to 11%.

- CIG committed to additional funding of up to $15 million to cover transaction costs, and CIG and NBCU agreed to cover their own fees for legal counsel and financial advisors.

D. ION Rejects Other Competing Proposals

Between January and May 2007, the Special Committee considered at least nine different proposals submitted by NBCU and Citadel, an anonymous third party, and an Ad Hoc Committee representing holders of the 14¼% Preferred Stock. For example, on February 16, 2007, certain Plaintiffs and other holders of 14¼% Preferred Stock proposed a recapitalization of ION that provided $100 million in new money to the Company. * * * In April 2007, the anonymous third party made a proposal to purchase ION through a $2.13 billion all-cash bid.

The Special Committee perceived significant execution risks with the alternative proposals made by the Ad Hoc Committee and the third party. * * * In addition, the Special Committee's investment advisor, Lazard, found it very difficult to come up with a transaction that did not require NBCU's consent, based on the contract rights NBCU obtained in the November 2005 settlement.

In part due to the fact that the call option was scheduled to expire on May 6, 2007, the Special Committee unanimously recommended on May 1, 2007 that the Board agree to the latest proposal made by Citadel and NBCU. The ION Board approved the transaction on May 3, 2007.

E. The Master Transaction Agreement

ION, NBCU, and CIG executed the MTA on or about May 3, 2007. The MTA summarizes the Company's agreement to an approach that would take ION private under the control of CIG or NBCU. The MTA contemplates several transactions. In general terms, NBCU assigns the call option to CIG and CIG exercises the option. A new call option is then issued from CIG to an affiliate of NBCU. CIG lends $100 million to ION by purchasing newly issued notes and promises to lend up to an additional $15 million to cover the expenses relating to the transaction. CIG tenders for the remaining shares of Class A common stock of ION at approximately $1.46 per share (the "Tender Offer"). The MTA also requires ION to commence "[a]s soon as reasonably practicable" an Exchange Offer and Consent Solicitation ("Exchange Offer" or "Exchange") for exchanges of Senior Preferred Stock. Following the closing of the call option, ION, which is expected to be substantially or completely controlled by CIG, would institute a reverse stock split. Thereafter, an NBCU affiliate could exercise the call option to acquire majority control of CIG. Ultimately, the MTA preserves NBCU's ability to gain control of the Company through a new stockholder agreement between NBCU and CIG.

On May 4, 2007, CIG commenced the Tender Offer for the ION Class A common stock in accordance with the MTA. As of June 4, 2007, approximately 40.6 million shares, or 62.1% of the Class A common stock, had been tendered to CIG. By June 15, that number had increased to over 88%.

F. The Exchange Offer and Consent Solicitation of the 14¼% Preferred Shares

ION commenced the Exchange Offer and Consent Solicitation on June 8, 2007. In the Exchange Offer, ION is offering to exchange for its outstanding 14¼% Preferred Stock newly-issued 11% Series A Mandatorily Convertible Senior Subordinated Notes due 2013 and, depending upon participation levels in the Exchange Offer, either newly issued 12% Series A–1 Mandatorily Convertible Preferred Stock or 12% Series B Mandatorily Convertible Preferred Stock. ION has conditioned the Exchange Offer upon the percentage of shares tendered. If more than 50% of the shares are tendered, each tendered share of 14¼% Preferred Stock will receive $7,000 principal amount of Series A Notes (subordinated debt) and $1,000 initial liquidation preference of the Series A–1 Convertible Preferred Stock, which would rank senior to any unexchanged Preferred Stock. If holders of 50% or less of the Senior Preferred Stock tender in the Exchange Offer, tendering holders will receive $7,500 principal amount of Series A Notes and $500 initial liquidation preference of Series B Convertible Preferred Stock, which would rank junior to any unexchanged Preferred Stock ("Minority Exchange Consideration"). The 14¼% holders who choose to participate in the Exchange also consent to, among other things, amending the existing certificate of designations to eliminate restrictive covenants, such as ION's obligation to repurchase the 14¼% Preferred Stock upon a change of control, and all voting rights provided for in the original certificates.

After the Exchange Offer commenced, ION announced on June 26, 2007, that the Company had extended the Exchange Offer generally for one day until 12:01 a.m. on July 11, 2007, and for ten business days if holders are to receive the Minority Exchange Consideration. If, during that time, a majority of shares of the Senior Preferred Stock have been tendered, holders will still receive the Minority Exchange Consideration, but have to give the covenant consents.

* * *

H. Parties' Contentions

In their motion for a preliminary injunction, Plaintiffs largely seek to enjoin the allegedly coercive aspects of the Exchange Offer based on equitable grounds rooted in Delaware law that make it actionable to "wrongfully coerce" shareholders into making investment decisions. Plaintiffs first argue that the Contingent Exchange aspect of the Exchange Offer is actionably coercive because it impermissibly induces the Preferred Stockholders to participate in the Exchange Offer, by "linking" to a decision not to participate the Elevation of junior preferred stock of NBCU and CIG to debt with priority over the Senior Preferred Stock, if less than 90% of the 14¼% Preferred Stock accept the Exchange Offer. Plaintiffs also argue that the Exchange Offer is actionably coercive because it calls for the removal of certain protective covenants from Senior Preferred Shares that are not tendered in the event that a majority (but less than 90%) of the shares decide to participate in the Exchange Offer. * * *

* * *

II. ANALYSIS

* * *

B. Likelihood of Success on the Merits

The first prong of a preliminary injunction analysis requires that I look to the merits of Plaintiffs' claims. In support of their motion for a preliminary injunction, Plaintiffs argue that the Exchange Offer is coercive with respect to its terms and the accompanying disclosures in the June 8 Solicitation. In particular, Plaintiffs argue that under Section 5.04(a) of the MTA, entitled "Contingent Exchange," if, at the close of the Exchange Offer, tendered shares are between 50 and 90 percent (*i.e.*, sufficient to be a majority of the shares but not for the Company to employ a short-form merger), the non-participating holders are required to give up the protective covenants present in the current Certificate of Designations ("CD") for the 14¼% Preferred Shares. Among the protections that would be eliminated are the requirement that ION redeem the shares upon a change of control and the voting rights to appoint Board directors triggered by, among other things, a failure to redeem the shares. Additionally, the Contingent Exchange triggers the Elevation of up to $470.6 million of NBCU and CIG holdings from junior preferred shares under the 14¼% Preferred Stock to subordinated debt above that stock in the Company's capital structure. The number of junior preferred shares so elevated is inversely proportional to the number of shares of 14¼% Preferred Stock tendered into the Exchange.

If tendered shares fall below 50% (*e.g.*, zero to minimal participation), closer to $470.6 million of NBCU and CIG holdings of junior preferred shares will be elevated to debt. Plaintiffs emphasized that the fairness opinion relied upon by the ION Board as to the MTA transactions in general, given by investment bank Houlihan Lokey Howard & Zukin ("Houlihan"), reports the enterprise value of ION to be between $1.61 to $2.01 billion. Before the Exchange Offer, the Company had $1.13 billion in senior secured debt. Thus, although the 14¼% Preferred Shares are currently within the enterprise value of the Company, the Elevation provided for in the Contingent Exchange would subordinate the 14¼% to such a degree that the exchange of NBCU and CIG shares would completely or substantially push the 14¼% shareholders "out of the money." Plaintiffs characterize their situation as one of a "prisoner's dilemma" of being forced to make a choice without knowing what choice is made by others where each others' choice directly affects the potential outcomes. Specifically, they contend:

> Here, Plaintiffs must choose between: (a) refusing to exchange and facing the devaluation caused by the NBC/CIG Elevation, or (b) participating in the Exchange and accepting its punitive redistribution of debt and stripped down preferreds, in the hope that over 90 percent of holders will also participate. Of course, this dilemma is increased exponentially by the possibility that 90 percent will not be reached, but more than 50 percent will. In such a case, non-participants face the

doubly punitive result of: (a) devaluation through the NBC/CIG Elevation, and (b) the stripping of all material rights from the Certificate governing their holdings.

In that regard, Plaintiffs argue that they are prevented from choosing the status quo and must select between two punishments in terms of loss of value in their securities.

Defendants respond that claims of preferred shareholders are almost exclusively based in contract. According to Defendants, therefore, any cognizable claims Plaintiffs might have stem from the contract rights they have under their CD, and not from any fiduciary duty owed to them by a Defendant. Moreover, Defendants argue that the sole remedy under the CD for any and all of the alleged violations presented in this case is the ability to elect two directors to ION's Board. Thus, Defendants urge the Court to deny a preliminary injunction because the CD effectively precludes Plaintiffs from obtaining such relief.

Defendants also dispute Plaintiffs' claim of being "pushed out of the money" because Plaintiffs still retain the ability to make a purely economic decision. Although the circumstances may make one choice more compelling than the other from a specific Plaintiff's point of view, Defendants argue that influencing a transaction so that one option is more attractive than another hardly makes such a transaction actionably coercive or "coercive in a legal sense." Defendants point to months of deliberations by the Special Committee of ION, with extensive advice from financial and legal advisors, before they recommended the MTA, a disinterested board who voted in favor of the overall series of transactions contemplated by the MTA, and a fairness opinion provided by Houlihan relating to the transaction as a whole to underscore the overall benefit provided to ION and all its shareholders, including common shareholders.

1. Applicable legal principles to coercion claims

As a general rule, preferred shareholders' rights are primarily contractual in nature.[32] Therefore, those rights are governed broadly by the express provisions of the company's certificate of incorporation[33] and specifically through the document designating the rights, preferences, etc. of their special stock. Where, however, a right asserted is not to a preference but rather a right shared equally with the common, the existence of such right and the scope of the correlative duty may be measured by equitable as well as legal standards.

In that regard, this Court has recognized that preferred shareholders share the same right as common shareholders to be free from wrongful

---

32. *Rothschild Int'l Corp. v. Liggett Group, Inc.,* 474 A.2d 133, 136 (Del. 1984).

33. *Id. See also Jedwab v. MGM Grand Hotels, Inc.,* 509 A.2d 584, 593 (Del. Ch. 1986) ("Generally, the provisions of the certificate of incorporation govern the rights of preferred shareholders, the certificate ... being interpreted in accordance with the law of contracts, with only those rights which are embodied in the certificate granted to preferred shareholders.") (quoting *Judah v. Del. Trust Co.,* 378 A.2d 624, 628 (Del. 1977)).

coercion in a stockholder vote.[36] In so holding, Delaware courts have determined that "the standard applicable to the [preferred shareholder's] claim of inequitable coercion is whether the defendants have taken actions that operate inequitably to induce the preferred shareholders to tender their shares for reasons unrelated to the economic merit of the offer."[37] In other words, the ordinary definition of "coercion," something akin to intentionally persuading someone to prefer one option over another is not the same as saying that the persuasion would so impair the person's ability to choose as to be legally actionable.[38] The challenged conduct must be "wrongfully" or "actionably" coercive for a legal remedy to ensue.[39] Thus, an action is not coercive unless a shareholder is wrongfully induced to make a decision for reasons unrelated to merit. On the other hand, an action is "actionably coercive" if, in the context of a tender offer, it "threatens to extinguish or dilute a percentage ownership interest in relation to the interests of other stockholders."

In *In re General Motors Class H Shareholders Litigation*,[42] Vice Chancellor Strine clarified the distinction between coercion (*i.e.* circumstances that lead to a preference in voting but are not legally actionable) and "wrongful" or "actionable" coercion. In that case, GM issued GMH stock, which represented rights in equity and assets in the parent company, GM, but which tied dividends to the financial performance of Hughes Electronics, a GM subsidiary that consisted of Hughes Defense, Hughes Telecom, and Delco. In an effort to recapitalize, the GM board proposed and approved a spin off of Hughes Defense to Raytheon and, in doing so, transferred Delco into the parent GM. The transactions also included a $1 billion infusion of money by Raytheon into the remaining portion of Hughes Electronics, Telecom. Upon approval of the transaction by shareholders, GMH shareholders would have economic interests as direct stockholders in Raytheon, as the purchaser of Hughes Defense, through a dividend interest in Hughes Telecom, as the holder of recapitalized GMH shares, and through a tenuous economic interest in Delco, now a division of GM.

---

36. *Eisenberg v. Chicago Milwaukee Corp.*, 537 A.2d 1051, 1061 (Del. Ch. 1987) (quoting *Ivanhoe Partners v. Newmont Mining Corp.*, 533 A.2d 585, 605, *aff'd*, 535 A.2d 1334 (Del. 1987)).

37. *Id.*

38. *Lacos Land Co. v. Arden Group, Inc.*, 517 A.2d 271, 277 (Del. Ch. 1986).

39. *Id.* As Chancellor Allen stated:

For purposes of legal analysis, the term "coercion" itself—covering a multitude of situations—is not very meaningful. For the word to have much meaning for purposes of legal analysis, it is necessary in each case that a normative judgment be attached to the concept ("inappropriately coercive" or "wrongfully coercive," etc.). But, it is then readily seen that what is legally relevant is not the conclusory term "coercion" itself but rather the norm that leads to the adverb modifying it.

Id. (quoting *Katz v. Oak Indus.*, 508 A.2d 873, 880 (Del. Ch. 1986)).

42. *In re Gen. Motors (Hughes) S'holders Litig.*, 734 A.2d 611 (Del. Ch. 1999).

The recapitalization efforts needed majority approval from both the GM and the GMH shareholders. As part of the consent process, GM informed GMH holders that a vote to approve the transactions would have the effect of waiving any possible application of certain covenant amendments contemplating GMH remedies upon a recapitalization. The solicitation also disclosed that the transactions, as contemplated, were entitled to tax-free treatment but that, because of recently enacted federal tax legislation that would become effective after the closing of the transactions, a future recapitalization involving Hughes Defense, if consummated, would be subject to taxable gains.

The GMH shareholders alleged that they were actionably coerced by having to choose between giving up recapitalization covenants intentionally tied to an affirmative vote or blocking the transactions and squandering potentially enhanced values realized from those transactions. The GMH shareholders also alleged that the board actionably coerced them by disclosing that the Hughes recapitalization would receive favorable tax treatment, but that future transactions might not.

The court found no actionable coercion in the board's actions regarding the waiver of the recapitalization provision. First, the court noted that neither allegation stated a claim that the coercive actions were "unrelated to the merits of the Hughes Transactions." As the court quipped, "you can't have your cake and eat it too"; by alleging coercion, plaintiffs attempted to take the benefit of a company's recapitalization and, notwithstanding that benefit, insure their position by seeking, in addition, recapitalization covenant protection. However, "the opportunity to make this choice by vote carried with it a concomitant obligation on the part of the voters to accept responsibility for the outcome."[45]

Second, and perhaps more importantly, the court looked at the board's rationale for relating the covenant stripping to the transactions and determined that the "GMH stockholders had a free choice between maintaining their current status and taking advantage of the new status offered by the Hughes Transactions."

* * *

A board's decision to construct a recapitalization without triggering contractual covenants is not, the court concluded, actionably coercive.

In making that determination, the court in *GM* focused on the *manner* in which the board used covenant stripping. In particular, the court held

---

45. *Id.* [at 621] Other cases have reached the same conclusion. *See, e.g., Katz v. Oak Indus.,* 508 A.2d 873, 881 (Del. Ch. 1986) (upholding transaction that conditioned exchange offer to bondholders on receipt of exit consents); *Cantor Fitzgerald, L.P. v. Cantor,* 2001 WL 1456494, at *8–9 (Del. Ch. Nov. 5, 2001) (exchange offer coupled with vote for amendments that would reduce economic protections to non-tendering holders not coercive, despite "compelling economic incentives for participating in the Exchange Offer"); *In re Marriott Hotel Props. II Ltd. P'ship Unitholders Litig.,* 2000 WL 128875, at *19 (Del. Ch. Jan. 24, 2000) (holding that it was not wrongfully coercive to make tender offer conditional on obtaining sufficient consents for allegedly unfair amendments to partnership agreement).

that a board's choices to formulate a business decision are given deference by the courts unless it impacts unfairly, or "strong-arms" the vote so as to force a shareholder, for reasons outside of the economic merit, to tender into the offer. The court concluded that the board's use of the covenant stripping did not amount to actionable coercion because the stockholders, if they chose not to tender, would still be in the same position they had been before the vote.[48]

* * *

A vote, by its nature, forces shareholders to suspend artificially the present circumstances in a snapshot economic situation. It is not, however, the same as suggesting that the economic world itself does not move forward. Keeping the shareholders in the "same" position, then, does not require an "identical" position, economic or otherwise. Instead, a shareholder is actionably coerced when he is forced into "a choice between a new position and a compromised position" for reasons other than those related to the economic merits of the decision.

An application of this analysis can be seen in *AC Acquisitions*.[51] Over the course of several months, shareholders of Anderson, Clayton attempted to bring the company to the bargaining table. Having failed to do so, they formed a new corporation, AC Acquisitions, to make a cash tender offer for any and all shares of Anderson, Clayton at $56 per share. One day later, Anderson, Clayton announced the commencement of a self-tender offer for 65.5% of its outstanding stock at $60 per share cash. The company also announced that, in connection with the closing of its tender offer, the company would sell stock to a newly-formed employee stock ownership plan ("ESOP") amounting to 25% of all issued and outstanding stock following such sale. AC Acquisitions sought preliminary injunctive relief against the company to, among other things, prohibit it from purchasing any shares pursuant to its self-tender offer. Plaintiffs alleged actionable coercion and cited the timing of the Anderson, Clayton offer and the decision to tender for 65.5% of the outstanding stock as elements of the self-tender reflective of the defendants' motives to actionably coerce shareholders into taking the company's offer.

Chancellor Allen remarked that, "if all that defendants have done is to create an option for shareholders, then it can hardly be thought to have breached a duty." The company, however, artificially manufactured circumstances surrounding the initial shareholder decision under which "no rational shareholder could afford not to tender into the company's self-

---

48. Presumably, in *GM*, if a majority of the shareholders voted to approve the transaction, it would have occurred and all the shareholders would have had the benefit of the transaction. The situation in this case is slightly different. If a majority of the 14¼% Preferred Shares are tendered into the Exchange, they no longer will own 14¼% shares. Those who do not accept will retain their 14¼% shares, but have them stripped of various covenants based on the consents of the tendering shareholders. In this sense, the current dispute is more analogous to *Katz v. Oak Industries*, 508 A.2d 873 (Del. Ch. 1986).

51. *AC Acquisitions Corp. v. Anderson, Clayton & Co.*, 519 A.2d 103 (Del. Ch. 1986) (examining coercion in the context of a *Unocal* analysis).

tender offer at least if that transaction is viewed in isolation." The Chancellor explained that:

> What is clear [from both parties' expert testimony on the value of the shares], is that a current shareholder who elects not to tender into the self-tender is very likely, upon consummation of the company transaction, to experience a substantial loss in market value of his holdings. The only way, within the confines of the company transaction, that a shareholder can protect himself from such an immediate financial loss, is to tender into the self-tender so that he receives his *pro rata* share of the cash distribution that will, in part, cause the expected fall in the market price of the company's stock.

In structuring such an option, the company precluded as a practical matter shareholders from choosing to accept the AC Acquisitions tender offer based on its economic merits. No reasonable investor would be able to choose between two tender offers; instead, and because of the board's actions, the shareholder effectively was forced to take the corporation's self-tender *regardless* of the economic merits of each proposal. Thus, the court held that the company moved the shareholders into a compromised, or actionably coercive, situation.

* * *

In the case at hand, Plaintiffs allege three actionably coercive actions. First, Plaintiffs allege that the Board's June 8 Solicitation omits material information relevant to the shareholders' decisionmaking. These allegations are discussed *infra*. Second, Plaintiffs suggest that the Board's requirement that tendering preferred shareholders consent to the elimination of certain existing rights of their preferred shares ("exit consents") is actionably coercive. Third, Plaintiffs allege that the Elevation, or the Contingent Exchange, is actionably coercive. I turn first to the exit consents.

2. Exit consents

Based on the evidence adduced to date, I am not persuaded that the exit consents in the Exchange Offer are actionably coercive. Consequently, Plaintiffs have not shown a reasonable likelihood of success as to this aspect of their challenge to the Exchange Offer. Under the Exchange Offer, a holder of 14¼% Preferred Stock who decides to tender her shares also must provide an exit consent to the stripping of various covenants from the remaining 14¼% shares. If more than 50 percent of the 14¼% shares tender, the covenant stripping will take effect.

As discussed above, this allegation, as *In re General Motors* explains, manifests Plaintiffs' attempt to put one foot in a new bargain, and still keep the other foot in the previous game by hedging, through the related covenant protection, the original bargain. A majority of 14¼% shareholders can either take the offered exchange of debt, thus removing themselves from their originally bargained for position, or choose to hold on to their 14¼% Preferred Stock. Plaintiffs contend that the non-tendering shareholders are then placed in an economically disadvantaged position. Although linking the vote on the covenants to the decision to tender threatens to reduce economic protections to non-tendering holders, the shareholders, in the aggregate, are free to choose between accepting the new debt securities (by tendering one's shares), or staying in one's place (and refusing to tender). Should a majority of the 14¼% Preferred Stock choose to support the Company's decision to recapitalize in this manner, the elimination of the non-tendered shares' covenants is merely an effect of the reality that a majority of the 14¼% peers have disagreed with the non-tendering share-holders and concluded that accepting the Exchange Offer is in their best interest. The amendment of the CD for the 14¼% Preferred Stock by the holders of a majority of that class of stock is authorized by the CD.

Further, ION's Board had no duty to structure these transactions in a way to trigger the contractual covenants. To suggest that the Board must fashion an imitative recapitalization or favor one group of shareholders over the overall benefit to the corporation here would contravene the fundamental principle that a board may freely make decisions that benefit ION as a whole. Thus, I provisionally conclude that ION's conditioning of a 14¼% Preferred Shareholder's acceptance of the Exchange on that share-holder's also providing a consent to delete certain covenants of the 14¼% Preferred Stock is not actionably coercive.

3. The Elevation provisions

Additionally, on the current record, I do not find the Elevation feature of the Exchange Offer actionably coercive. Accordingly, I conclude that Plaintiffs do not have a reasonable likelihood of success of prevailing on that aspect of their claims.

The Contingent Exchange aspect of the Exchange Offer is an integral part of the economics of the exchange and is, broadly, one aspect of a larger Exchange Offer designed to delever ION over time. The Exchange Offer results initially in only a modest reduction of fixed claims and fixed charges against the Company. Over time and with maximum participation, howev-er, mandatory conversion of the newly issued convertible securities would create a major benefit in terms of "deleveraging" the Company. This benefit also would inure to Plaintiffs and their class.

Defendants saw the Exchange Offer as part of a larger transaction designed to confer economic benefit on ION. For example, Frederick Smith, a member of the ION Board and the Special Committee, expressed the view that, under the CIG/NBCU Proposal, "the Corporation's preferred stock-holders would be offered a meaningful premium to incentivize participation in the proposed exchange offer" and provide an economic choice to partici-pate. As a representative of NBCU explained, NBCU and Citadel intention-ally "set up a structure where everyone in the capital structure would be incented to take a discount."

The Special Committee appreciated the economics of the Exchange Offer and sought to improve the premiums offered to the Senior Preferred Stock. "From the standpoint of the Special Committee, our goal was to negotiate the best transaction for the Company and to increase the likely

participation in the exchange by improving the recoveries for the 14¼%
Preferred Stock." Through its discussions and negotiations, the Special
Committee analyzed anticipated levels of participation by the Preferred
Stockholders as well as the integrated economic incentives structurally
built into the proposed Exchange Offer. Investment banks provided to the
Special Committee trading data, enterprise values, and valuations to assist
them in trying to provide economic benefit to the 14¼% Preferred Shareholders. Before the Special Committee vote on May 1 and even on the day
the MTA was approved, members of the Special Committee sought to
negotiate better recovery values for the Preferred Shareholders.[71] These
few excerpts from the extensive negotiating history of the Exchange Offer
and MTA are illustrative only. The evidence presented convinces me that
all the parties recognized the economic aspects of the decision presented to
the 14¼% Preferred Stock to either tender into the Exchange Offer or
decline to do so and have the Elevation occur.

No party disputes that the Elevation, in part, was included as a
deliberate attempt by NBCU and Citadel to induce tendering. Even Lazard
recognized that "there is a significant likelihood that the Citadel/NBC
exchange offer, if launched, would not be highly subscribed." The issue,
however, is whether linking the Elevation to the shareholder's decision to
tender "strong-arms" the vote in such a manner that Plaintiffs are precluded from making a decision on the economic merits of the offer. To use
Chancellor Allen's language in *AC Acquisitions,* does the Contingent Exchange aspect of the Exchange Offer prevent the Preferred Shareholders
from making a decision in the sense that "no rational shareholder" could
afford not to tender into the Company's offer? The Exchange Offer, while
perhaps complicated, still preserves the ability of the Senior Preferred
Shareholders to decide based on the economic merits of each alternative
whether to tender their shares into the Exchange or retain them and
endure the Elevation and possible covenant stripping.

At argument, Plaintiffs seemed to argue that, to use a "carrot and
stick" analogy for inducements, a company may employ carrots or sticks in
creating a security or other asset that it then offers to some or all of its
stockholders, but may not as part of the same offer intentionally attach
sticks or adverse aspects to a stockholder's decision to stay put, and not
accept the offer. In oversimplified terms, Plaintiffs argue that a stockholder
should have the right, as one of its options, to maintain the status quo.
Based on my review of numerous coercion cases previously decided, I do not
believe our law or the cases support such a sweeping proposition. Further,
in the circumstances of this case, Defendants' actions in "linking" the
Elevation provisions to the Exchange Offer and, specifically, to the situation in which significant numbers of Senior Preferred Shareholders reject

---

71. Fay Aff. Ex. A (F. Smith Dep. Ex. 9). As Plaintiffs emphasized at argument, there is
no evidence that the Special Committee obtained any concessions from NBCU or Citadel
regarding the Elevation-related terms of the Contingent Exchange. The various concessions
they did obtain pertained more to the terms of the debt securities offered to the Senior
Preferreds.

the Exchange, appears to be logical and consistent with the legitimate objectives of ION to improve its capital structure and begin reducing its debt in terms of both fixed claims and fixed charges. Moreover, the result is that the 14¼% Preferred Stock must choose between at least two possible alternatives, both of which have pros and cons depending on each investors' views as to the future prospects for the Company. These are the types of risks and analyses sophisticated investors, like the holders of ION's Senior Preferred Stock appear to be, must deal with everyday.

Defendants aver that the Contingent Exchange portion of the overall transactions was inserted as a mechanical adjustment of their risk, based on the number of tendering 14¼% shares. Plaintiffs, then, challenge the Exchange Offer by presenting evidence they contend shows that NBCU and CIG arranged the transaction this way to strong arm the Preferred Share-holders into taking the Exchange or to reap a windfall, if they did not. I provisionally find that the evidence does not support so sinister an inference.

Frederick Smith, a member of the Special Committee, testified that he understood from Citadel and NBCU's presentation that the Elevation of NBCU stock was

> an effective way of having a successful recap. Because it would induce, if you will, or provide added inducement to the senior preferreds to in fact exchange. And that if they didn't exchange, that NBC wanted to take advantage of that [debt] basket [i.e. the Elevation of the junior preferred shares into subordinated debt].

Todd Gjervold of Citadel stated, "I believe that [the manner in which the sliding scale in the Exchange Offer is constructed] is the most effective way to distribute value and to induce the exchange." And as ION's brief underscores, the Elevation present in the Exchange Offer "was insisted upon" by NBCU and Citadel.

Adding color to their claim of coercion, Plaintiffs assert that the Exchange Offer forces them to choose between two evils: (a) new debt and preferred shares they contend are valued at only 71% of the 14¼% Preferred Stock and reflect interest rate reductions of as much as 325 basis points; or (b) keep the 14¼% shares but "endure punitive effects" of the Elevation which, according to Plaintiffs, is improperly favorable to NBCU. Plaintiffs also stress that Defendants failed to obtain a fairness opinion relating to the Exchange Offer that might otherwise substitute for or buttress the Board's accumulated analysis of the NBCU–CIG offers. On the record available at this stage, however, I am not convinced that Plaintiffs are not likely to succeed in proving that the economic terms of the Exchange Offer are unfair to them.

Although there is sharp conflict over the fairness of the Exchange Offer among the witnesses, I find Defendants' evidence slightly more convincing. Plaintiffs, supported by their expert, Lloyd A. Sprung, say that no premium constituting fair consideration to the Senior Preferred Stock-holders existed at the time of the June 8 Solicitation because, "even if it is assumed that the new securities offered in the Exchange traded at their face value (*i.e.,* 80 percent), the *current* market price for the 14¼% Senior Preferred Shares is 89.7 percent." Plaintiffs further assert that any premium claimed by Defendants "was gone by May 4, 2007—the day the MTA was announced." In response, Defendants aver that the ION Board received extensive advice on May 1, 2007, from both UBS and Lazard that the Exchange Offer "provided a clear premium to the preferred stockholders based on the *then* trading ranges of their respective securities." In its presentation, UBS advised ION's Board that the premium to 14¼% Preferred Stockholders represented "a 10.7%–41.8% premium to the unaffected trading price on January 17, 2007, and a 6%–35.7% premium to the *then-current* trading price." Plaintiffs' focus on whether a premium existed on June 8, 2007, the date ION launched the Exchange Offer, seems misplaced. To determine whether the Exchange Offer provided a premium to Senior Preferred Stockholders, this Court more likely would consider whether such a premium existed in relation to the unaffected stock value, using a date before news of the MTA or the terms of the Exchange Offer became known in or about early May 2007, Defendants' witnesses used a similar approach.[83]

NBCU and Citadel included the Elevation in the Exchange Offer to control their risk in a transaction aimed at delevering ION. The risk of their bargain is directly tied to the degree of acceptance (or non-acceptance) of the Exchange Offer by the Senior Preferred Shares. Conversely, Defendants contend that the Elevation provision does not preclude Plaintiffs from making a decision rooted in the economic merits of the available alternatives and their view of ION's prospects after implementation of the MTA.

I also believe that Plaintiffs misinterpret the case law as it relates to the ability to "be in the same position." Merely choosing to remain in a position does not mean maintaining an equal and guaranteed economic position, particularly in the context of preferred shares. The ION Board, analogous to GM, informed the Preferred Stockholders that, should the Shareholders collectively approve the Exchange Offer, non-tendering Shareholders should not expect to be in the same position because the Company will have begun to implement the process set forth in the Offer. Those simply are the realities the Senior Preferred Stockholders and the

---

83. The economic merits of the Contingent Exchange are less clear. For example, James Millstein, a managing director at Lazard, testified that the Elevation "stepdowns were inconsistent with sort of the traditional step-downs in our business. Step-downs being the relative recovery rates offered to different classes of security holders based on their relative priority." Fay Supp. Aff. Ex. B (Millstein Dep.) at 10–12. Further, Millstein considered unique a transaction where a company purchased at par junior equity interests that were trading at 35% of their accreted claim. In his experience at Lazard, Millstein had never participated in such a transaction. According to ION's Answering Brief, at more than 90 percent participation in the Exchange Offer, the anticipated recovery for NBCU on their junior preferred was only 20 to 30 percent of the face value plus accrued dividends, and, at zero percent participation, NBCU's recovery through the Elevation would be about 54 percent.

Company must contend with upon the successful closing of the Exchange Offer.

Consistent with *AC Acquisitions, Kahn v. United States Sugar Corp.,* and *Eisenberg* and as discussed above, I do not, at this preliminary stage, find persuasive Plaintiffs contention that the Exchange Offer with the Elevation feature they criticize is actionably coercive. Unlike the cases that have held defendants' actions to be actionably coercive, Plaintiffs here merely allege the *risk* of being "put out of the money." Such a risk is inherent in the bargain a preferred shareholder makes, which, as in this case, generally includes the possibility that the company later can issue more senior debt or other securities without the preferreds' consent.

The Certificate of Designations between the 14¼% Preferred Stockholders and ION confirm this conclusion. In the CD, the parties have, under Section f, provided for specific remedies in certain situations that involve issuance of debt or payments to certain third parties (such as the Exchange Offer contemplates). In such situations the CD specifies the exclusive remedy between the parties to be the election of "the lesser of two directors and that number of directors constituting 25% of the members of the Board of Directors."

For all of these reasons, I find that Plaintiffs are not likely to succeed on their claim that the Exchange Offer, by its terms, is actionably coercive.

[The court rejected other claims of the plaintiffs.]

III. CONCLUSION

For the reasons stated, the Court denies Plaintiffs' motions for preliminary injunction in both CA. Nos. 3021 and 3043.

QUESTIONS

1. What are the holders of the 14¼% Preferred getting if the exchange succeeds in getting over 90% acceptance?

2. What are the holders of the preferred giving up in value if they accept?

3. Would this exchange leave them better or worse off than before?

4. If the holders don't accept at over 90%, but over 50% accept so the covenants are waived, what rights are left to them after NBCU and CIG exchange junior preferred for $470 million in debt?

5. Does this leave them better off or worse off than before?

6. How does the court define the areas where preferred shareholders are owed some fiduciary obligations?

7. A "prisoner's dilemma" in game theory is defined as a two-person non-communication game where each party is offered two unattractive choices, one even worse than the other. Acceptance of the less bad one by one party imposes even worse consequences on the other party. Worse yet, if both succumb and take the less bad choice, each of them receives the worst alternative. This game was played in hostile take-

overs, where a bidder would offer a tempting takeover price to those who accepted, with the threat that those who didn't accept would be frozen out at a much lower value—less than they would voluntarily accept for their shares. The court refers to *AC Acquisitions Corp. v. Anderson, Clayton & Co.*, 519 A.2d 103 (Del. Ch. 1986), where, in response to an attractive hostile bid for all shares, Anderson Clayton management made a higher bid, but only for 65% of its shares. So little wealth would be left in the company that the remaining shares would be worth much less, with a total value of the combined package worth less than the bidder was offering. The problem was that the bidder required receipt of at least a majority of the company's stock as a condition of acceptance, and if the outside bid failed while Anderson Clayton was closing its higher bid, those who tried to accept the outside bid would wind up holding Anderson Clayton shares worth much less. Concluding that no rational shareholder could afford to pass up the Anderson Clayton bid, even if the total value were less, the court concluded that the Anderson Clayton bid was impermissibly coercive, leaving shareholders with no effective choice. How does this court conclude that the Ion transaction is not coercive?

8. What does it take for an offer with choices, where one is better than the other, to be coercive?

CHAPTER EIGHT

OPTIONS AND CONVERTIBLE SECURITIES

1. INTRODUCTION

A. THE USES OF OPTIONS AND OPTION THEORY

This chapter once again utilizes the concept of substitution, but more broadly than before. We will learn that option contracts can be employed as substitutes for a wide (perhaps infinite) number of positions in other securities. Where the cost of transacting in options is sufficiently low, they can also serve as hedging devices to reduce the risk associated with positions in securities or currencies (or commodities, in other settings). Options are one form of a *derivative* security, in that the value of an option is derived from (depends on) the value of some other security or commodity.

We begin with some basic definitions:

i. An *Option* is a contract giving the holder the right to buy or sell an asset at (or before) a future date at a specified price.

ii. A *Call Option* is a contractual right to buy an asset at a specified price on (or before) a specified date.

iii. A *Put Option* is a contractual right to sell an asset at a specified price on (or before) a specified date.

iv. The *Expiration Date* is the last date on which the option may be exercised; after that it carries no rights.

v. An *American Option* is a contract that allows the holder to buy or sell an asset on or before the Expiration Date.

vi. A *European Option* is a contract that allows the holder to buy or sell an asset only on the Expiration Date.

vii. *Exercise or Strike Price* is the price at which the holder of an option can buy or sell the asset.

viii. A *Warrant* is a call option issued by a company with respect to its own securities.

The uses of options are so varied it is difficult to mention them all. As discussed below, options are often written to allow the participating parties to hedge other investment positions they have—to reduce their exposure to risk. On the other hand, options can be used to heighten risk and returns. Options are also used as compensation to executives, often to encourage them to take prudent risks on behalf of shareholders. The motivation for these options is entirely different—to provide performance incentives for executives, in order to reduce agency costs, as discussed in Chapter Four. In some cases options that provide high potential returns have encouraged extremely risky behavior, as in the case of Enron, where executives engaged in criminal fraud to falsify financial statements in order to profit from their options.

Options can be used to hedge various kinds of risks. A U.S.-based multinational company that enters into a profitable contract in a foreign country may be content to deal with the normal risks of contract performance and payment on behalf of the other party, but be concerned with the risk that the foreign country's currency may decline against the dollar before the price is paid. In this case the multinational may want to hedge its currency risk, which it can do by buying an option to sell the currency at or near the current price (a put option).

While risk-reducing options that are traded in markets have relatively short time limits—not more than nine months—other options may last for ten years, in common practice, as in the case of stock options granted to corporate executives. Real estate developers frequently use options to assemble parcels of land for a major project, because they entail less cost and less risk for the developer at a time when successful development is uncertain, either because of doubts about ability to acquire all necessary parcels, or because of doubts about rezoning, financing, or other contingencies.

Options also arise in the context of other financial instruments, such as preferred stock and issues of corporate debt. In some cases corporations issue warrants in connection with issues of other securities, but in others the option takes the form of a right to convert preferred stock or debt into common stock of the issuer at a fixed conversion ratio. These convertible securities are simply options with a higher purchase price and a commitment to pay dividends or interest until exercise. These forms of options are in common usage in venture capital financing. The conversion right has a value that allows the venture capitalist to accept a non-dividend paying cumulative preferred stock, and allows a lender to consider the value of the purchase option as an additional benefit that allows a reduction in the interest rate on the debt.

Sidebar: Forward Contracts

A *Forward Contract* is simply a contract for delivery of a good that is executory on both sides. For example, assume that Farmer Jones is nervous that today's price of wheat ($3.00 per bushel) may decline before the harvest in September. Because Farmer Jones is undiversified, being wholly invested (long) in wheat, he may prefer to sell now. At the same time, assume that a cereal manufacturer, such as Kellogg's, is concerned that the price of wheat may rise, and its costs may rise, while the makers of rice and oat cereals won't face such a cost increase. Both parties may benefit from a forward contract, in which Farmer Jones agrees to deliver his wheat to Kellogg's on September 15 at $3.00 per bushel. Each has managed to reduce a risk that faced each of them.

Sidebar: Futures Contracts

Futures Contracts are written on organized exchanges, and utilize a clearing house. Thus, Farmer Jones may write a futures contract to deliver September wheat at $3.00, which he can deliver at any date during September. When he decides to deliver, he notifies the exchange clearing house, which then selects, at random, a buyer of a September futures contract at $3.00, and notifies her to prepare to take delivery. If the buyer is Kellogg's, Kellogg's may take actual delivery. But if the buyer is Susan Smith, she may have no use for the wheat. In that case, she will resell her contract to someone, such as Kellogg's, that needs the wheat, in an anonymous exchange transaction.

Sidebar: Marking Futures Contracts to Market

Suppose that the price of September wheat declines to $2.98, and Farmer Jones and Susan Smith have each written the opposite sides of futures contracts. Ms. Smith has just lost two cents per bushel, since she has agreed to pay $3.00 for September wheat. The exchange on which the contract was traded will notify her broker, and she will be required to remit that sum through her broker to the exchange. Farmer Jones, who has just made a two cent profit as a seller, will receive two cents per bushel. The new quoted price on September futures contracts is $2.98. This prompt settling up dramatically reduces risk of major defaults by either party, which is vital in anonymous markets. Forward contracts (see below) are not marked to market, which creates an important default risk. They are not traded on anonymous exchanges, but generally between parties who know and trust each other.

Sidebar: Derivatives

Options are derivative securities, in the sense that their value is derived from the value of the underlying stock. You have seen how this operates in forward and futures contracts. But they are by no means the only derivative securities, and students of corporate finance should be aware of some of them. Broadly defined, a derivative is any security whose value depends upon the value of something else.

B. REAL OPTIONS

There are many economic arrangements that are the equivalent of options, and it is useful to think of them in that manner. Use of options theory to evaluate financial decisions is called "real options" theory. In any investment decision there may be a degree of flexibility that allows managers to make changes to the project during its life. This project flexibility, or real options, is ignored in DCF analysis and can significantly increase the value of the project by taking into account the value of being able to alter a project in response to unexpected market developments. Real Option Valuation complements traditional valuation methods by applying financial option theory to capital budgeting. Lawyers have engaged in this kind of reasoning for a very long time, without identifying it as a finance tool. For example, when a lawyer and client calculate potential liabilities if a client decides not to perform a contract, and compares this with the cost of performance, they are engaging in one form of real options analysis. Should litigation ensue, the lawyer will assist the client in appraising the value of various options available, between settlement and continuing the litigation.

Many investments have an option embedded in them. Many corporate investments in new projects have an option in the future to continue the investment or bail out if things don't go well. When a manufacturing company buys a vacant parcel of land next to a plant, it is creating the option to expand in the future. When an inventor files a patent application, she is creating an exclusive option to exploit the invention in the future.

For a heavily indebted corporation, where shareholders have limited liability, it is often helpful to think of shareholders as holding an option to buy the company by paying off the debt, or an option to sell it to the creditors if the firm value drops below the amount of corporate indebtedness. Assume that a company has fallen on hard times. Originally it sold stock for $100 and $100 worth of bonds. But now its assets are valued at only $110. If the firm's value drops below $100 when the bonds become due and payable, the stockholders will let the corporation default, and in effect sell its assets to the bondholders for the value of its assets (say $90). But if the value of the assets drops to $90 before the maturity of the bonds, will the stock's value fall to zero? Probably not, if the due date is some time in the future. This is because something good may happen to the firm, raising the value of its assets above $100. In this case the stockholders will cause the firm to pay off the bonds for $100. In effect, they have exercised their option to purchase the firm's assets from the bondholders at $100. As we noted in Chapter Six, this situation creates incentives for the stockholders to cause the firm to take more chances than would an all-equity firm. Stockholders are like option holders—if the value of the underlying asset falls below the exercise price, they are indifferent about how far below it falls.

The author once encountered a business that had lost money for seven years because of a particular combination of market and crop conditions. The major stockholder had guaranteed loans for the corporation to keep it in operation, so its debts exceeded the value of its assets. Why did the stockholder continue to do this rather than abandon the assets to the corporate creditors? Apparently because the stockholder believed that the right to claim ownership of the assets when conditions improved had a positive value—and guaranteeing the loans was a valuable real option to continue to control the assets. Declining to guarantee corporate debt would cause creditors to seize the corporate assets, thus effecting a sale to the creditors for the amount of the loans.

Oil and gas leases are another example of real options. The typical lease on undeveloped mineral rights calls for a nominal "delay rental," often $1.00 per acre per year, for as long as the lessee does not produce oil and gas. Typically the lease is for an indefinite duration, which only terminates when the lessee stops making the payments. This, in effect, is an option to the lessee to develop the mineral rights by drilling at the time of its choice (at which time higher royalty payments replace the delay rentals). What does the mineral interest owner get in exchange? An initial payment (called a "bonus"), which is really a payment for the option rights.

C. LONG AND SHORT POSITIONS AND POSITION DIAGRAMS

Because the options we are about to discuss are related to a particular stock (rather than mineral rights, commodities, or real estate), we begin with a discussion of transactions available in stock. Assume a stock currently trading at $100, say IBM common stock. When an investor buys a share, we describe her as having a "long" position in the stock. Presumably this investor expects that it is more probable than not that the value of the stock will increase. There is no upper bound on potential profits from the long position, but there is an upper bound on losses—the purchase price of the stock. A position diagram describes the value of the investor's long position in all possible future states of the world. The horizontal axis represents the stock price, while the vertical axis represents the value of the investor's long position. This is illustrated in Figure 8–1, below:

Figure 8-1 - Value of a Long Stock Position

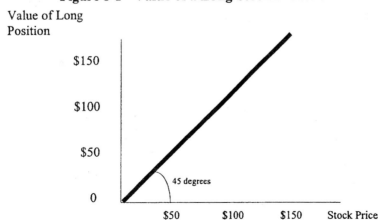

Not everyone believes that the stock is likely to increase in value. Under these circumstances, those holding long positions can sell, some doubters can simply avoid the stock, while those with stronger beliefs in the likelihood of a stock's decline can take a "short" position in the stock. She does this by borrowing the stock, usually from a broker, and selling it into the market, usually at today's price. (The broker typically will retain the proceeds or demand other collateral as security for the loan of the borrowed stock, and the short seller will have to compensate the lender for the dividends paid on the borrowed stock.) The customer, who now has cash in her account, is obligated to close out the short position by returning the share of stock at some time in the future. The customer expects that she can "cover" her position by buying the stock in the market at a lower price, and thus earn a profit on the decline. Of course, this short position is just as risky as the long position, if the market price moves against the short seller's expectations. This position diagram, in Figure 8–2, is the flip side of the long position:

Figure 8-2 - Value of a Short Position

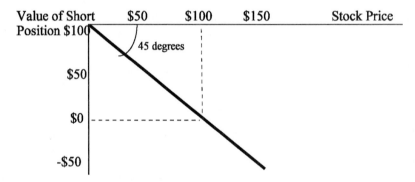

This diagram is easier to understand if one recalls that the short seller has already pocketed the proceeds of a sale. Thus, if the short seller has sold the stock at $100, and it declines to $50 at the time the short seller replaces it ("covers" his position), his $50 payment leaves him with a net gain of $50. One important feature of a short position is that there is no upper bound on one's potential losses; the higher the stock price rises, the greater the losses the short seller suffers. An investor with a long position can lose no more than her initial investment—$100, in our example. On the other hand, the short seller's possible gains are limited. This can be expressed as:

Value of Short = Proceeds of short sale – Replacement Cost

Thus, if the value of IBM stock drops to $50, our investor's short position is worth $50. This means it only costs her $50 to replace the stock she sold for $100. On the other hand, if IBM stock rises to $100, she has no gain: the total proceeds of the short sale, $100, were precisely the amount required to replace the stock.

2. How Options Operate

Options are binary contracts: in one outcome, their value is zero; in another their value is more (or less) than zero. Thus, if one holds a call option (discussed below) that allows one to purchase a stock at a particular price, the option is either worthless at expiration if the stock trades below that price or has a positive value in excess of the exercise price. Similarly, if one holds a put option (discussed below) to sell a stock at a certain price, it is worthless at expiration if the stock rises above that price, but worth the difference between the option price and the current market price of the stock if the stock price falls below the option price. In many cases the obligation of the writer of an option is unlimited. Thus, if you sell a call option, upon exercise the writer is obligated to deliver shares no matter how high the market price has risen.

Options are also bilateral agreements, and they are necessarily zero-sum games, where one pays and the other receives, depending on the value of the referenced asset. Whoever bears the risk of paying demands a price for bearing this risk, and the option price represents an informed view of the present value of that risk. Why would parties incur transaction costs to play a zero-sum game? In some cases one party has a large investment that is risky, and feels uncomfortable bearing the entire amount of the risk. Consider a person who has a very large investment in a volatile asset, such as stock in a drug company still in the early stages of developing new drugs, which may succeed spectacularly over time, or fail completely. As drug tests reach certain critical points, the company will have to decide whether to proceed on or kill the drug. An investor might decide to purchase "put options" to sell her shares at these critical times, thus insuring against a dramatic loss of value on announcement of results. Who would write and sell such an option? One possibility is an investor with a greater tolerance for risk, perhaps because of diversification, willing to profit from writing the contract and hoping for the best on the drug tests. Such an investor may write numerous put contracts, thus diversifying the risk of bad news.

A. Call Options

Call options are both the most common and the easiest to understand of the derivatives (although valuation is complex). When a trader issues a call option on a stock, the trader may or may not own the underlying shares that he agrees to sell pursuant to the terms of the option. When a corporation issues such an option on its own shares (a warrant), it typically has either treasury shares or authorized but unissued shares available with which to honor the exercise of the option, but this is not a necessary condition for the issuance of warrants, as long as the company has the ability to buy shares in the market to cover the exercise of the warrant.

Where options are traded on U.S. exchanges, such as the Chicago Board of Options Exchange ("CBOE"), a unit of the Chicago Board of

Trade ("CBOT") their terms must be standardized. Currently all traded options are American options, but some stock index options are European options. There are limits on the term of such options. The Options Clearing Corporation ("OCC") is the clearinghouse for all exchange-traded options. For example the terms of options traded on the CBOE cannot exceed three years* Options not traded on exchanges are called over-the-counter options.

An American call option on IBM stock might be issued on July 1, 2005, with an expiration date of December 31, 2005. Assume that on July 1, 2005 IBM's stock is trading for $100, and that the exercise price in the option is $100. This option has value if there is some probability that IBM's stock price will exceed $100 in the next six months. If IBM's stock price rises above $100 before the expiration date, the option is said to be *in the money*. The option is *out of the money* at any time the exercise price is higher than the stock price—that is, no one would exercise the option under these conditions. But it is important to remember that an option will still have a positive value if there is *any* chance that the stock will rise above $100 in the remaining portion of the life of the option.

i.   LONG POSITIONS IN CALL OPTIONS

Just as with stock, someone who purchases a call option is said to have a long position in the option. Why would anyone buy an option under these conditions? Note that the option-holder has no obligation to purchase the shares; she can simply *walk away* from the option if the stock price remains below the exercise price up to and including the expiration date. But the option holder has made a bet about IBM's stock price at the time of purchase of the option—that there is some probability that it will rise significantly. The option holder could have made the same bet by purchasing IBM stock at its current price of $100, of course, but the buyer incurs two costs not incurred by the option holder.

First, the buyer of stock bears the risk that its price will decline, rather than increase. In that case, the entire $100 purchase price would be at risk, rather than just the option price. Second, the buyer has to commit a much greater amount of capital to buy IBM shares than to buy an option on them. The option holder does risk the amount invested to purchase the call option, because the value of the option contract goes to zero if the stock price never rises above the exercise price by the expiration date, and the expires without exercise.

Options are settled by delivery. A call option is settled by tendering the exercise (strike) price and receiving the underlying security, but brokerage costs may be avoided by settling up, where the option writer simply delivers the holder's profit in cash (the stock price less the exercise price).

The payoff from a call option on its expiration date is a function of the stock price and the exercise price. Simply, if the exercise price is $100, and the value of the stock is less than $100, the option is worthless, while if the

---

* Zvi Bodie & Robert C. Merton, Finance, 385 (Upper Saddle River, N.J.: Prentice Hall, 2000).

stock price is greater than $100, the option is worth the stock price minus the exercise price. We can show this in the following chart:

Call Option Payoff on Expiration Date

Contingent States:	If stock price < $100	If stock price > $100
Call Option Value:	0	Stock price − $100

Notice that there is no upper limit to the potential value of a call option at maturity; no matter how high the price of the underlying stock rises, the strike value of the option rises accordingly. Sometimes the value of an option is expressed as if it were expiring immediately. Assume, in our example, that IBM stock is trading at $105 and the call option is exercisable at $100. The *"intrinsic value"* of the option, sometimes also called the *"intangible value"* is $5.00. If the option has a significant period of time left before its actual maturity, it should trade above the difference between exercise price and intrinsic value. This is because there remains some probability of a further increase in the value of IBM stock before maturity. The difference between intrinsic value and market value is called the option's *"time value."* An American option's time value is higher than that of a European option, if the option has a significant period of time to run, because it can be exercised at any time, rather than exclusively on the expiration date.

We now introduce a position diagram that shows the value of an option on the expiration date (a European option), which we use for simplification. The vertical axis represents the value of the option at maturity, in the dollars the investor will gain from exercise on that date. The horizontal axis represents the stock's price on the same date. The bold line represents the value of the option at various stock prices. Note that once the stock price reaches and exceeds the exercise price, the strike value of the option rises with the value of the stock on a dollar-for-dollar basis. Using the example given above, Figure 8–3 represents this relationship:

Figure 8–3   Value of Call Option at Expiration

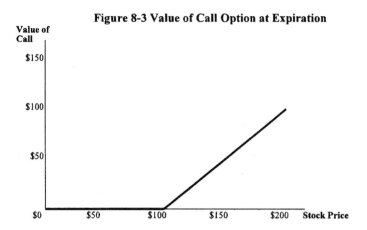

Figure 8-3 Value of Call Option at Expiration

The buyer of an option runs the risk that the option will be worthless at the expiration date. This defines the extent of the buyer's risk of loss. In the event of exercise, the buyer's gain potential is finite in the case of a put option. In the case of a call option, the buyer's potential gain is infinite. Regardless of how high the value of the underlying asset climbs, the buyer can obtain it for the exercise price. Thus, in Figure 8–3 there is no upper bound on the diagonal line. The advantage of a call option for a speculator who is confident that the underlying asset's price will rise is similar to leverage: the call option buyer can capture the potential gain on a larger number of underlying IBM shares, for example, by buying options rather than the stock itself. This is similar to borrowing to buy the shares. Of course, buying a large number of options increases the risk that one will lose all of the money invested. While the stock itself is unlikely to fall to a zero price, it is much more likely not to rise sufficiently to give the call option value at the exercise date.

ii.   SHORT POSITIONS IN CALL OPTIONS

For every buyer of a call option (long), there is someone who has written the option, and thus has taken a short position, by receiving the proceeds of the initial price of the call option and bearing the risk of having to deliver the stock (or the value of the option on exercise) if its price rises. The investor who writes a call option may hold IBM stock, and might believe that it is a good long-term investment, but that, for some reason, he does not expect the stock to do so well in the short run. Indeed, the investor might even believe IBM's stock price will decline over the next six months. The investor could, of course, sell IBM stock now with an intent to repurchase it in the future. But the investor will incur two sets of transaction costs—both selling and buying IBM stock. In addition to brokerage costs, some investors may incur tax costs as well. But our gloomy investor can hold the IBM stock and write a call option on it, and sell the call option. The option price represents a profit on the IBM stock, if it is not exercised. In short, our call option writer profits from the option if IBM stock declines or does not rise (above $100). Thus our option writer has hedged the risk of a decline in IBM stock. At the same time, the call option writer has foregone some of the gain if the stock price rises above $100 during the life of the option (although the writer can purchase more IBM shares at any time).

It is not necessary to be an IBM stockholder to write a call option; other investors holding the same expectations about the short term can write call options as well. (We include a discussion of "covered options," in which the writer owns the stock, later in this chapter.) Now we can diagram the position of a writer of a call option, in Figure 8–4:

Figure 8-4   Value of Position of Writer of Call Option at Expiration

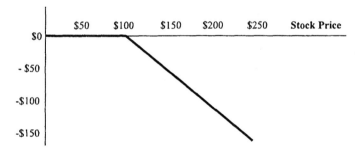

You will notice the reciprocal relationship between figures 8–3 and 8–4. This is because options represent a zero-sum game, standing alone: whatever one side gains, the counter-party loses. Note that there is no upper bound to the potential losses for the call option writer: the higher the stock price, the greater the losses of the call option writer. For most investors who are risk averse, options are only attractive when they provide an offset, or hedge, against some other risk the investor must accept.

What would cause the call option writer to undertake the risk shown? Only an initial payment for the option sufficient to compensate for the risk. We will leave the more difficult question of how to value a call option before the expiration date for a later point in this Chapter.

B. Put Options

A put option is the opposite of a call option. A put option gives the holder the right to sell (put) the underlying asset to the writer of the option at a previously specified price. In our previous example, if our IBM stockholder fears a decline in IBM's stock price, she can hedge that risk by buying an option giving her the right to sell IBM stock for $100 at any time up to and including the expiration date (once again, a European Option). Thus, if IBM stock turns out to be worth $50 at maturity, the payoff from holding the put option is $50; if IBM stock turns out to be worthless, the maximum value of the option is $100. In both cases the option should be exercised. If the price of IBM stock is at $100 or more, it should not be exercised. In this case, the relationship between the strike value of the put option and the value of the common stock is inverse; for every dollar that IBM stock falls below $100 on the expiration date; the value of the put option increases by the same amount. The value of the put option can be expressed as:

Value of Put Option = Exercise Price - Market Price of Stock

The value of the put option can never be less than zero.

This relationship is illustrated in Figure 8–5:

Figure 8-5 Value of Put Option to Holder at Expiration

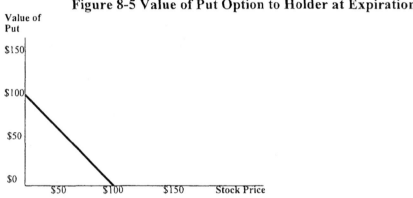

Quick Check Question 8.1

Using long and short positions in the other financial instruments, can you synthesize the position of the writer of a put option, to achieve the position shown in Figure 8–5? Keep in mind that some instruments have unlimited upsides and downsides, while the put option is confined to the space shown.

The reciprocal is the position of the seller (writer) of a put option, who has the obligation to buy the stock at the stated price ($100, in our examples). Figure 8–6 illustrates the value of a put option at various stock prices to the writer:

Figure 8–6   Value of Position of Writer of Put Option at Expiration

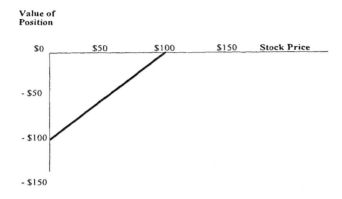

Summary: Option Outcomes at Expiration

Value of Underlying Stock	Winners	Losers
High (relative to exercise price)	Call Holder Put Writer	Call Writer Put Holder
Low (relative to exercise price)	Call Writer Put Holder	Call Holder Put Writer

C.   Combining Options, Stocks and Bonds; Put-Call Parity

Now we can proceed to combine stock ownership with various option contracts to create more complex positions for investors. You will see how various positions in financial instruments become substitutes for others. Assume, for example, that our IBM investor decides to buy IBM stock at today's price of $100. Assume also that she does this because she believes the long-term value of IBM stock will be much higher, perhaps $150. But she is concerned about the short run: she fears that the stock may fall below $100 in the next few months. Under these circumstances she can buy a put option on IBM stock with a $100 exercise price. Under these circumstances, she can sell the stock for $100 if the price falls, or hold it and lose the purchase price of the option if the stock rises. In effect, she has bought insurance against a price decline. The range of possible outcomes for her at the expiration date is shown in Figure 8–7:

Figure 8–7   Value of Stock Plus Put Option at Expiration

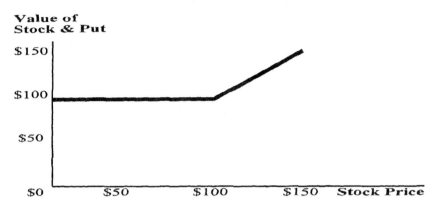

You will now observe that this figure is identical to Figure 8–3, the value of the call option, with the bold line moved upward along the vertical axis by $100, representing the original value of the stock. In this case, our investor's position is protected from loss, because she has sold a put option enabling her to obtain $100 cash if the stock price declines. (We have ignored the original price of the put option in this analysis.)

Now suppose our stockholder buys a put option at $100 and sells a call option at $100, with both being European options exercisable on the expiration date in one year. In this situation, her investment becomes the equivalent of a zero coupon bond,* with absolute certainty about her returns and the value of her investment at the expiration of the options.

Another way to see this with a chart. Suppose the exercise price of a call option and a put option are both $100, and they are European options, that can only be exercised on the expiration date, which occurs in one year. Assume in one year the stock price will be either $50 or $150. If you buy the stock now at $100, here are your choices:

Strategies on Expiration Date of European Option

Stock Price Rises to $150		*Stock Price Falls to $50*	
You let put expire.	0	Call expires	0
Call is exercised against you,		You exercise put,	
obligating you to sell your		selling the stock you own	
stock, to receive exercise		at the exercise	
price of	$100	price of	$100
TOTAL	$100		$100

---

* A zero coupon bond pays a stated principal obligation at maturity. Its current value is represented by its discounted present value, using the appropriate discount rate. (See Chapter Three, Table 3–4.)

This is illustrated in Figure 8–8:

Figure 8–8   Value of Stock Plus Holding Put and Call Options

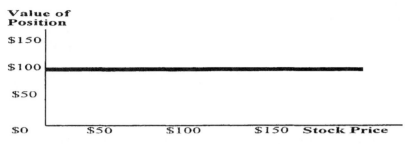

Whether the stock rises or falls, the investor's position is the same as holding a zero coupon bond. In either case, the investor expects to earn the risk-free rate of return, because the investment in both cases is riskless. By the Law of One Price, we know that the investor can earn no more than if she held a risk-free bond. This can be expressed as follows:

$$Stock\ Price + Price\ of\ Put = \frac{Exercise\ Price}{(1 + risk\text{-}free\ rate)^{Maturity\ of\ Option}} + Price\ of\ Call$$

This assumes that the costs of purchasing a call option and selling a put option are sufficient to wipe out any gains in excess of the risk-free rate. If they were not, arbitrage would occur until their prices were equivalent. This is another way of saying the values of a put and a call with the same exercise date and the same expiration date are precisely related to each other. This result is called *put-call parity*.*

The put-call parity theorem begins with four types of financial instruments: (1) a riskless zero-coupon bond, (2) a share of stock, (3) a call option on the stock, and (4) a put option on the stock. All can either be bought (long) or sold (shorted). The put-call parity theorem then states that with any three of these instruments, the fourth instrument can be replicated. We have illustrated the first example in Figure 8–8. We now illustrate how you can create a synthetic share of stock, using our previous assumptions. Assume you have $100 cash to invest. You can place it in a stock currently trading at $100, or in a bank deposit at the risk-free rate and deal in the following options. In this case we sell a put option on the common stock at its current price of $100, and buy a call option on the stock at $100. Using our previous assumptions that the stock may either fall to $50 or rise to $150 on the expiration date in one year, here are the results:

---

* For a formal proof of this, see Michael S. Knoll, Put–Call Parity and the Law, 24 Cardozo L. Rev. 61 (2002).

Strategies on Expiration Date of European Option

Stock Price Rises to $150		*Stock Price Falls to $50*	
Starting Cash	$100	Starting Cash	$100
You let put expire	0	You let call expire	0
You exercise call option at $100	($100)	You buy stock @$100 on exercise of put against you	($100)
Value of stock purchased	$150	Value of stock purchased	$50
TOTAL	$150	TOTAL	$50

If you had invested the $100 in a risk-free bond, you would have earned the risk-free rate of return during the year. In addition you would have had the net proceeds of selling the put option and buying the call option, which we will discuss later. Figure 8–9 illustrates this strategy:

Figure 8–9   Writing a Put and Buying a Call Option

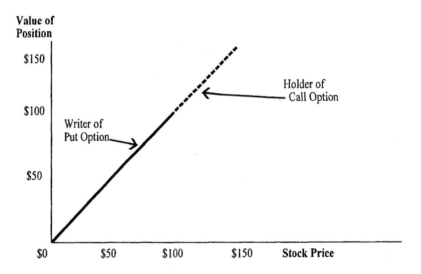

The observation to be drawn from put-call parity is that financial transactions can be broken down into components, and that no matter what we call them, the same cash flows must have the same price (the Law of One Price). There are six basic synthetic positions relating to the combination of put options, call options and their underlying stock:

1. Synthetic Long Stock = Long Call + Short Put
2. Synthetic Short Stock = Short Call + Long Put
3. Synthetic Long Call = Long Stock + Short Put
4. Synthetic Short Call = Short Stock + Short Put
5. Synthetic Short Put = Short Call + Long Stock
6. Synthetic Long Put = Long Call + Short Stock

In order for these relationships to work, all options used together must be of the same expiration, strike price and represent the same amount of shares used in combination.

Quick Check Question 8.2

How can you replicate a call option on the stock? Our investor can borrow $100 in cash (the equivalent of selling a zero coupon bond short), and buy a European call option to purchase IBM stock at $100. If the stock rises above $100, the investor exercises the option using the borrowed funds. If the stock falls below $100, the investor lets the call option expire and repays the loan with the borrowed $100 (ignoring interest for the moment). Can you demonstrate this in a payoff matrix? Can you diagram it?

D. USES OF OPTIONS

Brane v. Roth

590 N.E.2d 587 (Ind. App. 1992).

■ RATLIFF, C.J.

STATEMENT OF THE CASE

Paul H. Brane, Kenneth Richison, Ralph Dawes, and John Thompson (collectively "directors") appeal the award of $424,038.89 plus interest for Porter Roth, et al. (collectively "shareholders"), in an action against them as directors of the LaFontaine Grain Co-op ("Co-op"). We affirm.

* * *

This case involves a shareholders' action against the directors of a rural grain elevator cooperative for losses Co-op suffered in 1980 due to the directors' failure to protect its position by adequately hedging in the grain market. Paul Brane, Kenneth Richison, Ralph Dawes, and John Thompson were directors of Co-op in 1980. Eldon Richison was Co-op's manager that year who handled the buying and selling of grain. Approximately ninety percent of Co-op's business was buying and selling grain. The directors met on a monthly basis reviewing the manager's general report and financial reports prepared by Virginia Daihl, Co-op's bookkeeper. The directors also discussed maintenance and improvement matters and authorized loan transactions for Co-op. Requests for additional information on the reports were rare. The directors did not make any specific inquiry as to losses sustained in 1980.

The records show that Co-op's gross profit had fallen continually from 1977. After a substantial loss in 1979, Co-op's CPA, Michael Matchette, recommended that the directors hedge Co-op's grain position to protect itself from future losses. The directors authorized the manager to hedge for Co-op. Only a minimal amount was hedged, specifically $20,050 in hedging contracts were made, whereas Co-op had $7,300,000 in grain sales.

On February 3, 1981, Matchette presented the 1980 financial statement to the directors, indicating a net profit of only $68,684. In 1982, Matchette informed the directors of errors in his 1980 financial statement and that Co-op had actually experienced a gross loss of $227,329. * * * The directors consulted another accounting firm to review the financial condition of Co-op. CPA Rex E. Coulter found additional errors in Matchette's 1980 financial statement, which increased the gross loss to $424,038. * * * Coulter opined that the primary cause of the gross loss was the failure to hedge.

The court entered specific findings and conclusions determining that the directors breached their duties by retaining a manager inexperienced in hedging; failing to maintain reasonable supervision over him; and failing to attain knowledge of the basic fundamentals of hedging to be able to direct the hedging activities and supervise the manager properly; and that their gross inattention and failure to protect the grain profits caused the resultant loss of $424,038.89. The court ordered prejudgment interest of 8% from December 31, 1980 to the judgment date.

DISCUSSION AND DECISION

* * *

[W]e find that there was probative evidence that Co-op's losses were due to a failure to hedge. Coulter testified that grain elevators should engage in hedging to protect the co-op from losses from price swings. One expert in the grain elevator business and hedging testified that co-ops should not speculate and that Co-op's losses stemmed from the failure to hedge.

Further evidence in the record supports the court's findings and its conclusions that the directors breached their duty by their failure to supervise the manager and become aware of the essentials of hedging to be able to monitor the business which was a proximate cause of Co-op's losses. Although the directors argue that they relied upon their manager and should be insulated from liability, the business judgment rule protects directors from liability only if their decisions were informed ones.

In W & W Equipment Co. v. Mink (1991), Ind. App., 568 N.E.2d 564, trans. denied, we stated that "a director cannot blindly take action and later avoid the consequences by saying he was not aware of the effect of the action he took. A director has some duty to become informed about the actions he is about to undertake." Id. at 575 (citation omitted). Here, the evidence shows that the directors made no meaningful attempts to be informed of the hedging activities and their effects upon Co-op's financial position. Their failure to provide adequate supervision of the manager's actions was a breach of their duty of care to protect Co-op's interests in a reasonable manner. The business judgment rule does not shield the directors from liability.

* * *

Affirmed.

_____

The following article appeared in the Wall Street Journal on October 8, 2002, p. D–1, after a long decline in stock prices.

Who Says You Can't Make Money Off Stalled Stocks? More Investors Use Options, Trading Upside for Steady Gains

By Jeff D. Opdyke.

Victor Schiller is generating steady income off a stock portfolio ravaged by the bear market.

His trick: Writing covered-call options contracts*

Options—which give investors the right to buy or sell stocks at a certain price by a specific date—are generally thought of as complex tools for the pros. But covered-call options are regularly used by individual investors and are much less risky than more exotic option strategies, which can subject you to huge losses. Covered calls work best in a sour market, not unlike today's.

In Mr. Schiller's case, the Culpeper, Va. investor sells contracts that give other investors the right to purchase his shares at a set price. In return, Mr. Schiller is paid anywhere between 20 cents and a couple of dollars a share. If the stock goes down, Mr. Schiller keeps the payment. If it goes up sharply—something that hasn't happened much this year, he makes less profit on the stock than he would have if he hadn't sold the calls.

Covered calls have been around for years, but they're gaining popularity amid a down market. At OtpionsXpress, the largest online options-trading firm, 37% of customers are using a covered-call strategy these days, up from 12% a year ago. Big financial institutions like J.P. Morgan Chase and Merrill Lynch also report a surge in covered calls from both institutional and individual investors. "Since the market decline in 2000, [this technique] has become much more popular," says Heiko Ebens, derivatives strategist at Merrill Lynch.

The increased popularity of covered calls underscores how the bear market has transformed options trading. During the tech boom, investors

_____

* A "covered call option" is a call option written by someone who actually owns the stock subject to the call. A "naked call option" is written by someone who does not own the stock, but is prepared to "cover" the call by buying the stock, or settling up with the holder.—Ed.

often traded options instead of actual shares, gaining control of more shares for the same dollars—to supercharge their profits as stocks surged. Nowadays, many of the speculators are gone, and investors are using options to generate income, protect their portfolio and lower the volatility of the stocks they do own.

You can trade options either through brokers or online. Commissions can be as low as $15 a trade at discount brokers.

Here's how covered calls work: Suppose you own 500 shares of Wal–Mart Stores stock, recently in the $50 range. You can sell December contracts that give other investors the right to buy the 500 shares from you at $55 a share on or before Dec. 20. Those contracts were recently selling for $1.70 per share, meaning your 500 shares would have brought in an $850 premium.

Comes Dec. 20, one of two outcomes unfolds. If the stock remains below $55, the options contracts expire worthless, since the buyer who owns them has no interest in paying $55 for stock that is worth less. So, you keep the $850 and you keep the stock.

If Wal–Mart shares move to, say, $60 a share, the options buyers will exercise their rights to buy the stock at $55 a share. You probably lose the stock, but you keep the $850 from writing the contracts as well as $2,500 profits from the stock's $5–per-share move to $55 from $50.

"You're basically owning a stock and generating a return that can be greater than bond yields," says Steven Silverman, senior vice president at Connors Investor Services, a money-management firm specializing in covered-call-options investing in Wyomissing, Pa. Some of the firm's clients, Mr. Silverman notes, "are living off the options income we generate every month in their account. It's a very attractive alternative in a low-interest-rate environment."

Of course, there's a big downside to covered calls. By selling a Wal–Mart call, you risk having to sell the shares if the option is exercised, thereby triggering a tax hit. Even more important, you limit your potential upside. If Wal–Mart moves to, say $70, you still must sell at $55, forsaking much larger profits.

What's more, writing covered calls isn't a hedge against a stock tanking. Carmelo Montalbano, a Washington, D.C. investor who has been writing such calls for years, last month bought shares of power company Calpine. At the same time he sold calls. But the stock collapsed. He got to keep the premium from selling the calls, but the share-price loss erased that gain. Now he's holding a stock price at $2.11 a share, too low to bother selling calls.

Not everyone is a fan of writing covered calls. "The problem is you take away your upside and you don't protect your downside," says Ross Levin, a financial planner in Minneapolis. Even proponents of the options say they aren't for every market and every stock. Volatile stocks tend to bring in the highest premiums. But there's a greater chance their shares will move substantially higher, and most of the profits will go to the options buyer.

———

There are many other uses for options. We have discussed some of them in the beginning section of this chapter. The existence of preemptive rights in a close corporation is the creation of call options for the existing shareholders. Because preemptive rights slow down the process of raising capital for public companies, by requiring the corporation to wait to see how many rights will be exercised, preemptive rights are almost never used by public corporations. Stock options have formed a major part of the compensation of many corporate executives, in effect giving them the rewards of a call option without investing in the stock. Corporations looking to enter into joint ventures, often with smaller companies, may finance their participation through exercise of a series of options, which allow them to evaluate the progress of the enterprise at each stage before investing additional funds.

Venture capitalists investing in convertible preferred stock use options in a variety of ways. First, they invest less than the full amount needed by a start-up, giving them an option to continue to invest more only if the project shows signs of success. Second, they receive the option to convert their preferred shares into common stock of the company at any time. Third, they give the company the power to force conversion (they sell a put) when the company makes its initial public offering of common stock. Fourth, in the event they wish to sell the company, they often obtain the right to force minority shareholders to sell with them ("drag-along rights"). Finally, in the event the founders or other venture capitalists agree to sell their shares to a third party, they often obtain the right to sell their shares to the buyer on the same terms ("tag-along rights").

Recall that in Chapter Two we discussed stating earnings per share on a fully diluted basis. Options issued by the company (warrants) have the effect of assuring that more shares will be issued if the value of the stock rises. They also have the effect of assuring some dilution of the value of existing shareholders' investment at the time of exercise, since options will only be exercised if the market price exceeds the exercise price.

Even options written by traders (whether covered or not) will have some impact on the stock's price. The Law of One Price, and Put–Call Parity mean that the value of a synthetic share (see Figure 8–9 above) cannot diverge from the value of an actual share.

Problem

Your client is a minority stockholder in a business engaged in fishing for Menhaden, a herring-like fish used for its protein in fish and animal feed. Like the Biblical tale, fishing for Menhaden is a story of feast and famine. There are years, sometimes several in a row, when

Menhaden simply cannot be located in the ocean in commercial numbers. Then suddenly they reappear in huge quantities. Under normal circumstances prices would rise when Menhaden are scarce, and decline when they are plentiful. But the story is more complicated: soybeans are a close substitute for Menhaden, so that when soybeans are plentiful, that places downward pressure on Menhaden prices, regardless of their availability. The majority shareholder has guaranteed bank loans for the corporation, which is presently insolvent, standing on its own. The majority shareholder is prepared to guarantee further loans for the company, but is upset by your client's unwillingness to join in the guarantees. As a result, the majority shareholder has taken action to freeze your client out of the business, through a reverse stock split, in which all fractional shares (your client's) would be repurchased at their "fair value." Unfortunately, the majority shareholder has obtained an appraisal that suggests the fair value of the shares is zero, because liabilities exceed assets, and there is little or no salvage value for the fishing fleet, given the lack of Menhaden currently being caught. What alternative argument can you make about value?

3. VALUATION OF OPTIONS

The prices of options formerly were quoted daily in THE WALL STREET JOURNAL. Today one must use a web page to view option prices. Yahoo! Finance contains such quotes. Here are quotes for six separate call options of IBM stock, viewed on January 29, 2010, when the price of IBM Stock was $122.39. (The stock price changed constantly when the author clicked between months.)* This chart is a composite of several pages. There are a few pricing anomalies on the tails of some results, probably explained by the small amount of trading activity in these options.

---

* http://finance.yahoo.com/q/ops?s=IBM & m=2010 (last visited Jan. 29, 2010, at approximately 4:00 p.m.).

Table 8-1	Quotations on IBM Call Options					
View by Expiration:						
	Feb. 10	Mar. 10	April 10	Jul. 10	Jan. 11	Jan. 12
Strike	Last	Last	Last	Last	Last	Last
65.00			61.45		63.40	
70.00			57.50	57.05	60.00	
75.00						
80.00			46.73	51.40	44.50	
85.00			44.60	46.45	42.75	42.70
90.00	35.78		41.25	33.40	33.15	38.72
95.00	36.20	31.45	27.90	29.34	30.25	34.70
100.00	22.00	24.00	23.69	23.60	25.00	28.50
105.00	17.69	17.80	19.60	19.25	21.35	
110.00	12.70	12.58	13.85	15.50	17.99	21.65
115.00	7.60	8.65	10.10	11.90	14.70	
120.00	3.65	5.30	6.30	8.50	11.40	16.30
125.00	1.20	2.75	3.70	6.20	9.16	
130.00	0.29	1.16	2.01	4.20	7.40	11.50
135.00	0.10	0.40	0.90	2.65	5.29	
140.00	0.04	0.12	0.38	1.69	4.05	8.25
145.00	0.02	0.07	0.14	0.95	2.81	
150.00	0.02		0.06	0.51	1.95	5.50
155.00			0.05	0.34	1.51	
160.00			0.03	0.19	0.98	3.80
165.00			0.01	0.10	0.75	
170.00			0.13	0.15	0.51	2.12
175.00			0.08	0.11	0.30	
180.00				0.05	0.21	1.38

Now we turn to the theory that explains how these option values are determined. We have previously discussed the value of options at the expiration date. We did this primarily in the context of options with a relatively short life that are traded on organized exchanges. But options may have much longer durations, as in the case of convertible securities or options issued to corporate managers to motivate them to think like stockholders. The previous section described some uses of options and the prices (premiums) obtained by option writers. Now we must formalize the model of option pricing.

What we struggled to learn about discounted cash flow methods of valuation in Chapter Three just won't work here. There are several reasons. First, finding the opportunity cost of capital is impossible, because the risk of an option changes every time the price of the stock changes. Second, when you buy a call option, you're taking a position in the stock, but using less money. As a result the option is riskier than the underlying stock, with a higher beta. The result is that the expected rate of return investors expect varies constantly, as the stock price changes.

In this part we will focus on call options, because thinking about the valuation of put options becomes relatively easy once we have done the heavy lifting of call option valuation. There are six factors that enter into option pricing.

i. *Exercise Price.* It should be obvious that, all other things being equal (*ceteris paribus*), the higher the exercise price in relation to the market price of the underlying stock, the lower the value of a call option. Thus, using our previous example, if IBM stock is trading at $122, a short-term call option with an exercise price of $180 isn't likely to have any real value. On the other hand, if today's stock price of $122 for IBM is set in an efficient market, and the exercise price on the call option is $122, there is roughly a 50–50 chance that the price will rise above the exercise price, or fall below it. Since the holder of a call option can just let the option expire if IBM's price doesn't exceed $122, there is no down side (except the loss of the option price). Thus, the option will have a positive value.

ii. *Stock Price.* Other things being equal, the higher the stock price relative to the exercise price, the more valuable the call option will be. As you will see, this relationship holds even when the stock price is below the exercise price ("out of the money" or "under water"), because of the probability that it will rise above the exercise price. Where the exercise price is equal to the current market price, the option has value because of the 50% probability that the stock price will rise during the remainder of the option's life. Once the stock prices rises above the exercise price, the excess of the stock price over the exercise price represents the minimum value of an option. That is, if IBM's stock price rises to $132, the value of a $120 call option cannot be significantly less than $12. If it were, investors would rush to buy these options and bid up the price of an option until it reached at least $12. This is a simple arbitrage move by investors. Thus, if one can buy a $120 call option at $9 and exercise at $120, one has an immediate $3 profit. If you return to Table 8–1, you will see this, with a small exception: On January 29, 2010, the price of a call option exercisable at $120 expiring in February was $3.65, while the difference between the exercise price and the market price was $2.39. This difference must be explained by the month remaining in which to exercise, when the stock could rise in price (it was $126.46 on February 23, 2010).

We have already seen a position diagram showing the value of a European call at its expiration date in Figure 8–3. The valuation of an American call, exercisable at any time up to expiration, is a bit more complicated. Keep in mind that the intrinsic value, the amount by which the market price presently exceeds the exercise price, represented by the heavy diagonal line in Figure 8–10, is the minimum value of an American call. The maximum value of a call is always the price of the stock, represented by the light diagonal line arising from a zero price. That is, even if the exercise price were zero (free shares), no one would pay more for the call option than for the shares themselves. Finally, the value of an American call falls somewhere in between these two lines, represented by the broken line in Figure 8–10. The line is curved, unlike any line we have observed before. This represents an important fact about American calls: their value increases as the stock price rises, and the increase in the call's value is greater at high stock prices than at low stock prices. As the stock price rises, the option value approaches the stock price, less the present value of the exercise price. This is because at sufficiently high stock prices, exercise becomes virtually certain.

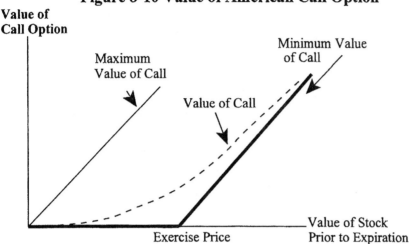

Figure 8-10 Value of American Call Option

iii. *Expiration Date.* The longer the life of the option, the greater its value, all other things being equal. Table 8–1 demonstrates this for options at all prices, ranging from $65 to $180. Each option at a particular exercise price has identical rights, except some last longer than others, thus increasing the chance that IBM's stock price will rise above the exercise price. Thus $115 IBM call options are priced at $7.60 for February, $8.65 for March, and $14.70 for January 2011. Figure 8–10 illustrates that the higher the stock price the closer the option value moves to the stock price, because the option's exercise price is discounted to present value. This illustrates that the longer the life of the option, the greater the convergence of option and stock prices.

iv. *Variance of the Underlying Stock's Value.* This is the most important factor in determining option values. Simply put, the greater the variance in the value of the underlying asset, the more valuable the call option will be. Using our previous example of IBM stock, suppose that, one year from now there is a 50% chance that "Stock A" will be worth $90 and a 50% chance it will be worth $110. If the strike price is $110, the call option will have no value, because there is no way the stock price will exceed the strike price. The expected value of the stock is:

(.5 × $90) + (.5 × $110) = $45 + $55 = $100

Now let's introduce greater variance into our expectations for the stock, and call it "Stock B." We will subtract $20 from the low end and add

$20 to the high end, so the stock will be worth either $70 or $130. Now there is some chance the call option will be in the money, so it will have a positive value. But note that the "expected value" (the weighted value of probable outcomes) hasn't changed:

$$(.5 \times \$70) + (.5 \times \$130) = \$35 + \$65 = \$100$$

Table 8–2 illustrates this:

Table 8–2   Expected Values of Stock

Value					Expected Value	
Stock A	Stock B	×	Probability	=	Stock A	Stock B
$90			0.5		$45	
$110			0.5		$55	
	$70		0.5			$35
	$130		0.5			$65
					$100	$100

What has changed, of course, is our old friend from Chapter Three, Part 3, variance, and the corresponding standard deviation. Figure 8–11, below, also illustrates this relationship:

Figure 8-11   **Payoffs from Options on Stocks A and B**

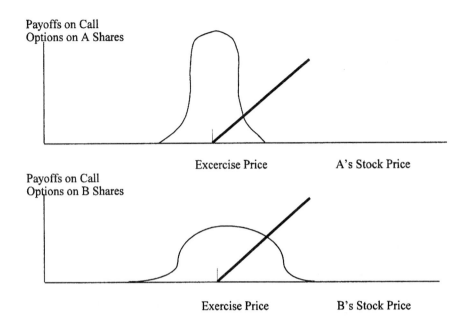

Once again, the heavy line represents option payoffs at various stock prices. The odds that B's price will rise above the exercise price are considerably greater than for A. You can see that while stocks A and B have the same expected values, stock B has a much greater probability of having its call option be in the money. While stockholders may wish to avoid variance, because it increases the chances of big losses, to a call option holder, variance is good. For a call option holder there is no difference between a price a little bit below the exercise price and a large amount below the exercise price. In either event, the option is worthless. You can now see why the expiration date becomes important—it generally increases the expected variance of stock price as the time period lengthens.

v. *Interest Rate.* An option that is in the money represents the chance to make a delayed payment for a valuable stock. Would you rather buy IBM stock now and hold it, or have the opportunity to buy it later at today's price, if it increases in value? Thus the value of the option is partially related to how much interest you can earn on your money investing it somewhere else during the life of the option. The higher current interest rates, the more valuable the call option. (But you may be missing out on IBM dividends, which would offset some of the interest benefits.) Thus, as always, paying later is better than paying earlier for an asset, if you wind up with the same value. This means that the higher the applicable interest rate, the greater the value of the option.

vi. *Dividend Rate.* The other side of delaying a purchase is that the call option holder foregoes the dividends that would have been received had the option holder simply bought the stock outright. Thus an increase in the dividend results in a decrease in the price of a call option.

In summary, the value of a call option is a function of the following:

i.   The current price of the underlying asset (the price of stock, in the case of stock options);
ii. The exercise price;
iii. The time to the expiration date;
iv. The variance of the price of the underlying asset;
v.   The risk-free interest rate; and
vi. The dividend rate.

All of these factors enter into the famous Black–Scholes option pricing model. This is not the place for a technical explanation of the Black–Scholes option pricing model. It was developed using mathematical techniques from disciplines as remote (and difficult) as physics and rocket science.* But fear not: there are numerous sites with calculators using the Black–Scholes model some of which are listed below. A caution: many of these calculators eliminate the dividend rate. This model calculates option values as if they were European options.

Chicago Board Options Exchange:

http://www.cboe.com/LearnCenter/Software.aspx

Professor Campbell R. Harvey, Fuqua School of Business, Duke University:

http://www.duke.edu/?charvey/applets/PriceDynamics/test.html

Numa Financial Systems:

http://numa.com/derivs/ref/calculat/option/calc-opa.htm

Economic Research Institute:

http://www.erieri.com/scripts23/blackscholes/blackscholes.exe/main

Biobek AB:

http://www.blobek.com/black-scholes.html

TradingToday.com:

http://www.tradingtoday.com/black-scholes

We now move from a qualitative description of option pricing toward a quantitative method. The put-call parity relation allows us to express the price of a call option in terms of the price of the underlying stock and the risk-free interest rate.

We offer a simplified model involving only two periods which illustrates some of the principles involved.

---

* Thomas A. Smith, Real Options and Takeovers, 52 Emory L. J. 1815, 1817 (2003) (citing Peter L. Bernstein, AGAINST THE GODS: THE REMARKABLE STORY OF RISK 305–12 (1996)).

The option price is money with an opportunity cost. The best way to see this is to compare two investments.

Assume IBM's stock is currently trading at	$100
IBM offers a 1–year call option to buy its stock at	$110
The stock can only do 2 things:	
Low price:	$80
High price:	$120
Also assume the interest rate is 10%.	

Alternative 1:

Buy one option:

	Stock price = $80	Stock price = $120
1 option @ $110:	$0	$10

Alternative 2:

Buy one share of stock at its current price of $100 and borrow $72.73 from the bank at 10% interest for one year:

	Stock price = $80	Stock price = $120
1 share of stock	$80	$120
Repayment of loan + interest	–80	–80
Total payoff	0	$40

The payoff from the levered investment ($40) is the same as the payoff from four call options. Therefore, under the Law of One Price, the investments must have the same value.

Thus: value of 4 calls = current value of share − $72.73 bank loan

Thus: value of 4 calls = $100 − 72.73 = $27.27

And value of 1 call = $6.82

The number of shares needed to replicate one call option is often called the *hedge ratio* or the *option delta*. In our IBM example four calls are replicated by a levered position on one share. The option delta is therefore ¼. We can express this as an equation:

$$\textit{Option delta} = \frac{\textit{spread of possible option prices}}{\textit{spread of possible share prices}} = \frac{10-0}{120-80} = \frac{10}{40} = \frac{1}{4}$$

Thus, using put-call parity, you have learned that borrowing and buying stock now is the equivalent of buying a call option. We might call this a home-made option. The difficulty with our example is that in truth, IBM stock can have more than two prices one year from now, as illustrated by our bell-shaped curves in Figures 8–12 and 8–13. Recall that as the price of the stock rises, the value of the option also rises. In the real world, there might be changes daily in our expectations about IBM's stock price at the end of the year. Each change in the current price, for example, might lead us to calculate new highs and lows to be expected at the end of the year. This is called the *Binomial Model* of option pricing. Unlike Black–Scholes, it can calculate periodic values for American options. Numerous calculators are available on-line. The Black–Scholes Model manages to capture these possible day-to-day changes in a formula and to duplicate the borrowing strategy at each stage to determine the value of a European call. The complexity of their model, developed with Robert Merton, was such that Scholes and Merton were awarded the 1997 Nobel Prize in Economics (Fisher Black having died). Complex as the formula is, options dealers use a specially programmed calculator or a set of tables to find the value of an option.

4. Disclosure Issues With Options

Prior to 2005 there was considerable debate about whether awards of officer and employee stock options should be reported as a current expense. Until the post-Enron and WorldCom era, the subject was not raised seriously by either the SEC or the accounting profession, although there had been growing criticism of the generosity of grants of options to executives. Beginning in 2002 some corporations announced that they would now treat the grant of options as a current expense. This raised the question of how to value these options. Typically employee stock options are not identical to call options written in trading markets. Frequently all of the options granted do not become immediately exercisable (so they are not pure American options). Further, in most cases all of the options granted will not vest immediately, so that if the executive leaves the corporation, those unvested options are lost. Hence, unvested options must be discounted to present value, and further discounted for the uncertainty of vesting.

One argument made by many corporate managers was that option grants should not be treated as a current expense at all. Harvey Golub, retired chairman and CEO of American Express, made this argument in The Wall Street Journal for August 8, 2002. His argument was that the grant of options costs the corporation nothing—there is no flow of value from the corporation to the executive. "The value inherent in a stock option, when exercised, is value taken from the other shareholders—without that value flowing through the company's books." He then argued that shareholders are adequately informed of the cost of option grants when earnings are reported on a fully diluted basis. Earnings are now spread over a larger number of shares once the exercise of all options are assumed, and "[t]he effect of options is accurately reflected in the EPS number—where it belongs."

The other argument was that there is no accurate way to value these options for financial reporting purposes. This is set out below:

Five Ways of Valuing Options
Of these possible methods, only one results in reliable, tamperproof, financial results

BusinessWeek online, July 29, 2002.

To determine the bottom-line impact of the various methods for valuing options, *BusinessWeek* used a hypothetical grant of 5.3 million options. That's the median number of options granted by 7 S & P 500 companies in 2001, and approximately the number granted by several well-known companies, including Aetna, Walgreen, Scientific–Atlanta, and CVS.

We plotted two different performance scenarios: In one, the stock price increases 15% a year over three years. In the other, it decreases 15% a year. For each scenario, we examined the impact on earnings from using two types of accounting: fixed accounting, which values options on the grant date and expenses them over time regardless of changing stock price and options value, and variable accounting, which values and expenses options every year.*

Black–Scholes

How it works: Uses formula based on dividend yields, volatility, and other factors to estimate option value.

Advantage: Accounts for most factors affecting future option value.

Disadvantage: Doesn't discount for vesting and other restrictions, so it overestimates option value.

Impact on earnings:

If stock increases in value: $66.5 million (fixed), $96.6 million (variable).

If stock decreases in value: $66.5 million (fixed), $31.7 million (variable).

Verdict: Thumbs down. Companies would overpay for underwater options; formula easily manipulated to boost earnings.

Binomial

How it works: Uses Black–Scholes variables, but assumes options will be exercised when optimally profitable.

Advantage: Reflects how options really are exercised.

Disadvantage: If company pays dividends, this model results in bigger hit to earnings than Black–Scholes.

Impact on earnings:

If stock increases in value: $67.3 million (fixed), $97.3 million (variable).

---

* The key to the use of fixed cost accounting for options is that the number of shares to be granted and the exercise price are both known at the time of grant. In that event the grant date becomes the measuring date for determining the cost of options. But where either number of shares or exercise price is not known at the time of grant, the award must be measured at each reporting date, with adjustments for number of shares and exercise price.— Ed.

If stock decreases in value: $67.3 million (fixed), $31.8 million (variable).

Verdict: Thumbs down. No improvement over standard Black–Scholes.

Note: For the purposes of this illustration, *BusinessWeek* assumed the options were granted on June 30, with the exercise price set at a current stock price of $30, and vested in equal installments on the grant date anniversary in 2003, 2004, and 2005. Calculations assume 40% volatility, 1.5% dividend yield, 1.1 beta, 4.5% risk-free rate, and 10.5% market return. Impact on earnings is the cumulative earnings reduction over three years, not adjusted for taxes.

The debate was followed by a FASB revision of its previous "no expense" policy in December of 2004, in FASB Statement No. 123R, that in the future stock options would be expensed at "fair value."* The SEC followed this with adoption of disclosure rules to this effect in 2005.**

FASB Statement No. 123R requires an employer to measure the cost of option awards over the period of service required to earn the award—normally the period required for vesting of the option rights. While the initial measure of the fair value of the award will be at the time of the grant, fair value must be remeasured at each subsequent financial reporting date, as the value of options changes with some of the elements discussed in Section 3, above. Appendix A, which discusses valuation, uses arms' length transactions as the measure of value, with reference to observable market prices of similar instruments, where available. Where these are not available, fair value "shall be estimated by using a valuation technique that ... (b) is based on established principles of financial economic theory and generally applied in that field...." (¶ A8) While the Business Week critique of using Black–Scholes argues that it does not take account of vesting requirements and restrictions on transfers of options, Appendix A, ¶ A9 responds that "... the measurement objective in this Statement is to estimate the fair value at the grant date of the equity instruments that the entity is obligated to issue *when employees have rendered the requisite service and satisfied any other conditions necessary to earn the right to benefit from the instruments.* Therefore, the estimated fair value of the instruments at grant date does not take into account the effect on fair value of vesting conditions and other restrictions that apply only

---

* FASB: Summary of Statement 123 (revised 2004) at http://www.basb.org/st/summary/stsum123r.shtml.

** Press release, U.S. Sec. & Exch. Comm'n, Statement of Chairman Cox Regarding Use of Market Instruments in Valuing Employee Stock Options, SEC Release 2005–129 (Sept. 9, 2005), available at http://www.sec.gov/news/press/2005–129.htm [hereinafter Cox Statement]; See FASB and SEC Guidance on Applying Statement 123R, Defining Issues (KPMG LLP, New York, N.Y.), Sept. 2005, available at http://www.us.kpmg.com/services/content.asp?l1id=30&l2 id=730&cid=1137#92. See also Regulation S–K, Item 402(c)(1)(vi), 17 CFR § 229.402(c)(1)(vi).

during the requisite service period." (Emphasis supplied.) The Statement allows use of a binomial or Black–Scholes model (¶ A13).

How would a company that has recently registered its stock on the public market calculate volatility, when there has not been a market for its stock until the time of registration? Pharmasset, Inc., a pharmaceutical development company, first listed its stock on NASDAQ in April of 2007. Here is the description of its methodology in its Form 10Q dated August 10, 2009:

> ***Stock–Based Compensation—*** The Company accounts for share-based payment(s) in accordance with SFAS No. 123R, *Share-Based Payment* ("SFAS 123R"). SFAS 123R requires companies to recognize stock compensation expense for awards of equity instruments to employees based on grant-date fair value of those awards (with limited exceptions). The Company adopted SFAS 123R on October 1, 2006, using the modified prospective method, which results in recognition of compensation expense for all share-based awards granted or modified after October 1, 2006 as well as all unvested awards outstanding at the date of adoption. Stock options granted to consultants are periodically valued as they vest in accordance with EITF 96–18, *Accounting for Equity Instruments That Are Issued to Other Than Employees for Acquiring, or in Conjunction with Selling, Goods or Services*, using a Black–Scholes option pricing model.
>
> Stock-based compensation expense is included in both research and development expenses and in general and administrative expenses in the statements of operations and comprehensive net (loss) income. Since the Company's stock was not publicly traded prior to April 27, 2007, the expected volatility was calculated for each date of grant prior to having a publicly traded stock based on the "peer method." The Company identified companies that trade publicly within the pharmaceutical industry that have similar SIC codes, employee count and revenues. The Company had chosen the weekly high price volatility for these companies for a period of five years. Effective October 1, 2006 the Company has used the weekly high price for these companies for a period of six years to coordinate with the expected term calculated pursuant to SAB No. 107 ("SAB 107"), relating to share-based payment, issued by the SEC.

NOTE

In some cases large grants of options (Enron and Worldcom) may have caused misbehavior and fraud on the part of top executives, who may want to inflate stock prices in order to profit from option grants. One might also be concerned that options may reward executives who have not performed especially well when overall stock market price levels rise, and an underperforming company's stock rises as well, albeit not as much as the overall market or the stocks of its industry group. Some consultants have developed measures of the value added by management (as opposed to market movements. One such method is the "Economic Value Added" or "EVA" method, which attempts to measure the cost of capital for a firm, and the gains added by management over and above the cost of capital (whether management has successfully undertaken positive net present value projects). See Joel M. Stern, G. Bennett Stewart III and Donald H. Chew, The EVA Financial Management System, 8, No. 2 BANK OF AMERICA JOURNAL OF APPLIED CORPORATE FINANCE 32 (1995). Recent attacks on stock options have suggested that managers be required to retain ownership of all stock acquired through their compensation for the duration of their term with the company, so that they would suffer any adverse long-run effects of short-term management designed to allow them to profit from the exercise and quick sale of the shares obtained through their options.

5.   CONVERTIBLE SECURITIES AND DEAL PROTECTION

Options can be written by any investor or trader. When options are written by issuers, they are often called "warrants." Issuers commonly issue warrants to underwriters in connection with securities offerings, or to lenders as additional consideration for borrowing. Issuers also issue options in the form of conversion rights, when companies issue either corporate debt (convertible debentures or bonds) or convertible preferred stock. The next cases examine the contractual issues involved in such convertibles. These issues fall into two areas: destruction of the option and dilution of the rights represented by the option.

A.   DESTRUCTION OF THE OPTION

There are a number of voluntary corporate actions (leaving aside corporate disasters such as operating losses, defaults and bankruptcy) that can destroy the value of options or conversion rights. Mergers in which the company does not survive cause its common stock to disappear, to be replaced by some other asset, either cash or securities of the surviving corporation. This causes a total destruction of the value of options and conversion rights, absent some contractual protection. Finally, while options have a specified term, the term of conversion rights may be rendered uncertain by the ability of the issuing corporation to call the underlying securities for redemption. This kind of redemption right makes the value of the conversion right relatively uncertain.

John Parkinson v. West End Street Railway Company

173 Mass. 446, 53 N.E. 891 (1899).

■ HOLMES, J.

This is an action to recover damages for a refusal to deliver preferred stock of the defendant road to the holder of certain bonds of the Highland Street Railway, upon demand at maturity. The bonds are not convertible into stock upon their face, but after they were issued the Highland Street

Railway was "authorized" to increase its stock to a million dollars, by St. 1879, c. 151, and by § 2 of the act it was provided that "three hundred thousand dollars of said stock shall be applied to the payment or redemption of" certain bonds, including these, "and the issue of said bonds is hereby legalized and made valid, and the holders thereof may convert them into stock as said bonds mature." The company voted to issue the new stock, but before it had issued the stock appropriated to this set of bonds, it consolidated with the Middlesex Street Railway, under St. 1886, c. 229, the new company being "subject to all the duties, restrictions, and liabilities" to which the old one was subject. The stock for these bonds never was issued. Subsequently this new company was bought up by the defendant corporation, under St. 1887, c. 413, the defendant being subject to "all the duties, restrictions, and liabilities" of the selling company.

* * *

When an option is given to take stock instead of receiving payment of a bond, the contract is not exactly what it was supposed to be in the argument for the plaintiff. Even when embodied in the contract, it imposes no restriction upon the obligor in regard to the issue of new stock, although the issue may be upon such terms as to diminish the value of the right. It leaves the management of the company in accordance with its other interests unhampered. It is simply an option to take stock as the stock may turn out to be when the time for choice arrives. The bondholder does not become a stockholder by his contract in equity any more than at law. So, if the corporation which made the bond finds it for its interest to go out of existence at or before the maturity of the obligation, the option given to the bondholder will not stand in the way. The option gives him merely a spes,* not an undertaking that the corporation will continue for the purpose of making it good. This being so, we are not prepared to admit that, if the corporation should be dissolved at the time fixed for the bondholder's choice, he would be entitled to claim a proportionate share of the assets of the company. We do not decide the question, but we do not think it clear that the contract operates except in the event of the corporation happening to remain a going concern, so that the promise can be fulfilled in a literal sense by the delivery of a certificate of stock.

However this may be, the contract does not prevent the corporation from consolidating with another in such a way as to make performance impossible, any more than it prevents the issue of new stock in such a way as to make performance valueless. Still more clearly is this true when, as here, the right to take stock is created, not by a contract of the company, but by a subsequent act of the Legislature, and is a pure gratuity as between the company and the obligee. The bondholder's right, if he had one, is subject to the condition that the corporation shall not have vanished in such a way that to enforce the option manifestly would run counter to the legislative plan. It is uninstructive to say that the consolidations preserve all obligations. The question is whether this obligation is not of

---

* "Hope" in Latin.—Ed.

such a nature that by its own terms it ceases to operate in the event which has happened. In this case, as in so many others, the general principles involved are reconcilable with either result, and the decision really turns upon the particular facts. * * * A consolidation which makes no arrangement for furnishing stock in the new company, and which ends the existence of the old ones, as a general rule may be presumed to put an end to the right of bondholders to call for stock, not because the law has not machinery for keeping such a right alive, but because, not being bound to do so, it has made dispositions which manifestly take no account of the right.

Perhaps we rather should say, not that the present case is to be decided on the particular facts, but that it is to be decided on the absence of particular facts, such as in the other cases were thought to show that the scheme of union contemplated the plaintiff's demand. Leaving on one side the first consolidation between the Highland and Middlesex roads, the second one, by which the West End bought up the consolidated road and others, was to be effected by exchanging the preferred stock of the West End for the stock of these roads, whereupon the rights and liabilities of the other roads were to be transferred to the West End. Or the preferred stock might be sold for cash for the purchase of the same property, first offering it to the West End stockholders at par, as usual when stock is increased. The preferred stock could be used for no other purposes. The West End was authorized to issue an amount of preferred stock equal to the stock of these roads, and no more. The West End was a stranger to the Highland Street road. The consolidation was under an act applicable to all the Boston roads. * * *

We do not mean to change or qualify the general views expressed in the former cases, but we are driven to the conclusion that in the case at bar there is no indication that the Legislature, when it authorized this consolidation, kept the identity of the Highland Street Railway so far alive under an altered name as to impose on the West End the duty of giving its preferred stock in a different ratio for the Highland Street bonds, when it imposed no such duty upon the West End toward the stockholders of the consolidated road, and expressly limited the uses of the West End preferred stock to purposes of which this was not one. It simply has extinguished the Highland Street Railway in this respect, and that is an act of which the plaintiff cannot complain.

Simons v. Cogan

542 A.2d 785 (Del. Ch. 1987), affirmed, 549 A.2d 300 (Del. 1988).

■ ALLEN, CHANCELLOR.

It has now become firmly fixed in our law that among the duties owed by directors of a Delaware corporation to holders of that corporations' debt instruments, there is no duty of the broad and exacting nature characterized as a fiduciary duty. Unlike shareholders, to whom such duties are owed, holders of debt may turn to documents that exhaustively detail the rights and obligations of the issuer, the trustee under the debt indenture, and of the holders of the securities.

Such documents are typically carefully negotiated at arms-length. In a public offering, the underwriter of the debt, and to some extent the indenture trustee, have an interest in negotiating in that fashion; in a private placement, the purchaser has a similar interest. More importantly, the purchaser of such debt is offered, and voluntarily accepts, a security whose myriad terms are highly specified. Broad and abstract requirements of a "fiduciary" character ordinarily can be expected to have little or no constructive role to play in the governance of such a negotiated, commercial relationship.

Accordingly, it is elementary that rights of bondholders are ordinarily fixed by and determinable from the language of documents that create and regulate the security. In a publicly distributed debenture the notes themselves and a trust indenture serve this function, but other documents such as a note agreement or, in the case of secured bonds, security agreements may be involved. Of course, in some circumstances bondholders may have rights against an issuer that are not expressly created by the indenture or other original documents. Most palpably this is the case where a statute has been violated or when bondholders allege and prove fraud in the inducement of the purchase of the bonds. In addition, the contractual documents creating the debenture and the duties of the issuer may, in narrow circumstances, be held to imply obligations arising from an implied covenant of good faith and fair dealing. See, e.g., Katz v. Oak Industries, Inc., Del. Ch., 508 A.2d 873, (1986) note 7 (1986); Van Gemert v. Boeing Co., 520 F.2d 1373, 1383 (2d Cir.1975) (applying New York law).

This case is a purported class action brought on behalf of the holders of 8–1/8% Convertible Subordinated Debentures of Knoll International, Inc. The complaint seeks various relief against the issuer of these bonds, and, among others, its controlling shareholder. Central to the theories of recovery urged is the contention that the defendants, in the particular circumstances presented, do owe a fiduciary duty to the bondholders[2] and have breached that duty. In addition, as amplified at oral argument, plaintiffs' position is that the facts alleged also state a claim for fraud, and for breach of contract, including a breach of an implied contractual duty of good faith.

Defendants have moved to dismiss the complaint for failure to state a claim upon which relief may be granted. For the reasons set forth below, I conclude that, assuming the well-pleaded factual allegations of the complaint to be true, those facts do not state a legal wrong to the class of bondholders. The pending motion will therefore be granted.

I.

The debentures here involved were issued in 1983 pursuant to a public offering and had an original maturity of twenty years. As issued, they were

---

2. For purposes of this opinion, I use the term "bonds" and "debentures" interchangeably, overlooking for the moment their technical differences relating to whether or not the note is secured.

convertible at the option of the holder into the Company's Class A Common Stock at a rate of one share for each $19.20 principal amount of debentures and were redeemable, at the Company's option, after August 15, 1985, at a stated premium which decreased as the securities matured. The bonds were subordinated and bore interest at 8-1/8%.

The issuer of these convertible debentures, Knoll International, Inc. ("Knoll"), is controlled through a series of subsidiaries by defendant Knoll International Holdings, Inc., which, in turn, is controlled by defendant Marshall S. Cogan. The gist of the complaint is that defendants caused the minority shareholders of Knoll to be eliminated through a two-stage transaction involving a $12 cash tender offer followed by a cash for stock merger at the same price. The merger that culminated this process occurred on January 22, 1987 and left Knoll, the issuer, as the surviving corporation and a wholly-owned subsidiary (indirectly) of Holdings. In connection with that merger, a Supplemental Indenture was executed by the issuer and the indenture trustee providing that, instead of each $19.20 of principal amount of the debentures being convertible into one share of Knoll Class A Common Stock, such principal amount would henceforth be convertible into the consideration received by the public Class A shareholders in the merger $12 cash. The core complaint is that the substitution of a right to convert to $12 in lieu of a right to convert to Class A Common Stock is unfair and a wrong.[3]

The complaint states that the issuer owes a fiduciary duty to the holders of its convertible debentures and asserts a lengthy list of facts that are said to constitute violations of that duty. For example, it is said that the self-dealing merger transaction was effected at a particularly disadvantageous time from the point of view of the minority stockholders; it was not negotiated by an independent committee; and the offering circular in connection with the tender offer leg of the transaction contained false and misleading information. Twelve dollars per share is said to be an unfairly low price, and inadequate consideration for loss of a Class A share; the right to convert to $12, thus, is seen as an inadequate substitute for the right to convert into a Class A share.

It is concluded (para. 17) that, "the defendants have ignored and breached the fiduciary duty of fair dealing they owe Knoll's debenture holders in structuring and proposing the Merger."

While it is not the principal theory of the complaint, a breach of contract theory can be detected in that pleading. Paragraph 13 asserts that the First Supplemental Indenture—which changed the conversion right from Class A Common Stock to cash—was entered "without the consent of the debenture holders as provided in § 15.02 of the original Indenture." At oral argument a somewhat different breach of contract theory—breach of a contractual obligation of good faith—was alluded to.

---

3. Knoll's Class A common was trading at 9¼ on the day before announcement of the $12 cash-out transaction; the 8-⅛% debentures were trading at 86 at that time. Complaint para. 15(g). The debentures, however, allegedly declined in value upon announcement of the supplemental indenture, trading at 73-¼ immediately thereafter.

Finally, it is also asserted that the complaint states a claim of common law fraud. Various assertions of inadequate disclosure in the tender offer document and in the 1983 prospectus published in connection with the original distribution of the debentures, are urged in support of this theory, although a reading of the complaint makes it utterly clear that, when drafted, those allegations were intended not to make out a claim of fraud but to bolster plaintiffs' principal, roll-it-all-into-a-ball, theory of breach of a fiduciary duty of entire fairness.

The complaint seeks, among other relief, rescission of the merger or the establishment of a new conversion rate and damages.

II.

I turn first to an evaluation of plaintiff's principal contention—that defendants owe to him as a holder of convertible debentures a fiduciary duty of loyalty and fairness. The answer to that central contention begins with a recognition that the courts of this state have consistently recognized that neither an issuer of debentures nor a controlling shareholder owes to holders of the company's debt securities duties of the special sort characterized as fiduciary in character. Those cases establish in this jurisdiction "that (i) a debenture holder has no independent right to maintain a claim for breach of fiduciary duty, and (ii) in the absence of fraud, insolvency or a statutory violation, a debenture holder's rights are defined by the terms of the indenture." In so holding, of course, our cases are directed to claims against an issuer not to those directed against an indenture trustee.

Under this traditional approach, it has no particular significance that the debentures in question are convertible into stock at the option of the holder. As early as 1889 Justice Holmes noted that such a conversion right is:

> ... simply an option to take stock as it may turn out to be when the time for choice arrives. The bondholder does not become a stockholder by his contract, in equity any more than at law ...

Parkinson v. West End Street Railway Co., Mass. Supr., 173 Mass. 446, 53 N.E. 891 (1899). This court made the same observation in Harff v. Kerkorian, Del. Ch., 324 A.2d at 219 in concluding that holders of a corporation's convertible debt were not stockholders in equity entitled to act as corporate representatives in derivative litigation. The implication of Harff was, of course, that, as creditors, holders of such debt were not the beneficiaries of fiduciary duties.

In so holding, the courts of this state have announced and applied well-established, conventional legal doctrine:

> Courts traditionally have directed bondholders to protect them-selves against ... self-interested issuer action with explicit contractual provisions. Holders of senior securities, such as bonds, are outside the legal model of the firm for protective purposes: a heavy black-letter line bars the extension of corporate fiduciary protections to them.

Bratton, The Economics and Jurisprudence of Convertible Bonds, 1984 Wisc.L.Rev. 667, 668 (1984). See also American Bar Foundation, Commentaries on Model Debenture Indenture Provisions (1971) at 527 (hereafter "ABF Commentaries").

This traditional view, which continues to be applied in other jurisdictions as well as in Delaware has not gone altogether unchallenged in the modern cases. In Broad v. Rockwell International Corp.,[6] a panel of the Fifth Circuit Court of Appeals held that an issuer of convertible debentures does owe a duty of fidelity to holders of such securities, although at its critical point, the doctrinal analysis of that point fails rather completely. See 614 F.2d at 430–31.[7] In all events, on en banc review, that opinion was vacated and, while the full court assumed for purposes of its decision the existence of such a duty, one cannot fairly read the later opinion except as an endorsement of the traditional conceptualization of the basis for the legal relationship between an issuer of convertible bonds and the holders of such securities. In Van Gemert v. Boeing Co., 520 F.2d 1373 (2d Cir. 1975), the Second Circuit Court of Appeals, applying New York law, found a covenant of good faith and fair dealing implied in a convertible debenture indenture. Judge Oaks alone on that panel indicated a willingness to go further and find an "underlying duty of fair treatment ... owed by the corporation or majority stockholders or controlling directors and officers" to bondholders. 520 F.2d at 1385. But another panel of that court, in a later phase of that same case has made clear that the rationale for the result reached in Van Gemert was contractual, not fiduciary. See 553 F.2d 812 (2d Cir. 1977).

And in Pittsburgh Terminal Corp. v. Baltimore & O.R. Co., 680 F.2d 933 (3d Cir. 1982), Judge Gibbons of the Third Circuit Court of Appeals noted, without citation of authority or elaboration, that he "would be very much surprised if Maryland or any other state would today hold that no [fiduciary] obligations were owed by an issuer of [convertible] securities and its directors." The two other members of that panel, however, specifically disavowed any such conclusion.

Finally, in a case relied upon by plaintiff here, the United States District Court for the Southern District of New York purported to find in our Supreme Court's reversal in part of this court's opinion in Harff v. Kerkorian authority for the imposition of fiduciary obligations running

---

6. 614 F.2d 418 (5th Cir. 1980) ["Broad I"] vacated, 642 F.2d 929 (5th Cir. 1980) (en banc) ["Broad II"] cert. denied 454 U.S. 965, 70 L. Ed. 2d 380, 102 S. Ct. 506 (1981).

7. Reliance by the panel in Broad I on identical dicta of Justice Douglas in two cases (Pepper v. Litton, 308 U.S. 295, 311, 60 S. Ct. 238, 84 L. Ed. 281 (1939) and Superintendent of Insurance v. Bankers Life & Casualty Co., 404 U.S. 6, 12, 92 S. Ct. 165, 30 L. Ed. 2d 128 (1971)) surely provides too frail a support for the conclusion reached. I need not now dilate upon those cases (although they are cited by plaintiff here) except to say that they were actions brought by a trustee in bankruptcy (not creditors) on behalf of a bankrupt corporation against a controlling shareholder for breach of fiduciary duty. They were properly maintained under perfectly conventional principles of fiduciary duty and legitimately raise no question about the existence of such a duty towards creditors. Pepper acknowledges as much. See 308 U.S. at 307.

from the issuer and its directors to holders of convertible securities. See Green v. Hamilton, S.D.N.Y., 76 Civ. 5433 (July 13, 1981).

Thus, there exists a body of judicial opinion willing to extend the protection offered by the fiduciary concept to the relationship between an issuer and the holders of its convertible debt securities. These seeds, however, have fallen upon stones. None of the appellate opinions actually represent a holding so extending that concept and, indeed, each of those cases evidence the fact that prevailing judicial opinion remains to the contrary.

* * *

That a convertibility feature of a debt security creates an economic interest in the issuer's stock price that the holder of a straight debt instrument would not have is plain. But, it does not follow at all that from such additional economic interest, fiduciary duties of loyalty, etc. necessarily or properly flow. Such duties and the restriction on self-dealing, etc. that they entail have been imposed upon those to whom property has been entrusted to manage for the benefit of another. Trusts are the prototype, but the concept has long been extended to corporate officers and directors, agents, partners. But it has not been extended to negotiated commercial transactions where the original property owner transfers it with a contractual right to repayment. Thus, for example, no case holds that the relationship between a bank and its borrower involves a fiduciary duty running from the borrower; nor, indeed, in the case of a deposit relationship from the bank to its depositor.

While the convertibility feature of convertible bonds creates an economic interest in an issuer's stock price, so long as the right to convert is not exercised, it remains merely an option, and the holder of it retains all of the benefits of his creditor status. Until the moment of exercise, his investment is not held subject to the risks that the fiduciary duty concept was designed to address, but is held pursuant to a negotiated contract detailing rights and duties and conferring upon the creditor a legal right to repayment. Thus, what Justice Holmes said in 1899 in Parkinson v. West End Street Railway remains true; the holder of a convertible bond is and only is a corporate creditor to whom contractual but not fiduciary duties are owed unless he acts to end his entitlement to the legal protections his contract affords him and to assume the risks of stockholder status through exercise of the power of conversion.

Accordingly, were I free to pass upon the question presented in Harff and Norte & Co. for the first time, I could find nothing in Green or in the other federal opinions cited above to suggest that an alteration in the traditional structure governing the legal relationship between corporations and holders of their convertible debt is warranted. That traditional approach has not been shown to be inadequate in any important way. Underwriters of convertible securities do have an interest in negotiating protections on points regarded as material by ultimate purchasers of those securities. The development of elaborate anti-destruction and anti-dilution provisions in indentures attests to the relative effectiveness of this mechanism of defining rights and obligations of issuers. See ABF Commentaries at 290–301.

The tide has no doubt long run away from a world of hard and fast rules with predictable outcomes and towards a world in which it is common for courts to evaluate specific behavior in the light cast by broadly worded principles.[10] Working amid such flows, however, courts must be wary of the danger to useful structures that they entail. To introduce the powerful abstraction of "fiduciary duty" into the highly negotiated and exhaustively documented commercial relationship between an issuer of convertible securities and the holders of such securities would, or so it now appears to me, risk greater insecurity and uncertainty than could be justified by the occasional increment in fairness that might be hoped for. See generally Bratton, The Economics and Jurisprudence of Convertible Bonds, *supra,* at 730–739. I conclude that plaintiff has failed to state a claim of breach of fiduciary duty upon which relief may be granted.

* * *

For the foregoing reasons, defendants' motion to dismiss the complaint shall be granted.

QUESTIONS

1. Why doesn't Chancellor Allen treat debt covenants as contracts of adhesion? Underwriters are hired by the issuer to market the debt securities. Why would they provide protection to investors?

2. Does the right to convert each $19.20 of principal amount of debenture into the merger consideration have any value to debenture holders?

3. In footnote 3 Chancellor Allen notes that the debentures were trading at $86 before announcement of the cash-out merger, and allegedly declined in value upon the announcement of the supplemental indenture to $73¼. The expectation of an event that would affect the value of a debt security typically results in bond rating agencies placing the debentures on immediate "credit watch," followed shortly by a downgrade. Markets typically respond more quickly. If the bonds were formerly convertible into common stock at $19.20 per share, what value does that attribute to the conversion right per share? If you were the defendant, what kind of evidence might you offer that the entire decline was not attributable to the announcement of the supplemental indenture?

4. Why does Chancellor Allen say that fiduciary duties aren't constructive here?

---

10. Professor P. S. Atiyah has brilliantly captured the zeitgeist in his inaugural lecture at Oxford University, which has been reprinted by the Iowa Law Review. See Atiyah, From Principles to Pragmatism: Changes in the Function of the Judicial Process and the Law, 65 Iowa L. Rev. 1249 (1980).

5. If you represented Knoll and Cogan, what response might you make to plaintiff's assertion that the cash-out merger "was effected at a particularly disadvantageous time from the point of view of the minority shareholders"?

6. Chancellor Allen holds that holders of convertible debentures aren't entitled to the benefit of fiduciary duties until they exercise their conversion rights. Is this pure formalism, or can you think of other reasons that might justify such a rule? Are there real differences in the situations of shareholders and holders of convertible debentures? What would happen if directors owed duties to both shareholders and convertible debenture holders?

NOTE ON BROAD v. ROCKWELL INTERNATIONAL CORPORATION

Similar issues arose in Broad v. Rockwell International Corporation, 642 F.2d 929 (*en banc*, 5th Cir.), cert. denied 454 U.S. 965 (1981). Collins Radio Company had issued debentures convertible into its common stock at $72.50 per Collins share, at a time when Collins stock was trading at around $60. But Collins then fell on hard times, and its stock price declined as low as $9.75, when Rockwell stepped in. At first Rockwell invested in convertible preferred stock of Collins, but then proceeded with a tender offer and cash-out merger at $25 per Collins share, a premium over the market. The indenture governing Rockwell's convertible debentures provided that upon a merger in which Collins disappeared, the conversion rights would become exercisable for the same consideration received by a Collins shareholder in the merger—in this case $25 cash. (No mention is made of the benefit of having Rockwell succeed as the obligor on the debentures, which had been trading at $600 because of looming bankruptcy before the merger.) After discussing the long history of primary emphasis on contractual language in determining bondholders' rights, the court found that the debenture holders had been provided exactly what the contract required—the right to convert each $1,000 debenture into $344.75 in cash, and that this "adequately accords to the holders of Debentures their valid rights under the Indenture." The court then proceeded to reject plaintiff's argument that an implied covenant of fair dealing under New York law required more for the debenture holders, stating ". . . this implied covenant of good faith and fair dealing cannot give the holders of Debentures any rights inconsistent with those explicitly set out in the Indenture. '[W]here the instrument contains an express covenant in regard to any subject, no covenants are to be implied with respect to the same subject.' "

STANDARD ANTI–DESTRUCTION LANGUAGE

The following is a fairly typical provision providing some protection for options or conversion rights against destruction:

> In case at any time the Company shall be a party to any transaction . . . in which the previously outstanding Capital Stock shall be changed

into or exchanged for different securities of the Company or common stock or other securities of another corporation ... then, as a condition of the consummation of the Transaction, lawful and adequate provisions shall be made so that each holder of Conversion Rights, upon the exercise thereof at any time on or after the Consummation Date, shall be entitled to receive, and such Conversion Rights shall thereafter represent the right to receive, in lieu of the Capital Stock issuable upon such exercise prior to the Consummation Date, the highest amount of securities or other property to which such holder would actually have been entitled as a shareholder upon the consummation of the Transaction if such holder had exercised such Conversion Rights immediately prior thereto....

PROBLEM

Poison pill rights plans are designed to "flip over" into stock of a hostile bidder, to preserve the value of the rights, and to dilute the bidder, even where the target company disappears in a freeze-out merger or similar transaction. Typically these rights provide for a bargain purchase of shares at a 50% discount from the market value of the issuer. Can you alter this language (from a poison pill's flipover rights provision) to protect the remaining value of options where the underlying stock is destroyed through merger, and option holders are given the right to convert into what the shareholders got in the merger, as in Simons v. Cogan? Note that those who hold long-term options, with a life of up to ten years, that have been issued at current market value, lose the expected gains from potential growth over that period.

"(a) In the event that ...:

"(i) the Company shall consolidate with, or merge with and into, any other Person other than a consolidation with, or merger with and into, a wholly-owned Subsidiary, and the Company shall not be the continuing or surviving corporation of such consolidation or merger; ... then, and in each such case, promptly following the occurrence of each such Section 13 Event [a merger or other reorganization], proper provision shall be made so that:

"(A) each holder of record of a Right ... shall thereafter have the right to receive, upon the exercise thereof at a price equal to the then current Purchase Price ... for which a Right was exercisable (whether or not such Right was then exercisable) ... such number of ... shares of Common Stock of the Principal Party (as defined herein) not subject to any liens, encumbrances, rights of first refusal or other adverse claims, as shall be equal to the result obtained by (1) multiplying the then current Purchase Price by the number of shares of for which a Right was exercisable immediately prior to the time that any Person first became an Acquiring Person ... and (2) dividing that product by 50% of the then current per share market price of the Common Stock of such Principal Party on the date of consummation of such consolidation, merger, sale or transfer; provided that the Purchase Price and the number of shares of Common Stock of such

Principal Party issuable upon exercise of each Right shall be further adjusted as provided in Section 11(f) of this Agreement to reflect any events occurring in respect of such Principal Party after the date of the such consolidation, merger, sale or transfer ..."

Is there a simpler way to protect the long-term value of rights?

Andaloro v. PFPC Worldwide, Inc.

830 A.2d 1232 (Del. Ch. 2003).

■ STRINE, VICE CHANCELLOR.

This is an appraisal action brought by petitioners John J. Andaloro and Robert J. Perslweig against respondent PFPC Worldwide, Inc. The petitioners seek appraisal of the value of the shares and options they owned in PFPC before it was merged with an acquisition vehicle of PFPC's indirect parent, PNC Financial Services Group, Inc., in a short-form merger under 8 Del. C. § 253 in which PFPC was the surviving entity. Both of the petitioners were PFPC executives before the merger.

The issue now before the court is a discrete one that is purely legal in nature: Can the petitioners seek appraisal under § 262 to receive the "fair value" of the options they were forced to give up in the merger in exchange for certain other consideration? The petitioners argue that the equities demand recognition of such a right. In support of that contention, the petitioners have filed affidavits suggesting that PFPC failed to provide the petitioners with adequate information or otherwise make fair provisions for the petitioners to convert their options into stock before the effective time of the merger, despite the fact that the relevant option agreements provided that the petitioners' options would vest upon the occurrence of a change of control, including a § 253 merger. For example, the petitioners have provided evidence to demonstrate that the PFPC board did not undertake a fair valuation process for the options but simply imposed a take-it-or-leave-it value on the petitioners in an offer that required them to waive a host of legal rights.

Without contesting in this action that the petitioners might have equitable or contractual claims regarding the treatment of their options, the respondent PFPC has moved for partial summary judgment advancing a simple proposition: § 262 is a limited statutory remedy that is available only to stockholders. Under the settled authority of Lichtman v. Recognition Equipment, Inc.,[2] the right of appraisal is not available to option holders. "It is limited to stockholders of the merged corporation."

---

2. 295 A.2d 771 (Del. Ch. 1972). One of the major treatises on Delaware law treats Lichtman as having settled the question of whether options can be appraised under § 262 by providing an authoritative negative answer. See 2 Rodman Ward, Jr. et al., Folk on the Delaware General Corporation Law § 262.2.1, at GCL–IX–182 (4th ed. Supp. 2002–1).

I see no proper basis to deviate from the holding in Lichtman, which tracks the language of § 262 itself. The statute by its own terms own applies to "shares of stock,"[4] a definition that excludes options.

Nor do the equities require straining the linguistic reach of the statute's words. In this case, for example, the petitioners have advanced arguments that, if true, might well constitute a breach of the relevant option agreements. In a breach-of-contract action, the petitioners would be free to show that they were deprived of their options (or of their contractual rights of vesting and conversion) in violation of their contractual rights. A fitting remedy for such a breach might well be an award of damages that equals a judicial assessment of the fair value of the options that the petitioners lost.[5] In this sense, the petitioners would have access to what in some equitable corporate cases is referred to as a "quasi-appraisal" award of damages.[6]

But, as a predicate to such an award, the petitioners would be required to make an independent showing that is not contemplated within a § 262 proceeding; namely, a showing that the petitioners suffered a contractual or equitable injury at the hands of the respondent, PFPC. Importantly, that type of case might well involve claims against parties other than the surviving corporation, which is the only proper respondent to a § 262 action. In fact, the petitioners have brought just this type of action against PFPC and other parties in this court and that action has also been assigned to me for resolution.

The reality that the petitioners have to prove a predicate breach of duty (of some kind) before getting to the point where a damages award would be assessable against PFPC demonstrates that the petitioners' desire for appraisal of their options cannot be squared with § 262. Shoehorning their claims into § 262 would distort the statute's intended focus as a limited and efficient remedy focused solely on the fair value of stock.[7]

For these same reasons, I reject the petitioners' alternative argument that under principles of equity, their options should be treated as having already been exercised before the merger and converted into "stock," and that the resulting (hypothetical) "stock" should be included in the appraisal action. It is undisputed that the petitioners did not actually exercise their options before the merger. The petitioners argue, however, that they "would have" exercised the options before the merger had PFPC provided

---

4. 8 Del. C. § 262(a) ("The words 'stock' and 'share' mean and include what is ordinarily meant by those words...."). See also id. § 262(d)(2) ("Appraisal rights are available for any or all shares of such class or series of stock of [the] constituent corporation....").

5. The parties have not discussed whether the petitioners believe that the directors of their former corporation owed them fiduciary duties as option holders in connection with the merger. I therefore concentrate on the obvious rights of the petitioners as option holders—their contract rights.

6. See, e.g., Erickson v. Centennial Beauregard Cellular, L.L.C., 2003 WL 1878583, at *3 (Del. Ch. Apr. 11, 2003); Tansey v. Trade Show News Networks, Inc., 2001 WL 1526306, at *7 n.30 (Del. Ch. Nov. 27, 2001); Weinberger v. UOP, Inc., 457 A.2d 701 (Del. 1983).

7. See Lichtman, 295 A.2d at 772 (stating that permitting option holders to seek appraisal would inject collateral issues not contemplated by § 262 into appraisal proceedings).

certain requested information, and that PFPC "treated" the options as stock in various ways during the transaction. This argument, however, is precisely the kind of breach-of-duty question that has no place in a statutory appraisal, and that must be raised in a separate plenary action. The petitioners cite no relevant authority for the proposition that equitable breach-of-duty claims may be raised in an appraisal proceeding,[9] and I decline to interpret § 262 to permit consideration of issues unrelated to the appraisal of the fair value of actual stock. To do otherwise would be to dishonor the General Assembly's determination of the proper scope of a § 262 action.

Finally, because the petitioners have the right to and, as noted, have already filed a separate plenary action seeking relief for breach of contract and fiduciary duty in connection with the treatment of their options, other judicial tools exist that can facilitate an efficient resolution of all of their claims. To the extent that the petitioners are able to prove a breach of contract or fiduciary duty, the remedy might well be one in the nature of an appraisal determination. After hearing from the parties to this action and the separate plenary action, the court might also conclude that the actions should be consolidated for many or all purposes. The option to consolidate eliminates any need to distort the § 262 remedy in the name of equity or efficiency.

For all these reasons, therefore, PFPC's motion for partial summary judgment is granted and the petitioners' claim for appraisal of their options is dismissed. IT IS SO ORDERED.

NOTE ON EMPLOYEE OPTIONS

Employee stock options typically have a long duration, being exercisable for a ten-year term from the time of the grant. Giving high-level officers

---

9. The petitioners cite various cases in their surreply brief for the proposition that it is necessary in an appraisal proceeding to determine what stock is validly at issue in the appraisal. Without quibbling with that statement, I note that these cases do not support the proposition that equity may require this court to ignore the simple fact that petitioners are seeking appraisal for options, not stock. Indeed, in all of the cases cited by petitioners that involve appraisal proceedings, the petitioners actually held, in some form or another, shares of stock for which appraisal was being sought. See Salomon Bros., Inc. v. Interstate Bakeries Corp., 576 A.2d 650 (Del. Ch. 1989) (holding that stockholder who purchased shares with notice of merger plans was not foreclosed from seeking appraisal); Neal v. Alabama By–Prods. Corp., 1988 WL 105754 (Del. Ch. Oct. 11, 1988) (holding appraisal demand by beneficial holder of stock invalid because demand was not by or on behalf of record holder as required by § 262); Engel v. Magnavox Co., 1976 WL 1705, at *5 (Del. Ch. Apr. 22, 1976) (holding that stockholder's submission of blank proxy constituted vote in favor of merger and therefore barred appraisal); Scott v. Arden Farms Co., 26 Del. Ch. 283, 28 A.2d 81 (Del. Ch. 1942) (holding that voting trustee's vote in favor of merger precluded stockholder from seeking appraisal). Other of the cases cited by petitioners deal with proceedings under other statutes in which the consideration of equitable claims is necessarily contemplated by the very nature of the statutory right of action, such as 8 Del. C. § 225, and are therefore irrelevant. See Agranoff v. Miller, 1999 WL 219650, at *17–18 (Del. Ch. Apr. 12, 1999) (explaining proper scope of § 225), aff'd & remanded, 737 A.2d 530 (Del. 1999) (TABLE).

and directors this long to exercise serves a valuable purpose. It provides them an opportunity to profit from decisions that take a long time to pay off, and aligns their interests with those of shareholders generally. What happens if the company is acquired and the options can no longer be exercised in company stock? There are at least two solutions. One approach is to accelerate vesting of unvested options, and allow the employee or director to exercise the options before the merger that destroys the company's stock. This allows the officer to obtain the same benefits as the other shareholders. But does it? If options were issued recently and have nine years of remaining life, the officer loses the anticipated gains from a rising stock price over the next nine years. Another approach, probably the most commonly used one, is to convert the options into the right to receive the same consideration that the shareholders will receive at the merger. If it's a cash merger, this is subject to the same criticism as allowing acceleration of vesting. But what if it converts into the right to receive a specified number of shares of the acquiring corporation's stock? Set out below is typical language to implement this approach:

> In case at any time the Company shall be a party to any transaction . . . in which the previously outstanding Capital Stock shall be changed into or exchanged for different securities of the Company or common stock or other securities of another corporation . . . then, as a condition of the consummation of the Transaction, lawful and adequate provisions shall be made so that each holder of an option, upon the exercise thereof at any time on or after the Consummation Date, shall be entitled to receive, and such option rights shall thereafter represent the right to receive, in lieu of the Capital Stock issuable upon such exercise prior to the Consummation Date, the highest amount of securities or other property to which such holder would actually have been entitled as a shareholder upon the consummation of the Transaction if such holder had exercised such option rights immediately prior thereto. . . .

If the consideration is stock, this gets the employee the right to purchase stock in the acquiring firm. If the option's duration remains unchanged, the employee has the opportunity to profit from increases in the acquiring firm's stock price over time. In AT & T, Inc.'s acquisition of BellSouth Corporation in 2006, this provision was made more explicit, in § 4.4 of the Merger Agreement, quoted below:

> (a)   At the Effective Time, each outstanding option to purchase Company Shares (a "Company Option") under the Company Compensation and Benefit Plans identified in Section 5.1(b) of the Company Disclosure Letter as being the only Company Compensation and Benefit Plans pursuant to which Company Shares may be issued or benefits measured by the value of Company Shares may be obtained (the "Company Stock Plans"), whether vested or unvested, shall be converted into an option to acquire a number of shares of Parent Common Stock equal to the product (rounded up to the nearest whole number) of (x) the number of Company Shares subject to the Company Option

immediately prior to the Effective Time and (y) the Exchange Ratio, at an exercise price per share (rounded down to the nearest whole cent) equal to (A) the exercise price per Company Share of such Company Option immediately prior to the Effective Time divided by (B) the Exchange Ratio; * * * Except as specifically provided above, following the Effective Time, each Company Option shall continue to be governed by the same terms and conditions as were applicable under such Company Option immediately prior to the Effective Time. At or prior to the Effective Time, the Company shall adopt appropriate amendments to the Company Stock Plans, if necessary, and the Board of Directors of the Company shall adopt appropriate resolutions, if necessary, to effectuate the provisions of this Section 4.4(a). Parent shall take all actions as are necessary for the assumption of the Company Stock Plans pursuant to this Section 4.4, including the issuance (subject to Section 4.4(c)) and listing of Parent Common Stock as necessary to effect the transactions contemplated by this Section 4.4.

Does this provide officers with equivalent value for their options?

B. DILUTION OF OPTION RIGHTS

Dividends on common stock generally have the effect of reducing the market price of the common stock in the amount of the dividend. This includes not only regular cash dividends, but also such events as dividends in partial liquidation, where a company sells off a major asset and declares an extraordinary dividend on its common stock, in effect returning capital to shareholders. Further, events that are the equivalent of dividends, such as stock dividends or stock splits, that increase the number of outstanding shares, also reduce the value of shares and decrease the percentage of shares represented by the options or conversion rights. Spin-off transactions, in which the company dividends the shares of a subsidiary to its shareholders, have the same effect. Issuance of new shares of common stock has two effects. First, even where the new shares are issued at the current market price, and thus do not adversely affect the value of the underlying stock, they do dilute the percentage of stock ownership represented by the options. Where potential control (or at least a veto) is important to the option holder, this by itself is a damaging event. Second, where new shares are issued at prices that reduce the value of the common stock, the value of the option is reduced, quite aside from control issues.

The issuance of new shares will always dilute the percentage ownership of the option holders upon exercise, but as we discussed in Chapter Five, Part 2, that type of dilution is only of concern where control of the entity is at stake, which most frequently will be in close corporations. The more global concern of investors in options and convertible securities is with issuance of new shares at "too low" a price. What is "too low?" One definition would be at a price lower than the price of the stock at the time of issuance of the options. Two authors point out that this problem is most common in closely held enterprises, where valuation is difficult and investors may be at an informational disadvantage in assessing the value of the company. Michael A. Woronoff and Jonathan A. Rosen, Understanding Anti–Dilution Provisions in Convertible Securities, 74 Fordham L. Rev. 129 (2005). The general assumption is that in efficient capital markets the stock price of any public company fairly reflects a consensus about the value of the company. In most cases public issuers resist anti-dilution clauses in options and convertibles, and argue that the purchaser of an option or a convertible is buying the right to participate in changes in the market value of the common stock, which can change in either direction for many reasons.

For these reasons anti-dilution protection is typically limited to structural changes in the common stock, such as a cash dividend. Large issuers resist dilution protection for ordinary dividends, even though they may reduce the value of the common stock when it trades ex dividend—without the right to the dividend attached—after the record date. In some cases they may agree to protection for any dividend that significantly exceeds the regular dividend, perhaps by some percentage, to capture special dividends. Structural changes, such as a stock split, a stock dividend or a recapitalization have similar effects—generally the creation of more shares without receipt of equivalent value by the issuer, thus reducing the value of the common stock after the event. These events are typically covered by antidilution provisions. There are several ways to handle this problem: (1) a formula reduction in the purchase price; (2) a flat prohibition on any such distributions, (3) a clause that requires prior notice to holders of options and convertibles, so they can convert in advance of the event and participate in the distribution, or (4) a participation feature giving holders an amount equal to that they would have received had they exercised or converted immediately prior to the distribution. They can be entitled to this amount either immediately or upon exercise or conversion. As you will see, defining these events to provide full protection for option holders can be a challenge. These transactions typically occur with existing shareholders, who can benefit at the expense of the holders of options and convertibles from issuance of free or underpriced shares. Large issuers resist protection.

NOTE: THE RESTRUCTURING OF MARRIOTT CORPORATION

Marriott Corp. had invested heavily in hotels during the 1970s and 1980s, and had expanded rapidly. The expansion was financed with large amounts of borrowing. In the late 1980s real estate values declined nationwide, including hotel values. The increased debt service began to reduce net profits for the stockholders. By the early 1990s real estate values were depressed, and lenders were only interested in high quality borrowers. Marriott, with its large debt load on its hotels, wasn't a high quality borrower able to borrow more to expand its management and services business.

Marriott couldn't sell the hotels and pay off the debts they carried. The solution, from the perspective of Marriott's managers and common stockholders, was to think of debt as an option to sell the company. Frequently debt is referred to in this way, but usually this connotes that the shareholders of a business that has borrowed heavily have the option to walk away from the business if its assets are worth less than the corporate debts. The price the creditors will "pay" for these assets is higher than the price anyone else will pay, so there is no point for the shareholders to continue to struggle to enhance the value of the business. In this case, however, Marriott tried a new strategy—to sell its real estate assets to the creditors through a spin-off. Marriott corporation would create a new corporation, Marriott International ("International"), which would hold Mariott's lodging, food services and facilities management and senior living service businesses. The existing Marriott Corporation would change its name to Marriott Host Corporation ("Host"), and would retain Marriott's real estate, airport, toll road and stadium concessions and some other properties.

The object of the restructuring was to get the profitable growing businesses—hotel management and services—out from under the load of debt. The result of the restructuring was to leave the service business—International—with $20 million in debt and $7.4 billion in revenues and $500 million in cash flows.* Host, on the other hand, would have over $2 billion in debt, $1.7 billion in revenues and cash flow of $368 million. Interest expense for Host would be $196 million. Host would show losses because of large depreciation expenses. Presumably some of the remaining cash flow of approximately $172 million would be used for debt retirement.

The price of Marriott's common stock jumped 12% on the date of announcement. The price of Marriott's bonds dropped 30% in 2 days.** Bond rating services downgraded the Marriott bonds from investment grade to junk bonds. The bonds had no covenants to prevent this distribution. Marriott also had convertible preferred stock outstanding.

HB Korenvaes Investments, L.P. v. Marriott Corporation

1993 WL 257422; FED. SEC. L. REP. (CCH) ¶ 97,773 (1993).

■ ALLEN, CHANCELLOR.

In this action holders of Series A Cumulative Convertible Preferred Stock of Marriott Corporation seek to enjoin a planned reorganization of the businesses owned by that corporation. The reorganization involves the creation of a new corporate subsidiary, Marriott International, Inc., ("International"), the transfer to International of the greatest part of Marriott's cash-generating businesses, followed by the distribution of the stock

---

* Eric W. Orts, The Complexity and Legitimacy of Corporate Law, 50 Wash. & Lee L. Rev. 1565, 1607–08 (1993).

** *Id.*

of International to all of the holders of Marriott common stock, as a special dividend.

Plaintiffs assert that the proposed special dividend would leave the residual Marriott endangered by a disproportionate debt burden and would deprive them of certain rights created by the certificate of designation that defines the special rights, etc., of the preferred stock. More particularly, they claim: (1) that the proposed transaction, taken together with a recently declared intention to discontinue the payment of dividends on the preferred stock, constitutes coercive action designed wrongfully to force them to exercise their conversion privilege and thus surrender their preference rights; (2) that the planned payment of cash dividends on International's common stock, while plaintiffs' preferred dividend will have been suspended, violates the preferred stock's dividend preference; (3) that the authorization by the directors of Marriott of the spin-off transaction, without the affirmative vote of the holders of preferred stock, violates the voting rights of the preferred conferred by the certificate of designation; and (4) that the distribution of the dividend will violate the provisions of Section 5(e)(iv) of the certificate of designation of the preferred stock. Section 5(e)(iv) is designed to protect the economic interests of the preferred stock in the event of a special dividend. Finally, plaintiffs allege (5) that defendants have made false statements upon which they have relied in buying preferred stock in the market and that defendants are liable for fraud.

The Series A Cumulative Convertible Preferred Stock is Marriott's only outstanding issue of preferred stock. Plaintiffs are four institutional investors who have acquired more than 50% of the preferred stock. They present their case as one involving manipulation, deception and a legalistic interpretation of rights, which, if permitted and generalized will impose a material future cost on the operation of capital markets.

Defendants assert that the reorganization, and more particularly the special dividend, constitutes a valid, good faith attempt to maximize the interests of Marriott's common stockholders. Marriott asserts the right to deal with the preferred stock at arm's length,[1] to afford them their legal rights arising from the certificate of designation, but also to take steps not inconsistent with those rights to maximize the economic position of Marriott's common stock. It claims that this is what the proposed special dividend does. Defendants also deny that they have intentionally misled plaintiffs.

Pending is plaintiffs' motion for a preliminary injunction prohibiting the distribution of the special dividend. It is presently anticipated by defendants that the holders of Marriott's common stock will approve the proposed transaction at the Company's annual meeting now scheduled for

---

1. Plaintiffs contention that, with respect to this transaction Marriott owes to the holders of its preferred stock fiduciary duties was rejected and a claim based on the existence of such a duty has been dismissed.

July 23, 1993 and that the distribution, if not enjoined, will occur in August or September of this year.

* * *

For the reasons that follow, I conclude that plaintiffs have not shown a reasonable likelihood of success with respect to those aspects of their claims that appear to state a claim upon which relief might be granted. Certain theories plaintiffs advance do not appear to state such a claim and will be dismissed.

I.

Except as otherwise indicated, I take the following background facts to be non-controversial.

(a) The Company

Marriott Corporation, as presently constituted, is in the business (1) of owning and operating hotels, resorts, and retirement homes, (2) of providing institutional food service and facilities management, and (3) of operating restaurants and food, beverage and merchandise concessions at airports, tollway plazas and other facilities. Its common stock has a present market value of approximately $2.6 billion. In December 1991 Marriott issued $200,000,000 face amount of convertible preferred stock bearing an 8¼% cumulative dividend, the stock owned by plaintiffs. Marriott has substantial debt, including Liquid Yield Option Notes ("LYONS") with an accreted value of $228 million;[2] and long-term debt of $2.732 billion. According to its proxy statement, the book value of Marriott's assets is $6.560 billion.

In the fiscal year ending January 1, 1993 Marriott's sales were $8.722 billion; earnings before interest, taxes, depreciation and amortization (EBITDA) was $777 million; earnings before interest and corporate expenses was $496 million; and net income was $85 million. Each common share has received an annual cash dividend of $0.28 per share and the preferred stock dividends have been paid over its short life.

(b) The terms of the preferred stock in brief

The preferred stock is entitled to an 8¼% cumulative dividend and no more. It ranks prior to the common stock with respect to dividends and distribution of assets. It has in total, a face amount of $200,000,000 and that, plus the amount of any unpaid cumulated dividends, "and no more" is the amount of its liquidation preference. The corporation may, at its option, redeem any or all of the preferred stock after January 15, 1996, at prices set forth in the certificate.

The preferred stock is convertible at the option of the holder into common stock at a conversion price set forth in the certificate. Generally

---

2. A leading finance text notes that "a liquid yield option note (LYON) is a callable and retractable, convertible zero coupon bond (and you can't get much more complicated than that)." An example set forth in that text explains the security. See Richard A. Brealey and Stewart C. Myers, Principles of Corporate Finance, 3d ed. (1988) at p. 586.

that means that every $50.00 face amount share of preferred stock may be converted into 2.87 shares of common stock. The certificate provides a mechanism to adjust the conversion price "in case the Corporation shall, by dividend . . . distribute to all holders of Common Stock . . . assets (including securities). . . ."

The value of the right to convert is protected by a notice provision. The certificate provides that "in the event the Corporation shall declare a dividend . . . on its Common Stock payable otherwise than in cash or out of retained earnings," the Corporation shall give written notice to the holders of the preferred stock 15 days in advance of the record date.

There are no express restrictions on the payment of dividends other than the requirement that the quarterly dividend on the preferred must be paid prior to the distribution of dividend payments to common stock.

(c) Announcement of the proposed transaction

On October 5, 1993, Marriott announced a radical rearrangement of the legal structure of the Company's businesses. The restructuring was said to be designed to separate Marriott's "ownership of real estate . . . and other capital intensive businesses from its management and services businesses." The latter constitute Marriott's most profitable and fastest growing business segments. As indicated above, following this transfer Marriott intends to "spin-off" this new subsidiary by distributing all its stock as a dividend to Marriott's common stockholders.

(d) Marriott International

International is anticipated to be highly profitable from its inception and to be well positioned for future growth. It is expected to pay to its common stockholders the same dividend that has been paid to Marriott's common stock. Marriott's proxy statement describes International's proposed business activities as follows:

> Pursuant to existing long-term management, lease and franchise agreements with hotel owners, and [similar] . . . agreements to be entered into with Host Marriott with respect to lodging facilities and senior living properties to be owned by Host Marriott, Marriott international will operate or franchise a total of 242 Marriott full service hotels, 207 Courtyard by Marriott hotels, 179 Residence Inns, 118 Fairfield Inns and 16 senior living communities. Marriott International will also conduct the Company's food and facilities management businesses, as well as the Company's vacation timesharing operations.

According to its pro forma balance sheet for the quarter ending March 26, 1993, after the distribution (and assuming the Exchange Offer described below is effectuated) International will have assets of $3.048 billion, long-term debt of $902 million, and shareholders equity of $375 million.

Had International, with all the assets it will hold, been operated as a separate company in 1992, it would have had sales of $7.787 billion, earnings before interest and corporate expenses of $331 million and net income of $136 million. Marriott's adviser, S.G. Warburg & Company, has estimated that in 1993 International will have sales of $8.210 billion, and EBIT of $368 million.

(e) Host Marriott

Marriott's remaining assets will consist of large real estate holdings and Marriott's airport and tollway concession business. Marriott will be renamed Host Marriott ("Host"). The assets retained by Host have a value of several billion dollars but will be burdened with great debt and produce little cash-flow after debt service.

> Host Marriott will retain [ownership of] most of the Company's [Marriott's] existing real estate properties, including 136 lodging and senior living properties. Host Marriott will also complete the Company's existing real estate development projects and manage the Company's holdings of undeveloped real estate. Host Marriott will seek to maximize the cash flow from ... its real estate holdings ... Host Marriott ... will also be the leading operator of airport and toll-road food and merchandise concessions in the U.S., holding contracts at 68 major airports and operating concessions at nearly 100 toll-road units.

Assuming the Exchange Offer is effectuated, after the special dividend Host will have, according to its pro forma balance sheet as of March 26, 1993, assets of $3.796 billion, long-term debt of 2.130 billion and shareholders' equity of $516 million. Host's pro forma income statement for the fiscal year ending January 1, 1993, would reflect sales of $1.209 billion, earnings before corporate expenses and interest of $152 million, interest expense of $196 million, corporate expenses of $46 million, and a net loss of $44 million.

When he announced the spin-off transaction on October 5, 1992, Stephen Bollenbach, Marriott's Chief Financial Officer stated, with respect to the future of Host:

> Net cash flow of Host Marriott will be used primarily to service and retire debt. The Company does not plan to pay dividends on its common stock ... I am very comfortable with the way Host Marriott has been structured. I believe this approach represents the best way for Marriott shareholders to unlock the value of our long-term assets. Secondly, the transaction gives Host Marriott the staying power needed if the recovery is slower than anticipated in arriving. I am convinced Host Marriott has the financial means to meet all its obligations to employees, suppliers, lenders and other stakeholders.[6]

---

6. Plaintiff has put forth substantial documentary support for their assertion that at the time this statement was made it was the expectation of the senior Marriott executives that the preferred stock dividend would not be paid following the distribution. This alleged undisclosed fact forms an important part of the predicate for their fraud claim in this lawsuit. Defendants deny that Marriott's responsible officers had at that time made the determination, which was later (March 15, 1993) announced, that preferred dividends would be discontinued. This factual dispute cannot be settled on this motion. For present purposes I assume that in October 1992 Marriott's responsible officers knew that no final decision on preferred dividends had been made, but expected such dividends to be discontinued; thus the lawyerly use of the term "obligation."

Mr. Bollenbach reiterated this position two weeks later at a meeting of securities analysts.

* * *

(g) Bondholders' suits lead to modified transaction

Despite Mr. Bollenbach's assurances of October 5, Marriott's bondholders reacted strongly against the proposed special dividend. The transaction will of course remove very substantial assets and even more cash flow from their debtor and will, in the circumstances, substantially increase the risk associated with the bondholders' investment, or so it was thought.

Ten class-action lawsuits seeking to block the dividend were filed by various classes of bondholders. They have been consolidated in the United States District Court for the District of Maryland.

On March 11, 1993, Marriott reached a settlement with the bondholder class action plaintiffs. The settlement if effectuated, would require Marriott to cause the Host subsidiary HMH to offer to exchange for existing bonds new bonds (Exchange Bonds) with a longer average maturity and bearing an interest rate 100 basis points higher than the existing bonds. The Exchange Bonds will include restrictive covenants that greatly limit opportunities for HMH to transfer cash to Host. Host's airport and toll road concession businesses, representing the preponderant part of its operating assets, and 40% of its cash-flow, will be transferred to a subsidiary of HMH. A $630 million credit line will be provided by International to HMH, but it cannot be drawn on to pay preferred dividends. One effect of the Exchange Offer, and the transfers it contemplates, is to restrict further Host's ability, as a practical matter, to pay dividends to the preferred stock.

Shortly after the Exchange Offer settlement Marriott announced for the first time that it was intended that, following the special dividend, Host would not pay dividends on its preferred stock. On March 15, 1993, Host announced in an S.E.C. filing that:

> It is the Company's present intention following the Distribution to declare dividends on its preferred stock only to the extent earnings equal or exceed the amount of such dividends. Since Host Marriott is expected to report book losses following the Distribution, this policy would lead to an indefinite suspension of dividends on the Company's preferred stock.

(h) Plaintiffs' acquisition of preferred stock and short sales of common

Plaintiffs began for the first time to purchase substantial amounts of Marriott's preferred stock following the announcement of the special dividend.

Since the preferred stock is convertible at the option of the holder into 2.87 shares of Marriott common stock and bears a dividend of 8¼% on its stated (liquidation) value of $50 per share, the market value of a share of preferred stock includes two possible components of value: the value of the conversion right and the value of the preferences. The presence of a presently exercisable conversion right will assure that the market value of the preferred will not fail below the market value of the security or property into which the preferred might convert, in this case 2.87 shares of common stock (less transaction costs of the conversion). The stated dividend, the dividend preference and the liquidation preference and other features of the preferred will ordinarily assure that the preferred trades at some premium to the value of the conversion right.

In this instance plaintiffs have acquired a majority of the shares of the preferred stock. Plaintiffs, however, did not simply acquire preferred stock. The record shows that each of the plaintiffs, except one, have hedged their risk by entering short sales contracts with respect to Marriott common stock. In this way plaintiffs have isolated their risk to that part of the preferred stock trading value represented by that stock's preference rights. Any change in the market price of the preferred stock caused by movement in the value of the underlying common stock will in their case be offset by change in the extent of their obligations under the short sales contracts.

(i) Marriott common and preferred stock price changes

The prices of both Marriott common stock and Marriott preferred stock have increased substantially since the announcement of the special dividend. On the last trading day before the announcement of the transaction Marriott's common stock closed at $17.125 per share. The day of the announcement the price increased to $19.25 and by June 4, 1993 it had reached $25.75, for a total increase of approximately 50.3%.

The price of Marriott preferred stock closed on the last trading day before the announcement at $62.75, which represented a premium of $13.54 over the value of the 2.8736 common shares into which each preferred share could convert. The day of the announcement the preferred stock increased to $68.875. On June 4, 1993 the price of the preferred stock closed at $77.00 per share, an increase of 22.8% over the pre-announcement market price. The premium that the preferred stock commanded over the common into which it could convert (i.e., the market value of the preferences) however, had by June 4th, shrunk, to $3.00.

Thus while both common stock and preferred stock have experienced substantial increases in the market value of their securities, because of the impact of their hedging strategy, plaintiffs are in a different position than are non-hedged holders of preferred stock. The reduction of the premium at which the preferred stock trades has resulted in losses on their short sales, leading some plaintiffs, as of June 4, 1993, to net unrealized losses on their investments.

For example, plaintiff, The President and Fellows of Harvard College, ("Harvard") as of June 4, 1993 owned 480,300 shares of preferred stock, which were purchased for $33,580,108 and which had a market value on that day of $37,724,801. Thus, this plaintiff has an unrealized profit of $4,144,693 on its investment in the preferred stock. Harvard also entered into short sales of 1,338,300 shares of Marriott common stock, approximately 2.8 times the number of preferred shared it purchased. It received

$30,949,383 on these short sales. The cost to cover these short sales, however, has increased to $34,609,056, or $3,659,673 more than was received on the sales, representing an unrealized loss in that amount. Thus, as of June 4, 1993, although the value of the preferred stock owned by this plaintiff has increased in value by over $4 million, the total value of its investment position has increased by only $485,020.[9]

II. Plaintiffs' Account

The foregoing set forth much of the factual background of the pending motion as it now appears. It does not set forth those contested facts that form an important part of plaintiffs' account of the case.

Plaintiffs take a dark view. They see themselves being forced by defendants to relinquish their preferences at a time when defendants cannot call or redeem their stock. This coercion is arranged for them, plaintiffs say, because the Marriott family is motivated to assure its continuing control over Host following the spin-off. That such a concern exists is evidenced by certain internal Marriott documents as well as by the existence of certain agreements that will give International the right to purchase 20% of Host's stock in the event that any person (as defined in S.E.C. Rule 13(D)) acquires 20% or announces a tender offer for 30% of Host's shares.

Working from the premise that control over Host is very important to the Marriott family, plaintiffs point out that after the special dividend (and after the adjustment of the preferred stock conversion rate that it will require) the preferred stock (if none of it is converted before the distribution) would be in a position to convert into more than 50% of the Host common stock. Thus, on this view, given the size of the special dividend, the existence of the conversion right transforms the preferred stock into a threat to Marriott family control of Host. The answer to this problem that plaintiffs say was hit upon was to force the preferred to convert into Marriott common stock before the record date for the special dividend. How could this be done? The principal means, according to plaintiffs, was to announce as early as the filing of Marriott's preliminary proxy on March 15, 1993 that Host would suspend dividends on the preferred stock indefinitely and would not reinstitute payment of the dividend until the Company's "earnings equal or exceed the amount of such dividends."

The scheme that plaintiffs detect has other elements (some of which may constitute independent wrongs). For example, in order to make post-distribution conversion less attractive, plaintiffs assert that defendants are intending to deviate from the conversion rate adjustment formula in the certificate of designation.

---

9. At least two other plaintiffs have entered into similar transactions. AKT Associates L.P., bad as of June 4, 1993, an unrealized profit on its preferred stock of $2,033,495 and increased cost to cover short sales of $2,036,777 for an unrealized loss of $3,282. HB Korenvaes Investments, L.P. had an unrealized gain of $3,555,648 on its preferred and a loss of $3,793,089 on its short position for an unrealized loss of $237,441. * * *

Plaintiffs' theory has another, more Machiavellian aspect. According to plaintiffs, defendants knew in October 1992 that Host would not pay a dividend on its preferred stock, but withheld that information, and even implied the contrary in public statements. The first question that this assertion raises is the following: If knowledge of the discontinuation of dividends would promote the posited scheme to force conversions, why would defendants in October withhold knowledge of the planned suspension of dividends? This is where the plaintiffs' account gets Machiavellian. According to plaintiffs, defendants understood that institutional investors would move into the preferred stock following the October 5 announcement and that these investors would hedge their position by short-selling Marriott common. Investors in this position (who isolate their risk in the preference rights) are, it is said, particularly sensitive to the "coercive" effect of a suspension of dividends. Therefore in delaying the announcement of the preferred dividend suspension defendants intended to cause these especially susceptible holders to move into the preferred stock before they sprang their trap.

III. Plaintiffs' Legal Theories

Plaintiffs see the planned spin-off and the suspension of Marriott preferred stock dividends that is planned to follow it as constituting wrongs of several sorts.

First, they complain that the proposal violates a fiduciary duty running from the board of directors of Marriott to them as stockholders of the company. For the reasons expressed in an earlier opinion I concluded, with respect to the spin-off transaction, that the Marriott directors owed no fiduciary duty to the holders of preferred stock.

Secondly, plaintiffs assert that the proposed transaction and the suspension of dividends constitute multiple violations of the contractual rights of the preferred stock. The most plausible of these allegations is the claim that the special dividend violates the certificate of designation because it distributes such a large proportion of the value of Marriott that the certificate of designation provision designed to protect the economic value of the preferred, in the face of a special dividend, cannot work.

Lastly, plaintiffs assert that defendants have engaged in fraudulent conduct by making untrue statements upon which plaintiffs relied in acquiring Marriott preferred stock and that plaintiffs will be financially injured should the special dividend not be enjoined. Their injury, they say, will result from the loss of the value of the preferred stock premium over conversion value. That loss will irretrievably occur when they are coerced into converting. They will be coerced in this way, they assert, because neither they nor others can afford to own a preferred stock that pays no dividend. Therefore unless an injunction is entered defendants' scheme will be brought to a successful conclusion.

* * *

V. The Section 5(e)(iv) Claim

I turn now to analysis of that which I regard as the centrally important certificate provision, Section 5(e)(iv). That section affords protection against dilution of the conversion component of the market value of the preferred stock by providing an adjustment to the conversion price when the corporation declares a dividend of assets, including securities. The principle that appears embedded in Section 5(e)(iv) is that when the assets of the Firm are depleted through a special distribution to shareholders, the preferred will be protected by the triggering of a conversion price adjustment formula. Under Section 5(e)(iv) the number of shares into which the preferred can convert will be proportionately increased in order to maintain the value of the preferred's conversion feature. The principle seems clear enough; the realization of it will inevitably involve problems.

> (a) Section 5(e)(iv) of the certificate of designation requires Marriott, when effectuating a special dividend, to leave sufficient net assets in the corporation to permit that Section to function as intended to protect the predisposition value of the preferred stock.

The language of the certificate of designation is as follows:

5. *Conversion Rights.* The holders of shares of Convertible Preferred Stock shall have the right at their option, to convert such shares into shares of Common Stock on the following terms and conditions:

(a) Shares of Convertible Preferred Stock shall be convertible at any time into fully paid and nonassessable shares of Common Stock at a conversion price of $17.40 per share of Common Stock (the "Conversion Price").

* * *

(e) The conversion Price shall be adjusted from time to time as follows:

(iv) In case the Corporation shall, by dividend or otherwise, distribute to all holders of its Common Stock ... assets (including securities ...), the Conversion Price shall be adjusted so that the same shall equal the price determined by multiplying the Conversion Price in effect immediately prior to the close of business on the date fixed for the determination of stockholders entitled to receive such distribution by a fraction of which the numerator shall be the current market price per share (determined as provided in subsection (vi) below) of the Common Stock on the date fixed for such determination less the then fair market value (as determined by the Board of Directors, whose determination shall be conclusive and shall be described in a statement filed with the transfer agent for the Convertible Preferred Stock) of the portion of the evidences of indebtedness or assets so distributed applicable to one share of Common Stock and the denominator shall be such current market price per share of the Common Stock, such adjustment to become effective immediately prior to the opening of business on the day following the date fixed for the determination of stockholders entitled to receive such distribution. (emphasis added).

Thus, stated simply, whenever Marriott distributes assets to its common stockholders this provision protects the value of the preferred conversion right by reducing the conversion price. Protection of this type may be important to the buyer of preferred stock and presumably its inclusion will permit an issuer to arrange the sale of preferred stock on somewhat more advantageous terms than would otherwise be available. What is intuitively apparent is that in a narrow range of extreme cases, a dividend of property may be so large relative to the corporation's net worth, that following the distribution, the firm, while still solvent,[16] will not represent sufficient value to preserve the pre-dividend value of the preferred's conversion right.

Appended to this opinion are three hypothetical cases in which the Section 5(e)(iv) formula is employed. Case 1 involves a dividend of 40% of the issuing corporation's net asset value. Case 2 is a dividend of 90% of net asset value. Case 3 displays the consequences of a dividend of 95% of asset value. Given the assumptions of the examples (i.e. preferred conversion rights equal 9.1% of total pre-distribution value), only in the last case does the Section 5(e)(iv) formula fail to function.

In light of the mathematical effect demonstrated in the appended examples, a court that must construe Section 5(e)(iv) is required to conclude, in my opinion, that Marriott has voluntarily and effectively bound itself not to declare and distribute special dividends of a proportion that would deprive the preferred stockholders of the protection that that provision was intended to afford. In providing a mechanism to maintain pre-distribution value (putting to one side for the moment, how pre-distribution value is determined) the issuer impliedly but unmistakably and necessarily undertook to refrain from declaring a dividend so large that what is left in the corporation is itself worth less than the pre-distribution value of the preferred stock. No other interpretation of the certificate of designation gives the language of Section 5(e)(iv) its intended effect in all circumstances. Thus, were the facts of Case 3 the facts of this case, I would be required to find that the special dividend violated the rights of the preferred stockholders created by the certificate of designation.

Such a holding would not be inconsistent with those cases that hold that rights of preference are to be strictly construed. This strict construction perspective on the interpretation of certificates of designation has long been the law of this jurisdiction and others. While that principle does define the court's approach to construction and interpretation of the documents that create preferred stock, that principle does not excuse a court from the duty to interpret the legal meaning of the certificate of designation. Thus where the necessary implication of the language used is the existence of a right or a duty, a court construing that language is duty bound to recognize the existence of that right or that duty.

---

16. Traditionally preferred stockholders have not been treated as creditors for the amount of the liquidation preference and the preference does not count as a "claim" for fraudulent conveyance purposes.

(b) Plaintiffs have failed to introduce evidence from which it could be concluded at this time that it is reasonably probable that they will prevail on a claim that the special dividend violates Section 5(e)(iv).

    (i) The value that Section 5(e)(iv) intends to protect is the market value of the conversion feature at the time the board authorizes a special dividend transaction.

The determination that Section 5 of the certificate creates by necessary implication an obligation on the part of the corporation to leave sufficient value in the corporation following a special dividend to permit the protections it creates to function with the intended effect, raises the further question, what value does Section 5 intend to protect. Plainly it is the value of the conversion feature, that is what all of Section 5 is about, but measured at what point in time?

On the last day of trading before the announcement of the special dividend, Marriott's common stock closed at $17.125. The preferred's conversion feature, (its right to convert into 11,494,400 common shares) had a value at that time of $196,842,000. Beginning the first trading day after the announcement of the special dividend, Marriott common stock rose greatly in price. By May 21, 1993, it had increased to approximately $26.00 per share and the value of the preferred's conversion right had increased to $298.5 million.

Plaintiffs' position is that this value, as effected by the prospect of the dividend attacked, is the value that must be left in the corporation.

I cannot accept this interpretation of what good faith adherence to the provisions of the certificate requires of Marriott. Section 5(e)(iv) operates to prevent the confiscation of the value of the preferred conversion right through a special dividend. By necessary implication it limits the board's discretion with respect to the size of special dividends. But that limitation is one that has its effect when it is respected by the board of directors at the time it takes corporate action to declare the dividend. If, when declared, the dividend will leave the corporation with sufficient assets to preserve the conversion value that the preferred possesses at that time, it satisfies the limitation that such a protective provision necessarily implies. That is, Section 5(e)(iv) does not, in my opinion, explicitly or by necessary implication grant the preferred a right to assurance that any increase in the value of their conversion rights following the authorization of a special dividend be maintained.

    (ii) Plaintiffs have failed to introduce evidence that establishes a reasonable probability of their proving that the net value remaining in Host after distribution of the special dividend is or is reasonably likely to be insufficient to maintain the pre-distribution value of the preferred's conversion right.

In attempting to demonstrate that the special dividend will confiscate some part of their property, plaintiffs rely on the affidavit of Charles R. Wright, a certified public accountant. Mr. Wright states that following the special dividend the value of Host's equity will not exceed $200 million.

This opinion is based upon analyses conducted by Wolfensohn, Inc. in October 1992, concerning the transaction as planned at that time. But the transaction of October 1992 reflected a very different financial structure than that now planned; it contemplated Host bearing substantially more debt than the transaction currently envisioned. Mr. Wright's conclusions are also based upon analyses conducted by S.G. Warburg, but under the assumption that the Exchange Offer will not be effectuated. Mr. Wright stated that he did not consider later valuations of the transaction developed by Wolfensohn and S.G. Warburg to be relevant because they were based upon the assumption that the Exchange Offer would close, an assumption plaintiffs regard as unfounded. I do not accept this premise. For present purposes I assume that the Exchange Offer will close. It is an integral part of the complex transaction that is under review. Any part of that transaction could, in theory, be abandoned or modified. My analysis proceeds on the belief both that preliminary review on this application is nevertheless appropriate and that the transaction now planned is the transaction that forms the basis of that preliminary review.

The later projections by Wolfensohn and S.G. Warburg, provide a different picture of Host's financial status than the earlier ones upon which Mr. Wright relies. On May 7, 1993, Wolfensohn provided Marriott's board with current valuations of Host and International. Wolfensohn concluded that, assuming the Exchange Offer closes, Host will have a total equity value of between $371 million and $556 million.

A discounted cash flow valuation of Host produced by Wolfensohn on April 20, 1993 and based on the assumption that the Exchange Offer will be effectuated, produced a range of values from $270 million (assuming a 14% discount rate; and a multiple of 7 times EBITDA) to $884 million (assuming a 12% discount rate and a multiple of 9 times EBITDA) with a middle case of $567 million (assuming a 13% discount rate and a multiple of 8 times EBITDA.)

S.G. Warburg's valuation of Host, dated May 6, 1993, estimated the trading value of Host, assuming the Exchange Offer closes, at $1.38 to $2.84 per share or an aggregate of $179 million to $368 million. Warburg also estimated that the summary business value of Host would be in the range of $551 to $830 million or $4.25 to $6.40 per share.

The lower end of S.G. Warburg's estimate of the likely range of trading values for Host stock falls below the $196.8 million that represents the value of plaintiffs' conversion rights prior to the announcement of the distribution. Unspecified assertions by plaintiffs' expert that "major assumptions used in the discounted cash flow analysis are inappropriate" and that companies used for comparison are not comparable to Host, do not, however, provide a basis upon which to conclude that it is more likely that Host's common stock will have a value in the lower end of this range of values rather than in the higher part. The mere possibility that this will be the case is not enough to support the grant of a preliminary injunction. I assume the shape of a graph of the probabilities of any of these values in the range being "correct" would form a bell shaped curve. That is to say it is more likely that, upon more exhaustive analysis or with a more definitive valuation technique, the intrinsic value of Host would be the mean number of these ranges rather than either expressed limit of them. These higher probability mean estimates are all in excess of $196 million.

Thus, I am unable to conclude that plaintiffs have shown a sufficient probability of demonstrating that the protective functions of Section 5(e)(iv) will be frustrated by the size of the special dividend to justify the issuance of an injunction preventing the effectuation of the planned reorganization of Marriott.

> (c) Plaintiffs have not shown that defendants have breached (or are about to breach) the agreed upon formula for implementing Section 5(e)(iv).

In its June 19, 1993 proxy statement, Marriott described the process that it intends to employ with respect to the operation of Section 5(e)(iv) of the certificate. After paraphrasing the certificate language quoted above, the proxy statement states:

> The Board currently intends to determine the "fair market value" of the Distribution, for purposes of this calculation, by ascertaining the relative, intrinsic values of Host Marriott and Marriott International (with reference to all factors which it deems relevant) and by designating the allocable portion of the Current Market Price attributable to Marriott International as the fair market value of the Distribution.

In this litigation defendants have amplified their proposed method for determining fair market value of the individual distribution. Marriott intends to first determine "with reference to all relevant factors" the "intrinsic values" of International and Host. Then the fraction of the value of a Marriott share represented by International would be determined by dividing International's "intrinsic value" by the sum of the intrinsic values of International and Host. This fraction would then be multiplied by the current trading value of Marriott to determine the fair market value (per share) of International and thus of the distribution. Therefore, the fair market value of the distribution (i.e., International) is treated by the board's proposed valuation method as fraction of the market value of Marriott prior to the distribution of the dividend. The premise of this methodology is the assertion that as long as Host common stock trades at some positive value, the fair market value of International for purposes of applying Section 5(e)(iv) must he less than the current market value of Marriott; the whole (Marriott) cannot be less than the sum of its parts (International plus Host).

Defendants claim that this method of determining fair market value is consistent with the certificate and that it reaches a determination of the fair market value of the distribution that can meaningfully be compared to the current market value of Marriott. Indeed, they assert that any alternative technique which yields a value for International that is higher than the market value of Marriott must (as long as Host trades at a positive value) be faulty.

Plaintiffs contend that defendants' approach is inconsistent with the contract language. They say that it is designed to hide the fact that the special dividend is so large that the conversion price adjustment formula cannot work properly with respect to it.

Plaintiffs point out that the conversion price adjustment formula requires as a numerator the current per share market price of Marriott (determined over a 30 day period) less the "then fair market value" (expressed as a per share figure) of the assets distributed. This number can be well estimated, it is claimed, by reference to the "when-issued" market which will, for a week or so before the distribution, establish a good proxy for the market value of the assets distributed.

Plaintiffs claim that the method of determining the fair market value of International which defendants propose to employ is an attempt to manipulate Section 5(e)(iv), by artificially limiting the "fair market value" of the assets to be distributed (International's common stock) to a fraction of Marriott's total value despite the fact that Section 5(e)(iv) makes no mention of such a limitation. Plaintiffs rely on the language of the certificate which states explicitly that the board must determine the fair market value of the assets to be distributed, to support their argument that the board is required to determine this value without placing a ceiling on it of the value of Marriott.

In my opinion, Marriott's proposed technique for determining the values to employ in the contractual formula is one valid way to do what the company is contractually bound to do. It follows that this claim presents no grounds to justify the issuance of a preliminary injunction.

It is, of course, the case that plaintiffs' alternative technique might seem superior to some, in that it looks to a direct market measure of the value of the distribution. While that has appeal, it is also true that the different measuring times that this technique implies itself makes it possible that it would cause the adjustment formula to produce a negative number. Given the multiple factors that affect public securities markets, this could be true, even if far more equity were left in Host than the value of the preferred. Thus, there is good reason to reject plaintiffs' proposal even though it has appealing aspects.

Defendants' intended technique for estimating the "fair market value applicable to one share" would appear to serve the purpose of the section. As explained above, the equation is intended to operate to reduce the conversion price by the same percentage that the total assets of the company are being reduced. Assuming again that Host will have some positive net worth, it is clear that less than 100% of the assets of Marriott are being distributed. Therefore, in such a case the conversion price should be reduced by less than 100%. The method adopted by the company for determining applicable fair market value would, if fairly and competently applied, provide for the adjustment of the conversion price in a manner that effectuates the purposes of the clause. The certificate of course confers broad discretion on Marriott in implementing the formula of Section 5(e)(iv) and makes its choices "conclusive." While that grant may too imply a duty of commercial good faith, the facts adduced do not suggest that the employment of the formula by defendants has been other than in good faith.

Thus, I am unable to conclude that plaintiffs have shown a reasonable probability of success on the merits of their claim that the method of determining the fair market value of the assets to be distributed "applicable to one share of [Marriott] common stock", that defendants have announced they will employ, violates Section 5(e)(iv).

* * *

APPENDIX

The following three hypotheticals demonstrate how section 5(e)(iv) operates to preserve the economic value of the conversion rights of the preferred when the company's assets are distributed as dividends to the common stockholders, and how at extreme levels it could fail.

CASE I

Assume a company, Corporation Y, with $1 billion in assets and no debts. It has 10 million shares of common stock and 1 million shares of cumulative convertible preferred stock having a face amount and liquidation preference of $100 million. The preferred is convertible into common stock at a price of $100 face amount per common share or into 1 million common shares, in total. The certificate of designation contains a provision identical to Section 5(e)(iv).

Assume further that the capital markets operate efficiently and the common stock trades at price reflecting Corporation Y's asset values on a fully diluted basis.

Under these assumptions at time T[1], Current Market Price ("CMP") is determined as follows:

CMP = $1 billion × 1/11 million shares = $90.9091 per share

Preferred Conversion Value = 1 million shares × $90.9091/1 share = $90,909,100

At time T[2] Corporation Y declares a dividend of assets with a fair market value of $400 million or $40 per outstanding common share, leaving the company with $600 million in assets.

The conversion price would be adjusted by the same formula as applies in section 5(e)(iv)

ACP = CP × CMP − FMV/CMP

Where: ACP = Adjusted Conversion Price

CP = Conversion Price;

FMV = Fair Market Value

CMP = Current Market Price common stock

ACP = 100 × $90.9091 − $40/$90.9091 = $56.0000

The preferred would become convertible into 1,785,710 common shares, $100,000,000 × 1 common share/$56.0000 = 1,785,870 common shares with an aggregate value of $90,908,900, $600,000,000 × 1,785,710 converted shares/11,785,710 common shares = $90,908,900

Thus in this case the anti-dilution provision of the certificate would serve to preserve the economic value of the preferred stock despite the diversion of 40% of Corporation Y's net worth out of the company.

CASE II

Now assume alternatively that Corporation Y declares a special dividend to its common stockholders of $900 million of its assets or $90 per outstanding share.

The conversion price adjustment formula would work to adjust the conversion price from $100 to 1.00 per share:

ACP = $100 × $90.9091 − $90/$90.9091 = $1.0000

The preferred would become convertible into 100,000,000 shares, (91% of all common stock) at T[2].

$100,000,000 × 1 common share/$1.0000 = 100,000,000 shares

But the aggregate value of the preferred portion would remain unchanged at $90,909,091:

100,000,000 converted shares/110,000,000 common shares × $100,000,000 = $90,909,091

Thus, on these assumptions, even if 90% of Corporation Y's assets are distributed to the common stockholders, the conversion value of the preferred is maintained at its pre-distribution level by the Section 5(e)(iv) gross-up provision.

CASE III

When the special dividend is so large that insufficient equity remains in Corporation Y to maintain the value of the preferred upon conversion the gross up provisions will fail to work.[1] In such a situation the gross-up equation provides for a negative adjusted conversion price and is therefore meaningless.

For example: If Corporation Y declared a dividend of $950 million of its assets, the gross-up equation would give the following result:

ACP = CP × CMP − FMV/CMP

ACP = $100 × $90.9091 − $95.00/$90.9091 = −($4.499)

Thus, a distribution of $950 million leaves only $50 million in assets in the corporation, making it impossible for the preferred to maintain its pre-

---

1. They may also fail, in the specific case of Section 5(e)(iv) because the measurement period for "current market price" is somewhat historical while the measurement period for "fair market value" of assets distributed is current. Thus, it may happen, given the potentials for fluctuating market prices, for a negative number to be generated simply as an artifact of the formula.

distribution conversion value of $90.909 million. For that reason it also causes Section 5(e)(iv) to fail to work meaningfully.

QUESTIONS

1. What is a short sale?

2. What did plaintiffs expect to achieve by selling Marriott common stock short?

3. If the announcement of the special dividend meant that no dividends were likely to be paid on the preferred stock, why did the market value of the preferred stock increase from $62.75 to $77.00 on June 4, 1993?

4. The court explains that the plaintiffs haven't profited very much from the rise in the value of both the common and preferred stock of Marriott. Why not?

5. What does the court mean when it says that "the premium that the preferred stock commanded over the common into which it could convert (i.e., the market value of the preferences) however, had by June 4th, shrunk, to $3.00"?

6. The opinion states that on the last trading day before announcement of the special dividend, the right to convert the preferred into 11,494,400 common shares, had a value of $196,842,000. This represents the market value of the common. Is that the correct measure of the conversion right's value? Is it the correct measure under the certificate of designation for the preferred? Is there a difference between the market value of the conversion right of the preferred and its value on the date of a hypothetical conversion?

7. Plaintiffs argue that the Marriott family wants the preferred to convert before the dividend, because a conversion after the dividend would give the preferred shareholders a majority of the Host common stock, thus taking control away from the Marriott family. How can this be?

8. Chancellor Allen holds that Marriott must leave enough assets in Host to preserve the conversion value of the preferred. What is the source of this holding?

9. If Chancellor Allen is correct that Marriott owes a contractual obligation to preserve the conversion value of the preferred, what language does he look to in the Certificate of Designation?

10. Could the certificate of designation provided specific protection against large distributions that lowered the conversion value of the preferred?

11. Why does the court pick the conversion value of the day before the distribution was announced? Why is that value the one that sets a ceiling on Marriott's distribution?

12. Some experts (namely S.G. Warburg, plaintiffs' expert), found potential trading values of the common stock between $179,000,000 and $368,000,000, with the lower end below the conversion value of

$196,000,000 used by the court as a minimum. Why doesn't the court hold that this breaches the implied covenant?

13. The Plaintiffs complain about how Marriott calculated the formula for valuing the distribution. What is the nature of their complaint? Marriott argues that the fair market value of International must be less than the current market value of Marriott. Is this necessarily true?

NOTE ON ANTI–DILUTION CLAUSES

All anti-dilution clauses cover such things as stock splits, and there is little variation in these clauses. Some adjust for stock dividends, but these clauses are more variable, because the problem is more complex. Small stock dividends may be the equivalent of a cash dividend in terms of their effect on the value of the outstanding shares, and may not be covered by these clauses. Larger stock dividends become the equivalent of stock splits, and generally are covered. The *Stephenson* case, infra, at footnote 2, contains an example of language that covers all stock dividends. The adjustment in that provision provides "then the number of shares of capital stock which may thereafter be purchased upon the exercise of the rights represented hereby shall be increased in proportion to the increase through such dividend or subdivision and the purchase price per share shall be decreased in such proportion." In some cases provision may be made for extraordinarily large cash dividends, as well as other dividends in kind, such as the dividend of shares of a subsidiary corporation found in the *Korenvaes* case.

As Jerome S. Katzin pointed out: "These anti-dilution clauses are designed to treat the convertible holder as though he were a shareholder and protect his pro-rata position." Jerome S. Katzin, Financial and Legal Problems in the Use of Convertible Securities, 24 Business Lawyer 359 (1960).

More difficult problems arise when new shares are sold. What happens when the market price of a publicly traded stock declines and the company can only sell shares at a market price that is below the exercise price? Typically no adjustment occurs. Common stockholders have suffered from the decline in the price of the common stock, and this is a risk that holders of options and conversion rights will also expect to bear. In some cases, shares may be sold above the exercise price but below the current market price of the stock. Obviously such an issue is dilutive for existing shareholders. Should it also be treated as a dilutive event for option holders, if the sale price is above the exercise price? If the reasoning is to treat the option holder as if he were a shareholder, then no protection should be provided. Option holders get their protection in these cases from the fiduciary duties owed to shareholders not to dilute their interests unless there is a good (presumably long-term) business purpose for the dilution, such as engaging in an attractive acquisition. (An exception may exist where a company makes a below-market offering to its own shareholders, in the form of a rights offering.)

Different rules are generally provided where the stock is not publicly traded, as in the case of development stage companies financed with convertible preferred stock. When new shares are sold at prices below the exercise price of options or convertibles, anti-dilution language generally kicks in. After the NASDAQ market index dropped from over 5,000 in early 2000 to a low of below 1500 in 2002, valuations for many small companies that had been anticipating public offerings plummeted, and public offerings were no longer feasible. These companies were forced to engage in new rounds of private financing through venture capitalists at lower valuations than before. These transactions, called "down rounds," triggered antidilution clauses where conversion rights on earlier rounds of convertible preferred stock were at higher prices. Venture capitalists often have considerable bargaining power in negotiating the terms of these clauses, especially in down rounds.

The toughest of these clauses is called the "full ratchet" clause. Here the conversion price is reduced to give the holders the same lower price paid by the most recent investor (there is no upward ratchet if stock is sold for a higher price). The tough part of this clause is that the conversion price ratchets down to this price regardless of how many shares are sold in the down round. This can be extremely favorable to investors. Consider the following example. A company has one million shares of common stock owned by founders, who paid one penny per share. The company also has outstanding 250,000 shares of convertible preferred stock outstanding, which convert into common stock at $1.00 per share. Thus, if all the preferred were converted, the venture capital investors would own 20% of the company. Now assume that the Company's board of directors invites a new person to join the board, and votes to issue him one share of common stock for one cent. At this point the rights adjust so the venture capitalists are now entitled to buy new shares at $0.01 per share, so their 250,000 shares of $1.00 preferred now convert into 25,000,000 shares of common stock. Now the venture capitalists own 25,000,000 out of 26,000,001 shares, or over 96% of the common stock!

The clause that is more desirable for the company and existing shareholders is the "weighted average" clause, which takes into account the number of shares issued. This clause works as follows:

Number of shares previously outstanding times conversion price
Plus consideration for additional shares

Divided by
Number of shares outstanding after additional issue

Under this formula, which is much more widely used, the results in the first example would be as follows:

$$\frac{(1,000,000)\,(\$1.00) \;+\; \$0.01}{1,000,001} \;=\;\;\; \$0.999999$$

Finally, when issuers have more bargaining power, they may insist that holders of convertibles must "pay to play" in any subsequent down round of financing. Under this scheme, convertible holders must purchase a pro rata share of any down round before the anti-dilution protection becomes applicable.

The worst case is discussed in Part 6—so-called "death spiral" financing, used by some smaller publicly-traded companies, which ratchets the exercise price down to the market price should it be below the stated price at the time of exercise. As Part 6 points out, some companies that went public before the NASDAQ crash, only to need new capital at a time when public markets were not accessible, resorted to private financing with convertibles containing these onerous terms.

Stephenson v. Plastics Corporation of America, Inc.

276 Minn. 400, 150 N.W.2d 668 (1967).

■ Sheran, Justice.

Action was instituted by plaintiffs against defendants on the theory that defendant Plastics Corporation of America, Inc., (hereafter called Plastics) breached contract obligations springing from stock purchase warrants issued by it, and that defendant United Fabricators and Electronics, Inc., (hereafter called United) participated in the resulting wrong to the plaintiffs by conduct constituting willful and malicious interference with the contract relationship. Defendant Plastics denied the claimed breach of contract and cross-claimed for indemnity as against United in the event plaintiffs should prevail. United denied the alleged breach of contract and the asserted unlawful interference. Each defendant moved for judgment on the pleadings. United's motion was granted; Plastics' was denied.

* * *

The Warrants

The stock subscription warrants are dated December 16, 1960. It will be helpful, at the outset, to place their provisions in these compartments:

(A) The principal object of the agreements.

(B) Corporate changes conceived as affecting the principal object of the agreements.

(C) Mechanisms provided for preserving the principal object of the agreements in the event of such changes.

(D) Provisions for notice of such corporate changes.

A. Principal Object

The principal object of the agreements was to afford the holders or their assigns (such as these plaintiffs) the option for a period of 5 years to obtain 30,000 shares of the "capital" stock of the company at the price of $1 per share. It is specifically provided that the warrants were not to entitle the holders to any voting rights or other rights as a stockholder of the company.

B. Anticipated Corporate Changes

In an apparent effort to prevent a defeat of the basic purpose of the warrants by a change in corporate circumstances, 12 different possible situations are anticipated in paragraph 3 of the agreements:

(1) A distribution upon capital stock payable in capital stock, i.e., a "stock dividend."[2]

(2) A division ("split") of the outstanding capital stock.[2]

(3) A combining ("reverse split") of outstanding capital stock.[2]

(4) A cash dividend upon stock not payable from net earnings or earned surplus.[3]

(5) *Such a dividend upon stock but not payable in cash.*[3]

(6) *A capital "reorganization."*[4]

---

2. 3(a). "In case the Company shall declare any dividend or other distribution upon its outstanding capital stock payable in capital stock or shall subdivide its outstanding shares of capital stock into a greater number of shares, then the number of shares of capital stock which may thereafter be purchased upon the exercise of the rights represented hereby shall be increased in proportion to the increase through such dividend or subdivision and the purchase price per share shall be decreased in such proportion. In case the Company shall at any time combine the outstanding shares of its capital stock into a smaller number of shares, the number of shares of capital stock which may thereafter be purchased upon the exercise of the rights represented hereby shall be decreased in proportion to the decrease through such combination and the purchase price per share shall be increased in such proportion."

3. 3(b). "In case the Company shall declare a dividend upon the capital stock payable otherwise than out of earnings or surplus (other than paid-in surplus) or otherwise than in capital stock, the purchase price per share in effect immediately prior to the declaration of such dividend shall be reduced by an amount equal, in the case of a dividend in cash, to the amount thereof payable per share of the capital stock or, in the case of any other dividend, to the fair value thereof per share of the capital stock as determined by the Board of Directors of the Company. For the purposes of the foregoing a dividend other than in cash shall be considered payable out of earnings or surplus (other than paid-in surplus) only to the extent that such earnings or surplus are charged an amount equal to the fair value of such dividend as determined by the Board of Directors of the Company. Such reductions shall take effect as of the date on which a record is taken for the purpose of such dividend, or, if a record is not taken, the date as of which the holders of capital stock of record entitled to such dividend are to be determined."

4. 3(c). "If any capital reorganization or reclassification of the capital stock of the Company, or consolidation or merger of the Company with another corporation, or the sale of all or substantially all of its assets to another corporation shall be effected, then, as a condition of such reorganization, reclassification, consolidation, merger or sale, lawful and adequate provision shall be made whereby the holder hereof shall thereafter have the right to purchase and receive upon the basis and upon the terms and conditions specified in this Warrant and in lieu of the shares of the capital stock of the Company immediately theretofore purchasable and receivable upon the exercise of the rights represented hereby, such shares of stock, securities or assets as may be issued or payable with respect to or in exchange for a number of outstanding shares of such capital stock equal to the number of shares of such capital stock immediately theretofore purchasable and receivable upon the exercise of the rights represented hereby had such reorganization, reclassification, consolidation, merger or sale not taken place, and in any such case appropriate provision shall be made with respect to the rights and interests of the holder of this Warrant to the end that the provisions hereof (including without limitation provisions for adjustment of the purchase price per share and of the number of shares purchasable upon the exercise of this Warrant) shall thereafter be applicable, as nearly as may be in relation to any shares of stock, securities or assets thereafter deliverable upon the exercise hereof." (Italics supplied.)

(7) A reclassification of stock.[4]
(8) A consolidation with another corporation.[4]
(9) A merger with another corporation.[4]
(10) *The sale of all or substantially all of the assets of the corporation to another corporation.*[4]
(11) An offer to holders of capital stock for pro rata subscription for additional shares of stock or any other rights.[5]
(12) A voluntary or involuntary dissolution.[5]

C. Contemplated Adjustment

In the event of the occurrence of situations 1 to 3 (stock dividends; splits; reverse splits) the warrants provide for adjustment by decrease or increase in the number of shares purchasable and the price per share to be paid.[6]

In situations 4 and 5 (depleting dividend) the adjustment is to be accomplished by reducing the purchase price per share (i.e., $1 per share) by (a) the amount of the dividend, if paid in cash, and (b) the fair value of distributed assets other than cash.[7]

In situations 6 to 10 (reorganization; stock reclassification; consolidation; merger; sale of all or substantially all assets) it is required by paragraph 3(c) of the agreement that "appropriate provision" be made for the protection of the rights and interests of the warrant holders.[8]

Paragraph 3(c) which deals with situations 6 to 10 concludes with this sentence:

> " * * * Any such shares of stock, securities or assets which the holder hereof may be entitled to purchase pursuant to this paragraph (c) shall be included within the term 'capital stock' as used herein."

This sentence becomes significant when considered in conjunction with paragraph 2 of the agreements which concludes with this sentence:

> " * * * The Company further covenants and agrees that during the period within which the rights represented by this Warrant may be exercised, the Company will at all times have authorized, and reserved, a sufficient number of shares of capital stock to provide for the exercise of the rights represented by this Warrant * * *." (Italics supplied.)

We interpret these provisions, considered together, to impose on Plastics an obligation to have reserved a sufficient number of shares of United stock to provide for the exercise of the rights represented by the warrants if the arrangement planned and executed by the seven directors of the two corporations, described hereinafter, amounted to a reorganization; stock reclassification; consolidation; merger; or a sale of all or substantially all of Plastics' assets to United.

---

5. Reference to situations 11 and 12 is to be found in the notice provision set out in footnote 11.

6. See footnote 2, supra.

7. See footnote 3, supra.

8. See footnote 4, supra.

Paragraph 3(c) provided with respect to situations 8 to 10 (consolidation; merger; sale of all or substantially all of assets) that the successor corporation should be required to assume "the obligation to deliver to such [warrant] holder such shares of stock, securities or assets as, in accordance with the foregoing provisions, such holder may be entitled to purchase."[9]

D. Notice Provisions

In situations 1 to 3 (stock dividends; splits; reverse splits) set out above, the company obligates itself to give notice to the warrant holder stating "the purchase price per share resulting from such adjustment and the increase or decrease, if any, in the number of shares purchasable at such price upon the exercise of this Warrant."[10]

In situations 1 (stock dividend) and 4 to 12 (dividends; reorganization; reclassification; consolidation; merger; sale of all or substantially all of assets; subscription offer; dissolution) a 20–day notice to the warrant holder is required by paragraph 3(e) which notice in situations 4 and 5 (dividends), 11 (subscription offer), and 12 (dissolution) at least, must specify "the date on which the holders of capital stock shall be entitled thereto," and in situations 6 (reorganization), 7 (reclassification), 8 (consolidation), 9 (merger), 10 (sale) and 12 (dissolution) must specify "the date on which the holders of capital stock shall be entitled to exchange their capital stock for securities or other property."[11]

---

9. 3(c). " * * * The Company shall not effect any such consolidation, merger or sale, unless prior to or simultaneously with the consummation thereof the successor corporation (if other than the Company) resulting from such consolidation or merger or the corporation purchasing such assets shall assume by written instrument executed and mailed or delivered to the holder hereof at the last address of such holder appearing on the books of the Company, the obligation to deliver to such holder such shares of stock, securities or assets as, in accordance with the foregoing provisions, such holder may be entitled to purchase."

10. 3(d). "Upon any adjustment of the number of shares of capital stock which may be purchased upon the exercise of the rights represented hereby and/or of the purchase price per share, then and in each such case the Company shall give written notice thereof, by first class mail, postage prepaid, addressed to the holder of this Warrant at the address of such holder as shown on the books of the Company, which notice shall state the purchase price per share resulting from such adjustment and the increase or decrease, if any, in the number of shares purchasable at such price upon the exercise of this Warrant, setting forth in reasonable detail the method of calculation and the facts upon which such calculation is based."

11. 3(e). "In case at any time:

"(1) the Company shall pay any dividend payable in stock upon its capital stock or make any distribution (other than regular cash dividends paid at an established annual rate) to the holders of its capital stock;

"(2) the Company shall offer for subscription pro rata to the holders of its capital stock any additional shares of stock of any class or other rights;

"(3) there shall be any capital reorganization, or reclassification of the capital stock of the Company, or consolidation or merger of the Company with, or sale of all or substantially all of its assets to, another corporation; or

"(4) there shall be a voluntary or involuntary dissolution, liquidation or winding up of the Company; then, in any one or more of such cases, the Company shall give to the holder of this Warrant (aa) at least twenty days' prior written notice of the date on which the books of the Company shall close or a record shall be taken for such dividend, distribution or subscription

The Corporate Change

In the latter part of 1964 and at a time when the warrants analyzed above were outstanding, Plastics was controlled and governed by a board of seven directors who agreed among themselves:

(1) A part of the assets of Plastics then devoted to the production of thermoplastic products by one of the divisions of Plastics should be transferred to a newly created corporation; the newly created corporation should, in exchange, transfer all of its stock to Plastics. (The new corporation, United Fabricators and Electronics, Inc., which we refer to as "United," was incorporated March 11, 1965.)

(2) All of the stock of the newly created corporation to be transferred to Plastics should be distributed to Plastics shareholders of record on February 22, 1965, and warrant holders exercising their stock options by March 16, 1965. (This agreement to distribute all of the stock of the newly created corporation to Plastics shareholders of necessity made it impossible for Plastics to reserve a sufficient number of shares of United's stock to provide for the exercise of an option with respect to such stock after March 16, 1965, but before expiration of the 5–year option period.)

(3) Three of the seven directors then in control of Plastics should resign and become the directors of United. The four remaining should continue in control of Plastics.

(4) The United stock to be acquired by the four directors of Plastics as a result of the distribution contemplated by step (2) above should be exchanged for the Plastics stock held by the three departing directors so that the one group would be in control of United and the other in control of Plastics when the transaction was completed.

Agreements were made intending to bind the seven directors and the corporations (Plastics and United) to this plan, and these agreements have been fully executed.

On February 24, 1965, Plastics gave notice to holders of stock purchase warrants, including plaintiffs, reading as follows:

"You are hereby notified that the Directors of Plastics Corporation of America, Inc. have authorized a distribution on March 31, 1965 to the common shareholders of said corporation of one (1) share of United

---

rights or for determining rights to vote in respect of any such reorganization, reclassification, consolidation, merger, sale, dissolution, liquidation or winding up, and (bb) in the case of any such reorganization, reclassification, consolidation, merger, sale, dissolution, liquidation or winding up, at least twenty days' prior written notice of the date when the same shall take place. Such notice in accordance with the foregoing clause (aa) shall also specify, in the case of any such dividend, distribution or subscription rights, the date on which the holders of capital stock shall be entitled thereto, and such notice in accordance with the foregoing clause (bb) shall also specify the date on which the holders of capital stock shall be entitled to exchange their capital stock for securities or other property deliverable upon such reorganization, reclassification, consolidation, merger, sale, dissolution, liquidation or winding up, as the case may be. Each such written notice shall be given by first class mail, postage prepaid, addressed to the holder of this Warrant at the address of such holder as shown on the books of the Company."

Fabricators & Electronics, Inc. for each two (2) shares of Plastics Corporation of America, Inc. held of record on February 22, 1965.

"Inasmuch as the holders of Stock Purchase Warrants of Plastics Corporation of America, Inc. are entitled to twenty days' notice of such distribution, the Directors have established March 16, 1965 as the record date for such distribution for the holders of Stock Purchase Warrants who shall hereafter become a shareholder by reason of the exercise of such Warrants."

Plaintiffs did not undertake to exercise their option to purchase Plastics stock until December 1965. We assume for present purposes (but do not decide) that they made an effective exercise of the option embodied in the warrants before the expiration of the 5–year period specified in it.

The theory of plaintiffs' pleading is that they are entitled upon exercise of their option before the expiration of the 5–year period to have the shares of Plastics stock specified in the warrants and in addition that number of the shares of United stock which would have been distributed to plaintiffs had they been stockholders when the distribution of United stock was in fact made; and that if specific performance is impossible, damages should be awarded.

1. In our opinion, the order of the trial court granting judgment for United against plaintiffs on the pleadings can be sustained if, but only if, any one of these legal conclusions follow from the facts summarized:

(a) The warrants created no right in plaintiffs to share in the distribution of United stock in any event.

* * *

2a. If the distribution of United stock was a dividend not charged to net earnings or earned surplus, plaintiffs would have no right as against United because in such event, by the terms of the warrants, plaintiffs' position was to be protected by reducing the purchase price per share of Plastics stock by the fair value of the United stock determined as of the date of distribution. In our opinion, it cannot be held on the present record that the parties to the warrants intended a transaction of this kind to be treated as a dividend.

* * *

There is a difference between the transactions involved in the present case and a "dividend" in the usual sense of that word. In Hoberg v. John Hoberg Co., 170 Wis. 50, 173 N.W. 639, 173 N.W. 952, it was held that a corporation's pro rata distribution to its stockholders of recently acquired stock of another corporation was not a dividend, emphasizing that no attempt was made to meet a dividend obligation by the transfer. In determining whether a transaction constitutes a "dividend," consideration must be given to the context in which the term "dividend" is used; the consequences that turn upon the answer to the question; and the facts of the particular case. We believe that it would be premature to rule as a matter of law upon the limited record now before us that the present transaction was intended to be a "dividend" within the meaning of the warrants.

Ordinarily the object of a dividend is to enable the shareholders to enjoy the fruits of a corporate operation. It is at least inferable that the purpose of the distribution of United's stock to Plastics shareholders was intended primarily (a) to enable the directors who remained with Plastics to acquire the stock of that corporation distributed to the three directors who were taking over the management of United and (b) to give the three departing directors control of the newly created corporation through exchange of their Plastics stock for the distributed shares of United coming into the hands of the four Plastics directors who remained. In fact it is reasonable to infer that this exchange of United's stock for Plastics after the distribution was an essential part of the agreement between the seven directors and that but for this understanding the "spin-off" would never have taken place. So considered, we cannot say that the warrants declare clearly and unambiguously that a transaction of this character was intended to be treated as a "dividend" within the meaning of the language of the warrants.

We do not disagree with United's contention that a "spin-off" can involve or be executed by a means of a dividend of a new company's stock to the old company's shareholders. See, Rockefeller v. United States, 257 U.S. 176, 42 S. Ct. 68, 66 L. ed. 186; Siegel, When Corporations Divide: A Statutory and Financial Analysis, 79 Harv. L. Rev. 534. We hold only that the question cannot be resolved in the present situation without the aid of extrinsic evidence.

2b. If the transaction does not represent a "dividend" within the meaning of the warrants, then what was it? Plaintiffs contend that it was a capital reorganization (situation 6 above) or a sale of all or substantially all of the assets of the corporation to another corporation (situation 10 above). If so (unless the notice set out above served to accelerate the time within which plaintiffs' option was exercisable with respect to the distribution), the corporation was obligated by the terms of the warrants to reserve a sufficient number of shares of United stock to permit the exercise of the right of the warrant holders to acquire it for the full 5–year term of the warrants. This is so because paragraph 3(c) of the agreement provides that, in the event of any capital reorganization or the sale of all or substantially all of the corporate assets to another corporation, "lawful and adequate provision shall be made whereby the holder hereof shall thereafter have the right to purchase and receive * * * such shares of stock, securities or assets as may be issued or payable with respect to or in exchange for a number of outstanding shares of such capital stock equal to the number of shares or such capital stock immediately theretofore purchasable and receivable upon the exercise of the rights represented hereby had such reorganization, * * * or sale not taken place." The obligation to hold the required number of shares of United in reserve follows from the concluding sentence of paragraph 3(c)[12] requiring that any such shares of stock or assets be included within the term "capital stock" as used in the warrants.

2c.   Although not free from ambiguity, we believe it would be possible for the plaintiffs to establish that the transaction here involved was a "capital reorganization" within the meaning of the warrants. The net result was that each Plastics shareholder held an interest represented by stock in exactly the same assets after the transaction as before. Before the transaction this interest was represented by stock in one corporation only; after the transaction the interest was represented by stock held in two corporations. All that was changed was the "organization."

The pertinent Federal and Minnesota income tax provisions declare transactions of this kind to be "reorganizations."[13]

* * *

United points out that the warrant contracts provide that upon reorganization a warrant holder is entitled to receive "*in lieu of* the shares of the capital stock of the Company immediately theretofore purchasable and receivable" certain stock or other assets of the transferee corporation. (Italics supplied.) It asserts that this shows that the parties to the warrant contracts contemplated that upon the reorganization a new corporation would take over and completely supersede the old one.

However, this provision does not compel the interpretation defendant would give it. It may simply mean that the warrant holder is entitled to a certain amount of stock of the old corporation, and in addition thereto (and in lieu merely of more stock of the old corporation), a certain amount of stock of the new corporation. Especially is this interpretation justifiable in

---

12.   The sentence, to which reference has been made, reads: "Any such shares of stock, securities or assets which the holder hereof may be entitled to purchase pursuant to this paragraph (c) shall be included within the term 'capital stock' as used herein."

13.   Section 368(a) of the 1954 Internal Revenue Code, 68A Stat. 120, 26 USCA, § 368(a), provides in part:

"(a) Reorganization.—

"(1) In General.—For purposes of parts I and II and this part, the term 'reorganization' means—

* * *

"(D) a transfer by a corporation of all or a part of its assets to another corporation if immediately after the transfer the transferor, or one or more of its shareholders (including persons who were shareholders immediately before the transfer), or any combination thereof, is in control of the corporation to which the assets are transferred; but only if, in pursuance of the plan, stock or securities of the corporation to which the assets are transferred are distributed in a transaction which qualifies under section 354, 355, or 356."

Section 355 covers, inter alia, a corporation's distributions to its shareholders of stock of a corporation which it controlled immediately before the distribution.

Minn. St. 290.136, subd. 9(a)(1)(D), is identical to the Federal provision.

United asserts that the present transaction was taxed as an ordinary dividend rather than as a reorganization, but this fact does not establish that it was a dividend as the term is used in the warrant.

light of the fact that the words in question also control where there has been a sale of "all or substantially all" of Plastics' assets. In the event of a sale of only substantially all of Plastics' assets, the agreement probably contemplates the warrant holder receiving both Plastics stock and stock of the vendee.

Defendant points out that the stock warrants' reference to Plastics' duty to require the "successor corporation" to assume the duty to honor the stock warrants covers only situations of consolidation, merger, or sale of all or substantially all of Plastics' assets and urges that this must mean that "capital reorganization" comprehends only situations involving a structural change within Plastics. But a change in Plastics' structure resulting in the birth of a new corporation is not necessarily excluded from the term "capital reorganization" by this language. The same may be said of the fact that the warrants referred to the giving of 20–day notice of the date that the books would close and a record would be taken "for determining rights to vote in respect of any such reorganization." Defendant insists this means that only "reorganizations" upon which shareholders vote in accordance with § 301.55 are included. Again, the argument is persuasive, but not so clear that plaintiffs should not be allowed to present evidence on the matter.

2d. In the alternative, plaintiffs urge that the evidence may establish that the transaction was a sale of "all or substantially all" of Plastics' assets. The complaint does not allege any particular proportion of Plastics' assets as having been transferred, merely stating that "the assets of its United Fabricators and Electronics Division, and certain other assets" were transferred.[15] Thus, at this stage of the proceedings, no proper evidence has been adduced on such matters as the proportion of Plastics' assets which were transferred; the nature of those assets (as compared to that of the assets retained); the relationship of the assets transferred and of those retained to Plastics' past and present objects and purposes; or the degree to which the transfer was unusual and out of the ordinary course of Plastics' business.

* * *

Conclusion

The difficulty we have had with this case comes from the fact that the provisions of the warrants do not seem to deal specifically with a situation such as that described in the pleadings where, in an apparent effort to resolve a conflict in business judgment as between the directors, the assets of the original corporation are divided with one group given operating control of one phase of the corporate activity and the other assuming

---

15. Defendant asserts that the claim that transfer was of substantially all of Plastics' assets "is clearly refuted by facts contained in the pleadings which make it clear that the spin-off involved something less than one-half of PCA's net worth," citing a portion of the complaint and certain documents made part of Plastics' pleadings. Plastics' pleadings are not to be considered as admitted on this motion on the pleadings; moreover, the portions cited do not clearly support defendant's assertion.

control of the balance. It is reasonable, in view of the elaborate effort to anticipate all possible changes that might affect the rights of warrant holders, to attribute to Plastics a general intent that the option rights of persons in the position of these plaintiffs should not be diminished by an arrangement which seems to have been particularly responsive to the needs of those in control of the corporation. But the language of the warrants is not so clear and unequivocal as to give a solution to the present problem without affording the parties an opportunity to present such evidence as may be available to clarify the ambiguities which have been discussed.

* * *

Reversed and remanded.

QUESTIONS

1. Why isn't this a dividend not payable in cash, covered by Paragraph 3(b) of the agreement?

2. Does this opinion suggest that no spin-off transaction, in which shareholders receive shares in a former subsidiary, would ever be covered by the adjustment for dividends other than in cash?

3. If the court had treated this transaction as a dividend not payable in cash, what provision would have been made to protect the warrant holders?

Wood v. Coastal States Gas Corporation

401 A.2d 932 (Del. 1979).

■ DUFFY, J.

This appeal is from an order of the Court of Chancery dismissing the complaints in a consolidated class action filed by the owners of two series of preferred stock[1] in Coastal States Gas Corporation (Coastal), a Delaware corporation. The suit is against Coastal, two of its subsidiaries and its chief executive officer. While this litigation is part of a complex controversy in a mosaic of many persons and disputes, it is entirely between the owners of Coastal's preferred stock and the owners of its common stock.

I

The facts out of which the dispute arises involve the sale and delivery of natural gas to many cities and corporate users in the State of Texas and, although our involvement is limited, we must recite some of them to put the appeal into context. For that purpose, the relevant facts are these:

---

1. One series is designated, "$1.83 Cumulative Convertible Preferred Stock, Series B," and the other, "$1.19 Cumulative Convertible Preferred Stock, Series A." The certificate of rights and preferences for each series is identical and thus what is said herein of one is applicable to both. We will refer to the stock in the singular as "Series A," or "Series B," or the "preferred stock."

A significant part of Coastal's business is the gathering, transporting and marketing of natural gas, all of which is conducted by a subsidiary, Coastal States Gas Producing Co. (Producing), also a defendant in this action. Producing, in turn, has a subsidiary, Lo–Vac. Gathering Co. (Lo–Vac.), another defendant, which supplies the gas to intrastate customers in Texas, including the Cities of Austin, Brownsville, Corpus Christi and San Antonio.

As a result of several factors associated with the "energy crisis" in the early 1970s, the wellhead price of natural gas increased significantly (from about 20 cents per 1000 cubic feet to about $2.00 for the same quantity) and Lo–Vac. was unable to honor its obligations to deliver gas to its customers at contract prices. In 1973, Lo–Vac. sought and obtained interim permission from the Railroad Commission of Texas (the agency vested with jurisdiction over intrastate utilities in Texas) to increase its rates; that authorization permitted Lo–Vac. to pass to its customers certain of its own cost increases. After the higher rates went into effect, a large number of Lo–Vac. industrial and municipal customers filed suits against Lo–Vac., Producing, Coastal and Oscar Wyatt (Coastal's chief executive officer, the owner of the single largest block of its common stock and a defendant in this suit) for breach of contract.

In December 1977, the Commission entered a final order denying Lo–Vac.'s original petition for rate relief and, in effect, rescinding the interim order which had authorized the increase. The Commission then directed Lo–Vac. to comply with the contract rates and ordered Coastal, Producing and Lo–Vac. to refund the rate increment which had been charged to customers under the 1973 interim order. It is estimated that the refundable amount exceeds $1.6 billion—which is about three times Coastal's net worth.

Given this state of affairs, with its obvious and enormous implications for a large section of Texas, settlement negotiations were undertaken and, eventually, a complex plan evolved. It is unnecessary for us to detail the plan, but the following summary states its substance:

(1) The substantial litigation and disputes between the natural gas sales customers of Lo–Vac. and Coastal, Producing, Lo–Vac. and Wyatt, which developed as a result of the "Lo–Vac. problem," will be settled;

(2) Producing will be renamed "Valery Energy Corporation," restructured into a corporate enterprise and spun off from Coastal; it will consist principally of Producing's present gas utility pipe-line and extraction plant operations, including Lo–Vac., and a Texas retail gas distribution division of Coastal;

(3) There will be transfers to a trust for the benefit of the customers who adopt the settlement plan ("Settling Customers") of: (a) approximately 1,196,218 shares (or about 5.3%) of the voting securities of Coastal; (b) a one-year interest-bearing promissory note of Valery in the principal amount of $8,000,000; (c) 13.4% of the outstanding shares of the common stock of Valery; and (d) 1,150,000 shares ($115,000,000

aggregate liquidation value) of Valery Preferred Stock, $8.50 Cumulative Series A;

(4) Coastal will issue to Valery approximately 805,130 shares (with approximately $80,513,000 aggregate liquidation value) of Coastal's $8.50 Cumulative Preferred Stock, Series D, $.33 1/3 par value (which is a new class of stock);

(5) A long-term program will be established providing for the expenditure of $180,000,000 to $230,000,000 (subject to certain increases or decreases, with a maximum commitment estimated at $495,000,000), by Coastal to find and develop gas reserves to be made available to the Lo–Vac. System and to be offered for sale by Coastal to Valery at discounted prices and, in turn, resold to Lo–Vac. (or, in some instances, to third parties) at higher prices, with the net proceeds (in excess of the cost of gas) received by Valery on such resale to be paid to the trust for the benefit of certain Settling Customers;

(6) There will be a new gas sales rate structure for Lo–Vac. designed to stabilize it as a viable public utility.

In addition, there will be a distribution by Coastal, in the form of an extraordinary dividend chargeable to earned surplus, to its common stockholders (except Wyatt) of the balance (86.6%) of the Valery common stock not transferred to the trust referred to in (3)(c) above.[2] Shareholders will receive one share of Valery for each share of Coastal common held at the time of the spin-off. It is this distribution which is at the center of this litigation between the preferred and common stockholders of Coastal. And Coastal's dividend history of annual payments to the preferred but none (with one exception) to the common suggests a reason for this. Coastal has paid regular quarterly dividends of $.2975 per share on the $1.19 Series A and $.4575 per share on the $1.83 Series B since each was issued. Only one dividend of $.075 per share has been paid on the common in the last twenty years.

Coastal's Board of Directors unanimously approved the settlement[3] and, in August 1978, the Commission gave its approval. The Coastal management then submitted the plan for approval at a special meeting of its stockholders called for November 10. * * *

* * *

Holders of the Series A and Series B preferred stock, (plaintiffs), filed an action in the Court of Chancery to enjoin the special shareholders

---

2. The Valero shares trade on a "when issued" basis at $6.50 to $7.00 per share (against an assumed market value of $6.50 per share).

3. Fletcher Yarbrough, who had been nominated by the Securities and Exchange Commission to serve as a director on the Coastal Board, testified at trial that the

"... complex of problems relating to Lo–Vaca, both before the Railroad Commission and in the litigation, simply had to be settled, that there was a truly unacceptably high risk that this problem could destroy the corporation and the value of the shares of the corporation...."

meeting. They alleged that the settlement plan breaches the "Certificate of the Designations, Preferences and Relative, Participating Optional or other Special Rights" (Certificate) of the Series A and Series B preferred stock. In essence, plaintiffs say that the plan violates their Certificate rights because the preferred will not receive any of the Valery shares, that is, the 86.6% to be distributed entirely to the Coastal common.

After a trial on the merits, the Vice Chancellor entered judgment for defendants and ordered plaintiffs to pay the costs of giving notice to the members of the class of the pendency of the action. The Court determined that the settlement plan and, more specifically, the spin-off of Producing and the distribution of Valery stock to the common stockholders of Coastal, is not a "recapitalization" within the meaning of the Certificate. (If it is, all parties concede that the preferred is entitled to participate in the distribution of the Valery shares.) The Vice Chancellor reasoned that a key phrase, "in lieu of," in the Certificate implies that the existing shares of Coastal common must be exchanged for something else before there is a "recapitalization" which creates rights in the preferred. And he found support for that conclusion in another Certificate provision which permits Coastal to pay a dividend to holders of common stock, in other than its own common, without affecting the rights of the preferred.

The Court also ruled that the holders of the preferred stock were not entitled to vote as a class on the settlement plan, because the requirements of the Certificate for such a vote had not been met.

Finally, the Court considered plaintiffs' claims that the settlement plan is unfair to the preferred, unjustly enriched the common and did not have a proper business purpose, and concluded that the rights of the preferred are found, under the circumstances of this case, solely in the Certificate, not in concepts of fairness or fiduciary duty.

On appeal, plaintiffs challenge each of these rulings, as well as the order requiring them to pay the costs of giving notice to the class.

II

Before discussing the merits of the controversy, we emphasize that this lawsuit is not a general attack upon the settlement plan. On the contrary, plaintiffs say that they approve the plan and hope to see it executed. As we have observed, the case involves a dispute between the preferred vis-a-vis the common over participation rights in the Valery stock to be distributed as part of the spin-off. As we understand it, that is the extent of plaintiffs' attack upon the plan.

The preferred has a conversion right to exchange for the common on a one-to-one basis. Briefly stated, the preferred argues that a distribution of Valery stock to the common only, and without provision for permitting the preferred to share therein now or at the time of conversion, violates its Certificate rights. We now examine those rights in some detail.

* * *

B.

For most purposes, the rights of the preferred shareholders as against the common shareholders are fixed by the contractual terms agreed upon when the class of preferred stock is created. And, as to the conversion privilege, it has been said that the rights of a preferred shareholder are "least affected by rules of law and most dependent on the share contract." Buxbaum, "Preferred Stock—Law and Draftsmanship," 42 Cal.L.Rev. 243, 279 (1954).

Our duty, then, is to construe the contract governing the preferred shares. In so doing, we employ the methods used to interpret contracts generally; that is, we consider the entire instrument and attempt to reconcile all of its provisions "in order to determine the meaning intended to be given to any portion of it." More to the point, we must construe the several qualifications of the conversion privilege which are stated in Sections (c)(4)–(7) of the Certificate.

C.

The basic conversion privilege is stated in Section (a) of the Certificate: at the option of the holder, each share of preferred is convertible into one share of common. * * * But, assuming silence on the subject in the conversion contract (as here), the preferred has no right to any particular market price ratio between the shares. However, the preferred is ordinarily given (as here) anti-dilution or anti-destruction rights in the conversion contract.

Section (c)(4) in the Coastal Certificate is such an "anti-dilution" clause. It provides for a proportionate change in the conversion ratio in the event of a stock split or a stock combination (that is, a reverse split). In each of those events, the number of outstanding shares of Coastal common would change so, in order to preserve the parity relationship, a proportionate adjustment to the conversion ratio is essential.[4] In brief, (c)(4) prohibits the common from diluting the conversion right by requiring a proportionate adjustment if the number of outstanding shares is increased (and a similar adjustment if there is a decrease resulting from a reverse split).

Section (c)(6) is directed to the same antidilution purpose. While (c)(4) applies to subdivisions and combinations (which enlarge or decrease the number of outstanding shares), (c)(6) is directed to a stock dividend, that is, the issuance of Coastal shares to its stockholders as a dividend. That, too, is a circumstance which, by definition, would dilute the prior parity relationship and, to prevent that, the conversion ratio is "proportionately increased" by (c)(6).

Since Coastal is neither splitting nor reverse-splitting its shares, nor distributing them as a dividend, (c)(4) and (6) do not directly apply to this case.

---

4. For example: if the Coastal common were split three for one, the number of outstanding shares would be tripled and, upon conversion thereafter, a preferred stockholder would be entitled to receive three shares of common for each share of preferred surrendered.

D.

This brings us to (c)(5) which plaintiffs contend is the heart of the matter. The short of it is that unless the plaintiffs can find something in this paragraph which, directly or by implication, prohibits Coastal from distributing the Valery stock to the holders of its common, without giving its preferred a right to participate therein (now or at the time of conversion), then, under our settled law, restated only eighteen months ago in Judah and running back at least to 1929 in Gaskill v. Gladys Belle Oil Co., Del. Ch., 16 Del. Ch. 289, 146 A. 337, 339, the preferred has no such right. The Vice Chancellor found none. Nor do we.

Given the significance of (c)(5) in the dispute, we quote it again, this time omitting the references to consolidations, mergers, sales, and so on, which are not directly germane here. Thus:

> "In the event that the Corporation shall be recapitalized, [consolidated with or merged into any other corporation or shall sell or convey to any other corporation all or substantially all of its property as an entirety], provision shall be made as part of the terms of such recapitalization, ... so that any holder of ... Preferred Stock may thereafter receive in lieu of the Common Stock otherwise issuable to him upon conversion of his ... Preferred Stock, but at the conversion ratio stated in this Article ... which would otherwise be applicable at the time of conversion, the same kind and amount of securities or assets as may be distributable upon such recapitalization, ... with respect to the Common Stock of the Corporation."

After noting that the "recapitalization" has no generally accepted meaning in law or accounting, the Vice Chancellor focused on the phrase, "in lieu of," as it appears in (c)(5) and concluded that, before the Section becomes applicable, the "Common Shares of Coastal must cease to exist and something [must] be given in lieu of them." Since the Coastal shares will continue in being after the spin-off, he concluded that the plan is not a recapitalization within the meaning of the Certificate.

Plaintiffs contend that Section (c)(5) is the key to analysis of the Certificate. They say that the settlement plan constitutes a "recapitalization" of Coastal, which triggers the adjustment called for in that section.

Relying on the significant changes which the plan will effect in Coastal's capital structure, plaintiffs argue that there will be a recapitalization in fact and law.

Section (c)(5) contains what is typically considered to be "anti-destruction" language. Transactions listed therein—a merger or consolidation, for example—are the kind of events that will not merely dilute the conversion privilege by altering the number of shares of common but, rather, may destroy the conversion privilege by eliminating the stock into which a preferred share is convertible. We focus, however, on the preferred's claim of right if Coastal "shall be recapitalized."

At trial, both sides offered the testimony of experts as to what "recapitalization" means. Professor Sametz noted that there is not a precise or specific definition, but the term implies a "fundamental realignment of relationships amongst a company's securities" or a "reshuffling of the capital structure."

The parties have also cited cases[7] from other jurisdictions, but we are not persuaded that such cases considered language reasonably comparable to that at issue here; so they are of little help. And the same is true of general financial terminology. The point is that we must decide the controversy under the facts in this case and, for present purposes, that means the Certificate language.

We agree with plaintiffs that the changes which the plan will bring to Coastal's financial structure are enormous. And it may be concluded that, collectively, these amount to a "reshuffling of the capital structure" under the general definition to which Professor Sametz testified. But that is not the test. The critical question concerns what is said in the contract.

Section (c)(5) provides that in the event of "recapitalization" one of the provisions shall be that a holder of preferred may "thereafter" receive— something. When he may receive it is clear: he may receive it "upon conversion" after the recapitalization has taken place. After that event, he may receive, not what he would have received before recapitalization; that was the common stock which was "otherwise issuable to him upon conversion." Certainly this clause is meaningless if the common share remains issuable to him after recapitalization. And so is the remainder of the paragraph which requires that the same conversion ratio be retained by distributing to the preferred, upon conversion, the "same kind and amount of securities or assets as may be distributable upon said recapitalization . . . with respect to the Common." The "same kind and amount" would be distributable to the common only if the common had been exchanged for something else. This was the situation the draftsman contemplated by the provision that the preferred "may receive" the "same kind and amount" of property "in lieu of the Common Stock."

Since the settlement plan does not include an exchange of the common and, given the added circumstances that the dividend or liquidated preference of the preferred is not threatened and that earned surplus is ample to support the distribution of the Valery shares to the common, the settlement plan does not include a recapitalization within the meaning of Section (c)(5).

E.

We turn now to (c)(7) which, we think, is related to what is said in (c)(5) and our construction of it; (c)(7) states:

"No adjustment of the conversion ratio shall be made by reason of any declaration or payment to the holders of the Common Stock of the Corporation of a dividend or distribution payable in any property or

---

7. See, for example, Stephenson v. Plastics Corporation of America, Minn. Supr., 276 Minn. 400, 150 N.W.2d 668 (1967); United Gas Improvement Co. v. Commissioner of Internal Revenue, 3 Cir., 142 F.2d 216, 218 (1944); Commissioner of Internal Revenue v. Neustadt's Trust, 2 Cir., 131 F.2d 528 (1942).

securities other than Common Stock, any redemption of the Common Stock, any issuance of any securities convertible into Common Stock, or for any other reason, except as expressly provided herein."

This section, plainly and clearly, lists transactions which do not call for an adjustment to the conversion ratio. Thus an adjustment is not made for:

(1) a dividend payable to holders of the common in property other than Coastal common,

(2) a redemption of the common,

(3) an issuance of securities convertible into common,

(4) "any other reason."

Section (c)(7) concludes with the phrase, "except as expressly provided herein," which creates an ambiguity that must be resolved.

Plaintiffs contend that the phrase relates to all of Section (c), including (c)(5), and thus if a property dividend (the Valery stock) is regarded as a "recapitalization," the latter section controls. It is somewhat difficult to follow that argument but, as we understand it, plaintiffs contend that (c)(7) does not apply here.

In our opinion, the phrase, "except as expressly provided herein," refers to those paragraphs of Section (c) which "expressly ... [provide]" for a change in the conversion ratio. In so doing, the phrase does modify the preceding phrase, "any other reason" (which is all-encompassing). But the transactions referred to are those in (c)(4) and (c)(6), and thus they are the exceptions "expressly provided" for. There are no exceptions provided for in (c)(7) and, therefore, the phrase would be meaningless if it were construed as applying to (c)(7).

Section (c)(7) states flatly that an adjustment shall not be made in the conversion ratio in the event any of the three specified events occurs: a dividend in property other than Coastal common, a redemption of the common or the issue of securities convertible into common. And the three specifics are enlarged by the general reference to "any other reason." Given what we believe to be mandatory language ("[no] adjustment ... shall be made") prohibiting a change in the conversion ratio, we conclude that such a change may be made only if it is "expressly provided" in Section (c), and, as we have said, that means by the anti-dilution provisions of (c)(4) and (c)(6), i.e., by a stock split, reverse split or a stock dividend. It is only in those paragraphs that provisions are found for an adjustment in the conversion ratio.[8] Section (c)(5), on the other hand, is not directed merely to an adjustment in the exchange ratio; it is directed toward maintaining parity between the common and the preferred after a specified event has occurred: thus a conversion after recapitalization, merger or consolidation shall be "at the conversion ratio stated in this Article." The

---

8. The adjustment called for is an increase or decrease, as the case may be, of the number of shares of common to be received for each share of preferred which is converted.

"conversion ratio" referred to here is the parity referred to throughout the Article (i.e., the Certificate).[9]

But even if one were to find some inconsistency or contradiction between (c)(5) and (c)(7), then, under familiar and well-settled rules of construction, the specific language of (c)(7) (as applied to the Valery stock) controls over any general language in (c)(5) regarding recapitalization.

F.

We have reviewed Sections (c)(4) through (c)(7) independently but failed to find therein any merit to the contentions which plaintiffs argue. And considering the paragraphs together, * * * So viewed, the basic scheme is that parity between the common and preferred is maintained through any changes in the number of outstanding shares which are unaccompanied by other balance sheet changes: thus a stock split, reverse split or stock dividend changes only the number of shares outstanding without any change in corporate assets. Sections (c)(4) and (c)(6) provide for continuing parity by making the appropriate adjustment to the conversion ratio (that is, what will be given for one share of preferred) in such instance. But it appears that a reduction in assets by distribution to the common may be made without adjustment to that exchange basis. Thus a cash dividend is permissible under (c)(7),[10] or other corporate assets (stock in a listed company, for example) may be distributed under that paragraph. And if the distribution of assets is in the form of a redemption of the common, that, too, is permissible. In short, dividends and other distribution of corporate assets are permissible without change in the exchange basis. Speaking generally, such distributions are the ordinary and permissible way in which the holders of common stock share in the earnings of the enterprise. In saying this, we emphasize once more that there is not a charge here that the liquidation preference or the dividend of the preferred is in any way threatened. Nor is fraud involved.

* * *

In summary, we conclude that a distribution of the Valery stock to the holders of coastal common is permissible under Section (c)(7) and may be made without adjustment to the conversion ratio; such distribution is not a recapitalization under Section (c)(5).

* * *

Affirmed.

QUESTIONS

1. In footnote 7 the court distinguishes the Stephenson case by saying that because of language differences it (and other cases) is of little help.

---

9. Assuming Section (c)(5) could possibly be interpreted to contemplate an adjustment of the conversion ratio, none would be appropriate under our view of these facts since we have concluded that the settlement plan here does not include a recapitalization within the meaning of Section (c)(5).

10. Mr. Katzin testified that Coastal has a substantial earned surplus to which the Valery distribution is to be charged.

Can you determine what language differences might be critical to the court's decision?

2. Does the language governing the preferred's conversion rights represent a drafting error?

3. Why does section (c)(5) cover sales of all or substantially all of Coastal's property (for which Coastal would presumably receive equivalent value), but not a dividend of stock of a subsidiary, for which Coastal receives nothing? What is the effect of section (c)(7)?

4. If you were drafting to protect the preferred stockholders, what kind of protective language would you suggest? Would paragraph 3(b) in the warrants of Plastics Corporation of America (footnote 3 in the Stephenson case, supra) have solved the problem?

5. These provisions, as interpreted by the court, provide a large hole in the protection of the preferred's conversion rights. Why would holders of preferred accept such provisions?

NOTE ON LOHNES v. LEVEL 3 COMMUNICATIONS, INC., 272 F.3d 49 (1st Cir. 2001)

Lohnes, as trustee of a real estate trust, had leased office space to a corporation later acquired by Level 3, and had obtained warrants to purchase common stock. After the acquisition, the warrants were adjusted to be exercisable in Level 3's stock. When Level 3 engaged in a two for one stock split, Lohnes insisted on an adjustment of the warrants to cover twice as many shares, and Level 3 declined. Lacking language that directly addressed stock splits, Lohnes argued that his rights were governed by the terms "capital reorganization" and "reclassification of stock." "Capital reorganization" was not a defined term in the warrant, and the court looked to Wood v. Coastal States Gas Corp., *supra*, and other cases to conclude that "capital reorganization" is a " 'general term describing corporate amalgamations or readjustments occurring, for example, when one corporation acquires another in a merger or acquisition, a single corporation divides into two or more entities, or a corporation makes a substantial change in its capital structure.' Black's Law Dict. 1298 (6th ed. 1990). The first two prongs of this definition are clearly inapposite here. That leaves only the question of whether a stock split entails a 'substantial change in [a corporation's] capital structure.' We think not."

Turning to the phrase "reclassification of stock," the court concluded that the "sine qua non of a reclassification of stock is the modification of existing shares into something fundamentally different," a test not met by a stock split.

Coffman v. Acton Corporation

958 F.2d 494 (1st Cir. 1992).

■ Aldrich, Senior Circuit Judge.

Twelve partnerships, hereinafter Partnerships, having equal claims against defendant Acton Corporation, engaged in settlement negotiations of a prior suit. Acton offered $60,000; ($5,000 apiece); Partnerships countered with $180,000, and Acton responded with $120,000. Partnerships were agreeable to $120,000 if there were an added "sweetener," and suggested stock warrants, but Acton did not wish this complication. Instead, Section 2.2 was added to each of the twelve settlement contracts; hereinafter the agreement:

> The Partnership shall be entitled to receive, upon written demand made within the three years following the execution of the Settlement Agreement (the "Exercise Date"), the following one time payment: the sum of "X" times a multiple of 7,500 where "X" equals the "price" of one share of Acton Corporation's common stock on the Exercise Date less $7.00. The "price" on the Exercise Date shall be equal to the average closing price of one share of the common stock of Acton Corporation on the American Stock Exchange for any period, selected by the Partnership, consisting of thirty (30) consecutive trading days prior to the Exercise Date. Acton CATV shall make such payment as necessary within 30 days after receipt of the written demand. The Partnership's rights hereunder shall expire three years after the date of this Agreement and shall not be assignable.

The manifestly implicit concept, quite apart from the parol evidence, is that if Acton did better, presumably reflected in its stock, it could afford to pay more for the settlement. At the same time, the chances that this would bear much fruit, if any, were not considered large, as Acton was not doing well, and its stock was fluctuating between $1.50 and $3.12. These circumstances are to be considered with the contract language regardless of the parol evidence rule.

About a year after the making of the agreement, Acton's stock not having increased in price, it concluded that there were psychological market advantages in artificially shrinking the number of outstanding shares, and thereby increasing the per share price. It accordingly executed a so-called reverse stock split, as the result of which each stockholder owned one-fifth the original number of shares, with the new shares having five times the par value and, at the outset, approximately five times the immediately preceding price on the Stock Exchange, viz., substantially more than the $7.00 figure in the agreement.

Surprisingly, Acton did not consult Partnerships before engaging in this maneuver; it merely sent a letter explaining that it was of no consequence.

> This is to advise you that the stockholders of Acton Corporation have authorized a one-for-five reverse stock split of Acton Corporation's common shares effective June 25, 1987. This means that one share of stock will represent five shares of Acton Corporation's common stock prior to that date. The reverse stock split will affect Section 2.2 of the above-referenced Agreement such that the price $7.00 as referenced in such Section shall become $35.00.

Partnerships immediately rejected this conclusion. At the same time their present contention that Acton's letter, sent the very day of the change, was a recognition of its substantive effect on the agreement, and an "attempted amendment," is a flight of fancy.

The fight was on. Under Partnerships' interpretation of the agreement the twelve Partnerships together are owed $1,218,600 for their abandoned $60,000, based on a per share price of $20.54, although, had the number of shares not been reduced by the reverse split the per share price would have been some $4.11, sparking nothing. After a bench trial the court, in an opinion reported at 768 F. Supp. 392 (D. Mass. 1991), found for defendants. Partnerships appeal. We affirm.

Partnerships' position is simple and straightforward. This is precisely the way the agreement reads; it is unambiguous, and integrated,[3] and even were parol evidence admissible, which they deny, there was no prior discussion suggesting exceptions. The court, taking up this last fact, stated that the agreement "did not address an eventuality such as a reverse stock split," and the very fact that the parties had not considered it supplied the answer. "An expression may be complete ... and yet ambiguous. Indeed, human limitations make it inevitable that every expression will be less than complete in a thoroughly comprehensive sense. Ambiguity will remain about some matters that might have been addressed and were not."[4] 768 F. Supp. at 395. Finding that the parties had not thought about dilution—a finding that binds Partnerships here—the court found the omission was an ambiguity in the agreement, and resolved it by concluding that the reasonable provision would have been that stock splits would have no effect.

We might turn one of Partnerships' arguments back on them in support of this result. The agreement provided that Partnerships had three years in which to pick a thirty day high price. During the negotiations Partnerships inquired what would happen if, during that period, Acton went private, as a result of which business success would not be reflected on the Exchange. Interestingly enough, while Partnerships are normally hostile to pre-agreement evidence, they narrate this. Acton "refused to give them any protection if Acton went private ... the Partnerships were 'at risk' on that issue." (Emphasis in original.) During trial—not subsequently repeated—the court suggested that this indicated Partnerships also took the risk if Acton made a stock split increasing the number of shares. Partnerships assert this implication. If there is any inference, we would draw just the opposite. Inclusio unius, exclusio alterius. But certainly this did not mean that Partnerships were accepting any and all defeating actions that Acton might take.

---

3. Integration. This Agreement contains the entire agreement between the parties hereto with respect to the transactions and matters contemplated herein and ... supersedes all prior agreements, if any, between the parties hereto....

4. More simply put, "Paragraph 6 is not self-interpreting—no form of words is—and the evidence could be received and used to elucidate its meaning in context." See Antonellis v. Northgate Construction Corp., 362 Mass. 847, 851, 291 N.E.2d 626 (1973). (Emphasis supplied).

The court ultimately so concluded. "It defies common sense" that Partnerships would have agreed that Acton could effectively escape the specified consequences of a rising market price by increasing the number of shares. And if Partnerships would not suffer from any increasing, it would follow, since a contract must be construed consistently, Acton should not suffer from any decreasing.

No doubt recognizing this symbiosis, when the district court inquired, as later did we, whether Acton could have avoided all liability under the agreement simply by increasing the number of shares, counsel answered affirmatively. The court characterized his proffered concession as "gallant." We can only say that if this particular counsel would have been too gallant to make a claim, surely some less chivalrous could have been found. How could so meaningless an undertaking have been considered a sweetener? It is a fundamental principle that a contract is to be construed as meaningful and not illusory. As the court said in Clark, 270 Mass. at 153,

> The construction of a written instrument to be adopted is the one which appears to be in accord with justice and common sense and the probable intention of the parties. It is to be interpreted as a business transaction entered into by practical men to accomplish an honest and straightforward end.

It is true that contracts cannot be rewritten simply to "rescue a firm from a sinkhole of its own design." Adding a whole new provision is normally permissible only when additional terms are "essential to a determination." Assuming that rule applicable, which we need not decide, Partnerships contends there was no necessity here; they may have been affirmatively content at the time of contracting to there being no antidilution provision. There are two answers to this. The first is that the court has found the parties gave no thought to dilution, and this finding cannot be said to be plainly wrong. Second, this is precisely a case where to read the contract as meaning that Partnerships should not suffer by dilution—and hence Acton by reverse dilution—is a necessity, or "essential to a determination." There is every reason to presume Partnerships did not intend to acquire nothing,[5] and saving from unenforceability ranks as a necessity.

Whether we reach that result by implying a provision to meet a circumstance not envisaged by the parties, or by construing the word "share" as including following the res, is immaterial. "[A] legal instrument is to be construed with reference to all of its language and to its general structure and purpose and in the light of the circumstances under which it was executed. These factors may qualify and control the literal signification of particular terms and phrases as effectually as if express qualifying words

---

5. We do not pause over Partnership's sought analogy to convertible debentures, where the rule is that anti-dilution must be expressly stated. Broad v. Rockwell International Corp., 642 F.2d 929, 940–45 (5th Cir.) (en banc), cert. denied, 454 U.S. 965, 70 L. Ed. 2d 380, 102 S. Ct. 506 (1981); Parkinson v. West End Street Ry., 173 Mass. 446, 53 N.E. 891 (1899). These are formal, and complicated commercial structures, prepared with care for the general public. Purchasers have the bonds in any event. Here we have a simple agreement between individuals, not even assignable.

were found in the instrument." In any event, the rules of construction do not call for Partnership's wooden interpretation.

Affirmed.

QUESTIONS

1. How does the court in Coffman v. Acton Corporation distinguish its case from the previous decisions involving conversion rights?

2. How does Judge Winter's reasoning in Sharon Steel Corporation v. Chase Manhattan Bank, 691 F.2d 1039 (2d Cir. 1982) in Chapter Six about interpreting indentures apply here?

3. If you were drafting on behalf of Acton, what kind of adjustment clause would you want to include in these agreements?

4. Does giving no thought to a subject in drafting always lead to its automatic insertion? Should it? See Ayres and Gertner, "Filling Gaps in Incomplete Contracts: An Economic Theory of Default Rules," 99 Yale L. J. 87 (1989), who argue that such contracts ought to be construed against the more knowledgeable and experienced party, thus providing incentives for such parties to disclose their real intentions. How would that argument apply here?

5. You've seen all the references to contract language being controlling in prior cases, including circumstances not addressed in the documents. Why doesn't the Acton court follow the reasoning of those cases? What's different here?

NOTE

Reiss v. Financial Performance Corp., 764 N.E.2d 958 (N.Y. 2001) involved warrants granted to a director that contained no adjustment provision whatever, including a reverse stock split that eventually occurred. The only evidence to support the trial court's conclusion involved company disclosures made after the reverse split, which took the position that the options had been adjusted. The Appellate Division affirmed, but on contextual grounds, that an adjustment clause was an essential term of the warrants that the court could supply, regardless of the parties' intent. 715 N.Y.S.2d 29 (App. Div. 2000). In justifying its approach, the Appellate Division declined to "disregard common sense and slavishly bow to the written word where to do so would plainly ignore the true intentions of the parties in making the contract." 715 A.2d at 34. Criticizing this approach (and implicitly that of the court in the previous case), Miriam Albert argues that the Restatement of Contracts 2d § 204 (1981) does not permit supplying an omitted term as a matter of interpretation, but only where it is necessary to effectuate the contract. Miriam Albert, Common Sense for Common Stock Options: Inconsistent Interpretation of Anti-Dilution Provisions in Options and Warrants, 34 Rutgers L.J. 321 (2003).

In contrast, in Sanders v. Wang, 1999 WL 1044880, 25 Del. J. Corp. L. 1036 (Del. Ch. 1999), a Key Employee Stock Option Plan provided for grants to participants of up to 6 million shares if the company's stock reached a price of $180 for at least 60 trading days. The plan contained no adjustment clause for stock splits, but after several splits the compensation committee of the board determined that the stock had reached the required price, after adjusting for the splits. It proceeded to issue options for 20.25 million shares, in order to adjust for the splits. In a derivative action brought by shareholders to challenge the grants, the court held for the plaintiffs, that there was no authority for an adjustment in the number of optioned shares to account for the splits, despite explicit language that allowed the compensation committee to adjust the performance target to reflect any stock splits.

QUESTIONS

1. Should it matter whether the options are individually negotiated with employees, or part of a plan adopted for a larger number of employees, or issued to the public?

2. Should it make any difference that the terms of the Key Employee Stock Option Plan in Sanders v. Wang would have been described in the company's filings with the SEC?

CL Investments, L.P. v. Advanced Radio Telecom Corp.

2000 WL 1868096 (Del. Ch. 2000).

■ JACOBS, VICE CHANCELLOR.

This action is brought to enforce the terms of a stock purchase warrant that entitles the plaintiff, who is the warrant-holder, to purchase a specific number of shares of the issuer upon exercising the warrant. Importantly, the warrant also requires two different kinds of adjustments of the type and number of shares the warrant-holder is entitled to purchase. The first type of adjustment occurs if the issuer of the warrant merges with another corporation. In that event the exercising warrant-holder becomes entitled to purchase the same securities it would have received in the merger if it were a shareholder. The second type of adjustment occurs if the company engages in specified transactions that dilute its shares. In that event, an adjustment is made to offset the effect of the dilution.

Both types of adjustments are implicated in this case. After the warrant was issued, the issuer merged with another corporation and as a result, the stock of the issuer was canceled and exchanged for stock of the acquiring corporation. It is undisputed that the merger triggered the first type of adjustment, thereby entitling the plaintiff warrant-holder to purchase stock of the acquiring corporation when the warrant is exercised.

What is disputed is the number of shares that the plaintiff, upon exercising the warrant, would be entitled to purchase. That dispute arises because after the merger, the acquiror entered into various dilutive transactions in its own stock. The plaintiff claims that those transactions triggered its right to the second type of adjustment, under the "anti-dilution" provision of the warrant. The defendant acquiror contends that in these circumstances the anti-dilution adjustment provision is not applicable. That dispute led to the filing of this action to enforce the warrant's anti-dilution provision. The defendants have moved to dismiss the complaint for failure to state a claim, and the plaintiff has cross-moved for partial judgment on the pleadings. This Opinion decides both motions.

I. FACTUAL BACKGROUND

* * *

B. The Merger

On October 28, 1996,[5] seven months after the Warrant was issued, Telecom entered into a Merger Agreement and Plan of Reorganization (the "Merger Agreement") with the co-defendant, Advanced Radio Telecom Corp. ("ART"). Under the Merger Agreement, ART acquired Telecom in a transaction in which (i) a wholly owned shell subsidiary of ART (the "merger-subsidiary") was merged into Telecom, (ii) Telecom became the surviving corporation,[6] (iii) all of Telecom's shares were exchanged for ART shares, and (iv) the Telecom shares were canceled.

C. Subsequent Dilutive Transactions

ART acknowledges that as a result of the Merger, the plaintiff, upon exercising the Warrant, would be entitled to purchase ART common stock instead of Telecom stock.[7] After the Merger took place, however, ART issued to third parties, in various transactions, ART common stock, securities convertible into ART common stock, and warrants and options to purchase ART common stock. These transactions diluted the ART stock to which the plaintiff would be entitled upon exercising the Warrant. The plaintiff claims that unless it receives an adjustment under the Warrant's anti-dilution provision (Section 7), those dilutive ART stock transactions will have improperly diminished the value of its Warrant. The defendants took the position, however, that the Warrant, by its own terms, does not entitle the plaintiff to any Section 7 adjustment to offset the dilutive effect of these transactions.

In its amended complaint, (the "Complaint"), the plaintiff alleges two Causes of Action that embody three separate claims: (1) breach of contract (i.e., the Warrant) for refusing to acknowledge the plaintiff's entitlement to the Section 7 adjustments, (2) breach of the Warrant for refusing to produce an Accountants' Certificate, and (3) unjust enrichment.

II. THE APPLICABLE STANDARDS AND THE PARTIES' CONTENTIONS

A. The Procedural Standards

The defendants have moved to dismiss the Complaint under Court of Chancery Rule 12(b)(6) for failure to state a claim upon which relief can be

---

5. The plaintiff purchased the Warrant as part of bridge financing to help defendants ART and combine their businesses and then offer common stock to the public. At that time, ART was named Advanced Radio Technologies Corporation.

6. ART and Telecom are collectively "the defendants."

7. All of Telecom's stock is now owned by ART.

granted. The plaintiff, in response, has cross-moved under Rule 12(c) for partial judgment on the pleadings on its claim that the defendants have breached the Warrant.

* * *

B. The Contentions

The plaintiff contends that it is entitled to judgment on the pleadings on its claim the defendants breached the Warrant. The alleged contractual breaches consist of the defendants' (i) failure to acknowledge the plaintiff's right to an anti-dilution adjustment under Section 7, and (ii) refusal to deliver an Accountants' Certificate. The bases for the claim are that as a result of the Merger the plaintiff became entitled to purchase ART common stock upon exercising the Warrant, and that ART's dilutive stock transactions after the Merger entitle the plaintiff to a dilution-offsetting adjustment under Section 7 of the Warrant.

* * *

The defendants respond that all of the plaintiff's claims must be dismissed as a matter of law, for three reasons. First, to the extent the breach of contract claim is based upon Section 7 of the Warrant, that claim is legally deficient because under the terms of the Warrant itself, the ART stock transactions in question could not, and did not, implicate Section 7. Second, to the extent the breach of contract claim rests on ART's alleged failure to deliver an Accountants' Certificate, that claim is invalid on its face and is also time-barred. * * *

III. ANALYSIS

* * *

B. The Breach of Contract Claim

1. The Issues

* * *

The parties agree that the dispute is governed by Sections 6 and 7 of the Warrant. Section 6 provides:

> In case the Company after the Original Issue Date shall (a) effect a reorganization, (b) consolidate with or merge into any other person, or (c) transfer all or substantially all of its properties or assets to any other person under any plan or arrangement contemplating the dissolution of the Company, then, in each such case, the holder of this Warrant, upon the exercise hereof as provided in Section 3 at any time after the consummation of such reorganization, consolidation or merger or the effective date of such dissolution, as the case may be, shall be entitled to receive (and the Company shall be entitled to deliver), in lieu of the Common Stock (or Other Securities) issuable upon such exercise prior to such consummation or such effective date, the stock and other securities and property (including cash) to which such holder

would have been entitled upon such consummation or in connection with such dissolution as the case may be, if such holder had so exercised this Warrant immediately prior thereto, *all subject to further adjustment thereafter as provided in Sections 5 and 7 hereof.*

And Section 7 provides:

Where *the Company* shall issue or sell shares of its Common Stock after the Original Issue Date without consideration or for a consideration per share less than the Purchase Price in effect pursuant to the terms of this Warrant at the time of the issuance or sale of such additional shares ... then the Purchase Price in effect hereunder shall simultaneously with such issuance or sale be reduced to a price determined by [a formula specified in the Warrant].

Section 7 is (to repeat) an "anti-dilution" provision designed to offset any dilution of the issuer's stock caused by stock issuances made for consideration less than the stipulated "Purchase Price." Section 7 accomplishes that by lowering the purchase price per share that an exercising warrant-holder would pay, which would thereby increase the number of shares to be purchased. But, because in this case the dilutive transactions involved stock issued by ART, Section 7 would not apply to those transactions unless ART is "the Company" referred to in the above quoted first line of Section 7. That is the key question upon which the pending motions turn.

"The Company" is a defined term in the Warrant. The definition, found in the Warrant's preamble, states:

As used herein the following terms, unless the context otherwise requires, have the following respective meanings:

(a) The term "Company" includes any corporation which shall *succeed to or assume* the obligations of the Company [Telecom] hereunder.

As earlier stated, the applicability of Section 7 turns on whether ART is "the Company" within the meaning of that Section. As that term is defined, there are only two ways that ART could be deemed "the Company." The first is if ART "succeed[ed] to or assumed" the obligations of Telecom under the Warrant in the Merger. The second is if the "context" of the term "the Company" in Section 7 "otherwise requires" that ART be deemed "the Company." The plaintiff contends that under either prong of the definition ART must be deemed "the Company." The defendants argue that the pled facts alleged in the Complaint implicate neither prong. Because both prongs of the definition are in issue, each must be separately analyzed.

   2.   Did ART Succeed to or Assume Telecom's Warrant Obligations?

The defendants argue that ART neither succeeded to nor assumed any obligations of Telecom, including its obligations under the Warrant, because nothing in the Merger Agreement provides for an assumption of those obligations. Indeed, the defendants urge, under Section 3(f) of the

Merger Agreement Telecom is the surviving corporation. Nor, defendants say, did ART assume Telecom's liabilities by operation of law, because the Merger Agreement states that "the corporate existence, franchises and rights of Telecom ... shall continue unaffected and unimpaired by the Merger."

In response, the plaintiff urges that ART "succeed[ed] to or assumed" Telecom's obligations under the Warrant by agreeing to a merger involving the exchange of Telecom's stock for ART stock and the cancellation of all Telecom stock. As support, the plaintiff points to Section 4(c) of the Merger Agreement, which provides that: "At the Effective Time ... each 2.75 issued shares of Telecom Common Stock ... shall be converted into the right to receive one share of ART Common Stock." The plaintiff also relies upon the language of Section 6(b), that: "after the Effective Time each certificate which represented outstanding shares of Telecom Common Stock ... prior to the Effective Time shall be deemed for all corporate purposes to evidence the ownership of the shares of ART Common Stock ... provided in Section 4." By virtue of the exchange of Telecom stock for ART stock and the cancellation of Telecom stock, the plaintiff concludes that ART must necessarily (albeit implicitly) have assumed Telecom's obligations in the Merger.

Having considered the arguments raised by both sides, I determine that in the Merger, ART did not succeed to or assume Telecom's Warrant obligations. Section 3(f) of the Merger Agreement explicitly provides that Telecom will continue as a functioning entity after the Merger. Nowhere does the Merger Agreement expressly provide for any assumption by ART of the liabilities and obligations of Telecom. Nor, given the structure of the Merger, did ART assume the obligations of Telecom by operation of law. As a purely structural matter, had Telecom merged into the merger-subsidiary so that the latter became the surviving corporation, then Telecom would no longer exist. In that case, ART would necessarily have "succeed[ed] to or assumed" the obligations of Telecom by virtue of 8 Del. C. § 259. Here, however, Telecom was the surviving corporation in the Merger, and therefore ART did not by operation of law "succeed to or assume" Telecom's Warrant obligations under § 259.

Because ART did not "succeed to or assume" the obligations of Telecom under the Warrant, the only way that ART could be deemed "the Company" under Section 7 of the Warrant is if the "context otherwise requires." I turn to that issue.

3. Does "the Context Otherwise Require" That ART Be Deemed "the Company For Purposes of Section 7 of the Warrant?"

a. *The Contentions*

The plaintiff urges that this Court must find as a matter of law that ART is "the Company" under the Warrant, as provided in the second prong of the definition of "the Company." The Court must so conclude (the plaintiff argues) for three reasons.

First, plaintiff contends, the context of "the Company" as used in Section 7 requires that "the Company" be read to mean ART. The argument runs as follows: By application of Section 6 of the Warrant and as a result of the Merger, the plaintiff, upon exercising the Warrant, can purchase only ART stock. But Section 6 does more than merely substitute ART stock for Telecom stock as the security the Warrant-holder is entitled to purchase. Section 6 also expressly makes that stock subject to "further adjustment . . . as provided in . . . Section 7." Because ART common stock is the only stock the plaintiff may now purchase upon exercising the Warrant, and because the Warrant defines Common Stock as "the common stock of the Company and its successors," the term "Common Stock" as used in Section 7, must mean ART common stock. Otherwise, the provision of Section 6 that (i) entitles the exercising Warrant-holder to purchase the stock or other securities received in a merger, and then (ii) makes that stock subject to adjustment under Section 7, would become meaningless and effectively be read out of the Warrant contract.

Second, the plaintiff argues that to read that Warrant in any different way would be inequitable. Because of the Merger, Telecom can no longer discharge its original obligation under the Warrant to deliver Telecom shares—adjusted for any dilutive transactions—to exercising warrant-holders. Now those warrant-holders can receive only ART shares. Unless ART is "the Company" under Section 7 of the Warrant, those ART shares could be diluted with impunity—a result that would be legally prohibited if the shares being purchased were the Telecom shares for which the ART shares were substituted. Under the defendants' interpretation, the plaintiff Warrant-holder, will be deprived of the anti-dilution protections that it bargained for.

* * *

Third, the plaintiff urges that its reading of "the Company" is the only interpretation that is faithful to "the rules of construction of contracts [which] require us to adopt an interpretation which gives meaning to every provision of a contract or, in the negative, no provision of a contract should be left without force and effect." Section 6 entitles the plaintiff to receive ART stock, and also expressly makes that stock "subject to further adjustment thereafter as provided in Sections 5 and 7 hereof." Only if "the Company" in Section 7 means ART, can a Section 7 adjustment occur. Any different construction would render the "further adjustment" provision in Section 6 meaningless. For these three reasons, the plaintiff concludes, it is entitled to judgment on the pleadings on its breach of contract claim.

The defendants respond by arguing, also as a matter of law, that ART is not "the Company." Therefore, the plaintiff's contractual claim of entitlement to an adjustment under Section 7 is not legally cognizable and must be dismissed, for two reasons.

The defendants first argue that it cannot be implied either from the Merger or from the context of Section 6 of the Warrant, that ART succeeded to or assumed the Warrant obligations of Telecom, which still exists as a wholly-owned subsidiary of ART. To find that ART implicitly assumed Telecom's obligations as a matter of "context" would contravene the established principle that a parent-subsidiary relationship, without more, cannot render a parent corporation liable for the obligations of its subsidiary even where the subsidiary is wholly owned. Nothing in the Merger Agreement alters this basic principle. On the contrary, defendants say, that Agreement provides that "the corporate existence, franchises and rights of Telecom, with its purposes, powers and objects, shall continue unaffected and unimpaired by the Merger."

Second, the defendants contend that the context in which the term "Company" appears does not "otherwise require" that "the Company" be read to mean ART. Rather, the definition of that term means that "the Company" is (i) Telecom, and that (ii) unless the context otherwise requires, "the Company" also means an entity that succeeds to or assumes Telecom's obligations under the Warrant. To put it differently, the defendants contend that the definitional language "unless the context otherwise requires," operates to limit, not expand, the universe of entities that could be "the Company." Accordingly, defendants conclude, nothing in the "context" of the Warrant justifies reading the term "the Company" broadly to include any other entity except one that expressly succeeds to or assumes liabilities of Telecom under the Warrant. Because ART did not succeed to or assume Telecom's Warrant liabilities, it cannot be "the Company."

b. *Discussion*

Having considered the parties' colliding views, I conclude as a matter of contract construction that ART must be deemed "the Company," as that term is used in Section 7 of the Warrant. Both legally and equitably, the "context" requires that result. The defendants rely essentially upon the technical structure they chose for the Merger as their reason for not recognizing a Section 7 adjustment that Sections 6 and 7 on their face expressly require.

Assume (counterfactually) that the Merger had resulted in ART's merger-subsidiary swallowing up Telecom and becoming the surviving corporation. In that case, the subsidiary would have, "succeeded to or assumed" the obligations of Telecom by operation of law under 8 Del. C. § 259, and a Section 7 adjustment would be required. Here, however, the merger-subsidiary was merged into Telecom, leaving Telecom as the surviving corporation. Under that structure, no obligations of Telecom were assumed by operation of law. But that does not end the analysis, because the definition of "the Company" also permits the Court to consider the "context." The definition of "the Company" is not narrowly confined to entities that succeed to or assume Telecom's liabilities under the Warrant. Indeed, that reading impermissibly conflates both prongs of the definition into only one prong. Nor does Section 6 (which makes the ART stock "subject to further adjustment under . . . Section 7") distinguish between mergers where the original issuer of the Warrant is—or is not—the surviving corporation. If Section 6 made such a distinction, then one would have expected the defendants to argue that the plaintiff is not entitled to receive ART stock when the Warrant is exercised. Yet the defendants concede that the plaintiff would be entitled to purchase ART stock.

In this case the relevant "context" is this: the plaintiff bargained for certain anti-dilution protections, and for other protections in the event of a merger that converted the stock the Warrant-holder was originally entitled to purchase into securities of the acquiring company. Both protections are mandated by the same Section—Section 6—which directs that adjustments be made to the stock received by reason of a merger under Sections 5 and 7. Unless the "context" from which both of these protections arise is respected, the defendants will be permitted to use the structure of the Merger self-servingly as both a shield and a sword—a sword to force the plaintiff warrant-holder to accept ART stock upon exercising the Warrant, and a shield to prevent that warrant-holder from enforcing anti-dilution provisions that are part and parcel of the same package of contractual protections. That simply cannot be.

The defendants respond that despite the linkage (in Section 6) between the Section 6 and Section 7 adjustments, and despite the plaintiff's entitlement under Section 6 to purchase ART stock when it exercises the Warrant, the plaintiff is not entitled to the anti-dilution adjustments under Section 7. The reason, defendants say, is that Telecom continues, post-Merger, as a viable entity capable of satisfying its obligations under the Warrant. But that argument is hopelessly flawed. To make it, the defendants must first de-couple Sections 6 and 7, and then assert that a Section 7 adjustment need not necessarily or inevitably follow or accompany a Section 6 adjustment.[25] The flaw is that unless "the Company" means ART in this context, Section 7 will essentially be read out of the Warrant contract. Unless the stock of "the Company" received by virtue of a Section 6 (merger) adjustment is the same as the stock of "the Company" that is adjusted (for dilution) under Section 7, then no post-merger dilution of the stock underlying the Warrant would ever trigger a Section 7 adjustment. That result would violate the explicit command of Section 6, which makes the stock received in the Merger "subject to adjustment under Section 7." Only by interpreting "the Company" in Section 7 as the same "Company" whose stock will be received by the warrant-holder under Section 6, can the Court avoid a construction that would render Section 7 superfluous and disregard a critical provision in Section 6. The defendants' interpretation would contravene New York's rule of construction, which prohibits a reading that would render a provision of a contract superfluous as "unsupportable under standard principles of contract interpretation."

In short, the context requires that ART be deemed "the Company" under Section 7. First, the anti-dilution adjustment formula in Section 7 works only if the stock triggering the anti-dilution adjustment is the same as the stock that is the subject matter of the Warrant. Second, at present

---

25. The defendants cite as an example, a Section 6 merger for cash. It is true that in that case, there would be no Section 7 adjustment. But the example is irrelevant, because cash need not be "adjusted" to prevent stock dilution, since the warrant-holder would not be receiving any stock that is capable of dilution.

the subject matter of the Warrant is, by virtue of the Merger, and Section 6, ART stock. Third, transactions involving ART stock are the only transactions that are capable of diluting the value of the Warrant. If ART is not "the Company" after its stock has been substituted for that of Telecom, then what entity can be? It cannot be Telecom. Logically and by process of elimination, the "context requires" that "the Company" be ART.

* * *

IV. CONCLUSION

For the foregoing reasons, (1) with respect to the plaintiff's claims for breach of contract (including its claim of right to receive an Accountants' Certificate), the plaintiff's motion for judgment on the pleadings is granted and the defendants' motion to dismiss is denied; and (2) with respect to the plaintiff's claim for unjust enrichment, the defendants' motion to dismiss is granted.

QUESTIONS

1. How does the court determine that ART, which was not one of the merging corporations, "*succeed[s] to or assume[s]* the obligations of the Company [Telecom]" under the merger agreement?

2. Section 6 provides antidestruction provisions so that Telecom warrant holders will be entitled to exercise in the same stock they would have received had they exercised their rights prior to the merger. What does the word "thereafter" in section 6 cover?

3. Section 7 provides antidilution protection where "the Company" issues or sells its shares at a price below the "Purchase Price" (which is surely a defined term). How could this apply to ART after the merger of its subsidiary with Telecom?

NOTE ON ANTIDESTRUCTION PROTECTIONS IN RIGHTS PLANS

Rights plans, or poison pill plans, represent some of the most careful corporate drafting possible, designed to protect certain rights under all conceivable states of the world. In that respect, a drafter trying to protect holders of warrants or conversion rights might well wish to start with the protective provisions found in a modern rights plan. The American Bar Foundation, COMMENTARIES ON MODEL DEBENTURE INDENTURE PROVISIONS (1971) contain antidilution provisions in Article 13, but contain no antidestruction provisions, suggesting their fairly recent evolution. Recall that poison pills provide shareholders of a company with the right to purchase additional shares of its common stock at a bargain price (usually 50% of current market value) if a hostile bidder gains a significant ownership interest in the "target" firm. (See Chapter Five, Part 2.C.) These rights are protected by extensive antidilution provisions, which are virtually always found in section 11 of the rights agreement (plagiarism being the sincerest form of flattery for drafting attorneys). But provisions are also required to protect the value of these rights from destruction in the event the target's shares disappear before the rights are exercised. Accordingly, section 13 of the standard rights agreement provides that if the rights are not exercised and the corporation disappears through a merger or similar transaction, the rights "flip over" to become rights to purchase shares of the bidder's common stock on the same bargain terms. Drafters face the same problems as drafters of other rights, including those discussed in the Advanced Radio Telecom Corp. decision. One solution is to define the acquiring corporation quite broadly, so that if a bidder uses an acquisition subsidiary to merge with the target, the rights flip over to become rights in the parent corporation's stock. This is accomplished through a definition (usually found in section 1 of the rights agreement) that defines a "principal party" to the merger as the one whose shares are issued:

" '*Principal Party*' shall mean

"(1) in the case of any transaction described in clauses (i) or (ii) of the first sentence of Section 13(a) hereof,

"(2) the Person that is the issuer of any securities into which shares of Common Stock of the Company are converted in such merger, consolidation, or share exchange or, if there is more than one such issuer, the issuer the shares of Common Stock of which have the greatest aggregate market value of shares outstanding, or

"(3) if no securities are so issued, the Person that is the other party to such merger, consolidation, or share exchange, or, if there is more than one such Person, the Person the shares of Common Stock of which have the greatest aggregate market value of shares outstanding, or

"(4) if the Person that is the other party to the merger does not survive the merger, the Person that does survive the merger (including the Company if it survives), or

"(5) the Person resulting from the consolidation; and

"(i) in the case of any transaction described in clause (iii) of the first sentence of Section 13(a) hereof, the Person that is the party receiving the greatest portion of the assets or earning power transferred pursuant to such transaction or transactions, or if each Person that is a party to such transaction or transactions receives the same portion of the assets or earning power so transferred or if the Person receiving the greatest portion of the assets or earning power cannot be determined, whichever of such persons that is the issuer of Common Stock having the greatest aggregate market value of shares outstanding; provided, however, that in any such case described in the foregoing Section 1(y)(i) or 1(y)(ii),

"(ii) if the Common Stock of such Person is not at such time and has not been continuously over the preceding twelve (12) month period registered under Section 12 of the Exchange Act, and such Person is a direct or indirect Subsidiary of another Person the Common Stock of which is and has been so registered, 'Principal Party' shall refer to such other Person, and "(iii) in case such Person is a Subsidiary, directly or indirectly, of more than one Person, the Common Stocks of two or more of which are and have been so registered, 'Principal Party' shall refer to whichever of such Persons is the issuer of the Common Stock having the greatest aggregate market value of shares outstanding, and

"(iv) if such Person is owned, directly or indirectly, by a joint venture formed by two or more Persons that are not owned, directly or indirectly, by the same Person, the rules set forth in clauses (A) and (B) above shall apply to each of the owners having an interest in the venture as if the Person owned by the joint venture was a subsidiary of both or all of such joint venturers, and the Principal Party in each case shall bear the obligation set forth in Section 13 hereof in the same ratio as its interest in such Person bears to the total of such interests."

The next step in the process is to make certain that all of the antidilution protections of section 11 of the typical rights agreement apply to the principal party. This is typically accomplished in section 13 of the rights agreement with language such as this:

"* * * then, and in each such case, promptly following the occurrence of each such Section 13 Event, proper provision shall be made so that:

"(1) Each holder of a Right, except as provided in Section 7(e) hereof, shall thereafter have the right to receive, upon the exercise thereof at the then current Purchase Price in accordance with the terms of this Agreement, such number of validly issued, fully paid, non-assessable and freely tradeable shares of Common Stock of the Principal Party (as such term is defined in Section 1(y) hereof), not subject to any liens, encumbrances, rights of first refusal or other adverse claims, as shall be equal to the product of eight times the result obtained by dividing the Current Market Price of a share of Common Stock as of the date immediately preceding the first public announcement of such Section 13 Event by the Current Market Price of a share of Common Stock of the Principal Party on such announcement date multiplied by a fraction the numerator of which is the number of shares of Common Stock outstanding on the Stock Acquisition Date with respect to such Right, and the denominator of which is the number of shares of Common Stock that are not Beneficially Owned by the Acquiring Person or its Affiliates or Associates, provided, however, that the Purchase Price and the number of shares of Common Stock of such Principal Party issuable upon the exercise of each Right shall be further adjusted as provided in Section 11(d) of this Agreement to reflect any events occurring in respect of such Principal Party after the date of such Section 13 Event;

"(2) such Principal Party shall thereafter be liable for, and shall assume, by virtue of such Section 13 Event, all the obligations and duties of the Company pursuant to this Agreement;

"(3) the term 'Company' shall thereafter be deemed to refer to such Principal Party, it being specifically intended that the provisions of Section 11 hereof shall apply only to such Principal Party following the first occurrence of a Section 13 Event;

"(4) such Principal Party shall take such steps (including, but not limited to, the reservation of a sufficient number of shares of its Common Stock in accordance with Section 9 hereof) in connection with the consummation of any such transaction as may be necessary to assure that the provisions hereof shall thereafter be applicable, as nearly as reasonably may be, in relation to its shares of Common Stock thereafter deliverable upon the exercise of the Rights, provided that, upon the subsequent occurrence of any merger, consolidation, share exchange, sale or transfer of assets or other extraordinary transaction in respect of such Principal Party, each holder of a Right shall thereupon be entitled to receive, upon Exercise of a Right and payment of the Purchase Price as provided in this Section 13(a), such cash, shares, rights, dividends, warrants and other property which such holder would have been entitled to receive had such holder, at the time of such transaction, owned the Common Stock of the Principal Party receivable upon the exercise of a Right pursuant to this Section 13(a); and

"(5) the provisions of Section 11(a)(ii) hereof shall be of no effect following the first occurrence of any Section 13 Event, except as they apply to determination of the Purchase Price."

Would these provisions have covered the claims of the Telecom warrant holders if they had been included in the warrants?

---

6. LAST PERIOD FINANCING: DEATH SPIRALS

After the NASDAQ high technology bubble of 2000 collapsed, many high tech companies were left with stock trading at depressed levels relative to their initial public offering (IPO) prices. The public market dried up for these companies, and early-stage companies, often with no profits or relatively small profit levels, found themselves unable to borrow, either in public debt markets or from conventional commercial sources. These companies were limited to novel means of raising funds. One such measure involved "private issues of public equity," ("PIPEs"), in which these companies sold their stock (often at discounts from the trading price of their shares) to privately managed funds willing to take high risks. In many cases the issuance of equity was indirect, because the investors purchased convertible debt or preferred stock in the company.

In some cases the "antidilution" provisions of the conversion feature protected the buyers not only from the risk of dilutive new issues, but from the risk that the market price for the issuing corporation's stock would decline further. This made the convertibles resemble traditional non-convertible debt in the sense that creditors don't bear the market risk associated with an issuer's common stock. Normally conversion rights impose some of this risk on the holders of the conversion rights. But this was a buyer's market, and all of the market risk could be shifted to the existing shareholders. In some pending litigation, it is alleged that short selling by the lenders was followed by conversion demands, to provide shares to cover the short sales. If the short sales were large enough and the market illiquid, these sales could drive stock prices sharply downward in a thin market, thus vastly increasing the number of shares issuable upon conversion. In some cases it is alleged that short sales drove the stock's price down by 90% or more, and that the final conversions were for sufficient shares to give the lender majority control of the corporation. Many of these companies were traded on the NASDAQ Over the Counter Bulletin Board, and trading was sufficiently small in volume that traders could apparently affect the stock's price with short sales.

Under the Securities Act of 1933 all shares of stock must be registered under Section 5 before they can be sold, unless an exemption is available for the sale. Sales to a sophisticated investor would typically be exempt as sales under the "private offering" exemption of section 4(2) of the Securities Act, while sales to a larger group of investors would typically seek their exemption under Rule 506 of Regulation D, 17 CFR 240.506, a "safe harbor" under section 4(2), typically employed when the investor group contains "accredited investors," either wealthy individuals (with incomes of $200,000 or more, or net worths in excess of $1 million) or specified corporate investors. In both cases these investors must give "investment representations" that they are purchasing for investment and not for distribution, and must accept legends to this effect on their securities. Where these exemptions are employed, investors in stock of a publicly traded company generally must hold their shares for six months before reselling. These resales must be in limited amounts every three months, into the market (no more than the greater of the average weekly trading volume or 1% of the outstanding shares of the class). Securities Act Rule 144. Because of these limitations, a buyer seeking to deliver shares to cover short sales after conversion must secure the borrower's (issuer's) commitment to register the underlying shares of common stock. Given the potential for issuance of increasing numbers of shares of common, the issuer might have to register virtually all of its authorized but unissued shares to honor this commitment.

Buyers who hold large amounts of the issuer's shares may be deemed to be "affiliates" of the borrower for purpose of these rules. Generally speaking, the SEC staff and practicing lawyers will presume that any holder of 10% or more of the stock is an "affiliate," which is defined as a person who "controls" the issuer. Where the lender becomes an "affiliate" by virtue of large stock ownership, its resales of the borrower's stock are restricted in volume and amount as described above.

Similarly, a person with the right to acquire a substantial amount of the shares of a reporting company may be subject to certain disclosure rules. For example, under the Williams Act amendments to the Securities

Exchange Act, every person who is the beneficial owner of more than 5% of an outstanding class of equity security must file a disclosure on Form 13D. Securities and Exchange Act § 13(d)(1); Rule 13d–3(d) provides that a person shall be deemed beneficial owner of securities which it has the right to acquire within 60 days. Thus, as short selling increases the number of shares that the holder of the convertible has the right to acquire, this disclosure obligation will be triggered. Similarly, the short swing sales provisions of § 16 apply to beneficial owners of more than 10% of a class of equity security, and Rule 16b–1 applies the Williams Act definition of beneficial ownership to these rules. Being subject to § 16 subjects the beneficial owner both to separate disclosure filings and capture by the issuer of profits from short-swing trades.

It has been alleged in some death spiral financing cases that the lenders have sold the borrower's stock short before entering into the loan, thus providing the cash for the loan from the short sales themselves. These short sales would allow the prospective lender to test the market's liquidity, and thus the ability of short sales to drive prices down. Below is a statement of facts describing allegations subject to a motion to dismiss in the following case.

Internet Library, Inc. v. Southridge Capital Management LLC

223 F.Supp.2d 474 (S.D.N.Y. 2002).

"Formerly known as Internet Law Library, Inc., plaintiff ITIS Inc. ('ITIS') and its CEO, Hunter Carr, along with several of its shareholders, bring this action against defendants Southridge Capital Management LLC ('Southridge'), Stephen Hicks, Daniel Pickett, Christy Constabile, Thomson Kernaghan & Co., Ltd. ('Thomson Kernaghan'), Mark Valentine, TK Holdings, Inc. ('TK'), and Cootes Drive LLC ('Cootes Drive') alleging their involvement in a scheme to defraud plaintiffs and to manipulate downward the price of ITIS stock in violation of federal and state laws. Defendants now move to dismiss the Amended Consolidated Complaint with prejudice pursuant to Rule 12(b)(6), F.R. Civ. P. for failure to state a claim and Rule 9(b), F.R. Civ. P. and the Private Securities Litigation Reform Act of 1995 ('PSLRA') for failure to plead fraud with sufficient particularity. For the reasons set forth below, defendants' motion is granted in part and denied in part.

"BACKGROUND

"This action is the by-product of the consolidation of several related actions originally filed in this court. ITIS, a Delaware corporation owning subsidiaries that operate Internet sites specializing in legal and other types of research and litigation support services, is a publicly-traded company whose stock trades on the NASDAQ over-the-counter bulletin board. In March, 2000, ITIS was in the process of seeking out capital in fulfillment of its business plan and, to that end, CEO Carr was referred to defendant

Southridge. Negotiations between Carr, acting on behalf of ITIS, and Hicks, Pickett, and Constabile, acting on behalf of Southridge and later Cootes Drive, ensued throughout March and April, 2000.

"During these negotiations, plaintiffs allege that defendants Hicks, Pickett, and Constabile made a number of misrepresentations, including that capital of up to $28 million, as needed by ITIS, consisting of a $3 million convertible preferred stock purchase and a $25 million equity line agreement, would be provided to ITIS, that defendants would refrain from selling ITIS stock for a year after the closing because they had a long-term investment interest in ITIS, that they would not manipulate ITIS stock with the intention of depressing its price, that they would not engage in the short-selling of ITIS stock, that Southridge was an accredited investor able to satisfy its funding commitment, that ITIS stock was being acquired for investment purposes and not for distribution or resale, that the stock of other companies funded by entities affiliated with the defendants had appreciated, and that defendants were not the subject of any active lawsuits. Throughout the negotiations, Carr, according to plaintiffs, continually inquired of Southridge and its agents about concerns regarding short-selling and stock manipulation and was repeatedly assured by Hicks, Pickett, and Constabile that no person associated with Southridge or its agents was engaged in short sales or manipulating ITIS stock, that no person would engage in such activities in the future, and that no sales would take place for a year after any closing. On the eve of the close of negotiations, however, defendants insisted that the no-short-sale period be reduced to six months.

"In reliance on the misrepresentations described above, on or about May 11, 2000, ITIS entered into a Convertible Preferred Stock Purchase Agreement ('Stock Purchase Agreement') with Cootes Drive, inserted in lieu of Southridge as a signatory at the last minute.[1]

"Pursuant to the terms of the Stock Purchase Agreement, ITIS submitted registration statements to the Securities and Exchange Commission to enable common shares to be issued to Cootes Drive upon conversion. Some time before the second registration statement became effective, defendant Thomson Kernaghan, acting for itself and on behalf of the defendants, allegedly sold ITIS stock short and otherwise manipulated the stock, despite representations that it would not do so. Specifically, the Amended Consolidated Complaint alleges that on July 18, 2000, Thomson Kernaghan sold 1,500 shares of ITIS stock short; on July 19, 2000, it sold 5,000 shares short; on July 27, 2000, it sold 10,000 shares short; on October 5, 2000, it closed 19,306 shares short; on October 6, 2000, it closed 29,306 shares short; and on October 10, 2000, it closed 61,806 shares short. A similar pattern of short sales continued until Thomson Kernaghan's short position had increased to nearly a million and a half shares by January 19, 2001 and back down to 876,894 shares by February 2, 2001, three days

---

1. Plaintiffs allege, on information and belief, that Cootes Drive is, in reality, only a "straw man" created for the purpose of funding the transaction between the parties and under the control of the defendants.

before Cootes Drive filed suit against ITIS in this court for breach of contract and fraud.*

"In general, plaintiffs allege that this short-selling activity was part of a larger strategy that defendants have repeatedly employed to manipulate the stock price of companies in which they have invested. According to plaintiffs, defendants Hicks, Pickett, and Valentine are seasoned practitioners of 'death spiral' funding schemes in which they provide financing to a target company and proceed to aggressively short-sell its stock in the hope that such short sales will drive down its price. This price drop, in turn, enables the defendants to obtain more shares of common stock upon conversion by virtue of an arrangement known as a 'toxic convertible' that allows the company's preferred stock to be converted at a discount to the present market value of the common stock issuable upon conversion. Defendants then use the additional shares obtained upon conversion to cover their short positions, profiting handsomely from the difference between the price at which the stock was sold short and at which it was converted. There are even times, according to plaintiffs, when defendants need not cover at all, typically when they have succeeded in driving down the stock price of the target company practically to zero. Moreover, the defendants use the stock from the conversion to push the stock price still lower, hence the characterization 'death spiral.' Plaintiffs have listed over 25 other companies in their Amended Consolidated Complaint that they believe have been the victims of toxic convertible or similar financing schemes orchestrated by defendants.

"Plaintiffs allege that ITIS was the victim of one such toxic convertible financing scheme at the hands of Hicks, Pickett, Valentine, and Southridge or entities associated with them. After holding a short position that had ballooned to almost a million and a half shares by January 19, 2001, the Amended Consolidated Complaint alleges that Thomson Kernaghan set out to cover its short position, despite knowing or having reason to know that the Stock Purchase Agreement was being materially breached by such action, by issuing conversion notices to ITIS, requesting that ITIS issue shares to Cootes Drive, with Thomson Kernaghan acting as an agent for Cootes Drive. In all, Thomson Kernaghan sent ITIS 12 notices of conversion and succeeded in converting 139.02 shares of preferred stock into 3,137,907 shares of common stock. The Amended Consolidated Complaint further alleges, on information and belief, that Thomson Kernaghan, acting on behalf of itself and other defendants and with their involvement and knowledge, made use of a multitude of manipulative techniques including, without limitation, 'painting the tape,' 'hitting the bids,' and 'dumping' large amounts of ITIS stock on the market, with an eye towards artificially affecting the price of ITIS stock, in violation of federal laws and regulations. The daily trading volume in ITIS stock mushroomed from 15,000

---

* At the beginning of 2000 ITIS had approximately 25 million shares outstanding, of which 70% were owned by insiders, leaving 7.5 million publicly owned shares for the "float." Thus, at one point Thomson Kernaghan had sold short approximately 20% of the float.—Ed.

shares a day before the closing to an average of 365,157 in the period between September 29, 2000 and October 27, 2000.

"As a result of such manipulation, plaintiffs allege that they have been damaged, that the price of ITIS stock was artificially depressed to the detriment of ITIS and its shareholders, both those present in this suit and elsewhere. The toxic convertible financing scheme, they allege, has been successful in running the price of ITIS stock into the ground, from a high of almost $7 to approximately 18 cents. Additionally, on account of defendants' manipulation of ITIS stock and the resulting price drop in the stock, Cootes Drive was excused from funding the $25 million equity line since the Stock Purchase Agreement conditioned funding on the stock of ITIS trading above a $1.50, further damaging plaintiffs. Accordingly, plaintiffs seek, among other things, the rescission of all agreements between ITIS and the defendants, declaratory relief excusing ITIS from honoring any future conversion notices by the defendants, damages of $200 million representing the decline in ITIS's market value caused by defendants' stock manipulation, damages of $100 million representing the decline in ITIS stock owned by Carr, damages for each of the individual plaintiffs equal to his/her losses in ITIS stock, an accounting for and disgorgement of all profits made by defendants in transactions involving ITIS stock, and attorney's fees."

GFL Advantage Fund, Ltd. v. Colkitt

272 F.3d 189 (3d Cir. 2001).

■ GREENBERG, CIRCUIT JUDGE:

This matter comes on before this court on defendant Douglas R. Colkitt's appeal from the district court's order for summary judgment in favor of plaintiff GFL Advantage Fund, Ltd. against Colkitt entered on April 25, 2000, and on appeal from an order entered on July 17, 2000, denying reconsideration of the April 25 order. For the reasons stated herein, we will affirm the orders of the district court.

I. BACKGROUND

A. FACTUAL HISTORY

Douglas Colkitt, who earned both his medical degree and MBA from the University of Pennsylvania in 1979, is the founder and majority shareholder of two small capitalization medical services businesses— EquiMed, Inc. ("EquiMed") and National Medical Financial Services Corporation ("National Medical"). As of February 1996, Colkitt held 20,783,-633 (73%) of EquiMed's 28,589,717 outstanding shares of common stock, and as of May 1996, he owned 2.8 million (38%) of National Medical's 7,426,844 outstanding shares of common stock. [Colkitt sought financing for various business ventures of his own, and borrowed funds from GFL Advantage Fund, Ltd., with conversion rights into shares of EquiMed and National Medical Financial Services in separate transactions. In each case, the conversion right was at a discount from the current market price of the stocks. Colkitt alleged that within a few months of each loan, GFL began a series of short sales and conversions to fund covering these sales, thus driving the price of both stocks downward and increasing the number of shares that he was required to deliver. These short sales occurred in rapid succession once begun, but did not involve the magnitude of shares sold short in the Internet Library case, above. At a point after several demands for conversion shares, Dr. Colkitt refused to deliver more shares, and GFL filed this action. The trial court granted GFL's motion to dismiss, and Dr. Colkitt filed this appeal.]

The theory of Colkitt's case, however, is that GFL sold National Medical and EquiMed shares short in an effort to depress the prices of the stocks. Indeed, Colkitt contends that the market price of National Medical dropped 17.5% between GFL's first and last short sales of National Medical stock, and that the market price of EquiMed declined by 18.5% between GFL's first short sale of EquiMed stock and GFL's first exchange demand.[1] Colkitt argues that GFL purposely depressed the stock prices so that Colkitt would be forced to exchange more shares to retire the same amount of debt. He asserts that GFL was able to obtain an additional 27,882 shares of EquiMed and an additional 11,658 shares of National Medical due to the respective declines in the stocks' prices.

As noted above, Colkitt refused to honor GFL's exchange request for EquiMed shares on January 3, 1997. Instead, Colkitt notified GFL in December 1996 and early January 1997 that he intended to prepay all unpaid principal and interest in cash. Colkitt contends that GFL improperly rejected his request to prepay the unpaid balance, even though the notes contemplated such prepayment. GFL responds that it did not reject outright Colkitt's offer to prepay, but rather refused to allow Colkitt to dictate the terms of any prepayment and disagreed with Colkitt about the amounts due. GFL admits that it does not believe that Colkitt had a right to prepay, but insists that it "accepted Colkitt's offer to prepay whatever amount Colkitt believed was then due, reserving for itself the right to contest the disputed balance." GFL claims that Colkitt neither responded to its overtures nor attempted to prepay or pay any amounts to GFL.

* * *

III. DISCUSSION

A. RESCISSION OF THE NOTES PURSUANT TO SECTION 29

Colkitt contends that the National Medical and EquiMed notes are unenforceable by reason of Section 29 of the Securities Exchange Act of

---

1. Inexplicably, Colkitt measures the price decline of EquiMed stock during the period between GFL's first short sale on November 8, 1996, and GFL's first exchange demand on November 27, 1996, rather than between GFL's first short sale on November 8, 1996, and its last short sale on November 22, 1996. As GFL points out, however, if the price decline of EquiMed stock is measured during the period between GFL's first and last short sales, EquiMed's price drop would be approximately 2. More specifically, the price of EquiMed on the day of the first short trade on November 8 was $5.25 per share, whereas the price on the day of the last short sale on November 22 was $5.13. This $.12 drop represents only a 2.3 decrease.

1934 ("Exchange Act") because GFL violated the anti-fraud provisions under Section 10(b) of the Exchange Act and Rule 10b–5 promulgated thereunder. Section 29(b) provides in relevant part that:

> Every contract made in violation of any provision of this chapter or of any rule or regulation thereunder, ... [or] the performance of which involves the violation of, or the continuance of any relationship or practice in violation of, any provision of this chapter or any rule or regulation thereunder, shall be void.

15 U.S.C. § 78cc(b) (emphasis added). Colkitt argues that GFL violated Section 10(b) and Rule 10b–5 when it engaged in market manipulation by short selling National Medical and EquiMed stock in an effort to depress the share prices, and when it engaged in fraudulent deception by concealing its plan to short sell National Medical and EquiMed stock. See Br. of Appellant at 24. Colkitt asserts that the notes are void and unenforceable under Section 29(b) because the notes were "made in violation of" Section 10(b) and Rule 10b–5 insofar as (1) they were part of GFL's scheme to manipulate the market prices of National Medical and EquiMed stock and (2) they contain omissions of material fact about GFL's short selling strategy.

* * *

B. MARKET MANIPULATION

Colkitt argues that the district court erred in rejecting his affirmative defense that the notes are void pursuant to Section 29(b) due to GFL's alleged market manipulation, as there exist genuine issues of material fact regarding whether GFL's short sales constituted market manipulation in violation of Section 10(b) and Rule 10b–5. GFL argues, however, that Colkitt has not presented enough evidence to create triable issues on any of the elements of market manipulation.[5]

---

5. GFL also insists that Colkitt cannot obtain reversal of summary judgment with respect to GFL's alleged manipulation of National Medical's price because Colkitt abandoned his market manipulation and securities fraud claims with respect to National Medical by conceding that GFL's short sales of National Medical stock did not violate any securities laws. To support its contention, GFL quotes a passage from Colkitt's opposition to GFL's motion for summary judgment, which states that "the short selling of National Medical presents an interesting contrast to the short selling of EquiMed." GFL claims that this statement, along with other unspecified passages in Colkitt's opposition and his motion for reconsideration, led the district court to limit its rulings to only the EquiMed note.

GFL's argument is without merit. A review of the district court's April 25, 2000 Memorandum reveals that the court addressed Colkitt's market manipulation and securities fraud claims as to both EquiMed and National Medical. Indeed, National Medical is mentioned throughout the district court's summary judgment and reconsideration rulings. There is no indication in the district court's rulings that Colkitt abandoned these claims or that the court limited its rulings to only the EquiMed note.

GFL also distorts the meaning of the above-quoted passage by taking it out of context. When Colkitt admitted that the short sales of National Medical differed in some respects to the short sales of EquiMed, he was referring only to GFL's contention that it engaged in the short sales as a hedging strategy. As will be explained in more detail below, see infra pp. 28–30, Colkitt's expert maintains that selling short prior to the five-day period before the

1. Elements of Market Manipulation Under Section 10(b) and Rule 10b–5

As an initial matter, the parties disagree about the specific elements of market manipulation under Section 10(b) and Rule 10b–5. To complicate matters further, we seemed not to have addressed squarely what elements are required to establish a claim of market manipulation, particularly in the context of a Section 29(b) affirmative defense, and the case law from other courts of appeals and district courts on this issue provides limited guidance. Section 10(b) states in relevant part that "it shall be unlawful for any person . . . to use or employ, in connection with the purchase or sale of any security . . ., any manipulative or deceptive device or contrivance in contravention of such rules and regulations" promulgated by the SEC. Rule 10b–5 provides in relevant part that "it shall be unlawful for any person . . . to employ any device, scheme, or artifice to defraud."

Noting that Section 10(b) outlaws but does not define a "manipulative or deceptive device or contrivance," Colkitt turns to Section 9(a) of the Exchange Act to determine the elements of the offense of market manipulation. Section 9(a) prohibits individuals from effecting "a series of transactions in any security registered on a national securities exchange . . . creating actual or apparent active trading in such security, or raising or depressing the price of such security, for the purpose of inducing the purchase or sale of such security by others." 15 U.S.C. § 78i(a)(2). Based on this passage and the Supreme Court's decision in Aaron v. SEC, 446 U.S. 680, 695, 100 S.Ct. 1945, 1955, 64 L. Ed. 2d 611 (1980), in which the Court recognized scienter as an element of a Section 10(b) claim, Colkitt maintains that summary judgment was improper because he created genuine issues with respect to each of the following elements of market manipulation: (1) GFL engaged in a series of transactions in the registered securities; (2) the purpose of GFL's short sales was to induce others to sell the securities; (3) GFL's short sales created "actual or apparent active trading" in the securities or depressed the prices of the securities; and (4) GFL acted with scienter.

GFL responds that Colkitt has mischaracterized the elements of market manipulation by applying an overly broad description of prohibited activities set forth under Section 9(a) and by ignoring the specific requirements of market manipulation that have evolved over time. GFL points out that market manipulation is "virtually a term of art when used in connection with the securities market. It connotes intentional and willful conduct

---

exchange demand is not a legitimate hedging strategy, but instead an attempt to profit from declining stock prices. The expert insists that if GFL were only trying to hedge against a possible drop in price after the exchange demand (so-called "delivery risk"), GFL could have eliminated that risk by selling short during the five-day period before the exchange demand— in essence, locking in the sale price during the same period the average closing price would be calculated. Colkitt's statement was simply an "acknowledgment that, unlike the EquiMed shorts, the National Medical shorts, by their timing, could at least qualify as a hedge strategy" because they were made within the days immediately preceding GFL's exchange demands for National Medical stock. This narrow admission cannot be construed as a complete waiver of his counterclaims and affirmative defenses with respect to the National Medical note.

designed to deceive or defraud investors by controlling or artificially affecting the price of securities." Ernst & Ernst v. Hochfelder, 425 U.S. 185, 199, 96 S.Ct. 1375, 1384, 47 L.Ed.2d 668 (1976). GFL asserts that Colkitt disregards two necessary elements of a market manipulation claim—that "GFL injected inaccurate information into the marketplace" and that GFL's conduct "affected the price" of National Medical and EquiMed stock.

The first disputed element is whether Colkitt must demonstrate that GFL injected inaccurate information into the marketplace or created a false impression of market activity. Like the district court, GFL relies on Olympia Brewing, 613 F.Supp. at 1292, in which the district court emphasized that the "essential element" of a market manipulation claim is the injection of "inaccurate information" into the market. GFL observes that even the cases cited by Colkitt "recognize that market manipulation requires an additional element, something beyond otherwise legal trading, which specifically injects false information into the market and/or creates an artificial demand for the underlying security." Colkitt responds, however, that he is not required to present evidence that "GFL injected affirmative misinformation into the market," but only needs to demonstrate that "GFL's short trades were made for the undisclosed purpose of artificially depressing share prices."

Notwithstanding Colkitt's assertion to the contrary, the parties appear to be in accord on this point. Indeed, the difference between their positions seems to be one without distinction. Both GFL and Colkitt focus on the need to demonstrate that some action was taken to artificially depress or inflate prices, whether by purposely making false statements or by employing illegitimate, deceptive trading techniques that mislead investors about the price or demand for a stock.

To the extent that the parties' respective positions are at odds, however, GFL advances a sounder construction of a Section 10(b) market manipulation claim, for it is less vague than Colkitt's. The Supreme Court has indicated that market manipulation "generally refers to practices, such as wash sales, matched orders, or rigged prices, that are intended to mislead investors by artificially affecting market activity." Santa Fe Indus. v. Green, 430 U.S. 462, 476, 97 S.Ct. 1292, 1302, 51 L.Ed.2d 480 (1977). "The gravamen of manipulation is deception of investors into believing that prices at which they purchase and sell securities are determined by the natural interplay of supply and demand, not rigged by manipulators." Gurary v. Winehouse, 190 F.3d 37, 45 (2d Cir. 1999). In that vein, courts must distinguish between legitimate trading strategies intended to anticipate and respond to prevailing market forces and those designed to manipulate prices and deceive purchasers and sellers. Although Colkitt's construction properly reflects the aspiration of Section 10(b) of preventing market activities that artificially depress prices, it provides little guidance on which activities artificially affect prices and which activities legitimately impact prices.

Requiring a Section 10(b) plaintiff to establish that the alleged manipulator injected "inaccurate information" into the market or created a false impression of market activity cures this problem. Such a construction permits courts to differentiate between legitimate trading activities that permissibly may influence prices, such as short sales, and "ingenious devices that might be used to manipulate securities prices," Santa Fe Indus., 430 U.S. at 477, 97 S.Ct. at 1303, such as wash sales and matched orders. As the court in Olympia Brewing, 613 F.Supp. at 1292, stated, "regardless of whether market manipulation is achieved through deceptive trading activities or deceptive statements as to the issuing corporation's value, it is clear that the essential element of the claim is that inaccurate information is being injected into the marketplace."

The second disputed element is whether Colkitt must establish that GFL's allegedly manipulative conduct actually depressed the prices of National Medical and EquiMed stock. GFL argues that market manipulation in violation of Section 10(b) and Rule 10b–5 requires that the allegedly unlawful conduct impact a security's price. GFL cites three cases to support its position, but all three are unhelpful. * * *

Colkitt's position is somewhat inconsistent on this point. On the one hand, he takes great pains to argue that GFL's short sales depressed the price of National Medical by 17.5% and the price of EquiMed by 18.5%. On the other hand, when confronted with evidence that the prices of the stocks were on a sharp downward trend before and after GFL's short sales, thus raising serious doubts about the true reason for the declining prices, Colkitt reverses course and argues that he need not prove that GFL's alleged scheme was successful in depressing prices. Colkitt insists that he only must establish that GFL attempted to depress prices by selling shares short. To muddy the waters even more, Colkitt appears to make a concession that an impact on price must be established when he states in his reply brief: "A jury must also decide whether GFL's short trades had an affect [sic] on share prices."

Despite his flip-flopping on the issue, Colkitt appears to be correct that he need not prove that GFL's manipulative conduct actually depressed prices. The Court of Appeals for the Fifth Circuit concluded in Chemetron Corp. v. Business Funds, Inc., 718 F.2d 725, 728 (5th Cir. 1983), that Section 10(b), unlike Section 9(a), does not require that a plaintiff prove the allegedly unlawful activities had an effect on the price of the stock. Although any damages that Colkitt would be entitled to recover under his Section 10(b) and Rule 10b–5 counterclaim would be contingent on proving that GFL's conduct actually depressed prices, proof of price movement is not necessary to establish a violation of Section 10(b) and Rule 10b–5 and therefore is not necessary to support his assertion of an affirmative defense under Section 29(b).[1]

---

1. Although maintaining a private right of action under Section 10(b) requires a plaintiff to prove reliance and damages (usually reflected in the stock's price movement), Section 29(b) only requires a violation of Section 10(b), not the maintenance of a private suit under Section 10(b). Therefore, looking to the statutory language of the anti-fraud provision, we note that an individual violates Section 10(b)—and therefore triggers Section 29(b)—when he or she employs manipulative or deceptive devices in connection with the purchase or sale of

We are satisfied that, at bottom, neither party properly articulates the elements of market manipulation under Section 10(b) in the context of a Section 29(b) affirmative defense. Because we have not squarely addressed this issue, we must set forth the necessary elements for such a claim. In this regard, we conclude that to establish a Section 29(b) affirmative defense of market manipulation in violation of Section 10(b) and Rule 10b–5, Colkitt must present evidence that (1) in connection with the purchase or sale of securities, (2) GFL engaged in deceptive or manipulative conduct by injecting inaccurate information into the marketplace or creating a false impression of supply and demand for the security (3) for the purpose of artificially depressing or inflating the price of the security.

2.   Evidence Supporting Colkitt's Claim of Market Manipulation

Colkitt's affirmative defense based upon GFL's alleged market manipulation fails because he cannot demonstrate that GFL engaged in any deceptive or manipulative conduct by injecting false inaccurate information into the marketplace or creating a false impression of supply and demand for the stock. As the district court explained repeatedly in its two rulings, Colkitt has not presented any evidence that GFL did anything but lawfully engage in short sales of National Medical and EquiMed stock. The fact that these short sales may have contributed to a decline in the stocks' prices is not evidence of deceptive or manipulative conduct, for there is no reason to believe these prices were depressed artificially. See Sullivan & Long, Inc. v. Scattered Corp., 47 F.3d 857, 864 (7th Cir. 1995) (concluding that defendant's "unprecedented massive short selling" did not create "a false impression of supply and demand" because on the other side of defendant's

---

securities. This situation is analogous to a government prosecution under Section 10(b), in which the government is not required to meet the normal standing requirements imposed on those asserting a private remedy, inasmuch as the government need not demonstrate that the defendant's conduct induced reliance by investors or affected the price of the security. See, e.g., United States v. Haddy, 134 F.3d 542, 549 (3d Cir. 1998) (holding that reliance is not an element of the crime of stock manipulation).

Even if we were to embrace the position of GFL and the district court that proof of an effect on price is necessary to establish a claim of market manipulation, the district court still erred in concluding that Colkitt failed to create a genuine issue of material fact with respect to price movement. As already noted, Colkitt claims that the price of National Medical dropped 17.5% and the price of EquiMed plummeted 18.5% during the period of GFL's short sales. The district court concluded, however, that these statistics are "not evidence that the value of the shares was affected by the short sales: the free fall began before the short sales and continued well after the short sales." The district court observed that the price of EquiMed declined steadily from $15.00 on February 1, 1996, to $2.4583 on January 2, 1998, including a dramatic drop of 27.6%, from $7.25 to $5.25, during the 24–day period immediately preceding GFL's short sales. The court also noted that National Medical plummeted from $12.875 on May 1, 1996, to $0.4375 on January 2, 1998. Based on these long-term, downward trends in the stocks' prices, the district court concluded that Colkitt could not prove that GFL's short sales had an effect on the price of either National Medical or EquiMed stock. Although the court was correct that other factors clearly were contributing to the slide in prices, it was not within the court's province to weigh the evidence as a finder of fact. Whether and how much GFL's alleged unlawful conduct contributed to the downturn in prices would have been issues for the jury if Colkitt's case had survived GFL's motion for summary judgment. Contrary to the district court's conclusion, Colkitt clearly created genuine issues as to whether GFL's short sales affected the prices of National Medical and EquiMed.

transactions were "real buyers, betting against [defendant], however foolishly, that the price of [the] stock would rise"); Olympia Brewing, 613 F. Supp. at 1296 (stating that "short selling is simply not unlawful, even in large numbers and even if the trading does negatively affect the purchase price"). Indeed, the district court stated it well when it wrote that it is unreasonable "to infer unlawful intent from lawful activity alone."

In the cases Colkitt cites in which courts concluded that a party's short selling was part of a scheme to manipulate stock prices, the short selling was in conjunction with some other deceptive practice that either injected inaccurate information into the market or otherwise artificially affected the price of the stock. See Russo, 74 F.3d at 1387, 1390, 1391 (defendants used short sales in concert with "unauthorized placements" and "parking" of stock in customers' accounts to generate false credits that funded their "stock-kiting scheme" designed to artificially inflate stock prices); United States v. Regan, 937 F.2d 823, 829 (2d Cir. 1991) (defendants sought to depress temporarily the price of stock by arranging to have 40,000 shares sold short secretly to a broker-dealer without disclosing to the dealer the identity of the seller or the moving party behind the deal); United States v. Charnay, 537 F.2d 341, 344 (9th Cir. 1976) (to facilitate a take-over bid, defendants artificially depressed stock prices by getting others to sell 86,100 shares short and "guaranteeing these sellers by secret understanding a recovery of $22 per share irrespective of the price obtained on the Exchange"); Advanced Magnetics, Inc. v. Bayfront Partners, Inc., No. 92 CIV. 6879 (CSH), 1996 WL 14440 (S.D.N.Y. Jan. 16, 1996) (defendant attempted to depress stock prices through short sales that contravened Section 10(a) of the Exchange Act and Rule 10a–1 thereunder, which prohibits a short sale "below the price at which the last sale" of the security was reported), vacated in part on other grounds, 106 F.3d 11 (2d Cir. 1997).

The remaining cases of market manipulation Colkitt cites likewise involved either injection of inaccurate information into the market or creation of a false impression of supply and demand for a stock. See Santa Fe Indus., 430 U.S. at 467, 97 S.Ct. at 1298 (defendant obtained "fraudulent appraisal" of stock that severely undervalued its worth "in order to lull the minority stockholders into erroneously believing that [its cash-exchange offer] was generous"); Crane Co. v. Westinghouse Air Brake Co., 419 F.2d 787, 792–93 (2d Cir. 1969) (in an effort to inflate prices and thwart a corporate take-over, defendant "painted the tape" by purchasing large blocks of stock in the open market at inflated prices while simultaneously making large secret and unreported sales at lower prices to partially finance the purchases); Blech, 928 F.Supp. at 1286, 1298 (defendant arranged "sham transactions" to inflate prices by improperly directing trades into and out of brokerage accounts at the firm without the authorization of the owners of the accounts); SEC v. Kimmes, 799 F.Supp. 852, 856–57 (N.D. Ill. 1992) (defendant maintained artificially high stock prices by buying and selling stock through "undisclosed nominee accounts," distributing "false and misleading registration statements," and filing "false and materially misleading period reports" with the SEC), aff'd sub nom., SEC v. Quinn, 997 F.2d 287 (7th Cir. 1993); SEC v. Malenfant, 784 F.Supp. 141, 144–45 (S.D.N.Y. 1992) (defendant arranged "matched buy and sell orders" to "create a misleading appearance of active trading in the Texscan common stock" and thus drive up the price of the stock). Once again, Colkitt fails to proffer any evidence that GFL engaged in any such inappropriate conduct.

Colkitt attempts to overcome this dearth of evidence of deceptive or manipulative conduct on the part of GFL by claiming that short sales, by their very nature, "convey to market participants negative information about the prospects of the firm." Colkitt's argument misses the mark, however, because conveying negative information about a firm does not constitute market manipulation unless the information is untruthful. Indeed, legitimate short sales often convey negative information about a company insofar as short sales suggest that a stock's price is overvalued, but that does not mean that such sales distort the market. To the contrary, short selling can help move an overvalued stock's market price toward its true value, thus creating a more efficient marketplace in which stock prices reflect all available relevant information about the stock's economic value. See Sullivan & Long, 47 F.3d at 861–62.

Colkitt maintains that National Medical and EquiMed were not overvalued. He insists that, because GFL did not argue before the district court that it sold short because it believed the stocks were overvalued, Colkitt is entitled to the inference that "the short sales were made at least in part to convey to the market the false impression that the stocks were overvalued so as to result in a decline in share prices." It would not be reasonable to draw such an inference, however, for to do so would fly in the face of uncontradicted evidence that the prices of National Medical and EquiMed were on a dramatic slide before and after GFL's short sales. If we were to draw any inference from the record evidence about the value of National Medical and EquiMed, it would be that the market considered the stocks to be overvalued and that GFL simply was responding to market forces, rather than distorting them, by engaging in short sales.

An examination of Colkitt's other requested inferences exposes Colkitt's claims for what they are—nothing more than a general attack on the lawful practice of short selling. For instance, Colkitt's first two inferences—that GFL had a "unique financial incentive" to depress the prices of National Medical and EquiMed because its profits increased as the market prices decreased,[8] and that short selling "conveys negative information"

---

8. Colkitt believes that GFL's incentive to depress prices is "unique" because the structure of the convertible notes allows GFL to receive more shares—and thus higher profits—as the stocks' prices decline. This incentive, however, is not unique to GFL's situation. All short sellers receive higher profits as the stock's price declines. Indeed, these higher profits in the face of declining prices are why traders engage in short sales. They are betting that the stock's price will decline, and if it does so, they will have to spend less money buying replacement stock to cover the borrowed shares, thus allowing them to pocket the difference.

Colkitt's differentiation between GFL and other short sellers based on the structure of the National Medical and EquiMed notes is misguided. Whether GFL acquires $100,000 worth of

about the company being short sold and contributes to a drop in share prices—are general criticisms of short selling. These inferences, even if granted, are of no help to Colkitt in trying to prove market manipulation, inasmuch as short selling is a lawful investment strategy. Colkitt's next three requested inferences—that GFL's short sales constituted a large percentage of shares sold on a daily basis, that GFL's short sales caused a 17.5% decline in National Medical and an 18.5% decline in EquiMed, and that these price slumps allowed GFL to obtain an additional 11,658 shares of National Medical and an additional 27,882 shares of EquiMed from Colkitt—are equally unavailing. Once again, short selling, even in large volumes, is not in and of itself unlawful and therefore cannot be regarded as evidence of market manipulation. That short selling may depress share prices, which in turn may enable traders to acquire more shares for less cash (or in this case, for less debt), is not evidence of unlawful market manipulation, for they simply are natural consequences of a lawful and carefully regulated trading practice.[10]

* * *

At bottom, the core of Colkitt's argument is premised on his belief that short selling artificially depresses prices and presumably should be banned as a market manipulation. Unfortunately for Colkitt, however, short selling is lawful, and courts have held that short selling, even in massive volume, is neither deceptive nor manipulative when carried out in accordance with SEC rules and regulations. See Sullivan & Long, 47 F.3d at 864–65. Therefore, to make out a claim of market manipulation, Colkitt must present evidence that GFL engaged in some other type of deceptive behavior in conjunction with its short selling that either injected inaccurate information into the marketplace or created artificial demand for the securities. Colkitt has offered nothing but evidence that GFL engaged in lawful short sales of National Medical and EquiMed, which alone is insufficient to prevail on a claim of market manipulation in violation of Section 10(b) and Rule 10b–5.

---

shares from Colkitt in exchange for debt (as GFL did here) or in exchange for cash (as short sellers normally do when they cover) is irrelevant. In either situation, GFL will be able to obtain more shares from Colkitt if prices decline. Thus, if this "unique" incentive to depress prices is evidence that GFL engaged in market manipulation, then all short traders are likewise guilty of manipulating markets in violation of Section 10(b). Of course, this position is untenable, for as already explained, short selling is perfectly lawful.

10. A passage in Colkitt's reply brief further undermines his theory that short sales are manipulative because they depress prices. He writes: "It is reasonable and makes economic sense to infer that short selling drives down share prices, because each short sale is, itself, a 'sale,' increasing supply. . . ." In other words, Colkitt believes that short sales are manipulative because they increase the stock's supply and drive down its price. This, of course, is true (assuming demand remains constant), but it is also true for all stock sales, whether they are from long positions or short positions. The rationale of Colkitt's theory would lead to the absurd result of outlawing any sales practice that increases a security's supply and consequently may affect its price. Colkitt fails to understand that increasing the supply of stocks by selling them on the open market in legitimate transactions to real buyers does not artificially affect prices and therefore cannot be manipulative.

Another reason why Colkitt's market manipulation claim fails is because he has not met the scienter requirement by offering evidence that GFL engaged in short sales for the purpose of artificially depressing the prices of National Medical and EquiMed stock. Citing our opinion in In re Advanta Corp. Securities Litigation, 180 F.3d 525, 535 (3d Cir. 1999), Colkitt argues that he has met the recklessness standard for liability under Section 10(b). He contends that GFL's conduct constitutes "an extreme departure from the standards of ordinary care" and "presents a danger of misleading buyers and sellers that is either known to the defendant or is so obvious that the actor must have been aware of it." According to Colkitt, evidence of GFL's alleged recklessness includes: GFL's "powerful economic incentive" depress the stocks' prices; "voluminous scholarly evidence" that GFL's short sales would convey a "negative impression" of the companies; the dramatic drop in the stocks' prices during the period of GFL's short selling; the additional 39,540 shares that GFL "extracted" from Colkitt because of the declining prices; GFL's use of four brokers to conceal his short sales; the conclusion of Colkitt's expert that GFL's short sales were not part of a legitimate hedging strategy; and GFL's having been sued twice for similar conduct.

In essence, Colkitt recycles his arguments that he advanced in support of his contention that GFL's short trades were manipulative and deceptive. Some of this evidence and the requested inferences to be taken therefrom already have been discredited—GFL's use of multiple brokers, whether GFL's short sales were a legitimate hedge strategy, and the alleged lawsuits against GFL for engaging in short selling—and the rest of the evidence and inferences are, once again, general attacks on the practice of selling short— the powerful incentive to depress prices, the negative impression of the company conveyed by short sales, the actual drop in National Medical and EquiMed prices, and the additional shares GFL obtained because of the declining prices. All that this information proves is that GFL engaged in the lawful practice of selling stock short and that these short sales may or may not have affected the price of National Medical and EquiMed stock. This evidence neither establishes that GFL's short sales were manipulative nor demonstrates that GFL executed the trades for the purpose of depressing the stocks' prices. Perhaps, if Colkitt had offered evidence that GFL's short sales violated SEC rules (for instance, if GFL failed to cover properly the short sales in violation of Rule 10a–2, or if GFL made short sales below the last sales price in violation of Rule 10a–1), Colkitt might have been able to establish that GFL's conduct was intentionally or recklessly manipulative or deceptive. In the absence of evidence that GFL engaged in any wrongful conduct, however, Colkitt's claim of market manipulation must fail. Therefore, we will affirm summary judgment in favor of GFL with respect to the market manipulation claim.

C. SECURITIES FRAUD

Colkitt also claims that the notes should be voided pursuant to Section 29(b) on the grounds that GFL committed securities fraud in violation of Section 10(b) and Rule 10b–5 when it failed to disclose its intent to manipulate the prices of National Medical and EquiMed stock through short sales. GFL responds that it had no duty to disclose its intent to engage in short sales and that Colkitt has not established that he either relied on this alleged omission of fact or suffered a cognizable injury as a result of the reliance.

1. Elements of Securities Fraud Under Section 10(b) and Rule 10b–5

It is well settled that a claim of securities fraud under Section 10(b) requires proof "that the defendant (1) made misstatements or omissions of material fact; (2) with scienter; (3) in connection with the purchase or sale of securities; (4) upon which plaintiffs relied; and (5) that plaintiffs' reliance was the proximate cause of their injury." Weiner v. Quaker Oats Co., 129 F.3d 310, 315 (3d Cir. 1997) (citation and internal quotations omitted). The parties apparently agree that the third element has been established, as there is no dispute that the alleged fraud was related to the purchase or sale of National Medical and EquiMed securities. Therefore, Colkitt must establish genuine issues with respect to the following elements: omissions of material fact, reliance, cognizable injury, and scienter.[13]

2. Evidence Supporting Colkitt's Claim of Securities Fraud

Colkitt asserts that GFL concealed from him two critical pieces of information that constitute omissions of material fact: (1) GFL's intention to sell short National Medical and EquiMed stock; and (2) GFL's actual short sales of the stock. Colkitt maintains that GFL had an affirmative duty to disclose this information because it was material and he would not have entered into the contracts with GFL if he had known it planned to sell the stocks short.

Analysis of a securities fraud claim under Section 10(b) and Rule 10b–5 includes two steps: "First, was the defendant under a duty to disclose at the time at issue? Second, was the alleged omission or misstatement material? If, under the facts of this case, no duty to disclose exists, or if the undisclosed facts are not material, there is no liability under Rule 10b–5." Staffin v. Greenberg, 672 F.2d 1196, 1202 (3d Cir. 1982). A duty to disclose arises only when one party to a transaction has material information that the other party is entitled to have because of some relationship of trust and confidence between the parties, such as when one party is a fiduciary, corporate insider, or "tippee." See Chiarella v. United States, 445 U.S. 222, 229, 100 S.Ct. 1108, 1115, 63 L.Ed.2d 348 (1980). The Supreme Court has determined that "an omission of fact is material if there is a substantial likelihood that a reasonable shareholder would consider it important in deciding" whether to invest. Basic, Inc. v. Levinson, 485 U.S. 224, 231, 108 S.Ct. 978, 983, 99 L.Ed.2d 194 (1988) (quoting TSC Indus., Inc. v. Northway, Inc., 426 U.S. 438, 449, 96 S.Ct. 2126, 2132, 48 L.Ed.2d 757 (1976)). Materiality is a mixed question of law and fact and should be decided as a matter of law "only when the disclosures or omissions are so clearly

---

13. Colkitt submits the same evidence of scienter in support of both his securities fraud claim and his market manipulation claim.

unimportant that reasonable minds could not differ." In re Craftmatic Sec. Litig., 890 F.2d 628, 641 (3d Cir. 1989).

Colkitt's securities fraud claim falters for at least one and possibly two reasons. To start with, he failed to present any evidence that GFL intended to engage in short sales at the time it loaned the money to Colkitt. See In re Phillips Petroleum Secs. Litig., 881 F.2d 1236, 1245 (3d Cir. 1989) (stating that "a statement of intent need only be true when made; a subsequent change of intention will not, by itself, give rise to a cause of action under Section 10(b) or Rule 10b–5"). More significantly, even if we can draw an inference that GFL had such a plan, it did not have a duty to disclose its intentions.

Colkitt argues that GFL had a duty to disclose its intentions because such a disclosure was necessary to clarify GFL's "implicit" representations that the debt-for-stock exchange price would be "based upon the accurate, unbiased and untainted market price quoted by the stock market." Colkitt explains that Section 10(b) and Rule 10b–5 impose a "duty to disclose any material facts that are necessary to make disclosed material statements, whether mandatory or volunteered, not misleading." Craftmatic, 890 F.2d at 641. He asserts that GFL's implicit guarantee that the exchange price would be based upon prevailing market forces "was rendered grossly misleading by GFL's failure to disclose that it intended to short sell EquiMed and National Medical."

We must reject Colkitt's argument for it is premised on the misguided notion that short sales distort markets and thus produce inaccurate, biased, and tainted market prices. As already explained, short sales executed in accordance with SEC rules and regulations not only are lawful, but also do not distort markets or create a false impression of supply and demand because they are legitimate transactions with real buyers on the other side of the sale who are betting that the stock's price will rise. See Sullivan & Long, 47 F.3d at 864. Contrary to Colkitt's assertion, GFL's short sales did not render its guarantee misleading, and GFL consequently did not have a duty to disclose to Colkitt its intention to engage in short selling. Therefore, because Colkitt failed to create a genuine issue with respect to GFL making an omission of material fact, we will affirm summary judgment in favor of GFL with respect to the securities fraud claim.

* * *

IV. CONCLUSION

For the foregoing reasons, we will affirm the orders of the district court entered on April 25, 2000, and July 17, 2000.

QUESTIONS

1. Would Colkitt state a claim for violation of Rule 10b–5 if he linked the short sales with an agreement that allowed GFL to cover its short sales by acquiring new shares through exercise of conversion rights at prices below the then market price for the stocks?

2. If you represented a company seeking financing under these circumstances, what covenants would you want from the investor about resales of converted securities? Keep in mind that restricting resales (and thus the lender's liquidity) reduces the attractiveness of the conversion feature, and thus may raise the price demanded by the investor, either in the form of a higher dividend rate on the preferred stock or a greater discount on the shares upon conversion.

3. If you represented such a corporation, what other kinds of representations and/or covenants would you want from the prospective investor?

4. If suit were brought by an issuing corporation, does it have standing to complain about the dilution of its own shares? What theories would a plaintiff have to argue that a claim belongs to the corporation rather than exclusively to its shareholders?

5. Are facts alleged in Internet Law Library, Inc., *supra*, that would distinguish it from the holding in the *Colkitt* case?

6. In note 10 the court states: "Colkitt believes that short sales are manipulative because they increase the stock's supply and drive down its price. This, of course, is true (assuming demand remains constant), but it is also true for all stock sales, whether they are from long positions or short positions. The rationale of Colkitt's theory would lead to the absurd result of outlawing any sales practice that increases a security's supply and consequently may affect its price." Is there a difference between short sales that increase apparent supply and other actions that increase actual supply? Consider that short sales are disclosed as the "short interest" in a stock. Is such trading deceptive? Does it send a signal about the expectations of some investors for a stock's price? Does it send a countervailing signal that at some point persons holding short positions will be forced to buy stock to cover their short positions if the stock's price rises? What if the short seller can cover his short sales without buying in market transactions? See Crane Co. v. Westinghouse Air Brake Co., 419 F.2d 787 (2d Cir. 1969), where a court found that a defendant had engaged in a manipulation by doing the reverse—buying large amounts of stock in the market while selling off the market. The court rejected this case as authority for Colkitt's claim. Why?

7. If one were obtaining covenants against short-selling, obviously an absolute prohibition of short sales by the investors would be the best protection. But would it protect against options transactions that might have the same effect? Recall our discussion of put-call parity in Part 2.C of this Chapter. What transactions could duplicate a short sale that should also be prohibited?

NOTE

"Daniel Drew, one of the nineteenth century financial buccaneers, was the author of the jingle:

"He that sells what isn't his'n,

"Must buy it back or go to prison".

See Deepa R. Nayini, Comment, The Toxic Convertible: Manipulation and Short Sales, 54 Emory L. J. 721 (2005). Short sales have generally been acknowledged as a valuable tool to allow markets to self-correct for waves of bullish enthusiasm. At the same time, concerns about abuses of short selling have always lingered. For a long time the SEC limited short selling by allowing short sales only on an "up-tick"—a previous transaction that involved a sale at a price higher than its predecessor. This rule was replaced early in the 21st century by Regulation SHO, which expressed less fear of short sales. The rule required prompt delivery of borrowed shares, and imposed strict limits on shares that were identified as "hard to borrow" where the short seller had to locate shares to be borrowed in advance of the short sale. Nevertheless, many failures to deliver continued, and the problem was exacerbated by hedge funds, which frequently used massive short sales as a trading strategy. Because these hedge funds were such lucrative clients of major brokerage houses, these brokers did not take action to close out the transaction by buying in the stock, but rather carried these accounts for their customers.

While cases such as those treated in this chapter indicate that some corporations and their shareholders were concerned about this activity, the SEC exhibited no concern about it until the financial crisis of 2008, when massive short sales began depressing the price of stocks of both brokerage houses and banks. This created fears that there would be "runs" by fearful customers and depositors seeking the return of their securities and deposits, which could lead to their failure. Accordingly, the SEC reinstated the up-tick rule for a limited number of financial institutions for a limited period until rescue activities assured customers and depositors that their funds were safe. This was followed by a rule-making proceeding that proposed permanent restoration of the up-tick rule. These actions do not address the issue of naked short sales, however. As this manuscript was completed the SEC had held discussions with interested parties about further reform and rule-making.

CHAPTER NINE

DIVIDENDS AND DISTRIBUTIONS

1. DISTRIBUTIONS AND INVESTOR WEALTH

We use the word "distributions" rather than "dividends" in parts of this chapter to emphasize that there are a variety of ways that shareholders can obtain cash from their investments in companies. Dividends generally come to mind first when we think of distributions, but there are several other ways. A special form of dividend is the spin-off transaction, in which a corporation declares a dividend of the shares of a subsidiary company. In other cases companies may choose to return cash to shareholders by repurchasing shares, which allows a self-selection process among those shareholders willing to bear the tax consequences of realizing capital gains or losses.

A. DIVIDEND PRACTICES

The following article is the seminal study of dividend practices in the second half of the twentieth century. For those with a background in economics, it is interesting to note how empirical work has changed over that period.

Distribution of Incomes of Corporations Among Dividends, Retained Earnings, and Taxes

By John Lintner.
46 American Economic Review 97 (1956).

* * *

What then can be said in any general way regarding the dividend policies of this diverse group of 28 companies? Several features stand out clearly. With the possible exception of 2 companies which sought a relatively fixed percentage pay-out, consideration of what dividends should be paid at any given time turned, first and foremost in every case, on the question whether the existing rate of payment should be changed. [W]e found no instance in which the question of how much should be paid in a given quarter or year was considered without regard to the existing rate.... Rather, there would be serious consideration of the second question of just how large the change in dividend payments should be only after management had satisfied itself that a change in the existing rate would be positively desirable. Even then, the companies' existing dividend rate continued to be a central bench mark for the problem in managements' eyes. * * *

707

It was equally clear that these elements of inertia and conservatism—and the belief on the part of many managements that most stockholders prefer a reasonably stable rate and that the market puts a premium on stability or gradual growth in rate—were strong enough that most managements sought to avoid making changes in their dividends that might have to be reversed within a year or so. This conservatism and effort to avoid erratic changes in rates very generally resulted in the development of reasonably consistent patterns of behavior in dividend decisions. The principal device used to achieve this consistent pattern was a practice or policy of changing dividends in any given year by only part of the amounts which were indicated by changes in current financial figures. Further partial adjustments in dividend rates were then made in subsequent years if still warranted. This policy of progressive, continuing "partial adaptation" tends to stabilize dividend distributions and provides a consistency in the pattern of dividend action which helps to minimize adverse stockholder reactions. At the same time it enables management to live more comfortably with its unavoidable uncertainties regarding future developments—and this is generally true even during at least a considerable part of most cyclical declines, since the failure of dividends to reflect increasing earnings fully and promptly during the preceding upswing leaves more cushion in the cash flow as earnings start to decline.

Within this context of the decision-making process, it became clear that any reason which would lead management to decide to change an existing rate—and any reason which would be an important consideration in determining the amount of the change—had to seem prudent and convincing to officers and directors themselves and had to be of a character which provided strong motivations to management. Consequently, such reasons had to involve considerations that stockholders and the financial community generally would know about and which management would expect these outside groups to understand and find reasonably persuasive, if not compelling. Current net earnings meet these conditions better than any other factor. Earnings are reported frequently and receive wide publicity in the financial press. Most officers and directors regarded their stockholders as having a proprietary interest in earnings, and many urged the stockholders' special interest in getting earnings in dividends, subject to their interest in regularity of payment. The managements we interviewed very generally believed that, unless there were other compelling reasons to the contrary, their fiduciary responsibilities and standards of fairness required them to distribute part of any substantial increase in earnings to the stockholders in dividends. Even the executives in the minority who were most inclined to view the interests of the company as distinct from those of the stockholders, and who seemed least concerned with their responsibility to frame dividend policy in the best interests of the stockholders as such, were generally concerned with the decline in favorable proxies and in the weakening of their personal positions which they believed would follow any failure to reflect a "fair share" of such added earnings in dividends.

* * *

We also found that the relationship between current earnings and the existing dividend rate was very generally much the most important single factor determining the amount of any change in dividends decided upon. In describing the character of this dependence, it is convenient to divide the companies into two groups. In the first group are two-thirds of the companies studied, each of which had a rather definite policy regarding the ideal or target ratio of dividends to current earnings. In all but two of these companies, however, for reasons already indicated, this normal pay-out ratio was considered to be a target or an ideal toward which that company would move, but not a restrictive requirement dictating a specific percentage payment within each year. Moreover, most of these companies also had somewhat more flexible but nevertheless reasonably well-defined standards regarding the speed with which they would try to move toward a full adjustment of dividends to current earnings. In a majority, these standards took the form of a formal policy or a rather clear understanding that dividends should be adjusted by some fraction of the difference between the last period's payment and the rate which would be indicated by applying the target pay-out ratio to current earnings, or a policy to make a full adjustment rather regularly over some stated period of years. * * *

The target pay-out ratios varied from a low of 20 per cent to a high of 80 per cent, with 50 per cent the most common figure and most of the other companies aiming at 40 or 60 per cent. With respect to speed of adjustment, two companies sought to make a reasonably full adjustment in dividends within each year, while most of the others generally sought to move some part of the way within each year.

* * *

The different target pay-out ratios and adjustment rates in the various companies reflected a large number of different factors in the companies' experience, objectives and pattern of operations. In some cases management had weighed and in some manner "balanced out" these considerations at some time in the earlier history of the company; in most companies a growing body of experience and precedents accumulated out of numerous decisions individually made on an *ad hoc* basis gradually became more rationalized and formalized in a reasonably fixed and definite policy. Among the more important factors which had more or less consciously and rationally entered into these standards were: the growth prospects of the industry and, more importantly, the growth and earnings prospects of the particular company; the average cyclical movement of investment opportunities, working capital requirements, and internal fund flows, judged by past experience; the relative importance attached by management to longer term capital gains as compared with current dividend income for its stockholders, and management's views of its stockholders' preferences between reasonably stable or fluctuating dividend rates, and its judgment of the size and importance of any premium the market might put on stability or stable growth in the dividend rate as such; the normal pay-outs and speeds of adjustment of competitive companies or those whose securities were close substitutes investmentwise; the financial strength of the company, its access to the capital market on favorable terms , and company policies with respect to the use of outside debt and new equity issues; and management's confidence in the soundness of earnings figures as reported by its accounting department, and its confidence in its budgets and projections of future sales, profits, and so on.

* * *

Special comment is required, however, regarding the bearing of the magnitude and profitability of current investment opportunities and the ease or stringency of current liquidity positions on each year's dividend decisions within the framework of these two standards. As already indicated, each company's target pay-out ratio and speed-of-adjustment factor reflected the cyclical movements of investment opportunities, working capital requirements, and fund flows in its previous experience along with the other considerations mentioned. Moreover, the standards ran in terms of net earnings as reported to stockholders and many used LIFO accounting for much of their inventories. Generally speaking, after these standards had been established or embodied in informal understandings, the company lived with them and undertook all of its financial planning and capital budgeting in the light of these standards of dividend behavior. Managements deliberately planned ahead so that carrying through their established dividend policy would not involve them in unduly short liquidity positions. Management was generally in a position and was willing to draw down on working capital to help meet such requirements. In general, management's standards with respect to its current liquidity position appear to be very much more flexible than its standards with respect to dividend policy, and this flexibility frequently provided the buffer between reasonably definite dividend requirements in line with established policy and especially rich current investment opportunities. If investment opportunities were particularly abundant and could not be financed with the funds currently available after dividends had been increased in line with established policies, the remaining investment projects which could be undertaken only through outside financing were re-examined to make sure that they were sufficiently desirable as to justify as to justify the company in having recourse to outside capital. If so, the necessary capital was raised and the projects were undertaken; if not, the projects were abandoned. In the companies which as a matter of policy would not go to the outside market except in the most extreme circumstances, the capital budget year by year was simply cut to fit the available funds.

In this connection it must be recognized that net earnings generally increase much more than in proportion to increased volume (and similarly on declines). Even though dividend rates are increased somewhat in line with policy described, the current pay-out ratio will decline with increased profits and under this pattern of behavior retained earnings fluctuate still more than in proportion. Marked fluctuations in working capital requirements and investment outlays are consequently "automatically" provided for under this form of conservative dividend behavior to a very considerable extent at least.

Disappearing Dividends: Changing Firm Characteristics or Lower Propensity to Pay?

By Eugene Fama and Kenneth R. French.
60 Journal of Financial Economics 3 (2001).

1. Introduction

Dividends have long been an enigma. Since they are taxed at a higher rate than capital gains, the common presumption is that dividends are less valuable than capital gains.* In this view, firms that pay dividends are at a competitive disadvantage since they have a higher cost of equity than firms that do not pay. The fact that many firms pay dividends is then difficult to explain.

Using CRSP and Compustat, we study the incidence of dividend payers during the 1926–99 period, with special interest in the period after 1972, when the data cover NYSE, AMEX, and NASDAQ firms. The percent of firms paying dividends declines sharply after 1978. In 1973, 52.8% of publicly traded non-financial non-utility firms pay dividends. The proportion of payers rises to a peak of 66.5% in 1978. It then falls rather relentlessly. In 1999, only 20.8% of firms pay dividends.

The decline after 1978 in the percent of firms paying dividends raises three questions. (i) What are the characteristics of dividend payers? (ii) Is the decline in the percentage of payers due to a decline in the prevalence of these characteristics among publicly traded firms, or (iii) have firms with the characteristics typical of dividend payers become less likely to pay? We address these questions.

* * *

The summary statistics provide details on the nature of dividend payers, former payers, and firms that have never paid. Former payers tend to be distressed. They have low earnings and few investments. Firms that have never paid dividends are more profitable than former payers and they have strong growth opportunities. Dividend payers are, in turn, more profitable than firms that have never paid. But firms that have never paid invest at a higher rate, do more R & D, and have a higher ratio of the market value of assets to their book value (V_t/A_t, a proxy for Tobin's Q) than dividend payers.** The investments of dividend payers are on the

---

* Effective in 2003, dividends are taxed at the same rate as long-term capital gains (15%) rather than at marginal rates as high as 35%, thus eliminating for the first time the differential in tax treatment. There is evidence of prompt corporate responses to this change in the form of increases in dividend rates and initiation of dividend payments by corporations that had not previously paid dividends. Ken Brown, As Taxes Fall, Dividends Rise–and Executives Reap Big Gains, THE WALL STREET JOURNAL, A1, Aug. 11, 2003.—Ed.

** Tobin's Q, named after Nobel Laureate James Tobin, is the relationship between the market value of firm assets and their estimated replacement cost. For the market value of assets it uses the market value of all the firm's securities, both debt and equity. It uses the estimated replacement cost of assets rather than book value because in many periods inflation has made all assets worth more than book value. Until 1985 firms were required to report current replacement costs, but since that time, as inflation subsided, such reporting became

order of pre-interest earnings, but the investments of firms that have never paid exceed earnings.* Finally, payers are about 10 times as large as non-payers.

The decline after 1978 in the percent of firms paying dividends is due in part to an increasing tilt of publicly traded firms toward the characteristics of firms that have never paid—low earnings, strong investments, and small size. This tilt in the population of firms is driven by an explosion of newly listed firms, and by the changing nature of new firms. The number of publicly traded non-financial non-utility forms grows from 3,638 in 1978 to 5,670 in 1997, before declining to 5,113 in 1999. Newly listed firms always tend to be small, with extraordinary investment opportunities (high asset growth rates and high V_t/A_t). What changes after 1978 is their profitability. Before 1978, new lists are more profitable than seasoned firms. In 1973–77, the earnings of new lists average a hefty 17.79% of book equity, versus 13.68% for all firms. The profitability of new lists falls throughout the next 20 years. The earnings of new lists in 1993–98 average 2.07% of book equity, versus 11.26% for all firms.

The decline in the profitability of new lists is accompanied by a decline in the percent of new lists that pay dividends. * * *

It is perhaps obvious that investors have become more willing to hold the shares of small, relatively unprofitable growth companies. But the resulting tilt of the publicly traded population toward such firms is only half of the story for the declining incidence of dividend payers. Our more striking finding is that firms have become less likely to pay dividends, whatever their characteristics. We characterize the decline in the likelihood that a firm pays dividends, given its characteristics, as a lower propensity to pay. What we mean is that the perceived benefits of dividends (whatever they are) have declined through time.

* * *

Share repurchases jump in the 1980s, and it is interesting to examine the role of repurchases in the declining incidence of dividend payers. We show that because repurchases are largely the province of dividend payers, they leave the decline in the percent of payers largely unexplained. Instead, the primary effect of repurchases is to increase the already high earnings payouts of cash dividend payers.

* * *

2.   Time trends in cash dividends

* * *

voluntary. For this reason many estimates must use book value rather than replacement value in calculating Tobin's Q.—Ed.

   * *Query*: How could dividend-paying firms invest an amount equal to their pre-interest earnings? What are the possible sources of funds for such investments?—Ed.

The proportion of NYSE non-financial non-utility firms paying dividends falls by half during the early years of the Great Depression, from 66.9% in 1930 to 33.6% in 1933 (Fig.2). Thereafter, the percent paying rises. In every year from 1943 to 1962, more than 82% of NYSE firms pay dividends. More than 90% pay dividends in 1951 and 1952. With the addition of AMEX firms in 1963, the proportion of payers drops to 69.3%. The addition of NASDAQ firms in 1973 lowers the proportion of payers to 52.8%, from 59.8% in 1972. It then rises to 66.5% in 1978, the peak for the post–1972 period of NYSE–AMEX–NASDAQ coverage. The proportion paying declines sharply after 1978, to 30.3% for 1987. It continues to decline thereafter, though less rapidly. In 1999, only 20.8% of firms pay dividends.

* * *

3.2. *Investment opportunities*

Like profitability, investment opportunities differ across dividend groups. Firms that have never paid dividends have the best growth opportunities. Table 3 shows that they have much higher asset growth rates for 1963–98 (16.50% per year) than dividend payers (8.78%) or former payers (4.67%). V_t/A_t (the ratio of the aggregate market value to the aggregate book value of assets) is also higher than for firms that have never paid (1.64) than for payers (1.39) or former payers (1.10). The R & D expenditures of firms that have never paid are on average 2.76% of their assets, versus 1.61% for dividend payers and 1.03% for former payers. Thus, though firms that have never paid seem to be less profitable than dividend payers, they have better growth opportunities. In contrast, former payers are victims of a double whammy—low profitability and poor investment opportunities.

* * *

3.3. *Size*

Dividend payers are much larger than non-payers. During 1963–67, the assets of payers average about eight times those of non-payers (Table 3). In the non-payer group, former payers are about three times the size of firms that have never paid.

* * *

Finally, firms that do not pay dividends are big issuers of equity. During 1971–98 (when data on stock purchases and issues are available on Compustat), the aggregate net stock issues of non-payers average 2.80% of the aggregate market value of their common stock, versus a trivial –0.05% for dividend payers.

* * *

5.4. *Propensity to pay: entrails from the portfolio approach.*

[In prior sections the authors have divided the studied stocks into separate portfolios based on profitability, investment opportunities, and size. Within each group they created separate portfolios based on the strength or size of each factor.]

At the 1978 peak, most big stocks pay dividends whatever their characteristics. When dA_t/A_t^* is used to measure growth opportunities, the 1978 proportion of payers exceeds 85.0% in all nine big-stock portfolios, and it is above 92% in seven of the nine (Table 9). But even among big stocks, the propensity to pay declines sharply after 1978. When dA_t/A_t is used to measure growth opportunities, the 1998 proportion of payers never reaches 80.0% in any big-stock portfolio, it is below 65.0% for five of the nine, and the 1998 proportion of payers is 40.6% or less in three big-stock portfolios.

The decline in the propensity to pay dividends is even larger among small stocks. * * *

6.   Share repurchases

Declining propensity to pay suggests that firms have become aware of the tax disadvantage of dividends. Consistent with this view, Table 11 confirms earlier evidence ... that share repurchases surge in the mid–1980s. For 1973–77 and 1978–82, aggregate share repurchases average 3.37% and 5.12% of aggregate earnings. For 1983–98, repurchases are 31.42% of earnings. Bagwell and Shoven (1989) argue that the increase in repurchases indicates that firms have learned to substitute repurchases for dividends in order to generate lower-taxed capital gains for stockholders. But subsequent tests of this hypothesis produce mixed results....

For our purposes, repurchases turn out to be rather unimportant. In particular, we show that because repurchases are primarily the province of dividend payers, they leave most of the decline in the percent of payers unexplained. Instead, the primary effect of repurchases is to increase the already high cash payouts of dividend payers.

We first address a problem. Previous papers treat all share repurchases as non-cash dividends, that is, a repackaging of shareholder wealth that substitutes capital value for cash dividends. There are two cases where repurchases do not have this effect: (i) repurchased stock is often reissued to employee stock ownership plans (ESOPs) and as executive stock options, and (ii) repurchased stock is often reissued to the acquired firm in a merger. An acquiring firm repurchases stock when it wishes to finance a merger with retained earnings or debt but the acquired firm (for tax reasons) prefers stock. Repurchases to complete mergers simply help finance this form of investment. Like other investments, mergers allow firms to transform earnings into capital value rather than dividends. But repurchases of stock to finance a merger are not a source of additional capital value, beyond what is produced by the merger.

A better measure of repurchases that qualify as non-cash dividends is the annual change in treasury stock. Treasury stock captures the cumulative effects of repurchases and reissues, and it is not affected by new issues of stock (seasoned equity offerings). * * *

---

* This is the change in assets divided by firm assets.—Ed.

During 1983–98, the annual change in Treasury stock, dT_t, is less than half of the gross share repurchases, SP_t; specifically, dT_t and SP_t average 14.95% and 31.42% of earnings (Table 11). Cash dividends are 45.24% of earnings, so if gross repurchases are treated as an additional payout of earnings, the total payout for 1983–98 averages 76.66% of earnings. Substituting the more appropriate annual change in treasury stock drops the payout to (a still high) 60.19% of earnings.

* * *

7. Conclusions

* * *

The evidence that, controlling for characteristics, firms become less likely to pay dividends says that the perceived benefits of dividends have declined through time. Some (but surely not all) of the possibilities are: (i) lower transaction costs for selling stocks for consumption purposes, in part due to an increased tendency to hold stocks via open end mutual funds; (ii) larger holdings of stock options by managers who prefer capital gains to dividends; and (iii) better corporate governance technologies (e.g., more prevalent use of stock options) that lower the benefits of dividends in controlling agency problems between stockholders and managers.

B. How Do Dividends Relate to Firm Value?

In Chapter Three we assumed, for purposes of developing a valuation model for stocks, that investors would capitalize either earnings or some variant, such as EBITDA. But investors don't own firm earnings; dividends of such earnings, as we shall see, are paid at the discretion of the directors. Fama and French show that dividend payout ratios have been declining over the past twenty-five years. Does this mean that investors don't value dividends? This would contradict many earlier views. As one writer responded in 1969:

"The answer here is that investors buy the firm's dividends, not its earnings. The intuitive rationale is quite straightforward: dividends constitute the only cash flows produced by the firm for its shareholders and therefore represent the one observable return they receive on their investment. They put up a sum of money to purchase a share of stock—i.e., they forego present consumption—in order to lay claim to a series of subsequent payments that will permit future consumption at a higher level. This trade-off, as perceived by the multitude of individuals who populate the capital markets, is in fact the essence of the community's collective investment decision. Such individuals cannot spend a firm's retained earnings on goods and services; they can spend only the dividends—the *cash* payments—they receive. Retained earnings are not necessarily irrelevant, but they are relevant only insofar as they generate higher *future* dividends. Unless some incremental cash flow eventually occurs, a corporation's retentions have absolutely no value to its stockholders."

Wilbur G. Lewellen, The Cost of Capital 88–89 (J. Fred Weston & Allan Meltzer eds., 1969)

Retained earnings irrelevant to value? Does this suggest that managers simply waste retained earnings rather than spend them to create new earnings and thus higher dividends? This suggestion also appears in the work of perhaps the leading academic investment guru of the twentieth century, Benjamin Graham, who wrote (with co-authors):

"**Historical Primacy of Dividends**. For the vast majority of common stocks the dividend record and prospects have always been the most important factor controlling investment quality and value. The success of the typical concern has been measured by its ability to pay liberal and steadily increasing dividends on its capital. In the majority of cases the price of common stocks has been influenced more markedly by the dividend rate than by the reported earnings. The 'outside,' or noncontrolling, stockholders of any company can reap benefits from their investment in only two ways—through dividends and through an increase in the market value of their shares. Since the market value in most cases has depended primarily upon the dividend rate, the latter could be held responsible for nearly all the gains ultimately realized by investors."

Benjamin Graham, David L. Dodd & Sidney Cottle, SECURITY ANALYSIS: PRINCIPLES AND TECHNIQUE (4th ed. 1962) 480.

Graham, Dodd and Cottle suggested that multipliers should be applied to dividends and earnings of companies in the following way:

- For growth shares, reliance should be placed solely on expected earnings;

- For average companies, they suggest somewhat less weight on earnings, and greater reliance on dividends.

- For below average companies, they suggest that the earnings multiplier should be applied to the expected dividend plus one-third of expected earnings.*

At the time these authors were writing a revolution was brewing, which they acknowledged in a footnote (although it is not clear they recognized the full importance of the change).

Franco Modigliani and Merton Miller (now both Nobel laureates) revolutionized thinking about dividends as much as they did about capital structure. Miller & Modigliani, "Dividend Policy, Growth and the Valuation of Shares," 34 Journal of Business 411 (1961). They argued that dividends

---

* Graham, Dodd & Cottle, at p. 518, give examples to illustrate this. Using a multiplier of 12 as the base multiplier, they posit some "average" companies, A and D for our purposes, each with earnings of $6 per share. They value each company at 12 times its dividend plus 12 times one-third of its earnings. Company A pays a $4 dividend while Company D pays $6. They would value these companies as follows:

Company A: $V = 12 \times 4 + 12 \times 2 = 72$

Company D: $V = 12 \times 6 + 12 \times 2 = 96$

were irrelevant to the value of the firm, and offered mathematical proofs of their assertion. They used simplifying assumptions in their model:

- All traders have perfect and costless access to information about the company and its stock price.

- There are no transaction costs, such as brokerage fees or transaction taxes.

- There are no tax differentials between distributed and undistributed profits and between dividends and capital gains. (It's easiest to think of this as a world of zero taxes, but it could also occur with equal tax rates on dividends and capital gains. For the first time in the author's memory this situation exists for the years 2003 and thereafter. At this writing the tax rate on dividends is scheduled to return to ordinary individual income tax rates after five years.)*

- Investors are rational wealth seekers—indifferent about how they hold their wealth—whether in cash or shares, assuming compensation for risk.

Modigliani and Miller broaden their valuation model by showing that a share should be valued on the basis of its entire stream of future benefits to the shareholders, which includes both the discounted present value of dividends and the discounted present value of the proceeds from selling the investment.

Their essential insights are two:

- Firm values depend on investment policies, not dividend policies. That is, investment policies that obtain returns in excess of the firm's cost of capital will create more value for investors, whether in the form of higher current dividends or higher terminal values for the shareholder's investment when sold. If the firm's investments simply earn the firm's cost of capital, investors will be indifferent between allowing the firm to grow its earnings annually by reinvesting retained earnings or investing the dividends the shareholders received to obtain the same return. In the latter case, the firm can only grow by selling new capital, and new investors will demand the same return on their capital, so the value of their claims will exactly equal the capitalized value of the new earnings from expansion.

- Shareholders can "home-make" dividends by selling shares.

Let's examine how the M&M irrelevance hypothesis works. Assume that a firm decides it wants to pay a dividend of one-third of its total value

---

* Where corporations own shares and receive dividends from another corporation, dividends have long been tax favored with a dividends received deduction. Under IRC § 243, the general rule is that 70% of dividends received are deductible. For a corporation that owns 20% or more of a dividending corporation's shares, the deduction is 80%. For a corporation that owns more than 80% of a dividending company's shares, the deduction is 100%. Dividends are tax-free for non-profit corporations such as universities and charities, and for pension funds and mutual funds that pass through their earnings to investors. Of course capital gains are also tax free for these entities.

to its shareholders, but that it also has a project that pays a return equal to the firm's cost of capital, that it would like to finance. Further assume that the cost of the new project is precisely equal to the proposed dividend. Now, if the firm declares the dividend, the moment the shares trade "ex dividend" (on the date when a record transfer of the shares on the firm's books can only be made after the record date for the determination of shareholders entitled to receive the dividend), the market value of the shares will drop by precisely one-third. At this point, to finance the project the firm has to sell new shares equal to the amount of the dividend. Because the firm is now worth one-third less than before, it must raise an amount equal to one-half of its remaining value. In short, the new investors must replace the funds paid out in the dividend. Assuming the new project will earn the cost of the firm's capital, the firm must sell new shares equal to one-half of the currently outstanding shares. This leaves the new investors with one-third of the total shares outstanding after the financing is completed. Each share is now worth the value of shares ex dividend, which is one-third less than before the dividend. In short, the original shareholders have swapped cash for share value. This is illustrated by Figure 9–1:

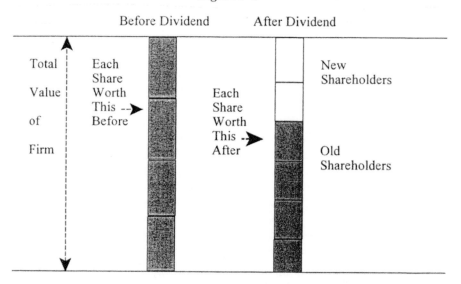

Figure 9-1

We can illustrate this numerically as well: Consider that our firm starts with 100 shares originally valued @ $10 each, for a total market value of $1,000. Assume that the firm earns $100 annually, which is capitalized at a 10% rate. Now our firm declares a $333 dividend. After the dividend is paid, the firm has one third fewer assets, and we will assume that the firm's earning power has been reduced pro rata, so it now earns $66.67. The situation of the shareholders can be described as follows:

Total firm value   = $667
Shareholders cash   = $333
Shareholder wealth: = $1,000

Note that each share is now worth $6.67. If the firm has a new project that will generate $33.33 in earnings it must calculate how many shares it must sell at $6.67 each in order to raise $333:

$$\frac{\$333}{\$6.67} \quad = \quad 50 \text{ new shares}$$

Thus the new shareholders must hold one third of total outstanding shares after completion of the financing. This leaves the old shareholders with their shares worth $667 and $333 in cash. Presumably they can reinvest that cash in another firm with a similar level of risk and a similar cost of capital. So the old shareholders are exactly where they were before. And paying the dividend has no effect on firm value, if new funds are raised to replace the dividended funds.

Now let's see what happens if the firm retains the $333 cash and reinvests the retained earnings in a new project. A shareholder who prefers to receive his pro rata share of the cash as a dividend can achieve the same result by selling off some of his shares. Assume a shareholder owns 10 shares, trading at $10 and can sell fractional shares in the market.

Sale of 3⅓ shares at $10 per share produces $33.33
Remaining value of 6⅔ shares   = $66.67
Total $100.00

Another way to think of this is that shareholders can raise cash from outside investors by selling them shares in the marketplace, or they can raise cash by receiving a dividend and having the firm sell new shares to outside investors. Figure 9–2 illustrates these choices:

Figure 9-2

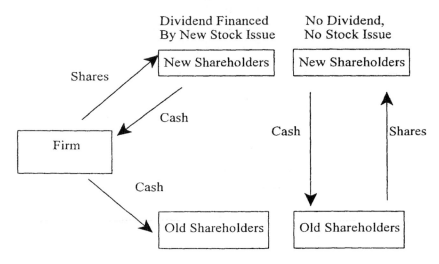

We close this section with the observation that under the conditions Miller and Modigliani have posited, investors should be indifferent about whether corporations pay dividends or not. This is sometimes referred to as the Indifference Proposition. It is important to observe that there is no link between dividend policy and investment policy: a firm may raise capital in capital markets as easily as it may retain earnings for reinvestment.

While Miller and Modigliani have established these relationships with formal proofs, we (and they) know they worked with simplifying assumptions. And we know that dividends exist in the real world. We also know that the proportion of companies paying dividends has been declining for the past quarter century. Do M&M help us understand why companies pay dividends, and why some companies decide not to pay them? Those questions are the focus of the following section. They help us see the Miller and Modigliani model as a device for understanding the causes and consequences of dividends in the real world, as we unpack their simplifying assumptions below.

Sidebar: Are Dividends Irrelevant?

We have shown that dividend policy is irrelevant to firm value. Are dividends also irrelevant? No. Clearly, investors prefer higher dividends to lower dividends, all other things being equal. This requires that future dividends not be affected by current dividends. Thus, if today's dividend is higher and future expected dividends don't change, the stock's price will rise. On the other hand, if dividends are withheld, will the stock price fall? Not necessarily. This depends on expected future dividends. If dividends will increase sufficiently so that the present value of the increase equals or exceeds the value of the missed dividend, the stock price will not fall; it might even rise. But this depends upon the investment policy of the firm, not its dividend policy, according to M&M.

C.   Explaining Dividend Practices

The Miller–Modigliani model provides a way to think about explaining why corporations continue to pay dividends in a more formal manner. We now begin the process of relaxing some of the assumptions in their model.

i.   CLIENTELE EFFECTS AND EXPECTATIONS

It should be obvious that investors have very different preferences about dividends. We start with the observation that some pay taxes and others do not. Individuals are generally tax payers. While corporations are also tax payers, corporations receive special treatment for receipt of corporate dividends. The general rule is that 70% of dividends received are deductible for a corporation. For a corporation that owns 20% or more of a dividending corporation's shares, the deduction is 80%. For a corporation that owns more than 80% of a dividending company's shares, the deduction is 100%. Dividends are tax-free for non-profit corporations such as universities and charities, and for pension funds and mutual funds that pass through their earnings to investors. Of course capital gains are also tax free for these entities. As more of our national savings have flowed from individuals to financial institutions such as pension funds, mutual funds and insurance companies, the impact of taxes on dividends has decreased. This doesn't provide an explanation for the decline of dividends observed by Fama and French.

But we return to individuals, who are still an important part of the stock market. Based on Franco Modligiani's famous life cycle theory of investing, we expect younger investors to be saving for long-term goals, such as providing higher education for children and providing for their own retirement.* Older investors will, when they retire, prefer investments that yield current income to support them in retirement. This may offer a partial explanation of why public utilities, a relatively safe form of investment in stocks, tend to pay relatively large dividends, since these two features are attractive to retirees. Indeed, some utilities have paid out more than their net earnings, dipping into cash flows generated from depreciation expense, so they often return capital to their shareholders on a regular basis. But wait—Miller and Modigliani's model has something to say about this, at least about dividends. (We already know from the discussion of CAPM in Chapter Three that an investor can achieve the desired level of safety with a diversified portfolio of virtually any beta and some risk-free Treasury bonds.)

Let's return to our model of the dividend-paying corporation Recall our shareholder who wanted cash when the company chose not to declare a dividend, who "home-made" his own dividend? Now assume a shareholder who prefers to remain fully invested in the company, when the company declares a dividend of $33.33, so the shareholder's investment is reduced to $66.67, and she now holds $33.33 cash. Each share is now worth $6.67. She can use her cash to buy new shares. How many? $33.33/$6.67 = 5 new shares, so she now owns 15 shares with a market value of $100. There are two problems with this strategy, as we shall discuss in the following subsections—the costs of selling and the costs of taxes.

ii.   TRANSACTION COSTS OF SELLING SHARES

In the M&M model it would be possible for the firm to sell new shares to fund new investments if the firm decided to pay dividends. While this is

---

* For a literature review, see Franco Modigliani, Life Cycle, Individual Thrift, and the Wealth of Nations, 76 AMERICAN ECONOMIC REVIEW 297 (1986). This description omits part of Modigliani's description. Younger adults, such as college and law students, often borrow funds, not only to pay tuition but also to provide living expenses, as they invest in their human capital. Once they complete this phase and move into the employment market, they may borrow to buy capital assets—homes, autos and appliances. Modigliani's theory is that individuals borrow and save in an effort to level out their standard of living throughout their lives, which maximizes total lifetime utility.

true, it is obvious that selling stock is not cost-free, entailing underwriting commissions and professional fees, and that most firms will find it cheaper to retain earnings rather than sell shares for such purposes. There is a second cost: the sale of new shares is typically greeted with a decline in the market price of stock, as investors infer that managers believe the stock must be overpriced, and wish to take advantage of investor ignorance. Under these circumstances, managers seeking outside financing may prefer to issue new debt, which, while it incurs transaction costs, is unlikely to cause the stock price to fall because of a negative signal that managers believe stock prices have reached a peak.

Similarly, shareholders incur transaction costs if they wish to reinvest dividends in the company. There are brokerage fees to start with. Some companies solve this with dividend reinvestment programs that allow investors to avoid brokerage fees. But there may be psychological costs for individual shareholders as well. Receipt of cash I don't need for consumption faces me with a decision—should I reinvest in the same firm, or would I do better elsewhere? If the firm pays no dividend, I'm not prompted to think about investment alternatives (through selling shares in this firm and buying shares in another) as directly.

iii.   TAXES

You've probably spotted another obvious real-world error in the previous example of using a dividend payment to buy more shares. Our shareholder's cash dividend is subject to a personal income tax, so after paying taxes she has less than $33.33 to reinvest in company stock. If her marginal tax rate is 35%, she will pay $11.67 in taxes, leaving her with only $21.66 to reinvest in shares. This will only buy her 3.25 shares at $6.67 each. Thus she will wind up with 13.25 shares with a market value of $88.33. Notice she bears this tax loss regardless of whether she simply keeps the cash dividend or reinvests it. (This ignores the 15% tax rate that expires in 2010, and the increase in the top marginal rate to 39.6%).

But now assume that the company pays no dividends, and reinvests the $333 in new productive resources earning its cost of capital, so the firm retains its value. If our shareholder who wished to receive cash engages in a sale of 3.33 shares to raise cash, what is the tax impact here? This, of course, depends on the size of the shareholder's gain from the sale. If the shareholder paid $33.33 for his shares, then there is no gain and no tax on the transaction. The worst case would be that the shareholder paid nothing for the shares, and thus has a zero basis and gains of $33.33. If the shares have been held for one year or more, they are taxed at the long-term capital gains rate, which, until 2003 was 20%. Now our shareholder's tax burden is only $6.67, and that is the worst case scenario! Thus for many investors home-made dividends have looked a lot more attractive than cash dividends. Does this start to explain the long-term trend toward fewer dividends that Fama and French have observed since 1978?

There was an important change in 2003. It will provide economists with a natural experiment about the importance of taxes in determining dividend policy. Tax legislation in 2003 reduced the long-term capital gains rate to 15% beginning in 2003, and it also reduced the tax rate on dividends to 15%! (These rates expire in 2010.) This is the first time in this author's memory that dividend and capital gains rates have been identical, so investors may be less concerned about the tax consequences of cash dividends. Of course, the shareholder who sells shares will generally have a positive tax basis for the shares, so the taxable gain will be less than the proceeds of the sale. If the proceeds of sale are the same as our hypothetical dividend, the home-made dividend is still less costly in terms of taxes. Thus corporate reinvestment that allows shares to appreciate in value will remain more attractive than dividends for tax purposes.

There is one more piece to this puzzle. Notice that when shares are sold, only that part of the proceeds which exceeds the shareholder's tax basis (the amount she paid for the shares) is subject to the capital gains tax, while the entire dividend is subject to tax. Or is it? In the special case of some public utilities with huge current investments in plant and accelerated depreciation deductions, taxable income may be much lower than free cash flow available for dividends. In these cases a substantial part of the cash dividend may be a "return of capital" to the shareholder, which is non-taxable. In these cases there may be a real equivalence between cash dividends and home-made dividends for tax purposes.

The historic relationship has been that capital gains have been taxed at significantly lower rates than cash dividends, at least for high-bracket taxpayers. Over the past 50 years the top marginal federal income tax rate for individuals began at 90%, was reduced to 70% , and has fallen more or less steadily for the past 25 years to a current rate of 35% for 2010. (Don't forget that state income taxes are an added burden for taxpayers.) This has pushed high-bracket individual investors in the direction of non-dividend paying stocks with attractive investment opportunities that promised appreciation of stock prices and the opportunity for capital gains. In contrast, many retirees on limited incomes will seek dividend-paying stocks such as public utility stocks, if they hold any stocks at all in their retirement portfolios.

The tax situation means that a corporation should never pay cash dividends if it has positive net present value projects that earn more than the cost of capital. Indeed, it should use retained earnings to invest in projects that simply return the cost of capital. What should the firm do if it lacks such projects? What is the tax-favored method of returning unneeded cash to shareholders, dividends or share repurchases?

Negative net present value projects. We will explore the reasons why firms might forego dividends to invest in negative net present value projects in a subsequent section about agency costs, but the fact is that some firms have invested in such projects. They may do so because of faulty projections about future returns, or to build empires to manage, etc.

Acquisitions. Firms with surplus free cash flow sometimes decide to expand by acquiring other firms. On its face this may be a rational strategy. Managers sometimes explain acquisitions as involving complementary assets that will create synergies, either lowering costs or increasing revenues. But acquisitions often involve considerable uncertainty about how firms will meld, and considerable transaction costs. There is a literature that suggests firms often overpay for acquisitions. See, e.g., Bernard Black, Bidder Overpayment in Takeovers, 41 STANFORD LAW REVIEW 597 (1989), and Richard Roll, The Hubris Hypothesis of Corporate Takeovers, 59 JOURNAL OF BUSINESS 197 (1986). For a general survey of returns to bidders and targets, see Michael C. Jensen and Richard S. Ruback, The Market for Corporate Control: The Scientific Evidence, 11 J. FIN. ECON. 5 (1983). These acquisitions may represent agency costs in the same way as investing in the firm's own negative net present value projects rather than paying dividends.

Acquiring Financial Assets. Assume for the moment that the firm can invest $1,000 in Treasury bonds yielding 5%, or it can pay the $1,000 cash to its shareholders as a dividend.* Assume that shareholders will also invest in Treasuries at 5% if the dividend is paid. If the corporate tax rate is lower than the personal tax rate, firms have incentives to retain earnings and reinvest at the corporate level; while if the personal tax rate is lower than the corporate rate, shareholders will be better off receiving dividends now and reinvesting on their own, assuming comparable rates of return on similarly risky projects. The following illustrates this principle, with purely hypothetical rates, for a decision on whether to pay a dividend now or reinvest for five years before paying a dividend that includes the com-pounded interest. Assume in both cases that interest is not realized (and thus not taxed) until the end of the fifth year. In cases (1) and (2) the corporate tax rate is higher than the individual rate (40% vs. 35%). Thus the net returns to the shareholder are (1) $767 and (2) $757, respectively. Here it makes sense to pay dividends promptly (choice #1) and let the individual invest the funds. In cases (3) and (4) the rates are reversed, and the opposite is true, so corporate reinvestment is preferred. Thus the net returns from the immediate dividend are $699 and $707 from the deferred dividend after corporate reinvestment. So it makes sense for the corpora-tion to reinvest the funds (choice #4). Does the fact that top individual marginal tax rates have long exceeded top corporate rates help explain why dividends have been declining?

Available Cash	$(1.05)^5$	Corp. Tax	Dividend to Shareholder	Ind'l Tax	To Share-holder*	$(1.05)^5$	Tax on Gain**	Net Gain
Corporate rate higher than individual rate:								
(1) $1,000	n/a	n/a	$1,000	35%	$650	$830	$63	$767
(2) $1,000	$1,276	40%***	$1,165	35%	$757	n/a	n/a	$757
Individual rate higher than corporate rate:								
(3) $1,000	n/a	n/a	$1,000	40%	$600	$765	$66	$699
(4) $1,000	$1,276	35%***	$1,179	40%	$707	n/a	n/a	$707

* The shareholder's tax is calculated on the entire dividend when received.

** The tax on gain is the tax on the appreciation over the 5 years the shareholder holds the dividend, where it is received at the start of the first year.

*** The corporate tax is applied to the appreciation over the original $1,000.

---

* Since the return on Treasury bonds will always be less than a firm's cost of capital, this is never a desirable long-term strategy. Generally corporate investments in Treasuries are only justifiable as a short-term strategy to hold funds the firm knows it will need in the near future, where the returns foregone by holding Treasuries are less than the transaction costs of raising new capital following a dividend. Recall Morgan Stanley & Co. Inc. v. Archer Daniels Midland Co. in Chapter Six, Part 3.G, where ADM was borrowing at 16% and investing in lower-yield government bonds?

iv.   IMPERFECT CAPITAL MARKETS AND THE SIGNALING VALUE
OF DIVIDENDS

M&M assumed perfect capital markets in which all traders have equal
and costless access to all relevant information about shares. But you will
recall from Chapter Three that traders act *as if* markets were not perfect;
they continue to engage in research in order to locate valuable information
not yet observed by other traders, and thus not yet reflected in stock prices.
Indeed, that leads to the Efficient Capital Markets Paradox: that it is the
disbelief of traders in market efficiency that keeps markets efficient. Of
course corporate frauds such as those at Enron and Worldcom, to name
only two, demonstrate that capital markets cannot be perfectly (strong
form) efficient—efficiency is only a relative concept. Similarly, traders
recognize that corporate managers frequently have superior information
about firm prospects. For example, when companies sell stock, traders infer
that managers believe stock prices have peaked, and that the next news
may be less optimistic than the current news, and depress prices. As a
result new issues generally depress current stock prices for the issuer.
Another way of saying this is that traders infer that managers believe their
company's stock is currently overvalued. This is a negative "signal" that
traders will operate on. So what kind of signal does announcing that
corporate dividends will increase send? Often it is read as a signal that
management expects earnings or cash flows to increase, so it can "afford"
to pay a higher dividend while maintaining its target payout rate. Recall
Lintner's observations that managers prefer consistent dividends, and that
they are likely to increase dividends only gradually when earnings are
rising, and when they believe they are sustainable. So perhaps a dividend
increase predicts management's expectations about future earnings increases. On the other hand, recall that management should invest in all new
positive net present value projects. Under this view, a dividend increase
could be read as an announcement that the company's markets have
matured, and fewer exceptional investment opportunities are expected in
the future. Which story is more consistent with the decline in dividends
observed by Fama and French? Typically a dividend decrease announcement appears to be read as a signal that management expects earnings to
decline, and that the company will not be able to "afford" to continue the
dividend at its current level. Typically stock prices decline on the announcement of a dividend reduction. One study reports a 6% price decline
on the announcement of a dividend decrease. David J. Denis, Diane K.
Denis & Autlya Sarin, The Information Content of Dividend Changes: Cash
Flow Signaling, Overinvestment, and Dividend Clienteles, 29 Journal of
Financial and Quantitative Analysis 567 (1994).

D.   ALTERNATIVE EXPLANATIONS OF DIVIDENDS.

Two Agency–Cost Explanations of Dividends

74 American Economic Review 650 (1984).
By Frank H. Easterbrook.

The economic literature about dividends usually assumes that managers are perfect agents of investors, and it seeks to determine why these agents pay dividends. Other literature about the firm assumes that managers are imperfect agents and inquires how managers' interests may be aligned with shareholders' interests. These two lines of inquiry rarely meet. Yet logically any dividend policy (or any other corporate policy) should be designed to minimize the sum of capital, agency, and taxation costs. The purpose of this paper is to ask whether dividends are a method of aligning managers' interests with those of investors. It offers agency-cost explanations of dividends.

I.   The Dividend Problem

Businesses find dividends obvious. Boards declare them regularly and raise them from time to time or face disquiet from investors, or so they think. Many managers are sure that higher dividends mean higher prices for their shares. There is a substantial body of law that controls when boards may (sometimes must) declare dividends, in what amount, and using what procedures. Firms enter into complicated contracts with creditors and preferred stockholders that govern the permissible rates of payouts. Dividends are paid (and regulated) at considerable cost to the firms involved.

Economists find dividends mysterious. The celebrated articles by Merton Miller and Franco Modigliani declared them irrelevant because investors could home brew their own dividends by selling from or borrowing against their portfolios. Meanwhile the firms that issued the dividends would also incur costs to float new securities to maintain their optimal investment policies.[4] Dividends are, moreover, taxable to many investors, while firms can reduce taxes by holding and reinvesting their profits. Although dividends might make sense in connection with a change in investment policy—when, for example, the firms are disinvesting because they are liquidating or, for other reasons, shareholders can make better use of the money than managers—they are all cost and no benefit in the remaining cases of invariant investment policies.[5]

---

4. See Miller and Modigliani, Dividend Policy, Growth and the Valuation of Shares, 34 Journal of Business 411 (1961); also Modigliani and Miller, The Cost of Capital, Corporation Finance and the Theory of Investment, 48 American Economic Review 261 (1958); Joseph Stiglitz, On the Irrelevance of Corporate Financial Policy, 64 American Economic Review 851 (1974).

5. See Modigliani, Debt, Dividend Policy, Taxes, Inflation and Market Valuation, 37 Journal of Finance 255 (1982), for an argument to this effect that modifies the M–M irrelevance model by considering taxes and uncertainty. Compare Miller and Myron Scholes,

Dividends are hard enough to explain when they occur in isolation; a combination of dividends and simultaneous raising of new capital is downright inexplicable. Yet the simultaneous or near-simultaneous payment of dividends and raising of new capital are common in business. Sometimes firms issue new stock at or around the time they pay dividends. More frequently they issue new debt, often in the form of bank loans that are almost invisible to finance economists. Why does this occur?

The problem with the irrelevance proposition is that dividends are costly yet ubiquitous. Something causes them. Even if most investors are irrational most of the time, dividends would go away if their costs exceeded their benefits to investors. Firms that reduced payouts would prosper relative to others; investors who figured out the truth also would prosper relative to others; and before long—certainly before now in light of the large costs of floating new capital issues and the large differences between income and capital gains tax rates—dividends would be infrequent occurrences characterizing failing or disinvesting firms.

The existence of dividends despite their costs has inspired a search for explanations. Some of the efforts have been obvious failures. Take the argument that investments are risky and that dividends hedge against the possibility that the firms will go bankrupt before distributing the saved-up assets to the shareholders. The argument goes: investors value a steady stream of dividends over the uncertain prospect of a large return when the firms liquidate or are sold as going concerns and the investors are cashed out, and firms pay dividends to cater to that preference. The problem here is that dividends are matched by reinvestments: so long as dividends do not affect firms' investment policies, they do not represent any withdrawal of capital from risky ventures. New investors bear the risk that the dividend-receiving investors avoid, and these new investors must be compensated. The new investors may well turn out to be the old ones; shareholders do not usually use the dividends for consumption or to purchase Treasury bills. If they reinvest the proceeds in the same or a different firm, they commit their cash (less taxes paid) to the same risks as if there had been no dividends. In sum, there is no bird-in-the-hand effect unless the firm also changes its investment policy.

Other arguments are only slightly more plausible. Consider the argument that dividends "signal" the well-being of the firm to investors and so promote confidence (and, one supposes, higher stock prices and a flow of investment capital).[8] The problem here is that it is unclear just what

---

Dividends and Taxes: Some Empirical Evidence, 90 Journal of Political Economy 1108 (1982), applying their earlier analysis Miller and Scholes, Dividends and Taxes, 6 Journal of Financial Economics 333 (1978) to extend the irrelevance hypothesis to a world with taxes. Miller and Scholes argue that taxes need not, and do not appear to, determine dividend policy; all the same, their analysis does not show why there are dividends in a world of costly flotation.

8. See, for example, Bhattacharya, Imperfect Information, Dividend Policy and "The Bird in the Hand Fallacy," 10 Bell Journal of Economics 259 (1979); Nils Hakansson, To Pay or Not to Pay Dividend, 37 Journal of Finance 415 (1982); Steven Ross, The Determination of Financial Structure: The Incentive Signalling [sic] Approach, 8 Bell Journal of Economics 23 (1977). Compare Miller and Rock: in this model, dividends may permit inference of sources

dividends signal, how they do so, or why dividends are better signals than apparently cheaper methods. Firms could and do issue disclosures of their prospects and profits. True, investors may be disinclined to believe the self-serving statements of managers about the firms' endeavors, but managers' usual response to this is to hire outsiders who examine the firms' books and other materials and opine on whether the managers are telling the truth. These outsiders work for many firms and acquire reputational capital so large that they become unbribable. No firm could offer them enough for a false (or slipshod) verification to make up for their losses on business with other firms. Auditors serve this function yearly or more often; even judges may serve this function in suits charging the managers with making false statements or omitting material facts.

Dividends would be desirable only if they added to the efficacy of these methods of disclosure. The beauty of a "signal" is that it is self-verifying. People believe the signal because sending the message is rational for the signaler only if the message is or is believed to be accurate. Thus one could say that a Ph.D. from the University of Chicago is a good signal of intelligence and diligence (two notoriously hard-to-verify qualities) because persons of inferior intellect could not obtain one. But dividends do not directly reveal the prospects of the firms, so the message they convey may be ambiguous. Unless the cost of issuing dividends is uniformly lower for prosperous firms, no signal is possible.

Prosperous firms may withhold dividends because internal financing is cheaper than issuing dividends and floating new securities. Worse, dividends do not distinguish well-managed, prospering firms from others. They are not irrational for poorly managed or failing firms. Quite the contrary, such firms should disinvest or liquidate, and their managers may choose dividends as a method of accomplishing this. Someone who observes an increase in the dividend has no very good way to tell whether this signals good times or bad. (This is consistent with both the finding that dividends are poor predictors of future net earnings and the finding that stock prices are poor predictors of future dividends.).[11] Doubtless only a prospering firm can continue to pay dividends year in and year out, but a firm with a long record of prosperity also would not need the verification available from the dividend signal. The persistent reports of auditors and securities dealers, its securities' prices, and the apparent marketing success of the firm would do as well in verifying the managers' tales.

The explanations based on clientele effects also are unsatisfactory. It is easy enough to see that if some investors are in different tax positions from others (for example, some hold tax-sheltered funds while others are taxed

---

and uses of funds; this achieves many of the effects of a signaling model but by direct revelation or inference.

11.   Stephen Penman, The Predictive Content of Earnings Forecasts and Dividends, 38 Journal of Finance 1181 (1983) finds that knowledge of dividends adds little or nothing to earnings forecasts as predictors of future earnings. See also, for example, Robert Shiller, Do Stock Prices Move Too Much to be Justified by Subsequent Changes in Dividends?, 71 American Economic Review 421 (1981).

at ordinary rates), the different groups will have different preferences for dividends. The taxed group would prefer to take profits as capital gains; the untaxed group would be indifferent. Some equilibrium would develop in which firms adopted different payout policies to cater to the different clienteles.[12] It is much harder, though, to use clientele effects to demonstrate why the current dividend structure exists. Why do most firms pay significant dividends, given the costs of paying them (and raising new capital), and given that all investors either prefer capital gains or are indifferent between dividends and capital gains?

II. Two Explanations

The dividend puzzle has been stated as: "what is the effect of a change in cash dividends paid, *given the firm's capital budgeting and borrowing decisions?*"[14] This statement of the problem makes it insoluble, because the irrelevance hypothesis and the growing body of evidence say that dividends do not matter so long as the firm's financing and investment policy is unaffected. The existence of dividends in the face of this, and despite the costs of paying them out and raising new money, suggest that it is appropriate to ask a different question: "what is the effect of a consistent policy of paying dividends?" This question leads to what could be called a naive explanation of dividends. Dividends exist because they influence the firms' financing policies, because they dissipate cash and induce firms to float new securities. Let us suppose that managers are not perfect agents of the other participants in the corporate venture, but that they pursue their own interests when they can. Because the managers are not the residual claimants to the firm's income stream, there may be a substantial divergence between their interests and those of the other participants. Managers, investors, and other participants will find it advantageous to set up devices, including monitoring, bonding, and ex post readjustments that give managers the incentive to act as better agents. The costs of monitoring, bonding, and the residual losses from slippage are agency costs borne by investors.[15]

One form of agency cost is the cost of monitoring of managers. This is costly for shareholders, and the problem of collective action ensures that shareholders undertake too little of it. Although a monitor-shareholder would incur the full costs of monitoring, he would reap gains only in proportion to his holdings. Because shares are widely held, no one share-

---

12. See Fischer Black and Scholes, The Effects of Dividend Yield and Dividend Policy on Common Stock Prices and Returns, 1 Journal of Financial Economics 1 (1974) and Alan Auerbach, Stockholder Tax Rates and Firm Attributes, Working Paper No. 817, National Bureau of Economic Research (1982). But see Miller and Scholes, *supra* note 5 (1982).

14. Richard Brealey and Stewart Myers, Principles of Corporate Finance (1981, p. 324, italics in original).

15. Michael Jensen and William Meckling, Theory of the Firm: Managerial Behavior, Agency Costs, and Capital Structure, 3 Journal of Financial Economics 305 (1976); Eugene Fama, Agency Problems and the Theory of the Firm, 88 Journal of Political Economy 288 (1980); Bengt Holmstrom, Moral Hazard in Teams, 13 Bell Journal of Economics 324 (1982); *JLE* Symposium on the Theory of the Firm, 26 Journal of Financial Economics 237 (1983).

holder can capture even a little of the gain. Shareholders would be wealthier if there were some person, comparable to the bondholders' indenture trustee, who monitored managers on shareholders' behalf.

A second source of agency costs is risk aversion on the part of managers. The investors, with diversified portfolios of stocks, will be concerned only about any nondiversifiable risk with respect to any one firm's ventures. Managers, though, have a substantial part of their personal wealth tied up in their firms. If the firms do poorly or, worse, go bankrupt, the managers will lose their jobs and any wealth tied up in their firms' stock. Managers therefore will be concerned about total risk, and their personal risk aversion will magnify this concern.

The risk-averse managers may choose projects that are safe but have a lower expected return than riskier ventures. Shareholders have the opposite preference. Riskier ventures enrich shareholders at the expense of creditors (because shareholders do not pay any of the gains to bondholders, yet bond-holders bear part of the risk of failure), and shareholders would want managers to behave as risk preferrers. Of course, creditors recognize this and try to control it in advance through bond indentures and other instruments; they also adjust the rate of interest they demand. Debtholders assume that given the limits set by their contracts, shareholders prefer to take the maximum advantage. But the question is not whether the riskiness of projects can be controlled through indentures or other legal devices. It is, rather, whether costs of control (including the costs of control and residual agency costs) can be reduced by a method that includes dividends.

Managers can change the risk of the firm not only by altering its mix of projects, but also by altering its debt-equity ratio. The lower the ratio of debt to equity, the lower the chance of bankruptcy of the firm. Once again, debtholders consider this in deciding what rate of interest to demand. Once again, given the existence of debt, managers can control the amount of risk. One way they can do this is by picking a dividend policy. If managers first issue debt and then finance new projects out of retained earnings, the debt-equity ratio will fall. The lower it falls, the lower the managers' risk and the greater the boon bestowed on the debtholders, who receive their contracted-for interest but escape the contracted-for risk. Financing projects out of retained earnings—if unanticipated by bondholders—transfers wealth from shareholders to debtholders. Just as bondholders want to limit dividends, to prevent advantage-taking by shareholders once a rate of interest has been set, so shareholders want to increase dividends to the extent possible in order to avoid being taken advantage of by bondholders.

Shareholders therefore would like to induce managers to take more risks, so that they do not give away wealth to bondholders. The shareholders would prefer that managers go to the limit authorized by contract in imposing risks on the firm's creditors. Yet it is hard to give managers the right incentives to do this. There is little one can do to get rid of their risk aversion. They will remain undiversified, because of the nature of their human capital, no matter what; indeed, the lack of diversification in managers' holdings has other benefits. Unless there is some form of ex post settling up with managers, which will be difficult (costly) to achieve, shareholders' payoffs will be lower, with consequences for the level of investment.

Both the monitoring problem and the risk-aversion problem are less serious if the firm is constantly in the market for new capital. When it issues new securities, the firm's affairs will be reviewed by an investment banker or some similar intermediary acting as a monitor for the collective interest of shareholders, and by the purchasers of the new instruments. The same occurs when the firm issues new debt, including bonds, commercial paper, and syndicated bank loans. Managers who need to raise money consistently are more likely to act in investors' interests than managers who are immune from this kind of scrutiny. Moreover, when it issues new securities, the firm can adjust the debt-equity ratio (and obtain a new rate of interest for its debt) so that neither shareholders nor bondholders are taking advantage of the other group. (It can, of course, make this adjustment in other ways, including making more frequent trips to financial markets for smaller sums of new cash, but because flotation costs decrease with the size of the offering, such alternatives may be more costly than combining infrequent flotation with dividends.)

The principal value of keeping firms constantly in the market for capital is that the contributors of capital are very good monitors of managers. The firm's existing investors can influence the managers' actions only by voting (which suffers from a collective choice problem) and by selling. Purchasers of stock will pay no more than the value of future profits under current management unless they are prepared to wage a takeover contest of some sort, which can be very costly. Managers of firms with fixed capital structures may well have substantial discretion to be slothful, consume perquisites, or otherwise behave in their own interests rather than the investors' interests.

New investors do not suffer under the collective choice disabilities of existing investors. They can examine managers' behavior before investing, and they will not buy new stock unless they are offered compensation (in the form of reduced prices) for any remediable agency costs of management. Managers who are in the capital market thus have incentives to reduce those agency costs in order to collect the highest possible price for their new instruments. New investors are better than old ones at chiseling down agency costs.

Of course, new investors need information, and that may be hard to come by. Neither auditors nor the managers themselves are perfectly reliable unless there is a foolproof legal remedy for fraud. Other forms of information gathering, such as shareholders' inquiries and stock brokers' studies, suffer from the problem that none of the persons making inquiry can capture very much of the gain of this endeavor, and thus there will be too little information gathered. There would be savings if some information gatherers had larger proportionate stakes, and if the verification of information could be accomplished at lower cost. Underwriters of stock and large lenders may supply the lower-cost verification. These firms put their own money on the line, and any information inferred from this risk-taking behavior by third parties may be very valuable to other investors. This form of verification by acceptance of risk is one of the savings that arise when dividends keep firms in the capital market.

The role of dividends in starting up the monitoring provided by the capital market is easy to see. An example of the role of dividends in making risk adjustments may help. Suppose a firm has an initial capitalization of 100, of which 50 is debt and 50 equity. It invests the 100 in a project. The firm prospers, and earnings raise its holdings to 200. The creditors now have substantially more security than they started with, and correspondingly the residual claimants are paying the creditors a rate of interest unwarranted by current circumstances. They can correct this situation by paying a dividend of 50 while issuing new debt worth 50. The firm's capital continues to be 200, but the debt-equity ratio has been restored, and the interest rate on the original debt is again appropriate to the creditors' risk.[23]

Expected, continuing dividends compel firms to raise new money in order to carry out their activities. They therefore precipitate the monitoring and debt-equity adjustments that benefit stockholders. Moreover, even when dividends are not accompanied by the raising of new capital, they at least increase the debt-equity ratio so that shareholders are not giving (as much) wealth away to bondholders. In other words, dividends set in motion mechanisms that reduce the agency costs of management and that prevent one group of investors from gaining, relative to another, by changes in the firm's fortunes after financial instruments have been issued. The future is always anticipated imperfectly in these contracts, so there will always be some need for ex post adjustments and supervision, and dividends play a role in these adjustments.

This obviously is not altogether different from information or signaling explanations of dividends. One could recharacterize part (but not all) of this treatment as an assertion that investment bankers and other financial intermediaries send signals to investors by putting their reputations (and, in underwritten offerings, money) on the line and certifying that the new securities are backed by the represented earnings potential. The information interpretation of this agency-cost treatment at least offers a plausible explanation why dividends (rather than, say, earnings announcements) carry essential information.

There is a further problem because the explanations I have offered are not unique explanations of dividends. Nothing here suggests that repurchases of shares would not do as well as or better than dividends. The issuance of debt instruments in series, so that payments and refinancings are continuous, serves the same function as dividends. I have "explained" only mechanisms that keep firms in the capital market in ways that

---

23. Some cases contain an implicit recognition of this function of dividends. For example, *Randall v. Bailey,* 23 N.Y.S.2d 173 (N.Y. Sup. Ct. 1940), aff'd mem., 262 App. Div. 844, 29 N.Y.S.2d 512 (1st Dep't 1941), aff'd, 288 N.Y. 280, 43 N.E.2d 43 (1942) (permitting dividend out of unrealized appreciation, financed by new debt).

instigate consistent monitoring and consistent readjustment of the risk among investors.

The explanation I have offered also is open to the objection, along the lines of Fischer Black, that shareholder-creditor conflicts may be resolved by negotiation after any change in the fortunes of the firm. The investors could agree to new payoffs or shares of control rather than to a dividend policy. This may well be true, but such ex post negotiation raises a bilateral monopoly problem, and the costs of the negotiation could be substantial even if (contrary to my assumption) there were no agency problems. Unless ex post negotiation is very costly, the existing pattern of complex bond indentures that provide for most contingencies makes little sense. I therefore think we must assume that in some decently large number of cases, accommodation through dividends and financing decisions set by the residual claimants is cheaper than accommodation through ex post negotiation. This is, however, an empirical matter, which raises the question whether the agency-cost explanations are testable.

* * *

IV. Conclusion

The economics literature has yet to integrate the study of corporate finance and the theory of the firm. This paper is a small step toward understanding whether, and how, dividends may be useful in reducing the agency costs of management. I suggest that dividends may keep firms in the capital market, where monitoring of managers is available at lower costs, and may be useful in adjusting the level of risk taken by managers and the different classes of investors. Such an explanation offers a hope of understanding why firms simultaneously pay out dividends and raise new funds in the capital market. It does not, however, explain dividends (as opposed to the set of all devices that have the effect of keeping firms in the capital market), and it will be difficult to test.

2. RESTRICTIONS ON DIVIDENDS AND OTHER DISTRIBUTIONS TO SHAREHOLDERS

Recall that in Chapter Six we discussed the role of indenture covenants and loan agreements in protecting creditors from shareholder attempts to strip all of the assets from the debtor corporation. A variety of approaches were explored—restricting dividends to some defined portion of earnings or retained earnings, requiring maintenance of some minimum net worth, or tangible net worth, or requiring maintenance of certain ratios that impose an indirect limit on dividends, such as current ratios or debt-equity ratios. These restrictions protect not only the lenders obtaining these covenants, but other creditors as well, both unsecured contract and tort creditors, who can free ride on the conservative behavior imposed on the debtor by covenants in bond indentures and loan agreements.

Since the Statute of 13 Elizabeth c. 5 (1571), there have been general prohibitions against conveyances by debtors that were either designed to or had the effect of removing debtor assets from the reach of creditors. The modern version of that act is the Uniform Fraudulent Transfer Act. Set out below are selected provisions:

§ 4.   Transfers Fraudulent as to Present and Future Creditors

(a) A transfer made or obligation incurred by a debtor is fraudulent as to a creditor, whether the creditor's claim arose before or after the transfer was made or the obligation was incurred, if the debtor made the transfer or incurred the obligation:

(1) with actual intent to hinder, delay, or defraud any creditor of the debtor; or

(2) without receiving a reasonably equivalent value in exchange for the transfer or obligation, and the debtor:

(i) was engaged or was about to engage in a business or a transaction for which the remaining assets of the debtor were unreasonably small in relation to the business or transaction; or

(ii) intended to incur, or believed or reasonably should have believed that he or she would incur, debts beyond his or her ability to pay as they became due.

(b) In determining actual intent under subsection (a)(1), consideration may be given, among other factors, to whether:

(1) the transfer or obligation was to an insider;

(2) the debtor retained possession or control of the property transferred after the transfer;

* * *

(7) the debtor removed or concealed assets;

(8) the value of the consideration received by the debtor was reasonably equivalent to the value of the asset transferred or the amount of the obligation incurred;

(9) the debtor was insolvent or became insolvent shortly after the transfer was made or the obligation was incurred;

(10) the transfer occurred shortly before or shortly after a substantial debt was incurred; and

(11) the debtor transferred the essential assets of the business to a lienor who transferred the assets to an insider of the debtor.

§ 5.   Transfers Fraudulent as to Present Creditors

(a) A transfer made or obligation incurred by a debtor is fraudulent as to a creditor whose claim arose before the transfer was made or the obligation was incurred if the debtor made the transfer or incurred the obligation without receiving a reasonably equivalent value in exchange for the transfer or obligation and the debtor was insolvent at that time or the debtor became insolvent as a result of the transfer or obligation.

(b) A transfer made by a debtor is fraudulent as to a creditor whose claim arose before the transfer was made if the transfer was made to an insider for an antecedent debt, the debtor was insolvent at that time, and the insider had reasonable cause to believe that the debtor was insolvent.

§ 7.   Remedies of Creditors

(a) In an action for relief against a transfer or obligation under this article, a creditor . . . may obtain:

(1) avoidance of the transfer or obligation to the extent necessary to satisfy the creditor's claim;

* * *

(3) subject to applicable principles of equity and in accordance with applicable rules of civil procedure:

(i) an injunction against further disposition by the debtor or a transferee, or both, of the asset transferred or of other property;

(ii) appointment of a receiver to take charge of the asset transferred or of other property of the transferee; or

(iii) any other relief the circumstances may require.

(b) If a creditor has obtained a judgment on a claim against the debtor, the creditor, if the court so orders, may levy execution on the asset transferred or its proceeds.

§ 8.   Defenses, Liability, and Protection of Transferee

(a) A transfer or obligation is not voidable under Section 4(a)(1) against a person who took in good faith and for a reasonably equivalent value or against any subsequent transferee or obligee.

(b) Except as otherwise provided in this section, to the extent a transfer is voidable in an action by a creditor under section 7(a)(1), the creditor may recover judgment for the value of the asset transferred, or the amount necessary to satisfy the creditor's claim, whichever is less. The judgment may be entered against:

(1) the first transferee of the asset or the person for whose benefit the transfer was made; or

(2) any subsequent transferee other than a good faith transferee or obligee who took for value or from any subsequent transferee or obligee.

(c) If the judgment under subsection (b) section is based upon the value of the asset transferred, the judgment must be for an amount equal to the value of the asset at the time of the transfer, subject to adjustment as the equities may require.

(d) Notwithstanding voidability of a transfer or an obligation under this article, a good faith transferee or obligee is entitled, to the extent of the value given the debtor for the transfer or obligation, to:

(1) a lien on or a right to retain any interest in the asset transferred;

(2) Enforcement of any obligation incurred; or

(3) A reduction in the amount of the liability on the judgment.

* * *

As you read the following materials, ask whether any of the specific corporate law rules described below are truly necessary, in view of contractual practices and the general rules on fraudulent transfers. Indeed, another important question is whether the "legal capital" rules of some statutes provide any useful creditor protection at all (quite aside from the question of redundancy).

Recall that in Chapter Five we discussed the older "legal capital" rules designed to assure the initial contribution of value to a corporation in exchange for its shares. Creating and identifying a fund of capital to protect creditors is one thing; preserving it is another. Older U.S. rules restricted payments of dividends to profits. While the current Model Act no longer takes this approach, it persists in some states, and thus is worthy of mention.

Here is some important nomenclature from § 2 of the Model Business Corporation Act ("MBCA") (1950):

"Stated capital" means par value times the number of shares outstanding, or the amount of consideration for no-par shares assigned to stated capital. (The default rule is the whole amount goes to stated capital under MBCA § 19 (1950).)

"Net assets" means assets minus liabilities.

"Surplus" means the excess of the net assets over stated capital.

"Surplus" can be broken down into two kinds:

"Earned Surplus," which is the accumulated net profits not paid to shareholders, minus accumulated losses (more commonly called "retained earnings" in accounting and finance).

"Capital Surplus" is the rest of the surplus (sometimes called paid-in surplus).

MBCA § 19 (1950) provided that the excess paid for shares over par value (or the amount paid for no-par shares over the amount allocated to stated capital) is "capital surplus." Even today, Del. GCL § 154 comes to about the same result. These Model Act rules remained in effect until 1980. As of 1998 thirty states had adopted the 1980 revisions of the legal capital rules, while most other states still had a form similar to that of the 1950 Model Act.

Formerly the Model Act followed the general European approach—capital was a fund to be preserved.* Dividends could only be paid from current or past profits. MBCA § 40 (1950), provided that dividends could be paid "only out of the unreserved and unrestricted earned surplus of the corporation...." Section 40, 1st paragraph, contained another limitation: dividends could be paid "except when the corporation is insolvent or when the payment thereof would render the corporation insolvent...."

Even today, Delaware G.C.L. § 170 takes the same approach:

> "(a) The directors of every corporation ... may declare and pay dividends upon the shares of its capital stock ... either (1) out of its surplus, as defined in and computed in accordance with §§ 154 and 244 of this title, or (2) in case there shall be no surplus, out of its net profits for the fiscal year in which the dividend is declared and/or the preceding fiscal year. * * * "

Unlike Europe, U.S. laws did not treat amounts paid for shares in excess of par value as part of permanent capital. See MBCA § 41 (1950). Distributions (a return of capital) could be made from these funds (capital surplus), either upon approval of shareholders, or with advance authorization in the articles of incorporation. This is subject to the same insolvency limitation—§ 41(a). Couple these rules with the use of low par or no par stock, authorized under all U.S. statutes, and formal legal capital rules (aside from insolvency limitations) preserved very little capital.

Evasions were possible. Thus, under the older MBCA, capital could be reduced by reducing par value through a shareholder vote that amended the articles of incorporation. MBCA § 53 (1950) permitted amendments of the articles that would reduce par value of both issued and unissued shares. Under MBCA § 55 (1950), this required a vote of the affected class. MBCA § 62 (1950) permitted a reduction by board action without a shareholder vote, provided that stated capital remained equal to the aggregate par value of all outstanding shares—small comfort when the common stock was no-par stock. The resulting funds were capital surplus (MBCA § 63 (1950)), which could be paid out to shareholders. The same result is possible in Delaware. See Del. GCL § 244, which is comparable to MBCA § 62 (1950).

"Nimble Dividends" were the next evasion: MBCA § 45(a) (alternative) (2d ed. 1967) provided as follows:

> "(a) Dividends may be declared and paid in cash or in property only out of the unreserved and unrestricted earned surplus of the corporation, *or out of the unreserved and unrestricted net earnings of the current fiscal year and the next preceding fiscal year taken as a*

---

* For a critical view of the European approach, see Luca Enriques & Jonathan R. Macey, Creditors versus Capital Formation: The Case against the European Legal Capital Rules, 86 Cornell L. Rev. 1165 (2001). In 2006 the European rules were liberalized, while still preserving a legal capital approach.

single period, except as otherwise provided in this section." (Emphasis added.)

The result was that even if a corporation had negative earned surplus it could pay dividends if it had two good years. Del. GCL § 170(a)(2), quoted above, contains a similar provision.

This is slightly more flexible than the old MBCA provision. Even if the negative earned surplus exceeds capital surplus (funds paid in excess of par value for shares or resulting from reduction of par value), the corporation can pay dividends under these circumstances.

Accordingly, the former MBCA rules represented a maze that was navigable by corporations determined to pay dividends or capital surplus to their shareholders, regardless of deficits in the earned surplus account. The only real restriction was insolvency (Recall the provisions of the Uniform Fraudulent Transfer Act?). Former MBCA § 40(a) (1950), dealing with dividends being paid only from surplus, allowed payment "except when the corporation is insolvent or when the declaration or payment thereof would render the corporation insolvent ..." Former MBCA § 41(a) (1950), dealing with distributions from capital surplus (in partial liquidation) provided:

> "(a) No such distribution shall be made at a time when the corporation is insolvent or when such distribution would render the corporation insolvent."

Del. GCL § 170(a) provides in part:

> "(a) * * * If the capital of the corporation, computed in accordance with §§ 154 and 244 of this title, shall have been diminished by depreciation in the value of its property, or by losses, or otherwise, to an amount less than the aggregate amount of the capital represented by the issued and outstanding stock of all classes having a preference upon the distribution of assets, the directors of such corporation shall not declare and pay out of such net profits any dividends upon any shares of any classes of its capital stock until the deficiency in the amount of capital represented by the issued and outstanding stock of all classes having a preference upon the distribution of assets shall have been repaired. Nothing in this subsection shall invalidate or otherwise affect a note, debenture or other obligation of the corporation paid by it as a dividend on shares of its stock, or any payment made thereon, if at the time such note, debenture or obligation was delivered by the corporation, the corporation had either surplus or net profits as provided in clause (1) or (2) of this subsection from which the dividend could lawfully have been paid." (Emphasis added.)

These statutes applied the same approach to share repurchases, which also return money to shareholders. MBCA § 5 (1950) authorized share repurchases, "but it shall not purchase, either directly or indirectly, its own shares except out of its earned surplus or, with the affirmative vote of the holders of at least two-thirds of all shares entitled to vote thereon, out of its capital surplus."

Del. G.C.L. § 160(a)1. suggests the same result:

> "(a) Every corporation may purchase, redeem, receive, take or otherwise acquire, own and hold, sell, lend, exchange, transfer or otherwise dispose of, pledge, use and otherwise deal in and with its own shares; provided, however, that no corporation shall—
>
> > "1. Purchase or redeem its own shares of capital stock for cash or other property when the capital of the corporation is impaired or when such purchase or redemption would cause any impairment of the capital of the corporation...."

Section 7 of the Uniform Fraudulent Transfer Act provides that creditors of a transferring debtor may avoid the transfer, seek to enjoin further transfers, or seek a receiver to take charge of the transferred assets. Corporate laws go further. MBCA § 8.33(a) provides:

§ 8.33 Directors' Liability for Unlawful Distributions

(a) A director who votes for or assents to a distribution in excess of what may be authorized and made pursuant to section 6.40(a) or 14.09(a) [distributions in liquidation] is personally liable to the corporation for the amount of the distribution that exceeds what could have been distributed without violating section 6.40(a) or 14.09(a) if the party asserting liability establishes that when taking the action the director did not comply with section 8.30.

Del. G.C.L. § 174 provides in part:

§ 174 Liability of Directors for Unlawful Payment of Dividend or Unlawful Stock Purchase or Redemption; Exoneration From Liability; Contribution Among Directors; Subrogation

(a) In case of any willful or negligent violation of the provisions of sections 160 [share repurchases] or 173 [dividends] of this title, the directors under whose administration the same may happen shall be jointly and severally liable, at any time within six years after paying such unlawful dividend or after such unlawful stock purchase or redemption, to the corporation, and to its creditors in the event of dissolution or insolvency, to the full amount of the dividend unlawfully paid, or to the full amount unlawfully paid for the purchase or redemption of the corporation's stock, with interest from the time such liability accrued.

Where dividends are to be paid in shares of the company's stock (a "stock dividend") stock exchange rules add another layer of regulation. These rules are discussed in Part 4.B of this Chapter.

Klang v. Smith's Food & Drug Centers, Inc.

Delaware Supreme Court.
702 A.2d 150 (1997).

■ Veasey, Chief Justice:

This appeal calls into question the actions of a corporate board in carrying out a merger and self-tender offer. Plaintiff in this purported class action alleges that a corporation's repurchase of shares violated the statutory prohibition against the impairment of capital. Plaintiff also claims that the directors violated their fiduciary duty of candor by failing to disclose material facts prior to seeking stockholder approval of the transactions in question.

No corporation may repurchase or redeem its own shares except out of "surplus," as statutorily defined, or except as expressly authorized by provisions of the statute not relevant here. Balance sheets are not, however, conclusive indicators of surplus or a lack thereof. Corporations may revalue assets to show surplus, but perfection in that process is not required. Directors have reasonable latitude to depart from the balance sheet to calculate surplus, so long as they evaluate assets and liabilities in good faith, on the basis of acceptable data, by methods that they reasonably believe reflect present values, and arrive at a determination of the surplus that is not so far off the mark as to constitute actual or constructive fraud.

We hold that, on this record the Court of Chancery was correct in finding that there was no impairment of capital and there were no disclosure violations. Accordingly, we affirm.

Facts

Smith's Food & Drug Centers, Inc. ("SFD") is a Delaware corporation that owns and operates a chain of supermarkets in the Southwestern United States. Slightly more than three years ago, Jeffrey P. Smith, SFD's Chief Executive Officer, began to entertain suitors with an interest in acquiring SFD. At the time, and until the transactions at issue, Mr. Smith and his family held common and preferred stock constituting 62.1% voting control of SFD. Plaintiff and the class he purports to represent are holders of common stock in SFD.

On January 29, 1996, SFD entered into an agreement with The Yucaipa Companies ("Yucaipa"), a California partnership also active in the supermarket industry. Under the agreement, the following would take place:

(1) Smitty's Supermarkets, Inc. ("Smitty's"), a wholly-owned subsidiary of Yucaipa that operated a supermarket chain in Arizona, was to merge into Cactus Acquisition, Inc. ("Cactus"), a subsidiary of SFD, in exchange for which SFD would deliver to Yucaipa slightly over 3 million newly-issued shares of SFD common stock;

(2) SFD was to undertake a recapitalization, in the course of which SFD would assume a sizable amount of new debt, retire old debt, and offer to repurchase up to fifty percent of its outstanding shares (other than those issued to Yucaipa) for $36 per share; and

(3) SFD was to repurchase 3 million shares of preferred stock from Jeffrey Smith and his family.

SFD hired the investment firm of Houlihan Lokey Howard & Zukin ("Houlihan") to examine the transactions and render a solvency opinion. Houlihan eventually issued a report to the SFD Board replete with assurances that the transactions would not endanger SFD's solvency, and would not impair SFD's capital in violation of 8 Del. C. § 160. On May 17, 1996, in reliance on the Houlihan opinion, SFD's Board determined that there existed sufficient surplus to consummate the transactions, and enacted a resolution proclaiming as much. On May 23, 1996, SFD's stockholders voted to approve the transactions, which closed on that day. The self-tender offer was over-subscribed, so SFD repurchased fully fifty percent of its shares at the offering price of $36 per share.

Disposition in the Court of Chancery

This appeal came to us after an odd sequence of events in the Court of Chancery. On May 22, 1996, the day before the transactions closed, plaintiff Larry F. Klang filed a purported class action in the Court of Chancery against Jeffrey Smith and his family, various members of the SFD Board, Yucaipa, Yucaipa's managing general partner Ronald W. Burkle, Smitty's and Cactus. On May 30, 1996, plaintiff filed an amended complaint as well as a motion to have the transactions voided or rescinded, advancing a variety of claims, only two of which are before us on appeal. First, he contended that the stock repurchases violated 8 Del. C. § 160[1] by impairing SFD's capital. Second, he alleged that SFD's directors violated their fiduciary duties by failing to disclose material facts relating to the transactions prior to obtaining stockholder approval.

* * *

Plaintiff's Capital–Impairment Claim

A corporation may not repurchase its shares if, in so doing, it would cause an impairment of capital, unless expressly authorized by Section 160. A repurchase impairs capital if the funds used in the repurchase exceed the amount of the corporation's "surplus," defined by 8 Del. C. § 154 to mean the excess of net assets over the par value of the corporation's issued stock.

Plaintiff asked the Court of Chancery to rescind the transactions in question as violative of Section 160. As we understand it, plaintiff's position

---

1. Section 160(a) provides in part:

(a) Every corporation may purchase, redeem, receive, take or otherwise acquire, own and hold, sell, lend exchange, transfer or otherwise dispose of, pledge, use and otherwise deal in and with its own shares; provided, however, that no corporation shall:

(1) Purchase or redeem its own shares of capital stock for cash or other property when the capital of the corporation is impaired or when such purchase or redemption would cause any impairment of the capital of the corporation, except that a corporation may purchase or redeem out of capital any of its own shares which are entitled upon any distribution of its assets, whether by dividend or in liquidation, to a preference over another class or series of its stock, or, if no shares entitled to such a preference are outstanding, any of its own shares, if such shares will be retired upon their acquisition and the capital of the corporation reduced in accordance with §§ 243 and 244 of this title.

breaks down into two analytically distinct arguments. First, he contends that SFD's balance sheets constitute conclusive evidence of capital impairment. He argues that the negative net worth that appeared on SFD's books following the repurchase compels us to find a violation of Section 160. Second, he suggests that even allowing the Board to "go behind the balance sheet" to calculate surplus does not save the transactions from violating Section 160. In connection with this claim, he attacks the SFD Board's off-balance-sheet method of calculating surplus on the theory that it does not adequately take into account all of SFD's assets and liabilities. Moreover, he argues that the May 17, 1996 resolution of the SFD Board conclusively refutes the Board's claim that revaluing the corporation's assets gives rise to the required surplus. We hold that each of these claims is without merit.

SFD's balance sheets do not establish a violation of 8 Del. C. § 160

In an April 25, 1996 proxy statement, the SFD Board released a pro forma balance sheet showing that the merger and self-tender offer would result in a deficit to surplus on SFD's books of more than $100 million. A balance sheet the SFD Board issued shortly after the transactions confirmed this result. Plaintiff asks us to adopt an interpretation of 8 Del. C. § 160 whereby balance-sheet net worth is controlling for purposes of determining compliance with the statute. Defendants do not dispute that SFD's books showed a negative net worth in the wake of its transactions with Yucaipa, but argue that corporations should have the presumptive right to revalue assets and liabilities to comply with Section 160.

Plaintiff advances an erroneous interpretation of Section 160. We understand that the books of a corporation do not necessarily reflect the current values of its assets and liabilities. Among other factors, unrealized appreciation or depreciation can render book numbers inaccurate. It is unrealistic to hold that a corporation is bound by its balance sheets for purposes of determining compliance with Section 160. Accordingly, we adhere to the principles of Morris v. Standard Gas & Electric Co.[7] allowing corporations to revalue properly its assets and liabilities to show a surplus and thus conform to the statute.

It is helpful to recall the purpose behind Section 160. The General Assembly enacted the statute to prevent boards from draining corporations of assets to the detriment of creditors and the long-term health of the corporation. That a corporation has not yet realized or reflected on its balance sheet the appreciation of assets is irrelevant to this concern. Regardless of what a balance sheet that has not been updated may show, an actual, though unrealized, appreciation reflects real economic value that the corporation may borrow against or that creditors may claim or levy upon. Allowing corporations to revalue assets and liabilities to reflect current realities complies with the statute and serves well the policies behind this statute.

---

7. Morris v. Standard Gas & Electric Co., 31 Del. Ch. 20, 63 A.2d 577 (1949).

The SFD Board appropriately revalued corporate assets to comply with 8 Del. C. § 160.

Plaintiff contends that SFD's repurchase of shares violated Section 160 even without regard to the corporation's balance sheets. Plaintiff claims that the SFD Board was not entitled to rely on the solvency opinion of Houlihan, which showed that the transactions would not impair SFD's capital given a revaluation of corporate assets. The argument is that the methods that underlay the solvency opinion were inappropriate as a matter of law because they failed to take into account all of SFD's assets and liabilities. In addition, plaintiff suggests that the SFD Board's resolution of May 17, 1996 itself shows that the transactions impaired SFD's capital, and that therefore we must find a violation of 8 Del. C. § 160. We disagree, and hold that the SFD Board revalued the corporate assets under appropriate methods. Therefore the self-tender offer complied with Section 160, notwithstanding errors that took place in the drafting of the resolution.

On May 17, 1996, Houlihan released its solvency opinion to the SFD Board, expressing its judgment that the merger and self-tender offer would not impair SFD's capital. Houlihan reached this conclusion by comparing SFD's "Total Invested Capital" of $1.8 billion—a figure Houlihan arrived at by valuing SFD's assets under the "market multiple" approach—with SFD's long-term debt of $1.46 billion. This comparison yielded an approximation of SFD's "concluded equity value" equal to $346 million, a figure clearly in excess of the outstanding par value of SFD's stock. Thus, Houlihan concluded, the transactions would not violate 8 Del. C. § 160.

Plaintiff contends that Houlihan's analysis relied on inappropriate methods to mask a violation of Section 160. Noting that 8 Del. C. § 154 defines "net assets" as "the amount by which total assets exceeds total liabilities," plaintiff argues that Houlihan's analysis is erroneous as a matter of law because of its failure to calculate "total assets" and "total liabilities" as separate variables. In a related argument, plaintiff claims that the analysis failed to take into account all of SFD's liabilities, i.e., that Houlihan neglected to consider current liabilities in its comparison of SFD's "Total Invested Capital" and long-term debt. Plaintiff contends that the SFD Board's resolution proves that adding current liabilities into the mix shows a violation of Section 160. The resolution declared the value of SFD's assets to be $1.8 billion, and stated that its "total liabilities" would not exceed $1.46 billion after the transactions with Yucaipa. As noted, the $1.46 billion figure described only the value of SFD's long-term debt. Adding in SFD's $372 million in current liabilities, plaintiff argues, shows that the transactions impaired SFD's capital.

We believe that plaintiff reads too much into Section 154. The statute simply defines "net assets" in the course of defining "surplus." It does not mandate a "facts and figures balancing of assets and liabilities" to determine by what amount, if any, total assets exceeds total liabilities. The statute is merely definitional. It does not require any particular method of calculating surplus, but simply prescribes factors that any such calculation must include. Although courts may not determine compliance with Section

160 except by methods that fully take into account the assets and liabilities of the corporation, Houlihan's methods were not erroneous as a matter of law simply because they used Total Invested Capital and long-term debt as analytical categories rather than "total assets" and "total liabilities."

We are satisfied that the Houlihan opinion adequately took into account all of SFD's assets and liabilities. Plaintiff points out that the $1.46 billion figure that approximated SFD's long-term debt failed to include $372 million in current liabilities, and argues that including the latter in the calculations dissipates the surplus. In fact, plaintiff has misunderstood Houlihan's methods. The record shows that Houlihan's calculation of SFD's Total Invested Capital is already net of current liabilities. Thus, subtracting long-term debt from Total Invested Capital does, in fact, yield an accurate measure of a corporation's net assets.

The record contains, in the form of the Houlihan opinion, substantial evidence that the transactions complied with Section 160. Plaintiff has provided no reason to distrust Houlihan's analysis. In cases alleging impairment of capital under Section 160, the trial court may defer to the board's measurement of surplus unless a plaintiff can show that the directors "failed to fulfill their duty to evaluate the assets on the basis of acceptable data and by standards which they are entitled to believe reasonably reflect present values." In the absence of bad faith or fraud on the part of the board, courts will not "substitute [our] concepts of wisdom for that of the directors." Here, plaintiff does not argue that the SFD Board acted in bad faith. Nor has he met his burden of showing that the methods and data that underlay the board's analysis are unreliable or that its determination of surplus is so far off the mark as to constitute actual or constructive fraud.[12] Therefore, we defer to the board's determination of surplus, and hold that SFD's self-tender offer did not violate 8 Del. C. § 160.

* * *

The judgment of the Court of Chancery is affirmed.

QUESTIONS

1. While the opinion isn't exactly clear on this subject, what do you think Houlihan Lokey Howard & Zukin did to determine the value of assets through a "market multiple" approach?

2. Does SFD's balance sheet constitute exclusive evidence of capital impairment? How could it show a negative net worth while Houlihan Lokey is giving an opinion that capital isn't impaired?

3. Plaintiffs argued that the definition of "net assets" in § 154, "the amount by which total assets exceed total liabilities," requires a calcu-

---

12. We interpret 8 Del. C. § 172 to entitle boards to rely on experts such as Houlihan to determine compliance with 8 Del. C. § 160. Plaintiff has not alleged that the SFD Board failed to exercise reasonable care in selecting Houlihan, nor that rendering a solvency opinion is outside Houlihan's realm of competence. Compare 8 Del. C. § 141(e) (providing that directors may rely in good faith on records, reports, experts, etc.).

lation of total assets and total liabilities as separate variables, and that Houlihan Lokey failed to do this. Why do Plaintiffs make this argument, and how does the court respond?

4. The court says "net assets" is "merely definitional." What does that mean?

The revolution in legal capital rules: MBCA § 6.40.

In 1979 the Model Act abandoned the legal capital approach. See the Report of the Committee on Corporate Laws, 34 Bus. Law. 1867 (1979):

> "It has long been recognized by practitioners and legal scholars that the pervasive statutory structure in which 'par value' and 'stated capital' are basic to state corporation statutes does not today serve the original purpose of protecting creditors and senior security holders from payments to junior security holders, and may, to the extent security holders are led to believe that it provides some protection, tend to be misleading."

> "In light of this recognized fact, the Committee on Corporate Laws has, as part of a fundamental revision of the financing provisions of the Model Act, deleted the mandatory concepts of stated capital and par value. In the Model Act as in effect prior to the amendments, dividends and stock repurchases could not lawfully be made by a corporation if, after giving effect thereto, the corporation would be insolvent in the equity sense, i.e., unable to pay its obligations as they become due in the ordinary course of business. The committee concluded that this is the fundamentally important test and should be retained without change. * * *

> "Upon elimination of par value and stated capital, the committee considered at length the question of what, if any, new or different standards should control dividends and share repurchases in addition to the equity-insolvency test. The Committee concluded that the Model Act should also contain a balance sheet test, which is also included in section 45. In a departure from existing statutory provisions, the balance sheet test is explicitly authorized to be determined on the basis of either financial statements prepared under accounting practices and principles that are reasonable in the circumstances, or, in the alternative, a fair valuation or other method that is reasonable in the circumstances."

BALANCE SHEET TEST

Set out below is MBCA § 6.40, which is the current version of that reform:

§ 6.40. Distributions to shareholders

> "(a) A board of directors may authorize and the corporation may make distributions to its shareholders subject to restriction by the articles of incorporation and the limitation in subsection (c).

"(b) If the board of directors does not fix the record date for determining shareholders entitled to a distribution (other than one involving a purchase, redemption, or other reacquisition of the corporation's shares), it is the date the board of directors authorizes the distribution.

"(c) No distribution may be made if, after giving it effect:

"(1) The corporation would not be able to pay its debts as they become due in the usual course of business; or

"(2) The corporation's total assets would be less than the sum of its total liabilities plus (unless the articles of incorporation permit otherwise) the amount that would be needed, if the corporation were to be dissolved at the time of the distribution, to satisfy the preferential rights upon dissolution of shareholders whose preferential rights are superior to those receiving the distribution.

"(d) The board of directors may base a determination that a distribution is not prohibited under subsection (c) either on financial statements prepared on the basis of accounting practices and principles that are reasonable in the circumstances or on a fair valuation or other method that is reasonable in the circumstances.[13]

"(e) Except as provided in subsection (g), the effect of a distribution under subsection (c) is measured:

"(1) in the case of distribution by purchase, redemption, or other acquisition of the corporation's shares, as of the earlier of (i) the date money or other property is transferred or debt incurred by the corporation; or (ii) The date the shareholder ceases to be a shareholder with respect to the acquired shares;

"(2) in the case of any other distribution of indebtedness, as of the date the indebtedness is distributed; and

"(3) in all other cases, as of (i) the date the distribution is authorized if payment occurs within 120 days after the date of authorization; or (ii) the date the payment is made if it occurs more than 120 days after the date of authorization.

"(f) A corporation's indebtedness to a shareholder incurred by reason of a distribution made in accordance with this section is at parity with the corporation's indebtedness to its general, unsecured creditors except to the extent subordinated by agreement or except to the extent secured.

---

13. The official commentary to MBCA § 6.40(d) states that:

"The board of directors should in all circumstances be entitled to rely upon reasonably current financial statements prepared on the basis of generally accepted accounting principles in determining whether or not the balance sheet test of section 6.40(c)(2) has been met, unless the board is then aware that it would be unreasonable to rely on the financial statements because of newly-discovered or subsequently-arising facts or circumstances."

"(g) Indebtedness of a corporation, including indebtedness issued as a distribution, is not considered a liability for purposes of determinations under subsection (c) if its terms provide that payment of principal and interest are to be made only if and to the extent that payment of a distribution to shareholders could then be made under this section. If the indebtedness is issued as a distribution, each payment of principal or interest is treated as a distribution, the effect of which is measured on the date the payment is actually made."

Hullender v. Acts II

153 Ga. App. 119, 264 S.E.2d 486 (1980).

■ Shulman, Judge.

As a part of a divorce settlement, appellee–Acts II, a corporation whose sole stockholders were appellant–Mrs. Hullender and appellee–Mr. Hullender, agreed to purchase all the common stock owned by appellant–Mrs. Hullender. In accordance with this agreement, Mrs. Hullender transferred her stock to Acts II in return for a debenture note and a personal guaranty from Mr. Hullender. When the corporation defaulted on this obligation and Mrs. Hullender's demands for payment were refused by appellees, appellant–Mrs. Hullender commenced this action seeking to collect on the debenture note and guaranty. This appeal follows the grant of appellees' and the denial of appellant's respective motions for summary judgment. For the reasons which follow, we affirm the judgment as to appellee–Acts II and reverse the judgment as to appellee–Mr. Hullender.

1. In granting appellee–Act II's motion for summary judgment, the trial court sustained Act II's contention that the purchase agreement was void ab initio under Code Ann. § 22–513 (e), which provided in pertinent part as follows: "No purchase of or payment for its [i.e., the corporation's] own shares shall be made for any purpose at a time when the corporation is insolvent or when such purchase or payment would make it insolvent ...."* Although appellant concedes that Acts II was insolvent when the debenture note was issued (in fact, Acts II has never been solvent), appellant insists that Acts II should not be permitted to take advantage of its own insolvency to avoid liability for its obligations where, as here, no creditor is involved. See, e.g., Dalton Grocery Co. v. Blanton, 8 Ga. App. 809 (70 SE 183), involving a situation where a solvent corporation was not permitted to take advantage of laws for the protection of creditors to repudiate a transaction where no creditors were complaining.

While we recognize that there is foreign authority to the effect that a corporation is estopped to assert its own insolvency as a defense to its obligations where no complaints by creditors are involved, Code Ann. § 22–513 (e) contains an absolute prohibition and does not provide exceptions for its application. We conclude, therefore, that the trial court properly held

---

* This language appears in § 6 of the 1968 Model Business Corporation Act. —Ed.

the insolvency defense available to Acts II in this litigation involving an insolvent corporation and a stockholder.

We are unpersuaded by appellant's argument in a related enumeration of error that an analysis of interrelated provisions of the Georgia Business Corporation Code requires the conclusion that the debenture note is not void ab initio. Since the issuance of the debenture was prohibited by law (Code Ann. § 22–513(e)), it follows that the repurchasing contract was void (Code Ann. § 20–501) and cannot be enforced.

[The court held that Mr. Hullender's personal guaranty was valid and enforceable.]

QUESTIONS

1. This case was decided under the pre–1980 version of the MBCA. Would this agreement have been enforceable against the corporation under MBCA § 6.40?

2. Would this agreement be enforceable against the corporation under Del. G.C.L. § 160?

3. If the corporation isn't currently solvent when the husband and wife wish to arrange a buyout of her shares with a corporate note, can you make it enforceable if the company later becomes solvent, under MBCA § 6.40?

4. Assume that a corporation that is the subject of a hostile takeover bid wants to distribute rights to each shareholder to be able to resell his or her shares to the corporation for a large promissory note in the event a bidder gains control. If the rights were triggered at the present time, the corporation would be rendered insolvent (in the balance sheet sense that assets were less than liabilities) by the issuance of notes for 49% of its shares. Can the corporation validly issue such rights now under § 6.40? Can you write the payment terms of the corporation's payment obligations to come within subsection (g)? Could you achieve this result under Del. G.C.L. § 170(a)?

Stock Repurchase Agreements in Bankruptcy: A Tale of State Law Rights Discarded

by Dennis F. Dunne.
12 Bankruptcy Developments Journal 355 (1996).

I.   Introduction

The classification and treatment of installment stock repurchase claims[1] in bankruptcy have been caught in the crossroads of two conflicting legal trends. On one side, a majority of states have amended their corporate

---

1. These claims usually arise under a note that was issued by a company to a former shareholder in exchange for his shares, frequently as a result of the retirement or the death of a principal. See, e.g., Scherling v. Ehrenkranz (In re Eljay Jrs.), 123 B.R. 961 (S.D.N.Y. 1991); In re Stern–Seligman–Prins Co., 86 B.R. 994 (Bankr. W.D. Mo. 1988).

statutes within the past decade to provide that debt incurred by a company in exchange for delivery of its shares is a valid obligation for all purposes, if the company was sufficiently capitalized at the time of the transaction and could have paid the entire obligation at that time without impairing its capital. Under this modern trend, the indebtedness incurred by the company in exchange for the repurchase of its shares is "at parity" with the company's indebtedness to its general unsecured creditors.[4] Simultaneously with this development, but in unrelated contexts, the United States Supreme Court has directed federal courts sitting in bankruptcy to defer to and enforce state law rights.[5]

A conflicting trend, however, pre-dates the current Bankruptcy Code and has crystallized into a bankruptcy canon: Thou shalt not allow a claim with an equity ancestry to share equally with a claim of other creditors. While there is a certain visceral appeal to this rule, upon closer inspection there is often little reason to ignore state law and creditor expectations. For instance, if the enforcement of stock repurchase claims were left to state courts, former shareholders could be relatively certain that their rights under state law would be protected. Should there be a different result if the stock repurchase claim is filed in a bankruptcy case?

A substantial body of case law decided under the Bankruptcy Code's predecessor statute almost uniformly subordinated such claims to all other debt obligations of the company. As discussed below, these cases were usually decided when no contrary state statute existed. Accordingly, those cases should be—but generally are not—afforded less precedential weight today, when intervening state statutes and Supreme Court directives control. Following these former Bankruptcy Act cases, most cases decided under the Bankruptcy Code have subordinated installment stock repurchase claims. Some of these courts have ignored the relevant state statute completely while others have consciously engrafted a judicial gloss onto it, even if patently contrary to the state statute's intent.

* * *

C. Treatment of Claims Arising From Installment Stock Repurchase Agreements Under the Bankruptcy Code

As discussed above, many courts have correctly subordinated claims arising from stock repurchases when the underlying state law prohibits payment at any time after the corporation becomes insolvent.[107] Cases that

---

4. See, e.g., Ala. Code section 10–2B–6.40(f) (1994); Ariz. Rev. Stat. Ann. section 10–640(f) (1994, eff. as of Jan. 1, 1996). See also Model Business Corp. Act section 6.40(f) (1991).

5. See, e.g., BFP v. Resolution Trust Corp. 114 S. Ct. 1757, 1765–66 (1994); Butner v. United States, 440 U.S. 48, 54–55 (1979); see also Barnhill v. Johnson, 503 U.S. 393, 398 (1992) ("In the absence of controlling federal law, [rights against estate] are creatures of state law."); Ohio v. Kovacs, 469 U.S. 274, 286 (1985) ("The classification of Ohio's interest" as secured, unsecured, or otherwise "depends on Ohio law.") (O'Connor, J., concurring).

107. See, e.g., La Grand Steel Prods. Co. v. Goldberg (In re Poole, McGonigle & Dick, Inc.), 796 F.2d 318, 323 (9th Cir.) modified, 804 F.2d 576 (9th Cir. 1986) (subordinating claim of former shareholder because Installment Test applied under Oregon law at time of repur-

are more difficult to reconcile—apart from the deep-seated sense that former equity claims should not share equally with creditors—are those that either ignore state law or find reasons to supplant state law.[108]

1. The SPM Case

A good example of the latter is In re SPM Manufacturing Corp.[109] At issue in that case was the validity of a former shareholder's installment stock repurchase claim. . . . SPM was financially healthy at the time of the stock repurchase and issuance of the note, and could have paid the note in full at that time without impairing its capital. Seven years after issuance of the note, SPM filed for reorganization.

The court found that Massachusetts ... "would not require current solvency for enforcement of the obligation." The court, however, did not end its analysis there. The court acknowledged that equitable subordination usually requires inequitable conduct by the claim holder and noted that the former shareholder in the case before it was guilty of no such misconduct. Nevertheless, troubled by the debt's equity origins, the court saw a direct conflict between Massachusetts state law and section 510(c) of the Bankruptcy Code.

The SPM court reasoned that the congressional purpose in codifying equitable subordination standards would be thwarted unless the claims of this former shareholder were subordinated. The court recognized it was also subordinating concerns of federalism and the enforcement of undisputed state law expectations and entitlements to the amorphous, evolving, and discretionary requirements of equitable subordination:

> It makes no difference that the purpose of [the state law] may be to promote certainty in the enforcement of a contract reflecting a significant business transaction. It is enough that the effect of the statute's application is to conflict with federal law.

As the SPM case shows, equitable subordination, a tool developed to deal with claimant misconduct and the dilution of compensatory claims by punitive damage and penalty claims, has become a vehicle under the

---

chase). Cf. Saltzman v. Noroton Heights Enters (In re Noroton Heights Enters.), 96 B.R. 11, 14 (Bankr. D. Conn. 1989) (finding proofs of claim deficient because they failed to allege that company was solvent at the time notes were delivered for stock, as required by Connecticut law).

108. See, e.g., Liebowitz v. Columbia Pkg. Co. (In re Columbia Pkg. Co.), 56 B.R. 222, 224 (D. Mass. 1985) (subordinating claim arising from installment stock repurchase agreement without discussing state law, and citing only former Bankruptcy Act cases), aff'd, 802 F.2d 439 (1st Cir. 1986); Envirodyne Indus., Inc. v. American Express (In re Envirodyne Indus., Inc.), 176 B.R. 825, 835 (Bankr. N.D. Ill. 1995) (subordinating claims because of equity heritage); In re Dino & Artie's Automatic Transmission Co., 68 B.R. 264, 269–70 (Bankr. S.D.N.Y. 1986) (subordinating repurchase claim with no discussion of state law). See also In re Micro–Acoustics Corp., 34 B.R. 279, 284 (Bankr. S.D.N.Y. 1983) (reasoning that standards under section 510(c) need not be met because a stock repurchase claim could be separately classified without violating absolute priority rule).

109. 163 B.R. 411 (Bankr. D. Mass. 1994). See also Ferrari v. Family Mutual Savs. Bank (In re New Era Pkg. Inc.), 186 B.R. 329, 337 (Bankr. D. Mass. 1995) (following SPM).

Bankruptcy Code by which bankruptcy courts can continue to follow former Bankruptcy Act cases notwithstanding the changing state law landscape. SPM is best understood as a case suspicious of attempts to transform equity interests into debt claims. End runs around the absolute priority rule should not and will not be tolerated. As discussed herein, there are many fact patterns that raise these concerns and justify equitable subordination, but the facts in SPM and the Hypothetical, on balance, do not.

* * *

3. The Stern–Slegman Case

Not all bankruptcy courts have subordinated claims arising under installment stock repurchase agreements. In In re Stern–SlegmanPrins Co.,[138] the court refused to subordinate an installment stock repurchase claim that was valid under state law.

The Stern court first addressed the issue of which test .. , Missouri had adopted. * * * Like Delaware and most states, however, Missouri had adopted the Outset Test.*

Since the claim was valid under state law, the Stern court proceeded to determine whether any reason existed under section 510(c) to subordinate the claim. Unlike SPM and its progeny, the court in Stern found no legitimate reason to subordinate the former shareholder's claim arising under a stock repurchase agreement that was executed more than ten years before the company's insolvency, reasoning:

> The stock repurchase transaction was not invalid under state law. Turning to the question of fraud, the [objecting party] has not submitted any evidence suggesting fraud or inequitable conduct. Nor has it suggested what facts give rise to even the slightest inference of fraud or inequitable conduct.... The option to purchase the shares ... was exercised ... more than a decade before [the debtor] experienced the severe financial problems that ultimately led to bankruptcy. Further the Court finds that the reasons for debtor's ultimate financial demise had nothing to do with repurchase of the stock by the company.[143]

The court did not revisit the issue of whether a claim arising from a installment stock repurchase agreement should be treated as debt or equity. The state legislature's policy decision foreclosed that analysis, and

---

138. 86 B.R. 994 (Bankr. W.D. Mo. 1988). See also In re Motels of Am., Inc., 146 B.R. 542, 544 (Bankr. D. Del. 1992) (finding stock repurchase claim to be valid and enforceable because it did not violate Outset Test adopted by Delaware). Cf. In re Wyeth Co., 134 B.R. 920, 922 (Bankr. W.D. Mo. 1991) (refusing to subordinate repurchase claim under section 510(b) because it is a valid debt claim).

* The author distinguishes the "Outset" test, which applies the capital surplus test only on the date the note is issued and the indebtedness is incurred, and (ii) the "Installment" test, which applies the capital surplus test each time a payment under the note is made.—Ed.

143. Stern, 86 B.R. at 1000–01 (brackets in original). See also Williams v. Nevelow, 513 S.W.2d 535, 538 (Tex. 1974) (Texas law) (allowing claim arising from installment stock repurchase agreement to share with other creditors's claims, despite intervening insolvency, when agreement was valid when executed and there was no evidence of bad faith).

the role of the bankruptcy court, according to the Stern–Slegman case, was merely to enforce Missouri's corporate laws. Once the equity versus debt question was removed, the reason for no-fault subordination disappeared, and the former shareholder shared pari passu with general creditors absent fraud or misconduct.[144]

4.   Ancillary Problems Created by SPM and Similar Cases

Perhaps the most significant unintended consequence of SPM and related cases is their application to the public markets.[145] Corporations may exchange shares for debentures to afford greater control to the remaining shareholders or to leverage the company so that future "dividends" to former shareholders will be tax deductible as interest payments on debt. The rationale supporting subordination of such claims, once equity, always equity, applies with equal force regardless of whether the company is publicly or closely held. If a debt obligation has an equity ancestor, the debt must be subordinated under SPM's logic. Thus, publicly issued stock that is held by thousands of investors and is subsequently converted into or exchanged for a debt instrument is subject to challenge in a subsequent bankruptcy. It does not matter how many years preceded the company's financial demise or how many times the securities have changed hands in the public markets.[147]

* * *

QUESTIONS

1.   In the context of hostile takeovers, some companies have used so-called "poison put" rights (a form of "poison pill"), that provide, in the event

---

144.   See also Libco Corp. v. Leigh (In re Reliable Mfg. Corp.), 703 F.2d 996, 1002 (7th Cir. 1983) (refusing to apply Installment Test to transaction governed by Delaware's Outset Test) The court found that:

> [The debtor] was adequately capitalized on the day its stock was transferred.... From the date of the sale [the sellers] ceased to be shareholders and stood purely in a creditor relationship to the corporation. Prior creditors were not defrauded by the transaction ... and all future creditors were on notice.

Id. (brackets in original).

145.   See, e.g., McConnell v. Butler, 402 F.2d 362, 367 (9th Cir. 1968) (finding that employees who held shares under employee stock option plan which were later converted to debentures could not share ratably with general creditors in subsequent bankruptcy).

147.   At least one state legislature has amended its law to except negotiable instruments from application of the Installment Test. In California, for example, if a corporation issues a negotiable debt security (as defined in section 8–102 of the Uniform Commercial Code) in exchange for repurchased stock, the Outset Test and not the Installment Test will apply. See Cal. Corp. section 511 (West 1990) ("A negotiable instrument issued by a corporation for the purchase or redemption of shares shall be enforceable by a holder in due course ... without notice that it was issued for that purpose."). Similarly, some courts have struggled to enforce such negotiable instruments. See, e.g., Triumph Smokes, Inc. v. Sarlo, 482 S.W.2d 696, 698 (Tex. Ct. Civ. App. 1972) (holding that debentures issued to repurchase stock were enforceable despite fact that no earned surplus was available and statute was violated; such violation meant that repurchase was ultra vires, but not illegal and unenforceable). It remains to be seen, however, whether courts such as SPM will enforce such state law.

that a hostile bidder gains control, the remaining public shareholders can put their shares to the corporation, which is required to repurchase them for a price previously determined by the target corporation's board to represent fair value. These rights represent a dividend to the target shareholders. Are these rights valid and enforceable if their exercise would render the company insolvent?

2. In other cases target corporations have adopted more conventional poison pill rights plans, that allow target shareholders, other than a bidder, to purchase additional shares at a discount (typically 50%) from the market price, thus diluting the bidder's investment. These plans typically require a company to have an amount of authorized but unissued shares at least four or five, and in some cases ten or twenty, times the number of outstanding shares. Because many companies lack such huge numbers of authorized but unissued shares, many of these plans have several fall-back positions. One fall-back provides that to the extent the company can't deliver the shares upon exercise of the rights, it will pay liquidated damages to the rights holders, in an amount equal to the difference between the exercise price and the value of the shares the company can actually deliver. Again, the amount of liquidated damages may exceed the market value of the company's currently outstanding stock. Can you think of a strategy to prevent such obligations from being voidable in bankruptcy?

3. BOARD DISCRETION AND DUTIES IN DECLARING DIVIDENDS

We begin our discussion with some basics. Statutes generally reserve dividend decisions for the board of directors. See Del. G.C.L. § 170(a) ("The directors of every corporation ... may declare and pay dividends upon the shares of its capital stock. . . .") and RMBCA § 6.40(a) ("A board of directors may authorize and the corporation may make distributions to its shareholders. . . ."). Every jurisdiction treats a declared dividend as an indebtedness of the corporation. But when does it accrue, and who owns it? These questions become critical when ownership is transferred, and in publicly traded corporations hundreds of thousands of shares may be transferred daily.

Caleb & Co. v. E. I. Dupont de Nemours & Company

615 F. Supp. 96 (S.D.N.Y. 1985).

■ SWEET, D.J.

This securities action, arising from the tender offer by E. I. DuPont de Nemours and Co. ("DuPont") for Conoco ("Conoco"), returns as the result of an amended complaint and a renewed motion to dismiss pursuant to

Fed.R.Civ.P. 12(b)(6). The motion is granted in part and denied in part, as set forth below.

* * *

Facts

DUPONT BUYING CONOCO

[On July 15, 1981, DuPont issued its prospectus to all Conoco share-holders, including Caleb, offering them a choice of $95 cash or 1.7 DuPont shares for every Conoco share tendered in accordance with the offer. Two weeks later, because DuPont's tender offer was hotly contested by two other bidders, Joseph E. Seagram & Sons, Inc. and Mobil Oil Corporation, DuPont increased the number of shares it would accept for cash, and on August 4, DuPont increased its cash offer to $98.00 per share, prompting Mobil to increase its offer to $120.00 per share.]

[I]t is alleged that the Board of Directors of Conoco declared a dividend on July 31, 1981, payable to shareholders of record as of August 14, 1981. * * *

The Complaint

On the facts alleged, Caleb asserts four causes of action. * * *

The fourth cause of action alleges that DuPont and First Jersey violated contractual and fiduciary obligations owed to Caleb by prematurely transferring the shares to DuPont thereby permitting DuPont wrongfully to receive the dividend payable to shareholders of record on August 14, 1981.

DuPont and First Jersey have moved to dismiss each of the four counts of the amended complaint, and the counts will be addressed sequentially.

* * *

Count Four: Entitlement to the Dividend

I MISSED RECEIPT OF DIVIDENDS

The amended complaint alleges that First Jersey improperly permitted DuPont to acquire the tendered shares, prior to payment, before the August 14 record date for the $0.65 quarterly Conoco dividend, thereby permitting DuPont improperly to receive the dividend. It is undisputed that Conoco declared a $0.65 per share dividend on July 31, 1981, payable on September 14 to stockholders of record on August 14. DuPont accepted and purchased the shares on August 5, although it did not pay for them until after August 14. The issues that must be resolved are first whether DuPont's acceptance without payment on August 5 made it the record owner on August 14, and second, which holder has the right to a cash dividend when the dividend is declared before a sale of stock but the shares are sold before the record date but after the declaration.

ISSUES?

A. DuPont's August 5 Acceptance

DuPont's acceptance of tendered shares on August 5 vested in DuPont the right to be considered the record owner on August 14, even though payment for the shares postdated August 14. The principle was explained and held to be uniformly applicable by Professor Williston, who stated:

> The uniform statutes, in force in all of the states in one form or another, definitely provide ... that legal title to stock passes to the buyer upon delivery of the certificate in proper form. But the passing of legal title may, or may not, be coterminous with the passing of the risks, and the rights of ownership, in the shares. Moreover, all of the rights, or obligations, of ownership may not pass at the same time. Thus, the purchaser of shares, absent any agreement to the contrary, is generally entitled to dividends, rights and all the privileges of a shareholder, except voting power, from the time he makes the purchase contract, whether or not he has made payment, has taken legal title or has been registered on the corporation records as a shareholder.

8 Williston on Contracts § 953 at 320–21 (1964) (footnotes omitted) (emphasis added).

In *Lafountain & Woolson Co. v. Brown*, 91 Vt. 340, 101 A. 36, 37 (1917), the court explained that "the principle of equitable assignments applies. The purchaser of shares of corporate stock is held to acquire an equitable interest in the stock before the transfer is completed, if the agreement of purchase and sale is binding between the parties." *Id.* The contract between the tendering shareholders and DuPont became binding on August 5, and DuPont thereby could benefit from the principle of equitable assignments in order to be considered the owner of record.

B. Declaration Date v. Record Owner

An examination of the Delaware authorities, recognized by both parties to be binding here, establishes that an owner as of the record date but not the declaration date is the beneficiary of the dividend. A sale between the declaration and record dates causes the dividend to inure to the benefit of the purchaser.

The tension between the declaration date and the record date results from the desire of corporations to clarify their own liability for dividend payments. Before the record date problem arose the courts with very few exceptions held that dividends belonged to the owner of the stock on the date the dividend was declared. However, the practice of most corporations today is to declare the dividend to be payable to shareholders on a date of record between the declaration date and the date set for payment. The original purpose of such a practice was undoubtedly to protect the corporation, so that when it paid a dividend to the person registered on the books on the record date no liability would fall on the corporation if such person were not the actual owner on that date. However, many courts have held that the record date is the effective date of the dividend and the actual owner on the date of record is entitled to the dividend even though he may not be the owner registered on the books of the corporation. Some courts have not accepted this view and retain the rule that title vests on the date of the declaration. The numerical majority follows the reasoning of the

Connecticut Supreme Court in Richter & Co. v. Light, whereas the minority in number is led by New Jersey.

"It would seem clear that the majority of states, both in number and importance, favors the Connecticut rule, and that the trend is increasingly in that direction."

Note, Dividends—To Whom Payable When Record Date Is Given, 7 Ohio St. U.L.J. 431, 437–39 (1941) (footnotes omitted).

When there is both a declaration date and a record date, the declaration of the dividend creates a debtor-creditor relationship between the corporation and the owner of the stock on the date of declaration:

It seems to be true that upon the declaration of a lawful dividend by a Board of Directors that the relation of debtor and creditor is set up between the corporation and the stockholder. In most cases the right set up in the stockholder is an irrevocable right and the declaration of the lawful dividend creates an obligation of the corporation and there exists a right to action on the part of the stockholder to enforce its payment. The right of action is in the nature of a contract and grows out of the declaration of a lawful dividend. The actual wording of the Resolution, the physical minutes, constitute mere matter of Record.

Selly v. Fleming Coal Co., 37 Del. 34, 180 A. 326, 328 (1935).

The theory [is] that when a dividend is declared, it is, in effect, set aside by the corporation, as money in hand, for the benefit of the stockholder entitled, though it is not then payable. Wheeler v. Northwestern Sleigh Co., C.C., 39 F. 347; Cogswell v. Second Nat'l Bank, 78 Conn. 75, 60 A. 1059; 38 Harv. Law. Rev. 247. This creates a debtor and creditor relation, and if such dividend is not paid when due it may be recovered in an appropriate action by the stockholders.

Wilmington Trust Co. v. Wilmington Trust Co., 25 Del. Ch. 193, 15 A.2d 665, 667 (1940). However, the ultimate beneficiary of the dividend will still be controlled by owner of the stock on the record date. As the court explained in Wilmington Trust, supra, the debtor-creditor relationship between the corporation and stock owner arising at the time of declaration of the dividend was not ultimately controlling.

The general rule is that the estate of the life beneficiary of the income is entitled to all regular cash dividends that have been declared during her lifetime, for the benefit of the stockholders of record on dates prior to her death, though such dividends are not actually payable or receivable by the trustees until dates subsequent thereto.

The Delaware Code also establishes the supremacy of the record date over the declaration date for the establishment of shareholder rights:

(a) In order that the corporation may determine the stockholders entitled to notice of or to vote at any meeting of stockholders or any adjournment thereof, or to express consent to corporate action in writing without a meeting, or entitled to receive payment of any dividend or other distribution or allotment of any rights, or entitled to exercise any rights in respect of any change, conversion or exchange of stock or for the purpose of any other lawful action, the board of directors may fix, in advance, a record date, which shall not be more than 60 nor less than 10 days before the date of such meeting, nor more than 60 days prior to any other action.*

See Fletcher, Cyclopedia of the Law of Private Corporations § 5379 (citing Del. Code Title 8, § 213 as statutory alteration of rule of declaration date entitlement); 12 Del. Code Ann. Title 12 § 6104(e) (establishing priority of corporate specified record date over declaration date).

* * *

Even though neither Wilmington Trust, supra, nor the Delaware Code section cited above, directly resolve the confrontation here, I conclude that their clear implication is that the owner as of the record date is the proper recipient of the dividend. Caleb's final cause of action is therefore dismissed.

QUESTIONS

1. Why would the transfer agent for Conoco's stock, First Jersey, transfer title to the shares before the receipt of the purchase price?

2. Williston states that legal title to stock passes to the buyer upon delivery of the certificate in proper form. This means that the selling shareholder has executed a stock transfer form (which is always found on the back of stock certificates, but which may be executed separately) and delivered the stock certificate to the buyer. Is this enough to entitle the buyer to the dividends, if the record date is subsequent to the delivery of the certificate, properly endorsed? Or does it take something more when the board has declared a record date for determining shareholders entitled to payment?

Berwald v. Mission Development Company

185 A.2d 480 (Del. 1962).

■ SOUTHERLAND, CHIEF JUSTICE

Plaintiffs, owners of 248 shares of the stock of Mission Development Corporation, brought suit to compel the liquidation of Mission and the distribution of its assets to its stockholders. Mission answered and filed a motion for summary judgment, based on affidavits and depositions. Plaintiffs tendered no contradictory proof. The Vice Chancellor granted the motion and the plaintiffs appeal.

The facts are as follows:

Defendant, Mission Development, is a holding company. Its sole significant asset is a block of nearly seven million shares of Tidewater Oil Company. Tidewater is a large integrated oil company, qualified to do

---

* Del. G.C.L. § 213(a)—Ed.

business in all the States of the Union. It is controlled, through Mission Development and Getty Oil Company, by J. Paul Getty.

Mission Development was formed in 1948 for the purpose of acquiring a block of 1,416,693 shares of Tidewater common stock.... * * * The shares of both Mission Development and Tidewater are listed on the New York Stock Exchange.

From 1948 to 1951 Mission acquired an additional 1,050,420 shares of Tidewater. Thereafter, and by 1960, Mission's holdings of Tidewater, through a 100% stock dividend and annual stock dividends of five per cent, increased to 6,943,957 shares.

In 1954 Tidewater discontinued the payment of cash dividends, thus effecting a discontinuance of Mission's income. Mission, as above noted, received thereafter until 1960 an annual 5% stock dividend, but Mission's proportionate ownership of Tidewater was not thereby increased, and its management accordingly deemed it unwise to distribute the shares as a dividend, since to do so would have decreased its proportionate ownership of Tidewater.

As hereafter shown, Tidewater's discontinuance of cash dividends was prompted by the adoption in 1954 of a policy of corporate expansion and modernization. The use of its available cash for this purpose left it without funds for dividends.

* * *

All of the foregoing facts were reported to Mission stockholders by letter of J. Paul Getty, President of the corporation, dated April 11, 1955.

We pause to note that some of the plaintiff's stock in Mission Development was bought in 1956 and 1959.

* * *

From September 1960 to and including August 1961 Getty Oil Company acquired 510,200 shares of Mission. Some of these were purchased off the market.

In November 1960 this suit was filed.

As above indicated, plaintiffs seek to compel a complete or partial liquidation of the defendant and the distribution of its assets, either through the medium of a winding-up receivership, or by means of a court order compelling the management to distribute, or to offer to distribute, at least part of the Tidewater shares in exchange for Mission shares.

The extreme relief of receivership to wind up a solvent going business is rarely granted. To obtain it there must be a showing of imminent danger of great loss resulting from fraud or mismanagement. Like caution is dictated in considering an application to compel a corporation to make a partial distribution.

Since no showing is made of fraud or mismanagement inflicting injury upon the corporation, what is the basis of plaintiff's case?

Plaintiff's argument proceeds as follows:

There is an inherent conflict of interest between the controlling stockholder of Mission, Mr. J. Paul Getty, and the minority stockholders. This arises out of the dividend policy of Tidewater. Because of high income taxes, Mr. Getty, it is said, is not interested in receiving dividends; he is interested in acquiring more shares of Tidewater. To achieve this end, it is charged, he has caused Tidewater to discontinue all dividends and to announce, in 1960, that no dividends could be expected for five years. The necessary effect of this policy, plaintiffs say, was to depress the market value of Mission shares, and enable Mr. Getty to buy more Mission shares at an artificially low price, at the expense of Mission's minority stockholders. This, plaintiffs charge, is just what he has done, as is proved by Getty Oil's purchases of stock in 1960 and 1961. Thus he and Mission have inflicted a serious wrong upon the minority stockholders.

It is quite true that in some cases the interests of a controlling stockholder and of the minority stockholders in respect of the receipt of dividends may conflict, because of the existence of very high income taxes.* And in some cases this may work hardship on the minority. But we find no such situation here.

It is plain that the whole argument based on a charge of conflict of interest rests upon the claim that Tidewater's dividend policy, and its public announcement of it, were designed to serve the selfish interest of Mr. Getty and not to further its own corporate interests. If the opposite is true—if Tidewater's policy was adopted in furtherance of its own corporate interest—then Mission's stockholders have not been subjected to an actionable wrong and have no complaint. The fact of Mr. Getty's purchase of Mission Development stock then becomes irrelevant.

What does the record show with respect to Tidewater's dividend policy?

In the ten years prior to 1953 Tidewater's expenditure for capital improvements did not exceed $41,100,000 in any one year. Shortly prior to 1954 Tidewater began to expand and modernize its facilities. In February 1955 it closed and subsequently sold its obsolete refinery at Bayonne, New Jersey, and built a new and modern refinery in New Castle County, Delaware at a cost in excess of $200,000,000. Also, it commenced and still continues the expansion and modernization of its refinery facilities at Avon, California, and the increase of its crude oil and natural gas resources. As of November 3, 1960, the budget for new capital projects to be begun in 1961 was $111,000,000.

It is unnecessary to elaborate the point. It is entirely clear from the facts set forth in the affidavits that Tidewater's cash has since 1960 been largely devoted to capital improvements and that, in the opinion of management, funds were not available for dividends. These facts are uncontradicted, and they constitute a refutation of the basic argument of plaintiffs

---

* During this era the maximum marginal Federal Income Tax rate for individuals was 90%.—Ed.

that dividends were discontinued to enable J. Paul Getty to buy Mission stock at a depressed price.

Some point is sought to be made of the unusual action of the Tidewater management in announcing that dividends could not be expected for five years. As defendant's counsel says, this was done out of common fairness to its stockholders and to prospective purchasers of its stock.

It is earnestly argued that plaintiffs should be allowed to go to trial and adduce testimony on the issue of the selfish motives of the controlling stockholder. Plaintiffs say that they could show by expert testimony that the market price of Mission common was artificially depressed.

It is first to be noted that the record of market prices put in by the plaintiffs themselves fails to show any drop in prices coincident with or closely following the announcement of the cessation of dividends. Plaintiffs reply that this fact is meaningless because at that time the market was steadily going up, and say that expert testimony will establish this. The answer to this argument is that if plaintiffs had such proof they should have come forward with it. "In such a situation, a duty is cast upon the plaintiff to disclose evidence which will demonstrate the existence of a genuine issue of fact * * * if summary judgment * * * is to be denied." Frank C. Sparks Co. v. Huber Baking Co., 9 Terry 9, 48 Del. 9, 96 A.2d 456, 459.

There are other facts in this case that support the conclusion above indicated. The sole corporate purpose of Mission is and has been to hold Tidewater stock. Any investor in its shares could readily ascertain this fact. Because of this he knows, or should know, that he is buying for growth and not for income.

Some point is made of the exclusion of Mission from the exchange offers made by Tidewater to its stockholders in 1954 and 1960. Obviously, for Mission Development to have been included in the exchange would have defeated the very purpose of its corporate existence.

However the various arguments are put they come to this: Plaintiffs are in effect seeking to wind up the corporation, either wholly or partially, because it is doing exactly what it was lawfully organized to do.

We think the plaintiffs have failed to make a case.

The judgment below is affirmed.

———————

QUESTIONS

1. One of the requests for relief of the plaintiffs was for Mission to distribute part of the Tidewater shares in exchange for Mission shares. Both Mission and Tidewater were listed on the New York Stock Exchange. How would this relief have benefitted the plaintiffs?

2. If you represented the defendants, what argument could you make from finance in response to plaintiff's claim that the Tidewater divi-

dends were eliminated to depress the market value of Mission shares, and thus to allow Getty to buy more Mission shares at a depressed price?

3. The court concedes that the interests of minority and majority shareholders may conflict because of high tax rates, and that in some cases this may work a hardship on the minority. Would you expect this to be a problem in a large publicly traded corporation? Why or why not?

4. The court notes that Tidewater had business reasons for ceasing dividend payments and reinvesting its profits in new plant. Would the same reason work if Mr. Getty had caused Mission to do the same? The author recalls a case where the majority shareholder, a similarly wealthy individual, was asked on deposition why he wanted to gain control of another corporation, and he responded by citing the provisions of the Internal Revenue Code that impose a penalty on accumulated corporate earnings for which there is no corporate use.

5. Misson's stock price did not fall in reaction to the announcement of the dividend cut. The plaintiff attributes this to a generally rising stock market. Does CAPM suggest a more refined way to examine the effect of the announcement?

NOTE

Many readers will recall Dodge v. Ford Motor Co., 204 Mich. 459, 170 N.W. 668 (1919), where Henry Ford, as controlling shareholder, caused the company drastically to reduce dividend payments in the face of efforts by the Dodge brothers, 10% shareholders, to start their own automobile company. Henry Ford testified that he thought profits were too large, and that he wanted to reduce car prices and increase sales to employ more workers. While the court rejected Ford's "charitable" justifications for the company's decisions, it declined to interfere with investments in an expanded plant, saying:

> "We are not, however, persuaded that we should interfere with the proposed expansion of the business of the Ford Motor Company. In view of the fact that the selling price of products may be increased at any time, the ultimate results of the larger business cannot be certainly estimated. The judges are not business experts. It is recognized that plans must often be made for a long future, for expected competition, for a continuing as well as an immediately profitable venture. The experience of the Ford Motor Company is evidence of capable management of its affairs...."

The court did order Ford to declare a dividend of surplus funds for which it had no planned use, however.

A more recent example of board discretion is Gabelli & Co. Profit Sharing Plan v. Liggett Group, Inc., 479 A.2d 276 (Del. 1984). Gabelli, a stockholder in Liggett, sued because the Liggett board declined to pay its regular quarterly dividend on its common stock after it had agreed to be acquired by Grand Metropolitan Limited. Grand Met completed a tender offer that obtained 87% of Liggett's common stock, and then prepared for a cash-out merger at the same price. The Chancery Court granted summary judgment for the defendant directors and was affirmed on appeal. The Supreme Court found no fraud or gross abuse of discretion, which it stated must be shown before the courts would interfere with a dividend decision. The court found two justifications for the failure to declare this dividend:

> On the record before us, the non-payment of a final dividend by the Liggett Board in the final stages of the cash-out merger, is reasonably "explicable" ... for at least 2 reasons: (1) It would have been unfair to the holders of 87% of the stock who accepted the tender offer upon the recommendation of the Board, to reward by a "farewell" or "bonus" dividend the holders of the remaining 13% who, for some unannounced reason, declined to accept the tender offer and held out for the merger cash-out with the risk-free assurance of receiving the same price per share; and (2) It would have been unreasonable to supplement the $69 per share, which had been approved by the Board as a fair price for Liggett and all of its assets, by a last minute dividend declared in the final stages of the merger cash-out process.

Some readers will also recall Sinclair Oil Corp. v. Levien, 280 A.2d 717 (Del. 1971), where a minority shareholder in a subsidiary of Sinclair's complained that the corporation was paying out excessive dividends, rather than causing the subsidiary to invest in new opportunities. He complained that Sinclair was causing the subsidiary to pay these dividends because of Sinclair's need for funds for its investments—a conflict similar to that in Berwald. Once again, the top marginal individual tax rate was 90%, and Sinclair, as owner of more than 80% of the subsidiary's stock, received a deduction for 100% of the dividends received (facts not discussed in the opinion). Recall that the court dismissed the dividend claim since all shareholders were treated alike—it was not important that the impact of receipt of dividends on them was quite different. Is this a good rule?

Decisions in the area of close corporations vary somewhat from this deferential rule. Many cases involve the same response as the cases above. Gottfried v. Gottfried, 73 N.Y.S.2d 692 (N.Y.Sup. 1947) involved the typical falling out between brothers, with one brother's employment terminated while the other held control. The controlling family members continued to draw salaries and, in one case, receive a share of the profits of a major subsidiary as compensation, and received loans from the corporation. Other funds were spent on expansion, and the court could not conclude that the failure to pay dividends, or to pay modest dividends, was in bad faith, and denied relief. In other cases courts have held that they lacked power to order payment of a dividend, and have held that the only remedy for oppressive conduct by a majority was dissolution or appointment of a receiver. White v. Perkins, 213 Va. 129, 189 S.E.2d 315 (1972).

Some courts have been willing to order the payment of dividends. See Miller v. Magline, Inc., 76 Mich. App. 284, 256 N.W.2d 761 (1977). Two of the three officers and directors left full-time employment with the company, and thereafter received neither salaries nor dividends, while the remaining officer-director took larger and larger compensation as the corporation prospered over the next six years. Earned surplus grew to over $2.5 million. The court ordered dividend payments for the most recent five years. Citing Dodge v. Ford Motor Co., 204 Mich. 459, 170 N.W. 668 (1919), the court noted that the controlling officer-director was taking a share of profits as compensation, while denying the other shareholders any part of the profits, and characterized it as "inequitable in not giving consideration properly to the needs and requirements of all of the stockholders of the corporation." The court rejected the defendant's arguments that a dividend was inappropriate because the company had a working capital shortage, had outmoded equipment that needed replacement, and was in a cyclical business. The controlling officer-director had not cut back his own compensation because of these concerns. To the same effect is Cole Real Estate Corp. v. Peoples Bank & Trust Co., 160 Ind. App. 88, 310 N.E.2d 275 (1974), except in this case the court took a more traditional approach in authorizing either dissolution or a mandatory buyout.

The most highly publicized dispute over non-payment of dividends in the past few decades did not reach the courts, but generated an attempt at a takeover of the company. Chrysler Corporation had come perilously close to bankruptcy in the late 1970s, due to a series of unsuccessful models. Under the new leadership of Lee Iacocca, Chrysler restructured its debt and obtained government guarantees for this new debt. Iacocca led a successful revival of Chrysler in the 1980s, so that by the 1990s the company was once again solvent. Iacocca was succeeded as Chrysler CEO in 1992 by Robert Eaton, who was hired from General Motors. Financier Kirk Kerkorian began accumulating Chrysler stock in 1990, and increased his holdings to nearly 10% by 1994. As profits increased, Chrysler had increased its dividends only modestly, retaining most of its earnings. Chrysler's management explained that it needed to retain cash because it was in a cyclical business, where large profits could be followed by equally large losses, but the need to introduce new models continued. One suspects that this buildup of cash was in part a residue of its previous financial crisis, and that Chrysler management was uncertain about its ability to go to the capital markets for funding during hard times. By the end of 1994 Chrysler projected that its cash reserves would be $7.5 billion, and $11.5 billion by the end of 1996. At the same time, Chrysler's stock fell from $63.50 in January 1994 to $45 by mid-November of that year. Kerkorian (now allied with the retired Iacocca) urged Chrysler increase its dividends and engage in large stock repurchases to return cash to shareholders. At the same time he urged the board to eliminate Chrysler's poison pill so he could acquire more than 15% of its stock and force a change in management. In December of 1994 Chrysler raised its dividend and announced a $1 billion stock buy-back program, which was completed in 1995. In 1995 Kerkorian, still unsatisfied, launched a $20 billion hostile takeover attempt, which aborted over doubts about his ability to finance the transaction. During this period Chrysler's stock rose as high as $52.50 on the first announcement of the initial offer, and fell to $44 after the second bid and the announcement of a possible proxy fight. In response, Chrysler raised its dividend again, from $1.20 to $2.00 per share. Following this he raised his stake from 9.2% to 13.6% through a $700 million dollar tender offer, and threatened a proxy fight for control. In September 1995 the Chrysler board doubled the size of its stock buy-back program to $2 billion. Ultimately, in the course of this battle Chrysler raised its dividend five times, and ultimately entered into a settlement with Kerkorian in which he agreed to keep his holdings below 13.7% and Chrysler agreed to an additional share repurchase program and placement of a Kerkorian representative on the board.

Smith v. Atlantic Properties, Inc.

12 Mass. App. Ct. 201, 422 N.E.2d 798 (1981).

■ CUTTER, JUSTICE.

In December, 1951, Dr. Louis E. Wolfson agreed to purchase land in Norwood for $350,000, with an initial cash payment of $50,000 and a mortgage note of $300,000 payable in thirty-three months. Dr. Wolfson offered a quarter interest each in the land to Mr. Paul T. Smith, Mr. Abraham Zimble, and William H. Burke. Each paid to Dr. Wolfson $12,500, one quarter of the initial payment. Mr. Smith, an attorney, organized the defendant corporation (Atlantic) in 1951 to operate the real estate. Each of the four subscribers received twenty-five shares of stock. Mr. Smith included, both in the corporation's articles of organization and in its by-laws, a provision reading, "No election, appointment or resolution by the Stockholders and no election, appointment, resolution, purchase, sale, lease, contract, contribution, compensation, proceeding or act by the Board of Directors or by any officer or officers shall be valid or binding upon the corporation until effected, passed, approved or ratified by an affirmative vote of eighty (80%) per cent of the capital stock issued outstanding and entitled to vote." This provision (hereafter referred to as the 80% provision) was included at Dr. Wolfson's request and had the effect of giving to any one of the four original shareholders a veto in corporate decisions.

Atlantic purchased the Norwood land. Some of the land and other assets were sold for about $220,000. Atlantic retained twenty-eight acres on which stood about twenty old brick or wood mill-type structures, which required expensive and constant repairs. After the first year, Atlantic became profitable and showed a profit every year prior to 1969, ranging from a low of $7,683 in 1953 to a high of $44,358 in 1954. The mortgage was paid by 1958 and Atlantic has incurred no long-term debt thereafter. Salaries of about $25,000 were paid only in 1959 and 1960. Dividends in the total amount of $10,000 each were paid in 1964 and 1970. By 1961, Atlantic had about $172,000 in retained earnings, more than half in cash.

For various reasons, which need not be stated in detail, disagreements and ill will soon arose between Dr. Wolfson, on the one hand, and the other stockholders as a group.[3] Dr. Wolfson wished to see Atlantic's earnings

---

3. At least one cause of ill will on Dr. Wolfson's part may have been the refusal of the other shareholders to consent to his transferring his shares in Atlantic to the Louis E. Wolfson Foundation, a charitable foundation created by Dr. Wolfson.

devoted to repairs and possibly some improvements in its existing buildings and adjacent facilities. The other stockholders desired the declaration of dividends. Dr. Wolfson fairly steadily refused to vote for any dividends. Although it was pointed out to him that failure to declare dividends might result in the imposition by the Internal Revenue Service of a penalty under the Internal Revenue Code, I.R.C. § 531 et seq. (relating to unreasonable accumulation of corporate earnings and profits), Dr. Wolfson persisted in his refusal to declare dividends. The other shareholders did agree over the years to making at least the most urgent repairs to Atlantic's buildings, but did not agree to make all repairs and improvements which were recommended in a 1962 report by an engineering firm retained by Atlantic to make a complete estimate of all repairs and improvements which might be beneficial.

The fears of an Internal Revenue Service assessment of a penalty tax were soon realized. Penalty assessments were made in 1962, 1963, and 1964. These were settled by Dr. Wolfson for $11,767.71 in taxes and interest. Despite this settlement, Dr. Wolfson continued his opposition to declaring dividends. The record does not indicate that he developed any specific and definitive schedule or plan for a series of necessary or desirable repairs and improvements to Atlantic's properties. At least none was proposed which would have had a reasonable chance of satisfying the Internal Revenue Service that expenditures for such repairs and improvements constituted "reasonable needs of the business," I.R.C. § 534(c), a term which includes (see I.R.C. § 537) "the reasonably anticipated needs of the business." Predictably, despite further warnings by Dr. Wolfson's shareholder colleagues, the Internal Revenue Service assessed further penalty taxes for the years 1965, 1966, 1967, and 1968. * * * An examination of these decisions makes it apparent that Atlantic has incurred substantial penalty taxes and legal expense largely because of Dr. Wolfson's refusal to vote for the declaration of sufficient dividends to avoid the penalty, a refusal which was (in the Tax Court and upon appeal) attributed in some measure to a tax avoidance purpose on Dr. Wolfson's part.

On January 30, 1967, the shareholders, other than Dr. Wolfson, initiated this proceeding in the Superior Court, later supplemented to reflect developments after the original complaint. The plaintiffs sought a court determination of the dividends to be paid by Atlantic, the removal of Dr. Wolfson as a director, and an order that Atlantic be reimbursed by him for the penalty taxes assessed against it and related expenses. * * *

The trial judge made findings (but in more detail) of essentially the facts outlined above and concluded that Dr. "Wolfson's obstinate refusal to vote in favor of ... dividends was ... caused more by his dislike for other stockholders and his desire to avoid additional tax payments than ... by any genuine desire to undertake a program for improving ... [Atlantic] property." She also determined that Dr. Wolfson was liable to Atlantic for taxes and interest.... She also ordered the directors of Atlantic to declare "a reasonable dividend at the earliest practical date and reasonable dividends annually thereafter consistent with good business practice." In addition, the trial judge directed that jurisdiction of the case be retained in the Superior Court "for a period of five years to [e]nsure compliance." Judgment was entered pursuant to the trial judge's order. * * *

1.   The trial judge, in deciding that Dr. Wolfson had committed a breach of his fiduciary duty to other stockholders, relied greatly on broad language in Donahue v. Rodd Electrotype Co., 367 Mass. 578, 586–597 (1975), in which the Supreme Judicial Court afforded to a minority stockholder in a close corporation equality of treatment (with members of a controlling group of shareholders) in the matter of the redemption of shares. The court relied on the resemblance of a close corporation to a partnership and held that "stockholders in the close corporation owe one another substantially the same fiduciary duty in the operation of the enterprise that partners owe to one another" (footnotes omitted). That standard of duty, the court said, was the "utmost good faith and loyalty." The court went on to say that such stockholders "may not act out of avarice, expediency or self-interest in derogation of their duty of loyalty to the other stockholders and to the corporation." Similar principles were stated in Wilkes v. Springside Nursing Home, Inc., 370 Mass. 842, 848–852 (1976), but with some modifications, mentioned in the margin,[5] of the sweeping language of the Donahue case.

In the Donahue case the court recognized that cases may arise in which, in a close corporation, majority stockholders may ask protection from a minority stockholder. Such an instance arises in the present case because Dr. Wolfson has been able to exercise a veto concerning corporate action on dividends by the 80% provision (in Atlantic's articles of organization and by-laws) already quoted. The 80% provision may have substantially the effect of reversing the usual roles of the majority and the minority shareholders. The minority, under that provision, becomes an ad hoc controlling interest.

* * * In the present case, Dr. Wolfson testified that he requested the inclusion of the 80% provision "in case the people [the other shareholders] whom I knew, but not very well, ganged up on me." The possibilities of shareholder disagreement on policy made the provision seem a sensible precaution. A question is presented, however, concerning the extent to

---

5.   The court said (at 850–852) that it was "concerned that [the] untempered application of the strict good faith standard . . . will result in the imposition of limitations on legitimate action by the controlling group in a close corporation which will unduly hamper its effectiveness. . . . The majority . . . have certain rights to what has been termed 'selfish ownership' in the corporation which should be balanced against the concept of their fiduciary obligation to the minority. . . . [W]hen minority stockholders . . . bring suit . . . alleging a breach of the strict good faith duty . . . we must carefully analyze the action taken by the controlling stockholders in the individual case. It must be asked whether the controlling group can demonstrate a legitimate business purpose for its action. . . . [T]he controlling group in a close corporation must have some room to maneuver in establishing the business policy of the corporation. It must have a large measure of discretion, for example, in declaring or withholding dividends" (emphasis supplied) and in certain other matters. "When an asserted business purpose . . . is advanced by the majority, however, . . . it is open to minority stockholders to demonstrate that the . . . objective could have been achieved through an alternative course . . . less harmful to the minority's interest."

which such a veto power possessed by a minority stockholder may be exercised as its holder may wish, without a violation of the "fiduciary duty" referred to in the Donahue case, 367 Mass. at 593, as modified in the Wilkes case.

The decided cases in Massachusetts do little to answer this question. The most pertinent guidance is probably found in the Wilkes case, 370 Mass. at 849–852 (see note 5, supra), essentially to the effect that in any judicial intervention in such a situation there must be a weighing of the business interests advanced as reasons for their action (a) by the majority or controlling group and (b) by the rival persons or group. It would obviously be appropriate, before a court-ordered solution is sought or imposed, for both sides to attempt to reach a sensible solution of any incipient impasse in the interests of all concerned after consideration of all relevant circumstances.

2. With respect to the past damage to Atlantic caused by Dr. Wolfson's refusal to vote in favor of any dividends, the trial judge was justified in finding that his conduct went beyond what was reasonable. The other stockholders shared to some extent responsibility for what occurred by failing to accept Dr. Wolfson's proposals with much sympathy, but the inaction on dividends seems the principal cause of the tax penalties. Dr. Wolfson had been warned of the dangers of an assessment under the Internal Revenue Code, I.R.C. § 531 et seq. He had refused to vote dividends in any amount adequate to minimize that danger and had failed to bring forward, within the relevant taxable years, a convincing, definitive program of appropriate improvements which could withstand scrutiny by the Internal Revenue Service. Whatever may have been the reason for Dr. Wolfson's refusal to declare dividends (and even if in any particular year he may have gained slight, if any, tax advantage from withholding dividends) we think that he recklessly ran serious and unjustified risks of precisely the penalty taxes eventually assessed, risks which were inconsistent with any reasonable interpretation of a duty of "utmost good faith and loyalty." The trial judge (despite the fact that the other shareholders helped to create the voting deadlock and despite the novelty of the situation) was justified in charging Dr. Wolfson with the out-of-pocket expenditure incurred by Atlantic for the penalty taxes and related counsel fees of the tax cases.

* * *

5. The judgment is affirmed so far as it (par. 1) orders payments into Atlantic's treasury by Dr. Wolfson. * * *

So ordered.

QUESTIONS

1. Why would Dr. Wolfson oppose receiving dividends? How might his interests vary from those of the other shareholders?

2. Who is the "cause" of the corporation's tax penalties? Think about the application of the Coase Theorem to this problem.

3.　Should it make a difference that the parties had bargained for the minority veto over the decisions involved here?

4.　If two of the other shareholders were attorneys and understood that Dr. Wolfson was a high-bracket taxpayer who might prefer capital gains on the sale of his stock to dividends, what grounds for complaint do they have when Dr. Wolfson did his best to avoid paying dividends?

5.　The court states that the business interests advanced by each group should be weighed. Is this a departure from the Business Judgment Rule? In view of Dr. Wolfson's "obstinance" in ignoring tax advice, is any departure required to reach the result in this case?

4.　Stock Dividends and Stock Splits

A.　The Economics of Stock Dividends and Stock Splits

Cash dividends are easy enough to understand. A company has more cash than it has good investment opportunities. But sometimes companies declare stock dividends, which simply distribute more stock certificates *pro rata* among existing shareholders. Necessarily, the market value of each share must decline in proportion to the percentage of new shares issued. Nothing on the company's balance sheet has changed except the number of shares outstanding—shareholders' equity remains the same. And each shareholder has the same proportion of equity as before. Corporate statutes generally don't concern themselves much with stock dividends—they aren't "distributions" under the Model Act, and thus aren't subject to the restrictions on distributions.

The obvious question about a stock dividend is "why bother?" But there is another situation that raises the same question—stock splits. A split involves subdividing the existing shares. A two-for-one stock split involves issuing one new share for each outstanding share. The effect is exactly the same as that of a 100% stock dividend—the market price of the stock should decline by one-half. The 1984 version of the Model Act eliminated any references to stock splits, and simply provides stock dividends as the sole means of issuing new shares pro rata to shareholders, in M.B.C.A. § 6.23. Stock splits can still be accomplished through amendments of the articles of incorporation, and the M.B.C.A. § 10.05(4) permits stock splits by board action alone, even though this requires an amendment of the articles of incorporation. From a corporate law perspective, this isn't a significant change requiring a shareholder vote. Again, with respect to stock splits, the question is "why bother?"

A stock dividend or stock split may be a way of announcing a permanent increase in dividend payments. If the dividend rate per share remains unchanged, a 10% stock dividend is effectively a 10% increase in cash dividends. But it would be just as easy to raise the cash dividend by 10%, wouldn't it? One important study (indeed the seminal article on event study methodology) looked at the cumulative abnormal returns to stocks at the time of stock splits. They found substantial positive returns (33%) in the 30 months leading up to a stock split, and none after the date of the split. Gains continued after the announcement, which generally would be a month or two before the actual split date. Eugene F. Fama, Michael Jensen and Richard Roll, The Adjustment of Stock Prices to New Information, 10 International Economic Review 1 (1969). This suggests that the decision to split the stock was a product of the price rise, and that once announced it caused a further rise. One explanation given for this is that splits signal future dividend increases, even though the dividend increases weren't announced at the time of the stock split. Mason and Shalor, Stock Splits: An Institutional Investor Preference, 33 Finance Review 33 (1998) finds that institutional investors are attracted to stocks that are about to split. Lakonishok and Lev, Stock Splits and Stock Dividends: Why, Who and When, 42 Journal of Finance 913 (1987), find that stock dividend announcements are followed by large cash dividend increases.

One explanation given for the use of these devices is premised on the idea that there is a "popular price range" for trading stocks. When a stock's price rises too far above this level, some companies become concerned that many investors may be reluctant to buy a "round lot" of 100 shares, the most common trading unit. (Brokerage commissions on odd-lots, less than 100 shares, are higher.) Keeping stocks in the popular price range may assure greater "retail" ownership of the stock by individual investors. Keeping more investors interested in a stock produces greater liquidity, and thus greater value, the story goes. There is support for this story. See Lamoureux and Poon, The Market Reaction to Stock Splits, 42 Journal of Finance 1347 (1987) (finding that the number of shareholders increases after a split) and Lakonishok and Lev, *supra* (finding that stocks that split have been priced above control firms). But the counter-story is that this really doesn't matter: more and more stocks are held by institutional investors, who usually buy far more than 100 shares at a time, and don't worry about odd lots. Would managers care whether their shares are held by individuals or institutions? They might. Individual investors tend to be more passive as voting stockholders than some institutions, which have become relatively active participants in corporate governance in recent years.

One author suggests that stock splits (and implicitly, stock dividends) raise several costs for investors. Thus brokerage fees tend to be a higher percentage of value for lower-priced stocks; some trading costs are relatively fixed, and don't go down with the price of the stock. Similarly, in over-the-counter stocks, the bid-ask spread may rise as a percentage of the value of the stock. Thus, if a dealer offers to buy a stock for $49.50 and to sell the same stock for $50.00, the spread is $0.50. But if the dealer offers to buy a stock for $9.50 and sell it for $10.00, the $0.50 spread is a much greater percentage of value. T. Copeland, Liquidity Changes Following Stock Splits, 34 Journal of Finance 115 (1979).

B. ACCOUNTING FOR DIVIDENDS AND SPLITS

Accounting principles require the assignment of some amount of the consideration paid for shares to a permanent capital account, typically called "paid in capital." This is the price paid for the shares. What is "paid" for shares issued as a stock dividend? In one sense, nothing is paid, since shareholders transfer no new value to the corporation. But in another and very real sense, shareholders pay with an opportunity. They surrender the previous market value of their shares in exchange for a larger number of shares, albeit with a reduced market value per share. As a result, GAAP requires the corporation to transfer from surplus accounts (retained earnings) to paid-in capital accounts an amount equal to the value of the newly issued shares. Accounting Research Bulletin No. 43. The remaining question is how to measure the value represented by the stock dividend. One measure would be the pre-dividend market value of the shares, while the competing measure would be the diluted post-dividend market value. In a relatively small stock dividend, the difference between these numbers will be relatively small, and the corporation may use the pre-dividend value of the shares. This is the procedure to be used for stock dividends of no more than 20–25%. (And you thought accounting was precise? Remember these are principles, not rules.)

Once the size of the stock dividend reaches the 20–25% range, accountants are required to wear glasses to reduce their myopia about the effect of a stock dividend on market value. But this is where accounting departs from economic reality. The larger the dividend, the greater the dilution of market value per share. Under these circumstances, the value of the stock dividend, measured post-dividend, will decline substantially. For example, assume a hypothetical corporation with one million shares outstanding, with a market value of $100 each, that declared a stock dividend of 30%, or another 300,000 shares. The issuance of new shares means a reallocation of the shareholders' equity accounts. Some amount must be moved from surplus accounts into the permanent capital account to reflect these shares. If we used post-dividend market value, we would now have a corporation with a shareholders' equity of $100 million, with 1.3 million shares outstanding. Under these circumstances, the per share value is calculated as:

$$\frac{\$100,000,000}{1,300,000} = \$76.92$$

Using the diluted value of the shares post-dividend, the value of the dividend is $76.92 × 300,000 = $23,076,923.* If we had used pre-dividend values, the dividend would have been $100 × 300,000 = $30,000,000. But accounting principles employ neither of these numbers. Instead, they require a transfer from retained earnings of the par value of the shares or the amount required by corporate law to be transferred. In the case of no-par shares, this will be the pro rata share of paid-in capital. If par value is $1.00 per share, the amount transferred from retained earnings will be $300,000. Delaware G.C.L. § 173 also requires this amount to be trans-

---

* Obviously the post-dividend number is an arbitrary assumption that stock dividends create no new value. To the extent that value is added, this assumption isn't entirely realistic. But absent perfect information about how markets will react to any particular stock dividend announcement, this assumption is not unreasonable.

ferred. The Model Act is silent, leaving this to the accountants. Where no-par shares are involved, Del. G.C.L. § 173 requires transfer of "such amount as shall be determined by the board of directors."

No matter what method is employed, shareholders' equity remains unchanged. Only the allocation between paid-in capital and retained earnings will change. Total firm value would remain unchanged; each shareholder's wealth would also remain unchanged. The only difference before and after is a transfer of some funds from the Retained Earnings account to the Paid-in Capital account.

In all cases, whether a dividend or split, shareholders receive more pieces of paper representing ownership of the same firm assets. In the case of dividends, this only requires directors' approval. In the case of stock splits, an amendment of the charter is required. In Delaware, § 242 requires a stockholder vote for such an amendment. In Model Act states, the procedure is not treated as seriously, for reasons previously mentioned:

§ 10.05 Amendment by Board of Directors

Unless the articles of incorporation provide otherwise, a corporation's board of directors may adopt amendments to the corporation's articles of incorporation without shareholder approval:

* * *

(4) if the corporation has only one class of shares outstanding:

(a) to change each issued and unissued share of the class into a greater or lesser number of whole shares of that class; or

(b) to increase the number of authorized shares of the class to the extent necessary to permit the issuance of shares as a share dividend; . . . .

M.B.C.A. § 6.23(a) permits the board to issue shares as a dividend:

§ 6.23 Share Dividends

(a) Unless the articles of incorporation provide otherwise, shares may be issued pro rata and without consideration to the corporation's shareholders or to the shareholders of one or more classes or series. An issuance of shares under this subsection is a share dividend.

Because there are no legal capital rules, the board has authority to do this without restriction, unless the articles of incorporation so provide. And because there are no legal capital rules in the M.B.C.A., no surplus has to be allocated to par value (stated capital). Thus large numbers of shares can be issued as a dividend, equivalent to a stock split under the M.B.C.A., without a shareholder vote (if there are enough authorized but unissued shares).

Delaware law still takes legal capital seriously. Del. G.C.L. § 173 provides that dividends may be paid in cash, property or shares of the corporation's stock. If they are paid in authorized but unissued stock, the board shall designate as capital an amount at least equal to the par value of the shares being dividended (presumably from surplus):

§ 173. Declaration and Payment of Dividends

No corporation shall pay dividends except in accordance with this chapter. Dividends may be paid in cash, in property, or in shares of the corporation's capital stock. If the dividend is to be paid in shares of the corporation's theretofore unissued capital stock the board of directors shall, by resolution, direct that there be issued as capital in respect of such shares an amount which is not less than the aggregate par value of par value being declared as a dividend and, in the case of shares without par value shares being declared as a dividend, such amount as shall be determined by the board of directors. No such designation of capital shall be necessary if shares are being distributed by a corporation pursuant to a split-up or division of its stock rather than as a payment of a dividend declared payable in stock of the corporation.

A stock split, which changes the number of shares, requires a shareholder vote to amend the certificate of incorporation under Del. GCL § 242(a):

§ 242 Amendment of Certificate of Incorporation After Receipt of Payment for Stock; Non–Stock Corporation

(a) After a corporation has received payment for any of its capital stock, it may amend its certificate of incorporation, from time to time, in any and as many respects as may be desired, so long as its certificate of incorporation as amended would contain only such provisions at it would be lawful and proper to insert in an original certificate of incorporation filed at the time of the filing of the amendment; and if a change in stock or the rights of stockholders, or an exchange, reclassification, subdivision, combination or cancellation of stock or rights of stockholders is to be made, such provisions as may be necessary to effect such change, exchange, reclassification, subdivision, combination or cancellation. In particular, and without limitation upon such general power of amendment, a corporation may amend its certificate of incorporation, from time to time, so as to:

* * *

(3) To increase or decrease its authorized capital stock or to reclassify the same, by changing the number, par value, designations, preferences, or relative, participating, optional, or other special rights of the shares. . . .

The principal concern with stock dividends is deception—fear that shareholders will either believe that a stock dividend somehow represents a distribution of profits or believe that a stock split is a sign of good things to come. The rules come from several sources. NYSE Listed Company Manual § 703.02 provides general guidance about stock splits, and attempts to provide a distinction between stock splits and stock dividends:

703.02 (part 1) Stock Split/Stock Rights/Stock Dividend Listing Process

(A) Introduction

Stock Splits—There are many factors which a company must consider in evaluating the merits of splitting its stock. Studies by the Exchange indicate that a properly timed stock split can contribute to an increase in and broadening of the shareholder base and can also be an important means of improving market liquidity. Generally speaking, a properly timed stock split, when effected under appropriate circumstances, serves as an excellent means of generating greater investor interest. Postsplit price is also an important consideration, especially when a company is competing in the financial marketplace for investor attention with other high quality securities.

Exchange statistics indicate a preferential price range within which a significant percentage of Exchange round-lot volume is generated. This preference tends to be strongly reinforced when demand for a particular security is supported by a strong corporate image, widely recognized product lines, a strong financial picture and a good dividend history.

Furthermore, a stock split can present an opportunity for long-term holders to consider the possibility of selling a portion of their position. This could have the effect of creating additional round-lot holders and thereby act as an aid in obtaining additional liquidity, thus assisting in broadening the floating supply of the stock.

A stock split also acts as a means of converting odd-lot holders into round-lot holders. It is the round-lot holder that plays a very important role in a stock's marketability and liquidity on the Exchange.

Today, liquidity is probably the most important element in the investment decision, other than the financial condition or suitability of the security under consideration. Optimum liquidity is measured by the relative ease and promptness with which a security may be traded with a minimum price change from the previous transaction. Accordingly, a further objective of a stock split is to lower the market price sufficiently in order to broaden marketability.

Consideration of a stock split is therefore justified when a company's shares are selling at a relatively high price, and when such action is accompanied by healthy operating results and a strong financial condition. When these factors are further supported by anticipated growth as evidenced by a steady increase in earnings, dividends, book value and revenue, a strong foundation is in place for a stock split decision.

While not having any fixed formula for determination of the appropriate ratio for a stock split, the Exchange is of the view that a stock split in a ratio of less than two shares for one (i.e., one additional share for each share outstanding), is not likely to achieve, to a satisfactory degree, the constructive purposes of a stock split. Experience has shown that frequently, when a stock split in a lesser proportion has been effected, the company has felt it necessary to follow it up with a further small stock split within a relatively short period in order to obtain the desired result. Adjustments of that nature, following each other too closely, may have effects upon the market not consistent with the best interests of the company, of its shareholders, or those of the general investing public.

As it appears to the Exchange, a stock split should be effected on a basis designed to produce, in one step, and to the full extent deemed beneficial, the adjustments of price and distribution indicated by current and anticipated conditions. If those conditions do not indicate clearly that a stock split of at least two-for-one proportion is warranted, it is questionable whether they warrant any stock split at all.

Furthermore, recurring stock splits in a ratio less than two-for-one may give rise to the question of whether such stock splits are not, in effect, periodic stock dividends to which the accounting requirement and other phases of the Exchange's stock dividend policy apply.

Preliminary Discussion Suggested—

Any company contemplating a stock split should discuss the matter with the company's Exchange representative before taking definitive action.

A preliminary discussion would be mutually helpful not only in clarifying matters of policy, but in arranging a schedule which will ensure the necessary coordination of the different actions to be taken by both the company and the Exchange. Such discussion will not result in premature disclosure of the company's plans.

Stock Dividends—

Many listed companies find it preferable at times to pay dividends in stock rather than cash, particularly in those cases in which a substantial part of earnings is retained by the company for use in its business. In order to guard against possible misconception by the shareowners of the effect of stock dividends on their equity in the company, and of their relation to current earnings, the Exchange has adopted certain standards of disclosure and accounting treatment.

Distinction between a Stock Dividend, a Partial Stock Split, and a Stock Split in Exchange Policy:

Stock Dividend—A distribution of less than 25% of the outstanding shares (as calculated prior to the distribution).

Partial Stock Split—A distribution of 25% or more but less than 100% of the outstanding shares (as calculated prior to the distribution).

Stock Split—A distribution of 100% or more of the outstanding shares (as calculated prior to the distribution).

Accounting Treatment—

In accordance with generally accepted accounting principles, the following accounting treatment is required for the various distributions:

Stock Dividend—Capitalize retained earnings for the fair market value of the additional shares to be issued. Fair market value should closely approximate the current share market price adjusted to give effect to the distribution.

Partial Stock Split—Requires capitalization of paid-in capital (surplus) for the par or stated value of the shares issued only where there is to be no change in the par or stated value. In those circumstances where the distributions of small stock splits assume the character of stock dividends through repetition of issuance under circumstances not consistent with the intent and purpose of stock splits, the Exchange may require that such distributions be accounted for as stock dividends, i.e., capitalization of retained earnings

Stock Split—Requires transfer from paid-in capital (surplus) for the par or stated value of the shares issued unless there is to be a change in the par or stated value.

Avoidance of the Word "Dividend"—

A stock split is frequently effected by means of a distribution to shareholders upon the same authority, and in the same manner as a stock dividend. However, in order to preserve the distinction between a stock split and a stock dividend, the use of the word "dividend" should be avoided in any reference to a stock split when such a distribution does not result in the capitalization of retained earnings of the fair market value of the shares distributed. Such usage may otherwise tend to obscure the real nature of the distribution. Where legal considerations require the use of the word "dividend", the distribution should be described, for example, as a "stock split effected in the form of a stock dividend."

Notice to Shareholders with Stock Dividend Distribution—

A notice should be sent to shareholders with the distribution advising them of the amount capitalized in the aggregate and per share, the relation of such aggregate amount to current earnings and retained earnings, the account or accounts to which such aggregate has been charged and credited, the reason for issuance of the stock dividend, and that sale of the dividend shares would reduce their proportionate equity in the company.

———————

In 1968 the SEC proposed Rule10b–12, which would have codified the NYSE's approach. It would have made it fraudulent under Section 10(b) to declare a stock dividend without capitalizing surplus equal to the fair market value. In the case of partial splits, the same rule would have applied, unless the issuer could show that the partial split wasn't part of a program of recurring pro rata distributions (thus designed to look like dividends). The rule was never adopted. Given what you know about modern understandings of securities markets, can you provide an explanation? Accounting Research Bulletin No. 43 takes the same approach as the NYSE.

American Stock Exchange Company Guide contains the following:

§ 505 Stock Dividends or Forward Splits of Lower Priced Issues

The Exchange does not view favorably a stock dividend or forward split of a stock selling in a low price range or a substantial stock dividend or forward split which may result in an abnormally low price range for shares after the split or stock dividend. Any company considering a forward split (or a stock dividend of more than 5%) which would result in an adjusted price of less than $3 per share for its stock should consult with the Exchange in advance of taking formal act. (See also § 970 for information regarding reverse splits.)

C. Reverse Stock Splits

Reverse stock splits are barely mentioned in standard finance texts. (Note the reference to "forward" splits in the AMEX Company Guide quoted above.) In a reverse stock split, the number of issued and outstanding shares is reduced, as in a one-for-three reverse split, where one new share is issued for every three shares outstanding.

There are a number of rules that disfavor low-priced shares, that can be overcome through reverse stock splits. For example, if a share's average trading price drops below $1.00 on NYSE or if the averge minimum bid on NASDAQ is below $1.00, NYSE Listed Company Manual ¶ 802.01C and NASD Manual Rule 4310(c)(2)(b) provide that this is a ground for delisting. The American Stock Exchange Rule is both more general and more educational. AMEX Company Guide § 1003(f)(v) provides:

(v) *Low Selling Price Issues*—In the case of a common stock selling for a substantial period of time at a low price per share, if the issuer shall fail to effect a reverse split of such shares within a reasonable time after being notified that the Exchange deems such action to be appropriate under all the circumstances. In its review of the question of whether it deems a reverse split of a given issue to be appropriate, the Exchange will consider all pertinent factors including, market conditions in general, the number of shares outstanding, plans which may have been formulated by management, applicable regulations of the state or country of incorporation or of any governmental agency having jurisdiction over the company, the relationship of other Exchange policies regarding continued listing, and, in respect of securities of foreign issuers, the general practice of the country of origin of trading in low-selling issues.

So-called "penny stocks" get harsher treatment from Congress and the SEC as well. Securities Exchange Act § 3(51)(A) authorizes the SEC to define a "penny stock." The SEC has adopted Exchange Act Rule 3a51–1, which defines a penny stock as any stock trading below $5.00. Section 15(g) of the Securities Exchange Act requires brokers to provide customers with warnings about the risks of penny stocks, and descriptions of dealer markets not required for other securities. Section 21E(b) excludes penny stocks from the benefits of the safe harbor created for forward-looking statements.

Some commentators mention transaction costs as a factor—that brokerage fees fall as a percentage of the trading price as stock prices rise. On the other hand, reducing the number of shares outstanding may reduce liquidity and the proportion of stock held by retail customers—individual investors. Finally, companies can reduce the cost of serving shareholders— the costs of shareholder mailings, etc., by eliminating holders of small amounts through a reverse stock split.

Applebaum v. Avaya

812 A.2d 880 (Del. 2002).

■ VEASEY, CHIEF JUSTICE:

In this appeal, we affirm the judgment of the Court of Chancery holding that a corporation could validly initiate a reverse stock split and selectively dispose of the fractional interests held by stockholders who no longer hold whole shares. The Vice Chancellor interpreted Section 155 of the Delaware General Corporation Law to permit the corporation, as part of a reverse/forward stock split, to treat its stockholders unequally by cashing out the stockholders who own only fractional interests while opting not to dispose of fractional interests of stockholders who will end up holding whole shares of stock as well as fractional interests. In the latter instance the fractional shares would be reconverted to whole shares in an accompanying forward stock split.

We hold that neither the language of Section 155 nor the principles guiding our interpretation of statutes dictate a prohibition against the disparate treatment of stockholders, for this purpose. We also hold that the corporation may dispose of those fractional interests pursuant to Section 155(1) by aggregating the fractional interests and selling them on behalf of the cashed-out stockholders where this method of disposition has a rational business purpose of saving needless transaction costs.

A further issue we address is whether, as an alternative method of compensation, the corporation may satisfy the "fair price" requirement of Section 155(2) by paying the stockholders an amount based on the average trading price of the corporation's stock. Here, the Vice Chancellor properly held that the trading price of actively-traded stock of a corporation, the stock of which is widely-held, will provide an adequate measure of fair value for the stockholders' fractional interests for purposes of a reverse stock split under Section 155.

Facts

Avaya, Inc. is a Delaware corporation that designs and manages communications networks for business organizations and large non-profit agencies. The enterprise is a descendant of the industry standard-bearer, AT & T. Avaya was established as an independent company in October of 2000 when it was spun off from Lucent Technologies. Lucent itself is a spin-off of AT & T. Because its capital structure is the product of two spin-off transactions, the outstanding stock of Avaya is one of the most widely-held on the New York Stock Exchange. Over 3.3 million common stockholders own fewer than 90 shares of Avaya stock each.

Although a large number of stockholders hold a small stake in the corporation, Avaya incurs heavy expenses to maintain their accounts. Avaya spends almost $4 million per year to print and mail proxy statements and annual reports to each stockholder as well as to pay transfer agents and other miscellaneous fees. Stockholders who own their stock in street names cost Avaya an additional $3.4 million in similar administrative fees.

Since the cost of maintaining a stockholder's account is the same regardless of the number of shares held, Avaya could reduce its administrative burden, and thereby save money for its stockholders, by decreasing its stockholder base. In February of 2002, at the corporation's annual meeting, the Avaya board of directors presented the stockholders with a transaction designed to accomplish this result. The Avaya board asked the stockholders to grant the directors authorization to engage in one of three alternative transactions:

(1) a reverse 1–for–30 stock split followed immediately by a forward 30–for–1 stock split of the Common stock

(2) a reverse 1–for–40 stock split followed immediately by a forward 40–for–1 stock split of the Common stock

(3) a reverse 1–for–50 stock split followed immediately by a forward 50–for–1 stock split of the Common stock.

We refer in this opinion to all three of these alternative transactions as the "Proposed Transaction" or the "Reverse/Forward Split." Regardless of the particular ratio the board chooses, at some future date the Reverse Split will occur at 6: 00 p. m., followed by a Forward Split one minute later. Once selected, the effective date of the Split will be posted on Avaya's website.

The transaction will cash out stockholders who own stock below the minimum number ultimately selected by the directors for the Reverse/Forward Split pursuant to those three alternative options. Stockholders who do not hold the minimum number of shares necessary to survive the initial Reverse Split will be cashed out and receive payment for their resulting fractional interests (the "cashed-out stockholders" or "targeted stockholders"). Stockholders who own a sufficient amount of stock to survive the Reverse Split will not have their fractional interests cashed out. Once the Forward Split occurs, their fractional holdings will be converted back into whole shares of stock.

Avaya will compensate the cashed-out stockholders through one of two possible methods. Avaya may combine the fractional interests and sell them as whole shares on the open market. In the alternative, the corporation will pay the stockholders the value of their fractional interests based on the trading price of the stock averaged over a ten-day period preceding the Reverse Split. * * *

To illustrate the Proposed Transaction through a hypothetical, assume Stockholder A owns fifteen shares of stock and Stockholder B owns forty-five shares of stock. If Avaya chooses to initiate a Reverse 1–for–30 Stock Split, Stockholder A will possess a fractional interest equivalent to one-half a share of stock. Stockholder B will hold one whole share of Avaya stock and a fractional interest equivalent to one-half a share. Using the provisions of Section 155(1) or (2) of the Delaware General Corporation Law,[2] Avaya would cash out Stockholder A since he no longer possesses a whole share of stock. Stockholder A would no longer be an Avaya stockholder. Stockholder B will remain a stockholder because Avaya will not cash out the fractional interest held by her. Stockholder B's fractional interest remains attached to a whole share of stock. When Avaya executes the accompanying Forward 30–for–1 Stock Split, Stockholder B's interest in one and one-half shares will be converted into forty-five shares of stock, the same amount that she held prior to the Transaction.

At the annual meeting, Avaya stockholders voted to authorize the board to proceed with any one of the three alternative transactions. Applebaum, a holder of twenty-seven shares of Avaya stock, filed an action in the Court of Chancery to enjoin the Reverse/Forward Split. Under any one of the three alternatives Applebaum would be cashed out because he holds less than thirty shares.

---

2. 8 *Del. C.* § 155 provides: Fractions of shares. A corporation may, but shall not be required to, issue fractions of a share. If it does not issue fractions of a share, it shall (1) arrange for the disposition of fractional interests by those entitled thereto, (2) pay in cash the fair value of fractions of a share as of the time when those entitled to receive such fractions are determined or (3) issue scrip or warrants in registered form (either represented by a certificate or uncertificated) or in bearer form (represented by a certificate) which shall entitle the holder to receive a full share upon the surrender of such scrip or warrants aggregating a full share. A certificate for a fractional share or an uncertificated fractional share shall, but scrip or warrants shall not unless otherwise provided therein, entitle the holder to exercise voting rights, to receive dividends thereon and to participate in any of the assets of the corporation in the event of liquidation. The board of directors may cause scrip or warrants to be issued subject to the conditions that they shall become void if not exchanged for certificates representing the full shares or uncertificated full shares before a specified date, or subject to the conditions that the shares for which scrip or warrants are exchangeable may be sold by the corporation and the proceeds thereof distributed to the holders of scrip or warrants, or subject to any other conditions which the board of directors may impose.

Proceedings in the Court of Chancery

Applebaum asked the Court of Chancery to enjoin the Proposed Transaction, alleging that Avaya's treatment of fractional interests will not comport with the requirements set forward in Title 8, Section 155 of the Delaware Code. Applebaum argued that Section 155 does not permit Avaya to issue fractional shares to some stockholders but not to others in the same transaction. Even if Avaya could issue fractional shares selectively, Applebaum contended that the methods by which Avaya plans to cash-out the smaller stockholders do not comply with subsections (1) and (2) of Section 155.

After considering cross-motions for summary judgment, the Court of Chancery denied Applebaum's request for an injunction and held that the Reverse/Forward Split would comply with Section 155 and dispose of the cashed-out stockholders' interests in a fair and efficient manner. Applebaum appeals the final judgment entered for the defendants. We affirm.

Issues on Appeal

Applebaum claims the Court of Chancery erred by: (1) holding that Title 8, Section 155 permits Avaya to issue fractional shares to the surviving stockholders but not issue fractional shares to the cashed-out stockholders; (2) holding that Avaya can combine the fractional interests and sell them on the open market; (3) holding that Avaya can instruct nominees to participate in the Split even if a particular nominee holds a sufficient amount of stock on behalf of all of its beneficial holders to survive the Split; (4) granting summary judgment and holding that the payment of cash for fractional interests based on a ten-day average of the trading price of Avaya stock constitutes "fair value" under Section 155; and (5) holding that the meaning of "fair value" in Sections 155(2) is different from Section 262 and thus failing to value the fractional shares as proportionate interests in a going concern.

Section 155 Does Not Prevent Avaya From Disposing of Fractional Interests Selectively

Applebaum questions the board's authority to treat stockholders differently by disposing of the fractional interests of some stockholders but not others. Applebaum contends that Avaya will issue fractional shares in violation of Section 155. According to this view of the transaction, during the one minute interval between the two stock splits the corporation will not issue fractional shares to stockholders who possess holdings below the minimum amount. Those stockholders will be cashed out. Stockholders who hold stock above the minimum amount, by contrast, will be issued fractional shares that will be reconverted in the Forward Split into the same number of whole shares owned by those stockholders before the Reverse Split.

Applebaum argues that Section 155 prevents Avaya from achieving this disparate result by providing that:

A corporation may, but shall not be required to, issue fractions of a share. If it does not issue fractions of a share, it shall (1) arrange for the disposition of fractional interests by those entitled thereto, (2) pay in cash the fair value of fractions of a share as of the time when those entitled to receive such fractions are determined. . . .

Applebaum reads Section 155 to mean that Avaya can employ the cash-out methods provided in Section 155 only if the corporation "does not issue fractions of a share."

This Court reviews de novo the Court of Chancery's decision to grant Avaya's motion for summary judgment. We need not reach the merits of Applebaum's interpretation of Section 155 because he has based his argument on the flawed assumption that Avaya will issue fractional shares. Since the Reverse/Forward Split is an integrated transaction, Avaya need not issue any fractional shares. The initial Reverse Split creates a combination of whole *shares* and fractional *interests*. Avaya will use either Section 155(1) or (2) to cash out the fractional interests of stockholders who no longer possess a whole share of stock. Fractional *interests* that are attached to whole *shares* will not be disposed of. Nor will they be represented by fractions of a share. Fractional shares are unnecessary because the surviving fractional interests will be reconverted into whole shares in the Forward Split.

Applebaum correctly notes that Avaya stockholders are not treated equally in the Proposed Transaction. The disparate treatment, however, does not arise by issuing fractional shares selectively. It occurs through the selective disposition of some fractional interests but not others. The provisions of Section 155 do not forbid this disparate treatment. While principles of equity permit this Court to intervene when technical compliance with a statute produces an unfair result, equity and equality are not synonymous concepts in the Delaware General Corporation Law. Moreover, this Court should not create a safeguard against stockholder inequality that does not appear in the statute.[10] Here there is no showing that Applebaum was treated inequitably. From all that appears on this record, the proposed transaction was designed in good faith to accomplish a rational business purpose-saving transaction costs.[11]

Our jurisprudence does not prevent Avaya from properly using Section 155 in a creative fashion that is designed to meet its needs as an on-going

---

10. *See, e.g., Williams v. Geier*, 671 A.2d 1368, 1385 n. 36 (Del. 1996) (noting "Directors and investors must be able to rely on the stability and absence of judicial interference with the State's statutory prescriptions"); *Nixon*, 626 A.2d at 1379–81(absent legislation there should be no "special, judicially-created rules for minority investors"); *American Hardware Corp. v. Savage Arms. Corp.*, 37 Del. Ch. 59, 136 A.2d 690, 693 (Del. 1957) (rejecting argument based on an interpretation that would "import serious confusion and uncertainty into corporate procedure").

11. *See Sinclair v. Levien*, 280 A.2d 717, 720 (Del. 1971) (board action presumed valid if it "can be attributed to any rational business purpose"); *see also Williams* [*v. Geier*], 671 A.2d at 1377–78 (board action in recommending charter amendment for stockholder action covered by business judgment rule in the absence of rebuttal demonstrating violation of fiduciary duty).

enterprise.[12] The subsections listed in Section 155 merely require the corporation to compensate its stockholders when it chooses not to recognize their fractional interests in the form of fractional shares.[13] Based upon this record, we conclude that Avaya is free to recognize the fractional interests of some stockholders but not others so long as the corporation follows the procedures set forth in Section 155.

Avaya May Proceed with Any of Its Alternative Plans to Dispose of the Fractional Interests

The balance of Applebaum's appeal challenges the alternative methods by which Avaya proposes to dispose of the fractional interests. The Court of Chancery concluded that Avaya could proceed under Section 155(1) by aggregating the fractional interests and selling them on behalf of the cashed-out stockholders. The Court also held that Avaya could employ Section 155(2), which requires payment of the "fair value" of the fractional interests, by paying the cashed-out stockholders an amount based on the average trading price of Avaya stock. We agree with the decision of the Court of Chancery and address separately the issues based on each subsection of the statute.

Section 155(1) Permits Avaya to Sell the Factional Interest on Behalf of the Stockholders

The stockholders have authorized Avaya to compensate the cashed-out stockholders by combining their fractional interests into whole shares and then selling them on the stockholders' behalf. Section 155(1) permits Avaya to "arrange for the disposition of fractional interests by those entitled thereto."

Applebaum claims that Avaya cannot use Section 155(1) because the corporation will sell whole shares rather than "fractional interests." According to this rendition of the transaction, the fractional interests held by the targeted stockholders must be reconverted into whole shares in the Forward Split. Otherwise, their fractional interests will be diluted. Avaya must reconvert the interests back to their initial value as whole shares in order to sell the combined fractional interests. Thus, Avaya would be selling whole shares rather than fractional interests.

Applebaum's argument incorrectly assumes that Avaya must issue fractions of a share in the Proposed Transaction. After the Reverse Split

---

12. *See Grimes v. Alteon Inc.*, 804 A.2d 256, 266 (Del. 2002) (noting that corporations "should have the freedom to enter into new and different forms of transactions") (citations omitted).

13. *See* WARD, WELCH & TUREZYN, FOLK ON THE DELAWARE GENERAL CORPORATION LAW § 155.1 (4th ed. 2002) (stating "a corporation may refuse to issue share fractions ... [but] If the corporation chooses to ignore share fractions, it must elect one of the three alternatives authorized by Section 155 ...").

takes place, the stockholders holding shares below the minimum amount will be cashed out. The fractional interests will not be represented as shares and are therefore not involved in the Forward Split. Avaya will then aggregate the fractional interests and repackage them as whole shares which the corporation will sell on the open market. The statute does not mandate any set procedure by which the fractional interests must be disposed of so long as those interests are sold in a manner that secures the proportionate value of the cashed-out holdings.

Applebaum also contends that Avaya cannot sell the fractional interests on behalf of the cashed-out stockholders. If Avaya sells the interests for the stockholders, Applebaum argues that the corporation will not comply with Section 155(1) because the interests are not disposed of by "those entitled thereto." As the Vice Chancellor noted, Applebaum presents a strained reading of Section 155(1). The Court of Chancery correctly reasoned that "In the eyes of equity, such sales would be 'by' " the stockholders.

Applebaum's interpretation also ignores the corporation's responsibility under Section 155(1) to "arrange" for the disposition of fractional interests. Since fractional shares cannot be listed on the major stock exchanges, the corporation must arrange for their aggregation in order to sell them. Aggregation is normally performed by

> affording to the stockholder an election to sell the fractional share or to purchase an additional fraction sufficient to make up a whole share. The elections are forwarded to a trust company or other agent of the corporation who matches up the purchases and sales and issues certificates for the whole shares or checks for payment of the fractional shares. . . .

The general practice requires the corporation to act as an intermediary to package the fractional interests into marketable shares. If the corporation were not permitted to do so, the fractional interests of the cashed-out stockholders would be dissipated through the transaction costs of finding other fractional holders with whom to combine and sell fractional interests in the market.

* * *

The Ten–Day Trading Average by which Avaya Proposes to Compensate the Cashed–Out Stockholders Constitutes "Fair Value" under Section 155(2)

As an alternative to selling the fractional interests on behalf of the stockholders, Avaya may opt to pay the stockholders cash in an amount based on the trading price of Avaya stock averaged over a ten-day period preceding the Proposed Transaction. To do so, Avaya relies on Section 155(2), which provides that a corporation may "pay in cash the fair value of fractions of a share as of the time when those entitled to receive such fractions are determined."

The corporation owes its cashed-out stockholders payment representing the "fair value" of their fractional interests. The cashed-out stockholders will receive fair value if Avaya compensates them with payment based on the price of Avaya stock averaged over a ten-day period preceding the Proposed Transaction. While market price is not employed in all valuation contexts,[28] our jurisprudence recognizes that in many circumstances a property interest is best valued by the amount a buyer will pay for it.[29] The Vice Chancellor correctly concluded that a well-informed, liquid trading market will provide a measure of fair value superior to any estimate the court could impose.

Applebaum relies on two instances where the Court of Chancery intimated that a Section 155(2) valuation may be similar to a going concern valuation employed in an appraisal proceeding. In *Chalfin v. Hart Holdings Co.*,[31] the Court of Chancery rejected a market price offered by a majority stockholder because the stock was not traded in an active market. In *Metropolitan Life Ins. Co. v. Aramark Corp.*,[32] the Court of Chancery declined to apply a private company discount presented by a controlling stockholder seeking to squeeze out the minority stockholders. Neither case applies here.

The court cannot defer to market price as a measure of fair value if the stock has not been traded actively in a liquid market. In *Chalfin*, for example, the Court of Chancery held that the controlling stockholder could not offer as "fair value" in a reverse stock split the same amount alleged to be the past trading value because the stock had not been publicly traded for "some time." The "market price" offered by the controlling stockholder was based on stale information. An active trading market did not exist to monitor the corporation's performance. Thus, a more thorough valuation would have been necessary.

Avaya stock, by contrast, is actively traded on the NYSE. The concerns noted in *Chaflin* are not pertinent to the Proposed Transaction because the market continues to digest information currently known about the compa-

---

28. *See e.g.*, 8 *Del. C.* § 262(h) (" In determining . . . fair value," in an appraisal proceeding, "the Court shall take into account all relevant factors."); *Smith v. Van Gorkom*, 488 A.2d 858, 876 (Del. 1985) (holding that a decision by the board of directors to approve a merger did not fall within the proper exercise of business judgment because the directors failed to consider the intrinsic worth of the corporation where the stock traded at a depressed market value).

29. *Cf.* 8 *Del. C.* § 262(b)(1) (denying appraisal rights for stock listed on a national securities exchange, interdealer quotation system by the National Association of Securities Dealers, Inc. or held of record by more than 2,000 holders); *Revlon, Inc. v. MacAndrews & Forbes Holdings*, 506 A.2d 173, 182 (Del. 1986) (noting that an auction for the sale of a corporation is an appropriate method by which to secure the best price for the stockholders); *Baron v. Pressed Metals of America, Inc.*, 35 Del. Ch. 581, 123 A.2d 848, 854 (Del. 1956) (noting that the "best price" a corporation could hope to obtain for the sale of a corporate asset "was what someone would be willing to pay" for it).

31. *Chalfin v. Hart Holdings Co.*, 1990 WL 181958 (Del. Ch.).

32. *Metropolitan Life Ins. Co. v. Aramark Corp.*, 1998 Del. Ch. LEXIS 70 (Del. Ch.).

ny. The value of Avaya's stock is tested daily through the purchase and sale of the stock on the open market.

In a related argument, Applebaum contends that the trading price cannot represent fair value because the stock price is volatile, trading at a range of prices from $13.70 per share to $1.12 per share over the past year. The volatility in trading does not necessarily mean that the market price is not an accurate indicator of fair value. Avaya stock is widely-held and actively traded in the market. The ten-day average has been recognized as a fair compromise that will hedge against the risk of fluctuation. Corporations often cash out fractional interests in an amount based on the average price over a given trading period.

Applebaum also misunderstands the appropriate context for which a going-concern valuation may be necessary under Section 155(2). In both *Chalfin* and *Aramark*, the Court of Chancery recognized that a transaction employing Section 155 may warrant a searching inquiry of fair value if a controlling stockholder initiates the transaction. When a controlling stockholder presents a transaction that will free it from future dealings with the minority stockholders, opportunism becomes a concern. Any shortfall imposed on the minority stockholders will result in a transfer of value to the controlling stockholder. The discount in value could be imposed deliberately or could be the result of an information asymmetry where the controlling stockholder possesses material facts that are not known in the market.[41] Thus, a Section 155(2) inquiry may resemble a Section 262 valuation if the controlling stockholder will benefit from presenting a suspect measure of valuation, such as an out-dated trading price, or a wrongfully imposed private company discount.

Although the Reverse/Forward Split will cash out smaller stockholders, the transaction will not allow the corporation to realize a gain at their expense. Unlike the more typical "freeze-out" context, the cashed-out Avaya stockholders may continue to share in the value of the enterprise. Avaya stockholders can avoid the effects of the proposed transaction either by purchasing a sufficient amount of stock to survive the initial Reverse Split or by simply using the payment provided under Section 155(2) to repurchase the same amount of Avaya stock that they held before the transaction.

The Reverse/Forward Split merely forces the stockholders to choose affirmatively to remain in the corporation. Avaya will succeed in saving administrative costs only if the board has assumed correctly that the stockholders who received a small interest in the corporation through the

---

41. *See, e. g., Glassman v. Unocal Exploration Corp.*, 777 A.2d 242, 248 (De. 2001) (a fair value determination must be based on "all relevant factors" in a short-form merger because the transaction presented by the controlling stockholder may be "timed to take advantage of a depressed market, or a low point in the company's cyclical earnings, or to precede an anticipated positive development...."). *See also* Robert B. Thompson, *Exit, Liquidity, and Majority Rule: Appraisal's Role in Corporate Law*, 84 Geo. L.J. 1, 36 (1995) (arguing that an appraisal valuation may be necessary in a squeeze-out context if "the minority does not have a choice and is being forced out, perhaps because of an anticipated increase in value that will only become visible after the transaction, [in which case] exclusion [of the minority stockholders] can easily become a basis for oppression of the minority").

Lucent spin off would prefer to receive payment, free of transaction costs, rather than continue with the corporation. The Transaction is not structured to prevent the cashed-out stockholders from maintaining their stakes in the company. A payment based on market price is appropriate because it will permit the stockholders to reinvest in Avaya, should they wish to do so.

The Meaning of "Fair Value" under Section 155(2) is not Identical to the Concept of "Fair Value" in Section 262

The Court of Chancery correctly interpreted "fair value" in Section 155 to have a meaning independent of the definition of "fair value" in Section 262 of the Delaware General Corporation Law.[44] Relying on the maxim that the same words used in different sections must be construed to have the same meaning, Applebaum argues that "fair value" under Section 155(2) requires the court to perform a valuation similar to an appraisal proceeding. Borrowing from appraisal concepts that require that shares of stock be valued as proportionate interests in a going concern, Applebaum contends that the average trading price would be inadequate because the market price possesses an inherent discount that accounts for the holder's minority stake in the company.

The Delaware General Assembly could not have intended Section 155(2) to have the same meaning as the fair value concept employed in Section 262.[47] The reference to fair value in Section 155 first appeared in 1967. The General Assembly did not place the term fair value in Section 262 until 1976. Furthermore, the case law developing the concept of fair value under the appraisal statute did not acquire its present form until this Court discarded the Delaware block method and underscored the necessity of valuing a corporation as a going concern. This Court has not suggested similar valuation guidelines for the right to receive "fair value" under Section 155(2). Finally, Section 262(b)(2)(c) expressly excludes fractional interests from the appraisal remedy when the stock is traded on a national exchange. When applied in the context of a merger or consolidation, Applebaum's interpretation of "fair value" under Section 155(2) would accord the stockholder of a constituent corporation an appraisal of fractional interests to which the stockholder is not entitled under the "market out" exception provided in Section 262.[51]

---

44. 8 *Del. C.* § 262(a) (providing that "Any stockholder of a corporation of this State who holds shares of stock on the date of the making of a demand pursuant to subsection (d) . . . who continuously holds such shares through the effective date of the merger or consolidation . . . who has neither voted in favor of the merger or consolidation nor consented thereto . . . shall be entitled to an appraisal by the Court of Chancery of the fair value of the stockholder's shares of stock. . . .").

47. *Hariton v. Arco Electronics, Inc.*, 41 Del. Ch. 74, 188 A.2d 123, 124 (Del. 1963) ("[t]he general theory of the Delaware Corporation Law that action taken pursuant to the authority of the various sections of that law constitute acts of independent legal significance and their validity is not dependent on other sections of the Act.") (quoting *Langfelder v. Universal Laboratories*, 68 F. Supp. 209, 211 (D. Del. 1946)).

51. Section 262(b)(1) denies appraisal rights to stockholders of a merging corporation if their stock is listed on a national securities exchange, interdealer quotation system, or held of

As this Court noted in *Alabama By–Products v. Cede & Co.*, the right to an appraisal is a narrow statutory right that seeks to redress the loss of the stockholder's ability under the common law to stop a merger. The Reverse/Forward Split permitted under Section 155 does not present the same problem and is ill-suited for the same solution provided for in Section 262.

The valuation of a stockholder's interest as a "going concern" is necessary only when the board's proposal will alter the nature of the corporation through a merger. When a corporation merges with another corporation, the dissenting stockholder is entitled to the value of the company as a going concern because the nature of the corporation's future "concern" will be vastly different. In a merger requiring an appraisal, the dissenting stockholder's share must be measured as a proportionate interest in a going concern because the proponents of the merger will realize the full intrinsic worth of the company rather than simply the market price of the stock. Thus, when a minority stockholder is confronted with a freeze-out merger, the Section 262 appraisal process will prevent the proponents of the merger from "reaping a windfall" by placing the full value of the company as a going concern into the merged entity while compensating the dissenting stockholder with discounted consideration.[54]

Avaya will not capture its full going-concern value in the Reverse/Forward Split. As the Vice Chancellor noted, if the cashed-out stockholders were awarded the value of the company as a going concern, they, rather than the corporation, would receive a windfall. The cashed-out stockholders could capture the full proportionate value of the fractional interest, return to the market and buy the reissued stock at the market price, and realize the going concern value a second time should Avaya ever merge or otherwise become subject to a change of control transaction.

QUESTIONS

1. Avaya could have achieved the same result through a merger with a newly created corporation under Del. G.C.L. § 151, in which Avaya shareholders would receive one share of the new corporation for each 30, 40 or 50 shares, and those holding fewer shares were cashed out or given appraisal rights under Del. G.C.L. § 262. Why do you suppose Avaya didn't choose this method?

2. How does the court determine that the meaning of "fair value" in section 155 is different from its meaning in the appraisal section of the Delaware Act, § 262? Does this make economic sense?

---

record by more than 2,000 holders. 8 *Del. C.* § 262(b)(1). Similarly, under Section 262(b)(2)(c), those same stockholders are not afforded an appraisal right for cash they receive "in lieu of fractional shares" of the stock. 8 *Del. C.* § 262(b)(2)(c).

54. *See Cavalier Oil*, 564 A.2d at 1145 ("To fail to accord to a minority shareholder the full proportionate value of his shares imposes a penalty for lack of control, and unfairly enriches the majority shareholder who may reap a windfall from the appraisal process by cashing out a dissenting shareholder, a clearly undesirable result.").

3. Applebaum argued that section 155 permitted cashing out fractional shareholders only if Avaya didn't issue fractional shares, and that holders of one whole share received fractional shares while holders of fewer shares did not, which wasn't authorized by section 155. How does the court respond to this objection?

4. One of the basic principles of corporation law is equality of treatment of similarly situated shareholders. Here Applebaum objects that his fractional shares will be treated differently from fractional shares held by those with more than 30, 40 or 50 shares. How does the court deal with this equality argument?

5. Why does the court accept a ten-day average market price as a "fair valuation" under § 155 in this case when the Chancery Court declined to do so in a case involving a cash-out of minority shareholders in Metropolitan Life Ins. Co. v. Aramark Corp., 1998 WL 34302067 (Del.Ch. 1998)? Do these distinctions make economic sense?

5. Stock Repurchases

A. The Economics of Share Repurchases

For creditors, share repurchases perform precisely the same function as dividends, by causing the corporation to pay funds to its shareholders. For that reason the RMBCA doesn't define "dividend," but rather defines "distribution" as a "transfer of money or other property (except its own shares) . . . to or for the benefit of its shareholders in respect of any of its shares." RMBCA § 1.40(6). This is an economically realistic way to look at share repurchases, because, absent taxes and transaction costs, shareholders in the aggregate will be indifferent between receiving a cash dividend and having a portion of their shares repurchased.

Dividends must always be paid pro rata. 11 Fletcher Cyclopedia Corporations § 5352 (2003 Rev. Vol.). In contrast, a corporation can repurchase its shares from some, but not all of its shareholders. It is the possibility for differential treatment of shareholders that creates most of the conflicts and law in this area, as we will see in succeeding sections of this Chapter.

Assume a corporation has a market value of $1,100 with 100 shares outstanding, each trading at $11. Now assume that the corporation has $100 surplus cash from last year's earnings, not required to continue the business at its current level of profits. If it declares a dividend of $1 per share, the value of the stock ex dividend will drop to $10, and each shareholder will have $1 cash, for a total of $11. Now assume the corporation distributes the $100 by buying back 9 shares at $11 each. The remaining 91 shares now own a firm still worth $1,000, because its earnings remain $100 annually, capitalized at 10%. In effect, the value of the firm has dropped by $99 after the repurchase.

	Share Repurchase	Dividend
Before:	100 shares outstanding @ $11	100 shares outstanding @ $11
Distribution to shareholders	$99	$100
After:	91 shares outstanding	100 shares outstanding
Value:	$\frac{\$1001}{91} = \$11.00$	$\frac{\$1000}{100} = \$10 + \$1$ cash = $11.00
Shares outstanding	91	100

So the shareholders remaining after the share repurchase have received a 10% increase in value, or $1.00, compared to their situation had they received a $1 dividend. Note that in the repurchase, earnings per share (EPS) have increased from $1 per share to $1.10. Thus the capitalization rate remains 10% in both cases. Sometimes the financial press focuses on the EPS as if it were a real benefit for the remaining shareholders, and would increase the value of the firm. Obviously in efficient markets with no transaction costs or taxes this cannot be so. Cases such as Applebaum v. Avaya illustrate some of the benefits of repurchasing shares, while others will be examined later in this section.

Taxes can make a large difference in the desirability of repurchases over dividends, if dividends are taxed at a higher rate than capital gains realized on repurchase. Assume a corporation with $100 it wishes to distribute to shareholders. Further assume individual tax rates of 40% and capital gains rates of 20%:

Dividend: $100 less $40 taxes = $60.
Repurchase: $100 less $20 taxes = $80.

But this example is unrealistic in that it assumes the entire $100 is capital gain—that the shareholder had paid nothing for her shares, and thus had no tax basis. The repurchase is even more beneficial if the shareholder has a substantial basis in the shares. For example, assume the shareholder's basis was $50, so the tax on the capital gain of $50 was $10:

Repurchase if basis is $50: gain = $100 less $10 taxes = $90.

As of 2010, the tax rate on dividends was identical to the capital gains rate—15%, so stockholders will be indifferent from a tax perspective if their capital gains are the entire amount received. To the extent they have a basis, so capital gains recognized would be less than the taxable dividend received, taxpayers will still prefer repurchases from a tax perspective, but the gap is not as wide. These rates expire at the end of 2010.

One effect of a repurchase of shares can be a capital restructuring. Given the "tax subsidy" of debt, repurchases can keep corporate debt at desired levels, thus enhancing efficiency by reducing agency costs and increasing total cash flows available to investors in the firm.

Sometimes managers explain share repurchases by stating that they believe their company's shares are a "good investment." In efficient markets, how can this be so? For a skeptical view of management's arguments that its stock is undervalued, see Vice Chancellor Strine's opinion in Chesapeake Corp. v. Shore, 771 A.2d 293 (Del. Ch. 2000). One way to explain this "good investment" rationale is that management believes the company has no positive net present value investments at present, so the board has simply decided to return cash to the shareholders. Why not use a dividend? Indeed, some companies that pay dividends also repurchase shares, and the obvious question is why they don't simply raise the dividend rate. The answer, at least in part, seems to be that raising the dividend is regarded as a more permanent commitment, and a subsequent dividend reduction would be viewed as a negative signal. Large bank holding companies provide a good example: in 1997 they paid out just under 40% of their earnings as dividends, and at the same time repurchased $16 billion of their own shares.

Repurchases are likely to signal that management lacks good investment opportunities now, but believes it will have better opportunities in the future. Is this likely to be the case, or are managers myopic when they do this? Recent studies have shown that stock prices don't rise rapidly after a repurchase, but often rise several years later. S. S. Stewart, Jr., Should a Corporation Repurchase Its Own Stock?, 31 Journal of Finance 911 (1976); L. Dann, Common Stock Repurchases: An Analysis to Bondholders and Stockholders, 9 Journal of Financial Economics 113 (1981); T. Vermaelen, Common Stock Repurchases and Market Signaling, 9 Journal of Financial Economics 139 (1981); David Ikenberry, Josef Lakonishok and Theo Vermaelen, Market Underreaction to Open Market Share Repurchases, 39 Journal of Financial Economics 181 (1995). Stock repurchases were very common in late 1987 and 1988, following a market crash of more than 20% in October, 1987. Many companies believed the market decline in the price of their shares was unwarranted, that their shares were currently trading at bargain prices, and began repurchasing their shares as soon as possible. Repurchases remain quite common. In 1997 over $120 billion of shares were repurchased by American corporations. See Chapter Four, Part 3 for Michael Milken's criticism of excessive stock repurchases that left companies undercapitalized in the downturn of 2008.

There are three major ways to repurchase stock in a public corporation. A corporation can repurchase its shares in the market in trading transactions, just like any other investor (subject to disclosure rules set out in the next subsection). A company can also make a "self-tender offer," in which it publicly offers to buy back a certain amount of its stock, generally at a premium over the market. In the past, a company could also engage in a "targeted repurchase," which usually involved buyout of a large shareholder that was threatening a hostile takeover. This often carried the pejorative name "greenmail," and was effectively outlawed by punitive tax treatment.

B.   Legal Authority for Share Repurchases

The leading English case of Trevor v. Whitworth, 12 App. Cas. 409 (1887) held that a corporation lacked the power to purchase its own shares; if it bought them to resell them, it would "trafficking in shares" rather than engaging in the business for which it was organized. If it bought them to reduce equity capital, it would be reducing capital without the court approval required by the English Companies Act. It is probably for this reason that all American statutes expressly grant corporations the power to repurchase their own shares, subject to the legal capital restrictions discussed earlier in this chapter. See, e.g., Del. G.C.L. § 160 and R.M.B.C.A. § 6.31.

C. REGULATION OF SHARE REPURCHASES

i. MARKET REPURCHASES

Market repurchases always run the risk of being made when a company is in possession of material inside information, and thus violating Rule 10b–5. Rule 10b5–1 now provides a solution: if the company adopts a repurchase plan at a time when it is not in possession of such information, purchases subsequently made in accordance with the plan are deemed not to be made "on the basis of" that information. The issuer must enter into a written plan for buying the stock. The conditions can be technical. Rule 10b5–1(c)(1)(B) provides that the plan must either (1) specify the amount of securities to be purchased, the purchase price and the date of purchase— a requirement that would limit the repurchase essentially to a one-time action; (2) include a formula or algorithm or computer program for determining the amount, price and date for the securities to be bought or (3) leave the agent executing the plan to exercise any discretion about how, when and whether to effect purchases, provided that agent was not in possession of material nonpublic information. Of course this does not address state law concerns about asymmetric information in repurchases, alluded to in Applebaum v. Avaya, although it may well be persuasive.

Market repurchases can also be manipulative. Companies may be tempted to repurchase at times that affect the price of their shares. In one sense, this appears to conflict with CAPM, which teaches that all stocks are fungible, and that they are priced fairly in relation to each other because they are only tools in building a portfolio. But purchases and sales can have signaling effects; substantial sales by insiders generally lead to a price decline, apparently because uninformed traders believe these insiders have superior information about the company's prospects. Myron Scholes, "The Market for Securities: Substitution versus Price Pressure and the Effects of Information on Share Prices," 45 J. Bus. 179 (1972). Further, our learning about how stock prices behave depends upon stocks trading in what the Supreme Court has called "open and developed" securities markets. Basic Inc. v. Levinson, 485 U.S. 224, 241 (1988). Recall that Judge Easterbrook emphasized the need for plaintiffs to prove the presence of such markets in West v. Prudential Securities, Incorporated, 282 F.3d 935 (7th Cir. 2002), set out in Chapter Three. Thin markets, where trading is infrequent, and the stock is not widely followed by analysts and traders, are generally understood to be susceptible to manipulation. Are there times when even the market for a widely traded stock might act as if it were thin? The SEC has thought so, and acted accordingly.

Securities and Exchange Commission v. Georgia–Pacific Corporation

U.S. District Court for the Southern District of New York, 66 Civil Action No. 1215, April 27, 1966. Excerpts from Complaint. Federal Securities Law Reporter (CCH) (1964–66 Decisions) ¶ 91,680.

COUNT ONE

Section 10(b) of the Securities Exchange Act and Rule 10b–5 thereunder

11. Since on or about May 26, 1961 GP has merged with other corporations or has acquired substantially all of the stock or assets of other corporations in return for stock in GP pursuant to agreements which provided that the total number of shares of GP stock to be issued in return for the interests in such other corporations would be dependent on the price of GP common stock on the NYSE at certain times or during certain periods of time (hereafter referred to as valuation periods).

12. During and immediately prior to certain of such valuation periods the defendants GP, CHEATHAM and PAMPLIN (individually and as trustees of the Georgia–Pacific Stock Bonus Trust), and MRS. BROOKS, intentionally caused GP common stock to be bid for and purchased for the Stock Bonus Plan and for the GP treasury on the NYSE in a manner which would and did, directly and indirectly, cause the price of GP common stock on the NYSE to rise in order that GP's obligations to issue additional shares of its common stock in return for the interests in other corporations would be avoided or reduced.

13. In making such purchases for the Stock Bonus Plan the defendants CHEATHAM, PAMPLIN, and MRS. BROOKS did not attempt to have them executed in a manner which would have tended to result in purchases at the lowest prices possible and thus did not act exclusively in the interest of the Stock Bonus Plan participants.

* * *

THE ST. CROIX PAPER COMPANY

16. From January 17, 1963 to about February 27, 1963 GP made an offer to exchange a maximum of 587,714 shares of GP common stock for the common stock of St. Croix Paper Company (St. Croix), a Maine corporation, which then had approximately 2,700 shareholders. The offer provided that up to 470,172 shares of GP common stock would initially be issued to the St. Croix shareholders at the rate of $^8/_{10}$ of a GP share for each St. Croix share. The offer further provided that GP was obligated to issue additional GP shares, up to the limit of $^2/_{10}$ of a GP share for each St. Croix share exchanged, to make up any difference should the last sale price on the NYSE of GP common stock not average $50 per share for a period of 30 consecutive trading days next preceding any date to be later selected by GP within the next 2½ years. The offer also provided that GP was obligated to

issue the additional $^2/_{10}$ of a GP share for each St. Croix share exchanged if within 2½ years GP did not select such a date.

17.   On March 7, 1963 GP acquired 94.6% of the St. Croix stock under this offer, and on April 10, 1963 GP acquired an additional 4.16% of the St. Croix stock under the same terms.

18.   On nine occasions between February 15 and April 9, 1963 the three trustees of the Stock Bonus Plan passed resolutions authorizing purchases of a total of 23,100 shares of GP common stock to be made at the discretion of either CHEATHAM or PAMPLIN. Pursuant to these authorizations, 22,900 shares of GP common stock (or 50.66% of the GP common stock purchased for the Stock Bonus Plan in 1963) were purchased for the Stock Bonus Plan on the NYSE on 25 of the 36 trading days from February 21 through April 15, 1963. Such purchases were effected at the discretion of MRS. BROOKS under the general direction of CHEATHAM.

19.   During this period, CHEATHAM, PAMPLIN, and MRS. BROOKS did not attempt to have such purchases executed in a manner which would have tended to result in purchases at the lowest prices possible. Instead, such purchases were caused to be executed predominantly through the use of several orders at the market* on the same day (on one occasion as many as 11 separate orders on the same day), sometimes through two or more brokerage firms on the same day and at the same times during one day and on most occasions without placing any price limit on such orders. In addition, such purchases were caused to be concentrated near the close of the market on many days during this period.

20.   Purchases of 9.6% of the GP stock made for the Stock Bonus Plan from March 28 through April 15, 1963 were executed at prices higher than those on the preceding transactions (on "plus ticks") or at the same price as the preceding transactions, the last change in price having been upward (on "zero plus ticks"). Consequently, the prices at which such purchases were executed led advances and retarded declines in the price of GP common stock on the NYSE. Between March 28 and April 15, 1963 such purchases accompanied an advance in the market price of GP common stock from 49 to 52¾. When the price of GP common stock appeared to be averaging above the price required to eliminate GP's obligation to issue additional shares under the St. Croix offer, such purchasing was discontinued, although funds still remained in the Stock Bonus Plan. In addition, on April 2, April 9, and April 10 such purchases (on plus and zero-plus ticks) were the last purchases of the day. In summary, such purchases were intentionally effected in a manner which would and did, directly and indirectly, cause the last sale price of GP common stock on the NYSE to rise in order that GP's obligation to issue additional shares of its common stock under the St. Croix offer would be avoided or reduced.

---

* A purchase "at the market" is an order to a broker to purchase at the best price currently available in the market.—Ed.

Georgia Pacific entered into a consent decree with the SEC which, in the words of SEC Litigation Release No. 3511 (May 23, 1966), provided as follows:

> In addition, the judgment enjoins Georgia–Pacific and the individual defendants (so long as they are associated with Georgia–Pacific) from bidding for or purchasing any Georgia–Pacific security (1) during serious negotiations looking toward the acquisition of another company in exchange for Georgia–Pacific securities, (2) during or within 10 business days immediately prior to any period of time during which the market price of any security of Georgia–Pacific is to be used to determine the amount of Georgia–Pacific securities to be issued in connection with an acquisition, (3) during a distribution of Georgia–Pacific securities, and (4) at any other time except in accordance with specified limitations intended to minimize the impact of such purchases on the market price of Georgia–Pacific stock and to cause such purchases to follow rather than lead changes in the market price of Georgia–Pacific stock.

The ultimate resolution of the SEC's concerns in this area is Securities Exchange Act Rule 10b–18, 17 C.F.R. 240.10b–18. Does it adequately address the problem identified above? Does it make sense in terms of what we know about efficient capital markets and CAPM? If so, why?

A slightly different problem arises when a company engages in a fixed price public offering. By definition, a fixed price offering means that all shares will be offered and sold to the public at a single offering price. To do otherwise would be fraudulent and deceptive, and create liability under section 11 of the Securities Act of 1933 as well as under Section 10(b) and Rule 10b–5. When shares are first sold in an initial public offering, trading begins immediately, whether on NASDAQ or elsewhere. There is no guarantee that the trading price will remain identical to the stated offering price. If the trading price falls, how can underwriters sell the remainder of the offering at the stated price, when investors can obtain the stock more cheaply in the market? In syndicated offerings, anticompetitive practices are used to assure that all shares can be sold at the original offering price. Selling dealers must abide by a resale price maintenance agreement, not to cut their price, and thus not to shave their selling dealers' commission to meet the current market price. The NASD is allowed to enforce these agreements as not violating the antitrust laws thanks to a dubious decision in United States v. Morgan, 118 F.Supp. 621 (S.D.N.Y. 1953) (Medina, J.)

But more is sometimes required. The "more" is permission from the SEC to engage in manipulation designed to put a floor under the market price during the offering period. See Securities Exchange Act Regulation M, 17 CFR § 242.100–105. These rules prohibit issuers, underwriters and others associated with them from bidding for or buying securities during or shortly before a distribution, with limited exceptions. The major exception is for stabilizing activities, regulated under Rule 104. This rule permits an underwriter to make a "stabilizing" bid for the stock, which can be no higher than the opening or most recent ask quotation for the stock or the last independent transaction price. A stabilizing bid cannot be increased in price beyond the highest independent bid for the stock or the last market transaction price. A stabilizing bid must be identified as such to the market in which it is made. The prospectus for the offering must disclose the possibility of stabilizing transactions as well.

ii.   GOING PRIVATE TRANSACTIONS

Transactions to cash out public shareholders, and to return companies to non-public status, first achieved prominence in the early 1970s. A bull market in the late 1960s was followed by a market drop in 1969 and 1970. Many companies that had "gone public" during the 1960s discovered that being a public company was not producing the benefits expected, in terms of a highly valued stock, liquidity, and providing a medium for stock options to retain employees. As a result some of these companies where the former owners remained controlling shareholders engaged in takeout mergers in which the public shareholders received cash for their stock. While the cash-outs were generally at premiums over prevailing market prices, in some instances they were below the initial public offering prices. Many commentators railed against these transactions, most notably A.A. Sommer, Jr., who described the "going private" transaction as "serious, unfair, and sometimes disgraceful, a perversion of the whole process of public financing, and a course that inevitably is going to make the individual shareholder even more hostile to American corporate mores and the securities markets than he already is." in a speech at Notre Dame Law School, "Going Private": A Lesson in Corporate Responsibility, reprinted in (1974–1975 Transfer Binder) Fed. Sec. L. Rep. (CCH) ¶ 80,010 (1974).

We will not repeat the Delaware jurisprudence on "going private" transactions here, except to note the concern of the Delaware Supreme Court that the terms of these transactions are set unilaterally by a controlling shareholder that dominates the board of the subject corporation, which has led the Delaware court to impose a duty of "entire fairness" on the controlling shareholder, which includes both fair dealing (candor and full disclosure) and fair price. Weinberger v. UOP, Inc., 457 A.2d 701 (Del. 1983). This duty is avoidable if the bidding corporation engages in a tender offer for public shares that results in acquisition of at least 90% of the target's stock, and follows this with a statutory short form merger under Del. G.C.L. § 253. See In re Siliconix Incorporated Shareholder Litigation, 2001 WL 716787 (Del. Ch. 2001) and Glassman v. Unocal Corp., 777 A.2d 242 (Del. 2001). In other states, appraisal is treated as the exclusive remedy of shareholders in a going private merger. See, e.g., M.B.C.A. § 13.02(d) and Grace Bros. v. Farley Industries, Inc., 450 S.E.2d 814 (Ga. 1994).

In 1977 the SEC proposed a rule dealing with going private transactions. Exchange Act Release No. 14185 (Nov. 17, 1977). The initial version of the proposed rule contained substantive regulation of going private transactions, providing that it would be a fraudulent, deceptive or manipulative act or practice to purchase securities in a going private transaction if it "is unfair to unaffiliated securityholders." After much debate a final version of the rule was adopted in 1979 which did not contain such substantive fairness requirements. As adopted, Rule 13e–3, 17 C.F.R. 240.13e–3, was a disclosure rule. It requires issuers subject to the Exchange Act which are about to engage in a going private transaction to file Schedule 13E–3. Schedule 13E–3 requires the issuer to disclose to share-holders all of the conventional financial information about an issuer, but also requires a discussion of the fairness of the transaction (Item 8) and a disclosure of any reports, opinions or appraisals received by the issuer or its affiliates relating to the fairness of the transaction.

Howing Co. v. Nationwide Corporation

826 F.2d 1470 (6th Cir.1987), cert. denied, 486 U.S. 1059 (1988).

■ MERRITT, CIRCUIT JUDGE.

Under § 13(e) of the Securities Exchange Act of 1934, a Williams Act provision enacted in 1968, a company that has issued publicly traded stock is prohibited from buying it back unless the issuer complies with rules promulgated by the SEC. This appeal raises issues concerning the existence of a private right of action under § 13e–3, the nature of the disclosure duty imposed by Rule 13e–3, and the interrelationship of this provision with other antifraud rules.

Pursuant to its authority under § 13e–3, the SEC has issued Rule 13e–3 and Schedule 13e–3, a long and detailed set of disclosure requirements governing such "going private" transactions. Schedule 13e–3 accompanying the Rule requires that numerous items of information about the transaction be filed with the Commission, including three items pertinent to this case, i.e., Items 7, 8 and 9. Item 7 covers the "reasons" for the transaction; Item 8 requires a statement concerning the fairness of the transaction; and Item 9 requires disclosure of appraisals and other information concerning the value of the stock. The Rule also provides that this same information be disclosed to the selling shareholders.

The basic questions presented in this case are: (1) whether the plaintiffs have a private right of action under § 13e–3 to police non-compliance with Rule 13e–3; (2) and if so, whether the disclosure requirements of Rule 13e–3 have been met; and (3) if those requirements have not been met, whether defendant's conduct in violating Rule 13e–3 also gives rise to liability under the antifraud provisions of Rules 10b–5 and 14a–9.

Parties and Summary of Disposition Below

Defendant Nationwide Corporation is one of the largest life insurance holding companies in the United States. Originally incorporated in 1947 as Service Insurance Agency, the company has enjoyed steady growth since its affiliation with the Nationwide group of insurance companies in September 1955. As a result of this affiliation, the company adopted its present name and issued a special class of common stock (Class B common) which was held entirely by two Nationwide companies: Nationwide Mutual Insurance Company and Nationwide Mutual Fire Insurance Company. The Class A common stock continued in the hands of individual shareholders.

* * *

Nationwide Mutual and Nationwide Mutual Fire began to eliminate public ownership of Nationwide Corporation in December 1978 when these companies made a tender offer to buy the Class A shares for $20.00 per share net in cash. By January 1979, Nationwide Mutual and Nationwide Mutual Fire had purchased 4,074,695 Class A shares through this offer. After the tender offer, Nationwide Mutual and Nationwide Mutual Fire continued to purchase shares in the open market at prices ranging between $22.50 and $24.62 per share. These transactions ultimately gave Nationwide Mutual and Nationwide Mutual Fire ownership of 85.6% of the Class A common stock formerly held by the public.

In November 1982, the Board of Directors of Nationwide Corporation approved a transaction in which Nationwide Mutual and Nationwide Mutual Fire would acquire the remaining Class A shares at $42.50 per share. As a result, Nationwide Corporation would become a wholly-owned subsidiary of the two mutuals, and would have no public ownership. This transaction was approved by 94.7% of the Class A shares. Plaintiffs in the present litigation abstained from voting their shares respecting the merger or seeking their appraisal remedy under state law.

The present class action began with an action by Belle Efros, a Nationwide shareholder, seeking a preliminary injunction with respect to a vote on the proposed merger. Following the denial of the Efros motion for a preliminary injunction, the merger was approved by 94.7% of the voted public shares. The District Court ultimately consolidated the Efros action with an action brought by the Howing Company and Douglas McClellan, two former shareholders of Nationwide. The District Court also later conditionally certified the case as a class action. The final amended complaint in this action raised claims under the Securities Exchange Act of 1934 §§ 10(b), 13(e), and 14(a) and rules promulgated thereunder as well as state law claims based on a breach of fiduciary duty.

The defendants moved for summary judgment and plaintiffs filed a cross-motion for partial summary judgment. The District Court granted defendants' motion, denied plaintiffs' cross-motion, and dismissed the amended complaint.

* * *

The District Court concluded overall that the proxy statement satisfied the requirements of Rule 13e–3. The District Court stated:

> Most important, there was sufficient information disclosed in the proxy statement to enable the stockholders to make an informed decision on what to do. It is the conclusion of the Court, therefore, that there is no genuine issue of material fact concerning the adequacy of the proxy statement when measured against the standards set forth in Rule 13e–

3, and that any omissions pointed out by plaintiffs were not material as defined by the Court in TSC Industries, Inc. v. Northway, Inc., 426 U.S. at 449, 96 S. Ct. at 2132.

* * *

Rule 13e–3 Compliance

Going private transactions raise unique problems because of their inherently coercive nature: minority shareholders are forced to exchange their shares for cash or other consideration. The coercive effect of these transactions is reinforced by the fact that the majority shareholders control the timing and terms of the transaction.

* * *

Rule 13e–3 does not require that the issuer's Schedule 13e–3 filing with the Commission be reproduced in its entirety in the communication with shareholders. Most items from that Schedule may be summarized. However, Items 7, 8 and 9 must be disclosed verbatim. The rationale behind complete disclosure of these items is that they go to the essence of the transaction. Item 7 requires full disclosure of the purposes, alternatives, reasons, and effects of the transaction; Item 8 requires a statement as to the fairness of the transaction and the factors upon which such belief is based; and Item 9 requires disclosure of reports, opinions, appraisals and certain negotiations.

* * *

B.   *Item 8 Disclosure*

The instructions accompanying Schedule 13e–3 are quite definite in the level of specificity required in certain disclosures.[5] The Instruction to Item 8 states that "conclusory statements, such as 'The Rule 13e–3 transaction is fair to unaffiliated security holders in relation to net book value, going concern value and future prospects of the issuer' *will not be considered sufficient disclosure in response to Item 8(a)*." (emphasis added.)

The Commission has expressed special concern with disclosures under Item 8(b) of Schedule 13e–3, the Item concerning the factors underlying a

---

5. The Instructions to Item 8(b) of the Schedule identify the following factors to be discussed in the disclosure:

Instructions. (1) The factors which are important in determining the fairness of a transaction to unaffiliated security holders and the weight, if any, which should be given to them in a particular context will vary. Normally such factors will include, among others, those referred to in paragraphs (c), (d) and (e) of this Item and whether the consideration offered to unaffiliated security holders constitutes fair value in relation to: (i) Current market prices, (ii) Historical market prices, (iii) Net book value, (iv) Going concern value, (v) Liquidation value, (vi) The purchase price paid in previous purchases disclosed in Item 1(f) of Schedule 13e–3, (vii) Any report, opinion, or appraisal described in Item 9 and (viii) Firm offers of which the issuer or affiliate is aware made by any unaffiliated person, other than the person filing this statement, during the preceding eighteen months . . .

belief as to the fairness of the transaction. The Commission has issued the following guidance to prospective issuers:

> The Division is concerned that in many instances the Item 8(b) disclosure being made to security holders is vague and non-specific and is therefore of limited utility to security holders.... Each such factor which is material to the transaction should be discussed and, in particular, if any of the sources of value indicate a value higher than the value of the consideration offered to unaffiliated security holders, the discussion should specifically address such difference and should include a statement of the bases for the belief as to fairness in light of the difference.

Exchange Act Release No. 34–17719, at 17,245–42.

The most serious problem in defendants' proxy statement concerns Item 8(b) compliance. Our review of the proxy statement indicates that defendants have made precisely the kind of conclusory statements prohibited by the Rule. In describing the fairness of the transaction as required by Item 8(b), defendants have done nothing more than provide a laundry list of factors considered by their investment banker.[6]

This kind of non-specific disclosure runs counter not only to the SEC's position taken in the Commission release discussed above but also to the Instruction to Item 8(b) of Schedule 13e–3. The Instruction states that the issuer shall "discuss in reasonable detail the material factors upon which the belief stated in Item 8(a) is based and, to the extent practicable, the weight assigned to each factor." (emphasis added). Thus, the proxy statement is incomplete in that we are not provided with any indication of the weights given the various factors as required by Rule 13e–3, incorporating Schedule 13e–3. Moreover, we therefore have no indication as to whether any of the "sources of value indicate a value higher than the value of the consideration offered to unaffiliated security holders." Exchange Act Release No. 34–17719, at 17,245–42.

Instead of providing this itemized disclosure called for by Rule 13e–3, defendants rely heavily on the First Boston opinion letter to discharge their disclosure obligations.[7] Indeed, the proxy materials state specifically, "Although the Evaluation Committee did not give specific weight to each of the various factors considered in evaluating the fairness of the proposed merger, particular emphasis was placed upon the receipt of the opinion of First Boston."

While the Commission has stated that an issuer in a going private transaction can rely on an investment banker's opinion to meet its disclosure obligations, such opinion itself must fully analyze the factors enumerated in Item 8(b) as well as be "expressly adopted" by the issuer. Exchange Act Release No. 34–17719, at 17,245–42. The issuer in this case did not conduct its own investigation but chose to rely on the expertise of First

---

6. See Appendix A for the relevant language from the proxy statement.

7. See Appendix B for the language from the First Boston opinion letter which appears in the proxy statement as Exhibit II.

Boston. The problem with defendants adopting the First Boston opinion letter as their disclosure to shareholders is that this one-page letter is itself woefully inadequate when measured against the specific disclosure requirements of the Rule. An issuer cannot insulate itself from 13e–3 liability by relying on an investment banker's opinion letter which itself does not comply with the specific disclosure requirements of the Rule. Therefore, defendants' conclusory statements are not cured by conclusory statements made by First Boston in its opinion letter.

Somewhere in the proxy materials the Nationwide shareholders should have received a reasonably detailed analysis of the various financial valuation methods discussed by the Rule and the weights attached thereto. Even if certain valuation methods were not particularly relevant, this should itself have been noted and explained. See Exchange Act Release No. 34–17719, at 17,245–42. Without this disclosure, Nationwide shareholders did not possess the information necessary to make an informed decision concerning the going private transaction.

* * *

The Antifraud Claims

In addition to liability under subsection (b)(2) of Rule 13e–3, plaintiffs also contend that the defendants breached the antifraud provisions of Rules 10b–5, 13e–3(b)(1), and 14a–9. In essence, plaintiffs contend that a failure to disclose information required by Rule 13e–3 ipso facto constitutes an "omission" actionable under the antifraud provisions. They argue that Rules 10b–5 and 14a–9 incorporate Rule 13e–3 by reference in the going private context.

The three antifraud provisions at issue here spring from distinct statutes which have unique texts and histories. All three, however, parallel the common law of fraud and deceit. Absent special circumstances, an action for deceit would lie at common law for both falsehoods and half-truths, but not for a complete failure to disclose. See III L. Loss, Securities Regulation at 1433–35. As was noted by this circuit almost fifty years ago with regard to a similarly worded antifraud provision in the Securities Act of 1933:

> The statute did not require appellant to state every fact about stock offered that a prospective purchaser might like to know or that might, if known, tend to influence his decision, but it did require appellant not "to obtain money or property by means of any untrue statement of a material fact *or any omission to state a material fact necessary in order to make the statements made, in the light of the circumstances under which they were made, not misleading.*"

Otis & Co. v. SEC, 106 F.2d 579, 582 (6th Cir.1939) (emphasis in original) (construing § 17(a)(2) of the Securities Act of 1933).

The second clauses of Rules 10b–5 and 13e–3(b)(1), and similar language in Rule 14a–9, adopt the common law rule and prohibit silence only where the omitted information is necessary to prevent inaccuracy in existing disclosure. As a result, these provisions have been considered by commentators and the courts alike to be concerned with half-truth rather than omissions per se.

The essence of plaintiff's claim is that a failure to provide items of disclosure required by Rule 13e–3(e) always constitutes a material omission under the antifraud rules. This is tantamount to incorporating the disclosure provisions of the securities laws into the antifraud provisions. No longer would omissions be actionable only where a half-truth resulted. Instead, any failure to comply with SEC disclosure obligations would be actionable by private litigants under the antifraud provisions.

Although the antifraud rules are the "catch-all" provisions of the securities laws, the Supreme Court has emphasized in the Rule 10b–5 context that they apply only where some fraud has been committed. See Chiarella v. United States, 445 U.S. 222, 234–35, 63 L. Ed. 2d 348, 100 S. Ct. 1108 (1980). Congress did not enact sections 10(b), 13(e), or 14(a) to give private litigants the same enforcement powers granted to the Commissioner of the SEC. Allowing private suits based on any non-disclosure, without regard to the "half-truth" limitation, would contravene the congressional intent behind these statutes. Therefore, we hold that omission of disclosure required by Rule 13e–3(e) will constitute a violation of the antifraud provisions of sections 10(b), 13(e), and 14(a) only where the information is necessary to prevent half-truth. The violations of Rule 13e–3, Item 8, itemized above, do not constitute "fraud" under sections 10(b) and 14(a) but should be considered as violations only of the specific rule in question.[11]

* * *

Accordingly, the judgment of the District Court is reversed and remanded for proceedings consistent with this opinion.

APPENDIX A

The proxy statement provides in pertinent part:

The members of the Evaluation Committee believe that, from a financial point of view, the terms of the proposed merger are fair to the public shareholders of the Corporation. The committee members considered important, as an indication of the fairness of the proposed merger, the receipt of the written opinion of First Boston. The committee members also considered important a number of other factors discussed with the representatives of First Boston. These factors are the current market price of the Class A Common shares as compared with stock prices of other comparable entities; past and current earnings of the Corporation; past and current price/earnings ratios of the Corporation and other companies having similar operations; past and current price/equity ratios of the Corporation (as computed in accordance with generally accepted accounting principles); and

---

11. Under certain circumstances, violations of Rule 13e–3 may be indicative of a "scheme or artifice to defraud" which would violate the antifraud provisions. Such is not the case here, however, where non-disclosure is claimed to be a violation standing alone.

the premium over market price offered to the public shareholders in other similar transactions as well as in other recent acquisitions in the life insurance industry generally. In its discussions with the representatives of First Boston, upon whose opinion the Evaluation Committee has concluded that it is appropriate to rely, these representatives stated that in addition to the above noted factors they had also considered the current overall level of the stock market; historical market prices of the Class A Common shares as compared with market prices for the stock of other comparable entities; going concern value of the Corporation; net book value of the Corporation; liquidation value of the Corporation; various financial ratios; present revenues, expenses, earnings and dividends of the Corporation and trends with respect thereto; the purchase price paid to holders of Class A Common shares by Nationwide Mutual in connection with the December 1978 tender offer for the Class A Common shares; present value of projected future cash flows of the Corporation; replacement value of the Corporation; off balance sheet items of the Corporation; significant trends in the insurance business; competitive environment of the insurance industry; regulatory environment of the insurance industry; and the impact of inflation on the Corporation.

APPENDIX B

The First Boston opinion letter reads in its entirety as follows:

November 1, 1982

Board of Directors
Nationwide Corporation
One Nationwide Plaza
Columbus, Ohio 43216

Gentlemen:

You have asked us to advise you as to the fairness to the shareholders of Nationwide Corporation, other than Nationwide Mutual Insurance Company and Nationwide Mutual Fire Insurance Company, of the financial terms of a proposed merger whereby the owners of 685,545 publicly held Class A common shares would receive cash for their shares and Nationwide Mutual Insurance Company and Nationwide Mutual Fire Insurance Company would become the only shareholder of Nationwide Corporation. The terms of the merger transaction are that Nationwide Corporation shareholders will be entitled to receive $42.50 for each share of Nationwide Corporation Class A common shares.

In connection with our review, Nationwide Corporation furnished to us certain business and financial data concerning Nationwide Corporation. This information was furnished specifically for the purpose of our advising you as to the fairness of the financial terms of the proposed merger, and our Corporation's representation that the information is complete and accurate in all material respects. We have not independently verified the information. We have also reviewed certain publicly available information that we considered relevant and have had discussions with certain members of Nationwide Corporation's management.

In arriving at our opinion we have also considered, among other matters we deemed relevant, the historical financial record, operating statistics, current financial position and general prospects of Nationwide Corporation and the stock market performance of the Class A common shares of Nationwide Corporation. In addition, we have considered the terms and conditions of the proposed transaction as compared with the terms and conditions of comparable transactions.

Based on our analysis of the foregoing and of such other factors as we have considered necessary for the purpose of this opinion and in reliance upon the accuracy and completeness of the information furnished to us by Nationwide Corporation, it is our opinion that the financial terms of the proposed transaction are fair to the minority shareholders of Nationwide Corporation.

Very truly yours,
THE FIRST BOSTON
CORPORATION

QUESTIONS

1. The court found that the proxy statement did not comply sufficiently with Item 8(b) of Schedule 13e–3. If you were advising corporate officials after this decision, what kinds of disclosures would you want to explore?

2. Why didn't the First Boston letter satisfy the obligations of the Board on fairness disclosures? Why can't you rely on the recommendation of experts concerning the fairness of the price offered? Suppose the Board really has no idea about what price is fair except the information they obtain from its investment bankers, who provide a letter like that provided by First Boston. What else can the Board say about fairness? Is there a reason why First Boston has provided such a short letter on a complex topic? Would a lawyer be well advised to provide a short opinion letter on a complex legal question?

3. Why doesn't a failure to comply with Item 8(b) constitute fraud under Rule 10b–5 and related statutes?

---

iii. REPURCHASES DURING HOSTILE TENDER OFFERS

In a hostile tender offer, a target company may decide to repurchase its own shares in the market. These transactions are governed by the disclosure requirements of Securities Exchange Act Rule 13e–1, 17 CFR 240.13e–1, set out below.

Rule 13e–1. Purchase of securities by the issuer during a third-party tender offer.

An issuer that has received notice that it is the subject of a tender offer made under Section 14(d)(1) of the Act (15 U.S.C. 78n), that has commenced under § 240.14d–2 must not purchase any of its equity securities during the tender offer unless the issuer first:

(a) Files a statement with the Commission containing the following information:

(1) The title and number of securities to be purchased;

(2) The names of the persons or classes of persons from whom the issuer will purchase the securities;

(3) The name of any exchange, inter-dealer quotation system or any other market on or through which the securities will be purchased;

(4) The purpose of the purchase;

(5) Whether the issuer will retire the securities, hold the securities in its treasury, or dispose of the securities. If the issuer intends to dispose of the securities, describe how it intends to do so; and

(6) The source and amount of funds or other consideration to be used to make the purchase. If the issuer borrows any funds or other consideration to make the purchase or enters any agreement for the purpose of acquiring, holding, or trading the securities, describe the transaction and agreement and identify the parties; and

(b) Pays the fee required by § 240.0–11 when it files the initial statement.

(c) This section does not apply to periodic repurchases in connection with an employee benefit plan or other similar plan of the issuer so long as the purchases are made in the ordinary course and not in response to the tender offer.

————————

An alternative means for a target to battle a hostile tender offer is through its own tender offer for its shares, at a higher price than the bidder offers. "Self-tenders" are regulated by the disclosure requirements of Securities Exchange Act Rule 13e–4, 17 CFR 240.13e–4, not included here because of its length. Delaware has its own rules for the fiduciary duties of boards of directors of such companies.

AC Acquisitions Corp. v. Anderson, Clayton & Co.

519 A.2d 103 (Del.Ch.1986).

■ ALLEN, CHANCELLOR.

This case involves a contest for control of Anderson, Clayton & Co., a Delaware corporation ("Anderson, Clayton" or the "Company"). Plaintiffs,

Bear, Stearns & Co., Inc., Gruss Petroleum Corp. and Gruss Partners ("BS/G") are shareholders of Anderson, Clayton who, through a newly formed corporation—AC Acquisitions Corp.—are currently making a tender offer for any and all shares of Anderson, Clayton at $56 per share cash. That offer, which may close no earlier than midnight tonight, is subject to several important conditions as detailed below. BS/G has announced an intention, if it succeeds through its tender offer in acquiring 51% of the Company's stock, to do a follow-up merger at $56 per share cash.

BS/G publicly announced its tender offer on August 21, 1986, having failed to bring defendants to the bargaining table despite attempts over several months. On the following day, Anderson, Clayton announced the commencement of a self-tender offer for approximately 65% of its outstanding stock at $60 per share cash. The Company also announced that, in connection with the closing of the self-tender offer, the Company would sell stock to a newly-formed Employee Stock Ownership Plan ("ESOP") amounting to 25% of all issued and outstanding stock following such sale. This alternative transaction (the "Company Transaction") itself is a continuation in another form of a recapitalization of the Company that had been approved by the Company's Board in February, 1986.

* * * Pending before the Court at this time is plaintiffs' motion for an order preliminarily enjoining the Company from (1) buying any shares of the Company's stock pursuant to its pending self-tender offer, (2) selling any of the Company's stock to the newly-established ESOP and (3) taking any steps to finance the self-tender offer or (4) attempting to apply or enforce a "fair price" provision contained in Article 11 of the Company's restated certificate of incorporation to any BS/G second-step merger at $56 per share.

In summary, plaintiffs contend that this relief is justified because the Company Transaction is an economically coercive transaction that deprives shareholders of the option presented by the BS/G offer, which provides demonstrably greater current value than is offered in the Company Transaction; and that in structuring the Company Transaction and in its timing the Board has breached its fiduciary duties of care and loyalty to the shareholders because the Company Transaction is designed and effective to deprive shareholders of effective choice, to entrench the existing Board and protect it from the discipline of the market for corporate control.

* * *

[Anderson, Clayton was faced with the prospect that four aging stockholders, owning 30% of its shares, would need to sell some of their stock for estate planning purposes. Accordingly, the AC board retained First Boston & Co. to explore alternatives. A management buyout foundered, and First Boston was asked to explore the sale of the company. Plaintiffs alleged that First Boston's efforts in this respect were weak, since neither it nor another obvious candidate were contacted. Instead of a sale or liquidation of the company, First Boston recommended a recapitalization, involving a merger and a shareholder vote, that would result in a partial liquidation, involving payment of substantial amounts of cash to shareholders and the issuance of large amounts of debt by the recapitalized company. First Boston estimated the value of this transaction at between $43 and $47 per share. When the recapitalization transaction was approved by the AC board and recommended to the shareholders, BS/G offered $54 per share all cash. The AC board never entered into meaningful negotiations with BS/G. Instead, it revised the transaction in the form of a share repurchase at $60 per share, coupled with the sale of a substantial portion of stock to the company's ESOP. The results were essentially the same as the previous recapitalization, but would not require a shareholder vote. First Boston was able to raise its estimate of the value of the Company Transaction to a range of $52.34 to $57.34, depending on the value of the remaining common stock (the "stub shares.")]

III.

* * *

Ordinarily when a court is required to review the propriety of a corporate transaction challenged as constituting a breach of duty or is asked to enjoin a proposed transaction on that ground, it will, in effect, decline to evaluate the merits or wisdom of the transaction once it is shown that the decision to accomplish the transaction was made by directors with no financial interest in the transaction adverse to the corporation and that in reaching the decision the directors followed an appropriately deliberative process. This deference—the business judgment rule—is, of course, simply a recognition of the allocation of responsibility made by section 141(a) of the General Corporation Law and of the limited institutional competence of courts to assess business decisions.

* * *

Because the effect of the proper invocation of the business judgment rule is so powerful and the standard of entire fairness so exacting, the determination of the appropriate standard of judicial review frequently is determinative of the outcome of derivative litigation. Perhaps for that reason, the Delaware Supreme Court recognized in Unocal Corp. v. Mesa Petroleum Co., Del.Supr., 493 A.2d 946 (1985) that where a board takes action designed to defeat a threatened change in control of the company, a more flexible, intermediate form of judicial review is appropriate. In such a setting the "omnipresent specter that a board may be acting primarily in its own interests," 493 A.2d at 954 (emphasis added), justifies the utilization of a standard that has two elements. First, there must be shown some basis for the Board to have concluded that a proper corporate purpose was served by implementation of the defensive measure and, second, that measure must be found reasonable in relation to the threat posed by the change in control that instigates the action. See Unocal, 493 A.2d at 955;. . . .

* * *

It is this standard of review applicable to corporate steps designed to defeat a threat to corporate control that I believe is applicable to the pending case. While this proposed stock repurchase derives from an earlier proposed recapitalization that itself may be said to have been defensive only in a general, preemptive way, there are elements of the present Company Transaction that are crucial to this case and that do not derive from the abandoned recapitalization. These elements are unmistakably reactive to the threat to corporate control posed by the BS/G $56 cash offer. Specifically, the timing of the self-tender offer and the decision to tender for 65.5% of the outstanding stock at $60 per share (rather than, as just one example, distributing the available $480,000,000 through an offer for 69% of the Company's 12,207,644 shares at $57) are elements of the transaction that go to the heart of plaintiff's complaint about coercion and that were obviously fixed in reaction to the timing and price of the BS/G offer.

I turn then to the two legs of the Unocal test.

A.

The first inquiry concerns the likelihood that defendants will be able to demonstrate a "reasonable ground for believing that a danger to corporate policy or effectiveness" exists by reason of the BS/G offer. Unocal, 493 A.2d at 955. Stated in these precise terms, the Company Transaction may seem not to satisfy this aspect of the Unocal test. There is no evidence that the BS/G offer—which is non-coercive and at a concededly fair price—threatens injury to shareholders or to the enterprise. However, I take this aspect of the test to be simply a particularization of the more general requirement that a corporate purpose, not one personal to the directors, must be served by the stock repurchase. As so understood, it seems clear that a self-tender in these circumstances meets this element of the appropriate test.

Unlike most of our cases treating defensive techniques, the Board does not seek to justify the Company Transaction as necessary to fend off an offer that is inherently unfair. Rather, Defendants account for their creation of the Company Transaction as the creation of an option to shareholders to permit them to have the benefits of a large, tax-advantaged cash distribution together with a continuing participation in a newly-structured, highly-leveraged Anderson, Clayton. The Board recognizes that the BS/G offer—being for all shares and offering cash consideration that the Board's expert advisor could not call unfair—is one that a rational shareholder might prefer. However, the Board asserts—and it seems to me to be unquestionably correct in this that a rational shareholder might prefer the Company Transaction. One's choice, if given an opportunity to effectively choose, might be dictated by any number of factors most of which (such as liquidity preference, degree of aversion to risk, alternative investment opportunities and even desire or disinterest in seeing the continuation of a distinctive Anderson, Clayton identity) are distinctive functions of each individual decision-maker. Recognizing this, the Board contends that "the decision in this fundamentally economic contest lies properly with the shareholders" and that the Board "has preserved the ability of the stockholders to choose between these two options."

The creation of such an alternative, with no other justification, serves a valid corporate purpose (certainly so where, as here, that option is made available to all shareholders on the same terms). That valid corporate purpose satisfies the first leg of the Unocal test.

B.

The fatal defect with the Company Transaction, however, becomes apparent when one attempts to apply the second leg of the Unocal test and asks whether the defensive step is "reasonable in relation to the threat posed." The BS/G offer poses a "threat" of any kind (other than a threat to the incumbency of the Board) only in a special sense and on the assumption that a majority of the Company's shareholders might prefer an alternative to the BS/G offer. On this assumption, it is reasonable to create an option that would permit shareholders to keep an equity interest in the firm, but, in my opinion, it is not reasonable in relation to such a "threat" to structure such an option so as to preclude as a practical matter shareholders from accepting the BS/G offer. As explained below, I am satisfied that the Company Transaction, if it proceeds in its current time frame, will have that effect.

If all that defendants have done is to create an option for shareholders, then it can hardly be thought to have breached a duty. Should that option be, on its merits, so attractive to shareholders as to command their majority approval, that fact alone, while disappointing to BS/G, can hardly be thought to render the Board's action wrongful. But plaintiffs join issue on defendants' most fundamental assertion that the Board has acted to create an option and to "preserve the ability of the stockholders to choose." Plaintiffs contend to the contrary that the Company Transaction was deliberately structured so that no rational shareholder can risk tendering into the BS/G offer. Plaintiffs say this for two related reasons: (1) Stockholders tendering into the BS/G offer have no assurance that BS/G will take down their stock at $56 a share since that offer is subject to conditions including a minimum number of shares tendered and abandonment of the Company Transaction; and (2) Tendering shareholders would thereby preclude themselves from participating in the "fat" front-end of the Company Transaction and risk having the value of all their shares fall very dramatically. In such circumstances, plaintiffs say, to characterize the Board's action as an attempt to preserve the ability of shareholders to choose is a charade. They claim the Company Transaction is coercive in fact and in the circumstances presented, improperly so in law.

May the Company Transaction be said to be coercive in the sense that no rational profit-maximizing shareholder can reasonably be expected to reject it? If it is concluded that the Company Transaction is coercive in this sense, one must ask why it is so and if, in these particular circumstances, this coercive aspect precludes a determination that the action is reasonable in light of the "threat" posed by the BS/G offer.

I conclude as a factual matter for purposes of this motion that no rational shareholder could afford not to tender into the Company's self-tender offer at least if that transaction is viewed in isolation. The record is uncontradicted that the value of the Company's stock following the effectuation of the Company Transaction will be materially less than $60 per share. The various experts differ only on how much less. Shearson, Lehman opines that the Company's stock will likely trade in a range of $22–$31 per share after consummation of the Company Transaction. First Boston is more hopeful, informally projecting a range of $37–52. What is clear under either view, however, is that a current shareholder who elects not to tender into the self-tender is very likely, upon consummation of the Company Transaction, to experience a substantial loss in market value of his holdings. The only way, within the confines of the Company Transaction, that a shareholder can protect himself from such an immediate financial loss, is to tender into the self-tender so that he receives his pro rata share of the cash distribution that will, in part, cause the expected fall in the market price of the Company's stock.[11]

I conclude that an Anderson, Clayton stockholder, acting with economic rationality, has no effective choice as between the contending offers as presently constituted. Even if a shareholder would prefer to sell all of his or her holdings at $56 per share in the BS/G offer, he or she may not risk tendering into that proposal and thereby risk being frozen out of the front end of the Company Transaction, should the BS/G offer not close.[12]

Thus, I conclude that if the Board's purpose was both to create an option to BS/G's any-and-all cash tender offer and to "preserve the ability of the shareholders to choose between those options" it has, as a practical matter, failed in the latter part of its mission.

The creation of an option of the kind represented by the Company Transaction need not have the collateral effect of foreclosing possible acceptance of the BS/G option by those shareholders who might prefer that alternative. The problem and its solution is one of timing. It would, in my opinion, be manifestly reasonable in relation to the limited "threat" posed by the BS/G any-and-all cash offer, for the Company to announce an

---

11. As a matter of fairly rudimentary economics it can readily be seen that a self-tender, being for less than all shares, can always be made at a price higher than the highest rational price that can be offered for all of the enterprises stock. See Bradley and Rosenzweig, Defensive Stock Repurchases, 99 Harv. L. Rev. 1378 (May, 1986).

12. BS/G could, by making its tender offer subject to no conditions, cure the coercive aspect of the Company Transaction, but it has no legal duty to extend an unconditional offer whereas the Board does have a legal duty to its shareholders to exercise its judgment to promote the stockholders' interests. Thus, in assessing the legal consequences in these circumstances of the conclusion that the Company Transaction has a coercive impact, I do not consider it relevant that plaintiffs, were they willing to do so, could counter that coercive effect by assuming additional risk.

alternative form of transaction (perhaps even a "front-end loaded" transaction of the kind the self-tender doubtlessly is)[13] to be available promptly should a majority not tender into the BS/G offer. An alternative timed in such a way would be a defensive step, in that it would make the change in control threatened by the BS/G offer less likely; it would afford to shareholders an alternative that, due to the non-coercive nature of the BS/G offer, would be readily available to shareholders if a majority of the shareholders in fact prefers it; and it would leave unimpaired the ability of shareholders effectively to elect the BS/G option if a majority of shareholders in fact prefers that option. A board need not be passive, Unocal, 493 A.2d at 954, even in the face of an any-and-all cash offer at a fair price with an announced follow up merger offering the same consideration. But in that special case, a defensive step that includes a coercive self-tender timed to effectively preclude a rational shareholder from accepting the any-and-all offer cannot, in my opinion, be deemed to be reasonable in relation to any minimal threat posed to stockholders by such offer.

What then is the legal consequence of a conclusion that the Company Transaction is a defensive step that is not reasonable in relation to the threat posed? The first consequence is that the Board's action does not qualify for the protections afforded by the business judgment rule. In the light of that fact, the obvious entrenchment effect of the Company Transaction and the conclusion that that transaction cannot be justified as reasonable in the circumstances, I conclude that it is likely to be found to constitute a breach of a duty of loyalty, albeit a possibly unintended one. (I need not and do not express any opinion on the question of subjective intent.) Where director action is not protected by the business judgment rule, mere good faith will not preclude a finding of a breach of the duty of loyalty. Rather, in most such instances (which happen to be self-dealing transactions), the transaction can only be sustained if it is objectively or intrinsically fair; an honest belief that the transaction was entirely fair will not alone be sufficient.

[The court determined it would issue a preliminary injunction, but ordered further hearings on its form.]

QUESTIONS

1. What can cause a court to abandon the deference of the business judgment rule in reviewing a transaction and impose a "more flexible, intermediate form of judicial review" under Unocal Corp. v. Mesa Petroleum Co.? What is the rationale for this shift?

2. Were there strategic reasons for abandoning a recapitalization plan in favor of a self-tender offer? If so, what were they?

3. Note that the AC board had previously adopted a recapitalization plan to create shareholder value. Here, as in Paramount Communications,

---

13. That is the $60 cash consideration offered is of greater current value than the stock with which a non-tendering shareholder will be left following consummation of the Company Transaction.

Inc. v. Time, Inc., 571 A.2d 1140 (1989), this decision was made without the pressure of a pending tender offer. In that case, the court held that the Time board was entitled to defend its earlier decision. Was this original decision (the recapitalization) eligible for protection under the business judgment rule?

4. If AC was offering $60 per share in its tender offer and BS/G offered $56 per share, how could AC's offer possibly be inferior to the BS/G offer?

5. What was coercive about AC's repurchase offer? Why couldn't shareholders simply decide the deal offered by BS/G was superior, and reject the AC offer?

6. How could the board have made the Company Transaction non-coercive? Would this have provided shareholders a meaningful choice?

iv. TARGETED REPURCHASES

Perhaps the most controversial repurchases of the 1980s involved repurchases of blocks of stock held by a stockholder who threatened a takeover. Stock repurchases can be used to persuade a potential hostile bidder to abandon its takeover efforts, if the shares are repurchased from the bidder at an attractive price, often above the current market price. These repurchases are called "greenmail." See Heckmann v. Ahmanson, 214 Cal. Rptr. 177 (1985), in Chapter Four, Part 5. The incidence of greenmail declined to zero in the 1990s, most likely due to an effective tax rate of 84% imposed on greenmail payments by Internal Revenue Code § 5881, adopted in 1987. Prior to this time there was a vigorous debate about whether greenmail could ever benefit target company shareholders. See Macey and McChesney, A Theoretical Analysis of Corporate Greenmail, 95 Yale L.J. 13 (1985) and Gordon and Kornhauser, Takeover Defense Tactics: A Comment on Two Models, 96 Yale L. J. 295 (1986). The transaction described in the following case was not covered by the greenmail provisions of IRC § 5881, which requires that the stockholder have made takeover threats before being bought out.

Grobow v. Perot

539 A.2d 180 (Del. 1988).

■ HORSEY, JUSTICE.

In these consolidated shareholder derivative suits, plaintiffs-shareholders appeal the Court of Chancery's dismissal of their suits for failure of plaintiffs to make presuit demand under Court of Chancery Rule 23.1. The Court of Chancery held that plaintiffs' complaints as amended failed to allege particularized facts which, if taken as true, would excuse demand under the demand futility test of Aronson v. Lewis, Del. Supr., 473 A.2d 805 (1984). The Court interpreted Aronson's "reasonable doubt" standard for establishing demand futility as requiring plaintiffs to plead particularized facts sufficient to sustain "a judicial finding" either of director interest or lack of director independence, or whether the directors exercised proper business judgment in approving the challenged transaction, placing the transaction beyond the protection of the business judgment rule. We find the Vice Chancellor to have erred in formulating an excessive criterion for satisfying Aronson's reasonable doubt test. Moreover, the Vice Chancellor erred in his statement that fairness is a "pivotal" question under an Aronson analysis. Unless the presumption of the business judgment rule is overcome by the pleadings, questions of fairness play no part in the analysis. However, applying the correct standard, we conclude that the complaints (singly or collectively) fail to state facts which, if taken as true, would create a reasonable doubt either of director disinterest or independence, or that the transaction was other than the product of the Board's valid exercise of business judgment. Therefore, we affirm the decision below, finding the Court's error to have been harmless.

I

* * *

A.

In 1984, General Motors Corporation ("GM") acquired 100 percent of Electronic Data Systems' ("EDS") stock. Under the terms of the merger, H. Ross Perot, founder, chairman and largest stockholder of EDS, exchanged his EDS stock for GM Class E stock and contingent notes. Perot became GM's largest shareholder, holding 0.8 percent of GM voting stock. Perot was also elected to GM's Board of Directors (the "Board") while remaining chairman of EDS.

The merger proved mutually beneficial to both corporations and was largely a success. However, management differences developed between Perot and the other officers and directors of GM's Board over the way GM was running EDS, and Perot became increasingly vocal in his criticism of GM management. By mid–1986, Perot announced to GM that he could no longer be a "company man." Perot demanded that GM allow him to run EDS as he saw fit or that GM buy him out. Perot then began publicly criticizing GM management with such statements as: "Until you nuke the old GM system, you'll never tap the full potential of your people"; and "GM cannot become a world-class and cost-competitive company simply by throwing technology and money at its problems." Thereafter, GM and American Telephone and Telegraph entered into exploratory negotiations for AT & T's purchase of EDS from GM allegedly as a means of GM's eliminating Perot. However, their negotiations did not proceed beyond the preliminary stage.

By late fall of 1986, Perot, anxious, for tax reasons, for a definitive decision before year-end, offered to sell his entire interest in GM. GM responded with a purchase proposal. Perot replied, suggesting additional terms, which Perot characterized as "a giant premium." When a definitive agreement was reached, the Board designated a three-member Special Review Committee ("SRC"), chaired by one of the Board's outside directors to review its terms. The SRC met on November 30, 1986 to consider the repurchase proposal and unanimously recommended that GM's Board approve its terms. The following day, December 1, 1986, the GM Board of Directors met and approved the repurchase agreement.

Under the terms of the repurchase, GM acquired all of Perot's GM Class E stock and contingent notes and those of his close EDS associates for nearly $745,000,000. GM also received certain commitments, termed "covenants," from Perot. In addition to resigning immediately from GM's Board and as Chairman of EDS, Perot further agreed: (1) to stop criticizing GM management, in default of which Perot agreed to pay GM damages in a liquidated sum of up to $7.5 million;[3] (2) not to purchase GM stock or engage in a proxy contest against the Board for five years; and (3) not to compete with EDS for three years or recruit EDS executives for eighteen months.

At all relevant times, a majority of the GM Board of Directors consisted of outside directors. The exact number and composition of the GM Board at the time is not clear. However, from the limited record, it appears that the Board was comprised of twenty-six directors (excluding Perot), of whom eighteen were outside directors.

The GM repurchase came at a time when GM was experiencing financial difficulty and was engaged in cost cutting. Public reaction to the announcement ranged from mixed to adverse. The repurchase was sharply criticized by industry analysts and by members within GM's management ranks as well. The criticism focused on two features of the repurchase: (1) the size of the premium over the then market price of GM class E stock;[4] and (2) the hush mail provision.

B.

Plaintiffs filed separate derivative actions (later consolidated) against GM, EDS, GM's directors, H. Ross Perot, and three of Perot's EDS associates. The suits collectively allege: (i) that the GM director defendants breached their fiduciary duties to GM and EDS by paying a grossly excessive price for the repurchase of Perot's and the EDS associates' Class E stock of GM; (ii) that the repurchase included a unique hush mail feature

---

3. This commitment by Perot would later be characterized as the "hush mail" feature of the agreement. The colloquial term is not defined in the pleadings but is assumed by this Court to combine the terms "green mail" and "hush money" to connote a variation on an unlawful and secret payment to assure silence. Here, the commitment is cast in the form of an explicit liquidated damage clause for future breach of contract. See infra section III B.

4. Plaintiffs allege that the total repurchase price per share ($31.375) was double the market price of the GM class E stock on the last day of trading before consummation of the repurchase ($61.90) [Sic. The trial court opinion makes clear that the "total sell-out price" was $61.90 per share, or double the stock's market value. 526 A.2d 914, 919, n. 6 (Del. Ch. 1987)]. However, the extent of premium over market cannot be mathematically calculated with any precision without disregarding the value of the contingent notes. The total repurchase price per share includes not only the price paid for the class E stock, but also the price paid for the contingent notes and the value of the special interest federal tax compensation. See infra note 7.

to buy not only Perot's resignation, but his silence, and that such a condition lacked any valid business purpose and was a waste of GM assets; and (iii) that the repurchase was entrenchment motivated and was carried out principally to save GM's Board from further public embarrassment by Perot. The complaints charge the individual defendants with acting out of self-interest and with breaching their duties of loyalty and due care to GM and EDS.

* * *

III

* * *

As previously noted, the business judgment rule is but a presumption that directors making a business decision, not involving self-interest, act on an informed basis, in good faith and in the honest belief that their actions are in the corporation's best interest. Thus, good faith and the absence of self-dealing are threshold requirements for invoking the rule. Assuming the presumptions of director good faith and lack of self-dealing are not rebutted by well-pleaded facts, a shareholder derivative complainant must then allege further facts with particularity which, "taken as true, support a reasonable doubt that the challenged transaction was [in fact] the product of a valid exercise of business judgment." The complaints as amended do not even purport to plead a claim of fraud, bad faith, or self-dealing in the usual sense of personal profit or betterment. Therefore, we must presume that the GM directors reached their repurchase decision in good faith.

* * *

A.   Disinterest and Independence

* * *

Having failed to plead financial interest with any particularity, plaintiffs' complaints must raise a reasonable doubt of director disinterest based on entrenchment. Plaintiffs attempt to do so mainly through reliance on Unocal Corp. v. Mesa Petroleum Co., Del. Supr., 493 A.2d 946 (1985); Unocal, however, is distinguishable. The enhanced duty of care that the Unocal directors were found to be under was triggered by a struggle for corporate control and the inherent presumption of director self-interest associated with such a contest. Here there was no outside threat to corporate policy of GM sufficient to raise a Unocal issue of whether the directors' response was reasonable to the threat posed.

Plaintiffs also do not plead any facts tending to show that the GM directors' positions were actually threatened by Perot, who owned only 0.8 percent of GM's voting stock, nor do plaintiffs allege that the repurchase was motivated and reasonably related to the directors' retention of their positions on the Board. Plaintiffs merely argue that Perot's public criticism of GM management could cause the directors embarrassment sufficient to lead to their removal from office. Such allegations are tenuous at best and are too speculative to raise a reasonable doubt of director disinterest. Speculation on motives for undertaking corporate action are wholly insufficient to establish a case of demand excusal. Therefore, we agree with the Vice Chancellor that plaintiffs' entrenchment theory is based largely on supposition rather than fact.

Plaintiffs' remaining allegations bearing on the issue of entrenchment are: the rushed nature of the transaction during a period of GM financial difficulty; the giant premium paid;[7] and the criticism (after the fact) of the repurchase by industry analysts and top GM management. Plaintiffs argue that these allegations are sufficient to raise a reasonable doubt of director disinterest. We cannot agree. Not one of the asserted grounds would support a reasonable belief of entrenchment based on director self-interest. The relevance of these averments goes largely to the issue of due care, next discussed. Such allegations are patently insufficient to raise a reasonable doubt as to the ability of the GM Board to act with disinterest. Thus, we find plaintiffs' entrenchment claim to be essentially conclusory and lacking in factual support sufficient to establish excusal based on director interest.

* * *

B. Director Due Care

Having concluded that plaintiffs have failed to plead a claim of financial interest or entrenchment sufficient to excuse presuit demand, we examine the complaints as amended to determine whether they raise a reasonable doubt that the directors exercised proper business judgment in the transaction. By proper business judgment we mean both substantive due care (purchase terms), and procedural due care (an informed decision).

With regard to the nature of the transactions and the terms of repurchase, especially price, plaintiffs allege that the premium paid Perot constituted a prima facie waste of GM's assets. Plaintiffs argue that the transaction, on its face, was "so egregious as to be afforded no presumption of business judgment protection." * * *

The law of Delaware is well established that, in the absence of evidence of fraud or unfairness, a corporation's repurchase of its capital stock at a premium over market from a dissident shareholder is entitled to the protection of the business judgment rule. We have already determined that plaintiffs have not stated a claim of financial interest or entrenchment as the compelling motive for the repurchase, and it is equally clear that the complaints as amended do not allege a claim of fraud. They allege, at most,

---

7. The formula plaintiffs use to establish the existence of a "giant premium" is ambiguous, making the allegation conclusory. The total repurchase price includes not only the price paid for the class E stock, but also the price paid for the contingent notes and the value of the tax compensation. Ambiguity is caused when these items are factored in, especially the contingent note discounts. For example, in their complaints, plaintiffs appear to discount the contingent notes by $16.20, reflecting present value ($62.50–$46.30). The GM directors, however, discount the notes by $6.00. This disparity appears to be due to plaintiffs' use of a base figure of $46.30, which is $16.20 less than that used by the defendants. The plaintiffs fail to explain this disparity with particularity, thus failing to satisfy their burden under Aronson.

a claim of waste based on the assertion that GM's Board paid such a premium for the Perot holdings as to shock the conscience of the ordinary person.

Thus, the issue becomes whether the complaints state a claim of waste of assets, i.e., whether "what the corporation has received is so inadequate in value that no person of ordinary, sound business judgment would deem it worth that which the corporation has paid." By way of reinforcing their claim of waste, plaintiffs seize upon the hush-mail feature of the repurchase as being the motivating reason for the "giant premium" approved by the GM Board. Plaintiffs then argue that buying the silence of a dissident within management constitutes an invalid business purpose. Ergo, plaintiffs argue that a claim of waste of corporate assets evidencing lack of director due care has been well pleaded.

The Vice Chancellor was not persuaded by this reasoning to reach such a conclusion and neither are we. Plaintiffs' assertions by way of argument go well beyond their factual allegations, and it is the latter which are controlling. Plaintiffs' complaints as amended fail to plead with particularity any facts supporting a conclusion that the primary or motivating purpose of the Board's payment of a "giant premium" for the Perot holdings was to buy Perot's silence rather than simply to buy him out and remove him from GM's management team. To the contrary, plaintiffs themselves state in their complaints as amended several legitimate business purposes for the GM Board's decision to sever its relationship with Perot: (1) the Board's determination that it would be in GM's best interest to retain control over its wholly-owned subsidiary, EDS; and (2) the decision to rid itself of the principal cause of the growing internal policy dispute over EDS' management and direction.

* * *

In addition to regaining control over the management affairs of EDS, GM also secured, through the complex repurchase agreement, significant covenants from Perot, of which the hush-mail provision was but one of many features and multiple considerations of the repurchase. Quite aside from whatever consideration could be attributed to buying Perot's silence, GM's Board received for the $742.8 million paid: all the class E stock and contingent notes of Perot and his fellow EDS directors; Perot's covenant not to compete or hire EDS employees; his promise not to purchase GM stock or engage in proxy contests; Perot's agreement to stay out of and away from GM's and EDS' affairs, plus the liquidated damages provision should Perot breach his no-criticism covenant.

Plaintiffs' effort to quantify the size of the premium paid by GM is flawed, as we have already noted, by their inability to place a dollar value on the various promises made by Perot, particularly his covenant not to compete with EDS or to attempt to hire away EDS employees. (See supra notes 2, 4, and 7.) Thus, viewing the transaction in its entirety, we must agree with the Court of Chancery that plaintiffs have failed to plead with particularity facts sufficient to create a reasonable doubt that the substantive terms of the repurchase fall within the protection of the business judgment rule.

* * *

[The court also rejected plaintiff's claim that the directors did not make an informed decision.]

IV.   Conclusion

Apart from whether the Board of Directors may be subject to criticism for the premium paid Perot and his associates for the repurchase of their entire interest in GM, on the present record the repurchase of dissident Perot's interests can only be viewed legally as representing an exercise of business judgment by the General Motors Board with which a court may not interfere. Only through a considerable stretch of the imagination could one reasonably believe this Board of Directors to be "interested" in a self-dealing sense in Perot's ouster from GM's management. We view a board of directors with a majority of outside directors, such as this Board, as being in the nature of overseers of management. So viewed, the Board's exercise of judgment in resolving an internal rift in management of serious proportions and at the highest executive level should be accorded the protection of the business judgment rule absent well-pleaded averments implicating financial self-interest, entrenchment, or lack of due care. These complaints fall far short of stating a claim for demand excusal.

* * * We hold that the complaints as amended fail to allege facts sufficient to create a reasonable doubt that the GM Board-approved repurchase transaction is not within the protection of the business judgment rule; thus, the plaintiffs have failed to establish the futility of demand required under Aronson and Pogostin for casting reasonable doubt thereon. The Trial Court, therefore, correctly dismissed the suits under Del. Ch. Ct. R. 23.1 for failure of plaintiffs to make presuit demand upon the GM Board.

Affirmed.

QUESTIONS

1. Are there any allegations of bad faith that would excuse demand?

2. If the way to assign a value to the premium paid for the class E stock is to separately value the other consideration, what methodology would you use to assign a value to the Contingent Notes. Each contingent note, on maturity, entitles the holder to the difference between (i) $62.50 and (ii) the then-current market price per share of Class E stock, for each Class E share received in the merger, plus "Special Interest" to offset certain federal tax consequences.

3. How would you value a covenant not to compete?

4. Can you put a value on what GM paid Perot to stop criticizing GM management?

5. What price do you suppose GM paid Perot for the standstill agreement?

6. What business purpose could GM have possibly had for getting Perot to agree to "stand still" and not purchase GM stock or engage in a proxy fight for 5 years?

7. What business purpose could GM have had for getting Perot to resign from the board?

8. Why, in a demand excused case, does the court require plaintiffs to show that the Board failed to exercise "sound business judgment 'in the honest belief that the action taken was in the best interest of the company' "?

9. Is getting a covenant not to compete a good business purpose?

D. DUTIES IN SHARE REPURCHASES

Nixon v. Blackwell

626 A.2d 1366 (Del. 1993).

■ VEASEY, CHIEF JUSTICE:

In this action we review a decision of the Court of Chancery holding that the defendant directors of a closely-held corporation breached their fiduciary duties to the plaintiffs by maintaining a discriminatory policy that unfairly favors employee stockholders over plaintiffs. The Vice Chancellor found that the directors treated the plaintiffs unfairly by establishing an employee stock ownership plan ("ESOP") and by purchasing key man life insurance policies to provide liquidity for defendants and other corporate employees to enable them to sell their stock while providing no comparable liquidity for minority stockholders. We conclude that the Court of Chancery applied erroneous legal standards and made findings of fact which were not the product of an orderly and logical deductive reasoning process. Accordingly, we REVERSE and REMAND to the Court of Chancery for proceedings not inconsistent with this opinion.

I. Facts

[The corporation was founded in 1928 by E. C. Barton. He set up two classes of common stock: Class A voting stock and Class B non-voting stock. Mr. Barton's purpose was to keep voting control of the company in the hands of its employees, and upon his death some of the Class A stock was bequeathed directly to employees, while the balance, along with 14% of the Class B stock, was placed in a trust for the same eight employees. The Class B stock was bequeathed to his second wife, and to his daughter and granddaughter from his first marriage. In order to assure that the Class A stock remained in the hands of employees, Mr. Barton caused the corporation to purchase "key man life insurance" policies on the lives of the key executives and directors, part of the proceeds of which were to be used to repurchase Class A shares from decedents' estates, so Class A shares would not be held by non-employee descendants. At times the premiums on this insurance were quite large, exceeding the dividends paid by the company.

To further assure retention of the A stock by employees, the company also had the right to exchange the Class A stock for Class B stock in the event of death or termination of employment.

Mr. Barton also caused the company to create an Employee Stock Ownership Plan ("ESOP") for the benefit of employees. The ESOP held Class B shares, and upon termination of employment employees were entitled to take either Class B shares or cash.

There was no public market for either the A or B shares, but from time to time the company had made repurchase offers for the Class B stock. In 1985 the company made a tender offer for 48,000 shares of Class B stock, at a price that the Class B shareholders rejected.]

* * *

F. Dividend Policy and Compensation

The Board from time to time paid modest dividends. Because the earnings were solid in many years and dividends relatively low, the retained earnings of the Corporation continued to increase at a relatively high level. Plaintiffs challenged these corporate decisions as unfair to the minority. There was also a challenge at trial by plaintiffs to the compensation level of the defendants. In view of the ruling of the Vice Chancellor in defendants' favor on the dividend policy and against the plaintiffs on the claim of excessive compensation, from which rulings no appeal was taken by plaintiffs, there is no need to detail the facts relating to those issues, except to the extent, hereinafter discussed, that the trial court referred to the dividend policy in connection with other issues or fairness generally.

II. Proceedings in The Court of Chancery

* * *

At trial, the plaintiffs charged the defendants with (1) attempting to force the minority stockholders to sell their shares at a discount by embarking on a scheme to pay negligible dividends, (2) breaching their fiduciary duties by authorizing excessive compensation for themselves and other employees of the Corporation, and (3) breaching their fiduciary duties by pursuing a discriminatory liquidity policy that favors employee stockholders over non-employee stockholders through the ESOP and key man life insurance policies. The plaintiffs sought money damages for past dividends, a one-time liquidity dividend, and a guarantee of future dividends at a specified rate.

The Vice Chancellor held that the Corporation's low-dividend policy was within the bounds of business judgment, that the executive compensation levels were not excessive, and ruled in favor of defendants on these issues. The Vice Chancellor further held, however, that the defendant directors had breached their fiduciary duties to the minority. The basis for this ruling was that it was "inherently unfair" for the defendants to establish the ESOP and to purchase key man life insurance to provide liquidity for themselves while providing no comparable method by which the non-employee Class B stockholders may liquidate their stock at fair value. Holding that the "needs of all stockholders must be considered and addressed when providing liquidity," the court ruled that the directors breached their fiduciary duties, and granted relief to plaintiffs. The trial court ruled against the plaintiffs on all the other issues. Since plaintiffs have not appealed those rulings, they are not before this Court.

* * *

III.   Rationale of the Vice Chancellor's Decision

* * *

The only issue before this Court is the ruling by the trial court as implemented in its judgment and final order that the defendants breached their fiduciary duties by failing to provide a parity of liquidity. The theory of the trial court on this issue is based upon the fact that, as directors, defendants approved the ESOP and the key man life insurance program, both of which had the effect of benefiting them as employees, with no corresponding benefit to plaintiffs. Thus, the trial court reasoned, defendants are on both sides of the transaction and the business judgment rule does not apply. Therefore, defendants have the burden of showing the entire fairness of their actions on these issues, which burden the Vice Chancellor held they had not carried.

The following portions of the opinion of the trial court are crucial to the determination of the issues on appeal:

> The inquiry does not end, however, with a finding that defendants have not been overcompensated. They have paid low dividends over the years and have attempted to justify high levels of retained earnings in part as a means of promoting the company's growth. If defendants' focus is on appreciation in the value of the company's stock as opposed to the payment of more than minimal dividends, it would be logical to assume that defendants had or were developing a plan that would enable the company's stockholders to realize the increased value of their shares. No such general plan has been adopted, however, and the few steps defendants have taken demonstrate the validity of plaintiffs' claim of unfair treatment.

> All Barton stockholders face the same liquidity problem. If they are to sell their shares, they must persuade defendants to authorize a repurchase by the company. The stockholders have no bargaining power and must accept whatever terms are dictated by defendants or retain their stock. If the stockholder is pressed for cash to pay estate taxes, for example, as has happened more than once, the stockholder is entirely at defendants' mercy. Defendants recognized their employee stockholders' liquidity needs when they established the ESOP. As noted previously, employees have the option of taking cash in lieu of the shares allocated to their accounts. Moreover, the disparity in bargaining position is eliminated for employee stockholders because the cash payment is determined on the basis of an annual valuation

made by an independent party. *No similar plan or arrangement has been put into place with respect to the Class B stockholders. There is no point in time at which they can be assured of receiving cash for all or any portion of their holdings at a price determined by an independent appraiser.*

Defendants have gone one step farther in addressing their own liquidity problems. Their ESOP allocation may be handled in the same manner as other employees. However, defendants are substantial stockholders independent of their ESOP holdings. *In order to solve defendants' own liquidity problem, the company has been purchasing key man life insurance since at least 1982. The proceeds will help assure that Barton is in a position to purchase all of defendants' stock at the time of death.* In 1989, the premium cost for the key man insurance was slightly higher than the total amount paid in dividends for the year.

While the purchase of key man life insurance may be a relatively small corporate expenditure, it is concrete evidence that defendants have favored their own interests as stockholders over plaintiffs'. It also makes one wonder whether the decisions to accumulate large amounts of cash and pay low dividends were not also at least partially motivated by self-interest. The law is settled that fiduciaries may not benefit themselves at the expense of the corporation, Guth v. Loft, Inc., 23 Del. Ch. 255, 5 A.2d 503, 510 (1939), and that, when directors make self-interested decisions, they must establish the entire fairness of those decisions. Weinberger v. UOP, Inc., Del. Supr., 457 A.2d 701, 710 (1983).

I find it inherently unfair for defendants to be purchasing key man life insurance in order to provide liquidity for themselves while providing no method by which plaintiffs may liquidate their stock at fair value. By this ruling, I am not suggesting that there is some generalized duty to purchase illiquid stock at any particular price. However, the needs of all stockholders must be considered and addressed when decisions are made to provide some form of liquidity. Both the ESOP and the key man insurance provide some measure of liquidity, but only for a select group of stockholders. Accordingly, I find that relief is warranted.

Blackwell v. Nixon, Del.Ch., C.A. No. 9041, Berger, V.C. (Sept. 26, 1991) (Sept. 26, 1991) (footnotes omitted; emphasis supplied).

* * *

V.   Applicable Principles of Substantive Law

Defendants contend that the trial court erred in not applying the business judgment rule. Since the defendants benefited from the ESOP and could have benefited from the key man life insurance beyond that which benefited other stockholders generally, the defendants are on both sides of the transaction. For that reason, we agree with the trial court that the entire fairness test applies to this aspect of the case. Accordingly, defendants have the burden of showing the entire fairness of those transactions. Sinclair Oil Corp. v. Levien, Del. Supr., 280 A.2d 717 (1971) ("Levien"); Weinberger v. UOP, Inc., Del. Supr., 457 A.2d 701 (1983) ("Weinberger").

* * *

Weinberger explains further the two aspects of entire fairness, fair price and fair dealing: * * * Id. at 711. The case before us involves only the issue of fair dealing.

It is often of critical importance whether a particular decision is one to which the business judgment rule applies or the entire fairness rule applies. It is sometimes thought that the decision whether to apply the business judgment rule or the entire fairness test can be outcome-determinative.

Because the effect of the proper invocation of the business judgment rule is so powerful and the standard of entire fairness so exacting, the determination of the appropriate standard of judicial review frequently is determinative of the outcome of derivative litigation.

Application of the entire fairness rule does not, however, always implicate liability of the conflicted corporate decisionmaker, nor does it necessarily render the decision void.

The entire fairness analysis essentially requires "judicial scrutiny." In business judgment rule cases, an essential element is the fact that there has been a business decision made by a disinterested and independent corporate decisionmaker. When there is no independent corporate decision-maker, the court may become the objective arbiter.

The trial court in this case, however, appears to have adopted the novel legal principle that Class B stockholders had a right to "liquidity" equal to that which the court found to be available to the defendants. It is well established in our jurisprudence that stockholders need not always be treated equally for all purposes. See Unocal Corp. v. Mesa Petroleum Co., Del. Supr., 493 A.2d 946, 957 (1985) ("Unocal") (discriminatory exchange offer held valid); and Cheff v. Mathes, 41 Del. Ch. 494, 199 A.2d 548, 554–56 (1964) (selective stock repurchase held valid). To hold that fairness necessarily requires precise equality is to beg the question:

> Many scholars, though few courts, conclude that one aspect of fiduciary duty is the equal treatment of investors. Their argument takes the following form: fiduciary principles require fair conduct; equal treatment is fair conduct; hence, fiduciary principles require equal treatment. The conclusion does not follow. The argument depends on an equivalence between equal and fair treatment. To say that fiduciary principles require equal treatment is to beg the question whether investors would contract for equal or even equivalent treatment.

Frank H. Easterbrook and Daniel R. Fischel, The Economic Structure of Corporate Law 110 (1991) (emphasis in original). This holding of the trial court overlooks the significant facts that the minority stockholders were not: (a) employees of the Corporation; (b) entitled to share in an ESOP; (c) qualified for key man insurance; or (d) protected by specific provisions in the certificate of incorporation, by-laws, or a stockholders' agreement.

There is support in this record for the fact that the ESOP is a corporate benefit and was established, at least in part, to benefit the Corporation. Generally speaking, the creation of ESOPs is a normal corporate practice and is generally thought to benefit the corporation. The same is true generally with respect to key man insurance programs. If such corporate practices were necessarily to require equal treatment for non-employee stockholders, that would be a matter for legislative determination in Delaware. There is no such legislation to that effect. If we were to adopt such a rule, our decision would border on judicial legislation. See Providence & Worcester Co. v. Baker, Del. Supr., 378 A.2d 121, 124 (1977).

Accordingly, we hold that the Vice Chancellor erred as a matter of law in concluding that the liquidity afforded to the employee stockholders by the ESOP and the key man insurance required substantially equal treatment for the non-employee stockholders. Moreover, the Vice Chancellor failed to evaluate and articulate, for example, whether or not and to what extent (a) corporate benefits flowed from the ESOP and the key man insurance; (b) the ESOP and key man insurance plans are novel, extraordinary, or relatively routine business practices; (c) the dividend policy was even relevant; (d) Mr. Barton's plan for employee management and benefits should be honored; and (e) the self-tenders showed defendants' willingness to provide an exit opportunity for the plaintiffs.

In a case where the court is scrutinizing the fairness of a self-interested corporate transaction the court should articulate the standards which it is applying in its scrutiny of the transactions. These standards are not carved in stone for all cases because a court of equity must necessarily have the flexibility to deal with varying circumstances and issues. Yet, the standards must be reasonable, articulable, and articulated. While the court is not expected to substitute its business judgment for that of the directors in areas where particular business expertise is an ingredient of the decision, the reasonableness of the business judgment of the conflicted directors' decision must be examined searchingly through a principled and disciplined analysis. The decision of the trial court did not plainly delineate and articulate findings of fact and conclusions of law so that this Court, as the reviewing court, could fathom without undue difficulty the bases for the trial court's decision. The court's decision should not be the product solely of subjective, reflexive impressions based primarily on suspicion or what has sometimes been called the "smell test."[17]

---

17. We are mindful of the elasticity inherent in equity jurisprudence and the traditional desirability in certain equity cases of measuring conduct by the "conscience of the court" and disapproving conduct which offends or shocks that conscience. Yet one must be wary of equity jurisprudence which takes on a random or ad hoc quality.

> Equity is a roughish [sic] thing. For law we have to measure, know what to trust to; Equity is according to the conscience of him that is Chancellor, and as that is larger or narrower, so it Equity. 'Tis all one as if they should make the standard for the measure we call a "foot" a Chancellor's foot; what an uncertain measure would this be. Once

We hold on this record that defendants have met their burden of establishing the entire fairness of their dealings with the non-employee Class B stockholders, and are entitled to judgment. The record is sufficient to conclude that plaintiffs' claim that the defendant directors have maintained a discriminatory policy of favoring Class A employee stockholders over Class B non-employee stockholders is without merit. The directors have followed a consistent policy originally established by Mr. Barton, the founder of the Corporation, whose intent from the formation of the Corporation was to use the Class A stock as the vehicle for the Corporation's continuity through employee management and ownership.

Mr. Barton established the Corporation in 1928 by creating two classes of stock, not one, and by holding 100 percent of the Class A stock and 82 percent of the Class B stock. Mr. Barton himself established the practice of purchasing key man life insurance with funds of the Corporation to retain in the employ of the Corporation valuable employees by assuring them that, following their retirement or death, the Corporation will have liquid assets which could be used to repurchase the shares acquired by the employee, which shares may otherwise constitute an illiquid and unsalable asset of his or her estate. Another rational purpose is to prevent the stock from passing out of the control of the employees of the Corporation into the hands of family or descendants of the employee.

The directors' actions following Mr. Barton's death are consistent with Mr. Barton's plan. An ESOP, for example, is normally established for employees. Accordingly, there is no inequity in limiting ESOP benefits to the employee stockholders. Indeed, it makes no sense to include non-employees in ESOP benefits. The fact that the Class B stock represented 75 percent of the Corporation's total equity is irrelevant to the issue of fair dealing. The Class B stock was given no voting rights because those stockholders were not intended to have a direct voice in the management and operation of the Corporation. They were simply passive investors—entitled to be treated fairly but not necessarily to be treated equally. The fortunes of the Corporation rested with the Class A employee stockholders and the Class B stockholders benefited from the multiple increases in value of their Class B stock. Moreover, the Board made continuing efforts to buy back the Class B stock.

* * *

[The court rejected judicial adoption of the "equal opportunity" rule of cases such as Donahue v. Rodd Electrotype Corp. of New England, Inc., 328 N.E.2d 505 (Mass. 1975) as modified by Wilkes v. Springside Nursing Home, Inc., 353 N.E.2d 657 (Mass. 1976). The court noted the availability contractual solutions when a shareholder enters a relationship to provide

---

Chancellor has a long foot, another a short foot, a third an indifferent foot. 'Tis the same thing in the Chancellor's conscience.

John Selden, 1584–1654. "Equity," Table–Talk, 1689. The Quotable Lawyer 97. (David S. Shrager and Elizabeth Frost eds., 1986)

liquidity, and held that the special remedies of the close corporation chapter preempted the field in Delaware.]

QUESTIONS

1. The opinion emphasizes that the plaintiff shareholders took their shares subject to plans for the ESOP and key man insurance that Mr. Barton had chosen. What does this say about the bundle of rights they obtained? Would the outcome have been different if they had purchased shares at the creation of the corporation, and Mr. Barton, as dominant stockholder, had caused the creation of these devices?

2. Would the outcome have been different if the corporation paid no dividends at all? What arguments could you make if you represented the Class B shareholders?

3. What opportunities did the B shareholders have to bargain about the terms of their relationship with the company? Note that Class B stock was bequeathed in trust to Mr. Barton's wife and daughter and grandaughter. Employees who terminated employment got B shares either from the Company or the ESOP or both.

6. LEVERAGED BUYOUTS

Review sections 4–8 of the Uniform Fraudulent Transfer Act, at the beginning of Part 2 of this chapter.

At first blush leveraged buyouts don't seem to belong in a chapter on distributions—a third party buys the corporate shares from the existing shareholders in a leveraged buyout, or LBO. The buyer raises the funds for the purchase largely through borrowings that are ultimately secured by the subject corporation's assets. Prime candidates for LBOS are companies with steady and predictable cash flows that enable the company to service its debt, and companies with relatively large proportions of fungible and marketable assets that can be liquidated quickly in the event of default. These are the most attractive kinds of assets for lenders, because a security interest in them has real value.

The prototypical LBO that spawns cases such as the two that follow involves the buyer's creation of an Acquisition Subsidiary, which is wholly owned by the buyer, into which the buyer's shareholders have invested some equity—whatever amount is demanded by the prospective lenders. The Acquisition Subsidiary then secures loan agreements from lenders, and agrees to pledge all of its property to secure the loans. The Acquisition Subsidiary and the "Target" corporation then merge, with the surviving corporation succeeding to all of the obligations of the constituent corporations—including the Acquisition Subsidiary's loans, security agreements and mortgages. The cash proceeds are paid to the Target shareholders, who then exit the scene.

This transaction leaves the pre-existing unsecured creditors of the Target with very large amounts of secured debt having a priority over their claims. Review section 4(a)(2) of the Uniform Fraudulent Conveyance Act again. We exclude for purposes of this discussion the possibility that the debtor incurs the debts with actual intent to hinder, delay or defraud its creditors under subsection (1)—all participants hope the debtor prospers, and is able to repay all of its obligations on schedule. Note that subsection (2) requires that the debt be incurred without receiving reasonably equivalent value in exchange for the debt incurred or the property transferred. The lenders are quite clear that they have given reasonably equivalent value for the loan obligations and pledges—they have lent cash. The shareholders are equally clear that they have given value for the cash they receive—they have surrendered their shares. Thus finding a fraudulent transfer in an LBO involves some doctrinal difficulties. The following case is the seminal case in working out the new doctrine.

United States of America v. Tabor Court Realty Corp.

803 F.2d 1288 (3d Cir. 1986).

■ ALDISERT, CHIEF JUDGE.

We have consolidated appeals from litigation involving one of America's largest anthracite coal producers.... Ultimately, we have to decide whether the court erred in entering judgment in favor of the United States in reducing to judgment certain federal corporate tax assessments made against the coal producers, in determining the priority of the government liens, and in permitting foreclosure on the liens. To reach these questions, however, we must examine a very intricate leveraged buy-out and decide whether mortgages given in the transaction were fraudulent conveyances within the meaning of the constructive and intentional fraud sections of the Pennsylvania Uniform Fraudulent Conveyances Act (UFCA), and if so, whether a later assignment of the mortgages was void as against creditors.

* * * We are told that this case represents the first significant application of the UFCA to leveraged buy-out financing.

We will address seven issues presented by the appellants and an amicus curiae, the National Commercial Finance Association, and by the United States and a trustee in bankruptcy as cross appellants:

* whether the court erred in applying the UFCA to a leveraged buy-out;

* whether the court erred in denying the mortgage assignee, McClellan Realty, a "lien superior to all other creditors";

* whether the court erred in "collapsing" two separate loans for the leveraged buy-out into one transaction;

* whether the court erred in holding that the mortgages placed by the borrowers on November 26, 1973 were invalid under the UFCA;

* whether the court erred in holding that the mortgages placed by the guarantors were invalid for lack of fair consideration;

* in the government's cross-appeal, whether the court erred in determining that the mortgage assignee, McClellan Realty, was entitled to an equitable lien for municipal taxes paid; and

* in the government's and trustee in bankruptcy's cross-appeal, whether the court erred in placing the mortgage assignee, McClellan Realty, on the creditor list rather than removing it entirely.

We will summarize a very complex factual situation and then discuss these issues seriatim.

I.

These appeals arise from an action by the United States to reduce to judgment delinquent federal income taxes, interest, and penalties assessed and accrued against Raymond Colliery Co., Inc. and its subsidiaries (the Raymond Group) for the fiscal years of June 30, 1966 through June 30, 1973 and to reduce to judgment similarly assessed taxes owed by Great American Coal Co., Inc. and its subsidiaries for the fiscal year ending June 30, 1975.

* * *

Raymond Colliery, incorporated in 1962, was owned by two families, the Gillens and the Clevelands. It owned over 30,000 acres of land in Lackawanna and Luzerne counties in Pennsylvania and was one of the largest anthracite coal producers in the country. In 1966, Glen Alden Corporation sold its subsidiary, Blue Coal Corporation, to Raymond for $6 million. Raymond paid $500,000 in cash and the remainder of the purchase price with a note secured by a mortgage on Blue Coal's land. Lurking in the background of the financial problems present here are two important components of the current industrial scene: first, the depressed economy attending anthracite mining in Lackawanna and Luzerne Counties, the heartland of this industry; and second, the Pennsylvania Department of Environmental Resources' 1967 order directing Blue Coal to reduce the amount of pollutants it discharged into public waterways in the course of its deep mining operations, necessitating a fundamental change from deep mining to strip or surface mining.

Very serious problems surfaced in 1971 when Raymond's chief stockholders—the Gillens and Clevelands—started to have disagreements over the poor performance of the coal producing companies. The stockholders decided to solve the problem by seeking a buyer for the group. On February 2, 1972, the shareholders granted James Durkin, Raymond's president, an option to purchase Raymond for $8.5 million. The stockholders later renewed Durkin's option at a reduced price of $7.2 million.

Durkin had trouble in raising the necessary financing to exercise his option. He sought help from the Central States Pension Fund of the International Brotherhood of Teamsters and also from the Mellon Bank of Pittsburgh. Mellon concluded that Blue Coal was a bad financial risk. Moreover, both Mellon and Central States held extensive discussions with Durkin's counsel concerning the legality of encumbering Raymond's assets for the purpose of obtaining the loan, a loan which was not to be used to repay creditors but rather to buy out Raymond's stockholders.

After other unsuccessful attempts to obtain financing for the purchase, Durkin incorporated a holding company, Great American, and assigned to it his option to purchase Raymond's stock. Although the litigation in the district court was far-reaching, most of the central issues have their genesis in 1973 when the Raymond Group was sold to Durkin in a leveraged buy-out through the vehicle of Great American.

A leveraged buy-out is not a legal term of art. It is a shorthand expression describing a business practice wherein a company is sold to a small number of investors, typically including members of the company's management, under financial arrangements in which there is a minimum amount of equity and a maximum amount of debt. The financing typically provides for a substantial return of investment capital by means of mortgages or high risk bonds, popularly known as "junk bonds." The predicate transaction here fits the popular notion of a leveraged buy-out. Shareholders of the Raymond Group sold the corporation to a small group of investors headed by Raymond's president; these investors borrowed substantially all of the purchase price at an extremely high rate of interest secured by mortgages on the assets of the selling company and its subsidiaries and those of additional entities that guaranteed repayment.

To effectuate the buy-out, Great American obtained a loan commitment from Institutional Investors Trust on July 24, 1973, in the amount of $8,530,000. The 1973 interrelationship among the many creditors of the Raymond Group, and the sale to Great American—a seemingly empty corporation which was able to perform the buy-out only on the strength of the massive loan from IIT—forms the backdrop for the relevancy of the Pennsylvania Uniform Fraudulent Conveyance Act, one of the critical legal questions presented for our decision.

Durkin obtained the financing through [a loan from IIT, in which the assets of the Raymond Group companies were pledged to secure repayment.] * * * We must decide whether the borrowers' mortgages were invalid under the UFCA and whether there was consideration for the guarantors' mortgages.

* * *

When the financial dust settled after the closing on November 26, 1973, this was the situation at Raymond: Great American paid $6.7 million to purchase Raymond's stock, the shareholders receiving $6.2 million in cash and a $500,000 note; at least $4.8 million of this amount was obtained by mortgaging Raymond's assets.

Notwithstanding the cozy accommodations for the selling stockholders, the financial environment of the Raymond Group at the time of the sale was somewhat precarious. At the time of the closing, Raymond had multi-million dollar liabilities for federal income taxes, trade accounts, pension fund contributions, strip mining and back-filling obligations, and municipal real estate taxes. The district court calculated that the Raymond Group's existing debts amounted to at least $20 million on November 26, 1983. [The trial court found this exceeded the fair salable value of its assets.]

Under Durkin's control after the buy-out, Raymond's condition further deteriorated. Following the closing the Raymond Group lacked the funds to pay its routine operating expenses, including those for materials, supplies, telephone, and other utilities. It was also unable to pay its delinquent and current real estate taxes. Within two months of the closing, the deep mining operations of Blue Coal were shut down; within six months of the closing, the Raymond Group ceased all strip mining operations. Consequently, the Raymond Group could not fulfill its existing coal contracts and became liable for damages for breach of contract. The plaintiffs in the breach of contract actions exercised their right of set-off against accounts they owed the Raymond Group. Within seven months of the closing, the Commonwealth of Pennsylvania and the Anthracite Health & Welfare Fund sued the Raymond Group for its failures to fulfill back-filling requirements in the strip mining operations and to pay contributions to the Health & Welfare Fund. This litigation resulted in injunctions against the Raymond Group companies which prevented them from moving or selling their equipment until their obligations were satisfied. * * *

[There were subsequent assignees of the obligations, followed by foreclosure sales of the secured property to the lienholders.]

* * *

II.

The instant action was commenced by the United States on December 12, 1980 to reduce to judgment certain corporate federal tax assessments made against the Raymond Group and Great American. The government sought to assert the priority of its tax liens and to foreclose against the property that Raymond had owned at the time of the assessments as well as against properties currently owned by Raymond. The United States argued that the IIT mortgages executed in November 1973 should be set aside under the Uniform Fraudulent Conveyance Act and further that the purported assignment of these mortgages to Pagnotti should be voided because at the inception Pagnotti had purchased the mortgages with knowledge that they had been fraudulently conveyed.

As heretofore stated, after a bench trial, the district court issued three separate published opinions. In Gleneagles I the court concluded, inter alia, that the mortgages given by the Raymond Group to IIT on November 26, 1973 were fraudulent conveyances within the meaning of the constructive and intentional fraud sections of the Pennsylvania Uniform Fraudulent Conveyances Act. In Gleneagles II the court further held that the mortgages to McClellan Realty were void as against the other Raymond Group creditors. * * *

The Raymond Group ... has appealed. * * * For the purpose of this appeal, we shall refer to the Raymond Group as "appellants", or "McClellan".

* * *

III.

McClellan initially challenges the district court's application of the Pennsylvania Uniform Fraudulent Conveyances Act to the leveraged buy-out loan made by IIT to the mortgagors, and to the acquisition of the mortgages from IIT by McClellan. The district court determined that IIT lacked good faith in the transaction because it knew, or should have known, that the money it lent the mortgagors was used, in part, to finance the purchase of stock from the mortgagors' shareholders, and that as a consequence of the loan, IIT and its assignees obtained a secured position in the mortgagors' property to the detriment of creditors. Because this issue involves the interpretation and application of legal precepts, review is plenary.

In applying section [3](a) of the UFCA, the district court stated:

> The initial question ... is whether the transferee, IIT, transferred its loan proceeds in good faith.... IIT knew or strongly suspected that the imposition of the loan obligations secured by the mortgages and guarantee mortgages would probably render insolvent both the Raymond Group and each individual member thereof. In addition, IIT was fully aware that no individual member of the Raymond Group would receive fair consideration within the meaning of the Act in exchange for the loan obligations to IIT. Thus, we conclude that IIT does not meet the standard of good faith under Section [3](a) of the Act.

McClellan argues that "the only reasonable and proper application of the good faith criteria as it applies to the lender in structuring a loan is one which looks to the lender's motives as opposed to his knowledge." McClellan argues that good faith is satisfied when "the lender acted in an arms-length transaction without ulterior motive or collusion with the debtor to the detriment of creditors."

Section [4] of the UFCA is a "constructive fraud" provision. It establishes that a conveyance made by a person "who is or will be thereby rendered insolvent, is fraudulent as to creditors, without regard to his actual intent, if the conveyance is made ... without a fair consideration." Section [3] defines fair consideration as an exchange of a "fair equivalent ... in good faith." Because section [4] excludes an examination of intent, it follows that "good faith" must be something other than intent; because section [4] also focuses on insolvency, knowledge of insolvency is a rational interpretation of the statutory language of lack of "good faith." McClellan would have us adopt "without ulterior motive or collusion with the debtor to the detriment of creditors" as the good faith standard. We are uneasy with such a standard because these words come very close to describing intent.

Surprisingly, few courts have considered this issue. In Epstein v. Goldstein, 107 F.2d 755, 757 (2d Cir. 1939), the court held that because a transferee had no knowledge of the transferor's insolvency, it could not justify a finding of bad faith, implying that a showing of such knowledge would support a finding of bad faith. In Sparkman and McLean Co. v.

Derber, 4 Wash. App. 341, 481 P.2d 585 (1971), the court considered a mortgage given to an attorney by a corporation on the verge of bankruptcy to secure payment for his services. The trial court found that the transaction had violated section 3 of the UFCA ... because it had been made in bad faith. On appeal the Washington Court of Appeals stated that "prior cases ... have not precisely differentiated the good faith requirement ... of fair consideration [in UFCA section 3] from the actual intent to defraud requirement of [UFCA section 7]." The court then set forth a number of factors to be considered in determining good faith: 1) honest belief in the propriety of the activities in question; 2) no intent to take unconscionable advantage of others; and 3) no intent to, or knowledge of the fact that the activities in question will, hinder, delay, or defraud others. Where "any one of these factors is absent, lack of good faith is established and the conveyance fails."

We have decided that the district court reached the right conclusion here for the right reasons. It determined that IIT did not act in good faith because it was aware, first, that the exchange would render Raymond insolvent, and second, that no member of the Raymond Group would receive fair consideration. We believe that this determination is consistent with the statute and case law.

McClellan and amicus curiae also argue that as a general rule the UFCA should not be applied to leveraged buy-outs. They contend that the UFCA, which was passed in 1924, was never meant to apply to a complicated transaction such as a leveraged buy-out. The Act's broad language, however, extends to any "conveyance" which is defined as "every payment of money ... and also the creation of any lien or incumbrance." [UFCA § 1]. This broad sweep does not justify exclusion of a particular transaction such as a leveraged buy-out simply because it is innovative or complicated. If the UFCA is not to be applied to leveraged buy-outs, it should be for the state legislatures, not the courts, to decide.

In addition, although appellants' and amicus curiae's arguments against general application of the Act to leveraged buy-outs are not without some force, the application of fraudulent conveyance law to certain leveraged buy-outs is not clearly bad public policy.[2] In any event, the circum-

---

2. A major premise of the policy arguments opposing application of fraudulent conveyance law to leveraged buy-outs is that such transactions often benefit creditors and that the application of fraudulent conveyance law to buy-outs will deter them in the future. See Baird and Jackson, Fraudulent Conveyance Law and Its Proper Domain, 38 Vand. L. Rev. 829, 855 (1985). An equally important premise is that creditors can protect themselves from undesirable leveraged buy-outs by altering the terms of their credit contracts. Id. at 835. This second premise ignores, however, cases such as this one in which the major creditors (in this instance the United States and certain Pennsylvania municipalities) are involuntary and do not become creditors by virtue of a contract. The second premise also ignores the possibility that the creditors attacking the leveraged buy-out (such as many of the creditors in this case) became creditors before leveraged buy-outs became a common financing technique and thus may not have anticipated such leveraged transactions so as to have been able to adequately protect themselves by contract. These possibilities suggest that Baird and Jackson's broad proscription against application of fraudulent conveyance law to leveraged buy-outs may not be unambiguously correct.

stances of this case justify application. Even the policy arguments offered against the application of fraudulent conveyance law to leveraged buy-outs assume facts that are not present in this case. For example, in their analysis of fraudulent conveyance law, Professors Baird and Jackson assert that their analysis should be applied to leveraged buy-outs only where aspects of the transaction are not hidden from creditors and the transaction does not possess other suspicious attributes. See Baird and Jackson, Fraudulent Conveyance Law and Its Proper Domain, 38 Vand. L. Rev. 829, 843 (1985). In fact, Baird and Jackson conclude their article by noting that their analysis is limited to transactions in which "the transferee parted with value when he entered into the transaction and that transaction was entered in the ordinary course." Id. at 855 (footnote omitted). In the instant case, however, the severe economic circumstances in which the Raymond Group found itself, the obligation, without benefit, incurred by the Raymond Group, and the small number of shareholders benefited by the transaction suggest that the transaction was not entered in the ordinary course, that fair consideration was not exchanged, and that the transaction was anything but unsuspicious. The policy arguments set forth in opposition to the application of fraudulent conveyance law to leveraged buy-outs do not justify the exemption of transactions such as this.[3]

IV.

* * *

E.

McClellan next contends that the district court erred in not crediting McClellan for that portion of the IIT loan that was not passed through to Raymond's shareholders: although "the District Court acknowledged that $2,915,000, or approximately 42 percent, of the IIT loan proceeds originally went for the benefit of . . . creditors, IIT and McClellan received no credit therefor in regard to the partial validity of their liens." McClellan argues the district court determined that "the wrong committed upon the creditors . . . [was] the diversion of some 58 percent of the loan proceeds from the IIT loan to [Raymond's] shareholders." It concludes that to invalidate the entire mortgage would be to provide Raymond's creditors with a "double recovery." We understand the dissent to agree with McClellan's analysis when noting that " 'creditors have causes of action in fraudulent conveyance law only to the extent they have been damaged.' "

McClellan and, by implication, the dissent mischaracterize the district court's findings and conclusions regarding the fraudulent nature of the IIT

---

3. It should also be noted that another basic premise of the Baird and Jackson analysis is that as a general matter fraudulent conveyance law should be applied only to those transactions to which a rational creditor would surely object. Baird and Jackson, at 834. Although a rational creditor might under certain circumstances consent to a risky but potentially beneficial leveraged buy-out of a nearly insolvent debtor, no reasonable creditor would consent to the intentionally fraudulent conveyance the district court correctly found this transaction to be. Thus, the application of fraudulent conveyance law to the instant transaction appears consistent even with Baird and Jackson's analysis.

loans. The district court did not determine that the loan transaction was only partially—or, to use McClellan's formulation, 58%—fraudulent. Nor did the district court conclude that Raymond's creditors had been wronged by only a portion of the transaction. Instead, the district court stated that:

> McClellan Realty's argument rests on the incorrect assumption that some portions of the IIT mortgages are valid as against the Creditors. In Gleneagles I, 565 F. Supp. at 580, 586, this Court found that IIT and Durkin engaged in an intentionally fraudulent transaction on November 26, 1973. The IIT mortgages are therefore invalid in their entirety as to creditors.

In essence, the district court ruled that the aggregate transaction was fraudulent, notwithstanding the fact that a portion of the loan proceeds was allegedly used to pay existing creditors.

This determination is bolstered by the fact that most of the $2,915,000 allegedly paid to the benefit of Raymond's creditors went to only one creditor—Chemical Bank. In Gleneagles I, the district court found that $2,186,247 of the IIT loan proceeds were paid to Chemical Bank in satisfaction of the mortgage that Raymond had taken to purchase Blue Coal (a Raymond subsidiary). The purpose of this payment is of critical significance:

> The Gillens and the Clevelands [Raymond's selling shareholders] required satisfaction of the Chemical Bank mortgage as a condition of the sale of their Raymond Colliery stock at least in part because Royal Cleveland had personally guaranteed repayment of that loan.

McClellan does not challenge this finding on appeal. Thus, of the $2.9 million allegedly paid to benefit Raymond's creditors, $2.2 million were actually intended to benefit Raymond's shareholders and to satisfy a condition for the sale. The remaining amounts allegedly paid to benefit Raymond's creditors were applied to the closing costs of the transaction.

On this record, the district court's characterization of the transaction as a whole as fraudulent cannot reasonably be disputed. The court's consequent determination that the "IIT mortgages are . . . invalid in their entirety as to creditors" is supported by precedent. See Newman v. First National Bank, 76 F.2d 347, 350–51 (3d Cir. 1935).

* * *

V.

McClellan, joined by the amicus, next argues that the district court erred "by collapsing two separate loans into one transaction." The loan arrangement was a two-part process: the loan proceeds went from IIT to the borrowing Raymond Group companies, which immediately turned the funds over to Great American, which used the funds for the buy-out. McClellan contends that the district court erred by not passing on the fairness of the transaction between IIT and the Raymond Group mortgagors. * * *

Contrary to McClellan's contentions, the district court did examine this element of the transaction, stating "We find that the obligations incurred by the Raymond Group and its individual members to IIT were not supported by fair consideration. The mortgages and guarantee mortgages to secure these obligations were also not supported by fair consideration."

Admittedly, in the course of its determination that the IIT–Raymond Group transaction was without fair consideration under section 353(a), the court looked beyond the exchange of funds between IIT and the Raymond Group. But there was reason for this. The two exchanges were part of one integrated transaction. As the court concluded: "the $4,085,000 in IIT loan proceeds which were lent immediately by the borrowing companies to Great American were merely passed through the borrowers to Great American and ultimately to the selling stockholders and cannot be deemed consideration received by the borrowing companies."

The district court's factual findings support its treatment of the IIT–Raymond Group–Great American transaction as a single transaction. * * *

Appellant cannot seriously challenge these findings of fact. We are satisfied with the district court's conclusion that the funds "merely passed through the borrowers to Great American." This necessitates our agreement with the district court's conclusion that, for purposes of determining IIT's knowledge of the use of the proceeds under section 353(a), there was one integral transaction.

VI.

McClellan next faults the district court's determination that the Raymond Group was rendered insolvent by "the IIT transaction and the instantaneous payment to the selling stockholders of a substantial portion of the IIT loan in exchange for their stock." McClellan disputes the method of computation used by the district court. The question of insolvency is a mixed question of law and fact. * * *

A.

Section [2] of the UFCA defines insolvency as "when the present, fair, salable value of [a person's] assets is less than the amount that will be required to pay his probable liability on his existing debts as they become absolute and matured." As heretofore stated, the district court calculated the Raymond Group's existing debts as "at least $20,000,000 on November 26, 1973." The court then compared Raymond's debt to the "present, fair, salable value" of its assets and found the Group insolvent. In doing so, the court relied on Larrimer v. Feeney, where the Pennsylvania Supreme Court stated:

> A reasonable construction of the . . . statutory definition of insolvency indicates that it not only encompasses insolvency in the bankruptcy sense i.e. a deficit net worth, but also includes a condition wherein a debtor has insufficient presently salable assets to pay existing debts as they mature. If a debtor has a deficit net worth, then the present salable value of his assets must be less than the amount required to

pay the liability on his debts as they mature. A debtor may have substantial paper net worth including assets which have a small salable value, but which if held to a subsequent date could have a much higher salable value. Nevertheless, if the present salable value of [his] assets [is] less than the amount required to pay existing debts as they mature the debtor is insolvent.

Guided by this teaching, the court found that: (1) the Raymond Group's coal production, which had been unprofitable since 1969, "could not produce a sufficient cash flow to pay the company's obligations in a timely manner"; (2) the sale of the Raymond Group's surplus lands, which had provided a substantial cash flow, was "abruptly cut off" by the terms of the IIT agreement; and (3) sale of its equipment could not generate adequate cash to meet Raymond's existing debts as they matured.

* * *

We conclude that McClellan has not demonstrated that this finding was clearly erroneous. We are satisfied that the district court followed the guidance of Pennsylvania courts in analyzing the Raymond Group's insolvency. Its application of the law was not clearly in error, nor were its factual determinations clearly erroneous.

QUESTIONS

1. At one point the court (at the start of Part III of its opinion) that IIT "obtained a secured position in the mortgagors' property to the detriment of [general unsecured] creditors." Isn't this always the case in secured lending? What more does it take to make the security interest a fraudulent conveyance?

2. The opinion went on to state that IIT knew that "no individual member of the Raymond Group would receive fair consideration within the meaning of the [Fraudulent Conveyance] Act in exchange for the loan obligations to IIT." If IIT actually lent and paid out the funds, what further step is necessary to make sense of this sentence?

3. If the the Raymond Group had essentially no funds before the loan, did the pass-through of the funds create or exacerbate its insolvency?

4. The district court found that Raymond was indebted by at least $20 million at the time of the IIT loan and mortgage, and found that the present fair, salable value of its assets meant it was insolvent. Further, the court found that its coal production was insufficient to produce a cash flow to meet Raymond's debts in a timely manner. Why would Durkin seek to acquire control of an insolvent corporation, that he had just caused, through the IIT mortgage, to become more heavily indebted?

5. If you are an attorney representing prospective LBO lenders after this decision, what can you do to protect your client from subsequent charges of fraudulent transfers?

6. Compare the valuation methods used here with those in Klang v. Smith's Food & Drug Centers, INc., in Part 2 of this chapter. Is the Klang methodology dead for all purposes in calculating solvency for LBOs?

7. How does the court deal with the problem that the lenders gave value for their loans?

8. Does the court address the fact that the shareholders gave up their valuable shares in the LBO?

9. Why hadn't any creditors obtained contractual protection against LBOs? Could they have done so economically? If one creditor has such protection, what is the effect upon other creditors?

For an interesting discussion of fraudulent conveyance law in the context of leveraged buyouts, see Douglas Baird and Thomas Jackson, "Fraudulent Conveyance Law and Its Proper Domain," 38 Van. L. Rev. 829 (1985). See also Sherwin, Creditors' Rights Against Participants in a Leveraged Buyout, 72 Minn. 449 (1988) and Richard Kummert, State Statutory Restrictions on Financial Distributions by Corporations to Shareholders: Part I, 55 Wash. L. Rev. 359 (1980) and ... Part II, 59 Wash. L. Rev. 185 (1984).

Matter of Munford, Inc., d.b.a. Majik Market, Debtor

97 F.3d 456 (11th Cir.1996).

■ Hatchett, Chief Judge:

In this corporate leveraged-buy-out merger case, we affirm the district court's ruling that Georgia's stock distribution and repurchase statutes apply.

FACTS

In May 1988, the Panfida Group offered to purchase Munford, Inc., a public company on the New York Stock Exchange, through a leverage buy out (LBO) structured as a reverse triangle merger for $18 per share. Under the terms of the proposed merger agreement, the Panfida Group agreed to create Alabama Acquisition Corporation (AAC) and a subsidiary, Alabama Merger Corporation (AMC), and through AAC or AMC deposit the funds necessary to purchase Munford, Inc.'s outstanding stock with Citizens & Southern Trust Company. As evidence of its commitment to purchase Munford, Inc., the Panfida Group bought 291,100 shares of Munford, Inc.'s stock. In June 1988, the Panfida Group also told Munford, Inc.'s board of directors that it, upon the sale of Munford, Inc., intended to put additional capital into Munford, Inc. but would only invest as much as Citibank required to finance the proposed merger.

After consulting its lawyers and financial experts at Shearson Lehman Brothers (Shearson), the board of directors accepted the Panfida Group's offer pending shareholder approval of the purchase agreement. Prior to the directors seeking shareholder approval, the Panfida Group learned that Munford, Inc. had potential environmental liability. Consequently, the Panfida Group reduced the purchase price from $18.50 a share to $17 a share. On October 18, 1988, the shareholders approved the merger plan. On November 29, 1988, the sale of Munford, Inc. to the Panfida Group closed. Pursuant to the purchase agreement, the LBO transaction converted each share of common stock into the right to receive the merger price of $17 per share and extinguished the shareholders' ownership in Munford, Inc. On January 2, 1990, thirteen months after the merger, Munford, Inc. filed for Chapter 11 proceedings in bankruptcy court.

PROCEDURAL HISTORY

On June 17, 1991, Munford, Inc. brought an adversary proceeding in bankruptcy court in the Northern District of Georgia on behalf of itself and unsecured creditors pursuant to 11 U.S.C. §§ 544(b) and 1107(a) (1988), seeking to avoid transfers of property, disallow claims and recover damages against former shareholders, officers, directors, and Shearson. In Count III of its complaint, Munford, Inc. asserted that the directors violated legal restrictions under Georgia's distribution and share repurchase statutes in approving the LBO merger. Specifically, Munford, Inc. asserts that the LBO transaction constituted a distribution of corporate assets that rendered Munford, Inc. insolvent. The directors moved for summary judgment contending that the Georgia distribution and repurchase statutes did not apply to LBO mergers. On August 10, 1994, the district court, adopting the bankruptcy court's report and recommendation in part, denied the directors' motion for summary judgment on Munford, Inc.'s stock repurchase and distribution claim, ruling that Georgia's stock distributions and repurchase restrictions applied to LBO transactions. The district court also found that a genuine issue of material fact existed as to whether the LBO merger rendered Munford, Inc. insolvent in violation of Georgia law. On August 26, 1994, the district court amended its order and entered final judgment pursuant to Federal Rules of Civil Procedure 54(b) to permit this appeal. Fed.R.Civ.P. 54(b).

CONTENTIONS

The directors contend that the district court erred in concluding that the LBO merger constituted a distribution of assets within the meaning of Georgia's distribution and repurchase statutes. They contend that these statutes do not apply to an arm's-length sale of a company to a third party through an LBO merger. In the alternative, the directors contend that they should not face personal liability for alleged violations of Georgia's distribution and repurchase statutes because they approved the LBO merger in good faith with the advice of legal counsel.

Munford, Inc. contends that the district court properly denied the directors' motion for summary judgment on this claim.

ISSUE

The sole issue on appeal is whether the district court erred in ruling that Georgia's stock distribution and repurchase statutes apply to a leverage acquisition of a corporation.

DISCUSSION

We review the denial of summary judgment de novo applying the same legal standard that controlled the district court in rendering its decision. Brown v. Crawford, 906 F.2d 667, 669 (11th Cir.1990), cert. denied, 500 U.S. 933 (1991).

Georgia's capital surplus distribution statute provides, in pertinent part:

> (a) The board of directors of a corporation may from time to time distribute to shareholders out of capital surplus of the corporation a portion of its assets in cash or property subject to the following [provision]:

>> (1) No such distribution shall be made at a time when the corporation is insolvent or when such distribution would render the corporation insolvent[.]

Similarly, Georgia's stock repurchasing statute prohibits directors of a corporation from repurchasing the corporation's shares when such purchase would render the corporation insolvent. Under both statutes, directors who vote for or assent to a corporate distribution or stock repurchase in violation of these statutes are jointly and severally liable for the amount distributed or paid to the extent the payments violated the restrictions.

The directors appeal the district court's denial of summary judgment contending that Georgia's distribution and share repurchase statutes do not apply to LBO mergers. The directors argue that Georgia's distribution and repurchase statutes only apply in circumstances where the directors take assets of the corporation and either distribute them to shareholders or use them to repurchase shares. In both cases, the directors assert, control of the company does not change hands and the directors determine the source of the assets used. The directors note that in this case the Panfida Group owned Munford, Inc. at the completion of the LBO merger and thereafter ran the company. The directors therefore argue that only Georgia's merger statutes apply to this transaction.

The district court denied the directors' motion for summary judgment adopting the reasoning of the bankruptcy court. The bankruptcy court, in analyzing the LBO merger, considered the substance of the transaction and equated the LBO merger to a stock distribution or repurchase, disregarding the fact that Munford, Inc. had new owners and stockholders as a result of the merger at the time the shareholders received the LBO payments. The bankruptcy court specifically found that: (1) the directors "approved or assented to the underlying merger agreement which structured and required payment to the shareholders"; (2) the merger agreement contemplated the Panfida Group's pledging of "virtually all of Munford[, Inc.]'s assets as collateral" for the loan that funded the LBO payments made to the shareholders; and (3) the directors knew or should have known "the source, purpose, or use of" Munford, Inc.'s assets prior to or at the time the directors approved the merger plan. Based on these findings, the bankruptcy court concluded that a reasonable jury could conclude that the merger rendered Munford, Inc. insolvent in violation of Georgia's distribution and stock repurchase statutes.

In reaching its conclusion, the bankruptcy court rejected a Fourth Circuit case that refused to apply Virginia's corporate distribution statute to recapture payments made to shareholders pursuant to an LBO merger. See C–T of Virginia, Inc. v. Barrett, 958 F.2d 606 (4th Cir.1992).

In C–T of Virginia, the Fourth Circuit held that the LBO merger did not constitute a distribution within the meaning of Virginia's share repurchase and distribution statutes reasoning that Virginia's distribution statute

> [was] not intended to obstruct an arm's-length acquisition of an enterprise by new owners who have their own plans for commercial success. The reason for this distinction is simple: a corporate acquisition, structured as a merger, is simply a different animal from a distribution.

C–T of Virginia, 958 F.2d at 611. The court in C–T of Virginia further reasoned that because such distribution statutes derive from the regulation of corporate dividends courts should limit their restriction to situations in which shareholders after receiving the transfer from the corporation retain their status as owners of the corporation.

The bankruptcy court, in this case, rejected this line of reasoning, reasoning that the legislature enacted the distribution and share repurchase statutes of the Georgia Code to protect creditors "by prohibiting transfers at a time when a corporation is insolvent or would be rendered insolvent." Such intent, the bankruptcy court noted, "furthers the long-standing principle that creditors are to be paid before shareholders." We agree with the district court and the reasoning of the bankruptcy court and decline to join the Fourth Circuit in holding that "[a] corporate acquisition, structured as a merger, is simply a different animal from a distribution." C–T of Virginia, Inc., 958 F.2d at 611.

We note that the LBO transaction in this case did not merge two separate operating companies into one combined entity. Instead, the LBO transaction represented a "paper merger" of Munford, Inc. and AMC, a shell corporation with very little assets of its own. To hold that Georgia's distribution and repurchase statutes did not apply to LBO mergers such as this, while nothing in these statutes precludes such a result, would frustrate the restrictions imposed upon directors who authorize a corporation to distribute its assets or to repurchase shares from stockholders when such transactions would render the corporation insolvent. We therefore affirm the district court's ruling that Georgia's restrictions on distribution and stock repurchase apply to LBO.

In the alternative, the directors argue that their approval of the LBO merger should not subject them to liability under the distribution and repurchase statutes because they approved the merger in good faith and with the advice of legal counsel. Because we are not aware of any Georgia courts that recognize good faith or reasonable reliance on legal counsel's advice as an affirmative defense to liability under Georgia's distribution and repurchase statutes, we reject this argument.

CONCLUSION

For the reasons stated above, we affirm the district court's denial of the directors' motion for summary judgment on Munford, Inc.'s stock distribution and repurchase claim.

Affirmed.

QUESTIONS

1. Georgia adopted the Revised Model Business Corporation Act effective in 1989. Would RMBCA § 6.40(d) have changed the outcome in this case?

2. The Court of Appeals characterized the LBO transaction as merely a "paper merger" that did not escape the regulation of the distribution statutes. O.C.G.A. § 14–2–103, as it became effective in 1989, after the Munford transaction, provides "Each provision of this chapter shall have independent legal significance." The notes to this section state an intent to adopt the rule of construction of Delaware, under such cases as Hariton v. Arco Electronics, 188 A.2d 123 (Del. Supr. 1963). Would the presence of this statute make a difference in future cases?

3. In C–T of Virginia, Inc. v. Barrett, 958 F.2d 606 (4th Cir.1992), cited in Munford, the Court of Appeals noted that at the time of the cash payment, the recipients were "former shareholders" rather than shareholders of the corporation, because their shares had been canceled in the merger. Is this a persuasive distinction? Is it more persuasive because the merger created new shareholders—those in the merging corporation, whose shares survived the merger?

4. Should it make a difference if an LBO is undertaken by outside third parties or by management?

5. Should it matter that the merger provisions of the statute provide no creditor protection against highly leveraged mergers?

6. If directors have decided to sell the company, and a proposed LBO offers the highest price for the company, how can directors satisfy their *Revlon* duties without running a risk of liability under distribution provisions?

7. Assuming that the directors resign at the effective time of the merger, what causes the subsequent insolvency, the decision to borrow against

the corporation's assets or the manner in which the corporation is financed and operated subsequent to the merger?

8. Should an infusion of new working capital by the buyers make a difference in directors' liability if the company still becomes insolvent? What about an infusion of new and better management?

7. SPIN-OFFS AND TRACKING STOCK

A. SPIN-OFFS

Spin-off transactions involve another form of dividend—this time of the stock of a subsidiary. Corporations may dividend out the stock of an existing subsidiary, or may take an operating division, put its assets into a newly created subsidiary, and then dividend out the shares of the newly created subsidiary.

There are a variety of reasons for spin-off transactions. The excesses of the conglomerate movement of the 1960s and 1970s left many companies with operations that did not fit well with the rest of the businesses owned, in terms of creating operating synergies. Remember, diversification can be home-made, so investors won't value it within a firm without a good reason. In many cases these "misfits" were ignored by top management, and received little in the way of new capital to exploit opportunities, even when the expected rates of return were higher than those on projects in more favored divisions. In some cases top management had little knowledge or understanding of these divisions. See David J. Denis, Diane K. Denis and Atulya Sarin, Agency Problems, Equity Ownership, and Corporate Diversification, 52 Journal of Finance 135 (1997). Many of these divisions were sold off during the 1980s. In some cases divisional management would seek outside financing and engage in a leveraged buyout of the division. In others, competitors might be the buyers. Finally, a corporation without such offers might simply spin the subsidiary's shares off to its own shareholders. The finance literature suggests that spinning off divisions is generally a value-enhancing strategy for shareholders. See James A. Miles [ALTERNATIVE TO SELLING] and James D. Rosenfeld, The Effect of Voluntary Spin-off Announcements on Shareholder Wealth, 38 Journal of Finance 1597 (1983) and James D. Rosenfeld, Additional Evidence on the Relation Between Divestiture Announcements and Shareholder Wealth, 39 Journal of Finance 1437 (1984).

One other use of the spin-off was less benign. Beginning in the early 1970s asbestos claims began to be brought in large numbers against makers of asbestos, makers of products containing asbestos, and makers of products that used asbestos in their manufacturing process. The largest maker of asbestos was Johns Manville Corporation, which was also one of the first to file for Chapter 11 reorganization in 1982, followed in the next several years by manufacturers of products containing asbestos. The number of claims against these companies continued to grow throughout the 1980s, and the number of companies that were forced to file for Chapter 11 grew, and continues to grow in the 21st century, as the identity of defendants changed as bankruptcy eliminated many of the early defendants in these cases. By the mid–1980s the handwriting was on the wall: any association with asbestos was likely to bankrupt many companies. Some dealt with this issue through corporate reorganizations. In these cases the companies would reorganize into a structure in which the shareholders first received shares in a holding company that owned all of the stock of the potential bankrupt. The parent corporation would then proceed to purchase the non-asbestos businesses from the potential bankrupt, placing them in newly created subsidiaries. The parent corporation could then dividend out the shares of the new subsidiaries to the parent's shareholders, thus separating the asbestos assets from the other assets. Litigation then centered around whether these transactions were fraudulent conveyances, which depended on the potential insolvency of the defendant and the intent of its management in creating this series of transactions. For one variation on this technique, in which the parent then sold the defendant entity and retained the viable enterprises, see Raytech Corp. v. White, 54 F.3d 187 (3d Cir. 1995). See also Edward S. Adams and Arijit Mukherji, Spin–Offs, Fiduciary Duty and the Law, 68 Fordham L. Rev. 15 (1999); Richard M. Cieri, Lyle G. Ganske and Heather Lennox, Breaking Up Is Hard to Do: Avoiding the Solvency–Related Pitfalls in Spinoff Transactions, 54 Bus. Law. 533 (1999) and Kevin M. Warsh, Corporate Spin–Offs and Mass Tort Liability, 1995 Colum. Bus. L. Rev. 675.

One advantage of the spin-off is that unlike many other distributions, it is tax free under I.R.C. § 355, if certain conditions designed to frustrate tax avoidance of distribution of earnings are met. These conditions center on the existence of a legitimate business purpose for he spin-off.*

---

* Revenue Procedure 96–30 spelled out permissible business purposes:

1. To provide an equity interest in either the distributing or controlled corporation to a key employee. In general, the Service would require that the employee receive a "significant" equity interest, in terms of percentage and value, within one year of the IRC Section 355 transaction.

2. To facilitate a stock offering. In general, the Service would require that the stock offering be completed within one year.

3. To facilitate corporate borrowing. In general, the Service would require that the borrowing be completed within one year.

4. To produce significant cost savings. In general, the Service would require that the projected after-tax cost savings of the distributing and controlled corporations (net of the IRC Section 355 transaction costs) over the three (or five) years following the transaction equal at least one percent of the net after-tax income of the distributing and controlled corporations over the three (or five) years preceding the transaction.

5. To resolve management, systemic or other problems.

6. To satisfy a customer or supplier who objects to either the distributing or controlled corporation being associated with a competing business.

7. To facilitate a subsequent tax-free acquisition of the distributing corporation by another corporation. In general, the subsequent acquisition should be completed within one year.

B. Tracking Stock

Tracking stock is a variation on a spin-off. It generally involves the creation of a new subsidiary, into which a corporation pours the assets of an operating division, although an existing subsidiary could also be used. The parent remains owner of 100% of the subsidiary's stock, but issues a tracking stock to its shareholders.

Tracking stock is a class of common stock of the parent corporation, with special rights. The subsidiary's assets and businesses would be segregated, and separate financial statements would be prepared and published.* The parent board would declare such dividends as it chose on each class of stock. The dividends on the tracking stock would, by contract, be limited to the amount that would be legally available if the subsidiary were a separate corporation and the tracking shares were actually shares in the subsidiary. In some cases it appears that voting rights of the tracking shares vary depending on the relative value of the parent and the subsidiary, treated separately. Similarly, liquidation rights are generally allocated on the basis of the relative market values of the two businesses, although the tracking shares have no separate claim on the subsidiary's assets. Thus, in bankruptcy, the holders of the tracking stock have no priority over the parent's common stockholders to the assets of the subsidiary.

General Motors was the first corporation to issue tracking stock in 1984, when it acquired Electronic Data Systems from Ross Perot and the public stockholders of EDS, and issued a new Class "E" common stock tied to the earnings of the EDS operations. Subsequently it used the same technique when it acquired Hughes Aircraft in 1985, and issued "H" common. USX, formerly United States Steel Corporation, had acquired a

---

8. To facilitate a subsequent tax-free acquisition of another corporation by the distributing or controlled corporation. In general, the subsequent acquisition should be completed within one year.

9. To significantly reduce risk.

* This creates potential tax issues, about whether the tracking stock is really stock of the parent or the subsidiary. If the IRS treats it as stock of the parent, the following tax consequences will exist:

1. A distribution of tracking stock to stockholders of the parent will qualify as a nontaxable stock dividend under IRC § 305(a).

2. Such a distribution will be tax-free to the parent under IRC § 311.

If, on the other hand, the IRS treats it as stock of the subsidiary, here are the major tax consequences:

1. If the tracking stock transaction doesn't qualify as a § 355 spin-off, tracking stock distributed to the parent's stockholders would be taxable as dividends under § 301.

2. If the tracking stock transaction doesn't qualify as a § 355 spin-off, the difference between the fair market value and the basis of the tracking stock would be recognized as gain to the parent under § 311 of the Code.

See Hass, supra, 94 Mich. L. Rev. at 2111, citing Harold R. Handler & Dickson G. Brown, Tracking Stock, in 6 Tax Strategies for Corporate Acquisitions, Dispositions, Spin-Offs, Joint Ventures and Other Strategic Alliances, Financings, Reorganizations and Restructurings 1993, at 369 (PLI Tax Law and Estate Planning Course No. J–346, 1993).

business of approximately equal size (and ultimately greater value) when it acquired Marathon Oil in the 1980s. Carl Icahn, noted financier, bought 13% of USX's stock and demanded that the company spin off shares of its steel operations. Icahn might have foreseen future financial difficulties for steel that would reduce the value of the remaining oil and gas operations. In response, USX decided to issue tracking stock for each division. Other companies have also issued tracking stock. For an account of these transactions, see Julia D'Souza and John Jacob, Why Firms Issue Targeted Stock, 56 Journal of Financial Economics 459 (2000).

Distributing tracking stock is claimed to have some advantages over spin-offs. By remaining one large diversified corporation, all businesses owned by the entity benefit from the lower cost of capital sometimes available to large international corporations. Second, overhead costs are spread over one, not two entities. Third, the larger entity is better protected from unsolicited takeover bids, although a corporation created before a spin-off can be well protected in advance.

Tracking stock creates conflicts between the parent and subsidiary boards and shareholders. The parent's directors would elect the board of the subsidiary, with all the difficulties for independent dealing between the two corporations that entails. The other difficulty is that the parent board would owe fiduciary duties to two discrete groups—holders of its own common stock and holders of its tracking stock. These difficulties are discussed in Jeffrey J. Hass, "Directorial Fiduciary Duties in a Tracking Stock Equity Structure: The Need for a Duty of Fairness," 94 Mich. L. Rev. 2089 (1996). The EDS transaction illustrated one of the difficulties with tracking stock. If General Motors acquired EDS at least in part to provide services to General Motors, how can one set a price for those services that is fair to both GM and the E shareholders? Despite those difficulties, another study finds gains for shareholders of companies that announce the prospective issuance of tracking stock. D'Souza and Jacob, *supra*. These authors view tracking stock as a substitute for the spin-off transaction. For one thing, it does not create the problems for creditors than spin-offs may entail. The authors speculate that using tracking stock may increase value because it enhances the transparency of financial reporting, since the corporation must now separate its financial results by division quite clearly.

INDEX

References are to pages.

ACCOUNTING PRINCIPLES BOARD (APB)
Generally, 5-6

ACCOUNTING SERIES RELEASES (ASRS)
Securities and Exchange Commission, 5

ACCOUNTS AND ACCOUNTING
Financial reports, accounting periods, 8
Financial Statements, this index
Stock dividends and stock splits, 769-776

ACCOUNTS RECEIVABLE
Balance sheet, assets, 12
Capital structure, 215
Corporate debt, security for lines of credit, 364
Turnover ratio, financial statements, 56

ACCRUAL METHOD
Financial reports, 8

ACID-TEST RATIO
Financial statements, 54-55

ACQUISITIONS
Dividends and distributions, taxes, 723-725

ACTIVITY RATIOS
Financial Statements, this index

AGENCY COSTS
Capital structure, 243-248

AMENDMENTS
Charter, dividends and distributions, 771-772
Corporate debt, 435-445

AMERICAN INSTITUTE OF CERTIFIED PUBLIC ACCOUNTANTS (AICPA)
Generally, 5

AMERICAN OPTIONS
Generally, 583

ANGEL INVESTORS
Public securities markets and regulation, new issues market, 356

ANNUITIES
Valuation, 98-100

ASSET BACKED FINANCING
Corporate debt, 467-471

ASSET TURNOVER RATIO
Financial statements, 55-56

AUDITS AND AUDITING
Generally, 7

AVAILABLE-FOR-SALE SECURITIES
Parent and subsidiary corporations, consolidated returns, 7

BALANCE SHEETS
Financial Statements, this index

BANK LOANS
Capital structure, 214-215

BANKRUPTCY
Stock repurchase rights, 748-753

BETA
Capital assets pricing model, 119-125

BLANK CHECK PREFERRED STOCK
Generally, 477-478

BOND RATING AGENCIES
Corporate debt, 364

BONDS AND DEBENTURES
Corporate Debt, this index

BOOK VALUE
Generally, 88-89

CALL OPTIONS
Options and Convertible Securities, this index

CALL PROTECTION
Corporate debt, 426-433

CAPITAL ASSETS PRICING MODEL
Valuation, 118-130, 172-194

CAPITAL LEASES
Generally, 217-218
Balance sheets, 16-17, 466-467
Corporate debt, 465-467

CAPITAL STRUCTURE
Generally, 211-308

CAPITAL STRUCTURE—Cont'd
Accounts receivable financing, 215
Bank loans, 214-215
Bonds. Corporate Debt, this index
Capital leases, 217-218
Close corporations and disallowance of interest deductions, 290-296
Commercial paper, 216
Common stock, 212
Convertible preferred stock, 214
Corporate Debt, this index
Creditor liability, 279-290
Debentures. Corporate Debt, this index
Debt and agency costs, 243-248
Debt and taxes, 237-238
Deepening insolvency doctrine, liability of affiliated parties under, 296-306
Excessive debt, 262-308
Fiduciary duties to creditors, 270-279
Floating rate preferred stock, 214
Fraudulent transfers and obligations, 270
Inventory financing, 215
Irrelevance hypothesis
    Generally, 226-236
    Net income perspective, 226-228
    Net operating income approach, 228-231
    One-owner corporations, 231-233
Letters of credit, 216
Leveraged buyouts, 307-308
Lines of credit, 215
Long term commercial loans, 215-216
Net income perspective, irrelevance hypothesis, 226-228
Net operating income approach, irrelevance hypothesis, 228-231
One-owner corporations, irrelevance hypothesis, 231-233
Participating preferred stock, 214
Preferred stock, 212-214
Range of financial choices, 212-226
Real world, generally, 236-248
Releveraging, 240-242
Short term commercial loans, 215
Structural response to threat of insolvency, 307-308
Structured financing, 216
Subordination, 262-270
Substitutability postulate, 211
Unleveraging, 242-243
Warrants, 212
Weighted average cost of capital, 238-240

CASH FLOW STATEMENTS
Financial Statements, this index

CASH RATIO
Financial statements, 55

CHIEF EXECUTIVE OFFICERS
Certification of accuracy of corporate financial statements, 6

CHIEF FINANCIAL OFFICERS
Certification of accuracy of corporate financial statements, 6

CLASS VETO POWER
Preferred stock, 521-538

CLOSE CORPORATIONS
Capital structure, disallowance of interest deductions, 290-296

COMMERCIAL PAPER
Capital structure, 216

COMMON STOCK
Generally, 309-363
Capital structure, 212
Dilution
    Generally, 313-363
    Equitable doctrines governing dilutive stock issues, 323-328
    Flip-in plans, 345-346
    Flip-over rights, 335-345
    Legal capital or nominal value, 346-351
    Misrepresentation theory, 347-348
    Penalty dilution, 315-316
    Poison pills, 328-346
    Preemptive rights to purchase portion of any new issue, 316-323
    Statutory obligation theory, 348
    Sweat equity problem, 348-351
    Trust fund theory, 347
    Watered stock theory, 348
Equitable doctrines governing dilutive stock issues, 323-328
Flip-in plans, 345-346
Flip-over rights, 335-345
Legal capital or nominal value, 346-351
Limited liability of stockholders, 309-313
Misrepresentation theory, dilution, 347-348
New issues market, 355-359
Penalty dilution, 315-316
Poison pills, 328-346
Preemptive rights to purchase portion of any new issue, 316-323
Public securities markets and regulation
    Generally, 351-363
    New issues market, 355-359
    Securities Act of 1933, 351-353
    Securities Exchange Act of 1934, 351, 353-355
    Trading markets, 359-363
Securities Act of 1933, 351-353
Securities Exchange Act of 1934, 351, 353-355
Sweat equity problem, 348-351
Trading markets, 359-363
Trust fund theory, 347
Valuation, 101-103
Watered stock theory, 348

COMPARABILITY
Financial reports, 8

COMPOUNDING
Valuation, 90-95

CONSERVATIVENESS
Financial reports, 8

CONSIGNMENT SALE CONTRACTS
Financial statements, 30-36

CONSISTENCY
Financial reports, 8

CONSOLIDATED RETURNS
Generally, 7

CONTINGENT LIABILITIES
Balance sheets, 17, 62-70

CONTROL PREMIUMS
Valuation, 194-210

CONVERSION RIGHTS
Corporate debt, substitutes for covenants, 423-424

CONVERTIBLE PREFERRED STOCK
Capital structure, 214

CONVERTIBLE SECURITIES
Options and Convertible Securities, this index

CORPORATE DEBT
    Generally, 1, 214, 217, 364-476
Accounts receivable as security for lines of credit, 364
Alteration of risks, 409-415
Amendments, 435-445
Asset backed financing, 467-471
Asset dispositions, restrictions on, 414
Bond rating agencies, 364
Call protection, 426-433
Capital leases, 465-467
Consolidation or merger only on certain terms, 413
Contract interpretation, 371-382
Contract terms, 382-409
Conversion rights as substitutes for covenants, 423-424
Corporate existence, 422
Debentures, generally, 216-217, 218-226
Default, duties of trustees, 458-464
Distributions, 415-420
Dividends and redemptions, restrictions on, 419-420
Enforcement of bondholder rights, 445-448
Factors, sale of accounts receivable to, 364
Insurance, 422-423
Investments, 414-415
Leveraged buyouts, 389-407
Lines of credit, 364
Maintenance of assets, 420-423
Monitoring compliance, 433-434
New York bonds, 368-369
Renegotiation, 364
Revised Model Simplified Indenture, 474-476
Securitization of assets, 467
Sinking funds, 424-426
Successor corporation, substitution of, 413-414
Trust Indenture Act
    Amendments to indentures, 436-437

CORPORATE DEBT—Cont'd
Trust Indenture Act—Cont'd
    Trustees, 449-450
Trustees
        Generally, 448-464
    Default, duties in, 458-464
    Nature of trustee and duties, 448-458
    Trust Indenture Act, 449-450
Underinvestment, 420-423
U.S. exchange bonds, 367-369

COST EFFECTIVENESS
Accounting reports, 6

COST PRINCIPLE
Generally, 6

CURRENT OR NON-CURRENT
Assets, 12
Liabilities, 13

CURRENT RATIO
Financial statements, 54

CYCLE OF CASH FLOW
Financial statements, 42

DEATH SPIRAL FINANCING
Options and convertible securities, 653, 687-706

DEBT TO EQUITY RATIO
Financial statements, 54

DEBT TO TOTAL ASSETS RATIO
Financial statements, 53-54

DEEPENING INSOLVENCY DOCTRINE
Capital structure, liability of affiliated parties, 296-306

DEFERRED INCOME TAXES
Balance sheet, assets, 14, 16

DEFINED BENEFIT PENSION PLANS
Contingent liability statements, 65-70

DEPLETION
Financial statements, 27-28

DEPRECIATION
Financial statements, 27-28, 46-49

DERIVATIVES
Options and convertible securities, 585

DILUTION
Common Stock, this index

DIRECTORS
Unlawful dividends or distributions, liability for, 739

DISCLOSURE ISSUES
Options, valuation of, 612-616

DISCONTINUED OPERATIONS
Income statements, extraordinary items, 29

DISCRETION OF BOARD
Dividends and distributions, 753-768

DISTRIBUTIONS
Dividends and Distributions, this index

DIVERSIFICATION
Valuation, cost of capital, 116-118

DIVIDEND PAYOUT RATIO
Financial statements, 57

DIVIDEND YIELD
Financial statements, 57

DIVIDENDS AND DISTRIBUTIONS
Generally, 707-844
Accounting for stock dividends and stock splits, 769-776
Bankruptcy, stock repurchase rights in, 748-753
Clientele effects and expectations, 720-721
Corporate debt, 415-420
Declaration, 772
Directors, liability for unlawful dividends or distributions, 739
Discretion and duties of board, 753-768
Economics
    Stock dividends and stock splits, 768-769
    Stock repurchases, 788-790
Explanations for dividend practices, 720-733
Financial statements, 57
Fraudulent transfers, 734-736
Going private transactions, stock repurchases, 795-803
Greenmail, stock repurchases, 790, 811-818
Historical primacy of dividends, 716
Hostile tender offers, stock repurchases during, 803-811
Imperfect capital markets and signaling value of dividends, 725
Irrelevance hypothesis, 716-720
Leveraged buyouts, 825-841
Listing process, stock dividends and stock splits, 773-775
Market stock repurchases, 791-795
Options, valuation of, 610
Payment, 772
Preferred Stock, this index
Relation to value of company, 715-720
Restrictions on dividends and distributions, 733-753
Reverse stock splits, 776-788
Spin-off transactions, 707, 841-842
Stock dividends and stock splits
    Generally, 768-788
    Accounting, 769-776
    Economics, 768-769
    Listing process, 773-775
    Reverse stock splits, 776-788
Stock repurchases
    Generally, 788-825
    Duties of directors, 818-825
    Economics, 788-790
    Going private transactions, 795-803

DIVIDENDS AND DISTRIBUTIONS
    —Cont'd
Stock repurchases—Cont'd
    Greenmail, 790, 811-818
    Hostile tender offers, repurchases during, 803-811
    Legal authority, 790-791
    Market repurchases, 791-795
    Regulation, 791-818
    Targeted repurchases, 790, 811-818
Targeted stock repurchases, 790, 811-818
Taxes, 722-725
Tracking stock, 843-844
Transaction costs of selling shares, 721-722
Two-agency explanations for dividends, 726-733

DOUBLE DECLINING BALANCE
Depreciation, accounting options, 48-49

DOWN ROUNDS
Convertible securities, dilution of option rights, 652

DUTCH AUCTIONS
Valuation, 150-152, 158

EARNINGS BEFORE INCOME, TAXES, DEPRECIATION AND AMORTIZATION (EBITDA)
Cash flow statements, 41

EARNINGS BEFORE INCOME AND TAXES (EBIT)
Cash flow statements, 40-41
Income statements, 28-29

EARNINGS PER SHARE
Financial statements, 51

ECONOMIC ENTITIES
Accounting reports, 7

ECONOMIC VALUE ADDED
Financial statements, 53

EFFICIENT CAPITAL MARKETS
Valuation, this index

EFFICIENT CAPITAL MARKETS HYPOTHESIS MODEL
Valuation, 131-135

ENHANCED INCOME SECURITIES (EIS)
Capital structure, structural response to threat of insolvency, 307-308

EQUITABLE DOCTRINES
Common stock, dilutive stock issues, 323-328

EQUITY METHOD
Parent and subsidiary corporations, consolidated returns, 7

EQUITY PREMIUM
Capital assets pricing model, 124

EUROPEAN OPTIONS
Generally, 583

EUROPEAN UNION
Common stock, minimum capital, 347

EXCHANGE RATE FLUCTUATIONS
Cash flow statement, operating activities, 39

EXERCISE PRICE
Options, valuation of, 606

EXTRAORDINARY ITEMS
Income statements, 29-30

FACTORS
Accounts receivable, sale of, 364

FIDUCIARY DUTIES
Capital structure, 270-279

**FINANCIAL ACCOUNTING STAN-
DARDS BOARD (FASB)**
Generally, 6

FINANCIAL LEVERAGE RATIOS
Financial Statements, this index

FINANCIAL STATEMENTS
Generally, 4-87
Accounting, purpose of, 4
Accounting options
Generally, 44-50
Depreciation accounting, 46-49
Expense vs. capitalization, 49-50
Inventory accounting, 44-46
Net profit interest, 50
Activity ratios
Generally, 50, 55-56
Asset turnover ratio, 55-56
Inventory turnover ratio, 56
Receivables turnover ratio, 56
Analysis of financial statements, 43-61
Asset turnover ratio, 55-56
Assets, balance sheet, 11-12
Balance sheets
Generally, 10-26
Assets, 11-12
Capital leases, 16-17, 466-467
Liabilities, 12-13
Stockholders' equity, 13-14
Capital leases, balance sheet, 16-17, 466-467
Cash flow statements
Generally, 36-42
Cycle of cash flow, 42
Financing activities, 39-40
Free cash flow, 42, 102
Investing activities, 39
Operating activities, 38-39
Cash ratio, 55
Changes in stockholders' equity, statement
of, 42-43
Consignment sale contracts, 30-36
Contingent liability statements, 17, 62-70
Current ratio, 54
Cycle of cash flow, 42
Debt to equity ratio, 54

FINANCIAL STATEMENTS—Cont'd
Debt to total assets ratio, 53-54
Depreciation accounting, 46-49
Dividend payout ratio, 57
Dividend yield, 57
Earnings per share, 51
Economic value added, 53
Expense vs. capitalization, accounting op-
tions, 49-50
Extraordinary items, income statement,
29-30
Financial leverage ratios
Generally, 50, 53-54
Debt to equity ratio, 54
Debt to total assets ratio, 53-54
Financing activities, cash flow statement,
39-40
Form 10-K, 10
Form 10-Q, 26
Forms of financial reports, 10-43
Free cash flow, 42, 102
Gross profit percentage, 51
Income statement
Generally, 26-36
Consignment sale contracts, 30-36
Extraordinary items, 29-30
Inventory accounting, 44-46
Inventory turnover ratio, 56
Investing activities, cash flow statement, 39
Liabilities, balance sheet, 12-13
Liquidity ratios
Generally, 50, 54-55
Cash ratio, 55
Current ratio, 54
Quick (acid-test) ratio, 54-55
Times-interest earned (interest cover) ra-
tio, 55
Market to book ratio, 58
Market value ratios
Generally, 50-51, 56-58
Dividend payout ratio, 57
Dividend yield, 57
Market to book ratio, 58
Price-earnings ratios, 56-57
Net profit interest, accounting options, 50
Operating activities, cash flow statement,
38-39
Price-earnings ratios, 56-57
Profit margin, 51-52
Profitability ratios
Generally, 50
Earnings per share, 51
Economic value added, 53
Gross profit percentage, 51
Profit margin, 51-52
Return on assets, 52
Return on equity, 52-53
Return on sales, 52
Quick (acid-test) ratio, 54-55
Ratios
Generally, 50-61, 71-87
Activity ratios, above
Analysis of ratios, 58-61
Financial leverage ratios, above

FINANCIAL STATEMENTS—Cont'd
Ratios—Cont'd
    Liquidity ratios, above
    Market value ratios, above
    Profitability ratios, above
Receivables turnover ratio, 56
Return on assets, 52
Return on equity, 52-53
Return on sales, 52
Standardization, 5
Stockholders' equity, balance sheet, 13-14
Times-interest earned (interest cover) ratio, 55
Translating financial statements, 26

FIRM RISK
Capital assets pricing model, 119

FIRST-IN, FIRST-OUT
Inventory, accounting options, 44-45

FITCH'S
Corporate debt, rating of, 367

FLIP-IN PLANS
Common stock, 345-346

FLIP-OVER RIGHTS
Common stock, 335-345

FLOATING RATE PREFERRED STOCK
Capital structure, 214

FORM 10-K
Financial statements, 10

FORM 10-Q
Financial statements, 26

FORWARD CONTRACTS
Options and convertible securities, 584-585

FRAUD
Securities Exchange Act of 1934, 354-355

FRAUDULENT TRANSFERS AND OB-LIGATIONS
Capital structure, 270
Dividends and distributions, 734-736

FREE CASH FLOW
Financial statements, 42, 102

FULL RATCHET CLAUSES
Convertible securities, dilution of option rights, 652

FUTURES CONTRACTS
Options and convertible securities, 585

GENERALLY ACCEPTED ACCOUNTING PRINCIPLES (GAAP)
Generally, 5

GERMANY
Corporate debt, 364

GOING CONCERNS
Balance sheet, 15-16

GOING CONCERNS—Cont'd
Financial reports, 8

GOING PRIVATE TRANSACTIONS
Stock repurchases, 795-803

GOOD WILL
Balance sheet, 14-15
Depreciation, financial statements, 28

GREENMAIL
Stock repurchases, 790, 811-818

GROSS PROFIT PERCENTAGE
Financial statements, 51

HOSTILE TENDER OFFERS
Stock repurchases, 803-811

IMPORTANCE OF CORPORATE FINANCE
Generally, 1

INCOME DEPOSIT SECURITIES (IDS)
Capital structure, structural response to threat of insolvency, 307-308

INCOME STATEMENT
Financial Statements, this index

INITIAL PUBLIC OFFERINGS
Public securities markets and regulation, new issues market, 356-358

INSIDER TRADING
Valuation, 131-133

INSURANCE
Corporate debt, 422-423

INTANGIBLE ASSETS
Balance sheet, 14-15

INTEREST RATE
Options, valuation of, 609-610

INTERNAL RATE OF RETURN
Valuation, 105-106

INVENTORY ACCOUNTING
Financial statements, 44-46

INVENTORY FINANCING
Capital structure, 215

INVENTORY TURNOVER RATIO
Financial statements, 56

INVESTMENTS
Cash flow statements, investing activities, 39
Corporate debt, 414-415

IRRELEVANCE HYPOTHESIS
Capital Structure, this index
Dividends and distributions, 716-720

JAPAN
Corporate debt, 364

JUNK BONDS
Generally, 365

LAST-IN, FIRST-OUT
Inventory, accounting options, 45

LETTERS OF CREDIT
Capital structure, 216

LEVERAGE
Valuation, 194-210

LEVERAGED BETAS
Valuation, cost of capital, 128-129

LEVERAGED BUYOUTS
Capital structure, 307-308
Corporate debt, 389-407
Dividends and distributions, 825-841

LINES OF CREDIT
Capital structure, 215
Corporate debt, 364

LIQUIDITY
Financial Statements, this index

LISTING PROCESS
Stock dividends and stock splits, 773-775

LONG TERM COMMERCIAL LOANS
Capital structure, 215-216

LUMP SUM SETTLEMENTS
Generally, 1

MANAGEMENT'S DISCUSSION AND ANALYSIS
Financial statements, 26

MARKET TO BOOK RATIO
Financial statements, 58

MARKET VALUE RATIOS
Financial Statements, this index

MATERIALITY
Accounting reports, 6

MINORITY DISCOUNTS
Valuation, 194-210

MISREPRESENTATION THEORY
Common stock, dilution, 347-348

MONETARY BASIS
Financial reports, 8

MOODY INVESTORS' SERVICES
Generally, 472-473
Corporate debt, rating of, 367

MORTGAGES
Asset backed financing, 471
Subprime mortgages, 3

NEGATIVE NET PRESENT VALUE PROJECTS
Dividends and distributions, taxes, 723

NET INCOME FROM CURRENT OPERATIONS
Income statements, extraordinary items, 29-30

NET INCOME PERSPECTIVE
Capital structure, irrelevance hypothesis, 226-228

NET OPERATING INCOME APPROACH
Capital structure, irrelevance hypothesis, 228-231

NET PRESENT VALUE
Valuation, 104-106

NET PROFIT INTEREST
Financial statements, accounting options, 50

NEW ISSUES MARKET
Common stock, 355-359

NEW YORK BONDS
Corporate debt, 368-369

NIMBLE DIVIDENDS
Generally, 737-738

NORTH AMERICAN INDUSTRY CLASSIFICATION SYSTEM (NAICS)
Financial statements, analysis of ratios, 58-59

ONE-OWNER CORPORATIONS
Capital structure, irrelevance hypothesis, 231-233

OPERATING ACTIVITIES
Cash flow statements, 38-39

OPTIONS AND CONVERTIBLE SECURITIES
Generally, 583-706
Call options
Generally, 583, 589-593
Long positions, 590-592
Short positions, 592-593
Combining options, stocks and bonds, 595-599
Convertible securities
Generally, 616-687
Destruction of options, 616-631
Dilution of option rights, 631-687
Poison pill rights plans, 626-627
Standard anti-destruction language, 625-626
Death spirals - last period financing, 687-706
Definitions, 583
Derivatives, 585
Dilution of option rights, convertible securities, 631-687
Disclosure issues, valuation of options, 612-616
Dividend rate, valuation of options, 610
Exercise price, valuation of options, 606
Expiration date, valuation of options, 607
Forward contracts, 584-585
Futures contracts, 585
Interest rate, valuation of options, 609-610
Long and short positions and position diagrams, 587-588
Long positions on call options, 590-592
Marking futures contracts to market, 585

OPTIONS AND CONVERTIBLE SECU-RITIES—Cont'd
Poison pill rights plans, 626-627
Put options, 583, 593-595
Put-call parity, 595-599
Real options, 586-587
Short positions on call options, 592-593
Stock price, valuation of options, 606-607
Uses of options and option theory, 583-585, 599-604
Valuation of options
    Generally, 604-616
  Disclosure issues, 612-616
  Dividend rate, 610
  Exercise price, 606
  Expiration date, 607
  Interest rate, 609-610
  Stock price, 606-607
  Variance of underlying stock's value, 607-609
Variance of underlying stock's value, valuation of options, 607-609

PARENT AND SUBSIDIARY CORPORATIONS
Consolidated returns, 7

PARTICIPATING PREFERRED STOCK
Capital structure, 214

PATENTS
Depreciation, financial statements, 28

PAYBACK PERIODS
Valuation, 105

PAYMENT
Dividends and distributions, 772

PENALTY DILUTION
Common stock, 315-316

PENNY STOCKS
Reverse stock splits, 777

PERPETUITIES
Valuation, 101

POISON PILLS
Common stock, 328-346
Options and convertible securities, 626-627

PORTAL
Corporate debt not registered under securities laws, 365

PREEMPTIVE RIGHTS
Common stock, right to purchase portion of any new issue, 316-323

PREFERRED STOCK
  Generally, 477-582
Altering the preferred contract
    Generally, 508-538
  Class veto power, 521-538
  Voting rules and voting rights, 508-521
Blank check preferred stock, 477-478
Board duties

PREFERRED STOCK—Cont'd
Board duties—Cont'd
    Generally, 538-565
  Duties of preferred-controlled board, 548-565
  Duties to preferred shareholders, 538-548
Capital structure, 212-214
Class veto power, 521-538
Defined, 477-480
Dividends
    Generally, 482-508
  Property rights in dividends, 494-508
  Straight and cumulative dividends, 489-494
  Varieties of dividends, 482-489
Property rights in dividends, 494-508
Redemptions and repurchases of shares, 565-582
Sham preferred stock, 479-480
Straight and cumulative dividends, 489-494
Uses of preferred stock, 481-482
Voting rules and voting rights, 508-521

PRESENT VALUE
Generally, 95-98

PRICE-EARNINGS RATIOS
Financial statements, 56-57

PRIVATE ISSUES OF PUBLIC EQUITY (PIPES)
Death spirals - last period financing, 687

PROFIT MARGIN
Financial statements, 51-52

PROFITABILITY RATIOS
Financial Statements, this index

PUBLIC COMPANY ACCOUNTING OVERSIGHT BOARD (PCAOB)
Generally, 6

PUBLIC SECURITIES MARKETS AND REGULATION
Common Stock, this index

PUT OPTIONS
Options and convertible securities, 583, 593-595

PUT-CALL PARITY
Options and convertible securities, 595-599

QUICK (ACID-TEST) RATIO
Financial statements, 54-55

RATIOS
Financial Statements, this index

REDEMPTION OF STOCK
Balance sheet, 17-25

REGISTRATION
Securities Act of 1933, 352-353

RELEVERAGING
Capital structure, 240-242

RELIABILITY
Accounting reports, 6

RENEGOTIATION
Corporate debt, 364

REPORTS AND REPORTING
Securities Exchange Act of 1934, 353-355

RETURN ON ASSETS
Financial statements, 52

RETURN ON EQUITY
Financial statements, 52-53

RETURN ON SALES
Financial statements, 52

REVERSE STOCK SPLITS
Generally, 776-788

**REVISED MODEL BUSINESS CORPO-
RATION ACT**
Financial reports, 10

**REVISED MODEL SIMPLIFIED INDEN-
TURE**
Corporate debt, 474-476

SARBANES-OXLEY ACT
Generally, 6
Directors, knowledge of accounting and fi-
nance, 2

SEC REGULATION S-X
Generally, 6
Form and content of filings, 5, 10

SECURITIES ACT OF 1933
Common stock, 351-353

SECURITIES EXCHANGE ACT OF 1934
Common stock, 351, 353-355

SECURITIZATION OF ASSETS
Corporate debt, 467

SELF-TENDER OFFERS
Stock repurchases, 790

SHAM PREFERRED STOCK
Generally, 479-480

SHELF OFFERINGS
Public securities markets and regulation, new
issues market, 358-359

SHORT TERM COMMERCIAL LOANS
Capital structure, 215

SINKING FUNDS
Corporate debt, 424-426

SPECIAL PURPOSE ENTITIES (SPES)
Asset backed financing, 467-471
Balance sheet, assets, 11

SPIN-OFF TRANSACTIONS
Dividends and distributions, 707, 841-842

STANDARD & POOR'S
Generally, 473
Corporate debt, rating of, 367

STANDARD DEVIATION
Valuation, cost of capital, 115

STANDARDIZATION
Financial statements, 5

**STATEMENTS OF FINANCIAL AC-
COUNTING STANDARDS**
Generally, 6
No. 2, 5

STOCK AND STOCKHOLDERS
Generally, 1
Balance sheets, stockholders' equity, 13-14
Common Stock, this index
Dividends and Distributions, this index
Options and Convertible Securities, this in-
dex
Preferred Stock, this index

STOCK REPURCHASES
Dividends and Distributions, this index

STOCK SPLITS
Dividends and Distributions, this index

STRAIGHT LINE
Depreciation, accounting options, 48

STRUCTURED FINANCING
Capital structure, 216

STRUCTURED SETTLEMENTS
Generally, 1

SUBORDINATION
Capital structure, 262-270

SUBPRIME MORTGAGES
Generally, 3

SUBSTITUTABILITY POSTULATE
Capital structure, 211

SUCCESSOR CORPORATIONS
Corporate debt, 413-414

SUM OF THE DIGITS
Depreciation, accounting options, 48

SWEAT EQUITY PROBLEM
Common stock, 348-351

**SYSTEMATIC AND UNSYSTEMATIC
RISK**
Capital assets pricing model, 119

TAKEOVER DEFENSES
Valuation, 144-149

TARGETED STOCK REPURCHASES
Generally, 790, 811-818

TAXATION
Capital leases, 465-466
Capital structure, 237-238

TAXATION—Cont'd
Dividends and distributions, 722-725
Stock repurchases, 789

TIMES-INTEREST EARNED (INTEREST COVER) RATIO
Financial statements, 55

TRACKING STOCK
Dividends and distributions, 843-844

TRADING MARKETS
Common stock, 359-363

TRADING SECURITIES
Parent and subsidiary corporations, consolidated returns, 7

TREASURY INFLATION-PROTECTED SECURITIES (TIPS)
Generally, 99

TRUST FUND THEORY
Common stock, 347

TRUST INDENTURE ACT
Corporate Debt, this index

TRUSTEES
Corporate Debt, this index

UNDERINVESTMENT
Corporate debt, 420-423

UNDERWRITING
Corporate debt, commissions, 367

UNIQUE RISK
Capital assets pricing model, 119

U.S. EXCHANGE BONDS
Corporate debt, 367-369

VALUATION
Generally, 88-210
Agreement on the implication of current information for stock prices, 134
All available information is costlessly available to market participants, 134
Annuities, 98-100
Book value, 88-89
Capital assets pricing model, 118-130, 172-194
Challenges to capital assets pricing model, 129-130
Challenges to Efficient Capital Markets Hypothesis, 135-152
Common stock, 101-103
Compounding, 90-95
Cost of capital
Generally, 106-130
Beta, 119-125
Capital assets pricing model, 118-130, 172-194
Challenges to capital assets pricing model, 129-130
Diversification and risk, 116-118
Leveraged betas, 128-129

VALUATION—Cont'd
Cost of capital—Cont'd
Measurement of risk, 111-116
Price of risk, 106-111, 118-128
Standard deviation, 115
Variance, 114-115
Diversification and risk, cost of capital, 116-118
Dutch auctions, 150-152, 158
Efficient capital markets
Generally, 131-172
Agreement on the implication of current information for stock prices, 134
All available information is costlessly available to market participants, 134
Challenges to Efficient Capital Markets Hypothesis, 135-152
Dutch auctions, 150-152, 158
Efficient Capital Markets Hypothesis model, 131-135
Insider trading, 131-133
Measuring market efficiency in regulatory setting, 156-157
Sufficient capital to engage in risky arbitrage, 135
Takeover defenses, 144-149
Zero transactions costs in securities, 134
Efficient Capital Markets Hypothesis model, 131-135
Frequency of compounding, 93-95
Insider trading, 131-133
Internal rate of return, 105-106
Investments with different cash flows at different times, 103-104
Leveraged betas, cost of capital, 128-129
Measurement of market efficiency in regulatory setting, 156-157
Measurement of risk, cost of capital, 111-116
Minority discounts, control premiums and leverage, 194-210
Net present value, 104-106
Options and Convertible Securities, this index
Payback periods, 105
Perpetuities, 101
Present value, 95-98
Price of risk, cost of capital, 106-111, 118-128
Standard deviation, cost of capital, 115
Sufficient capital to engage in risky arbitrage, 135
Takeover defenses, 144-149
Variance, cost of capital, 114-115
Venture capital financing, 209-210
Zero transactions costs in securities, 134

VARIANCE
Valuation, cost of capital, 114-115

VENTURE CAPITAL
Generally, 1
Public securities markets and regulation, new issues market, 355-356
Valuation, 209-210

VOTING RULES AND VOTING RIGHTS
Preferred stock, 508-521

WARRANTIES
Balance sheet, assets, 14, 16

WARRANTS
Generally, 583

WARRANTS—Cont'd
Capital structure, 212

WATERED STOCK THEORY
Common stock, 348

WEIGHTED AVERAGE METHOD
Inventory, accounting options, 45-46

†